T0393031

ROUTLEDGE HANDBOOK OF TRANSNATIONAL TERRORISM

This handbook provides contributions by some of the world-leading experts in the field on recent phenomena and trends in transnational terrorism.

Based on the methodological approach of a trend-and-key-factor analysis of transnational terrorism and processed on the virtual platform Foresight Strategy Cockpit™ (FSC), the volume seeks to examine what potential future variants of transnational terrorism may evolve. Focusing on the latest structural developments in the sphere of politically or religiously motivated violence, this handbook considers the tactical, strategic, and not least the systemic dimension of terrorism. Divided into seven thematic sections, this handbook's contributions cover a wide range of issues, dealing, among others, with strategic and hybrid terrorism, the systemic dimension of extremist violence, prevalent actors, counter-narratives, the crime terror-nexus, the role of digitalization and the spiral dynamic between Islamist and right-wing terrorism. The expert contributions provide a condensed overview of current developments, structural linkages and important academic debates centering around transnational salafi-jihadi terrorism, but also right-wing terrorism and counter-terrorism. A key objective of the work is to make the effects of prevention/ preemption, (de-) radicalization and (non-) intervention both transparent and assessable. As such, it contributes well-founded strategies, feasible solutions and options for policy-makers and counter-terrorism experts.

This volume will be of great interest to students of terrorism and counter-terrorism, and political violence and security studies.

Nicolas Stockhammer is Director of the Research Cluster Counter-Terrorism, CVE (Countering Violent Extremism) and Intelligence™ at Danube-University Krems (Austria).

ROUTLEDGE HANDBOOK OF TRANSNATIONAL TERRORISM

Edited by Nicolas Stockhammer

Routledge
Taylor & Francis Group

LONDON AND NEW YORK

Cover image: © Devrimb

First published 2024
by Routledge
4 Park Square, Milton Park, Abingdon, Oxon OX14 4RN

and by Routledge
605 Third Avenue, New York, NY 10158

Routledge is an imprint of the Taylor & Francis Group, an informa business

British Library Cataloguing-in-Publication Data
A catalogue record for this book is available from the British Library

Library of Congress Cataloging-in-Publication Data
Names: Stockhammer, Nicolas, editor.
Title: Routledge handbook of transnational terrorism /
edited by Nicolas Stockhammer.
Description: Abingdon, Oxon ; New York, NY : Routledge, 2023. |
Includes bibliographical references and index.
Identifiers: LCCN 2022061754 (print) | LCCN 2022061755 (ebook) |
ISBN 9781032353197 (hardback) | ISBN 9781032353203 (paperback) |
ISBN 9781003326373 (ebook)
Subjects: LCSH: Terrorism. | Transnational crime.
Classification: LCC HV6431 .R6854 2023 (print) |
LCC HV6431 (ebook) | DDC 363.325--dc23/eng/20230526
LC record available at https://lccn.loc.gov/2022061754
LC ebook record available at https://lccn.loc.gov/2022061755

ISBN: 978-1-032-35319-7 (hbk)
ISBN: 978-1-032-35320-3 (pbk)
ISBN: 978-1-003-32637-3 (ebk)

DOI: 10.4324/9781003326373

Typeset in Bembo Std
by KnowledgeWorks Global Ltd.

E·I·C·T·P

This edition was realized in close cooperation with EICTP, the European Institute for Counter Terrorism and Conflict Prevention, headquartered in Vienna, Austria.

EICTP, as an independent security policy think-tank, conducts projects with renowned research partners in Europe and abroad, maintaining close relationships with high-level research organizations and networks of worldwide acknowledged key experts on transnational (counter-)terrorism, hybrid conflicts and P/CVE measures.

CONTENTS

FIGURES AND TABLES

Figures

Tables

NOTE ON EDITOR

Nicolas Stockhammer, Ph.D., has an academic background in political theory, studying conflict and terrorism. Following government related research positions in the field of security policy, he is currently in charge of the Research Cluster "Counter-Terrorism, CVE (Countering Violent Extremism) and Intelligence" in the Department of Law and International Relations at Danube-University Krems, which is dedicated to basic research on counter-terrorism, CVE and intelligence.

Nicolas Stockhammer's research is centered around security policy issues with a strong focus on transnational (counter-)terrorism. He is the author of *Das Prinzip Macht* (Nomos 2009). Recently he has published (selection) *Die Morphologie des hybriden Terrorismus. Plädoyer für eine vernetzte Terrorismusabwehr,* in: Stefan Hansen/Joachim Krause (Hrsg.): *ISPK Jahrbuch Terrorismus 2015/16,* Bd.7, Opladen/Berlin/Toronto 2017. Since 2020 several EICTP (European Institute for Counter Terrorism and Conflict Prevention) studies: EICTP Policy Brief (May 2020) *COVID-19: Is Bioterrorism on the Rise Now?* together with Peter R. Neumann Stockhammer issued "Preliminary lessons learnt from the Vienna Terror attack", EICTP Policy Brief, Vol.1/February 2021. His *Al-Qaida – 20 Jahre danach: Zwischen Abdriften in die Bedeutungslosigkeit, systemischer Konsolidierung und strategischer Resilienz,* appeared in: Journal for Intelligence, Propaganda and Security Studies (JIPSS) VOL.15, Nr.2/2021; together with Stefan Goertz *Corona-Maßnahmen-Gegner. Rezente Akteure, Ideologieelemente und ihr stochastisches Gewaltpotenzial,* EICTP Expert Paper, December 2021, as well as *"Taktische Erkenntnisse zum Wiener Terroranschlag vom 2. November 2020",* EICTP Expert Paper, March 2022.

He has contributed numerous national and international commentaries and media appearances on issues of transnational terrorism and extremism. Stockhammer regularly appears in Austrian and international news broadcasts and is considered an expert on terrorism and security policy related issues. He tweets at @nic_stockhammer.

NOTES ON CONTRIBUTORS

Gary A. Ackerman, PhD., is an Associate Professor in the College of Emergency Preparedness, Homeland Security and Cybersecurity at SUNY, Albany, where his research focuses on assessing emerging threats and understanding how terrorists and other adversaries make tactical, operational, and strategic decisions, particularly regarding innovating in their use of weapons and tactics. Much of his work in this area is centered on the motivations and capabilities for non-state actors to acquire and use chemical, biological, radiological, or nuclear weapons, as well as other emerging technologies. In addition to his faculty position at Albany, he is Associate Dean for Research in the College, and the founding director of the Center for Advanced Red Teaming (CART).

Aljoscha Albrecht, M.Sc., is a Research Assistant in the Africa and Middle East Research Division at the German Institute for International and Security Affairs (Stiftung Wissenschaft und Politik, SWP) in Berlin. He holds degrees from the School of Oriental and African Studies (SOAS) in London and Freie Universität Berlin (FU Berlin). His research interests include non-state violence and civil wars in Africa and the Middle East.

Randy Borum, Ph.D., is a Professor, Director of the School of Information (iSchool), and Director of Intelligence and National Security Studies at the University of South Florida. Before coming to USF, he was an Assistant Professor Medical Psychology at Duke University School of Medicine. Borum supported three Directors of National Intelligence (DNI) on the Intelligence Science Board (ISB) and served on the Defense Science Board Task Force on Understanding Human Dynamics. He is Board Certified and fellowship-trained in forensic psychology and has served as an instructor with the BJA State & Local Anti-Terrorism Training (SLATT), a Senior Consultant to the US Secret Service, advisor to the FBI's Behavioral Analysis Unit-1 (Threat Assessment & National Security), Senior Behavioral Scientist in the National Security Directorate at Pacific Northwest National Laboratory (PNNL), and is listed on the United Nations' Roster of Experts in Terrorism. He has previously served as a sworn police officer and as Chief Psychologist for the acute admission unit of a regional state psychiatric hospital.

Daniel Byman, Ph.D., is a professor at Georgetown University and a senior fellow at the Center for Middle East Policy at the Brookings Institution, where his research focuses on counterterrorism and Middle East security. He previously served as the research director of the center. Byman also served as a staff member with the National Commission on Terrorist Attacks on the United States ("The 9/11 Commission") and the Joint 9/11 Inquiry Staff of the House and Senate Intelligence Committees. Prior to that, Byman was a policy analyst and the director for research in the Center for Middle East Public Policy at the RAND Corporation and worked for the U.S. government. His most recent book is *Road Warriors: Foreign Fighters in the Armies of Jihad* (Oxford University Press, 2019). He is the author of several other books on counterterrorism, state sponsorship of terrorism, and conflict and terrorism in the Middle East.

Colin P. Clarke, Ph.D., is the director of Policy and Research at The Soufan Group. Clarke's research focuses on domestic and transnational terrorism, international security, and geopolitics. Prior to joining The Soufan Group, Clarke was a professor at Carnegie Mellon University, and a senior political scientist at the RAND Corporation, where he spent a decade researching terrorism, insurgency, and criminal networks. Clarke is also an Associate Fellow at the International Centre for Counter-Terrorism (ICCT) – The Hague, a non-resident Senior Fellow in the Program on National Security at the Foreign Policy Research Institute (FPRI), an Associate Fellow at the Global Network on Extremism and Technology (GNET), and a member of the "Network of Experts" at the Global Initiative Against Transnational Organized Crime.[1]

Blyth Crawford, M.A., is a research fellow at the International Centre for the Study of Radicalisation where she specialises in far-right online social movements. She is also a PhD candidate at King's College London where she studies far-right radicalisation within online forums utilising an ethnographic method. She has published work for the Centre for Research and Evidence on Security Threats, CTC Sentinel, and the George Washington University Programme on Extremism, and has presented to both academic and government bodies. Previously she has worked in Hostile Threat Replication. She also holds an MA in Terrorism, Security and Society from King's College London and an undergraduate degree in Social Anthropology from the University of Edinburgh.

Catrina Doxsee, M.A., is an associate director and associate fellow for the Transnational Threats Project at the Center for Strategic and International Studies (CSIS), where she analyzes international and domestic terrorism and the irregular activities of countries such as Iran, Russia, and China. Outside of CSIS, she is a member of the editorial board for the Irregular Warfare Initiative at the Modern War Institute at West Point and was the 2021 counterterrorism fellow at Young Professionals in Foreign Policy. Prior to joining CSIS, Ms. Doxsee worked as an associate policy analyst at the Migration Policy Institute. She has also conducted research at the Philip Merrill Center for Strategic Studies at Johns Hopkins and the U.S. Treasury Department's Middle East and North Africa Office. She previously served for two years in AmeriCorps as a refugee resettlement caseworker in Pittsburgh. Ms. Doxsee holds a BA in history, with a concentration in military history, from the University of Chicago and an MA in strategic studies and international economics from the Johns Hopkins School of Advanced International Studies.

Ali Fisher, Ph.D., is an advisor, strategist and author who delivers strategic insight into complex information ecosystems, often containing extreme or illegal content. Ali has a dual specialism in Strategic Communication and Data Science and has worked on Strategic Communication projects for European and US Government Departments. His analysis has helped organisations build or disrupt networks of influence and impact the flow of information through a community across a diverse range of fields commercial and governmental sectors including Strategic

Communication, Public Diplomacy, Counter Terrorism and Child Protection. Now Director and Explorer of Extreme Realms of Human Cognition, Ali created BlackLight, the cloud-based system that provides strategic insight into the spread of extremist digital content. His books include *Collaborative Public Diplomacy* (2012), *The Connective Mindshift* (2013), and *Trails of Engagement* (2010), Fisher's 2015–2017 CPD Research Fellowship project was titled, *Netwar in Cyberia: Decoding the Media Mujahedeen and the Jihadist Swarmcast.*

James J.F. Forest, Ph.D. is a professor in the School of Criminology and Justice Studies at the University of Massachusetts Lowell, and also a Visiting Professor at the Fletcher School of Law and Diplomacy, Tufts University. He is co-editor of the peer-reviewed scholarly journal *Perspectives on Terrorism,* and has published over 20 books on several aspects of international security.

Dirk Freudenberg, Ph.D., is a political, state and social scientist with several years of professional experience as senior consultant and operations manager in a consulting agency for crisis and security management. Since 2002 he is lecturer at the Federal Office of Civil Protection and Disaster Assistance (BBK). Freudenberg has participated at the Manfred-Wörner seminar of the armed forces team, as well as the "security policy" seminar BAKS. In his capacity as colonel of the parachute regiment he has taken part in several foreign missions abroad of the German Armed Forces. He is lecturer at several academic institutions, among them the renowned Berlin School of Economics and Law (HWR), member of the Clausewitz Society, and author of numerous articles and books on security policy-related and military scientific topics, as well as on civil protection and corporate security. Freudenberg received his PhD in 2004 from the Bundeswehr University Munich.

Boaz Ganor, Ph.D., is the founder and executive director of the International Institute for Counter-Terrorism (ICT) and the Ronald S. Lauder Chair for Counter-Terrorism at the Interdisciplinary Center (IDC), Herzliya, Israel. He previously served as the Dean of the Lauder School of Government, Diplomacy & Strategy at IDC. Prof. Boaz Ganor was Aaron and Cecile Goldman Visiting Israeli Professor and Israel Institute Fellow at Georgetown University, and a Koret Distinguished Visiting Fellow at Stanford University, U.C. Berkeley, the Hoover Institution and held further academic positions in other universities around the world. He has published numerous articles on terrorism and counterterrorism, including his books *The Counter-Terrorism Puzzle – A Guide for Decision Makers* (Transaction Publishers, 2005), or *Global Alert: Modern terrorism rationality and the challenge to the democratic world* (Columbia University Press., 2015). Prof. Ganor has given briefings and testimonies to the United Nations Counter- Terrorism Executive Directorate (CTED), the Australian Parliament, the United States Congress, the US Army, the FBI, the US Department of Homeland Security, as well as numerous intelligence, security and police services throughout the world.

Stefan Goertz, Ph.D., is a high official of the German Federal Police, lecturer at the German Federal University of Applied Administrative Sciences in Lübeck (specialization in federal police work) and researcher in the fields of Islamism, Salafism, terrorism, organized crime and extremism/radicalization research. In his capacity as official of the German Armed Forces Goertz was deployed abroad in Bosnia and Lebanon (EUFOR and UNIFIL). He studied social and political sciences in Syria, Canada and Germany and received his doctorate in the field of Islamist terrorism.

Carolin Görzig, Ph.D., is a research group leader at the Max Planck Institute for Social Anthropology in Halle/Saale, Germany, where she and her group primarily deal with how terrorists learn and whether and how states should learn to negotiate with terrorists. Görzig has worked as an assistant professor at L. Douglas Wilder School of Government and Public Affairs at the Virginia Commonwealth University (VCU) in the United States from 2013–2015, and was Visiting Research Scholar at John Hopkins University within the Conflict Management Program in Washington D.C. from 2011–2012, among other positions. She held a transatlantic Post-Doc Fellowship for International Relations and Security at the EU Institute for Security Studies in Paris as well as at RAND Corporation in Arlington. Görzig has held several presentations, conferences and workshops on topics around terrorism, religion and terrorists' learning and unlearning. Previous to her PhD in Philosophy received from the Ludwig Maximilians-University of Munich, Carolin Görzig finished her M.A. in International Conflict Analysis at the University of Kent, Brussels School of International Studies.

Heiko Heinisch, M.A., studied history at the University of Vienna and was a staff member of the Ludwig Boltzmann Institute for Historical Social Science and the Institute for Theological Islamic Studies at the University of Vienna. For 20 years he has been researching and publishing on the topics of anti-Semitism and National Socialism, integration of Muslim immigrants, Islamism, as well as on the complex of topics of Europe, human rights and Islam. He is a member of the scientific advisory board of the Documentation Center for Political Islam. His most recent publication, co-authored with Nina Scholz, is: *Alles für Allah. Wie der politische Islam unsere Gesellschaft verändert*, Molden Verlag Wien 2019.

Bruce Hoffman, Ph.D., is professor and political analyst specializing in the study of terrorism and counter-terrorism and insurgency and counter-insurgency. He is a tenured professor in Georgetown University's Edmund A. Walsh School of Foreign Service where until recently he was the director of both the Center for Security Studies and of the Security Studies program. In addition, Hoffman is visiting professor of terrorism studies at St Andrews University, Scotland. Prof. Hoffman previously held the corporate chair in counter-terrorism and counterinsurgency at the RAND Corporation and was also director of RAND's Washington, DC, office as well as vice president for external affairs.

Brian Michael Jenkins, M.A., is an american expert on terrorism and transportation security. He is a senior adviser to the president of the RAND Corporation and author of numerous books, reports and articles on topics around terrorism, including *Will Terrorists Go Nuclear?* (2008) and *Unconquerable Nation* (2006). He formerly served as chair of the Political Science Department at RAND and has advised governments, private corporations, the Catholic Church, etc. on terrorist threats for nearly four decades now. His research focus is on peacekeeping and stability operations, as well as terrorism.

Seth G. Jones, Ph.D., is an academic, political scientist, author and currently Director of the Transnational Threats Project at the Center for Strategic and International Studies (CSIS), where he holds the Harold Brown Chair. He teaches at Johns Hopkins University's School of Advanced International Studies (SAIS) and the Center for Homeland Defense and Security (CHDS) at the U.S. Naval Postgraduate School. Prior to joining CSIS, Jones was the director of the International Security and Defense Policy Center at the RAND Corporation. Before that, he was a plans officer and adviser to the commanding general, U.S. Special Operations Forces, in Afghanistan (Combined Forces Special Operations Component Command–Afghanistan). In 2014, Jones served on a congressionally mandated panel that reviewed the FBI's implementation of counterterrorism recommendations contained in the 9/11 Commission Report. Jones specializes in counterterrorism, counterinsurgency, unconventional warfare, and covert action. He is the author of several papers, articles and books, including *A Covert Action: Reagan, the CIA, and the Cold War Struggle in Poland* (W.W. Norton, 2018), *Waging Insurgent Warfare: From the Vietcong to the Islamic State* (Oxford University Press, 2016), and H*unting in the Shadows: The Pursuit of Al Qa'ida Since 9/11* (W.W. Norton, 2012). Jones is a graduate of Bowdoin College and received his M.A. and Ph.D. from the University of Chicago.

Rüdiger Lohlker, Ph.D., is professor of Islamic Studies at the Institute for Oriental Studies, University of Vienna, various academic activities, and affiliations; also, adjunct professor at Northwest University Xi'an (PR China). His current research fields are modern Islamic phenomena, jihadism, history of Islamic thought and history of science in the Islamic world.

Sophia Moskalenko, Ph.D., is a social and clinical psychologist studying mass identity and inter-group conflict. After she received her Ph.D. from the University of Pennsylvania in 2004, her research has focused on the psychology of radicalization, self-sacrifice and martyrdom. Moskalenko's work has been presented at scientific conferences, government briefings, radio broadcasts and international television newscasts. As a research fellow at the National Consortium for the Study of Terrorism and Responses to Terrorism (NC-START) she has worked on research projects commissioned by the Department of Defence, Department of Energy, Department of Homeland Security, and Department of State. She serves as a consultant to the United Nations' Counterterrorism Hub, Harry Frank Guggenheim Foundation, the European Commission and the Evidence-based Cyber Security Group at Georgia State University. She has written several books, including award-winning Friction: How conflict radicalizes them and us; The Marvel of Martyrdom: The power of self-sacrifice in the selfish world; and Pastels and Pedophiles: Inside the Mind of QAnon.

Herfried Münkler, Ph.D., is a former professor for Political Science (Political Theory) at the Humboldt University in Berlin and a member of the Academy of Sciences of Brandenburg. Most of his books are considered standard works, such as *Die neuen Kriege* (2002) or *Die Deutschen und ihre Mythen* (2009), which was awarded the Prize of the widely acclaimed Leipziger Buchmesse. Prof. Münkler is a regular commentator on global affairs in the German-language media and a renowned expert of history, political ideas, state-building and the theory of war.

Sam Mullins, Ph.D., is a professor at the Daniel K. Inouye Asia-Pacific Center for Security Studies (DKI APCSS) in Hawaii, and an honorary principal fellow at the University of Wollongong, Australia. Previously, he was a professor of counter-terrorism at the George C. Marshall European Center for Security Studies in Germany, where he was awarded the Superior Civilian Service Award in March 2019. Mullins has presented his work for a variety of government agencies including the Federal Bureau of Investigation, the New York Police Department, the Canadian Security Intelligence Service and many more. He holds an MA (Hons) in Psychology from the University of Glasgow, Scotland; an MSc in Investigative Psychology, with distinction, from the University of Liverpool, UK; and a PhD from the University of Wollongong, Australia. He is the author of two books: *'Home-Grown' Jihad: Understanding Islamist Terrorism in the US and UK, and Jihadist Infiltration of Migrant Flows to Europe: Perpetrators, Modus Operandi and Policy Implications.*

Petter Nesser, Ph.D., is a senior researcher at the Norwegian Defence Research Establishment's Terrorism Research Group (FFI), the prime institution responsible for defence-related research in Norway, and an associate professor with BI Norwegian Business School. He is a political scientist, historian and Arabist, educated at the University of Oslo (UiO) and The American University in

Cairo (AUC). Nesser has conducted extensive research on European jihadism for more than a decade while concentrating on radicalization, why and how terrorist cells emerge, and how they operate. His research focuses currently on jihadism worldwide in the post-IS era, while working on a book about entrepreneurs of transnational terror networks. Nesser acts as advisor to Norwegian authorities on issues related to counterterrorism and the prevention of extremism. He has communicated research findings in Norway and internationally, through academic conferences and teaching, speeches before public sector and NGOs, and via media. He is author of *Islamist Terrorism in Europe* (Hurst/Oxford University Press, 2015, 2018).

Peter R. Neumann, Ph.D., is a German proessor of Security Studies at the War Studies Department at King's College London (KCL), and also serves as Director of the International Centre for the Study of Radicalization (ICSR) which he founded in 2008. He teaches several courses at KCL and the School of Foreign Service at Georgetown University, and he authored a great number of acclaimed books, including *Old and New Terrorism* (2009) and *The Strategy of Terrorism* (2008). His research focuses on radicalization and counter-radicalization, terrorism and counter-terrorism, insurgency and counter-insurgency.

Raffaelo Pantucci, M.A., is a senior fellow in the International Centre for Political Violence and Terrorism Research (ICPVTR) at the S. Rajaratnam School of International Studies (RSIS) in Singapore and a Senior Associate Fellow at the Royal United Services Institute for Defence and Security Studies (RUSI) in London. He has previously worked at prominent strategic studies think tanks in London (IISS and RUSI), Washington (CSIS) and Shanghai (SASS). He is the author of *We Love Death As You Love Life: Britain's Suburban Terrorists* (London: Hurst, April 2015/ US: Oxford University Press, September 2015), described by *The Financial Times* as "the most articulate and carefully researched account of Britain's 'suburban terrorists" to date.' His writing has appeared in the New York Times, Financial Times, Wall Street Journal and Foreign Policy amongst others, and his work on lone actor terrorism in particular has been cited in two iterations of the UK's Counter-terrorism strategy Contest.

Nico Prucha, Ph.D., is chief content curator at Human Cognition. He is a fluent Arabic speaking specialist in Jihadist theology and strategy. His work has covered the use of the internet by Jihadist groups from the mid-2000s to the present and documented shifts in strategy from Forum to Twitter to Telegram. Main aspects of his research cover the relationship of textual and audio-visual content of jihadist activity online, specifically focusing on the extremist definition of applying theology. Another major focus is the understanding and analysis of the social media strategies used by groups such as the Islamic State and al-Qa'ida in theory and practice. His blog is available at www.onlinejihad.net

Olivier Roy, Ph.D., is presently professor at the European University Institute (Florence): he is the scientific adviser of the Middle East Directions programme at the Robert Schuman Centre for Advanced Studies and headed the ReligioWest research project (funded by the European Research Council with a grant of 1,8 million euro). Prof. Roy has been a Senior Researcher at the French National Center for Scientific Research (since 1985), professor at the Ecole des Hautes Etudes en Sciences Sociales (since 2003), and visiting professor at Berkeley University (2008/2009). He headed the OSCE's Mission for Tajikistan (1993–1994) and was a Consultant for the UN Office of the Coordinator for Afghanistan (1988). Prof. Roy also worked as a part-time consultant for the Policy Planning Staff of the French Ministry of Foreign Affairs (1984–2009).

Giray Sadik, Ph.D., is a Professor and Director of European Studies Research Center at Ankara Yıldırım Beyazit University, Turkey. ORCID: 0000-0002-4099-7840. The author would like to thank the Research Division of NATO Defense College (NDC), where he conducted part of this research as an Eisenhower Fellow. The views expressed in this article are the responsibility of the author and do not reflect the opinions of the NDC or NATO.

Marc Sageman, M.D., Ph.D., is an independent scholar on terrorism who is a psychiatrist and a political sociologist. He was a CIA case officer supporting the mujahedin during the Afghan Soviet War in the 1980s, a consultant for the U.S. Secret Service, a scholar-in-residence at the New York Police Department, and an advisor for the U.S. Army Deputy Chief of Staff (Intelligence). He has testified before the 9/11 Commission and the Beslan Commission in Russia. In the last decade he has been an expert witness in terrorism trials in the United States. He has written five books on terrorism and lectured at more than 80 universities worldwide.

Behnam Heidenreuter, Ph.D., is a German expert for Islamic Studies and has been a consultant at the German Municipal Office of Justice in Hamburg since 2018. He previously worked as an intelligence-based analyst. Said is an expert on Islamism, Salafism, Jihadism and has published numerous academic books and articles on his research. His investigations and analyses of jihadist hymns and poems (under the perspective of the social movement-theory as means of mobilization within jihadist movements) encountered particularly great public interest.

Alex P. Schmid, Ph.D., is a distinguished fellow at the International Centre for Counter-Terrorism (ICCT) in The Hague. He is Editor-in-Chief of *Perspectives on Terrorism* and former Co-Editor of *Terrorism and Political Violence* – both leading journals in the field of Terrorism Studies. Until 2009, Schmid held a chair in International Relations at the University of St. Andrews where he was also Director of the Centre for the Study of Terrorism and Political Violence (CSTPV). Previous positions include Officer-in-Charge of the Terrorism Prevention Branch of the UN Office on Drugs and Crime in Vienna (1999–2005) and a chair in Conflict Resolution at Erasmus University, Rotterdam (1991–1999). Between 1978 and 2018 he also held various positions at Leiden University and at its The Hague Campus. He is Director of the Vienna-based Terrorism Research Initiative (TRI), a consortium of institutes and individual scholars seeking to enhance human security through collaborative research. Prof. em. Schmid has more than 200 publications and reports to his name, including the award-winning volume *Political Terrorism* (1984, 1988, 2006) and the acclaimed *Routledge Handbook of Terrorism Research* (2011, 2013). His most recent major publication is the *Handbook of Terrorism Prevention and Preparedness* (The Hague: ICCT Press, 2021), a volume with 35 chapters, 6 of them from the editor Alex P. Schmid.

Nina Scholz, political scientist, author. Studied political science at the Free University of Berlin. Research work at the Ludwig Boltzmann Institute for Historical Social Science. Since 2007 freelance work. Research and publications on National Socialism and anti-Semitism, on the thematic complex of Europe, human rights and Islam, on organizations and ideology of political Islam in Europe, with a special focus on Austria and Germany. Member of the advisory board of the Graz prevention project "HEROES – against oppression in the name of honor" and of the scientific advisory board of the Raif Badawi Foundation for Freedom. Most recently published: Peter R. Neumann/Nicolas Stockhammer/Heiko Heinisch/Nina Scholz, Lagebild Extremismus und Migration: Fallstudien aus vier österreichischen Migrations-Communitys (2022).

Karolin Schwarz is a freelance journalist and author who focuses primarily on the far right and their use and abuse of the Internet and digital disinformation. She has spoken as an expert on disinformation in the Bundestag and testified as an expert witness in the trial of the Halle terrorist. In February 2020, her first book *Hasskrieger: Der neue globale Rechtsextremismus* (*Hate Warriors – the New Global Right-Wing Extremism*) was published. She gained international recognition and attention in February 2016 when she founded the Hoaxmap.org project, which maps misinformation about refugees.

Andrew Silke, Ph.D., is professor of Terrorism, Risk and Resilience at Cranfield University. He has a background in forensic psychology and criminology and has worked both in academia and for government. He is the author/editor of many books on terrorism and counterterrorism, including *Prisons, Terrorism and Extremism: Critical Issues In Management, Radicalisation and Reform* (2014) and *The Routledge Handbook of Terrorism and Counterterrorism* (2019). He is a member of the UK Government's Cabinet Office National Risk Assessment Behavioural Science Expert Group.

Joshua Sinai, Ph.D., is chair and professor, Intelligence and Security Studies, at Capitol Technology University, in Laurel, Maryland. He develops and teaches distance learning courses on intelligence analytic methods, homeland and international security, terrorism and counterterrorism, at the undergraduate and Master's levels. He also serves as Chair for several doctoral dissertation students in these areas. His more than 30-year career in Washington, DC, has included working as a contractor at the Department of Homeland Security's National Operations Center (when it was first stood up) and DHS's Science & Technology Directorate, as well as at the FBI's Foreign Terrorist Tracking Force (FTTTF) and the Federal Protective Service's (FPS) Training Branch. He also serves as Book Reviews Editor of the online bimonthly academic journal *Perspectives on Terrorism*, for which he writes the "Counterterrorism Bookshelf" review column.

Guido Steinberg, Ph.D., is a senior fellow at the German Institute for International and Security Affairs (Stiftung Wissenschaft und Politik, SWP) in Berlin, specializing in Middle East Politics and Terrorism. He has worked as a research coordinator at the Free University Berlin (2001) and as an advisor on international terrorism in the German Federal Chancellery (2002–2005). Since 2006, he has been a frequent expert witness in terrorism trials in Germany, Austria, the United States, Denmark, and Canada. His publications include: *German Jihad. On the Internationalization of Islamist Terrorism*, New York: Columbia University Press 2013.

Nicolas Stockhammer, Ph.D., is a political scientist with focus on security policy and terrorism research. From 2004 to 2006 he was research fellow and university lecturer at the chair for Political Theory (Herfried Münkler, Ph.D.) at Humboldt-University Berlin, Germany. From 2014 to 2021, Stockhammer has been working as senior post-doc researcher of the research group Polemology and Legal Ethics at the Institute for Legal Philosophy of the University of Vienna. With numerous publications in academic journals, articles published in print media as well as many media appearances as an expert for terrorism and terrorist developments, Stockhammer's expertise on security policy-related issues continues to meet great interest in Austria and abroad. Currently Nicolas Stockhammer is in charge of the Scientific leadership and coordination of the Research Cluster "Counter-Terrorism, CVE (Countering Violent Extremism) and Intelligence" in the Department of Law and International Relations at Danube-University Krems.

Jean-Luc Vannier is a French psychoanalyst professor also working as a clinician. He is graduated from Panthéon-Sorbonne University Paris I in Political Sciences and now lecturing at Nice Côte d'Azur University and at Edhec and Ipag p.g. Business School (Nice & Paris). He belongs to Therapyroute Association and is a member of the Editorial Committee of The Psychreg Journal of Psychology (London). He is Auditor of the Institut des Hautes Etudes de la Défense Nationale (IHEDN).

Lorenzo Vidino, Ph.D., is the director of the Program on Extremism at George Washington University. An expert on Islamism in Europe and North America, his research over the past 20 years has focused on the mobilization dynamics of jihadist networks in the West; governmental counter-radicalization policies; and the activities of Muslim Brotherhood-inspired organizations in the West.

Charlie Winter, Ph.D., is co-founder and director of Research at the threat intelligence platform ExTrac. His research on terrorism has been funded by Facebook, various bodies of the UK government, the US Central Intelligence Agency, and the Department for Homeland Security (among others). Having left academia in 2021 to focus solely on ExTrac, he leads in the development and deployment of its data and methodologies.

Katherine Zimmerman, M. A., is a fellow at the American Enterprise Institute (AEI), where she focuses on the global Salafi-jihadi movement and counterterrorism. She also studies the al Qaeda network and related trends in the Middle East and Africa, including al Qaeda in the Arabian Peninsula and Yemen, al Shabaab in Somalia, and al Qaeda in the Sahel. She is also an adviser to AEI's Critical Threats Project.

Ms. Zimmerman has testified before Congress about the threats to US national security interests emanating from al Qaeda and its network. In addition, she has briefed members of Congress, their staff, and US military, diplomatic, and intelligence community personnel.

Her commentary and analyses have been widely published, including in CNN.com, Foreign Affairs, Foreign Policy, FoxNews.com, The Hill, The Huffington Post, The Wall Street Journal, and The Washington Post. She is often interviewed, and her appearances include the Associated Press, BBC News, Bloomberg News, CNBC, CNN's "The Situation Room", Fox News Channel's "Special Report with Bret Baier", Voice of America, and Yahoo Finance. Ms. Zimmerman is a term member of the Council on Foreign Relations and a member of the RESOLVE Network Research Advisory Council. She holds an MA in terrorism, security and society from King's College London and a BA in political science and modern Middle East studies from Yale University.

ACKNOWLEDGMENTS

An edited volume always reflects a plurality of views and approaches. This multitude enriches an academic handbook in particular. It is the result of a common effort, first and foremost by its contributors, who did a phenomenal job and deserve a deep gratitude from the editor. I consider myself exceptionally fortunate and privileged that so many excellent researchers followed my invitation. As editor I want to explicitly thank each contributor, all of them internationally recognized experts in their academic field, who in my humble opinion delivered outstanding research papers for this volume. My sincere thanks to you all for your trust and generosity!

A book like this always depends on a great publisher which I was happy to find in Routledge. My special thanks go to Andrew Humphrys and Devon Harvey, who facilitated this publishing project from the very beginning with their great patience, broad experience and valuable practical assistance.

This publication is rooted in a research project, which I have developed together with the European Institute for Counter Terrorism and Conflict Prevention (EICTP) since 2019. Therefore, I am indebted to the EICTP, first of all its President, former minister of defence of Austria, H.E. Herbert Scheibner and Brig. Gen. (ret.) Gustav Gustenau, Secretary General of EICTP, who from the very beginning supported this project enthusiastically and generously. Thank you for your support!

Mag. Franziska Höller of EICTP was a driving force behind this edition, making many things possible and assisting me to keep everything "under control" with her pragmatic approach. Thank you very much Franziska and Heidrun!

Last but not least, I would like to thank my own team from my Research Cluster "Counter-Terrorism, CVE (Countering Violent Extremism) and Intelligence" at Danube-University Krems, in particular, Simone Jungwirth, Ph.D., during the first stage and MMag. Florian Liepold respectively Barbara Gruber, Ph.D., during the process of the volume's final compilation. Their work has proven essential for the genesis of this volume.

Note

1 https://www.soufangroup.com/team-member/colin-p-clarke

1

INTRODUCTION

Nicolas Stockhammer

Terrorists resemble a fly that tries to destroy a china shop. The fly is so weak that it cannot move even a single teacup. So how does a fly destroy a china shop? It finds a bull, gets inside its ear, and starts buzzing. The bull goes wild with fear and anger, and destroys the china shop.[1]

Yuval Noah Harari on the subversive instrumentalization strategy of terrorists

Terrorism has its own grammar *and* its own logic.

With analogous reference to Clausewitz' famous dictum[2]

Introduction

War and terrorism as the eminent phenomena of conflict structurally share common grounds. The nature of war is violence. The same applies to terrorism. In chapter one of his unfinished eternal classic *On War*, the Prussian military theorist Carl von Clausewitz argued that the nature of *polemos* (i.e., war) would perpetually remain stable, given the underlying proposition of enhancing political purposes by other means. What is according to him subject to continuous transformation, however, is the character of war(fare), as it is determined by what means and intensity such violence is exerted by the parties of conflict. The same may analogically be assumed for terrorism as ideologically (politically and/or religiously) motivated violence. In a similar approach, it is necessary to distinguish between the nature and the character of terrorism. While its violent nature in essence remains unchanged, its volatile operative character is permanently adapting tactically to its multiple security environments. With reference to another Clausewitzian metaphoric comparison, terrorism in its pluriverse manifestations is nothing less than a "true chameleon"[3] that aligns with its surrounding. This alignment includes the manifold immediate stages, where terrorist violence takes place, as well as structures, key players on both sides, political stakeholders and various governmental efforts to counter-terrorism, but also the wider security environment such as the "euro-strategic" or the overall geopolitical framework. A globalized extension and enlarged outreach of almost every aspect of human existence has impacted the phenomenon of terrorism substantially. The internet being probably the most significant catalyst, the multitude of possibilities for extremist actors to engage has been further amplified, particularly in the first two decades of the 21st century.

DOI: 10.4324/9781003326373-1

Terrorism Has Gone Global

Globalization has brought with it not only unprecedented opportunities and all manner of progress but also exponential risks. Interdependent structures such as international economies can eventually affect each other in real time just like in the social, cultural and political spheres, where "local" more and more means "global". Transnational terrorism has gradually evolved and even more tremendously flourished in the era of globalization.[4] By virtue of its claim to transcend boundaries by uniting advocates of common ideologies and aspirations, it has profited from the ongoing interdependence encompassing almost any aspect of cross-border (mostly social) networking, essentially ranging from propaganda to agitation, recruitment and assistance (e.g., in plotting attacks). Considered as a shadow side of globalization, intensified cross-border activities of subversive terrorist groups and sub-conventional network structures provide these groups with the ability to spread their messages and to enlarge the scope of their operations. The impact of transnationalization alters not only the organizations *per se*, but also terrorist groups' respective approach to methods, their intention to acquire necessary capabilities and the handling of their resources.[5] Furthermore, this symptomatically concerns their motivational repertoire and ideological fundamentals or positions. Under these conditions, we have seen the "proliferation of transnational terrorist groups with globalized agendas" whose operations involve many countries or have ramifications that transcend national borders.[6]

Following Martha Crenshaw, transnational terrorism "involves actions in which victims, perpetrators, and sites of violence represent different states and nationalities".[7] Moreover, "transnational terrorist attacks may be initiated by local actors against foreign targets in the geographic conflict space, or by radicalized local residents or transnational networks against targets outside the combat zone".[8] In a wider organizational context, "transnational" reflects a network's core ability to operationally transcend borders. It addresses the organization's intention to bundle strengths in order to subsequently promote a collective extremist purpose. In that light, cross-border support can either target ideology, comprise logistical or tactical assistance, or consist of any measure appropriate to substantiate the pursuit of common ideological or strategic goals. However, all these have to be regarded through a geostrategic lens.

Key geopolitical dynamics and shifts in the sphere of international relations deeply impact transnational security and our perhaps all-too-Western perception of it. It is well possible that the political age of borders and related geopolitical framing of territorial boundaries are slowly coming to an end. At least in the strategic thinking of globally relevant key decision-makers they have lost some of their original significance. That does not imply that geopolitics is disappearing, rather it tends to appear on a different stage. Quite similar to terrorism, the phenomenon of global interdependence has become more complex, subversive and clandestine in its structures and inter-operational ties. And, therefore, less visible. There are strong arguments for a systemic transformation from archaic "telluric" toward postmodern "fluid" geopolitics.[9] Carl Schmitt's concept of the "telluric partisan" represents a backward-oriented figure bound to fight outside the normative boundaries of conventional war, just as prototypical terrorist actors, in defense of their homeland and the traditional identities that are rooted in it.[10]

In his paradigmatic "*Kriegssplitter*" Herfried Münkler (2015) stresses fluidity as the most significant feature of future warfare[11] and also, as I believe, of terrorism: Conflicts, according to this theoretical approach, would become less centered around territorial gains (the current war in Ukraine may be a last symptom of an eroding telluric strategy rooted in a traditional geocultural, in a sense very Russian foundation) but generically rather around the "*control of streams*" ("*Kontrolle der Ströme*"). This comprises the flow of energy resources, cyber-dynamics, capital streams, flexible services, sophisticated technologies, human migration, etc. To illustrate that, Herfried Münkler differentiates between "virtual" and "real" streams: "By analogy, we have to imagine the "stream-based" spatial control of a present or future empire, distinguishing two types of streams: the virtual ones, where communication and information transfer take place, and the physically real ones, which are the major transport lines for raw materials and finished products; these can be pipelines, railroads, or sea lanes, and significantly, both are also the targets of attack for anti-imperial actors. Partisans, saboteurs, pirates, and hackers are the security challenge of the 21st century".[12] As are terrorists. The latter could well benefit from that meta-development in various forms, exploiting emerging tactical weaknesses of their targets. Thus, we may justifiably assume that conventional and, even more so, sub-conventional actors will increasingly employ tactics that evolve from and correspond with this new fluid transnational strategy and its accelerating digital manifestations. Particularly, the use of social media for propaganda (creating narratives) and recruiting purposes indicates a comprehensive understanding of the necessity to seize control over (information) streams.

An increasing use of virtual (communication, weapon etc.) technologies and drones as means of terrorist activities indicate this phenomenological shift away from traditional tactical patterns related to an old-fashioned telluric, binary friend-or-foe thinking. The cyberspace with its fluid dynamics reflects the entire value chain of terrorism, from first contact with extremist ideology to the plotting of terrorist attacks. Against this backdrop, an ongoing erosion of the binarity of conflicts that goes hand in hand with an ambiguity about the concepts of "war and peace", "friend and enemy", or "war and crime" may further shape a meta-strategically advanced understanding of terrorism. Blurred conceptual lines and unclear semantics pave the way for hybrid, i.e., convergent forms of conflict that must consequently materialize in adapted counter-terrorist responses. These could either follow the more European "crime paradigm" or the long-held "war paradigm" as initially propagated by the G.W. Bush administration. In the fight against terrorists, as several unclear asymmetric warfare constellations in Iraq, Afghanistan and elsewhere have indicated, it is sometimes hard to distinguish between combatants and non-combatants. Neither the ultimate objectives nor their several advocates, let alone the ideological origins and their extremist proponents, remain discriminable. In that light, a "war on terror" will become more of a war against an elusive phantom. Waging a war of attrition (against terror), according to this monolithic proposition, puts the parties of conflict in a simple logic of victory and defeat, where the terrorists win as long as they do not lose. However, the crime paradigm structurally tends to oversee the military-based approach of major terrorist organizations as relates to training, tactics and logistics. In the long run, the requirement for adaption to shifting realities will probably to some degree cause a "constabulization" of the military, where armed forces will be increasingly used for police-like tasks, or a "militarization" of police, where police forces will fulfill tasks of the armed forces and adopt their armament or tactics. This could further lead to overlapping competences and a loss in specific operative capabilities on both sides of the executive branches.

Geopolitics matter – more than ever. Beyond dispute, the character of future transnational terrorist violence is more intensely embedded in the wider context of geopolitics and global conflicts following these parameters. Most terrorist attacks beyond the locally manifested low-level scenarios will in some form be related to transnational conflicts and structures. This ultimately concerns the immanent international political dimension, as well as the extremist narratives, such as those of Salafi-jihadists, that often draw upon conflicts in other regions such as the Greater Middle East. But far-right extremists also spawn and cultivate narratives such as the "Great Reset" that substantiate, in their flawed, globally oriented perceptions, that our societies have to be rebuilt according to their racist views. Transnationalization plays a major role in all these developments.

Key Trends and Developments

However, given all this transnational interdependence, it is still a difficult task for terrorism research to identify the main indicators and define key trends that will very likely set the scene for the next 3–5 years – and sometimes even beyond – in advance. Moreover, the examination of these strategic foresight-based scenarios, the ability to predict near-future developments is more an art than a craft. Involving a strong component of software-based operationalization ("*Foresight Strategy Cockpit*",[13] henceforth "FSC") and expert contributions evolving from both conventional and unconventional, i.e., software-processed/tool related social science research approaches, makes in many ways this book a unique compilation.

Some of the world-leading scholars in the field of terrorism studies and other relevant disciplines elaborate on recent phenomena and key trends that will very likely shape the character of transnational extremist violence.

Successively, much of their expert input is methodologically processed by the help of various FSC tools (environment scanning, idea analysis, trend analysis, key factor analysis, cross-impact analysis, uncertainty and risk analysis and trend scenarios) and reassessed by selected experts.

This unique three-step method allows a different perspective on long-held research propositions, where some of them are verified, whereas others are proven wrong in the course of a multi-factor analysis. On a cautionary note, however, it is crucial to be aware of the deeply explorative and constructivist character of this research method. Still, it provides a high degree of innovation and, as editor, I sincerely hope that the readers will appreciate the, in many ways, different approach and the specific emphasis of this publication. Structurally addressing diverse questions and indicators such as the ongoing dominance of low-level terrorist scenarios, a manifest virtualization of terrorism, a continuous transnationalization, structural fragmentation (organizational fluidity) and hybridity is expected to make the book a solid strategic compass through the jungle of terrorism.

In sum, all this entails a very specific, tailored response from counter-terrorism institutions. Without doubt, as counter-terrorism in the West is deeply rooted in a tactical day-to-day business approach, where practitioners do their best to anticipate and foil terrorist plots, a keen strategic outlook is what matters most in order to identify future threats and challenges. Foresight is a keen javelin thrown into a widely unknown future. A strategic necessity, trend scenario projections can help decision makers in the field to adjust or adapt their counter-terrorism structures and measures to what is deemed to be the most likely developments and scenarios. Their symptomatic dilemma is to weight probability against impact and to define their own threat scenarios, perhaps including aspects of the insights generated by some of the eminent scholars dedicating their research to sketch out possible futures.

Outline of This Volume

We are, as Andrew Silke rightly pointed out, amid an "important and transformational phase" in our understanding of terrorism and counter-terrorism.[14] Studying terrorism and extremist violence, particularly in a transnational nexus, requires, more than ever, transdisciplinary efforts and a strong commitment to methodological open-mindedness. Multiple angles and access points, various different backgrounds and multi-disciplinary skills have paved the way from a fusty, sometimes obscure 1970s occupation of a few real pioneers and all too many nerds to a widely accepted, 21st century research discipline that is still controversial, but rooted in substantial academic grounds. Terrorism research's skillful interplay between theory, comprehensive quantitative analysis and practical relevance for counter-terrorism makes it a unique endeavor. In that sense, the large and steadily growing, unprecedented amount of high qualitative research in the field has raised the level of sheer expectation with relation to scope, depth and, notably, output. But also in terms of applicability with regard to fieldwork experience of practitioners, new standards have been established. Bearing all this in mind, a well-researched and yet accessible collection of contributions by outstanding experts in the field, including some international authors whose mother tongue is not English, bringing the excellent work of some eminent scholars to the awareness of an anglophone audience, has become a long overdue desideratum. Together with already existing Routledge Handbooks on the broader topic and selected other publications, this volume is intended to shed light on new phenomena and current security relevant affairs in global politics (e.g., the pandemic, the Western withdrawal from Afghanistan, the current Ukraine war, etc.) that to a large extent impact politically motivated, extremist violence in all its different forms. Geographically, this volume strongly focuses on regions that are predominantly relevant for European and US security, bearing in mind that transnational terrorism in other large regions, such as Latin America, the Middle East, Sub-Saharan Africa or South Asia, will be of more particular interest for terrorism research in the near future. It is intended to address these regions in a subsequent edition of this Handbook.

For a good reason, like a baseball catcher, the *Routledge Handbook on Transnational Terrorism* does not intend to catch everything that it comes across along the analytical path dealing with terrorism in its many appearances, but rather to catch what is likely to play a significant role in the near future. Therefore, its scope is intentionally kept open and ready to absorb cutting-edge fact-finding, an FSC-based analysis of key trends and developments, as well as emerging threats and challenges. In a nutshell, this handbook is meant to provide overall insight, a comprehensive compendium on what is important to know about transnational terrorism, reflecting state-of-the-art research and its skillful translation into hopefully very readable chapters.

Section I: The Strategic and Systemic Dimension of Terrorism

Under this headline, both the manifold strategies of terrorism as well as the instrumental dimension of terrorism as a strategy are addressed. Herfried Münkler opens the floor by investigating the essential strategic logic of terrorism. In the course of his pivotal reflections the functional dynamics of the phenomenon are laid out under the assumption that the volatile character of terrorism is subject to permanent change. Terrorism, whether ethno-separatist, vigilantist, left-wing extremist, right-wing extremist, or jihadist, has first and foremost a tactical function. In essence, any terrorist act is intended to be the initial spark for a revolutionary process of upheaval, at the end of which stands the strategic goal of transforming society according to the specifications of the extremist ideology. The realization of exclusive social utopias (a caliphate, white majority society, an ethnic isolation, etc.) is *in nuce* the paradigm on which all terrorism is based in its genesis. However, the causality of terrorism is diverse. A multifaceted root cause analysis of jihadist terrorism is therefore conducted by a key expert in the field, Alex P. Schmid, who seeks to explain the "revival of jihad in the Arab and Muslim world since the 1980s". This is preceded only by Daniel Byman's account on "geopolitical game changers and triggers" ("conflict-terror-nexus"), where he sketches eight plausible geopolitical game changers that could substantially reshape the transnational terrorism and counter-terrorism landscape. Plausibility here means that the occurrence of these trend developments is neither inevitable, nor necessarily likely, but still plausible enough that any counter-terrorism efforts should consider their implications. Bruce Hoffman, a doyen of terrorism research, examines both emerging and persisting players on the scene of Salafi-jihadists violence. In his state-of-the-art assessment the remarkable resiliency of both ISIS and al-Qaeda is discussed against the backdrop of their incontestable weakening, degrading and diminishment. Dispersive franchise strategies of devolving command authority and an ongoing local approach are key to their longevity, as Hoffman conclusively explains. Consequently, emphasis is put on hybrid systemic developments in the sphere of terrorist networks and single actor terrorism ("atomization of political violence"), which conclude the structural reflections of the first section. Marc Sageman starts, by suggesting a "new model of terrorism violence built on self-categorization theory" in his chapter. Following a dialectical relation between a political protest community on the one side and the state on the other side, this confrontation may boil down to violence under three conditions, which he elucidates thoroughly. Based on recent developments and trends, Brian M. Jenkins, who has contributed some groundbreaking pioneer work in the discipline, is deeply convinced that a transformative security environment is promoting a particular mode of low-level terrorism, the "atomization" of political violence, in which "individuals – not groups – motivated partly by ideology, partly by personal grievances, untethered or only loosely affiliated with an organization, are increasingly carrying out violent attacks on their own initiative, without central direction". This entails miscellaneous challenges for counter-terrorism, in particular with regards to prevention. In my own account I try to derive systemic lessons from some of the major European jihadist terrorist plots since 2015. What I call "hybrid terrorism" could likely emerge as a dominant form of transnational jihadist violence.

Approaching the phenomenon in this first, more theoretical, part of the book from various disciplinary angles should further contribute to providing a broad picture of the systemic foundations, as well as the strategic dimension of terrorism that may be considered as promotive factors for its overall development.

Section II: Technology and Radicalization

The increasing permeation of technology in our society is rapidly changing every aspect of our lives, providing society with amazing opportunities, but also dramatically increasing our vulnerabilities and making us a target for extremist violence. Threat actors, including terrorists, could misuse technology to conduct a wide range of activities, from sabotage to organizing complex operations involving people from different countries. Terrorists and extremist organizations could (and already do) use technology for a wide variety of purposes, from propaganda, psychological warfare, recruitment and training, fundraising, data mining, information gathering, intelligence gathering, secure communication, cyberattacks, software distribution (e.g., mobile apps), acquisition of false documents to physical attacks. In his sober analysis, Gary A. Ackerman identifies and describes the major technological trends of concern for counter-terrorism and how these might facilitate terrorism. In the light of prevention, he makes prudent suggestions on how to mitigate the risk of potential exploitation of new technologies by terrorist actors.

Technology and particularly virtualization is the most effective driver of terrorism and counter-terrorism. Being not only a means but also a stage, it encompasses and impacts practically all spheres along the entire value chain from radicalization to plotting terrorist attacks. Digitalization has widely increased the scope and shifted the groundwork of extremism. Being not only a generational phenomenon, the internet has become the primary place where radicalization, recruitment and propaganda take place. As Nico Prucha and Ali Fisher argue, the "Islamic State" as a terrorist organization increasingly takes advantage of dispersed and constantly reconfiguring forms of digital network organization that permanently reorganizes, much the way a swarm of bees does during flight. According to the authors, this marks a "shift" from obsolete broadcast models of communication to a new fast moving, and resilient form, the user-curated jihadi

"Swarmcast", a Web3 dissemination channel for religiously motivated, extremist propaganda. Charlie Winter and Blyth Crawford stress similar aspects by addressing the virtualization of violent extremism from three perspectives: strategy, tactics and platforms. Together, these three contributions contextualize the probably fastest moving aspect of transnational terrorism: technology and digitalization/virtualization. These technological developments and their exploitation serve the purpose of transferring extremist content and enabling frictionless conversation among like-minded networks. In that capacity they are kind of a carrier, maybe even a conveyor belt, of radicalization.[15]

Focusing on recent aspects like hybrid radicalization, Sophia Moskalenko takes us on a swift tour exploring the heterogenous landscape of radicalization. Following her thoughtful conception, radicalization is increasingly becoming a mass phenomenon, centered around but not restricted to extremist identitarian or conspiracist communities. According to Olivier Roy, radicalization is embedded in a broader context of a youth culture whose common features are a fascination for death, the aesthetics of violence and a lack of prospects in society. Jihad becomes an allure for young Muslim radicals, particularly when it is constructed as a narrative. These dynamics result in the phenomenon of lose jihadist franchise networks henceforth referred to as "McJihad". Correspondingly, there is a significant nexus between petty crime and terrorism. What Peter R. Neumann thoughtfully describes as the "crime-terror-nexus" reflects the preponderance of criminal backgrounds among a sample of 130 Western European jihadists. In his contribution, Neumann discusses the redemption-driven radicalization processes of "ordinary" criminals who turn to terrorism. His findings are highly relevant for the configuration and implementation of P/CVE measures. The same can be said of the effective tool of counternarratives that Behnam Heidenreuter elaborates on and which he considers as enormously appropriate means of countering terrorist propaganda. Moreover, he asks under which conditions the implementation of counter-narratives can be undertaken.

Conclusively, this section intends to provide a clear picture of current dynamics and interdependences in the sphere of temporary, predominantly jihadist, radicalization.

Section III: Right-Wing Extremism and Stochastic Terrorism

The West is continuously facing a "revival of militant right-wing extremist groups, networks, and incidents in recent years, with a surge of anti-immigration and Islamophobic violence, as well as anti-government attacks and assaults on political opponents, ethnic minorities, and homosexuals".[16] This section focuses on the various dynamics and impact of these particular phenomena from different viewpoints. A driving force behind these developments is an extremist ideology based upon a mechanism of deepening social and "racial" cleavages. Herfried Münkler emphasizes ideological polarization and societal disruption as root causes for extremism. In his seminal political-theoretical examination he addresses the question of what divides societies and what unites them. Münkler's assessment of the actual degree of the ideological polarization and societal disruption in the West will embed these reflections into a greater context. Stefan Goertz addresses the spiral of right-wing extremism and jihadism in his contribution. Identifying similarities, he argues that both reject Western democratic systems and strive for a revolutionary system change. According to him, they share anti-Semitism and anti-pluralism as ideological common ground. Carolin Goerzig analyzes recent trends and catalysts such as the prominence of "Generation Z"[17] in far-right extremism, as well as new emerging actors and the structural linkage between Corona-protesters,[18] anti-vaxxers, conspiracy theorists and right-wing extremists/militias. Given the very recent dramatic rise of right-wing-extremism on both sides of the Atlantic and elsewhere, the ongoing emergence of stochastic terrorism is a defining tactical pattern, as Karolin Schwarz points out. Stochastic terrorism means indirect "activation" and incitement using mass media to provoke random acts of ideologically motivated violence that are statistically predictable but individually unpredictable. The case of the violent Capitol riot on January 6, 2021, is symptomatic in both aspects. Events like these were no coincidence, according to Catrina Doxsee, who, using very recent data, suggests that in the early 2020s US domestic terrorism has "dramatically grown and fundamentally changed". Not surprisingly, the number of US terrorist attacks and plots reached its highest levels in the last three decades. This assessment is pretty much congruent with the latest European developments, as Stefan Goertz pessimistically exposits in his account. He identifies entirely new forms of right-wing extremism such as right-wing networks operating on the internet, self-radicalizing lone wolf terrorists, but also foremost right-wing extremist movements such as the "Identitarian movement" and state-deniers who aim to popularize right-wing extremism. In this regard, far-right homegrown terrorism as a permanent threat has to be reviewed under the auspices of extremist-ideological diversification and stakeholder-specific heterogeneity.

Section IV: Forecast, Trends, Scenarios and Tactics

A clear picture of the situation and a fact-based understanding of the specific dynamics of the extremist phenomenon in question are prerequisites for any form of anticipation. Anticipation means the learned ability to recognize trends as early as possible and to project scenarios into the future. This is done in structured processes and increasingly with the help of proprietary software tools and applications such as the "Foresight Strategy Cockpit". Forecast as a research method offers generic ways to transmit the multiple variables into a solid process that allows keen but cautious future predictions as relates to terrorist violence in its manifold facets. In this section, against the backdrop of theoretical conclusions, experts seek to distill fundamental, maybe paradigmatic shifts in terms of terrorist strategies and tactics. Derived from that, and also reciprocally circling back, distinct key developments in the sphere of terrorism such as potential future attack scenarios as well as major systemic trends are thoroughly assessed and put into an inter-subjective, transparent research context. Foresight-relevant key drivers are those expected to constitute transnational terrorism over a period of at least three to five years in the wider security-political, be it geopolitical or otherwise surrounding field. My chapter methodologically draws on a cross-impact-analysis that examines the interdependence of the identified key-factors and seeks to outline the extent to which they influence and "drive" each other in terms of their reciprocity and ramifications.

Joshua Sinai lays out that it is a structural mistake to confound forecasting and predicting terrorist warfare. He consequently presents a ten indicator-based early warning methodology to forecast and predict future terrorist warfare by a terrorist group under examination with the aim of providing an effective early warning methodology for adequate CT ambitions. This is the keyword for James J.F. Forest, whose chapter is dedicated to the question of how recent developments in transnational terrorism impact counter-terrorism.

In the light of current operational and tactical trends in global terrorism, including the increase in lone actors using easily available weapons, Forest explores the inherent implications for future counter-terrorism policies and strategies. Colin Clarke's fact-based scenario threat assessment of transnational Islamist terrorism takes all that into consideration. Based on his research, global jihadism is expected to become further decentralized, presenting "myriad threats" to the West. Adding to this, Petter Nesser stresses the importance of including foiled plots in terrorism research. This is difficult, since data availability may be restricted or subject to confidentiality.

However, CT can only draw fundamental lessons learnt for prevention if foiled terrorist attacks are also taken into account. In his contribution Dirk Freudenberg understands jihadism as a hybrid threat and a borderless phenomenon. Not only in the sense of a transnational capacity, but even more so when it comes to culture and laws. Homeland security resiliency needs to be strengthened in the face of potential digital decapitation strikes that could lead to complete infrastructural system failures (blackouts etc.). Rooted in a similar threat awareness, Giray Sadik postulates in his description a stronger commitment of NATO in CT and therefore aims to explore how the alliance could expand its strategic cooperation and develop effective countermeasures against terrorism and hybrid threats.

The section centers around paradigmatic developments and systemic trends which include (not exhaustively) an ongoing virtualization, transnationalization (conflict-terror-nexus), decentralization (loose terrorist franchise-networks), ideological polarization, simplification (modi operandi) and a manifest hybridization (structural convergence). Moreover, lessons-learnt processes from foiled attacks, the role of forecast and thinking in scenarios are put in reference of current counter-terrorism approaches.

Section V: Political Islam, Jihadism, Psychology and Counter-Terrorism

Drawing on the non-violent extremist phenomenon of "Political Islam", the structures, goals and manifestations of the so-called "legalistic" variant of Islamism, one that "uses liberal democratic freedoms to advance illiberal and undemocratic ends",[19] are examined. Nina Scholz and Heiko Heinisch argue that while the world's attention was focused on Islamist terrorism, practically unobserved, legalistic Islamists had "set out to transform democratic societies from within". All they had to do was to "prove that they were not bin Laden", Scholz/Heinisch conclude in their crucial piece referring to a quote of former Muslim Brother Ahmed Akkari.

In addition, the question whether there is a transition toward or nexus vis-à-vis jihadism is discussed. Accordingly, a discourse analysis of the supposed relation between jihadism and "true Islam" is contrasted by Rüdiger Lohlker with the "realities" on the ground. Lohlker remarks on an "intense competition among several groups of exclusivist Islam". Another focus in this section is on the specifics of Salafi-jihadist violence, in particular in its Western real and virtual, i.e., online, appearance. The current Western jihadist environment is, as Lorenzo Vidino points out in his conclusions, determined by mobilizing external factors such as conflicts in the Muslim world and internal factors like the "socio-economic marginalization of local Muslim communities". As a symptom of this microcosm, jihadist actors in the West are "extremely heterogeneous" (Vidino). Radicalized individuals include both genders; recent immigrants to the West, third generation Western Muslims and converts; well-integrated and highly educated individuals and those at the margins of society; individuals who belong to structured networks with solid connections to ISIS, al-Qaeda or other groups operating outside of the West; and "individuals or small groups [that] are observed to self-radicalise, principally on the internet, without being part of wider networks".[20] The psychoanalytical pathology of Islamist perpetrators and the psychology of terrorist offenders are analyzed from different disciplinary angles.[21] Jean-Luc Vannier sheds light on the entire articulations of the psychoanalytical dimension involved in the process of enrolling an individual in jihadist terrorism. Vannier's reflections are engaged with the problem of how adolescents, in search of new heroic identifications at this difficult period of life, become the privileged targets of jihadist internet recruiters. The psychological approach of Randy Borum criticizes earlier disciplinary attempts to identify a terrorist personality profile. He advocates the position that the answer to the questions of "how and why people become involved in violent extremism" is a complex and dynamic process dependent on important social and psychological factors. Particularly the concept of (multiple) identities could be a useful theoretical i.e., explanatory framework to understand that "vulnerabilities and propensities can affect individuals' pathways and decisions about engaging in violent extremism". In two compelling further contributions, both theoretical and practical insights into CVE and counter-terrorism (risk assessment) are generated. Andrew Silke examines the threat emerging from terrorist offenders released from detention and the different European risk management systems related to it. His account provides a critical overview of three significant risk assessment frameworks which are currently used in Europe: VERA-2R, ERG and TRODA. Joshua Sinai introduces a distinctive model to assess effectiveness in governments' countering violent extremism (CVE) programs to deradicalize violent ideological extremists and their supporters based on a scoring system, which is applied to measure programmatic effectiveness on a scale of 1 to 100. The various practically relevant insights derived from the papers of this important section undoubtedly could and should be of great interest for governments and authorities involved in P/CVE and counter-terrorism.

Section VI: COVID-19, Resilience and Terrorism

In his contribution, Herfried Münkler pleads for a clear differentiation between catastrophe and crisis, since, according to him, the "erosion of the semantic order has for instance brought conspirative narratives to the center of society and politics". Societies may only cope with threats and tackle challenges when these are properly identified and categorized. The COVID-19 pandemic has been a game changer also in the sphere of extremism and terrorism, wielding great influence on many other global processes that reciprocally impact extremist violence. Not only the tremendous multifaceted impact of the global health crisis but also the various strategies to cope with it and the question of resilience have been reconsidered according to the many different propositions about SARS-CoV2. Boaz Ganor elaborates on COVID-19 and terrorism in the sense of "two pandemics". Without doubt, there are structural similarities and parallels regarding the pandemic and terrorism, as both "cause and foster indiscriminate fear" (in the case of the pandemic at least in its initial phase) and are promoted by contagion. The pandemic infection equals the ideological inspiration to extremist violence. Both challenge and subvert the public's trust in its governments and decision-makers, destabilize law and order and may cause severe economic harm. To tackle SARS-CoV2 and transnational terrorism alike, a functioning cross-border cooperation is crucially needed. The importance of enlisting the public to fight these crises adequately and the provision of further valuable suggestions for counter-terrorism are further claimed. In the final part of the section, a slight glimpse into the future post-COVID-19 era has been ventured, contrasted by a possible trend scenario for transnational terrorism. Seth Jones discusses Salafi-jihadists' attempts to take advantage of the COVID-19 pandemic alongside the intention of conducting five main types of activities: "increase terrorist attacks around the globe, conduct biological warfare, expand recruitment and other support, outperform local regimes, and weaken the West". Luckily, according to Jones, major terrorist organizations in the jihadist spectrum, al-Qaeda and the "Islamic State", generally failed to achieve most of these objectives, and their statements remained largely rhetorical. Sam Mullins agrees with the proposition that violent extremists and terrorists have tried to exploit the pandemic to their advantage ever since the outbreak began. However, he disagrees with the assertion that their endeavor was not too successful after all. In this context Mullins analyzes evidence for the thesis of jihadist groups' effective exploitation of the pandemic, particularly when it comes to jihadist recruitment efforts during the pandemic, fundraising bids, health-related governance and the aspiration to conduct attacks. Both Jones and Mullins offer stringent analyses with, in some aspects slightly different results. For Brian M. Jenkins pandemics expose or reinforce existing problems: "poor governance, societal divisions, prejudices, inequality, corruption. Existing social and political cleavages intensify". This causes an increase in political violence in various forms, also terrorism, that goes hand in hand with a "legacy of disorder, desperation, and defiance", as Jenkins concludes. Raffaello Pantucci asks which implications the pandemic could have on terrorism and terrorist threats. For Pantucci, constraints and restrictions sometimes led to fully-fledged resentments against governments that can range from discontent in unexpected niches in societies to outright rejections. Accordingly, anti-governmental and anti-establishment movements might resort to violence, as he adds. The trend scenario "Hybrid Jihad", which I drafted during the pandemic and certainly also under its impression, is based upon the subjective combination of the seven most likely future projections for the next five years. *Hybrid Jihad* is rooted in assumptions like operative simplicity, tactical practicability and both effectiveness and efficiency from a terrorist network's or individual perpetrator's perspective. Among other aspects its underlying rationale is that jihadists increasingly seek tactical and operative success by reducing complexity. The same applies for the Taliban authority in Afghanistan, that strives for the least complex way to achieve its main goal: stabilizing its rule and preserving the supporting system of governance.

Section VII: Afghanistan, Al-Qaeda and Beyond

Afghanistan under a Taliban regime is very likely to create several security challenges for the West, especially considering the potential emergence of a terrorist safe haven.[22] The section sheds a light on recent developments in Afghanistan following the Western retreat, discusses the possible ramifications for the failing/failed (?) Taliban state and its impact on international security policy. From the necessity of averting its inner collapse with the help of financial aid from the West to the risk of supporting an authoritarian regime collaborating with terrorist groups – all these aspects keep the transatlantic security community alert.[23] With ongoing challenges like potentially increased opium production and the creation of exploding migrant flows to Europe and elsewhere, as well as the creation of a breeding ground or operative basis for terrorist organizations, Afghanistan remains to be observed with growing apprehension. For Herfried Münkler it all starts with a proper assessment or whether the West's intervention should be considered a failure or success. According to him, such an evaluation amounts to a "complete failure", if regime change or nation building had been core objectives. If one emphasizes the destruction of al-Qaeda as the actual purpose of the intervention, it is more appropriate to speak of a "partial success", Münkler adds. Finally, he asserts, the goal of preventing Afghanistan becoming a sort of retreat or a deployment area for global terrorism has been achieved. Seth Jones contradicts this last judgment. For him Afghanistan as a failing state is again becoming a safe haven for terrorist groups. Network ties would already exist. Moreover, he argues that US and other Western intelligence agencies assess that al-Qaeda and IS Khorasan (IS-K) will likely have the ability and willingness to conduct external attacks over the next 1–2 years, including in the West. Guido Steinberg and Aljoscha Albrecht consider the Western withdrawal from the Hindu Kush a major success for the global jihadist movement and they fear that this will likely boost its morale for years to come. For them ISIS-K, the local branch in Afghanistan, is not only a powerful competitor for al-Qaeda, but also for the Taliban, which it has chosen as its main opponent right from the start. Katherine Zimmerman considers Afghanistan now as "the primary battlefield between al-Qaeda and the Islamic State". She notes that Afghanistan is the place where the Taliban and al-Qaeda have celebrated their victory, one the Islamic State dismisses as hollow. Zimmerman also recognizes the force of "inspiration" of this "success" for global jihadi organizations. Much of this will depend on the capacities of al-Qaeda. Bruce Hoffman examines the "state and condition of al-Qaeda today –over two decades since the war on terror commenced". In his analysis Hoffman considers the repercussions of the Taliban's re-conquest of Afghanistan and what that augurs for al-Qaeda's future. His substantial conclusion may well be anticipated: al-Qaeda will remain a serious threat for international security with a potential to increase. Nico Prucha and Ali Fisher see commonalities between the Taliban and al-Qaeda: Both share an understanding of core theological components, ranging from a commitment to jihad against occupying forces and their allies inside Afghanistan to the parameters of shari'a law and the essentials of an Islamic state. Both groups have shared the battlefield in Afghanistan and continue to share the global online space where content is published and pushed. This originally deeply internalized alliance between the Taliban and al-Qaeda has shaped the history of the Afghan jihadist movement practically since Bin Laden returned to Afghanistan. Al-Qaeda's manifold difficulties have surely been compounded by the emergence of ISIS(-K) as a powerful extremist competitor in Afghanistan. The section reassesses status and impact of current al-Qaeda, ISIS(-K) and the infamous Haqqani network from various angles and a global perspective. Most interestingly, some of the defining factors that account for these terrorist movements' resilience and longevity are submitted to analysis. Afghanistan may without doubt be considered as a crucial security-relevant hotspot, whose further development impacts the overall evolution of transnational terrorism.

Notes

1 Harari, Yuval Noah (2018). *21 Lessons for the 21st Century* (London: Vintage Press), p. 144.
2 Clausewitz, Carl von (1991): *Vom Kriege,* 19th Ed., Book VIII, Chap. 6B, p. 991, Clausewitz argued that war had "its own grammar, but not its own logic".
3 "War is, therefore, not only a true chameleon, because it changes its nature in some degree in each particular case, but it is also, as a whole, in relation to the predominant tendencies which are in it, a wonderful trinity, composed of the original violence of its elements, hatred and animosity, which may be looked upon as blind instinct [...]", Carl von Clausewitz, *On War*, ed. and trans. Michael Howard and Peter Paret (1984), ed. (Princeton: Princeton University Press), p. 89.
4 Institute for Economics & Peace (March 2022). *Global Terrorism Index 2022: Measuring the Impact of Terrorism*, Sydney, available at: https://www.visionofhumanity.org/wp-content/uploads/2022/03/GTI-2022-web_110522-1.pdf (accessed October 13, 2022).
5 Brown, Katherine E. (2022). "Transnational Terrorism", in: McGlinchey, Stephen, ed.: *International Relations* (Bristol: E-International Relations Publishing), p. 152.
6 Ibid p. 152.
7 Crenshaw, Martha (February 2020). "Rethinking Transnational Terrorism: An Integrated Approach", in: *Peaceworks (No. 158)* (Washington, D.C.: United States Institute of Peace), p. 4, available at: https://www.usip.org/publications/2020/02/rethinking-transnational-terrorism-integrated-approach (accessed October 13, 2022).
8 Ibid p.4.
9 Tan, Yeling (2019). *Shifting Strategies in a Fluid Geopolitical Context*, US-China Dialogue on Global Issues (Georgetown University), available at: https://uschinadialogue.georgetown.edu/responses/shifting-strategies-in-a-fluid-geopolitical-context (accessed October 13, 2022).
10 Schmitt, Carl (2004). *The Theory of the Partisan.* (Michigan: Michigan State University Press); Slomp, Gabriella (2005): "The Theory of the Partisan: Carl Schmitt's Neglected Legacy", in: *History of Political Thought*, pp. 502–19.
11 See Münkler, Herfried (2015). *Kriegssplitter. Die Evolution der Gewalt im 20. und 21. Jahrhundert* (Berlin: Rowohlt Berlin), p. 325.
12 Ibid., p. 325 (translation NS).
13 See Chapter 24, p. 240.
14 Silke, Andrew (2019). "The Study of Terrorism", in: Silke, Andrew ed.: *Routledge Handbook of Terrorism and Counterterrorism* (London/New York: Routledge), p. 6.

15 Baran, Zeyno (2005). "Fighting the War of Ideas", in: *Foreign Affairs*, Volume 84, Number 6, p. 68; Baran, Zeyno (2006): "Countering Ideological Support for Terrorism in Europe: Muslim Brotherhood and Hizb ut-Tahrir? Allies or Enemies?", in: *Connections: The Quarterly Journal*, Volume 5, Number 3, p. 24.

16 Koehler, Daniel (2016). "Right-Wing Extremism and Terrorism in Europe Current Developments and Issues for the Future", in: *PRISM*, Volume 6, Number 2, p. 85.

17 Görzig, Carolin (July 2020). Konjunkturen der Gewalt: Die Generation Z und die fünfte Welle des Terrorismus, in *FAZ*, available at: https://www.faz.net/aktuell/politik/die-gegenwart/die-generation-z-und-die-fuenfte-welle-des-terrorismus-16877108.html (accessed October 13, 2022).

18 Goertz, Stefan/Stockhammer, Nicolas (2021). *Corona-Maßnahmen-Gegner–Rezente Akteure, Ideologieelemente und ihr stochastisches Gewaltpotenzial*, EICTP Expert Paper, Vienna, available at: https://www.eictp.eu/wp-content/uploads/2022/01/FINAL_EICTP_Expert-Paper_Coronamassnahmengegner.pdf (accessed October 13, 2022).

19 Jenkins, John (February 2021). The German Debate on Islamism Continues (Policy Exchange), available at: https://policyexchange.org.uk/blogs/the-german-debate-on-islamism-continues/ (accessed October 13, 2022).

20 Europol TE-SAT (2020). "*EU Terrorism Situation and Trend Report*" (The Hague, Netherlands: Europol), p. 33.

21 For a general overview see: Victoroff, Jeff (February 2005): "The Mind of the Terrorist. A Review and Critique of Psychological Approaches", in: *Journal of Conflict Resolution*, Volume 49, Number 1, pp. 3–42.

22 https://carnegieendowment.org/2021/08/18/afghanistan-under-taliban-pub-85168 (accessed October 13, 2022).

23 Malkasian, Carter (March 2022). "The West Still Doesn't Understand the Taliban. How to Engage with the New Afghan Regime", Review Essay, in: *Foreign Affairs*, available at: https://www.foreignaffairs.com/reviews/review-essay/2022-03-21/west-still-doesnt-understand-taliban (accessed October 13, 2022).

PART I

The Strategic and Systemic Dimension of Terrorism

2

STRATEGIC TERRORISM

Herfried Münkler

The many types of terrorism are usually differentiated according to their political goals. Two main approaches can generally be identified: social revolutionary terrorism and ethnic separatist terrorism. Social revolutionary terrorism aims at revolutionizing a state's interior affairs and at re-shaping the social order in doing so; or, roughly speaking, it aims at overthrowing the powerful and bringing power to the hitherto powerless. Anarchist groups in Western Europe as well as Russian Narodniks were the first movements of this type of terrorism during the last decades of the 19th century.[1] A temporary end of this first social revolutionary terrorism came in the 1970s to 1980s, with representatives such as the Red Brigades in Italy, the Red Army Faction in Western Germany and the Weathermen in the United States. The beginnings of ethnic separatist terrorism lie in the 19th century as well, when attempts to push forward secessions from national minorities in the multinational great empires were made. This terrorism covered a broad range, at least in Europe, extending even to Basque separatists of ETA (Euskadi ta Askatasuna). Although both types of terrorism had their beginnings in Europe, they are today, however, emerging all over the world; and since social marginalization often goes hand in hand with national oppression, they have been interconnected over the years. For example, the Irish Republican Army (IRA) claimed the combination of social revolutionary motivations with ethnic-religious interests for itself and is therefore considered a hybrid, composed of social revolutionary and nationalist terrorism.

However, in the light of the political aims that are both extensive and only to be achieved over a long period of time, terrorism has no strategic but rather tactical functions in the cases of social revolutionary and ethnic separatist terrorism. Terrorism should serve as a starter for a process at the end of which is the formation of a new society, the establishment of a new state must be. Even if terrorism is not restricted to remain within the early stage of this political process, it only continues to play an accompanying role, rather than a critical one in the overall strategy. No new society or state can grow from terrorist attacks.

Terrorism embedded in an overall strategy to fundamentally change a society and/or to establish a new state primarily aims at spreading a message of power and capability of reaching an end goal, and that the fight for said goal has now begun. According to this self-description, terrorist attacks should overcome apathy and resignation within a society and show that the governing regime is not as powerful and invincible as many believe. The violence of terrorist attacks should prevent anyone from missing this message or its dissemination by the state apparatus. The more

DOI: 10.4324/9781003326373-3

spectacular the attack, the more sustainable the message. As soon as a political mass movement has emerged, or a guerrilla army has developed out of terrorist cells, the phase of terrorist attacks should end and the decisive battle for political power begins. "Using" terrorist attacks then becomes only an option when the battle is at risk of being lost – or at least this is the intention of social revolutionary and ethnic separatist terrorist strategies.

As a tactical element, terrorism is not only a way of communication but also a kind of provocation.[2] Terrorist attacks aim at forcing a state authority to perform certain actions that confirm the slogans of the attackers and at the same time the wrong social order the authority has hitherto defended. For instance, this happens when state authorities apply reinforced control and repression measures on any third party in whose interest terrorist groups allegedly carry out attacks; or it happens whenever violent actors and potential supporters (sympathizers) are separated from one another, which eventually leads to even more supporters sympathizing with violent actors. Terrorism can insofar be described as a particularly savvy tactic, which seeks to provoke reactions of the state by carrying out attacks.[3] Those reactions should ideally provide political legitimacy and increase the number of supporters – and it should be noted that the supporters also represent the logistic base of a group that commits acts of terrorism. In this way, terrorism reaches a strategic level that goes way beyond a mere opening tactic but it also remains a certain element of the political *grand strategy*. Terrorism as a tactic is used to provide legitimacy and logistics. A glance back at the history of the states founded since World War II shows how often state authorities under attack fell into the trap of terrorism.

The dual function of terrorism – on the one hand, as a message to "supposedly interested third parties" and as "a provocation of the attacked state authority" on the other – means that the defenders of the existing order are well-advised to maintain a de-escalating role as long as possible, in order to prevent terrorists from achieving their wanted effects and to substantially marginalize terrorist actors in public. In doing so, the attacks committed by terrorists can be categorized as accidents and criminal acts in general, or the attackers might even be provoked to escalate their actions even further, to which their "interested third parties" eventually fall victim. This might in turn lead to the entire legitimacy of terrorist groups being called into question and a growing dissociation of their third-party supporters.

At this stage of growing conflict two different strategies collide, both striving for political legitimacy, loyalty and support: the principles of violent acts on one side, and the intention of preventing an escalation of violence of the attacked party on the other. This strategic struggle is highly complex, as terrorists are at risk of either not reaching strong, communicative or provocative messages if their attacks are too small, or of failing totally if their attacks are too far-reaching and hurt relatives of their "third party "supporting group. The state apparatus must deal with challenges arising from its de-escalation measures, which can be understood as weakness by some parts of the population. This can produce a lot of pressure increased by the media and also growing demands of an "iron fist policy approach", which could in turn play into the hands of an escalation the terrorists have in fact been seeking. This shows that a battle of legitimacy is being fought, where both violence and the renunciation of using violence are tactical means. For both of the two opposing sides a tendency of the violence becoming more and more independent and tactical means becoming an end in themselves must be expected.

For example, in the case of a state this would be the demand for strong counter-measures against the real, potential or supposed supporters of terrorist groups, brought forward by parts of the media acting as the true (or alleged) voice of the people. A consequence thereof is a change of paradigm, meaning that counter-terrorism activities develop into combating crime and eventually into fighting wars. This development is a rather semantic or rhetorical one at the beginning, but slowly turns into a strategy. In the case of terrorists, this would be the groups' tendency of increasing the dimension of attacks even further, which means the excessive character of violence is put on a level with the effectiveness of attacks and violence campaigns become an end in itself. In other words: If the military arm of the movement becomes independent from the political arm, terrorism stops being a subordinate tactic and evolves into a strategy. This means that the initially dominant tactics of political communication and provocation diminish steadily through effective attacks and their escalating dynamics. This is exactly the trap social revolutionary and ethnic separatist groups tend to fall into over and over again, eventually leading to their failures. They abandon their grand strategy and thus their policy of committing attacks for tactical reasons. The opposing side under terrorist attacks, on the other hand, obviously turns such developments into a strategy in order to be able to defeat terrorism on this level, should it not have been able to counter and marginalize terrorism during its early phase.

All this is very different when it comes to the so-called *vigilante terrorism*, a third type of terrorism next to the aforementioned social revolutionary and ethnic separatist forms. The most prominent example for this type of terrorism is the violence against Black people committed by the Ku Klux Klan in the southern states of the United States during the 1950s and 1960s. Their violence aimed at preventing Black people from making use of their civic rights and to retain them even more strongly in their marginal social status. The term "vigilantism "derives from the Latin term *vigilia*, meaning "night watch". This terror-creating violence is applied to uphold an existing order, with the "night watchers "acting as its defenders. It is necessary to mention that terror as a means of creating fear and carrying out violent acts appears as a strategy and not as tactical means, because as soon as terror has managed to cause a certain behavior of endangered social groups, violence wins. Vigilante terror does not necessarily have a conservative function (as is the case with the Ku Klux Klan) but can serve as a mean of establishing new behavioral standards (as is the case with jihadist terrorism sometimes).

It can generally be noticed that jihadist terrorism, which has dominated our minds and debates throughout the past two decades, escapes this underlying threefold pattern.[4] This is due to the fact that it does pursue both social revolutionary and ethnic separatist goals, but also adopts a vigilante character (depending on the respective political constellations) and, on top of everything, is used for altering the global order, either by driving away foreign influences from the Islamic world – mainly al-Qaida's goal in their confrontation with the United States – or by establishing a caliphate/state that encompasses the entire Islamic community, as it was the declared goal of ISIS. With regard to the raised issue of the tactical and strategic dimension of terrorist action, Islamist terrorism holds a special position.[5]

One peculiarity of vigilante terrorism is the fact of the communicative function being almost fully identical with the strategic dimension of its ultimate objective. Any aforementioned obstacles and traps do not play a significant role for this type of terrorism. The closer vigilante terrorism comes to reaching its goals, the greater its horror appears to become. This can inversely be applied for the opposition, the party under terrorist attack: there are not many options available or counterproductive effects. The opposing side must rather try to prevent attacks by implementing legal and police means. This is possible within the crime paradigm. Consequently, the opposition has no relevant reason for differentiating between strategy and tactic. The special position of vigilante terrorism actually stems from its lacking necessity of having to win an "interested third party" over, as it primarily aims at intimidating certain groups within a society.

As social revolutionary and ethnic separatist terrorism have become less important in Europe throughout the past years, both jihadist and right-wing extremist terrorism are more and more stepping forward, mainly in their vigilante forms (in Europe at least). Following the reflections outlined in this paper, this means that local police and constitution protection authorities are dealing with terrorism as a strategy, and not with a complex mesh of tactics and strategy. This does not mean that such authorities are entitled to choose any available defense measures without safety concerns, as the defense of a liberal and pluralist order is at stake and this must not be undermined by the defense measures used. Temporary and socio-spatial limits can deprive the enemies of freedom of certain civil liberties, but they must not question the basic nature of the democratic, social order. Such measures taken must remain limited and provide comprehensible justifications. This simplification of actions does not only concern counter-measures by the state but also includes terrorist attacks. It can be observed that there are increasing attacks carried out by individuals who do not belong to a clandestine, hierarchically structured organization, but who become radicalized through the internet and, based on their internet-based knowledge, spring into action and commit attacks on their own.[6] This applies for both jihadist and right-wing extremist terrorism. The wide range of terrorists has become, as a consequence of this, very complex and unpredictable. Therefore, when dealing with vigilante terrorism the state has to face very different challenges compared to social revolutionary and ethnic separatist terrorism, as both act on diverse levels due to their far-reaching political goals, which often contradict each other. This is almost never the case with vigilante terrorism.

In its immediate effect, vigilante terrorism as a strategy-based phenomenon is more solid and has higher subversive potential than social revolutionary and ethnic separatist terrorism forms, which are both more generally aiming at certain long-term goals. Among other things this is evident from the fact that both forms manage largely without accompanying commands and explanations that clarify certain goals and purposes. Their violent attacks stand for themselves as messages. This is even more evident in far-right extremist terrorism than jihadist terrorism, which has recently turned into the greatest threat for the political order of Western democracies. This is also due to the fact that right-wing extremist terrorism shows the closest proximity between terrorist attacks and rampage killings, which increases the possibility of attacks and makes their execution less difficult.

The force of jihadist terrorist attacks results from the non-selectivity of its victims, since they do not require any complex or diligent selection.[7] Considering the Paris attacks in November 2015, the 2016 truck attack in Nice at the promenade, or the 2016 Berlin truck attack at the Christmas market, it is obvious that the attackers' main goal was to achieve the largest number of casualties and severely injured persons. Carrying out attacks using trucks, bombs and automatic weapons is not too complex both in planning and logistics, which is why we must expect them at any time. Such attacks – if carried out very frequently – are ideal for putting societies in a state of fear from which they are unable to free themselves by using police-related support but rather forcing them to rely on civic measures. In this regard, the Republican marches caused by the *Charlie Hebdo* shooting ("Je suis Charlie" slogans) are a recent example. This shows that this type of terrorism can cause permanent stress for any social order, and counter-measures may not be possible to be performed by specialized state institutions. Such type of terrorism distinguishes itself from social revolutionary and ethnic separatist terrorism by the simple fact that anyone feels threatened and that this feeling of undifferentiated danger is not without reason, whereas the other two forms aim at certain groups of people and professions.

Right-wing terrorism directed at certain groups of people, such as migrants from the global South or politicians of parties supportive of integration measures including their followers, must be clearly distinguished from this type of terrorism, even though its philosophy is based on vigilante principles. This terrorism directly targets the fundamental basis of democracy and liberal societies. Terrorist acts committed against migrants are tools for preventing their social integration, and terrorist acts against (local) politicians who try to push forward the integration of migrants can eventually lead to a slow death of democracies – because there is no one else willing to intervene and become engaged.

Dealing with the different forms of the use of violence predominantly aimed at certain mental consequences rather than physical ones (which is how you can describe terrorism in general) shows how the name "terrorism" represents a collective rather than a precise description of specific strategies and tactics. Additionally, authoritarian regimes such as Russia, Turkey or China use the term "terrorism" as an instrument to denounce political opponents, who can subsequently be excluded from the legal opposition framework within the political system. Therefore, renewed efforts to clarify the typology of anything "terrorism"-related are necessary.

Notes

1 Miller, Martin A. (2015): Entangled Terrorisms in Late Imperial Russia, in Randall D. Law (ed.): *The Routledge History of Terrorism*, Oxfordshire/NY: Routledge, pp. 92–107.
2 Cf. Waldmann, Peter (1998): *Terrorismus. Provokation der Macht*, München: Gerling Verlag.
3 Münkler, Herfried (2004): *The New Wars*, Cambridge: Polity Press, p. 99.
4 Juergensmeyer, Mark (2017): *Terror in the Mind of God: The Global Rise of Religious Violence*, Berkeley: University of California Press.
5 Hoffman, Bruce (2019): *Inside Terrorism*, New York, NY: Columbia University Press, p. 328.
6 Cf. Crenshaw, Martha/Pimlott, John (1997) (eds.): *Encyclopedia of World Terrorism*, 3 vols., Armonk: Sharpe.
7 Hoffman, Bruce (2019): *Inside Terrorism*, p. 313.

3

GEOPOLITICAL GAME CHANGERS AND THEIR IMPACT ON GLOBAL TERRORISM

Daniel Byman

Terrorism changes as politics, society, and technology change. The anarchist exploitation of the invention of dynamite at the turn of the century, the rise of jihadist violence in the 1980s with the return of political Islam, the collapse of left-wing terrorism with the end of the Cold War, the changing nature of state-sponsored terrorism as highly ideological regimes became more pragmatic, and the reinvigoration of white supremacist violence all mirrored transformations occurring in the world at large.

How might the global terrorism threat evolve in the years to come? This chapter focuses on eight geopolitical game changers that could reshape the terrorism and counterterrorism landscape. None of these are inevitable, or even necessarily likely, but they are plausible enough that counterterrorism analysts and government officials should consider their implications when designing programs for the future. The game changers include

1   the collapse of another Muslim-majority state and a resulting civil war;
2   a more substantial U.S. military withdrawal from the greater Middle East;
3   an increase in terrorism abroad driven by China's mistreatment of its Muslim population and its growing global role;
4   the reemergence of left-wing violence;
5   an increase in Russian sponsorship of terrorism;
6   a rise in Palestinian international terrorism;
7   a contested election in the United States where the leader plays on anti-government fears; and
8   a U.S. military campaign against Iran.

Muslim–Majority State Collapse

The collapse of another government in the greater Muslim world and any accompanying civil war would offer several opportunities for jihadist groups to grow stronger after several years of setbacks.[1] Not all civil wars produce international terrorism, of course. However, in the last decades, civil wars in Iraq, Libya, Mali, Nigeria, Somalia, Syria, and Yemen have proved fertile ground for terrorist groups, and strife in Afghanistan, Pakistan, the Philippines, and other countries also generated or worsened terrorism. Even more limited civil strife that produces ungoverned spaces in part of a country, as in the Sinai today, can worsen terrorism.

DOI: 10.4324/9781003326373-4

The civil wars have several dangerous effects. First, the collapse of the government offers an opportunity for small terrorist groups to operate and to expand their operations with little or no interference. Libya had largely defeated jihadist groups in the country before Qaddafi fell and civil war broke out in 2011, and Al Qaeda in Iraq was on the ropes before the 2011 civil war next door in Syria broke out. In these and other cases, small terrorist groups found a haven in which to operate, as the government was too weak and too focused on more immediate threats emanating from the civil war to fight terrorism.[2] Second, the war itself can be an inspiration and a magnet. Communities involved in local disputes may see the terrorist group as an ally and protector against the government, an occupying power, or a rival community, and even if they do not feel this way initially, the to and fro of attacks on the terrorist group and the community may drive them together.[3] Internationally, some wars become causes célèbres, attracting hundreds, thousands, or even tens of thousands of volunteers to fight – Syria attracted 40,000 foreigners, and conflicts in Afghanistan, Chechnya, and other countries attracted thousands of foreign recruits. These foreign fighters become more skilled and more radical in the war zone and can prove a terrorism danger to their home countries upon return.[4]

The civil wars also make Western counterterrorism more complex. One of the most common, and most effective, ways to fight international terrorism is to work with allied intelligence services to disrupt the group at hand. Despite uneven relations in the best of times, the United States cooperated with Libya, Syria, and other countries on counterterrorism when their governments were intact and had close partnerships with a host of other countries in the region. When a civil war breaks out, the government often cannot act against the group in question, and the brutality of the war makes even limited cooperation morally repellent and politically difficult.[5] This leaves the United States and its allies with the choice of allowing the terrorist group a high degree of operational freedom or intervening in a local war via drones or with their own forces. Limited intervention often has only limited impact, and carries the risk that a nationalist backlash against the intervention will aid the terrorists.

A More Substantial U.S. Withdrawal from the Greater Middle East and Africa

Since the 1990–1991 Gulf War, the United States has played a dominant military role in the Middle East, and after 9/11 the United States increased it security role in Africa. In addition to going to war with Iraq twice, the United States has intervened in Libya and Syria, confronted Iran with limited military strikes and broad sanctions, played a leading, if unsuccessful, role in negotiating peace between Israel and the Palestinians, and otherwise tried to shape the region. To this end, the United States has maintained a network of military bases throughout the Middle East, deploys tens of thousands of troops there, and has regularly made the region's problems a foreign policy priority.[6] Africa has traditionally been less important to U.S. interests, but as part of the struggle against terrorism, the United States has increased its role there, helping allies fight the affiliates of Al Qaeda and the Islamic State in Chad, Nigeria, Somalia, and other countries.

Under President Obama, and later under President Trump, the United States attempted to move away from the Middle East and Africa, shifting its focus to other regions (in the case of Obama) or calling for more retrenchment in general, but especially away from troubled regions like the Middle East (under Trump).[7] The Trump administration began downgrading the U.S. role in Africa, with little protest from Democrats, and repeatedly considered withdrawing U.S. forces from Syria and Afghanistan. Under President Biden, the United States has withdrawn forces from Afghanistan and, in general, has focused foreign policy on Europe and East Asia.

It is possible, indeed probable, that future administrations will continue to attempt to move the United States out of these troubled regions. European states, beset by their own problems at home and Russian aggression, are not eager to fill the resulting void.

Such a shift has both risks and benefits for counterterrorism. On the positive side, the removal of troops reduces a longstanding jihadist grievance that the United States (or France, or other Western countries) are occupying Muslim land and one that proved an effective rallying cry. However, the salience of this concern has declined as other issues, such as the sectarian war in Syria and the desire to live under an Islamic government, have risen to the fore as motivations.

A reduced U.S. presence would also come with less U.S. influence. U.S. security support and aid give the United States more pull with allies, and the allies recognize more counterterrorism cooperation is often the price of support. Because the United States plays an important role in training allied military forces to fight terrorism, the capacity of allied security forces may also suffer from a U.S. withdrawal even if their will is undiminished. In addition, in some conflicts, the United States has provided logistics, intelligence, and other forms of direct support to bolster the raw capacity of allies. Should this be lacking, allies will be less effective in fighting terrorism.

Perhaps most important, the lack of U.S. support for regional allies may lead to more strife. This could take several forms. First, a decline in U.S. support may make unrest more likely, as allied security forces are less able to protect the regime. Second, adversaries of U.S. allies might be more willing to meddle, and supporting rebel and terrorist groups is a time-honored means of gaining influence.[8] This may even occur among U.S. allies the bitter rivalry between Saudi Arabia and the UAE with Qatar has often played out with each side backing rival factions, such as in Libya. In the absence of a U.S. presence, groups may find state patrons as well as more operational space as a result. Allies are also less likely to coordinate their activities with one another even when they are not in direct opposition.

A Greater Terrorism Focus Associated with China[9]

China currently faces a limited terrorism threat, but this danger could increase as China's global presence expands. Beijing is concerned about the domestic threat posed by the East Turkestan Islamic Movement and the Turkestan Islamic Party, and as China has become an international economic and political actor, its nationals and facilities overseas have become potential targets of a range of terrorist groups. Some of those targeting China have international links, but the most common dangers are from disgruntled members of Muslim minorities in China who have only loose ties to established terrorist organizations like the Islamic State.

Despite facing at most a modest threat, Beijing considers terrorism a threat to the integrity and legitimacy of the Chinese state, not just a limited danger to individual citizens.[10] The result has been a series of massive crackdowns, with China now becoming the world's largest jailor of Muslims, particularly those of its Turkic ethnic minority.[11] In addition, Beijing has implemented a comprehensive surveillance system, enabling it to track its citizens both to stop crime and any political violence before it spreads.[12] A longer-term approach, and one that also provokes considerable resentment, is the use of policies designed to encourage cultural assimilation and internal migration to areas where Turkic minorities predominate. Over time, Chinese leaders hope, Muslim cultures will simply be swallowed up and dissipate, and, in the meantime, they must be carefully controlled.[13]

Counterterrorism, for now, is not an important shaper of China's foreign policy. China is not involved in wars against terrorist groups. In addition, Beijing has shown a willingness to work with an array of countries, such as Saudi Arabia, whose policies foster the spread of Salafi ideas that China opposes at home, as well as other countries like Iran that the United States considers a sponsor of terrorism. For now, neither the United States nor other countries have shown more than token concern for China's mass incarceration and surveillance programs. Indeed, China is even selling its surveillance methods to other countries.

Although China's current terrorism risk, both at home and internationally, is low, several factors may change this in future years. This change is particularly likely abroad as China becomes a global power and because China has less ability to repress dissent abroad than it does at home. The most likely risk is simply to Chinese nationals and commercial interests overseas. Many Chinese commercial initiatives are in countries like Nigeria and Pakistan that have a significant jihadist terrorist presence. Al Qaeda, the Islamic State, and like-minded groups have a presence in Southeast Asia, South Asia, Central Asia, and Africa where China is active, and governments are often weak or have limited reach. Chinese nationals may also prove victims of "collateral damage" from other attacks, targets of kidnapping for ransom, or other risks.

Because China is providing investment and may provide military support should its nationals be threatened, local partners may also try to exploit a terrorism problem to gain additional Chinese help. After 9/11, countries around the world realized they could play up any group with links to Al Qaeda to attract U.S. attention and support. Similarly, local actors may seek to play up the anti-Chinese nature of the violence, the level of the threat, or otherwise try to gain more from China.

The biggest question is whether China's gross mistreatment of its own Muslim community could become an issue among the world's Muslims. For now, important states like Saudi Arabia and Egypt have played down any criticism of China. In addition, the Gulf states increasingly look to China as the United States proves to be an erratic partner that openly discusses withdrawal from the Middle East. These governments usually exert considerable control over their domestic media environments and are otherwise able to shape or suppress discourse: part of the reason Syria became a jihadist *cause célèbre* was because Saudi Arabia, Qatar, and other countries opposed the Assad regime and allowed preachers and propagandists to whip up religious and sectarian hatred against it, even though this eventually benefited groups like the Islamic State. China historically has not been an important part of the Islamic world's discourse, but high-profile events there could change this, perhaps quite quickly. China is the world's largest jailor of Muslims, an atheistic and (nominally) communist regime, and an increasingly assertive international actor. Each of these characteristics could, in theory at least, put it in the crosshairs of a jihadist movement. Since its modern development following the anti-Soviet jihad in the 1980s, the movement has focused on supposed apostate regimes in the Muslim world, sectarian rivalries with Shiite Muslims and their Iranian champion, and non-Muslim powers like Russia, Israel, India, and the United States.[14] China might be next.

The scale of China's mistreatment has begun to attract attention from jihadist groups. Some groups have dozens or more Uighur members, as well as many others from Central Asia or other areas where China is increasingly present and ascendant. Thus, through person-to-person contact, they have individuals who are likely to press an anti-Chinese agenda and otherwise publicize China's abuses. Regional regimes may also be more critical. Turkey's leader, Recep Tayyip Erdoğan, seeks more influence in Turkish-populated areas of Central Asia. His government blasted China's actions as "a great shame for humanity."[15] He may continue to try to keep this on the global agenda in order to expand his own influence. Other countries and leaders may follow suit, using Chinese abuses not only to gain more influence themselves but also to undercut rivals that might move close to China: Saudi Arabia, for example, is locked in a bitter rivalry with both Iran and Qatar, and it is easy to imagine any of these countries seizing on another's relationship with China to criticize their adversary.

Much depends on whether terrorists can successfully provoke China and whether China's response further grabs the attention of terrorists. Terrorism is often likened to theater, with hostage-taking, beheadings, and other dramatic forms of violence designed to grab media attention and thus help the terrorists further put themselves on the global agenda. In an age of social media, terrorists do not need coverage from outside media sources or even a sophisticated media capacity of their own; rather they can use existing commercial platforms to publicize issues related to their cause. Theatrical violence against China may create popular anger and force the government to respond strongly. China's response might create a cycle, where any violence or high-profile activity makes China more of an enemy and raises it on the terrorists' priorities list. In addition, the death of Chinese workers or others may lead China to increase cooperation with the regime in charge, deploy its own forces, or otherwise increase its global security role, and thus its risk of a terrorism reaction.

The Reemergence of Left-Wing Violence

During much of the Cold War, Marxist and other left-wing groups such as the Red Brigades and the Popular Front for the Liberation of Palestine played an important, and often leading, role in international terrorism, fomenting unrest in Europe, Africa, Latin America, and other regions. In addition, they often professed loyalty to Moscow or Beijing, adding to geopolitical tensions. When the Soviet Union collapsed and Beijing moved away from its revolutionary foreign policy, many of these leftist groups collapsed or withered. The withdrawal of foreign financial and logistical support and the discrediting of Marxist ideology seemed like a death blow.

A number of issues have emerged that could reinvigorate the violent left, although it is not likely to approach its strength during the Cold War. The growing inequality within countries such as the United States is one such issue, as are concerns about the environment and racial justice. Perhaps even more important, white supremacist and other right-wing violence is growing, and the reaction to that may trigger leftist violence. Movements like Antifa in the United States are not terrorist groups, but they do use violence in reaction to right-wing violence, and imagining further radicalization is not difficult.[16]

The growth of and response to left-wing violence could further polarize politics. A cycle may develop as right-wing groups respond to the violence. If the state cracks down on left-wing violence without a similar crackdown on the right, it will be accused of bias and siding with conservative forces.

Russia Increases Its Sponsorship of Terrorism

Russia has killed dissidents in multiple countries, which is a form of international terrorism in that it involves violent activity outside Russia, a political motive, and a broader goal of intimidating other dissidents. In Syria, Russian military forces have worked closely with the Lebanese Hezbollah, which the United States has long described as one of the world's leading terrorist groups, to fight the enemies of the Assad regime.[17] In Ukraine, Russia has backed anti-regime separatist militias with money, training, weapons, and direct military support, and some of these groups have used violence against civilians notably the downing in 2014 of a Malaysian commercial flight that killed all 298 people aboard.[18] Russia also directly and indirectly aids or tries to inspire an array of white supremacist and other right-wing groups and individual terrorists in Europe and the United States. These efforts in the West serve Moscow's goal of dividing and discrediting Western governments and societies.[19]

For the most part, such efforts have worked for Moscow, which might increase its support for and use of terrorism or at least continue to use it, especially as its confrontation with the United States and its allies has grown more intense in the aftermath of the February 2022 invasion of Ukraine. Relative to its global aspirations, Moscow is weak militarily and economically, and ties to terrorist groups give it greater reach and influence than it would have otherwise. In addition, the Putin regime is obsessed with silencing dissidents, and it has instilled fear in many potential critics. In the future, Moscow could provide an array of clandestine support to groups operating in the former Soviet states or Europe as a whole, greatly increasing their capacity.

A Rise in Palestinian Terrorism

The Arab-Israeli and Palestinian-Israeli disputes produced numerous international terrorist groups, such as Black September, Hamas, and the Popular Front for the Liberation of Palestine. Some of these groups are now defunct, while others have moved away from terrorism, especially international terrorism. Groups like Hamas and Palestine Islamic Jihad, which still use terrorism, largely do so in the West Bank, Gaza Strip, and Israel proper, keeping the violence localized.

Broader Palestinian terrorism that targets Israel internationally or the United States or other non-Israeli targets could resume for several reasons. Important Palestinian organizations like Fatah abandoned terrorism in favor of peace negotiations in the late 1980s, but if the peaceful path is no longer viable, the argument for violence becomes stronger. The Israeli-Palestinian peace talks have sputtered for over a decade and observers on both sides see them as dead.[20] Indeed, much of the Arab world seems to be ignoring the Palestinian problem, as evidenced by the 2020 Abraham Accords – a peace agreement between Israel and the UAE and Bahrain that eventually included Morocco and Sudan – which went forward despite the lack of progress on the Palestinian issue. Although any violence is likely to continue to focus on Israeli targets in the West Bank and perhaps Israel itself, attacking non-Israeli targets is a particularly high-profile way to grab the world's attention. In the past, groups like the PFLP argued that international attacks were necessary for the Palestinian issue to be on the world's agenda, even if it produced negative publicity in the short-term.

Disputes within the Palestinian nationalist community may also increase the incentives for international terrorist attacks. During the 1970s and 1980s, terrorist attacks on Israel were a way for Palestinian groups to outbid their rivals, attract recruits to their group, and otherwise compete. When the Second Intifada raged from 2000 to 2005, attacks on Israel proved the dedication of the groups to recruits and funders and helped them compete for supremacy in the Palestinian nationalist movement.[21] Mahmoud Abbas, the head of the Palestinian Authority and leader of the peace camp, cooperates with Israel on counterterrorism and has long been engaged in a bitter rivalry with Hamas. Born in 1935, Abbas' leadership may end soon, and there is no clear successor. New leaders may be reluctant to cooperate with Israel when the political track for peace and a Palestinian state does not appear viable. So, there may be rivalries within Abbas' faction and between it and groups like Hamas, all exacerbated by the political weakness of the peace camp.

Regional political trends may also increase terrorism related to the Palestinian conflict. Iran has close ties to the Lebanese Hezbollah and Palestine Islamic Jihad and also relations with Hamas. Tehran is ideologically committed to Israel's destruction. In addition, because Iran's regional enemies like the UAE are allying with Israel, Iran may seek to foment unrest, highlighting Palestinian issues and, in so doing, discrediting its rivals. High-profile Israeli responses may increase the political impact of Palestinian terrorism in the Arab and Muslim worlds.

A Contested Election Where the Leader Plays on Anti-Government Fears

President Trump's response to his loss at the polls in 2020 should give us pause when it comes to the interplay of right-wing terrorism and elections. Trump incited a crowd to contest the results, leading to the storming of the U.S. Capitol on January 6, 2020. This occurred with apparent co-ordination by groups like the Proud Boys and the Oathkeepers, along with many less-organized supporters.

After a future election defeat in 2024, one could imagine President Trump or a like-minded candidate claiming that "people say" voting machines were fixed, Democrats suppressed Republican ballots, or other absurd statements as a way to justify their defeat. Trump is also likely to try to discredit any opponent. Even if a future Republican nominee is more gracious than President Trump, many of his or her supporters may see the new administration as illegitimate from the start. Add such discrediting of his successor to conspiracy theories about a stolen election and you have a powerful cocktail of righteous anger and potential violence.

In contrast to jihadists, right-wing terrorists draw on a significant number of Americans who share at least some of their views. Jihadists in the United States are not only few in number, but their ideas have little or no support among the broader American Muslim community. In contrast, issues Americans consider to be right-wing, such as skepticism of the federal government, gun rights, and so on, are often championed by legitimate, peaceful, organizations. Almost half of Republicans see immigrants as a burden on America, and half of Americans see Muslims as outside the mainstream of American society.[22] A 2017 poll found that 14 percent of Americans hold anti-Semitic (though not necessarily violent) views, up from 10 percent in 2015.[23] Far more Americans are accepting of Jews, but this number means that almost 50 million Americans hold hateful views – hardly a fringe belief. Many Americans hold even more extreme racist views. A poll found 4 percent of Americans agree with the white supremacy movement, almost 15 million people.[24] More than half of Republicans believe the 2020 election was stolen.[25] With the encouragement of senior leaders like President Trump, these hateful views are more likely to produce violence.

Because of these ties to the mainstream, right-wing violence has far more potential political impact than does jihadist violence. Especially when combined with attempts to delegitimize the election, this can undermine faith in U.S. institutions. This will make domestic counterterrorism more difficult, as at least some communities will be less likely to work with the police and FBI to identify extremists in their midst. In addition, it would make efforts by technology and financial firms to repress violent voices more difficult politically, as they would be seen as taking sides in a political dispute rather than fighting violence.[26]

A Military Campaign against Iran

Under President Trump, the United States rejected the nuclear deal forged by President Obama, killed the leader of the Islamic Republican Guard Corps, Qasem Suleimani, and tried to increase economic pressure on Iran. In addition, close regional allies such as Israel, Saudi Arabia, and the UAE have pressed for America to take a tough stance on Iran. So far, this has not boiled over into outright war, although Iranian proxies continue to target U.S. forces in Iraq and threaten regional peace. President Biden is trying to renegotiate the Iran nuclear deal, but its fate remains uncertain as of April 2022.

Should a confrontation occur over continued Iranian nuclear activity or another issue, Iran is likely to turn to terrorism to strike back at the United States, in part because it has few other options. Tehran's military is weak, and its economy is in freefall. The regime's legitimacy is battered by poor economic performance, corruption, a lack of fair elections, and a disastrous response to the COVID-19 epidemic. On the other hand, Iran has a vast network of proxies in Afghanistan, Iraq, Syria, and Yemen as well as ties to militants in other countries.[27]

Because Iran's network is regional, its most likely responses will be regional. This might involve attacking U.S. forces in Afghanistan and especially Iraq, where Iran's proxies are strongest. It also might mean using terrorism against foes like Saudi Arabia and the UAE. Striking Israel is a constant possibility as Iran may try to use such attacks to highlight its resistance credentials to Muslims while casting its enemies as the allies of the unpopular Jewish state. Terrorism against the U.S. homeland or against European targets is likely to be held in reserve as a deterrent, but it could occur if a limited military conflict starts to threaten the regime's hold on power.

In addition to any deaths from terrorism itself, the potential back and forth between terrorist acts and U.S. and allied military responses could fuel a broader war. Depending on the political circumstances in Iran and in the target countries, leaders may feel unable to back down, with dangerous escalation as a result.

Conclusions

The terrorism threat is constantly evolving, and the contingencies noted above are only a few possible ways in which the danger might change. One of the biggest unknowns is technological: new forms of communication, advances in synthetic biology and artificial intelligence, or the spread of accessible weapons technologies all could increase the terrorist threat in numerous ways. Some technological changes might also help counterterrorism: China, for example, has used improvements in biometrics and artificial intelligence to strengthen its police state and, in so doing, reduce any danger from Muslim militancy (while also crushing legitimate resistance of all sorts).

The picture is further complicated by the poor relations among the great powers and the uncertainty regarding U.S. foreign policy in particular. Growing rivalries, or fluctuations in U.S. policy, could change the conditions for both terrorist groups and their supporters.

Effective counterterrorism will be vital for keeping the danger limited. Policing, intelligence liaison, and other instruments are necessary to disrupt terrorist networks and limit their overall capacity. So too is gaining the support of technology and financial companies as well as civil society to ensure that terrorists cannot easily recruit, communicate, raise money, or gain broader support. Too harsh a response, in contrast, can polarize society, alienate minority groups, and otherwise create fertile ground for the terrorists. The last decade saw both impressive success and dramatic failures, and it is likely that the record in the years to come will also prove mixed.

Notes

1 For data on the setbacks, see START, "Global Terrorism Overview: Terrorism in 2019" (July 2020), https://www.start.umd.edu/pubs/START_GTD_GlobalTerrorismOverview2019_July2020.pdf.
2 Jessica A. Stanton, "Terrorism in the Context of Civil War," *The Journal of Politics* 75, no. 4 (2013): 1009-1022.
3 David Kilcullen, *The Accidental Guerrilla: Fighting Small Wars in the Midst of a Big One* (Oxford University Press, 2011).
4 Daniel Byman, *Road Warriors: Foreign Fighters in the Armies of Jihad* (Oxford University Press, 2019); Thomas Hegghammer, "Should I stay or should I go? Explaining variation in Western jihadists' choice between domestic and foreign fighting," *American Political Science Review* 107, no. 1 (2013): 1-15.
5 Daniel Byman, "The Intelligence War on Terrorism," *Intelligence and National Security* 29, no. 6 (2014): 837-863.

6 Rashaan Ayesh, "Where U.S. Troops and Military Assets are Deployed in the Middle East," *Axios*, January 8, 2020, https://www.axios.com/where-us-troops-deployed-middle-east-5e96fdb2-c7ba-4f26-90b4-7bf452f83847.html; For base locations as of 2020, see "U.S. Bases in the Middle East," American Security Project, last modified January 8, 2020, https://www.americansecurityproject.org/national-security-strategy/u-s-bases-in-the-middle-east/.

7 For Obama's thinking, see Jeffrey Goldberg, "The Obama Doctrine," *The Atlantic*, April 2016, https://www.theatlantic.com/magazine/archive/2016/04/the-obama-doctrine/471525/; Kenneth M. Pollack, "Mid East Update: Kenneth M. Pollack on the Region in the Era of Trump," interview by Albert Stern, *Jewish Federation of the Berkshires*, November 4, 2019, https://www.jewishberkshires.org/community-events/berkshire-jewish-voice/berkshire-jewish-voice-highlights/kenneth-m-pollack-on-the-regions-upheavals-in-the-era-of-trump

8 Daniel Byman, *Deadly Connections: States that Sponsor Terrorism* (Cambridge University Press, 2005).

9 This section draws on my longer work with Israa Saber. See Daniel Byman and Israa Saber, "Is China Prepared for Global Terrorism? Xinjiang and Beyond" (Washington, DC: The Brookings Institution, September 2019), https://www.brookings.edu/research/is-china-prepared-for-global-terrorism/

10 Sheena Chestnut Greitens, Myunghee Lee, and Emir Yazici. "Counterterrorism and preventive repression: China's changing strategy in Xinjiang." *International Security* 44.3 (2019): 9-47.

11 Ben Blanchard, "China says 13,000 'terrorists' arrested in Xinjiang since 2014," *Reuters*, March 17, 2019, https://www.reuters.com/article/us-china-xinjiang/china-says-13000-terrorists-arrested-in-xinjiang-since-2014-idUSKCN1QZ08T.

12 Philip Wen and Olzhas Auyezov, "Tracking China's Muslim Gulag," *Reuters*, November 29, 2018, https://www.reuters.com/investigates/special-report/muslims-camps-china/.

13 For a longer examination, see Sheena Chestnut Greitens, Myunghee Lee, and Emir Yazici, "Counterterrorism and Preventive Repression: China's Changing Strategy in Xinjiang," *International Security* 44, no. 3 (2020): 9-47.

14 Daniel Byman, *Al Qaeda, the Islamic State, and the Global Jihadist Movement: What Everyone Needs to Know* (Oxford, 2015).

15 Matthew Bell, "Turkey Changes Its Tune On China's Crackdown Against Muslims," *The World*, February 14, 2019, https://www.pri.org/stories/2019-02-14/turkey-changes-its-tune-chinas-crackdown-against-muslims.

16 Michael Kenney and Colin Clarke, "What Antifa Is, What It Isn't, and Why It Matters," *War on the Rocks*, June 23, 2020, https://warontherocks.com/2020/06/what-antifa-is-what-it-isnt-and-why-it-matters/.

17 For my thoughts, see Shelby Butt and Daniel Byman. "Right-wing extremism: The Russian connection." *Survival* 62.2 (2020): 137-152.
Alexander Corbeil, "Russia is Learning About Hezbollah," *Sada* (blog), Carnegie Endowment for International Peace, January 11, 2017, https://carnegieendowment.org/sada/67651.

18 "Ukraine Conflict: Russia Accused of Terrorism and Discrimination at ICJ," *BBC News*, March 6, 2017, https://www.bbc.com/news/world-europe-39177504.

19 Shelby Butt and Daniel Byman, "Right-wing Extremism: The Russian Connection." *Survival* 62, no. 2 (2020): 137-152. This essay also draws on Daniel Byman, "Russia is a State Sponsor of Terrorism -- But Don't Treat it That Way," *Lawfare Blog*, April 30, 2018, https://www.lawfareblog.com/russia-is-state-sponsor-terrorism-but-dont-treat-that-way.

20 Khaled Elgindy, "The Israeli-Palestinian Peace Process is Dead. An Expert Explains Why," interview by Alexia Underwood, *Vox*, April 15, 2019, https://www.vox.com/world/2019/4/15/18306224/palestinians-israel-khaled-elgindy-blind-spot.

21 Mia M. Bloom, "Palestinian Suicide Bombing: Public Support, Market Share, and Outbidding," *Political Science Quarterly* 119, no. 1 (2004): 61-88.

22 Kristen Bialik, "State of the Union 2019: How Americans See Major National Issues," *Fact Tank* (blog), Pew Research Center, February 4, 2019, https://www.pewresearch.org/fact-tank/2019/02/04/state-of-the-union-2019-how-americans-see-major-national-issues/; "How the U.S. General Public Views Muslims and Islam," Pew Research Center, July 26, 2017, https://www.pewforum.org/2017/07/26/how-the-u-s-general-public-views-muslims-and-islam/.

23 "14 Percent of Americans Hold Anti-Semitic Views, 52 Percent Concerned About Violence Against Jews ADL Polls Find," *Jewish Telegraphic Agency*, April 6, 2017, https://www.jta.org/2017/04/06/united-states/few-americans-hold-anti-semitic-views-but-most-concerned-about-violence-against-jews-poll-finds.

24 C. K. "Racist Behaviour is Declining in America," *The Economist*, September 1, 2017, https://www.economist.com/democracy-in-america/2017/09/01/racist-behaviour-is-declining-in-america.

25 Lane Cuthbert and Alexander Theodoridis, "Do Republicans Really Believe Trump Won the 2020 Election?" *Washington Post,* January 7, 2022, https://www.washingtonpost.com/politics/2022/01/07/republicans-big-lie-trump/

26 Jessica Guynn, "Conservatives accuse Twitter of liberal Bias," *USA Today,* November 18, 2016, https://www.usatoday.com/story/tech/news/2016/11/18/conservatives-accuse-twitter-of-liberal-bias/94037802/

27 Seth G. Jones, "War by Proxy: Iran's Growing Footprint in the Middle East," (Washington, DC: Center for Strategic and International Studies, March 11, 2019), https://www.csis.org/war-by-proxy.

4

THE SYSTEMIC DIMENSION OF JIHADIST VIOLENCE

A Root Cause Analysis of Jihadist Terrorism

Alex P. Schmid

Introduction

Since the Peace of Westphalia (1648), the international system increasingly consists of states (193 sovereign states by 2019 in the United Nations), some of them based on ethnicity, others based on religion and yet others on other characteristics like a common history or a particular geographic territory. The system is not stable but held together by normative rules agreed upon in international treaties and, more pragmatically, by temporary coalitions of member states which seek to stabilise it by creating balances of power against unilateral attempts to establish hegemony. Much of the world's territorial history can be viewed as a succession of competing rising and falling great and not so great powers. Some of the more successful ones expanded mainly over land and others mainly overseas and a few expanded in both ways to form empires, based on military might, religious missionary zeal, commercial or technological superiority or a combination of such factors. The term colonialism has been associated mainly with the expansion of European states since 1492 (Spain, Portugal, England, France, Belgium, the Netherlands, Germany, Italy, etc.). Land-based expansion has historically been more frequent but has politically received less condemnation, perhaps because it was often more incremental and linked to greater population settlements.

A major example of the land-based type is the expansion of Islam between the conquest of Mecca by Mohammad in 629 and the abolition of the caliphate in 1924. The gradual decline and ultimate rapid final fall of the last Islamic empire – the one of the Ottomans (1299–1922) – has been experienced as a humiliation by many Muslims and contrasted to the rapid rise under the first Caliphs after Prophet Mohammed himself had united the tribes on the Arab peninsula.[1]

To understand the root cause of contemporary jihadist terrorism, one has to look at the distant past. Many Muslims have seen the rapid military expansion of early Islam as an expression of a divine favour. After the death of the Prophet in 632, one of his successors, Caliph Omar, conquered Damascus in 635, Jerusalem in 637, Egypt in 641, and Iran and Azerbaijan in 643. After Omar's death in 644, subsequent Caliphs continued this series of conquests. By 670, North Africa had been conquered and in 677 Constantinople was besieged (but it was taken only much later by Mehmed the Conqueror). By 711, Andalusia had been conquered. One hundred years after the death of the Prophet, Islamic rule stretched from Spain to China. Muslim soldiers were

DOI: 10.4324/9781003326373-5

also trying to advance over the Pyrenees into France, but Karl Martell managed to stop them in 732 in the battles of Tours and Poitier. In the Islamic tradition, these early conquests came to be regarded as the "quintessential jihads".[2]

There was an attempt by Christians, initiated mainly from France, to undo one of these conquests. In November 1095, Pope Urban II had called for a military campaign (much later termed "crusade") to liberate the Holy Land. It resulted in the reconquest of Jerusalem in July 1099. However, Jerusalem was lost again in 1187 to Saladin and Islamic rulers pushed back Christian rulers, conquering in 1453 Constantinople and renaming it Istanbul. Subsequently Muslim soldiers were advancing into the Balkans, and then under Suleiman the Magnificent (who ruled from 1520 to 1566) into Ukraine and Hungary. Twice, in 1529 and 1683, Ottoman armies stood at the gates of Vienna.[3] By that time, Islam had also reached deep into Sub-Saharan Africa, into Central and South West Asia and reached as far east as the southern Philippines. Although the hold of Islam over its more distant conquests started to weaken in the 18th century and although in the 19th century Christian countries like Greece (1832), Serbia (1878) and Bulgaria (1908) regained their freedom, the religion of Islam and a nominal Caliphate outlived the loss of political control until 1924 when the institution of the Caliphate was abolished by Mustafa Kemal Atatürk who had replaced the last Sultan in 1922 when becoming president of the secular republic of Turkey.[4]

By the end of World War I, the Caliphate had been no more than a symbol of Islamic unity. It had, in fact, ceased to be a *political* institution with the Mongol conquest of Baghdad in 1258, 626 years after the death of the Prophet for which Caliphs (khalifah = successor) had to be found after his death. Nonetheless, the idea of a Caliphate as a political-religious dominion uniting the Muslim community, not only in religious but also in political terms lingered on. And its formal abolishment in March 1924 was, and continues to be, seen by many as a painful break with a glorious history. Yet, as a belief system, Islam is still strong and in fact growing.

Islam Today

Today, Islam has nearly 1,600,000,000 believers in seven geographic spheres. In the words of Ed Husain, author of *The House of Islam*[5]:

(i) The first is the Arabic-speaking domain from Iraq to Mauritania, home of approximately 400 million Muslims. (...)

(ii) The Persian sphere, consisting of modern-day Iran, Afghanistan and Tajikistan, is the second zone of the House of Islam. Here, the 100-million-strong population speaks Farsi, Dari or Tajik – different dialects of the same language (...)

(iii) Sub-Saharan Africa, home to some 250 million Muslims, is the third zone.

(iv) The fourth sphere is the Indian subcontinent (...) Today, Pakistan, India, Bangladesh, Burma, Nepal and Sri Lanka make up this domain, which has...around 400 million. (...)

(v) The fifth concentration is Turkic. It spans around 170 million Muslims who speak mostly Turkish, but also include others of backgrounds such as Azeri, Chechens, Chinese Uighur, Uzbek, Kirghiz and Turkmen. (...)

(vi) Sixth is the Malay area of South East Asia, which consists of Indonesia, Malaysia, Brunei, and sizeable minorities in Thailand and the Philippines. More than 200 million Muslims live here. (..)

(vii) The seventh and final home for Muslims is in the West. Roughly 60 million of today's Muslims live in the West as minorities and new immigrant communities.....

Today, 80%of all Muslims live outside the Arab world and as many as one in five human be-ings are considered Muslims. With their higher fertility rate, Muslims might, if present trends continue, number 3,000,000,000 by 2050.[6] However, their demographic strength is not matched by similar political, economic, cultural or military strength.

Yet religion is very much alive in Muslim-majority countries, much more than Christianity in those countries that were not so recently considering themselves Christian nations. The main push factor behind the recent spread of a literalist version of Islam has been Saudi Arabia, which came into existence in 1932 and regards itself as an Islamic state and calls the Quran its constitu-tion. In more than five decades the Saudi Kingdom has spent an estimated $200 billion of its oil money on strengthening Wahhabism – its particular version of Salafism – in the world.[7] It had also supported, together with the United States and the Afghan Mujahideen resistance against the Soviet occupation (1979–1989).

The withdrawal of Soviet troops from Afghanistan under President Mikhail Gorbachev was portrayed by Arab foreign fighters who had joined the resistance of local mujahedeen as a victory over one of the two superpowers of the Cold War period, encouraging some of them to challenge the other remaining superpower, America, in its wake. Ten years before, in 1979, a Shi'ite theocracy had come to power in Iran. It has also challenged the United States and, in recent years, managed to extend its influence into Iraq, Syria, Lebanon and Yemen, while secretly seeking to become a nuclear power threatening Israel and Saudi Arabia – two Western allies. A further threat to the West arose in Syria and Iraq when the so-called Islamic State, an ultra-militant Sunni jihadist movement, strengthened by former intelligence and military ele-ments of Saddam Hussein's deposed regime, sought to resurrect the institution of the Caliphate in mid-2014. This attempt by the Islamic State was greeted with enthusiasm by some of the world's 1.6 billion Muslims – especially by many of the 50 million Salafists among them – and led to an influx of some 42,000 foreign fighters from more than 80 countries before this self-proclaimed Caliphate was militarily defeated as a coherent territorial unit in 2018 by a coalition of more than 60 states, led by the United States.

The American-British intervention in Iraq to overthrow Saddam Hussein in 2003 and the proxy wars in Syria by Turkey, Saudi Arabia, Iran, Russia and some Western states as well after 2011 have destabilised an already volatile region, producing millions of refugees, dozens of non-state armed groups of which most are religiously inspired. The hostility between Sunnis and Shi'ites, the rivalry between Iran and Saudi Arabia, the vying for influence by Russia and the United States, the Israeli-Palestinian conflict, and the concern of the international community about the safety of shipping in a region that supplies much of the world's oil and gas and the lack of significant economic development in much of the Middle East combined with the repressive-ness of most of its regimes are some of the main factors that form a backdrop to the rise of Salafi Jihadism since the end of the Cold War.

While other regions, notably China but also India, have become world players, Muslim countries – except those lucky few who have enough oil and gas to export – have played no major role in recent world history and, given the declining role of fossil fuels in the world economy, are unlikely to catch up with other world regions due to the generally low levels of education of their populations and the lack of industrial or technological infrastructures. Poverty is widespread, the number of young people unable to find adequate gainful employment is very high, as is corrup-tion and inequality. Good governance is largely absent, as are widespread state welfare provisions in all but a few oil-rich states. All these factors combine to make armed rebellion under the ban-ner of Islamist jihad a tempting option. This option to break this blocked development had been placed on the table long before 9/11.

Jihad as Instrument to (Re-)Gain Political Power for Islam

Ninety years had passed between the abolition of the Caliphate by Mustafa Kemal Atatürk (1881–1938) and its attempted resurrection by Abu Bakr al-Baghdadi in mid-2014. However, the idea to restore Muslim power first came to the fore only four years after the abolition of the Caliphate in 1924. A semi-secret society – the Muslim Brotherhood (MB – "al-Ikhwan al-Muslimeen") – had been set up in March 1928 in Egypt by Hassan al Banna (1906–1949), a school teacher. He propagated *jihad* as an instrument to restore Islam's past glory, summarizing the mission of the MB in the formula: "Allah is our objective, the Qur'an is our constitution, the Prophet is our leader, jihad is our path, and death in the name of Allah is our goal".[8] He even managed to shorten this battle cry into "Islam is the solution"("*Al-Islam huwa al-hall*").[9] But what was the problem? Partly it was colonialism – Great Britain still controlled directly (until 1956) the Suez Canal and, indirectly, much of Egypt's domestic politics, although the country had nominally gained independence in 1922. Next to colonialism, Western secularism had been seen as a threat ever since Napoleon Bonaparte had arrived in Alexandria in 1798, bringing to Egypt ideas from the French revolution. Most of all, however, the problem was that while Muslims consider Islam to be the last and the best of all religions, most followers of Islam did generally less well than the infidels in the world – a humiliating experience hurting the dignity of many Muslims.

In 1928, the Muslim Brotherhood begun to gain ground in Egypt, at a time when Fascism and National-Socialism were gaining strength in Europe. Like Mussolini and Hitler, Hassan al-Banna created within the Muslim Brotherhood a paramilitary organisation (*Kata'ib* – "*battalions*")[10] that served to protect him and attack his enemies. It would later assassinate Nokrashy Pasha, the Egyptian Prime Minister. In response Hassan al Banna was killed by the Egyptian secret police in 1949. However, his organisation, numbering some two million members by the time it was outlawed in Egypt in December 1948, lives on and today it has an overt or covert presence in more than seventy countries.[11] Many, if not most, of recent and present jihadist leaders have passed through the Muslim Brotherhood organisation. After al-Banna's assassination, another Egyptian member of the Muslim Brotherhood, Sayyf Qutb (1906–1966), author of a 30-volumes commentary on the Qur'an, carried the torch of jihad further. His hanging by President Nasser in 1966 made him a martyr, amplifying the reach of his teachings. At the time of Qutb's death some Arab rulers still used nationalism, and to some extent socialism, as their ideological tools. The turn towards religion came only in 1979, most decidedly in Iran, a non-Arab Muslim country that had been under American control ever since the CIA and British MI6 staged a coup in 1953, forcing Iran's liberal president Mohammad Mosaddegh to resign and making the Shah their willing tool.

Today, most of the countries in the Middle East and North Africa are ruled by autocrats – kings or generals who at best pay lip service to some rudimentary democratic principles. These rulers tend to present themselves as sole bulwark against the rise to power of jihadists, after having successfully repressed (except in Tunisia) the rise of the democratic forces of the Arab Spring of 2011. With no choice between repressive dictatorships and extremist jihadist groups, many Muslims see no future in their homelands. A recent Gallup poll held in 120 countries asked people whether they want to emigrate; more than 30%of the respondents in the Middle East and Africa expressed such a wish.[12] Their desired destinations are, however, not other Muslim countries but Western democracies. However, since 2015 when more than one million refugees arrived in Western Europe from Syria and other Muslim countries, Western democracies have become much less than welcoming, partly due to the cultural baggage many of these Muslims bring with them, including their disrespect for infidels and their treatment of women as second class people.

Today, most of the more than 70 million refugees and internally displaced persons hail from Muslim-majority countries.[13] In Europe, in response to this influx, right-wing populist parties have booked electoral gains with their nationalist and xenophobic slogans. After the financial crisis and a worldwide recession originating in the United States in 2008, liberal democracies have come under attack for other reasons as well: inequality has grown sharply and the welfare state has come under stress as the very rich manage to hide much of their income and wealth in foreign tax shelters. The link between democracy and economic growth by means of social market capitalism, taken for granted in Europe for much of the post-World War II period, has become strained. Outside Europe liberal democracy is no longer seen as a model for development since the authoritarian Communist Party of China, with an aggressive authoritarian model of mercantile state capitalism has outperformed other economies and replaced Russia as the only other superpower able to successfully challenge the United States. While also home to a large Muslim population, China has managed to suppress Islamist challenges with draconian policies of forced re-education of more than a million mostly Uighur Muslims in closed camps. In defence of these drastic de-radicalisation measures, the Chinese authorities claimed to have been facing thousands of attacks from jihadists in recent years.[14] Yet, China has not been the main target of jihadists.

The Global Salafi Jihadist Movement

In recent years, hardly a day has passed without jihadist attacks.[15] According to a publication of the Tony Blair Foundation, 121 Islamist terrorist groups conducted 7,841 attacks in 2017 – on average 21 every day – killing 84,000 people in 66 countries, of whom nearly 22,000 were civilians [16,17]. In the period 2011–2016, Al-Qaeda alone conducted 5,887 attacks while ISIS conducted 4,343 attacks worldwide.[18] By late 2018, some 230,000 Salafi Jihadists have, according to a study by Anthony Cordesman, been operating in nearly 70 countries. They have the support of many more Muslims and the sympathy of tens of millions of others.[19]

So far, most of the jihadist attacks have taken place outside Europe but in recent years Western societies have also experienced more terrorism, including vigilante terrorism from white right-wing extremists reacting (and provoking) violent extremism from Islamists. Although there has been an increase in right-wing terrorism in recent years, the dominance of Islamist terrorism remains unchallenged: almost one-third of all major active terrorist groups (some 120 out of some 370) are Islamist.[20] Most of the terrorist violence takes place in the Middle East and Northern Africa, that is, in Muslim majority states.[21]

The main driver behind these attacks is the ideology of Salafi Jihadism.[22] Salafism as a reform movement within Islam emerged in the 18th and 19th centuries and was revived again in the 1970s. It comes in three variants, (i) a quietist, almost apolitical version, (ii) a political assertive variant and (iii) an aggressive jihadist variant.[23] Jihadism has become the most aggressive social movement in contemporary Sunni Islam. It claims to be in possession of a blueprint to break the political paralysis caused by the repressive, corrupt and foreign-supported regimes of many Arab and Muslim countries. The structure of this ideology is threefold:

1 There is a basic grievance – the Muslim world is in chaos and a Zionist-Christian alliance is held responsible for most, if not all, that is wrong in Muslim countries and the way Muslims are humiliated, discriminated and/or (mis-) treated in the world. The collusion of corrupt Muslim rulers with the West keeps Muslims impotent and those who follow them have turned away from "True Islam" by allowing Western ways in Muslim lands.

2 *There is a vision of the good society*: a single political entity – the Caliphate – that replaces corrupt, apostate rulers under Western influence, by a rule under *sharia* wherever there are Muslims so that Allah's will shall be done and order is restored; and

3 *There is a path to the realisation of the vision*: the eradication, in a violent *jihad,* led by a heroic vanguard, to get rid of Western influence in the Muslim world. However, great sacrifices are needed to turn the tables. Every true Muslim has to engage in a violent jihad against the invading Crusaders to defend their faith and Muslim lands from enemies near and far in order to achieve victory and humiliate the oppressors".[24]

Currently, Al Qaeda and the Islamic State are the vanguards of the jihadist movement. Their goals reach beyond the Muslim world alone. In an essay with the title "Moderate Islam is a Prostration to the West", the late Osama bin Laden wrote:

[O]ur talks with the infidel West and our conflict with them ultimately revolve around one issue, and it is: Does Islam, or does it not, force people by the power of the sword to submit to its authority corporeally if not spiritually? Yes. There are only three choices in Islam: either willing submission [i.e. conversion]; or payment of the jizya [poll-tax paid by non-Muslims], thereby bodily, though not spiritual, submission to the authority of Islam; or the sword – for it is not right to let him [an infidel] live. The matter is summed up for every person alive: either submit, or live under the suzerainty of Islam, or die [...] Such, then, is the basis of the relationship between the infidel and the Muslim. Battle, animosity, and hatred – directed from the Muslim to the infidel – is the foundation of our religion.[25]

While some analysts have considered bin Laden "moderate" in comparison to ISIS' leader Abu Bakr al-Baghdadi (a.k.a. Caliph Ibrahim), both share a similar interpretation of the role of Islam. Abu Bakr:

Islam was never a religion of peace. Islam is the religion of fighting. No-one should believe that the war that we are waging is the war of the Islamic State. It is the war of all Muslims, but the Islamic State is spearheading it. It is the war of Muslims against infidels.[26]

We find such an offensive line of thought not only with jihadists like Bin Laden and Abu Bakr, but, in milder forms, also with other Islamists who themselves are not directly engaging in violence. Islamist extremists have built their ideology on foundations that are not far removed from Wahhabism as practiced and propagated by Saudi Arabia, which portrays itself as the social carrier of mainstream Islam. While Saudi Arabia has used petro-dollars and missionary work (dawah) as the main instruments to bring people to a fundamentalist (i.e. literalist) version of Islam,[27] violent extremists rely on jihad, seen by Islamist extremists as the "sixth pillar" of Islam.[28]

Jihad and Terrorism

According to John Esposito, editor of the Oxford Dictionary of Islam "Jihad is the only legal warfare in Islam, and it is carefully controlled in Islamic Law".[29] According to Shahab Ahmed, a Harvard scholar, the orthodox and majoritarian understanding of jihad is that jihad means, above all, "fighting the infidel".[30] However, there are also other interpretations, e.g. that there is a "greater jihad" and a "lesser jihad", with the "greater jihad" being the fight in every human soul against negative, socially or religiously harmful impulses, and the "lesser jihad", being the armed struggle in defence of Islam. This particular distinction of greater and lesser jihad is, however, not Quranic, but based on one single hadith – out of many thousands of sayings later attributed to the Prophet.[31] The specific hadith referring to the "greater jihad" surfaced only centuries after the death of the Prophet and is widely regarded as "weak" in terms of being an authentic statement of the Prophet.[32]

Literally, jihad means "struggle in the path of God" (*jihad fi sabil Allah*), and jihadists are those who embrace jihad as their calling.[33] The Quran promises those who die in the jihad that they will get direct access to paradise.[34] There is among Islamic scholars some dispute as to whether this type of struggle is legitimate only when it is defensive or whether jihad is also legitimate when it is offensive.[35] There is also controversy in Islam whether only a legitimate authority like the ruler of a state can declare jihad or – as today's jihadists who follow the Palestinian theologian and militant Abd Allah Azzam (the mentor of Osama Bin Laden) hold – that it is an individual obligation (*fard al-'ayn*) for each Muslim, indeed the sixth pillar of Islam, as the current generation of Salafi Jihadists claim.[36] The acceptance of the idea that jihad is an individual obligation for every Muslim if a Muslim country is attacked, has ideologically justified the phenomenon of "foreign fighters".[37] Most of them are Salafi Jihadists. In his book, "Salafi-Jihadism the History of an Idea", Shiraz Maher offers a detailed history of the rise of Salafist Jihadism (*al-Salafiyya al-jihadiyya*). Summarizing Maher's argument, Salafist Jihadism can be defined as

> Militant, Islam-based ideology involving the violent rejection of non-sharia-based states and the existing international order, calling for holy war against external non-Muslim enemies, seeking recovery of lands formerly Muslim and the overthrow of those local rulers in Muslim-majority countries who are not considered to be true Muslims and the replacement of their apostate regimes with strict sharia-based governance.[38]

This definition focuses on ends rather than means of warfare. Today, jihadism is mainly associated with terrorism, a means to an end involving such tactics as (suicide) bombings, hostage takings, kidnappings and the massacres of civilians. While jihadists also attack military and police forces, they prefer soft, civilian targets with higher news value. There is therefore considerable overlap between acts of terrorism and war crimes as defined in the laws of war. International humanitarian law identifies a number of methods of conflict waging as "war crimes":[39]

1. Wilful killing of civilians and prisoners;
2. Taking of hostages;
3. Intentionally directing attacks against the civilian population as such or against individual civilians not taking direct part in hostilities;
4. Attacking and bombarding, by whatever means, towns, villages, dwellings or buildings which are undefended and which are not military objectives;
5. Intentionally directing attacks against buildings dedicated to religion, education, art, science or charitable institutions.

There can be little dispute that many, if not most, armed attacks of Al-Qaeda and ISIS and other violent Islamist extremists engaging in a jihad constitute acts of terrorism, war crimes and, in some cases, crimes against humanity and in at least one case (IS' attack on Yazidis) amount to genocide. All this also falls under the broad category of "violent extremism".

Not only the means of these jihadist groups are extreme, their objectives are too, since their ambitions involve revolution and overthrow of heretic regimes in the Muslim world, the destruction of Israel, the abolition of national borders created in the Middle East after World War I, the reconquest of lands once under Muslim rule (e.g. Spain, 711–1492) and the establishment of a caliphate ultimately ruling over both Muslims and non-Muslims worldwide. In the case of the Islamic State, the end goal even includes bringing about the End of Times in an apocalyptic struggle.[40] All in all, a totalitarian agenda for world rule.

Conclusion

Based on a survey and analysis of major opinion polls in Muslim-majority countries as well as some diasporas in the West, I noted in 2017 that there is a substantial extremist milieu sympathizing, and in some cases actively supporting, Islamist extremism. I concluded that

> Salafist Jihadism (*al-Salafiyya al-Jihadiyya*) has managed to establish itself as the dominant ideology of rebellion in the early 21st century…. For a brief moment in 2011, the Arab Spring with its non-violent mass demonstrations, seemed to offer an alternative model of rebellion in the absence of democratic regimes but when these mass uprisings were crushed in all countries except Tunisia, jihadism as a non-mass based method of fighting repression and foreign intervention gained the upper hand in the minds of many militant youths. Young Muslims with rising expectations but low chances of realising them also have emerged in diasporas outside the Muslim world, especially among disgruntled young Muslims in Western Europe where militant Islamism forms a small but significant subculture among some 25 million Muslims.[41]

While in the 20th century, Fascism and Communism were the main violent extremist challenges to the international system, in the beginning 21st century Salafist Jihadism has become the main manifestation of violent extremism. It seeks to abolish the existing system of (nation-) states and replace it with a theocratic Islamic empire, thereby challenging the current global order. Despite the loss of the short-lived caliphate (2014–2018), the spirit of jihadism seems unbreakable as long as Muslim governments and Western democracies cannot offer Muslims realistic and practical alternatives to jihad as a method to improve their position. As Ed Husain, author of *The House of Islam* (2018) has rightly observed:

> The House of Islam is on fire. Anger and hate are fanning the flames from room to room. We must act before it suffocates us.[42]

Notes

1 Hamed Abdel-Samd. Mohamed. Eine Abrechnung. München: Droemer, 2015, pp. 228–230.
2 Jalil Roshandel and Sharon Chadha. Jihad and International Security. New York, NY: Palgrave Macmillan, 2006, p. 40.
3 David Nicolle. Historical Atlas of the Islamic World. New York, NY: Checkmark Books, 2003, p. 166.
4 Dan Smith. The State of the Middle East. An Atlas of Conflict and Resolution. London: Earthscan, 2006, p. 16.
5 Ed Husain. The House of Islam. A Global History. London: Bloomsbury Publishing, 2018, pp. 32–34.
6 Idem, p. 40, p. 1 and p. 34.
7 Idem, p. 162, p.13.
8 Cit. Efraim Karsh. Imperialismus im Namen Allahs. Von Muhammad bis Osama Bin Laden. Müunchen: Deutsche Verlags-Anstalt, 2007, p. 314.(orig. published as Islamic Imperialism. A History. New Haven: Yale University Press, 2006).

9 Cit. Ed Husain, op. cit., p. 120.

10 Ed Husain, op. cit., pp. 125–126.

11 Cf. American Foreign Policy Council. World Almanac of Islamism. Lanham: Rowman & Littlefield, 2014, pp.1010–1026.

12 The Figure of 31% for the Middle East and North Africa was cited in *The Economist*, September 7th, 2019, p. 77.

13 Cf. unhcr.org/figures-at-a-glance.html. 70.8 million forcibly displaced persons worldwide.

14 Cf. Informationsbüro des Chinesischen Staatsrats. Kommentar: Weissbuch über Erfolg von Berufsaus-bildung in Xinjiang entlarvt westliche Lügen. 16 August 2019.

15 For a daily overview of such attacks in one specific year (2017) around the world, see: Paul Cliteur. In Naam van God. Elke dag een aanslag. Antwerp: Houtekiet, 2018, pp. 115–251 (Dagboek van de terreuraanslagen 2017).

16 Tony Blair Institute for Global Change. Global Extremism Monitor., 2017; cit. *CBS News*, 13 September 2018. URL: https://www.cbsnews.com/news/islamist-extremism-caused-84000-deaths-worldwide-in-2017-a-new-report-says/; however, another data source, the Global Terrorism Database (GTD) re-corded "only" 10,900 terrorist attacks in 2017 that killed more than 26,400 people worldwide–but not by jihadist alone. Cf. URL: https://www.start.umd.edu/gtd/.

17 Eric Schmitt. "Two Decades After 9/11, Militants Have Only Multiplied". *New York Times,* 20 November 2018, quoting a study by the Center for Strategic and International Studies in Washington, D.C.; URL: https://www.nytimes.com/2018/11/20/us/politics/terrorism-islamic-militants.html; the CSIS study can be found at: https://www.csis.org/analysis/evolution-salafi-jihadist-threat.

18 Anthony H. Cordesman. Rethinking the Threat of Islamic Extremism: The Changes Needed in U.S. Strategy. Washington, DC: Center for Strategic & International Studies, 2017; DOI: https//doi.org/10.1515/Sirius-2017-0094; URL: https//www/csis.organalysis/rethinking-threat-islamic-extremism-changes-needed-us-strategy.

19 Alex P. Schmid, "Data to Measure Sympathy and Support for Islamist Terrorism: A Look at Muslim Opinions on Al Qaeda and IS", *The International Centre for Counter-Terrorism – The Hague* 8, no. 2 (2017), pp. 25–26; URL: https://www.icct.nl/sites/default/files/import/publication/ICCT-Schmid-Muslim-Opinion-Polls-Jan2017-1.pdf

20 The number of 120 terrorist organisations is from the Tony Blair Institute; the one of 370 such groups is from START, University of Maryland; URL: www.start.umd.edu/gtd/.

21 Cf. Global Terrorism Database, maintained by START at the University of Maryland.

22 Shiraz Maher. Salafi-Jihadism. The History of an Idea. London: Penguin, 2017. Ed Husain concluded: "Jihadism is the logical conclusion of Salafism"- Op. cit., p.142. Both Husain and Maher are former Islamic fundamentalists.

23 Cf. Quintan Wiktorowicz. Radical Islam Rising: Muslim Extremism in the West. Lanham: Rowman and Littlefield, 2005.

24 Alex P. Schmid. The Importance of Countering Al-Qaeda's "Single Narrative". In: National Coordi-nator for Counterterrorism. Countering Violent Extremist Narratives. The Hague: NCTb, 2010, p. 47.

25 Cit. R. Ibrahim. The Al Qaeda Reader, p. 32.

26 Cit. Frank Gardner, "Islamic State Releases 'al-Baghdadi message". *BBC Middle East Service*, 14 May 2015; URL: http://www.bbc.com/news/world-middle-east-32744070.

27 Dawah refers to missionary work whereby persuasion is used to Islamise non-Muslim individuals, com-munities and the states they live in. Dawah is also used for efforts to revitalise the faith of lukewarm Muslims. Cf. Lemma "Dawah" in John Esposito, The Oxford Dictionary of Islam. Oxford: Oxford University Press, 2003, p.64.

28 The traditional five pillars of Islam are: (i) declaration of faith [shahadah] (ii) observance of the five pre-scribed daily prayers [salat], (iii) almsgiving [zakah], (iv) fasting during Ramadan [sawn], (v) performance of the pilgrimage to Mecca at least once in a life-time [hajj]. – John L. Esposito, op. cit., pp. 247–248.

29 John L. Esposito., op. cit., p.160.

30 Shahab Ahmed. What is Isla m? The Importance of Being Islamic. Princeton: Princeton University Press, 2016, pp. 318–319.

31 Cf. URL: http://www.bbc.co.uk/religion/religions/islam/beliefs/jihad_1.shtml.

32 None of the four main schools of Sunni jurisprudence nor the Shi'ite tradition make a reference to the "greater jihad".– WikiIslam, as quoted in Shahab Ahmed, op.cit., p. 318.

33 Shahab Ahmed, op. cit., pp. 318–319.

34 Ruud Peters. Djihad tussen wettig gezag en revolutie. De Heilige Oorlog in de heedendaagse Islam. In: Martin Gosman & Hans Bakker (Eds.). Heilige Oorlogen. Een onderzoek naar historische en hedendaagse vormen van collectief religieus geweld. Kampen: Kok Agora, 1991, pp. 176–178.

35 Aaron Y. Zelin. "Your Sons Are at Your Service": Tunisia's Missionaries of Jihad. Dissertation, London, King's College, December 2017, p.195.

36 In his booklet "Defending the Land of the Muslims Is Each Man's Most Important Duty", Azzam claimed that "If the enemy has entered Muslim lands, the jihad becomes an individual obligation according to all doctors of the law, all commentators of the Sacred Texts, and all the scholars of tradition (those who assembled the words and deeds of the Prophet". – Cit. Gilles Kepel. Jihad. The Trail of Political Islam. 4th edition. London: I.B. Tauris, 2006, p. 146.

37 Ibid.

38 Shiraz Maher. Salafi Jihadism. The History of an Idea. London: Penguin, 2016, pp. 8–19.

39 Cf. Dieter Fleck (Ed.). The Handbook of Humanitarian Law in Armed Conflicts. Oxford: Oxford University Press, 1995; Roberta Arnold. The ICC as a New Instrument for Repressing Terrorism Ardsley, NY: Transnational Publishers, 2004, pp. 66–69.
Peter Romaniuk and Naureen Chowdhury Fink. From Input to Impact. Evaluating Terrorism Prevention Programs. New York: Center for Global Counter-Terrorism Cooperation, 2012, p. 5.

40 Based on Daniel Byman. Al Qaeda, The Islamic State, and the Global Jihadist Movement. What Everyone Needs to Know. Oxford: Oxford University Press, 2015, pp. 47–50 & pp. 170–172.

41 Alex P. Schmid, "Data to Measure Sympathy and Support for Islamist Terrorism: A Look at Muslim Opinions on Al Qaeda and IS", *The International Centre for Counter-Terrorism–The Hague* 8, no. 2 (2017), pp. 25–26; URL: https://icct.nl/wp-content/uploads/2017/02/ICCT-Schmid-Muslim-Opinion-Polls-Jan2017-1.pdf

42 Ed Husain, op. cit., p. 284.

5

JIHADIST VIOLENCE

New Terrorist Actors/Groups Emerging – Who will be the Key Players in the Next Decade?

Bruce Hoffman

Two conclusions emerge from any examination of contemporary jihadist violence. ISIS is here to stay, at least for the foreseeable future; and al-Qaeda hasn't gone away. Accordingly, it is unlikely that new terrorist actors or groups will emerge any time soon and that what new developments we see will be more in the realm of the creation by both terrorist movements of new franchises or branches and their appearance in new, fertile grounds for expansion in hitherto atypical jihadi operational grounds.

Terrorism and territory have never been coterminous. Terrorists historically have been able to prosecute sustained violent campaigns absent the accoutrements of governance, possession of vast geographical expanse or control over populations that the Islamic State once exercised. Continued access to sanctuary and safe haven, sufficient finances, a compelling ideology, and an enduring appeal have always been the fundamental requirements of terrorist organizations. Accordingly, ISIS's unremitting capacity for violence remains. Its battlefield defeats and the demise of the short-lived Islamic State have astonishingly neither eroded ISIS's appeal nor undermined its trans-national reach. Indeed, while the physical caliphate was crumbling, ISIS was nonetheless spreading to new locales – such as the Democratic Republic of the Congo, Cameroon, Chad, Sri Lanka, and Mozambique, among other places.

The 2019 Easter Sunday suicide bombings underscore ISIS's undiminished allure to extremists even in places where ISIS hitherto had little to no presence. Sri Lankan authorities, for example, attribute the six simultaneous attacks on churches and luxury hotels that claimed the lives of 259 persons and wounded twice that number to two local groups – the National Thowheeth Jama'ath (NTJ or National Monotheism Organization) and Jammiyathul Millathu Ibrahim (JMI, Organization of the Faith of Ibrahim). Neither had any known, prior connection to ISIS nor had they evidenced a capacity for the magnitude of violence unleashed that tragic day. The NTJ had previously been linked to the vandalization of Buddhist statues following anti-Muslim disturbances in 2018; with the JMI having emerged from complete obscurity.

According to a 2019 United Nations report, the attacks were apparently carried out without the knowledge or approval of ISIS's senior leadership. This only deepens the mysteries of the operation's genesis; the surprising rapidity with which both groups acquired the expertise to construct the devastatingly effective improvised explosive devices; and the operational and logistical mastery required to execute coordinated attacks.[1] Historically, even a single successful suicide

DOI: 10.4324/9781003326373-6

bombing has involved a long logistical "tail" involving many people, including: recruiters to radicalize and maintain the resolve of the bomber-martyrs; skilled bomb makers to fabricate the IEDs used in the assaults; and operatives to identify and surveil potential targets without arousing suspicion. This is a formidable undertaking and one typically accomplished by persons with prior operational experience relying on an already existing organizational network.

Planning for so complex a terrorist operation likely predates the shootings at two mosques in Christchurch, New Zealand just weeks before. Nonetheless the fact that two entirely local collections of militants, with a hitherto limited capacity for violence, saw advantage in allying themselves with ISIS – despite the group's declining fortunes – establishes a worrisome precedent: that is unlikely to prove unique. A key dimension of the attacks may have been the terrorist cell's ability to harness the experiences of at least one member who had left Sri Lanka in 2014 to join ISIS.[2] Jameel Mohammed Abdul Latheef reportedly traveled to Raqqa, Syria in 2014, where he is believed to have come into contact with the infamous British ISIS commander, Mohammed Emwazi, also known as "Jihadi John" – the person responsible for the mistreatment, and ultimately the beheadings, of the American journalists James Foley and Steven Sotloff that same year (Emwazi was killed in November 2015 by a U.S. airstrike).

Latheef's survival and escape from Syria is by no means atypical. Only about 10,000 of the 40,000 foreign fighters who came to fight with ISIS in the Levant and Iraq in fact were killed. At least 15,000 were reportedly able to flee the caliphate before its collapse. Of this number, approximately 7,500 returned home – of whom only about half are imprisoned or being actively monitored by local authorities; 5,000 others were deported by Turkey without notification given either to the recipient governments or those countries of whom they are citizens; 2,500 more found sanctuary in Sudan; and about 2,700 others migrated to ISIS branches elsewhere. Approximately 8,000–10,000 are believed to be fighting in the remaining pockets of Syria where ISIS has a presence or in western Iraq where the group has launched a new insurgency.[3]

The 2018 trial in Denmark of a former foreign fighter who is alleged to have ties to the ISIS cell responsible for the previous year's suicide bombing of a Manchester, England concert venue underscores the challenges that security and intelligence services and law enforcement agencies face in tracking these individuals. This person was born in Somalia, lived in Britain, held a Finnish passport, went off to fight with ISIS in Syria, but then was arrested in Denmark during a police roundup of illegal immigrants that he was inadvertently swept up in.[4]

The odyssey that eventually led this former foreign fighter to Denmark suggests that the European network of ISIS's external operations arm is still active. It was organized at least two years before the November 2015; having been created by the Amniyat Khalifa – also known also by its Turkish acronym, Enmi, and its Arabic one, Anmi – the secretive ISIS unit serves as both its internal security force and the unit responsible for external operations. In the latter context, it appears to have continued to function despite ISIS's declining military and territorial fortunes. According to U.S. intelligence and defense officials quoted by Rukmini Callimachi in her revealing August 2016 *New York Times* article, ISIS had already deployed "hundreds of operatives" into the European Union with "hundreds more" having been dispatched to Turkey before the caliphate fell. This investment of operational personnel was doubtless designed to ensure that ISIS retained an effective international terrorist strike capability.[5] Whether the perpetrators of the aforementioned May 2017 suicide bombing of an Ariana Grande concert in Manchester, that killed 22 persons, and of the pair of attacks three months later in Barcelona and Cambrils Spain, where 16 persons perished, were part of this network is not known. What does seem apparent is that ISIS retains a powerful ability to inspire and motivate attacks regardless of any diminution of its stature caused by its battlefield defeats in Syria and Iraq and the caliphate's demise.

Another noteworthy feature of both the Sri Lanka attacks and other ISIS operations in recent years is the frequency that siblings are involved. Two brothers, who were the sons of a wealthy Sri Lankan spice trader, were among the Easter Sunday bombers. Four sets of brothers comprised the ten-person terrorist cell in Catalonia responsible for the Barcelona and Cambrils attacks. Two brothers participated in the November 2015 Paris attacks and two brothers also carried out the March 2016 dual suicide bombings at the Brussels international airport and at subway station in the city. Admittedly, siblings have long been involved in al-Qaeda as well as ISIS terrorist incidents. Two sets of two brothers were among the 19 hijackers on September 11 2001. Two brothers were also implicated in the 2000 attack on the USS Cole in Aden; in the 2015 shootings at the Paris offices of Charlie Hebdo, the French satirical newspaper; as well as in the 2013 Boston Marathon bombing.

But ISIS has consistently turned terrorism into a family activity. A husband and wife, for instance, were responsible for the mass shooting in San Bernardino, California in December 2015. Three brothers were implicated in a plot to blow up an Etihad Airways passenger plane en route from Sydney to Abu Dhabi in July 2017. And three sets of families were implicated in the May 2018 suicide bombings of three churches in Surabaya, Indonesia, the country's second largest city. Among them was a family of six – including a 9-year old daughter and her three brothers, ages 18, 16, and 12; another family of six with four children, ages 10 through 17; and a family of five, among whom was their 8-year-old daughter. Penetrating an ISIS terrorist cell not comprised of close-knit family is arguably already sufficiently challenging for the authorities in any of these countries. But gaining access to an intimate, nuclear family presents different operational security challenges of an entirely more formidable magnitude.

Another aspect of ISIS's perverse embrace of family is the role women played as proponents of jihad. The situation of some tens of thousands of displaced persons, mainly women and children, still detained in the Kurdish-run Al-Hol camp, has focused increased attention on the women, both indigenous and from elsewhere, who supported the Islamic State and indeed continue to do so.[6] There is no clear profile of even a small subset of these detainees: the European women who traveled to Syria to join ISIS and help build that state. Most are devout Muslims whose motivations reflect those of men who joined ISIS to fight: concern over the plight of Muslims worldwide and a profound sense of responsibility to defend the ummah against all threats – internal as well as external. The former include fears of local Shi'a domination and the latter Iranian domination and Western interference and influence. The same sense of adventure and perhaps personal rebellion that animated male foreign fighters were also factors with the women. In some instances, there was a salient desire to ensure their place in heaven (Jannah) by becoming part of the Islamic State – an intention also shared by the men who journeyed to the caliphate. Foreign women, like their male volunteer counterparts, also sought to be part of something bigger than themselves and to collectively help to build a community united under Shar'ia law and sharing a common identity and purpose. There were other female volunteers, however, who were enthralled by a highly romanticized version of the Islamic State conveyed via social media and the Internet. In this context, the prospect of marriage to a fighter and the status it brought was still another enticement – especially to become the wife of a martyr.[7]

Meanwhile, the danger from so-called lone actor attacks remains. The late ISIS commander Abu Muhammad al-Adnani's famous September 2014 summons to battle has long proven far more compelling than al-Qaeda's longstanding efforts to motivate and inspire individuals to engage in violence in support of its aims. In December 2001, for example, al-Qaeda's current leader and then number two, Ayman al-Zawahiri, issued a similar call in his treatise titled, *Knights Under the Prophet's Banner*. Published in a London-based Arabic-language newspaper, it explained that

> Tracking down Americans and the Jews is not impossible. Killing them with a single bullet, a stab, or a device made up of a popular mix of explosives or hitting them with an iron rod is not impossible. Burning down their property with Molotov cocktails is not difficult. With the available means, small groups could prove to be a frightening horror for the Americans and the Jews.[8]

But al-Zawahiri was using an anachronistic media platform that was in the process of being rendered irrelevant by more immediate and pervasive 21st century technology. His print message consequently was thus seen by few and ignored by most. By comparison, al-Adnani's plea reverberated in a self-sustaining echo chamber that acquired its own momentum. "If you are not able to find an IED or a bullet," al-Adnani memorably declared, "then single out the disbelieving American, Frenchman, or any of their allies. Smash his head with a rock, or slaughter him with a knife, or run him over with your car, or throw him down from a high place, or choke him, or poison him."[9] Hence, despite al-Adnani's 2016 killing, his words still resonate given the cumulative power of the Internet and social media: reaching an audience both faster and more effectively than al-Zawahiri could ever have achieved, much less imagined.

ISIS's cultivation of lone actors became even more critical as the military operations of the global coalition of 84 countries mobilized to defeat it progressed.[10] In response to this historically unprecedented onslaught, ISIS actively embraced the lone actor strategy to ensure its survival. Thus, far from the battlefields in Mosul and Raqqa, ISIS inspired its disciples to independently carry out vehicular, stabbing and shooting attacks in France, Finland, England, Australia, the United States and Canada, among other countries.

Although these lone actor attacks are less sophisticated and their perpetrators less capable than their more professional, trained counterparts – such as the Paris November 2015 attacks – they can be just as homicidal. The truck driven into a crowd of Bastille Day celebrants in Nice the following summer, that killed 86 persons, is an especially heinous example of this now commonplace threat.

In sum, ISIS today appears unbowed by its battlefield defeats and the loss of its caliphate. As one of the last messages communicated by the group's founder and leader Abu Bakr al-Baghdadi – only weeks before he was killed in a U.S. military special forces operations – had promised,

> the wheel of attrition is running smoothly, by the grace of Allah, and on a daily basis and on different fronts. After the protector of the Cross America and its apostate proxies in the region were stepped upon and their faces dragged over the land of Afghanistan and Iraq, the dog of the Romans, America … is drowning in the quagmire …[11]

In this respect, it is perhaps worth recalling that the 2015 Paris attacks was the biggest terrorist attack on a Western city in over a decade. They occurred with no advance warning and in defiance of the prevailing analytical assumption that ISIS wasn't interested in mounting external attacks and moreover lacked the capability to do so. Moreover, just two weeks earlier, ISIS was able to perpetrate the single most significant attack against commercial aviation in more than a decade. Over two hundred persons perished when a bomb exploded shortly after take-off aboard a Russian charter jet. That this incident, like recent operations linked to ISIS, was undertaken by its comparatively less-technologically sophisticated Sinai Wilayat (province) perhaps in cooperation with its counterpart in North Africa and not by core ISIS, points to the longstanding capacity of the movement's branches to independently execute highly consequential terrorist attacks regardless of senior leadership guidance or direct orders. These incidents, like the 2019 Easter Sunday attack in Sri Lanka that similarly surprised everyone, should make us very circumspect that we have any better understanding of ISIS's post-caliphate capabilities and intentions today than we did when the group first emerged.

While ISIS has dominated the headlines and preoccupied our attention for the past several years, al-Qaeda has been quietly rebuilding. Al-Qaeda today is numerically larger and present in more countries than at any other time in its history. From northwest Africa to southeast Asia, al-Qaeda has maintained a global movement of some two dozen local networks. It is entrenched in Libya, where groups such as Ansar al-Sharia and the Benghazi Defense Brigades as well as Shura Councils in Benghazi, Darnah, and Sirte, advance the parent movement's interests. Al-Qaeda in the Islamic Maghreb is meanwhile active in surrounding countries: targeting Western aid workers and tourists. Al-Quaeda of the Arabian Peninsula (AQAP), long the movement's most threatening and consequential franchise, as previously noted, controls ports and highways along Yemen's coastline ensuring itself a continuous source of revenue from smuggling that is used to coopt local communities through the provision of goods and services that the shattered central government cannot provide. Not surprisingly, AQAP's ranks have quadrupled in recent years. Al-Shaabab in Somalia has similarly expanded and regained lost momentum as it has beaten back attempts by ISIS to challenge al-Qaeda's dominant position in east Africa. Thanks to its Taliban allies in Afghanistan, al-Qaeda has expanded its operations in that country. The movement has made new inroads in Bangladesh – in addition to its most recently announced franchise dedicated to the liberation of Kashmir. Among the multitude of Salafi-Jihadi factions present in Syria's Idlib province, al-Qaeda retains an albeit smaller presence and reduced influence. In all, al-Qaeda now has tens of thousands of fighters – with potentially as many as 20,000 worldwide.

Indeed, with a remarkably resilient senior command structure still in place, al-Qaeda seeks to position itself to exploit ISIS's weakened military position and territorial losses and once again claim its pre-eminent position at the vanguard of the violent Salafi-Jihadi struggle. ISIS has long been stronger than its rival in three key aspects: name recognition and the power of its brand coupled with ISIS's presumed ability to mount spectacular terrorist strikes in Europe. But the latter, it should be noted, is a product of al-Zawahiri's strategic decision to prohibit external operations in the West so that al-Qaeda's rebuilding can continue apace. The handful of aberrations to this policy – such as the 2015 Charlie Hebdo attacks in Paris, the 2017 St Petersburg Metro bombing in Russia, and a massive plot that was disrupted in Lucknow, India in July 2021 – evidence that al-Qaeda's own external operations capabilities have not completely atrophied and can likely be reanimated when the timing is deemed propitious.

Moreover, AQAP's longstanding expertise in targeting commercial aviation[12] has now clearly spread to the movement's franchises. Even the comparatively technologically unsophisticated al-Shabaab nearly succeeded in downing a Dallo Air passenger jet departing Mogadishu in February 2016 with an improvised explosive device concealed in a laptop computer. The late AQAP master bomb-maker Ibrahim al-Azziri's ordnance craftsmanship has thus migrated to other al-Qaeda partners – including groups that hitherto never targeted commercial aviation.

Al-Qaeda's success in resurrecting its global network is the result of three, key strategic decisions taken by al-Zawahiri. The first was strengthening the movement's decentralized, franchise approach that has ensured al-Qaeda's survival since the dark days following the commencement of the U.S.-led global war on terrorism. Over the years, the leaders and deputies of al-Qaeda's disparate franchises have been integrated into the movement's deliberative and consultative processes. Today, al-Qaeda is truly "glocal" – having effectively melded local concerns into an all-encompassing worldwide grand strategy that homogenizes global/local distinctions across the movement.

The second key decision, as previously noted, was the order given by al-Zawahiri in 2013 to avoid mass-casualty operations, especially those that might kill Muslim civilians and innocent women and children. At a time when ISIS was soon running rampant, with fresh atrocities succeeding one another, the new al-Qaeda leader's move prove an enormously prescient strategic gambit. Al-Qaeda, accordingly, has been able to present itself, paradoxically, as "moderate extremists" – an ostensibly more palatable rival to ISIS. The fact that al-Qaeda is just as ambitious but far more patient and calculating than ISIS is thus lost on many who not only actively support and assist it, but seek to partner with what they perversely regard as a more acceptable and reasonable alternative.

This development reflects al-Zawahiri's third key strategic decision of letting ISIS take all the heat and absorb all the blows from the coalition arrayed against it while al-Qaeda unobtrusively re-builds its military strength and basks in its new-found cachet as moderate in contrast to the unconstrained ISIS. Anyone inclined to be taken in by this ruse would do well to heed the admonition of Theo Padnos (née Peter Theo Curtis), the American journalist who spent two years in Syria as a Nusra Front hostage. Padnos relates how the group's senior commanders "were inviting Westerners to the jihad in Syria not so much because they needed more foot soldiers – they didn't – but because they want to teach the Westerners to take the struggle into every neighborhood and subway back home."[13]

Accordingly, with ISIS lamentably still active and al-Qaeda clearly resurgent, today we arguably face the most parlous security environment since 2001 – with serious threats emanating from not one but two terrorist movements who both have cultivated a myriad of branches and affiliates, thereby enhancing their capabilities and ensuring their longevity.

Notes

1 Analytical Support and Sanctions Monitoring Team, Twenty-Fourth report, United Nations Security Council, July 15, 2019, p. 5 at: https://documents-dds-ny.un.org/doc/UNDOC/GEN/N19/199/15/PDF/N1919915.pdf?OpenElement.

2 See Niharika Mandhana, Rob Taylor and Saeed Shah, "Sri Lanka Bomber Trained in Syria with Islamic State," Wall Street Journal, 29, 2019, at: https://www.wsj.com/articles/sri-lanka-attacks-show-isiss-reach-even-after-defeat-11556561912.

3 Data made available courtesy of Dr. R. Kim Cragin, National Defense University, Washington, DC. The most recent United Nations monitoring team report also cites the number of surviving foreign fighters as 30,000. See Analytical Support and Sanctions Monitoring Team, Twenty-Fourth report of the Analytical Support and Sanctions Monitoring Team submitted pursuant to resolution 2368 (2017) concerning ISIL (Da'esh), Al-Qaida and associated individuals and entities New York, NY: United Nations Security Council, July 15, 2019, p. 6 at: https://digitallibrary.un.org/record/3813209?ln=zh_CN.

4 "Danish terror trial may have connections to UK attack: reports," Ritzau/The Local dk, February 19, 2018 https://www.thelocal.dk/20180219/danish-terror-trial-may-have-connections-to-uk-attack.

5 Rukmini Callimachi, "How a Secretive Branch of ISIS Built a Global Network of Killers," *New York Times*, August 3, 2016.

6 Vivian Yee, "Guns, Filth and ISIS: Syrian Camp Is 'Disaster in the Making,'" *New York Times*, September 3, 2019.

7 See Edwin Bakker and Seran de Leede, "European Female Jihadists in Syria: Exploring an Under-Researched Topic, ICCT Background Note (The Hague: International Centre for Counter-Terrorism, 2015), pp. 4–7; and, Mia Bloom, "How ISIS is Using Marriage as a Trap," *Huffington Post*, March 2, 2015 at: https://www.huffpost.com/entry/isis-marriage-trap_b_6773576?guccounter=1&guce_referrer=aHR0cHM6Ly93d3cuZ29vZ2xlLmNvbS8&guce_referrer_sig=AQAAAHr8Lw-44_6N4hbMKEU5S

gIwUmp5tiHHGTHQue3KM2oAUBfzTY0eD_5JdO0RzxCcTKycU0HAk7qeIDXBUeKD2f82f-
Vo8SICsWhoYYyVUTxSjC9pDEvGA9-lv0VW0xDLmU8FOF2_zPdxsPaQdUyiaKLXCcpz4ZT-
91kcwLaZVYOeq8; and, Suhartini Samsudin and Anitawati Mohd Lokman, Women and Emotion:
The Themes and Narratives of the 'Diary of a Muhajirah' Tumblr Page," Proceedings of the 7th International Zconference on Kansei Engineering and Emotion Research (2018), pp. 187–195. at: https://
link.springer.com/chapter/10.1007/978-981-10-8612-0_21.

8 Ayman al-Zawahiri, Knights Under the Prophet's Banner, translated and published in FBIS, "Al-
Sharq Al-Awsat Publishes Extracts from Al-Jihad Leader al-Zawahiri's New Book," Document
ID: GMP20020108000197, January 8, 2002, p. 86. See also the excerpt reprinted in Walter Laqueur,
ed., Voices of Terror: Manifestos, Writings, and Manuals of Al-Qaeda, Hamas, and Other Terrorists
from Around the World and Throughout the Ages (New York: Reed Press, 2004), pp. 431–32.

9 See text of the statement in ibid., pp. 95–96.

10 Global Coalition homepage at: https://theglobalcoalition.org/en/mission/.

11 "Translated Text: IS Leader Abu Bakr al-Baghdadi Orders Fighters Redouble Efforts at All Levels,
Promotes Religious Activism," September 16, 2019.

12 Eric Schmitt and Saeed Al-Batati, "The U.S. Has Pummeled Al Qaeda in Yemen. But the Threat Is
Barely Dented," New York Times, December 30, 2017 at Eric Schmitt and Saeed Al-Batati, "The U.S.
Has Pummeled Al Qaeda in Yemen. But the Threat Is Barely Dented," *New York Times*, December 30,
2017 at: https://www.nytimes.com/2017/12/30/world/middleeast/yemen-al-qaeda-us-terrorism.html.

13 Theo Pados, "My Captivity,' *New York Times Magazine*, October 29, 2014.

6

FROM NETWORKS TO SOCIAL IDENTITY

A Dialectical Model of Terrorism

Marc Sageman

I was invited to submit an essay on terrorist networks and bottom-up jihadism, the subjects of my first two books.[1] It was a reasonable request as my first book is still highly cited by terror network analysts. However, despite having worked with a dozen prominent teams of social network analysts over the past decade and a half, I have become disappointed with the promise of this perspective for understanding the phenomenon of terrorism. It has not produced significant new insights that may have led to policies minimizing the threat of terrorism in modern society. In addition, the nature of terrorist attacks in the West has changed to the point where the majority is carried out by loners with no link to other terrorists, limiting the usefulness of this perspective. Nevertheless, social network analysis still has value. For instance, a 2004 graph of the links between terrorists based on press reporting showed that the global neo-jihadi network formed four clusters.[2] At the time, I had no real explanation for this finding. Since then, I discovered from new primary sources that what I had called the Maghrebi network was in fact different from al Qaeda and formed a rival network linked to the Khalden training camp. Here, this perspective was helpful in separating different networks of global neo-jihadis that had mistakenly been lumped as al Qaeda. However, I have found that most social network analyses of the global neo-jihad are inaccurate because they rely on speculative and flawed press reports of either insignificant or non-existent links among terrorists and incorporate these errors into their underlying databases.

Self-Categorization Theory

After I got access to all classified U.S. databases and sensitive discovery material in criminal and civil litigation in the United States and was able to interview extensively more than sixty global neo-jihadis, I was intrigued by how they thought of themselves and their roles in their communities. At the same time, as a member of the U.S. government counterterrorism and intelligence community, I noticed how my colleagues viewed themselves and their role in protecting U.S. society. The parallel self-views of their respective roles and functions gave me the idea to analyze terrorism through the prism of self-categorization theory[3] combined with new developments in social movement and cognitive research.[4]

In brief, the theory postulates that we make sense of the social world by breaking it down into simple contrasting categories according to what we perceive we have in common with some

DOI: 10.4324/9781003326373-7

people but not others in a given situation. A person always self-categorizes in contrast to an out-group (them) that in turn helps define his in-group (us). This self-categorization creates a social identity, which is just the feeling of belonging to or being a member of a given group.[5] There are many potential social categories or in-groups to which one potentially belongs. Common groups are race, religion, gender, occupation, nation, political party, and social class. The salience of a specific in-group/out-group duality depends on many factors at the time of self-categorization. In-groups are not fixed or static, but evolve all the time, relative to salient out-groups at a given time, and have fluid boundaries according to specific circumstances. A violent threat against one of the multiple in-groups increases its salience and demands one's attention. The feeling of belonging to a threatened group automatically leads to two natural processes: accentuation of in-group homogeneity and out-group difference; and bias in favor of fellow in-group members, which may degenerate into discrimination against out-group members.

Self-categorization theory includes a theory of social influence. Since one does not know how to think, feel, and act as a new member of an in-group, one usually looks for a model for guidance and imitation. This model is one of the most representative members of the in-group and most different from the out-group. Such models exert a disproportionate influence on other members and their behaviors, feelings, and ideas and shape group norms. Some models even attract outsiders to join the group: deliberate recruitment is not necessary. There can be several possible models in a group, and they don't need to be the formal group leaders. They often change according to a group's relationship with its salient out-group. If this relationship is good, the most credible models are friendly to out-group members. If it is bad, the most credible models are correspondingly antagonistic to out-group members. In-group/out-group self-categorization is not static but evolves over time and can lead to changes in boundaries for the respective groups.

As group members, people see themselves as just part of their group, not as individuals. They engage in-group activities for group, not personal, motives. They do what they do because of who they believe they are, namely group members. There is no need for indoctrination or coercion to acquire a given social identity or act as a group member. This self-perception contrasts with that of out-group members, often reduced to a stereotype of who in-group members are not. This reduction erases out-group members' individual differences into a one-dimensional stereotype and may lead to their depersonalization and even dehumanization during strong group hostility.[6]

Self-categorization theory treats the in-group/out-group interaction as the most important independent variable affecting the dependent variables of group and individual behaviors. This implies that any analysis of social groups in society must be interactive and dialectical, especially with respect to salient out-group behavior. The emerging dynamic of group and individual members' behaviors are reactions to their salient out-group's actions.[7]

Politicized Self-Categorization

So far, the paradigm described normal group processes, but it can help conceptualize political or group violence. Let's assume that a grievance divides people into two contrasting sides, an in-group and an out-group. The macro level of analysis – social, economic, structural, and historical factors – comes into play in the genesis of this grievance. In a Weberian state that has a monopoly of legitimate violence within its territory, unfair and forceful state intervention politicizes the victimized group, adding complaints of the state to its original grievance. Often, the original grievance may even fade away to be replaced by a more emotional grievance against state brutality. A new in-group automatically emerges from the protestors' perception of a common fate at the hands of state agents. They self-categorize in contrast to these aggressive state agents, who, from their perspective, attacked or threatened them in a discriminatory and illegitimate manner. In a non-Weberian state, intervention of armed militia or vigilantes may play the same role.

The collection of active protestors, or people sharing the same politicized social identity in contrast to state agents, creates an imagined discursive political protest community. It is imagined in the sense that a nation is an imagined community.[8] It is discursive because constant discussions among members try to make sense of their common experience, sharpen distinctions between them and their salient out-group, and drive the process of becoming violent on behalf of the group. People drift in and out of this new in-group, which is amorphous, fluid with porous boundaries, akin to a social blob. Radicalization is simply the process of increasing commitment, dedication, loyalty, or devotion to this new in-group.[9]

Given enough time, these continuous discussions gradually breed a counterculture with its own lifestyle: they generate their own symbols and manners of speaking; develop their own shared ways of behaving, thinking and feeling about the world; and adopt common references (narratives and heroes), standards, rituals, and fashions, such as dress codes or diets. Commitment to this community – in other words, "radicalization" – is multifaceted. It is important not to reduce this devotion to just its cognitive or ideological dimension. Conversations evaporate but documents espousing this ideology survive. The prominence of written records in the surviving historical data tempts many scholars to rely exclusively on them and to assume that this ideological dimension is the most important explanatory variable for members' behavior. The model proposed here suggests instead a more complex explanation for the emergence of political violence.

So far, this political protest community is still not violent, but a few members may become so under the following three conditions.

Escalation of Conflict

The first condition is an escalation of conflict between the two groups. This escalation involves a rhetorical escalation to extreme positions. Extreme concepts such as war metaphors frame the way actors think about their conflict and narrow the range of available solutions to extreme ones, which in turn decreases the threshold of violence. So, it is not extremist ideology but extreme concepts and speech that are important. Group beliefs may or may not be "radical," in the sense of their rejection of hegemonic ideas in the rest of society.[10] New technology such as social media now amplifies this polarization of discourse: a limit of 140 characters in Twitter texts is not conducive to thoughtful calm analysis in trying to resolve an escalating conflict.

This dynamic results in a polarization or extremity shift within each group.[11] Militant models are now seen as more credible in each group and, as they generate group norms, both groups become more militant. Given the pro-in-group bias, members within each group ignore their own extremist discourse and the out-group's moderate voices. On the contrary, they believe that the most extremist out-group voices are representative of the out-group. In-group members also neglect their own aggression and violence toward the out-group and blame the out-group for all the escalation of the conflict, like "unprovoked attacks" on the in-group.

Disillusionment with Legal Protest

The second condition is progressive disillusionment with legal protest. Group members complain that leaders on both sides "talk, talk, talk, and nothing happens." The large majority in in-group members becomes disappointed when they get no result and lose their belief that they can legitimately affect their grievances. As they lose their belief in self-efficacy,[12] they exit the protest community. A few continue to voice their protest, but, as nothing happens, they also eventually leave.[13] Eventually, very few in-group members remain, accounting for the extremely low base rate of terrorism (from one thousand original committed protestors, perhaps only one may end up being violent).[14] The remaining protestors are the most committed, loyal, and devoted[15] to their comrades and cause, and often escalate their protest efforts.[16] They maintain their sense of self-efficacy, and blame all their grief on the out-group, which loses its legitimacy in their eyes. In a Weberian state, this out-group is usually the state, which represents society. As a result, the state and then society in general undergo a process of delegitimation in the eyes of these very committed protestors.[17] This process comes at the end of a political protest campaign, which explains the common observation that violence usually breaks out at the end of a political protest campaign.

Moral Outrage at Unexpected Out-Group Aggression

The third condition is a feeling of moral outrage at egregious out-group aggression against the in-group. This feeling is a reaction to out-group killings of in-group members; out-group threat to eradicate the in-group; out-group unfair punishment against in-group members; or out-group insults against symbols of in-group social identity, like the cartoons of the Prophet. As the conflict escalates, political protest becomes high-risk activism in which participation may severely harm participants.[18] In this dangerous circumstance, treason within a group, which of course not only undermines the meaning of group membership but also physically threatens each member, elicits disproportionate punishment from group members. This "black sheep effect"[19] of punishing a treasonous group member is sometimes the first instance of violence within a group. Moral outrage, the emotional engine driving the turn to violence, comes from strong identification with innocent in-group victims. The few remaining in-group members think, "enough is enough," and realize the need to defend themselves against out-group aggression.

Martial Self-Categorization

Under these three conditions, a few of the small number of remaining activists volunteer as soldiers to defend their imagined community against out-group attacks, crossing the threshold of violence. In other words, they acquire a martial social identity. Most of the time, these militants just drift into the role of soldiers and killing is what soldiers do. This process may be short or long: there are no real stages. These self-appointed soldiers start to act out their new social identity and participate in paramilitary activities, which reinforce their social identity. Loners, who carry out violence by themselves, are no different from small groups: they do not warrant a special label, like lone wolves, as they are all soldiers, part of an imagined community and willing to sacrifice themselves for comrades and cause.

Over time, they gradually separate themselves from former protestors and become a new violent group. They band together as they feel more comfortable socializing with like-minded companions. At the same time, former protestors not sharing their martial social identity avoid them to stay clear of potential legal problems. These soldiers often redraw the boundary of their new in-group to exclude society and even their former non-violent friends and lumping them with their original out-group. In their mind, this expanded out-group becomes a legitimate target of violence. These soldiers start to feel special and different from the original political protest community: they view themselves as the vanguard of the revolution, creating history.[20]

The actual form of the resulting violence depends on the repertoire of collective action available to the mind of these self-appointed soldiers, which itself depends on their traditions, rituals, innovations, opportunities, and organizations.[21]

Dynamics of Violence

Bunches of violent guys and gals emerge gradually, which makes them difficult to detect before the outbreak of violence. They arise from clusters of trust, usually based on kinship and friendship, that egg each other on during their discussions. These informal groups are often unstable as they recognize no authority to resolve inevitable disputes among rivals, whose personality conflicts end up masquerading as ideological conflicts. There is a spectrum of involvement: from a small active core, which initiates and drives plots; to associates, who fully participate in the violence, but would not have initiated them on their own; and to peripherals, who know something but not all. These peripherals may not share their friends' readiness to use violence but feel a sense of loyalty toward them and can't let them down when they ask for small favors, such as temporary shelter or money.

Newcomers voluntarily join the bunch of violent guys, attracted by these new models who "do something." There is no need for recruitment, "grooming," "brainwashing," or "indoctrination." Active participation in this imagined violent community is not static: some people participate at one time but not at another. Group participation in political violence demands intense dedication and time commitment to the in-group. Therefore, these violent guys must be biographically available: they are often in a period of life transition and have no competing career or family commitment. So, involvement in political violence is fluid and depends on individual opportunity (often chance meetings with violent guys) and lack of meaningful outside commitment.

This violent struggle generates intense emotional bonds, an *esprit de corps*, forged in adversity: violent models are deeply attractive to fellow members, especially those of the opposite sex. Sexual promiscuity is a prominent feature of the bunch of violent guys and gals. At this point, devotion to the group tolerates no challenge and even an attempt to understand their enemies may be seen as a betrayal: "Whose side are you on?"

Violent loners further complicate this description. Some undergo martial self-categorization through virtual interactions with other soldiers while others do so in isolation, but still on behalf of this imagined community. Although social media facilitates this identification with a threatened but violent community,[22] it is by no means necessary as anarchists in the 1890s already underwent this process and carried out attacks in the name of their comrades without having any physical contacts with them.

Campaigns of Political Violence

The above process describes the emergence of political violence. For most groups, their first attack is their last: they are either killed, captured or, more rarely, shocked by their own action, they simply disappear into society. Society is especially vigilant against this type of violence, and its police clearance rate is much higher than that for ordinary crimes. State repression drives the surviving soldiers underground to escape arrest. If they survive, the dynamics of the situation favor a continuation of the violence. Informal leaders must carry out new attacks to fend off more extreme rivals and keep up the morale of followers, who might exit without new operations negating the boredom of clandestine life.

Violence brings similar shifts to extremity in both belligerent groups. As violence produces casualties, in-group members start to see themselves as avengers of victims of out-group aggression.

State agents no longer view themselves as peacekeepers but avengers of society's victims. As violence continues, a real cult of violence emerges on both sides, which legitimates all means to achieve a group's goals, including large-scale detention, torture, persecution, and indiscriminate killings of suspected out-group members. *Esprit de corps* on each side trumps ideology or abstract political goals. With the bunch of violent guys, this process may degenerate into plain banditry.[23]

State repression of the original non-violent protest community drives many of its members underground, inadvertently increasing the pool of potential violent guys, who adopt a clandestine life. The relative isolation of this type of life, lack of interaction with non-fugitive friends, and the significance of the sacrifice they endure have important psychological consequences: obsession with the enemy and narrowing of their cognitive horizons[24] (they only talk with each other about their common concerns); hardening of their beliefs (constant self-confirmation from fellow fugitives); and over-estimation of their own popularity (all the people they now know support them). Therefore, these violent guys appear irrational because of the opacity of their beliefs; fanatic because of the strength of these beliefs; and rigid because of their resistance to outside arguments. Clandestine life reduces complex group dynamics to apparent personality traits, constructed as "pathological hatred." Survival requires the adoption of necessary tactics of secrecy, security, and discipline. With time, some remaining clusters consolidate into disciplined, clandestine, and hierarchical organizations.

The Global Neo-Jihad

In the context of the current global neo-Jihad, the violent community is the neo-ummah, which is the collection of global neo-jihadis, who claim to represent the "real ummah."[25] Since it is an imagined community, while some of its organizations like al Qaeda or the Islamic State may be physically shrinking, people identifying with it may still increase worldwide. The size of the neo-ummah in the West fluctuates according to factors that make neo-jihadi self-categorization more salient, like the vividness of the threats against it illustrated by images of Muslim victims of Western aggression.

Bombing these organizations abroad may increase attacks at home. Military action may eliminate organizations, like al Qaeda or the Islamic State, that can carry out attacks in the West. However, morally outraged people in the West, who identify with the victims of their own state military actions abroad, may volunteer to retaliate at home. So, while eradication of neo-jihadi organizations abroad may eliminate direct attacks from abroad, it may temporarily increase the probability of homegrown neo-jihadi attacks at home. As the fighting in Syria and Iraq winds down, emotionally laden images that had elicited moral outrage gradually fade away on the Internet, decreasing the probability of retaliatory violence in the West.

In the past decade, Western states have all started to preach the mantra of countering violent extremism (CVE) or the global neo-jihadi "narrative." This narrative is actually very simple: "Make Islam Great Again." Global neo-jihadis, like any group members, interpret information through the prism of their social identity. They reject out-group (state) propaganda out of hand without paying much attention to it. CVE programs seem pointless for these targeted groups. On the other hand, they feed societal self-confirmatory bias against neo-jihadis and harden public prejudice against them. So, CVE programs may worsen the situation by further escalating the conflict between global neo-jihadis and the rest of society.

The role of women in the global neo-jihad is unusual. In other campaigns of political violence, women were full participants in all group activities, including the execution of attacks. Indeed, women are generally as dedicated and devoted as men to their comrades and cause but their contribution to violence depends on their group's repertoire of action, especially its gender roles. Up to now, the tradition of the current global neo-jihad assigns them only support responsibilities, with very few exceptions. This may change as new traditions may emerge according to circumstances.

Global neo-jihadi loners may be physical loners but are very much part of the imagined neo-ummah, often linked through virtual communications. There is no need for a physical contact with organizations like al Qaeda, or the Islamic State. In the United States, there is usually no link between these loners and the Islamic State except for a last-minute message on social media swearing allegiance to its leader. In Europe, where neo-jihadis can commute to the battlefields of Syria and Iraq, there is a mixture of loner and Islamic State controlled or directed attacks. For this second type, social network analysis can be a useful tool to detect neo-jihadis coming back home to carry out attacks. But most attacks in the West are carried out by loners with imagined rather than physical links to the neo-ummah, limiting the usefulness of social network analysis to detect them.

Implications of the Suggested Model

This model emphasizes the dialectical nature of group conflict and argues that the interaction between two conflicting groups is the major contributing factor to political violence. This implies that both groups contribute to the outbreak of violence. In other words, the behavior of the state, one of these two contentious groups, contributes to the emergence and persistence of a protest group's violence. This state contribution to non-state political violence is a neglected area of research as the great majority of terrorism studies focus exclusively on non-state groups, acting as if they exist in a vacuum. Such a narrow focus cannot explain the outbreak and persistence of contentious political violence.[26]

Another implication of this model is that it provides us with a new conceptualization of terrorism, which is the categorization of deliberate and unexpected out-group political violence, or its threat, targeting people and property not involved in the conflict between two groups. This self-reflexive definition solves the conundrum that one man's terrorist is another's freedom fighter: the labeling of a group's violence depends on where one stands with respect to it. Allies call this type of violence virtuous (freedom fighters) while enemies call it terrorism, a term that carries disapproval and condemnation. Society's strong reaction to terrorism may be partly due to the facts that it is deliberate, totally unexpected ("comes out of the blue"), and targets strangers, regular members of society, who are not party to the conflict between the two groups. This contrasts with the violence between the police and large crime syndicates that avoids targeting outsiders. The implication is that terrorism is meaningful only during domestic peacetime as wartime violence that may terrorize the population would be considered a war crime rather than terrorism.

This model argues that terrorism, as political violence, is first and foremost the product of a political process and not that of personal pathology or ideology. In fact, pathology is low in-group violence because high-risk activists do not trust people with bizarre behavior and eliminate them from their group. However, computer-mediated communications reduce communication to a single dimension, hiding disturbing behavior (for example, lack of eye contact) that previously might have caused their rejection, and allow participation of loners uncomfortable in-group settings. As loner violence becomes more common, the incidence of mental disorders among politically violent actors may increase.

In general, in the process of becoming violent, social identity trumps ideology and self-interest: there is no radicalization without self-categorization. This model involves a combination of normal social psychological processes. This means that turning to political violence is part of human nature and not an aberration. Fortunately, the frequency of lethal violence has decreased over the past few centuries despite huge paroxysms of murder during global wars. Nevertheless, avoiding political violence requires constant vigilance from all concerned to prevent the escalation of ubiquitous social conflicts.

In this model, the process of exit from political violence is relatively understudied. Most of the subjects of the sample informing this analysis were still in prison and committed to their political community. Their detention had stopped the violence. The few formerly violent people interviewed had simply given up on the fight as the cost and sacrifices they endured led to a gradual disillusionment with the effectiveness of their violent actions without a corresponding abandonment of former comrades or ideals. Their exit from violence was more akin to a military demobilization ("the war is over for you") than some mysterious process of de-radicalization. In fact, none had gone through a program of disengagement.

Finally, this model suggests the main paradox of political violence. The emergence of violence drowns any other grievances as a focus of human attention. Once violence breaks out, it becomes the exclusive focus of public attention to the complete neglect of the original grievance. The use of violence to address a grievance generally undermines the prospect of its resolution. The exception comes from an oppressed society's identification with a populist challenger to a small minority-ruled state. The strategy of national liberation movements under colonial domination was to trigger large-scale state repression against the overwhelming majority of the native population, which gradually identified and supported the challengers, eventually resulting in the overthrow of colonial rule. Self-categorization with popular challengers was the key to success as it was for social revolutions in countries ruled by small unpopular elites. Otherwise, the paradox applies, and political violence fails to achieve its goals.

Recommendations: What Can Be Done?

The usefulness of a model lies in its policy implications. This model's four factors that combine to activate a martial social identity, or the readiness to use political violence, suggests a range of recommendations on how to prevent the outbreak of political violence, or once started, how to break its cycle.

Prevention

The first set of recommendations is to avoid the politicization of private disputes. Specific recommendations include taking care not to scapegoat or stigmatize a protest community; establishment of procedures to address valid grievances in legitimate ways; and education of the public about legitimate grievances. Since it is often state intervention that politicizes an aggrieved community involved in a private dispute, if state intervention is necessary, it must be even-handed and non-violent.

The second set of recommendations is to avoid escalation in the face of a non-violent political protest. The state cannot confuse and lump together legitimate peaceful protestors with violent ones but must clearly distinguish between them since punishing peaceful activists may turn them into violent guys. The state must be careful not to escalate the tone of its discourse and vilify protestors by using war metaphors in describing its relationship with them.

Many states now try to pre-empt future violence through detection of potentially violent actors with "indicators" of "radicalization." The most striking feature of political violence is its extremely low base rate. Because of the rarity of terrorism, scholars find it necessary to select on the dependent variable (terrorism), giving the impression that terrorism is more common than it is. On the contrary, it is extremely rare. This means that any indicator to detect potentially violent actors that is not itself extremely specific will generate a huge number of "false positives," people wrongly branded as terrorists.[27] In the process, the state stigmatizes and often persecutes these falsely suspected non-violent protestors. Attempts to pre-empt violence by using such indicators may on the contrary escalate the conflict, increasing the probability of the violence that the state tries to avoid, a tragic example of self-fulfilling prophecy.

The third set of recommendations is to avoid the process of disillusionment and delegitimation. This can be achieved through procedural justice[28] that builds trust in the protest community. Procedural justice relies on fair principles. The state must allow protestors to voice their legitimate grievances (voice). It must be viewed as a neutral third party in the original private dispute and, in dealing with each party, establish fair, transparent, and neutral procedures that are carefully explained to them (neutrality). It must treat each person with dignity and courtesy (respect). And finally, it must show that it is acting in good faith, concerned about everyone's welfare (trustworthiness). By endorsing this strategy of voice, neutrality, respect, and trustworthiness, the state reinforces its legitimacy among protestors, who still feel meaningfully engaged in legitimate protest and society in general, precluding their disillusionment with peaceful means to address their grievances.

The final set of recommendations is to avoid any egregious aggression against protestors. The state must be fair in its dealing with them and avoid excessive use of force especially in crowd control during large scale protest demonstrations. If police cause physical harm to protestors, they must be held accountable for their brutality through transparent procedures.

Containment and De-Escalation

Once political violence breaks out, the state strategy depends on whether the threat to society comes from abroad or home.

Proportional Reaction and Containment of Foreign Threat

In the face of a foreign threat, the model suggests a strategy of proportional reaction and containment of the threat. The state must not conflate multiple local foreign threats into a coordinated global one. It is normal for states to conflate such threats like the alleged anarchist international committee in the 19th century that never existed, or the alleged Comintern orchestration of national liberation movements in Asia and Africa in the 20th century. In the last instance, while there were Comintern attempts to control such movements, in reality, they quickly shed Moscow's influence when their interests clashed with Soviet ones.

Disproportionate measures to control native populations' presumed susceptibility to "foreign" influence completely alienated them and boosted their determination to achieve independence. As previously mentioned, disproportionate military operations abroad may stimulate retaliatory violence at home from people identifying with victims abroad. Instead, containment abroad of trained fighters attempting to return and attack the homeland through travel denial at entry points is more proportional and relatively easier to achieve than the search for returnees hiding at home.

De-Escalation in the Face of a Domestic Threat

In the face of a domestic threat, the dialectical model suggests that the most appropriate strategy is to break the cycle of violence through de-escalation of the conflict with justice and fairness. This strategy is predicated on the education of scholars, state agents, politicians, and the public about the dialectical nature of political violence, especially the state's own contribution to its outbreak and persistence.

The first element of this strategy is focused and proportional repression of the violence. It is important to bring only violent actors to justice, people with actual blood on their hands. Punishing people for just verbal and other low-level support of their violent friends (i.e., helping a friend with temporary shelter) may seem excessive to non-violent sympathizers and turn some of them into violent guys. Unfortunately, the trend in Western countries is to criminalize these non-violent small acts of support, and therefore escalate the conflict.

The second element is to isolate the violent guys from the rest of the political protest community, to facilitate this community's rejection of their violent former comrades, and to bring it back into the societal fold. To accomplish this task, political leaders must craft a sense of inclusive national identity that trumps the protest community's more parochial identity. This sense of inclusiveness is critical because a feeling of exclusion leads to a search for an alternate social identity, which may oppose the national social identity. In addition, the state must avoid the criminalization of trivial acts of support for it creates a permanent barrier preventing now criminalized but still non-violent protestors' return to society. Again, it is crucial to be very focused and proportional in terms of repression.

The third element is resisting gratuitous self-promotion for political gain at the expense of the protest community. Heralding minor arrests as major accomplishments in the so-called war on terror leads to public alarm and further escalation. In the process, the state may also inadvertently promote the defendants as heroes to protestors, creating wrong models for them to imitate. Minor participants suffering disproportionate punishment for activities not considered crimes except in terrorist cases may become martyrs to their comrades and inspire a few morally outraged ones to become violent in retaliation of this perceived injustice.

The fourth element is the absolute necessity of fair policing. There must be no brutality toward peaceful protestors and no stigmatizing profiling against them since it invariably leads to some form of persecution, escalating the conflict. As the model suggests, there is no objective social or psychological profile of violent actors. Their profile is a subjective one: each imagines himself or herself to be a soldier defending his or her attacked community. There is no easy mind biopsy that allows police to detect a martial social identity. The use of non-extremely specific indicators of "radicalization" needlessly escalates the conflict.

As part of fair policing, the state must resist the temptation to use entrapment tactics to arrest suspected violent actors. Fortunately, such tactics are still banned in most Western countries. Although undercover operations are legitimate police tactics to gather information not otherwise available, state agents must be careful not to become agents provocateurs. Aggressive undercover operations in the United States have crossed the line into sting operations entrapping suspects under the influence of an agent provocateur. In these operations, an undercover agent or informant is introduced to the suspect. Since this person is often older than the usually young and naïve suspect and claims to be a veteran neo-jihadi to establish his credibility, the paradigm suggests that the agent becomes a model for the suspect to imitate. In order to prove himself to his model, the suspect will act in a way to show that he belongs to the community of soldiers. So, even when the agent is careful not to encourage the suspect to commit a crime, the suspect will still do something that he probably would not have done absent the agent (remember the extremely low base rate of terrorism). Most of the time, these cases are not so subtle, and the agent provocateur encourages the suspect to commit a crime outright. At this point, the uncover operation becomes an unfair sting operation and should be banned because such police tactics are incompatible with a liberal democracy.

Another dimension of breaking the cycle of violence is the adoption of procedural justice already mentioned. Laws and procedures used in conflict resolution must be viewed as fair and just. This means that the state must demonstrate impartial and transparent procedural justice with fair punishment to regain legitimacy with the protest community. Terrorism enhancements in sentencing, which are trending across the Western world, should be abandoned for they needlessly escalate the conflict. They do not act as deterrence: terrorists just see them as pure spite from prosecutors acting as public avengers, increasing their sense of outrage. Instead, these enhancements play to the public at large to illustrate that the state is being tough on terrorism. In some instances, prosecutors want to win their case at all costs and are willing to engage in unfair tactics that are clearly seen by defendants. Furthermore, judges share a common background with prosecutors and often identify with their former colleagues, leading to a potential bias against defendants. Both prosecutors and judges must be vigilant against these natural tendencies that unfairly influence proceedings to prevent any further escalation of conflict.

All these recommendations are derived from the dialectical model. They constitute the essence of a Western liberal democracy, as it had gradually evolved before the recent global neo-jihadi challenge. I am simply proposing that Western liberal democracies stay true to their long experiences and traditions in continuing to enact fair and just laws and procedures.

Notes

1 Marc Sageman, 2004, *Understanding Terror Networks*, Philadelphia: University of Pennsylvania Press and Marc Sageman, 2008, *Leaderless Jihad*, Philadelphia: University of Pennsylvania Press.
2 Sageman, 2004: 138.
3 For a good summary, see Alexander Haslam, Stephen Reicher, and Michael Platow, 2020, *The New Psychology of Leadership: Identity, Influence and Power, Second Edition*, London: Routledge.
4 See Marc Sageman, 2017, *Turning to Political Violence: The Emergence of Terrorism*, Philadelphia: University of Pennsylvania Press: 1–47; 2019, *The London Bombings*, Philadelphia: University of Pennsylvania Press.
5 This acquisition of a social identity is quick and automatic and must not be confused with the philosophical concept of identity (often defined in terms of values) based on a complex process of reasoning about what it means to be part of a group, or the psychological concept of identity based on an individualist perspective distinguishing oneself from all others.
6 Albert Bandura, 1999, "Moral Disengagement in the Perpetration of Inhumanities," *Personality and Social Psychology Review* 3: 193–209.
7 This is similar to Clausewitz's metaphor of the nature of war, as "a pair of wrestlers. Each tries through physical force to compel the other to do his will." Carl von Clausewitz, 1976, *On War*, Princeton, NJ: Princeton University Press: 75.
8 Benedict Anderson, 1991, *Imagined Communities: Reflections on the Origin and Spread of Nationalism, Revised Edition*, London: Verso.
9 Kenneth Keniston, 1968, *Young Radicals: Notes on Committed Youth*, New York, NY: Harvest Book.
10 Egon Bittner, 1963, "Radicalism and the Organization of Radical Movements," *American Sociological Review* 28(6): 928–940 for a more formal definition of radicalism.
11 Roger Brown, 1986, *Social Psychology: The Second Edition*, New York, NY: Free Press: 200–249.
12 Albert Bandura, 1989, "Human Agency in Social Cognitive Theory," *American Psychologist* 44(9): 1175–1184.
13 Albert Hirschman, 1970, *Exit, Voice, and Loyalty: Response to Decline in Firms, Organizations, and States*, Cambridge, Mass: Harvard University Press.
14 Marc Sageman, 2021, "The Implication of Terrorism's Extremely Low Base Rate," *Terrorism and Political Violence*, 33(2): 302–311.
15 This concept of group commitment is similar to Scott Atran's notion of devoted actor. Scott Atran, Hammad Sheikh, Angel Gomez, 2014, "For Cause and Comrade: Devoted Actors and Willingness to Fight," *Cliodynamics* 5: 41–57.
16 This escalation of commitment in the face of adversity is an example of cognitive dissonance. Leon Festinger, Henry Riecken, and Stanley Schachter, 1964, *When Prophecy Fails: A social and psychological study of a modern group that predicted the destruction of the world*, New York, NY: Harper Torchbooks.

17 Ehud Sprinzak, 1991, "The Process of Delegitimation: Towards a Linkage Theory of Political Terrorism," *Terrorism and Political Violence* 3: 50–68.

18 Doug McAdam, 1986, "Recruitment to High-Risk Activism: The Case of Freedom Summer," *American Journal of Sociology* 92(1): 64–90.

19 Jose Marques, Vincent Yzerbyt, and Jacques-Philippe Leyens, 1988, "The 'Black Sheep Effect': Extremity of judgments towards ingroup members as a function of group identification," *European Journal of Social Psychology* 18: 1–16.

20 This feeling of personal significance is a result of this process and not one of its causes as argued in Arie Kruglanski, Xiaoyan Chen, Mark Deschesne, Shira Fishman, and Edward Orchek, 2009, "Fully Committed: Suicide Bombers' Motivation and the Quest for Personal Significance," *Political Psychology* 30(3): 331–357.

21 Charles Tilly, 1986, *The Contentious French: Four Centuries of Popular Struggle*, Cambridge, Mass: Harvard University Press.

22 Jacquelien van Stekelenburg, Dirk Oegema, and Bert Klandermans, 2010, "No radicalization without identification: How Ethnic Dutch and Dutch Muslim Web Forums Radicalize Over Time," in Assaad Azzi, Xenia Chryssochoou, Bert Klandermans, and Bernd Simon (eds), *Identity and Participation in Culturally Diverse Societies: A Multidisciplinary Perspective*, Oxford: Blackwell Wiley: 256–274.

23 This describes the process of degeneration into banditry for politically violent people with no criminal past. However, in the real world, many violent guys had such a past, which decreases their threshold for violence. See Jean-François Gayraud, 2017, *Théorie des Hybrides: Terrorisme et crime organisé*, Paris: CNRS Éditions.

24 Donatella Della Porta, 2013, *Clandestine Political Violence*, New York, NY: Cambridge University Press: 204–262 refers to this phenomenon as ideological encapsulation and militant enclosure.

25 I call the present violent global threat to the West, the neo-jihad because it is not jihad as traditionally understood by Muslims, but neo-jihadis claim it is jihad. Likewise, I call their imagined community the neo-ummah because it is not the ummah (the large worldwide Muslim community), but global neo-jihadis claim to carry out violence in its defense.

26 Welcomed exceptions are Tilley, 1986, and Della Porta, 2013.

27 See Sageman, 2021.

28 Tom Tyler, 1990, *Why People Obey the Law*, New Haven, CT: Yale University Press.

7

THE ATOMIZATION OF POLITICAL VIOLENCE

Brian Michael Jenkins

When Dr. Stockhammer asked me to write a chapter for this volume, the question he put to me was: Is low-level terrorism a permanent threat to society? To talk about the future course of terrorism is always risky. The focus of my research is political violence – I am not recognized in the field of prophecy. Moreover, forecasts seem especially perilous at the moment. This chapter is being written against a backdrop of dramatic events that could have profound effects on the future course of terrorism: the Taliban takeover of Afghanistan; the potential long-term effects of a still-raging pandemic on economic inequality, political polarization, and security issues; the recent rise in ideological extremism, mainly but not exclusively on the far right.

Yet even before these events, I had been watching long-term trends that suggested changes in the course of terrorist violence, which Dr. Stockhammer's invitation would give me an opportunity to explore. "Explore" is the operative word here. Research on a phenomenon like terrorism should take the form of rigorous analysis of past events, groups, individuals, circumstances, the effects of various responses, strategies, and countermeasures to reach empirically supported conclusions.

Sometimes, however, it is important to look for more subtle trends or changes in the fashions of political violence – yes, highly publicized terrorist attacks inspire imitation, creating contagion effects, even fads. As I wrote in the 1970s, *terrorism is theater*, violence is aimed at the people watching. The audience includes those who are the objects of the fear and alarm that terrorists want to create, but terrorist actions are also intended to inspire and instruct others, including the terrorists' own followers. With the development of social media, this impact is now more immediate. Like most wartime communications, terrorists' "propaganda of the deed" is aimed at the home front. The message of every terrorist action is "Do as we do, here's how."

Looking at what might occur instead of analyzing what has happened is, of course, a more speculative line of inquiry, and conclusions are necessarily more tentative. It is always tempting to extrapolate from recent events, but it is obviously more difficult to chart a trajectory into the future.

My hypothesis is that the employment of terrorist tactics will persist as a mode of political expression and a form of armed conflict – an easy forecast, given the long history of terrorism. However, I also believe that changing circumstances are promoting a particular mode of low-level terrorism.

DOI: 10.4324/9781003326373-8

We are witnessing what could be called the *atomization* of political violence, in which individuals – not groups – motivated partly by ideology, partly by personal grievances, untethered or only loosely affiliated with an organization, are increasingly carrying out violent attacks on their own initiative, without central direction.

Most of these attacks involve simple tactics employing easily accessible weapons. The attacks are directed against unprotected, virtually random targets. The trend is not a departure from the historical attributes of terrorist violence – simple tactics, easily accessible weapons, soft targets, and violence as performance art to achieve broader goals are the hallmarks of terrorism. What we are seeing now is an extension of terrorist violence to its end point – "pure terrorism" – essentially, killing *anyone* to make a point.

Terrorist Violence Normalized

When terrorism in its contemporary form began to emerge in the late 1960s and early 1970s – airline hijackings and sabotage of commercial aircraft, kidnappings of diplomats and takeovers of embassies, individual assassinations, indiscriminate bombings – a primary policy objective of concerned governments was that terrorism should not become *normalized* as a mode of political expression or armed conflict. Despite the ability of the international community to eventually achieve a measure of consensus on the tactics and classes of targets that made terrorists enemies of all, terrorism nonetheless became a permanent feature of the political environment, a continuing threat.

Terrorism has evolved over the past half-century. Through inspiration and imitation, terrorist tactics spread across the globe. Terrorists standardized their playbook, although techniques were refined and innovations appeared. Terrorist tactics were melded into terrorist strategies. Terrorists exploited technological advances that offered new capabilities or created new vulnerabilities. These developments in terrorism tradecraft occurred independently of the identity of perpetrators or the reasons for which they adopted terrorist tactics. Each group was unique, but the tactics tended to be generic.

At the same time, however, new groups took the field, killing on behalf of new causes. The worldwide volume of terrorist violence increased overall, but the brutalization that comes with long campaigns, the necessity of carrying out ever more spectacular attacks to ensure continued impact and attention, and changes in motivations led to the escalation of terrorism. Terrorists fighting on behalf of defined groups to achieve concrete political goals were constrained by self-imposed limits to their violence – going too far might alienate perceived constituents. Terrorists driven by vague ideologies or answering only to God were freed from political calculations or considerations of morality. They were more determined to kill in quantity and willing to kill indiscriminately.

Death Tolls into the Thousands and Beyond

Escalation appeared to be a continuing trend. The worst incidents of terrorism in the 1970s resulted in tens of fatalities. This ascended to the hundreds in the 1980s. That remained the ceiling during the 1990s, although large-scale attacks grew more frequent. On September 11, 2001, terrorist violence crossed over into thousands killed in a coordinated attack. In 30 years, the upper register of terrorist violence had increased by two orders of magnitude.

It was not surprising when, in the shadow of 9/11, political leaders as well as terrorism analysts anticipated that future terrorist attacks could reach casualties in the tens of thousands, even hundreds of thousands. Extrapolation is always a perilous form of analysis, but the 9/11 attacks had fundamentally altered perceptions of plausibility. Scenarios that would have been dismissed as far-fetched the day before 9/11 became operative presumptions the day after.

The only way these higher levels of violence could be achieved would be by employing weapons of mass destruction. And many asserted that terrorist use of nuclear or biological weapons was inevitable – "not if, but when," to use the now-famous phrase. Osama bin Laden's interest in acquiring nuclear weapons was known. Discoveries of notes in al Qaeda training camps and later at Islamic State sites seemed to confirm fears that terrorists were exploring nuclear, biological, and chemical weapons. Although the notes provided evidence of ambition rather than of capability, scenarios of mass destruction proliferated in government and on the airwaves. Government officials and government commissions warned that future terrorist attacks would almost certainly involve weapons of mass destruction.

Horizontal Rather than Vertical Escalation

The 9/11 attack turned out to be a statistical outlier – a high point in death and destruction rather than a harbinger of worse to come. Instead of the anticipated vertical escalation, the post-9/11 environment saw what might be called "horizontal escalation" – a proliferation of low-level attacks. Even as concerns about terrorists using weapons of mass destruction increased in the years immediately following the 9/11 attacks, the operational capabilities of al Qaeda and its jihadist allies, who were regarded as the main threat, were being degraded.

Al Qaeda was under heavy pressure after 9/11. The American invasion of Afghanistan deprived the organization of its bases and training camps and scattered its leaders. A number of them, including the architect of the 9/11 operation, were killed during the initial fighting or were captured soon after. Al Qaeda's central command was disrupted. An unprecedented global intelligence effort rendered the terrorists' operating environment more hostile. Forced to lie low, al Qaeda lacked the organization and logistics to plan and support further large-scale attacks.

Although jihadist extremists were able to carry out some spectacular terrorist attacks around the world between 9/11 and 2006, these appear to have been largely local initiatives, although inspired by al Qaeda and in some cases involving alumni of its training camps. Some of the attacks caused heavy casualties. A 2002 bombing killed 202 persons in Bali, a bomb aboard a ferry boat killed 118 in the Philippines in 2004, and bombs on commuter trains in Madrid killed 191 persons later that year, but these death tolls were at pre-9/11 orders of magnitude, not the higher orders that had been feared. Other attacks, although still deadly, resulted in even fewer fatalities.

The attacks provoked strong responses from local governments. While they were not necessarily supportive of America's "Global War on Terror," other governments could not tolerate jihadist challenges to their own survival. Gradually, the capabilities of al Qaeda's allies and their offshoots were ground down, with the exception of Iraq, where the American invasion in 2003 created a new opportunity for the local jihadist enterprise. Iraqi jihadists would later emerge as the Islamic State of Iraq and Syria (ISIS), which ten years later would split from al Qaeda to launch a rival global jihad.

By the tenth anniversary of 9/11, no one would claim that al Qaeda had been defeated, even after the death of its leader Osama bin Laden. But the organization no longer had accessible training camps and a continuing flow of recruits to draw upon. Its ability to launch large-scale terrorist operations had been destroyed. It was reduced to exhortation, which would become its major strategy.

In the late 1970s, I participated in an effort to identify weapons that future terrorists might add to their arsenal. We looked at new weapons being deployed to military arsenals around the world to see what might be applicable to terrorist operations. The possibility that terrorists might acquire and use man-portable surface-to-air missiles against commercial airliners was a source of great concern. In our focus on military weapons, however, we missed what would turn out to be the most important "weapon" in the terrorist arsenal – the Internet, then still in its infancy. The Internet would enable terrorist organizations to communicate directly with their target audiences without mediation. Cyberspace would become another theater of terrorist operations.

Remote Recruiting

The Internet would come to be exploited by jihadists to create slick online magazines designed to *inspire* (the name of al Qaeda's online production) acts of terrorism and instruct readers on how to carry out various kinds of attacks. Online exhortation, augmented soon after by direct communications using social media, became the jihadists' primary vehicle for radicalization and recruitment.

Violent right-wing extremists followed a parallel trajectory. Wary of infiltration by informants and undercover agents, many right-wing extremist groups adopted a strategy of "leaderless resistance." The concept was popularized by Louis Beam, an American white supremacist who argued that traditional hierarchical organizations were vulnerable to government penetration and prosecution under conspiracy laws. He proposed an enterprise in which the center would inspire like-minded individuals to carry out operations, but without close communication or coordination.[1]

Remote recruiting changed the profile of terrorist recruits. Before the Internet, joining an urban guerrilla group or terrorist organization meant going underground—being accepted into a usually small, clandestine organization. The groups were fearful of admitting possible infiltrators or unreliable members, so any volunteer would be already known to other members or carefully vetted, even tested, before admission.

Remote recruiting, in contrast, entails little risk to an organization. Even if they are in direct contact via the Internet, remotely recruited volunteers have little information to give to authorities. Those who carry out an action on the group's behalf are applauded and awarded membership *ex post facto*, if the group wants to embrace them.

To mount an effective terrorist campaign based upon remote recruiting requires mobilizing a high volume of activity – many small attacks instead of large-scale operations. Remote recruiting offers low-yield ore. Exhortations can reach vast audiences, but only a handful of the listeners respond. Many individuals self-radicalize, few take action. Virtual armies remain virtual.

Moreover, interactions on the Internet tend to be solitary activities. Communicating threats and reaching out to others raise the risk of being identified. Many terrorist plots have been thwarted by overzealous recruits who wanted to be noticed or signaled their intentions to others.

Those who act are self-selectors. The absence of vetting means that there is no quality assurance. Some are attracted more by the prospect of engaging in violence than by their devotion to the cause. The ideology of the recruiting organization may be a conveyer for personal discontents. The attraction to violence may also reflect psychological disorders.

Personal problems were undoubtedly also an attribute of many of those who joined terrorist organizations in the traditional way. This was particularly true of cohorts of individuals who joined groups after the groups had already begun terrorist campaigns. The first cohort, or founders, tended to be ideologues who turned to violence. The second generation tended to be foot soldiers who were attracted once the violence was under way. The status they derived from their participation in the terrorist campaign was as meaningful to them as devotion to the cause. The third generation included thugs who were very low on ideological commitment but who saw participation as a license to kill. Remote recruiting leads immediately to the third-generation types.

The resources of individuals recruited remotely are limited, as their planning skills also usually are. With no group, each attack is a "one-off." There is no institutional learning. Tactics are primitive, although they can be lethal. A jihadist gunman with a semi-automatic rifle killed 49 people at a nightclub in Orlando, Florida. A jihadist with a rented truck killed 86 people in Nice, France. For the most part, however, primitive attacks cause fewer fatalities. The spectacular nature of terrorist attacks leads to a tendency to overestimate the overall lethality of terrorism. Nevertheless, the fear that it creates is real.

Trends in Lethality

Focusing on the deadliest incidents of terrorism can be misleading. Many terrorist attacks are symbolic, meant to attract publicity, but without killing people. The Global Terrorism Database (GTD), maintained by START at the University of Maryland, recorded a total of 201,183 terrorist incidents between 1970 and 2019, of which 93,014 (or 46 percent) resulted in fatalities. The total number of fatalities recorded in the GTD is 456,249 – approximately 2.3 fatalities per incident overall, or 4.9 fatalities per incident with fatalities.[2] While the number of events is large, most of them were recorded in war zones. Despite some spectacular events, the volume of terrorist activity in Europe, North America, and other advanced countries is much lower.

The RAND Corporation's Database of Worldwide Terrorism, which covers the years from 1968 to 2009, records a total of 40,129 terrorist incidents, of which 15,532 (39 percent) resulted in fatalities. The total number of fatalities was 64,236 – approximately 1.6 fatalities per incident, or 4.1 fatalities per fatal attack.[3]

The two databases have different collection criteria, which explains the different numbers of incidents. The RAND database focuses on international incidents of terrorism in which terrorists attacked foreign targets or went abroad to carry out their attacks. This was the primary concern of the international community in the 1970s and 1980s. In contrast, the GTD includes domestic terrorist activity where terrorists operating in their own country attacked fellow citizens. RAND researchers have also been cautious about how terrorist acts were recorded in war zones, where levels of violence are already high and isolating acts of terrorism is more difficult.

The difference can be seen in the following GTD statistics. The GTD recorded 131,350 incidents between 2000 and 2019, of which 66,316 (50 percent) resulted in 315,982 fatalities. This gives us 2.4 fatalities per attack, or 4.8 per attack with fatalities. However, Afghanistan, Iraq, Syria, Yemen, and Somalia, which were war zones for much of the period, account for 55,662 incidents (42 percent of the total number of incidents), reflecting the disproportionate effect that these five countries have on the total numbers. Of the remaining 75,688 incidents, 31,062 (41 percent) resulted in 137,482 fatalities.[4] This reduces the fatalities per attack to 1.8 overall, or 4.4 per attack with fatalities. While these differences may seem modest, given the small number of fatalities per attack, they are statistically significant.

The Mineta Transportation Institute (MTI) database of attacks on public surface transportation systems (passenger trains, metros, stations, buses, bus depots, etc.) provides further insights into trends in terrorism. Attacks in surface transportation venues can be a good indicator of broader trends. These venues are highly accessible, often crowded public spaces, making them attractive targets for terrorists seeking to cause casualties and disruption. Public transportation is an easy target.

The MTI database records 4,200 attacks between 1970 and the end of 2020 resulting in a total of 11,923 fatalities,[5] an average of 2.8 fatalities per attack. This level of lethality, which is higher than the rate seen in attacks overall,[6] reflects the fact that some of the terrorists carrying out the attacks saw public transportation venues primarily as killing fields.

This is underscored by the large-scale death tolls seen in the 1980 Bologna train station bombing, which killed 85; a 2003 arson attack on Daegu, South Korea, which killed 192; the 2004 Moscow metro bombing, which killed 41; the 2004 Madrid commuter train bombing, which killed 191; the 2005 London tube and transport bombings, in which 52 persons died; the 2006 bombing of a commuter train in Mumbai, which killed 209; and the 2010 Moscow metro bombing, which killed 40.[7] Numerous additional terrorist plots aiming at causing mass casualties in surface transportation attacks were uncovered and thwarted by authorities. The fact that many of the high-fatality attacks took place in Europe rather than in war zones in the developing world is also noteworthy.

The MTI database shows a declining rate of fatalities per attack. For the three decades between 1970 and 2000, the database records 825 attacks, with an average fatality rate of 3.8 deaths per attack. In the first decade of the 2000s, there was an average fatality rate of 3.0 fatalities per attack. In the most recent decade, from January 2011 to the end of 2020, there was a further decline, to 2.3 fatalities per attack.[8]

Correcting Reporting Biases

Caution is warranted in attributing too much importance to the fatality rate in the years between 1970 and 2000. Collecting data during this period was far more difficult than it is today. The world's news media had not yet been digitized on the Internet. The higher lethality rate may reflect the fact that lower-level incidents simply did not get the kind of international news-media coverage that would enable them to be captured by researchers. The most spectacular attacks, those with many casualties and those taking place in Europe and North America, were more likely to be identified and recorded. In other words, part of the growth in the volume of incidents may simply reflect improved reporting, which could also affect the lethality rate, since more lower-level incidents have been recorded in more recent decades. This problem arises in all long-term databases that include incidents from the pre-Internet age.

One easy way to check this is to eliminate all non-fatal attacks and count only incidents with fatalities, on the presumption that attacks with fatalities were less likely to have been missed in the earlier counts. Doing so for the GTD shows a clear increase in the number of attacks with fatalities, suggesting that the worldwide increase in terrorism over the past half century is real.

A second corrective approach is to rely solely on more recent data, for example, data on incidents in only the past 20 years, to see what trends they suggest. Comparing the reports of attacks and attacks with fatalities in the first decade of this century with the numbers reported in the second decade in the MTI database, we see that both numbers increase, with the number of attacks with fatalities nearly doubling, suggesting that the increase in volume is not merely the result of better reporting but is real. At the same time, the fatality rate for the incidents with fatalities shows a decline from an average of 8.8 fatalities per attack between 2001 and 2010 to 6.0 between 2011 and 2020. This suggests fewer high-fatality events, which is a fact, or a greater number of fatal events, but with fewer fatalities per event. A detailed examination of the chronology and the narratives of the individual attacks indicates that both conclusions are correct.

More Individual Attackers

Since 9/11, the majority of terrorist attacks outside of conflict zones has been carried out by a single individual. We are not referring here to a single operative of a larger terrorist enterprise – a suicide bomber recruited, trained, equipped, and deployed by a terrorist group – but cases in which a single individual planned, prepared, and carried out the attack. The only external involvement was encouragement and, in some cases, advice from an online contact.

All but three of the 31 jihadist attacks that occurred in the United States between 9/11 and 2020 were carried out by a single individual, although one of the individuals traveled to Pakistan to learn how to construct explosive devices before returning to carry out a bombing. His device did not work.[9] The three exceptions included two brothers who carried out the 2013 bombing at the Boston Marathon; two individuals who participated in a 2015 shooting in Garland, Texas; and a husband and wife team who opened fire on office workers in San Bernardino, California. The vast majority of the jihadist terrorist plots that were uncovered also involved a single individual, although in some cases, additional subjects were arrested for lying to the authorities during the investigation.

Single actors were responsible for most of the jihadist attacks in Europe, as well, although a number of them had traveled to Syria, where they were recruited, trained, and returned to Europe as terrorist operatives. The deadliest attacks – the 2004 bombings in Madrid, the 2005 bombings in London, the 2015 attacks in Paris, and the 2016 attacks in Brussels – were carried out by larger groups.

The news media glorify individual attackers by calling them "lone wolves," but the lone actors often turn out to be disturbed individuals with limited capabilities and resources. There are questions about whether a number of the incidents should be seen as terrorist attacks and whether the attackers were even mentally competent to stand trial.

In the 20 years after 9/11, American jihadists killed 105 persons, but nearly half of these deaths resulted from one attack in Orlando, and more than half of the attacks involved no fatalities (other than the death of the attacker). This is far fewer fatalities than analysts feared in the dark days immediately after 9/11. In Europe, the majority of the fatalities from terrorist attacks resulted from attacks by groups, not individual jihadists.

An Increase in More-Primitive Tactics

Recent terrorism research suggests some developments that are not statistically significant within the total volume of terrorist violence but that nonetheless suggest a broader trend. There appears to be a recent increase in less-sophisticated attacks involving readily accessible "weapons" – knives in stabbing attacks and motor vehicles in vehicle ramming attacks. Both tactics have increased significantly since 2014.

Terrorist attacks are generally not sophisticated. Defining sophistication as reliance on inside information or specialized skills, the use of sophisticated explosive devices or sabotage techniques, the penetration of active security measures, or involving complex operations with simultaneous attacks against multiple targets, MTI researchers noted that only 11 of 346 attacks (3 percent) met at least one of the criteria, and only four (1 percent) met at least two.[10]

Terrorist attacks are seldom sophisticated, simply because they don't have to be. As an MTI report concluded, "Unlike sophisticated criminals or wartime commandos who must penetrate often daunting security measures to reach a specific target, often within a narrow time frame, terrorists can attack anything, anywhere, any time. This means that they can choose the easiest targets to attack…. Attacks in public places obviate the need for inside information. If presented with security barriers, terrorists can shift their sights to easier targets or merely carry out an attack in the vicinity of a desired symbolic target and still gain the publicity they seek…. Or they can exploit the extreme dedication of their operatives and plow through security, using suicide attackers. Sophisticated terrorist attacks are therefore rare because, quite simply, they are unnecessary."[11]

Since the invention of dynamite, bombs have historically been the favored weapon of terrorists. In the 1970s, bombs accounted for 70 to 80 percent of the terrorist attacks in the United States and Europe. Bombings continued to account for a majority of terrorist attacks worldwide, being used in an average of about 51 percent of the annual incidents in the GTD between 2000 and 2019; however, the share of bombings among terrorist attacks dropped to an annual average of 44 percent between 2015 and 2019.[12]

Again, including terrorist violence in conflict zones in the statistics has a significant effect. Omitting Afghanistan, Iraq, Syria, Yemen, and Somalia reduces the average annual share of bombings by about 5 percentage points. Outside of these conflict zones, the average annual share of bombings between 2015 and 2019 drops to 36 percent – an even sharper decline than that shown in the worldwide figures.[13] Lacking the experienced bomb-makers and organizational structure that sustained the bombing campaigns carried out by groups like the Irish Republican Army or Spain's Basque separatist group (*Euskadi Ta Askatasuna*) during the final decades of the 20th century, it has become more difficult to obtain explosives, build explosives devices that work, and continue terrorist bombing campaigns.

Since 9/11, bombs and guns have accounted for a majority of the deaths resulting from terrorist attacks in both Europe and the United States, but bombings declined as a tactic after the spectacular attacks in Europe in 2004 and 2005. Jihadists in Europe continue to build bombs and target public places in an attempt to achieve high body counts, but in 2019, all of their bombing attacks failed because the plots were discovered or because the explosive devices failed.[14] In the 20 years since 9/11, only four terrorist attacks in the United States have involved bombs. The devices in two of these cases worked only partially, and only the bombing at the Boston Marathon caused fatalities. Three persons were killed in that event, although hundreds were injured.[15]

Stabbing Attacks

Stabbing attacks are not an uncommon form of violent crime. In the United States, where guns are readily available, stabbings account for between 11 and 13 percent of all homicides; guns are used in approximately three-quarters of the homicides. In Europe, knives are used in one-third of the murders, while guns are used in only 13 percent. Overall, knife crime appears to be increasing.[16]

There are a number of explanations for the increase in stabbing attacks. Some observers see growing knife crime as a component of increasing violent crime. Both gun crime and knife crime have increased in England and Wales, and French authorities have noted a similar increase. Some analysts suggest that stabbings reflect the increasing flow of drugs into the continent, while others assert that knife crime is most prevalent in areas of poverty and marginalization. Still others see knife crime as a manifestation of a broader change in public behavior. Those who hold this view assert that an increasing number of people are angry and frustrated with life, ready to explode with rage via violent crime. The inhibitions to organized violence – i.e., war – are greater, while individual inhibitions are lower. Mental disorder is offered as yet another reason.[17]

Our focus here is on stabbings as a terrorist tactic. On April 4, 2020, an assailant stabbed seven shoppers and pedestrians along the streets of Romans-sur-Isère, a town in southeastern France. The attacker killed two people and wounded five others. The attack was the third public stabbing in France in 2020. Other stabbing attacks were carried out by terrorists or mentally unstable individuals in Germany and the United Kingdom. As this chapter was being written, a jihadist extremist stabbed seven people at a supermarket in Auckland, New Zealand.

Recent trends in Europe, North America, and Australia would seem to validate an increase in politically or racially motivated stabbing attacks (although these sometimes blur with attacks by mentally disordered assailants). Of the 31 terrorist attacks that have been carried out by jihadist extremists in the United States since 9/11, 13 involved guns and 10 involved attacks with knives, machetes, or hatchets – all of the latter occurred since 2014.[18]

Stabbing attacks take place in public places – such as tourist sites, train stations, churches – and are unprovoked attacks, usually by a single individual, on members of the public or security personnel guarding them. Some of the attacks are beheadings.

Vehicle Ramming Attacks

Terrorists have only recently resorted to vehicle ramming attacks. None of the terrorist groups that appeared in the late 1960s and early 1970s utilized this tactic – they saw bombs and guns as the legitimate weapons of revolution and war. Ramming attacks became a terrorist tactic in the 1990s, when Palestinians started carrying out vehicle assaults in Israel, but they did not become a significant feature of Palestinian tactics until a decade later.[19]

Jihadist websites began calling for vehicle ramming attacks in 2010. Since then, both al Qaeda and ISIS have urged their followers abroad to carry out such attacks, although their initial exhortations produced no discernible response. A cluster of car ramming attacks appeared to follow the November 2016 issue of the online ISIS magazine *Rumiyah*, which urged them. However, the attack in Nice, France, that killed 86 persons and preceded the exhortation in *Rumiyah* by four months, may have inspired both the author of the article and other attackers.[20]

The chronology of vehicle ramming attacks shows a contagion effect that reaches beyond political extremism. One event inspires another. Attacks occur in clusters. The publicity surrounding these attacks seems also to attract mentally unstable persons. The categories of "terrorist" and "mentally unstable" are blurred in both the stabbing and vehicle attacks. Mentally unstable persons may express themselves in ideological terms, and terrorist attackers may have histories of mental health problems.

With few exceptions, the lethality achieved in stabbing and vehicle ramming attacks is very low. Stabbing attacks have averaged fewer than one person killed per attack (not counting the attackers). The nine stabbing attacks in the United States resulted in one fatality, although others were injured. Vehicle ramming attacks have caused an average of 2.6 fatalities per attack, but that figure includes the high-fatality incident in Nice. Setting aside this incident, the average number of fatalities per vehicle ramming drops to 2.1.[21]

Growing Antisocial Behavior

As a final observation, antisocial behavior – violence between strangers in public places unconnected with terrorism or ordinary crime such as robbery – appears to be a growing problem. Airline passengers are increasingly unruly and sometimes violent. People have been attacked at random on trains and in train stations. Individuals have been punched, stabbed, pushed off platforms in the path of oncoming trains. Bus drivers are now protected behind plastic shields.

The extent of the increase is unknown and may in part be an artifice of reporting. But it appears to be real, and there is no single obvious explanation for the violence. Is it a manifestation of a broader societal problem? Are people more anxious and angry now than they were in the past? Does the violence reflect problems of substance abuse, mental illness, chronic homelessness? Racial tensions? Political polarization? The loss of comity? Anomie? The pandemic may be responsible for some of the encounters – angry disputes over wearing or not wearing masks have turned violent in a number of cases – but the phenomenon precedes the pandemic.

Whatever its sources, antisocial behavior blurs the bottom edge of low-level terrorist violence with the upper edge of social aggression, making it difficult to define, isolate, and quantify, let alone offer solutions.

Conclusions

Circling back to the original question of whether low-level terrorism is a permanent threat to society: It is. Current trends suggest that low-level terrorism will remain a threat for the foreseeable future. Terrorism has persisted for decades, indeed centuries. And most terrorist activity is, in fact, low level, in that attacks are unsophisticated, fewer than half of the attacks cause any fatalities, and those that do cause fatalities cause few per incident.

The operational capabilities of some of the large organizations that were active in the past, including al Qaeda, have been ground down. (Whether the Taliban takeover of Afghanistan will allow an al Qaeda comeback is not clear yet.) Because of changes in how terrorists are recruited, especially in the West, we are seeing more lone actors with limited resources. There are fewer bombings, especially outside of conflict zones, and instead more shootings, stabbings, and vehicle ramming attacks. Shootings and vehicle ramming attacks can cause large numbers of casualties, although on average they are less lethal than large-scale bombings.

Motivations are becoming more complex, with jihadists and ideological extremists on both ends of the political spectrum being joined by individuals disturbed by changing social norms, sexual frustration, or conspiracy theories promoted on the Internet, or simply competing to demonstrate their prowess by outdoing others in slaughter – mass murderers with manifestos.

The atomization of violence can be seen as progress – driving terrorism down to the level of individual perpetrators is sort of an improvement. However, it complicates counterterrorism and has important policy implications. Addressing root causes will not likely dissuade today's solo extremists. Community-based prevention programs will not reach them. Autonomous actors, relying on primitive methods, are harder to identify and are especially hard to protect against. Blurring low-level terrorism with increasing antisocial behavior could further confound definitions and countermeasures.

The conclusion that terrorism is likely to persist at low levels does not preclude large-scale attacks. The present tumultuous state of the world and growing domestic extremism could produce dramatic changes in the future trajectory of political violence.

Notes

1 Louis Beam, "Leaderless Resistance," *The Seditionist*, 1992. http://www.armyofgod.com/Leaderless-Resistance.htm
2 Statistical data derived from the National Consortium for the Study of Terrorism and Responses to Terrorism (START), *Global Terrorism Database* (GTD), College Park, MD: University of Maryland. https://www.start.umd.edu/gtd/
3 The RAND Corporation, *RAND Database of Worldwide Terrorism Incidents* (RDWTI). https://www.rand.org/nsrd/projects/terrorism-incidents.html
4 GTD, op. cit.
5 Mineta Transportation Institute (MTI), *MTI Database of Terrorist and Serious Criminal Attacks Against Public Surface Transportation*, San Jose, CA: Mineta Transportation Institute. https://transweb.sjsu.edu/
6 Ibid.
7 Brian Michael Jenkins and Bruce R. Butterworth, *Long-Term Trends in Attacks on Public Surface Transportation in Europe and North America,* San Jose, CA: Mineta Transportation Institute. https://transweb.sjsu.edu/research/Long-Term-Trends-Attacks-Public-Surface-Transportation-Europe-and-North-America

8 *MTI Database of Terrorist and Serious Criminal Attacks Against Public Surface Transportation,* op.cit.
9 Brian Michael Jenkins, *The Origins of America's Jihadists,* Santa Monica, CA: The RAND Corporation, 2017. https://www.rand.org/pubs/perspectives/PE251.html; and Brian Michael Jenkins, *Paths to Destruction: A Group Portrait of America's Jihadists—Comparing Jihadist Travelers with Domestic Plotters,* Santa Monica, CA: The RAND Corporation, 2020. https://www.rand.org/pubs/research_reports/RR3195.html
10 Brian Michael Jenkins and Bruce R. Butterworth, *How Sophisticated are Terrorist Attacks on Passenger Rail Transportation,* San Jose: CA: Mineta Transportation Institute, 2020. https://transweb.sjsu.edu/research/SP0520-Terrorist-Attacks-Passenger-Rail-Transportation
11 Ibid.
12 *Global Terrorism Database,* op. cit.
13 Ibid.
14 Europol, *European Union Terrorism Situation and Trend Report (TE-SAT) 2020.* June 23, 2020. https://www.europol.europa.eu/activities-services/main-reports/european-union-terrorism-situation-and-trend-report-te-sat-2020
15 Jenkins, *The Origins of America's Jihadists,* Op.cit.
16 Brian Michael Jenkins, Bruce R. Butterworth, Jean-Francois Clair, and Joseph E. Trella III, *An Exploration of Terrorist Stabbing Attacks,* San Jose, CA: Mineta Transportation Institute, 2019. https://transweb.sjsu.edu/research/SP0319-Terrorist-Stabbing-Attacks-Public-Transportation
17 Ibid.
18 Ibid.
19 Brian Michael Jenkins and Bruce R. Butterworth, *An Analysis of Vehicle Rammings as a Terrorist Threat,* San Jose, CA: Mineta Transportation Institute, 2018. https://transweb.sjsu.edu/research/Analysis-Vehicle-Ramming-Terrorist-Threat
20 Ibid.
21 Ibid.

8

THE CASE OF HYBRID TERRORISM

Systemic Lessons from Recent European Plots

Nicolas Stockhammer

A hybrid threat is a phenomenon resulting from convergence and interconnection of different elements, which together form a more complex and multidimensional threat.[1]

Today's terrorist leaders think strategically. They have benefitted from decades of experience, observing their predecessors, enabling them to create new kinds of organizations and formulate strategies that exploit the disadvantages of the democratic state. Intellectually states have not kept up, and radical rethinking is in order.[2]

Brian Jenkins

Prologue

The devastating Paris terror attacks of November 13, 2015 may well be regarded as "Europe's 9/11". They mark the beginning of a breaking new wave[3] of Islamist terrorism against the soft centers of Europe.[4]

Three squadrons of terrorists had simultaneously staged coordinated attacks on six locations throughout Paris, including the Bataclan concert hall, the Stade de France, and at least two restaurants, with 137 killed and some three hundred seriously injured. Promptly ISIS claimed responsibility for the massacres. The Western world was left in a state of shock, and for a good reason. As Thomas Hegghammer rightly observed, this was "one of the most complex terrorist operations ever carried out in Europe".[5]

But already the Charlie-Hebdo attacks of January 2015 involved "an intricate interplay between personal factors and group dynamics, between extremists in Europe and groups overseas, between social grievances and religious-political ideology".[6] In some way, this incident falsely indicated operational contingency with neither an elaborated strategy nor a generic system behind it.

Not only a specific European phenomenon, society's saturated volatile *Aufmerksamkeitsökonomie* (economy of attention; Franck/Honneth) had apparently led to a profound shift of awareness. All eyes were then directed to Ukraine and sporadic intra- European crises such as the recurring Grexit and Brexit debates. This also applies to the media's growing interest in the considerable wave of refugees rolling toward Europe that had by then slowly started to emerge. Fatally, in 2015 neither the political decision-makers nor the media really contextualized the refugee crisis with the dramatic security-political developments at the continent's contested Southern

DOI: 10.4324/9781003326373-9

periphery ("ring of fire") in the Middle-Eastern-Northern-African region. Notwithstanding, there were already then well-informed observers who considered Europe to be mainly a side-show on the global terrorist theatre and consistently jihadist attacks largely as spin-offs and re-percussion of the civil wars, repression and insurgencies in the Arab world. Regardless, without doubt, Europe was in the focus of Islamist terrorism.

These shocking attacks were no unforeseeable "black swan" incident, but rather the inevitable consequence of a dangerous persistent trend.

A Jihadist Apocalypse?

Eventually an unprecedented type of hybrid attack scenario, both in scope and scale, had been executed on European soil.[7] For David Kilcullen the Parisian November attacks of 2015 "represent the start of a sustained urban guerilla campaign".[8] They "signaled the existence of a paramilitary underground – a better organized, more capable version of the ISIS internationale though not yet at the level of a full-blown wilayat – operating in cities within France, Belgium and Germany, and possibly also Denmark and the Netherlands".[9]

The assaults were planned, coordinated, and executed by a team of returnees ("homebounds"), i.e. returning foreign fighters from the jihad in Syria and Iraq. James R. Clapper, then director of US-National Intelligence, stated in the aftermath of the attacks in 2016: "Foreign fighters who have trained in Iraq and in Syria might potentially leverage skills and experience to plan and execute attacks in the West. Involvement of returned foreign fighters in terrorist plotting increases the effectiveness and lethality of terrorist attacks".[10] This was surely an accurate analysis, but unfortunately too late.

The jihadist perpetrators merged established *modi operandi* combining the meanwhile proven and tested "Mumbai style" tactics[11] (referring to the "running gun battle" attacks in Mumbai in 2008 – a kinetic form of desperado terrorism utilizing rifles)[12] simultaneously with a non-kinetic one that is based on the use of improvised explosive devices (IEDs).[13] Kilcullen attests them a "high degree of battle discipline".[14] ISIS adopted what had been some sort of an al-Qaeda trade-mark: synchronized and well-coordinated, brutal terrorist attacks against the "soft belly" of the West. Independently and meticulously prearranged and staged, this well executed staccato of projected (=organized and directed) attacks overburdened Parisian police forces' limited reactive capacities and transcended their ability to keep up efforts stabilizing the difficult security situation. Suddenly, the government's counter-terrorist mission was at once about (further) prevention, protection, persecution and reaction. Then French president Hollande did not hesitate to proclaim a state of emergency in France, which formally entitled his government to involve the armed forces in its counter-terrorist measures.[15]

It appeared evident that this kind of carefully designed plot was rather an attack on the sovereignty of the state than just on indiscriminate victims. Moreover, this projected terrorist incident resembled in its quality more a military strike than an ordinary crime. In such a constellation rather conceived as an act of warfare than a criminal deed, the question was whether to react with means according to the crime (law enforcement and prosecution) or the war paradigm ("war on terror") in countering this adaptive form of extremist violence.[16] If projected terrorism is understood as a type, or at least, a means of warfare, then this proposition necessarily entails implications on the twofold character of terrorism. When it comes to inspired single actor plots that are substantiated in occasional terrorist assaults, for good reasons a criminal typology can be prepended. A distinction between projected or occasional terrorism can only be drawn following thorough investigation, since the differences can be in some cases minimal.

In particular, within the last decade, transnational terrorism has apparently undergone a considerable morphological transformation.[17] As the separating lines between war and crime have disappeared or at least become blurred in the beginning of the 21st century, it can occasionally be difficult to detect what rationale (i.e. intrinsic motivation) lies behind a terrorist attack. By taking advantage of this obvious lack of conceptual and institutional clarity (albeit not everywhere in Europe), the jihadist mindset deliberately aims with its activities at the small interface between internal and external security, which directly affects a major vulnerability of European security architecture. Therefore, some EU member states currently discuss the idea of implementing a homeland security system inspired by the existing US model.[18] Have Western states and even scholars missed a trend with relation to transnational terrorism and its recent multi-dimensional phenomenology? Perhaps to some extent.

Hybridity as Patchwork: "Hybrid Terrorism"

The academic discussion on hybrid forms of warfare has now been around approximately since 2007. However, there is yet no clear consent on either purpose or usefulness of this vague concept to describe an elusive phenomenon. Most of the conflicts in history have been defined by the use of asymmetries to exploit an opponent's weaknesses. To achieve this end, simultaneously regular/irregular and conventional/unconventional tactics have been employed further leading to complex conflict constellations. Similarly, the rise of cyber warfare has not fundamentally changed the nature of warfare as a whole, but rather mutated its character and expanded it into a new dimension.

Asymmetry

Asymmetry is the "key concept for understanding hybrid warfare". Irregular warfare has always been the preferred tool of the weak and a "method of offsetting imbalances between forces and capabilities".[19] At the "strategic level, the enemy using asymmetrical tactics exploits the fears of the populace, thereby undermining the government, compromising its alliances, and affecting its economy. To achieve this, the protagonist uses tactics like guerrilla warfare, hit-and-run attacks, sabotage, terrorism, and psychological warfare. By these means, the weak seeks to deny victory to the strong, who already loses if he doesn't win".[20] One could assert that groups using terrorist means and strategies are usually inferior to the state's police and military potential in terms of logistics and personnel. On the other hand, they operate out of the clandestine and have the tactical element of surprise on their side, which compensates the initial instrumental inferiority.[21]

Asymmetry is just one end of a scale on the spectrum of a conflict typology, not reduced to a one-dimensional scheme, as Herfried Münkler prominently highlighted.[22] Terrorism is according to this categorization hence the "purest form of asymmetry".[23] It is important to add that the fundamental characteristic of asymmetry is the willful breach of common norms or ethical standards and the consequent denial of reciprocity by one (irregular) party: The purpose of a (predominantly) non-state actor is to exploit the vulnerabilities of the enemy by intentionally breaking rules that the adversary feels bound to or that are morally impossible to be given up by the latter. Superiority is not only a result of applying superior means, but taking advantage of the conventional foe's major drawback: the self-imposed obligation to follow rules and laws. This unsolicited commitment is at once a tactical weakness but also a strength. Terrorists, however, constantly aim at provoking democracies to overreact, inducing them to enforce restrictive security measures and limit freedom. Attacked states may exaggerate in their reactions and could even be incited to wage war against a phantom. Then such a provocation turns out to be successful.[24]

It's About Convergence, Stupid!

Asymmetry presupposed, the evolving dynamic of versatile conflict is best characterized by convergence. This includes the convergence of the physical and psychological, the kinetic and non-kinetic aspects, as well as that of combatants and noncombatants. Moreover, one may observe the convergence of military force and the interagency community, of states and non-state actors, and of the capabilities they are armed with. Of greatest relevance are the converging modes of war. This implies that any future conflict will be multi-variant rather than one single form of warfare. Resulting from that, greater attention should be drawn to increasingly blurring and blending forms of war in combination with incrementing frequency and lethality. This conglomerate constitutes "hybrid warfare", in which the adversary will most likely resort to unique combinational threats specifically targeting vulnerabilities of a superior enemy: "Modern adversaries make use of conventional/unconventional, regular/irregular, overt/covert means, and exploit all the dimensions of war to combat the Western superiority in conventional warfare. Hybrid threats exploit the "full-spectrum" of modern warfare; they are not restricted to conventional means".[25]

Is hybrid warfare thus the continuation of warfare by other means? Only partially. Convergence may however add a new dimension to warfare. It is about comprehensiveness. Tactics will be combined, readapted and employed as a mixture thus multiplying the threat. Instead of separate challengers with fundamentally different approaches (conventional, irregular, or terrorist), we can expect to face enemies who will employ all forms of war and tactics, perhaps even simultaneously. "In practice, any threat can be hybrid as long as it is not limited to a single form and dimension of warfare. When any threat or use of force is defined as hybrid, the term loses its value and causes confusion instead of clarifying the "reality" of modern warfare".[26] Scholars and practitioners alike nowadays use the term "hybrid warfare" in different ways: From "grey zone strategies", "competition short of conflict", "active measures", to "new generation warfare" or "postmodern warfare". Despite subtle differences, all these terms point to the same thing: Actors using multiple instruments of power, with an emphasis on non-military tools, to pursue their national interests outside their borders – often at the expense of other actors' interests and those of their allies.

Herfried Münkler, stresses in his recent works upon "fluidity" as the most significant feature of future warfare: It's not about seizing control over territory anymore. Prospective conflicts will be mostly about the control of streams and waves (cyber-dynamics, capital streams, "waves" of migrants, flow of energy resources, etc.).[27] So we may well assume that engaged players will more and more refer to tactics that evolve from and correspond with this new fluid logic. Also, sub-conventional organizations like major terrorist groups have pretty much adjusted to the fluidity that specifies our decade. Particularly, the use of social media for propaganda (creating narratives) and recruiting purposes indicates a comprehensive understanding of the necessity to seize control over (information) streams.

Hybrid Terrorism

Brian Jenkins argues that structurally there could be nothing "new" about terrorism: "Terrorists blow up things, kill people or seize hostages. Every terrorist incident is merely a variation on these three activities".[28] Jenkins is right in his basic approach regarding the types of operations – obviously, as the reservoir of operative options gradually remains the same. But when it comes to motivation (why?), means (what?), execution (how?) and targeting (against what and whom?), the setting has significantly changed over the years.[29]

Bearing this in mind, is hybrid somewhat new? When it comes to the character of terrorism-yes, regarding its nature probably not. Nowadays a lot of things are called "hybrid". Car engines, robots, software and even wristwatches. Why then coin the inflationary term "hybrid" as the significant attribute of transnational terrorism? Does this terminological entry have something to do with "hybrid warfare"? Only conditionally, because both of them make use of tactical advantages resulting from asymmetry, however, access and means vary. The term "hybrid" rather refers to a structural interdependency, the intentional merging of different forms, which in sum creates something new. Elements of preexisting patterns prevail and are recombined with previously unrecognized elements and thus re-established. For the most part, it is about pooling different "ingredients" to produce more effective results, or to create a new form, probably the preliminary stage of a paradigmatic development.

In the specific context of Islamist terrorism, this means the genesis of a more or less modified form of violence which deliberately absorbs known procedures, but at the same time, triggers special dynamics, such as the creation of a loose franchise network, which in turn results in a shift of emphasis under the primacy of unconditional systemic adaptation – and a formerly unknown ability to learn from experience. It is primarily about tactical innovation.

A hybrid threat thus arises from the convergent interaction of various elements of violence, which together manifest a considerably more substantial threat. Explosives, for example, develop their complete destructive potential only when combined with the appropriate substances. This is exactly the case for the currently dominant form of jihadist terrorism. Petter Nesser called (European manifestations of) jihadi terrorism since 2011 a "heterogeneous threat".[30] His nomenclature points to the multidimensional aspect covering recent expressions of transnational terrorism combining group or individual attacks, "homebounds" or "homegrowns" involved, connections with abroad or none, etc. Also the deliberate combination of different building blocks, the "LEGO principle" of terrorist action (assassins, scenarios, armament, etc.) renders current organized terrorist attacks more complex in terms of their anticipation, and thus more dangerous. On that account, suitable adaptive responses from defense authorities must be complex as well. At a first glance, seemingly unorthodox connections (target selection, tactical approach, armament, effects, etc.) are made, taken into account for tactical preparation, and used by commandos (or single actors). These scenarios, however, reveal in their effectiveness and lethality, an unprecedented, negative quality.

Two "major" European terrorist assaults in 2016, in Nice and Berlin, that have exacerbated insecurity and a subjective high threat perception among the population, can serve as meaningful examples of this. Not to forget the symbolic dimension of the attacks (the French national holiday of July 14 and a Christmas market). "Violence and symbolic value seem to have merged" in recent jihadi-salafist plots.[31]

Against the backdrop of this convergence, the traditional framing of Islamist terrorism of the 2010s has to be structurally questioned and re-classified. Resulting from a hybrid phenomenology, counter-terrorism ambitions face an increased difficulty in adjusting to flexible dynamics of a lose network terrorism. There is justified criticism that institutions in charge of combatting terrorism have not caught up yet with these developments and were only prepared for the "wars of yesterday". Terrorists have meanwhile also recognized this fact. Therefore, they consciously practice a hybrid, violent "double game" performing organized networked plots and inspired single actor attacks alike.

Multidimensional Warfare

From the perspective of counterterrorism research, this latest alarming development toward an ambivalent overall approach of jihadist terrorism could even mean a profound systemic shift.[32]

At least a new understanding of transnational terrorism is crucial, bearing in mind that the nature of terrorism may indeed be timeless but its characteristics are constantly changing.[33] Martha Crenshaw emphasizes that "Today's terrorism is not a fundamentally or qualitatively new phenomenon", draws upon the "evolving historical context" and criticizes that emerging differences are "of degree".[34] This observation is basically not wrong. Bruce Hoffman, in opposition to this view, perceives terrorism as "constantly changing and evolving- indeed, far more rapidly and consequentially during the period of time since September 11, 2001…(today)…we face a different enemy than we confronted in 2001 and 2002, and in 2011 and 2012".[35]

In this light the "new" includes or even absorbs older forms. But significant and continuous systemic change is unquestionable. Maybe it is not a manifest revolution, but it indicates an apparent tactical evolution, as modified parameters seem to emerge. Recent developments suggest a turn toward convergence of different elements concerning rationale, planning, *modi operandi*, organization, perpetrators, etc. This interdependence massively impacts the quality of attacks and thus affects the character of transnational terrorism. Likewise, Boaz Ganor focusing on prevailing forms of terrorism, introduced the term "multidimensional warfare".[36] Ganor argues, that modern terrorism has to be understood as a dynamic type of warfare, that has "many facets". Accordingly, "various modi operandi", used against a "variety of targets" in "multiple arenas" at "varying levels of intensity" causing anywhere "from a few to tens of thousands of casualties" come into play under such circumstances.[37] Islamist terrorists capitalize on this multidimensional approach, as the sheer plurality of options makes their tactics hard to anticipate and even harder to prevent. Much of this reshaping is primarily based on the terrorist organizations' strong anarchical ability to adapt to changing security environments. This leads to an increasing flexibility in execution and the imagined omnipresence of a serious, at once elusive and amorphous threat. Also with regard to motivation, intention and ideology, it is difficult to grasp current jihadist groups as there are multiple heterogeneous influences that are individually construed.

Layers of Hybridity

Hybrid Motivation

What are the root causes underlying the ongoing spread of jihadist terrorism in the past decade? ISIS, for instance, can be regarded as a symptom and a catalyst of nine major problems and trends[38] that are driving jihadist terrorism around the globe and will continue to do so, even though ISIS as a terrorist militia seems to be largely defeated. Its other operative terrorist branch will nonetheless persist and may even expand its ruthless activities. According to a recent New America study, the major drivers for transnational jihadism are:

1 the regional civil war in the Middle East between Sunni and Shia;
2 the collapse of Arab governance around the region;
3 the collapse of economies in war torn Muslim states;
4 the population bulge in the Middle East and North Africa;
5 the tidal wave of Muslim immigration into Europe;
6 the marginalization of Muslims in Europe;
7 the rise of European ultranationalist parties;
8 the spread of militant Salafism;
9 social media's amplification of anger caused by all of these trends.[39]

These generic foundations of jihadism strongly suggest that a successor of ISIS is likely to emerge in the coming years. At least its violent ideology and multidimensional warfare principles will live on. Moreover, a jihadist organization requires, as any other extremist group, a clear enemy concept. Historically, the "near enemy-far enemy" distinction was often used to differentiate between organizations that primarily target local, in most cases Muslim, regimes and groups that focus on Western targets. Hybrid terror organizations like ISIS have contributed to render this antagonism obsolete. "Many jihadist groups are displaying ambiguous rhetoric and behavior with regard to who they consider as their main enemy", as Thomas Hegghammer underlines.[40] And: "When enemy hierarchies become unclear, undefined, or heterogeneous, then this is most often a sign of increasing radicalization and political isolation".[41] More importantly, Hegghammer registers a dynamic toward a "hybrid ideology" among jihadist groups. An ideologically hybridized group is one, as he asserts, whose "behavior and ideological discourse display influences of more than one type of ideal rationale in near equal measure".[42]

There is evidence that during the peak-phase of ISIS when the organization was rising to power, gathering control over an extensive territory, it seized "sovereignty of interpretation" over the jihad, in the sense that fighting the close enemy in the "caliphate" was prioritized. Along with a forthcoming recession, facing a superior coalition of enemies and an unfolding erosion of the "caliphate", the distant enemy (Europe) was set more and more in the focus of the organization's activities. Hand in hand with this turn toward the distant enemy goes a relatively heterogeneous targeting behavior. Attacks could likewise focus on a highly symbolic target such as a Christmas market, or just on a random place such as a regional commuter train in Germany. There was no clear evidence as to a tactical preference, although the strategic value of attacking the symbols of the foe was obvious to the planning elite of ISIS. Such perfidious deeds were meant to consolidate the ideological foundations of the then perceived legitimate jihadist successor of al-Qaeda.

Their specific archaic and immanent interpretation of jihad was the core of what had somewhat become a global jihadist ideology. It was conveyed by a "social movement" and disappointed, young Muslims all over the world could hook–up with this modern style of jihad, that now ultimately had a face. Other than Usama bin Laden's approach, daily propaganda and footage from the fight against the "infidel aggressors" fueled the idea of jihad. This had the taste of adventure and incorporated the apocalyptic ideology of the ultimate battle against the infidels, the *kuffār.* When the source of jihadist inspiration, the vision of a caliphate, seemed to run dry, the jihadist tactics had to be adapted accordingly. Terrorism was regarded as a cheaper and yet not less effective alternative to guerilla warfare. ISIS had without doubt learned from al-Qaeda's successes and failures, and constantly attempted to outperform its predecessor organization. Hence, for ISIS' operative leaders the first thing to tackle was to develop an appropriate, multidimensional terrorist strategy that would be both cost-efficient and effective.

Hybrid Strategy

According to Bruce Hoffman the basic "principle of jihad is the ideological bond that unites this amorphous movement, transcending its lose structure, diverse membership, and geographic separation".[43] A common ideological foundation allows the cultivation of a loose network. Fluid terrorist organizations like ISIS are more or less structured like a "franchise of terror".[44] Herfried Münkler raises the question, whether ISIS has a strategic plan that is more than the indiscriminate spread of fear and terror. His consideration: "This is difficult to find under the conditions of a franchise system, as anyone who is willing to kill can choose targets and victims according to their own preference and opportunity".[45] Maybe there is no strategic plan or even a "grand strategy" behind a lose organization such as ISIS, but there are definitely some "mosaics" of strategic orientation that can be detected. In their groundbreaking study "The Strategies of Terrorism" Andrew H. Kydd and Barbara F. Walter filtered out five principal strategic principles, predominantly relevant for 21st century terrorist campaigns: [1] *attrition*, [2] *intimidation*, [3] *provocation*, [4] *spoiling*, and [5] *outbidding*.[46] An attrition strategy, is merely about terrorists seeking to "persuade the enemy that the terrorists are strong enough to impose considerable costs if the enemy continues a particular policy".[47] Intimidation is the attempt to "convince the population that the terrorists are strong enough to punish disobedience and that the government is too weak to stop them, so that people behave as the terrorists wish".[48] A provocation strategy seeks to "induce the enemy to respond to terrorism with indiscriminate violence, which radicalizes the population and moves them to support the terrorists".[49] Spoilers attack in an effort to "persuade the enemy that moderates on the terrorists' side are weak and untrustworthy, thus undermining attempts to reach a peace settlement".[50] Last but not least, "groups engaged in outbidding use violence to convince the public that the terrorists have greater resolve to fight the enemy than rival groups, and therefore are worthy of support".[51] Without doubt, understanding these five distinct strategic motivations of transnational terrorism is crucial for designing effective anti-terror-policies. Currently, the imperatives of attrition, which comprises exhaustion, as well as intimidation and provocation seem to overlap spoiling and outbidding strategies. Attrition and exhaustion are achieved by a strategy of ceaseless violence, whereas provocation is rather subject to a strategy of communication.

Multidimensional Communication

With reference to communication, terrorists aim at conveying a message of violence and fear to the various intended recipients: the wider national and international public, governments, the media, supporters and competitors, and in particular their own group. Contents and intentions, however, vary. While the public and the media should be shocked, supporters should be motivated to continue with their endorsement and financial aid, and also be reaffirmed in their allegiance, competitors should be deterred – governments and executive branches should be provoked to inconsiderate counter-action. This multitude of different simultaneous messages reflects a multidimensional communicative approach of a terrorist campaign as executed by al-Qaeda and more recently by ISIS. Terrorism is an instrument to address different audiences, a pathological form of communication. Violence reinforces the claims of the terrorists as it attracts attention of media and the populace. Subjective, sometimes paranoid anxiety generated by exaggerated media coverage often becomes larger than the objective threat. This can be seen as a psycho-cultural phenomenon.

Creating fear, just like the use of violence has meanwhile become an end in itself for jihadist terrorists. This caused: "...a new, dangerous knock-on effect to emerge: a pull of empowerment that encourages extremists in the West to commit attacks in their homeland. They should stir up fear and mistrust among the population. ISIS still uses fear as a strategic weapon, only the goals change".[52]

Boundless Violence

A shocking terrorist incident in early June 2016 can be categorized as paradigmatic for this trend toward boundless violence. In Magnanville, a suburb west of Paris, a self-radicalized jihadist brutally stabbed a police officer and subsequently his partner, also a member of a police commissariat, in front of their three-year-old son. The entire horrific act was live-streamed via the

Internet.[53] At the same time the Islamist expressed his loyalty to ISIS and the jihad on Facebook. Of course, communicating by means of violence is still in the focus of such atrocities, but the stark expressive display of violence seems very disturbing: The terrorist is made delirious by his deed – even while it is in progress – and the feeling of situational omnipotence is a condensate of this beastly violence. All that happened before the eyes of the heavily traumatized child of the victims. By this incredible deed moral borders that have long been regarded as taboo had been deliberately transcended. Quite evidently the focus seems to have shifted now to brute violence as a statement, not a message wrapped with force. The act itself has become the message. The ethos of the "economic use of force"[54] (Peter Waldmann) that had determined past waves of terrorism, has somehow eroded: It is no longer consciously calculated what extent of violence is necessary to achieve the goal – predominantly there is a randomness and arbitrariness concerning the targeting, the selection of victims, expected casualties and any collateral damage. For quite some time, at the latest with the emergence of ISIS as a key player in the field of transnational terrorism, the ruthless use of force has evidently developed into an end in itself. That aspect reflects the performative dimension of terrorism.

In the aftermath of the Manchester plot in 2017, when jihadists staged a suicide bombing attack during an Ariana Grande pop- concert killing several teenagers, Kenan Malik observes

> increasingly blurred lines between ideological violence and sociopathic rage. There is now what we might call a 'jihadi state of mind', in which some mixture of social disengagement, moral dissolution, unleavened misanthropy and inchoate rage drives some to see the most abhorrent expressions of violence as a kind of revolt.[55]

All these aspects go together, creating a deadly bundle of motivations, leading to boundless, indiscriminative violence against particularly young victims. The message was clear: Anybody can become a victim. The initially constituting factors like age, origin, religion, social status and other possible determinants for targeting, do not play a significant role anymore for the current generation of lone acting jihadist perpetrators.

The Anarchy of the Chameleon

The main objective of terrorist organizations or single actors with allegiance to such groups, is to destabilize and to create disorientation. Perpetrators multiply terrorist violence and are able to tactically "learn anarchically " (Herfried Münkler): They act in the sense of a "trial and error procedure" and in principle they are not bound by any rules, which manifests real asymmetry. Through a constant testing, the "strategists" of terror identify structural weaknesses of the defensive system. Like a chameleon they adapt to permanently changing security precautions and are tactically highly flexible. Terrorists want to provoke a "false counteraction" by the security authorities, such as a drastic intensification of security measures: "Terrorism is a strategy that works through the mechanism of provoking a reaction, terrorists are trappers, and the more likely it is that the state gets caught in the trap, the faster it gets provoked and reacts 'blindly'".[56] Within their tactical disposition lies a core ambivalence: Terrorists want to attract attention and recruit followers, but also sustainably split the attacked societies. Following such a hybrid approach, not only radical elements are in the terrorist's focus, but above all, moderate forces that gradually feel marginalized. According to this intentionality, a sustainable spiral of violence is triggered, that can hardly be encountered by one-dimensional, often ineffective de-radicalization campaigns.

Hybrid Radicalization

In his recent work Peter Neumann describes five building blocks or risk factors that play a more or less important role in radicalization in different ways: "grievance, needs, ideas, people and violence".[57] At the beginning of every radicalization process is a frustration and thus the susceptibility to a (violent) ideology, which promises to satisfy certain, generally quite justified human needs, such as the urge for orientation, a sense of community, identity or sheer thirst for adventure. The underlying frustration coupled with these needs is consciously directed by the ideology into a political or religious project, usually associated with revanchist claims. In addition, the social environment and the influence of other individuals (amplifiers, catalysts) as well as violence, either as one's experience or transitive against others are important. This process can unfold gradually and manifests itself differently, just as the inhibition threshold for violence in individuals is different in each case. The so-called "turbo" or "flash" radicalization, an individual short-time development process leading to extremist views, which is often subject to media reporting, however, seems to be a myth.

In the aftermath of the November 2015 attacks there was a broad, not solely academic discussion in France, on radicalization and if there was a significant development toward more radical forms within Islam or whether Islam was just misused as a religious stalking-horse for violence. A protagonist, the French political scientist Olivier Roy considers the religious component of the attacks to be just a pretext. Unlike his intellectual adversary, Gilles Kepel, a scholar of Islamic Studies, he doesn't recognize a "radicalization of Islam" but rather an "Islamization of radicalism".[58] According to Roy, the young French "banlieue-terrorists" usually have no idea about the Qur'an or the Algerian War (1954 to 1962). But these young men (it is mostly a male phenomenon) tend to adopt the religious or anti-colonial slogans after their indoctrination by Syrian recruiters. They smoked, consumed alcohol, drugs and pornography, often being converts, as Roy claims. Many of the jihadist terrorists have an actual background and even a judicial track record as petty criminals. As Peter Neumann points out

> One of the most significant facts about IS recruits in Europe is their close proximity to 'ordinary' crime. In most Western European countries, more than half of the group's recruits have criminal pasts, often as members of gangs, drug dealers, thieves or burglars. For many of these young men, joining IS was a way of seeking redemption. In the words of a Danish fighter, 'it's not good enough just praying with all the shit I've done'[59]

What is rightly summarized under the "crime –terror- nexus" is probably a most significant characteristic of hybrid terrorism.[60] Peter Neumann and his research team discovered that it

> is not the merging of criminals and terrorists as organizations but of their social networks, environments, or milieus. Criminal and terrorist groups have come to recruit from the same pool of people, creating (often unintended) synergies and overlaps that have consequences for how individuals radicalize and operate. This is what we call the new crime-terror nexus.[61]

The inhibition threshold for such predisposed criminals to morph into jihadist perpetrators is relatively low. Given this undeniable dynamic, which is detached from any spiritual roots even of an extremist religious interpretation of political Islam, Olivier Roy's aforementioned hypotheses of an "Islamization of radicalism" gains further credibility. The perpetrators' nihilism, even their reflexes of violence are in stark contradiction to the Sunni tradition that still served as spiritual or ideological fundament for the 9/11 attackers. What about their mental constitution? The forensic psychologist Jerome Endrass carved out four attacker prototypes:

> The first category concerns the mentally ill – for example schizophrenics; secondly, people with personality disorders (e.g. narcissistic personality disorders); thirdly, those who feel drawn to the authoritarian and belligerent character of jihad; and fourthly Muslims who feel despised and discriminated against in Europe and perceive jihad as an invitation to avenge themselves.[62]

Again, despite clear categorization, we are facing a mixed typology of perpetrators. Seldom there is a linear, monolithic psychopathology. The same rule seems to apply for terrorist organizations.

Hybrid Organization

According to Boaz Ganor's prevalent classification, ISIS is a "hybrid organization" of violence.[63] It is widely conceived as a "popular terrorist organization", that comprises "thousands of activists, who are buoyed on waves of support from an extensive community".[64]

A hybrid terrorist organization "subsumes two, and sometimes three, components: a militant-terrorist wing, a political wing, and a wing devoted to providing social welfare services. All three wings are directly or indirectly subject to the organization's leadership and operate according to the policies it delineates".[65] ISIS is at once a classic terrorist militia with a longtime focus on the "near" enemy in the territory of interest, the meanwhile eroded "caliphate" in the Levant and on the other hand a fully-fledged and newly proportioned terrorist organization whose proponents practice a mixture of "state terror" and insurgent terrorism against vulnerable European metropolises. This structural ambivalence is highly dangerous, which can be very well documented by the still ongoing jihadist migration ("homebound jihadists") from the war zone in Syria and Iraq. Attacks against soft targets in the homeland of many of these returning jihadist foreign fighters become foreseeable. Hardly anyone dares to predict the threat Europe is facing, considering the relatively large number of returning jihadists, regardless of them being traumatized or further radicalized.

But especially homegrown jihadism (i.e. mostly self-radicalized and individual offenders) has become virulent as recent plots in France, Sweden, Germany, UK and Spain seem to prove. There is strong evidence that this is currently the endemic expression of the jihadist threat.

Hybrid Attack Scenarios

Since the Jewish Museum attack in Brussels in May 2014, "jihadists have been responsible for plotting more than a hundred attacks in Europe…" and "in 41 instances, they were successful", as Peter Neumann summarizes.[66] He concedes that both, the character and dynamics of Islamist terrorist assaults are likely to change. This refers to scope, composition and complexity. Jihadist terror nourishes fear by its immediacy, apparent randomness and demonstrative arbitrariness in target and victim selection. The logistics of transnational terrorism borrows from the principle of guerrilla warfare, seeking advantage of clandestineness, because a phantom is hard to fight. The current trend in terrorist attack scenarios in the West – whether projected or opportunity-induced- clearly portends toward structured planning, fast execution and appropriate arming of the assassins (rapid-fire rifles and explosives vests). However, one could assume "increasing complexity" of attack scenarios for the near future, as soon as returning foreign fighters, usually experienced and trained, become involved.[67] Following that complexity proposition, at the level of "projected terrorism", suitable attack targets will likely be rather selected according to the "Desperado scheme", possibly including IEDs or chemical agents. Just like in Paris 2015 and Brussels 2016. With reference to the simplicity hypothesis, at the level of opportunity-based terrorism, random, amok (e.g. vehicular terrorism), or explosives attacks, at the tourist hot spots of major European cities will continue to be in the focus of terrorist attackers.

Scholars should for different reasons take a closer look at recent cases of vehicular terrorism. The car rampage in Nice on 14 July 2016, carried out by the Tunisian Mohamed Lahouaiej-Bouhlel, killing 86 victims and injuring 458 persons, can be regarded as a symptom of a jihadist shift toward indiscriminative violence as an end in itself. An arithmetic of the highest possible number of victims is connected with the sinister claim to unfold maximum publicity. The fact that someone turns a truck into a bulldozer and randomly mows down people, mainly children and teenagers, indicates the perfidious nefariousness of the jihadists. A similar incident occurred on 19 December 2016, when the Tunisian Anis Amri, a failed asylum seeker, drove a heavy truck (20 tons) carrying steel beams into a crowded Christmas market on Breitscheidplatz next to the Kurfürstendamm, leaving 12 people dead and 56 injured. The latest noteworthy terrorist vehicular incident took place in Barcelona on the afternoon of 17 August 2017, when 22-year-old Moroccan Younes Abouyaaqoub drove a van into pedestrians on La Rambla promenade killing 13 people and injuring at least 130 others. Abouyaaqoub managed to escape the scene by foot, then killed another person trying to steal the victim's car. Nine hours later, five members of the same terrorist cell, drove into pedestrians in nearby Cambrils, killing one woman and injuring six others. All five attackers were killed by police forces.

As early as in 2014, former ISIS propagandist al-Adnani called for attacks against "disbelievers" in their own environment with even the simplest means: "Smash his head with a rock, or slaughter him with a knife, or run him over with your car, or throw him down from a high place, or choke him, or poison him".[68] Such vile assassinations can hardly be anticipated and certainly not prevented by the security authorities. They are sort of an Achilles' heel of counter-terrorism. The Islamists' tactical change of attitude corresponds to an operational shift toward low-tech scenarios. It no longer requires complex logistics to carry out a terrorist attack with great resonance. In addition, there is a current trend toward individual offenders decoupled from networks who attack soft destinations on their own initiative, such as the tranquil seaside resort on the Côte d'Azur. Not only the choice of a tourist destination as a target of attack, but also that of the French national holiday as a time for the rampage have quite a symbolic meaning: The "decadent" West should be hit where it most indulges in its liberal, relaxed lifestyle, when celebrating a national holiday. The signal effect is devastating.

Hybrid Perpetrators

Transnational terrorism in its present form is in principle indiscriminate. Attacks like in Paris, Brussels or Berlin could happen anywhere and anytime in Europe, but also abroad. Above all, however, assassinations that took place in a martyr style – i.e. at the expense of the perpetrator's own death such as e.g. the axe-attack in the German city Würzburg, indicate a perfidious form of "occasional terrorism" and a rampant free-rider problem. Virtually everyone can join this terror cooperative, it's like joining a franchise system.

Lone actors, who act arbitrarily and detached from command structures, often without direct affiliation to an Islamist network are a special case.[69] Spaaij defines "lone wolves" as persons who "(a) operate individually, (b) do not belong to an organized group or network; and (c) whose modi operandi are conceived and directed by the individual without any direct outside command or hierarchy."[70]

Declaring allegiance to a terrorist organization often happens at the assassins' own initiative and then mostly in connection with an attack already carried out. Unlike a decade ago, it's possible to observe a strong preference for relatively simple plots, especially among single actors.[71] These only require a suicide assassin, equipped with an AK-47 or driving a truck into a crowd, killing innocent people in a densely populated urban area.[72] Such manifestations of violence are becoming more likely and make effective anticipation infinitely more difficult. Still, some counter-terrorism experts fear that we may soon face attacks using chemical substances such as mustard gas or even biological agents (e.g. smallpox) in the near future. To get an idea of ongoing developments, it makes sense to shed a light on the prototypical perpetrator regarding their respectively preferred attack scheme.

Projected Terrorism

Coordinated terror plots (projected terror) will continue, as the major attacks in Paris and Brussels prove. Still we are facing an interchanging instrumentalization of projected terrorism and opportunistic terrorism (occasional terrorism). Under "Projected terrorism" we above all summarize pre-structured scenarios coordinated by group leaders like the jihadist "mastermind" of the Paris assassinations, Salah Abdeslam. Generally, this type of networked operation requires relatively static, less flexible logistics but also a demanding and complex preparation. Attackers, in most cases skilled homebound jihadists, were usually recruited and specifically trained by ISIS (related) commanders. After having gone through a terrorist boot camp, they were transferred to the underground of European cities. Under such a clandestine, hostile environment in the forefront of an attack, foreign fighters were "…sometimes part of attack cells, whereas in other instances they functioned as handlers or advisors of cells, leaving the scene before attacks were set in motion".[73] Therefore these attacks can be legitimately regarded as a form of expeditionary terrorism.

With reference to a study by Nesser/Stenerson/Oftedal it can be assumed that "…attack cells are built by entrepreneurs".[74] These jihadist mediators are trying to recruit "misfits and drifters" among their social networks for violent jihad. Entrepreneurs are typically "resourceful, politicized and activistminded, and they serve as a link with groups in conflict zones".[75] Moreover, they "socialize, politicize and manipulate the misfits and drifters that commonly involve criminals and socially deprived people, and turn them into tools for terrorist groups".[76] For the Norwegian researcher team this explains why "seemingly non-political and non-ideological people (such as petty criminals) end up engaging in political violence in accordance with the ideology of ISIS". It seems like a consistent trend in Europe. The major difference now is that interaction (recruitment, radicalization) takes place online. Unfortunately, we only know little about the structure of networks behind the latest wave of ISIS-terrorism in Europe. But certainly there is a hierarchical pattern: "mostly misfits and drifters as foot soldiers, while entrepreneurs are in coordinating roles, both within attack cells and surrounding networks".[77] Counter-terrorist approaches have to consider this entrepreneur-driven structure of contemporary projected, jihadist terrorism. A vivid example for such a dynamic is the "Abaaoud network", named after the planner of the Paris November attacks. Several members of this network such as the El-Bakraoui brothers, were "misfits known for criminal activity, and many of them did not appear to be particularly religious (e.g. smoking and drinking, doing drugs or keeping girlfriends outside of marriage). Many hailed from segregated suburbs or working class areas, had low education and survived on odd jobs".[78]

Somehow resuming the security-relevant developments in Europe between 2014 and 2016, Petter Nesser identifies two main changes concerning ISIS network dynamics and terrorist cell formation: "The first is an increase in the use of social media to recruit and instruct terrorist operatives and the second is the use of refugee streams to transfer operatives and recruitment efforts aimed at refugees".[79]

The latter aspect has gradually lost its significance due to an at least partial "containment" of the migrant influx to Europe. The role of social media as a catalyst of recruitment and channel for terrorist instruction has definitely remained constant.[80] What kind of instructions? Tactical instructions? These questions are worth a closer inspection and automatically lead to another: What are the tactical implications of projected terrorist attacks in their current expression?

Jihadi "Auftragstaktik"

Beginning with 13 November 2015 in Paris an essentially new pattern of convergent jihadist tactics had ultimately become evident and this disturbing impression was further confirmed by the March 2016 attack in Brussels. What are the tactical implications that came along with this type of terrorist assault? Within this range of a "projected", networked operation, the currently preferred jihad-salafist method for carrying out larger scale terrorist attacks in Europe, involves an adaptation of *Auftragstaktik*, an operational leadership doctrine with the highest possible degree of flexibility in order fulfilment. It is predicated on a strategic battlefield principle, deeply rooted in the legendary Prussian field marshal Moltke's (the Elder) classic combat doctrine of maximum situational flexibility.[81] A key component of this German command system was the comparably wide bandwidth in execution options given to combat officers in fulfilling a mission. According to these tactical guidelines, commanders prescribe their subordinates a goal and a framework (time and/or target) to help them achieve this, endowing them with the greatest possible freedom of action. Symptomatically, the nowadays dominating form of hybrid terrorism provides assassins with a new operational toolkit regardless of them being directly mandated, acting entirely or partially on their own, they will be much more flexible than they have been up to now. The 9/11-like micro-management with detailed pre-structured processes has obviously been replaced in favor of a more efficient, free-floating (fluid) military procedure. Jihadist terrorists have gradually deviated from operationally and logistically complex attack scenarios in order to remain unpredictable for counterterrorism approaches, due to augmented spontaneity derived from unspecific orders. Plots are usually arranged by a sub-unit of the terrorist network, a self-sufficient operating cell, whose integral part is the individual assassin. Under such circumstances, a perpetrator turns into an "appendage" of the executive body – an extended, invisible hand of jihad. The assassin squads of Paris and Brussels were organized and briefed in such a manner.

Notably, ISIS conceded that the terrorist organization adopted *Auftragstaktik* to provide their recruits with "complete tactical autonomy", with few fingerprints that could be tracked back to the group, and "no micromanaging".[82] This deliberate turn to *Auftragstaktik* requires an adequate response by executive counterterrorism institutions – may it be intelligence based or planned beforehand on a tactical level.

Opportunity Terrorism

"McJihad"

Quite contrary to the network scheme of projected attack scenarios, there is "the prospect of continued attacks perpetrated by lone wolves or cells of individuals banding together to carry out entirely self-generated and self-directed incidents…",[83] what can be best summarized under inspired "occasional terrorism". The terrorist act itself results from the combination of the operational propaganda and a favorable (i.e. opportunistic) environment. Virtually every radicalized person without ever having appeared as Islamist before could join the "Jihad 3G" of the 2010 decade.[84] Why refer to a "third generation" of jihad? The first generation of jihadists were still a kind of self-proclaimed holy warriors in the sense of the classical "mujaheddin", who interpreted their activities primarily as a liberation struggle against occupying forces. The second generation of assassins, who before were responsible for the attacks of September 11, were organized hierarchically and thoroughly trained. They received tactical directives and instructions from the "top management" of al-Qaida, and at a strategic level there was a kind of jihadist "master plan" that envisaged weakening or destroying the main enemy, the United States. The birth of the third generation of jihad ("Jihad 3G" – Gilles Kepel) can be traced back to the youth protests of 2005, which set the Parisian banlieues on fire. As a reflex of the forgotten, a generation of chronically disadvantaged young people who do not shrink from violence, originally mostly of North African origin.[85] Most of them were young men between 15 and 25 years old who were looking for rituals to prove their masculinity, which was perceived as constricted and circumcised.

The second significant turning point was the widespread failure of the "Arab Spring", which must be understood as a rebellion of a Muslim youth against social inequality, unemployment, and lack of prospects. A veritable jihadist movement emerged from the numerous radicalized of the "generation of the forgotten", regardless of them being fanatical returnees of war from Syria or homegrown Islamists in European states. Hybrid terrorism of the third generation is dialectically constructed as a new "McJihad", a specific kind of franchise of terror, derived from the former cultural struggle in the sense of the antagonism "Jihad vs. McWorld" (Benjamin Barber).[86] This is to be understood as a sophisticated system that deliberately exploits (communication) technologies, the capitalist orientation of the West and its obvious vulnerability as an open, liberal system for its own terrorist purposes.

The radicalized proponents could become part of "Jihad 3G" anytime, without lengthy admission procedures or initiation rites. No more preliminary lead time or complicated instructions are needed beforehand and also membership of ISIS or another jihadist terrorist organization is no longer necessary. You don't even have to bring in a proven "track record" as a jihadist. Likewise, there is no requirement for prior expressions of solidarity with a terrorist network anymore. Such a loose franchise system has proven efficient. Terrorist action is handled under the primacy of spontaneity paired with an unprecedented simplicity in implementation. As paradoxical as this may sound, this is an indication of "democratization" of Islamist terrorism since the original "exclusivity" of the second generation of jihadists has been willingly given up. In the forefront of 9/11, among jihadist communities it has still been considered as a "privilege" to be selected for the "holy war". The Internet has created a simplified access to information and a social media communication platform which has extensively been used by Islamist proponents. They fertilize these channels for their ideology of violence to target or even recruit new assassins, to incite doubters and finally to call for terrorist attacks. Under such favorable circumstances a turn toward simple, immediate schemes of attack seems evident.

An involvement of foreign fighters is so far still widely regarded as an exception within the categories of homegrown cells or single actors, but it is possible that perpetrators had drawn inspiration (online) from them, prior to their attack.[87]

Jihadist Connections & Control

There is in such cases no direct connection with a terrorist organization like ISIS (neither direct contact, nor financial or material support, nor training). Recently, however, there is a trend toward "remote control", especially with self-radicalized assassins, without previous connections to any terrorist organization.

With reference to the aspect of remote control and connections, Hegghammer and Nesser proposed a typology that reflects the different link options between perpetrators and the relevant terrorist organization and the quality of preeminent relations[88]:

1 *Training and top-level directives.* This is the 9/11 attack example: The perpetrator is trained in a safe haven boot camp and tasked by an organization's top leaders to perform an attack in the West.
2 *Training and mid-level directives.* The perpetrator is trained in a safe haven boot camp and is encouraged by mid-level cadres to carry out a more or less specified attack in the West.
3 *Training.* The perpetrator is trained in a safe haven boot camp, but is not specifically instructed by anyone to attack in the West.
4 *Remote contact with directives.* The perpetrator communicates remotely (typically by telephone, email, or social media) and bilaterally with cadres of the organization and receives personal instructions to attack in the West.
5 *Remote contact without directives.* The attacker communicates remotely and bilaterally with members of the organization but does not receive instructions to attack in the West.
6 *Sympathy, no contact.* The attacker expresses ideological support for the group through his propaganda consumption, written or spoken statements, or some other aspect of his behavior, but does not communicate bilaterally with anyone in the organization.

The recent ISIS plots in Europe rather suggest prior connections according to a scheme as described under 4, 5 and 6. Again, in this context it is necessary to distinguish between opportunity-based assaults and those that are carefully planned projected scenarios, including two or more attack squads. In particular, the "sympathy no contact" mode of ideologically inspired assaults that has turned out to be a common practice among single actors during the last 2–3 years, poses a serious problem to counter-terrorism efforts, as in most cases there is no evident prior contact between a later perpetrator and the organization. Basically, any expression of sympathy for, and ideological support of jihadism by a suspect could manifest to a real threat. This is of course only one of the issues.

Lessons for Counter-Terrorism Ambitions

The Cyclic 5–Stages– Approach

Counter-terrorism

> refers to all measures aimed at thwarting terrorist plots and dismantling terrorist organizations. This typically includes the arrest of suspected members, the disruption of terrorist attacks, recruitment, propaganda, travel, and logistics, countering terrorist finance, the protection of potential targets, and the pooling and exchange of data with foreign countries.[89]

During all five cyclic CT stages (prevention-protection-prosecution-reaction-deterrence), whereas the order may change, the core business of intelligence is to gather information and use it accordingly against the terrorist threat.

(Counter-)Intelligence

Without doubt, an appropriate counter-terrorism strategy should be based on intelligence. Relevant information should be collected and distributed among international security agencies. Probably the most prominent and efficient policing method to detect, identify and consequently arrest terrorist suspects in Europe is the so-called "grid search". It is predominantly used to identify potential endangerers by collecting mass data from both, public and private databases. Such databases may include resident registrations, criminal record datasets, but also information on customers of public and private companies and most interestingly, communications data. By increasingly applying these "grids" to the search, investigators aim at generating a manageable amount of individuals, which can facilitate the potential identification of the suspect(s).

It is no secret however, that despite ongoing attempts to improve this situation, coordination between European intelligence services is relatively poor, with no comprehensive, shared list of suspected extremists. Several individual databases already exist, but so far there is no substantial overarching logic behind these efforts. Currently there already exist some meta-data based projects, that focus on comprehensiveness, accessibility and interpretation. Much research and development is invested in solutions that are meant to turn this huge bulk of collected data into actionable intelligence.

Intelligence, properly employed, "implies understanding the motivations, leadership structure, and modus operandi of terrorist organizations, and developing a plan that can anticipate and adapt to their constantly morphing operations. Importantly, the ideological dimension should not be ignored because it explains the extremes to which terrorists are willing to arrive".[90]

Any counter-terrorist measure must address both the terrorist's capability and intention (or "motivation"). These two factors are reciprocally intertwined. Boaz Ganor assumes that "Terrorism is likely to end if one of these factors is neutralized – that is, if a terrorist organization's operational capability is impaired or if its motivation diminishes".[91]

Tackling the terrorist's motivation is much more complex than thwarting their capabilities.

Prevention and De-radicalization

The terrorist's intention to resort to means of violence usually evolves in the course of the radicalization process (compare Peter Neumann's classification above) and comprises besides others, predominantly micro- and macro-sociological but also psychological or ideological aspects. As the Internet has become the major field of jihadist propaganda and communication, it is necessary to seize control over, infiltrate or even destroy these channels in order to prevent radicalization. This may include, but is not restricted to the following measures:

- Collecting and interpreting data
- Identifying potential ideological influences
- Closing, restricting or controlling the channels of (ideological) communication
- Fighting the catalysts (persons, propaganda) of extremist ideologies
- Weakening, undermining or infiltrating organizations that foster such ideologies
- Destroying networks (if necessary)
- Providing an adequate counter-narrative
- Addressing the (individual) root causes of radicalization
- Engaging in individual de-radicalization (if necessary)

The "measures" suggested here can only be a superficial account of what could be done. Countering terrorism and in particular its motivational core that is a product of a radicalization process is difficult and has to be tailored to the real, i.e. individual conditions. There is no patent solution after all.

Strengthening of Physical Security

A third and often underrated core principle in the European struggle against terrorism is the aspect of improvement of physical security. It goes without saying that this should primarily occur on a national basis. Measures include a further strengthening of police forces (personnel, equipment), but also, with regard to systemic terrorist attacks, the protection of critical national infrastructure, which is in most cases a task for the military. Attempts to implement community policing (similar to neighborhood watch), as well as public monitoring initiatives have been made in several European states. With respect to protection of urban environments, some European capitals have built up barriers and bollards as preventive measures to physically protect pedestrian zones and to preempt rampages. There have also been broad and considerable efforts to intensify CCTV surveillance in public areas. Quite a recent phenomenon is the increasing drone (UAV) "traffic" in public spaces and the inherent risk of a terrorist misuse of this new technology. Governments all over Europe have reacted to this new kind of threat and initialized a drone defense, in particular with regard to larger public events. In the face of latest developments, aviation security has somewhat become a major security concern throughout Europe and there are attempts to coordinately strengthen it.

The EU's Counter-Terrorism – A Paper Tiger?

Meanwhile, some European states have got an idea what kind of multidimensional terrorism they are facing. But how to respond to such a hybrid terrorism in a structured and organized manner? The EU's Counter-Terrorism Policy, often referred to as a "paper tiger",[92] is limited to grand announcements of a "comprehensive" security approach, while still heavily relying on classical investigative police work. One cornerstone of the EU's structural fight against terrorism, in addition to the previously mentioned preventive measures, is "elementary precaution" against attacks. For example, recently, as an immediate reaction to the Nice and Berlin rampage attacks, public areas such as shopping streets and open market areas in Germany and Austria have been "protected" by special constructions such as bollards, to avoid unauthorized access. This tactical approach to protection can be only a limited one, as terrorists can draw from an almost unlimited reservoir of attack scenarios, which require an equally wide range of counter-measures. Unfortunately, organizations in charge of protection will therefore always lag at least one step behind. Other parts of the EU Counter-Terrorism Policy deal with the prosecution of terrorists and with the response to such attacks: As these are reactive in character they can rightly be regarded as subsidiary.

Networked Counter-Hybridity

An effective counter-terrorism strategy, however, has to be set up broadly and needs to anticipate the realities of a virtually unlimited spectrum of attacks. This can only be properly done if the required interdepartmental and international cooperation between security authorities is implemented accordingly. The possibilities of military contributions at a European level have not yet been fully taken into account nor sufficiently discussed, and the field is deliberately left open to the respective interior departments, who still seem set in their conventional ways. Yet European authorities, as a manifestation of strict compliance with the rule of law, preferably tend to search for appropriate responses to terrorist attacks within the criminal justice paradigm. This is surely plausible, but not sufficient. What is being done in order to deter from future attacks? Not much, even though it is evident that deterrence is probably the best prevention.

With regard to prevention, counter-terrorist agencies and security authorities have often been publicly accused of having waited too long, as the future attacker had allegedly been under close surveillance or on a list of potential endangerers.[93] Probably the most prominent example is the case of Anis Amri, the Berlin attacker, who had been scrutinized by German police authorities long before his activities started. Despite concrete evidence that Amri could be involved in preparations of a terrorist plot they failed to foil the attack.[94] As in other constellations the reason for the authorities' failure was a frightening lack of cooperation. Also a lot of red tape made mistakes possible.

Former US–General Stanley McChrystal famously expressed that it *"takes a network to defeat a network"*.[95] This is all the more true with current terrorist networks. Networked hybrid terrorism can only be countered by a networked (i.e. cooperative and complementary) hybrid counter-terrorism. Comprehensiveness is the imperative of the hour and unrestricted international cooperation (e.g. common databases) is key to a successful counter-terrorism policy.

Ultimately, counter-terrorism is a game with, and against time. Time is the most important resource in the fight against terrorism. This principle should underlie any effort to prevent, protect, prosecute or react. Even concerning deterrence, the time factor is essential. Counter-terrorist ambitions and measures should follow their own timely agenda and not any requirements indicated by public (i.e. mostly media–driven) expectations. In opposition to conventional opinion, counter-terrorism should be a calm and opaque intelligence business. The adversary should intentionally be left insecure about possible (re-)actions, measures and procedures. The time factor can hence be a useful weapon in the fight against a phantom. All this is patchwork on the road to comprehensiveness. Nevertheless, some time will pass until the necessary steps in the direction of a fully comprehensive, international network against transnational terrorism are taken. Approaches, however, exist.

Notes

1 Patryk Pawlak (2015). *"Understanding Hybrid Threats"*, European Parliamentary Research Service; URL: https://epthinktank.eu/2015/06/24/understanding-hybrid-threats (accessed September 7, 2022).
2 Brian Jenkins, Endorsement of Boaz Ganor (2015). *Global Alert. The Rationality of Modern Islamist Terrorism and the Challenge to the Liberal Democratic World* (New York, NY: Columbia University Press), Backside Cover.
3 Jeffrey Kaplan (2008). *"Terrorism's Fifth Wave: A Theory, a Conundrum and a Dilemma"*, Perspectives on Terrorism, Vol. 2, Issue 2, pp. 12–25; Jeffrey D. Simon (2011). Technological and Lone Operator Terrorism: Prospects for a Fifth Wave of Global Terrorism, in: Jean E. Rosenfeld (ed.) *Terrorism, Identity and Legitimacy. The Four Waves Theory and Political Violence* (London: Routledge), pp. 66–84; Anthony N. Celso (2015). *"The Islamic State and Boko Haram: Fifth Wave Jihadist Terror Groups"*, Orbis, Vol. 59, Issue 2, pp. 249–268.
4 Petter Nesser (2015). *Islamist Terrorism in Europe. A History* (London: Hurst), p. 294.
5 Thomas Hegghammer (2016). *"The Future of Jihadism in Europe: A Pessimistic View"*, Perspectives on Terrorism, Vol. 10, Issue 6, p. 2; URL: http://www.terrorismanalysts.com/pt/index.php/pot/article/view/566/1122 (accessed September 7, 2022).
6 Nesser. *Islamist Terrorism in Europe*, p. 294.
7 President Hollande deplored *"terrorist attacks of an unprecedented scale"*: Adam Nossiter/Rick Gladstone: „*Paris Attacks Kill More Than 100, Police Say; Border Controls Tightened*", New York Times (13 November 2015), URL: https://www.nytimes.com/2015/11/14/world/europe/paris-shooting-attacks.html (accessed September 7, 2022).

8 David Kilcullen (2016). *Blood Year. The Unraveling of Western Counterterrorism* (Oxford: Oxford University Press), p. 220.

9 Ibid, p. 220.

10 James R. Clapper, Director of National Intelligence, "*Statement for the Record: Worldwide Threat Assessment of the US Intelligence Community,*" Senate Armed Services Committee, February 9, 2016, pp. 4–5.

11 Raffaelo Pantucci. "*Paris Terror Attacks: The Lessons of Mumbai were Learned–by the Jihadis. For Isis to Distinguish Itself from Al-Qaeda it Must Create Greater Misery*", Independent (November 14, 2015), URL: http://www.independent.co.uk/voices/paris-terror-attacks-the-lessons-of-mumbai-were-learned-by-the-jihadis-a6734836.html (accessed September 7, 2022).

12 Bruce Hoffman (2017). *Inside Terrorism.* 3rd ed. (New York, NY: Columbia University Press), p. 313.

13 Nesser. *Islamist Terrorism in Europe*, p. 59.

14 Kilcullen, *Blood Year,* p. 221.

15 https://web.archive.org/web/20151114092552/http://www.telegraph.co.uk/news/worldnews/europe/france/11995481/French-President-declares-state-of-emergency-following-Paris-shootings.html (accessed September 7, 2022).

16 Herfried Münkler. "*Terrorismus als ein Drittes zwischen Krieg und Frieden*", Heinrich-Böll-Stiftung (November 24, 2015); https://www.boell.de/de/2015/11/24/terrorismus-als-ein-drittes-zwischen-krieg-und-frieden (accessed September 7, 2022).

17 This transformation argument had already been formulated in the aftermath of 9/11. URL: https://www.research-collection.ethz.ch/bitstream/handle/20.500.11850/147420/eth-26433-01.pdf?sequence=1&isAllowed=y (accessed September 7, 2022).

18 Juliet Lodge (2007). "*EU Homeland Security: Citizens or Suspects?*", Journal of European Integration, Vol. 26 Issue 3, pp. 253–279; Elisabeth Braw. "*Scandinavia's Homeland Defence: A Model for Other Countries?*", Commentary (March 13, 2018)/RUSI Domestic Security; URL: https://rusi.org/explore-our-research/publications/commentary/scandinavias-homeland-defence-model-other-countries (accessed September 7, 2022).

19 Rob de Wijk (2014). *Hybrid Conflict and the Changing Nature of Actors,* in: Julian Lindley-French / Yves Boyer (eds.) *The Oxford Handbook of War* (Oxford University Press), p. 358.

20 Ibid.

21 Ulrich Schneckener (2006). *Transnationaler Terrorismus. Charakter und Hintergründe des neuen Terrorismus.* (Suhrkamp: Frankfurt a. M.), p. 25.

22 Herfried Münkler (2004). "*Symmetrische und asymmetrische Kriege*", Merkur, *58,* Vol. 664, pp. 649–659.

23 Ibid.

24 John Mueller (2005). "*Reactions and Overreactions to Terrorism*" "Presentation at the 25th Anniversary Conflict Studies Conference", *Terrorism in History: The Strategic Impact of Terrorism From Sarajevo 1914 to 9/11*", Centre for Conflict Studies, University of New Brunswick (October 14–15, 2005); URL: https://politicalscience.osu.edu/faculty/jmueller/NB.PDF (accessed September 7, 2022); also: Simon Jenkins. "*If We Overreact to this Attack on Paris then Terrorism Will 'Just Never End*", The Guardian (April 21, 2017); URL: https://www.theguardian.com/commentisfree/2017/apr/21/overreact-paris-attack-terrorism-just-never-end (accessed September 7, 2022).

25 Damien Van Puyvelde (2015). *Hybrid War–Does It Even Exist?,* NATO Review; URL: https://www.nato.int/docu/review/2015/Also-in-2015/hybrid-modern-future-warfare-russia-ukraine/EN/ (accessed September 7, 2022).

26 Ibid.

27 Herfried Münkler (2015). *Kriegssplitter. Die Evolution der Gewalt im 20. und 21. Jahrhundert* (Berlin: Rowohlt Berlin), p. 326.

28 Brian Michael Jenkins (1974). *International Terrorism: A New Kind of Warfare* (Santa Monica, CA: RAND), p. 4.

29 Peter R. Neumann (2009). *Old & New Terrorism. Late Modernity, Globalization and the Transformation of Political Violence* (London: Polity), p. 25; also David Tucker (2001). "*What is New About the New Terrorism and How Dangerous is It?*", Terrorism and Political Violence, Vol. 13, Issue 3 (Autumn 2001), pp. 1–14, here: p. 7.

30 Nesser. *Islamist Terrorism in Europe*, p. 267.

31 Neumann. *Old & New Terrorism*, p. 26.

32 French Counter-Terrorism expert Jean-Charles Brisard Called the Paris Attacks a "*Change of Paradigm*", see Kilcullen. *Blood Year,* p. 224; Also: Griff Witte/Loveday Morris. "*Failure to Stop Paris Attacks Reveals Fatal Flaws at Heart of European Security*", Washington Post (November 28, 2015); URL: https://www.

washingtonpost.com/world/europe/paris-attacks-reveal-fatal-flaws-at-the-heart-of-european-security/
2015/11/28/48b181da-9393-11e5-befa-99ceebcbb272_story.html?noredirect=on&utm_term=.f41b9978f760
(accessed September 7, 2022).

33 Martha Crenshaw explicitly warned about a premature proclaiming of a *"New Terrorism"*; see Martha
Crenshaw (2011). *Explaining Terrorism. Causes, Processes and Consequences* (London: Routledge), p. 53.

34 Ibid, p. 53.

35 Hoffman. *Inside Terrorism*, p. 330.

36 Boaz Ganor (2015). *Global Alert. The Rationality of Modern Islamist Terrorism and the Challenge to the Liberal
Democratic World* (New York, NY: Columbia University Press), p. 5.

37 Ibid, p. 5.

38 Peter Bergen/David Sterman/Albert Ford/Alyssa Sims: *Jihadist Terrorism 16 Years after 9/11: A Threat
Assessment*, New America: Policy Paper (September 11, 2017), p. 5; URL: https://www.newamerica.
org/international-security/policy-papers/jihadist-terrorism-16-years-after-911-threat-assessment/
(accessed September 7, 2022).

39 Ibid.

40 Thomas Hegghammer. *"The Ideological Hybridization of Jihadi Groups"*, Current Trends in Islamist Ideology, Vol. 9, Hudson Institute (November 18, 2009), p. 6; URL: https://www.hudson.org/national-
security-defense/the-ideological-hybridization-of-jihadi-groups (accessed September 7, 2022).

41 Ibid, pp. 6–7.

42 Ibid, pp. 6–7.

43 Hoffman. *Inside Terrorism*, p. 328.

44 http://www.sueddeutsche.de/politik/terror-die-franchise-dschihadisten-1.3086776 (accessed September 7,
2022).

45 Herfried Münkler. *"Die Falle ist gestellt. In Nizza und Würzburg ist eine neue Form des Terrors sichtbar
geworden: Jeder kann Opfer werden. Und jeder Täter"*, Die Zeit (31) 2016; URL: http://www.zeit.de/2016/31/
terrorismus-opfer-zielgruppe-nizza-wuerzburg (accessed September 7, 2022).

46 Andrew H. Kydd / Barbara F. Walter (2006). *"The Strategies of Terrorism"*, International Security, Vol. 31,
Issue 1, pp. 49–80, p. 51.

47 Kydd/Walter, *The Strategies of Terrorism*, p. 51.

48 Ibid.

49 Ibid.

50 Ibid.

51 Ibid.

52 Ehrhardt, Christoph: *"Angst schüren"*, Frankfurter Allgemeine Woche, 25/2016, p. 21.

53 Alissa J. Rubin / Lili Blaise: *Killing Twice for ISIS and Saying So Live on Facebook,* New York Times
(June 14, 2016); URL: https://www.nytimes.com/2016/06/15/world/europe/france-stabbing-police-
magnanville-isis.html (accessed September 7, 2022).

54 Peter Waldmann. *"Was kennzeichnet ihn?"*, FOKUS- Analysen und Perspektiven für Österreichs Sicherheit, p. 5.; URL: http://www.bundesheer.at/pdf_pool/publikationen/fokus_1602_terrorismus_online.
pdf (accessed September 7, 2022).

55 Kenan Malik. *"The Jihadi State of Mind"*, New York Times (May 24, 2017); URL: https://www.
nytimes.com/2017/05/24/opinion/the-jihadi-state-of-mind.html (accessed September 7, 2022).

56 Herfried Münkler. *Die Falle ist gestellt*, op.cit.

57 Peter R. Neumann (2016). *Der Terror ist unter uns. Dschihadismus und Radikalisierung in Europa* (Berlin:
Ullstein), p. 237; also: https://icsr.info/wp-content/uploads/2017/12/ICSR-Report-Countering-Vi-
olent-Extremism-and-Radicalisation-that-Lead-to-Terrorism-Ideas-Recommendations-and-Good-
Practices-from-the-OSCE-Region.pdf (accessed September 7, 2022).

58 Robert F. Worth. *"The Professor and the Jihadi"*, The New York Times Magazine (April 5, 2017); URL:
https://www.nytimes.com/2017/04/05/magazine/france-election-gilles-kepel-islam.html?_r=0 (accessed
September 7, 2022).

59 Peter R. Neumann (2018). *ICSR Insight – "ISIS And Terrorism In Europe: What Next?"*; URL: https://
icsr.info/2018/02/16/isis-terrorism-europe-next/ (accessed September 7, 2022).

60 Peter R. Neumann (2016). *"Criminal Pasts, Terrorist Futures: European Jihadists and the New Crime-Terror
Nexus"*, URL: http://icsr.info/wp-content/uploads/2016/10/crime-terror-report_20171214_web.pdf
(accessed September 7, 2022).

61 Ibid, p. 3.

62 Frederike Haupt: *"The Psychology of Radicalisation: Lego Islam",* Quantara.de; URL: http://en.qantara. de/content/preventing-jihadism-the-psychology-of-radicalisation-lego-islam?nopaging=1 (accessed September 7, 2022).

63 Ganor. *Global Alert,* op.cit., p. 73; Also Guido Steinberg, a German expert on jihadism, identifies a specific jihadist *"hybrid form of organisation",* even since 2005; Guido Steinberg (2014). *Al-Qaidas deutsche Kämpfer. Die Globalisierung des islamistischen Terrorismus ("German Jihad. On the Internationalization of Islamist Terrorism" Columbia University Press, 2013)* Hamburg: Edition Körber, p. 391.

64 Ganor, *Global Alert,* op.cit., p. 73.

65 Ibid., p. 74.

66 Peter R. Neumann, *ISIS And Terrorism In Europe: What Next? op.cit.*

67 Ibid.

68 Yara Bayoumy. *"ISIS urges more attacks on Western 'disbelievers'",* Independent (September 22, 2014); URL: https://www.independent.co.uk/news/world/middle-east/isis-urges-more-attacks-on-western-disbelievers-9749512.html (accessed September 7, 2022).

69 Mark S. Hamm and Ramón Spaaij (2017). *The Age of Lone Wolf Terrorism* (New York, NY: Columbia University Press); Ramon Spaaji (2010). *The Enigma of Lone Wolf Terrorism: An Assessment,* Studies in Conflict and Terrorism, Vol.33, Issue 9, pp. 854–870 provides an excellent overview on the issue. See also Ramón Spaaij and Mark S Hamm (2014). *Key Issues and Research Agendas in Lone Wolf Terrorism,* Studies in Conflict and Terrorism, Vol. 38, Issue 3, p. 168; Raffaelo Pantucci (2011). *A Typology of Lone Wolves: Preliminary Analysis of Lone Islamist Terrorists* (London: The International Centre for the Study of Radicalisation and Political Violence); Petter Nesser (2012). *Research Note: Single Actor Terrorism: Scope, Characteristics and Explanations,* Perspectives on Terrorism, Vol. 6, Issue 6.

70 Spaaji. *The Enigma of Lone Wolf Terrorism,* p. 856.

71 Stacy Meichtry, Joshua Robinson. *"Paris Attacks Plot Was Hatched in Plain Sight",* The Wall Street Journal (November 27, 2015); URL: http://www.wsj.com/articles/paris-attacks-plot-was-hatched-in-plainsight-144858730 (accessed September 7, 2022).

72 *"How to Respond to the New Tactics of Terrorism",* The Economist (November 20, 2015); URL: http://www.economist.com/news/middle-east-and-africa/21678907-deadly-style-suicidal-gun-assault-has-spreadacross-globe-how-respond (accessed September 7, 2022).

73 Nesser. *Islamist Terrorism in Europe,* p. 66.

74 Nesser, P./ Stenersen, A. / Oftedal, E. (2016). *Jihadi Terrorism in Europe: The IS-Effect,* Perspectives on Terrorism, Vol. 10, Issue6, p. 7; URL http://www.terrorismanalysts.com/pt/index.php/pot/article/view/553 (accessed September 7, 2022).

75 Ibid, p. 7.

76 Ibid, p. 7.

77 Ibid, p. 7.

78 Ibid, p. 7.

79 Ibid, p. 9.

80 Neumann. *Der Terror ist unter uns,* op.cit. p. 167.

81 Gunter Rosseels (2012). *Moltke's Mission Command Philosophy in the Twenty-First Century: Fallacy or Verity?* U.S. Army Command and General Staff College (Fort Leavenworth, Kansas); URL: http://www.dtic.mil/dtic/tr/fulltext/u2/a563054.pdf (accessed September 7, 2022).

82 Rukmini Callimachi. *How ISIS Built the Machinery of Terror Under Europe's Gaze,* New York Times (March 29, 2016); URL: https://www.nytimes.com/2016/03/29/world/europe/isis-attacks-paris-brussels.html (accessed September 7, 2022).

83 Hoffman. *Inside Terrorism,* p. 313.

84 Gilles Kepel (2017). *Terror in France: The Rise of Jihad in the West* (Princeton University Press: New Jersey).

85 Ibid.

86 Benjamin R. Barber: *Jihad vs. McWorld,* The Atlantic (March 1992 issue); URL: https://www.theatlantic.com/magazine/archive/1992/03/jihad-vs-mcworld/303882/ (accessed September 7, 2022).

87 Nesser. *Islamist Terrorism in Europe,* p. 66.

88 Thomas Hegghammer / Petter Nesser (2015). *Assessing the Islamic State's Commitment to Attacking the West,* Perspectives on Terrorism, Vol. 9, Nr.4, p. 22.

89 Peter R. Neumann. OSCE Report *"Countering Violent Extremism and Radicalisation that Lead to Terrorism: Ideas, Recommendations, and Good Practices from the OSCE Region";* URL: https://www.osce.org/chairmanship/346841?download=true (accessed September 7, 2022), p. 18.

90 Norman Loayza. *"How to Defeat Terrorism: Intelligence, Integration, and Development"*, Brookings Future Development (July 25, 2016); URL: https://www.brookings.edu/blog/future-development/2016/07/25/how-to-defeat-terrorism-intelligence-integration-and-development/ (accessed September 7, 2022).
91 Ganor. Global Alert, op.cit., p. 86.
92 Oldrich Bures (2011). *EU Counterterrorism Policy. A Paper Tiger?* (Ashgate: Surrey)
93 Lorenzo Tondo/Patrick Wintour/Piero Messina. *"Interpol Circulates list of 173 Suspected Members of Isis Suicide Brigade"*, Economist (July 21, 2017); URL: https://www.theguardian.com/world/2017/jul/21/isis-islamic-state-suicide-brigade-interpol-list (accessed September 7, 2022); see also: http://www.bbc.com/news/world-europe-38399561; http://www.bbc.com/news/world-europe-34866144 (accessed September 7, 2018).
94 http://www.spiegel.de/politik/deutschland/anis-amri-gravierende-fehler-der-behoerden-auf-allen-ebenen-a-1172661.html (accessed September 7, 2022).
95 Stanley McChrystal (2015). *Team of Teams. New Rules of Engagement for a Complex World* (New York, NY: Penguin), p. 93; Stanley McChrystal (2013). *My Share of the Task* (New York, NY: Penguin), p. 148.

PART II

Technology and Radicalization

9

THE EMERGING TERRORIST TECHNOLOGICAL LANDSCAPE

Gary A. Ackerman

Introduction

The early 21st century has witnessed remarkable and remarkably rapid technological advances in almost all areas of human activity. Hardly a day goes by where the media fails to report that a university, corporate or government laboratory has developed some novel mechanism, process or algorithm to revolutionize our lives.[1] Yet, as far back as Roger Bacon and Leonardo da Vinci, there has been the realization that new technologies can have a dark side, as these great inventors reportedly disguised certain of their discoveries so as to prevent malefactors from taking advantage of them. Similar concerns have arisen with many recent advances, especially when it comes to the violently asymmetric adversaries that constitute today's terrorists. As American President Obama stated in 2014, but is even more true today, "…the world is changing with accelerating speed. This presents opportunity, but also new dangers. We know all too well, after 9/11, just how technology and globalization has put power once reserved for states in the hands of individuals, raising the capacity of terrorists to do harm."[2]

A number of questions present themselves, questions that are made more urgent by the dramatic pace of technological developments: Will today's terrorists emulate the 19th-century Irish Fenians, who enthusiastically viewed the advent of dynamite as a "gift of science"[3]? With emerging applications in AI, synthetic biology, manufacturing, and much else besides, will we begin to see terrorist leaders that resemble Bondian supervillains who can bring governments to their knees by exploiting game-changing technologies or perhaps even super-empowered individuals who can cause mass destruction? On the other hand, will counterterrorist forces also be able to access these new technologies and, if so, will their ability to harness novel technologies be sufficient to offset any advantages that the same or other technologies bestow upon terrorists?

This chapter attempts to bring some sober analysis to these questions by first describing the major technological trends of concern and how these might facilitate terrorism and counterterrorism. It will also, however, address the sociological aspects of technology diffusion to terrorists that might serve to temper some of the more superficially frightening implications of terrorists adopting emerging technologies. Last, it will provide some broad recommendations for counterterrorist forces on how to mitigate the degree to which new technologies can be exploited by terrorists.

DOI: 10.4324/9781003326373-11

Technological Dynamics for Terrorists and Counterterrorists

Before addressing particular technologies and how they might interact with the phenomenon of terrorism, it is necessary to trace certain broad technological currents that become particularly salient in the context of terrorism. Perhaps the most important of these is that the pace of technological development is accelerating. As Ray Kurzweil has pointed out, this does not only imply that *technology is changing faster than ever before*, but that it will continue to grow even faster.[4] So, for instance, if it took several hundred years for gunpowder weapons to become effective, three decades for the Internet to dominate global communication and only a few years after its discovery before CRISPR-Cas9 was being widely used to manipulate genomes, future technological innovations might appear, mature and be widely available for use within a few short months – or even less. This means that policymakers cannot take it for granted that an incipient technology will take decades to mature or that they will have plenty of time to respond if an emerging technology displays the potential for dangerous applications.

The second major trend is that recent technologies are *deskilling* what were formerly highly technical and often arcane and resource intensive activities. This is a combination of two factors. The first is the consumerization of technologies, where innovations migrate out of the laboratory and become user-friendly and widely available over time. For example, the drones of today are equipped with GPS and flight control systems that make them far easier to fly and require little to no knowledge of aeronautics compared to the remote-controlled airplanes of, say, the 1980s. The other side of the coin is the rise in digitally-based education, such as MOOCs (massive open online courses) which, while a boon with respect to economic and human development, means that highly technical skills – including those that can be turned towards destructive aims – can be developed and accessed from the most remote locations by almost anyone, terrorists included.

The third trend is the *rapid penetration of technologies*, which is a byproduct of globalization and the information revolution, and entails the swift diffusion of technologies worldwide. There are of course the legitimate channels of academic collaboration, cross-national commercialization, and international licensing. Yet, in addition, illicit diffusion from rampant smuggling, the theft of intellectual property and the illegal replication of products makes it difficult for any entities – be they governments or private corporation – to prevent the spread of technological innovations, even when this is desired. With the ability to split many new technologies into both digital and physical manifestations, controlling diffusion is likely to become even more difficult, if not impossible, when the digital designs for a new product can be distributed widely over email and then reproduced using 3D printers and similar production technologies by the recipients. This conversion from the digital to the physical is even becoming true for complex substances like pharmaceuticals and biological organisms.

The final trend to consider is the *miniaturization and intangibility* of many technologies. Production processes (e.g., for chemical agents or weapons components) that used to require large workshops, sizeable equipment and involve multiple individuals can now be performed on a benchtop or even on a microchip, while other processes (such as training and testing) have now become increasingly digital and thus more intangible. These dynamics are well-suited for actors whose activities are mostly clandestine and who seek to minimize their operational footprint in order to evade authorities and security measures.

Against the backdrop of these critical dynamics, almost any new technology can be expected to move quickly from its first appearance to, at least theoretically, fall within the reach of terrorists, ranging from urban guerillas operating out of Western cities to apocalyptic cults in isolated compounds. Although technology can be broadly defined as "knowledge applied for a practical purpose in order to affect and control the user's environment,"[5] the following discussion will focus on the subset of technologies that constitute physical or digital tools rather than abstract systems or knowledge processes.

There is a wide array of technologies that could potentially be exploited by terrorists to increase their capabilities, but these can be broadly divided into those related to *weapons, targets, logistics* and *organizational growth*. Some of these technologies could provide new tactical possibilities, while others function more as adjunct technologies that might allow terrorists to accomplish existing activities more easily, cheaply, or with lower risk of interdiction. A comprehensive survey is beyond the scope of this chapter, but Table 9.1 provides a list of some of the more prominent technologies in this regard, together with illustrative scenarios of how some of these technologies could conceivably be leveraged by terrorists.

Table 9.1 Emerging Technologies Potentially Facilitating Terrorism

Category of Terrorist Activity	*Examples of Potentially Empowering Technologies*	*Illustrative Applications in Terrorism*
Weapons	• Autonomous vehicles • Swarm algorithms • Chemical microreactors • Synthetic biology★ • "Maker" tools, including 3D printers, computer controlled lathes, etc. • New highly energetic materials★ • Neurological weapons (E)★	• A small cell of terrorists uses 3D printers to produce >100 drones equipped with explosives and then employs swarm algorithms, GPS and autonomy to precisely deliver individual payloads to specific targets at the same time. • A terrorist organization utilizes microreactors to produce an extremely toxic chemical agent with almost no production footprint and then disseminates it widely using novel energetic materials that cannot be identified with existing detectors.
Targets	• IoT devices and systems★ • Online identities / reputations	• A solipsistic lone actor inserts a virus into automated insulin pumps that scrambles readings and dosages across thousands of patients. • "Superdoxxing": a group of extremists hacks into, collects and then publishes the browsing history of hundreds of thousands of corporate personnel.
Logistics	• Augmented / virtual reality • AI + simulation software • Quantum encryption (E) • Active camouflage materials (E)	• Terrorists use machine learning and simulation software to discover unrecognized vulnerabilities in defensive systems. • Terrorists utilize augmented / virtual reality to conduct low-cost, inconspicuous, decentralized training for their operations.
Growth	• Augmented / virtual reality • Gamification • Social media manipulation (e.g., bots and disinformation campaigns)	• Extremist movements inject radicalizing memes and "hooks" into popular games designed to identify and attract vulnerable youth and then actively recruit anyone who "bites". • Terrorists emulate state disinformation campaigns, including the use of botnets and unwitting influencers, to covertly disseminate their ideological narratives on a large scale.

(E) = Incipient technology not yet widely available.
★ = Intentionally described at a high level of abstraction for security reasons.

Table 9.2 Emerging Technologies Potentially Facilitating Counterterrorism

Category of CT Activity	Examples of Potentially Empowering Technologies	Illustrative Applications in Counterterrorism
Direct Kinetic Action	• AI • Autonomous vehicles	• Autonomous drones using facial recognition software locate high-profile terrorists for capture or targeted killing.
Plot / Attack Detection	• AI • Hazardous materials detectors	• Machine learning algorithms sift through masses of open-source data detecting anomalies that indicate terrorist attack precursor activities.
Attack Effect Mitigation	• Medical countermeasures • Improved blast-resistant materials	• Using transgenic animals (e.g., mutant goats) to produce an enzyme that prophylactically counteracts the effects of nerve agents.[8]
Countering Violent Extremism	• Simulation and gaming as a preventative strategy • Automated radicalization prevention	• Using targeted advertising (e.g., Moonshot's "Redirect"[9]) to identify individuals at risk for radicalization and provide alternative narratives and positive engagement.

Emerging technology is not a one-sided street, however, and can provide opportunities for counterterrorist forces as well as for terrorists. Some of the technologies that could assist counterterrorism and their applications are described in Table 9.2. These developments set up a co-evolutionary dynamic, in what Bruce Hoffman has described as a "technology treadmill,"[6] where the terrorist offense and the counterterrorist defense compete to get ahead of one another. As Harry Turney-High has famously observed: "[t]he offense thinks up new weapons or improves the old ones so that the defence's genius must think up new defence or be crushed out of existence. There is nothing new nor old in this. The entire history and prehistory of weapons is summarized in this cycle."[7]

Yet, while a full analysis of the strategic and tactical efficacy of technologies for terrorism and counterterrorism relative to one another remains to be conducted, there are reasons to suspect that, on balance, technology will present more opportunities for terrorists than those acting to counter them. The first indication of this emerges from an in-depth horizon scan that my colleagues and I conducted in two particular technological domains – the future chemical and biological threat landscapes – which concluded that defensive advances would not be sufficient to counteract the broader and more foundational developments that are driving the threat side of the equation.[10] The second is that the defense often only adapts to offensive innovations after a substantial time lag. For instance, it took several decades for Renaissance engineers to come up with the new fortifications of the *trace italienne* as an answer for the bronze cannon that assailed the Italian kingdoms at the beginning of the sixteenth century. Given the destructive potential of some of the technologies listed in Table 9.1, and the malignant mass-casualty intent of many of today's terrorist actors, any delay between an offensive technology-driven innovation and a counteracting defensive adaptation could have dire consequences for the safety and security of civilians the world over. Overall, therefore, there is an argument to be made that technology is lengthening the terrorists' levers of asymmetry rather than making it easier for authorities to counter them.

Defying Determinism

While an exclusive focus on the technologies themselves and their potential advantages for terrorists paints a rather bleak picture, one must avoid falling into the trap of technological determinism; i.e., that the mere existence of a dangerous technology that could be adopted by terrorists automatically implies an increased threat. The reason for not succumbing to such determinism is that there are three "gates" that a terrorist actor (organization or individual) needs to pass through in order to adopt a new technology:

1 **Awareness**: Clearly terrorists must be aware of a technology's existence or they will not even attempt to obtain it, but this gate goes further and requires that at least one member of a terrorist organization is also *aware of the potential applications of that technology* in the organization's activities. In other words, terrorists must recognize that the technology is relevant to terrorist operations.
2 **Decision**: Adoption of a new technology always involves at least some costs and is highly unlikely to occur spontaneously. Therefore, a terrorist organization or individual must make *a positive decision to pursue* the acquisition of that technology.
3 **Success**: The final gate requires the would-be terrorist adopter to successfully acquire and use the new technology. Success here is partly defined subjectively by the adopter, but usually requires that the *use of the technology is not only viable and relatively reliable, but also is able to achieve its intended operational effects*. Note that this applies only to the "tactical" performance of the technology and not whether the adoption of the technology actually advances the terrorists' broader political or social goals.

A terrorist actor needs to pass through all three gates, sequentially, for a new technology to become a threat and add to its capabilities – failure to proceed through any of the gates means that the technology, while theoretically useful to terrorists, does not constitute a practical threat. How likely are terrorists to do so for new technologies like the ones listed in Table 9.1? The answer is not a simple one and will be determined by characteristics of both the terrorist actor and the technology itself. Moreover, there is not a single possible route through each gate – there are multiple causal pathways by which an enterprising terrorist can find their way through. Indeed, there are several dozen factors that either facilitate or obstruct a terrorists' progress through each gate, almost none of which are strictly necessary or sufficient. Some of the factors relate to preconditions that determine how fertile the ground is for successful adoption, while others relate to more direct precipitants (drivers or barriers) for adopting a given technology. It is the sum total of the effects of all these factors in a particular context, time and place which will determine whether or not a terrorist will be able to leverage the new technology. A full examination of each of these factors is beyond the scope of this essay, but I will briefly discuss some of the overall dynamics at each gate below, as well as provide some examples of potentially relevant factors.

Beginning with the *Awareness* gate, some of the factors that can facilitate the type of awareness I have outlined above include extensive publicity or hype surrounding a new technology, demonstration of the technology in a similar context by other violent actors, the presence of an educated, technically proficient cadre, and the presence of an institutionalized "quartermaster" or R&D function within a terrorist organization, as seen in the case of groups like the Provisional Irish Republican Army, Hizb'allah and the Islamic State. Some factors that might retard awareness are an overall low level of technical literacy within the terrorist group, extreme isolation (e.g., on a cult-like compound or hiding in remote areas), and certain cognitive biases amongst key decision makers that cause them to overlook potential technological opportunities.

However, modern society is saturated with a massive online volume of dedicated websites, media stories, and blog posts devoted to discussing new scientific and technical developments, not to mention the widespread reach of remote education. It is thus doubtful that any reasonably engaged terrorists will be completely unaware of new technologies and that some member of an organization will not contemplate potential uses for the technology in the organization's operations. So, with the exception of a narrow range of extremely sensitive military-related technologies, such as nuclear weapons or precision munitions, it is likely that most new technological innovations will come to the attention of the majority of halfway capable terrorists and will at least, however fleetingly, be considered for adoption. To strengthen the case, it is instructive to observe that even in the 1970s and 1980s, prior to the Internet, most of the major terrorist groups were at least minimally aware of technological developments. To quote just two examples, Provisional Irish Republican Army (PIRA) bombmakers used to scour printed catalogs for new products that might assist their operations, and leaders of the Order, a far-right extremist group in the United States, were interested in laser weapons.[11]

When it comes to the *Decision* phase, it should be recognized that most terrorists are conservative and imitative in their tactics.[12] Adopting new technologies will invariably entail costs with at least some uncertainty about outcomes, while most terrorists face limited resources, pressures to act and targets that are still vulnerable to traditional weapons and tactics like guns and bombs. Borrowing from general theories of innovation, it is therefore only when the performance of existing methods and technologies is perceived to be insufficient to achieve the terrorists' aims (the so-called "performance gap") that terrorists are likely to diverge from the status quo. Even when they do so, there are many other possible innovations besides adopting a new technology, from merely changing operational tactics to internal organizational changes. So, what factors will tend to push terrorists either towards or away from innovation in general and which of these will make it more or less likely that they will seek to adopt new technologies to address any perceived shortcomings in performance?

With respect to underlying factors, a sample of characteristics that make a positive adoption decision more likely includes possessing a lot of resources, a leader who seeks prestige or has a high risk tolerance, and having technically proficient members. Among the underlying preconditions that can in general inhibit a positive decision are the presence of guardians of the status quo and a lack of intra-organizational cohesiveness. Then there are more immediate and direct factors, which often operate powerfully, that can drive an adoption. Some of the key drivers associated with a positive decision to adopt are: a need to overcome countermeasures; proselytization for the technology, whether from inside the group or from respected elements within the group's wider social network; and inter- or intra-organizational rivalries. The more accessible the technology is perceived to be (e.g., the lower the financial cost or the easier the terrorists believe it is to acquire), as well as the extent to which the technology is trialable (i.e., testable at small scale before needing to commit to full adoption), are two factors associated with the specific candidate technology that are important at this stage. Examples of direct barriers that can make rejection of (or failure to even properly consider) adoption more likely are an ideological or cultural incompatibility with the technology and near-term demands (e.g., being on the run) that make it impossible to devote resources or attention to an adoption process.

To pass through the ultimate gate, that of achieving technology adoption *Success*, the overarching criterion is that the technical, organizational, and other capabilities possessed by the terrorist actor need to match or supersede those required to adopt the particular technology. This is obviously highly dependent on the technology itself, but there are still underlying organizational factors that can facilitate or impede the likelihood of a capability match. Examples of factors that can enhance the prospects of success are the possession of a safe haven and/or a specialized R&D unit, state support, connections with illicit networks, and technically proficient members, while factors that might impede successful adoption include operating in an area with underdeveloped infrastructure, security pressures, and low levels of resources (both human and material). Aspects of the technology itself that can promote success include that it has been commercialized or has matured, and that technical information about the technology is widely available, while aspects of the technology that hinder success include high financial costs and requirements for extensive testing during development.

A key requirement for success is knowledge acquisition. The terrorists must possess or be able to acquire the correct amount and type of knowledge needed to adopt the technology, which includes knowledge about how to obtain or produce the technology, how to maintain it as long as it is needed, and then how to properly deploy the technology to achieve its desired effects. The amount and type of knowledge required varies widely across technologies, ranging from relatively simple (such as learning to utilize social media) to the highly complex (e.g., applying swarming algorithms to direct a fleet of drones). They will also vary temporally, with knowledge requirements generally decreasing for a given technology over time. It is essential to recognize, however, that it is not merely the codified or "explicit" knowledge that the terrorist must gain, but also the more experiential, "tacit" knowledge that comes from hands-on experience and trial-and-error. The latter, which is much more difficult to capture in recordable media, is thus often more difficult to acquire, but can make all the difference to a successful adoption. It is probably one of the reasons that scholars have estimated that up to 30% of all would-be bombmakers blow themselves up.[13]

As a last note, there is the matter of terrorist technology transfer, whereby a terrorist actor is provided with a new technology wholesale by some benefactor or element of their network, whether this is a state sponsor, an affiliated terrorist group or merely a mercenary criminal trafficker. While being bequeathed a technology package can vitiate many potential hurdles to success, it still does not guarantee that adoption ultimately will be successful. First, there is the requirement for not only transferring the technology hardware, but also the accompanying "software" aspects of the technology (operating instructions, integration into existing systems, and training), which is often less straightforward. Then there is still the requirement for transferring both explicit and tacit knowledge about the hardware as well as the software. Finally, such transfers often involve middlemen, brokers, and the physical transport of materials across illicit networks, which create additional issues of trust, uncertainty, and potential exposure for the terrorist group. So, even in this case, passing through the success gate is not necessarily a trivial exercise.

Implications for CT Policy and Practice

Although it is likely that most modern terrorist actors will pass through the first gate and become aware of the possibility for exploiting new technologies, it is expected that substantially fewer will decide that the subjective benefits outweigh the costs and risks and that they will then proceed through the second gate to seriously pursue one or more of the advanced emerging technologies listed in Table 9.1. Of these terrorists, only a select few are likely to have the resources, expertise, and organizational infrastructure to make it through the third gate to successful adoption. The case for there being only a relatively small subset of actors who will be able to transform technological potential into a true terrorist threat is supported by the historical record; the number of terrorist groups over the past five decades that have succeeded in adopting new technologies in a way that appreciably advanced their goals and raised the danger they posed is quite small, including the PIRA, Hizb'allah, the PFLP and more recently ISIS, and to a lesser extent individuals like Ramzi Yousef and Ted Kaczynski, and the apocalyptic cult Aum Shinrikyo. The first policy implication of this is that counterterrorism policymakers and practitioners should not jump to conclusions about the terrorist threat posed by an emerging technology, at least not until conducting a proper analysis of how many and which extant terrorist actors are likely to pursue and successfully adopt a given technology of concern.

Yet there are bound to be certain terrorist actors who possess both the will and the capability to exploit new technologies to increase their influence and impact. The challenge thus becomes identifying which combination of terrorist actor and emerging technology poses a threat. Note that the problem may have already become simplified somewhat by recognizing that the key unit of analysis in this regard is the unique terrorist-technology pairing (or dyad). A second policy implication is that this recognition can help resolve the dual-use dilemma that bedevils much modern technology: if, for example, a new technology is capable of inflicting a substantial amount of harm but only a handful of terrorists are judged to be able to pass through all three adoption gates, then, rather than trying to monitor or control the technology everywhere around the globe (which is often difficult if not impossible), counterterrorism agencies can focus their efforts on observing that particular subset of terrorist groups for signs of interest in or pursuit of the particular technology. Efforts at more widespread monitoring and control can therefore be reserved for the (probably fairly limited) subset of emerging technologies which simultaneously hold high harm potential and are likely to be adopted widely by terrorist groups.

So, how then to identify the terrorist-technology dyads of greatest concern, especially when the determinants of terrorist technology adoption are so numerous and complex? As an initial step in this direction, a tool has been developed that simultaneously assesses and weighs the several dozen relevant variables involved. The Terrorist Technology Adoption Model (T-TAM)[14] is based on a set of observable indicators that are applied to a particular terrorist-technology dyad (or even across multiple terrorist groups for a single technology) and offers estimates for the relative likelihood of the terrorist actor passing through the three required technology adoption gates. It can be easily updated by counterterrorism analysts to account for changes in a terrorist group or changes in the characteristics of the technology and can thus provide an ongoing assessment of threat levels over time.

Although all of the factors in T-TAM have diagnostic value, there are certain factors where changes might be particularly indicative of a possibly increasing terrorist technology threat. Intelligence and law enforcement agencies involved in counterterrorism could pay particular attention to such developments. Besides the obvious signals that would be provided by intercepted intergroup communications detailing technology adoption plans, or interdicted attempts to acquire expertise, equipment or raw materials unique to a particular technology, these signals might include:

- Changes in organizational structure
- Changes in recruitment targets and practices towards "expert-oriented" recruitment
- Attempts to recruit, hire, coerce or otherwise acquire general technical expertise
- Acquisition of a safe haven or other changes in the security environment that allow the terrorist entity more operational freedom
- Setting up a specialized R&D unit
- Consistently successful defensive countermeasures or thwarted plots
- Use or attempted use of the particular technology for violent purposes by another actor
- A dangerous technology reaching COTS (commercial-off-the-shelf) status

While it is unlikely that awareness of new technologies can be curtailed, there is more scope for preventing terrorist transit through the decision and success gates. A third policy implication is therefore that there may be advantages to policies that seek to limit terrorist access to specific explicit (and even more importantly) tacit knowledge surrounding a new technology, and to the "software" rather than the hardware associated with it. An example would be the recent controversy regarding publishing studies that discuss experiments to increase the virulence of the influenza virus.[15] In this case, the results of the research could be published widely, but not necessarily the detailed blueprints for making the virus more deadly. The importance of knowledge transfer to technology adoption also lends weight to the argument that it is easier for a scientist to become a terrorist than for a terrorist to become a scientist, which emphasizes issues of personnel reliability. The cases of CERN physicist Adlene Hicheur, who reached out to AQIM, and Tunisian aeronautical engineer Mohammed al-Zawahri who volunteered to lead HAMAS' drone-building program, are instructive in this regard.

Overall, while it is important not to assume that every new technology will be twisted by terrorists to nefarious ends, it is equally important to recognize that certain of today's emerging technologies in the hands of certain terrorists can constitute a significant threat. To counter this, it will be necessary for policymakers and practitioners to combine counterterrorism analysis with technology foresight approaches and to move beyond simplistic threat assessment to achieve genuine threat anticipation.

Notes

1 For general descriptions of current technological change, see Kevin Kelley, *The Inevitable* (New York, NY: Viking, 2016) and James Canton, *Future Smart* (Philadelphia: Da Capo Press, 2015).

2 The White House, Office of the Press Secretary, *Remarks by the President at the United States Military Academy Commencement Ceremony* (May 28, 2014), accessed on September 7, 2021 at https://obamawhitehouse.archives.gov/the-press-office/2014/05/28/remarks-president-united-states-military-academy-commencement-ceremony

3 David Ronfeldt and William Sater, *The Mindsets of High-Technology Terrorists: Future Implications from an Historical Analog* (Santa Monica, CA: RAND, 1981), p.14 ftn. 23; Paul Wilkinson, "Editor's Introduction" in Paul Wilkinson (ed.), *Terrorism and Technology* (Portland, Oregon: Frank Cass, 1993).

4 Ray Kurzweil, *The Singularity is Near* (New York, NY: Penguin Books, 2005), pp. 96, 7–8, 12, and 25.

5 Gary A. Ackerman, *'More Bang for the Buck': Examining the Determinants of Terrorist Adoption of New Weapons Technologies* (PhD Dissertation: King's College London, 2014), p. 19, available at: *https://kclpure.kcl.ac.uk/portal/files/32901277/2014_Ackerman_Gary_0715371_ethes*.

6 Bruce Hoffman, *Inside Terrorism* (New York, NY: Columbia University Press, 2006), p. 252.

7 Harry H. Turney-High, *Primitive War: Its Practice and Concepts* (Columbia, SC: University of South Carolina Press, 1949), p. 7.

8 Nachon et al, "Progress in the Development of Enzyme-Based Nerve Agent Bioscavengers," *Chemico-Biological Interactions* 206:3 (2013), pp. 536–544.

9 See "The Redirect Method", accessed September 10, 2021 at https://moonshotteam.com/redirect-method/.

10 Gary A. Ackerman, Markus K. Binder and Crystal Watson, "Chemical and Biological Threats: The Emerging Strategic Landscape," Paper presented at the 2017 Meeting of the International Studies Association, Baltimore, Maryland (February 25, 2017).

11 Author Interview with Former PIRA Bombmaker, Athlone, Republic of Ireland (June 20, 2012); Singular, Stephen, *Talked to Death: The Life and Murder of Alan Berg* (New York, NY: Beech Tree Books, 1987), p. 239; Kevin Flynn and Gary Gerhardt, *The Silent Brotherhood: Inside America's Racist Underground* (New York, NY: Free Press, 1989), p. 299.

12 Brian Jenkins, "Defense Against Terrorism," *Political Science Quarterly*, Reflections on Providing for "The Common Good," 101:5 (1986), pp. 777–778; Bruce Hoffman, *Terrorist Targeting: Tactics, Trends, and Potentialities* (Santa Monica, California: RAND, 1992), p. 15; Adam Dolnik, *Understanding Terrorist Innovation: Technology, Tactics and Global Trends* (New York, NY: Routledge, 2007), p. 56.

13 Brian Jackson, "Technology Acquisition by Terrorist Groups: Threat Assessment Informed by Lessons from Private Sector Technology Adoption," *Studies in Conflict and Terrorism*, 24 (2001).

14 The theoretical make-up of T-TAM is contained in Ackerman (2014) and its integration into an assessment tool is described in Gary Ackerman and Anthony Barrett, "Risk-Based Prioritization of Technologies in Countering Weapons of Mass Destruction," Presented at the Society for Risk Analysis 2019 Annual Meeting, Arlington, Virginia (December 11, 2019).

15 For example, see Simon Wain-Hobson, "H5N1 Viral-Engineering Dangers Will Not Go Away," *Nature* (March 27, 2013).

10

ONLINE TERRITORIES OF TERROR

The Multiplatform Communication Paradigm and the Information Ecology of the Web3 Era

Ali Fisher and Nico Prucha

The battle for your reality begins in the fields of digital interaction[1]

Douglas Rushkoff

The Internet treats censorship as a malfunction and routes around it.[2]

John Perry Barlow

At the dawn of mass access to the internet, some, including legendary author of "Cyberia", Douglas Rushkoff,[3] foresaw that dissident groups would use technological innovation and the networks of our postmodern society in unconventional ways to pursue subversive goals. That time has come. Jihadi groups such as the Islamic State have developed a multiplatform distribution system which is based on emergent behaviour in complex systems – projecting a unique set of coherent content to its followers, sympathisers, and their target audiences. The Islamic State has fully adopted a similar approach to that which Rushkoff outlined.[4] For the Islamic State, the "battle for your reality" is one of religious identity.[5]

The documents and videos produced by the Islamic State project what they consider to be a real Sunni Muslim, on the path of God and acting in accordance with divine rule and the regulations which the early Muslims had under the leadership of Prophet Muhammad. Any release by IS – as much as by AQ – seeks to inform, educate and convince the consumer that the jihadis are the only "true" Muslims, following the correct "prophetic methodology"[6] This ideational content echoes an earlier prediction about an internet-enabled ideological struggle over the definition of reality. In this vision, warfare would be "conducted on an entirely new battleground; it is a struggle not over territory or boundaries but over the very definitions of these terms"[7], where IS seeks to maintain hegemony over concepts such as the "prophetic methodology" and other theological concepts expressed by key words.

The battle for these definitions occurs in the physical landscape and equally on the digital platforms that comprise the information ecosystem.

As Rüdiger Lohlker argued: "Without deconstructing the theology of violence inherent in jihadi communications and practice, these religious ideas will continue to inspire others to act,

DOI: 10.4324/9781003326373-12

long after any given organized force, such as the Islamic State, may be destroyed on the ground."[8] In doing so, he argues that neglecting the evidence that jihadi networks online are both agile and unified around coherent theological "narratives" risks breeding a sense of complacency, which allows the Islamic State (and other jihadi groups) to develop physical and digital locations to which they can retreat and regroup at. This is a real risk if the current shift in distribution strategy adopted by the Islamic State is viewed as decline, rather than a reconfiguration and refocusing of effort.

The Islamic State communicates its strategy to supporters predominantly in Arabic and often uses citations of legitimate mainly Arabic language scriptures, the Holy Qur'an and Hadith (deeds and sayings of Prophet Muhammad) as well as scholarly religious (historical and contemporary) writings.[9] These citations of historical as well as contemporary Islamic scholars are frequent in writings and are woven into the audio-visual productions of jihadis.[10] This cannon of material that jihadis have to hand justifies, from their perspective, their acts and seeks to provide a clear identity; defining what being a "Sunni Muslim" means to them.

To distribute this content, the Islamic State (and other Salafi-Jihadi groups) previously used Twitter for both communicating with sympathizers and to perform da'wa. However, late in 2015 the Islamic State reduced the emphasis on reaching sympathizers via Twitter, and, since early 2016, established a well-maintained presence on Telegram for this specific purpose.[11] As of 2022, the Salafi-Jihadi movement has turned its attention to expand on Web3.

The Electronic Footprint of the Salafi-Jihadi Movement

For over 20 years, the activity of the electronic Media Mujahidin has been in a state of constant evolution, as their multiplatform zeitgeist has continued to reconfigure.[12] Having been pioneers in using electronic communication, the Media Mujahidin are an established side of any real-life conflict and became of greater importance with the war in Afghanistan 2001 and Iraq 2003. As of now, Salafi-Jihadi groups have already fully embraced many of the characteristics of Web3, including decentralisation, in a self-governing distributed and robust multi-server and multiplatform network. While the Media Mujahidin have been forging ahead, exploiting new technologies and approaches, many researchers and 'embedded academics' in the transatlantic orthodoxy of Terrorism Studies have perpetuated a 'success narrative' about the online efforts against Salafi-Jihadi groups.[13] This success narrative has been around since 2014 and in many ways echoes elements of the wider War on Terror, where finding means to demonstrate policy success and announcing the decline, collapse, defeat, and demise of Salafi-Jihadi groups has taken centre stage. Unfortunately, the extent to which the Transatlantic orthodoxy of Terrorism Studies has defined these groups as defeated has little to do with their continued ability, willingness, and the theological drivers to wage their particular form of jihad.[14] Salafi-Jihadi groups remain undeterred by the Western claims of success against them.[15]

While the digital environment has gone through significant changes, much of the orthodox research landscape has focused on the same old places from the early Web 2.0 era, with any change in tactics made by the Media Mujahidin being ascribed to the success of Western pressure. One will often hear pundits and researchers use a version of the supposed truism that IS's presence 'it is not like it used to be' and indeed, it is not. The tech landscape has changed significantly, and the Media Mujahidin has evolved their tactics to maximise the impact of their efforts.

Web Ecology

Online information is disseminated within an ecosystem of different platforms. Previous studies have shown that the Media Mujahidin exhibit an emergent intelligence and swarm mentality as they operate in online information ecosystems. This enables the speed, agility, and resilience of the Swarmcast.

The Media Mujahidin have established resilient networks on their chosen platforms through which they create platform-specific ecosystems of accounts, channels or groups. In addition, a previous study has shown that the speed and agility of the Media Mujahidin which comprise the Swarmcast have allowed them to create a multiplatform ecosystem, in which each online platform contributes elements to the ecosystem, in the form of beacons, content stores, and aggregators.

This section examines the way in which the multiplatform communication paradigm (MCP) is particularly suited to the contemporary internet and the way users currently engage with content online. Specifically, the success of the MCP mode of content dissemination is that it is native to the way individuals now access information and use social media. At the end of 2021, the average user engaged with seven different platforms. This means internet users are increasingly familiar with engaging with all elements of life across numerous digital platforms and spaces. At a basic level, the more places where large groups of users congregate, the greater the opportunities the Salafi-Jihadi movement may have to reach individuals.

This development creates significant incentives for groups such as al-Dawlat al-Islamiyya and al-Qaeda to have multiple beacons and presence on multiple platforms. Such groups have adopted numerous hubs including Telegram, Element, Rocket, Chirpwire, and Whatsapp.

The Multiplatform Communication Paradigm

The Multiplatform communication paradigm has been one of the most important developments in the way the Salafi-Jihadi movement exploits the internet since the early recognition by thought leaders such as Yusuf al-Uyari[16] in the early 2000s to project their theology of violence. The theology of violence where al-jihad is the core theme, intimately intertwined with the commitment to da'wa – proselytizing –, is driving the Salafi-Jihadi movement to the internet, the most useful hub for content distribution. In 2013 AQ's number two, Abu Yahya al-Libi, clarified who the target audience is and why: "we are industrious in transforming our propagation to Islam (da'wa) into a general da'wa, with the ambition to reach the hearts of the people. We shall inject into their natural purified composition of their faith [our da'wa]."[17]

The recognition of this evolution in the mode of digital communication[18] made possible the categorisation of the role different platforms play within the information ecosystem. The categorisation of roles such as beacons, aggregators and content stores is now in use by industry groups such as Tech Against Terrorism and GIFCT, along with governments attempting to reduce the effectiveness of Salafi-Jihadi outreach.

At the same time, a Web3-enabled Swarmcast 2.0 has arrived. Swarmcast 2.0 is much more dynamic, secure, encrypted, decentralised, and resilient than the original version which emerged by 2014. It is native to the multiplatform communication paradigm (MCP) where the presence across many interconnected and even interoperable platforms and services provides the means for the Salafi-Jihad movement to continue reaching audiences despite the millions of dollars invested in the attempt to disrupt them.

There are two particularly important developments which make Swarmcast 2.0, built on a multiplatform communication paradigm, well suited to exploiting the contemporary internet. First, at the end of 2021, the average user engaged with seven different social platforms.[19] This means internet users are increasingly comfortable interacting with material across numerous digital platforms and spaces. During this shift to multiplatform-based interaction with social media, research produced by transatlantic orthodoxy of Terrorism Studies (OTS) has tended to focus on the study of single platforms.[20] While there is clearly value in understanding networks on a single platform, data must be interpreted in the wider context, accounting for the way that a platform contributes to the multiplatform communication paradigm and the overall da'wa effort.

At a basic level, the more spaces and platforms there are where large groups of users congregate, the greater the number of opportunities the Salafi-Jihadi movement has to reach individuals.

This development creates significant incentives for groups such as al-Dawlat al-Islamiyya and al-Qaeda to have multiple beacons and a presence on multiple platforms. Such groups have adopted numerous hubs including Telegram, Element, Rocket, Chirpwire, and Whatsapp. Furthermore, the ability to establish points of contact on multiple sites reduces the impact of disruption activity on a single platform, as users can always continue to engage with the Salafi-Jihadi movement through contacts on other platforms. Rather than relying on maintaining communication via accounts on the same platform, Swarmcast 2.0 maintains connections across the multiple platforms that users frequent.

Many of the CVE and tech industry commentary has been about a successful disruption of IS specifically and Salafi-Jihadi movements more broadly, following the 2019 EUROPOL-led day of action. That action was heralded as having "resolutely trashed the Islamic State's presence on Telegram".[21] Furthermore, this and later efforts, are often presented as fragmenting IS and Salafi-Jihadi movements online. However, the evidence of this fragmentation is undermined by researchers observing Salafi-Jihadi movements using a range of platforms. Using multiple platforms to engage users is a normal practice for organisations wanting to engage users online – as users tend to use multiple social media sites each month.

Second, technological developments have significantly eroded the notion of online and offline. While there are places where there is no or little internet access, there are many populations in which the concept of being offline is something from a bygone era. The flipside of which is that "online radicalization is a redundant concept".[22] This is particularly the case for people who spend their entire day carrying a device tracking their location, every heartbeat and footstep, and reporting these to a cloud server, while that same device also instantly receives the latest news, media content and alerts. While the notion of 'online vs. offline' persists in the orthodox Terrorism Studies (OTS) literature, the days of 'going on line' as if engaging in the late 1990s process of checking email are rooted in a dial-up mindset and increasingly do not reflect he mindset of internet users. At the same time, research into 'online radicalisation' frequently focuses on what is observable from a Western researcher's perspective, often with little if any reference to the networks of shared meaning that coordinate around theological concepts. This research often produces 'score keeping' accounts, which focus on counting channels, users, or messages, as if producing more messages is what Salafi-Jihadi da'wa is about.[23]

Conclusions drawn from this approach echo the 'survivor bias' often discussed in relation to Abraham Wald's work assessing where to place armour on a World War II aircraft.[24] An initial reaction to count where bullet holes appeared in planes, just like counting number of messages or channels, would, as Wald showed, lead to armour being placed incorrectly. This is because as it does not account for the possibility that there is a reason the researcher has only a partial view. In Wald's case, the planes that had crashed were not represented in the data. In the study of the Salafi-Jihadi movement, the persistent exclusion of theology creates a Western caricature of the Salafi-Jihadi movement. It should be obvious that kittens, Nutella, rap music, crime, and vague Western notions of creating a 'jihadi utopia' on earth are insufficient to explain the ability of Salafi-Jihadi groups to continue in the face of a physical assault by some of the world's most powerful military organisations and repeated killing of their leaders.[25] However, there has been a persistent devaluation of Arabic; the focus is on logos, flags, and a limited number of motifs (often treated as a range of exotic corsage);

and the stated intent is to whittle away theology.[26] Such an approach inevitably creates only a partial view of the online activity, disconnected from the pathways through which users locate material and the networks congregating around shared meaning rather than logos and flags.

Take for example the claims amongst OTS and policy circles of IS being 'deplatformed' from Twitter[27], coming at a time when one third of known traffic to IS content originated from Twitter.[28] One has to conclude that users, likely within the primary target audience, were able to locate links to material in a manner Western researchers were not. The reality, of course, is that this material is produced as part of da'wa and therefore the study of such activities should focus on the meaning of the content as intended by the producer and understood by the primary target audience. It is in essence the patterns of behaviour exhibited by the humans behind the screens. Such a focus, along with the common practice of internet users, fundamentally erases the dial-up notion of online/offline.

The 'Swarmcast'

2016 started with talk of 'cyberbombs' and transatlantic whispers that the Islamic State (IS) would be wiped off the internet by the end of the year.[29] Years later, as of 2022, it is clear that IS maintains a persistent online presence through a mobile-enabled 'swarm' that rapidly reconfigures despite attempts to target key individuals and remove content – while the group managed to expand into Africa to spread their core theology and marking their enemies accordingly in combat zones ranging from Mali to Nigeria, Congo and Mozambique. IS continues to fight and maintain their online footprint from their traditional zones of operations in Syria and Iraq.

The original 'swarmcast' was defined by several features; specifically, the speed, agility, and resilience of the Salafi-Jihadi networks.[30] The next evolution, 'Swarmcast 2.0', has taken those features previously applied at a platform level and applied them within the multiplatform communication paradigm.

The Current Pillars of Swarmcast 2.0

The persistent presence produced by Swarmcast 2.0 relies on it being in tune with a multi-platform zeitgeist maintained by the speed, agility, and resilience of its networks. The Media Mujahidin, and the Salafi-Jihadi movement more broadly, currently operate across a vast range of platforms that make up their multiplatform communication paradigm (MCP).[31] The MCP and Swarmcast 2.0 have emerged with a similar structure and ethos to much of current thought about Web3. Within the MCP, some platforms fulfil the role of beacons around which the movement can regroup should their activity be disrupted on a single specific platform. These beacons are the pillars of Swarmcast 2.0, Telegram, Rocket and Matrix.

Telegram functions as the core of the movement where the entire Salafi-Jihadi ecosystem exists in one place. Since 2016, users have been able to access mainstream Salafi material alongside material from specific Salafi-Jihadi groups, including IS and AQ. All of this communication takes place via a mobile app that can facilitate communication in groups of over 100,000 users or encrypted one-to-one messaging.

Rocket.Chat servers have the role of static 'citadel' or 'factory' similar to the original bulletin board and forum sites from the first decade of the 21st century. The role of these sites was described by Abu Sa`d al-`Amili in a piece where he lamented the shift of "major [jihadi] writers and analysts" to social media and the decline in participation in jihadist online forums. He issued a "call (nida') to the Soldiers of the Jihad Media", demanding that they "return to their frontiers (thughur)", elevating their status as the driving force of the movement.[32] Rocket provides the modern version of these citadels, where access, participation, and publication are controlled by the server administrators loyal to AQ or IS.

Matrix operates as the final pillar, heavily promoted in online security briefings posted by groups aligned to IS. It is from a technical perspective the leading edge of the Salafi-Jihadi movement, already fully able to operate using Web3 approaches and ethos.

Telegram

What Is Telegram?

The Media Mujahidin have used Telegram to communicate since 2016.[33] According to Telegram developers, Telegram is a cloud-based instant messaging service, providing optional end-to-end encrypted messaging. Telegram lets users access their chats from multiple devices with messages that are heavily encrypted and can self-destruct. Telegram has no limits on the size of your media and chats, and groups can hold up to 200,000 members.[34] It is free and open, having an open API and protocol free for everyone, which has allowed users to build their own bots, and even their own clients to access Telegram.

Over the past years Telegram has been the most important social media platform for jihadist media operatives, to project influence, disseminate videos, text documents, pictures, audio, and torrent files. Since its adoption, Telegram has customarily been the first point where Salafi-Jihadi content is released into the information ecosystem.

Much of the transatlantic 'success narrative' has presented the adoption of Telegram as the result of disruption on Twitter forcing IS and AQ to use smaller platforms on the margins of the internet. From the perspective of the Media Mujahidin, Telegram has had much greater utility for their efforts to communicate with supporters. The ability to use one app to have encrypted conversations, share large files, broadcast content to thousands of users, large group text chat, now with the option to allow millions of users to chat live[35], along with one-to-one video, and automated features, including bots[36], to moderate groups or interact with users to share content.

It is important to note, while the move to Telegram by the Media Mujahidin has been mythologized within the transatlantic orthodoxy of Terrorism Studies as the result of a 'successful' effort to drive them from Twitter, there is another perspective. First, Telegram now has both a far larger user base than Twitter and a greater number of mobile downloads; current estimates place Telegram users at around 700 million, while Twitter is under 400 million. Second, even when Salafi-Jihadi groups such as the Taliban are able to use Twitter openly, they have Telegram groups with tens of thousands of users. Third, Telegram enables users to engage with the full range of groups and content across both sides of the Salafi-Jihadi nexus.[37] Fourth, on Telegram, large Salafi networks are well established. This is the primary target audience for Salafi-Jihadi groups to garner sympathizers and recruits, with the Media Mujahidin linking to Salafi-only channels and resharing salafi content within Salafi-Jihadi channels to demonstrate the application of theology at the centre of Salafi scholarship of the Salafi-Jihadi ambition of why they fight and what for.[38]

The URLs from Telegram highlight the type of platforms that make up the structure of the MCP.

The most shared domains on Telegram (Figure 10.1) include platforms fulfilling the main roles within the multiplatform communication paradigm; 'beacon', 'content aggregator', and 'file store'. In addition to Telegram, WhatsApp chat links are shared frequently. Justpaste. it and Telegra.ph are the most frequently used aggregators, with YouTube, archive.org, and

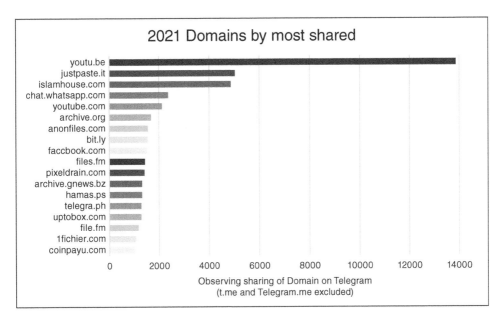

Figure 10.1 2021 Domains by Most Shared

Source: Author's Creation

annonfiles being prominent content stores. Three other particularly noteworthy domains; first, archive.gnews.bz is a subdomain from the former location of the AQ Rocket server, discussed in more detail below. Second, Coinpayu.com enables users to earn cryptocurrency and gives access to a number of cryptocurrency mining and exchange apps – cryptocurrency, NFT, and blockchain being prominent elements of current Web3 applications.[39] Third, Islamhouse.com describes itself as "the largest and the most authentic free reference to introduce Islam in the world languages on the internet".[40] That it is part of the Salafi-Jihadi nexus should not be surprising, given the theological nature of the movement and the tendency to use mainstream salafi material alongside branded IS or AQ content.[41] Islamhouse.com offers mainly books in Arabic, and in another 120 languages, while selected Arabic writings are free to read online and download as translations. The site hosts the writings of Sunni Islamic scholars – hence the writings are all theological and offer a wide range of shared meaning within the Salafi-Jihadi movement, ranging from hatred against Shi'ites to historical books framing it a divine obligation for any Muslim to kill anyone accused of blasphemy, especially of insulting God or Prophet Muhammad.

Through the Telegram app, with hundreds of millions of users, Salafi-Jihadi groups are able to target their primary target audience through the concurrence of salafi and Salafi-Jihadi material within a single interconnected online network.

Rocket

The makers of Rocket.Chat describe it as "the communications platform you can fully control and trust". It is offered as either Software as Service (SaaS) or as a "self-managed" install on an independent server. It is intended to "empower organizations to own their conversations by developing the world's most flexible and secure open-source communications platform".[42] Echoing the Web3 emphasis on decentralisation, Rocket.Chat is open source and the creators argue: "the future of communication is not on closed systems and will never be".[43] In fact, the Rocket.Chat code is hosted on Github, has over 31,000 stars (similar to Facebook 'likes') and has been forked[44] over 7,000 times.[45]

Both IS and AQ have access to their own self-managed Rocket.Chat installation. In Web3 style, this means they have all the capabilities of a mature communications platform, but without the centralised administration of Web 2.0 platforms, like Facebook or Twitter, that can suspend or remove IS/AQ accounts when reported by users or governments.

The AQ installation is primarily Arabic focused with some other languages from multiple AQ groups. These include JNIM (Sahel), HSM (Somalia), AQAP (Yemen), as-Sahab (global) and additional media via Thabat and Zallaqa, GIMF and Shahada News.

The IS Rocket server has a range of multilingual channels sharing branded IS news and releases, along with a range of media foundations, including al-Bayan, Ajnad, al-Taqwa, and Sunni Shield. There are also a series of groups on specific themes, from lives of the martyrs and Jihadi Scholars to Coronavirus as a soldier of God.[46]

On their Rocket.Chat servers IS has approximately twice as many groups and twice as many total messages, and the largest group is approximately twice as large as the largest group on the AQ server. It is beyond the scope of this discussion to analyse the number of unique users on each server, but the largest group indicates that there are at least this number of accounts on each server.

In addition to the updates on content releases and announcements available in the channels, both IS and AQ use other features which contribute to the multiplatform communication paradigm:

- Following well established protocol, lists of URLs are shared to content stored on filesharing sites as well as to lists of channels on other platforms, including Telegram, Matrix, and Whatsapp.
- The Rocket servers have an 'archive' subdomain where content is stored. Links to content in the Rocket archives appear in the lists of URL shared content releases and re-releases. These archives circumvent the content removal efforts, because even if all other links are removed, material is available via the Rocket archive link.
- The 'archive' subdomain provides integration with Nextcloud, free and open-source software which enables anyone to "install and operate it on their own private server".[47] Files can be transferred directly from the Rocket archive subdomain to an individual's self-hosted Nextcloud, links to which can then be shared. Nextcloud is "open source file sync and share software for everyone from individuals operating the free Nextcloud Server in the privacy of their own home, to large enterprises and service providers supported by the Nextcloud Enterprise Subscription".[48] Links to Nextcloud servers, which are shared within the Salafi-Jihadi movement, focus on specific groups or areas, including HSM material on an installation called "kataibdrive", or AQIM on "maghrebfiles", or in a specific language such as and installation known as "Banglafiles".[49] This combination of Rocket, an archive subdomain, and Nextcloud creates the dispersed storage that enables the Media Mujahidin to maintain a persistent presence as part of the Web3 approach to decentralisation.

Matrix

Matrix is an open network for secure, decentralized communication (the Matrix open standard).[50] Through using the Matrix open standard it *"is as simple to message or call anyone as it is to send them an email".* Users can *"communicate without being forced to install the same app"* and *"can choose who hosts your communication".* In addition, *"conversations are secured by E2E encryption".*[51]

Matrix is a network of interconnected 'federated' home servers – users initially register on a 'homeserver' and the matrix open standard enables communication between users on the same server and connects "home servers" to each other. Matrix likens it to having email servers; users can communicate across servers, but each server has its own specific nuances – just as in the email example, Gmail is different from Zoho, Outlook, Protonmail or Yahoo! Mail services. They talk to each other, but each gives the user a slightly different experience.

Matrix is heavily favoured in advice circulated within the Salafi-Jihadi movement, due to the utility, security, and anonymity. It can be accessed through clients such as Element (previously Riot), Ditto Chat, FluffyChat, Hydrogen for mobile, with Desktop clients including Nheko, Fractal, NeoChat, Mirage, Seaglass, and Spectral. Other options exist for Web, Terminal/Command Line, and even Nintendo 3DS.

The decentralised nature of Matrix makes it particularly useful to the Web3-enabled Swarmcast 2.0, and Matrix users are likely the leading edge of the Salafi-Jihadi online movement. Both IS and AQ have created channels on the main Matrix.org home server, while IS has also created its own homeserver. That now deactivated home server ran on an Nginx[52] web server, controlled by a pro-IS administrator. In the Web3 context, this gives IS the ability to provide content, and to control the content on their server (using their 'node prerogative'), in a decentralised and interoperable network.[53] All channels which appeared on this IS home server have the approval of the server admin, and had between 300 and 550 members.

In addition to having their own node in the Matrix network, using their node prerogative to host the material they choose, the home server also used the Matrix 'bridge' function, where content can be imported from other platforms. In the IS case, they had bridges from Telegram, so the material which appeared in their channels on Telegram also appeared in their Matrix channels. This extends the distributed network which made the Salafi-Jihadi network on Telegram so resilient to the "hyper-distributed, replicated, [and] resilient" network imagined in the Web3 ethos and the multiplatform communication paradigm which underpins Swarmcast 2.0.

Data archived from the IS Matrix home server in December 2021 demonstrate how the IS home server is used.[54]

The majority of the messages are text that includes URLs, but a third are images. The URLs which appear in the text of messages also facilitate the multiplatform communication paradigm. The most commonly linked-to domain is Telegram, shared over 1750 times. This enables users to reconnect with the core of the Salafi-Jihadi network on Telegram and is also driven by the links contained in material posted via the Matrix Telegram Bridge.

The range of domains shown in Figure 10.2 highlights the different roles platforms fulfil in the MCP, including the 'beacons' such as Telegram and Matrix, with many of the others being filesharing sites in the role of 'content stores'.[55] Most relevant to the emergence of Swarmcast 2.0 is the adoption of decoo.io, which brands itself as the "Entrance to Web 3.0".[56]

Web3 in Action

The Web3 technology currently in use already represents a significant circumvention of existing tactics and techniques intended to disrupt their online activity. From EthLink and IPFS pinning, to the integration of onion links which underpin the strategy to deliver a resilient surface web distribution infrastructure, Web3 is already in use. This final section provides evidence of specific Web3 approaches already in use by groups within the Salafi-Jihadi movement.

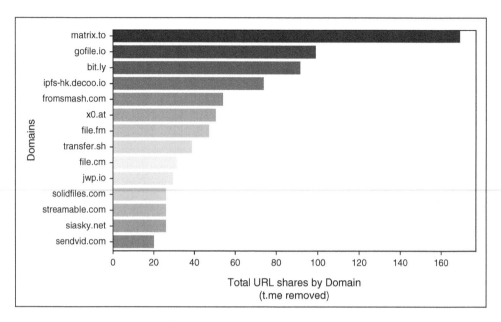

Figure 10.2 Top Domains by Total Shares during 2021

Source: Author's Creation

Ipfs

IPFS, the InterPlanetary File System.[57] IPFS is a distributed system for storing and accessing files, websites, applications, and data.[58] IPFS makes "it possible to download a file from many locations that aren't managed by one organization", producing the decentralisation central to Web3 and the modus operandi of the Media Mujahidin.[59] IPFS not only "supports a resilient internet", "it makes it harder to censor content".[60] The IPFS provides greater resilience: "files on IPFS can come from many places, it's harder for anyone (whether they're states, corporations, or someone else) to block things. We hope IPFS can help provide ways to circumvent actions like these when they happen".[61]

"IPFS is based on the ideas of possession and participation, where many people possess each other's files and participate in making them available", an approach which is very similar to both iterations of the Swarmcast, where members of the Salafi-Jihadi movement contribute to maintaining the persistent presence of Salafi-Jihadi material.[62] By being able to make content available via IPFS links, the Media Mujahidin can take advantage of the additional resilience on offer.

Decoo

Decoo is a Web3 service provider established by DCF (Decentralized Cloud Foundation). Decoo focuses on IPFS Pinning & Hosting Service, Decentralized Cloud Storage, Node Service and API Service. Decoo aims to create an easy-to-use entrance infrastructure into Web3 - a real decentralised, distributed cloud, for worldwide users.[63] It is built on the experience of projects such as Git[64], BitTorrent[65], Kademlia[66] (which contributed to the development of Ethereum[67]), and Bitcoin[68,69] Decoo, and other similar services allow users predominantly used to a web 2.0 experience to use IPFS.

Figure 10.3 Screenshot of IS video from West Africa available via IPFS

One of the groups to take advantage of IFPS services such as Decoo is IS.[70] Figure 10.3 shows an IS video from West Africa posted on IPFS and viewed via a Decoo gateway.

This means IS have adopted the technology to deliver a resilient surface web distribution infrastructure via Web3. As we have seen with many other developments once the practical details have been established by one group within the movement, that 'blue collar knowledge' rapidly spreads to other groups.

EthLink and Onion

EthLink is one of a range of approaches and services which can be leveraged to deliver a much more resilient, Web3-enabled distribution system. "EthDNS is a way to access information in the Ethereum Name Service (ENS) from DNS" and "EthLink is EthDNS for the .eth domain".[71]

> "Because .eth is not a registered DNS top-level domain it is normally inaccessible from DNS, but by appending .link to the domain the relevant information can be obtained. For example, a DNS A record request for mydomain.eth.link would look up the A records in ENS for mydomain.eth."[72]

This system makes users or material findable outside the current DNS system (that is usually required for making a website findable and which makes websites with regular domain names susceptible to disruption and removal. Salafi–Jihadi websites have been around for decades and their use has gained increased attention recently.[73]

While organisations including Tech Against Terrorism seek to draw governmental attention to the issue of individual websites, by using a single Ethlink, https://f####s.eth.limo,IS media operatives have created a system to circumvent the disruption effort of removing individual websites. The eth.link provides a regularly updated index page of their websites. Rather than return to the domain name for a website, the user just accesses the index page from their browser and selects the link to their desired website, wherever it is currently hosted. This capacity effectively renders the disruption through the removal of individual websites obsolete, at a time when the Western CVE industry is still grappling with developing potential mechanisms for the removal of individual websites.

To add an extra layer of resilience, a very similar approach has been deployed with an onion link.[74] Like the EthLink, this also provides the index of existing webpages. One need only bookmark the link in a Tor browser (or ethLink in any browser) and the whack-a-mole deletion of domain-named websites is circumvented almost in its entirety. This approach combines the elements of decentralisation with the structure of dispersed nodes that are hallmarks of Web3, with the utility of existing services, such as Tor, that have pursued this approach to security and resilience for well over a decade.[75]

There are two elements worthy of additional note, which are highlighted by the use of eth and onion. First, the ability of the Media Mujahidin to adapt to the changing tech landscape, and second, the commitment and technical competence these steps demonstrate.

Firstly, as observed previously, the tech landscape has changed significantly, and the Media Mujahidin has evolved their tactics to maximise the impact of their efforts. Tor was once thought of as relatively hard to use, and by 2013 had become "a focus of criticism, accused of facilitating a dangerous 'dark web' of paedophiles, drug dealers and arms traders",[76] or, as one an NSA document puts it: "Very naughty people use Tor".[77] In this mindset it became common to lump criminals using the dark web and Tor users into one category, with multiple stories surfacing of the National Security Agency based in the US and GCHQ in the UK attempting to attack the Tor network and undermine the anonymity of users.[78]

However, the current Tor browser, a variant of Mozilla Firefox, is as easy to download and install as Chrome, Edge, Safari, Opera or any of the many other browser options.[79] It is easy to use on Windows, macOS and Linux, with a version for Android and Onion Browser for iOS.[80] Tor can even be made 'portable' so an individual can take it with them and use it from a USB stick or SD Card on other computers.[81]

Far from being a service just used by 'naughty people', the way users interact online has evolved and many now use VPN and/or Tor as additional layers of protection for their identity and privacy. The Media Mujahidin have adapted to the new ways available to reach their target audience.

Secondly, the way Tor and Onion services are being used by the Media Mujahidin highlights the level of commitment and technical competence they have at their disposal. Onion links are usually random strings. Time and computing effort must be invested to create a custom or vanity string. This process takes a few seconds for the first three or four characters, but rapidly escalates to around thirty minutes for six characters, and from there reaches a day, a month, and approximately 40 years if ten characters were required.[82] The onion link starts with a six-character custom string which matches the EthLink. This effort comes at a time when advocates of the OTS 'success narrative' claim the Media Mujahidin are being degraded, are tiring, and have been worn down by having to create new pages and accounts on various social media platforms.

It is hard to square such assertions with the evidence-base which shows the Salafi-Jihadi movement innovating new ways of working and making the 'website' element of their distribution system more resilient, even when those websites are a "blind spot for policymakers, practitioners, and researchers", according to Tech Against Terrorism.[83] If all that were not enough to demonstrate their current capabilities, IS are then going the extra mile to give their onion link a custom identity.[84] The gap between the innovation and technical ability of the Media Mujahidin on the one hand and the OTS researchers claiming to be measuring the decline of IS and Salafi-Jihadi groups on the other, is vast and growing rapidly. It has already grown to such an extent that much of the Swarmcast 2.0 is effectively invisible to elements within OTS, who are reassuring rhetoric for policymakers.

Conclusion

We are now seven years after the claims that content distribution had been degraded, six years after the "purported resilience" of Salafi-Jihadi online networks was derided by those in the orthodoxy of Terrorism Studies, and three years after the supposed "full-fledged collapse" of IS media.[85] In this time, the tech landscape has changed, some of what are referred to as 'smaller' and 'niche' platforms have become new 'tech giants', a reality which poses a significant challenge to the orthodox notion of driving the movement to smaller platforms.

In addition, a Web3-enabled Swarmcast 2.0 has arrived. Swarmcast 2.0 is much more dynamic, secure, encrypted, decentralised, and resilient than the original version which emerged by 2014. Swarmcast 2.0 circumvents or renders obsolete many of the current tactics intended to disrupt the online activity of the Media Mujahidin.

As the Media Mujahidin have maintained a large network on Telegram, users can span the Salafi-Jihadi nexus and tap into material from a wide range of salafi and Salafi-Jihadi groups. The network of content sharing on Telegram during 2021 shows that over 90% of channels connect into a single giant network which includes both salafi and Salafi-Jihadi content. This means that while IS, AQ, Hamas, the Taliban and the Muslim Brotherhood may not connect together directly, they are all connected to the same network, and draw on the same ecosystem of content and theological material.

If careful consideration is not given to the theological references and strategic documentation in Arabic, the strategy of the Islamic State will not be fully understood. We must accept, if we like it or not, that the Islamic State attracts mainly Arab recruits and bases its "narratives" on complex theological constructs. As we have shown, it is vital that measurements of overall media production of the Islamic State (and other extremist groups) are produced based on an awareness of the strategy of those groups.

To deliver an accurate representation of the information environment and strategy of extremist groups, future research will need an interdisciplinary approach that combines the insight of Arabic speaking subject matter experts, versed in Islamic State theology and strategy, working in genuine collaboration with individuals who possess appropriate data analysis skills.

The need for a strategic level approach to disruption, and collaborative strategies, is increasingly pressing and can no longer be held back by the comfort and reassuring rhetoric of the OTS 'success narrative'.

The future of disruption efforts requires a Web3 strategy. The Salafi Jihadi movement is engaged in a battle for the reality of the humans behind the screens. They treat censorship as a malfunction and through Swarmcast 2.0 have consistently routed around it. The risk posed by relying on Web 2.0 disruption approaches in an increasingly Web3 world approaches the equivalence, to lean on Darcy DiNucci's analogy, of planning to play Pong but finding yourself in *The Matrix*.

Notes

1 Douglas Rushkoff (1995). Cyberia: Life in the Trenches of Hyperspace (New York, NY: Harpercollins Publishers), e-book version.
2 Uncensorable Wikipedia on IPFS (2017). IPFS Blog & News, https://blog.ipfs.tech/24-uncensorable-wikipedia/(accessed 26 June 2022).
3 Douglas Rushkoff (1995). Cyberia: Life in the Trenches of Hyperspace (New York, NY: Harpercollins Publishers), e-book version.
4 Ibid.
5 Further discussed in: Nico Prucha (2016). IS and the Jihadist Information Highway–Projecting Influence and Religious Identity via Telegram, Perspectives on Terrorism, Vol. 10, No 6, http://www.terrorismanalysts.com/pt/index.php/pot/article/view/556 (accessed 17 December 2016).
6 AQ often referred to 'aqida (creed) and minhaj (methodology) when outlining what defines a Sunni Muslim. This ranges from proper prayer conduct to destroying graves of holy men (awliya') whenever possible. The claim to re-enact the lives of early Muslims under the command of prophet Muhammad, acting on said "prophetic methodology" and applying divine laws as opposed to man-made laws is not new. Abu Mus'ab al-Suri (2004) romanticised about this as one of the objectives for any mujahid in his 1600 page long book "Global Islamic Resistance Call" (pages 42, 92). Al-Suri referenced a popular hadith, predicting "the return of the caliphate upon the prophetic methodology." Ayman al-Zawahiri in his "fourth open interview" (2007), conducted online and published by al-Sahab, demanded that Sunni jihadist organisations in Iraq ally with "the Islamic State in Iraq" to liberate territory and consequently re-establish the "abode of Islam" by introducing the "prophetic methodology".
7 Douglas Rushkoff (1995). Cyberia: Life in the Trenches of Hyperspace (New York, NY: Harpercollins Publishers), e-book version.
8 Rüdiger Lohlker, "Why Theology Matters–The Case of ISIS," *Strategic Review* July–September 2016, http://sr-indonesia.com/in-the-journal/view/europe-s-misunderstanding-of-islam-and-isis.
9 Among the tens of thousands of writings are prominent items such as "An Abbreviated Biography of the Prophet – Peace and Blessings upon him" by ISIS media foundation Maktabat al-Himma (2015, 335 pages) or the 1106 page long theological tractate by Khalid bin 'Ali al-Mardi on shirk – ascribing or the establishment of "partners" placed beside God, which is a frequent theological sanctioning used to execute "apostates" and Shiites within ISIS videos.
10 Linguistic problems are nothing new in the study of terrorism. See for example: http://foreignpolicy.com/2015/04/15/why-we-cant-just-read-english-newspapers-to-understand-terrorism-big-data/
11 Ali Fisher, "Interpreting Data about ISIS Online", USC Center on Public Diplomacy, 6 October 2016, https://uscpublicdiplomacy.org/blog/interpreting-data-about-isis-online
12 Prucha Nico, Ali Fisher (2013). "Tweeting for the Caliphate: Twitter as the New Frontier for Jihadist Propaganda." *CTC Sentinel* 6(6), 19–23.
Fisher Ali; Prucha Nico (2014, August). "The Call-up: The Roots of a Resilient and Persistent Jihadist Presence on Twitter." *CTX*, 4(3), 73–88.
Jamie Bartlett, Ali Fisher (2018). "How to beat the media mujahideen", DEMOS Quarterly, Issue #5, Winter 2014/15 Ali Fisher, Netwar in Cyberia: Decoding the media mujahidin, paper 5, USC Center on Public Diplomacy.
13 The role of 'embedded academics' in the transatlantic orthodoxy of Terrorism Studies, Jackson, RDW, 'The Case for a Critical Terrorism Studies' (2007) http://hdl.handle.net/2160/1945 https://pure.aber.ac.uk/portal/files/99753/APSA-2007-Paper-final2.pdf
14 The claims of victory over jihadi groups by the covered in depth in: Ali Fisher, Nico Prucha (2021), Understanding the Global Jihadist Movement–20 Years after 9/11, EICTP October 2021, https://www.eictp.eu/wp-content/uploads/2021/12/FINAL_EICTP_Expert-Paper_Jihadist-Movement.pdf.
15 And by the continued claim of their defeat. The claims of victory over jihadi groups by the covered in depth in: Ali Fisher, Nico Prucha (2021), Understanding the Global Jihadist Movement–20 Years after 9/11, EICTP October 2021, https://www.eictp.eu/wp-content/uploads/2021/12/FINAL_EICTP_Expert-Paper_Jihadist-Movement.pdf
16 Nico Prucha (2010). Die Stimme des Dschihad–Al-Qa'ida erstes Online-Magazin (Hamburg: Verlag Dr. Kovac), pp. 11–17.
17 Abu Yahya al-Libi (2013). Risala ila l-ikhwa fi thaghr al-i'lam al-jihadiyyi, Nukhbat al-I'lam-al-Jihadiyyi, August 11, 2013, http://justpaste.it/3djs (accessed 11 August 2013), p. 12.

18 Ali Fisher, Nico Prucha, Emily Winterbotham (2019). Mapping the Jihadist Ecosystem Ecosystem, RUSI Global Research Network on Terrorism and Technology, Paper no. 6, https://rusi.org/explore-our-research/publications/special-resources/mapping-jihadist-information-ecosystem-towards-next-generation-disruption-capability.

19 Simon Kemp, TikTok Hits 1 Billion Users—Faster Than Facebook (And More New Stats), October 21, 2021 https://blog.hootsuite.com/simon-kemp-social-media/

20 For earlier critique of OTS see: Jackson, R. D. W. (2007). The Case for a Critical Terrorism Studies. http://hdl.handle.net/2160/1945

21 Charlie Winter, Amarnah Amarasingam. "The decimation of Isis on Telegram is big, but it has Consequences", Wired, 2nd December 2019. https://www.wired.co.uk/article/isis-telegram-security.

22 Whittaker Joe (2022). "Rethinking Online Radicalization." *Perspectives on Terrorism* 16(4), 27–40.

23 Mohamedou, Mohammad-Mahmoud Ould. A Theory of ISIS: Political Violence and the Transformation of the Global Order. Pluto Press, 2017. (p. 9)

24 Mangel, Marc, and Francisco J. Samaniego (1984). "Abraham Wald's Work on Aircraft Survivability." *Journal of the American Statistical Association* 79(386), 259–267.

25 Ali Fisher, Nico Prucha (2021). Understanding the Global Jihadist Movement–20 Years after 9/11, EICTP October 2021, https://www.eictp.eu/wp-content/uploads/2021/12/FINAL_EICTP_Expert-Paper_Jihadist-Movement.pdf

26 Ingram, Haroro J., Craig Whiteside, and Charlie Winter. The ISIS Reader: Milestone texts of the Islamic state movement. Oxford University Press, USA, 2020. p. 7, 225

27 Conway, M. "Why Deplatforming the Extreme Right is a Lot More Challenging than Deplatforming IS" GNET, 15th January 2021, https://gnet-research.org/2021/01/15/why-deplatforming-the-extreme-right-is-a-lot-more-challenging-than-deplatforming-is/
Also see: Maura Conway, Moign Khawaja, Suraj Lakhani, Jeremy Reffin, Andrew Robertson, David Weir (2019). Disrupting Daesh: Measuring Takedown of Online Terrorist Material and Its Impacts, Studies in Conflict & Terrorism, 42(1–2), 141–160
https://www.tandfonline.com/doi/full/10.1080/1057610X.2018.1513984

28 Frampton, Martyn, Ali Fisher, Nico Prucha, and David H. Petraeus. The New Netwar: Countering extremism online. Policy Exchange, 2017

29 https://www.scientificamerican.com/article/how-u-s-cyber-bombs-against-terrorists-really-work/

30 Hub and spoke structures have tended to be the result of 'coordination games', where there is a specific strong reason for individuals to huddle around a central node. However, centralised 'hub and spoke' networks can be very fragile, because a loss of the central node, or the strong reason to coordinate around a specific point cause, others in the network to lose contact. This has been long known since simulations run by Paul Baran (published in 1964), showed that "the centralised network is obviously vulnerable as destruction of a single central node destroys communication between the end stations". However, Paul Baran concluded that "extremely survivable networks can be built using a moderately low redundancy of connectivity level ... The redundancy level required to survive even very heavy attacks is not great – on the order of only three or four times that of the minimum span network". Elements of the original Swarmcast are discussed in detail in: Ali Fisher (2015). "Swarmcast: How Jihadist Networks Maintain a Persistent Online Presence." *Perspectives on Terrorism* 9(3)http://www.terrorismanalysts.com/pt/index.php/pot/article/view/426/html.

31 Fisher A., et al. (2019). "Mapping the jihadist information ecosystem: Towards the 3rd generation of disruption capability." *Policy Brief, Royal United Services Institute, London.*

32 Prucha Nico, Ali Fisher (2013). "Tweeting for the Caliphate: Twitter as the New Frontier for Jihadist Propaganda." *CTC Sentinel* 6(6), 19–23.

33 Prucha, Nico (2016). "Is and the Jihadist Information Highway–Projecting Influence and Religious Identity via Telegram." *Perspectives on Terrorism* 10(6), 48–58.
Frampton, Martyn, Ali Fisher, Nico Prucha, and David H. Petraeus. *The New Netwar: Countering extremism online*. Policy Exchange, 2017.

34 https://telegram.org/

35 https://telegram.org/blog/voice-chats-on-steroids#limitless-voice-chats

36 https://core.telegram.org/bots

37 For detail on Salafi-Jihadi Nexus see: Fisher, Prucha, 'Understanding the Global Jihadist Movement 20 years after 9/11', *EICTP Expert Paper*, October 2021.

38 Ali Fisher Nico Prucha "Working and Waiting": The Salafi-Jihadi movement on Telegram in 2021

Sicurezza, Terrorismo e Società 15(1), 141–170 https://www.sicurezzaterrorismosocieta.it/wp-content/uploads/2022/05/SicTerSoc-15-2022-Working-and-Waiting-_-The-Salafi-Jihadi-movement-on-Telegram-in-2021-Ali-Fisher-Nico-Prucha.pdf

39 For example, current options promoted on the site include: KuCoin, Bitdeer, Binance, HOO, Indoex

40 http://islamhouse.com/en

41 For description of Salafi-Jihadi Nexus see: Fisher Prucha, 'Understanding the Global Jihadist Movement 20 years after 9/11', *EICTP Expert Paper*, October 2021. p. 23.

42 https://rocket.chat/company/about-us.

43 https://rocket.chat/company/about-us.

44 To 'Fork' means to take a copy of the source code from one software package and start the development of a distinct and separate piece of software.

45 About Github: "Millions of developers and companies build, ship, and maintain their software on GitHub—the largest and most advanced development platform in the world" https://github.com/about.

46 For an analysis thereof: Rüdiger Lohlker, Nico Prucha (2022). Jihadi Reactions to Covid-19, EICTP Expert Paper, March 2022, https://www.eictp.eu/wp-content/uploads/2022/03/Jihadi-Reactions-to-Covid19.pdf (accessed 19 April 2022).

47 https://nextcloud.com/.

48 https://docs.nextcloud.com/server/latest/user_manual/en/.

49 The full domain is intentionally not provided.

50 https://spec.matrix.org/latest/.

51 https://matrix.org/.

52 In addition to paid services, Nginx provides an open source web server that powers more than 400 million websites https://www.nginx.com/.

53 For node prerogative see: David Pierce, How IPFS is building a new internet from the ground up, Protocol, October 13 2021, https://www.protocol.com/ipfs-new-internet.

54 System messages not displayed in graph.

55 Fisher A., et al. (2019). "Mapping the jihadist information ecosystem: Towards the 3rd generation of disruption capability." *Policy Brief, Royal United Services Institute, London.*

56 https://decoo.io/ an IPFS Pinning service discussed in more detail below.

57 For FAQ relating to IPFS see: https://docs.ipfs.io/concepts/faq/.
    And History of the project see: https://docs.ipfs.io/project/history/#a-p2p-summer-1999-2003.

58 Examples of IPFS projects can be found: https://awesome.ipfs.io/.

59 For an extended introduction to IPFS, see: https://docs.ipfs.io/concepts/what-is-ipfs/.

60 https://docs.ipfs.io/concepts/what-is-ipfs/#decentralization.

61 https://docs.ipfs.io/concepts/what-is-ipfs/#decentralization.

62 https://docs.ipfs.io/concepts/what-is-ipfs/#participation.

63 https://wiki.decoo.io/general/gettingStarted.

64 https://git-scm.com/.

65 http://bittorrent.org/.

66 https://en.wikipedia.org/wiki/Kademlia.

67 https://eth.wiki/.

68 https://bitcoin.org/en/.

69 https://github.com/ipfs/ipfs#quick-summary

70 Screenshot taken 4th February 2022.

71 See: https://eth.link/.

72 See: https://eth.link/.
    For examples of use see: https://ens.domains/.

73 The Threat of Terrorist and Violent Extremist Operated Websites, Tech Against Terrorism, 28 January 2022.
    https://www.techagainstterrorism.org/wp-content/uploads/2022/01/The-Threat-of-Terrorist-and-Violent-Extremist-Operated-Websites-Jan-2022-1.pdf.

74 http://f####s4fw3s5bi3enjrompr6kxpywkscqmmcvyiyey3xamrv5zjllgad.onion.

75 https://www.theguardian.com/technology/2014/jul/29/us-government-funding-tor-18m-onion-router.

76 Stuart Dredge, What is Tor? A beginner's guide to the privacy tool, The Guardian, November 5th, 2013, https://www.theguardian.com/technology/2013/nov/05/tor-beginners-guide-nsa-browser.

77 Stuart Dredge, What is Tor? A beginner's guide to the privacy tool, The Guardian, November 5th, 2013, https://www.theguardian.com/technology/2013/nov/05/tor-beginners-guide-nsa-browser.

78 https://www.theguardian.com/world/2013/oct/04/nsa-gchq-attack-tor-network-encryption.

79 https://www.myrasecurity.com/en/what-is-the-darknet/.

80 See https://www.torproject.org/download/ and https://onionbrowser.com/.

81 https://tb-manual.torproject.org/make-tor-portable/.

82 The process is discussed here: https://opensource.com/article/19/8/how-create-vanity-tor-onion-address as with many things increased computing power can be used to shorten the process.

83 The Threat of Terrorist and Violent Extremist Operated Websites, Tech Against Terrorism, 28 January 2022. https://www.techagainstterrorism.org/wp-content/uploads/2022/01/The-Threat-of-Terrorist-and-Violent-Extremist-Operated-Websites-Jan-2022-1.pdf.

84 Custom element of the link obscured: http://f####s4fw3s5bi3enjrompr6kxpywkscqmmcvyiyey3xam rv5zjllgad.onion

85 Charlie Winter, Jade Parker. "Virtual Caliphate Rebooted: The Islamic State's Evolving Online Strategy", Lawfare (January 2018). https://www.lawfareblog.com/virtual-caliphate-rebooted-islamic-states-evolving-online-strategy
Berger, Jonathon M., Jonathon Morgan (2015). "The ISIS Twitter Census: Defining and Describing the Population of ISIS Supporters on Twitter." *The Brookings Project on US Relations with the Islamic World* 3(20), 4–1.

11

THE VIRTUALISATION OF TERROR

Violent Extremism on the Internet Today

Charlie Winter and Blyth Crawford

Introduction

The internet today is a pivotal tool and sphere of activity for extremist movements, violent and non-violent, across the ideological spectrum. While it has always been important – with extremists using it since its emergence as the "World Wide Web" to facilitate their outreach and planning efforts – today it is not just useful, it is essential.

As internet technologies have advanced in recent decades, so too have the ways in which they are exploited by radical groups and their supporters. Nowadays, the internet is not just a way to network and distribute doctrinal materials; it is its own complementary sphere of influence and activity, a new, overlapping arena in which extremist identities are amalgamated and extremist communities formed. Consequently, the old adage that there is a neat separation between on- and offline realms is become less and less relevant by the day. In reality, the two interact and overlap, often directly, with each other.

What we define as "online extremism" will always be subject to constant and rapid evolution, but there is no doubt that online environments, platforms, tools and capabilities will remain central to the pursuit of extremist agendas for decades to come. Try as social media companies and file-sharing platforms might, they cannot inoculate themselves from the continual shifting, nebulous nature of contemporary extremism. However, what they can do – and, indeed, have done very effectively in some contexts – is render themselves much less hospitable to malign actors, something that, short of stopping their activities altogether, simultaneously has had the effect of displacing them and hastening the evolutionary process. This means that extremist communities – and their online activities – are now more diffuse, more diverse, and more difficult to lastingly disrupt than they have ever before been.

This article considers, from a comparative perspective, the implications of how online extremism has evolved in recent years. Focusing in particular on the online outreach strategies of religiously motivated violent extremist (RMVE) and ideologically motivated violent extremist (IMVE) movements, it comprises three thematically grouped sections. After we have defined what we mean by the term "online extremism", the first section addresses the undergirding principles that govern how each constellation of RMVE and IMVE groups and individuals approaches, in general, the field of strategic communication and outreach online. The second

DOI: 10.4324/9781003326373-13

section assesses how RMVE and IMVE organisations manoeuvre in online spaces, addressing their tactics, techniques and procedures (TTPs). The third and final section considers where these activities take place and why, tracking how RMVE and IMVE platform preferences have evolved in the way they have in recent decades.

Defining "Online Extremism"

We define the term "online extremism as internet activism that is related to, engaged in, or perpetrated by groups or individuals that hold views considered to be doctrinally extremist".[1] This definition thus includes the first two of Wibtrope's categories – i.e. the activities of non-violent extremists, violent extremists, and terrorists.[2] This definition is consciously context-specific, and relevant only to where it stands in relation to social convention at the time in which the group or individual in question exists. While imperfect, this concession to historical context is necessary.

As we demonstrate below, however we choose to define extremism, let alone the even thornier concept of radicalisation, the internet has become a central theatre of operations for the former and a key facilitator for the latter. While no causative relationship necessarily exists between it and either phenomenon, there is no question that extremist movements would not be where they are today without the adept use of virtual terrains.[3] This should not come as a surprise. Indeed, as Benson notes, "it would be strange if today's terrorist did not use the Internet, just as it would be strange if past terrorists did not use the postal service or the telephone".[4]

Strategies

Violent extremist (VE) organisations – whether religiously or ideologically motivated – deploy strategic communications in online spaces with a view to achieving a range of objectives, some targeted at supporters and others at adversaries.

Bockstette's 2008 work on extremist "marketing" strategies identifies propagation, legitimisation and intimidation as the three core objectives of extremist outreach.[5] Propagation refers to a movement's efforts to attract recruits, draw in donors, and expand the reach of its ideology. Legitimisation refers to its efforts to justify violence and situate its actions within a broad cultural-historic context. And intimidation refers to efforts to scare and provoke adversaries and motivate supporters, most often manifesting in propaganda of the deed (i.e., violence deployed to communicate socio-political/ideological intent) and propaganda of the virtual deed (i.e., footage or imagery of violence deployed to communicate socio-political/ideological intent). To this, an additional category of outreach can be added—instruction, or the provision of logistical advice regarding illicit VE-associated activities, anything from operational security to attack planning.[6]

All four of these objectives overlay on top of each another. Propagation-focused outreach establishes a basis for the ideology and agenda of the movement in question; legitimisation-focused outreach fends off counter-claims and/or adversary narratives; intimidation-focused outreach boosts morale and energises the rank and file, while psychologically attacking opponents; and instruction-focused outreach provides movement sympathisers with a means with which to turn supportive sentiments into supportive actions.

Tactics, Techniques, and Procedures (TTPs)

In the context of RMVE outreach, there are three main spheres of activity: propaganda production and distribution, directed recruitment, and logistics and planning.

For decades, RMVE organisations have invested a significant amount of time and energy in propaganda work. From the influence network of Abu Jandal al-Azdi, one of al-Qaeda's (AQ) most important internet ideologues in the late 2010s, to al-Shabab's sprawling covert media apparatus, online spaces have long been replete with examples of RMVE organisational outreach.[7] Importantly, while it is arguably the most prominent example of RMVE propagandising, the Islamic State (IS) is by no means the only RMVE organisation to have seen the value in resource-intensive strategic outreach. Hamas, Hizbullah, and the Afghan Taliban all preside over similarly sized (if not bigger) media networks, which they each deploy, like IS, to shape the narrative landscape and attract followers, legitimise their actions, and intimidate their opponents.[8] Alongside these official infrastructures – whether in the context of Sunni or Shi'i RMVE – operate a vast array of supporter-run media outlets and agencies which peddle the ideological line and amplify the message.

In the more tangible, tactically direct sphere of recruitment, RMVE outreach is characterised by a combination of hierarchical design and organic, volunteer-led activism. The role of social media platforms in formal enlistment to RMVE groups has been pivotal over the course of the last decade. Official operatives and unofficial advocates, the latter serving as connective tissue between communities and groups, use these spaces to directly engage with curious onlookers, drawing them in before furnishing them with the information they need to physically sign up – i.e., who to talk to, where to fly to, how to evade being apprehended, and so on.[9] While online interactions are important, however, a measure of face-to-face interaction is usually also required to facilitate the process of joining an RMVE movement, something that accounts for the prevalence of real world, social network-based recruitment patterns.[10]

Directed RMVE outreach is also central to attack planning. A small number of detailed yet exploratory studies have shown how, at an organisational level, online spaces are used to facilitate acts of terrorism.[11] Whether this is done through a "virtual entrepreneur" network, or some other form of semi-autonomous covert community structure, this sphere of activity usually relies on a convoluted logistical system that sees in-theatre RMVE operatives encouraging and motivating on the one hand and inciting and instructing on the other, occasionally providing operational advice in the form of technical literature or how-to videos.

By contrast, the structure of the IMVE outreach landscape differs fundamentally from that described above. In general, it is far less hierarchical. This is symptomatic of the fact that IMVE movements are generally more nebulous, not tied to specific organisations or formal membership arrangements. Rather, whether it is in relation to propaganda, recruitment or even attack planning, the IMVE outreach ecosystem instead consists of loosely defined groupings and key cultural figureheads.[12] Therefore, IMVE outreach activities, even if similarly orientated, usually occur as part of a bottom-up rather than top-down process. This means that rather than being formally recruited, enlisted, and furnished with "joining instructions" by specific recruiters, IMVE adherents more commonly become associated with extremist ideologies and activism through "radicalisation pipelines" that sees them being gradually exposed to, or "red pilled" on, increasingly extreme content within online IMVE echo-chambers.[13]

One of the clearest examples of this form of trajectory into extremism is that of the 2019 Christchurch shooter, Brenton Tarrant. On 15 March 2019, Tarrant initiated a firearms attack across two mosques in Christchurch, New Zealand, killing 51 people. He livestreamed the attack to Facebook, and uploaded a manifesto and link to the stream to the/pol/(politically incorrect) board of the online imageboard 8chan prior to the attack. A report on the incident, presented by the Royal Commission of Inquiry in New Zealand confirmed that Tarrant had not been a member of any IMVE of far-right groups, and had instead spent large amounts of time consuming extremist content online, which later interacted with his international travels. The report shows that he started visiting the imageboard 4chan at age 14, later moving on to the more extreme sibling site 8chan, and that he was majorly influenced by extremist content on YouTube. Thus, although Tarrant at various points donated to the Identitarian movement "Generation Identity" – as well as several far-right media outlets – his radicalisation trajectory was that of a so-called lone-actor, unattached to any formal organisations. Tarrant is representative of a large portion of the IMVE movement that operates largely outside the influence of structured groups with formal recruitment processes.

That being said, IMVE groups remain an important part of the broader extremist landscape, and some have attempted to formalise their media operations. One prominent way in which this manifests is in the form of "meme campaigns", wherein active members of IMVE movements share "edgy" memes on mainstream platforms to propagate their ideology and brand-build their agenda.[14] These efforts often deploy humour – something that we do not generally see in RMVE contexts – with a view to "disguise[ing] the loaded racism of their messaging" and sparking intrigue among people who may previously have been unreceptive to IMVE narratives.[15]

In particular, a number of such campaigns are targeted specifically towards young people. The organisation Jugendschutz has noted that some IMVE meme campaign strategies are tailored to be topic- or sector-driven, focusing on issues like school or homework in order to resonate particularly with young people.[16] Similarly, National Action, the UK-based proscribed far-right extremist group purposefully incorporated a focus on recruiting youth into the fabric of their organisation. In their 2014 "Year in Review Document", the organisation describes itself as a "youth movement" focused on creating the appropriate "social lubricant" to unite young racial nationalists.[17] As such, their propaganda is bold with strong flashes of colour, oftentimes incorporating a memetic style to appeal to young people.

Researchers Hannah Rose and AC expand on this dynamic and highlight a phenomenon they term "youth-on-youth" radicalisation. They study a selection of 10 European racial nationalist groups founded since 2018 with an average membership age of under 25 years old. Rose and AC stress that, not only are these groups composed of young people, but they are also run by them, with the transnational network Feuerkrieg Division, for example, being originally founded by a 13-year-old boy. Many of the movements studied also specifically branded themselves as "youth movements", representing young people as the onus of racial nationalist change in the West.[18] Thus a sizeable proportion of IMVE content and propaganda is being targeted towards, consumed by, as well as created by, young people.

Propaganda produced by IMVE movements is also utilised in the offline sphere. Postering and stickering campaigns are a popular tactic used by IMVE groups. Multiple propaganda videos produced by Atomwaffen Division feature masked group members plastering posters made by the group around their local areas. Notably, in three such videos members targeted university campuses, again indicating the group's interest in recruiting young people. This tactic has been utilised by many members of other IMVE groups, including 16-year-old Harry Vaughan, a member of the System Resistance Network (a National Action off-shoot), and supporter of Sonnenkrieg Division, who created his own posters to hang in and around his school in southwest London, England.[19]

More than just simply advertising the groups, these kinds of campaigns also have an online dimension. Firstly, most posters contain the email address of each group, encouraging those who see them to sign up and become a member. Secondly, many groups, such as Feuerkrieg Division, encourage supporters who carry out poster campaigns to document their efforts, later posting pictures of the campaign to their official group social media. In doing so, the group was both able to advertise their cause to newcomers who came across the posters, while also signalling to existing members on their social media channels that they were actively expanding their ranks, while not being caught by law enforcement.

Such campaigns have spread beyond proscribed terrorist groups, with a number of other IMVE movements, such as the online "Hundred Handers" collective embracing stickering as their main form of activism. The group posts regularly updated sticker designs with reactive IMVE slogans to their Telegram channel and encourages users to print them at home and anonymously spread them around their communities. While the Hundred Handers Telegram group only had around 4,000 subscribers as of mid-October 2021, forthcoming research by the International Centre for the Study of Radicalisation shows their stickers have already been posted across at least 168 cities in 13 countries.

In recent months, the online coronavirus-focused IMVE conspiracy movement, "The White Rose", has mimicked and subsequently innovated this stickering tactic, including links or QR codes to their Telegram channel on each of their stickers and so far amassing more than 50,000 unique subscribers. Once part of this channel, new users are directed to join the 12,000 members-strong "White Rose chat" discussion board, which hosts more explicitly extreme IMVE discussions. A similar "propaganda+" approach has been deployed by the likes of the neo-Nazi accelerationist collectives the Feuerkrieg Division and the Green Brigade, both of which append email addresses to official releases and encourage interested observers to make direct contact.

In general, then, RMVE outreach efforts online are markedly easier to define and delineate than those of their IMVE counterparts, which are both more diffuse – by design – and selective in who they target their wares at.

Platforms

In recent decades, extremist outreach has developed in leaps and bounds according to advances in technology and shifts in both the physical and information security environment. Much of the time, these developmental trends have been intuitive and borne of an iterative process of bottom-up innovation. However, occasionally – and often when the shifts they result in are most impactful – there is also evidence of top-down influence playing a role.

In the context of RMVE outreach, the late 1990s and early 2000s saw the most prominent organisations like the Global Islamic Media Front (GIMF) and AQ transitioning from static websites to closed forums.[20] These were, come the first half of the 2010s, supplanted by conventional social media platforms like Twitter and Facebook.[21] Nowadays, RMVE outreach efforts are principally tied to the encrypted broadcasting and chat platform Telegram, which, while it has become increasingly inhospitable to RMVE activism in recent years, remains a more open and functional space than sites like Twitter.

Telegram does not, however, have a monopoly on RMVE outreach. Other, similarly orientated and secured apps like WhatsApp, Element and Hoop have recently emerged as preferred platforms for sensitive communication between adherents of RMVE ideologies.[22] Since 2018 in particular, static websites have also become increasingly important spaces, especially in the context of propaganda archiving and distribution. Moreover, for more conventional state-based groups like Hamas, Hizbullah and, more recently, the Afghan Taliban, Twitter has never been more important.[23]

On the IMVE side of the spectrum, a similar set of diffusion dynamics can be observed. As far back as 1985 – that is, five years before the term "World Wide Web" had even been coined – right-wing supremacists in the United States had established the "White Aryan Resistance" static site, an online board devoted to sharing news, facilitating recruitment, and disseminating instructional materials.[24] Since then, IMVE movements have, like their RMVE equivalents, bounced from static online platforms to closed forums and then to mainstream social media, before eventually landing on smaller "alt-tech" platform like the Facebook and Twitter alternatives Gab and Minds. Gab in particular experienced a user resurgence in 2020 after the QAnon community breathed new life into it.[25] Similarly, Parler – particularly prior to the 6 January insurrection in Washington, D.C. – has served as a major recruitment "pipeline" for the likes of the Proud Boys, who amassed approximately 200,000 followers on the site before their activities on it were shut down.[26]

A recent report by Tech Against Terrorism notes that for both RMVE and IMVE ecosystems, static websites remain an important base for extremist content. It stresses that while violent far-right actors usually adopt a "multi-platform" approach, maintaining a presence on numerous platforms and disseminating content "largely via loosely affiliated ad hoc content creators", static websites have commonly gone unregulated. Groups like Atomwaffen and various neo-Nazis collectives have hosted their own websites with very little disruption. Having a dedicated website enables these groups to have authoritative control over the content they post, enabling them to display their mission statement, core ideology and various readings and propaganda on their own sites in one easily accessible space, outside the reach of mainstream platform moderation efforts.[27]

Besides the use of these mainstream equivalents, gaming platforms also remain important for IMVE movements – something that cannot be said in the RMVE context, at least at present. Steam, for example, hosts large quantities of extreme right-wing material, with some Steam groups openly encouraging young users to discuss extremist narratives.[28] Similarly, Discord is rife with IMVE content; it works particularly well for illicit politics because its servers can be either open access or private. The latter functionality means users can be vetted on open forums before being actively invited into private IMVE discussion boards. Although the platform has attempted to crack down on proscribed groups like Atomwaffen Division and openly extremist groups like Nordic Resistance Front organising on its platform, Discord remains a key organising and recruitment space for more nebulous IMVE movements.[29]

For its part, TikTok has also become an increasingly fertile ground for IMVE outreach in recent years, something that has gone hand-in-hand with recent surges of misinformation and conspiracy theorising on the app. Moderation efforts of IMVE content on TikTok are extremely inconsistent. Research by the Centre for Countering Digital Hate found that, of their sample of 119 videos they reported for anti-Jewish hate, just 13.5 percent were removed by TikTok's moderators. This chimes with findings from the Institute for Strategic Dialogue who found that of the 1,030 videos they coded as containing hateful or violent extremist content, just 18.5 percent of content was removed by TikTok.[30] This patchy moderation is extremely important, given IMVE movements' focus on recruiting young people, who are the main user demographic on TikTok.[31] The authors of this report have observed hard-line extremist content on the platform, such as violent excerpts from the Christchurch livestream, and snippets of official Atomwaffen videos, which have failed to be taken down after being reported. Smaller neo-Nazi movements like the National Socialist Legion have also openly disseminated propaganda posters on the platform, without being removed.

Importantly, users posting IMVE content on TikTok also occasionally link to affiliated Discord or Telegram groups in their videos, thereby channelling users into smaller, often more extreme "pipeline" communities. This therefore means that TikTok is currently catering to extremists on multiple levels, enabling them to advertise their cause to an existing captive audience of young users, and then directing them to more extreme channels where they may be more likely to organise.

With all that being said, as of mid-April 2022 at least, Telegram remained the main hub for IMVE outreach online. Notwithstanding its increasingly invasive moderation efforts, Telegram presently hosts thousands of groups and channels moderated by IMVE movements such as the Proud Boys and their white supremacist counterpart, "The Western Chauvinist", the channel of which boasts some 50,000 subscribers, as well as the National Socialist Network, and other more informal extremist collectives. Telegram is a particularly effective recruitment and radicalisation tool for extremists, as it enables members to reshare, and add to, content posted by other groups. This means that many IMVE groups frequently post and link to content from other extremist movements, making it easy for users to quickly find other IMVE collectives active on the platform.

Telegram is also a central hub for QAnon content, with over 3,500 documented groups referring directly to QAnon and a further 10,000+ channels linking directly to the networks.[32] This convergence of ideologies is important because, as QAnon followers have been pushed towards smaller platforms like Telegram as a result of social media takedowns, hard-line extremists already on the app have viewed their migration as an opportunity to recruit new members into more extreme IMVE ideologies like neo-Nazism and White Supremacy.[33]

Conclusion

Focusing in particular on the role(s) they play in the context of outreach, recruitment, and propaganda activism, this article has set out the centrality of internet technologies in the context of extremism today. We have shown that both RMVE and IMVE movements and their supporters engage in strategic communication in online spaces in pursuit of four core objectives: propagation, legitimisation, intimidation, and instruction. Whereas RMVE outreach is characterised by three main spheres of activity – propaganda production and distribution, directed recruitment, and logistics and planning – in which hierarchical design often plays a major role, IMVE outreach, by contrast, tends to be more nebulous and organically innovative. This is due to the fact that the IMVE ecosystem is generally more diverse and driven by grassroots activism. In any case, both RMVE and IMVE movements and their supporters have for the most part moved away from mainstream social media platforms in recent years, preferring the security guarantees of tools like Telegram. However, important exceptions remain, with Twitter, Facebook and YouTube in particular continuing to play a pivotal role for certain groups, something that is unlikely to change in the foreseeable future.

Notes

1 Winter, C., Peter, N., Alexander, M.-H., Magnus, R., Lorenzo, V., and Johanna, F. (2020). Online Extremism: Research Trends in Internet Activism, Radicalization, and Counter-Strategies. *International Journal of Conflict and Violence* 14(2), 2.

2 Wibtrope, R. (2012). *Rational extremism: the political economy of radicalism.* Cambridge: Cambridge University Press. 79.

3 Stevens, D. and O'Hara, K. (2015). *The devil's long tail: religious and other radicals in the internet marketplace.* London: Hurst Publishers; and O'Hara, K. and Stevens D. (2015). Echo Chambers and Online Radicalism: Assessing the Internet's Complicity in Violent Extremism. *Policy & Internet* 7(4). 401–422; Archetti, C. (forthcoming 2018). The unbearable lightness of strategic communication. In Pamment, J. and Biola, C. (Eds.). *Countering online propaganda and violent extremism: the dark side of digital diplomacy.* Abingdon: Routledge. 8.

4 Benson, D. (2014). Why the Internet Is Not Increasing Terrorism. *Security Studies* 23(2), 293–328.

5 Carsten B. (2008). "Jihadist use of strategic communication," Marshall Center.

6 Winter, C. (2020). Redefining "Propaganda": The Media Strategy of the Islamic State. *RUSI Journal* 165(1), 38-42.

7 Wagemakers, J. (2011). Al-Qa'ida's Editor: Abu Jandal Al-Azdi's Online Jihadi Activism. *Politics, Religion, and Ideology* 12(4); Anzalone, C. (2016). Continuity and Change: The Evolution and Resilience of Al-Shabab's Media Insurgency, 2006–2016. Hate Speech International, 9 November. 355–369.

8 See, for example, Khatib, L. (2013). *Image politics in the middle east: the role of the visual in political struggle.* London: I. B. Tauris; 2020. Mapping the Extremist Narrative Landscape in Afghanistan. Extract. https://public-assets.extrac.io/reports/ExTrac_Afghanistan_1120.pdf.

9 Hoffman, B. (2006). *Using the web as a weapon: the internet as a tool for violent radicalization and homegrown terrorism.* [Prepared Testimony]. Washington, DC: Committee on Homeland Security; Hoffman, B. (2008). The Myth of Grass-Roots Terrorism: Why Osama bin Laden Still Matters. *Foreign Affairs* 87(3), 133–138.

10 Conway, M. (2012). From Al-Zarqawi to Al-Awlaki: The Emergence and Development of an Online Radical Milieu. *CTX: Combating Terrorism Exchange* 2(4), 12–22.

11 See, for example, Hughes, S. and Meleagrou-Hitchens, A. (2017). The Threat to the United States from the Islamic State's Virtual Entrepreneurs. *Combating Terrorism Center Sentinel* 10(31), 1–8.

12 Manuela, C. and Linda, P. (2013). *European and American extreme right groups and the internet.* Farnham: Ashgate. 59.

13 Luke, M. (2019). "Alt-right pipeline: Individual journeys to extremism online", *First Monday.*

14 Jacob, D. and Julia E. (2017). "The Fringe Insurgency: Connectivity, Convergence and Mainstreaming of the Extreme Right", *Institute for Strategic Dialogue.* 21. https://www.isdglobal.org/wp-content/uploads/2017/10/The-Fringe-Insurgency-221017_2.pdf

15 Blyth, C. (2020). "The Influence of Memes on Far-Right Radicalisation", *Centre for Analysis of the Radical Right.* June 9, 2020 https://www.radicalrightanalysis.com/2020/06/09/the-influence-of-memes-on-far-right-radicalisation/

16 Jugendschutz. (2017). "Network of Hatred: How right-wing extremists use social media to court young people", *Jugendschutz.net.* 6.

17 National Action "Year in Review" August 2014

18 Hannah Rose and AC. (2022). "We are generation terror!": Youth-on-youth radicalisation in extreme-right youth groups", *The International Centre for the Study of Radicalisation and Community Security Trust* https://icsr.info/wp-content/uploads/2021/12/ICSR-CST-Report-We-are-Generation-Terror-Youth%E2%80%91on%E2%80%91youth-Radicalisation-in-Extreme%E2%80%91right-Youth-Groups.pdf

19 Lizzie D. "Neo-Nazi teenager admits encouraging terror attacks with propaganda poster campaign", *Independent* 16 October 2020 https://www.independent.co.uk/news/uk/crime/neonazi-terrorists-uk-teenagers-harry-vaughan-kingston-london-attacks-b1073965.html

20 Torres-Soriano, M. (2012). The Dynamics of the Creation, Evolution, and Disappearance of Terrorist Internet Forums, *International Journal of Conflict and Violence* 7(1), 164–178.

21 As detailed in: Berger, J. M., and Jessica Stern. (2015). *Isis: the state of terror.* New York, NY: HarperCollins.

22 Brantly, A. (2017). Banning Encryption to Stop Terrorists: A Worse Than Futile Exercise. *Combating Terrorism Center Sentinel* 10(5), 29–33.

23 Winter, C., Sayed, A. and Alrhmoun, A. (2021). The Taliban's vast propaganda machine has a new target, *Wired.*

24 Smith, L. (2017). In the early 1980s, white supremacist groups were early adopters (and Masters) of the internet, *Timeline*, 11 October.

25 Siladitya, R. (2021). "The far-right is flocking to these alternative social media apps–not all of them are thrilled", *Forbes*

26 Marc-Andre Argentino *et al* "Far from Gone". 28. https://icsr.info/wp-content/uploads/2021/04/ICSR-Report-Far-From-Gone-The-Evolution-of-Extremism-in-the-First-100-Days-of-the-Biden-Administration.pdf

27 Tech Against Terrorism. "The threat of terrorist and violent extremist-operated websites". January 2022 https://www.techagainstterrorism.org/2022/01/28/report-the-threat-of-terrorist-and-violent-extremist-operated-websites/20–22.

28 The Anti-Defamation League. (2020). "This is not a game: How steam harbors extremists", *ADL.*

29 Julia, A. "Discord is purging alt-right, white nationalist and hateful server", *Polygon*, 28 February 2018 https://www.polygon.com/2018/2/28/17061774/discord-alt-right-atomwaffen-ban-centipede-central-nordic-resistance-movement

30 Ciarán, O'Connor. (2021). "Hatescape: An in-depth analysis of extremism and hate speech on TikTok", *Institute for Strategic Dialigue.* https://www.isdglobal.org/isd-publications/hatescape-an-in-depth-analysis-of-extremism-and-hate-speech-on-tiktok/39.

31 "Distribution of TikTok users in the United States as of September 2021, by age group", *Statista* January 2022 https://www.statista.com/statistics/1095186/tiktok-us-users-age/

32 Jordan, W. and Marc-André, A. (2021). "QAnon is not dead: New research into telegram shows the movement is alive and well", *GNET.*

33 Marc-Andre, Argentino *et al.* (2021): Far from Gone: The Evolution of Extremism in the First 100 Days of the Biden Administration, ICSR, 28.

12

THE EVOLUTION OF HYBRID RADICALIZATION

From Small Group to Mass Phenomenon

Sophia Moskalenko[1]

Since the terrorist attacks of 9/11, terrorism and radicalization have taken a prominent role in mainstream political discourse around the world. Major state-funded research initiatives to understand, prevent and counter terrorist threats have contributed to a sizable literature in social sciences and policy analysis over the past 20 years. We now know a lot more about how and why individuals and groups become radicalized than we did before 9/11. During the same period, however, the nature of radicalization has been fundamentally transformed.

Here, I will discuss the state of the art of the psychology of radicalization. I will then present the overview of current trends in political radicalization, noting the opening gaps between the evolving phenomenon and our understanding of it. Finally, I will briefly outline the directions for future research and security efforts that can help to bridge these gaps.

Understanding Political Radicalization: Research Milestones

Jihadist terrorism became an inescapable reality for many Westerners with the deadly attacks of 9/11 in the USA, and the bombing of the London Underground of 07/07. Especially in the USA, the resulting "war on terrorism" has taken a central role in the news, with President George W. Bush setting the scene when he famously wondered, "Why do they hate us?"[2] His confusion represented the confusion of millions of people, as well as lack of research on the issue. In the aftermath of the tragedies caused by terrorist attacks, government money poured into research centers and consortia dedicated to answering this question.

Some of the early theories of radicalization centered on the idea of a "conveyor belt" (alternatively, "stairway "or "stage") model of radicalization (e.g., Moghaddam, 2005; Silber & Bhatt, 2005; Horgan, 2005). These theoretical models presented radicalization to terrorism as a gradual progression from political neutrality, to political activism, to political radicalism, with ideology playing a central role in transforming individuals into terrorists. The early theories of radicalization implied an almost inescapable transformation, like a seed is destined to grow into a tree or like stepping on a conveyor belt eventually brings one to the final destination – terrorism.

This theoretical narrative arc follows a pattern of personal transformation made familiar by folklore and literary fiction. In fictional storytelling, a person doesn't suddenly become a hero or villain: instead, they are gradually forged into that status by a series of increasingly trying

DOI: 10.4324/9781003326373-14

circumstances and realizations. This familiarity made the idea of a gradual progression from neutrality to radicalism intuitively appealing. The more familiar something is, the more positively it is perceived, a tendency captured by the "mere exposure" paradigm[3] in social psychology.

However, despite its appeal, the idea of gradual and predictable radicalization driven by ideology didn't find empirical support. In fact, as more data on terrorists became available, we learned that radicalization is far from linear. Many individuals become terrorists without ever having been political activists, effectively jumping over stages (or stairs) all the way to the apogee of radicalization.

This was the case, for example, with Major Malik Hassan, also known as Fort Hood Shooter. An Army psychiatrist, Hassan was facing imminent deployment into Afghanistan, which, in his mind, would force him to fight fellow Muslims. When his attempts to avoid this predicament were thwarted, he attacked his military base, killing thirteen people and injuring over 30 others. In his radicalization, Major Hassan was driven not by ideology but by emotions: fear of his pending deployment and anxiety stemming from his cognitive dissonance as potentially having to fight fellow Muslims. Further, Major Hassan's radicalization was not characterized by a series of smaller radical actions, such as donating to a radical cause, joining a radical group, or contributing to radical actions of others. Defying stage theories, Major Hassan radicalized precipitously.

Another infamous example of non-gradual, non-ideological radicalization was Dzhokhar Tsarnaev. Together with his older brother, Tamerlan, Dzhokhar carried out the deadly Boston Marathon bombing, which killed three people and injured hundreds of others, including 17 people who lost limbs in the attack.[4] Unlike his older brother, Dzhokhar did not have complaints about the USA, where he had immigrated with his family as a child: he was popular at school, didn't have an accent, and was successful as a college student. Dzhokhar's teachers and peers had a hard time believing he could have been involved in a jihadist attack, because he was so "normal" and so seemingly far from a jihadist lifestyle and rhetoric. Instead of going through stages or steeping in ideology, Dzhokhar became a terrorist because his older brother, a figure of importance and authority in Chechen culture, asked him to become part of his mission. Love and admiration for a brother turned a cheerful and sociable, Americanized college student into a lethal jihadist terrorist.

Researchers and security practitioners used to hope to develop something like a profile for terrorists, which would help identify them before they would ascend the final stair to terrorism. However, accumulating data made it clear that such a profile is not possible. Terrorism is not a personality trait that can be picked up by early testing. Rather, it is a strategy of the weak against the strong, or a reaction to perceived injustice, or a means to attain certain personal or political goals.[5]

From Stairs to Pathways

With the "stage" or "stairway" models of radicalization not standing up to empirical tests, researchers and practitioners turned to the view of radicalization as developing through "pathways" or "mechanisms." In this perspective, radicalization cannot be summarized as a gradual or linear process, but rather as a diverse and non-linear one.[6] What's more, this perspective emphasizes the social aspect of radicalization, including small, face-to-face groups. One example of the power of small group dynamics is radicalization of the 9/11 bombers, which seemed to have resulted from their joint isolation in a culture they perceived as hostile and morally deprived.[7]

Based on case studies of terrorists spanning over 100 years, several continents and multiple terrorist groups, McCauley and Moskalenko (2008)[8] identified 12 mechanisms of radicalization. These included individual mechanisms, such as Love, which radicalized Dzhokhar Tsarnaev, and Unfreezing, which radicalized Major Hassan. In addition to individual mechanisms of radicalization, McCauley and Moskalenko identified small group mechanisms, such as Group Isolation and Threat, which radicalized the 9/11 bombers. Finally, mechanisms of mass radicalization described entire mass public transitioning toward a greater acceptance of violence and radical action. Such was the case of Nazi Germany in the run-up to World War II, when dehumanizing propaganda, first against Jews and Communists, and later against anyone who was not Aryan, resulted in Hate, a mechanism that transitioned the whole country toward accepting the atrocities of the Holocaust and welcoming military action.

Mechanisms of radicalization are often nested, with an individual developing a political grievance at the same time as they are influenced by a small group's dynamics, while also being subject to the zeitgeist of mass radicalization. For example, the elder of the Boston Marathon bombers, Tamerlan Tsarnaev, developed a grievance against the United States, where he felt rejected as an immigrant unable to adapt to the local culture and language (individual level; Personal Grievance). On his trip to visit relatives in Russia's Caucasus region, Tsarnaev befriended members of radical jihadist groups, and became exposed to their radical rhetoric and high-risk activities (group level; Polarization and Competition). Upon his return from Russia's Caucasus region to the United States, Tamerlan continued to frequent websites and forums run by radical Islamist circles, exposing himself to jihadist videos viewed and shared by millions around the world (mass level; Hate and Martyrdom). This compounding of psychological mechanisms culminated in the mass casualty attack Tamerlan masterminded and carried out with his brother, Dzhokhar.[9]

The Role of Ideology in Radicalization

Another shift in understanding radicalization has to do with the role of ideology. Researchers and security practitioners used to assume that bad actions come out of bad ideas: that terrorists' transition from political inertia to political violence by first developing a radical ideology, which then leads them to radical action – like a "character arc" in narrative fiction. In our cultural narratives, villains tend to have their reasons – we expected no less from terrorists. However, research has proven this expectation wrong: ideology is not necessary for radicalization.

Individuals often seek out radical groups for companionship, camaraderie, or risk and status that group-based violence can offer – in other words, for reasons that have nothing to do with politics. Such was the radicalization vector of Abu Mussab al Zarqawi, "the butcher of Baghdad."[10] In his native Zarqa, he was known as a "bad Muslim," who never went to the mosque, drank alcohol, and covered his body with tattoos (a practice forbidden by Islam). Instead of learning about Islam, he spent his days looking for trouble. Zarqawi was implicated in several crimes, including attempted rape and violent assault. A local gang of Palestinian refugees offered al Zarqawi opportunities to indulge his love for violence and his hunger for social dominance. These propensities were further stoked when Zarqawi was imprisoned in a maximum-security jail. There, he became a de facto leader, controlling the wing of the prison where he was housed. Zarqawi's own understanding of Islam and Jihadism lacking, he befriended another inmate: a learned Islamic scholar, Abu Muhammad al Maqdisi. Upon their release, Maqdisi traveled with Zarqawi everywhere, adding ideology to Zarqawi's raw fierceness. When Zarqawi became the head of al-Qaeda in Iraq, his brutality against Muslims alarmed Usama bin Laden. Ayman al Zawahiri, al-Qaeda's second in command, wrote letters to Zarqawi, imploring him to remain faithful to al-Qaeda's goal of fighting for Muslims against infidels. But Zarqawi dismissed these ideological appeals. To him, al-Qaeda was only a vehicle to satisfy his lust for power and status. The only thing that would stop him was U.S. rockets that leveled the compound where he was hiding, killing him.

Zarqawi's case demonstrated that ideology was not necessary for radicalization. It is also not sufficient. Large surveys of representative samples from populations vulnerable to radicalization uncovered that the proportion of people who hold radical views is hundreds of times greater than the proportion of those who ever engage in radical actions. In repeated surveys of U.S. Muslims, about seven percent consistently endorsed the radical idea that suicide bombing of civilians is justified in the name of Islam.[11] Projected from the sample, seven percent adds up to about 70 thousand of U.S. Muslim adults. By comparison, only a few hundred U.S. Muslims were ever indicted for Jihadi violence. In other words, radical ideology is common, but radical action is rare and is not always connected with radical ideology.

As a result, policing radical ideas is a bad idea for several reasons. First, the number of people who become targets of surveillance or de-radicalization is far greater than the actual threat (hundreds of times greater, in the case of U.S. Muslims). Second, such efforts would miss those individuals whose radical actions are unconnected with radical ideas, like Zarqawi. Third, in the course of policing a large population, mistakes, misuse of power, and "collateral damage" are increasingly likely. Such "false positives" can create real grievances, likely to radicalize the targeted population. The false positives also provide rich material from which to create emotion-arousing narratives for malicious actors seeking to drive vulnerable individuals to radical action. This was the unfortunate outcome of the "War on Terror," in the United States, which overwhelmingly targeted American Muslims. As a result, the targeted minority felt persecuted, and came to view "the war on terror" as "the war on Islam."[12] Images from Abu Ghraib's prison and Guantanamo Bay, where U.S. officials humiliated and tortured Muslim prisoners, were used by jihadist terrorists to radicalize scores of Muslims around the world and recruit them into ISIS. The effort whose purpose was to reduce radical action did just the opposite. In short, policing radical opinions is impractical, imprecise, and often counter-productive.

Two Pyramids Model of Radicalization

To capture the disparity between radical opinions and radical action, the Two Pyramids model suggests two distinct representations of radicalization.[13] The radicalization of the opinion pyramid and the radicalization of the action pyramid. Each pyramid has four layers. At the apex of the radical opinion pyramid are those who believe radical action is a moral imperative. These individuals endorse statements like, "I believe jihad is a personal moral obligation." One layer below contains a larger proportion of the population who justify violent and illegal tactics in support of their cause or group, such as bombing of civilians in defense of Islam. Lower on the pyramid is an even more numerous proportion that sympathize with violent means of terrorists without justifying them. Finally, at the bottom of the opinion pyramid are the majority who are indifferent to the terrorists' cause.

Similarly, at the apex of the radical action pyramid are terrorists or violent extremists. One layer below are those who partake of radical but not terrorist action, including illegal break-ins or sit-ins or violent riots. Lower on the pyramid are those who participate in activism, legal and non-violent action in support of their cause or group. And at the bottom layer are the majority who do not participate in any politically motivated action.

The relationship between the two pyramids is tentative and in need of a systemic empirical exploration. To date, we know that terrorists are influenced by public opinions of their tactics, scaling violence up or down in response to changes in public support. For example, Palestinian suicide terrorism attacks against Israel slowed dramatically in the period after the Oslo Accords.[14] Hope of a peace agreement was associated with decreased support for terrorism, as reported in a polling of Palestinians. When the Palestinian Front for the Liberation of Palestine (PFLP) began to seem irrelevant in the second intifada, its standing in Palestinian polls dropped to near zero. As suicide attacks brought increased support for Hamas and Fatah, PFLP responded by deciding that it did after all support jihad, recruiting its own *shaheeds*. A few martyrdom operations restored PFLP's standing in the polls. It appears that terrorism varies with popular support for terrorism.[15]

We also know that a negative public view of specific countries and their leadership can predict terrorist attacks against those countries. One study[16] compared public opinion toward leadership of nine world powers (including the USA, UK, Russia, Japan, India, China, France, etc.) among residents of Middle Eastern and North African (MENA) countries. The results demonstrated that the more disapproval residents of a MENA country expressed against a world power, the more terrorist attacks against that world power originated from the MENA country. In other words, public opinion in country A about country B predicted rates of terrorism from country A toward country B.

However, our understanding of mass radicalization is still in its infancy. Especially as compared with individual and small group mechanisms, research on which is now abundant and methodology diverse and well-validated, mass radicalization remains *terra incognita*.

The Changing Face of Radicalization

As our understanding and policing of radical individuals and small groups has evolved, so has the nature of radicalization. Thus, since 9/11, 73% of all lethal ideological crimes in the United States have been carried out by right-wing militia groups[17] – not by jihadists who were the primary targets of policing and deradicalizing efforts of the U.S. security apparatus. At the same time, a similar rise in right-wing political violence was taking place in Europe,[18] perhaps most notoriously exemplified by Anders Breivik's shooting rampage. While we were learning about jihadist terrorists and getting better at identifying them and averting their attacks, the relative threat they posed grew smaller.

This was likely due to two reasons. First, the FBI and police have become exceedingly good at infiltrating jihadist circles, and at thwarting any planned attacks. Second, savvy political actors leveraged the threat of jihadist violence, utilizing public fear to maximize their political mandates. The result of this utilization of fear was a widespread increase in radical right-wing sentiments, in other words, mass radicalization against Muslims, immigrants, and minorities.

Evolution of biological traits is subject to the same pressures and the same outcomes as evolution of behaviors, including radical behaviors. The classic example of the British White Moth[19] helps to understand the parallel. The British White Moth's light coloring helped to camouflage it against the white bark of birch trees, protecting the moths from birds that fed on them. When the industrial revolution in Great Britain resulted in air pollution, British birch trees turned dark with soot and grime. The moths' white color that used to protect them turned into a vulnerability, making them stand out against the darkened birch trees, and marking them as easy prey. However, the moths didn't go extinct. There were enough individuals in their population with darker colored wings, which offered an unexpected survival advantage. As a result, over several years, as the lighter moths fell prey more frequently, and the darker moths were more likely to survive and reproduce, the British White Moth evolved enough to warrant a name change, becoming known as the British Black Moth. Then, in the 1900s, the British cleaned up the air. The birch trees became light again. The darker wings that used to save moths from birds' preying eyes were doing the opposite, and the evolutionary pressures have once again turned the moths' colors. They are now known as the Peppered Moth.

The case from biology exemplifies one of the central tenets of evolution: it prepares for the challenges of yesterday. This seems to also be true with radicalization research and security efforts. Over the past twenty years, we have gained great insights into the radicalization dynamics that no longer exist. The political and social landscape has changed, and, as a result, so has the nature of radicalization. Our understanding of the psychology of radicalization is insufficient, and the methods developed for policing and preventing terrorism are outdated.

In the past, jihadist terrorists typically had some direct ties to the Muslim world outside of the Western countries where they planned their attacks – by family connections, via personal travel or through their Internet contacts. This made it easier to identify and track them. But now right-wing and anarchist extremists operate within the fabric of the society, with little to help mark them as potentially dangerous.

Before, terrorists were forced deep into hiding, knowing they are social pariahs and outlaws. But now, right wing extremists enjoy support from prominent politicians. After a white supremacist rally "Unite the Right" in Charlottesville, N.C., turned deadly, with a white supremacist deliberately ramming his truck into a crowd of counter-protestors, killing one and injuring 35 others,[20] President Trump excused the incident, remarking, "there are very fine people on both sides."[21] This kind of open support from national leaders emboldens radical individuals and groups, giving them a sense of invincibility. And the problem is not isolated to the United States: Presently, 39 European countries have extreme right and nationalist parties represented in their parliaments.[22]

Not only the ideological roots of radicalization have shifted, but so has the medium through which it grows. The advent of the Internet and social media have completely reshaped communications, including those of extremists and radicalizing agents. Twenty years ago, in order to organize an attack, terrorists had to meet face-to-face and train or prepare attacks together in secret, as did the 9/11 terrorists or London Underground bombers. Radicalization of jihadist terrorists often took place in remote training camps, as it did for Tamerlan Tsarnaev. These activities, as well as financial transactions required for carrying out travel, lodging, and training, often revealed radical actors to security officials. But now, radicalizing rhetoric and emotion-stirring appeals to radical action can appear in the palm of one's hand, day or night. Communities of likeminded others can be found online with minimal effort, and with minimal exposure to police. As the storming of Capitol Hill in Washington, D.C., on January 6, 2021, demonstrated, mass radical action can be inspired, organized, and carried out by ill-intentioned individuals who have never met each other. This makes the task of tracing radicals' connections much more difficult for security practitioners.

While social media made radicalization more accessible and less detectable, mass migration and the COVID pandemic made it more likely.

The wars in Iraq, Afghanistan and Syria have pushed scores of Muslim refugees into Europe. In the United States, migrants were coming from South America, displaced by disastrous economic and political conditions in their native countries. The influx of brown-skinned strangers was often framed as a Realistic Group Conflict[23] by politicians and mass media, with immigrants portrayed as taking jobs while bringing crime and diseases into the established communities. This new reality opened the door to a new kind of radicalizing narrative, centered around the idea of "replacement" of White culture and values by minorities and immigrants. The perception of scarcity and competition is well-established in the social psychology research as causing an escalation of inter-group conflict, with all hallmarks of radicalization: dehumanization of the opponents, increased group cohesion, and increased support for authoritarian group leaders.[24]

The COVID pandemic added fear, uncertainty, and anxiety into this already tense social environment. While in lockdowns, people became increasingly lonely and isolated. With the

Internet as the only outlet for seeking answers about the many unknowns of the unprecedented times, the appeal of radical groups and narratives online grew manifold.

This increased traffic of radical messaging was not entirely spontaneous. Russia, China, and Iran have amplified and spread radical messages online, sowing discord among Americans and Europeans.[25] Similarly, radical right-wing groups took advantage of the COVID pandemic and the extraordinary exposure to online content that it effected, multiplying their efforts to spread radicalizing messaging.[26] Over the past two years, we have observed a geometric progression in radicalizing online content, and in the number of people who engage with it.

Identity Politics and Mass Radicalization

Perhaps the best-known spawn of mass radicalization online that was expedited by the COVID pandemic is QAnon. A baseless and debunked conspiracy theory, QAnon is a collection of far-fetched narratives: that the Earth is flat, that there are lizard-human hybrids living among us, that COVID is a hoax and the vaccines are vehicles for introducing tracking devices into human bodies, that a Satan-worshipping cabal of pedophiles and sadists have taken control over the world. QAnon followers often refer to their online content as "the rabbit hole" – echoing Alice in Wonderland's descent into an alternative reality. Mixing metaphors, they invite newcomers to "take the Red Pill" – evoking the Matrix, the Wachowski siblings' blockbuster movie where the main character was invited to take a red pill to see the true nature of the world. In QAnon's view, the world is ignorant of the horrific truths that are only available to those who would "do their own research" to uncover the conspiracy theory behind a world government, its design to enslave humanity, its perversion and pedophilia, etc.

QAnon followers number in tens of millions in the United States alone,[27] and it has sizable followings in over 70 countries around the world. Their radical beliefs have inspired a number of QAnon followers to radical action, including participation in the January 6 insurrection attempt in Washington, D.C. This is a new kind of a radical movement, and a new kind of threat.

Unlike a terrorist group, QAnon is a mass movement facilitated almost entirely online, with no leadership and no unified agenda or ideology. Some QAnon followers (in the United States) believe Hillary Clinton is the leader of the Global Cabal, while others (in Russia or Kazakhstan) think the leader is billionaire Rothschild; some believe COVID is a hoax, while others believe COVID is a potent biological weapon used to control the world economy.

In another distinction from terrorists, most QAnon followers have no intention to ever act on their beliefs. Out of about 30,000,000 U.S. adults who believe in QAnon, only about 60 were ever implicated in ideologically motivated crimes.[28] In fact, QAnon's greatest threat likely comes, not from guns or explosives, but from their ability to undermine fundamental institutions of democracy, impeding essential governance. In analyzing users' data, Facebook uncovered a correlation between exposure to QAnon content and COVID vaccine hesitancy.[29] QAnon radical rhetoric leads in a sizable proportion of the population to refusing the vaccines, which has real public health consequences, and real financial and existential costs to the society. Yet our existing tools for understanding, identifying and policing radicalization are largely useless against QAnon, a massive online movement with loose membership, no hierarchy and rare radical action.

Finally, in contrast to traditional terrorist groups, QAnon followers are overwhelmingly suffering from mental health problems.[30] Self-report and court records of QAnon followers in the United States revealed rates of diagnosed psychopathology among them of magnitudes greater than that found in average U.S. adults. A recent study on a large sample of Canadian adults found that psychological distress mediated the relationship between beliefs in conspiracy theories and radical intentions,[31] substantiating and clarifying the U.S. finding in QAnon followers. Mental health appears to play a much greater role in QAnon-based radicalization than it does in traditional, small face-to-face radical groups.

QAnon may be the most numerous, but it is not the only identity-based online radical movement that grew precipitously in the past few years. Another is "incels" – an acronym that stands for "involuntarily celibate." Incels are men who believe the society is prejudiced against them because of their inferior looks (a tendency they call "lookism"), such as short stature, weak chin, insufficient musculature, and/or penis size. Incels are especially aggrieved about feminism, which they see as having prejudiced women, making them arrogant and too selective about their mates. As a result, incels feel pre-destined to never find a sexual partner. Many also believe that the only way out of this predicament is to stage a rebellion through which they would redefine women's role in society, effectively enslaving them to assure their availability to every man, including incels. Attacks on women, particularly women of liberal, feminist attitudes, are also viewed as advancing incels' cause. This radical ideology behind inceldom is known as "Black Pill." In contrast to QAnon's "Red Pill," which is supposed to show the truth of the world's fundamental flaws, incels' Black Pill prescribes a course of deadly action to deal with the world's fundamental flaws. A number of incels have, in fact, attacked and killed women.[32]

Like QAnon, incels are a different kind of radical threat than more traditional terrorists. Like QAnon, the incel movement exists almost exclusively in online spaces, making it difficult to identify and track individuals who may present a security threat. Like QAnon, most incels are non-violent – despite their radical ideology. Finally, like QAnon followers, incels present an overwhelming rate of psychopathology, including autism-spectrum disorders, anxiety, depression and PTSD.[33]

To summarize, the new wave of radicalization seems to be spreading mainly online and through social media, is driven by identity politics, and is tapping into a mental health crisis that was greatly exacerbated by the COVID pandemic and the resulting lockdowns. This drastic change in the nature of radicalization (from individual and small groups to mass publics; from face-to-face to online; from political grievances to identity politics; and from few savvy operatives to many mentally unwell lay people) requires a similarly drastic change in our research and policing efforts. Below are three directions for counter-radicalization initiatives to address the current trends.

Counter-radicalization Initiatives

Develop a Systemic Study of Mass Radicalization

As mass radicalization is becoming an increasingly pressing problem, there is no parallel investment into research and theory of mass psychology. How do individuals come to feel as part of a large impersonal collective, so invested into a crowd of anonymous strangers that they are willing to spend money, time and risk their well-beings and even lives, as did those who stormed Capitol Hill in Washington, D.C., on January 6, 2021? What brain processes and structure maintain ideas about the mass collective? How do individuals derive an idea of mass opinion in the absence of instant polling, such as what "other X think about Y"? These are the kinds of questions we need to be researching to better understand mass psychology.

A variety of methods are now available to study mass psychology of radicalization. For example, we can analyze emotional and cognitive content of Tweets that originate from the same geographical area or that respond to the same political events. We can also observe mass psychology in the rates of public engagement with online content, including "likes" and "shares", helping to identify "viral" images, slogans or videos. Geo-location of personal phones can offer another insight into people's physical movements in response to political events, such as those of the crowd that travelled from a rally for Trump in Washington, D.C., to storm the Capitol Hill building. In short, the existing gap in our understanding of mass radicalization can be addressed with new and emerging methodologies.

Demand Social Media Transparency and Accountability

Even before the pandemic, social media had become an unregulated Wild West of social influence. The Cambridge Analytica Scandal[34] showcased how user data can be leveraged for micro-targeting vulnerable pockets of the population with strategically designed messages, resulting in measurable changes in behavior, from voter turnout to participation in civil unrest. At the same time as ill-intentioned players like Cambridge Analytica were able to capitalize on Facebook data collection efforts, these same data were off limits to researchers. Facebook, Twitter, YouTube and Instagram enjoy protections that are reserved for private companies, even though they have outgrown this role and became, effectively, public squares that that are unregulated, unmonitored, and not policed. During COVID lockdowns, for example, social media became the main modality of social interactions for most people.

There's now evidence of intrusions into the social media space by malicious foreign agents, such as Russia- and China-sponsored trolls and bots who promote content, including QAnon conspiracy theories, designed to foment radicalization and sow political discord.[35] In addition to foreign influences, ill-intended domestic actors have been shown to spread disinformation through social media. For example, after Donald Trump was de-platformed, the rate of engagement with disinformation-disseminating Tweets has declined by 73%,[36] showcasing the extent to which a single agent of disinformation can influence the online environment.

Pervasive and unregulated, social media is a convenient conduit for hybrid radicalization by foreign and domestic malicious actors. In order to curtail this mass radicalization that fuels identity-based social movements, we need to hold social media accountable for their increasingly central role in our day-to-day social functioning, demanding transparency that would allow us to identify radicalizing content as well as radicalizing influencers.

Prioritize Community Mental Health

In both QAnon and incel populations, mental health problems are rampant. Research into U.S. online-based right-wing radicalization found a similar correlation between extremist views and mental health problems.[37] It seems that either existing psychopathology drives individuals to radical online communities, or that participation in these communities, often associated with exposure to fear and anxiety-inducing radicalizing material, leads many to develop mental health problems. In either case, today's mass radicalization requires qualitatively new interventions that offer psychological support and/or treatment.

Given the number of people affected by mass radicalization, the cost and availability of individual psychotherapy would not be sustainable. Another limitation is the stigma often associated with mental health issues – even if we could provide traditional modalities of psychological treatments to everyone affected by both mass radicalization and mental health problems, many would reject them.

What are the alternatives?

One possibility is to leverage the reach of social media as well as their data collecting capacities, identifying disturbing content and limiting its spread, as well as curtailing social influence of especially influential spreaders of disinformation and radicalization. Social media can also be a vehicle for assessment of mental status, and even for targeting high-risk individuals with suggestions for diagnostics and treatment.

Another alternative would be something like a mentorship program, similar to the one used in the Aarhus deradicalization model,[38] with lay people providing companionship, support, and exposure to different psychological perspectives for vulnerable individuals. Mass radicalization through social media, greatly affected by loneliness and isolation, should be especially responsive to this kind of intervention.

One final idea is to broadly implement Mindfulness-Based Stress Reduction (MBSR).[39] MBRS is a group-based program that typically spans over 8 weekly meetings, each 3 hours long, during which participants learn about the physiology of stress, as well as practice meditation, mindful movement and moment-to-moment awareness. MBSR has been extensively validated, with cross-cultural success in long-term reduction of depression, anxiety, PTSD and other psychological problems.[40] Its group modality and short duration make MBSR much more cost-effective than individual therapy. Another advantage is that MBSR does not require self-disclosure, and thus avoids the stigma of traditional psychological or psychiatric treatments. Recent studies have demonstrated elements of MBSR, such as befriending meditation, successfully reducing political polarization.[41] Embedding MBSR courses at community centers, public libraries, schools, clinics, and colleges should go a long way toward both reducing mental health problems and mass radicalization.

In conclusion, this chapter has presented radicalization research milestones and state of the art research, highlighting the gaps between the field's knowledge and emerging threats. In recent years, broad availability of social media, social isolation, anxiety of the COVID pandemic, and malevolent political operatives' polarizing messaging have led up to mass-level radicalization. Identity-based political movements, such as QAnon and incel movements, require novel approaches to research, policing, and interventions. As social media introduced new ways to connect, it has also enabled new ways to radicalize. Researchers and security practitioners must act fast to adapt to this new reality of hybrid radicalization.

Notes

1 The author receives funding from Office of Naval Research (grant N000 14-21-275485). However, any opinions, findings, or recommendations expressed in this article are those of the author and do not reflect the views of the Office of Naval Research, the Department of the Navy or the Department of Defense.

2 Ray, N. (December 2002). Fear and Freedom: The Bush Administration and civil liberties. *Australasian Journal of American Studies*, *21*(2), 66–75.

3 Zajonc, R.B. (December 2001). "Mere exposure: A gateway to the subliminal". *Current Directions in Psychological Science*, 10(6), 224–228.

4 https://en.wikipedia.org/wiki/Boston_Marathon_bombing

5 Moskalenko, S., & McCauley, C. (2020). *Radicalization to Terrorism: What Everyone Needs to Know®*. Oxford University Press.

6 Horgan, J. (2008). From profiles to pathways and roots to routes: Perspectives from psychology on radicalization into terrorism. *The ANNALS of the American Academy of Political and Social Science*, *618*(1), 80–94.

7 Sageman, M. (2011). *Understanding Terror Networks*. University of Pennsylvania Press.

8 McCauley, C., & Moskalenko, S. (2008). Mechanisms of political radicalization: Pathways toward terrorism. *Terrorism and Political Violence*, *20*(3), 415–433.

9 Moskalenko, S., & McCauley, C. (2020). *Radicalization to Terrorism: What Everyone Needs to Know®*. Oxford University Press.

10 McCauley, C., & Moskalenko, S. (2011). *Friction: How Radicalization Happens to them and us*. Oxford University Press.

11 Fajmonová, V., Moskalenko, S., & McCauley, C. (2017). Tracking radical opinions in polls of US Muslims. *Perspectives on Terrorism, 11*(2), 36–48.

12 McCauley, C. R. (2018). Explaining homegrown Western jihadists: The importance of Western foreign policy, 2018. *International Journal of Conflict and Violence, 12*, 1–10.

13 McCauley, C., & Moskalenko, S. (2014). Toward a profile of lone wolf terrorists: What moves an individual from radical opinion to radical action. *Terrorism and Political Violence, 26*(1), 69–85.

14 Moskalenko, S., & McCauley, C. (2020). *Radicalization to Terrorism: What Everyone Needs to Know®*. Oxford University Press.

15 Maoz, I., & McCauley, C. (2009). Threat perceptions and feelings as predictors of Jewish-Israeli support for compromise with Palestinians. *Journal of peace research, 46*(4), 525–539.

16 Krueger, A. B., & Malečková, J. (2009). Attitudes and action: Public opinion and the occurrence of international terrorism. *Science, 325*(5947), 1534–1536.

17 Durbin, B., Booker, C., Coons, D., Harris, K., Klobuchar, M., Whitehouse, S., ... Reed. (2019). *116 S894 IS: Domestic terrorism prevention act of 2019 U.S. congress*. Retrieved from https://www.congress.gov/116/bills/s894/BILLS-116s894is.xml

18 https://www.opendemocracy.net/en/countering-radical-right/western-europe-right-wing-terrorism-rise/

19 https://en.wikipedia.org/wiki/Peppered_moth_evolution

20 https://en.wikipedia.org/wiki/Unite_the_Right_rally

21 https://abcnews.go.com/Politics/trump-defends-2017-fine-people-comments-calls-robert/story?id=62653478

22 https://cco.ndu.edu/PRISM/PRISM-Volume-6-no-2/Article/839011/right-wing-extremism-and-terrorism-in-europe-current-developments-and-issues-fo/

23 Sherif, M. (1988). *The robbers cave experiment: Intergroup conflict and cooperation.[Orig. pub. as Intergroup conflict and group relations]*. Wesleyan University Press.

24 Jackson, J. W. (1993). Realistic group conflict theory: A review and evaluation of the theoretical and empirical literature. *The Psychological Record, 43*(3), 395.

25 https://www.axios.com/coronavirus-misinformation-china-russia-iran-bdd7f45a-4212-497c-8c77-c00b4c7c2379.html

26 https://www.europol.europa.eu/newsroom/news/terrorists-attempted-to-take-advantage-of-pandemic-says-europol%E2%80%99s-new-eu-terrorism-situation-and-trend-report-2021

27 Bloom, M., & Moskalenko, S. (2021). *Pastels and Pedophiles: Inside the mind of QAnon*. Stanford University Press.

28 Moskalenko, S., & McCauley, C. (2021). QAnon. *Perspectives on Terrorism, 15*(2), 142–146.

29 https://thehill.com/policy/technology/543273-facebook-study-finds-overlap-between-vaccine-hesitancy-and-qanon

30 https://theconversation.com/many-qanon-followers-report-having-mental-health-diagnoses-157299

31 https://www.researchgate.net/publication/353454294_Conspiracy_Theories_Psychological_Distress_and_Sympathy_for_Violent_Radicalization_in_Young_Adults_during_the_COVID-19_Pandemic_A_Cross-Sectional_Study/references#fullTextFileContent

32 https://www.tandfonline.com/doi/abs/10.1080/1057610X.2020.1751459

33 Moskalenko, S. & Morton, J. (in prep) Miserable, Mistreated and Misunderstood: psychopathology and radicalization among in cels.

34 https://www.nytimes.com/2018/04/04/us/politics/cambridge-analytica-scandal-fallout.html

35 https://thehill.com/policy/technology/549077-study-china-russia-played-role-in-amplifying-qanon-conspiracy

36 https://www.washingtonpost.com/technology/2021/01/16/misinformation-trump-twitter/

37 https://www.tandfonline.com/doi/abs/10.1080/14789949.2020.1820067

38 Bertelsen, P. (2015). Danish preventive measures and de-radicalization strategies: The Aarhus model. *Panorama: Insights into Asian and European Affairs, 1*(241), 53.

39 Kabat-Zinn, J. (2003). Mindfulness-based interventions in context: past, present, and future.

40 Keng, S. L., Smoski, M. J., & Robins, C. J. (2011). Effects of mindfulness on psychological health: A review of empirical studies. *Clinical Psychology Review, 31*(6), 1041–1056.

41 https://journals.sagepub.com/doi/full/10.1177/13684302211020108

13

THE EMERGENCE OF DECOUPLED RADICALISATION AND FRANCHISE TERRORISM

McJihad

Olivier Roy

The debate about the roots of Islamic violence is usually focussed on one issue: the relation between religion (Islam of course) and violence. Hence the question at the centre of the debate: is jihadi violence rooted in Islam as a religion, or is it a larger and more recent phenomenon that frames itself in a religious narrative but has a more complex set of roots?

There is no question that the Islamic jihadists and terrorists, when they jump into action, believed that they are entering into the path of martyrdom and that they will thus achieve their personal salvation. Religion is shaping the way they decide to die. There is a great narrative of jihad and martyrdom that circulates on the Internet, where videos exhibit young and magnificent heroes who are theatrically staged through esthetical clichés taken from contemporary youth culture. In this sense, the jihadi narrative is one among other narratives readily available on the contemporary market of great narratives circulating on the Internet.

The key question is to know whether it is a religious process from the beginning, in a word, whether it is the radicalisation of religious practices and beliefs that push a category of believers (most often among disenfranchised second-generation immigrants) to choose martyrdom. Or is the process of radicalisation relatively autonomous from previous religious practices and learnings? To put it in other words, are the radicals attracted by religion first, and then, after a slow process of religious maturation through brainwashing and adhesion to a Salafi theology, come to the conclusion that true religion requests them not only to look for martyrdom but also to kill as many unbelievers or heretics as possible? Or is their fascination for death the main reason for why they are attracted not by a specific theological school of thought but by a great narrative centred around martyrdom and jihad?

It is not a useless and rhetorical issue, because what is at stake here is setting up a policy of countering radicalisation and terrorism. Beyond the usual intelligence gathering practices (spotting suspicious activities, infiltrating networks, tracing the circulation of weapons, etc.), the broader issue is to understand the milieu and the conditions of radicalisation. The issue of the debate is not so much to "save" Islam from Islamophobia, nor to avoid amalgaming Islam with violence, or Muslims with potential terrorists. The issue is efficiency: how to put an end to a specific cycle of violence that has begun in the mid-1990s.

There are consequently two opposed approaches: the first is vertical and genealogical, looking for the roots of Islamic radicalisation first in the Quran, then in the traditional theological schools

DOI: 10.4324/9781003326373-15

that would have developed in the course of history a "radical" view of religion, which flourishes now among contemporary preachers. The second is transversal: what is the relationship between jihadi violence and other forms of violence among the youth. What is the modernity of jihadism?

If the first vision is true, it means that to fight jihad one must check the mosques, the religious books, the sermons and theological debates among Muslims; one should check and censor "radical" religious theology while pushing for "liberal" forms of religiosity and theology. Counter terrorism starts from the mosques and the textbooks. Religious radicalisation (the adoption of fundamentalist and Salafi views of Islam) is the starting point of many forms of radicalisation. To detect would-be terrorists, one should first spot any sign of "extreme" forms of religious practices. That is for instance the policy implemented by the French government, requesting school authorities to spot and report "early signs of religious radicalisation "among pupils and students (prayers, sudden refusal to drink alcohol or shake a women's hand, etc.).

If it is the second view that prevails, the big problem is to spot early signs of fascination for death, suicidal attitudes, calls for jihad, gore videos. Spotting religious signs is at best a waste of time and manpower, at worst, it re-enforces the fascination for the "Islamisation" of radicalism among would-be desperados, who know that they could give far more impact to their suicidal attack if they claim to act for Islam. A quite significative issue illustrates the case.

Every time an unidentified attacker assaults people in the streets with a knife, the first question is "Did he or she shout 'Allah Akbar'?". If yes, it is a radical Muslim following the ideology of jihad, if not it is just a crazy individual who does not deserve to make the headlines in the newspapers and on TV screens. In this sense, what makes terrorism is not the action, but the meaning of the action. And the problem is that we analyse this meaning not by studying the person involved in the attack but by applying pre-determined categories: religiously motivated action that has a geo-strategic dimension (Islam versus the West) or individual crazy outburst with neither merit nor meaning, even if the number of dead and wounded is the same.

From Local to Global Jihad

Let's start with definitions of current terms used to qualify "radicals": a terrorist, a jihadist, somebody doing "hijra", a Salafi. Not all jihadists are terrorists: it depends on whether they join a territorial or a global jihad. In Afghanistan during the eighties, the West supported the "mujahidin" who were fighting the Soviet occupation. Most of them were in favour of implementing the Sharia and of establishing an Islamic state in Afghanistan, but none of them indulged in terrorist activities whether inside or outside Afghanistan (no Soviet civilians have been targeted by Afghan mujahideen).

Nevertheless, a group of foreign fighters (mostly Arabs under the leadership of Abdallah Azzam and Usama Bin Laden) who came to support the Afghan Jihad developed the concept of "global jihadists", which means training volunteers who could travel after the war in Afghanistan to different countries where Muslims were supposedly under threat. In this sense, there is a clear distinction between a "mujahid", who fights a local jihad in his own country, and a "jihadist" who joins the global jihad and travels from one jihad to the other. The distinction between the two terms is made as well in the different European languages (we speak of former Afghan "mujahidin", but of present ISIS-"jihadists") as in Arabic, where the neologism "jihâdi" applies to global jihadists as opposed to "mujahid" referring to those who participate in "classical" jihad, as for instance Algerian fighters did against the French army in the 1950s.

Two other terms are also used to qualify religious radicalism: "hijrah" and "Salafis". "Hijrah" means emigration for the sake of religion: a good practicing Muslim is supposed to make hijrah to a Muslim country if he or she cannot practice in the country where he or she lives as a minority.

The first hijrah was made by the Prophet himself when he left Mecca for Medina. At the end of the 19th century hundreds of thousands of Muslims left the Balkans and the Caucasus to settle in what remained of the Ottoman Empire. Nowadays, thousands of French citizens leave France for various countries that are supposedly more respectful of an Islamic religious way of life. European countries tend to merge "muhajirin" (people making "hijrah") and jihadists, particularly when they go to Syria. The two categories might overlap but are quite distinct, as shown by the favourite destination for a "hijrah": Dubai, where they hope to reconciliate devotion with business (in the 1990s many went to Egypt and Yemen but were constrained to leave either due to police pressure or civil war). Finally, a Salafi is, in the broad sense of the term, a Muslim that abides by a scripturalist and normative conception of religious life: Salafis strive to frame everyday life in an all-encompassing devotional system. This is certainly a "radical" vision of religion, comparable to the vision of a catholic monk or life in some Jewish ultra-orthodox communities. The two radicalisms nevertheless – religious and political – are never connected by a consequential link. Most violent radicals do not have a Salafi background and few Salafis join global jihad, in percentage of the supposed Salafi population.[1]

Let's go back to the concept of global jihad, which is undoubtedly the common point and main motto of the Islamic radicals (far more than the call to implement Sharia). It started during the war in Afghanistan (1979–1989). The promoter was Abdallah Azzam (a Palestinian Muslim Brother, who was replaced after his assassination in 1989 by Usama Bin Laden): he saw the Afghan war against the Soviets as the perfect battle field for foreign volunteers, not only to fight for the just cause but also as an opportunity to fabricate and train a sort of vanguard of international jihadists bound by an "esprit de corps" and cut off from their former familial, tribal, ethnic or national identities. Once again, during the leadership of Azzam, there was no story of perpetrating terrorist actions against the West.

The shift from "global jihad" to terrorism happened when Usama Bin Laden, back from Afghanistan into Saudi Arabia, proposed in 1990 to the Saudi King to send these volunteers to fight the Iraqi invasion of Kuwait, instead of calling the US troops for aid. Bin Laden's proposal was scornfully rebuked, and he subsequently broke with the Saudi Kingdom. That was the start of al-Qaeda as an international terrorist organisation in the name of global jihad; from that time different attacks occurred against the Americans, although the first attack against the World Trade Center in 1993 was not directed by Bin Laden: nevertheless, the surviving perpetrators joined al-Qaeda later.

The Western Roots of Radicalisation

In the mid 1990's members of al-Qaeda were Middle Easterners born and trained in the Middle East. But from 1995 onwards a new generation appeared: the Western "home grown" terrorists joining global jihad. The first was Khaled Kelkal, a French second generation Muslim from Lyon (1995). They perpetrated terrorist actions in the West while looking to join any kind of local jihad: Afghanistan, Bosnia, Chechnya, Iraq, Syria … At the beginning they went on their own, but from 1997 onwards they swore loyalty to a global jihad organisation, first al-Qaeda and then ISIS.

Interestingly, when Western authorities refer to "radicalisation", they almost exclusively target this category of "home grown" terrorists. It seems that there was something incomprehensible in these Western-educated young people who join a jihad in a country they have no connection with. Why would a second-generation French Algerian prefer in the 90s to go to Bosnia and Afghanistan to wage jihad, but not to the land of his parents, Algeria, where a real war was unravelling at that time? Why did so many young European men and women convert to Islam in order to join global jihad? Moreover, why did almost all Islamic terrorists choose to die in action?

After conducting research from 1995 to 2016 on the French radicals who perpetrated terrorist actions or went abroad for jihad,[2] I found a set of common patterns. Most of them (about 2/3) are second generation Muslims with their parents having come to France as migrants. They were then joined by converts (about 1/4) who are more numerous among jihadists than among terrorists.

Interestingly, over the course of 20 years we have the same percentage of second generations and almost no third generation, although the latter is now "on the market". This generational dimension is far more important than any kind of socio-economic background. Few of them had a real religious background, and around half of them went to jail for petty delinquency. If racism could be a factor, why are there so many converts among radicals? There is another interesting pattern: death. Most of them died either by using explosive belts or by waiting for the police to kill them. Why are suicide attacks the modus operandi of terrorist actions? This was not the case for the extreme-left terrorism of the 1970s or for the Palestinian attacks of the 1980s for instance. Moreover, suicide attacks are not necessarily very rational from a purely military approach. In the short term they create an effect of terror among the civil population: how to fight people who don't care about their own life and are very proud of it. The sentence "we love death as much as you love life" attributed to Bin Laden was mentioned by different terrorists (Merah in 2012, Leila B., arrested in Béziers on Easter weekend in 2021).

But in the longer term it deprived the organisation of its best-trained and professional fighters. In the series of attacks in Paris and Brussels in November 2015, 12 well-trained terrorists killed themselves. They had been preparing the attack for months and benefited from a good logistical network. All that was lost for ISIS. After that attack (and well before the fall of ISIS in Syria) all the terrorist attacks in Europe were made by isolated individuals, with makeshift weapons and no logistical support. The best militants died without even trying to flee to launch further attacks in the future. Whatever the strategy designed by the organisation, the militants view their action not in terms of a long-term war to establish an Islamic emirate, but as a way to stage their death in a little apocalypse. No future for them.

Strangely enough, I am one of the few experts that consider this fascination for death as central for the motivation of the suicide bombers. There is definitely something mystical and religious about that, but it has not been studied as such. Nevertheless, there is a feeling among experts that religion is central in the conduct of the terrorists although this centrality has been displaced from a mystical nihilist vision to theology, in the sense that theology is closer to ideology (a discursive Weltanschauung) and is thus more understandable for social scientists and intelligence officers. What is missing here is precisely what is "purely religious" in the vision of the suicide attackers. Interestingly enough, during the period of extreme-left terrorism in Europe, there has never been an approach to understand the process of radicalisation and to devise adapted techniques of "de-radicalisation". My guess is that the extreme-left terrorists were in fact familiar or at least came from a familiar history of class-struggle, revolution and anarchism. They were consequently treated as political activists, certainly dangerous but "readable". Conversely, there is something exotic, strange and unfamiliar with the Islamist radicals: they were perceived as "fanatics" and Islam, considered a backward religion, was easily seen as the root of their anachronistic kind of violence. But by isolating Islamic violence from other forms of violence among young Europeans, we miss both what is religious and profoundly modern in these radical Islamists.

The Bias in Methodology: The Obsession with Religious Radicalisation

There is obviously something about the European obsession with studying radicalisation and creating de-radicalisation projects that goes beyond the number of casualties inflicted by Islamist radicals. What is at stake is clearly Islam; the underlying real question is to know to which extent these radicals may either represent the vanguard of a migrant Muslim population that could have radicalised itself or are outcasts in the larger context of the European Muslim population. Terrorism seems to appear as the trial for the integration of Muslims in Europe, and that explains why the approach is so different from the precedent forms of terrorism that stuck Europe in the 1970s.

To sum up: is Islam at the core of radicalisation or is it the big narrative chosen by rebels in search of a cause? At stake is clearly the integration of Islam as a religion within Europe. And it is not enough to have gentle Muslim theologians claiming that Islam is a religion of peace. The problem is to understand why young radicals deliberately choose to see it as a call to violence. These guys will not be convinced by a better teaching of religion, but will dismiss the moderate imam as an ignorant or as traitor.

Probably hundreds of millions of euros have been devoted by different European institutions, governments, think tanks and universities to fund projects to study the process of radicalisation (I am myself also involved in some of them). The competition is strong: each expert or each team of experts wants to show that they provided the best results and have solved the conundrum of radicalisation. Interestingly enough, many consider that to win the competition, one has first to debunk the colleagues instead of capitalizing on previous research. But we all share at least some common methodological tools (as well as bias), at least when starting the project. The first thing is to come up with a sample of terrorists, or more exactly would-be terrorists, and then to create some statistics. The problem is that an accepted list of terrorists does not exist. Roughly speaking, the respective expert will first try either to constitute his or her personal pool or to use already existing lists of real or potential radicals from different authorities (counter terrorist agencies, police, ministry of justice, penitential authorities). In a second step, he or she will sort out their motivations through a close study of their biographies and declarations in order to find the "roots of radicalisation". This approach is supplemented by opinion polls, studies of police or justice files, questionnaires given to school children or students.

Nevertheless, it is very difficult to draw an objective list of "radicals" because since setting up such a list presupposes that we have an implicit definition of what a radical is. It is not enough to say that it should be a Muslim using violence. What about a Muslim who kills somebody in the street because he suffers from schizophrenia and delusion? And more importantly, what about a Muslim who never acted, but was arrested under the suspicion that he or she could have acted? On what is the suspicion based?

Let's take two examples from radicalisation studies. Both are written by competent professionals, a journalist and two sociologists, and are based on serious in-depth research. One of them is David Thomson's "Les Revenants" (the Returned) which includes 13 interviews with former jihadists. The other one is Olivier Galland and Anne Muxel's La tentation radicale, enquête auprès des lycéens.[3] Both studies claim to provide the key for understanding radicalisation.

The first book raises the problem of the sample of an odd group of people who deliberately had refused to commit suicide attacks and have since then abandoned jihad and have even been de-radicalised or at least disengaged from it. Even if they still support jihad, this only relates to a "good" jihad according to accepted rules. They therefore missed the "jump" into death as they did not act on their initial intentions. They help us understand why some people are fascinated by jihad, but not why some will become suicide bombers. The distinction between jihadists and terrorists is important but currently missing in the wider debate.

The second book is more controversial. The field work had been done with the support of the French Ministry of Education, and the questionnaire was presented by the teachers in schools during class. The aim was to spot early signs of radicalisation among schoolchildren. These signs were defined as "any deviance from the secular norms", as stated by the authors. They deliberately chose schools with a high percentage of Muslims, because they claim that Muslims are more prone to radicalisation. Thus, the answer had been provided before the question was asked. The consequence is dual:

1 Islam seems to be far more of an incentive for violence than Christianism or Judaism. Although this might be possible, it should have been deduced from a comparison with comparable samples of students belonging to the three religions.
2 Any sign of regular practice in a public space is identified as a potential first step towards violent action. However, there is no analysis showing that terrorists practice their religion more openly than others? There is no regular connection between real perpetrators and religious practices, indicating that "the more violence, the more devotion" is not a verified method of deduction.

Undoubtedly, the enquiry among school children shows that there seems to be a will among a significative proportion of nominal Muslims to practice their religion and to display it in school. Some remarks by the school children are interpreted as a rejection of the French way of life. For instance, when they state that "the law of God is above man's law" or that "a Muslim should follow Sharia", this is immediately interpreted as a sign of political radicalisation. However, while defending "non-negotiable principles" (rejection of abortion and same-sex marriage), Pope Benedict XVI also made clear that God's Law is above man's law. After Maréchal Pétain had signed a set of anti-Semitic laws in 1942, the head of the Protestant Federation of France wrote to Pétain that the church cannot do otherwise but object to these laws.[4]

By the same token, many Jews would say that a good Jew should follow the halakha, for which they will not be seen as being on the path of violence. Hence the premise of the enquiry seems to be that Sharia has not the same meaning as Halakha and that the Christian God is more benevolent than the Muslim one. Although this might be right or wrong, it is a theological prejudice that should have no place in a sociological inquiry, unless previously demonstrated.

If it were the case (that Sharia is leading to political violence), how should one explain why there are so few jihadists and terrorists compared to the number of second-generation Muslim migrants? If the milieu of Muslim schoolchildren seems so prone to religious radicalism, why do most of the terrorists after 2016 not belong to the category of second-generation Muslims? They are a heterogeneous group: Chechens, Pakistanis, Egyptians, Sudanese, converts, newcomers (mainly from Tunisia), older people and others. They are not troubled young people from a "Salafised" and destitute neighbourhood, but lone wolves with an undeniable psychiatric dimension coming from various milieus and are always associated with a makeshift lethal weapon (knife) and a suicidal attitude. In a word, there is a huge gap between the actual terrorists and the potential pool of radicalisation.

A Different Methodological Approach: Youth Culture Versus Salafism

There are only a few studies about real terrorists, who killed and were killed, because most of them died in action. My thesis here is that the bottom-up analysis (let's spot signs of radicalisation possibly leading to the jump into action) should give way to a top-down approach: what is particular with the guys who jump into action that could fascinate and motivate the candidates for terror action?

The first thing is fascination for death, as I mentioned above. There is absolutely no rationale for a terrorist organisation with a long-term strategy to systematically lose its best-trained fighters. Moreover, the decision to die is not imposed by their hierarchical superiors on the fighters (as it was for instance for the Japanese kamikazes of WWII). It was a free choice made by the terrorists. Prior to their attack, they were never involved in political or religious activities outside their objective of perpetrating a suicide attack. We have no examples of future terrorists preaching in mosques or canvassing from door to door to bring nominal Muslims back to the real faith. None of them was active in Islamic charities, communities or institutions. When joining ISIS in Iraq, they never use their skills to contribute to building a true Islamic society. They are often married and have children, although they never raise or educate them. In a word, they are without any future perspective, which is why I dubbed them "nihilist".

This fascination for death is rather modern: they belong to the generation of the juvenile mass-killers who rampaged in their schools. Such school mass killings started at around the same period as the suicide terrorist attacks in Europe (the school shooting of Columbine was done in 1999, four years after the attack by Kelkal in Lyon). From 1999 onwards, they both follow and use the development of the Internet, for instance, to announce and film the shootings. Many school killers referred to Satanism, a cult of death that is close to the image of the "martyr" (as Bin Laden supposedly said: "We love death as you love life"). In this sense, Western Islamist terrorists are part of a generational phenomenon that cuts across different ethnic and religious affiliations.

In France, there is a startling parallel between two cities: Marseille is a big city where entire neighbourhoods in the North of the town are populated by former migrants and their successive generations. They are poor and destitute. But they have almost never produced a terrorist. In the meantime, the small town of Lunel, west of Marseille, sent about 20 jihadists to Syria, with a population that is only 4% of that of Marseille. If we look only through religious lenses, it does not make sense. But if we take into consideration that Marseille is in France the deadliest place for killings between young second-generation Muslims involved in drug trafficking, it makes some sense: this new generation of drug traffickers, which has replaced older local mafias (often of Corsican or Italian origin) does not respect the traditional ways of settling feuds through negotiations and carefully planned assassinations. They easily kill not only rivals but even youngsters used as lookouts by other dealers: they kill and are killed. One of the most popular movies in the French suburbs was Scarface from Brian da Palma. This kind of "glorious bastard" is presented as a hero whose destiny is to die young. Death and Kalashnikov as a daily horizon: no need to go to Syria (and they make more money in Marseille).

Apart from the fascination for death, a central point for the young would-be suicide attackers (Columbine as well as Bataclan) is to frame their action in a big narrative while staging this narrative through videos they publish on the Internet. They stage their own action.

The strength of ISIS was communication: they had teams of experts, including many converts, who shot clips presenting the jihadists as modern heroes. Such videos were aesthetically far more elaborated than those by al-Qaeda: all present young Westerners, who joined the jihad and were thus physically and morally transformed, driving an SUV at full speed while brandishing their Kalashnikovs. They even played with the sexual attraction of jihad, implying that everyone joining will have immediate access to wives and sexual slaves. There is an aesthetic of violence comparable to many American movies: blood spilling, beheadings, massacres (see the Sam Peckinpah movie "The wild Bunch"). This aesthetic of violence is unknown to any Muslim religious tradition: it is sadistic, while the spiling of blood is traditionally associated with martyrdom and mortification (as the Shias practice during the processions of Ashura).

Fascination for death, aesthetics of violence, the feeling to have no place and no future in the present societies (including Muslims), the quest for adventures and sex: they are the common features of a "no future generation".

Local Jihads and McJihads

Presently, there is an interesting puzzle concerning France. France has probably seen the highest number of terrorist attacks in Europe during the last ten years. Overall, the profile of the terrorists is quite stable since 1995. But as argued for above, in 2016 we witnessed a shift.

The recent terrorists do not seem to share this youth culture, although they are still systematically suicidal. It is puzzling that this decrease in qualitative and quantitative terrorism happens at a time when France is engaged more than ever in a military counter-terrorist action in Mali. Even more important, France is the leading military force and is not acting just as an auxiliary for the Americans as in Afghanistan and Syria. This should have made France the prime target for jihadists and terrorists. Nevertheless, to my knowledge no terrorist before and after 2016 has ever mentioned the role of France in Africa, while still mentioning Syria and Charlie Hebdo.

There are two ways to explain that. The first is purely sociological: the second generation is greying, and the third generation is more acculturated. As I explained in my book,[5] the second generation is not rooted in the traditional religious culture of their parents, but plainly involved in the modern youth culture. They are unable to formulate Muslim faith and practices in the mainstream French culture and rely on a subversive youth culture. But often the children of a "radical generation" (as for instance the generation after Baader-Meinhof or the Red Brigades) are less rebellious than their parents, while being far more acculturated, more prone to accept what I called the "formatting" of religion into a new cultural landscape.[6] People who jump into action now have other reasons to be "deculturated" (primo-immigrants, mental illness, recent converts, etc.).

This explanation should certainly be taken into account. Nevertheless, it does not explain why the different jihadis in the Sahel region have so little impact on young French Muslims or converts, although there is a significative African diaspora in France. What is the difference between the jihadis of the Sahel region and al-Qaeda and ISIS?

It is not religion: the jihadists in the Sahel are also promoting the implementation of Sharia, the killing of apostates and infidels. The big difference is that they remain purely local and regional jihads. They do not construct a complex narrative of death, heroism and sexual power for young foreigners. They don't produce videos, life stories, songs, and the gore aesthetic that fascinate youngsters brought up in the West so much. They are not framed in a global aesthetics of youth culture. They don't address the global world. They are not McJihad enough.

Jihad fascinates young radicals only if it is constructed as a narrative through aesthetics connected to a global youth culture.

Notes

1 There is no data available because we have no idea about the total number of Salafis: first there is no agreement on the definition, second being a Salafi might concern only a period in the life of an individual. But in any case, the total number of jihadists joining ISIS was about 20 000 to 30 000 fighters coming from all over the world, while from Morocco to Indonesia people pretending to follow the "way of the *Salaf*" are in the millions and even tens of millions.

2 Olivier Roy (2017), *Jihad and Death*, Hurst/Oxford University Press.

3 David Thomson (2018), *The Returned*, Polity, Olivier Galland and Anne Muxel *La tentation radicale, enquête auprès des lycéens.* 2018 PUF.

4 "« Les Eglises chrétiennes, quelles que soient les diversités de leur confession, seraient infidèles à leur vocation première si elles n'élevaient, devant l'abandon de leurs principes, leurs douloureuses protestations. » https://www.reforme.net/religion/histoire/2020/08/20/20-aout-1942-le-pasteur-marc-boegner-proteste-contre-la-politique-du-marechal-petain/.

5 Oliver Roy (2017), *Jihad and Death: The Global Appeal of Islamic State*, Oxford University Press.

6 Olivier Roy (2010), *Holy Ignorance,* Hurst/Oxford University Press.

14

THE CRIME-TERROR NEXUS IN EUROPE AND ITS IMPLICATION FOR JIHADIST RADICALISATION

Peter R. Neumann

Our interest in terrorists with criminal backgrounds started in 2015, when it became obvious that a significant percentage of the approximately 5,000 young Muslims from Western Europe who had left their home countries in order to join Islamic State in Syria (so-called "foreign fighters") had previously been involved in (non-terrorist) crime. Although impossible to quantify, it seemed like their number and prominence had increased when compared to earlier jihadist mobilisations. This was echoed in the more brutal, gangster-like way in which Islamic State presented itself. Alain Grignard, a commissioner in the Belgian Federal Police, described the group as "a kind of super-gang".[1]

The research we have subsequently conducted has focused on the ways in which prior involvement in crime affects radicalisation and terrorist behaviour. Drawing on a sample of 130 Western European jihadists, who became affiliated with jihadist groups between 2012 and 2018, our aim was not merely to describe a sub-segment of European jihadists, but to use the preponderance of criminal backgrounds among them in order to extract wider lessons about "ordinary" criminals who turn to terrorism. How do radicalisation processes differ? Where are they recruited? Do they have specific "skills" and experiences that are useful in terrorism?

Our research shows that criminal backgrounds can have a profound impact on radicalisation and terrorist behaviour. Though not exclusive to former criminals, we found evidence that "redemption" is an especially powerful narrative among former criminals, and that prisons offer conditions that are conducive to their radicalisation. We also demonstrate that former criminals have contributed to terrorism through their ability to access weapons, stay "under the radar", and raise money through petty crime. One of the most significant findings is that (violent) criminals take less time to radicalise into terrorism than non-violent criminals.

The Data

The dataset we started creating in 2015 contains entries for Western European jihadists, who became involved in terrorism during the 2012–2018 period, and for whom there is evidence that they had previously engaged in (non-terrorist) criminality. To determine criminality, we relied on official statements by the police or prosecuting authorities, indicating that a person had committed criminal offences before their radicalisation. To qualify as someone involved in (jihadist)

DOI: 10.4324/9781003326373-16

terrorism, individuals had to have joined groups such as al-Qaeda and Islamic State as so-called "foreign fighters" (evidenced, for example, by their own statements, official indictments, or credible reports), or been charged and convicted of terrorism-related offences in Europe.

For each entry, we sought information in 142 categories, from basic demographic data (for example, age, nationality, place of residence, marital status, education, profession, death) to their criminal histories (for instance, date/time of crime, type of crime, number of offences known, motive, prison stays), radicalisation and recruitment (date of initial involvement, circumstances of introduction, recruiter, place and context, activities, etc.), and involvement in terrorism (group, length of involvement, roles played, state response, etc.). The information we relied on was gleaned from official documents, such as police reports and court judgments, the foreign fighter database at the International Centre for the Study of Radicalisation (ICSR), King's College London,[2] as well as media reports.

Based on these criteria, we identified 130 individuals for whom we found sufficient information to paint a detailed picture of their criminal activities, radicalisation, and terrorist involvement. All of them were male, with an average age of 24 at the time of their mobilisation into terrorism. They came from across Western Europe: Belgium (18), Denmark (11), France (35), Germany (17), Italy (11), Netherlands (13), Sweden (1), and the United Kingdom (24). Sixty per cent (78) were "foreign fighters" who had travelled to Syria, while forty per cent (52) had participated in planning, plotting, or promoting terrorist attacks in Europe.

In 2016, we also started creating a control group of jihadists with *no* criminal backgrounds. In addition to 48 jihadists, who we could be certain had no criminal backgrounds, we compared our findings to official statistical data from Western European countries, such as Germany and the Netherlands,[3] which had published comprehensive data on the nature and backgrounds of their jihadist populations during the 2012–18 period.

Radicalisation and Recruitment

One of the most important questions in relation to the crime-terror nexus is how criminal pasts contribute to processes of radicalisation, that is, the personal circumstances, experiences, narratives, networks and other factors that explain an individual's involvement in extremism and their mobilisation into violence.[4] The cases in our database offer some tentative answers. They suggest that the jihadist narrative – as articulated by the Islamic State – is surprisingly well-aligned with the personal needs and desires of criminals, and that it can be used to condone as well as curtail continued involvement in crime. Among the individuals in our database are cases in which becoming a jihadist justified and legitimised continued criminal activity, but also the opposite, that is, for radicalisation to serve as a means of "redeeming" past "sins". The most likely – and plausible – explanation for the high number of "gangster" jihadists remains the merging of criminal and jihadist milieus: both criminals and jihadists are recruited from the same demographics – and often in the same places.

Redemption

For up to 20 of the individuals in our database, we found evidence for what we labelled the "redemption narrative". These were criminals who had experienced what Quintan Wiktorowicz termed a "cognitive opening", a shocking event or personal crisis that prompted them to re-assess their entire life and become open for a radical change of values and behaviour.[5] In our case, they realised how their criminal behaviour had been harmful, that they needed to break with their past and make up for their "sins". This then provided the rationale for their turn to religion and justified the involvement with jihadist groups.

That they sought redemption in jihadism instead of other, more mainstream forms of religion or spirituality may be explained with the strong alignment of needs and narratives. In other words: involvement in jihadism offered redemption from crime while satisfying the personal needs and desires that led them to become involved in it. Just like the criminal gangs of which many of them used to be members of, jihadist groups offered power, violence, adventure and adrenaline, a strong identity, and – not least – a sense of rebellion and being anti-establishment. For criminals with a guilty conscience, the jihadism of the Islamic State could seem like a perfect fit.

Among the most prominent examples is Abderrozak Benarabe, locally known as "Big A", a long-time criminal from Copenhagen who decided to turn to jihadism after his brother had been diagnosed with cancer. Benarabe's radicalisation was prompted by a cognitive opening after his brother's diagnosis with cancer. When explaining why he had decided to become a foreign fighter, he referred to his criminal past:

> I really don't know what's gonna happen. Maybe I'm gonna die there... so what? Because, you know, some people have died of my hands. This is a big problem when I meet Allah ... I've gotta try and make a difference. I think about Judgement Day ... But at least I can say I went down there and did what I could... It's not good enough just praying with all the shit I've done.[6]

Others used very similar justifications. Ali Almanasfi, for example, a British-Syrian from West London, turned to jihadism after participating in the violent assault of an old man for which he received a long prison sentence. When telling a friend about his trip to Syria and his recruitment as a foreign fighter, he said: "I want to do something good for once. I want to do something pure".[7]

Legitimising Crime

While the jihadist narrative can be a source of redemption, several of our cases suggest that it may also serve as a *legitimiser* of crime. This is not entirely new. Anwar al-Awlaki, the radical cleric who helped to create al-Qaeda's online magazine *Inspire* and incited young Western Muslims to become jihadist "lone wolves" during the late 2000s, repeatedly told his followers that "stealing from your enemies" is not only permitted but, in certain cases, obligatory.[8] Islamic State draws on the same logic,[9] except that the current wave of jihadist mobilisation has produced more supporters that are capable of turning al-Awlaki's prescription into reality. Our database contains over a dozen cases in which this type of justification has played a role.

The best known example is the network around Khalid Zerkani. Born in Morocco in 1973, he moved to Belgium as an adult and made money as a small-time criminal. After becoming radicalised, he used his criminal "skills" (and considerable charisma) to recruit young men, mostly with Moroccan backgrounds, as jihadist foreign fighters. In particular, he encouraged them to commit thefts and robberies,[10] which he justified on religious grounds. As a witness in his trial testified, Zerkani told his recruits that "to steal from the infidels is permitted by Allah".[11] The proceeds were then redistributed amongst the group and used to fund their travel to Syria, leading to Zerkani's nickname of *Papa Noël* (Father Christmas).[12]

Prior to his 2014 arrest, Zerkani had become a hugely influential figure within the jihadist scene in Brussels, and was responsible for the recruitment and mobilisation of up to 72 foreign fighters.[13] More than any other example, the structures that he created illustrate the near-perfect merging of criminal and terrorist milieus that took place in Belgium and help explain why this small country has produced nearly 500 jihadist foreign fighters in just four years.

Prisons

That prisons are uniquely significant places for people with criminal pasts seems obvious. Over 50 per cent of our cases (69) had been incarcerated prior to their mobilisation, with sentences ranging from 1 month to over 10 years, for various offences from petty to violent crime. More significantly, at least 26 per cent of those who spent time in prison radicalised there, although – in the majority of cases – the process continued and intensified after their release. Given the recent surge in terrorism-related arrests and convictions, and the rapidly expanding number of convicted terrorists in custody, prisons are likely to become more – rather than less – significant as centres of gravity for the jihadist movement.

The cases in our database highlight two mechanisms. First, they are places of vulnerability in which extremists can find plenty of "angry young men" with criminal pasts who may experience cognitive openings and are "ripe" for extremist radicalisation and recruitment. And second, they bring together criminals and terrorists, and therefore create opportunities for collaboration and "skills transfers".

Vulnerability

For many new inmates, the very fact of imprisonment is a personal crisis, which raises profound questions about their lives while providing ample time to search for meaning. They are cut off from their immediate family, friends, and wider society, while finding themselves in an environment which is often hostile, unfamiliar, and tribal in nature, with divisions along religious or ethnic lines. Simply put, prisons are places in which new inmates are mentally and physically vulnerable, and may be more likely than elsewhere to experience "cognitive openings" – the willingness and desire to identify with new ideas, beliefs, and social groups.[14]

For the same reason, jihadist recruiters view prisons as places of opportunity. Not only are inmates vulnerable and experience cognitive openings, making them receptive to jihadist ideas, they also tend to be part of the demographic that jihadist groups are keen to attract: young men, often from Muslim backgrounds, who are unfamiliar with their own religion yet impulsive, confident, willing to take risks, and have been in conflict with the state and established authorities.[15] Far from being an obstacle, their criminal pasts have de-sensitised them to law-breaking and violence, and may in fact have provided them with skills that can be used in terrorism. In short, from the jihadists' perspective, prisons are the perfect "breeding ground".

A prominent example is Harry Sarfo from the northern German city of Bremen, who joined Islamic State in the spring of 2015.[16] His journey towards extremism began in prison, where he began serving a two year sentence for aggravated theft in 2011. It was during this time that he met René Marc Sepac, a well-known German jihadist who had been sentenced for terrorism-related offences. Sepac gave him Salafist books and sat down with him every day, working through the material and getting him excited about the "new" faith he was discovering. "The books explained everything", Sarfo later told his police interrogators, "very precise and to the point... And I thought, wow, I didn't know any of this stuff".[17] After his release, Sarfo became a regular at the *Islamischer Kultur- und Familienverein* (IKF), an extremist mosque on the outskirts of Bremen, and part of a group of 27 who eventually went to Syria.

Networking

More so than anywhere outside, prisons are places where criminal and terrorist milieus converge, and have the potential to produce more terrorists that are also better skilled and equipped. Unless extremists are entirely separated from the rest of the prison population, which may not always be possible or advisable, prison environments have the potential to enable the flow of information, people, and skills.[18] This is of greater benefit to the extremists than the criminals: not only do they get access to potentially fruitful opportunities and targets for radicalisation, they can also take advantage of the criminals' skills and underground connections.

The most significant example is that of Chérif Kouachi, Amedy Coulibaly, and Djamel Beghal. Kouachi and Coulibaly first met inside Fleury-Mérogis prison near Paris in 2007, and formed a friendship after spending seven months on the same wing.[19] Coulibaly had a history of armed robberies, and was imprisoned for aggravated theft, receiving stolen goods, and using false number plates.[20] Kouachi, meanwhile, was on remand awaiting trial over a 2005 attempt to travel to Iraq to become a foreign fighter.[21] The pair – one an "ordinary" criminal, the other an extremist – were then mentored and radicalised in prison by Djamel Beghal, an al-Qaeda recruiter.[22] In other words, prison allowed the initial network to be established, which culminated in Kouachi and Coulibaly coordinating the January 2015 Paris attacks, killing 17 people.

Criminal "Skills"

There are many "skills" that terrorists with criminal backgrounds may have developed as a result of their previous involvement in crime. In our dataset, we have found concrete evidence for four: access to weapons; the ability to "stay under the radar"; terrorist financing through "petty crime"; and a lower threshold for becoming involved in violence among formerly violent criminals.

Access to Weapons

Although Islamic State has frequently encouraged its supporters to use everyday objects, such as cars and knives,[23] guns and bombs continue to play a prominent role in jihadist operations. As early as 2013, Danish intelligence warned that the large numbers of criminals who were joining jihadists groups would lead to the proliferation of firearms among would-be terrorists.[24] Two years later, the warning came true. In February 2015, Omar el-Hussein attacked a free speech event and, later that day, a synagogue in Copenhagen. Between the two attacks, he went to his neighbourhood of Mjølnerparken, where he disposed of an M95 rifle that he had stolen during a home robbery and used during the first attack.[25] He then visited an internet café to meet with former gang associates who helped dispose of the rifle. In short: without his criminal past, el-Hussein would have found it much harder – if not impossible – to acquire the means with which he carried out his attacks.

The same is true for Amedy Coulibaly. The arms dealer that sold him his weapons had no idea that Coulibaly was a terrorist. Upon seeing the media reports that followed the attacks in January 2015, he pre-emptively turned himself in to the police, and confessed to supplying Coulibaly with Škorpion submachine guns, a rocket propelled grenade launcher, and the two AK-47s that the Kouachi brothers used.[26] He calculated that the attacks would eventually have led the police to him anyway. Indeed, had he known Coulibaly's true intentions, he might have been more hesitant in supplying the weapons.

Staying "Under the Radar"

In addition to procuring firearms, terrorists may benefit from criminals' ability to "stay under the radar", especially by gaining access to fake documents and access to safe houses. What matters in this regard are not specific abilities that former criminals may (or may not) possess themselves, but – rather – their access to (criminal) networks through which they can be mobilised. The production of forgeries, for instance, is difficult for terrorists to develop in-house. (Our database contains only three criminals who used identity theft prior to their radicalisation.)[27] Instead, it is more likely that terrorist networks would "out-source" this capability to people who are experts – and who can typically be found in criminal milieus.

In the case of the network that carried out the attacks in Paris in November 2015 and Brussels in March 2016, this clearly succeeded. The organisers used fraudulent documents throughout their attack planning in order to wire money, travel between countries, rent cars, and – crucially – acquire safe houses.[28] Yet here, as in other cases, the skills transfer consisted not of *manufacturing* forgeries, but of having access to a criminal network that was in a position to *acquire* forgeries. This is how they came across Djamal Eddine Ouali, an Algerian who ran a forgery operation in the Brussels district of Saint-Gilles. There is no evidence that Ouali knew of his customers' true intentions, or was even interested in them. As the Belgian investigator in charge of Ouali's case has said: "[He] was a professional document falsifier whose main goal was to make as much money as possible".[29]

Financing

If we accept that criminal backgrounds facilitate access to weapons and help obtain fraudulent documents, it may be no surprise that they also enable terrorist financing. Rigorous empirical examinations of this phenomenon are surprisingly rare, though two recent studies have started cataloguing the funding of jihadist activities in Europe. A report by Magnus Normark and Magnus Ranstorp focuses on how European foreign fighters have funded their travel to Syria: in addition to loans, private donations, bank fraud, and business fraud, they consistently emphasise the role of petty crime.[30] Emilie Oftedal's study examined the financing of 40 jihadist plots between 1994 and 2013: though nearly three-quarters generated at least some of their income from legal sources,[31] she shows that criminality played a significant role, with nearly 40 per cent of the plots drawing on the proceeds of crime.[32]

The principal difficulty in detecting crime as a means of terrorist financing is that it does not involve a change of behaviour, but merely of purpose: individuals with criminal pasts often continue what they were doing in their previous lives, except that profits are used to finance terrorism. As a result, it can be difficult to separate funds that were raised for terrorism from money that is spent on other, often entirely mundane purposes. Saïd Kouachi, for example, sold counterfeit goods, received money from AQAP, engaged in bank fraud, and was involved in theft.[33] Not all of his money went into the funding of the Charlie Hebdo attack, but some of it did. The same logic applied to a British jihadist Choukri Ellekhlifi, who had convictions for several robberies, and financed his trip to Syria by doing more of them.[34] In all these cases, the common thread was not any particular source of funding, but biographical continuity.

Familiarity with Violence

Such practical skills are supplemented by a more intangible "skill" or – rather – experience: that of familiarity with violence. Sixty-five per cent of the individuals in our database were involved in violent crime. Among the individuals that were involved in domestic plotting (as opposed to "foreign fighting"), this figure rises to 80 per cent. What we are hypothesising is that, having engaged in violence repeatedly and routinely as a criminal can lower the (psychological) threshold for becoming involved in violence as a terrorist. In other words: for someone who is familiar with using violence and has become de-sensitised to its use, the "jump" from cognitive to violent extremism will be smaller, and the process of mobilisation therefore quicker and less difficult.

The argument is hard to substantiate based on individual trajectories alone, given all the other potential influences that may have caused a person to engage in terrorism. Nevertheless, our database shows that the period of mobilisation – that is, the time between joining a jihadist group and becoming involved in violence – among the individuals involved in domestic plotting was, in many cases, extraordinarily short, often less than four months or even just a few weeks. Furthermore, while there was no "like-for-like" use of violence, the terrorist use of violence was always *more violent* than someone's criminal use of violence. These findings support the idea that familiarity with (criminal) violence produces terrorists that are not only more volatile but also more violent.

Conclusion

This chapter has shown that there is a significant aspect of the crime-terror nexus which many of the existing debates have almost entirely ignored: the radicalisation and involvement in terrorism of individuals with criminal backgrounds. Our findings challenge many assumptions about radicalisation. The individuals in our database often contradicted the notion that involvement in extremism correlates with religious behaviour. Some of them smoked cigarettes, drank alcohol, or took drugs. Others, in turn, observed religious rules but continued engaging in crime. Simply put: being pious is no guarantee that criminal behaviour has stopped, while acting like a "gangster" does not preclude involvement in terrorism.

As a consequence, policymakers have to make sure that relevant agencies become more effective at sharing relevant information across departments and "disciplines". Another priority are prisons. As this study has shown, prisons are like a microcosm of the crime-terror nexus where radicalisation, recruitment, networking and even terrorist plotting have taken place. With increasing numbers of terrorism-related arrests and convictions, the significance of prisons in terrorist trajectories is unlikely to diminish.[35]

On the other hand, countering jihadists' criminal behaviour should enable law enforcement agencies to operate a so-called "Al Capone approach" by bringing lesser charges against individuals in cases in which terrorism related offences are difficult to prove.[36] The mayor of the Brussels district of Molenbeek, where several of the terrorists that were involved in the Paris and Brussels attacks had lived, made precisely this point. She argued that "radicalisation thrives on other forms of criminality", and that "one way to tackle terrorism" was to begin by dealing with crime, and for states to engage with areas that, in many cases, they seem to have forgotten.[37]

Notes

1 Paul Cruickshank, "A view from the CT foxhole: an interview with Alain Grignard, Brussels Federal Police", *CTC Sentinel*, Vol 8, Issue 8, 2015, p. 8.
2 Foreign fighter database created and maintained by the International Centre for the Study of Radicalisation (ICSR), King's College London.
3 Bundeskriminalamt (Federal Criminal Police Office, BKA), Bundesamt für Verfassungsschutz (Federal Office for the Protection of the Constitution, BfV) and Hessisches Informations- und Kompetenzzentrum gegen Extremismus (Hessian Information and Competence Center against Extremism, HKE), "Analyse der Radikalisierungshintergründe und -verläufe der Personen, die aus islamistischer Motivation aus Deutschland in Richtung Syrien oder Irak ausgereist sind – Fortschreibung 2016",

2016; Anton W. Weenink, "Family, Crime, and Mental Health Problems in Jihadis in Police Files", presentation delivered at NSCR symposium "The Crime-Terror Nexus: Merging Criminological and Psychological Perspectives" in Amsterdam, 12 September 2017.

4 For a discussion of definitions, see Peter R. Neumann, "The Trouble with Radicalization", *International Affairs*, Vol 89, Issue 4, 2013, pp. 873–93.

5 Quintan Wiktorowicz, *Radical Islam Rising: Muslim Extremism in the West* (London: Rowman & Littlefield, 2005), p. 20.

6 Nagieb Khaja, "On the frontline in Syria: The Danish gangster who turned jihadi", *The Guardian*, 7 July 2014.

7 As relayed to Tam Hussein, quoted in Luke Harding, "From Acton to Aleppo: how one British Muslim's quest to Syria ended in death", *The Guardian*, 31 May 2013 (note: the reports of Almanasfi's death in May 2013 were incorrect).

8 Thomas Joscelyn, "Anwar al Awlaki: Jihadists should steal from disbelievers", *Long War Journal*, 17 January 2011.

9 See Rumiyah, Issue 8, *Al Hayat Media Center*, 2017, and Rumiyah, Issue 11, *Al Hayat Media Center*, 2017.

10 Patrick J. McDonnell, "'Papa Noel' – the militant recruiter in Brussels who groomed young men for violence", *Los Angeles Times*, 28 March 2016.

11 Andrew Higgins and Kimiko De Freytas-Tamura, "A Brussels mentor who taught 'Gangster Islam' to the young and angry", *New York Times*, 11 April 2016.

12 Pieter Van Ostaeyen, "Belgian radical networks and the road to the Paris attacks", *CTC Sentinel*, Vol 9, Issue 6, 2016, pp. 7–12.

13 Pieter Van Ostaeyen and Guy Van Vlierden, "Belgian fighters in Syria and Iraq – An important review of our data", published on https://pietervanostaeyen.com/2016/08/03/belgian-fighters-in-syria-and-iraq-an-important-review-of-our-data/, 3 August 2016.

14 Peter R. Neumann, "Prisons and Terrorism: Radicalisation and De-radicalisation in 15 Countries", *International Centre for the Study of Radicalisation (ICSR)*, 2010, p. 26. https://www.clingendael.org/sites/default/files/pdfs/Prisons-and-terrorism-15-countries.pdf

15 See Andrew Silke, "Holy Warriors: Exploring the psychological processes of jihadi radicalization", *European Journal of Criminology*, Vol 5, No 1, 2008, p. 107.

16 Jörg Diehl, Julia Jüttner, Fidelius Schmid, and Wolf Wiedmann-Schmidt, "Back from the 'Caliphate': Returnee Says IS Recruiting for Terror Attacks in Germany", *Der Spiegel*, 16 December 2015.

17 "Vernehmungsprotokoll der Beschuldigtenvernehmung vom 15. Dezember 2015", *Generalbundesanwalt*, 15 December 2015.

18 Peter R. Neumann, Prisons and Terrorism: Radicalisation and De-radicalisation in 15 Countries, *International Centre for the Study of Radicalisation (ICSR)*, 2010.

19 Angelique Chrisafis, "Charlie Hebdo attackers: Born, raised and radicalised in Paris", *The Guardian*, 12 January 2015.

20 Ibid.

21 Scott Bronstein, "Chérif and Said Kouachi: Their path to terror", *CNN*, 14 January 2015.

22 Angelique Chrisafis, "Charlie Hebdo attackers: Born, raised and radicalised in Paris", *The Guardian*, 12 January 2015.

23 Abu Muhammad Al-Adnani, "Indeed Your Lord Is Ever Watchful", 9 September 2014.

24 PET Center for Terroranalyse, "Truslen mod Danmark fra personer udrejst til Syrien", 23 October 2015, p. 3.

25 "Terrortiltalt hjalp Omar El-Hussein", *Berlingske*, 17 March 2016; Michala Rask Mikkelsen, "Riffel fra terrorangreb blev stjålet under hjemmerøveri", *Berlingske*, 18 February 2015. The rifle model is otherwise known as an RK 95 TP.

26 "Charlie Hebdo – Un Carolo se rend à la police prétendant avoir eu des contacts avec Amédy Coulibaly", *La Libre*, 14 January 2015.

27 Brahim Abdeslam (fraud/stealing IDs), Aria Ladjevardi (passport forgery) and Mohammed Merah (passport forgery). It is possible that the actual figure is higher.

28 Lori Hinnant, "Piecing together Salah Abdeslam's itinerary in Paris attacks: Days on end at the wheel and months of planning", *Associated Press*, 10 December 2015.

29 Maïa de la Baume and Giulia Paravicini, "Inside the Brussels flat where terrorists scored fake IDs", *Politico*, 31 March 2016.

30 Magnus Normark and Magnus Ranstorp, "Understanding terrorist finance: Modus operandi and national CTF regimes", *Swedish Defence University*, 18 December 2015.

31 Emilie Oftedal, "The financing of jihadi terrorist cells in Europe", *FFI Report, Norwegian Defence Research Establishment,* p. 3, 26.

32 Ibid., p. 19.

33 Emeline Cazi, Jacques Follorou, Matthieu Suc, and Elise Vincent, "La fratrie Kouachi, de la petite délinquance au djihad", *Le Monde*, 8 January 2015.

34 "The Al Qaeda fanatic from Britain who funded jihad trip to Syria by mugging Londoners with a Taser", *Mail Online*, 30 November 2013.

35 For concrete recommendations, see Peter R. Neumann, Prisons and Terrorism: Radicalisation and De-radicalisation in 15 Countries, *International Centre for the Study of Radicalisation (ICSR)*, 2010.

36 Al Capone is the name of the notorious American mobster who was eventually caught and convicted for tax crimes.

37 Quoted in Nikolaj Nielsen, "Molenbeek mayor opens new front on extremism", *EU Observer,* 9 September 2016.

15

COUNTER-NARRATIVES

Behnam Heidenreuter

The attack on democracy begins with an attack on language.

(Schaeffer 2018, p. 289)

Terrorism is frequently described as communication strategy aimed at provoking a reaction by the opposing side (Waldmann 2005, p. 34 ff.). Since terrorist groups tend to explicitly reflect upon their communication strategies and write about them, too, the significance of communication becomes obvious. The book published by ISIS in April 2016 titled *Media Operative. You Are a Mujahid, Too*, which has been analyzed thoroughly by Charlie Winter from the International Centre for the Study of Radicalization and Political Violence (ICSR) at King's College London (2017), serves as a good example here.

It is important to analyze any communication expressed directly by terrorist and extremist groups, such as letters of confession, flyers, essays or speeches, and to deal with them thoroughly, as each violent act in fact inheres communication, and even non-terrorist but also extremist groupings are making major efforts to disseminate their "world simplification formulae" (Schaeffer 2018, p. 204). Irrespective thereof, technical measures to limit terrorist and extremist propaganda have proven especially effective as has been shown regarding ISIS and their reduced amount of public releases.

Dealing with challenges in relation with terrorism – however ideology-based – is a difficult undertaking. This is definitely a lesson learnt after two decades of "war against terrorism" since September 11, 2001, and it should be applied to other phenomena and areas, in particular right-wing terrorism, as well. Counter-terrorism and counter-extremism strategies both include a set of diverse measures. Basically, distinctions can be drawn between the following categories:

- Weakening of terrorist structures and the increase of terrorists' planning efforts by
  - police investigations and law enforcement,
  - military interventions,
  - intelligence work,
  - technical safety measures at critical points, and
  - technical measures for curbing propaganda.

DOI: 10.4324/9781003326373-17

- Empowerment of society through

  - sharing information about the aims, intentions and ways used by terrorist and extremist groups,
  - collectively banning terrorist and extremist groups and their messages, and
  - identification with a positive collective-body-concept.

The measures of "counter-narratives"(a more detailed explanation of the term will follow in the next section of this chapter) belong to the second category, namely "empowerment of society", which describes the weakening of logic and argumentation by terrorist and extremist groups.

The intention is to enable their target groups to independently recognize terrorist and extremist narratives, to question them and to eventually not accept them. As regards the applicability and implementation as well as the effectiveness of counter-narratives, there are a number of important questions. The following paper will summarize the current discussion on counter-narratives and provide recommendations on how to properly use them.

Terminology

In this paper, *narratives* are considered a series of explanatory, inter-relating stories that provide answers to and recommendations for certain problems and also help to create and give meaning (cf. to the discussion of terminology Braddock & Horgan 2015, pp. 2–3 and GTAZ 2017, 4). While ideology can be comprehended as a set of connecting ideas and explanations as well as solutions, a narrative is a vehicle of ideology, like a transmission belt (Braddock & Horgan 2015, p. 3). A narrative used by jihadists would be, for instance: Western states have installed "puppet regimes" in Muslim societies in order to pursue their interests and to weaken and control Islam and Muslims in general (status description). Muslims are not able to defend themselves because they have deviated from the right path of "true Islam" (explanation). Not negotiations or reforms, but only "Jihad in the way of God" is the solution to the misery (solution). With regard to right-wing terrorism, the status description would include the fact that political and media elites have deliberately planned a population exchange in order to weaken entire nations and to let people from other cultures enter the respective countries in large numbers. This "status" can only be solved by violent campaigns against all persons responsible and immigrants, since any free expression is subject to repression.

In the context of the aforementioned narrative, we thus have to ask ourselves what "counter-narratives" actually are. Brigg and Feve (2013, p. 2) defined them as "measures used to directly deconstruct, discredit and demystify violent extremist messaging". Two years later, Braddock and Horgan (2015, pp. 1–2) defined the function of counter-narratives as "…] objections to the topics that fuel and uphold terrorist narratives, and that discourage from supporting terrorism encouraged by those topics and narratives produced by terrorist groups, in a broader sense".

Both definitions highlight the reactive/defensive nature of the term "counter-narrative". In this regard, Ingram and Reed (2016, p. 6) mention the following: "It is important to recognize that counter-narratives represent an inherently defensive way of messaging, that is messaging developed as a reaction to messaging of an opponent". Although this conclusion should remain value-free at this point, it is relevant for distinguishing counter-narratives as an instrument from other "offensive" strategic communication forms. These forms particularly include the "alternative narrative", which places special focus on its own strength instead of taking up the weakness of the opposing narrative. Strategic communication utilized by governments for reporting their goals and measures is another alternative narrative form (Brigg & Feve 2013, p. 2).[1]

The governments of the United States and the United Kingdom have both shown great commitment with respect to the creation and dissemination of counter-narratives and even established bodies specifically for this purpose (Brigg & Feve 2013, pp. 8–9). Following the work of both the United States and the United Kingdom, the respective authorities concerned with safety and security issues in Germany, and later also other public bodies, started dealing with this topic too (i.e. GTAZ 2007) and even carried out specific projects. Examples worth mentioning are the information video series on "Islam Terminology" by the German Federal Agency for Civic Education (FACE, BPB 2019) which were first published on October 12, 2015, and the video series titled "Jihadi Fool" by the North Rhine-Westphalian Office for Protection of the Constitution, which started in August 2019 as the first initiative by an official security body (Regional Government of North Rhine-Westphalia, August 22, 2019). Furthermore, a broad range of projects against extremism and hate speech were funded by governmental and non-governmental agencies in Germany and other European countries, such as Great Britain or France (cf. Winter & Fürst 2017).

Effective Narratives

With regard to the intended or actual effect the question arises as to what makes a good narrative. The answer to this question explains what elements of a counter-narrative must be regarded. In this context, the communication strategy of the Islamic State (IS) deserves a closer look, since IS is considered one of the most successful models of terrorist groups and like no other movement has managed to perfect and optimize its media use. In addition to the high number of daily, weekly and monthly reports, videos, pictures, hymns and anthems produced by IS (cf. Zelin 2015), as well as the fact that the whole terrorist group and its followers had countless online accounts on many different Social Media-platforms to spread the word, it has been the coherent and recognizable "brand image" of IS that explains its success. Part of this "brand" is a positive and optimistic basic message of the narrative, which puts more emphasis on alternatives to the existing systems (cf. Winter 2017, pp. 15–16). As a matter of fact, it seems that this aspect, highlighted by Winter, attracted sympathizers worldwide, along with the initial war success of IS. In his essay "The true believer" (1951) by American philosopher Eric Hoffer, which presents explanations for the rise of nationalist, left-wing and religious mass movements, he concluded that the power of presenting convincing arguments for an alternative future is a very important pull-factor, as this gives its sympathizers hope of becoming part of a swift and fundamental political change. Even though Hoffer's considerations were expressed 60 years before the rise of IS, they may help us understand what factors make up the "moment of success" and the attraction of (extremist) mass movements today. Furthermore, they provide indications on how possible counter-measures should be designed.

Based on Hoffer's description of the positive factors which inspire any mass movement, it seems plausible that elements focusing on the benefits of the society model at stake should be paramount when designing a counter-narrative. Also, considerations should be given to the broader historical framework, and opportunities for participation must be stressed more.

By now there are various concepts on counter-narratives of jihadist propaganda which have already been implemented. In its information video series project titled "Islam Terminology" the German Federal Agency for Civic Education (FACE) mainly focused on the discursive discussion on terms jihadists are claiming for their own. The free project "Date Assassins" tries to satirically question radicalization, much like years later the Office of Constitution Protection tried to do. Another project called "Jamal al-Khatib" was invented in Vienna and focuses on the narrative, biographical work and on creating alternative narratives to jihadist propaganda through the application of dramaturgic and didactic methods.

So far, there are only few research findings on the effect of counter-narratives. In this regard the research study carried out by the German Federal Criminal Office presents a notable exception (Frischlich et al. 2017). This particular study examined the effectiveness of different counter-narrative videos and found that the level of acceptance of single videos depends on various factors. According to Rutkowski et al. (2017, pp. 155–156) a high level of narrativity, hence a coherent narration, any entertaining narrative style, as well as tales of drop-outs and of change, received especially high approval ratings, whereas humorous and satirical videos were regarded as critical by the study participants, as they feared such videos might cause emotional injuries or, in the worst case, further radicalization of the target audience (ibid.). Such risk of further radicalization is even higher in cases where the copyright of videos is not owned by publicly independent distributors but by official authorities, or even security and safety authorities (which is the case with North Rhine-Westphalia). The aforementioned GTAZ-paper "Guideline for Dealing with Counter-Narratives" particularly stresses this fact by mentioning that "under certain circumstances it can be profitable for State authorities to support civic actors with creating their own counter-narratives", and that Counter-Narrative projects developed by State authorities should be implemented only with restrictions (GTAZ 2017, p. 7). The wordings of such recommendations in the paper are as follows:

> For the conceptual development and dissemination, suitable partners must be identified. For example, such partners could be prominent personalities who would receive a high level of acceptance by young people. Cooperations with political foundations, whose fundamental tasks include the promotion of democracy and who can provide the necessary structures and know-how, would also be possible.
>
> *(GTAZ 2017, p. 21)*

This clearly demonstrates the skeptical attitude of the authors of the paper towards public bodies running counter-narrative projects, and how they clearly prefer subcontracting independent third parties as it can be presumed that in doing so, both higher acceptance and improved effects may be achieved.

The position expressed by the GTAZ task force is also apparent in the survey of existing measures by Brigg and Feve (2013, p. 17). Based on experiences in the United States and the United Kingdom, the authors caution against government bodies playing a too active role in the creation of a dissemination of counter-narratives. This is due to the limited credibility among the target audience and also to possible contra-productive effects (ibid.).

Realization–What Are the Key Issues?

Counter-narratives can be edited and presented in various ways. However, a few key points should always be noted in order to not accidentally harm oneself and to not become a subject of public mockery. This, for instance, was the case of the video game "Slippery Slope" by the FBI, which received really bad press (cf. McCormick 2016; cf. Kohring 2016).

First, the message needs to be studied carefully, and it is necessary to clearly grasp the presentation of the arguments and their translation into a narrative. Reservations against government and society both require detailed explorations. Furthermore, the target audience should be studied thoroughly regarding demographic factors (age, gender, domicile, education, etc.) and also regarding their specific media use behaviors; various studies including the JIM study provide valuable information in this context. Only then will it be possible to create the ideal design and to address and virtually meet the target audience in the media. Each single piece of this preparatory work will set a certain framework for the way of presentation, the narrative style and imagery, the argumentation and the dissemination channels. In this regard it is essential to prepare precisely – even though this might result in high costs, especially when agencies are hired to carry out film projects, for instance. Based on experience, this is likely to be very costly and involve several hundred thousand Euro. Political decision-makers should be aware of this fact too whenever they demand the creation and implementation of a specific project by experts. In case of doubt this might require fundraising, which may considerably delay the entire planning and implementation process.

In the further evolution of the project the question as to who will be the messenger of the respective counter-narrative will arise. In the past, drop-outs have been "used" as authentic messengers (Brigg & Feve 2013, p. 17). However, in connection with IS it has become evident in Germany that drop-outs such as returnees from conflict zones are not ideal for this role, as their involvement in battle very often is not clear or requires further clarification. Also, in most cases such persons are subject of criminal investigations or even must serve prison sentences. This shows that authentic messengers do not necessarily need to have an extremist past, even though this might make sense in some cases. Other messengers acting as positive role models for their target audience might be prominent influencers, athletes and artists who allow their audience to identify themselves with them.

It must be pointed out that all reflections outlined here shall apply to new projects and that there are already sufficient projects dealing with right-wing extremism and Islamism, disposing of extensive experience in dealing with the respective narratives and still trying to provide and disseminate counter-arguments. In this sense, it is important to carry out a thorough control of already evolving projects before re-issuing counter-narrative projects. Also, it should be assessed whether the support of civic actors might serve better for creating a more sustainable counter-narrative than the creation of stand-alone projects, since their lasting effect may be more limited.

Conclusion

Narratives are like a glue holding together social movements, which also include extremist tendencies. This "social glue" not only fosters cohesion within an ideological framework, but it also supports an explanation for all world affairs and contributes to building a sense of identity. In this regard, the connection between the two levels of radicalization, namely cognitive radicalization and activist/social radicalization, emerges (please see Neumann 2013 for more information on the academic discourse on the significance of these levels). In order to be able to build up a counter-balance to extremist narratives, one should realize that no narrative only addresses the rational/cognitive level of any individual. Instead, it must always be considered within the larger context that empowers a narrative.

For this reason, counter-narratives are experiencing difficulties: on the one hand, they ought to deconstruct and present the inner contradictions of extremist perspectives and argumentations and are thus in danger of remaining on a merely discursive level. On the other hand, however, they must appropriately and emotionally appeal to the target audience and take into account its world perceptions with all their contents and designs, should they actually become effective. Therefore, the demands on successful counter-narratives are very high, and for effectively planning and implementing them all timely and appropriate, financial and human resources must be provided. Furthermore, the messages should not remain rhetorical but correspond with the real-life conditions. If jihadist narratives like "the war of the West against the Islamic world" are to be answered with religious freedom and participation opportunities for Muslims in Western societies, then they should in fact comply with the actual social practice and not be attacked with constant negative stigmatization discourses about Muslims, be it by politicians or media representatives. Another example is the Islamist narrative according to which society wants to systematically exclude Muslims. It is important to establish the necessary physical conditions in order to authentically counter such messages. Measures to compensate existing social disadvantages in economically underdeveloped regions, which are home to members of Muslim minorities in particular, may be instrumental.

Similarly, the situation concerning the right-wing extremist narrative can be dealt with as described above, however it is not completely congruent. In this case it is also important to connect messages to existing realities and to identify problems as such. Since, however, both government failure and systematical hoaxes, false reports or half-truths are put into circulation across the extreme right-wing spectrum very often (cf. Schaeffer 2018), it seems particularly important to demonstrate the governmental capacity to act in diverse policy areas and to openly explain the reasons for political decisions, including all previous considerations. Ideally, counter-narratives are tailored towards local circumstances and seize on regional examples.

As the discourse utilized by right-wing extremists especially stresses a distribution of resources to the disadvantage of the local population and the advantage of the newly arrived, examples of action could be used from within those discourse areas and be prepared accordingly.

Both the message and reality should ideally be consistent with one another or, provided that this requirement has not yet been fulfilled, the ways towards participation in connection with the call for activity should be demonstrated clearly, in order to be able to integrate oneself peacefully and within the framework of applicable law into socio-political life. It is always crucial to know the target audience well, and to integrate their language and life reality into the conceptual design.

Based on these assumptions it can be quite reasonable to oppose extremists with counter- or alternative narratives. Such narratives should not necessarily be set by state authorities, but rather it should be the goal of any public action to support civic actors who are already advocating against disinformation and agitation and developing counter-narratives in their daily lives themselves – although such narratives can hardly be designated as such – and who are acting in both real and virtual space.

Note

1 A critical reflection of the term according to German safety and security authorities is available in the report GTAZ-UAG titled "Counter-Narratives" (GTAZ 2017, pp. 4–6).

References

Braddock, Kurt und John Horgan (2015). "Towards a Guide for Constructing and Disseminating Counternarratives to Reduce Support for Terrorism", *Studies in Conflict & Terrorism*, (39:5), 2016, 381–404.

Brigg, Rachel und Sebastien Feve (2013). "Review of Programs to Counter Narratives of Violent Extremism. What works and what are the Implications for Government?", Institute for Strategic Dialogue. London.

Bundeszentrale für politische Bildung (o.D.) (2019). *Begriffswelten Islam*. http://www.bpb.de/lernen/digitale-bildung/medienpaedagogik/213243/webvideos-begriffswelten-islam (abgerufen am 22.08.2019).

Frischlich, Lena, Diana Rieger, Anna Morten und Gary Bente in Kooperation mit der Forschungsstelle Terrorismus/Extremismus (FTE) des Bundeskriminalamtes (Hrsg.) (2017). *Videos gegen Extremismus? Counter-Narrative auf dem Prüfstand*. Wiesbaden.

https://www.hamburg.de/contentblob/11233354/acebc6c39b4b7b32b878490671db22e1/data/leitfaden-counter-narratives.pdf (abgerufen am 24.08.2019).

Ingram, Haroro J. und Alastair Reed (2016). "Lessons from History for Counter-Terrorism Strategic Communications", The International Centre for Counter-Terrorism–*The Hague* (7:4).

Kohring, Birte (016). "Das FBI will Jugendliche mit einem Computerspiel über Extremismus informieren", *Bento*, fbi-spiel-wie-die-amerikanische-behoerde-jugendlichen-ueber-terrorismus-lehren-will-a-00000000-0003-0001-0000-000000341895 (abgerufen am 04.09.2019).

McCormick, Rich (2016). "The FBI made a very confusing game about preventing terrorism", *The Verge*, https://www.theverge.com/2016/2/12/10976914/fbi-anti-extremist-video-game-slippery-slope (abgerufen am 04.09.2019).

Neumann, Peter (2013). "The Trouble with Radicalization", *International Affairs* (89:4), 873–893.

Rutkowski, Olivia, Ronja Schötz und Anna Morten (2017). "Subjektives Erleben", in: Lena Frischlich, Diana Rieger, Anna Morten & Gary Bente in Kooperation mit der Forschungsstelle Terrorismus/Extremismus (FTE) des Bundeskriminalamtes (Hrsg.), *Videos gegen Extremismus? Counter-Narrative auf dem Prüfstand*. Wiesbaden.

Schaeffer, Ute (2018). *Fake statt Fakt. Wie Populisten, Bots und Trolle unsere Demokratie angreifen*. München.

Waldmann Peter (2005). *Terrorismus. Provokation der Macht*. Hamburg: Murmann Verlag.

Winter, Charlie (2017). *Media Jihad: The Islamic State's Doctrine for Information Warfare*. London: Institute for Strategic Dialogue.

Winter, Charlie und Johanna Fürst (2017). *Challenging Hate: Counter-speech Practices in Europe*. London.

Zelin, Aaron (2015). "Picture Or It Didn't Happen: A Snapshot of the Islamic State's Official Media Output", *Perspectives on Terrorism* (9:4), 85–97. The International Center for the Study of Radicalisation and Political Violence (ICSR).

16

IDEOLOGICAL POLARIZATION AND SOCIETAL DISRUPTION

Herfried Münkler

When asked for the conditions of social cohesion, political liberalism answers with a paradox by referring to the cohesive force of public conflict resolution. According to general conviction, social cohesion was not served by "sweeping them under the carpet" and giving the impression of perfect harmony as conflicts are part of any pluralistic society, no matter whether this concerned material interests or ideational values. These conflicts needed to be called by their name, politically marked, and settled according to a fair process that is acceptable to both sides. That might have led to compromises in which both sides could have recognized themselves but could have ended with the victory of one and the defeat of the other side as well. Those defeats, so the expectation, will be accepted by the losers, if the political constellations guarantee that the conflict line can be reactivated at a later point so that the defeat just suffered is not an eternal guarantee. Political decisions are in this form of democratic order under the reservation of their reversibility.

The concept of the reversibility of political decisions was and is the basic condition for the acceptance and the functioning of liberal orders. The changeability of the momentous constellations guarantees that social groups and classes will become accustomed to the rather endless process of the constantly re-arranged conflict resolution. There are two tremendous advantages to be gained from this procedure: On the one hand, it prevents the losing parties from sinking into a state of political resignation and thereby forming resentments against the social and political order in which they always – they at least feel – belong to the losers. On the other hand, it ensures that the resort to violence is not an attractive option for change as that would lead to an all-or-nothing-constellation, resulting in a civil war with unclear outcome. The organization of cohesion in the mode of proceduralized conflict resolution emphasizes the time factor, which relativizes the relentlessness of the moment.

The discussion on social cohesion that has arisen for some time can be seen as an indicator that the liberal mechanism of public conflict resolution does not function any more or that relevant groups do not have lasting trust in the capability of pacifying problem solving of society in the form of public conflict resolution. One of the reasons for this is the fear that a series of the taken decisions will turn out to be irreversible, ranging from nuclear energy to climate change and immigration.

It is about everything or nothing. The challenge for liberal democracy can also be re-formulated: The conviction that procedurality is the best mechanism for resolving political conflicts, both

DOI: 10.4324/9781003326373-18

for those which persist for a long time as well as for those which have just surfaced, has recently lost its binding force. A fundamentally altered conception of time can be identified as the main reason, with the perspective of long duration being condensed to short time spans. There is no more time for what needs to be done, according to the respective understanding, to proceduralize, to postpone it into the future and until the next opportunity, just as the generally provisional nature of all decisions does not exist anymore. The increasing transference of the "We" connects with this perspective loss of time through an "I" that pushes its way into the foreground. The individual lifetime takes the place of the future potential of political and social organizations.

The "society of singularities", as Andreas Reckwitz puts it,[1] and the change of socio-political time conception go hand in hand. At last, apocalyptic scenarios follow, seemingly demanding immediate action as the only prospect of rescue.[2] Apocalyptic scenarios are marked by the fact that after the occurrence of the feared, any possibility of reversing, stopping or undoing a course of events is excluded. The procedurality of liberal conflict resolution and the acceptance of its results, no matter how they turn out, is no generally accepted mode of problem solving anymore under these circumstances. Equally, the idea of social cohesion based on proceduralized conflict resolution can no longer be founded on it. The question is whether these changes constitute a societal change in perspective and mentality, which takes place time and again in modern societies, but changes again after some time, or whether it really has to do with a so catastrophic situation that all former forms of problem solving have become obsolete.[3] This question ultimately settles, whether liberal democracy has a future or not. The doubts that can already be observed about the problem-solving capacity of liberal democracy have already led to a considerably harsher political climate in which hostility and hate speech have increased.

Certainly, this is only a first and preliminary glance at the possible causes of social disruption and political extremism. Changes in the time horizon of a society, the sudden emergence of apocalyptic scenarios and the dissolution of community-building bonds have existed before as well, but apparently compensatory developments have taken place relatively fast, with whose help the society-endangering effects of such developments have been mitigated and certainly relativized. Retrospectively, we rather observe a reorganization of conceptions of time and the metamorphosis of disaster and crisis scenarios[4] instead of an actual dissolution of society. At the same time, a glance at social historiography shows that there has hardly been an era which in historic hindsight has not been described as a time of crisis, so that, defining the crisis term rather loosely, the history of society is depicted as a single sequence of crises. This is apparently the consequence of pronounced expectations for stability and continuity, which consistently perceive changes as disruptive, so that with contemporary crisis diagnoses and disaster prognoses, we are rather dealing with distortions of perspective than with observations in the form of protocols. The mediatized society focuses its attention on the disaster discourse, while it considers the postulation of stability and continuity as dull and does not thematize it anymore. This should be kept in mind as a warning sign, if subsequently the development of the last decades will be examined as one of disruption and dissolution.

The Ambivalence of Political Ideologies

Political ideologies are generally perceived as the cause and amplifier of societal divisions. If one understands by them a self-contained interpretation of the world that is immune to refutation, they undeniably provide social groups and classes with current diagnoses and future prospects, in which a certain socio-political development is highlighted as the only correct and promising one: normatively correct and possible in reality, so no mere pipe dream, supposedly scientifically secured and at the same time an effective answer to the diagnosed crises of society. Political ideologies since the French Revolution have appeared with this claim and shaped the political landscape. And as they appeared, with the exception of totalitarian societies, consistently in the plural, they have necessarily divided and polarized societies into irreconcilable opposing positions. The occupation with these ideological cleavages has led to the idea that under post-ideological conditions the cleavages would vanish, and social cooperation would come about on its own. The ideational expression of the problem is evident in this respect as the ideological interpretation of the societal divide has been confused with the problem itself, the divide. With the end of ideologies, as it had been proclaimed in 1989/90, the societal cleavages have in no way disappeared. Actually, they have only lost their former ideological coating.

This averts the gaze to the other side of ideologies where it is not about their contribution to the solidification of social cleavages, but about their community-building character. Ideologies power certain groups and classes of society with the conception of their similarities, solidarity and the therefrom resulting agency. A political ideology relativizes the feeling of individual impotence and insignificance by describing many individuals not only as victimized and suffering communities, but by postulating them as a political group capable of acting, if they make the ideologically prescribed to their binding self-image.

Ideologies are thus both crutches for orientation and confidence in a seemingly bleak world, but at the same time they are instruments, with which elites and also individuals give themselves more power and influence. Ideologies are thus ambivalent. This applied equally to nationalist and socialist ideologies, as well as for certain religions and confessions which push political community building, beyond individual life lessons and promises of salvation, as was recently described using the example of Islamism, Hindu nationalism, as well as Evangelicalism. The split of society into conflicting groups with irrefutable certainties and the overcoming of social isolation through narratives of belonging and future potential go hand in hand. Robert Putnam has taken this ambivalence into account by differentiating in his work between the dimensions of bonding and bridging in the area of social capital of trust.[5]

Now the political and economic breakdown of the regime of real socialism in large parts of the world has actually led to post-ideological societies, if one focuses on ideologies in which there is a strong bonding component. According to Jean-François Lyotard,[6] the era of the "great narrations" has come to an end. What remains are the rudimentary moveable pieces of these stories, from which members of society who have fallen back into their isolation put together their individual success or failure stories. Some achieve this quite well, they are at one with themselves and describe their situation as one of prosperity and freedom; others succeed less or not at all, and their self-description, including their judgment of society reflects this. The divisions thus emerge unexpectedly and without any ideological mitigation. The lack of the liberal model's usefulness is reflected in the circumstance that by now the term "cleavage" has replaced what formerly was categorized as "conflict", meaning that it does not connect to an expectation of its overcoming in the course of societal development or through political conflict resolution. It can also be described as an expiry of a dialectic deeply enrolled in history, in consequence of which the productive element has vanished from the observation of the negative. Accordingly, the division of society is perceived as one that yields neither anything new nor anything probably better. It is a mere split, and the only thing that can in perspective be said of it results is that it is an ever more deepening and widening split. It can only be about stopping this development or at least slowing it down. Politics will be described according to the requirements of the catechontic, delaying the path down into the abyss.

The narration of a division of society, being nothing but a division, is extremely conservative, and the hegemony of this narrative is primarily responsible for the dominance of conservative parties and policymaking in present times – ranging from socio-structural issues to the preservation of culture and identity to radical ecological ideas that require an immediate rerouting. Progress as a societal self-description has been discredited and wherever it still has a say, this then happens in the sense of a return to pre-industrial times or as a codification of identities someone wants to protect now and against any eventual change. Describing the spirit of the age thus does not imply that this description is viewed either positively or negatively. Initially, it is about the inspection of the dominant discourse. One should admit, however, that this description amounts to a pointed version of Francis Fukuyama's reflections on the "end of history". Those also state that we will have nothing substantially new to expect after the definitive victory of democracy and market economy.[7]

For some it amounts to getting as comfortable as possible in the present and ignoring the divisions in society as a political challenge (both stubborn structural conservatives and neoliberals); others indeed thematize these divisions and want to cushion and bridge them with the "integrated tools" of these societies (the remaining social democrats); again others see a structural need for change, which is primarily not about social divisions but about a fundamental change of the socioeconomic momentum that is being described as disaster-prone or culturally threatening (supporters of the Greens but also moderate populists). All of these perspectives forego a "strong" concept of progress and, if they belong to the political left, make use of a "weak" concept of progress, which stands for a dampening of divisions, the limitation of resource consumption and the turning away from natural destruction. All of these programs can be subsumed under the guiding concept of "conservation". They are positions that claim to be coming from the mainstream of society and deny having a political extremist character.

Proletariat and Precariat: The Terminology of Social Disruption

Disruption is a counter term to stability and continuity and thus also to what is designated as social cohesion. Disruption stands for break, division, inner turmoil without any implementation of productivity and future potential to turn prosperity into the opposite and conflicts, as was the case in the dialectic perception of history. The dialectic ascribes to negativity the power to promote progress. Naturally, this dialectic can be criticized as self-deception, with which Hegel and subsequently Marx have filled the empty spaces in the self-image of people after the decay of religious bonds in enlightened social classes. One such radicalized criticism of ideology (radicalized insofar as the criticism is making itself the object of criticism) meanwhile overlooks the socially integrating effects that are unique to dialectic views of history. They empower especially in their Marxist variation, the disadvantaged and disconnected, the oppressed and exploited by attesting their ability to redesign society, as an anti-thesis to the existing order. Or as the poet Georg Gerwegh puts it: "Working man, wake up!/And recognize your power!/All wheels stand still/When your strong arm wants it". Whoever belonged to such a social class, no matter how defenseless and helpless he felt, turned through the ideology of the proletariat to a historically significant figure and could believe that what could not be currently achieved can be achieved over a longer period, nevertheless. The awareness of this power became a socially integrative element. It was complementary to the idea of social cohesion based on proceduralized conflict resolution.

The "precariat" has replaced the "proletariat" in contemporary descriptions of society, describing a conglomeration of people in vulnerable and badly paid working conditions, of which anyone can be replaced by anyone else at any time.

Whereas the strength of the proletariat was its attributed solidarity, which ensured that the arbitrary treatment of an individual would be met by the resistance of the many, the precariat has no comparable narration of a self-empowerment through cohesion. The members of the precariat cannot assert themselves on their own, but rely on the fairness, possibly even care, of others who pity them and look after them. They do it not because they are on the same level with the precarious but because they are themselves so much better off and thus turn to them with concern. This can be named as solidarity in its patriarchal variant, meaning that it causes thankfulness and not rage because the ones affected find themselves in an undignified position, as well as a deeply seated resentment against those who treat them this way. Be that as it may: Precariat is the designation for those who experience themselves as helpless individuals and in whose case thankfulness and humiliation are very close.

The contrasting opposition of proletariat and precariat does not necessarily indicate the socially structural status descriptions but rather the cognitive and emotional effects of a terminology that is hegemonic for society, thus the dominant self-description. The ideologically charged self-description have vanished in the post-ideological era, and they have been replaced by a terminology, which expresses social marginality without the chance of self-empowerment. Herewith connected is the politically relevant conception. The ideologically laden term of the proletariat did not only transport the promise of political agency, but equipped it with long-term time perspectives as well: Even if the aspired change did not progress at the time, having had to deal with set-backs and defeats, this was superimposed by the optimism that the victory of one's own cause inevitably has to take place in the future. None of this is the case with the term of the precariat that has turned from an attribution by others to a self-characterization. The term addresses either the individual's resignation and despair or his unlimited rage and wild uprising. It puts him in the role of a social and political outsider – or within the vicinity of extremists.

Apocalypse, Revolt and Extremism

In retrospective, we thus encounter the paradoxical observation that especially the revolutionary ideology of socialist movements had both a substantial socially integrating and equally a non-violent dimension. This was the case while it managed to transform through those dissatisfied with the *status quo* an ideological story into a political vector. Its key element was the narrative of the revolution, which necessarily followed due to the momentum of capitalism, which could be promoted through prudent and cautious action. Meanwhile, this was connected to the indication that nothing should be rushed as it would only harm one's own cause. The legendary discipline of socialist organizations can be explained not least because of this idea. Weak phases of socialist organizations, mostly combined with a loss of plausibility of the big narration, was accompanied by a defibering of the formerly solid fabric of ideology and the future revolution dissolved into a multitude of uncoordinated revolts, in which smaller and mostly clandestine groups tried to take matters into their own hands. The most recent development, where left- and right-wing extremists try to trigger revolts through assassinations, sabotage and more, has a series of historical precursors with which models for the course of the current phase of violence-prone extremism can be developed.

Generally, it is striking that the practice of political revolt is connected to a condensed conception of time, following which immediate action is demanded in terms of radical acceleration or sudden stopping. If time runs short and developments seem irreversible this will be understood by some as a request, or even compulsion, to revolt. These are then constellations, in which the binding force of the conservative and progressive narratives, the idea of national unity and the creative power of political organizations decreases, and more and more single groups are formed at their edges, groups which break away from, as they explain, the attentism or quietism of old organizations. The reasoning for their separation nearly always resolves around the idea of "betrayal". The feeling of condensed time, which renders clinging to politics of calm waiting impossible, is supplemented with the accusation of moral failure. Both result in a self-empowerment to initiate, which can serve as an initial impulse for a wider movement.

Should the here presented observations on the change of the social climate, on the shrinking trust in proceduralized conflict resolution, on the dwindling binding force of the big narrations or ideologies and the advance of apocalyptically pointed disaster scenarios turn out to be true, it follows for the discussion about political extremists: Instead of dealing with the political extremes, more attention should rather be given to the socio-political mainstream, its confidence and assurance of being up to the emerging challenges. Connected therewith is the strategy for sequencing the problems that are to be dealt with in order to develop a perspective that is extended over time for overcoming them and to protect the mechanisms of procedural conflict resolution against overloading. All this culminates in the question of self-confidence in a society. This cannot be proclaimed but must be literally developed through experiencing solutions to problem. This confidence was dwindling in many democratically constituted societies and was connected to the changed communications structures and the intrusion of *décor* and marketing specialists into the centers of politics and society. The binding power of political narratives requires in addition to the mere promise also the experience of its stepwise implementation. Wherever that is missing, the disruptive power of the apocalyptic turns out to be stronger than the story of the glorious future.

Notes

1 Andreas Reckwitz, *Die Gesellschaft der Singularitäten. Zum Strukturwandel der Moderne*, Berlin 2017.
2 See Herfried Münkler/Marina Münkler, *Abschied vom Abstieg*, Berlin 2019, p.25ff.
3 The expectation of catastrophical future can be the result of a spreading disaster discourse; cf. Leon Hempel/Marie Bartels/Thomas Markwart (Ed.), *Aufbruch ins Unversicherbare. Zum Katastrophendiskurs der Gegenwart*, Bielefeld 2013.
4 See Herfried Münkler, "Crises and Catastrophes, Security and Resilience. On the Significance of Finding Definitions for Security Policy"; in Part VI of this volume.
5 Mention can be made of Putnam's books *Making Democracy Work: Civic Traditions in Modern Italy*, Princeton 1993, and *Bowling Alone. The Collapse and Revival of American Community*, New York, NY 2000.
6 Jean-François Lyotard, *Das Postmoderne Wissen. Ein Bericht*, Graz-Vienna 1986, p.87ff.
7 Francis Fukuyama, *The End of History and the Last Man*, New York, NY 1992.

PART III

Right-Wing Extremism and Stochastic Terrorism

17

THE CURRENT AND FUTURE THREAT POSED BY ISLAMIST AND RIGHT-WING EXTREMIST TERRORISM IN EUROPE

Stefan Goertz

Both the current right-wing extremist terrorist attacks in Germany – including the assassination of Walter Lübcke on 2 June 2019, a German politician, member of the CDU party and president of the governmental district of Kassel, as well as the attempted attack on the synagogue in Halle on 9 October 2019 which caused two casualties close to the synagogue – and the increasing number of Islamist terrorist attacks that have either been committed or prevented by security authorities since 2004 clearly illustrate the historic threat which is posed by right-wing extremist and Islamist terrorism in Europe at present and in the future. Since 2004, the year of the Islamist terrorist attack in Madrid, over 80 Islamist acts have been carried out or prevented by security authorities in Europe. In those cases in which attacks were successful, about 780 people were killed and nearly 3725 injured.[1] The attacks were registered mainly in Albania, Austria, Belgium, Bosnia and Herzegovina, Denmark, France, Germany, Italy, Kosovo, the Netherlands, Norway, Spain, Sweden, Switzerland and Great Britain.

According to EUROPOL, seven Islamist attacks were committed in Europe in 2018; all attacks were organized by individuals, killing 13 people in total. 16 Islamist attacks were prevented by security authorities or failed,[2] the latter including attacks with biological weapons that were thwarted by authorities (Paris, Cologne and Sardinia). This shows that not only omnipresent weapons such as knives, axes and vehicles are used for terrorist attacks, but also nuclear, biological and chemical weapons (CBRN warfare) that are harder to come by. Furthermore, the numbers provided by EUROPOL state that 511 individuals suspected of Islamist terrorism were arrested by security authorities in 2018; in the years before, 705 individuals (2017) and even 718 individuals (2016) were arrested.[3]

According to EUROPOL's information, the number of individuals suspected of right-wing extremist terrorism that were arrested by police authorities amounts to 34 (2014), 11 (2015), 12 (2016), 20 (2017) and 44 (2018).[4] In 2015, nine right-wing extremist motivated attacks were committed in Europe, one attack in 2016, five attacks in 2017 and one attack in 2018.[5]

Islamist and Right-Wing Extremist Individuals – Lone Wolves

Analysing Islamist attacks in Europe since 2004 leads to the conclusion that all attacks can be divided into two categories: one, there are major events or multiple tactical scenarios organized

DOI: 10.4324/9781003326373-20

by so-called "hit teams", and two, there is low level-terrorism committed by Islamist individuals or small cells. As regards the operative and tactical independence/autarky or the organizational/logistical control of Islamist individuals and/or terrorist cells, it can be noted that the difference between independently operating Islamist individuals/cells and loose members or supporters of jihadist organizations (jihadist movements) is rather blurred.[6]

An evaluation of the dozens of attacks committed by Islamist individuals since 2004 emphasizes this grey area between independently operating Islamist individual attackers and their links to the Islamist/Salafist scene or even to international jihadist organizations, such as the Islamic State (IS) and al-Qaeda. EUROPOL currently stated in this regard the following: "Lone actors, however, seldom act in total isolation. They often maintain relations in loose networks or small unstructured groups, and may receive material and/or moral support from like-minded individuals".[7]

Concerning the organization and logistics of terrorist attacks, politically motivated terrorist individuals usually operate independently from any organization, network or group. They are, however, inspired by the ideology or ideas of a terrorist organization, and therefore act in line with their strategy after all. According to the most recent state of investigations, the right-wing extremist attack in Halle, Germany, on 9th October 2019 – the day of the latest Yom Kippur holiday – was committed by right-wing extremist and terrorist individual attacker (*lone wolf*) Stephan Balliet. This attack resulted in two deaths and left two severely injured. The 27-year-old far-right extremist terrorist had planned to commit mass murder in the synagogue of Halle but failed due to the barricaded entrance door. He then shot a customer of a kebap shop. The German security authorities had no knowledge or information of any kind regarding previous far-right activities by Balliet. The suspect filmed the attack online with video and streamed it to the gaming website Twitch. The entire video stream can be compared to the far-right extremist Christchurch mosque shootings in New Zealand that killed 51 Muslims.[8]

It is difficult for security authorities to prevent terrorist attacks unless individuals communicate – virtually or in reality – their attacks before they carry them out. For this reason, constitution protection authorities must monitor both virtual networks of far-right extremists and terrorists and real-life groups. Of course, this creates various problems for security authorities.[9] Far-right extremist terrorism by so-called *lone wolves* stems from the neo-Nazi idea of a *leaderless resistance* which became popular in the 1990s and originated from American Ku Klux Klan-leader Louis Beam, who strongly promoted the tactics of small cells and individual attackers with no organizational or hierarchical structures. Experiences with far-right terrorist organizations in the United States teach us that the bigger and more centrally led a potentially violent neo-Nazi group appeared to be, the faster and easier it was for U.S. security authorities to detect and fight them.[10]

Anti-Semitism in Islamism and Right-Wing Extremism

Anti-Semitism is one of the core ideological elements for both Islamism/Islamist terrorism and right-wing extremism. The enemy image of Judaism forms a central pillar upon which the lines of arguments and agitation of Islamist and far-right groups are based.[11] The term "anti-Semitism" describes the politically, socially, racially or religiously motivated hostility towards Jews, according to German constitution protection authorities.[12] Expressions and behaviours aimed at one or several Jewish people (or entire Jewish communities) are considered anti-Semitic, and it is insignificant whether this person or community is united within the State of Israel or beyond. One characteristic element of all Islamist organizations is the so-called "Islamist anti-Semitism" developed by Egyptian Islamist Sayyid Qutb.

As a result, the key idea that "Jews are secretly seeking for global supremacy" or are already exerting such power and therefore in control of the world's politics and economy is a dominant element of Islamist ideology.[13]

Anti-Semitism continues to play an important role for European far-right extremists, as it poses a steady agitation potential and is a characteristic feature for this sort of ideology, even though all anti-Semitic agitation within the right-wing spectrum has been subject to the ups and downs of day-to-day political events for years. As of right now, the far-right propaganda is dominated by other enemy images and topics, and far-right agitators are currently expecting more connections to public discourse. "Foreigners", especially asylum seekers and Muslims, as well as political decision-makers, are part of such enemy images. According to evaluations by German constitution protection authorities, topics including "foreign infiltration" and a supposed threat of losing the national identity are the main focus of concern.[14]

On Social Media channels, blogs and online comments a significant increase of anti-Semitic statements has been registered. Very often, anti-Semitic stereotypes are being used and the hatred towards Jews is put into criticism of the State of Israel. The anonymity the Internet provides also induces anti-Semites to openly express their hatred towards Jews. Hatred-filled language goes beyond virtual spaces when offenders believe they are acting and speaking for the people and in accordance with parts of society.[15]

The Transition from Far-Right Extremism to Far-Right Terrorism in Germany: Current Cases

On 7 March 2018, and following a year-long trial, the Dresden Criminal Division of the fourth regional court of appeals (Saxony) sentenced eight Germans, aged between 20 and 40, to between four and ten years in prison for forming the far-right terrorist *Freital Group* in connection with attempted murder, producing explosive devices, causing grievous bodily harm and criminal property damage.[16] The Federal Prosecutor had initiated a second preliminary investigation proceeding against nine alleged supporters of the Freital Group in 2016, but had to hand this case over to the Public Prosecutor's Office in 2017. Not until 28 March 2018, did executive measures against the ten alleged supporters of the far-right terrorist *Freital Group* take place, when the police carried out searches in Bavaria, Lower Saxony and Saxony and seized data storage devices, weapons and National Socialist memorabilia. All defendants had met during protests against a new accommodation centre for asylum seekers in 2015 in Freital, Saxony, and within a very short time had formed the *Freital Group* in order to commit (terrorist) violent and criminal acts together.[17]

On 5 July 2018, the District Court of Neuruppin (Brandenburg) sentenced an accused far-right extremist to four years and six months in prison for attempted arson, and an accomplice to suspended time of two years. The principal defendant had caused a fire by throwing two self-made incendiary devices at a housing centre for asylum seekers in Kremmen (Brandenburg). The fire was extinguished by an employee of the security guard service at the housing centre, without causing any damages to the accommodation.[18]

The District Court of Dresden sentenced a 31-year-old far-right extremist to nine years and eight months in prison for attempted murder and arson and for producing an explosive device on 31 August 2018. The defendant had detonated a pipe bomb at the Turkish Fatih Camii Mosque and in the outer zone of the International Congress Center in the eastern German city of Dresden on 26 September 2016. At the time of the crime, the imam and his family were inside the Fatih Mosque. According to the German court's ruling, the sentence was carried out due to the defendant's xenophobic and racist inhuman attitude. This specific case is a good example for radicalization processes of individuals within a cloudy, xenophobic spectrum, at the end of which the engagement in a serious (violent) offence is very likely.[19]

The investigation of the Federal Public Prosecutor pursuant to Art. 192a StGB (German Criminal Code) against an alleged far-right extremist-terrorist group called *Nordadler* (Northern Eagle), that has so far mainly been communicating virtually, proves the possibility of easy transitions from right-wing extremism to right-wing terrorism. The members of this group supposedly exchanged information online on how to procure military equipment and arms and how to manufacture explosive devices. Additionally, the accused group members are suspected of creating lists of political opponents in order to hold those persons accountable in the event of a possible state collapse.[20]

On 12 September 2018, the police searched the homes and workplaces of six suspects who had been connected with the violent, far-right extremist, neo-Nazi group *Kameradschaft Aryans* (Camaraderie Aryans), which was founded back in December of 2016 in Bavaria, Hessia, North Rhine-Westphalia, Rhineland-Palatinate and Saxony-Anhalt, with about 15 founding members. The group was established with the aim of engaging in an armed struggle against the destruction of the German people, as instigated by German politics, according to the group's point of view. The searches took place within the framework of an investigation initiated by the Federal Public Prosecutor and grounded on suspicion of forming a terrorist organization pursuant to Art. 129a of the German Criminal Code.[21]

The National Socialist Underground (*Nationalsozialistischer Untergrund, NSU*) was a far-right extremist terrorist group responsible for nine counts of murder of small business owners with migration backgrounds, the murder of a police officer, two bomb attacks, 15 robberies and at least 43 attempted murders. On 11 July 2018, the Munich Higher Regional Court sentenced Beate Zschäpe to life imprisonment for her complicity in the offences, for her membership in a terror organization and arson. Ralf Wohlleben, Carsten Schultze, Holger Gerlach and André Eminger were convicted of aiding and abetting and received between two and a half to ten years in prison. All of the accused appealed; the Federal Prosecutor appealed only in the case of André Eminger.[22] The Higher Regional Court determined a particular severity of guilt in the case of the main accused Beate Zschäpe. This made imprisonment with ordinary parole after 15 years legally possible but almost impossible in practice. Although the Public Prosecutor demanded it, the court did not order a preventive detention following Zschäpe's imprisonment.[23]

In March 2017, the Munich Higher Regional Court sentenced four members of the far-right extremist terrorist group *Oldschool Society* (OSS) to prison for between three to five years for the forming of a terrorist organization pursuant to Art. 129a StGB. The court had come to the conclusion that this very group had aimed at expelling people of non-German origin from Germany by the use of violence. In pursuit of this aim, bomb attacks on asylum centres had been planned and the far-right organization would have accepted the deaths of potential victims their plans would have caused. Therefore, the judgment is final.[24]

On 27 April 2017, the Federal Prosecutor charged two more alleged members of the *Oldschool Society* right-wing terrorist group before the state security senate of the Dresden Higher Regional Court. Both were accused of forming a terrorist organization and also of the membership in a terrorist organization pursuant to Art. 192a StGB, as well as preparing acts to cause an explosion according to Art. 310 StGB. Together with members of the *Oldschool Society*, they had allegedly planned to prepare a bomb attack on a refugee accommodation centre in Borna, Saxony in May 2015. For this reason, on 6 May 2015, a police operation took place against this group, which stopped them from carrying out their terrorist action plan.[25]

On 24 August 2018, the Dresden Regional Court sentenced two members of the far-right extremist group *Freie Kameradschaft Dresden* (Free Camaraderie Dresden, FKD) for membership in a criminal organization, aggravated battery and for causing an explosion to prison for between eight months to three years. Both accused were found guilty of having been active members within the Camaraderie and of having participated in violent acts against asylum seekers and political opponents in this regard. All offences had been planned precisely and well in advance. The *Freie Kameradschaft Dresden* itself has now been dissolved.[26]

Aforementioned far-right extremist neo-Nazi group *Kameradschaft Aryans* (Camaraderie Aryans) is also another example of formations where violence can clearly be seen. For maintaining a uniform appearance in public and during meetings, *Aryans'* members usually wear clothes that include a logo of the group, represented as imperial eagle with black, white and red wings and the word "Aryans" surrounded by a laurel wreath. The group operates on a supra-regional level and can be associated with the German neo-Nazi spectrum.[27] Already in the 2016 Annual Report on the Protection of the German Constitution, the domestic intelligence service (*Bundesamt für Verfassungsschutz, BfV*) had warned against the continuous virulent danger of far-right terrorist potentials, which are especially apparent within the anti-asylum-agitation context.[28] Therefore, on 16 March 2016, the German Federal Minister of the Interior banned the right-wing extremist organization *Weisse Wölfe Terrorcrew* (White Wolves Terror Crew) in accordance with the Associations Act. The WWT-group's purpose and activities did both not comply with German Criminal Law and were contrary to the constitutional order of the Republic of Germany. The group first made an appearance in 2008 and became active nationwide later. Its members attracted negative attention with their neo-Nazi propaganda and violent crimes. At the peak of their spread, the group was represented in ten federal states and counted between 70 and 100 members, all characterized by a considerable propensity for violence and aggression towards people with migration backgrounds, (alleged) members of the extreme left and the police, their actions very often taking place in everyday situations.[29]

The Current Threat of Islamist Terrorism in Europe

According to the Austrian Office for the Protection of the Constitution and Counter-terrorism, the biggest current threat is posed by Islamist terrorism in Austria.[30] Although there have been less Foreign Terrorist Fighters returning to Austria than expected so far, this group of jihadist returnees poses a considerable risk which is highly difficult to predict for the internal security of the Austrian state. So-called *lone wolves* (individual attackers) and very small jihadist groups are substantial risks too, as they often carry out attacks by using cutting or stabbing weapons, firearms or motor vehicles.[31]

By the end of 2018, the Office for the Protection of the Constitution and Counter-terrorism was informed of the identity of 320 Austrians who had actively participated or are still participating in the wars in Syria and Iraq. It is presumed that about 58 Austrians lost their lives in Syria/Iraq and 93 persons have returned to Austria; another 62 persons of Austrian origin could be prevented from exiting the country and are still residing in Austria. It is estimated that 107 Austrian jihadists currently remain in Syria/Iraq.[32]

There are two main threat scenarios posed by jihadist organizations and actors right now and in the future: one, the big attacks and multiple tactical scenarios planned and carried out by international jihadist organizations such as IS and al-Qaeda, and two, there are low level-attacks committed by Islamist lone wolves. Greater attacks and multiple scenarios are usually planned and carried out according to a hierarchical, top-down-principle by global jihadist associations, and they can also be referred to as "Mumbai/Paris/Brussels-style attacks". Such acts are committed by hit-teams (with or without (para)military training and/or combat experience) and present a significant challenge for security authorities and rescue services of Western states, due to their simultaneousness and the time-displaced modus of the attacks.[33]

The death of Abu Bakr Al Baghdadi, the long-time caliph of IS who committed suicide with explosives during an operation by U.S. special forces in the northwestern town of Barisha near the Turkish border, was considered an important milestone in international security policy events, especially from the U.S.' point of view ("milestone in the war against the Islamic State – and, more generally, in the struggle against terrorism")[34]. However, the assumption that Al Baghdadi's death was also the end of the Islamic State as a terrorist organization with global reach must surely be questioned.

Islamist terrorism (jihadism) is the sustainable fight for jihadist goals that must be reached by committing attacks on life, limb and property, and therefore a strategic choice of a rational, sensibly acting agent. Within jihadism, terrorist violence is a tool in the form of a communication act, used for achieving religious/political goals. The current global jihadism is characterized by a decentralized network structure on sub-state level, with multiple private sources of money and logistics, a multi-national character of its members and – unlike the ethnic-national terrorism groups (ETA, IRA) – very internationally oriented due to its global reach and religious/ideological focus.

Jihadism of the 21st century benefits from the developments of globalization, open borders, weak or no controls of borders and new and modern communication tools. Arising groups and agents use both weak and failed states of the so-called second and third world (developing countries such as Syria, Iraq, Afghanistan, Somalia) and European states with strict codes of banking secrecy, such as Switzerland or Luxemburg. International jihadist organizations dispose of organizational structures like cells and sleepers in Western, democratic states, and by networking within the Islamist milieu they also have access in African and Caucasian regions, as well as the Near and Middle East. Their jihadist ideology serves as a Trojan horse by which they infiltrate conflicts which have originally grown from regional, political, economic and ethnic conflicts. In addition to al-Qaeda, the Islamic State (IS) is at present and in the future one of the two major jihadist organizations operating worldwide. IS has a broad base of supporters in both the Islamic and the Western world. These two Islamist-jihadist movements are historically very closely connected – because of the many possibilities the Internet provides for both, among other things – and share the same ideology.[35]

Conclusion: Possible Correlation

Both the Islamist and the far-right terrorism forms reject Western democracies and their constitutional systems. Instead, they both strive for a system change and share anti-Semitism and anti-pluralism as key ideological elements. The far-right attack on Muslims during the Christchurch mosque shootings (New Zealand) on 15 March 2019, which killed 51 people and injured dozens, clearly shows that far-right terrorists consider Muslims their enemies and potential attack targets on an ideological and tactical-operative level. This could lead to a future spiral of politically motivated violence. Also, as over a million Muslims have fled to different European states in the past years, especially to Germany, dealing with refugees is an issue which has been used and still is being used by far-right extremists and terrorists ideologically and propagandistically. In relation to the refugee issue, there is a strong connection with Islamophobia among far-right extremists worldwide. Islamophobic agitation and violence committed by far-right extremists pose a potential correlation with the growing number of Salafism supporters who are growing more and more violent throughout the past years in Europe.

Assemblages and demonstrations are potential targets for both Islamist and far-right extremist terrorists. The existence of thousands of websites originating from Islamist and far-right extremists is particularly worth mentioning, as they facilitate virtual radicalization processes. Even within the so-called gaming scene, Islamists/Islamist terrorists as well as far-right extremists/far-right terrorists have become active.

Finally, it should be noted that both Islamism and Islamist terrorism as well as far-right extremism and far-right extremist terrorism are currently and in the future posing threats for the public security of European states.

Notes

1 These figures are based on the following document, in which Islamist attacks until 18 March 2019, are collected: Bundesamt für Verfassungsschutz (2019): Übersicht ausgewählter islamistisch-terroristischer Anschläge; https://www.verfassungsschutz.de/DE/themen/islamismus-und-islamistischer-terrorismus/zahlen-und-fakten/zahlen-und-fakten_node.html#doc678982bodyText4 (accessed November 30, 2019). Perpetrated or prevented Islamist attacks since March 18, 2019, were self-collected.

2 EUROPOL (2019): European Union Terrorism Situation and Trend Report 2019, p. 6.

3 Ibid., p. 29.

4 Ibid., p. 61.

5 Ibid.

6 Cf. Goertz, S. (2018): Terrorismusabwehr. Zur aktuellen Bedrohung durch den islamistischen Terrorismus in Deutschland und Europa. Wiesbaden: Springer VS, pp. 23–24.

7 EUROPOL 2019, p. 32.

8 Vgl. Goertz, S. (2019): Rechtsextremismus und Rechtsterrorismus in Deutschland. In: Sicherheits-Berater 21/2019, p. 408.

9 Ibid.

10 Ibid.

11 Cf. Bundesamt für Verfassungsschutz (2019): Antisemitismus im Islamismus, p. 5.

12 Cf. ibid., p. 8.

13 Cf. ibid., p. 20.

14 https://www.verfassungsschutz.de/DE/themen/rechtsextremismus/begriff-und-erscheinungsformen/begriff-und-erscheinungsformen_artikel.html (accessed November 30, 2019).

15 Ibid.

16 Bundesministerium des Innern/Bundesamt für Verfassungsschutz (2019): Verfassungsschutzbericht 2018, pp. 58–60.

17 Ibid., p. 59.

18 Ibid.

19 Ibid.

20 Ibid.

21 Ibid., p. 60.

22 https://www.faz.net/aktuell/politik/inland/nsu-urteile-lebenslange-haft-fuer-beate-zschaepe-15685433.html accessed November 30, 2019); https://www.veko-online.de/archiv-ausgabe-05-2019/titel-rechtsextremismus-und-rechtsextremistischer-terrorismus-in-deutschland.html?highlight=WyJyZWNodHNleHRyZW1pc211cyJd (accessed November 30, 2019).

23 Ibid.

24 Bundesministerium des Innern/Bundesamt für Verfassungsschutz (2018): Verfassungsschutzbericht 2017, p. 55; https://www.veko-online.de/archiv-ausgabe-05-2019/titel-rechtsextremismus-und-rechtsextremistischer-terrorismus-in-deutschland.html?highlight=WyJyZWNodHNleHRyZW1pc211cyJd (accessed November 30, 2019).

25 Ibid.

26 Ibid., pp. 55–56.

27 Ibid., p. 58.
28 Bundesministerium des Innern/Bundesamt für Verfassungsschutz (2017): Verfassungsschutzbericht 2016, p. 43; https://www.veko-online.de/archiv-ausgabe-05-2019/titel-rechtsextremismus-und-rechtsextremistischer-terrorismus-in-deutschland.html?highlight=WyJyZWNodHNleHRyZW1pc211cyJd (accessed November 30, 2019).
29 Ibid., p. 44
30 https://www.bvt.gv.at/401/files/Verfassungsschutzbericht2018.pdf, p. 11 (accessed November 30, 2019).
31 Ibid.
32 Ibid.
33 Ibid., pp. 19–20.
34 https://www.brookings.edu/blog/order-from-chaos/2019/10/29/al-baghdadis-death-and-that-presidential-speech/ (accessed November 30, 2019).
35 Goertz, S. (2017): Der neue Jihadismus und seine Basis. In: Die Polizei 10/2017, p. 297; Goertz, S. (2018): Der "Islamische Staat". Sein Aufstieg, sein Niedergang, seine Zukunft. In: ÖMZ 2/2018, p. 205.

18

GENERATION Z
AND TERRORISM

Carolin Görzig

Introduction

Each generation is influenced by certain events and actors, be it "Hot Wars" or Cold Wars (or their endings), the Arab Spring and Arab Winter, or gentle seasonal changes that bring about changes of no less importance, introduced by actors such as Amazon, Google or YouTube. When I was studying in Brussels my fellow American students always talked about the September 11 attacks and how this day – and everything that happened afterwards – had become a dramatic, major experience for them. Members of Generation Z, also called Generation YouTube or Generation Digital Native, is a generation of people born in the late 1990s and early 2000s. Very often Generation Z has no memories of September 11, 2001, in contrast to their parents who usually belong to Generation X (people born between 1960 and 1980). For me and my fellow students – who belong to Generation X – 9/11 was a milestone in our lives. The 50th anniversary of the birth of the Red Army Faction (RAF) was in 2020, nearly 20 years after September 11.

What would Andreas Baader have said about the September 11 attacks? Almost 25 years after his death, Usama bin Laden led al-Qaeda to commit an attack right in the heart of US capitalism – would the former leader of the left-wing militant RAF have cheered full of joy? In 1971, RAF co-founder Ulrike Meinhof wrote in an essay called "The Concept of the Urban Guerrilla" that American imperialism is a "paper tiger" which can be defeated by anti-imperialist fighting all over the world. This was expressed just in the same way by bin Laden in an interview regarding the withdrawal of the United States from Somalia. But here is a scenario to think about: does this mean the RAF and al-Qaeda would have made common cause? Even though this might seem absurd at first glance, a more thorough consideration allows us to draw the conclusion that there are in fact parallels between people who have maneuvered themselves toward the underground and who are exposed to constraints and contradictions that seem almost impossible to bear. The facts that members of the RAF wanted to get rid of the fascist legacy of their parents and at the same time were being trained by two organizations that fight against Israel, namely the Popular Front for the Liberation of Palestine (PFLP) and the Palestine Liberation Organization (PLO), clearly show what sort of contradictions are inevitable when fighting from the underground.

Stephan B., the attacker of the Halle synagogue shooting on October 9, 2019, where two people were killed after he unsuccessfully tried to enter the temple, blames the Jews for being

DOI: 10.4324/9781003326373-21

responsible for the consequences of the "Great Replacement." In 2016, Renaud Camus published his book "Revolt against the Great Replacement," which is considered the ideological basis for right-wing terrorist attacks. The criticism of the elite in Camus' book presents a seemingly paradox parallel, as the author describes how a white population is being threatened by migration. According to Camus, so-called "replacist elites" are actively engaging in a population exchange within the framework of global capitalism. He stresses that the single individual is becoming more and more interchangeable within the capitalist system. Is this criticism of the elite and of capitalism in a new guise, with the Right learning from the Left?

Terrorism evolves very slowly and unexpectedly, ranging from the Red Army Faction (RAF) to Islamist and right-wing terrorism. All of the evolvement cycles depend on both the global political happenings and the state authorities and can bring certain particularities with them. However, it is possible to draw comparisons that show that violence and counter-violence always have something in common.

A Generation Perspective

One possibility of working out the common features between violence and counter-violence is to focus on the causes and motivations of terrorism. Quite often it has been assumed that poverty, lack of opportunities or no education are reasons for resorting to terrorism. However, several study projects have been able to weaken these arguments. For example, some researchers observed that a high level of education can even be related to a more radical approach.[1] Among the right-wing extremists in Germany there are individuals right from the middle of society, and separatist movements often operate in more prosperous regions. Even though separatism does not necessarily turn into terrorism, separatist movements often "form" a radicalization environment. But how come many attackers originally come from the very heart and middle of a society and an educated, prosperous environment? One could almost say that especially the more privileged tend to be committing terrorist attacks. Moreover, upon reversion, can the conclusion be drawn that terrorism is a privilege?

Very often, narratives of the past and of the future play decisive roles for terrorist groups: far-right extremists refer to old Knights Templar orders, Islamists speak of the glorious times of Islam, and the Left pick up ideas of anarchy. Other than legitimizing their existence by putting themselves within a wider, historic framework, it is the future visions of each group that aim at mobilizing others. Sometimes these visions are apocalyptic predictions, and sometimes the creation of a new world is the main goal.

What can we assume about terrorists who do not fit into a "standard" victim pattern (poverty and lack of perspectives) but who are rewriting time and space? Why do some people put themselves voluntarily in dangerous, illegal situations even though they are actually privileged? We all know these situations: We get caught in those little white lies and suddenly everything gets out of hand until we realize that unintentionally we have put ourselves in a dilemma. But does this explain how one becomes a terrorist and how they find themselves in life-threatening situations? We could almost state that terrorists are either really stupid or competent. Life in the underground actually demands a lot of competencies for example you must differentiate clearly between friend and enemy, which is not always an easy distinction. Furthermore, people who have put themselves in the middle of such controversies are being confronted with group dynamics that can exacerbate the situation even more.

Concluding from this, it is valid to question whether the way into such tricky situations can ever be a voluntary one. Anyone who is going down the path toward illegality does not chose a life full of restrictions and contradictions – but has been subjected to particular constraints and restrictions all his or her life. The motivation can be as diverse as the individuals themselves are. Going through the biographies of radicalized individuals, a high variance can be noted.

Usama bin Laden originally came from an entrepreneurial family of multimillionaires from Saudi Arabia. What did he miss, when it looks like he had everything? Andreas Baader had to leave high school and came into conflict with the law several times. Instead of starting a professional training he made pottery and painted. The question arises as to what really drove him, and also why did he have to leave the private school (financed by his mother) even though he was considered highly gifted? Stephan B., the perpetrators of the Halle synagogue shooting in October 2019, was unemployed, railed at everything and everyone, according to his own mother, and blamed "the Jews" for his situation. Did he see himself defeated by certain constraints, and if yes, what kind of constraints were those, and did he want to rebel against them?

Millionaires' son, highly gifted dropout and unemployed individual – looking for the common denominator is quite difficult and leads to the assumption that radicalization processes are as individual as the radicalized individuals themselves are. Among them there are the more or less privileged, highly and hardly educated, wealthy persons as well as those fighting for survival. For this reason, I want to go beyond the analysis of the motivations of individuals and also examine the development of organizations and movements within the framework of which individuals are acting. Considering individuals alone and without their greater framework, or putting the investigation's focus only on organizations and without their members, bears the risk of looking at only one side of the whole story. For this reason, it makes sense to concentrate on the connection between both the individuals and the organizations: the generations.

Differences between generations influence families, organizations, and societies and can cause conflicts but also result in learning effects. Some researchers believe that generational differences automatically bring about tensions among organizations and within a society.[2] Divergent worldviews or expectations could be reasons for this, and certain structures within organizations can intensify already existing tensions among generations,[3] as is the case when power falls into the hands of a minority whose leaders do not want to create any change, for example. Such factors can hinder the transfer of knowledge and resources between generations.[4] These effects that last over generations are closely connected to constraints lived out in families, and they often determine the lives of entire generations. These constraints are in most cases the result of traumata inherited by previous generations. In systemic therapy, the generation perspective suggests that problems, conflicts or certain tasks are passed on to subsequent generations: "It is assumed that everything that happened earlier, especially subconsciously, afflicted with conflict and unresolved, continues to be effective today and to have decisive influence on all patterns of experience and behavior.[5] Transfer processes and compulsive repetition within families means to stop to evolve."[6] We can still feel the legacy of the Nazi era until this day, for example. However, as children oftentimes rebel against their parents, we experience today that grandchildren are drawing nearer to their grandparents. The so-called RAF phenomenon of the 1970s originated in unsolved problems of the parents from the time of the Nazi regime. Now the Left is revolting against the Fascist ideology, while the Far-Right is beginning to take these ideas back on.

Rapoport's "Four Waves Theory" and Terrorism's Fifth Wave

The idea of the development of terrorism throughout generations also agrees with the theory of David Rapoport, political scientist and pioneer of the study of terrorism.[7] According to Rapoport, terrorism has evolved in four overlapping historical waves since the 1880s, namely the anarchist wave (1880s–1920s), the anti-colonial wave (1920s–1960s), the New Left wave (ca. 1960s–1990s) and the current religious wave that started to spread in the 1970s and 1980s. If we are to follow Rapoport's assumption that each wave of non-state terrorism has always lasted about 40 years, with the last one – the religious wave – emerging in 1979, we are at the threshold of a new wave right now. Does this in fact mean, that a fifth wave of terrorism is currently developing? And if that is the case, is it worth taking a look back at the beginnings of terrorism?

How does anarchy or anti-colonialism relate to Generation Z? If we assume a generational pattern of passing on certain constraints, they do have much in common. In this regard, it makes sense to check the theory of four waves by Rapoport for a possible generational pattern. Additionally, it might be useful to comprehend terrorism as a reply to state terrorism, in order to be able to see the bigger picture. Terrorist groups interact with whole states and provoke them to overreact, for instance. We might even use the term "co-escalation" in this regard. If we apply this idea to the Four Waves Theory, imperialism, colonialism, capitalism, and the war against terror can be understood as the state-side counterparts of the anarchist wave, the anti-colonialism wave, the New Left wave, and the religious wave. The pattern of action – reaction, as well as state violence – non-state violence, can be projected into the future. Therefore, we can imagine a fifth wave of terrorism as a reaction to globalization.

Looking closely at the four previous waves it is interesting to note that the first and the third waves are similar, just like the second and the fourth wave resemble one another. The anarchists of the first wave of terrorism and the New Left of the third wave propagated mainly their criticism of the political system; the second anti-colonial wave and the religious fourth one had territorial claims. Islamist groups want to free territories occupied by their enemies – very often in the form of Western occupiers – which is the case in Palestine, for example. Contrary to the opinion that groups pertaining to the religious wave only have faith-related concerns on their agenda, religion often only serves as legitimization or a cover-up of secular ambitions. According to the pattern of a wave-skipping generation effect, the socialist activists of the third wave can certainly be considered the "grandchildren" of the anarchist revolutionaries, and Arabic Islamists be understood as liberators of neo-colonial oppression. The fact that one wave resembles the penultimate wave suggests that we can actually speak of a generational pattern where grandparents pass on their heritage to the grandchildren.

While "children" rebel against their "parents" and do not continue on the paths of their waves, they take on the ideas of their grandparents' generation. What can we therefore deduce from our observations on repeating developments for the next and fifth wave of terrorism? If the grandparents-grandchildren-pattern is to continue, we must assume that the fifth wave will be based on the criticism of (political) systems, and if it will be a reaction to globalization – the expression of the dominant world order – then its answer could be in the withdrawal toward the local. The strengthening of anti-liberal and far-right extremist forces is a trend which has clearly been visible with the rise of populists such as Trump and Orbán, and also with the experience of recent attacks in Christchurch, Halle, and Hanau.

Far-right extremists rely on local traditions and customs such as the connection to Germanic neo-heathenism, the American frontier mentality, or even to Christian fundamentalisms, all of which show certain parallels to the religious wave. At the same time, activists of new far-right movements such as the Identitarian Movement or the alt-right movement in the United States see themselves as revolutionary actors and take over symbols and concepts of the Left. For example, they complain about language and thinking bans as a result of liberal anti-discrimination. While right-wing attacks are often dealt with as isolated events committed by lone wolves and without considering their transnational connections,[8] an increasing perception of the level of threat is fast developing, and it is repeatedly questioned how lonely those wolves really are.

Thanks to the Internet, far-right terrorists act very globally. This could already be seen in the Christchurch attack, where the perpetrator explicitly mentioned his American role-models, the discourses and even the Norwegian attacker Breivik. There is not only a connection between the different far-right attackers but also between far-right terrorism and other forms of terrorism and violence. Metaphorically speaking, when we examine today's far-right terrorism we could describe it as the grandchild of left-wing terrorism, the stepchild of religious terrorism and the little brother of right-wing populist regimes. In any case, we cannot examine the far-right phenomena without considering historical or global developments. Left-wing terrorism, religious terrorism, far-right terrorism – they all leave traces in the changes and developments toward a fifth, right-wing terrorist wave.

Dynamics between generations can also be closely connected with pressure and constraints, the latter being also related to operating in the dark. In the underground, any form of contact and each movement can turn into a threat. What are the constraints under which far-right terrorists are operating today? What can be said, is the fact that far-right extremism is becoming both more and less visible at the same time. Far-right extremist phenomena happening in elections are more visible, for instance. The most different movements originating on the right spectrum are merging into a mishmash of European political parties, and because they do not distance themselves clearly enough from the radical milieu, they are providing even more ground for extreme right-wing views than currently exists. Furthermore, so-called troll armies swamping social media channels with their fake profiles suggest that far-right radicals have become a huge movement. There is also a simultaneous development happening in the background, which is almost impossible to assess. The police and armed forces are being infiltrated, and tendencies toward "swarm attacks" entail unpredictable individual attackers. The possibilities of fast reactions are rather limited: Even though it is possible to react to the visible actions in politics by weakening their arguments or by taking preventive steps, repressions are always reactive and can even support the development of far-right extremist structures. The phenomenon of individual attackers can also be considered an adaptation by terrorist groups to state repressions. The actions of an individual are much less traceable. Now, what can we do, and what solutions can generation Z find to get rid of the constraints its previous generation has imposed upon it? How should we deal with the far-right extremist danger, and what counter-measures and responses can we formulate?

Generations as a Source of Problem Solving

You could always choose to turn a crisis into an opportunity. Generations do not only pass on their traumata and problems but can also become the source of problem solving. Intergenerational relations do not always have to be conflictual; they can also lead to mutual learning processes. Research indicates that the mixing of generations within the Irish Republican Army (IRA) has strongly contributed to the organization developing into a more political body. Young people who are full of energy and ready for action can change their views over the years. With their peace initiative, the leaders of the IRA wanted to protect the youth from making the same mistakes again. Another example is the Egyptian Gamaa Islamija, the organization responsible for the Luxor massacre in November of 1997, which is geographically and ideologically far away from the IRA but which also turned its back on violence. According to their own words, they consider themselves young and stupid whenever they are confronted with their violent past. In about 20 books the leaders of Gamaa Islamija reflect upon their change of heart and also describe what it means for them to admit faults – a confession anything but easy to make. It is one thing to lead thousands of people and to risk their lives and then realize that everything had been a mistake. It's another level of commitment to actually communicate this mistake to those people. What can we learn from the experiences of Gamaa Islamija? Maybe the fact that generations reflect upon their mistakes and are able to communicate them? Learning processes within terrorist organizations do lead to the questioning of violence in general more often than widely expected. Also, a certain deradicalization logic can be detected in search for patterns in the development of terrorism, namely that groups do question the means and values that define their goals. These considerations can arise from the discrepancy between set and actually achieved goals, or it can be the case that goals contradict themselves and the groups then try to solve this conflict.

In order to start the mechanisms of deradicalization, the groups have to address those contradictions and problems themselves first. In their work on organization learning, scientists Chris Argyris and Donald Schön developed the concept of double-loop learning in organizational structures[9] and describe how so-called double binds should be made more discussible. Those are situations characterized by incompatible requirements where your only option is losing, never winning. Very often, however, any such contradictions are never addressed in organizations, which is for example the case whenever a leader is not aware of double binds. If a co-worker or follower is not able to articulate certain issues too, the situation becomes even more desperate: "If one wanted to design a strategy to inhibit double-loop learning and to encourage error, a better one could not be found."[10]

Is it either cognitive abilities or perception errors that explain why organizations and their members are becoming incapable of learning? According to Argyris and Schön, the problems are defensive routines, which are often enabled when they are actually the most counterproductive. Such routines develop out of feelings of shame and fear of losing countenance. The leaders of Gamaa Islamija wrote in their books how they were able to track down the causes of their mistakes and how to remedy them. They found that a lack of self-criticism, ignorance and also self-glorification are the main problems that lead to the leaders being afraid of losing their members or followers, or doing very poorly against competitors. The Gamaa Islamija leaders overcome any such fears, admit their mistakes and deal with the contradictions that have formed out of their past counterproductive violence. Continuing to fight would only lead to more victims from within their own ranks and giving up was not an option at first. This apparently hopeless situation leads to the leaders' decision to prioritize and to choose the lesser evil and opt for the greater benefit.[11] This way, they were able to resolve several double-bind situations.

Together with my research group at the Max Planck Institute for Social Anthropology in Halle, Germany, I have investigated the learning processes of Islamist, ethno-separatist, and right wing terrorist groups and compared them to each other. I found that groups who openly question the values and norms of their goals and initiate new cognitive processes within their group structures, are, in doing so, the ones most capable of learning in general. Leaders must overcome themselves in particular, and also address and deal with taboos. Looking at how groups are communicating with one another over different continents with different worldviews, and still learning new things from each other this way, is especially revealing for our research. This is the case, for example, with the Northern Irish IRA learning from the African National Congress (ANC) how far they can possibly go in negotiations, or the IRA positioning itself alongside anti-colonial fighting in India, Vietnam and Palestine. It is also the case with the Gamaa Islamija sparking a debate within Islam and projecting its findings upon al-Qaeda with the result that the latter clearly has a lack of insight into reality, because the group looks at life itself as if it was a chemistry lab.[12]

Generations of terrorist groups are influenced by global events that connect them. When I was interviewing former IRA-members in Belfast last year, the influence of the South African ANC became obvious rather quickly. Representatives of the ANC had visited prisons in Northern Ireland in order to discuss a possible change of course with IRA-members. For the leaders of the Irish Republican Army the ANC provided significant arguments, since they had successfully closed their own negotiations amongst themselves. This example made it easier for the IRA to understand that non-violence is also a tool to "win" a fight, and that peaceful change is in fact possible. An interview partner of mine told me that the meeting with the ANC had been a crucial event in his life, which had led him to rethink his entire standards.[13] The concept of "ideas travel "shows its fruits with this example of the Northern Ireland conflict, where Catholics often consider themselves similar to the South African black population, and Protestants to the white one.

Sometimes terrorist groups learn something by separating themselves from one another. For instance, members of the IRA distance themselves from the German RAF by stating that they are not a group of six against six million; instead, the IRA really carries weight.[14] But actually, being invisible brings tactical advantages, because the hunt for catching the three criminal members of the RAF from the third generation would definitely have been a lot more difficult if the support network had been smaller, which could bust them. The more visible terrorist groups become, the more responsibility they have to assume and break the taboo which often dominates such groups, namely giving up the fight. For some a taboo break might mean protection from a taboo break for others. For example: there are strong reasons for some taboos, such as the ban of Nazi insignia in Germany or the drawing of Mohammed caricatures. Making the non-discussable discussable again can help to prevent the following generation from blundering into hopeless situations and restrictions.

Final Remarks: The Generation Z and Terrorism

What are the constraints the Generation Z is dealing with? What possibilities does it have? Generation Z is often named" Generation YouTube "or "Generation Digital Natives." Could it be the Internet itself that provides the necessary tools to make the unspeakable speakable? Or is it mainly hate that is being communicated via the global network? Both scenarios are possible. On the one hand, filter bubbles and likes can hinder your own capabilities of questioning information. Hate is also becoming more and more acceptable online thanks to certain dynamics, such as considering it "cool" to create extreme posts. On the other, new ways for communication and information are evolving that can bring transparency along with them too. Digital libraries could contribute to taking a new look at historical connections, for instance. The creation of new and common identities can reduce tensions. Historians could turn into agents of conflict transformation within conflict situations such as the current one between Israel and Palestine. Historiography has a lot to do with acknowledgement. Therefore, the digitalization of knowledge should play a role in this regard too.

The statements of members of terrorist groups can also turn into sources of cognitive processes and conflict transformation. In one of their books, the leaders of Gamaa Islamija mention that, unfortunately, all human beings only have one life instead of two – one life to collect experiences and a second to learn from these. But the reality is that both must take place within one lifetime only.[15] Each generation collects its experiences but can also learn from the past and future generations. Until the 20th century, intergenerational learning meant that the elders passed on their knowledge to the young. However, digitalization and modernization have led to the younger generation teaching the old one their knowledge and to the introduction of the new term of "life-long learning": "The different generations must in fact learn from one another and with each other, in order to deal with complex social challenges."[16] Whether it be conflict-ridden or solution-oriented: the effects of certain powers across generations influence and characterize individuals, organizations, and movements all the same.

What will Generation Z teach us about terrorism? Terrorist groups create visions of both the past and the future, maybe because their present means they have to spend their lives in secrecy and under pressure. But terrorist groups also learn in the here and now. Unexpected events may completely turn history upside down and influence entire generations. The coronavirus pandemic, for instance, which overran and has overwhelmed us since the beginning of 2020, can play into the hands of terrorists Wherever states are failing, terrorist groups fill this gap and offer their social services in order to mobilize as many members as possible. With terrorist groups filling new niches, the response of the state is decisive. Regarding COVID-19, the war rhetoric of some heads of state suggests that we are currently facing a fight with nature. The call from UN Secretary General Guterres for a global ceasefire shows that things can be handled and solved differently, a fact also shown by the efforts of the youngest generation in protecting the climate. What sort of past, present and future tenses will Generation Z create? What kind of historical footprint will the Digital Natives leave and what taboos will they break?

Generation Z is characterized not only by the Internet or the current coronavirus pandemic. It is also the result of its members' parents', grandparents' and great-grandparents' influence. Each and every one of us is a child of our time, following certain trails and leaving traces behind. Gamaa Islamija compared its renunciation of violence with flying a plane: with no communication, you are in danger of crashing. On the other hand, al-Qaeda was described by the Gamaa Islamija member with the image of a driverless car.[17] Gamaa Islamija's approach shows how easy it is to lose one's track, and how communication can help with finding the way back – sometimes such accidents even make history, when people set out on a journey and eventually find something else, as numerous examples of historical discoveries show. Terrorist groups also live with the unexpected. Witnessing members of terrorist organizations who end up in prison and who – against the assumption of further radicalization – undergo a process of self-education and reflection is especially revealing. Imprisoned Gamaa Islamija leaders and members did understand very well how counterproductive their fight had been, especially for themselves. In their books, they even warn other Muslim brothers against falling into the trap of the thesis of the clash of civilizations.[18] This means they have been using western narratives and exposed their radicalization potential.

Not all issues can be solved and corrected at any time. Sometimes we learn from the mistakes our role models have made, sometimes we make mistakes ourselves and sometimes we are shaking the status quo. If we dare to play an optimistic mental game, both digitalization and globalization could make the concepts of borders, identities, and enemy stereotypes obsolete. It is almost ironic that Gamaa Islamija – a former Islamist terrorist group – warns against the "Clash of Civilizations" trap. Peace must be worth it, as one member of the IRA mentioned: "We all wanted peace, but not at any price."[19] Just how high must any effort be in order to reshuffle the pack and for revolutions to become redundant? Members of terrorist groups not only want to physically leave prison one day, but to also leave their imprisonment mentally behind. Questioning the repetitive patterns of violence and counter-violence could contribute to breaking mental limits and to strengthening the imaginative power for creating a peaceful world. Breaking up generational borders could definitely support this quest.

Notes

1 Mark Sageman exposes myths on the causes of radicalization and focuses on group dynamics. See also: Mark Sageman (2020): *Turning to Political Violence. The Emergence of Terrorism* (University of Pennsylvania Press, Philadelphia).

2 Katrina Pritchard, Rebecca Whiting (2014): "Baby Boomers and the Lost Generation: On the Discursive Construction of Generations at Work", in: *Organization Studies* 35 (11), pp. 1605–26.; Vasanthi Srinivasan (2012): "Multi Generations in the Workforce: Building Collaboration", in: *IIMB Management Review* 24 (1), pp. 48–66.; Joseph R Gusfield (1956): "The Problem of Generations in an Organizational Structure", in: *Social Forces* 35, p. 323.

3 Joseph R. Gusfield (1956): "The Problem of Generations in an Organizational Structure", in: *Social Forces* 35, p. 323.

4 Kimberly A. Wade-Benzoni (2002): "A Golden Rule over Time: Reciprocity in Intergenerational Allocation Decisions", in: *Academy of Management Journal* 45 (5) pp. 1011–28.

5 Günter Reich, Almuth Massing, Manfred Cierpka: Die Mehrgenerationenperspektive und das Genogramm, in: Manfred Cierpka [ed.] (2003): *Handbuch der Familiendiagnostik* (New York, NY: Springer, Berlin, Heidelberg), pp. 223–258.

6 Eckhard Sperling, Almuth Massing et al. (1982): Die Mehrgenerationen-Familientherapie (Verlag für Medizinische Psychologie: Göttingen); Massing, Almuth., Reich, Günter., Sperling, Eckhard. (1994): *Die Mehrgenerationen-Familientherapie* (Göttingen: Vandenhoeck und Ruprecht)

7 David C. Rapoport: The four waves of modern terrorism, in: Cronin, Audrey. Kurth.; Ludes, James. M. [eds.] (2004): Attacking Terrorism: Elements of a Grand Strategy (Washington, D. C.: Georgetown University Press).

8 Chris Allen (2019): "Nur"einsame Wölfe"? Rechtsterrorismus als transnationales Phänomen, Bundeszentrale für politische Bildung: https://www.bpb.de/apuz/301134/nur-einsame-woelfe-rechtsterrorismus-als-transnationales-phaenomen (accessed on 01.09.2020).

9 Chris Argyris, Donald A. Schön (1978): *Organizational Learning: A Theory of Action Perspective* (Reading: Addison-Wesley Publishing Company), pp. 20–29; see also Chris Argyris, Donald A. Schön (1995): *On Organizational Learning II: Theory, Method, and Practice* (Boston: Addisson-Wesley); Chris Argyris, Donald A. Schön (2018): *Die lernende Organisation: Grundlagen, Methode, Praxis* (Stuttgart: Schäffer Poeschel).

10 Argyris and Schön, Organizational learning, pp. 3–4.: "If one wanted to design a strategy to inhibit double-loop learning and to encourage error, a better one could not be found."

11 Karam Zuhdi et al. (2002): *Al-Qaida's Strategy and Bombings: Errors and Dangers* (Istratijiyat wa Tafjirat al-Qa'ida: al-Akhta' wa al-Akhtar), Corrective Concepts Series (Cairo: Maktaba al-Turath al-Islami), p. 147.

12 Karam Zuhdi et al.: *Al-Qaida's Strategy and Bombings: Errors and Dangers* (Istratijiyat wa Tafjirat al-Qa'ida: al-Akhta' wa al-Akhtar), Cairo 2002, pp. 200–201.

13 Interview 8 in Belfast, 2017 (former PIRA member).

14 Interview 6 in Belfast, 2017.

15 Hamdi Abd-al-Rahman 'Abd al-Azim, Najih Ibrahim, and Ali Mohammad al-Sharif (2002): *Shedding Light on Errors Committed in Jihad* (Taslit al-adwa 'alama waga' fi' al-jihad min akhta'), Corrective Concepts Series (Cairo: Maktaba al-Turath al-Islami, 2002), p. 117.

16 Julia Franz (2014): *Intergenerationelle Bildung. Lernsituationen Gestalten und Angebote Entwickeln* (Bielefeld: W. Bertelsmann).

17 Interview in Cairo, 2006.

18 Karam Zuhdi et al.: *Al-Qaida's Strategy and Bombings: Errors and Dangers* (Istratijiyat wa Tafjirat al-Qa'ida: al-Akhta' wa al-Akhtar), Cairo 2002, p. 314.

19 Interview 8 in Belfast, 2017 (former PIRA member): "we all wanted peace, but not at any price".

19

STOCHASTIC TERRORISM

Mass Media Escalation Against Victim Groups as a Radicalization Platform for Terrorist Individual Perpetrators?

Karolin Schwarz

The attacks by right-wing extremist and Islamist alleged "lone wolves" in the 2010s put pressure on security agencies and academia to explain the killings. This is especially true of the right-wing terrorist attacks on a church in Charleston (South Carolina) in 2015 and a synagogue in Pittsburgh (Pennsylvania) in 2018 and the subsequent attacks in Christchurch, Poway (California), El Paso (Texas), Bærum and Halle in 2019. In all these cases, the perpetrators announced their attacks online on imageboards and, in one case, on the social media platform Gab. Almost all of them also published pamphlets in which they explained their motivations and ideology, sometimes in more, sometimes in less detail. Two of them succeeded in broadcasting their attack live on the Internet: Brenton T. in Christchurch and Stephan B. in Halle.

In response to the terrorists' deeds and obvious references to right-wing extremist online subcultures, which can be found in references and inside "jokes" in their writings, two lines of explanation were frequently discussed. On the one hand, the "gamification of terror",[1] which refers to terrorist fan communities on the Internet, in which, among other things, lists ranking perpetrators by the numbers of murders they committed are circulated. Stephan B., who killed two people during a terrorist attack targeting a synagogue and a kebab shop in Halle, also published a series of "achievements" that he considered desirable for his attack. He named possible victims and different methods of killing people. These references, which can be traced back to the world of gaming, led some experts to the conclusion that the killings were being gamified here. However, other references, for example to anime in Stephan B.'s pamphlet, can also be found in the writings of the perpetrators. Brenton T., on the other hand, made fun of the debate on the possible radicalization of terrorists and school shooters via games and gaming platforms in a document he published, claiming to have been radicalized by a children's game.

Another paradigm that is used to explain the attacks is "stochastic terrorism". The concept suggests that terrorist acts that appear randomly are the effect of mass media radicalization. Two characteristics of the terrorist attacks of recent years relate to this: First, there is the fact that the perpetrators are usually not formal members of any right-wing extremist or terrorist organizations. Moreover, mass media, especially digital platforms, play a central role:

1 For the radicalization of the terrorists, particularly through the construction and constant thematization of their "enemies" on the Internet.

DOI: 10.4324/9781003326373-22

2 For the dissemination of imagery of the attacks and the perpetrators and their propaganda material.

The Internet is used constantly to construct and reinforce the extremists' bogeymen. This is especially true on the platforms that Islamists and right-wing extremists have appropriated and built up themselves in recent years. But it also applies to the platforms that are frequented by the broad public and mass media, which have been massively used by hatemongers in recent years to place their ideology with a broad reach. Organized right-wing extremists had begun to strategically use the Internet as early as in the 1990s and 2000s. This applies both to addressing potential new supporters and to networking among themselves. Over the years, they developed new platforms and tools and formulated and perfected their strategies, so that today it is hardly surprising that they are often several steps ahead of public authorities and tech companies. For a long time, the deadly potential of their actions was simply not taken seriously enough.

Lone(ly) Wolves?

It usually follows the same pattern: after a terrorist attack, the focus of politics, security authorities and the media is first directed at the perpetrators. People want to know: How could this happen? What kind of person was the perpetrator? When and why did he decide to take action? It is also common to try to use psychological disorders to explain the causes of attacks. This is shown not least by the long struggle to classify David S.'s attack on the Olympia-Einkaufs-Zentrum in Munich in July 2016. The attack was only classified as right-wing years later. Many right-wing personalities often try to absolve themselves of any responsibility for violent acts by declaring the perpetrators to not be sane. However, this explanation is inadequate. On the one hand, because less than half of the perpetrators are considered to be mentally ill[2] and, on the other hand, because mental illness is not a sufficient explanation for why the perpetrators direct their hatred toward marginalized groups. The overwhelming majority of perpetrators acting alone are male. A majority of them are also unmarried, and while some can be described as socially isolated, others cultivated social contacts away from the Internet.[3]

The biographies of the perpetrators were analyzed and compared when possible in recent years. However, it is not possible to draw up a generally valid profile of lone-actor terrorists. Even though there are often similarities between them, a look at the perpetrators alone is not enough and carries the danger of individualizing right-wing terrorism. It is essential, however, to also include the digital communities to which they refer and which they want to impress with their actions.[4] In the digital age, those who incite hatred and violence online and normalize dehumanizing expressions are partly to blame for the violence.

A Look at the Digital Environment of the Perpetrators

The range of options for right-wing extremists on the Internet is overwhelmingly large. This not only applies to the sheer mass of accounts on mainstream platforms such as Facebook, Twitter, YouTube and Instagram. Additionally, many far-right actors use alt-tech platforms, a sphere of alternative platforms and apps that right-wing extremists have appropriated or created after mainstream platforms increasingly intervened by moderating content. Above all, this also applies to the different audiences that are being targeted today. Whether young or old, gamers, literature lovers, athletes or fans of conspiracy theories - the scene has become considerably more differentiated in recent years and is subject to constant change. The movement of refugees to Europe, especially to Germany, has benefited above all racist and Islamophobic actors since 2015 and 2016. The ongoing crisis triggered by the coronavirus pandemic in 2020 benefited conspiracy ideologues in particular, who were active as influencers on Telegram or other platforms or in anonymous communities like the conspiracy theorist movement QAnon.[5]

Right-wing extremist actors use the Internet in a targeted manner to attract new supporters and radicalize accordingly. The term "red pill" has become established in far-right circles, at least among some groups. The term is used as a reference to the film "The Matrix", in which the protagonist, Neo, is confronted with the choice of swallowing a blue pill that ensures that the world in which he used to live does not change for him. The red pill in turn causes Neo to recognize reality as such. Among right-wingers, the "red pill" is now used as a synonym for the appropriation of right-wing ideology.

Researcher Luke Munn has used videos, chat transcripts and posts by members of the Alt-Right to investigate their individual radicalization.[6] He found that the development can be divided into three phases, which, however, do not have to be distinctly linear, but can also overlap: Normalization, acclimatization, and dehumanization. Based on the results, it can be traced that radicalization is also by no means to be seen as a singular event, i.e., the symbolic taking of a single "red pill", but rather that different set pieces of right-wing extremist ideology are consumed and internalized progressively online. The dosage form varies: From YouTube videos to podcasts, from music to memes.[7]

In addition, time does not matter: in contrast to far-right concerts, trips and demonstrations off the Internet, content can be viewed and distributed at will, whenever the recipients want to. Communication can also be time-delayed, for example via chats or imageboards. Thus, the total amount of right-wing extremist propaganda available online – if it is not deleted – is continuously growing.

The terrorists of Christchurch, El Paso, Bærum and Halle used imageboards like 8chan, Endchan and Meguca to publish their pamphlets, photos and links to their live streams. It is no coincidence that these platforms were chosen. Hate and the glorification of violence are part of the tone of conversation on many of these forums. This is especially true for the subforums/pol/ and/b/, which are part of the repertoire on many imageboards. Studies confirm, for example, that 4chan has a significantly higher percentage of hate postings than other platforms. This also applies to antisemitism, which is cultivated there. The percentage of antisemitic and negatively stereotyping posts is higher on 4chan than on Reddit and Twitter, for example.[8]

The glorification of violence against minorities and women is part of the norm on imageboards. In threads about right-wing terrorist attacks, open denouncement of violence tends to be present in a minority of posts and is often linked to authors expressing fear that their forums will be shut down. If terrorists spread their announcements and propaganda PR packages on imageboards, the role of the recipients in these online communities is usually predefined by the perpetrators. One of the goals expressed by far-right terrorists is being included in the ranking of terrorists who have their own fan communities. In addition, their audience is supposed to spread terrorist propaganda by distributing the pamphlets, videos and photos not only on imageboards, but also on as many platforms and accounts as possible. After the Christchurch attack, Brenton T.'s propaganda strategy worked, at least for a while: The video showing his murders was uploaded in hundreds of different versions several million times on platforms like Facebook, YouTube and Twitter. The digital terrorist fan community became the terrorist's extended arm.

Terrorist Fan Communities Beyond Imageboards

In August 2019, right-wing terrorist Patrick C. carried out an attack on the premises of a supermarket in El Paso, Texas, in which 23 people died. Like Brenton T., he published a pamphlet on

8chan. As a consequence, several service providers terminated their contracts with 8chan, which ultimately resulted in the site being unavailable for a prolonged period of time. Many image-boards have backup forums that are kept ready in case of a possible shutdown. 8chan was also initially accessible via darknet and is now back online under a new name. Nevertheless, the fan scene of right-wing terrorists has sought another digital home by switching to Telegram. There has been a network of numerous channels on Telegram in which the terrorists are being wor-shipped. All in all, right-wing extremists have discovered Telegram as one of the most important platforms in recent years, following Islamist groups that had already discovered the messenger service for themselves earlier.

Many of the channels supporting terrorists include uploads of terrorist pamphlets. Neo-Nazi and antisemitic book classics such as "Siege", "The Turner Diaries" and the "Protocols of the Elders of Zion" can be found there, as well as instructions on how to build weapons and bombs and relevant music.

It can be expected that the scene on Telegram will continue to play an important role. Although Telegram has deleted several right-wing extremist channels, the operators of Telegram channels are very well interlinked, so that the operators of deplatformed channels can easily cre-ate new channels and advertise them. Just as right-wing extremists are represented online in a decentralized manner on all conceivable platforms, communities dedicated to glorifying terror-ism are also constantly diversifying their presence.

Sometimes Socially Isolated – but No Lonely Wolves

Although these right-wing terrorists of recent years are not formally members of right-wing extremist organizations, their attacks can be summarized into a series within which several similarities are striking:

1 announcements: The attacks were announced on relevant online platforms that are popular with right-wing extremists, such as imageboards and the Twitter alternative Gab.
2 "role models": The majority of the perpetrators reference other attacks in their pamphlets and posts, especially the attack by Anders B. in Oslo and on Utøya in 2011.
3 Community: The jargon of the perpetrators often suggests that the perpetrators have spent some time on the platforms where they leave announcements and pamphlets. In many cases, the users of the imageboards and alternative platforms are also addressed directly.

The perpetrators consider their possible fan base while writing their scripts and announce-ments. Often they have studied previous attacks in detail. For example, the court case against Stephan B. has demonstrated that he dedicated a considerable amount of time to studying the attacks in Christchurch, El Paso and Bærum.

The terrorists see themselves as a community, which in turn is embedded in the circle of their fan communities. The terrorist from Halle did not want to disappoint his potential fans: This became apparent when he repeatedly called himself a failure during the attack. The significance of the digital communities he frequented is demonstrated by the fact that he refused to provide any information about them in court. Stephan B. also wanted to contribute to future terrorist attacks: his stated goal was to demonstrate the use of self-made weapons.

It is essential to include the terrorists' digital contacts in the evaluation of their crimes and the elaboration of possible consequences and prevention programs. Beyond anonymous forums such as 4chan, there is sufficient evidence that relationships among right-wing extremists are established and maintained via the Internet – and possibly even beyond the Internet. Brenton T. sought contact to right-wing extremist organizations worldwide via the Internet, and David S. was celebrated online by William A. from the United States after the attack in Munich. A. shot two Hispanic students at a high school in New Mexico a few months after the Munich attack. The two murderers were operating a racist group on the gaming platform Steam.

The ideological references of the terrorists of recent years are by no means new. However, digital relationships, both one-sided and reciprocal, are becoming increasingly important. The digital communities are above all complementary to the existing networks and forms of organization that continue to spawn terrorists. These include the murderer of the German politician Walter Lübcke in June 2019, for example, as well as the terror cell of the National Socialist Underground, whose network was not disbanded after the core cell's self-exposure. And even if Stephan E., the murderer of Walter Lübcke, was well networked with other neo-Nazis for many years away from the Internet, the digital hate community still played a role for him. E. was present when Walter Lübcke addressed agitators present at a citizens' meeting and suggested to them that if someone could not identify with the values of a country, they could leave it. The meeting was held to discuss the admission of refugees into Germany. E. filmed the scene and later uploaded it to YouTube. It came to be the trigger for years of hatred, which unleashed itself towards Lübcke. Digital hatred was also a factor in the recent Islamist attack on a history teacher in France. Islamists had called for acts of violence in dozens of posts on the Internet.

The Internet has long served as a tool for forming and maintaining relationships. This also applies to right-wing extremists and Islamists. After the coronavirus pandemic only increased people's time being spent online, it is to be expected that violent far-right extremists will not lose interest in weaponizing digital tools to radicalize their audiences.

Notes

1 Robert Evans (2019): "The El Paso shooting and the gamification of terror"; Bellingcat; URL: https://www.bellingcat.com/news/americas/2019/08/04/the-el-paso-shooting-and-the-gamification-of-terror/ (accessed October 21, 2020).
2 Paul Gill & John Hogan (2013): "Bombing Alone: Tracing the Motivations and Antecedent Behaviors of Lone-Actor Terrorists"; *Journal of Forensic Sciences 59* (2), 2014, pp. 425–435; 431.
3 Ibid, 432.
4 Stefan Malthaner (2020): Einzeltäterschaft, relational betrachtet. Radikalisierungsszenarien. - In: Mittelweg 36. 29 (2020), 4/5, pp. 119–144.
5 Maik Fielitz & Karolin Schwarz (2020): "Hate not found", IDZ Jena, https://www.idz-jena.de/fileadmin//user_upload/Hate_not_found/IDZ_Research_Report_Hate_not_Found.pdf
6 Luke Munn (2019): "Alt-right pipeline: Individual journeys to extremism online"; First Monday; URL: https://firstmonday.org/ojs/index.php/fm/article/view/10108 (accessed October 21, 2020).
7 Richard Kearney (2019): "Meme frameworks. A semiotic perspective on internet memes"; URL: https://brill.com/view/journals/vjep/4/2/article-p82_82.xml?body=fullHtml-33150#FN000007 (accessed October 21, 2020).
8 Katie Cohen, Lisa Kaati, Björn Pelzer, Nazar Akrami (2020): "Antisemitiska stereotyper i digitala medier"; URL: https://www.foi.se/report-summary?reportNo=FOI%20Memo%207292 (accessed October 21, 2020).

20

THE HEIGHTENED THREAT OF U.S. DOMESTIC TERRORISM

Catrina Doxsee

Recent data on terrorist attacks and plots indicate that the threat of terrorism in the United States has both grown and fundamentally changed in nature in recent years—and now the government is struggling to keep pace. In 2020 and 2021, the number of U.S. terrorist attacks and plots reached its highest levels in at least three decades.[1] Despite the heightened threat from terrorism in the United States, the threat from individuals inspired by Salafi-jihadist ideologies—the primary focus of U.S. counterterrorism efforts since September 11, 2001—has decreased. Most recent U.S. terrorist attacks and plots have been perpetrated by individuals with violent far-right extremist views, including white supremacists and anti-government paramilitary networks. A smaller but growing number of incidents were conducted by individuals with violent far-left extremist beliefs, such as anarchists and anti-fascist extremists.

Efforts to counter domestic terrorism in the United States have historically been reactive, and the present is no exception. Within the past five years, political attention on coordinated violent far-right activity grew following the August 2017 Unite the Right rally in Charlottesville, Virginia, during which a counterprotester was killed in a vehicle ramming attack. More recently, the federal government began a series of reviews and policy efforts to improve its counterextremism capabilities in direct response to the January 6, 2021, attack at the U.S. Capitol.

Based on an analysis of terrorist attacks and plots in the United States between 1994 and 2021, the recent increase in domestic terrorist activity—primarily driven by perpetrators motivated by violent far-right ideologies—actually began around 2014.[2] Yet, as recently as 2019, the Department of Homeland Security (DHS) continued to prioritize Salafi-jihadist threats and even redirected funds intended to combat white supremacist extremism to support counter-jihadist activities.[3]

While a variety of factors contributed to the delayed governmental response to the growing threat from domestic extremists in the United States, it is particularly notable that the government does not currently have a centralized or standardized mechanism to track and analyze data on domestic terrorist incidents. Without this type of analysis, policymakers will continue to struggle to identify the most pressing threats and to shift their focus—including the allocation of resources—to the most appropriate counterterrorism activities.

This chapter analyzes a data set of terrorist incidents to identify trends in the nature and prevalence of domestic terrorism in the United States, and it assesses recent federal efforts to combat domestic violent extremism. Amid renewed focus on domestic terrorism in the United States,

DOI: 10.4324/9781003326373-23

policymakers have a rare opportunity to construct new, data-driven approaches to understand and prevent domestic terrorism.

The remainder of the chapter is divided into four sections. The first section provides a brief overview of the definitions of terrorism and terrorist ideologies used throughout the analysis. The second highlights key data trends in the characteristics of U.S. domestic terrorist incidents and their perpetrators. The third assesses ongoing U.S. government efforts to understand and counter domestic extremism. Finally, the fourth outlines brief implications for U.S. policymakers.

Definitions

Within this analysis, domestic terrorism is defined as deliberate acts or threats of violence by non-state actors within the 50 U.S. states, the District of Columbia, or Puerto Rico in order to achieve a political goal and create a broad psychological impact. This definition, particularly its focus on *violence*, is consistent with the U.S. government's definition of domestic terrorism. U.S. Code—the official compilation and codification of laws in the United States—defines domestic terrorism as "acts dangerous to human life" that occur primarily within U.S. territory and that are intended "(i) to intimidate or coerce a civilian population; (ii) to influence the policy of a government by intimidation or coercion; or (iii) to affect the conduct of a government by mass destruction, assassination, or kidnapping".[4]

This chapter addresses four broad categories of extremist ideologies: far-right, far-left, religious, and ethnonationalist. Far-right extremists are motivated by ideas of racial or ethnic supremacy; opposition to government authority; misogyny, including incels ("involuntary celibates"); hatred based on sexuality or gender identity; belief in the QAnon conspiracy theory; or opposition to certain policies, such as abortion.[5] Far-left extremists are motivated by an opposition to capitalism, imperialism, or colonialism; Black nationalism; support for environmental causes or animal rights; pro-communist or pro-socialist beliefs; or support for decentralized political and social systems, such as anarchism. Religious extremists are motivated by a faith-based belief system, such as Christianity, Hinduism, Islam, Judaism, or other faiths. In recent U.S. history, religious terrorism has predominantly involved individuals inspired by the Salafi-jihadist beliefs of international terrorist organizations such as al-Qaeda and the Islamic State. Finally, ethnonationalist extremists are motivated by ethnic or nationalist goals, including self-determination.

Trends

This analysis utilizes a data set of 1,040 terrorist attacks and plots in the United States between January 1, 1994, and December 31, 2021, compiled by the Transnational Threats Project at the Center for Strategic and International Studies (CSIS).[6] The following subsections examine recent trends in the number of U.S. domestic terrorist attacks and plots, the number of fatalities, and the most frequent targets.

Attacks and Plots

The recent escalation in U.S. domestic terrorist activity began in approximately 2014 and reached historic highs in 2020 and 2021.[7] There were 110 U.S. terrorist attacks and plots in 2020 and 77 attacks and plots in 2021—the largest numbers of annual terrorist incidents since the beginning of the data set in 1994. Of the 77 terrorist attacks and plots that occurred in 2021, violent far-right extremists conducted 38 incidents, violent-far left extremists conducted 31, religious

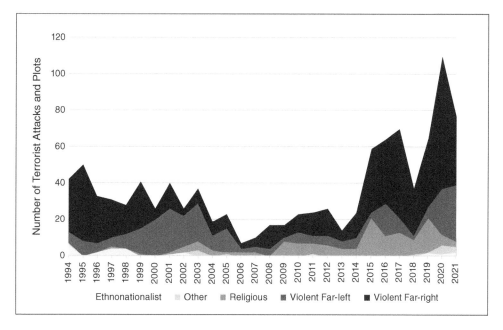

Figure 20.1   U.S. Terrorist Attacks and Plots by Ideology, 1994–2021

Source: CSIS Transnational Threats Project.

extremists (all of which were Salafi-jihadists) conducted 3, and ethnonationalists and individuals with other motives conducted 5 (Figure 20.1).

The large number of attacks and plots motivated by far-right beliefs is consistent with trends over the past five years. Violent far-right extremists such as white supremacists, militia members, and other anti-government extremists committed 62 percent of all U.S. terrorist attacks and plots between 2017 and 2021. In 2020—the year with the largest amount of domestic terrorist activity—violent far-right individuals conducted 66 percent of all domestic terrorist attacks and plots. Throughout 2020 and 2021, far-right extremist violence frequently occurred in response to racial justice demonstrations; federal, state, and local policy responses to the Covid-19 pandemic, which some anti-government extremists perceived as infringing on individual liberties; and the 2020 presidential election—both during the campaign and after the election, amid claims that the election had been "stolen" by then-president-elect Joe Biden.

Although less frequent than violent far-right incidents, the number of domestic terrorist attacks and plots committed by violent far-left perpetrators such as anarchists and anti-fascist extremists increased between 2019, when they composed 9 percent of domestic terrorist attacks and plots, and 2021, when they made up 40 percent of attacks and plots. With this recent increase included, violent far-left extremists committed 20 percent of U.S. terrorist attacks and plots in the past five years, from 2017 to 2021.

The growth in violent far-left activity was likely a response to the frequency of far-right violence in 2020. Far-left extremists cite concerns that the government cannot—or will not—respond adequately to far-right extremism, and they use this as justification for "direct action" campaigns, during which they seek to disrupt far-right demonstrations and activities, including through violence if deemed necessary. For example, Rose City Antifa—an anti-fascist network in Portland, Oregon, that is reportedly the oldest anti-fascist organization in the country—explains on its website that it does not rely on government protection because the "state upholds white supremacy at every level of government and the police frequently work with far-right aggressors to brutalize people opposing state oppression and violence. We cannot count on state actors to push forward the cause of justice, equity, and community safety. It's up to us to keep us safe".[8]

Furthermore, recent CSIS analysis found that amid the historically high levels of both far-right and far-left terrorism in 2020 and 2021, there was a significant increase in the portion of U.S. terrorist attacks and plots occurring at demonstrations in metropolitan areas—both committed by and against protesters.[9] As demonstrations and counterdemonstrations generate conflict, a security dilemma effect has developed, in which attempts by either "side" to protect itself threaten the security of its opponents, increasing tensions and the likelihood of violence.[10]

In a further indication of the changing nature of terrorism in the United States, Salafi-jihadist-inspired attacks and plots have decreased since 2019. Salafi-jihadists committed 29 percent (19 incidents) of terrorist attacks and plots in 2019, but this portion fell to 5 percent (6 incidents) in 2020 and 4 percent (3 incidents) in 2021.

Fatalities

Apart from 2020, the number of fatalities from terrorist attacks in the United States each year has remained high amid elevated levels of extremist violence (Figure 20.2). Between 2014 and 2021, there were, on average, 31 annual deaths from terrorism in the United States. The largest number of fatalities—66 deaths—occurred in 2016, making it the third deadliest year for terrorism fatalities in modern U.S. history, after 2001 and 1995.[11] Although the number of terrorism-linked fatalities in the United States fell to five in 2020—the lowest level since 2013—this appears to have been an anomaly. In 2021, the number of fatalities increased to 30.

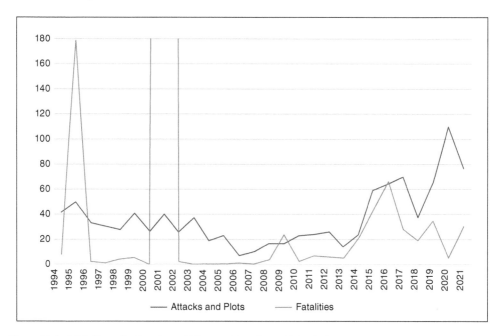

Figure 20.2 U.S. Terrorist Attacks and Plots and Fatalities, 1994–2021

Source: CSIS Transnational Threats Project.

Violent far-right extremists, including white supremacists, violent misogynists, and anti-government extremists, committed the majority of fatal terrorist attacks. Between 2017 and 2021, far-right terrorist attacks caused 73 percent (85 of 117) of terrorism-linked fatalities in the United States. For example, in March 2021, Robert Aaron Long shot and killed eight people during a shooting spree at three spas in the Atlanta, Georgia, metropolitan area. Long chose to target the spas because he believed that the women working in these businesses were the cause of sex addiction.[12]

During the same time period, Salafi-jihadist terrorist attacks resulted in 16 percent (19 of 117) of all terrorist fatalities, and far-left terrorist attacks produced 9 percent (11 of 117) of fatalities. In October 2017, for example, Sayfullo Habibullaevic Saipov drove a rental truck down a bike path in Manhattan, killing eight individuals. Saipov had pledged allegiance to the Islamic State and had intended to indiscriminately kill as many people as possible.[13] In August 2020, self-identified anti-fascist Michael Reinoehl shot and killed Aaron "Jay" Danielson, a member of the far-right group Patriot Prayer, at a demonstration in Portland, Oregon.[14]

Regardless of ideology, the perpetrators of most fatal domestic terrorist attacks in recent years killed their victims with firearms. Between 2017 and 2021, firearms caused 83 percent (97 of 117) of fatalities in U.S. terrorist attacks. The widespread availability of firearms in the United States is of substantial concern amid heightened political tensions and threats of domestic terrorism. Moreover, the number of firearms in the country increased more rapidly than usual during the Covid-19 pandemic with gun sales spiking in 2020.[15]

Targets

The most frequent targets of domestic terrorist attacks between 2017 and 2021, as well as in 2020 and 2021, were, individually, government, military, and law enforcement locations and personnel. These targets were commonly chosen by extremists of all ideologies. In 2021, government, military, and law enforcement targets were attacked in 33 of 77 incidents and were the most frequently selected targets by violent far-right, violent far-left, and Salafi-jihadist extremists.

Violent far-right extremists' most frequent targets across this five-year period, and second most frequent targets in 2021, were private individuals, often selected on the basis of their race, religion, ethnicity, or gender. For example, in August 2019, Patrick Crusius opened fire at a Walmart in El Paso, Texas, killing 23 individuals and wounding 23 others. Crusius specifically targeted Latino individuals and cited white supremacist conspiracy theories such as the Great Replacement as his rationale for the attack.[16]

Violent far-left extremists' second most frequent targets both throughout the five-year period and in 2021 (after government, military, and law enforcement targets) were businesses. For example, in October 2021, approximately 100 self-described anarchists smashed windows, destroyed property, and set fires at banks and stores in Portland, Oregon, following a "direct action march". The group caused over $500,000 in property damage and later publicized the event on several anarchist news platforms.[17]

Domestic Counterterrorism Efforts

U.S. domestic counterterrorism efforts historically have been reactive, conceived as a response to high-profile attacks and often advanced under political pressure and public scrutiny. Now, however, as the U.S. government once again considers revamping its domestic counterterrorism efforts in the wake of the January 6, 2021, attack at the U.S. Capitol, there may be unique opportunities to expand proactive and data-informed counterextremism strategies.

Policy reviews and updates following terrorist attacks are not new. For example, two high-profile terrorist attacks in 1995—the April bombing of the Alfred P. Murrah Federal Building in Oklahoma City, Oklahoma, by Timothy McVeigh, an anti-government extremist, and the December murder of a Black couple in Fayetteville, North Carolina, by three neo-Nazi-linked soldiers stationed at Fort Bragg—sparked a series of counterextremism policy reviews and clarifications, studies (albeit limited) of extremist ideology within the military, and congressional hearings.[18] Not long after, the September 11, 2001, terrorist attacks prompted a fundamental shift in U.S. national security policy toward combatting international, Salafi-jihadist extremism.

The latest event that sparked renewed interest in expanding or improving domestic counterterrorism efforts was the January 6, 2021, attack at the U.S. Capitol, during which individuals attempted to disrupt and prevent the certification of the results of the 2020 U.S. presidential election. Shortly after taking office a few weeks after the attack, the Biden administration initiated a domestic terrorism threat assessment, conducted by the Office of the Director of National Intelligence (ODNI), as well as a 100-day review of existing domestic extremism policy, led by the National Security Council (NSC). Simultaneously, the Department of Defense (DOD) required all personnel to participate in stand-downs to address the issue of extremism in the ranks and launched a working group to review DOD policy and generate mid- to long-term recommendations for combatting extremism in the military.[19]

The ODNI assessment, released in March 2021, found an elevated threat of domestic violent extremism (DVE) and assessed that "racially or ethnically motivated violent extremists (RMVEs) and militia violent extremists (MVEs) present the most lethal DVE threats, with RMVEs most likely to conduct mass-casualty attacks against civilians and MVEs typically targeting law enforcement and government personnel and facilities."[20]

At the conclusion of the NSC review, the administration released the nation's inaugural National Strategy for Countering Domestic Terrorism. The strategy did not establish new legal authorities, though it also did not preclude the possibility of new legislation in the future. Instead, it outlined four broad categories of action for the government and law enforcement at all levels to pursue: (1) understand and share information related to domestic terrorism; (2) prevent domestic terrorism recruitment and mobilization to violence; (3) disrupt and deter domestic terrorist activity; and (4) confront long-term factors that contribute to domestic terrorism.[21] The strategy echoed the community-focused language that the DHS used the month prior when it established the Center for Prevention Programs and Partnerships (CP3) to replace Office for Targeted Violence and Terrorism Prevention.[22] The CP3 stressed a whole-of-society approach to counterextremism that engages communities and incorporates public health interventions. This shift attempted to address past criticism of the government's counterterrorism efforts as violating civil liberties and discriminating against Muslim and Arab Americans; however, some advocates remained critical, warning that the change was simply a rebranding of the same flawed approaches.[23]

Both houses of Congress have hosted numerous discussions of domestic extremism since 2021, but partisan divisions and mistrust have hampered action. Committee hearings, for example, have addressed issues such as racially, ethnically, religiously, and politically motivated attacks and concerns over extremism among current and former military personnel.[24] Although the House passed new domestic terrorism legislation, the *Domestic Terrorism Prevention Act of 2022*, in May 2022, just days after a white supremacist terrorist attack in Buffalo, New York, the bill lacked the bipartisan support necessary to gain Senate approval.[25]

Policy Implications

The renewed focus on domestic counterterrorism within the U.S. federal government is a step forward in combatting the extremist threat, but this federal response is both overdue and limited by a lack of bipartisan political will and resources. However, this period of heightened attention and public pressure to address the growing domestic terrorism threat presents a unique opportunity to effect lasting change if political actors can reach consensus on ideology-agnostic counterterrorism efforts. This section outlines three recommendations for policymakers seeking to improve domestic counterterrorism efforts in a manner that is balanced, transparent, and responsive to evolving threats.

First, the U.S. government should track and publicly release comprehensive data on domestic terrorist attacks, plots, and perpetrators. The federal government should establish a central clearinghouse to compile and analyze data on terrorism in the United States, including facilitation of interagency data sharing and standardization. This data center, likely housed within the DHS or Department of Justice, should provide regular reports both to Congress and to the public that include analyses of recent terrorist activity such as attacks, disrupted plots, arrests, and indictments; the level and types of domestic terrorist threat in the United States; and new or recommended counterterrorism activities. These assessments would enable policymakers, law enforcement, and non-governmental actors to respond to emerging trends in a timely and proportionate manner.

This transparency could also support broader civics education and information literacy efforts. Recent polling from the Pew Research Center indicates that similar, high shares of U.S. adults from both major political parties view domestic extremism as a major problem to address and one that exceeds the threat of Salafi-jihadist terrorism—though they differ by party affiliation on the domestic ideology they most fear.[26] Despite this polarized threat identification, most U.S. adults may be open to learning more about domestic extremism and measures the government is pursuing to reduce the threat, as long as they can receive this information from a trusted source. This highlights the importance both of open communication about counterterrorism efforts and of efforts to counter disinformation and restore trust in democratic institutions.[27]

Second, policymakers should dedicate additional operational and training resources to support community interventions aimed at countering disinformation and radicalization, as well as to support well-evidenced law enforcement and intelligence operations to counter domestic terrorist activity "left of boom"—before an attack occurs. Resources and personnel for these efforts should be allocated in accordance with the data analysis described above to ensure that counterterrorism efforts are transparent, proportionate to the threat, and applied in an equal manner, regardless of the ideologies of individuals involved.

Finally, the U.S. government should expand efforts to track and respond to violent extremist activity on digital platforms, including through coordination with technology companies related to content moderation and threat monitoring. Domestic extremists, particularly those motivated by violent far-right ideologies, frequently use online platforms such as Facebook, Twitter, YouTube, Gab, Reddit, 4Chan, 8kun (formerly 8Chan), Endchan, Telegram, Vkontakte, MeWe, Discord, Wire, and Twitch to share extremist content, recruit followers, and coordinate their activities. In recent years, manifestos and livestream videos of attacks have become increasingly common, and online platforms have repeatedly failed to stop their spread.[28]

Inciting materials shared online may also include content related to incidents that do not meet the definition of terrorism, such as non-political mass shootings, but that may inspire extremist violence. For example, in June 2022 the DHS issued a National Terrorism Advisory System bulletin warning of a heightened threat of terrorist attacks in the United States following a series of violent incidents that could encourage copycat attacks and that both domestic extremists and foreign adversaries had begun using as propaganda to exacerbate political grievances. These incidents included both terrorist attacks, such as the Buffalo shooting, and attacks with no clear political motive, such as the May 2022 elementary school shooting in Uvalde, Texas.[29]

The urgent need for these counterterrorism efforts is reinforced as extremist views developed in the United States continue to proliferate abroad. One prominent example is the QAnon ideology—a "big tent" conspiracy theory that alleges that the government is controlled by a cabal of satanic pedophiles who control the Democratic party and mainstream media outlets.[30] The QAnon movement, which draws inspiration from older conspiracy theories such as the belief in the Zionist Occupied Government and the New World Order, originated in a U.S.-specific context: the secretive "Q" was allegedly a government operative whose online posts allegedly referenced classified knowledge, and his messages supported President Donald Trump while vilifying the Democratic Party.[31] However, as the conspiracy theory evolved and merged with other streams of violent far-right extremism, it also attracted adherents in other countries, such as Germany, who adapted the conspiracy theory's false allegations to fit their own political circumstances and to exploit anti-Semitic beliefs among local far-right networks.[32] Thus U.S. domestic terrorism—which other nations may have once dismissed as a U.S. problem—is increasingly becoming an international threat.

Despite the heightened levels of domestic terrorism in the United States and extremist networks' growing influence globally, there is some cause for optimism. Although U.S. domestic counterterrorism policy traditionally has been reactive, the country is currently facing a moment in which change is possible. With the federal and policy reviews conducted since early 2021 as a guide, policymakers must now seek common ground on the basis of an ideology-agnostic rejection of violence and pursue long-term solutions that prioritize proportionality, transparency, and public trust.

Notes

1 Catrina Doxsee et al., "Pushed to Extremes: Domestic Terrorism amid Polarization and Protest," *CSIS Briefs*, CSIS, May 17, 2022, https://www.csis.org/analysis/pushed-extremes-domestic-terrorism-amid-polarization-and-protest.

2 Ibid.

3 Molly O'Toole, "Trump Officials Have Redirected Resources from Countering Far-Right, Racism-Fueled Domestic Terrorism," *Los Angeles Times*, August 5, 2019, https://www.latimes.com/politics/story/2019-08-05/trump-officials-have-redirected-resources-from-countering-far-right-racism-fueled-domestic-terrorism.

4 *U.S. Code* 18 § 2331.

5 Jacob Aasland Ravndal et al., *RTV Trend Report 2019: Right Wing Terrorism and Violence in Western Europe, 1990–2018* (Oslo, Norway: Center for Research on Extremism, 2019), 3, https://www.sv.uio.no/c-rex/english/groups/rtv-dataset/trend-report-2019.pdf; Jacob Aasland Ravndal and Tore Bjørgo, "Investigating Terrorism from the Extreme Right: A Review of Past and Present Research," *Perspectives on Terrorism* 12, no. 6 (December 2018): 5–22, https://www.universiteitleiden.nl/binaries/content/assets/customsites/perspectives-on-terrorism/2018/issue-6/a1-ravndal-and-bjorgo.pdf; Ehud Sprinzak, "Right-Wing Terrorism in a Comparative Perspective: the Case of Split Delegitimization," *Terrorism and Political Violence* 7, no. 1 (1995): 17–43, doi:10.1080/09546559508427284; and Cas Mudde, "Right-Wing Extremism Analyzed: A Comparative Analysis of the Ideologies of Three Alleged Right-Wing Extremist Parties (NPD, NDP, CP'86)," *European Journal of Political Research* 27, no. 2 (1995): 203–24, doi:10.1111/j.1475-6765.1995.tb00636.x.

6 CSIS compiled incidents and details from the following databases and other sources: ACLED (2020–2021); the Anti-Defamation League's (ADL) Hate, Extremism, Anti-Semitism, and Terrorism (H.E.A.T.) Map (2002–2021); Janes Terrorism and Insurgency Events (2009–2021); START GTD (1994–2017); press releases and reports from the Federal Bureau of Investigation and Department of Justice; criminal complaints and affidavits; and local and national news sources such as the *New York Times*,

Washington Post, and *Los Angeles Times*. For a full methodology and codebook, see Catrina Doxsee et al, "Methodology and Codebook: Pushed to Extremes: Domestic Terrorism amid Polarization and Protest," CSIS, May 17, 2022, https://csis-website-prod.s3.amazonaws.com/s3fs-public/publication/220517_Doxsee_PushedtoExtremes_Methodology.pdf?RRRlmS5ysSXu3wII.sxKs9rq4LHx.3gZ. For some of the external databases referenced, see Clionadh Raleigh, Andrew Linke, Håvard Hegre, and Joakim Karlsen, "Introducing ACLED-Armed Conflict Location and Event Data," *Journal of Peace Research* 47, no. 5 (2010): 651–60, doi:10.1177/0022343310378914; "ADL H.E.A.T. Map," ADL Center on Extremism, https://www.adl.org/education-and-resources/resource-knowledge-base/adl-heat-map; and "Janes Terrorism and Insurgency Events," Janes, https://www.janes.com/military-threat-intelligence/terrorism-and-insurgency.

7 Although the number of terrorist attacks and plots increased across this period, there was a brief decrease in activity in 2018, when only 37 domestic terrorist attacks and plots occurred.

8 "About: Frequently Asked Questions," Rose City Antifa, accessed February 7, 2022; and Doxsee et al., "Pushed to Extremes: Domestic Terrorism amid Polarization and Protest."

9 Doxsee et al., "Pushed to Extremes: Domestic Terrorism amid Polarization and Protest."

10 Ibid. For more on the security dilemma as applied in international relations literature, see, for example, John Herz, "Idealist Internationalism and the Security Dilemma," *World Politics* 2, no. 2 (January 1950): 157–80, doi:10.2307/2009187; Robert Jervis, "Cooperation Under the Security Dilemma," *World Politics* 30, no. 2 (January 1978): 167–214, doi:10.2307/2009958; Charles L. Glaser, "Realists as Optimists: Cooperation as Self-Help," *International Security* 19, no. 3 (Winter 1994/95): 50–90, doi:10.2307/2539079; and Charles L. Glaser, "The Security Dilemma Revisited," *World Politics* 50, no. 1 (October 1997): 171–201, https://www.jstor.org/stable/25054031.

11 There were 2,984 fatalities from terrorist attacks in the United States in 2001 and 179 in 1995. These were primarily due to the September 11 attacks and the bombing of the Alfred P. Murrah Federal Building in Oklahoma City, respectively.

12 Kate Brumback, "Atlanta Spa-Shooting Suspect Pleads Not Guilty in 4 Killings," Associated Press, September 28, 2021, https://apnews.com/article/atlanta-spa-shootings-robert-aaron-long-a87456e5f25f34f0acc85c41f73ffbc6; "8 Dead in Atlanta Spa Shootings, With Fears of Anti-Asian Bias," New York Times, March 26, 2021, https://www.nytimes.com/live/2021/03/17/us/shooting-atlanta-acworth#the-suspect-in-the-spa-attacks-has-been-charged-with-eight-counts-of-murder; Alexis Stevens, "Cherokee DA Defends Plea Deal, Decision Not to Pursue Hate Crime," *Atlanta Journal-Constitution*, July 27, 2021, https://www.ajc.com/news/cherokee-da-defends-plea-deal-says-long-targeted-multiple-ethnicities-genders/WXOAD4JXHNGO3ML3WACU3NBV3E/; and Jina Moore, "How the Atlanta Shooting Shows the Dangers of American Evangelicalism's Trademark 'Purity Culture,'" Business Insider, March 20, 2021, https://www.businessinsider.com/the-atlanta-shooting-and-the-dangers-of-evangelical-purity-culture-2021-3.

13 *United States of America v. Sayfullo Habibullaevic Saipov*, Indictment, U.S. District Court Southern District of New York, 17 Cr. 722, November 21, 2017.

14 Lewis Kamb and Hal Bernton, "Portland Shooting Suspect Followed Right-wing Activists After Spotting Them Downtown, Unsealed Arrest Warrant Says," Seattle Times, September 5, 2020, https://www.seattletimes.com/seattle-news/portland-shooting-suspect-followedright-wing-activists-after-spotting-them-downtown-unsealed-arrestwarrant-says/; Neil MacFarquhar, Mike Baker, and Adam Goldman, "In His Last Hours, Portland Murder Suspect Said He Feared Arrest," New York Times, September 4, 2020, https://www.nytimes.com/2020/09/04/us/portland-shooting-michael-reinoehl.html; and Destiny Johnson and Cassidy Quinn, "Unsealed Documents Shed Light on Moments Before Fatal Downtown Portland Shooting," KGW8, September 4, 2020, https://www.kgw.com/article/news/local/multnomah-county-district-attorney-provides-new-information-inhomicide-case/283-629b983a-620a-469e-bc03-4b365a99a547.

15 "NICS Firearm Background Checks: Month/Year," National Instant Criminal Background Check System (NICS), November 30, 1998–May 31, 2022, https://www.fbi.gov/file-repository/nics_firearm_checks_-_month_year.pdf/view.

16 U.S. Attorney's Office, Western District of Texas, "Federal Grand Jury in El Paso Returns Superseding Indictment against Patrick Crusius," Press release, U.S. Department of Justice, July 9, 2020, https://www.justice.gov/usao-wdtx/pr/federal-grand-jury-el-paso-returns-superseding-indictment-against-patrick-crusius.

17 David Mann, "Police: Crowd Causes $500K in Damage to Downtown Portland During Memorial for Activist Killed in 2019," KGW8, October 13, 2021, https://www.kgw.com/article/news/local/portland-memorial-vandalism/283-e5171a7b-be9a-49b5-902a-34da286bb966; and "Protesters Commemorating Activist's Death Damage Downtown Portland Windows, Leave Graffiti," The Oregonian, October 13, 2021, https://www.oregonlive.com/news/2021/10/protesters-commemorating-activists-death-damage-downtown-portland-windows-leave-graffiti.html.

18 Catrina Doxsee and Michelle Macander, "Assessing the Pentagon's Progress on Countering Extremism in the Military," Critical Questions, CSIS, April 8, 2022, https://www.csis.org/analysis/assessing-pentagons-progress-countering-extremism-military.

19 U.S. Department of Defense, *Stand-Down to Address Extremism in the Ranks*, Lloyd James Austin III, memorandum (Washington, D.C., 2021), https://media.defense.gov/2021/Feb/05/2002577485/-1/-1/0/STAND-DOWN-TO-ADDRESS-EXTREMISM-IN-THE-RANKS.PDF; U.S. Department of Defense, "Stand-Down Training Materials to Address Extremism in the Ranks," Press release, February 26, 2021, https://www.defense.gov/News/Releases/Release/Article/2517651/stand-down-training-material-to-address-extremism-in-the-ranks/; and U.S. Department of Defense, *Immediate Actions to Counter Extremism in the Department and the Establishment of the Countering Extremism Working Group*, Lloyd James Austin III, memorandum (Washington, D.C., 2021), https://media.defense.gov/2021/Apr/09/2002617921/-1/-1/1/MEMORANDUM-IMMEDIATE-ACTIONS-TO-COUNTER-EXTREMISM-IN-THE-DEPARTMENT-AND-THE-ESTABLISHMENT-OF-THE-COUNTERING-EXTREMISM-WORKING-GROUP.PDF.

20 *Domestic Violent Extremism Poses Heightened Threat in 2021* (Washington, D.C.: Office of the Director of National Intelligence, March 1, 2021), https://www.dni.gov/files/ODNI/documents/assessments/UnclassSummaryofDVEAssessment-17MAR21.pdf.

21 *National Strategy for Countering Domestic Terrorism* (Washington, D.C.: National Security Council, June 15, 2021), https://www.whitehouse.gov/wp-content/uploads/2021/06/National-Strategy-for-Countering-Domestic-Terrorism.pdf; and Catrina Doxsee and Jake Harrington, "The First U.S. National Strategy for Countering Domestic Terrorism," Critical Questions, CSIS, June 17, 2021, https://www.csis.org/analysis/first-us-national-strategy-countering-domestic-terrorism.

22 "DHS Creates New Center for Prevention Programs and Partnerships and Additional Efforts to Comprehensively Combat Domestic Violent Extremism," press release, U.S. Department of Homeland Security, May 11, 2021, https://www.dhs.gov/news/2021/05/11/dhs-creates-new-center-prevention-programs-and-partnerships-and-additional-efforts.

23 Harsha Panduranga, "Community Investment, Not Criminalization," Brennan Center for Justice, June 17, 2021, https://www.brennancenter.org/our-work/research-reports/community-investment-not-criminalization; *Domestic Terrorism and Violent Extremism: Examining the Threat of Racially, Ethnically, Religiously, and Politically Motivated Attacks, Part II*, 117th Cong., sess. 1 (2021) (statement of Maya M. Berry, Executive Director, Arab American Institute), https://www.hsgac.senate.gov/imo/media/doc/Testimony-Berry-2021-08-05-REVISED.pdf; "The Problems with 'Violent Extremism' and 'Violence Prevention' Programs," ACLU, accessed May 21, 2022, https://www.aclu.org/other/problems-violent-extremism-and-violence-prevention-programs; and Odette Yousef, "Biden Team Promises New Approach to Extremism, but Critics See Old Patterns," NPR, January 27, 2022, https://www.npr.org/2022/01/27/1075790314/biden-team-promises-new-approach-to-extremism-but-critics-see-old-patterns.

24 See, for example, U.S. Senate Committee on Homeland Security and Governmental Affairs, *Violent Extremism and Terrorism: Examining the Threat to Houses of Worship and Public Spaces*, 117th Cong., 2nd sess. (March 16, 2022); U.S. Senate Committee on Homeland Security and Governmental Affairs, *Domestic Terrorism and Violent Extremism: Examining the Threat of Racially, Ethnically, Religiously, and Politically Motivated Attacks, Part I*, 117th Cong., 1st sess. (August 3, 2021); U.S. House Armed Services Committee, *Extremism in the Armed Forces*, 117th Cong., 1st sess. (March 24, 2021); and U.S. House Committee on Veterans' Affairs, *Helping Veterans Thrive: The Importance of Peer Support in Preventing Domestic Violent Extremism*, 117th Cong., 2nd sess. (March 31, 2022).

25 Congress.gov, "H.R.350 - 117th Congress (2021–2022): Domestic Terrorism Prevention Act of 2022," May 26, 2022, https://www.congress.gov/bill/117th-congress/house-bill/350; and Deirdre Walsh, "Days after Buffalo Mass Shooting, the House Approves a Bill to Fight Domestic Terror," NPR,

May 18, 2022, https://www.npr.org/2022/05/18/1099756134/days-after-buffalo-mass-shooting-the-house-approves-a-bill-to-fight-domestic-ter.

26 "Large Majority of the Public Views Prosecution of Capitol Rioters as 'Very Important,'" Pew Research Center, March 18, 2021, https://www.pewresearch.org/politics/2021/03/18/large-majority-of-the-public-views-prosecution-of-capitol-rioters-as-very-important/.

27 Suzanne Spaulding and Devi Nair, "Restore Trust in National Security Institutions," CSIS, Critical Questions, https://www.csis.org/analysis/restore-trust-national-security-institutions.

28 Jacob Ware, "Testament to Murder: The Violent Far-Right's Increasing Use of Terrorist Manifestos," ICCT Policy Brief, International Centre for Counter-Terrorism, March 2020; "Footage of Buffalo Attack Spread Quickly Across Platforms, Has Been Online for Days," ADL, May 20, 2022, https://www.adl.org/resources/blog/footage-buffalo-attack-spread-quickly-across-platforms-has-been-online-days; and Tech Against Terrorism, "Gap Analysis and Recommendations for Deploying Technical Solutions to Tackle the Terrorist Use of the Internet," Global Internet Forum to Counter Terrorism (GIFCT) Technical Approaches Working Group, July 2021, https://gifct.org/wp-content/uploads/2021/07/GIFCT-TAWG-2021.pdf.

29 National Terrorism Advisory System, "Summary of Terrorism Threat to the United States," Bulletin, U.S. Department of Homeland Security, June 7, 2022, https://www.dhs.gov/ntas/advisory/national-terrorism-advisory-system-bulletin-june-7-2022.

30 James Suber and Jacob Ware, "Examining Extremism: QAnon," Examining Extremism, CSIS, June 10, 2021, https://www.csis.org/blogs/examining-extremism/examining-extremism-qanon.

31 Ibid.

32 Katrin Bennhold, "QAnon Is Thriving in Germany. The Extreme Right Is Delighted," The New York Times, October 11, 2020, https://www.nytimes.com/2020/10/11/world/europe/qanon-is-thriving-in-germany-the-extreme-right-is-delighted.html.

21

RIGHT-WING EXTREMISTS AND STATE DENIERS IN EUROPE

Current Narratives, Trends and Actors

Stefan Goertz

Introduction

Right-wing extremism and terrorism currently constitute major threats to European democracies, and will potentially do so for many years to come. This is particularly evident in Germany, where the estimated number of right-wing oriented persons has reached an historic high and where several right-wing terrorist attacks have been carried out by terrorists, or have been prevented by national security agencies in recent years.

The trend away from the "old" right-wing extremism and toward the "new" right-wing extremism entails new actors who pose new challenges for the national security agencies.

In addition to the problem of organized structures of violent right-wing extremists – currently more than 13,300[1] in Germany – the internet poses a risk factor for national security agencies in Europe as an incalculable spectrum of potential right-wing lone wolf terrorists run the risk of being radicalized by conspiracy narratives/myths, and right-wing extremist ideological elements in narratives and propaganda. This causal factor for radicalization represents a tremendous present and future challenge for national security agencies, actors involved in prevention and deradicalization work as well as for civil societies.

Immediately after her inauguration on December 6, 2021, the German Federal Minister of the Interior, Nancy Faeser, wrote: "The fight for the open society and against its enemies will be a matter of great concern to me – right-wing extremism poses the greatest threat to our democracy, and as Minister of Interior I intend to combat this threat with the utmost vigor".[2] In her first statement to the German parliament, the new Federal Minister of the Interior stated: As "right-wing extremism is the greatest threat to our democracy", combating this threat is "top priority".[3] Right-wing extremism and terrorism are international and European in character. Yet, throughout Europe, right-wing extremism is especially strong in German-speaking countries.

Current Trends and Actors

We notice a new dynamic in the area of right-wing extremism. Thereby, national security agencies face – in addition to the old structures – entirely new forms [of right-wing extremism] such as right-wing networks operating in the internet or self-radicalizing lone wolf terrorists.[4]

Thomas Haldenwang, President of the German Bundesamt für Verfassungsschutz.

DOI: 10.4324/9781003326373-24

With respect to the spectrum of right-wing extremists in Germany, the German Bundesamt für Verfassungsschutz, the interior intelligence service of the German Federation, distinguishes between right-wing extremist parties, the category of "right-wing extremists in party-independent or party-unaffiliated structures", the "number of largely unstructured right-wing extremists", neo-Nazis, "subculturally influenced right-wing extremists", and other right-wing extremists. According to the German intelligence services, one in three of German right-wing extremists is currently violence-oriented, i.e.13,300 out of 33,300.[5]

The "New Right"

Under the umbrella term "the New Right", the German Bundesamt für Verfassungsschutz summarizes an informal network of groups, individuals and organizations, from right-wing radicals to right-wing extremists, which work together to promote their sometimes anti-liberal and anti-democratic positions in society and the political sphere. Thereby, actors of the "New Right" dovetail parliamentary and extra-parliamentary movements, meta-political theory formation and practice with protest and demonstration initiatives.[6] The German Bundesamt für Verfassungsschutz comes to the conclusion "that the various actors within this network perform different and partly complementary functions and roles, which are intended to serve the common goal of a 'cultural revolution from the right' and which are each directed at different target groups".[7]

The "Identitarian Movement Germany" (IBD) functions within these neo-right-wing networks as an action-oriented extra-parliamentary youth organization. The "Identitarians" cultivate an elitist self-image and focus on media-effective actions in the public sphere, which are directed in particular against migration, a perceived "Islamization" and an alleged "population exchange" (conspiracy narrative "the great replacement").

According to the German Bundesamt für Verfassungsschutz, the "COMPACT Magazin", published by "COMPACT-Magazin GmbH", as well as its associated extensive internet presence and its online video channel, popularize – additionally supported by events – neo-rightist contents, contents defaming the democratic system and its institutions and, especially, conspiracy ideological positions.[8]

"COMPACT-Magazin GmbH" was established in 2010. Already since December 2010, this GmbH has published the monthly magazine "COMPACT-Magazin", of which – based on its own information – 40,000 copies are sold per month. In addition, numerous special issues are published in several series on specific topics with titles such as "Corona Lies", "War, Lies, USA" and "Secret File Child Molesters". Meanwhile, "COMPACT" represents, according to the analysis of the German Bundesamt für Verfassungsschutz, a multimedia phenomenon. This includes extensive online offerings such as its own website, the YouTube channel "COMPACT TV" with approximately 148,000 subscribers, and presences in social networks.[9]

The German intelligence services describe the "Institut für Staatspolitik" based in Schnellroda (Saxony-Anhalt) as a "new right think tank with an intellectual façade". The main aim of the institute is "to develop ideological and strategic concepts and to underpin and legitimize, for instance, political positions that deny people from different ethnic backgrounds "the qualification for citizenship"/"the ability to belong to the German nation".[10]

The association "Ein Prozent e.V". is described by the German intelligence services on the one hand as a project support and networking agency, but on the other hand, this association also goes public with its own campaigns in which migrants are sweepingly disparaged. The association's primary goal is to provide material and immaterial support to projects of right-wing organizations, groups and individuals, as well as to network actors and thereby support them in their respective political objectives.

According to the German Bundesamt für Verfassungsschutz, the right-wing extremist "wing" of the Alternative für Deutschland (AfD), which was formally dissolved at the end of April 2020, continues to have an impact on the AfD party as a whole and can be described as the "parliamentary arm of the new-right network". The German Bundesamt für Verfassungsschutz sees evidence of this in statements by exposed "wing" protagonists on migration policy and Islam, which are made in the same tenor as those of the "Identitarian movement". As its official youth organization, the "Junge Alternative für Deutschland" (JA) supports the parent party AfD in its political work. According to observations by the German intelligence services, the JA also maintains informal and structural links to new-right actors and groups and reproduces their content through its own announcements and campaigns.[11]

The "Identitarians" in Europe

The "Identitarian movement" was founded in France and, with the Casa Pound movement in Italy as a role model, it soon found thousands of supporters throughout Europe. At the moment, the "Identitarian movement" officially has permanent organizational structures in Ireland, Great Britain, Denmark, Germany, France, Austria, the Czech Republic, Hungary, Slovenia and in Italy, backed by supporters and sympathizers throughout Europe.

The "Identitarian movement", or the "Identitarians", also belong to the New Right and have been classified as a right-wing extremist organization by the German intelligence services. The "Identitarian movement" exemplifies recent developments in right-wing extremism. The "Identitarians" not only stand out organizationally from classic party structures such as the NPD, but also differ from the neo-Nazi scene in their rhetoric and actions. According to Lower Saxony's Landesamt für Verfassungsschutz, the intelligence service of the federal state Lower Saxony, the "Identitarian movement" stands for a modern right-wing extremism that attempts to connect with broad social circles by building on a canon of anti-Islam, anti-Asylum and anti-establishment themes. Terms such as "race" and "nation" are replaced by innocuous concepts such as ethnicity, identity and culture, and reinterpreted in the European context as the concept of an "ethnocultural identity" that needs to be defended, according to the motto: "No to Islamization! Defend yourself, it is your country!"[12]

The "Identitäre Bewegung Deutschland" (IBD), founded in 2012 as a Facebook group, sees itself as the German offshoot of the "Identitäre Bewegung Österreichs" (IBÖ) and the French youth organization "Génération Identitaire" (GI). Especially the French GI served as a role model for the IBD's own activities in its initial phase. The GI is a New Right organization founded in 2003, which has attracted attention in France for its Islamophobic, xenophobic, racist and nationalist positions and which has repeatedly attracted attention through publicly promoted actions such as flash mobs and forms of civil obedience.[13]

In March 2021, the French government banned the Génération Identitaire France. The cabinet approved the dissolution of the group, as stated by Interior Minister Gérald Darmanin. The group acts like a "private militia" and calls for "discrimination, hatred and violence", Darmanin wrote on Twitter. Marine Le Pen, the leader of the right-wing populist party Rassemblement National, criticized the group's dissolution as a "violation of freedom of expression and the rule of law". The French Interior Ministry also justified the dissolution of Génération Identitaire by referring to links to the right-wing terrorist bomber of Christchurch, Brenton Tarrant, from whom the GI and the Austrian Identitarian Movement are said to have received donations.

Tarrant had shot dead a total of 51 people in right-wing terrorist attacks on two mosques in New Zealand in March 2019 and was later sentenced to life imprisonment.[14]

As a supposed youth movement, the "Identitarian movement" strives to develop its own trademarks and its own form of corporate identity. For instance, the colors black and yellow are dominant in their choice of colors, which are consequently also found in the symbolism of the "Identitarian movement". [15]

The "Identitarians" in Europe are engaged in a struggle against multiculturalism and immigration and for the preservation of "ethnocultural identity". According to the German intelligence services, the movement believes that "community" is derived from the transmission of supposed cultural achievements of the ethnically homogeneous self-group. For the ideological classification of the concept of "ethnocultural identity", social scientists also use the term "cultural racism" to emphasize the basic idea contained therein that people are devalued and excluded on the basis of their origin and/or ancestry. In this way, Islamophobia and the immigration debate go hand in hand in the "Identitarian movement" and are an expression of ideologically deeply rooted xenophobia that is combined with a fundamental criticism of the political system and the rejection of political correctness.[16]

According to the German intelligence services, the "Identitarian Movement Germany" presents itself in its publications and actions as a modern, Europe-wide youth movement, as the mouthpiece of a supposed community of fate of the (young) people in Europe, who are defenseless in the face of a "flood of people washed into the country" from the "Islamic cultural area and with hardly any education".[17] The consequences of this "policy of self-abolition" are "ethnic poverty ghettos, where violence and religious fanaticism flourish in a parallel society that cannot be integrated"[18].

One strategic goal of the "Identitarians" is to connect with broader social circles in Europe. They want to reach the mainstream of society. The strategy of the "Identitarians" is a "modern" right-wing extremism in order to distinguish themselves from the representatives and members of the NPD, neo-Nazis, skinheads and others.[19]

In Austria in October 2019, it almost came to a ban on the Identitarian Movement of Austria; ÖVP, NEOs and "Liste jetzt" voted in favor of it in parliament, SPÖ and FPÖ against it.[20] A few months earlier, an association with links to the IBÖ had almost been banned, but the association anticipated the authorities' plan and dissolved itself. On July 7, 2021, the Austrian parliament decided to ban the public use of the symbols of the "Identitarian movement" (IB).

State Deniers as Well as "Reichsbürger" and "Selbstverwalter"

According to the German Bundesamt für Verfassungsschutz, "Reichsbürger" and "Selbstverwalter" (lit. "citizens of the Reich" and "self-governors") are "groups and individuals who for various motives and on various grounds – e.g. by referring to the historical German Reich, lines of arguments used by conspiracy theorists or a self-defined law of nature – reject the existence of the Federal Republic of Germany and its legal system, deny the legitimacy of its democratically elected representatives or claim that the German legal order does not at all apply to them. Hence, there are concerns that they might infringe the law".[21]

With reference to information from the German intelligence services, "Reichsbürger" and "Selbstverwalter" are a phenomenon of extremism sui generis. According to the German Bundesamt für Verfassungsschutz, only a small percentage of "Reichsbürger" and "Selbstverwalter" are also right-wing extremists. Regardless of this, it is the anti-state and conspiracy-related arguments put forward by these individuals that facilitate compatibility with antisemitic ideas, which also play an important role in right-wing extremism. Thereby, the antisemitic attitudes and assertions of

"Reichsbürger" and "Selbstverwalter" range from accusations by individuals who blame "the Jews" for their unemployment, through openly antisemitic conspiracy theories often conveyed using codes and cyphers, according to which the First World War was planned by "the Jews", to Holocaust denial. To spread their ideology fragments and argumentation patterns, "Reichsbürger" and "Selbstverwalter" rely to a large extent on the internet and social networks. In the offline world, they also undertake various activities to propagate their views, most of which are legal nonsense. It is often difficult to distinguish between "Reichsbürger" and "Selbstverwalter": As regards territory and governing law, "Reichsbürger" refer to some kind of "German Reich", thus rejecting the Federal Republic of Germany. "Selbstverwalter" feel that they do not belong to the state and are not bound by its legal order. They declare their "secession" from the state and that they are "self-governors".[22]

The German intelligence services consider the entire scene of "Reichsbürger" and "Selbstverwalter" to be generally hostile to the state. At the moment, the scene is thought to comprise about 20,000 persons nationwide and about 1,000 of them can be considered right-wing extremists. Of these 20,000 persons nationwide, about 2,000 are thought to be violence-oriented. This number includes violent members of the scene as well as persons who have come to the attention of the authorities by making threats or statements approving violence and having the relevant ideological content. The scene of "Reichsbürger" and "Selbstverwalter" consists of about three quarters men. In Germany, there are around 28 groups, including the "Staatenbund Deutsches Reich" with "Gliedstaaten", "Bismarcks Erben" with the subdivision "Vaterländischer Hilfsdienst" (VHD) and the "Verfassunggebende Versammlung".[23]

State deniers, also called state rejectionists, reject the existence of the Republic of Austria, "refer to the state as a company and do not recognize its institutions".[24] At the end of December 2020, the former Austrian Federal Office for the Protection of the Constitution and Counterterrorism (BVT) assumed that there were 3693 state deniers in Austria known by name.[25]

In 2014, the Austrian Ministry of the Interior estimated that 20,000 to 22,000 people in Austria sympathize with these "state-denying" ideas. In mid-April 2017, the first sentences against state deniers were handed down in Austria. Among them were those involved in the first publicly known case from the summer of 2014. A small group of state deniers had wanted to hold a "people's tribunal" on a farm in Lower Austria, before the fictious "International Common Law Court of Justice Vienna" (ICCJV). A court sentenced six of the eight participants to fines and imprisonment. One of those Austrian state deniers, Monika Unger, had also linked texts denying the Holocaust on her website. Representatives of Germanic New Medicine joined her group. Germanic New Medicine believes, for example, that the majority of German oncologists are Jews who deliberately want to kill people via chemotherapy; furthermore, they deny the existence of AIDS.[26]

With about 3,000 members, the "State Union of Austria" was not small, considering that this "State Union" had only been founded in 2015 and its leadership was arrested in 2017. This leadership group had been on trial in Graz since September 2020. The members "were immensely radicalized", the Graz prosecutor admonished the jury as he read out the indictment against 13 state deniers: "This was the largest anti-state alliance that has ever existed in Austria. They wanted to take vigilante action against judges and politicians", the prosecutor elaborated in 2018. "This cannot be tolerated".[27]

Propensity to Violence and Violence of "Reichsbürger" and "Selbstverwalter"

The German police forces and intelligence services have identified a high potential for violence in the scene of "Reichsbürger" and "Selbstverwalter". For instance, "Reichsbürger" and "Selbstverwalter" repeatedly engage in verbal and physical aggression against public service employees.

In the context of the active participation of "Reichsbürger" and "Selbstverwalter" in demonstrations against the measures taken by the federal and state governments to combat the pandemic, there have been repeated incidents of violence by members of this scene. Criminally relevant actions were reported, especially against police officers, but also beyond the demonstrations. In this context, the police force and the intelligence services note that all state measures are or can be used by "Reichsbürger" and "Selbstverwalter" as an occasion for aggression and dangerous situations, including serious acts of violence.[28]

The German intelligence services describe it as worrying and significant that the murder and attempted murders by "Reichsbürger" and "Selbstverwalter" in 2016 in Reuden (Saxony-Anhalt) and Georgensmünd (Bavaria) in particular were "celebrated" within the "Reichsbürger" and "Selbstverwalter" scene as successful "resistance" against the state.[29]

The acts of violence committed by Adrian U. and Wolfgang P. are an indication that "Reichsbürger" and "Selbstverwalter" display an increased willingness to use violence, especially in connection with state measures. Due to their high affinity for weapons, "Reichsbürger" and "Selbstverwalter" also pose an increased potential threat. In the United States, several police officers have already been killed by individuals from a comparable spectrum ("sovereign citizens").[30]

In the view of the German intelligence services, various theses and elements of the worldview of "Reichsbürger" and "Selbstverwalter" are suitable for entangling people in a closed conspiracy-theory worldview, in which disenchantment with the state can turn into state hatred. This conspiracy-theory worldview can be the basis for radicalization processes that can even lead to violence. Members of the scene obstruct the courts, police and authorities in their work and threaten their employees. Any state intervention – especially the revocation of weapons permits – can trigger considerable aggression and dangerous situations.[31]

Right-Wing Extremist and State-Denying Ideology, Narratives and Conspiracy Narratives

Right-wing extremism is not a uniform phenomenon in Europe. According to the German Bundesamt für Verfassungsschutz, right-wing extremism is characterized, to varying degrees, by elements of nationalist, antisemitic, anti-Muslim/Islamophobic, racist and xenophobic ideology. Right-wing extremists allege that a person's value is determined by the ethnic group or nation to which they belong.[32] This notion is fundamentally incompatible with the basic laws of European countries.

Two essential elements of the neo-National Socialist ("neo-Nazi") ideology are nationalism and racism. Antisemitism plays a central role for most right-wing extremists. Antisemitism is expressed in various ways, for example, through the idea of a worldwide secret conspiracy by Jews or by holding Jews collectively accountable for the actions of the State of Israel.[33]

In addition to that, right-wing extremists usually believe in the concept of an authoritarian state, which often goes along with a rejection of the separation of powers that is typical of democracies. Referring to historical National Socialism and Adolf Hitler, neo-Nazis call for a "Führerstaat" ("leader state") in which all decisions are made by and all state power is concentrated in the hands of a single individual.[34]

Antisemitic, anti-Muslim/Islamic, racist, anti-democratic and revisionist ideological elements appear in various forms in right-wing extremism and among "Reichsbürger" and "Selbstverwalter", state deniers and "Querdenker". These ideological fragments are fundamentally incompatible with the basic laws of European countries.

Current Trend: Muslimo – and Islamophobia

At least since the "European refugee crisis" in 2015, European right-wing extremists have used the campaign themes "anti-Muslims", "anti-Islam". According to the Bavarian Landesamt für Verfassungsschutz (intelligence service of the state of Bavaria), "Islamophobes equate Islam as a world religion with Islamism as a political ideology across the board. They portray it as a totalitarian ideology that glorifies violence and poses a considerable threat to society. In their eyes, Muslims cannot be integrated into a democratic social order. Elementary fundamental rights, such as freedom of religion, should therefore not apply to them without restrictions".[35]

The German Bundesamt für Verfassungsschutz analyzes Islamophobia or Muslimophobia as a field of action for right-wing extremists, which has increased sharply since the "European refugee crisis". According to the German Bundesamt für Verfassungsschutz, Islamophobia among right-wing extremists "cannot be attributed solely to mere resentment and the adoption of right-wing populist theories, but rather is rooted in pronounced ideological basic convictions, in particular in the ideal of an ethnically homogenous "ethnic community" constructed by right-wing extremists. Right-wing extremists try to create fears of foreign infiltration or prejudices against the religion of Islam or Muslims or to stir up corresponding reservations to influence public opinion in their favor. They spread the thesis of a supposed "threatening Islamization" of Europe. The boundaries between extremist and populist Islamophobia are often blurred".[36]

The far-right scene in Germany used the rise in refugee numbers in Germany in 2014 and 2015 in the "European refugee crisis" for a large-scale anti-asylum agitation, linked to the far-right narrative of "der große Austausch/le grand remplacement/the great replacement" of the Identitarian movement/the New Right.

Xenophobic, anti-Muslim and Islamophobic narratives and ideological elements of the Identitarians and other members of the New Right but also other right-wing extremists in Europe are, for example:

- "Ethnopluralism", "End of the Islamization" and "Fortress Europe"
  The "Identitarian movement" calls for the "preservation of the diversity of peoples and cultures" and demands the "end of the Islamization of Europe". What is needed is the establishment of a "fortress Europe" that "defends its borders".[37]
- "Reconquista"
  In the ideology of the "Identitarian movement", Muslim immigrants are seen as a threat to the "Christian West", which must be actively fought with the help of the "Reconquista". Thereby, Islam is described as incompatible with the values of European culture and as a threat to the "ethno-cultural identity" of Europe.[38]
- "Great replacement"
  The "great replacement" refers to a demographic change caused by the alleged mass immigration, at the end of which "autochthonous Germans" or Northern Europeans "will be" a minority in Germany or Northern Europe. Moreover, this is said to be accompanied by an Islamization of Germany and Europe.[39]
- "Remigration"
  This term stands for the claim of the "Identitarian movement" to oppose alleged illegal immigration and to clearly commit to a "repatriation of all illegal entrants according to humane standards".[40]

The Conspiracy Narratives of QAnon, the "Deep State" and the "Great Reset"

Conspiracy narratives or conspiracy myths are – in addition to extremist ideological elements and narratives – a factor in radicalization processes of (evident) right-wing extremists, "Reichsbürger" and "Selbstverwalter" as well as state deniers. The spread of conspiracy narratives and myths has been the subject of intense public, media and political debate since the beginning of the Corona pandemic. Even centuries after the medieval plague conspiracy narrative that Jews poisoned the wells, conspiracy narratives with health-related issues are widespread. For example, psychological studies have shown that a conspiracy mentality is associated with a stronger rejection of scientific medicine and a greater openness to alternative healing methods. The stronger the conspiracy belief, the more likely people are to reject, for example, vaccinations.[41]

In an analysis of the special situation report "Danger and risk potential, especially from extremists and foreign services", which was discussed in the media after the fall meeting of the Conference of Interior Ministers (IMK) in December 2020, the Bundesamt für Verfassungsschutz warned against the QAnon movement and its conspiracy narrative. The association of conspiracy believers, which originated in the USA, is also finding followers in Germany. The core element of this conspiracy theory is the claim that "an international ring of pedophiles from secret services, politics and business, acting in secret, is murdering children in underground camps in order to obtain the life-rejuvenating substance adrenochrome from their blood. The conspiracy followers are under the delusion that a "deep state" is at work. At Corona protests in Berlin and other cities, QAnon supporters demonstratively wore clothing with the letter "Q" and the intelligence services state that both "right-wing extremists and a number of Reichsbürger adhere to the QAnon theory".[42] A gateway for right-wing extremists is the belief of the QAnon movement that the acting elites of the "deep state" are "leftists, of Jewish faith or controlled by Jews". Therefore, the German intelligence services see the danger that antisemitic acts of violence and/or acts of violence directed against politicians "would be legitimized with the claim of a threat from the 'deep state'".[43]

The actors of the New Right in Europe have been adapting their agitation themes, ideological elements, narratives and strategies in Europe since the beginning of the 21st century. Thus, "the anathema" of the New Right, "the great replacement" – dominant since the "European refugee crisis" in 2015 – was replaced by the theme of protests against the Corona measures of the Austrian federal government in 2020. Since 2020, the theory of "the great reset"[44] has replaced "the great replacement" as dominant narrative of the New Right in Austria and become the new propagandistic and conspiracy ideological focus of New Right groups, according to the Austrian Directorate of State Protection and Intelligence (DSN). In connection with the Corona pandemic, prominent representatives of the New Right referred to a book entitled "Covid-19: The Great Reset". This book describes, among other things, "how the novel corona virus could cause so much destruction and suffering, and what changes are needed for a more inclusive, robust, and sustainable world". From the perspective of the New Right, however, this concept is much more about the "perfidious plan" of the "global elites" and "globalists" to build a "new world" according to their ideas after an intentional destruction of the existing conditions. Representatives of the New Right used the Corona demonstrations in Germany to propagate these theories with publicity effect.

The Strategy of "the New Right" in the Corona Pandemic in Austria

At the anti-Corona measures demonstration in Vienna on December 4, 2021, about 42,000 people demonstrated against the Austrian federal government's Corona policy. In some cases, the heated situation escalated and police officers were pelted with "pyrotechnic objects"; two police officers were even injured during the process. Prominent representatives of the right-wing extremist "Identitarian movement" around its "figurehead" Martin S. also took part in the demonstration. Slogans such as "You'll never get us", "We are the people" and "No to compulsory vaccination" could be read on banners.[45]

The Austrian Directorate of State Protection and Intelligence (DSN) states in its current 2021 report on the protection of the constitution that, from the beginning of the Corona pandemic, New Right groups in Austria used "the cross-milieu COVID-19 measures rallies as a stage" to "implement their agitations and actions in a way that attracted public attention". Thus, from the very beginning, New Right activists showed a presence at the anti-Corona measures events and tried to give the protest a campaign character. Activists of the "Identitarian movement Austria" (IBÖ) and the grouping "Die Österreicher" (The Austrians) often appeared prominently in the demonstrations by the opponents of the COVID-19 measures with banners and posters in order to present themselves as the "right-wing movement of the street". According to the Austrian Directorate of State Protection and Intelligence, the "Identitarians movement Austria" (IBÖ) and "Die Österreicher" are the best-known representatives of New Right groups in Austria. The "Identitarian movement Austria" (IBÖ) and "Die Österreicher" overlap considerably in terms of both personnel and content.[46]

Furthermore, the Austrian DNS states that in the recent past it has been a well-known strategy of New Right ideologues to take up and occupy topics and discourses with a high emotional impact. For example, the signature of the leading ideologues of the IBÖ and „Die Österreicher "(DO5) was particularly visible in the protests against the Austrian federal government's Corona measures in 2020. The IBÖ and "Die Österreicher" (DO5) used the Corona pandemic strategically to position themselves in the emotionally driven discourse surrounding the Corona measures.[47] According to the DSN, the New Right succeeded in making their conspirational ideological patterns of interpretation of the pandemic accessible to a broader section of the population. Initially, the New Right groups stirred up fears and insecurities among the Austrian population and conflated the COVID-19 pandemic with false reports about an imminent next "migration wave". Furthermore, the DSN states that, during the pandemic, the leading cadres of the New Right are deliberately linking right-wing extremist ideological elements and narratives such as anti-asylum "the great replacement" and Islamophobia/Muslimophobia with criticism of Corona measures and instrumentalizing them. Thus, in this context, the New Right in Austria also thematized the danger of an alleged Austrian "surveillance state". In this context, the COVID-19 measures of the Austrian federal government were sharply criticized and calls were made for joint protest rallies against the "viral dictatorship". According to the DSN, the banners and conspiracy narratives of the IBÖ/DO5 had thus partly become the "slogan of the COVID-19 protest movement in Austria".[48]

Conclusion

The trend outlined above, which goes away from the "old" right-wing extremism, the right-wing extremism of violent neo-Nazis and apparently "subcultural right-wing extremists", toward the "new" right-wing extremism, by no means precludes an on-going transition from right-wing extremism to right-wing terrorism. On the contrary: The ideological fragments and narratives of the "new" right-wing extremism serve to familiarize the mainstream of society with right-wing extremist ideology. Thereby, the "new" right-wing extremism aims to address the mainstream throughout Europe.

The foregoing analysis of current trends, and right-wing extremist actors and state deniers shows that these actors gear their strategies and narratives closely to current political issues such as the "European refugee crisis" and the coronavirus pandemic, with the objective of polarizing the people.

For years, the number of right-wing extremists, state deniers, opponents of the state, "Reichsbürger" and "Selbstverwalter" has been rising continuously, a rise further exacerbated by the coronavirus pandemic. The "Querdenken" movement might be the beginning rather than the end. There is further potential for movements organized by radicalized fractions of society. In addition, there are open calls for armed resistance against democracy. Against the background of the coronavirus pandemic and the war in Ukraine, it can safely be stated that the deterioration of the economic situation in Europe will most likely result in a growing number of radicalized individuals, right-wing populists and right-wing extremists in numbers that have never been seen in European history since 1945.

Regarding the on-going Russian war of aggression against the European country Ukraine, the following can be noted: In recent years, a trend of internationalization, of networking within European right-wing extremism can be observed: in the real world, in the context of martial arts tournaments such as the "Battle of the Nibelungs" and right-wing extremist music concerts; virtually, on numerous websites with right-wing extremist content, as well as in social networks. European right-wing extremists agree that they reject Europe's liberal, pluralistic democracies, the European democratic value system. This hostility to democracy on the part of European right-wing extremists and this consensus could represent a strategic gateway for the Putin system to exert influence. For example, in the context of Fake News on the level of psychological warfare on the Internet, on websites, in social networks. But financial support of (violent) right-wing extremists in Europe by Russian players is also conceivable. European right-wing extremists and right-wing extremists worldwide reject liberal democracies. The Putin system now finds itself in a new East-West conflict, which has reached, at the moment, the escalation stage of a war of aggression on a sovereign European state, Ukraine. In this new East-West conflict, players of the Putin system could form strategic partnerships with European right-wing extremists. This should be countered by the governments of European countries, their security agencies, as well as academic institutes and the media with resources, measures, programs and research.

As illustrated above, the actors and trends of right-wing extremism and state deniers, as well as their virtual networking, currently pose a major challenge for policymakers, national security authorities, actors involved in prevention and deradicalization work, as well as for civil societies in Europe, and will potentially do so for many years to come.

Notes

1 Cf. https://www.bmi.bund.de/SharedDocs/downloads/DE/publikationen/themen/sicherheit/vsb-2020-gesamt.pdf?__blob=publicationFile&v=6 (accessed April 1, 2022).

2 https://twitter.com/nancyfaeser/status/1467834923880960000 (accessed April 2, 2022).

3 https://www.welt.de/politik/deutschland/article236207852/Bundestag-Faeser-sagt-Rechtsextremismus-mit-Aktionsplan-den-Kampf-an.html (accessed April 2, 2022).

4 https://www.verfassungsschutz.de/DE/themen/rechtsextremismus/rechtsextremismus_node.html.

5 Cf. https://www.bmi.bund.de/SharedDocs/downloads/DE/publikationen/themen/sicherheit/vsb-2020-gesamt.pdf?__blob=publicationFile&v=6, p. 53.

6 Cf.https://www.bmi.bund.de/SharedDocs/downloads/DE/publikationen/themen/sicherheit/vsb-2020-gesamt.pdf?__blob=publicationFile&v=6 (accessed April 3, 2022), p. 74.

7 Cf. ibid., p. 75.

8 Cf. ibid.

9 Cf. Bundesministerium des Innern, für Bau und Heimat (2021): Verfassungsschutzbericht 2020, pp. 79–80.

10 Cf. ibid.

11 Cf. ibid., p. 76.

12 Cf. Niedersächsisches Ministerium für Inneres und Sport/Verfassungsschutz: Identitäre Bewegung Deutschland (IBD). Ideologie und Aktionsfelder, 3rd edition, Hannover 2016, p. 6.

13 Cf. Niedersächsisches Ministerium für Inneres und Sport/Verfassungsschutz, 2016, p. 10; Goertz, S. (2021): Rechtsextremismus und Rechtsterrorismus in Deutschland. Hilden, pp. 62–63.

14 Cf. https://www.zeit.de/politik/ausland/2021-03/frankreich-generation-identitaire-rechtsextremismus-verbot-gerald-darmanin (accessed April 4, 2022).

15 Cf. Goertz, Rechtsextremismus und Rechtsterrorismus in Deutschland, 2021, pp. 63–64.

16 Qdt. in: Niedersächsisches Ministerium für Inneres und Sport/Verfassungsschutz, 2016, p. 23.

17 Qdt. in: ibid., p. 30.

18 Ibid.

19 Cf. Goertz, S. (2022): Extremismus und Sicherheitspolitik. Studienkurs für die Polizei und die Verfassungsschutzbehörden, Wiesbaden, pp. 73–75.

20 Cf. https://www.derstandard.de/story/2000124394268/verbot-der-rechtsextremen-identitaeren (accessed April 5, 2022).

21 https://www.verfassungsschutz.de/EN/topics/reichsbuerger-and-selbstverwalter/reichsbuerger-and-selbstverwalter_node.html (accessed April 5, 2022). https://www.verfassungsschutz.de/DE/themen/reichsbuerger-und-selbstverwalter/begriff-und-erscheinungsformen/begriff-und-erscheinungsformen_artikel.html (accessed April 6, 2022).

22 Cf. ibid. (April 6, 2022).

23 Cf. Bundesministerium des Innern, für Bau und Heimat (2021): Verfassungsschutzbericht 2020, p. 113; Goertz, S. (2022): Extremismus und Sicherheitspolitik. Studienkurs für die Polizei und die Verfassungsschutzbehörden, pp. 125–126.

24 https://www.derstandard.at/story/2000130478849/was-fuer-ein-bloedsinn-ein-staatsverweigerer-und-sein-wien-der / (accessed April 7, 2022).

25 Cf. https://www.sn.at/panorama/oesterreich/3693-staatsleugner-sind-bisher-bekannt-97272769 (accessed April 7, 2022).

26 Cf. https://www.zeit.de/politik/2017-04/staatsverweigerer-oesterreich-staatsleugner-gesetz-verbot/komplettansicht (accessed April 8, 2022).

27 Cf. https://kurier.at/chronik/oesterreich/staatsverweigerer-12-jahre-haft-fuer-praesidentin/401072787 (accessed April 8, 2022).

28 Cf. Bundesministerium des Innern, für Bau und Heimat (2021): Verfassungsschutzbericht 2020, p. 119.

29 Cf. Bundesministerium des Innern, für Bau und Heimat (2019): Verfassungsschutzbericht 2018, pp. 99–100.

30 Cf. ibid., pp. 137–138.

31 Cf. https://www.verfassungsschutz.de/DE/themen/reichsbuerger-und-selbstverwalter/begriff-und-erscheinungsformen/begriff-und-erscheinungsformen_artikel.html (accessed April 9, 2022).

32 Cf. ibid.

33 Cf. ibid.

34 Ibid.

35 https://www.verfassungsschutz.bayern.de/weitere_aufgaben/islamfeindlichkeit/index.html (accessed April 9, 2022).

36 Bundesamt für Verfassungsschutz: Kompendium des BfV. Darstellung ausgewählter Arbeitsbereiche und Beobachtungsobjekte, December 2018, p. 20; Goertz, S. (2022): Extremismus und Sicherheitspolitik. Studienkurs für die Polizei und die Verfassungsschutzbehörden, pp. 116–117.

37 Cf. Zentrum Innere Führung/Bundesamt für den Militärischen Abschirmdienst: Die Verteidigung unserer Werte: Gemeinsam gegen Extremismus, Koblenz 2020, pp. 24–25.

38 Cf. ibid.

39 Cf. ibid.

40 Cf. ibid.

41 Cf. Imhoff, R./Lamberty, P. (2020): A bioweapon or a hoax? The link between distinct conspiracy beliefs about the Coronavirus disease (COVID-19) outbreak and pandemic behavior. Social Psychological and Personality Science, 11, 8, pp. 1110–1118; Lamberty, P./Rees, J. (2021): Gefährliche Mythen: Verschwörungserzählungen als Bedrohung für die Gesellschaft. In: Schröter, 2021, Die geforderte Mitte, p. 287.

42 Cf. https://www.tagesspiegel.de/politik/eine-hoechst-dynamische-situation-verfassungsschutz-befuerchtet-folgen-durch-verschwoerungstheoretiker-fuer-superwahljahr-2021/26707722.html (accessed April 10, 2022); Goertz, S. (2021): "Corona-Proteste" und der Einfluss von Extremisten. In: Forum Kriminal-prävention, 2/2021, pp. 6–7.

43 Cf. ibid.

44 Cf. https://www.dsn.gv.at/501/files/VSB/VSB_2020_Webversion_BF.pdf, p. 20 (accessed April 10, 2022).

45 https://www.welt.de/politik/ausland/article235472546/Corona-Demos-40-000-Menschen-protestieren-in-Wien-Markt-in-Luxemburg-gestuermt.html (accessed April 10, 2022).

46 Cf. https://www.dsn.gv.at/501/files/VSB/VSB_2020_Webversion_BF.pdf (accessed April 11, 2022), p. 18.

47 Cf. ibid., p. 19.

48 Cf. ibid.

PART IV

Forecast, Trends, Scenarios and Tactics

22

HOW TO FORECAST AND PREDICT FUTURE TERRORIST WARFARE

Joshua Sinai

The field of counter-terrorism studies requires new conceptual frameworks, methodologies, and software tools to enable analysts in government and academia to forecast and predict new types of warfare and targeting likely to be employed by their terrorist adversaries. This is important because they are always surprised when terrorist adversaries resort to new types of warfare in terms of new motivations, types of operatives, tactics, weaponry, and targeting to launch attacks that were previously unforeseen, but should have been anticipated if upgraded analytic capabilities had been in place.

Al-Qaeda's catastrophic 9/11 attacks are considered the most infamous attack surprise in the modern history of terrorism with four passenger aircraft hijacked simultaneously in order to crash them into their intended targets in two major cities in the United States. Other unexpected surprises include the post-9/11 anthrax poisonous letter attacks by an allegedly single operative (who had subsequently committed suicide before he was expected to be arrested), the use of rockets by the Lebanese Hizballah and the Palestinian Hamas against Israel when everyone was expecting a continuation of suicide bombings by their operatives, and the exploitation by al-Qaeda and the Islamic State of self-radicalized and self-funded lone actor terrorists as opposed to groups in conducting attacks in Western countries.

In one of the latest trends, the prevalence of far-right-wing terrorist attacks in the United States has also come as a surprise, with the more than 800-strong insurrectionists' violent takeover of the U.S. Capitol Building on January 6, 2021, notable for the lack of preparedness by the Capitol Police and other law enforcement authorities, including the U.S. Secret Service.[1] It should be mentioned, nevertheless, that this insurrection was allegedly instigated and led by former President Donald Trump and his allies, so a number of additional factors were responsible for the lack of anticipation in preempting the Capitol Building's violent takeover. This issue has been under investigation by the U.S. House of Representatives' Select Committee, with the full extent of culpability for the January 6 violent insurrection revealed by its final report when it is published in early 2022.[2]

In other areas requiring prediction and forecasting of future terrorist warfare, although it was expected that the Taliban would take over Afghanistan once the United States and its NATO allies began to withdraw their military forces from the country in August 2021, the especially fast pace in which the Taliban took over the country came as a strategic surprise when it occurred.[3]

To empower government and academic counterterrorism communities to avoid the element of surprise by forecasting and predicting the next waves of terrorist warfare, at the strategic,

DOI: 10.4324/9781003326373-26

operational, and tactical levels and thereby proactively and preemptively prepare to respond to such new developments during the earliest pre-incident phases, this chapter presents a conceptual framework based on ten early warning indicators that can be utilized to estimate likely future warfare and targeting by one's terrorist adversary.

Prior to utilizing these ten indicators, it is necessary to define terrorism and the distinction between forecasting and prediction.

Defining Terrorism

To understand the magnitude of a terrorist threat, it is crucial to accurately define it. In this approach, terrorism is defined as violent attacks by sub-state groups for political reasons against civilian *and* military (and law enforcement) targets to coerce their targeted governments to give in to their various objectives. A problem with the "conventional" definition of terrorism that terrorism involves only attacks against unarmed civilians is that it overlooks the fact that terrorists also attack the armed military and law enforcement personnel (such as al-Qaeda's targeting of the U.S Pentagon), resulting in an undercounting of the magnitude of a terrorism threat facing a country when only attacking civilians is counted, thereby causing the targeted societies to be unprepared to effectively anticipate and defend against the full magnitude of the threats against them. To avoid such misconceptions, by properly defining terrorism as consisting of attacks by terrorists against civilians *and* the armed military (and law enforcement),[4] it will be possible for counterterrorism analysts and campaign planners to effectively anticipate the full spectrum of the types of new threats they are likely to face in the future, instead of being surprised that the terrorist adversary will intentionally attack a military or law enforcement target when only civilian targets are being focused on.

Prediction Versus Forecasting

To effectively anticipate future terrorist attacks, it is necessary to understand the difference between prediction and forecasting. Prediction, which is operational and tactical, is based on relatively accurate information, and asserts the occurrence of an event with a high degree of certainty, focusing on the where, how, and when of imminent terrorist attacks. Prediction at the operational and tactical level is possible when sufficient information is collected about a terrorist adversary, for instance, by penetrating it with human agents, intercepting its communications, or if they are pre-incident operational mishaps that give away its future attack plans.

Forecasting, on the other hand, is strategic and more general in nature. It focuses on a terrorist group's general warfare proclivity as opposed to predicting an imminent attack, or its likely weapons and targeting selection. When applied to terrorism, it is possible to forecast general trends about a group's overall warfare, such as whether it is likely to employ "conventional" weapons, suicide martyrdom tactics, weapons of mass destruction, or cyber weapons, as well as its likely areas of operations where the attacks are likely to take place.

Thus, in estimating a terrorist group's likely future warfare, it is important to understand whether the estimate is a prediction or a forecast, based on the type of information available to the estimator.

Ten Early Warning Indicators

Once analysts understand how to properly define terrorism and the distinction between forecasting and prediction, it will be possible to apply them to operationalizing the ten early warning indicators that might point to a potential imminent terrorist attack at the tactical level or a new strategic and operational direction by a terrorist group in its overall warfare.

Organizational Types

The first warning indicator is the nature of the terrorist adversary's organizational formation, which would determine whether it will be a group directed or a personal initiative type of attack. This is an important consideration because a large and well-funded terrorist organization will be able to carry out large-scale and complex attacks as opposed to a smaller and less resourced group, with a lone actor terrorist having to self-fund an attack. Also, a large terrorist group will be able to deploy several combat cells in an operation (such as al-Qaeda's 9/11 attacks, Lashka e-Taiba's November 2008 Mumbai attacks, or the Islamic State's November 2015 Paris attacks), as opposed to a lone actor who can mount only a single, one-person attack (such as Omar Mateen's June 2016 shooting rampage at the Pulse Nightclub, in Orlando, Florida). At the same time, as demonstrated by Mateen's shooting rampage, it is possible for a single actor to inflict mass casualties in a confined public space, with 49 people killed and 53 others wounded.[5] Finally, future attacks could consist of several organizational types of terrorists, such as a mix of groups and lone actors, so various possible combinations of terrorist adversary formations need to be anticipated.

Areas of Operations: Physical or Cybespace

Terrorists' areas of operations, whether current or future, need to be anticipated. Thus, will their attacks take place in physical space, i.e., on the ground, and, specifically, in urban, rural, or maritime areas? Moreover, with the advancement of new communications technologies available to terrorists, they now operate in physical space *and* in cyberspace, where they can launch cyber-attacks against their adversaries. Thus, in anticipating future warfare, will their attacks take place on the ground, in cyberspace, or as a combination of both?

Areas of Operations: Foreign or Local Presence

In estimating the terrorist threat, it is important to identity whether the terrorist adversary is foreign-based or locally-based, and, if it is foreign-based, is it capable of covertly transporting, housing, and equipping its attack team close to their intended targets in other countries. Notable examples of foreign-based attackers include those of the al-Qaeda's 9/11 attacks and the LeT attack teams in Mumbai, India, in November 2008. If the attack team is locally based, it will be easier for them to reach their intended target, so it is crucial to identify likely homegrown terrorist operatives in one's immediate area who might carry out attacks against their local targets, such as the Timothy McVeigh-led cell that carried out the Oklahoma City bombing in April 1995.

Leadership

Understanding the nature of the adversary group's leadership is crucial in anticipating its likely category of warfare at the strategic and operational levels. If a group's leader, for example, is an all controlling charismatic leader, who is not risk averse, and believes in using catastrophic violence to become a world-class perpetrator, then the group is likely to employ weapons of mass destruction types of attacks. For example, with Usama bin Laden regarding himself as a "world class destroyer," al-Qaeda hijacked four aircraft to employ them as weapons of mass destruction on 9/11, and, on March 20, 1995, Shoko Asahara directed his Aum Shinrikyo operatives to carry out a sarin gas attack against the Tokyo subway system, which killed 14 people, and wounded an estimated 5,500 others, with reports that he had contemplated acquiring and exploding a nuclear weapon as part of his apocalyptic vision for inaugurating a new millennium.[6]

Ideology

All terrorist group ideologies are extremist and have no moral constraints in seeking violent revenge against their demonized and dehumanized adversaries for alleged injustices against their perceived community. Like the leadership indicator, a warning indicator, at the strategic level of forecasting, that a group might be seeking to carry out an especially catastrophic attack is whether its ideology is millenarian and apocalyptic to usher in a new global order through the catastrophic destruction of the adversary. A group's ideology will not necessarily remain static and fixed, but its objectives may change. For example, over time a White Supremacist ideology, which might primarily be anti-black, might incorporate a Jihadi ideology's perceived enemies, thereby becoming anti-Semitic, as well, so it is crucial to identify such ideological changes in anticipating a group's future targeting direction.

Funding

Terrorists rely on funding to support their operations, so disrupting their flow of funding is crucial in degrading their operational capabilities. Terrorist groups operate covertly, so tracking new trends in the variations in their funding sources, methods of movement, and activities is crucial. As illicit organizations, many terrorist group also engage in a variety of criminal activities to raise funds, making it necessary to track their associations with criminal groups, which can also generate insights into trends in their areas of operations and types of funding they might require for future operations. The increasing use of cryptocurrencies, such as Bitcoin, by terrorist groups means that both official and cryptocurrencies need to be tracked. Finally, it is also necessary to discern whether the funds that are raised flow to groups or individual operatives to carry out operations.

Recruitment

Tracking new trends in the recruitment of operatives into terrorist groups is an important indicator in forecasting and predicting potential transformations in their warfare and targeting. Recruiting identifies potential operatives to provide crucial capabilities for terrorist groups. This includes acquiring new sets of skills, increasing operational capabilities, and replacing losses caused by the arrests or killings of operatives. Some recruiting is specialized, such as recruiting operatives who are sufficiently pliable to become suicide bombers, firearm shooters, engineers who can build improvised explosive devices (IEDs), scientists who can manufacture biological, chemical, radiological or nuclear weapons and devices, or computer scientists who can build cyber-weapons.

Modus Operandi

Modus operandi refers to the techniques, tactics, and procedures (TTPs) used by terrorists to execute their attacks. Identifying changes in their modus operandi, such as the resort to new types of weapons and tactics, can provide clues to how they might conduct their future attacks. One of the most noteworthy examples is the simultaneous hijacking of four civilian aircraft by al-Qaeda on 9/11, not to bargain over demands, as was the previous rationale for aircraft hijackings, but to use as suicidal weapons of mass destruction to destroy skyscrapers and inflict mass casualties. A potential new trend in terrorists' modus operandi might involve a combination of physical and cyber-attacks in an operation, or a cyber-attack that might be comparable to the use of a weapon of mass destruction against an adversary country's critical infrastructure. To avoid strategic, operational, and tactical surprises, therefore, forecasting and predicting new trends in terrorists' modus operandi require anticipating new ranges of options to the terrorists that might have been previously considered unthinkable.

Types of Weapons Technology

A variety of weapons technologies are available to terrorist groups. These range from firearms, improvised explosive devices (IEDs), edged weapons (such as knives), vehicles (to ram into pedestrians or use them as bombing platforms), weapons of mass destruction (such as chemical, biological, radiological, or nuclear – CBRN), and cyber weapons. It is important, therefore, to anticipate the types and combinations of current and new weapons and devices that terrorist adversaries are likely to employ in their future attacks. Will a terrorist adversary, for example, embark on attacks that are conventional low-impact (CLI), conventional high impact (CHI), chemical, biological, radiological, nuclear (CBRN), or cyber warfare – or a combination of these four categories of warfare, as well as ones that use new types of weapons technologies that are not yet known. A warning indicator that a group might be on the trajectory to using a CBRN or cyber weapon is the recruitment of engineering and scientific specialists with appropriate technological skills to develop and deploy them. Another warning indicator is the training of a group's operatives in using such weapons and devices to attain operational capability in their warfare and targeting.

Target Selection

To forecast and predict likely terrorist target selection, "target packages" can be prepared that identify targets that would correlate with a group's propaganda and objectives (including its value, such as whether it is iconic or not), its logistical capability to reach and access the target, the types of weapons used, the target's level of security, including whether it is a "hard" public facility or an unprotected public space "soft" target i.e., the target's vulnerability to attack), the consequences of attacking the target (in terms of casualties and physical damage), and the likelihood that the attackers would be able to escape from the scene of the attack.

Assessment

Once these ten warning indicators are correlated, analysts can assess the incubation periods, triggers, and timeframes for the future terrorist attacks of concern. Generally, terrorist operations are preceded by incubation periods of varying timeframes. It is important to identify them because they provide pre-incident observables that can be monitored and disrupted. Different types of operations involve varying incubation periods, so effective forecasting and prediction requires appropriate levels of awareness of the phases and components involved in mounting terrorist operations. Some incubation periods can be relatively short in duration, especially if a terrorist group becomes extremely desperate as a result of a government's counterterrorism campaign that pushes it "against the wall" and therefore decides to resort to catastrophic warfare to punish the "offending" state, or, as a last resort, to maintain its very survival. In other cases, a terrorist group that is confident in its warfare capability might accept a long incubation period to launch a major attack, such as al-Qaeda's long-planning period for 9/11, as opposed to other groups that feel weak, which causes them to launch numerous and frequent low-impact types of attacks.

It is also important to anticipate whether an attack might be carried out by a group or a lone actor. In the case of a long actor, they are difficult to identify during the pre-incident phases because their activities and communications are difficult to detect, as few or no associates of such perpetrators are informed of their imminent attack intentions.

Wild Cards

Counterterrorism analysts and campaign planners need to anticipate wild cards ("black swan" events) that might propel a terrorist adversary to suddenly and unexpectedly embark on a major attack. In the case of a resort to weapons of mass destruction, these would include sudden access by a terrorist adversary to the black/grey markets, theft of such weapons and devices, or provision by a state sponsor of CBRN weapons, devices, and delivery systems.

In another "wild card", it is important to be aware that a group's extremist ideology might change over time. As mentioned earlier, a far-right White Supremacist group's ideology might suddenly incorporate some jihadist elements, which would affect its choice of weaponry and targeting.

Conclusion

In a final consideration, although it is an example of forecasting success, Bill Gates, the founder and former Chairman of Microsoft, who became a public health philanthropist, had warned in a March 2015 TED Talk about the need to prepare to counter a future outbreak of a COVID-19 type deadly pandemic, which was likely to quickly spread around the world and kill millions of people.[7] However, his repeated warnings were ignored by government agencies around the world, which were unprepared to mitigate the deadly and economically devastating impacts of the hundreds of thousands of cases of infection spreading around the globe. This pandemic also has a terrorism component, with terrorist groups such as the Islamic State and White Supremacists calling on their adherents to further spread the pandemic on their own or to carry out terrorist attacks in order to significantly exacerbate civil unrest in the affected countries.

What can be done to improve the analytic capability to conduct forecasting/prediction of new trends in terrorist warfare as "realistically" as possible? While it is known that predictions are limited in their reliability because, unless they are based on covertly obtained intelligence, which is difficult to obtain about a group's – or a lone actor's – imminent attack planning, by adopting a more strategic level forecasting capability it will be possible to identify a terrorist group's future warfare intentions, particularly whether it is likely to embark on CLI, CHI, CBRN, or cyber warfare. This would be similar to Bill Gates's prescience in forecasting the potential outbreak of a catastrophic virus pandemic. Analytic tools such as Red Teaming, alternative competing hypotheses (ACH), social network analysis (SNA), geo-spatial analytics, artificial-intelligence (AI)-driven data-mining tools, and other software applications, can be utilized to collect relevant information that can be collated to forecast such terrorist warfare capability at more strategic levels of analysis.

Notes

1 See Joshua Sinai, "Assessing the January 6, 2021 Violent Takeover of the U.S. Capitol Building: The Threat and the Security Technology Response," Capitology Blog, March 18, 2021, https://www.captechu.edu/blog/assessing-january-6-2021-violent-takeover-of-us-capitol-building-threat-and-security.
2 See, https://www.twelvebooks.com/titles/the-january-6-select-committee/the-january-6-report/9781538742150/?utm_source=Social(Promo)&utm_medium=Google-Adwords&utm_campaign=TheJanuary6SelectCommittee_January6Report_Preorder_Traffic_GCP_9781538742150&utm_

content=Politics&utm_term=TopicInt_JanuarySix_GenPop_BrandAwareness&gclid=Cj0KCQiAyrac BhDoARIsACGFcS6dD_2iuCXHT0tBtvSDq3oMaq4TIJMfEhuhlViMrssiP_pQx5FUKQAa AuyfEALw_wcB.

3 Joshua Sinai, "How to Prevent Future Afghanistan-Like Disasters in a Post 9/11 World, The Washington Times, September 9, 2021, https://www.washingtontimes.com/news/2021/sep/9/how-to-prevent-future-afghanistan-like-disasters/.

4 Joshua Sinai, "How to Study Terrorism," Capitology Blog, December 15, 2020, https://www.captechu.edu/blog/how-study-terrorism.

5 "Terrorist Gunman Attacks Pulse Nightclub in Orlando, Florida," History.com, June 12, 2016, https://www.history.com/this-day-in-history/terrorist-gunman-attacks-pulse-nightclub-in-orlando-florida.

6 "Tokyo Subways Are Attacked With Sarin Gas," History.com, March 20, 1995, https://www.history.com/this-day-in-history/tokyo-subways-are-attacked-with-sarin-gas.

7 Bill Gates, "The Next Outbreak, We're Not Ready, Ted2015, April 3, 2015, https://www.ted.com/talks/bill_gates_the_next_outbreak_we_re_not_ready/transcript?language=dz.

23

RECENT TRENDS IN INTERNATIONAL TERRORISM AND THEIR IMPACT ON COUNTERTERRORISM AMBITIONS

James J.F. Forest

Terrorism is a constantly evolving form of criminal and deviant behavior. As a result, a snapshot of global terrorist activity is destined to become outdated rather quickly. Nonetheless, for the same reason we occasionally take family snapshots to capture a moment in time, a reflective exercise like this serves a useful purpose. So, at the risk of over-simplifying this complex and dynamic phenomenon, this essay will briefly describe current operational, technological and ideological trends in the global terrorism landscape and then examine implications for future counterterrorism policies and strategies.

Operational, Tactical, and Technological Trends

Of the major operational and tactical trends we see in terrorism today, the most prominent categories involve 1) the types of attack perpetrators, 2) their most frequent targets, and 3) the weapons chosen to use in their attacks. In terms of attack perpetrators, we have seen increases over the past decade in the number of terrorist groups using women and children for logistical support and to deliver a weapon (often an improvised explosive device) to the intended target. The most notable examples of this include al-Shabaab, Boko Haram and the Islamic State, while in Russia, a network of Chechen women called "Black Widows" have attacked airplanes and subways. Additionally, we see an increasing frequency of "do-it-yourself" (DIY) attacks throughout Europe, North America, Asia and the Middle East.[1] These are attacks in which the perpetrators have no known connections to any established terrorist network leaders or members, and there is no evidence of operational support or direction from anyone else. A lone actor (or sometimes a small team of individuals) has full control over the financial and logistical dimensions of the attack, including the choice of target, weapon and timing. These kinds of attacks are virtually impossible to prevent unless the perpetrator (often through careless, sloppy tradecraft) inadvertently reveals their intentions and preparations to intelligence or law enforcement.

This increase of lone actor DIY attacks emulates a pattern observed 120 years ago during a period of anarchist terrorism from the 1880s to the 1920s. Similarly, today's terrorists attack many of

DOI: 10.4324/9781003326373-27

the same kinds of targets that were chosen by anarchists and others years ago, such as government and commercial buildings, public gatherings, law enforcement, and political leaders. For example, while anarchists many years ago attacked a Spanish prime minister, Russian Tsar, and American president and in 2020 right-wing terrorists in the United States plotted to attack the Michigan State Capitol and to kidnap and kill the governor of Michigan. However, there are also key differences in terrorist targeting, particularly attacks against aviation and rail transportation. Recent decades have also seen a wide range of attacks against houses of worship, including Sunni mosques in Canada and New Zealand, Shia mosques in Iraq and Pakistan, synagogues in Pittsburgh and San Diego, a Sikh temple in Wisconsin, and Christian churches in South Carolina and Texas.

The weapons used in terrorist attacks have remained fairly consistent, even though terrorist networks—as with many other forms of human activity—are quite capable of adapting and innovating in order to achieve their objectives. Just like the anarchists of old, today's terrorists predominately use guns, knives, and homemade explosives in their attacks. Well-known recent examples include a mass casualty shooting attack in 2011 at a political youth gathering outside Oslo; knife attacks in Berlin, Wuerzburg, and several other German cities since 2015; a shooting and hostage incident at a nightclub in Orlando; a shooting attack at an office party in San Bernardino, and a shooting at a department store in El Paso. But modern perpetrators of terrorism have also added motor vehicles to their arsenal of weapons, often in combination with gun or knife attacks. For example: on July 14, 2016, Mohamed Lahouaiej-Bouhlel used a delivery truck to mow down 86 people celebrating Bastille Day in Nice, France. On November 28, 2016, Abdul-Razak Ali Artan rammed his car into several students at Ohio State University, then jumped out and stabbed others. In London, Khalid Masood drove a car into pedestrians on Westminster Bridge on March 22, 2017, killing five and injuring 45 others. Rakhmat Akilov used a hijacked truck on April 7, 2017 to kill five people in Stockholm, Sweden. On June 3, 2017, three attackers drove a car into pedestrians on London Bridge, then ran into a market and began stabbing people. On August 12, 2017, James Fields, Jr. rammed his car into a crowd of anti-racism protestors in Charlottesville, Va., killing a young woman. And on April 23, 2018, Alek Minassian drove a rented van onto a busy sidewalk in Toronto, killing 11 pedestrians and injuring 15 more. In comparison to these individual or small group attacks, more elaborate terrorist attacks involving multiple perpetrators, targets and high explosives (e.g., the post-9/11 attacks in Bali, Madrid, London, and Paris) are rare exceptions to the norm.

Meanwhile, when assessing the future threat of terrorism, some researchers focus on some of the worst-case scenarios involving chemical, biological, radiological, or nuclear (CBRN) weapons. The 1995 sarin nerve agent attack by Aum Shinrikyo in the Tokyo subway is frequently cited as a harbinger of things to come. In recent years we have observed dozens of chemical weapon attacks by the Islamic State of Iraq and Syria, while far-right extremists in the United States have aspired to use cyanide, anthrax, and ricin in several failed terrorism attempts.[2] And relatively new extremist movements—like Atomwaffen and Boogaloo—embrace an "accelerationist" ideology in which they argue that an apocalyptic destruction of society is necessary in order to create a more ideological (and racially) pure future.[3] This, in turn, suggests an ideological rationale for the use of CBRN weapons not unlike that of Aum Shinrikyo. However, throughout history, terrorist plots and attacks involving these kinds of weapons have been exceedingly rare. Instead, it is significantly likely overall that the future of terrorism will continue to be dominated by more low-tech weapons that are not difficult to acquire and use.

Terrorists of the modern era have also adapted their tactics and operations in other ways. For example, the Internet is used for recruitment, target surveillance, and for gathering information about the efforts of a government to combat the threat of terrorism. Tools and techniques for cyberattacks are widely available online, and some groups—like Hezbollah—have shown surprising information warfare capabilities.[4] And the so-called dark web offers an array of opportunities for terrorist networks in areas of operational planning, financing sources, weapons procurement and other logistical dimensions of their operations. In short, the globalization of information access and communication capabilities via the Internet has brought tremendous benefits to terrorists across the global landscape, as we'll address in more detail later in this essay.

Finally, other technologies that are being adapted by modern terrorists include the use of relatively small unmanned aerial vehicles (UAVs) for surveilling and attacking targets. Hamas, Hezbollah, Harakat Tahrir al-Sham and the Islamic State are among nearly two dozen groups that have demonstrated capabilities in this area.[5] As UAVs and robotics become less expensive and more ubiquitous in homes and industry, many experts expect that terrorists will find new ways to use these technologies for their purposes. Similarly, artificial intelligence could prove beneficial to terrorists in the future—for example, using pre-programmed autonomous vehicles to deliver explosives, or coordinating swarms of lethal autonomous drones in indiscriminate attacks against public gatherings. However, terrorist networks have most often been risk-averse, with a preference for "tried and true" tactics over riskier, more exotic options. Because no terrorist network has unlimited resources, the pressure to ensure "return on investment" will continue to impact how often and how effectively terrorist groups will be able to incorporate these and other new kinds of weapons or technologies into their operations. That said, terrorists' choices of targets and weapons will also continue to be driven by their specific ideological motivations and strategic objectives.

Ideological Trends

Throughout history, a majority of terrorist activity has been domestic in orientation. A group or movement in a given country was launched, fueled by grievances and goals specific to that country, and began attacking targets within that country. This has been the case particularly for certain types of terrorist ideologies, like ethno-nationalist, anti-colonial and left-wing terrorism. Many religiously-oriented terrorist attacks have also been directed exclusively against targets within the country of the group's origin: the Egyptian Islamic Group attacked targets within Egypt; the Army of God attacked family clinics in the United States; Jemmah Islamiyaa attacked targets in Indonesia; Abu Sayyaf Group attacked targets within the Philippines; and so forth.

But terrorism has also come in transnational forms as well, including the anarchist movements in Europe in the late 19th and early 20th centuries, and more recently the global jihadist movement in which al-Qaeda and the Islamic State play central roles. Here, unlike other kinds of Islamist extremism, the goal of global jihadism is not confined to a particular country or political regime, but instead seeks to reframe the entire Muslim world's relationship with non-Muslim civilizations. Adherents of the global jihadist movement eventually want to establish a transnational caliphate, uniting the Muslim world under a caliph (a spiritual and political leader), and their terrorist attacks are characterized as necessary steps toward that long-term objective.

The terrorist attacks against the United States on September 11, 2001, demonstrated how global jihadism threatens Western societies. Numerous high-profile attacks since then—in Bali, Madrid, London, Jakarta, New York, Boston, Paris, Brussels and many others—have continually reinforced the view among security professionals that global jihadists pose a significant terrorist threat to international security. Billions of dollars have been dedicated to a so-called "global war on terror," explicitly focused on countering this threat. In Iraq and Syria, the rise of the Islamic State over the previous decade signaled both expansion and peer competition within the global jihadist landscape. This landscape is now characterized by the evolution of two major jihadist networks of affiliate groups worldwide, some of whom have declared loyalty to the leaders of al-Qaeda and others to the Islamic State. Further, both al-Qaeda and the Islamic State have embraced the promotion of "do-it-yourself" jihadist attacks by individuals with no identifiable links to any established groups. Today, the ideology of global jihadism continues to inspire and motivate attacks worldwide, including in countries like Sri Lanka, where jihadists previously had no significant presence. This trend is likely to shape the security environment for many years to come.

And yet, despite the frequent assumption that global jihadists will continue to dominate the terrorist landscape worldwide for the foreseeable future, we have also seen a rapid growth of terrorist activity associated with another ideological category—far-right extremism—particularly in North America and Europe. While the July 2011 attack by Anders Breivik in Oslo, Norway, is perhaps the most notorious example in recent decades, significant right-wing attacks have taken place in dozens of countries from Canada to New Zealand. As Bruce Hoffman has noted, far-right extreme nationalists "span the globe from the Americas to Europe to East Asia."[6] Compared to other ideological categories, far-right extremism includes dozens of sub-types, from pro-nationalist militias to white supremacists to anti-government movements. According to one study, there are at least 26 definitions of far-right extremism, and the most common features mentioned in them—nationalism, racism, xenophobia, anti-democracy and the desire for a strong and encompassing state—are included in only half of these definitions.[7]

While many groups focus on local or national grievances and goals (e.g., the Soldiers of Odin in Canada, the Italian New Order, the English Defence League, and Russian National Unity[8]), others—like the neo-Nazi groups Blood and Honor and Atomwaffen—are transnational, with active chapters in multiple countries embracing a global "accelerationist" ideology (described earlier) that rejects liberal democracy and encourages an escalation of violence in order to hasten the collapse of society in order to build something entirely new.[9] Far-right nativist and nationalist ideologies are typically anti-foreigner and anti-immigration. Their violent attacks are frequently driven by insecurities and fear among members of a community, who believe that they are profoundly threatened by others (often defined by racial and ethnic differences) who are typically seen as having a lower moral or ethical status than the community members.[10] Similarly, as Pete Simi and colleagues explain, "[w]hite supremacists imagine they are part of an innately superior biogenetic race (i.e., a 'master race') that is under attack by race-mixing and intercultural exchange …[they] unite around genocidal fantasies against Jews, Blacks, Hispanics, gays, and anyone else opposed to white power. They desire a racially exclusive world where non-whites and other 'sub-humans' are vanquished, segregated, or at least subordinated to Aryan authority."[11]

The increasing threat of far-right terrorism in the United States has been recognized by scholars and government agencies. In April 2017, the U.S. Government Accountability Office released a report that examined domestic terrorist attacks between 9/11 and December 2016, concluding that "of the 85 extremist incidents that resulted in death since September 12, 2001, far-right violent extremist groups were responsible for 62 (73%), while radical Islamist violent extremists were responsible for 23 (27%)."[12] Similar reports by think tanks and academic researchers have found that compared to jihadists, right-wing terrorists have killed nearly twice as many people in the US over the past two decades.[13] From 2016 to 2020, the Trump administration facilitated access for far-right extremists to executive branch power and subsequent policy influence, with ultra-nationalist, anti-Muslim racist extremists serving in key White House positions. This in turn inspired an increase of far-right terrorist attacks throughout the United States as well as internationally. For example, in a manifesto published online shortly before his March 2019 attacks against mosques in Christchurch, New Zealand, the assailant praised Trump "as a symbol of renewed white identity and common purpose."[14]

Trump's loss in the 2020 election fueled a barrage of conspiracy theories, rage and hostility among those who lost this access. Then on January 6, 2021, a mob of angry Trump supporters stormed the U.S. Capitol Building in Washington, D.C., in an attempt to disrupt the Congressional certification of the election results. They attacked police officers and security guards, crashed through windows and doors, and threatened to harm or kill a number of elected politicians, including the Vice President. To date, nearly 740 people have been arrested for their involvement in the January 6 assault in Washington, D.C., some charged with sedition, others for violent attacks against police officers protecting the building and the elected leaders inside.[15] According to the Department of Justice, the Department of Homeland Security, and the Director of National Intelligence (among many other credible sources), nearly 100 of the most violent perpetrators in this attack were affiliated with U.S. far-right extremist groups, including the Oath Keepers, Proud Boys, and Three Percenters.

Further, there are political leaders whose beliefs and goals complement those of far-right extremists. One of the most disappointing facets of political life in the United States is that following the January 6, 2021, violent insurrectionist attack in Washington, D.C., certain elected politicians have shown a blatant disregard for criminal behavior when they agree with the sentiments motivating that behavior. Despite a mountain of factual evidence, they have sought to diminish the threat of far-right extremists, instead favoring violent rhetoric that vilifies and dehumanizes foreigners, immigrants, and members of the Democratic party while promoting pro-demagogue conspiracies like QAnon. By hiding behind the constitutional protections of free speech, they are not held accountable for providing inspiration and moral support to far-right extremists attacking Americans. As a result, they will contribute to a permissive political context in which more far-right extremist attacks are inevitable.

Comparing the Two Most Prominent Ideological Categories

While it is likely impossible to resolve the debate over which of these—global jihadism or far-right extremism—will serve as the top terrorist threat in the foreseeable future, it is important to recognize some key similarities and differences among them. To begin with, groups in both ideological categories express a desire for legitimate order and structure. They view the world through the framework of a superior in-group threatened by inferior out-groups, and they despise government officials (especially in democracies) for illegitimately protecting those out-groups. Both ideological categories are infused with conspiracy theories (e.g., a "war against Islam," "the great replacement," "Zionist Occupied Government," and "cultural Marxism"), particularly conspiracies that seek to weaken and subjugate them, or even annihilate their way of life.[16] They feel that there can be no political solution, have a strong hatred of perceived traitors enabling a corrupt system, and view terrorism as a form of purifying violence toward spiritual rejuvenation and society redemption. To them, violence is seen as legitimate and necessary in order to establish a utopian society in which their in-group reigns supreme.[17] These kinds of sociopolitical grievances, in turn, have led terrorists in both categories to attack a variety of unarmed civilian targets, including public gatherings and houses of worship.

Economic grievances are also prominent within both ideological categories. Shared frustrations about globalization (including economic interdependence, information technology, and migration patterns) and distrust of government policies have been further exacerbated by the economic effects of the COVID-19 pandemic. At the same time, both ideological categories have seen organic growth in transnational linkages formed both intentionally and via ad hoc opportunities. Some countries have provided notably hospitable environments in which to forge such links. For several years, Iraq and Syria attracted tens of thousands of global jihad-ists, while more recently Hungary has become an active hub of far-right extremist activity, hosting various international gatherings of anti-immigrant, anti-Muslim and white national-ist movements. These connections facilitate knowledge sharing, diverse sourcing of financial support, and active recruitment efforts both online and on the ground in various communities worldwide.[18]

Beyond these similarities in grievances and transnational linkages, there are some impor-tant differences to account for as well. For example, while global jihadists want to replace the Westphalian nation-state system with a transnational caliphate representing a united and newly empowered Muslim world, most far-right extremists have more regional or local agendas. A unique exception to this are accelerationists, who feel that only apocalyptic rebirth will make a better world, so their goal is to tear apart the fabric of modern society and provoke mass conflict. Another key difference is that global jihadism may have lost some momentum and ideological traction (particularly after the failure of the Islamic State's effort to establish a caliphate), while far-right extremism appears to be on the rise.

But perhaps the most consequential difference between these two ideological categories is that unlike global jihadists, the far-right violent movements have an established base of support within Western countries, allowing groups and individual adherents the freedom to recruit, or-ganize and operate in the open, in broad daylight. Several European far-right movements have formed political parties—like the National Rally in France (led by Marine Le Pen)—whose candidates have gained widespread public attention (and sometimes even political victories). In general, there appears to be more tacit acceptance or support of far-right grievances than global jihadist grievances, with certain political and media elites adding perceived legitimacy to far-right extremist narratives. More worrisome, far-right extremist groups have attracted for-mer military and law enforcement personnel, whose training and expertise may lead to serious "insider threat" consequences.[19]

The Challenge of Online Amplification

Terrorists' means of communication have evolved from printed manifestos, pamphlets and press releases to audio and video recordings (disseminated on disc and then online), digital magazines (like *Inspire* and *Dabiq*), and discussion forums like Stormfront and Iron March. Since the turn of the century, social media platforms (notably Facebook, Twitter, YouTube and Instagram) and encrypted messaging applications like Telegram and WhatsApp have become increasingly used by terrorist networks, not only to communicate with members and supporters but also to spread fear and uncertainty among target populations. In some instances (for example, the Christchurch attack), terrorists have even used live streaming capabilities to showcase their violence online in real time. By analyzing an individual's social media activity, terrorist networks can also use these platforms to identify potential sympathizers and recruits. Multi-player gaming platforms and private messaging forums are also commonly used by terrorist networks, while emerging tech-nologies in the field of "extended reality" (including augmented reality and virtual reality) can be used for indoctrination, training, attack simulation and other terrorist-related purposes. And computer algorithms built into search engines and social media platforms—which recommend content and resources based on user activity—help to surround an individual with only informa-tion sources that confirm what they already want to believe (even wholesale lies) and avoid any contradictory information (including factual evidence) that risks exposing them to the discomfort of cognitive dissonance.

Meanwhile, as noted above, the acceptance and promotion of far-right extremist narratives among major influential figures in Europe and North America represents a significant difference to the global jihadist ideology. Compared to global jihadist networks, the far right has a much greater presence on the open Internet, from entire sections of Reddit, 4chan, 8kun and other discussion boards to social media channels like Gab, Discord, and Parlor dedicated to promoting far-right ideologies, conspiracies, and outright hatred of others. Only in the past couple of years (and particularly after the events of January 2021) have we seen active efforts by social media platforms to address the spread of far-right extremist activity. Similarly, for several years YouTube has implemented various efforts to scrub their channels of global jihadist videos, but there has been significantly less focus on suspending or deleting videos that promote far-right ideas.

Another core difference between global jihadism and far-right extremism is the amount of online disinformation presently linked to the latter.[20] Of course, there is a great deal of propaganda produced and distributed online by adherents of both ideological perspectives, but there are many more blatant falsehoods, manipulated images and videos, gaslighting attempts and conspiracy theories associated with the far-right. Further, certain political groups and individuals in both Europe and the United States have tried to legitimate these conspiracy theories and encourage right-wing extremist movements. For example, members of Congress like Paul Gosar (R-AZ) and Marjorie Taylor Greene (R-GA), have disputed official government accounts about the Capitol insurrection, even arguing that the election was stolen—despite tons of video and documentary evidence proving they are wrong. They have also accused the government of conducting various conspiracies against Trump and his supporters, even claiming that the January 6th rioters were primarily non-violent, and those who engaged in violence were leftists in disguise, trying to cause trouble for true "patriotic Americans."

These claims have been further amplified not only by fringe right-wing media outlets like Gateway Pundit and Revolve, but also by more prominent media personalities like Fox News Network's Tucker Carlson. And unlike global jihadists, many far-right extremists have been very active in spreading disinformation about the COVID-19 pandemic and vaccines, particularly online. In sum, a range of longstanding socioeconomic and political grievances, fear and uncertainty surrounding the pandemic, a burning hatred of "others," and the spread of provocative disinformation on social media platforms have all combined to fuel the rise of far-right extremist activity. The culmination of recent political events in the United States and Europe, and the expanding reach of transnational far-right extremist movements, all point to a disturbing conclusion: the civilized world will be grappling with this deadly ideological cancer for the foreseeable future.

Summary and Implications for Counterterrorism

So, to summarize: the global terrorism landscape is framed by a combination of intersecting trends that suggest we are likely to see more lone actor terrorists motivated by either far-right extremism or global jihadism, using low-tech weapons (knives, guns and vehicles) in attacks against a variety of civilian targets. Terrorists in both of these ideological categories are motivated by in-group/out-group "othering"—they orient those shared socioeconomic and political grievances in ways that direct their anger and violence toward specific types of individuals based on ethnicity, religion, political beliefs, and other characteristics. By providing an "other" to vilify, these ideologies offer an attractive and convenient means for people to avoid the uncomfortable feeling of having nobody (or no one but themselves) to blame for their personal struggles.

Each of these major ideological categories requires different (and not often complementary) counterterrorism efforts. Further, counterterrorism efforts that may work against global jihadist groups may not work against far-right extremist groups. Policymakers and practitioners must identify and confront the ideological centers of gravity within each type of transnational terrorism described here, in order to stem the flow of recruits and financial support. Combating these kinds of transnational terrorism will require a whole of society effort—militaries and police forces are critical but insufficient for defeating ideologically-driven security threats. There are critical roles to play for educators and community leaders, religious authorities, prominent influencers (including journalists and popular social media accounts), prisons and courts, and of course political leaders. Unfortunately, politicians, media outlets and others pursuing a political agenda that ignores—or worse, encourages and emboldens—far-right extremists will make counterterrorism more difficult. In turn, they will bear some responsibility for the carnage and destruction wrought by right-wing extremists, though it is doubtful they will be held accountable, as seen most notably in the aftermath of the January 6, 2021, attack in Washington, D.C.

Similarly, we must confront the potential insider threat of far-right ideological support among members of military and law enforcement communities. Fortunately, existing research on this topic has found only a very small percentage of a nation's military or law enforcement harbor these sentiments, but because their position within a society authorizes them to carry weapons and use force to coerce the behavior of a civilian population, they should not be allowed to act as if certain members of the population are less worthy of protection than others. Allowing such sentiments to fester or flourish can fracture the kinds of trust between security forces and communities that are essential to effective counterterrorism.

Technological advances could add more complexity to the threat of terrorism over time. Alongside careful government monitoring of import and export activities, we will need private sector involvement to constrain terrorist acquisition of drone (and other) technologies. Attacks using CBRN weapons remain a possibility, particularly among far-right militant accelerationists. But it is equally likely that low-tech attacks (shooting, stabbing, vehicle ramming, use of rudimentary explosives) will continue to be the most common. Another area of technology regarding the terrorist threat involves the Internet. Both global jihadists and far-right extremists are using global communications infrastructure to inspire DIY lone attackers, and more generally to manipulate the emotional and behavioral responses of audiences worldwide. With the advances in deepfake technology, we will undoubtedly see increasingly realistic and believable videos and images used for these purposes. So, while it is already difficult to effectively counter the kinds of online propaganda and disinformation that can fuel terrorism, it will be increasingly essential to do so. Responding to this challenge will require public education efforts focused on digital media literacy, in order to equip individual consumers of information with the skills and sense of personal responsibility for recognizing and rejecting the online efforts of terrorist networks.

Finally, judging from the historical record, it is highly likely that in the broader landscape of national and international security, acts of terrorism will remain exceedingly rare events regardless of the ideological orientation of the perpetrators. This leads to the oft-cited maxim in counterterrorism that societies and governments must not over-react to this threat. A central strategy of terrorism is to provoke the kind of over-reaction that curtails civil liberties in the name of security, with the goal of producing a climate of fear, distrust and oppression that tears at the fabric of a society and threatens to undermine the perceived legitimacy of the government. We all must—as Tom Parker wisely counsels—"avoid the terrorist trap,"[21] through counterterrorism policies and educational efforts that replace sensationalism and fear-mongering with a more rational, evidence-based and contextually appropriate response.

Notes

1 For a detailed description and examples of this, see "Do-It-Yourself Terrorism," in James Forest (ed.), *The Terrorism Lectures* (Los Angeles, CA: Nortia Press, 2019), pp. 315–344.

2 Columb Strack, "The Evolution of the Islamic State's Chemical Weapons Efforts," CTC Sentinel (October 2017). Online at: https://ctc.usma.edu/the-evolution-of-the-islamic-states-chemical-weapons-efforts/; and Daniel Koehler and Peter Popella, Mapping Far-right Chemical, Biological, Radiological, and Nuclear (CBRN) Terrorism Efforts in the West: Characteristics of Plots and Perpetrators for Future Threat Assessment, Terrorism and Political Violence (August 2018).

3 JM Berger, "A Paler Shade of White: Identity & In-Group Critique in James Mason's Seige," Resolve Network (April 2021). Online at: https://doi.org/10.37805/remve2021.1.

4 Guermantes Lailari, "The Battle for Strategic Influence in the 2006 Israeli/Hizbollah Conflict," in James Forest (ed.) *Influence Warfare* (Santa Barbara, CA: Praeger, 2009), pp. 311–328.

5 Peter Bergen, Melissa Salyk-Virk and David Sterman, "World of Drones," updated (July 30, 2020). Online at: https://www.newamerica.org/international-security/reports/world-drones/.

6 Bruce Hoffman, *Inside Terrorism* (New York, NY: Columbia University Press), p. 237.

7 Cas Mudde, "Right-Wing Extremism Analyzed. A Comparative Analysis of the Ideologies of Three Alleged Right-Wing Extremist Parties," *European Journal of Political Research* 27, no. 2 (1995), p. 206.

8 Specific research case studies include Graham Macklin, "Extreme Right-Wing Terrorism in Britain: The Case of National Action," *Perspectives on Terrorism* 12, no. 6 (December 2018), pp. 104–122. Miroslav Mareš, "Right-Wing Terrorism and Violence in Hungary at the Beginning of the 21st Century," *Perspectives on Terrorism* 12, no. 6 (December 2018); Pietro C. Gattinara et al., "What Characterizes the Far-Right Scene in Europe and Beyond?" in Anders Ravik Jupskås and Eviane Leidig (eds.), *Knowing What's (Far) Right: A Compendium* (C-REX: University of Oslo, August 2020), pp. 45–49; Riccardo Marchi and Raquel da Silva, "Political Violence from the Extreme Right in Contemporary Portugal," *Perspectives on Terrorism* 13, no. 6 (December 2019), pp. 27–42. Kristy Campion, "A 'Lunatic Fringe'? The Persistence of Right-Wing Extremism in Australia," *Perspectives on Terrorism* 13, no. 2 (April 2019), pp. 2–20. Emil Archambault and Yannick Veilleux-Lepage, "Soldiers of Odin in Canada: Internal Conflicts and Transnational Dimensions," in Tore Bjørgo and Miroslav Mareš (eds.), *Vigilantism Against Migrants and Minorities* (London: Routledge, 2019) pp. 272–285; Cas Mudde, *Racist Extremism in Central and Eastern Europe* (New York, NY: Routledge, 2005).

9 Jacob Ware, "Siege: The Atomwaffen Division and Rising Far-Right Terrorism in the United States," The International Centre for Counter-Terrorism – The Hague (July 2019); Berger, "A Paler Shade of White"; Zack Beauchamp, "Accelerationism: The Obscure Idea Inspiring White Supremacist Killers around the World," Vox (November 18, 2019). Online at: https://www.vox.com/the-highlight/2019/11/11/20882005/accelerationism-white-supremacy-christchurch.

10 Victor Asal and R. Karl Rethemeyer, "The Nature of the Beast: Organizational Structures and the Lethality of Terrorist Attacks," *Journal of Politics* 70, no. 2 (2008), p. 437.

11 Pete Simi, Steven Windisch, and Karyn Sporer, *"Recruitment and Radicalization among U.S. Far Right Terrorists,"* (College Park, MD: START Center, 2016), p. 6.

12 U.S. Government Accountability Office, "Countering Violent Extremism," Washington, DC (April 2017). Online at: https://www.gao.gov/assets/690/683984.pdf.

13 David Neiwert et al., Homegrown Terror. Center for Investigative Reporting (June 2017). Online at: https://apps.revealnews.org/homegrown-terror/; David Sterman and Peter Bergen, "Study: Right-wing Terrorism has Killed 48 People in the U.S. Since 2001," New America Foundation (June 2015). Online at: https://www.newamerica.org/international-security/in-the-news/study-right-wing-terrorism-has-killed-48-people-in-the-us-since-2001/; Seth G. Jones, Catrina Doxsee, and Nicholas Harrington, "The Escalating Terrorism Problem in the United States," CSIS Brief (June 2020). Online at: https://www.csis.org/analysis/escalating-terrorism-problem-united-states.

14 Brenton Tarrant, "The Great Replacement: Towards a New Society," (March 2019).

15 The Program on Extremism at George Washington University provides a continually updated database and reports on the arrests of individuals charged with criminal activities related to the January 6th attack on the U.S. Capitol Building. Online at: https://extremism.gwu.edu/Capitol-Hill-Siege.

16 Alexander Meleagrou-Hitchens, Blyth Crawford, and Valentin Wutke, "Rise of the Reactionaries: Comparing the Ideologies of Salafi-Jihadism and White Supremacist Extremism," GWU Program

on Extremism (December 2021). Online at: https://extremism.gwu.edu/sites/g/files/zaxdzs2191/f/Rise%20of%20the%20Reactionaries.pdf.

17 Ibid.

18 Regarding the transnational nature of far-right extremism, see Jacob Aasland Ravndal and Tore Bjørgo (eds.), "Terrorism from the Extreme Right," A Special Issue of Perspectives on Terrorism Vol. XII, No. 6 (December 2018). Online at: https://www.sv.uio.no/c-rex/english/publications/2018/special-issue.html.

19 Michael German, "Hidden in Plain Sight: Racism, White Supremacy, and Far-Right Militancy in Law Enforcement," Brennan Center (August 27, 2020). Online at: https://www.brennancenter.org/our-work/research-reports/hidden-plain-sight-racism-white-supremacy-and-far-right-militancy-law; Cynthia Miller-Idriss, "When the Far Right Penetrates Law Enforcement," Foreign Affairs (December 15, 2020); Daniel Milton and Andrew Hines, "This is War: Examining Military Experience Among the Capitol Hill Siege Participants," GWU Program on Extremism and Combating Terrorism Center at West Point (April 12, 2021). Online at: https://ctc.usma.edu/this-is-war-examining-military-experience-among-the-capitol-hill-siege-participants/.

20 For a detailed examination of provocation, deception and other disinformation tactics, see James Forest, *Digital Influence Warfare in the Age of Social Media* (Santa Barbara, CA: Praeger/ABC-CLIO, 2020), pp. 67–152.

21 Tom Parker, *Avoiding the Terrorist Trap: Why Respect for Human Rights is the Key to Defeating Terrorism* (London: World Scientific, 2019).

24

KEY TRENDS IN TRANSNATIONAL TERRORISM

A Software-Based Key Factor Foresight Analysis

Nicolas Stockhammer

Methodology and Scope

The instant research design is based on an algorithm-processed (Foresight Strategy Cockpit- FSC)[1] trend- and key factor analysis of transnational terrorism. At the very beginning of the analytical process, current trends related with (predominantly Islamist) terrorism, partially rooted in aggregated expert analyses were identified and are expected to shape the phenomenon for around five years to come. Based on these trends, the overall-influencing "key factors" are determined, thoroughly described and operationalized according to criteria like probability, impact and stability of the trend. These are foresight relevant key drivers that will very likely constitute a period of 5–10 years in the surrounding field ("*Umfeldanalyse*") of transnational terrorism and the phenomenon itself. The methodological core process of this study is a cross-impact-analysis that examines the interdependence of the identified key-factors and outlines the extent to which they influence and "drive" each other. Also on the passive side, which relates to the degree to which they are affected and pushed. On a scale ranging from 1 (weak), 2 (moderate) to 3 (strong), the impact between the factors was estimated and weighted against each other. It goes without mentioning, that such kind of analysis rather attempts to paint the bigger picture, a kind of a "Bayeux Tapestry" of transnational terrorism, as strategic foresight is about sketching possible scenarios with a certain level of adaption. However, this methodology does not rule out a phenomenal description of key factors that encompasses etiology, outreach and interdependence alike. Given the timeliness of the pandemic, any such analysis has to start with the dominant topic that has occupied everything and everybody for the last two years: COVID-19.

COVID-19 and Terrorism

Situation Awareness

Without doubt, COVID-19 and its consequences can be regarded as a key driver for the development of transnational terrorism. The still ongoing global health crisis has a tremendous impact on security and terrorism in particular. By advancing a pandemic-related social division originating in the erosion of socioeconomic cohesion, it will most likely have an accelerating effect

DOI: 10.4324/9781003326373-28

on societal radicalization tendencies and consequently on politically motivated violence.[2] Not surprisingly, COVID-19 leverages almost any other key driver identified in the research matrix. According to the key factor cross-impact analysis, it indicates the highest active sum (3,0) when measuring degree of influencing other key factors among all examined items, whereas on the passive side, it is only affected partially by other key factors with an average degree of 1,6 on the scale.

In the slipstream of the ongoing COVID-19 pandemic, after a perceived détente phase, the Salafi-jihadi terrorist threat is reemerging in and around Europe. Islamist terrorism has never really disappeared from the scene; rather, it has remained under the clandestine surface, a fact that statistics on foiled plots, related arrests but also very recent attacks suggest. For Gilles de Kerchove, the former EU's counter-terrorism coordinator, the "*fact that the number of [Isis]-inspired attacks has declined in the EU does not mean that the threat has disappeared. It primarily means that we have got better at detecting and breaking up terrorist plots*".

While most states around the world are still concerned with containing the virus and attempting to limit its lasting damage, jihadist terrorist organizations such as ISIS, which is, in the aftermath of the collapse of the so-called "caliphate", considered to be fundamentally weakened, are trying to capitalize on the misery.[3]

In past ISIS propaganda, the novel coronavirus was called the "crusaders' biggest nightmare" and "Allah's scourge for the infidels".[4] At the same time, practical hygiene recommendations for Islamist adherents to protect themselves from the viral pathogen were provided there, as a concession to the high infection rate of the virus and a cautious admission that COVID-19 might not stop at the extremists. In addition, "Al-Naba" proclaimed a clear message to its fellow jihadist comrades-in-arms: The moment would be right to attack an enemy weakened by the effects of the pandemic.[5] The spread of Corona should hence be seen as an

> opportunity to capitalize on now and launch attacks on the west, in the west for the following reasons: (i) the peoples of the world and especially the "crusaders" (the west) allocate massive resources to fight the spread of the pandemic. Therefore, their security forces are tied to public safety and civilian assistance duties; (ii) the fear of an economic hardship that will hurt the poor as a result of the markets decline; (iii) the possibility of chaos and anarchy that will be manifested in an increase of attacks against people and property.[6]

According to this prescription, Islamists were supposed to carry out terrorist attacks and strike in metropolises such as Paris, London or Brussels,[7] especially since the local security authorities, as well as the respective health care system there, had often reached the limits of both their capacity and performance.

In the wake of COVID-19-related restrictions such as lockdowns or other measures to ban people from crowding the streets, one could confidently assume that sympathizers of ISIS or respective jihadi groups would lose simple targets due to the lack of large crowds and events. Likewise, the fact that the borders between the nation states had temporarily been largely sealed off and at least rigidly controlled for reasons of disease containment, contributed to the interim assessment that a further influx of former foreign terrorist fighters into the Schengen area could be transiently prevented, at least as a collateral effect of the (partial) border closures.

Neither assumption has been proven wrong, but there are three essential factors that must be taken into account that seemingly correspond with the logic of ISIS propagandists:

Shock and Awe Strategy

Firstly, terrorism strategically aims at provocation and attrition maintained by a general "shock and awe" effect, which is why terrorist attacks may have an even stronger psychological impact on the population during the pandemic. Especially after the first phase of what has been called the "new normality" (i.e. learning to live with the virus) was developing only gently like a delicate plant, the pandemic and its consequences may be considered as a major setback. Even small-scale attacks carried out by individual perpetrators, could under these circumstances unfold oversized fear effects and unleash disproportionate governmental reactions as desired by the terrorists. And yet, this is exactly what happened in Paris, Dresden and Nice in the summer/autumn of 2020.[8] All of them being lone actor attacks carried out using cut and thrust weapons; in the French cases the attackers did not even shy away from beheadings, a brutal form of execution associated with ISIS. Media reporting covering these terrorist incidents even overshadowed the extensive 24/7 crisis news regarding SARS-CoV2 all over Europe. The November 2, 2020 attack in Vienna, a projected single actor "plus" scenario[9] (inspired; logistic and planning support) with ties to the Islamist scene in Germany, Switzerland and very likely also the Balkans, even transcended this in terms of international attention and media coverage, as Vienna was long considered as not being in the imminent focus of jihadist violence. Before these attacks in Europe, Salafi-jihadist attacks appeared to be in decline. According to the EUROPOL reporting in 2019, there were 21 Islamist attacks in Europe, down from 24 in 2018 and 33 in 2017.[10] Drawing on Petter Nesser's research published in this volume, it may be assumed, that up to 56% of jihadi terrorist plots are usually successfully thwarted.[11] Obviously, the 2020 republishing of the Mohammed cartoons in the Charlie Hebdo satire magazine reignited the networks' terrorist ambitions and probably fueled the intent to start a campaign.

Pandemic-Driven Shift of Security Focus

Secondly, it is perceivable that the immediate focus of European security authorities at the moment may not entirely be dedicated to fighting terrorism. Besides the Russian invasion to Ukraine that has a strong impact on European security, major capacities to combat the societal, financial and also health policy consequences of COVID-19 are still being maintained as a governmental priority. In a recent CSIS commentary this popular trend to bundle security capacities and simultaneously split functionalities tackling COVID-19 is critically reflected concerning its several possible implications for the system:

> "As countries around the world continue to struggle to contain the spread of the novel coronavirus, governments may rely upon their security forces to perform a range of functions. While there are important, short-term benefits to leveraging security forces for crisis response, this approach can reinforce dependencies on the security sector for civilian competencies, exacerbate conflict drivers, and strengthen authoritarian tendencies in governments".[12]

This continuing concentration on the pandemic could result in a gradual weakening of interior security, as fiscal necessities may also further affect the security sector as a whole.

Awareness among Terrorists

Thirdly, it is no less relevant that any proper assessment of the current threat-potential of ISIS adherents already present in the Schengen area should take the multifaceted effects of COVID-19 on counter-terrorism into consideration. As mentioned above, when countering terrorism, European authorities – for good or worse – are forced to turn their attention to urgent public health and also economic matters. Terrorist organizations register that crisis-driven shift of security focus and consider this as a chance. Against the backdrop of an expected further consolidation of ISIS' terrorist network also in its safe haven in Iraq and Syria,[13] a declared intention to target Europe with terrorist attacks, and a capacity to implement it, especially by single supported actors, should not be underestimated, given the ramifications of COVID-19 on any field of security. The alert-level concerning Islamist-motivated attacks in Europe is furthermore high, what the recent plots seem to confirm.

Global Health

COVID-19 is exactly what forecast analysis usually calls a "disruption,"[14] an instantaneous phenomenon described as kind of "known unknown", something we knew that could happen, but we had practically no idea about the severity of its implications. The novel coronavirus is a game changer. It has triggered a serious global health crisis, one that has both short and long-term effects on a multitude of societal aspects. It is a fundamental truth that nowhere around the globe healthcare systems were designed to deal with this challenge appropriately.[15] In its consequences unpredictable, but certainly a large-scale health crisis, COVID-19 requires urgent mobilization of resources and significantly affects the whole population. What remains unchanged is that the health and social care systems' ability and efficiency to tackle the pandemic is in the focus. Only the intensity and strategies have been modified given the new dynamics. In a timely assessment Deloitte asserted that "leaders around the world are putting in place emergency measures to cope with this health crisis, adjusting in real-time and 'spending each day fixing errors they made yesterday'".[16]

According to Deloitte's in-depth analysis, healthcare systems will probably face major, additional, "collateral" issues like the physical and mental exhaustion of the healthcare workforce, along with worn-out hospital infrastructure.[17] Partly this has become true. In addition, local governmental containment measures, such as lockdowns and curfews, severely affected mental and physical health. Continuous progress concerning appropriate medical treatment and the "race" to provide an efficient vaccine may have given optimism. Then, not before summer 2021 any overall improvement regarding the overall health situation had to be expected.[18] Later pandemic waves and virus mutations like Omikron still had a handle on our health systems. And yet there is no definite end in sight.

Strategically, it remains crucial, to prepare also for future pandemics that are very likely to hit us in the near future. It goes without saying that COVID-19 increases governmental demands to update states' and international organizations' risk assessment based upon manmade threats that should be reflected in political guidelines such as national crisis response plans, and finally also in national strategies. Preparedness and measures to ensure resilience are key assets for the struggle against the pandemic as well as against terrorism.

Global Wealth

Without doubt, the novel Coronavirus poses significant challenges to national and international economic policy with protracted implications for all national budgets. The severity and extent of the global COVID- 19 recession that fully came into effect in 2022 is unprecedented.

According to Moody's Analytics' baseline economic forecast, real global GDP will decline by 4.5% due to COVID-19.[19] The baseline scenario for the US indicates that it will take until the middle of the decade for the economy to return to full employment.

> COVID-19 has caused massive damage to the global economy. Quickly reopening economies will boost growth by unleashing pent-up demand, but will also raise the specter of a re-intensification of COVID-19 and another economic downdraft, which could lead to a worldwide depression. We construct our economic forecasts to help market participants navigate this daunting uncertainty and make better decisions.[20]

In the course of almost all past global downturns, there has been at least one significant part of the world that has managed the economic problems with appropriate dedication and turned out to be critical to the subsequent recovery as a catalyst for global growth. China played this role during and after the 2008 financial crisis, using its considerable monetary and fiscal resources to support its large economy and, given its central role in the global supply chain, much of the rest of the world. No part of the world seems willing and able to play this leading role in this pandemic. While the pandemic has affected economies around the world, some may have weathered the storm better than others so far. The U.S. economy has at least temporarily suffered more than any other, at least in terms of the immediate rise in unemployment. The unemployment rate in the United States almost reached 15% in April 2020.[21] Canada came closest with an unemployment rate of 7.5%, and then Germany and Australia with an unemployment rate of almost 6%, while Japan's unemployment is still somewhere about 3%.[22] The extraordinary job losses in the United States were considered to be rooted largely in the Trump administration's poor management of the pandemic.[23] It was late in recognizing the threat of the virus and eventually handed over most of the crisis management to local government authorities, resulting in an uncoordinated patchwork of responses that was slow to get underway. By contrast, in much of Asia and Europe, the management of the health crisis was much more aggressive at an early stage and the subsequent contact tracing of infections was more comprehensive until a certain point. Asian and European economies were severely affected by the pandemic, but not nearly as seriously as North America's.

Fareed Zakaria has concluded there are ten "lessons" for the time after COVID-19.[24] In his account he argues that the economy will change fundamentally, inequality will grow, that digitalization will further advance and that crisis management will be determined largely by (health?) experts. Moreover, he predicts that the world will soon become bipolar.[25]

This may be true, however for the time being, neither the United States nor China can emerge as sole leading players in the theater of geopolitics, as Europe and Russia with different possibilities and ambitions are still competing in that arena.

Geopolitical Impact

Confrontative Multipolarity

The key factor "developments in global power", which comes down to a cross-referential analysis and assessment of geopolitical power projection and conversion capabilities of global players, is actively determining almost any other key factors (by a degree of 2,6). It is also influenced and driven by other key factors that the relatively high passive sum of 1,9 indicates. According to the FSC research matrix for the key factor "developments in global power", four possible scenarios were elaborated that should capture the actual global power constellations and at the same time incorporate the range of likely developments in geopolitics for the next years to come:

1 A cooperative unipolar model,
2 a confrontational unipolar model,
3 a cooperative multipolar model,
4 and a confrontational multipolar model.
5 A wild card scenario: anarchy in the global system (everything between an eroding, volatile and dysfunctional order structure and a global security vacuum)

Concerning the polarity, the distinction refers to unipolarity as a centripetal security architecture that is constructed around a single actor with a wide-ranging power projection capability (be it an empire or a hegemony). Multipolarity, in contrast, is centered on at least two (bipolar) or more state actors that struggle for dominance geopolitically. With respect to the cooperation vs. confrontation distinction, the aspects of belligerence, conflict-proneness and natural impetus to cooperate among great powers are weighted up against each other. The usual "wild card scenario" is rooted in the probability that none of the above scenarios may be sufficient to clearly describe ongoing power shifts and developments in global security.

A recent assessment of global power and geopolitical impact regards confrontational multipolarity as the likeliest scenario for the next 10 years to come.[26]

Yet, with recourse to the immediate geopolitical constellation it may be concluded that the long lasting phase of US-led unipolarity is probably over. However, there is an ongoing intense debate among international relations experts as to whether we currently find ourselves amidst a global security vacuum as elaborated in the "wild card scenario" or rather in a phase of ascending bipolarity (the United States vs. China).

Undoubtedly, we face growing instability in the global power structure due to a fundamental change in US foreign policy that culminated in the Trump administration's de-commitment policy in international relations according to the 45th president's "America-First-Strategy". Accordingly, a further disengagement of the United States as international crisis manager can be expected, also under the 46th president. In that context, the progressing abandonment of America's former role as "globo-cop" makes perfect sense. Any future US administration will continue the path of disengagement in order to reduce costs. The Europeans should not estimate or even hope that the current Biden administration will at any time, despite its initial announcement to foster international cooperation, ignore that strategic imperative of decoupling and focusing on self-interest. This recessive trend poses enormous new political challenges, especially for Europe, as European security must now be guaranteed autonomously. In general, an intensification of particularistic great power interests seems very likely. There are several international security-trends that suggest more of the same in the international arena for the next 4–5 years:

1 A possible (further) disengagement of the USA within NATO could contribute to a sustainable shift toward a multipolar balance of power (probably in favor of Russia) and encourage a bilateral confrontation with China, thus automatically enforcing a Sino-Russian security cooperation, sometimes referred to as the "dragon-bear"-scenario. Notwithstanding, the containment of the "dragon" (China) could turn out to be a viable foreign policy strategy for Biden. However, the latest developments related to the Ukrainian War suggest a temporary strengthening of NATO. Still the US may continue a disengagement and demand more European responsibility in collective defense.

2 An emerging, resurgent Anglo-Saxon transatlantic axis (USA/UK) in the wake of BREXIT could destabilize the Euro-Continental security architecture (NATO and EU).

3 The damaged transatlantic relations could be used as a pretext to promote the fragmentation of the EU to strengthen Washington's geopolitical position.

4 A continuation of the existing "Moneyball America" (Ian Bremmer) course (i.e. a primacy of the economy) could be set up under auspices by the Biden administration.

5 The enhancement of US unilateralist ambitions could tempt other global power actors (Russia, China) to give priority to their own immediate power interests. A lack of incentives for cooperation feeds a growing unilateralism among all key players. This in turn could lead to a further hardening of the geopolitical conflict lines, facilitate confrontation and perhaps lead to proxy wars in contested regions. There are some commentators that see the current Ukrainian War in that light.

6 A further serious weakening of international structures (IOs) is possible, even under the current Biden administration and could have a lasting negative impact on Europe, where the rule of law and international law take precedence in international relations.

7 Side actors and hotspots in the global power struggle, such as Ukraine, Turkey, Syria, Iran and Egypt, all on the European periphery, could become the cue-ball of these great power solo-efforts in geopolitics.

A growing geopolitical instability, which ties up and weakens Europe's power resources is associated with an increasing threat potential in global security policy. Strategic competition between and conflicting interests of the United States, Russia and China could continue to find their expression on playing fields at the periphery (e.g. throughout Africa, the Greater Middle East, currently also in the Ukraine) in the form of proxy wars or low intensity conflicts.

Conflicts in the Euro-Strategic Environment

Having said that, there is growing consent among security policy analysts that the European Southern periphery (from the Levant and the Maghreb to Sub-Saharan Africa and beyond), polemically referred to as the "ring of fire", will be the major "battlefield", where great power interests will be materialized.[27] European crisis management there is crucially needed, as Europe is routinely in the focus of refugee and illegal migration from these regions, sometimes resulting in welfare state or security challenges. Conflicts and instability in this surrounding geographical environment have a significant impact on European security and terrorism in particular.

Referring to a differentiated typology of conflicts, the Heidelberg Institute for International Conflict Research (HIIK) annually presents a "Conflict Barometer", which distinguishes between interstate, intrastate, substate and transstate conflicts.[28] Interstate conflicts involve recognized state actors, intrastate conflicts both recognized states and non-state actors, whereas substate conflicts are carried out solely by non-state actors. Transstate conflicts are a hybrid form – they involve state and non-state actors alike but are led under the patronage of at least two sovereign states (Figure 24.1).[29]

With respect to the Middle East and Maghreb area it refers to four "limited wars": Iraq (opposition), Israel (Hamas et al.), Libya (inter-tribal rivalry) and Syria (inter-opposition rivalry).[30] Conflicts defined as "wars" are identified in Afghanistan (Taliban et al.), Egypt (militant groups, Sinai peninsula), Libya (opposition), Syria/Iraq et al (ISIS), Syria (opposition), Syria (Turkey-SDF/Northern Syria), Turkey (PKK/TAK), and Yemen/Saudi Arabia (al-Houthi).[31] The same applies for Sub-Saharan Africa, where HIIK names eight conflicts as "limited wars" and five as "wars".[32] Most of these conflicts are geopolitically influenced, therefore more or less relevant for European security and consequently impact the Salafi-jihadist scene in Europe. Conflicts in the

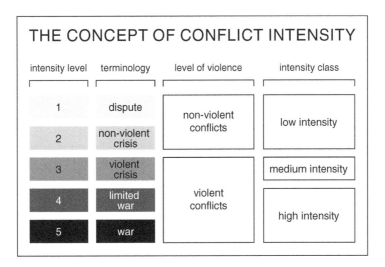

Figure 24.1 The Concept of Conflict Intensity

Source: Based on HIIK Conflict Barometer 2019.

Euro-strategic environment and their direct nexus with terrorist activity in Europe in particular, are according to the FSC cross-impact-matrix an important driver for Islamist terrorism in Europe- with a relatively high active score of 2,7 (passive sum score of 2,2), ranking second after the key factor "COVID-19", which is still a main driver in almost any sphere. Regularly, both returning foreign terrorist fighters but also homegrown radicals draw upon regional conflicts and possible intervention by Western governments or even armed forces in their narratives as a justification for violent extremism.[33]

Conflict Terror-Nexus

Geo-strategically, the significant three main poles of the Islamic world are located in South East Asia, the Middle East and North Africa. In terms of maritime security this includes highly strategic channels and straits, such as the Straits of Malacca, the Hormuz Strait in the midst of the middle-eastern Islamic countries, and the Bab al-Mandeb and the Suez Canal, as well as the Dardanelles and Bosporus straits, all waterways of international eminence. As Naji & Jawan (2013) emphasize in their study, the

> "…strategic role of these marine routes in pursuing strategic goals, international transportation and transfer of goods, as well as crude oil has been so critical that all great powers during the modern world systems have stressed the need to control these points".[34]

This may be the underlying "deeper reason" (Thucydides) for conflicts in the Islamic world, rooted in the Western intention to "control streams and waves", what could be termed as "fluid security".[35] In terms of their power projection and power conversion capability,[36] the Islamic world remains bound to regional influence, some states possibly emerging as hegemonic stakeholders.

With the exception of the "fortunate few" who have sufficient oil and gas resources for export, the majority of Muslim states has not played a significant role in recent geopolitics and, given the declining role of fossil fuels in the world economy, most of them will hardly be able to catch up with other global regions due to the lack of industrial or technological infrastructure. Poverty is widespread, the number of young people who cannot find adequate employment is very high, as are corruption and social inequality.[37] OECD countries *"appear to experience Islamist violence as a result of large numbers of economically and socially segregated immigrants from the Middle East and North Africa".*[38]

Good governance is largely absent, as is widespread state social legislation or a state social system in all but a few oil-rich states. All these factors make armed rebellion under the banner of Islamist jihad a tempting option.[39]

Turkish President Recep Tayyip Erdoğan claims a leading role for the Islamic world and has repeatedly underlined this pretension, evident in the dispute with French President Macron over the republishing of Charlie Hebdo's Mohamed cartoons, the beheading of a Parisian teacher who showed these in the classroom and the following debate in France whether a Western liberal society should allow this kind of satirical critique considered as blasphemy by Erdoğan. In the course of this discussion Erdoğan said: *"What else can one say about a head of state who treats millions of members from different faith groups this way: first of all, have a mental check".*[40] Very clearly he intended *"...to fashion himself as the voice of the Muslim world and defender of the faith".*[41] "In a series of tweets he added that *"by attacking Islam, clearly without having any understanding of it, President Macron has attacked & hurt the sentiments of millions of Muslims in Europe & across the world".*[42] Critical observers consider this an attempt to shift the attention abroad and to distract from economic and pandemic problems at home.[43]

However, this does not change the fact that neither Turkey nor any other regional players in the Greater Middle East are competing for more than limited regional hegemony, while the four eminent geostrategic powers – the USA, China, Russia and (gradually also) the EU – each with different ambitions and capabilities, are struggling for global dominance. This geopolitical side actor role of most Islamic countries with some gradual regional exceptions (e.g. Iran, Saudi Arabia, Egypt, Turkey and U.A.E.), that are more or less perceived as chess pieces in the Great Game, is cleverly interwoven into a "status quo-description"- narrative by Salafi-jihadi ideologists, where they call themselves *"heroic defenders of the Muslim world – the ummah (community of Muslims) – against Western colonisation and the domination of Arab and other Muslim lands by pro-Western Muslim rulers who are portrayed as puppets of the West".*[44] In the extremists' mindset, Muslims hence would not be sufficiently able to defend themselves, because they allegedly have deviated from the right path of 'true Islam'". ISIS falsely claims to stand for "pure and unadulterated Islam.[45] Islamist propagandists provide a simple solution: A way out of the "misery" is according to their extremist ideology not offered by negotiations or reforms, but exclusively by "jihad on the path of God".[46,47] Bearing in mind that a partially reconsolidating ISIS could fill the security gap in fragile states such as in Libya, Yemen, Lebanon or Afghanistan, given the consequent retreat of the US military in the Middle East, the terrorist threat in the region but also abroad ("the distant enemy") is likely to increase.[48] On a larger scale the Saudi-Iranian conflict plays into the reemergence of ISIS as it deliberately fosters an anti-Shiite narrative to recruit Arab Sunnites.[49]

To a certain extent, most of these factors and conflict relations suggest a direct connection between geopolitically relevant, regional conflicts (in particular in the Greater Middle East) and Islamist terrorism. Without doubt, there is noteworthy evidence for the claim that a manifest nexus between regional conflicts in the Islamic world and international Salafi-jihadist terrorism exists, at least concerning propaganda and motivation.[50] Jihadist perpetrators Regularly seek revenge for invasions, occupations or war in their home countries. Already in the aftermath of the US campaign in Iraq starting 2003, *it was found that "[...] the invasion and the occupation of Iraq has stirred a great deal of anger among jihadists in Europe".*[51] Ever since 2003 *"...proxy wars in Syria by*

Turkey, Saudi Arabia, Iran, Russia and some Western states as well after 2011 have destabilised an already volatile region, producing millions of refugees, dozens of non-state armed groups of which most are religiously inspired".[52] The inherent intentionality of this Salafi- jihadist propaganda is to draw attention to political issues related to conflicts allegedly "brought" to Islam-dominated regions and to exploit them in the sense of a "clash of civilizations"-narrative using exclusive rhetoric to ignite a spark of terrorist violence in the West. As a counter-terrorist measure it turns out to be crucial for Europe to identify reliable strategic partners in the Muslim world to successfully cooperate and tackle the emerging threat *ab origine* and *in situ*. Beyond all doubt, the "conflict-terror nexus", in its phenomenology not new, can be regarded as an essential characteristic of the current hybrid transnational terrorism.

"Erosion of Cohesion"

Polarization

COVID-19 like very recently the Ukrainian War, still contributes to intensifying centrifugal tendencies and strengthening the ideological, indeed extremist edges of society. Discourses will be shaped by fake news, conspiracy theories and a narrative that seeks to divide. A further polarization has to be expected. In general, the observation that extremist actors at any point of the ideological spectrum discursively associate the novel coronavirus with their respective agendas is not surprising at all. Given these uncertain times, conspiracy theories are abused in a targeted manner to present complex issues in a simple and ideological way and to strengthen enemy images. Furthermore, as has been shown, not all narratives presented by extremist groups in this context can be classified as extremist: Statements on everyday issues that are *per se* unproblematic are often linked to ideological positions. This applies to the discursive way in which these groups deal with the pandemic as well as with other events. However, if one looks at, reads or shares certain posts or content on social media platforms (such as YouTube, Facebook or Twitter), due to algorithms, similar content from other profiles or further posts by the same user are suggested to the user. A spiral is set off- by consuming such content; it can easily happen that increasingly radical messages are conveyed and offered on social media to the consumers. It seems likely that this process is influenced and accelerated by the pandemic: Due to the widespread restriction of public life, a large part of social interaction is shifting to the virtual world. As a result, at least some people spend more time on social media and are therefore more often confronted with narratives of all kinds. This would explain, for example, why some channels of right-wing extremist actors at the messenger service Telegram have gained hundreds of new subscribers within the last weeks. Some experts fear[53] that self-isolation could also increase individual susceptibility to extremist narratives and accelerate the spread of extremist content and conspiracy theories, especially via the Internet. Progressive polarization can symptomatically lead to what may be called the "erosion of cohesion", a wide-ranging societal divide that could spur extremism. Any kind of radicalization process has to be put into this context of the cohesive condition of a society. A stable center can withstand any kind of attack from the edges. From the perspective of ISIS, the pandemic has been regarded as an „*opportunity to exploit the divisions and weaknesses among its enemies that have arisen because of the pandemic*".[54] In the cross-impact matrix, the key factor "polarization" has a relatively strong passive sum (factor 2,6) and also an above average value on the active side (2,4 on the scale). It is mainly driven by economic factors as well as by radicalization, which is reciprocally also a manifest driver for polarization.

Hybrid Radicalization

The still ongoing French debate whether recent forms of radicalization should be regarded as Islamization of radicalism (Olivier Roy) or radicalization of Islam (Gilles Kepel) has a wide-ranging leverage not only on Islamic studies but even more on terrorism research.[55]

"Radicalization of (Within) Islam"

The French sociologist Gilles Kepel believes that the religious aspect of terrorist attacks is underestimated. Even the Parisian banlieue riots of 2005 (in which more than 10,000 cars burned out) flared up when a tear gas bomb was thrown into the entrance of a mosque. Already in the same year, the Syrian Abu Mussab al Suri called for "global Islamic resistance" and explicitly named satirical magazines, that publish cartoons vituperating the Prophet, such as "Charlie Hebdo", as targets. For Gilles Kepel, this was kind of a *"playbook for the atrocities of the Islamic State jihadists that have bedeviled France"*.[56] This was the starting signal for the new wave of jihadist violence in Europe that reached its preliminary climax in the Parisian terrorist attacks of 2015. Kepel defines the "religious" dimension broadly and in France this also includes an "anti-colonial" motive: Mohamed Merah, a petty criminal from Toulouse, killed Jewish school children on March 19, exactly 50 years to the day after the ceasefire of the Algerian war, which in French Algerian nostalgia is still regarded as a day of defeat.[57]

"Islamization of Radicalism"

Olivier Roy considers the religious component of the attacks only as a pretext and speaks unlike Kepel not of the "radicalization of Islam" but of the "Islamization of radicalism". The young banlieue terrorists in France usually had no idea about the Qur'an or the Algerian war (1954 to 1962); the religious or even anti-colonial slogans they had heard were all about their indoctrination by Syrian recruiters. They smoked, used drugs and were often converts. Their nihilism, even their violent reflexes, were in stark contrast to the Islamic tradition.

A political scientist, Olivier Roy, understands the radicalized, "home-grown" young people who follow ISIS or al-Qaeda in Europe and other regions outside the war zones in Afghanistan, Iraq or Chechnya as a violent "youth movement" that has much in common with other forms of violent protest or subversion and at best flirts with fundamentalist Islam. For him, the success of the Islamists does not consist in creating a modern and efficient Islamist political organization, but in inventing a narrative that allows "disenfranchised" rebels to associate with a "cause" for no reason. This legitimizes the nihilistic rebellion with an ostensible reason. Islamist terrorism, also through its demonization, serves this purpose, but it could ultimately be another reason that promises attention, radicalism and meaning.

In fact, both approaches, Roy's and Kepel's are justified in terms of methodology and explanatory value, and from the point of view of terrorism research, based on the findings of individual case analyses from recent years, there is quite strong evidence that each perspective is appropriate to retrace and classify individual radicalization processes of jihadist perpetrators. However, a combination of the two theses seems most useful to describe the current phenomenon. Actually a hybrid mix of "Islamization of radicalism" and "radicalization of Islam" may best describe how young men turn into Islamist terrorists, for it is most likely a whole set of causes and conditions that shapes the individual radicalization process. The case of the subsequent perpetrator from Belgian Molenbeek, Salah Abdeslam, shows that Islamist radicalization is to a large extent the culmination of religious and sociological affects and mechanisms. The logistical supporter of the Paris attacks of November 2015, Abdeslam, did not follow the strict directives of radical Islam, and as a petty criminal, he preferred to spend his time playing video games, smoking pot and going to gay clubs.[58] He also never grew a beard, he regularly drank alcohol and may not have ever prayed in a mosque. Unlike other attackers, Abdeslam may have never visited Syria. So far this plays into Roy's sociological argument. But if we supposed that his behavior could be regarded as an example of *taqiya*, i.e. a calculated pretense, in which the jihadi preparing for "martyrdom" melts in with the enemy, adopting a Western way of life, to avoid detection, this would suggest that Kepel's religious approach may be right.

In order to prevent violent extremism, it is a crucial task to properly study radicalization alongside these propositions, as effective counter-strategies will depend on a solid assessment of root causes, catalysts and processes.

New Active Areas?

Emerging Technologies

Technology is a main driver in any field. According to the cross-matrix analysis it actively influences all other key factors by a degree of 2,7. On the passive side it is influenced only at a level of 1,8. Technological progress is rapidly changing every aspect of our lives, offering amazing opportunities to society, but it also dramatically increases our vulnerability und poses a veritable threat to security. Criminal actors and terrorists as a special type thereof, systematically misusing any kind of digital technologies to carry out a wide range of activities, from sabotage to organizing complex operations involving people from different countries. Modern terrorism is monitoring emerging technologies with growing interest. In the perception of terrorists, technology is regarded a powerful amplifier of the scale of attacks. A field where this has gained significance is bio-terrorism and the terrorist weaponization of CBRN in general.[59] Jihadists are constantly assessing the strategic ramifications of using WMD. Whereas there is still a gap between motivation and capabilities, this may turn out a serious threat in the next decade and beyond.

Correspondingly, the planned tactical use of advanced digital technologies for terrorist purposes is an alarming trend. Scenarios based on the hacking of critical infrastructures (power plants, airports and the like) or the use of drones as terrorist weapons have been widely discussed. The "Internet of things" (traffic control systems, building services and engineering, etc.) also reveals security gaps that could be exploited by terrorists at a large cost to states.[60]

International networks and extremist groups increasingly use the Internet and digital communication media in order to disseminate jihadist propaganda and influence politics. During the last years, a migration of extremist content from websites, chat rooms and forums toward social media has occurred, as the latter are more flexible in terms of (dis-)appearance and also allow terrorist groups to address a much larger public. These groups hence use social media platforms for a deliberate dispersion of fake information, effective propaganda, hate speech and direct appeals to violence, as well as the publication of professionally produced media, in order to communicate to a very broad, global public within seconds.

"Most domestic extremists use the internet and social media platforms to release propaganda, coordinate training, raise funds, recruit members, and communicate with others. They have used various combinations of Facebook, Twitter, YouTube, Gab, Reddit, (...) Telegram, Vkontakte, MeWe, Discord, Wire, Twitch, and other online communication platforms".[61]

In this light it seems evident, that the Internet increasingly plays an important role in "online radicalization" of lone attackers and respective groups. Additionally, indoctrination and recruitment occur more and more online. Social media contribute to the spreading and amplifying of terrorist attacks, increase the media interest, with the negative effect that the world community spreads the terrorist messages, and favors radicalization. Attacks become even more instantaneous and unpredictable, they can happen anywhere, at any moment and thanks to digital media they can reach a wide, sometimes global audience. Technology brings terror into our homes, and thanks to mobile devices it can be followed everywhere.

Our networked society is even more vulnerable to cyber-attacks. Cyberspace is an environment without borders and it is easy for terrorists to find resources on the web and Dark Net, to carry out propaganda activities, to create communication channels and to gather information about potential targets.[62] In recent cases Dark Net channels have been successfully used to acquire guns or IEDs for later terrorist attacks.[63]

The conquering of cyber-space has given Salafi-jihadists access to domains that in the past were solely controlled by states.[64] The Global Internet Forum to Counter Terrorism, which includes industry giants such as Facebook, Microsoft, Twitter and YouTube, is cooperating intensively to remove any kind of terrorist information or propaganda. Particularly Google and Facebook are investing heavily in AI-based programs to prevent this extremist content but creators are often finding alternative ways to spread their messages. Laws have not been sufficient to keep extremists from using the Internet as a strategic asset.[65]

Cyber-Caliphate

In the vast literature on terrorism and violent extremism the essential role of the Internet has been emphasized for several years.[66] Relevant studies point to the key role of the Internet in information gathering, communication, and the dissemination of and agreement to extremist attitudes. Furthermore, the Internet allows radical and violent ideologies to be translated into political activism.[67] Social science has focused on describing the extremist and terrorist online landscape (actors, portals, networks, content). Case studies of extremist and terrorist biographies have also found clear evidence that Internet propaganda has played a significant role in individual radicalization processes.[68] However, the question of which propaganda content is actually effective, and how exactly it works, remains quite unresolved.

With regard to online radicalization, researchers have collected case study-based information on terrorist perpetrators concerning the following aspects: Acquiring technical knowledge via the Internet (e.g., bomb-making), communication channels (chat rooms, e-mail, etc.) and downloading ideological texts.[69] Individual radicalization process, ideological development, and the corresponding training were actually only made possible by the Internet, as recent studies suggest.[70]

The Web, with reference to Islamist propaganda functionally denominated as "cyber-caliphate", is the most important mobilization medium for groups, recruiters, and strategists of extreme movements. Angela Gendron noted that the Internet strengthens the bond between charismatic leaders and their followers.[71] These studies largely agree that extremist online content (e.g. texts, videos, music, etc.) contributes to ideologization and radicalization in general. To counter this dispersion of jihadist propaganda on social media it is crucial to implement automatic recognition based on algorithms and to cooperate with the platforms that involuntarily host any kind of extremist content.

Tactical Implication

In terms of radicalization, recruiting, plotting attacks and coordination the Internet offers the entire "value chain" for terrorist groups and affiliates. Nearly everything from the early stage idea until the execution of the attack, and even afterwards, the exploitative dissemination of the attack as *"propaganda of the deed"* can be maintained on the Internet. Very interestingly, regarding the plotting and carrying out of attacks, despite a usual preference for personal real-life communication of some perpetrators, the Internet has become sort of a virtual playground for preparation. According to a UNODC report, *"...the use of the Internet in furtherance of the execution of acts of terrorism may, inter alia, offer logistical advantages, reduce the likelihood of detection or obscure the identity of responsible parties. Internet activity may also facilitate the acquisition of items necessary for the execution of the attack. Terrorists may purchase individual components or services required to perpetrate violent acts of terrorism by means of electronic commerce. Misappropriated credit cards or other forms of compromised electronic payment may be used to finance such purchases"*.[72] On a tactical level also the phenomenon of what Robert Evans called *"The Gamification of Terror"* more and more plays a significant role for the modus operandi of jihadi perpetrators.[73] Using the combat style aesthetics of ego-shooter online games like "Counter-Strike" during their attacks, terrorists frequently stream their killings live in the Internet – from the moment they get to the scene until they are forcefully stopped by the intervention of security forces. In extremist chat fora a competition concerning the number of casualties between terrorist attackers has been sparked. Random social media networks are intensively used to propagandistically exploit the attacks. What was originally primarily associated with right-wing extremists is becoming popular among jihadist perpetrators (e.g. the attack in Magnanville 2016).[74]

This racing-fast virtualization of Salafi-jihadist terrorism has a tremendous impact on counterterrorism approaches. It is a space that can only partially be controlled by security services but that everybody has access to. And there is the DarkNet.

Hybrid Terrorism

In the first chapter of this volume the concept of "hybrid terrorism" has been elaborated in detail. According to the FSC cross-matrix-analysis, hybrid terrorism is a key driver that actively influences all other determinants with a relatively high factor of 2,9 on the scale and is equally driven to a surprising extent of 2,6. This, however unsurprisingly, suggests that it can be regarded as the fundamental development in the sphere of transnational terrorism for the years to come, as it practically touches upon any kind of relation among key factors and trends.

Hybrid terrorism as a concept refers to a structural interdependence, the intentional merging of different forms, methods and patterns seeking to create something new, a *"more or less modified form of violence which deliberately absorbs known procedures, but at the same time, triggers special dynamics, such as the creation of a loose franchise network, what in turn results in a shift of emphasis under the primacy of unconditional systemic adaptation- and a formerly unknown ability to learn from experience. It is primarily about tactical innovation"*.[75] In the light of constant transformation, we must expect an intensification and further acceleration of already prevalent dynamics in the field of tactics, *modi operandi* and radicalization. Most likely, hybrid operational tactics (*"Jihadist Auftragstaktik"*), hybrid organizations (terror militia and terrorist organization at once), hybrid perpetrators ("single actor plus" and/or lose franchise networks) and *modi operandi* (opportunity driven and/or projected attacks), hybrid radicalization ("Islamization of radicalism" and "radicalization of Islam") will shape and set the stage of Salafi-jihadist violence for the time to come.[76]

The ISIS-Effect

Due to the phenomenal binary development of hybrid terrorism (opportunity driven and projected scenarios) and the associated *"simplicity paradigm"* (for efficiency reasons simple plots with random targeting will be trending), the ongoing shift toward low-level single perpetrators (maybe single actor "plus") is expected to be sustainable. It no longer requires complex logistics to perpetrate scattered terrorist attacks with significant attention. In connection with the lose franchise dynamics – "act autonomously and get the credits" (McJihad)[77] – this creates what I would like to call the "ISIS-effect": *"Such a loose franchise system has proven efficient. Terrorist action is handled under the primacy of spontaneity paired with an unprecedented simplicity in implementation".*[78]

Tactically, we are currently confronted with opportunity driven attacks or hybrid forms between coincidental and planned (network) scenarios. The "low level" category actually includes very different constellations, which all have only one thing in common: terrorist attacks (mostly a single actor variant) result from the combination of operational propaganda and a favorable environment. In a very cautious assessment, it can be presumed, that if there is no direct connection with ISIS or other extremist groups, most likely there are still indications of inspiration, a prevalent contact with a terrorist organization or even "remote control". When it comes to jihadi operational thinking, lose network-affiliates may reduce the number of red flags retraceable by security authorities.

Counter-Approach

Looking at these specific hybrid forms of individual perpetrator jihadism in Europe it is crucial to try to understand the loose relationship between lone attackers and their social networks (physical and virtual). While physical networks (cells, radical mosques) have been in the focus of European security bodies for some time now, internet platforms have long been widely neglected or under the radar. This is expected to change in the near future, as attempts by international organizations in cooperation with industry giants such as Google or Facebook have been made to tackle this issue. Further measures imply new regulations for the providers and site owners to prevent dissemination of extremist content.[79]

The acting persons should nevertheless still remain in focus. Certainly, the awareness among citizens about the homegrown terrorist threat should be raised, to encourage early reporting of suspicious behavior.[80] That being said, predominantly lone attackers are at least inspired by or connected with a group: "Most of the terrorist acts initially believed to involve a 'lone wolf' turned out to be connected to extremist networks..."[81]

Conclusion

COVID-19 is without doubt a game changer. In the sphere of security, it has aggravated already symptomatic developments. The emerging erosion of cohesion in the aftermath of the pandemic crisis is expected to reinforce the gradual weakening of the political center with its recourse to democracy and the rule of law. Simultaneously the reinvigoration of the political edges will likely contribute to a renaissance of global extremism. Conflicts resulting from geopolitical tensions, that again are currently carried out in the Ukraine and potentially also in the Middle East or in the Arab world, will more than ever impact security, particularly in Europe. Also, warfare and terrorism as a hybrid of crime and war, will be shaped by new paradigms. Geo-strategically, fluid security may gain further significance, just as hybridity, asymmetry and low intensity conflicts will set the stage for the time to come. Terrorism, notably Salafi-jihadist violence, is expected to increasingly turn online. The entire terrorist "value chain" from a young radicalized person's first contact with propaganda to the preparation of the attack and its subsequent exploitation through dissemination can be maintained virtually. Terrorists are excessively trying to exploit state of the art technology in any possible way- be it drones, the internet of things or even CBRN scenarios. Last but not least, terrorism is going hybrid. Tactical innovation supports the development of new kinds of (preferably simple) attack scenarios, *modi operandi*, perpetrators and even radicalization, that emerge from convergence of formerly known and adapted forms in each context. And there is more to come, as technical innovation will phenomenologically impact any variation of terrorism, as its masterminds are anarchically adaptive.

Notes

1 For further information about the program please contact us at https://eictp.eu/#footer.
2 The UN Counter-Terrorism Committee Executive Directorate (CTED) has prominently argued the exploitation of COVID-19 by extremists; CTED (2020). The Impact of the COVID-19 Pandemic on Counter-Terrorism and Countering Violent Extremism, available at https://www.un.org/sc/ctc/wp-content/uploads/2020/06/CTED-Paper--The-impact-of-the-COVID-19-pandemic-on-counter-terrorism-and-countering-violent-extremism.pdf
3 Joseph Hincks. With the World Busy Fighting COVID-19, Could ISIS Mount a Resurgence?, in: Time Magazine (29 April 2020), available at https://time.com/5828630/isis-coronavirus/
4 Michael Barak (2020). The Corona Pandemic: An Opportunity for ISIS, in: ICT Papers, available at https://www.ict.org.il/images/Corona%20and%20ISIS%20-%20Eng.pdf; On the implications of COVID-19 on terrorism see also Ephraim Karsh (2020). The COVID-19 Crisis: Impact and Implications, The Begin-Sadat Center for Strategic Studies Bar-Ilan University, *Mideast Security and Policy Studies No. 176,* available at https://besacenter.org/wp-content/uploads/2020/07/MSPS176web.pdf
5 Barak (2020), p. 1.
6 ibid, p. 2.
7 ibid, p. 2.
8 https://www.ft.com/content/076e1b00-2d54-449a-bab5-09920a10f4f7, also https://www.economist.com/europe/2020/11/03/despite-the-horrors-in-vienna-and-paris-jihadism-has-declined
9 In a recent newspaper commentary, I briefly elaborated on this type of perpetrator, see Nicolas Stockhammer. "Dresden und Paris. *Vorschau auf den Terror, der kommt,*" in: Die Presse (28 October 2020), available at https://www.diepresse.com/5889034/dresden-und-paris-vorschau-auf-den-terror-der-kommt
10 https://www.europol.europa.eu/activities-services/main-reports/european-union-terrorism-situation-and-trend-report-te-sat-2020
11 See Petter Nesser's account in this volume. *"Foiled versus Launched Terror Plots: Some Lessons Learned"*
12 Melissa Dalton. *Providers or Enforcers? The Duality of Security Forces' Roles in Covid-19 Response Efforts,* in: CSIS Commentary (7 October 2020), available at https://www.csis.org/analysis/providers-or-enforcers-duality-security-forces-roles-covid-19-response-efforts
13 Colin Clarke discusses post-Caliphate options around ISIS in his recent account. Colin P. Clarke (2019). *After the Caliphate.* Cambridge (Polity), p. 150; Gayle Tzemach Lemmon. ISIS is Using Coronavirus to Rebuild Its Terrorism Network in Iraq and Syria, in: THINK (NBC News) (28 May 2020), available at https://www.nbcnews.com/think/opinion/isis-using-coronavirus-rebuild-its-terrorism-network-iraq-syria-ncna1215941
14 https://www.who.int/news/item/31-08-2020-in-who-global-pulse-survey-90-of-countries-report-disruptions-to-essential-health-services-since-covid-19-pandemic
15 Helen Lambert / Jaideep Gupte / Helen Fletcher et al. "COVID-19 as a Global Challenge: Towards an Inclusive and Sustainable Future," in: The Lancet "Comment" (August 2020), available at https://www.thelancet.com/action/showPdf?pii=S2542 5196%2820%2930168-6
16 https://www2.deloitte.com/fr/fr/pages/covid-insights/articles/impact-covid19-healthcare-systems.html
17 ibid.

18 https://www.bloomberg.com/news/articles/2020-04-27/vaccine-coalition-sees-potential-to-go-even-faster-in-covid-race

19 https://www.moodysanalytics.com/about-us/press-releases/2020-06-04-resurgence-of-covid-19-could-cause-global-economic-depression

20 ibid.

21 https://www.statista.com/statistics/273909/seasonally-adjusted-monthly-unemployment-rate-in-the-us/

22 https://www.statista.com/statistics/263696/unemployment-rate-in-canada/

23 John Dickerson. "What Trump Should Have Learned from His Predecessors. Presidents Who Have Successfully Navigated Crises Share a Key Quality," in: The Atlantic (July/August Issue 2020), available at https://www.theatlantic.com/magazine/archive/2020/07/trump-crisis-management/612226/

24 Fareed Zakaria (2020). *Ten Lessons for a Post-Pandemic World.* New York, NY: W.W. Norton.

25 Ibid., pp. 187–210.

26 Barbara Lippert / Nicolai von Ondarza / Volker Perthes (2019). *Strategische Autonomie Europas- Akteure, Handlungsfelder, Zielkonflikte,* SWP-Studie Nr. 2: Berlin, pp. 30–36.

27 Gilles Kepel (2019). *Chaos. Die Krisen in Nordafrika und im Nahen Osten verstehen.* München, pp. 11–23; et passim.

28 HIIK (2020). Conflict Barometer 2019, p. 8, available at https://hiik.de/wp-content/uploads/2020/03/CoBa-Final-überarbeitet.pdf

29 Ibid., p. 8.

30 Ibid., p. 10.

31 Ibid., p. 10.

32 Ibid., p. 10.

33 A recent brilliant account on (returning) foreign terrorist fightes is provided by Daniel Byman. See Daniel Byman (2019). *Road Warriors. Foreign Fighters in the Armies of Jihad.* Oxford University Press.

34 Saeid Naji / Jayum A. Jawan (2013). "Geopolitics of the Islam World and World Leadership in the Post-Cold War Geopolitical Developments," in: *Transcience,* Vol. 4, Issue 1, p. 5.

35 Herfried Münkler (2015). *Kriegssplitter. Die Evolution der Gewalt im 20. und 21. Jahrhundert.* Berlin: Rowohlt Berlin, p. 326.

36 This distinction was made prominent by Joseph Nye. See Joseph S. Nye (2011). *The Future of Power.* New York, NY: Public Affairs.

37 Gouda and Marktanner examine the nexus between youth unemployment and expat jihadism. See Moamen Gouda & Marcus Marktanner (2019). Muslim Youth Unemployment and Expat Jihadism: Bored to Death?, in: *Studies in Conflict & Terrorism,* Vol. 42, Issue 10, pp. 878–897

38 ibid., p. 880.

39 See Alex P. Schmid. "The Systemic Dimension of Jihadist Violence - A Root Cause Analysis of Jihadist Terrorism," in Part I of This Volume.

40 https://www.theguardian.com/world/2020/oct/26/macrons-clash-with-islam-sends-jolt-through-frances-long-debate-about-secularism

41 https://www.nytimes.com/2020/10/27/world/europe/French-Muslims-Turkey-crackdown.html

42 ibid.

43 ibid.

44 Alex P. Schmid (2015). Challenging the Narrative of the "Islamic State," ICCT Research Paper, p. 6.; https://www.icct.nl/sites/default/files/import/publication/ICCT-Schmid-Challenging-the-Narrative-of-the-Islamic-State-June2015.pdf

45 ibid, p. 4.

46 See ISIS online magazine Dabiq, issues 1–4, available at http://www.clarionproject.org/news/islamic-state-isis-isil- propaganda-magazine-dabiq.

47 See Behnam Heidenreuter. "Counter-Narratives" in Part II of This Volume.

48 Guido Steinberg (2020). "Der IS bleibt eine Gefahr," in: *Internationale Politik,* Vol. 6, pp. 12–14.

49 Ibid, p. 13.

50 Petter Nesser (2006). "Jihadism in Western Europe After the Invasion of Iraq: Tracing Motivational Influences from the Iraq War on Jihadist Terrorism in Western Europe," in: *Studies in Conflict & Terrorism,* Vol. 29, Issue 4, pp. 323–342.

51 ibid, p. 324.

52 See Alex P. Schmid. "The Systemic Dimension of Jihadist Violence - A Root Cause Analysis of Jihadist Terrorism," in Part I of This Volume.

53 Nikita Malik (2020). Self-Isolation Might Stop Coronavirus, but It Will Speed the Spread of Extremism, in: Foreign Policy (26 March 2020), available at https://foreignpolicy.com/2020/03/26/self-isolation-might-stop-coronavirus-but-spread-extremism/.

54 Aymenn Al-Tamimi (2020). Coronavirus and Official Islamic State Output: An Analysis, in: Global Network on Extremism and Technology, available at https://gnet-research.org/2020/04/15/coronavirus-and-official-islamic-state-output-an-analysis/

55 Adam Nossiter. "That Ignoramus': 2 French Scholars of Radical Islam Turn Bitter Rivals," in: New York Times (12 July 2016), available at https://www.nytimes.com/2016/07/13/world/europe/france-radical-islam.html; also: https://www.derstandard.at/story/2000034842070/der-clash-der-islamologen-in-frankreich; http://www.spiegel.de/spiegel/terror-frankreichs-prominenteste-islamforscher-streiten-ueber-ursachen-a-1104464.html; from a research perspective the case studies of Petter Nesser may give an illustration on radicalization of Islamist perpetrators. See Nesser Petter (2016). *Islamist Terrorism in Europe: A History*. London, p. 53.

56 Adam Nossiter. "That Ignoramus': 2 French Scholars of Radical Islam Turn Bitter Rivals," in: New York Times (12 July 2016), available at https://www.nytimes.com/2016/07/13/world/europe/france-radical-islam.html

57 https://www.derstandard.at/story/2000034842070/der-clash-der-islamologen-in-frankreich

58 Simon Cottee. Europe's Joint-Smoking, Gay-Club Hopping Terrorists, in: Foreign Policy (13 April 2016), available at https://foreignpolicy.com/2016/04/13/the-joint-smoking-gay-club-hopping-terrorists-of-molenbeek-abdeslam-radicalization/

59 Nicolas Stockhammer (2020). *COVID-19: Is Bioterrorism on the Rise Now?*, EICTP Policy Brief (May 2020), available at https://eictp.eu/wp-content/uploads/2020/05/EICTP_Policy_Brief_Bioterrorism.pdf

60 Roey Tzezana (2016). 'Scenarios for Crime and Terrorist Attacks Using the Internet of Things', in: *European Journal of Futures Research*, Vol. 4, Issue 1, p. 18.

61 Seth G. Jones et al. (2020). The Tactics and Targets of Domestics Terrorists, in: CSIS Briefs (July 2020), available at https://csis-website-prod.s3.amazonaws.com/s3fs-public/publication/200729_Jones_TacticsandTargets_v4_FINAL.pdf

62 Gabriel Weimann (2018). Wilson Center Report *Going Darker? The Challenge of Dark Net Terrorism*," available at https://www.wilsoncenter.org/sites/default/files/media/documents/publication/going_darker_challenge_of_dark_net_terrorism.pdf

63 Gabriel Weimann (2015). *Terrorism in Cyberspace: The Next Generation*. New York, NY: Columbia University Press.

64 Christina Schori-Liang (2017). *Unveiling the "United Cyber Caliphate" and the Birth of the E-Terrorist*. Georgetown Journal of International Affairs, 18/3, pp. 11–20.

65 Christina Schori-Liang (2020). *Hydra: The Evolving Anatomy of Extremism*, in: Institute for Economics & Peace. Global Terrorism Index 2019: Measuring the Impact of Terrorism, Sydney, November 2019, p. 85, available at http://visionofhumanity.org/reports

66 Nico Prucha et al. (2015). Detecting Jihadist Messages on Twitter. 2015 European Intelligence and Security Informatics Conference; Nico Prucha (2016). IS and the Jihadist Information Highway – Projecting Influence and Religious Identity via Telegram, in: *Perspectives on Terrorism*, Vol. 10, pp. 48–58; Ines von Behr et al. (2013). *Radicalisation in the digital era. The use of the internet in 15 cases of terrorism and extremism*, RAND Corporation; Maura Conway (2016). Determining the Role of the Internet in Violent Extremism and Terrorism: Six Suggestions for Progressing Research, in: *Studies in Conflict & Terrorism*, Vol. 40, pp. 77–98.

67 Daniel Koehler (2014). The Radical Online: Individual Radicalization Processes and the Role of the Internet, in: *Journal of Deradicalization*, Vol. 1, pp. 116–134.

68 Anne Aly et al.(2016). *Violent Extremism Online: New Perspectives on Terrorism and the Internet*. London: Routledge.

69 Paul Gill et al. (2015). *What are the roles of the Internet in terrorism? Measuring online behaviours of convicted UK terrorists*. VOX-Pol, available at: https://www.voxpol.eu/download/vox-pol_publication/What-are-the-Roles-of-the-Internet-in-Terrorism.pdf

70 Daniel Koehler (2014). The Radical Online: Individual Radicalization Processes and the Role of the Internet, in: *Journal of Deradicalization*, Vol. 1, pp. 116–134; Donald Holbrook (2015). A Critical Analysis of the Role of the Internet in the Preparation and Planning of Acts of Terrorism, in: *Dynamics of*

Asymmetric Conflict, Vol. 8, available at https://www.tandfonline.com/doi/abs/10.1080/17467586.2015.1065102?tab=permissions&scroll=top

71 Angela Gendron (2017). The Call to Jihad: Charismatic Preachers and the Internet, in: *Studies in Conflict & Terrorism*, Vol. 40, pp. 44–61, available at https://www.tandfonline.com/doi/abs/10.1080/1057610X.2016.1157406

72 United Nations Office on Drugs and Crime (2012). *The Use of The Internet for Terrorist Purposes,* p. 12.

73 Robert Evans (2019). *The El Paso Shooting and the Gamification of Terror,* in: Bellingcat, available at https://www.bellingcat.com/news/americas/2019/08/04/the-el-paso-shooting-and-the-gamification-of-terror/

74 Maura Conway & Joseph Dillon. *Case Study Future Trends: Live-Streaming Terrorist Attacks?* (VOX-POL), available at https://www.voxpol.eu/download/vox-pol_publication/Live-streaming_FINAL.pdf

75 See Nicolas Stockhammer. *The Case of Hybrid Terrorism – Systemic Lessons from Recent European Plots*, in: Part I of This Volume.

76 ibid, pp. 19–27.

77 ibid, p. 25.

78 ibid, p. 25.

79 https://www.consilium.europa.eu/en/press/press-releases/2018/12/06/terrorist-content-online-council-adopts-negotiating-position-on-new-rules-to-prevent-dissemination/?utm_source=dsms-auto&utm_medium=email&utm_campaign=Terrorist+content+online:+Council+adopts+negotiating+position+on+new+rules+to+prevent+dissemination

80 Petter Nesser (2012). Individual Jihadist Operations in Europe: Patterns and Challenges, in: *CTC Sentinel*, Vol. 5, Issue 1, p. 18, available at https://www.ctc.usma.edu/wp-content/uploads/2012/01/Vol5-Iss1.pdf

81 ibid, p. 18.

25

SCENARIOS OF TRANSNATIONAL TERRORISM

Trends and Developments – A Fact-Based Threat Assessment

Colin P. Clarke

Introduction

More than twenty years after the al-Qaeda attacks of September 11, 2001, many governments, security services, and intelligence agencies around the world are taking stock of the current threat while attempting to prepare for what could come next. The global terrorism landscape looks radically different than it did two decades ago. Al-Qaeda is larger in terms of overall numbers, but weaker in its ability to plan and execute spectacular attacks in the West. Its progeny, the Islamic State (IS), rose from the Levant in 2014, constructed a proto-state in the heart of the Middle East, and attracted tens of thousands of fighters from over 120 different countries. The self-proclaimed caliphate has been crushed and IS deprived of its physical territory, although its affiliates and franchise groups remain active in various regions of the globe.

Al-Qaeda today is nothing like the group that attacked the United States on September 11, 2001—it has evolved considerably, remains dangerous, and is more geographically dispersed. It maintains jihadist cells all over the Muslim world, no longer just relegated to operating in and around Taliban-controlled territory within Afghanistan, although its presence in Afghanistan is once again expected to grow following a U.S. troop withdrawal. The al-Qaeda of 2021/22 is more focused on local issues and continues to work through its branches, affiliates, and franchise groups. But al-Qaeda's focus could very well change, and a more recent devotion to the "near enemy" does not obviate attacks on the "far enemy," including the United States. A generation of jihadists has come of age gaining experience not in South Asia, where Bin Laden's generation honed its skills, but in the Levant, fighting against the regime of Bashar al-Assad and a range of other actors, including Iran, Russia, Lebanese Hezbollah, and an ever-shifting panoply of violent non-state actors.[1]

The Islamic State is experiencing its own setbacks and, at present, is following a similar evolution to that of al-Qaeda between the U.S.-led invasion of Afghanistan and the Arab Spring in 2011. IS' command-and-control has been attenuated, forcing it to rely more on its affiliate groups operating on the periphery. Africa is now at the center of IS' strategy to maintain an offensive posture, with its branches in West and Central Africa gaining more prominence.

DOI: 10.4324/9781003326373-29

The Future of Al-Qaeda and the Focus on Playing the "Long Game"

The United States has completed a troop withdrawal from Afghanistan, giving rise to concerns that the country will once again become a magnet for violent extremists and transnational terrorists. According to the most recent report from the United Nations Security Council, al-Qaeda's leader Ayman al-Zawahiri is assessed to be "alive but unwell."[2] When rumors of al-Zawahiri's demise began to swirl a few months ago, the counterterrorism community weighed in with projections of what that could mean for al-Qaeda and who would go on to be the organization's third emir.[3] A clumsy attempt by al-Qaeda's official media arm, al-Sahab, to quell concerns among al-Qaeda supporters by releasing audio clips of al-Zawahiri backfired.[4] Sound bites of al-Zawahiri addressing the plight of Rohingya Muslims in Myanmar failed to reference specific and recent events.[5] Accordingly, his boilerplate commentary fueled further speculation that the septuagenarian terrorist leader was in fact dead.

If al-Qaeda's septuagenarian leader is unwell and ultimately succumbs to what plagues him, it will be yet another blow to the organization's already thin bench.[6] Over the course of the past several years, al-Qaeda's senior leadership has been attenuated by a series of targeted assassinations and Zawahiri would not be easily replaced.[7] His death would likely lead to the promotion of veteran jihadist Saif al-Adel, a veteran Egyptian jihadist indicted by the United States for his role in the 1998 U.S. Embassy bombing in Kenya.[8] Adel is believed to be hiding out in Iran, where he has been based since 2002 or 2003. Leading al-Qaeda from Iran—a country that maintains a complicated relationship with the jihadist group—would pose serious limitations for al-Adel.[9] The relationship between al-Qaeda and Iran has been described as "antagonistic."[10] This is true even with a consistent track record of cooperation at various points over the past twenty years.[11] One obvious danger for al-Adel is whether he could remain beyond the reach of the Israelis, who were allegedly responsible for the assassination of another high-ranking al-Qaeda leader—Abu Muhammad al-Masri—in Tehran in August 2019.[12]

Last year was a particularly challenging year for al-Qaeda.[13] Once its flagship franchise, al-Qaeda in the Arabian Peninsula (AQAP) suffered a series of dissensions and desertions that left its ranks depleted.[14] This was the culmination of a steady drumbeat of targeted assassinations that methodically eliminated AQAP's top ideologues, bombmakers, and strategists over the course of the past decade. Abdelmalek Droukdel, a longtime al-Qaeda veteran and leader of al-Qaeda in the Islamic Maghreb (AQIM), was killed in a French-led operation in Mali.[15] Numerous leading figures in al-Qaeda's Syrian branch, Hurras al-Din, were killed in U.S. drone strikes.[16]

But it would be a mistake to underestimate the resolve of al-Qaeda or its affiliates. In December 2019, a Saudi airman stationed at a U.S. Navy base in Pensacola, Florida for military training shot and killed three U.S. sailors and wounded eight other Americans. The plot was linked back to AQAP in Yemen and Saudi Arabia.[17] Yet, across the U.S. government, the threat perception of al-Qaeda seems to be of a group with extremely limited capabilities to attack the U.S. homeland. In remarks delivered before the Senate Judiciary Committee in March 2021, Christopher Wray, the director of the Federal Bureau of Investigation (FBI), noted that while al-Qaeda "maintains its desire for large-scale, spectacular attacks," its current focus will likely remain occupied by local or regional issues in the Sahel and the Horn of Africa, while also "supporting small-scale, readily achievable attacks" in those regions.[18] Al-Qaeda's diminished capability to strike the U.S. homeland was assessed to result from continued counterterrorism pressure and recent leadership losses suffered by the group.

There is a divergence within the counterterrorism community over just how dangerous of a threat al-Qaeda still poses to the West.[19] Jihadist ideology seems to resonate far less with homegrown violent extremists in the United States, although as evidenced by a spate of attacks in Europe toward the end of last year, it bears close watching.[20] Those attacks were primarily committed by individuals with no established links to jihadist groups or organizations, including al-Qaeda.[21] Even if al-Qaeda and its overseas branches remain less capable of external operations, they are still able to destabilize entire regions, carve out territory within ungoverned spaces, and wreak havoc in weak and failed states. Two al-Qaeda affiliates in particular seem to have momentum—Jama'a Nusrat ul-Islam wa al-Muslimin (JNIM) in the Maghreb and al-Shabab in Somalia and East Africa. Both groups have displayed a penchant for resilience and the ability to maintain a steady operational tempo of attacks.[22]

As the United States and its allies like France reconsider military deployments and current commitments of troop levels, including throughout sub-Saharan Africa, the result could be power vacuums that jihadist groups move to fill.[23] Because African jihadist groups have not demonstrated the capability to attack the West, they have been deprioritized. Yet, there could be a change in the desire to attack the West, exemplified by a terror plot foiled in 2019 that led to the arrest of a Kenyan national and al-Shabab operative member planning to hijack an airplane in the United States and crash it into a building.[24]

"Remain and Expand" Continues to Guide the Islamic State's Evolution

More than two years after its physical caliphate was crushed, the Islamic State is still managing to wage a global insurgency, with an operational presence in at least 20 countries.[25] The diffusion of Islamic State affiliates and branches around the globe has been described, quite accurately, as an "adhocracy." In other words, a group of "structurally fluid organizations in which 'interacting project teams' work towards a shared purpose and/or identity."[26] This organizational structure is a deliberate design that allows the group's leaders to leverage the benefits of a transnational network.

What this model allows IS to do is to function akin to a venture capital firm.[27] As the primary investor, IS core provides expertise, materiel, and resources to its regional provinces and affiliates. In ideal scenarios, even a modicum of investment can have a worthwhile return, improving the capabilities of franchise groups to launch attacks against state security forces or regional militaries, conquer and hold territory, and establish influence among local populations. In return, IS gains the brand recognition of its name and can feature its branches in propaganda, portraying an image of success and momentum.[28] The arrangement is mutually beneficial—jihadist groups in sub-Saharan Africa or Southeast Asia that pledge allegiance to IS enjoy the benefits of the core group's operational and organizational capabilities, including financing, training, weapons, propaganda support, and advice on tactics and strategy.

According to the most recent report of the UN Security Council Monitoring Team, the most striking feature of the latest period under review was "the emergence of Africa as the region most affected by terrorism."[29] As mentioned above in the section on al-Qaeda, its affiliates JNIM and al-Shabaab are responsible for destabilizing parts of the Sahel and the Horn of Africa, respectively. But the Islamic State also has its sights set on the continent, particularly as a target for future expansion.[30] The Islamic State's affiliate in Somalia has been functioning as a "command center" for a "triad" of jihadist groups in the Democratic Republic of Congo and Mozambique, streamlining operations in East, Southern and Central Africa.[31] Regional conditions, including weak security forces, porous borders and a high availability of weapons make it easy for IS core to help improve the capabilities of armed groups.[32] Modest infusions of cash, weapons, and trainers can act as a force multiplier for jihadist groups, and translate to tangible gains on the battlefield.[33] But through its involvement, IS also seeks to impart its imprimatur, thus transforming the identity of affiliates to operate with a more global mindset and draconian approach. In Central Africa, the Islamic State's influence is already apparent, exemplified by ISCAP's beheading of foreigners, a signature tactic of the Islamic State.

Sub-Saharan Africa is likely to remain a focus of the Islamic State for the foreseeable future. IS affiliates have seized the opportunity to grow their presence in the region, and with Western countries pivoting away from counterterrorism and toward great power competition, it seems inevitable that jihadists will continue to refine their capabilities. Seven of the top 10 countries experiencing the most significant increase in terrorist attacks last year were located in sub-Saharan Africa—including Mozambique, Mali and Congo—all countries where al-Qaeda and IS maintain active affiliates.[34] Sub-Saharan Africa has been identified as a region where IS can achieve "breakout capacity," defined as the ability to generate and maintain a high frequency of attacks or operational tempo.[35] IS provinces in Central Africa and West Africa each have the potential to conquer and hold territory similar to what IS core achieved in Iraq and Syria between 2014 and 2019. With the momentum enjoyed by the Islamic State West Africa Province (ISWAP), including around the Lake Chad region, that area could be a prime candidate for the next experiment in jihadist governance.

The goal of IS sponsorship is to push jihadists focused on local issues to consider a more regional or transnational outlook. And even as some of these groups will remain motivated primarily by parochial grievances, as IS affiliates continue to develop their operational capabilities, this evolution could result in a global approach. After becoming IS affiliates, a number of African jihadist groups have demonstrated both tactical improvement and strategic evolution. The end result is that groups like ISWAP and ISCAP are now more capable of launching sophisticated attacks and thus have become more prominent in IS propaganda.[36] ISCAP in particular has undergone a significant transformation since its formal recognition by IS in April 2019.[37] By early 2020, ISCAP militants in Mozambique were noticeably operating in larger units and staging more complex operations against higher-value targets, including in some cases district capitals.[38] Even as groups like ISCAP adopt aspects of IS' approach, there is still a need to tailor the ideology to local conditions. At times, this includes balancing wanton violence with an effort to win the hearts and minds of locals that affiliates see as supportive or potentially supportive, with recent examples from northern Mozambique.[39] During a string of attacks in March 2020, jihadists went to great lengths to avoid collateral damage and even doled out looted supplies to local residents, including food, medicine, and fuel.

In a show of force, in August 2020 IS fighters in Mozambique captured the strategic port city of Mocimboa de Praia. In October of the same year, ISCAP jihadists displayed cross-border capabilities by launching attacks into southern Tanzania from northern Mozambique.[40] The deadly siege of the town of Palma in March 2021 left dozens dead and bore many of the hallmarks of IS attacks, including the beheading of foreigners and the symbolic targeting of Western economic interests.[41] As a result, the French energy behemoth Total suspended a $20 billion offshore natural gas project near Palma. This attack could be a harbinger of things to come in Mozambique. Reporting suggests that ISCAP received training and funding from IS central and that "battle hardened Arab Muslim volunteers" were embedded in fighting units in both the Democratic Republic of Congo (DRC) and Mozambique.[42] IS's African affiliates are "no longer a sideshow to its operational core in Syria and Iraq" as noted in a recent research paper in the *CTC Sentinel*, and indeed, IS core is currently assessed to be "dependent now more than ever on the military activities of its affiliates" throughout sub-Saharan Africa.[43]

With a war chest estimated between $25 million and $50 million, IS is still able to provide resources to its affiliates and branches, enhancing the capabilities of existing groups in an effort to keep the "caliphate" alive. There is an old maxim that can be summed up simply as, "insurgents win by not losing. The Islamic State's senior leadership is seeking to bide its time and rely on strategic patience to rebuild its networks, not only in the Iraqi-Syrian core conflict zone, but in other weak states and ungoverned regions that could provide IS with new opportunities to conquer territory, recruit new members, and carve out a safe haven from which to launch external operations against the West. Geopolitical events, including civil wars and shifting force posture of Western militaries could provide jihadist groups with new opportunities to rebuild. As we approach the two-decade anniversary of the al-Qaeda attacks of September 11, 2001, the world is once again focused on events in Afghanistan. Al-Qaeda's leadership could be staking the organization's future on what happens as a result of ongoing negotiations in Afghanistan involving the Afghan government and al-Qaeda's longtime partner, the Taliban.[44]

Afghanistan as a "Wild Card"

In April 2021, U.S. President Joseph Biden made the decision to withdraw all U.S. military troops from Afghanistan by September 11, 2021. In justifying the withdrawal, the President declared, "Bin Laden is dead and al-Qaeda is degraded in Iraq and Afghanistan."[45] Bin Laden is indeed dead, and has been for more than a decade. But al-Qaeda is not defeated, and the U.S. withdrawal could very well be the precipitating event that the jihadist group has been waiting for to accelerate a strategy of rebuilding in Afghanistan, Pakistan, and throughout South Asia more broadly. The Biden administration recognizes that the Taliban has not jettisoned al-Qaeda. By all accounts, a Taliban-led government in Afghanistan would provide al-Qaeda with the operational space it needs to regroup and rebuild jihadist networks throughout South Asia.[46]

The U.S. intelligence community assesses that both al-Qaeda and IS are still focused on striking the U.S. homeland. According to the 2021 Annual Threat Assessment released by the Office of the Director of National Intelligence, "ISIS and al-Qaeda remain the greatest Sunni terrorist threats to US interests overseas; they also seek to conduct attacks inside the United States, although sustained US and allied [counterterrorism] pressure has broadly degraded their capability to do so."[47] In the absence of a U.S. military presence in Afghanistan, high-ranking military officials, policymakers, and counterterrorism analysts are growing concerned that jihadist groups will further metastasize to the point of once again being able to pose a direct threat to the United States.[48] In an acknowledgment of the challenges that the U.S. withdrawal will present to the intelligence community, CIA Director William Burns publicly bemoaned a degraded ability to collect, analyze, and act on intelligence.[49]

It remains unclear what an offshore U.S. counterterrorism strategy will look like after the withdrawal is complete. To maintain a presence closer to Afghanistan, the United States could look to a Central Asian nation, or to neighboring Pakistan. But even if Washington is able to secure basing rights from Islamabad, any deal will be unable to address Pakistan's continued support for militant groups, which it sees as part of its national security strategy. If the Taliban secures political and military control of large swaths of Afghanistan, it could soon become difficult, if not impossible, to differentiate between the Taliban, al-Qaeda and the Haqqani network.

The Biden administration believes that the terrorist threat from Afghanistan is similar in nature to other jihadist threats in theaters where U.S. and allied counterterrorism efforts have contained or mitigated terrorist groups, including in Somalia, Yemen and Libya. But the recent string of Taliban military victories in Afghanistan, where in several instances Afghan National

Security Force (ANSF) troops fled and abandoned their vehicles, is eerily reminiscent to scenes from Iraq in 2011 following another calendar-based withdrawal of U.S. troops, which was swiftly followed by the rise of the Islamic State. And once again, the Islamic State, through its Afghan branch Islamic State Khorasan Province (ISKP), could receive a much-needed boost from a U.S. military withdrawal.

Upwards of 2,000 ISKP members remain in prisons, including much of the group's top leadership, many of whom were arrested following the group's near collapse in 2019–2020. As of 2022, ISKP is still on the rebound, moving into new provinces such as Nuristan, Badghis, Sari Pul, Baghlan, Badaskhshan, Kunduz, and Kabul.[50] It is also looking to regain influence in Nangarhar and Kunar provinces, considered among the most strategically important. ISKP is approaching a dual-track strategy, the first piece of which is moving away from holding territory to more clandestine activity. The group, which retains strong support among Afghanistan's Salafist community, has focused on targeting sectarian targets. If ISKP is afforded the opportunity to resurge, it is not inconceivable to see the group mushroom to thousands of members. Despite repeatedly having its leadership targeted and territory revoked, ISKP has managed to mount numerous comebacks.[51] Even without holding territory, ISKP has managed to cultivate a cadre of battle hardened fighters with the resources and training necessary to mount devastating terrorist attacks, including in the capital of Kabul.

Conclusion

How events unfold in Afghanistan is just one scenario with the potential to impact the trajectory of transnational Islamist terrorism. If the trend toward decentralization continues, the global jihadist movement could become less potent in the near term, while still posing a major security threat in the medium-to-long term. There are more jihadist groups operating in the contemporary environment than at any point in the past forty years.[52] It has been well-documented that the COVID-19 pandemic has served as an artificial suppressant for terrorist attacks, especially for plots in the West. As the pandemic begins to ebb and travel restrictions have been altogether lifted, it will inevitably invite more opportunities for terrorist groups to launch attacks against soft targets.

Another question is how the relationship between al-Qaeda and the Islamic State—and their respective affiliates—will continue to evolve over the course of the next several years. While the conflict is mostly localized at the moment, regional and even global dynamics could take on increased significance. The struggle for ascendancy in the Muslim world between moderates and radicals will likely have a substantial impact on how successful or unsuccessful jihadists ultimately are when it comes to recruiting, fundraising, and conquering new territory.

The global jihadist movement remains strong and is motivated by many of the same grievances that fueled its rise nearly three decades ago. Al-Qaeda, and now the Islamic State, have proven resilient, even as both groups suffer from mounting leadership losses.[53] If the rivalry between these jihadist heavyweights heats up, it could lead to a situation where one of the two groups attempt to "up the ante" and grab the attention of would-be supporters by plotting and executing a spectacular attack in the West. The attacks of September 11, 2001 demonstrated how airplanes could be used to create catastrophic terrorism. More recent advances in synthetic biology could allow an even smaller number of hardcore militants to perpetrate an attack of even greater magnitude.

Some scholars have speculated that the current religious wave of terrorism, epitomized by the global jihadist movement, might finally be starting to ebb. But the movement could very well roar back to life, catalyzed by a surge of activity in sub-Saharan Africa and South Asia, once again rising to the level of the threat posed by al-Qaeda more than two decades ago.

Notes

1 Tore Refslund Hamming, "Global Jihadism after the Syria War," *Perspectives on Terrorism,* Volume 13, Issue 3, June 2019, https://www.universiteitleiden.nl/binaries/content/assets/customsites/perspectives-on-terrorism/2019/issue-3/01—hamming.pdf; see also, Colin P. Clarke and Charles Lister, "Al Qaeda is Ready to Attack You Again," *Foreign Policy,* September 4, 2019, https://foreignpolicy.com/2019/09/04/al-qaeda-is-ready-to-attack-you-again/

2 United Nations Security Council, Twenty-Eighth Report of the Analytical Support and Sanctions Monitoring Team Concerning Islamic State in Iraq and the Levant (Da'esh), al-Qaeda and Associated Individuals, Groups, Undertakings and Entities, July 2021, https://undocs.org/S/2021/655

3 Daniel L. Byman, "The Death of Ayman al-Zawahiri and the Future of Al-Qaida," *Brookings Institution,* November 17, 2020, https://www.brookings.edu/blog/order-from-chaos/2020/11/17/the-death-of-ayman-al-zawahri-and-the-future-of-al-qaida/

4 Mina Alami, "'New' Al-Qaida Leader Message Fails to Offer Proof of Life," *BBC Monitoring,* March 13, 2021, https://monitoring.bbc.co.uk/product/c202fl5u

5 Thomas Joscelyn, "Al Qaeda Leader Threatens Myanmar in New Video," *Long War Journal,* March 12, 2021, https://www.longwarjournal.org/archives/2021/03/al-qaeda-leader-threatens-myanmar-in-new-video.php

6 Colin P. Clarke and Asfandyar Mir, "Al Qaeda's Leader is Old, Bumbling—and a Terrorist Mastermind," *Foreign Policy,* September 10, 2020, https://foreignpolicy.com/2020/09/10/zawahiri-bin-laden-al-qaedas-leader-terrorist-mastermind/

7 Barak Mendelsohn and Colin Clarke, "Al Qaeda is Being Hollowed to Its Core," *War on the Rocks,* February 24, 2021, https://warontherocks.com/2021/02/al-qaeda-is-being-hollowed-to-its-core/

8 Ali Soufan, "Al-Qa'ida's Soon-To-Be Third Emir? A Profile of Saif al-'Adl," *CTC Sentinel,* Volume 14, Issue 2, February 2021, https://ctc.usma.edu/al-qaidas-soon-to-be-third-emir-a-profile-of-saif-al-adl/

9 Cole Bunzel, "Is Ayman al-Zawahiri Dead?" *Jihadica,* March 17, 2021, http://www.jihadica.com/is-ayman-al-zawahiri-dead/

10 "Hearing before the Subcommittee on Counterterrorism and Intelligence of the Committee on Homeland Security, House of Representatives, May 22, 2013, https://www.govinfo.gov/content/pkg/CHRG-113hhrg85684/html/CHRG-113hhrg85684.htm

11 Asfandyar Mir and Colin P. Clarke, "Making Sense of Iran and al-Qaeda's Relationship," *Lawfare,* March 21, 2021, https://www.lawfareblog.com/making-sense-iran-and-al-qaedas-relationship

12 Adam Goldman et al., "Al Qaeda's No.2, Accused in U.S. Embassy Attacks, Was Killed in Iran," *New York Times,* November 13, 2020, https://www.nytimes.com/2020/11/13/world/middleeast/al-masri-abdullah-qaeda-dead.html

13 Aaron Y. Zelin, "Jihadis 2021: ISIS & al Qaeda," *Wilson Center,* March 17, 2021, https://www.wilsoncenter.org/article/jihadis-2021-isis-al-qaeda

14 https://undocs.org/S/2021/68

15 Julie Coleman and Meryl Demuynck, "The Death of Droukdel: Implications for AQIM and the Sahel," *International Centre for Counterterrorism (ICCT)–The Hague,* June 9, 2020, https://www.icct.nl/index.php/publication/death-droukdel-implications-aqim-and-sahel

16 Eric Schmitt, "U.S. Commandos Use Secretive Missiles to Kill Qaeda Leaders in Syria," *New York Times,* October 26, 2020, https://www.nytimes.com/2020/09/24/us/politics/missiles-al-qaeda-syria.html

17 Colin Clarke, "The Pensacola Terrorist Attack: The Enduring Influence of al-Qa'ida and its Affiliates," *CTC Sentinel,* Volume 13, Issue 3, March 2020, https://ctc.usma.edu/pensacola-terrorist-attack-enduring-influence-al-qaida-affiliates/

18 "Oversight of the Federal Bureau of Investigation: The January 6 Insurrection, Domestic Terrorism, and Other Threats," Statement by FBI Director Christopher Wray before the Senate Judiciary Committee, March 2, 2021, https://www.fbi.gov/news/testimony/oversight-of-the-federal-bureau-of-investigation-the-january-6-insurrection-domestic-terrorism-and-other-threats

19 Michael Hirsh, "Biden Team Engaged in 'Rigorous' Debate Over Ending Forever War," *Foreign Policy,* March 12, 2021, https://foreignpolicy.com/2021/03/12/biden-forever-war-drones-al-qaeda-september-11/

20 Colin P. Clarke, "As Right-Wing Extremism Rises, Jihadism Still Persists," *World Politics Review,* February 19, 2021, https://www.worldpoliticsreview.com/articles/29438/in-europe-terrorism-and-jihadism-remain-threats-as-right-wing-extremism-rises

21 Rafaello Pantucci, "End of Al Qaeda Era?" *RSIS,* December 8, 2020, https://raffaellopantucci.com/2020/12/08/end-of-al-qaeda-era/

22 Frank Gardner, "Is Africa Overtaking the Middle East as the New Jihadist Battleground?" *BBC News,* December 3, 2020, https://www.bbc.com/news/world-africa-55147863

23 Andrew Lebovich, "After Barkhane: What France's Military Drawdown Means for the Sahel," *European Council on Foreign Relations,* July 2, 2021, https://ecfr.eu/article/after-barkhane-what-frances-military-drawdown-means-for-the-sahel/

24 Department of Justice, Office of Public Affairs, "Kenyan National Indicted for Conspiring to Hijack Aircraft on Behalf of the Al Qaeda - Affiliated Terrorist Organization Al Shabaab," December 16, 2020, https://www.justice.gov/opa/pr/kenyan-national-indicted-conspiring-hijack-aircraft-behalf-al-qaeda-affiliated-terrorist

25 Haroro J. Ingram, Craig Whiteside, and Charlie Winter, "The Islamic State's Global Insurgency and its Counterinsurgency Implications," *International Centre for Counterterrorism (ICCT)–The Hague, Evolution in Counter-Terrorism,* Volume 2, November 2020, pp. 21–46, https://www.icct.nl/sites/default/files/2023-01/Special-Edition-2-2.pdf

26 Haroro J. Ingram, Craig Whiteside, and Charlie Winter, "The Routinization of the Islamic State's Global Enterprise," Hudson Institute, April 5, 2021, https://www.hudson.org/research/16798-the-routinization-of-the-islamic-state-s-global-enterprise

27 https://www.worldpoliticsreview.com/articles/29630/for-isis-africa-offers-best-hope-of-renewal

28 Christina Goldbaum and Eric Schmitt, "In Bid to Boost Its Profile, ISIS Turns to Africa's Militants," *New York Times,* April 7, 2021, https://www.hudson.org/node/43763

29 United Nations Security Council, Twenty-Eighth Report of the Analytical Support and Sanctions Monitoring Team concerning Islamic State in Iraq and the Levant (Da'esh), al-Qaida and Associated Individuals, Groups, Undertakings and Entities, July 2021, https://undocs.org/S/2021/655

30 Colin P. Clarke and Jacob Zenn, "ISIS and Al-Qaeda's Sub-Saharan Affiliates Are Poised for Growth in 2021," *Defense One,* February 26, 2021, https://www.defenseone.com/ideas/2021/02/isis-and-al-qaedas-sub-saharan-affiliates-are-poised-growth-2021/172313/

31 https://undocs.org/S/2020/53

32 Meryl Demuynck, Tanya Mehra, and Reinier Bergema, "ICCT Situation Report: The Use of Small Arms & Light Weapons by Terrorist Organisations as a Source of Finance in West Africa and the Horn of Africa," *International Centre for Counterterrorism (ICCT) – The Hague,* July 1, 2020, https://icct.nl/publication/icct-situation-report-the-use-of-small-arms-light-weapons-by-terrorist-organisations-as-a-source-of-finance-in-west-africa-and-the-horn-of-africa/

33 "Facing the Challenge of the Islamic State in West Africa Province," *International Crisis Group,* May 16, 2019, https://www.crisisgroup.org/africa/west-africa/nigeria/273-facing-challenge-islamic-state-west-africa-province

34 Frank Gardner, "Is Africa Overtaking the Middle East as the New Jihadist Battleground?" *BBC News,* December 3, 2020, https://www.bbc.com/news/world-africa-55147863

35 Jacob Zenn, "ISIS in Africa: The Caliphate's Next Frontier," *Newlines Institute,* May 26, 2020, https://newlinesinstitute.org/isis/isis-in-africa-the-caliphates-next-frontier/

36 Cris Chinaka, Lesley Wroughton, and Joby Warrick, "An Islamist Insurgency in Mozambique is Gaining Ground—And showing a Strong Allegiance to the Islamic State," *Washington Post,* November 13, 2020, https://www.washingtonpost.com/world/africa/mozambique-insurgents-islamic-state/2020/11/13/82d3bc8a-2460-11eb-9c4a-0dc6242c4814_story.html

37 Daveed Gartenstein-Ross, Emelie Chace-Donahue, and Colin P. Clarke, "The Evolution and Escalation of the Islamic State Threat to Mozambique," April 13, 2021, https://www.fpri.org/article/2021/04/the-evolution-and-escalation-of-the-islamic-state-threat-to-mozambique/

38 Amy Mackinnon, "Mozambique's Growing Insurgency Takes Strategic Port," *Foreign* Policy, August 14, 2020, https://foreignpolicy.com/2020/08/14/mozambique-growing-insurgency-take-strategic-port-mocimboa-praia-islamic-state/; see also, Jason Warner et al., "Outlasting the Caliphate: The Evolution of the Islamic State Threat in Africa," *CTC Sentinel,* Volume 13, Issue 11, November/December 2020, https://ctc.usma.edu/outlasting-the-caliphate-the-evolution-of-the-islamic-state-threat-in-africa/

39 Alex Vines, "The Insurgency in Northern Mozambique Has Got Worse. Why? *Mail & Guardian,* March 31, 2020, https://mg.co.za/article/2020-03-31-the-insurgency-in-northern-mozambique-has-got-worse-why/

40 Sunguta West, "Islamic State Fighters' First Claimed Attack in Tanzania: Strategic Calculations and Political Context," *The Jamestown Foundation, Terrorism Monitor,* Volume 18, Issue 22, December 3,

2020, https://jamestown.org/program/islamic-state-fighters-first-claimed-attack-in-tanzania-strate-gic-calculations-and-political-context/

41 Christina Goldbaum et al., "As Militants Seize Mozambique Gas Hub, a Dash for Safety Turns Deadly," *New York Times,* March 28, 2021, https://www.nytimes.com/2021/03/28/world/africa/mozambique-palma-hotel-insurgents.html

42 "Report: Islamic State Financier Paid Money to Eastern Congo Rebel Group," *Voice of America*, November 15, 2018, https://www.voanews.com/a/report-islamic-state-financier-paid-money-to-eastern-congo-rebel-group/4659982.html; Benoit Faucon et al., "Islamic State Seeks Revival in Christian Countries," *Wall Street Journal,* April 15, 2021, https://www.wsj.com/articles/islamic-state-seeks-revival-in-christian-countries-11618498283?mod=hp_lead_pos10

43 Tomasz Rolbiecki, Pieter Van Ostaeyen, and Charlie Winter, "The Islamic State's Strategic Trajectory in Africa: Key Takeaways from its Attack Claims," *CTC Sentinel,* Volume 13, Issue 8, August 2020, https://ctc.usma.edu/the-islamic-states-strategic-trajectory-in-africa-key-takeaways-from-its-attack-claims/

44 Candace Rondeaux, "The U.S. Must Prepare for the Worst in Afghanistan," *World Politics Review,* March 12, 2021, https://www.worldpoliticsreview.com/articles/29489/with-a-u-s-withdrawal-afghanistan-must-prepare-for-the-worst

45 "Remarks by President Biden on the Way Forward in Afghanistan," *The White House*, April 14, 2021, https://www.whitehouse.gov/briefing-room/speeches-remarks/2021/04/14/remarks-by-president-biden-on-the-way-forward-in-afghanistan/

46 Missy Ryan et al., "With Clock Ticking Before Exit Deadline, U.S. Appears Poised to Postpone Troop Withdrawal from Afghanistan," *Washington Post,* March 12, 2021, https://www.washingtonpost.com/national-security/us-afghanistan-troop-withdrawal-postponed/2021/03/12/cf92d51c-8296-11eb-bb5a-ad9a91faa4ef_story.html

47 Office of the Director of National Intelligence (ODNI), "2021 Annual Threat Assessment," https://www.dni.gov/index.php/newsroom/reports-publications/reports-publications-2021/item/2204-2021-annual-threat-assessment-of-the-u-s-intelligence-community

48 Eric Schmitt and Helene Cooper, "How the U.S. Plans to Fight from Afar After Troops Exit Afghanistan," *New York Times,* April 27, 2021, https://www.nytimes.com/2021/04/15/us/politics/united-states-al-qaeda-afghanistan.html

49 Patricia Zengerle and Jonathan Landay, "CIA Chief Highlights Loss of Intelligence Once U.S. Troops Leave Afghanistan," *Reuters,* April 14, 2021, https://www.reuters.com/world/asia-pacific/cia-chief-says-intelligence-will-diminish-once-us-troops-leave-afghanistan-2021-04-14/

50 United Nations Security Council, Twenty-Eighth Report of the Analytical Support and Sanctions Monitoring Team concerning Islamic State in Iraq and the Levant (Da'esh), al-Qaeda and Associated Individuals, Groups, Undertakings and Entities, July 2021, https://undocs.org/S/2021/655

51 Amira Jadoon and Andrew Mines, "Broken, but Not Defeated: An Examination of State-Led Operations against Islamic State Khorasan in Afghanistan and Pakistan (2015–2018), *CTC Sentinel,* March 23, 2020, https://ctc.usma.edu/broken-not-defeated-examination-state-led-operations-islamic-state-khorasan-afghanistan-pakistan-2015-2018/

52 Seth G. Jones et al., "The Evolution of the Salafi-Jihadist Threat: Current and Future Challenges from the Islamic State, Al-Qaeda, and Other Groups," Center for Strategic and International Studies (CSIS), November 2018, https://csis-website-prod.s3.amazonaws.com/s3fs-public/publication/181221_EvolvingTerroristThreat.pdf

53 Bruce Hoffman and Jacob Ware, "Al-Qaeda: Threat or Anachronism," *War on the Rocks,* March 12, 2020, https://warontherocks.com/2020/03/al-qaeda-threat-or-anachronism/

26

FOILED VERSUS LAUNCHED TERROR PLOTS

Some Lessons Learned

Petter Nesser

Introduction[1]

The common approach to measuring terrorism is to count attacks. Nearly all quantitative studies of terrorism rely on attacks as a metric for terrorist activity. Such studies typically draw upon the Global Terrorism Database (GTD), which is widely accepted as the gold standard for data on terrorism.[2] Attacks are also the focus of public debate on terrorism.

This focus on attacks is natural since they are the most tangible and measurable output of terrorist activity. Yet, to solely focus on launched terror attacks is problematic. The reason is that attacks constitute the "tip of the iceberg", what is left after security services have done their job at foiling attack plots.[3] Not considering the foiled plots comes with a risk of misrepresenting the scale and nature of terror threats.

To base analyses of terrorism on launched attacks only implies ignoring how countermeasures affect threat patterns. Many terror attacks are never completed, usually because the security apparatus intervenes. So for every launched attack there will be foiled ones, and these are seldom considered in scientific studies. If there was a fixed relationship between foiled and launched plots this problem would be limited. For example, if there were two foiled plots per attack, and the foiled plots pursued the same modus operandi as the attacks, it would usually suffice to study the latter. However, this is not the case.

Counterterrorism varies for different reasons, between countries, and over time. There is also variance in how security regimes prioritize different types of threat actors with different types of modi operandi. Since 9/11 western governments have prioritized countering jihadism, necessarily at the expense of other threats. Similarly, states will prioritize avoiding highly disruptive and lethal types of terrorism, such as attacks on aviation or WMD terrorism, over less lethal types, such as knife attacks. What this means is that attacks become a precarious measure for assessing terrorist threat patterns. The attacks may not be representative of the overall threat. The scale of a threat could be higher than it would seem based on the number of attacks, because of vigilant counterterrorism. A threat's modus operandi could also be more diversified than the attacks signal. Not considering foiled plots could also distort comparative analyses of the threat from actors, such as jihadis, nationalist-separatists, or right-wing militancy.

Both research and public discourse influence policy decisions on how to tackle political violence: how much resources should be allocated for this purpose, which types of countermeasures should

DOI: 10.4324/9781003326373-30

be put in place, and what types of threats should be prioritized. An effective counterterrorism policy hinges on an accurate understanding of the threat. It is therefore important to examine how analyses of attacks can misrepresent terrorism, and what can be gained by analyzing foiled plots. However, research on foiled plots involves methodological pitfalls. Therefore this untapped resource in terrorism research ought to be used with caution. Despite a growing awareness about the value added of foiled plots as a unit of analysis, there exist few databases that systematically include them.

This paper will discuss what can be gained from researching foiled plots. As a background it will present some lessons learned from a data collection project at the Norwegian Defence Research Establishment (FFI), mapping launched and foiled terror plots by jihadi terrorists in Western Europe. This section will highlight some of the methodological challenges of studying foiled terror plots. The paper then looks briefly at the state of research on foiled plots. Next it will show some examples on how the jihadi threat in Europe looks different when we include foiled plots than it does when we leave them out of the analysis. The paper concludes with a call for more data on foiled plots in terrorism research.

The Jihadi Plots in Europe Dataset (JPED)

In 2003 the Terrorism Research Group at the Norwegian Defence Research Establishment started mapping the activities of al-Qaeda in Western Europe based on open sources, such as media and judicial documents. Most of what al-Qaeda was doing in Europe at that time revolved around propaganda, recruitment, money laundering, and weapons smuggling. These activities were geared toward supporting jihadis in conflict zones.

However, there was also an emerging pattern of attack plotting. Cells linked to al-Qaeda attempted to strike US and Jewish targets in Europe but ended up being intercepted by counterterrorism. We decided to focus the data collection on this attack-geared activity, and to assemble as much information as possible about the foiled plots in a chronology. Closer analyses of these foiled plots showed that there was a well-organized, persistent effort by al-Qaeda to launch attacks in Europe. Then, following the 2003 invasion of Iraq, this effort resulted in the 2004 Madrid bombings and the 2005 London bombings. From that point FFI's data collection consisted of both foiled plots and attacks.[4]

We also decided to include historical data on jihadi terrorism in the region, tracing the beginning of the phenomenon to the mid-1990s, with the Algerian GIA's bombing campaign in France.[5] Over time the chronology has become a dataset, maintained through day-to-day monitoring of media, and other sources. At the time of writing the dataset contains a total of 341 observations of plots and attacks attributed to jihadis in Western Europe. JPED only looks at Western Europe and not former Eastern bloc states. There are two reasons for this. Firstly, it makes the data collection manageable. Secondly, it eases cross-country comparisons, because Western European states are similar in terms of political systems, access to sources, and history with jihadism. Broadly speaking JPED covers three waves of terrorist plotting: The GIA terror wave in France and Belgium in the mid-1990s, the al-Qaeda wave of the 2000s, and the IS wave from the mid-2010s. Each observation in the dataset is coded as a terrorist plot.

What Are Terror Plots?

There exists no unified definition of what constitutes a terrorist plot.[6] The concept is used to describe different phenomena ranging from an expressed idea or vague intention to conduct an attack, to very concrete acts of preparation and implementation. Sometimes the word "plot" is also used about actions by extremists which are not directly linked to attack planning, such as recruitment of foreign fighters. In JPED, the term "terrorist plots" narrowly refers to attacks and concrete plans thereof. This needs to be qualified though, as JPED can only include attack plans which are documented in publicly available sources. This means that there will be dark figures, as we must assume that security services make early interventions, and prevent some attack plans that the public never hears about. To use the ice-berg analogy, there will always be parts of the iceberg that cannot be captured by JPED. Still, because there are incentives for security services to report on what they have managed to stop, the dark figures are probably not huge.

In JPED terror plots are either foiled or launched. A plot is launched when perpetrators reach the stage where they physically attempt to hurt the target. A launched plot therefore equals an attack. A plot is foiled when an attack plan gets thwarted before the perpetrator can implement. This mostly happens because security services intervene, but sometimes because perpetrators run into problems during the planning process, or have a change of heart. One example of the latter pattern is the case of Sajjid Badat. He was supposed to bomb a trans-Atlantic airliner for al-Qaeda, but hid the bomb under the bed and tried to forget about the whole thing.[7] Each observation or "plot" in JPED is coded for more than twenty variables signifying outcome (e.g. the number of people killed or injured), perpetrator profiles (e.g. involvement of women, or minors), cell-configuration (group vs single actors), and modus operandi (weapons, tactics, and targets). JPED does currently not code for how plots are foiled, mainly because open sources offer limited information about the security services' methods.

The ambition for JPED is to give an updated and reliable overview of jihadi terrorist attack activity in Western European countries, and make the dataset available to academic researchers. There are three main challenges with the project. Firstly, since the dataset includes foiled terror plots, which are essentially non-events, there needs to be a continuous and critical assessment of which cases should be included and which cases should not. Secondly, because of the secret nature of terrorism and the many biases involved in the discourse on terrorism, it can be challenging to obtain reliable sources. Thirdly, maintaining this type of dataset is very labor-intensive.

Inclusion Criteria

With regards to the inclusion of cases, JPED applies a narrow definition of terrorism. The terror plots must involve some level of organization and sustained preparation, and be designed to spread a political message and fear, through killing people. This excludes, for example, sabotage against property or spontaneous hate crime, even though these can be highly politicized and the latter very lethal.[8] When identifying terror plots (launched or foiled) for JPED, and including them, there are three main criteria. Firstly, perpetrators must be "jihadi" in the way that they subscribe to the ideology of al-Qaeda and IS. Secondly, there must be information about a target or target type. Last, there must be concrete evidence, such as bomb-making material or reconnaissance. If all three aspects are well-documented the case is category 1 (C1). This applies to most attacks. If two aspects are well-documented it is category 2 (C2). This applies to most foiled plots. If there are uncertainties regarding all three, the case is defined as category 3 (C3).

JPED also sticks to the principle that perpetrators must be considered rational, meaning that plots by persons known to suffer from severe mental illness are either coded C3, or not included in the dataset at all. An example of such an assessment is the case of Mark T., a serial fraudster and former porn director, suffering from personality disorders.[9] He contemplated assassinating Prince Harry of Britain. Mark T. received a three-years-sentence for planning murder in 2014, but was released in 2015. The case was for a long time coded C2 in JPED, but was in the end categorized as C3. While technically this was at least a C2 plot, the circumstances and Mark T's background were just too bizarre. Last, JPED does not set as an absolute criterion that a verdict must have been reached on terrorism charges for a case to be included. A verdict strengthens the reliability of the case, but on the other hand a dismissal of a case does not necessarily mean that an attack was not in the making. Terrorism laws vary between countries, and are changing to deal with evolving threats. For data collection designed to capture trends in how the threat picture evolves, it makes sense to include cases based on how they are presented during investigation rather than applying a legalistic principle.

FFI's analyses of trends in jihadi terror plotting are based on C1 and C2 plots. The purpose of this classification system, is partly to not miss out on cases that may not seem terror-related at first, but become linked to terrorism as investigations proceed. More importantly the purpose is to avoid making generalizations based on cases that are dubious. Exploiting data on foiled plots comes with a risk of exaggerating the threat. However, because of the strict inclusion criteria, this risk is mitigated, and it can be argued that some level of over-reporting is less of a problem, than a high level of under-reporting when it comes to measuring terrorist attack activity. After having built a dataset containing both clear-cut, and not so clear-cut cases of terror plotting, the job is far from done. For the dataset to give an as accurate picture of the threat as possible, the cases need to be reassessed, and re-coded as new sources emerge.

Sources

Sources are a challenge in all types of terrorism research, but become even more of an issue when looking at foiled plots. Terrorism is secret activity and the information about foiled terror plots that reaches the public domain usually comes from law enforcement spokespersons, or leaks from investigations. It can be in the interest of states to manipulate information to justify countermeasures, or be able to disrupt an extremist milieu that might be considering attacks, but has yet to take the plans further. This problem is probably limited in well-functioning democracies, as there are institutionalized checks on what security services can, and cannot do. Still, it is a factor that cannot be ignored, and necessitates a careful assessments of the sources and triangulating them when possible.

Media sources have been the main tool in building JPED (especially local newspapers from European countries where plots have occurred). Looking at the attack activity by transnational terror networks, media sources are a highly effective tool. Yet, working with media sources has its challenges. The quality of the reporting varies across different publications, between countries, and between journalists. Sometimes reporters exaggerate to pursue an angle and make headlines. To the extent possible, we have tried to cross-check media against judicial documents, official reports, other research, and interviews with investigators or former extremists. All of these sources come with biases, so there will always be an element on uncertainty. A more recent challenge is that pay-walls are making the collection of sources and triangulation more difficult and costly. In sum, maintaining a dataset of both terror attacks and foiled plots has proved possible, yet labor-intensive and costly, something that helps explain why such datasets are few and far between.

Data on Foiled Terror Plots

Foiled plots have always been an object of analysis, both for security analysts and terrorism researchers. Security services have taken foiled plots into consideration when producing threat assessments, but they seldom share their data.[10] Europol obtains data on foiled plots from EU member states. Analyses based on these data are presented in their T-Sat report.[11] This report emerged in 2007 and lacks data before that. T-Sat's inclusion of foiled plots does not appear to have been systematic from its inception, but has become more so over the last few years.

Terrorism research has a tradition for examining foiled plots.[12] However, early terrorism studies tended to focus on foiled plots when looking at types of terrorism where few attacks materialized, such as chemical, biological or nuclear (CBRN) terrorism.[13] From the mid-2000s, jihadism research began to examine foiled plots systematically, primarily in qualitative studies.[14] Then in the 2010s, research on both right-wing and jihadi terrorism began using mixed methods in studies of foiled plots[15] Most of this research focused on modus operandi, perpetrator profiles, or effects of countermeasures. Studies of foiled plots remain sparse, however, compared to the vast body of quantitative terrorism research, which uses attacks as a metric.

The main reason for this, is that the main data databases used in quantitative terrorism studies, the *Global Terrorism Database* (GTD) and the *International Terrorism: Attributes of Terrorist Events* (ITERATE), never included foiled plots. GTD does include failed attacks according to the "out-the-door"-principle; when perpetrators are stopped on their way to launching an attack. It does not, however, include plots that were planned, prepared, and potentially very lethal, but intercepted at the last minute.

If we acknowledge that foiled plots are an essential part of the total attack activity, terrorism is therefore under-reported in the main database for quantitative studies. Because of this lack of data on foiled plots in databases, there has emerged separate data collections that include them. These collections are usually narrow with regards to actors, geographical and temporal scope. They tend to look at one type of terrorism (mostly jihadism, but also far-right violence and CBRN), in one country (mostly the US), over a limited time interval. They are typically published as chronologies of incidents rather than tabulated data.

As for full worthy datasets that include foiled plots, very few exist and none are openly available (although academics can apply for access to some of them). One such dataset is POICN, which contains CBRN incidents by non-state actors between 1993 and 2017.[16] Another is the RTV dataset which documents right-wing terrorism and violence in Western Europe since 1990.[17] The third, and closest thing to JPED, is a dataset by Crenshaw et al, which includes jihadi plots in NATO countries, EU countries, Australia and New Zealand between 1993 and 2017.[18]

Although systematic data on foiled plots are increasing, there is still a long way to go. The existing datasets cover different time periods and different actors, using different inclusion criteria, something that makes comparison across them challenging. Yet they provide an opportunity to assess the value added of including foiled plots in terrorism research. The following provides examples, based on preliminary data from JPED, on how the inclusion of foiled plots can inform threat analyses.

Examples on the Usage of Foiled Plots Data

By 2020, Islamic State was militarily defeated and two years had passed since Europe had seen the last mass casualty attack (plus 10 deaths). Although there were still smaller attacks by individuals linked to or influenced by jihadi networks, these received less attention from the public and policy makers. While security services and experts warned that jihadism still posed a threat, the general feeling was that it was time to concentrate on other security challenges such as hybrid warfare or terror from the far right. In late 2020 a series of grisly attacks by extremists in France, seemingly to avenge the re-publication of Mohammed cartoons, alerted the public to the fact that jihadism remained a potent threat.[19]

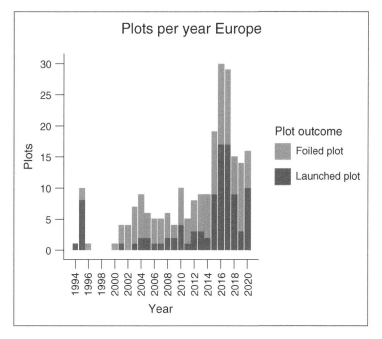

Figure 26.1   Foiled and Launched Plots per Year

Source: JPED dataset, 2020 version.

The Scale of the Threat

As shown in Figure 26.1, data from JPED demonstrate that the idea of a waning jihadi threat to Europe is premature at best. JPED currently includes 343 plots in total, whereas 227 plots are considered sufficiently documented for trend analyses. Statistics presented in this paper are based on the latter. Of the 227 well-documented plots, 99 cases (44 %) are launched attacks and 128 cases (56 %) are foiled. We have currently registered 652 deaths and 5616 injuries as a result of jihadi attack activity in the region.

The total attack activity (launched and foiled plots) has remained elevated after the collapse of IS and the historical trend also shows that al-Qaeda was able to uphold substantial levels of terrorist plotting after losing its Afghanistan camps in 2001. From 2018 onward the total attack activity plotted decreased some 50% compared to the unprecedented numbers in 2016–2017. Yet we notice that total attacks frequency after 2017 remained higher than any given year before 2015 (when al-Qaeda was targeting Europe).

Comparative Threats

Acknowledging that attacks constitute the "tip of the iceberg" complicates comparison across different terror trends. Data from GTD and Europol's T-Sat report have been invoked to show that jihadis are behind far fewer terror attacks in Europe than nationalist-separatists, such as IRA off-shoots, the Spanish ETA or the Corsican FLNC.[20]

Large-scale attacks by right-wing militants in Europe and elsewhere have created fears of a new wave of terror from the far right. The massacres by Anders Behring Breivik in Norway in 2011, and that of Brenton Tarrant in a New Zealand mosque in 2019, are cases in point. So are

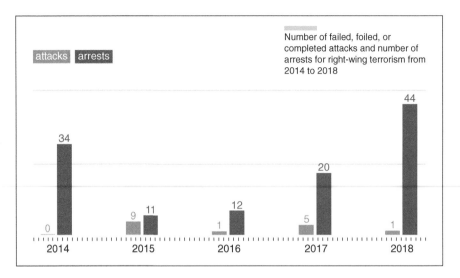

Figure 26.2 Right-wing Arrests and Terror Plots

Source: Terrorism Situation and Trend Report 2019 (T-Sat) Europol, 2019.

recent reports that right-wing terrorism is the fastest growing threat in some European countries.[21] At the same time, as shown in Figure 26.2, Europol's 2019 T-Sat report suggests that (despite an increase in extremist activity and arrests) right-wing terrorist plotting appears to be low compared to jihadism.[22]

Comparing the threat from jihadism with nationalist-separatist militancy, or right-wing terror is problematic for different reasons. Nationalist-separatist groups operate locally while jihadis constitute a transnational threat. Furthermore, nationalist-separatist groups tend to launch smaller-scale attacks against representatives of the state or sabotage, whereas jihadis often aim for large-scale, indiscriminate attacks. As for right-wing militancy, it differs from jihadism by being less embedded in armed conflicts.

The main problem, however is that comparisons between these three types of terrorism rarely account for the fact that European governments had a special focus on jihadism, and thereby stopped many mass atrocities, which rarely show up in databases such as the GTD. One famous example is the 2006 trans-Atlantic airliner plot, which could have killed people in the thousands.[23] More recently European security services have stopped multiple plans to launch mass casualty attacks in France, the UK, Germany, and the Netherlands (see below). To properly compare the scale and nature of nationalist, jihadi and right-wing terror, we need quality data for all of the actors, which also include foiled plots. A closer look at JPED data illustrates how launched attacks do not accurately represent the nature of the threat Europe is facing from jihadism.

The Nature of the Threat

Most of the jihadi attacks in Europe since IS came under severe military pressure, have been low-tech, conducted by single actors, using melee weapons or vehicles.[24] We have not seen complex, mass casualty attacks, like those in Paris in November 2015, which involved a group of attackers, employing different weapons and tactics, such as suicide bombings and mass shootings. An analysis based on launched attacks would therefore indicate a major change in the threat situation.

Low-tech, plots by individual attackers can be very lethal such as the truck attack in Nice in 2016 (which killed 87). In most instances, however, they kill fewer than complex, group-based attacks, and trigger different state responses. The large-scale ones are the ones that make states go to war, whereas the smaller attacks usually trigger more limited responses.

Tactics

Data from JPED show that even though single actors dominate the threat situation, this is not the whole picture. Among the foiled plots there are multiple plans by groups to launch large-scale attacks that receive limited media coverage compared to attacks. For example, in November 2019 a jihadi terrorist launched an attack with knives at a prisoners' rehabilitation event at Fishmonger's Hall, near London Bridge. He killed two people before he was overpowered by bystanders. One of them, also a prisoner, attacked the terrorist with a decorative narwhal tusk from Fishmonger's Hall. The case received worldwide attention because the terrorist had just been released from prison after serving time for involvement in an al-Qaeda linked attack plot in the UK, in 2012.[25] Although the attack had a tragic lethal outcome, it signified a very different threat pattern than the attacks on Bataclan and other locations in Paris in 2015.

At the same time, since the collapse of IS, there have been quite a few plots to launch big, group-based attacks by jihadis in Europe, that were foiled by vigilant counterterrorism. One example is an alleged Dutch terror cell, which was foiled in late September 2018. According to different sources this seven-member cell planned a so-called "Mumbai-style" attack (after the attacks in India in 2008) with guns and explosives at a public event, while setting off a car-bomb at another location. The cell had international connections to IS networks in the Middle East, as well an alleged terror cell in Denmark.[26] JPED codes plots for "cell configuration," to measure the ratio of group plots versus plots by single actors. Figure 26.3 shows the ratio of plots by groups versus single actors in launched plots only, whereas Figure 26.4 shows the ratio if we include foiled plots.

The data provide an interesting picture of the historical pattern. During the GIA-wave in the 1990s the terrorists were consistently operating in groups. Towards the end of the 2000s al-Qaeda-wave the share of plots involving single actors increased as the organization came under pressure, and urged followers to act on their own to avenge cartoons of the Prophet Mohammed. During the IS-phase (2010s) this trend has continued and intensified.[27] However, by including foiled plots we notice that the militants have persisted in pursuing group-based attacks, up until today. According to JPED data as much as 79 percent of group plots are foiled, whereas single actor plots are foiled at a rate of only 31 percent.

The logic explanation is that group-based plots involve more communication and coordination than single actor plots. The data suggest that, were it not for vigilant counterterrorism, Europe would have seen more large-scale attacks. They also suggest that there is urgent need for better protection against single actors.

Weapons

In addition to foiling group-based, "Mumbai-style", plots, European security services have foiled at least two plots to employ the deadly poison ricin, one in Germany and one in France.[28] These plots received massive media attention, because CBRN incidents always generate fear and headlines, but they do not appear in attack databases such as GTD. As shown in Table 26.1, data from JPED illustrates that in general, high-tech plots (bombs, CBRN) are foiled at a much higher rate than low-tech ones (knives, vehicles).

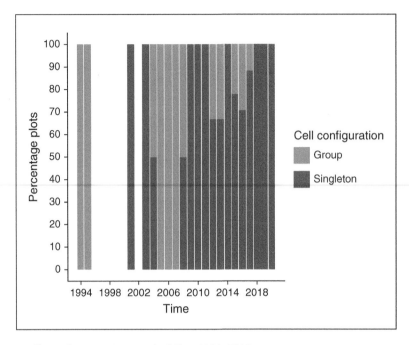

Figure 26.3　Cell Configuration in Launched Plots 1994–2020

Source: JPED, 2020.

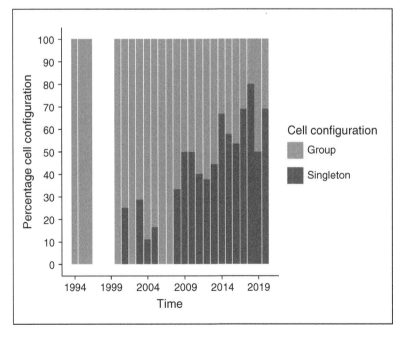

Figure 26.4　Cell Configuration in Launched and Foiled Plots 1994–2020

Source: JPED, 2020.

Table 26.1 Percentage Foiled Per Weapon

Weapon	Total	Foiled	Percentage
CBRN	9	8	90
Explosive	122	88	70
Firearms	53	29	70
Vehicle	20	8	40
Melee	61	15	25

Source: JPED, 2020.

On the one hand the data suggest that European counterterrorism regimes have been relatively effective in foiling plots that require procuring firearms and chemicals. On the other hand, they indicate that open societies are vulnerable to plots that can be implemented with items not considered weapons, such as a vehicle.

Foreign Fighters

Analyses of foiled plots can also add to our understanding of the threat posed by foreign fighters. JPED codes for whether or not plots involve at least one foreign fighter (defined as people who join jihadi groups in another country than they live in). Preliminary data indicate that plots involving at least one foreign fighter have a higher chance of being foiled than plots without foreign fighters. Looking at all plots from 1994 until today, in which sources say at least one foreign fighter took part, 73 percent have been foiled. For plots where available sources say no foreign fighter participated the percentage is 43 percent. The logical explanation is that foreign fighters draw attention from security services, and that there has been an increasing awareness over time that foreign fighters play a significant role in attack activity. Foreign fighters have been involved in massive attacks, such as those in France in November 2015, and in recent years, there are multiple examples that foreign fighters have recruited contacts back home for attacks, using communication apps.[29]

JPED also allows for examining year-by-year involvement of foreign fighters in plots, which can provide one metric for how the countermeasures work. In line with what we see regarding cell configuration and weapons, JPED shows a significant difference in foreign fighter involvement, when we compare launched plots and total plots. If we look at the IS wave from 2014 onward (see Figure 26.5), there is at least one foreign fighter in only 5 percent of launched plots. If we include foiled plots, involvement increases to 16 percent. Importantly, these numbers only represent direct participation by foreign fighters in plots, and not indirect forms of involvement, such as instructing attackers via communication apps.

We notice how there was a significant foreign fighter involvement at the beginning of the IS-wave in Europe, but that the share of foreign fighter plots fell once European states adapted its laws and counterterrorism regimes, to prevent the threat from returnees. In addition to misrepresenting the scale and nature of the threat, ignoring foiled plots can also lead to problematic inferences about causal mechanisms.

The Threat's Causes

A research note by Hegghammer and Ketchley compares datasets that only include attacks with datasets that also include foiled plots. According to their research note, counts of attacks and foiled plots correlate imperfectly.[30] It shows that one can get statistically different results when

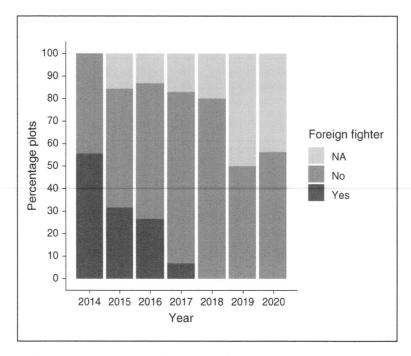

Figure 26.5   Foiled and Launched Plots with Foreign Fighter 2014–2020
Source: JPED, 2020.

measuring the effect of common variables such as economic factors, demographics, state characteristics, political grievances, and events on the number of attacks only, versus when foiled plots
are included. This potentially challenges the results of many statistical studies on terrorism.

As shown in Figure 26.6., data from JPED illustrates how counting just the attacks can blur
the vision when formulating hypotheses about what causes jihadi threats to Europe. For example,
if we only consider attacks, France towers as the main target for jihadism in Europe. This has led
many to highlight explanations specific to France: in particular its integration policy, aiming to
assimilate Muslim immigrants.

When foiled plots are included the difference between France and some other countries becomes less pronounced. We notice that the UK, for example, experiences a very high frequency
of plots, the difference being that the Brits foil more plots than the French. This is highly relevant
to the formulation of hypotheses regarding the threat's causes. The UK has a very different approach to integration than France, relying on multiculturalism rather than assimilation. That two
countries with opposite integration policies face a relatively similar threat, is a strong indicator
that the main causes lie elsewhere.

Conclusion

This paper has highlighted the importance of including foiled plots in terrorism research and offered some lessons learned from working with the Jihadi Plots in Europe Dataset (JPED). Analyses
that only use the launched attacks as a metric risk misrepresenting the scale and nature of terrorism, and could also produce faulty conclusions regarding what causes terrorism. As discussed

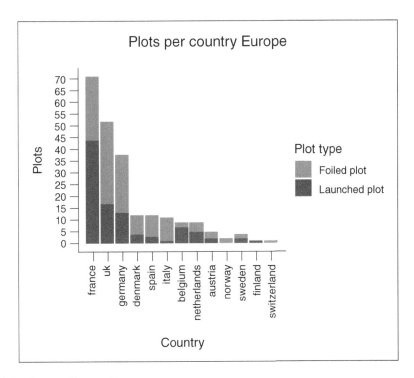

Figure 26.6   Plots per Country Europe

Source: JPED, 2020.

in the paper, a threat may seem smaller than it actually is, because the current counterterrorism regime foils the most lethal plots. Yet, it is the launched attacks that dominate research and public debate. Because research and public debate influence policy decisions, we may end up with counterterrorism designs that are not suited to meet tomorrow's threat.

Research on foiled plots remains sparse, but is increasing. There are efforts to build new datasets, such as JPED, Crenshaw et al, RTV and POICN. Building such datasets are challenging and labor-intensive because sources on foiled plots are rarer than for attacks and can be manipulated, or biased. At the same time, the value added of including foiled plots, makes the effort to exploit this data resource imperative. Ideally we should have a global database that includes foiled plots. This may not be feasible, however, as plot research requires trustworthy sources from counterterrorism investigations. In open democracies such sources are attainable. In authoritarian and failed states, however, it is more difficult to ascertain that sources are reliable. In the absence of a global plot database, researchers should seek to build local, or regional datasets like the ones discussed in this paper, for the main types of extremism.

Notes

1 The author thanks Thomas Hegghammer for key contributions to the chapter, and, Anne Stenersen, Vidar B. Skretting and Henrik Gråtrud for contributions to developing and maintaining the Jihadi Plots in Europe Dataset (JPED)
2 LaFree and Dugan (2007)
3 Crenshaw and LaFree (2017)

4 See for example, Nesser (2008)
5 Lia and Kjøk (2001)
6 For a closer discussion of how to define a foiled plot, consult Hegghammer and Ketchley (2020)
7 "Shoe-Bomber Supergrass Testifies in US" (2012)
8 There is no unified definition of terrorism, but there is progress toward an academic consensus Schmid (2012)
9 "Prince Harry Death Plot Man Was Kicked Out of British Army" (2014)
10 See for example FBI (1988), or a recent report by the Norwegian Police Security Service (PST) on how terror plots are foiled in Europe PST (2020)
11 Europol (2019)
12 Rapoport (1971)
13 Jenkins et al. (1983)
14 See e.g. Nesser (2004) and Sageman (2004)
15 Nesser and Stenersen (2014), "A Mixed Method Examination of Law Enforcement Investigatory Strategies Used in Jihadi and Far-Right Foiled Terrorist Plots Before and After 9/11" (2019), Simcox (2018)
16 Binder and Ackerman (2019)
17 Ravndal (2016)
18 Crenshaw, Wilson, and Dahl (2017)
19 "A Day After the Fatal Church Attack in Nice, Here's What We Know So Far" (2020)
20 Obeidallah (2015), "Terrorism in Europe Classified" (2019), "EU Sees Terror Attacks Record in 2015" (2016)
21 Dodd and Grierson (2019)
22 Europol (2019)
23 Sciolino and Grey (2006)
24 Silva (2017)
25 "UK to Introduce Tougher Jail Terms for Convicted Terrorists After London Bridge Attack" (2020)
26 Daragahi (2018)
27 Nesser, Stenersen, and Oftedal (2016)
28 Samuel (2018), "Cologne Ricin Plot Bigger Than Initially Suspected" (2018)
29 See e.g. Hamid (2018)
30 Hegghammer and Ketchley (2020)

References

Gruenwald, Jeff, Joshua Freilich, and Steven Chermak. 2019. "A Mixed Method Examination of Law Enforcement Investigatory Strategies Used in Jihadi and Far-Right Foiled Terrorist Plots Before and After 9/11." *Journal of Qualitative Criminal Justice & Criminology* 7: 29–58.

"A Day After the Fatal Church Attack in Nice, Here's What We Know so Far." 2020. *France* 24, October 30. https://www.france24.com/en/france/20201030-a-day-after-the-fatal-church-attack-in-nice-here-s-what-we-know-so-far

Binder, Markus K., and Gary A. Ackerman. 2019. "Pick Your POICN: Introducing the Profiles of Incidents Involving CBRN and Non-State Actors (POICN) Database." *Studies in Conflict & Terrorism* 44 (9): 730–754. https://doi.org/10.1080/1057610X.2019.1577541.

"Cologne Ricin Plot Bigger Than Initially Suspected." 2018. *Deutche Welle,* June 20. https://www.dw.com/en/cologne-ricin-plot-bigger-than-initially-suspected/a-44319328#:~:text=Federal%20prosecutors%20have%20found%20more,a%20biological%20weapon%20using%20ricin

Crenshaw, Martha, and Gary LaFree. 2017. *Countering Terrorism.* Washington DC: Brookings Institution Press.

Crenshaw, Martha, Margaret Wilson, and Erik Dahl. 2017. "Comparing Failed, Foiled, Completed and Successful Terrorist Attacks." College Park, MD: National Consortium for the Study of Terrorism and Responses to Terrorism.

Daragahi, Borzou. 2018. "Terror Cell Busts in Denmark and Holland Spark Fears of Isis Attacks." *The Independent*, September 29.

Dodd, Vikram, and Jamie Grierson. 2019. "Fastest-Growing UK Terrorist Threat Is from Far Right, Say Police." *The Guardian*, September 19.

"Record number of EU terror attacks recorded in 2015." 2016. *BBC News*, July 20. https://www.bbc.com/news/uk-36845647

Europol. 2019. "EU Terrorism Situation & Trend Report (Te-Sat)."

FBI. 1988. "Terrorism at Home and Abroad: The U.S. Government View." In *The Politics of Terrorism*, 295–316. New York, NY: Marcel Dekker.

Hamid, Nafees. 2018. "The British Hacker Who Became the Islamic State's Chief Terror Cybercoach: A Profile of Junaid Hussain." *CTC Sentinel* 11 (4): 30–36.

Hegghammer, Thomas, and Neil Ketchley. 2020. "Measuring Terrorism." SocArXiv.

Jenkins, Brian Michael, Bonnie Cordes, Karen Gardela Treverton, and Geraldine Petty. 1983. "*A Chronology of Terrorist Attacks and Other Criminal Actions Against Maritime Targets*." Santa Monica, CA: Rand.

LaFree, Gary, and Laura Dugan. 2007. "Introducing the Global Terrorism Database." *Terrorism and Political Violence* 19 (2): 181–204. https://doi.org/10.1080/09546550701246817.

Lia, Brynjar, and Åshild Kjøk. 2001. "Islamist Insurgencies, Diasporic Support Networks, and Their Host States: The Case of the Algerian GIA in Europe 1993–2000." Kjeller: FFI.

Nesser, Petter. 2004. "JIHAD IN EUROPE - A Survey of the Motivations for Sunni Islamist Terrorism in Post-Millennium Europe." FFI.

Nesser, Petter. 2008. "Chronology of Jihadism in Western Europe 19942007: Planned, Prepared, and Executed Terrorist Attacks." *Studies in Conflict & Terrorism* 31 (10): 924–946. https://doi.org/10.1080/10576100802339185.

Nesser, Petter, and Anne Stenersen. 2014. "The Modus Operandi of Jihadi Terrorists in Europe." *Perspectives on Terrorism* 8 (6): 2–24.

Nesser, Petter, Anne Stenersen, and Emilie Oftedal. 2016. "Jihadi Terrorism in Europe: The IS-Effect." *Perspectives on Terrorism* 10 (6): 3–24.

Obeidallah, Dean. 2015. "Are All Terrorists Muslims? It's Not Even Close." *The Daily Beast*, January 14.

"Prince Harry Death Plot Man Was Kicked Out of British Army." 2014. *Belfast Telegraph,* February. https://www.belfasttelegraph.co.uk/sunday-life/news/prince-harry-death-plot-man-was-kicked-out-of-british-army/30015091.html

PST. 2020. "Hvordan Avverges Terrorangrep." PST.

Rapoport, David. 1971. *Assassination & Terrorism*. Ottawa: Canadian Broadcasting Corporation. Canada.

Ravndal, Jacob Aasland. 2016. "Right-Wing Terrorism and Violence in Western Europe: Introducing the RTV Dataset." *Perspectives on Terrorism* 10 (3): 2–15.

Sageman, Marc. 2004. *Understanding Terror Networks*. Philadelphia: University of Pennsylvania Press.

Samuel, Henry. 2018. "Man Charged After French Police Foil Paris Ricin Terror Plot." *Telegraph*, May 18.

Schmid, Alex P. 2012. "The Revised Academic Consensus Definition of Terrorism." *Perspectives on Terrorism* 6 (2): 158–159.

Sciolino, Don Van Natta Jr, Elaine, and Stephen Grey. 2006. "Details Emerge in British Terror Case." *The New York Times*, August 28. https://www.nytimes.com/2006/08/28/world/europe/28plot.html

"Shoe-Bomber Supergrass Testifies in US." 2012. *BBC*, April 24. https://www.bbc.com/news/world-us-canada-17820810

Silva, Daniella. 2017. "London Terrorist Attack: Vehicle, Knife Incident Shows Threat of Low-Tech Terror." *NBC*, March.

Simcox, Robin. 2018. "The Asylum Terror Nexus: How Europe Should Respond." *The Heritage Foundation*.

"Terrorism in Europe Classified." 2019. *POLITICO*, October 10. https://www.politico.eu/article/terrorism-in-europe-classified-germany-halle-terrorist-attack-synagogue-yom-kippur-graphics-data-visualization/

"UK to Introduce Tougher Jail Terms for Convicted Terrorists After London Bridge Attack." 2020. *Reuters*, January 21. https://www.reuters.com/article/uk-britain-security-idUKKBN1ZK005

27

HYBRID LOANS AND TACTICS OF JIHADISM

Will Hybridity Remain the Narrative of Convergent, Politically Motivated Violence?

Dirk Freudenberg

Preliminary Remarks

This chapter's topic requires the author to draw some lines in order to be able to determine the position of approaching the subject of the paper, an endeavor which causes certain difficulties to the author. From a legal and political science-related perspective, the determination of the position is decisive since the great diversity of possible viewpoints brings with it a great diversity of research results, too.

The following explanations consider jihadism primarily an ideology in the sense of a political world view which is governed by religious conditions and strongly influenced and steered by both power and interests. This is why ideological movements disconnect from the rest of the world and exist and operate on their own. The same is true for Islamist and fundamentalist movements.[1] This jihadism – a phenomenon of Islamist movements – has put itself on the global stage militarily in the form of irregular wars.[2] The most important differentiating characteristics is the factor violence, even though the word "military" does not only suggest the use of violence in a selective, single way but describes violence as a comprehensively organized, strategic instrument. Furthermore, transnationally operative jihadists represent a completely new form of Islamism.[3] Thanks to their ability to project violence globally, consequently a new quality of power projection of irregular power has developed. Looking at the bigger picture we can conclude that there is dangerous, political moment that lies in the connection of religious views and social motives, because thanks to this connection religious views become the carriers of political ideologies. The effects such ideologies can have on individuals and societies must not be undervalued. Militant religions have always been the most successful politically.[4]

Therefore, not the "woolly thoughts" of the "mental insanities" are determinative factors for any action but rational considerations, which follow strategic-political goals in accordance with their world views in their operative concepts and tactical implementations, and these goals and views also produce their (own) rationale. Regarding the question of "hybridity" it is necessary to elaborate what the author actually means when using this term in his following explanations, in particular in relation to the approach used for this chapter. The linguistic term "hybridity" seems difficult to define, also because different authors try to explain the phenomenon from different perspectives or deal with it from unequal points of view. In general, it can be noted that

DOI: 10.4324/9781003326373-31

the understanding of what hybrid phenomena actually are and why they differ from other phenomena is very inconsistent. First of all, we can question whether this is merely about "old wine in new bottles"[5] or we can argue alongside Melanie Alamir who doubts whether the concepts behind the term "hybrid" are too generic and therefore, according to her approach, without any visible analytic value in a series of less blurry terms, such as "asymmetric warfare" or "irregular warfare."[6] The diffuse occurrence of hybrid threats as well as the fact that their causes and actors are too difficult and sometimes too late to identify accordingly further demonstrates the importance of this in particular.[7]

Therefore, this chapter aims at taking a closer look at what are the liabilities, effects and maybe even the consequences that result for the area of "civil defense," a field which has been rather neglected in literature but is a main part of a comprehensive defense system, next to military defense. From this kind of perspective we can argue and also justify the use of the word "hybrid" in an innovative sense. It is this concept we want to determine from different points of view of security policy-related factors and frameworks, also considering the possible innovative effects.[8]

Urbanity as a Security Policy Condition

The global population is growing constantly and will reach 10 billion by the middle of the 21st century.[9] The number of people living in large cities will also grow considerably, leading to a significant enlargement of cities and the assumption that by 2050, about two thirds of the world's population will be living in urban areas, with 10 million people living in each of the 43 so-called megacities.[10] The larger German cities are also considerably growing in population.[11] This has led to a concentration of people living in urban centers and, subsequently, a growing dependence of this population share on public services, in particular on so-called "critical infrastructures." From a security policy view this development creates huge challenges for civil defense, especially with view to hybrid threats and hybrid warfare.[12]

Terminology and Focus on Hybrid Warfare

The conception of what hybrid threats really are and how they differentiate from other phenomena is inconsistent throughout the respective literature. In his academic work, Johann Schmid focuses on the perspectives according to which hybrid threats target different gravity fields and also mentions those perspectives which do not necessarily aim at military war decisions.[13] Based on the arguments put forward here, hybrid warfare can be distinguished by the fact that its weapons and targets both mainly concern and aim at the civilian sector. This means that by the use of civilian effectors and operating from a civilian sphere, certain effects in civilian space are the target of action. As a result, a "void battlefield" could develop for conventional, military forces and capacities in a classic sense. This could simply happen by classic military forces being slowly used concomitantly at best in order to obscure, support or secure hybrid action, instead of an equivalent counterpart taking over the stage. The focus of vulnerabilities and of the effectors targeting them is therefore definitely put on the civilian sector. However, the significance of the dependencies of civilian critical infrastructures and their respective dependencies for the population and for Germany as an important business location has risen considerably throughout the past decades, and it has even led to the protection of critical infrastructures becoming a national security factor. From this, the demand to the approach toward civil defense and of considering it an additional competence – a rather tedious appendix of a primarily military defense system – opposite classic warfare has started to become louder. Right now it is becoming more and more important to consider civil defense as an equivalent pillar of a comprehensive defense system because in order to continue to maintain an entire social system, raising awareness for the significance of civil defense and strengthening its capacities are required.[14] Moreover, the Conception Civil Defense (*Konzeption Zivile Verteidigung, KZV*) already mentions the parallels between crises in times of peace and in times of defense.[15] In this respect the packages of measures – as developed from parts of the Conception Civil Defense – could possibly be the fundamental basis of a future, comprehensive crisis management concept.

Modern Weapons of Hybrid Warfare

Threats from and within cyber space belong to the negative downsides of modern information technology (IT), be it in form of criminal actions or cyber wars.[16] With the support of IT tools, they are accurate and politically motivated strikes that have strong effects on the lives and health of an entire population, and/or the economic or political capacity of states to act (not necessarily including the use of armed forces).[17] This means that hybrid warfare is about the penalization, penetration or even the "twisting "of electronically operated systems of an enemy – the strategically and existentially important information technology – and has disastrous consequences for a state apparatus, for a state's autonomy and for society as a whole.[18] From any point the targets within the virtual space of cyber war can be reached and deactivated within seconds, be it in motion, at sea or land level, out of the air and even from outer space.[19,20] This scenario of information warfare leads to space-related limits of war becoming less sizeable and lets war turn into a placeless phenomenon.[21] War becomes invisible within the special nowhere and without any differentiation between civilian and military spheres.[22]

The kinetic inferiority of an actor can be offset by a way of asymmetric warfare in order to cause damage electronically at the enemy's home front, especially for critical infrastructures, in the event of war.[23] Moreover, attacks can be committed from a distance via cyber space which means that the immediate presence of a perpetrator is no longer bound to the location of an attack.[24] Any attack is primarily about destroying or eliminating the information necessary for maintaining a military or civilian system, without actually targeting the material destruction of these goods.[25] States can be immobilized in some cases and services restored right after they surrender,[26] which shows that there are no considerable costs for reconstruction. Concurrently, the time of state re-activation is reduced, which makes the consequences for the entire social system and the population in general manageable considering the overall timeline.[27] In academia the term "digital first strike"[28] repeatedly comes up, since the dimension of cyber war makes the chance of reaching very quickly and completely supremacy through the act of a digital decapitation strike possible. This means a "victory" can happen without using conventional powers. The classic military principle of achieving and making use of the advantage of surprise receives in this new form of warfare a new chance, contrary to the growing comprehensive information according to conventional concepts.[29]

Effects on Urban Spaces

It is possible to assume that the failure of critical infrastructures is enormous for large cities and their inhabitants – as malfunctions during times of peace already prove – and in a sense the consequences of a digital decapitation strike can be anticipated. These are not limited locations such as parts of cities, whole cities or regions, but extensive failures that can even affect the entire national territory of a state. In the shortest possible time public services will collapse and not be available or accessible anymore to the people. If the urban population retreats to near rural areas that are less affected, the (rudimentary) infrastructures and resources still functioning there could also experience a collapse within a short period of time, and eventually be disturbed.[30]

Consequences

The hybrid possibilities within cyber space clearly show that a strict separation between internal and external security is constantly challenged,[31] gradually dissolves and proves that only military risks are actually a thing of the past.[32] These conclusions have effects on the use of armed forces or the military capacities of interior state affairs.[33] Therefore it is important to create solutions, protection and defensive measures in an appropriate variety.[34] This also includes the phases of threat analysis and the planning of how to deal with the challenges accordingly. Leaving the assessment of (military) threats mainly to the armed forces (as foreseen in the Concept of Civil Defense[35]), has become almost completely inconsistent seen from the perspectives of hybrid threats and the author's previous remarks.[36]

In total, territorial defense, homeland security and civilian defense and protection are affected by hybrid threats. Under these conditions, established ways (and tools) of reaction are in danger of not serving adequately and of taking full effects too late in order to bring about decisions, due to their traditional forms and original functions.[37] From this we can conclude that we should interconnect the capacities of a social, comprehensive prevention with national security-responsible actors according to their use.[38] The 2016 White Book establishes that hybrid threats demand hybrid analyses and defense preparedness, which in turn has consequences for both the character and understanding of state and alliance defense in the 21st century.[39] The abstract danger situation (meaning the mental work and materialization of the threat) already shows that there are demands for an efficient, civilian–military comprehensive defense system.[40] This demand also results from reversing the original explanation for the inferior supporting role civilian protection is experiencing, according to which civilian defense allots the decisive supportive role for military defense in times of crises and wars, which guarantees primarily the upholding of the defense capacity and operational freedom of the armed forces.[41] This one-sided priority, however, is no longer suitable considering the conditions of hybrid threats today,[42] on the contrary: the modern approach toward hybrid warfare as postulated by the Chief of General Staff of the Russian armed forces, Gerasimov, is based exactly on the idea of changing the fundamental rules of war by increasing the role of non-military means to achieve certain political and strategic goals, and by those means exceeding in many ways the effectiveness of weapons.[43] Furthermore, orienting hybrid threats toward and engaging in hybrid wars with non-military gravity centers does not necessarily require a military war of conflict decision.[44] The demand of adjusting the importance of civilian defense is therefore based on the fact that attacks with hybrid capacities can likely underrun a state's own military capabilities, making any defense and reaction only possible by using civilian means.[45] This concept can be explained also in a constitutional sense: civilian defense is a necessary factor which includes an effective comprehensive defense according to its constitutional mandate.[46] As a result, civilian defense and protection must be analyzed in a new way according to their comprehensive defense framework and for a wider population protection, and eventually both must be adapted and equipped with new capacities and means of military defense. [47]

Constant Factors of Warfare

Despite of all the changes and developments, the fundamental nature of war remains the same. War is politically motivated and does not follow an independent logic. The overall aim of war is reaching a state where specific interests can be ensured in the long run, and to make the enemy fulfil a certain will by using organized violence (according to the teachings of Clausewitz[48]).[49] Following the Clausewitzian analysis, the use of strategic instruments therefore serves exclusively the modification of the will of the political Other, because peace and conflict and war are all political phenomena.[50] Furthermore, he explains that "…the political mean as the original motif for war will become the measure for both the goal which must be achieved through an act of war as well as for the necessary efforts."[51] Corresponding with this assessment, Ihno Krumpelt explains that the measure of violence used in war will follow the level of conflicting interests on both sides and the level of the goal to be achieved.[52] Clausewitz puts this goal in connection with the political and real price that is to be paid for actually achieving it. This price also describes the extent and at the same time limits of the engagement of action by connecting the value with the risk. The smaller the sacrifice we demand from our enemy, the lesser will be the enemy's efforts to withhold it from us. Furthermore, the smaller our political aim the lesser the importance we place on it, and the more likely we will let it go. Our efforts, consequently, will be the lesser too.[53] Dangers and risks are connected with the goal, and the decisions taken according to the respective assessment of costs and benefits. This has remained valid until today. In order to impose one's own will on an enemy, one must put this enemy in a position which is more harmful than the sacrifice that is demanded.[54]

Importance of Resilience

It is society's own will – the will and the capacity of both society and its security structure – that must be strengthened in order to successfully counter hybrid threats.[55] One academic approach is to identify one's own level of vulnerability and to minimize it to increase society's resilience.[56] For providing a nationwide security precaution, strengthening resilience is particularly important and understood as an individual's capacity to successfully deal with difficult situations in this regard.[57][58] However, this raises the question of how high the level of resilience and society's will to actually endure any kind of threat and its consequences are, and whether they eventually give in if they do not actively oppose the threat they are experiencing.[59]

The term "resilience" first describes a system's capacity of dealing with any kind of disturbance in a useful, sensible way. However, "resilience" is not only about resistance or sturdiness, but also about adaptability, buoyancy and agility, which also includes going out of a crisis strengthen.[60] All this means that it is about a system's capacity to adapt to new conditions, meaning this very system replicates through change and inherits this capability of establishing itself after any kind of disturbance has happened during its daily routine, even though it may be established in a completely new form.[61] Hence, resilient systems are capable of returning to their original state or to even reach an improved, transformed state after a disturbance.[62] Finally, "resilience" also describes the capability of surviving in the eye of alien powers.[63] Still, this requires that the systems remain unharmed in their very core, which is a prerequisite for being able to repair their previous condition within an appropriate amount of time, or for a completely destroyed system to become so redundant that its functions can be transferred to other units. Therefore all those critical infrastructures whose breakdown cannot be tolerated in any way must be strengthened and protected to secure their resilience and survival.[64]

However, any measures directed only toward the inner affairs of a system cannot suffice for the general strengthening of resilience.[65] For this reason, increasing the complexity for enemies until reaching an overall overload and at the same time propagating resilience must become the central measure against hybrid threats.[66] The key to strategic success lies in confronting the enemy with multiple dilemmas,[67] meaning that the enemy party must reach a status of complete overload and disorientation through a complexity and great number of events overwhelming it. In this situation of confusion the enemy will no longer be capable of reacting accordingly and of sticking to priorities, and at the same time the system's own cohesion and upkeep of certain procedures must remain.[68] In a tactical sense this method corresponds to so-called *swarming*, or at least it contains some basic elements of this approach. This allows to consider the enormous danger and threat for the enemy, since this approach also means there is very likely only little time to react and counter threats reliably.

Here some thoughts on preventive and preemptive measures for actively getting involved can open up new possibilities. However, at the end of all considerations, a combination of capacities – in the sense of a comprehensive general approach of an interconnected security structure – and of the general defense will be most expedient, since on the one hand such an approach will increase social cohesion and protect from failure through resilience, and on the other it involves initiatives that provide active features that can be used effectively to counter hybrid threats. In any case it is necessary for the systems not to be completely destroyed or not too much affected in their core existence so that restoration and restarting are possible.[69]

Conclusion

At the end of all considerations, warfare is nothing less than the arrangement of violence and leadership within a fight, in all its individual and different facets. Within armed conflicts, the involved actors can use a whole range of conventional and irregular resources.[70] This also accounts for all forms of irregular powers which kind of increase from below their resources and ways.[71] Therefore, these rationales apply to the phenomenon of jihadism as a narrative of convergent, politically motivated violence.

Notes

1 Dirk Freudenberg, Theorie des Irregulären. Erscheinungen und Abgrenzungen von Partisanen, Guerillas und Terroristen im Modernen Kleinkrieg sowie Entwicklungstendenzen der Reaktion, 2. Bd., Von der Definitionsproblematik bis zu der Universalität der Methoden Irregulärer Kräfte, Berlin 2017, S. 49

2 Bassam Tibi, Der neue Totalitarismus. „Heiliger Krieg"und westliche Sicherheit, Darmstadt 2004, S. 121; vgl. David Kilcullen, Counterinsurgency, New York 2010, S. 169 ff.; vgl. Thomas Jäger und Ralph Thiele (Hrsg.), Der Politische Islamismus als hybrider Akteur globaler Reichweite. Die liberale demokratische Ordnung muss ihre Resilienz stärken, Berlin 2021

3 Olaf Farschid, Jihadismus – Ideologie, Kommunikationsstrategien, Wirkung, SIAK-Jounal – Zeitschrift für Polizeiwissenschaft und polizeiliche Praxis 2006, Heft 3, S. 3 ff.; 4

4 Konrad Lorenz, Das sogenannte Böse, München 1974, S. 252

5 vgl. Rob de Wijk, Hybrid Conflict and the changing Nature of Actors, in: Julian Lindley-French, Yves Boyer (Hrsg.), The Oxford Handbook of War, Oxford 2014, S. 358 ff.; 359 ff.; vgl. Timothy McCulloh, The Inadaquacy of Definition and the Utility of a Theory of Hybrid Conflict: Is the "Hybid Thread" New?, in: JSOU-Report 13-4, Florida August 2013, S. 1 ff.; vgl. Jürgen Ehle, Hybride Bedrohungen – Neue Bedrohungen oder neuer Wein in alten Schläuchen?, in: Ringo Wagner, Hans-Joachim Schaprian (Hrsg.), Komplexe Krisen – aktive Verantwortung. Magdeburger Gespräche zur Friedens- und Sicherheitspolitik, Magdeburg 2016, S. 80 ff

6 Fouzieh Melanie Alamir, „Hybride Kriegführung"– ein möglicher Trigger für Vernetzungsfortschritte?, in: Ethik und Militär 2015, Heft 2, S. 3 ff

7 Dirk Freudenberg, Theorie des Irregulären. Erscheinungen und Abgrenzungen von Partisanen, Guerillas und Terroristen im Modernen Kleinkrieg sowie Entwicklungstendenzen der Reaktion, 3. Bd., Von der heutigen Bedeutung des Kleinkrieges bis zu den strategischen Fällen, Berlin 2017, S. 158

8 Dirk Freudenberg, Hybride Bedrohungen, Zivilschutz und die Strategischen Fälle, in: Martin H.W. Möllers, Robert van Ooyen (Hrsg.), Jahrbuch Öffentliche Sicherheit 2018/2019, Frankfurt 2019, S. 557 ff.

9 Generalstab des Österreichischen Bundesheeres, Trends und Konfliktbild bis 2030, o. JA., S.4

10 Deutsche Stiftung Weltbevölkerung, Im Jahr 2050 werden zwei Drittel der Weltbevölkerung in Städten leben, in: DWS vom 16. Mai 2018; https://www.dsw.org/projektionen-urbanisierung/; Internet vom 12.06.2019; vgl. NN., Zwei Drittel der Weltbevölkerung werden 2050 in Städten leben, in: Zeit Online vom 17. Mai 2018; https://www.zeit.de/gesellschaft/zeitgeschehen/2018-05/vereinte-nationen-weltbevoelkerung-staedte-2050; Internet vom 12.06.2019

11 vgl. Bhuiyan, In diesen Städten wächst die Bevölkerung am stärksten, in: WELT vom 24.04.2018; https://www.welt.de/wirtschaft/article175761683/Bevoelkerungsstudie-In-diesen-Staedten-waechst-die-Bevoelkerung-am-staerksten.html; Internet vom 12.06.2016

12 vgl. Freudenberg, Hybride Kriegsführung in urbanen Zentren. Relevanz für die Zivile Verteidigung in: Wissenschaft und Frieden 2019, Heft 3, S. 27 f.; vgl. Dirk Freudenberg, Hybride Kriegsführung und ihre Relevanz für die Zivile Verteidigung – Innovative Aspekte moderner Konfliktaustragung in urbanen Zentren, in: Die Bundeswehrverwaltung 2019, Heft 12, S. 276 ff.; vgl. Sicherheitspolitik und Zivilschutz – Eine antizipatorische Analyse, in: Dirk Freudenberg, Marcel Kuhlmey (Hrsg.) Festschrift anlässlich 60 Jahre Bevölkerungsschutz in Deutschland. „Krisenmanagement – Notfallplanung – Zivilschutz"zugleich Supplementband der Lehrstoffsammlung Krisenmanagement – Bevölkerungsschutz, Berlin 2021, S.21 ff.

13 Johann Schmid, Der Archetypus hybrider Kriegführung. Hybride Kriegführung vs. militärisch zentrierte Kriegführung, in: ÖMZ 2020, S. 570 ff.; 974

14 Freudenberg, Hybride Bedrohungen unter besonderer Berücksichtigung Bevölkerungsschutzes, in: Ehrhart (Hrsg.), Krieg im 21. Jahrhundert. Konzepte, Akteure, Herausforderungen (2017) S. 346–373.; 372; vgl. Freudenberg, Theorie des Irregulären. Erscheinungen und Abgrenzungen von Partisanen, Guerillas und Terroristen im Modernen Kleinkrieg sowie Entwicklungstendenzen der Reaktion, 2. Bd., Von der Definitionsproblematik bis zu der Universalität der Methoden Irregulärer Kräfte, 2017, S. 260; vgl. Freudenberg, FN 5, S. 27; Hybride Kriegsführung und Urbanität – Die Bedeutung innovativer Aspekte moderner Konfliktaustragung für die Zivile Verteidigung, in: ÖMZ 2020, Heft 3, S. 314 ff.; vgl. Hybride Kriegsführung und ihre Relevanz für die Zivile Verteidigung – Innovative Aspekte moderner Konfliktaustragung in urbanen Zentren, in: Die Bundeswehrverwaltung 2019, Heft 12, S. 276 ff.

15 Bundesministerium des Inneren, Konzeption Zivile Verteidigung (KZV), Berlin 2016, S. 17

16 vgl. Die Bundesregierung, Weißbuch 2016. Zur Sicherheitspolitik und zur Zukunft der Bundeswehr, Berlin 2016, S. 36 ff.; vgl. Arne Schönbohm, Bedrohung im Cyber-Raum, in: Florian Hahn (Hrsg.), Sicherheit für Generationen. Herausforderung in einer neuen Weltordnung, Berlin 2017, S. 57 ff.

17 Reinhard Hutter, „Cyber-Terror": Risiken im Informationszeitalter, in: APuZ, B 10-11/2002, S. 31 ff.; 35; vgl. Glenn C. Buchan, Force Protection: One-and-a-Half Cheers for RMA, in: Thierry Gongora, Harald von Riekhoff (Hrsg.), Toward a Revolution in Military Affairs. Defense and Security at Dawn of the Twenty-First Century, Westport, London 2000, S. 139 ff.; 141 f.; vgl. Jacquelyn K. Davis, Michael J. Sweeney, Strategic Paradigms 2025. U.S. Security Planning for a new Era, Cambridge, Washington 1999, S. 190

18 Gustav Däniker, Die „neue"Dimension des Terrorismus – Ein strategisches Problem, in: Erich Reiter (Hrsg.), Jahrbuch für internationale Sicherheitspolitik 1999, Hamburg, Berlin, Bonn, S. 121 ff.; 128; vgl. Bundesministerium der Verteidigung, Generalinspekteur der Bundeswehr, Teilkonzeption Schutz von Kräften und Einrichtungen der Bundeswehr im Einsatz (TK Schutz), Bonn 2006, S. 13; vgl. James F. Dunnigan, How to Make War. A Comprehensive Guide to modern Warfare in the 21st Century, 4. Aufl., New York 2003, S. 363 f.; vgl. Dorothy E. Denning, Activism, Hacktivism, and Cyberterrorism: The Internet as a Tool for Influencing Foreign Policy, in: John Arquilla, David Ronfeldt (Hrsg.), Network and Netwars, Santa Monica 2001, S. 239 ff.; 239 f.

19 vgl. Dirk Freudenberg, Weltraumgeopolitik – Aspekte eines unterbelichteten Forschungsfeldes, in: ASMZ 2019 Heft 4, S. 14 ff.; vgl. Dirk Freudenberg, Weltraumgeopolitik – Sicherheitspolitische Aspekte eines (noch) wenig beachteten Forschungsfeldes, in ÖMZ 2019, Heft 4, S. 473 ff.; vgl. Dirk Freudenberg Sicherheitspolitische Aspekte der modernen Weltraumnutzung, in: Jahrbuch Öffentliche Sicherheit 2020/2021, Frankfurt 2021, S. 835

20 Erich Vad, Militär und die neuen Formen der Gewalt als Mittel der Politik, in: Gerhard P. Groß (Hrsg.), Führungsdenken in europäischen und nordamerikanischen Streitkräften im 19. und 20, Jahrhundert, Hamburg, Berlin, Bonn 2001, S. 57 ff.; 68

21 vgl. Steffen Martus, Marina Münkler, Werner Röcke, Schlachtfelder. Zur Codierung militärischer Gewalt im medialen Wandel, in: Steffen Martus, Marina Münkler, Werner Röcke(Hrsg.), Schlachtfelder. Zur Codierung militärischer Gewalt im medialen Wandel, Berlin 2003, S. 7 ff.; 15

22 Bernd Hüppauf, Das Schlachtfeld als Raum im Kopf. Mit einem Postscriptum nach dem 11. September 2001, in: Steffen Martus, Marina Münkler, Werner Röcke (Hrsg.), Schlachtfelder. Zur Codierung militärischer Gewalt im medialen Wandel, Berlin 2003, S. 207 ff.; 228

23 Alexander Niedermeier, Nicht(s) auf dem Radar: Cyberkrieg als komplexe Herausforderung für die hochgradig vernetzte Gesellschaft, in: Zeitschrift für Politik 2012 Heft 1, S. 39 ff.; 46 f.

24 Anton Dengg, Michael N. Schurian, Zum Begriff der Hybriden Bedrohung, in: Anton Dengg, Michael Schurian (Hrsg.), Vernetzte Unsicherheit – Hybride Bedrohungen im 21. Jahrhundert, Wien 2015, S. 23 ff.; 46

25 Stephan Blancke, Information Warfare, in: APuZ, 30-31/2005, S. 24 ff.; 25; vgl. Stephan Blancke, Geheimdienste und globalisierte Risiken. Rough States – Failed States – Information Warfare – Social Hacking – Data Mining – Netzwerke – Proliferation, Berlin 2006, S. 68

26 Erich Schweighofer, Konflikt im Cyberspace: Wo bleibt das Völkerrecht?, in: Erich Reiter (Hrsg.), Österreichisches Jahrbuch für internationale Sicherheitspolitik 1997, Graz, Wien, Köln 1997, S. 391 ff.; 392

27 Dirk Freudenberg, Theorie des Irregulären. Erscheinungen und Abgrenzungen von Partisanen, Guerillas und Terroristen im Modernen Kleinkrieg sowie Entwicklungstendenzen der Reaktion, 2. Bd., Von der Definitionsproblematik bis zu der Universalität der Methoden Irregulärer Kräfte, Berlin 2017, S. 353; vgl. Dirk Freudenberg, Hybride Kriegsführung in urbanen Zentren. Relevanz für die Zivile Verteidigung in: Wissenschaft und Frieden 2019, Heft 3, S. 27 ff.; 27

28 Frank Rieger, Der digitale Erstschlag ist erfolgt, in: FAZ.NET, http://www.faz.net/s/RubCEB-3712D41B64C3094E31BDC1446D18E/Doc~E8A0D43832567452FBDEE07AF579E893C~ATpl~Ecommon~Scontent.html, Internet vom 29.09.2010; vgl. Stefan Haubner, Der „digitale Erstschlag", in: Stuttgarter Zeitung vom 24.09.2010, http://www.stuttgarter-zeitung.de/stz/page/2640390_0_9223_-computervirus-stuxnet-der-digitale-erstschlag-.html, Internet vom 04.10.2010; vgl. Henrique Schneider, Cyberwar: Digitaler Erstschlag?, in: ASMZ. Heft 3, 2004, S. 6 f.

29 Dirk Freudenberg, Hybride Kriegsführung in urbanen Zentren. Relevanz für die Zivile Verteidigung in: Wissenschaft und Frieden 2019, Heft 3, S. 27 ff.

30 Dirk Freudenberg, Hybride Kriegsführung in urbanen Zentren. Relevanz für die Zivile Verteidigung in: Wissenschaft und Frieden 2019, Heft 3, S. 27 ff.; 28.

31 Susanne Dehmel, Hybride Kriegsführung 4.0, in: Ringo Wagner, Hans-Joachim Schaprian (Hrsg.), Komplexe Krisen – aktive Verantwortung. Magdeburger Gespräche zur Friedens- und Sicherheitspolitik, Magdeburg 2016, S. 91 ff.; 91 f.; vgl. Stefan Goertz, Cyberwar und Cyber-Terrorismus: Bedrohungen in Gegenwart und Zukunft, in: ASMZ 2017, Heft 4, S. 5 ff.; 5

32 Helmut Ganser, Sicherheitspolitik und Streitkräfte in einer künftig durchdigitalisierten Welt, in: Ringo Wagner, Hans-Joachim Schaprian (Hrsg.), Komplexe Krisen – aktive Verantwortung. Magdeburger Gespräche zur Friedens- und Sicherheitspolitik, Magdeburg 2016, S. 155 ff.; 155

33 *Hierzu siehe auch:* Harald Erkens, Neues Spiel – alte Regeln? Der Einsatz der Streitkräfte im Innern im Lichte der aktuellen Basisdokumente – Teil 1, in: BWV 2019, S. 73 ff.; vgl. Harald Erkens, Neues Spiel – alte Regeln? Der Einsatz der Streitkräfte im Innern im Lichte der aktuellen Basisdokumente – Teil 2, in: BWV 2019, S. 97 ff.

34 Anton Dengg, Michael N. Schurian, Zum Begriff der Hybriden Bedrohung, in: Anton Dengg, Michael Schurian (Hrsg.), Vernetzte Unsicherheit – Hybride Bedrohungen im 21. Jahrhundert, Wien 2015, S. 23 ff.; 34

35 Bundesministerium des Inneren, Konzeption Zivile Verteidigung (KZV), Berlin 2016, S. 12 f.; *Zur Konzeption Zivile Verteidigung vergleiche auch zusammenfassend:* Wolfram Geier, Das Konzept Zivile Verteidigung. Hintergründe, Aufgaben, Perspektiven, in: Crisis Prevention 2016, Heft 4, S. 4 ff.; vgl. Angela Clemens-Mitschke, KZV vom 24.08.2016, in: Bevölkerungsschutz 2017, Heft 4, S. 2 ff.

36 Dirk Freudenberg, Theorie des Irregulären. Erscheinungen und Abgrenzungen von Partisanen, Guerillas und Terroristen im Modernen Kleinkrieg sowie Entwicklungstendenzen der Reaktion, 2. Bd., Von der Definitionsproblematik bis zu der Universalität der Methoden Irregulärer Kräfte, Berlin 2017, S. 253; vgl. Dirk Freudenberg, Hybride Kriegsführung in urbanen Zentren. Relevanz für die Zivile Verteidigung in: Wissenschaft und Frieden 2019, Heft 3, S. 27 ff.; 28

37 Dirk Freudenberg, Hybride Bedrohungen und Bevölkerungsschutz, in: Sicherheit & Frieden 2016, Heft 2, S. 141 ff.; 145; vgl. Dirk Freudenberg, Hybride Bedrohungen unter besonderer Berücksichtigung Bevölkerungsschutzes, in: Hans-Georg Ehrhart (Hrsg.), Krieg im 21. Jahrhundert. Konzepte, Akteure, Herausforderungen, Berlin 2017, S. 346 ff.; 372; vgl. Dirk Freudenberg, Theorie des Irregulären. Erscheinungen und Abgrenzungen von Partisanen, Guerillas und Terroristen im Modernen

Kleinkrieg sowie Entwicklungstendenzen der Reaktion, 2. Bd., Von der Definitionsproblematik bis zu der Universalität der Methoden Irregulärer Kräfte, Berlin 2017, S. 259; vgl. Dirk Freudenberg, Hybride Kriegsführung in urbanen Zentren. Relevanz für die Zivile Verteidigung in: Wissenschaft und Frieden 2019, Heft 3, S. 27 ff.; 28

38 Dirk Freudenberg, Soziale Medien und Hybride Bedrohungen unter besonderer Berücksichtigung der strategischen Führungsebene, in: Notfallvorsorge 2016, Heft 2, S. 10 ff.; 14; vgl. Dirk Freudenberg, Resilienz als Schutzschild und Bindeglied zwischen ziviler und militärischer Verteidigung, in: Uwe Hartmann, Claus von Rosen (Hrsg.), Jahrbuch Innere Führung 2017. Die Wiederkehr der Verteidigung in Europa und die Zukunft der Inneren Führung, Berlin 2017, S. 93 ff.; 105; vgl. Dirk Freudenberg, Hybride Kriegsführung in urbanen Zentren. Relevanz für die Zivile Verteidigung in: Wissenschaft und Frieden 2019, Heft 3, S. 27 ff.

39 Bundesministerium der Verteidigung (Hrsg.), Weißbuch zur Sicherheitspolitik und zur Zukunft der Bundeswehr, Berlin 2016, S. 38

40 Florian Schraurer, Hans-Joachim Ruff-Stahl, Hybride Bedrohungen. Sicherheitspolitik in der Grauzone, in: APuZ 43-45/2016, S. 9 ff.; 10

41 vgl. Markus Kneip, Eine Untersuchung inwieweit die Rahmenrichtlinien für die Gesamtverteidigung – Stand: 15.05.1988 – Zielsetzung, Strukturen, Aufgaben und Kräfte, Zuständigkeiten und das Zusammenwirken in der Gesamtverteidigung der Bundesrepublik Deutschland darstellen, unveröffentlichte Jahresarbeit an der Führungsakademie der Bundeswehr, Hamburg 1989, S. 21

42 Dirk Freudenberg, Die zivile Sicherheitsarchitektur in Deutschland und ihre sicherheitspolitische Relevanz, in Reader Sicherheitspolitik 4/2017, S. 5 f.; vgl. Dirk Freudenberg, Hybride Bedrohungen unter besonderer Berücksichtigung Bevölkerungsschutzes, in: Hans-Georg Ehrhart (Hrsg.), Krieg im 21. Jahrhundert. Konzepte, Akteure, Herausforderungen, Berlin 2017, S. 346 ff.; 372; vgl. Dirk Freudenberg, Theorie des Irregulären. Erscheinungen und Abgrenzungen von Partisanen, Guerillas und Terroristen im Modernen Kleinkrieg sowie Entwicklungstendenzen der Reaktion, 2. Bd., Von der Definitionsproblematik bis zu der Universalität der Methoden Irregulärer Kräfte, Berlin 2017, S. 260; vgl. Dirk Freudenberg, Hybride Kriegsführung in urbanen Zentren. Relevanz für die Zivile Verteidigung in: Wissenschaft und Frieden 2019, Heft 3, S. 27 ff.; 28

43 Valery Gerasimov, The Value of Science Is into the Forsight. New Challanges Demand Rethinking The Forms and Methods of Creating Combat Operations, in: MILITARY REVIEW January-February 2016, S. 23 ff.; 24

44 Johann Schmid, Konfliktfeld Ukraine: Hybride Schattenkriegführung und das „Center of Gravity"der Entscheidung, in: Hans-Georg Ehrhart (Hrsg.), Krieg im 21. Jahrhundert. Konzepte, Akteure, Herausforderungen, Berlin 2017, S. 141 ff.; 155

45 Dirk Freudenberg, Hybride Bedrohungen unter besonderer Berücksichtigung Bevölkerungsschutzes, in: Hans-Georg Ehrhart (Hrsg.), Krieg im 21. Jahrhundert. Konzepte, Akteure, Herausforderungen, Berlin 2017, S. 346 ff.; 372; vgl. Dirk Freudenberg, Theorie des Irregulären. Erscheinungen und Abgrenzungen von Partisanen, Guerillas und Terroristen im Modernen Kleinkrieg sowie Entwicklungstendenzen der Reaktion, 2. Bd., Von der Definitionsproblematik bis zu der Universalität der Methoden Irregulärer Kräfte, Berlin 2017, S. 261; vgl. Dirk Freudenberg, Hybride Kriegsführung in urbanen Zentren. Relevanz für die Zivile Verteidigung in: Wissenschaft und Frieden 2019, Heft 3, S. 27 ff.; 28

46 Alexander Poretschkin, Bevölkerungsschutz als Verfassungsauftrag, in: Christoph Unger, Thomas Mitschke, Dirk Freudenberg (Hrsg.), Krisenmanagement – Notfallplanung – Bevölkerungsschutz. Festschrift anlässlich 60 Jahre Ausbildung im Bevölkerungsschutz dargebracht von Partnern, Freunden und Mitarbeitern des Bundesamtes für Bevölkerungsschutz und Katastrophenhilfe Berlin 2013, S. 513 ff.; 514; vgl. Alexander Poretschkin, Zivilverteidigung als Verfassungsauftrag, Rheinbach 1991, S. 114 ff.

47 Dirk Freudenberg, Hybride Bedrohungen und Bevölkerungsschutz, in: Sicherheit & Frieden 2016, Heft 2, S. 141 ff.; 145; vgl. Dirk Freudenberg, Die zivile Sicherheitsarchitektur in Deutschland und ihre sicherheitspolitische Relevanz, in Reader Sicherheitspolitik 4/2017, S.6; vgl. Dirk Freudenberg, Hybride Bedrohungen unter besonderer Berücksichtigung Bevölkerungsschutzes, in: Hans-Georg Ehrhart (Hrsg.), Krieg im 21. Jahrhundert. Konzepte, Akteure, Herausforderungen, Berlin 2017, S. 346 ff.; 372; vgl. Dirk Freudenberg, Theorie des Irregulären. Erscheinungen und Abgrenzungen von Partisanen, Guerillas und Terroristen im Modernen Kleinkrieg sowie Entwicklungstendenzen der Reaktion, 2. Bd., Von der Definitionsproblematik bis zu der Universalität der Methoden Irregulärer Kräfte,

Berlin 2017, S. 261; vgl. Dirk Freudenberg, Hybride Kriegsführung in urbanen Zentren. Relevanz für die Zivile Verteidigung in: Wissenschaft und Frieden 2019, Heft 3, S. 27 ff.; 28; vgl. Dirk Freudenberg, Katastrophenschutz, politische, gesellschaftliche und pragmatische Aspekte, in: Staatslexikon der Görres-Gesellschaft, Bd. 3, 8. Aufl., Freiburg im Breisgau 2019, Sp. 601 ff.; 604

48 vgl. Carl von Clausewitz, Vom Kriege, in: Werner Hahlweg (Hrsg.), Hinterlassenes Werk des Generals von Clausewitz, 16. Aufl., Bonn 1952, S. 71 ff.; 89 f.

49 Oliver Tamminga, Hybride Kriegführung, Zur Einordnung einer aktuellen Erscheinungsform des Krieges, in: SWP-Aktuell 27, Berlin März 2015, S. 4

50 Florian Schrauer, Hans-Joachim Ruff-Stahl, Hybride Bedrohungen. Sicherheitspolitik in der Grauzone, in: APuZ 43-45/2016, S. 9 ff.; 10

51 Carl von Clausewitz, Vom Kriege, in: Werner Hahlweg (Hrsg.), Hinterlassenes Werk des Generals von Clausewitz, 16. Aufl., Bonn 1952, S. 71 ff.; 98

52 Ihno Krumpelt, Gedanken über die Arten der Atomkriege und ihre Führung, in: ASMZ 1968, S. 124 ff.; 125

53 Carl von Clausewitz, Vom Kriege, in: Werner Hahlweg (Hrsg.), Hinterlassenes Werk des Generals von Clausewitz, 16. Aufl., Bonn 1952, S. 71 ff.; 98

54 Oliver Tamminga, Hybride Kriegführung, Zur Einordnung einer aktuellen Erscheinungsform des Krieges, in: SWP-Aktuell 27, Berlin März 2015, S. 4

55 Dirk Freudenberg, Hybride Bedrohungen und Bevölkerungsschutz, in: Sicherheit & Frieden 2016, Heft 2, S. 141 ff.; 144; vgl. Dirk Freudenberg, Hybride Bedrohungen unter besonderer Berücksichtigung Bevölkerungsschutzes, in: Hans-Georg Ehrhart (Hrsg.), Krieg im 21. Jahrhundert. Konzepte, Akteure, Herausforderungen, Berlin 2017, S. 346 ff.; 369

56 Oliver Tamminga, Zum Umgang mit hybriden Bedrohungen, in: SWP-Aktuell 92, Berlin November 2015, S. 1

57 vgl. Hubert Annen, Resilienz – eine Bestandsaufnahme, in: Military Power Revue der Schweizer Armee, 2017, Heft 1, S. 24 ff.; 24

58 Bundesministerium der Verteidigung (Hrsg.), Weißbuch zur Sicherheitspolitik und zur Zukunft der Bundeswehr, Berlin 2016, S. 50

59 Dirk Freudenberg, Hybride Bedrohungen und Bevölkerungsschutz, in: Sicherheit & Frieden 2016, Heft 2, S. 141 ff.; 144; vgl. Dirk Freudenberg, Hybride Bedrohungen unter besonderer Berücksichtigung Bevölkerungsschutzes, in: Hans-Georg Ehrhart (Hrsg.), Krieg im 21. Jahrhundert. Konzepte, Akteure, Herausforderungen, Berlin 2017, S. 346 ff.; 369

60 Hubert Saurugg, Hybride Bedrohungspotenziale im Lichte der Vernetzung und Systemischen Denkens, in: Anton Dengg, Michael Schurian (Hrsg.), Vernetzte Unsicherheit – Hybride Bedrohungen im 21. Jahrhundert, Wien 2015, S. 77 ff.; 106

61 Rüdiger Korff, Resilienz: Eine Frage von Biegen oder Brechen im Ausnahmefall, in: Kai von Lewinski (Hrsg.), Resilienz des Rechts, Baden-Baden 2016, S. 23 ff.; 23

62 Hubert Saurugg, Hybride Bedrohungspotenziale im Lichte der Vernetzung und Systemischen Denkens, in: Anton Dengg, Michael Schurian (Hrsg.), Vernetzte Unsicherheit – Hybride Bedrohungen im 21. Jahrhundert, Wien 2015, S. 77 ff.; 106

63 Josef Isensee, Resilienz von Recht im Ausnahmefall, in: Kai von Lewinski (Hrsg.), Resilienz des Rechts, Baden-Baden 2016, S. 33 ff.; 35

64 Dirk Freudenberg, Hybride Bedrohungen und Bevölkerungsschutz, in: Sicherheit & Frieden 2016, Heft 2, S. 141 ff.; 144; Dirk Freudenberg, Hybride Bedrohungen unter besonderer Berücksichtigung Bevölkerungsschutzes, in: Hans-Georg Ehrhart (Hrsg.), Krieg im 21. Jahrhundert. Konzepte, Akteure, Herausforderungen, Berlin 2017, S. 346 ff.; 369

65 Jürgen Ehle, Hybride Bedrohungen – Neue Bedrohungen oder neuer Wein in alten Schläuchen?, in: Ringo Wagner, Hans-Joachim Schaprian (Hrsg.), Komplexe Krisen – aktive Verantwortung. Magdeburger Gespräche zur Friedens- und Sicherheitspolitik, Magdeburg 2016, S. 80 ff.; 81

66 Uwe Hartmann, Hybrider Krieg als neue Bedrohung von Freiheit und Frieden. Zur Relevanz der Inneren Führung in Politik, Gesellschaft und Streitkräften, Berlin 2015, S. 45; *Der Gedanke, für den Gegner ein Chaos zu kreieren, dadurch, dass er durch die Anzahl der Lagen mit denen er konfrontiert wird, nicht mehr bewältigen kann, und dass man ihn in diesem Stadium hält wurde bereits während des 3. Golfkrieges umgesetzt.* (Tom Clancy, Fred Franks, Jr., Into the Storm. A Study in Command, New York 2004, S. 159; vgl. Harry Horstmann, Der rote Esel. Handbuch für den militärischen Stabsdienst und Führungsprozess, Norderstedt 2008, S.210 FN 179)

67 David G. Perkins, Preface from the Comanding General U.S.-Army Training and Doctrine Command, in: TRADOC (Hrsg.), The U.S.-Army Operating Concept. Win in a Complex World, 31. October 2014, S iii ff.; iii

68 Tom Clancy, Fred Franks, Jr., Into the Storm. A Study in Command, New York 2004, S. 159

69 Dirk Freudenberg, Hybride Bedrohungen und Bevölkerungsschutz, in: Sicherheit & Frieden 2016, Heft 2, S. 141 ff.; 145; vgl. Dirk Freudenberg, Hybride Bedrohungen unter besonderer Berücksichtigung Bevölkerungsschutzes, in: Hans-Georg Ehrhart (Hrsg.), Krieg im 21. Jahrhundert. Konzepte, Akteure, Herausforderungen, Berlin 2017, S. 346 ff.; 370

70 Oliver Tamminga, Hybride Kriegführung, Zur Einordnung einer aktuellen Erscheinungsform des Krieges, in: SWP-Aktuell 27, Berlin März 2015, S. 4

71 Uwe Hartmann, Hybrider Krieg als neue Bedrohung von Freiheit und Frieden. Zur Relevanz der Inneren Führung in Politik, Gesellschaft und Streitkräften, Berlin 2015, S. 12

28

TERRORISM AND HYBRID THREATS

Analyzing Common Characteristics and Constraints for Countermeasures

Giray Sadik

Introduction

Today's security atmosphere has been increasingly characterized as a hybrid environment. The lines between war and peace have been blurred more than ever before. Despite these circumstances, coined tellingly as gray-zone threats, terrorism and hybrid threats have mostly been studied in isolation. This chapter aims to bridge this gap by explaining their critical commonalities in terms of the similar characteristics and constraints they pose for political and military communities. Building on this ground of established commonalities, the chapter explores the venues for cross-breeding and strategic learning when developing effective countermeasures against terrorism and hybrid threats. Finally, the chapter highlights the implications of a hybrid security environment for the worlds of policymaking, the military, technology (i.e. AI/AR, CBRN/WMD, UAV, cyber security), and academia, which paves the way for an evolving roadmap for a research agenda that combines insight and experience from the related fields.

Hybrid Threat Definitions and Terrorism

As hybrid threats to international security have evolved, their analysis in scholarly and policy debates have become a source of on-going confusion. In addition to conceptual clarification, this section aims to put these terms into context. To this end, this commentary refers to NATO and EU definitions from official reports as primary sources, which reflect a consensus among respective member states about their understanding of these key terms. As NATO and the EU are the two core institutions organizing Euro-Atlantic cooperation against hybrid threats, their definitions present a meaningful starting point. In a 2011 report, NATO describes hybrid threats as follows:

> *Hybrid threat* is an umbrella term, encompassing a wide variety of existing adverse circumstances and actions, such as *terrorism*, migration, piracy, corruption, ethnic conflict... What is new, however, is the possibility of NATO facing the adaptive and systematic use of such means singularly and in combination by adversaries in pursuit of long-term political objectives, as opposed to their more random occurrence, driven by coincidental factors.
>
> *(Quoted by Bachmann and Gunneriusson 2015)*

DOI: 10.4324/9781003326373-32

This comprehensive definition of hybrid threats enables researchers to grasp the term's multi-faceted nature, while also presenting examples of hybrid threats such as terrorism and migration. The same report underlines that "hybrid threats are not exclusively a tool of asymmetric or non-state actors, but can be applied by state and non-state actors alike. Their principal attraction from the point of view of a state actor is that they can be largely non-attributable, and therefore applied in situations where more overt action is ruled out for any number of reasons" (Quoted by Bachmann and Gunneriusson 2015).

Common Characteristics of Terrorism and Hybrid Threats

As highlighted in the above definitions terrorism is listed under the "umbrella of hybrid threats". Therefore, there is at least an acknowledgement on paper that these two set of threats are inter-related. However, so far, only a few experts have observed that "despite the potential of ter-rorist violence as part of hybrid warfare, counterterrorism as a response or preventive measure has an unexpectedly low profile in NATO's policy on hybrid threats" (Mumford 2016, Braun 2019). Still, their observation is relevant today, and for the most part for other international or-ganizations such as the UN, EU, OSCE that can be critical partners in fostering international cooperation in countering terrorism and hybrid threats. For this reason, instead of dealing with extensive conceptual definitions and debates about these terms, which is another issue they have in common, this section focuses on the essential commonalities of these threats that require comprehensive consideration.

To begin with, in a strategic landscape, acts of terror function as components of hybrid threats. Therefore, by definition terrorism is among the key parts of hybrid strategy in a gray zone, where lines between state and non-state, domestic and international, civilian and military, physical and cyber domains are deliberately blurred. At times, terrorist attacks can be used to further compli-cate the relationship between these domains, so as to have a greater asymmetric impact against an adversary with superior conventional forces. Therefore, in this gray zone it is not practically feasible to isolate terrorism from hybrid threats. Braun highlights this end-means link on the role of terrorism in hybrid strategy as follows:

> The main objective of terrorist activity in a hybrid environment is to spread fear and terror, to intimidate populations and degrade the will of an adversary. When multiple terrorist activities follow a central strategy, they can destabilize a state or a society to a considerable degree, even if an individual acting alone may cause relatively little harm.
>
> *(Braun 2019).*

In addition to the critical role of terrorism as a key component of hybrid threats, there is also a growing trend which can be coined as the 'hybridization of terrorism', which can be used to describe the rising threat of terrorist organizations acquiring hybrid capabilities. Ongoing clashes in Syria demonstrate how these hybrid strategies can be violently pushed to the limits and pave the way for a number of unintended consequences. For example, "all factions are benefiting from material support from external actors, besides the plundering of pre-existent Syrian army depots. As relations between the factions are fluid, weapons often do not end up in the hands of the users for which they were intended" (Angelovski et al. 2017). The growing hybrid-capacity of terrorist organizations such as AQ, IS, PKK, and their regional variants can be illustrated as only the tip of an iceberg of this rising trend. Furthermore, "nation states may empower terrorists by making heavy weapons (e.g. anti-tank weapons or drones) available to them" (Braun 2019). These interrelated trends reduce the technological edge that states typically have against terrorists, and thus, decrease the risk for terrorists when attacking. Therefore, in theater these parallel trends of increasing use of terrorism in hybrid warfare and hybridization of terrorism can be viewed as the ying-and-yang of each other, paving the way for protracted conflicts (e.g. Afghanistan, Libya, Syria etc.), increasing civilian casualties and resulting in mass refugee outflows from wars with no end in sight. These common characteristics in the gray zone put forward a number of critical shared constraints when dealing with terrorism and hybrid threats, which need to be analyzed together.

Shared Constraints when Dealing with Terrorism and Hybrid Threats

The similar below-the-threshold-of-war nature of these threats confronts governments with a number of common constraints when dealing with terrorism and hybrid threats. First of all, "since, in a hybrid scenario, violence may occur solely within the borders of a state, attribution of responsibility is a major challenge" (Tertrais 2016). This would be especially true if a state actor waging hybrid warfare was to disguise its terrorist actions through disinformation (e.g. propaganda, mass manipulation, social media etc.) or if a terrorist campaign emerged exclusively within a country. Then, international organizations such as NATO are likely to have difficulty reaching consensus on whether an attack merits Article-5 Allied collective defense reaction, for example. In turn, this can put organizations' credibility at stake for its members, and thus, it can further encourage adversaries to further exploit the blurred lines in the gray zone. At national level, "even if conceived of, instigated and controlled from abroad, terrorist and hybrid threats usually emerge within a state. In conventional military operations, the crossing of geographical borders clearly indicates the origin of such an attack. In contrast, in a hybrid environment, it is difficult to attribute responsibility for the use of force with equal clarity"(Tenenbaum 2015). As a result, use of force against terrorism and hybrid threats raises concerns in light of attribution difficulties, and challenges to identify who is responsible for an attack.

Secondly, attribution difficulties at national and international levels, makes tailoring adequate countermeasures against terrorism and hybrid threats challenging. Coupled with the risk of spill-over from hybrid theatres to interveners' homelands further constrains policymakers. Currently, "a hybrid approach to warfare is primarily associated with Russia, making NATO's eastern member states and their neighborhood seem particularly exposed. However, terrorism as part of a hybrid campaign could also spill over from the South or South East to the Euro-Atlantic region "homegrown terrorism must be kept in mind too" (Santamato 2013). Recently, significant threats to European states' internal security have been growing as result of thousands of foreign terrorist fighters (FTFs) who have returned home from conflicts mostly in the wider Middle East and North Africa (MENA). Most of these fighters were born and raised in Europe, carrying their EU-passports when radicalized and joined various extremist groups in the region. Then, when they decided to come back home, where they officially belong, this raised concerns in many European capitals, especially, after shocking terrorist attacks in Brussels and Istanbul airports, as well as knife and bus attacks against crowds in Paris, Berlin, London etc.

These fighters often bring with them military training as well as a broad war-fighting experience, and they are used to extreme violence. For instance, ex-Jihadists trained in weapons, explosives and tactics could cause considerable damage, especially if operating in groups. Such activities – launched as a coordinated terror campaign – could have similar effects to a hybrid attack launched from outside Alliance territory (Braun 2019).

Therefore, transnational spill-over effects from ongoing violent hybrid environments in Libya Syria, Afghanistan etc. must be considered when developing counterterrorism strategies domestically and internationally. Increase in these attacks will not only worsen the domestic security of European states, but also contribute to growing concerns about use of force abroad, furthering the existing 'intervention fatigue' among many Europeans. Furthermore, growing number of refugees and sleeper cells can only add to these legitimate concerns of backfiring back home from ongoing hybrid theatres.

Effective Countermeasures Necessitate Thinking and Acting Together against Hybrid Threats

Above all, for effective countermeasures against terrorism and hybrid threats we need to think about them together and act against them collectively. Otherwise, if we keep adding new terms to an already exhaustive alphabet soup it is likely that this can only contribute to further complicating our limited understanding of these ongoing threats. In addition to conceptual limitations, "using different wording for identical content carries the risk of duplication and stove-piping" (Braun 2019). These are real risks that if not addressed in a timely fashion are likely to grow, and to be exploited by adversaries seeking asymmetric advantages such as terrorists. In a report prepared for NATO's Centre of Excellence for Defense Against Terrorism in August 2016, for instance, Andrew Mumford from the University of Nottingham concluded that "NATO counter-terrorism planning [...] needs to be fully integrated within the Alliance's overarching military planning as an acknowledgment of the centrality of terrorism to the waging of hybrid warfare" (Mumford 2016).

Although progress has been made in various areas since, Mumford's critical assessment still holds today. Moreover, this assessment needs to be considered by other international organizations such as the EU and OSCE with important roles in European security, when complementing NATO's military role with political mechanisms to enhance physical (i.e. infrastructure, energy security) and informational (i.e. cyber, AI/AR, media) resilience against hybrid threats. As a starter, these organizations can begin by "formulating a better-integrated strategy covering both threats, including an all-embracing threat description, followed by a comprehensive response across the full range of different modes of warfare" (Braun 2019). In light of this comprehensive strategy, we need to act together to this end, and not only among these organizations and their members, but also in tandem with the private sector and civil society, as their roles have become critical in sustaining resilience against hybrid threats in the long term. Recently, NATO Secretary General Jens Stoltenberg stressed the importance of unified efforts against hybrid threats and terrorism in a meeting with the Allied National Security Advisers (NSAs): "many of our countries have suffered from different types of hybrid attacks. In isolation we may not always see the pattern, but together we can connect the dots to see the full picture" (Quoted by Jane's Intelligence Review, July 2019). Therefore, we all need to connect the dots for meaning, while we need to work together for this meaning to be translated into effective countermeasures.

In Search of Hybrid Implications for Policy and Research

Threats in the gray-zone are designed to have asymmetrical political impact, therefore by definition any research on terrorism and hybrid threats is bound to address its policy implications. This exploratory study puts forward two sets of interrelated implications: one for policymakers, and the other for researchers.

Starting with the implications for policymakers, who have been under pressure to function in this gray-zone in recent years, the strategic landscape will only get more 'hybrid', where even so-called 'domestic terrorism' will have a global footprint in terms of audiences, recruits, and logistics. Therefore, assuming that terrorists only come from the South and hybrid threats only from the East is a dangerous form of strategic blindness. From Breivik in Norway to Russia in Syria, there are various instances where our assumptions have been bloodily wrong. In this strategic landscape of global terrorism and hybrid threats, challenging mindsets with fixed targets can be a good start for policymakers determined to avoid false assumptions.

False assumptions lead to misjudgments and policies that do more harm than good. It is time for a sober assessment of recent interventions in terms of their 'contributions' to global terrorism and its increasingly hybrid character. From Afghanistan to Libya and from Syria to Ukraine risks of over-reaction versus under-reaction remain. Conflicts are likely to last even longer and potentially with ever more backfires to homelands from returning FTFs to homegrown terrorist attacks by sleeping-cells, and cyber formations...

The above considerations are of more immediate concern for policymakers, who need to adapt their decisions to emerging strategic landscapes. For scholars, the need for a comprehensive research agenda remains, and not only for policy relevant research but also to keep up with the changing character of war, while engaging the key stakeholders in the policy, military, private sectors and in civil society. Therefore, we must practice what we preach when talking about the unity of efforts. Ultimately, it is this practice in academia and in policymaking that is going to make a meaningful difference toward more resilient societies facing hybrid threats.

References

Ivan Angelovski et al. "The Coyote's Trail – A Machine Gun's Path from Serbia to Syria", Balkan Insight and OCCRP, 9 May 2017. Available at: https://balkaninsight.com/2017/05/09/the-coyote-s-trail-a-machine-gun-s-path-from-serbia-to-syria-05-08-2017/

Sascha-Dominik Bachmann and Hakan Gunneriusson, "Hybrid Wars: The 21stCentury's New Threats to Global Peace and Security", *Scientia Militia, South African Journal of Military Studies*, Vol. 43, No.1, 2015, pp. 77–98.

Peter Braun, "Fighting 'Men in Jeans' in the Grey Zone between Peace and War", *NDC Policy Brief* No.18, NATO Defense College, Rome, August 2019.

Andrew Mumford, "The Role of Counter Terrorism in Hybrid Warfare", Report Prepared for NATO Center of Excellence Defense Against Terrorism (CEO-DAT), November 2016.

Robert Munks, ed., "NATO Seeks Better Collective Situational Awareness to Counter Hybrid Threats", *Jane's Intelligence Review*, July 2019.

NATO "Bi-strategic Command Capstone Concept, Hybrid Threats Description" in Description" in 1500/CPPCAM/FCR/10-270038 and 5000 FXX/0100/TT-0651/SER: NU 0040, 25 August 2010.

Giray Sadik, ed., *Europe's Hybrid Threats: What Kinds of Power Does the EU Need in the 21stCentury?* Cambridge Scholars Publishing, UK, 2017.

Giray Sadik, "Global Hybrid Threats and European Security in the Age of Trump, Growing Populism, and International Terrorism", *Europe Now Journal*, Vol. 2, November 2018. Available at: https://www.europenowjournal.org/2018/11/07/global-hybrid-threats-and-european-security-in-the-age-of-trump-growing-populism-and-international-terrorism/.

Stefano Santamato, "The New NATO Policy Guidelines on Counterterrorism: Analysis, Assessment, and Actions", *Institute for National Strategic Studies, Strategic Perspectives* No.13, National Defense University Press, Washington, DC, 2013, p.5.

Élie Tenenbaum, "Hybrid Warfare in the Strategic Spectrum: A Historical Assessment" Lasconjarias and Larsen (eds.), "*NATO's Response to Hybrid Threats*", 2015 pp. 99–101. Available at: https://www.files.ethz.ch/isn/195405/fp_24.pdf.

Bruno Tertrais, "Article 5 of the Washington Treaty: Its Origins, Meaning and Future", *Research Paper* No.130, NATO Defense College, Rome, April 2016.

PART V

Political Islam, Jihadism, Psychology and Counter-Terrorism

29

LEGALISTIC ISLAMISM

The Transition from Political Islam to Jihadism

Heiko Heinisch and Nina Scholz

By pondering the political and religious preconditions of Islamic world dominance, Hasan al-Banna did not solely create, in 1930s Egypt, the ideological foundations to which Islamists of various stripes still refer today; the founder and leader of the Muslim Brotherhood developed at the same time a grassroots movement strategy meant to be a counter-model to dominant ideologies of his time – secularism, democracy, and communism. From 1930s Egypt till today, according to the will of Islamists, societies were supposed to transform gradually into a normative Islamic order imagined as God-given.

Islamism is based on a dichotomous worldview that divides the world into believers and unbelievers, Muslims and enemies of Muslims, and invokes an idealized community of all Muslims. The building blocks of this ideology are quickly enumerated:

Islam is seen as a holistic system superior to all other religions and worldviews.

Men and women are considered equal before God, but their equality in this world is rejected as a violation of the different rights and duties given to them by God.

Muslims are victimized as a group; it is claimed that from the very beginning they have been oppressed and had to defend themselves.

Thus, contrary to the historical reality of Arab and later Ottoman imperialism, the ideological building blocks of Islamism include a victim myth. Islamic history of the past 1400 years is told through the perspective of an Islamic community in constant distress, defending itself against enemies till today.[1]

The modern ideology of Islamism or Political Islam – terms used synonymously in this contribution – devalues other religions, worldviews, and lifestyles, looking with despite on everybody non-Muslim. Since its elaboration by al-Banna, Islamism has possessed an antisemitic core that refers to anti-Jewish contents found in the Quran and Hadith.[2] Such basic tenets of the ideology are shared, with varying emphasis, by all currents of Political Islam. Likewise, the declared utopian goal on a distant horizon is the same for all: an Islamic world community (Ummah) united in a caliphate.

This evokes similarities with ideologies like Communism, where the world revolution functioned as the movement's "last stand" in fulfilling the utopia. In short, Political Islam is another totalitarian ideology, alongside Communism, Fascism, and National-Socialism, whose proponents seek to impose their intolerant ideas on a worldwide scale. The difference between violent

DOI: 10.4324/9781003326373-34

Jihadist currents and legalistically operating non-violent ones lies primarily in the strategy for achieving their goals.

Again, there are parallels with extra-parliamentary opposition forces in several European states during the 1960s: Some embarked on the famous "march through the institutions" to transform "the system" from within; others were impatient and tried to force the revolution through violence. There are, of course, differences between the various Islamist currents with respect to the "correct" interpretation of Islamic tradition and the concrete shaping of society and state. But we are familiar with such shadings from other ideological political movements, such as Communism, in the past.

Unlike the left-wing ideologues of the 1960s and 1970s, legalistic Islamist actors often disguise their goals; sometimes, they do not even publicly profess their support for Islamist causes. This behavior results primarily from the persecution Islamist movements faced in Egypt and Syria in the past. When those regimes turned oppressive, the development of clandestine structures proved necessary for Islamists' survival. While Salafists are usually easily recognizable by their outward appearance and open anti-democratic propaganda, supporters of the Muslim Brotherhood in Europe, with a few exceptions, do not present themselves as such. It is therefore difficult for politicians, the media, or NGOs to identify them and assess their associations and institutions. One of the leading and almost legendary Muslim Brothers, Kamal Helbawy, explained in March 2012 why he had left an organization to which he had devoted his whole life. According to Lorenzo Vidino, who conducted an extensive interview with him, Helbawy considered the secrecy of his organization and its activists to be fundamentally wrong: "We are not selling opium or drugs, we are propagating dawa. And I can't be ashamed of my selection [sic] or my dawa program. If it is followed right, it is a source of happiness, not sadness."[3]

To define Islamists who act in accordance with democratic principles as peaceful and opposed to violence would be too easy. The Muslim Brotherhood, for example, is not a pacifist organization. Rather, there exists a tactical relationship to violence. Violence is not the first choice of the Brotherhood and may not be used if the harm resulting from it outweighs the benefit. A 1980s strategy paper, for example, instructed Brotherhood supporters not to seek direct confrontations with opponents, lest they could provoke a backlash, endangering the movement and its mission.[4] Brotherhood cadres already knew this from their experience in 1950s Egypt, when such a government backlash following Brotherhood violence almost completely crushed the organization. In the early 1980s, this experience repeated itself in Syria. After several assassinations of regime representatives, the suppression of Muslim Brotherhood-initiated uprisings culminated in the Hama massacre, mass arrests, and executions of its members in February 1982.[5]

The Brotherhood, however, advocates the use of force for defensive purposes. If Muslims and Islam cannot be protected by other means, violence is deemed legitimate.[6] In the case of the Middle East conflict, they considered this case to have occurred. Therefore, almost all Islamist organizations support Hamas's armed struggle against Israel propagandistically, financially, and/ or logistically.

The tactical relationship to violence is evident in the Muslim Brotherhood's emblem too: two swords crossed under the Quran and the injunction "Be prepared!" written below. Hasan al-Banna, as the founder of the Muslim Brotherhood, wrote his own treatise on Jihad. It begins with the following sentences:

"Jihad is an obligation from Allah on every Muslim and cannot be ignored nor evaded. Allah has ascribed great importance to Jihad and has made the reward of the martyrs and the fighters in His way a splendid one. Only those who have acted similarly and who have modeled themselves upon the martyrs in their performance of Jihad can join them in this reward."[7]

Although ideologists of the Muslim Brotherhood as well as the Turkish *Milli Görüş* movement see Jihad as a means and even describe it as an obligatory religious act,[8] it would still be wrong to assume cooperation between the legalist and Jihadist organizations in Europe; legalists in Europe do not even refer positively to Jihadism. While organizations bound to the Muslim Brotherhood network sometimes covertly and sometimes openly support propagandistically or financially Jihadist organizations in the Arab world – especially Hamas, but also smaller groups in Syria, Iraq, or Egypt, such as the al-Nusra Front or Liwa al-Tawhid [9] – in Europe they resolutely and credibly reject violence.

Like that, representatives of Political Islamic organizations have succeeded over the past 60 years to occupy key positions in organized Islam in Europe, functioning as a kind of "hinge" between Muslim communities and political decision-makers. Almost ironically, they have especially taken advantage of the attacks of 11 September 2001 and the subsequent global Islamist terror wave.

"Not Being Bin Laden"

Ahmed Akkari, a former Muslim Brotherhood supporter from Lebanon who lives in Denmark, explained the strategy behind this success with a few words in an interview: "We understood that the West is short-sighted, and that it basically wants three things from us: money, votes, and not being Bin Laden."[10]

After 9/11, Jihadist terror attracted worldwide attention with attacks in Madrid (2004) and London (2005) and reached a sad peak in Europe between 2015 and 2017 with 311 deaths in 8 grave attacks and a series of smaller ones.[11] In 2014–2015, the Islamic State terrorist organization reached its largest territorial expansion in Iraq and Syria as well. Meanwhile, legalistic Islamists initiated, since the attacks in New York and Washington, a new phase for their establishment in Europe. During the last two decades, when interacting with political decision-makers, the media, and civil society, legalists successfully took up the role of representatives of peaceful Islam and allies in the fight against terrorism.

The Establishment of the Muslim Brotherhood in Europe

The establishment of the Muslim Brotherhood in Europe took place in three phases. When supporters of the Muslim Brotherhood first came to Europe in the 1950s, their activities were focused on their country of origin. After the military coup of the so-called "Free Officers" under Gamal Abdel Nasser in 1952, which had initially been supported by the Muslim Brotherhood, the Brotherhood was banned in Egypt in 1954. In response to the ban, an assassination attempt was made on Nasser, leading to massive persecution of Muslim Brotherhood supporters. Many Egyptian Muslim Brothers fled to Europe where they were granted political asylum. At the same time, students from Egypt and other Arab states, including Muslim Brothers, were drawn to Europe.[12]

Among the refugees was Said Ramadan, the son-in-law of the founder of the Muslim Brotherhood, Hasan al-Banna. After a brief imprisonment in Egypt, Ramadan initially found refuge in Geneva in 1954, before studying at the University of Cologne. There he received his doctorate in 1958 with a thesis on Islamic law.[13] Parallel to his studies, Ramadan built up the first structures of the Brotherhood in Europe and worldwide. For example, he was a founding member of the *Muslim World League* (MWL), an organization established in 1962 in cooperation with Saudi Arabia that still exists today.[14]

His participation in the founding of Islamic centers in Europe as hubs for the Muslim Brotherhood's work was of particular importance for further developments. In 1961, Said Ramadan founded the *Islamic Center in Geneva*, which is now headed by his son Hani Ramadan; then followed the *Islamic Center in Munich* in 1973.[15] The latter emerged from the *Munich Mosque Building Commission*, which had previously been founded by Muslims who had fled the Soviet Union. This organization was "hijacked" in the late 1950s by Said Ramadan and a group of students gathered around him.[16]

In this first phase, the Muslim Brotherhood's actors were primarily concerned with the survival of the organization, which had been banned in Egypt. The Brotherhood, largely crushed in its country of origin, was seeking a new basis from which to continue its interrupted "Islamic revolution" in the Arab world.

While the Muslim Brotherhood were established its first institutions in Europe, Germany and Austria concluded so-called recruitment agreements with states like Turkey (1961) and Yugoslavia (1968) to compensate for pressing labor shortages in industries rebuilt after WW2. From Turkey alone, around 900,000 workers came to Germany until the recruitment stop in 1973.[17] In the first two decades after their arrival, confessing Muslim migrants build up a religious infrastructure on their own, without the support of their countries of origin.[18] Initially, these were provisionary living room-, backyard-, and basement-mosques.[19]

Also, followers of the Islamist Turkish *Milli Görüş* movement who had migrated became active in Germany in the early 1970s. As the first Muslim Brothers, members of *Milli Görüş'* primary concern was to create a safe base in a democratic country to exert influence on Turkish politics. Necmettin Erbakan, the founder of the *Milli Görüş* movement, was strongly influenced by Muslim Brotherhood's thought and regarded Sayyid Qutb, the Brotherhood's leading ideologue of the 1950s and 1960s, as a role model.

The cadres of these first Political Islamic structures in Western Europe, both those of the Muslim Brotherhood and Milli Görüş, were without exception men who had been born, raised, and socialized in the Middle East. Their political interests were primarily focused on the conditions in their respective countries of origin: Egypt, Syria, and Turkey.

Second Phase: Looking to Europe

This changed in the 1980s and 90s. In the meantime, a generation born and socialized in Europe had grown up. Naturally, the focus of these organizations gradually shifted from concentrating on their countries of origin to Europe. For this, a partial reinterpretation of Islamic norms and jurisprudence (*fiqh*) was necessary. In classical Islamic jurisprudence, the world was divided into the area of Islam (*dar al-islam*) and the area of war (*dar al-harb*) or disbelief (*dar al-kufr*). The permanent presence of Muslims in non-Islamic countries was not envisaged in this concept, so a revision was needed. Through the concept of the "middle way" (*wasaṭiyya*) developed by, among others, the chief ideologist and spiritus rector of the Muslim Brotherhood, the Qatar-based Yusuf al-Qaradawi, and the so-called minority *fiqh*,[20] the geographical division of the world was extended to include a third area. European countries and North America, where Muslims can live their faith unhindered, were declared *dar al-da'wa*, the area of mission (*da'wa*).[21]

At the end of the 1980s, Europe was no longer just a safe haven for Muslim Brothers to support political work in their countries of origin but had become the target of political ambitions itself. The strategy paper of the Muslim Brotherhood from 1982, which was found during house searches following the attacks of 9/11 at the home of the well-known Muslim Brother Youssef Nada in Switzerland, proves this theological, political, and strategic reorientation. The paper describes the path to a "global strategy for Islamic politics." In twelve points, it outlines a plan for infiltrating societies and formulates the long-term goal of establishing a worldwide Islamic state.[22]

A kind of founding fever set in during the 1980s, with various national organizations of the Muslim Brotherhood emerging in Europe. In 1989, these organizations formed the *Federation of Islamic Organizations in Europe* (FIOE). This included the *Islamic Community in Germany* (IGD), now called *German Muslim Community* (DMG), which had been founded by Said Ramadan himself, and the Austrian organization *Liga Kultur*. This umbrella organization close to the Muslim Brotherhood initiated further foundations: In 1992, the *Institut Européen des Sciences Humaines* (IESH) was established in the French Chateau Chinon. Today, there are several offshoots of this university in various European countries, including Germany. Behind the innocuous name stands a private Islamic university run by the Muslim Brotherhood, which trains Imams and religious teachers from all over Europe.[23]

In 1996, the *Forum of European Muslim Youth and Student Organizations* (FEMYSO) was founded as an umbrella organization for youth organizations close to the Muslim Brotherhood. Finally, in 1997, the *European Council for Fatwa and Research* (ECFR) was founded under the direction of the Brotherhood mastermind Yusuf al-Qaradawi, now 97 years old. Based in Dublin with a branch in Frankfurt/Main, this organization is commonly known as the *"European Fatwa Council"*. It aims at applying Islamic norms to European conditions and providing advice to Muslims living there. The Fatwa Council can be described as the ideological basis of the Brotherhood in Europe. The fatwas of the ECFR, available to Muslims via their own app, are written in the spirit of the "middle way" (*wasaṭiyya*) and minority jurisprudence (*fiqh*) mentioned before.[24]

Parallel to this, according to the specifications of the strategy paper, various associations and organizations were founded in individual European states from the local to the transnational level. The goal of these activities has since then been to influence political decision-makers at all levels, from municipalities to regions, to state level, and the institutions of the EU, and to push the Muslim Brotherhood's ideological goals. The strategy paper states clearly under point 5: "To dedicate ourselves to the establishment of an Islamic state, in parallel with gradual efforts aimed at gaining control of local power centers through institutional action." And, furthermore: "To influence centers of power both local and worldwide to the service of Islam."[25]

Today, some 200 organizations in Europe can be attributed to the Muslim Brotherhood network, ranging from direct Muslim Brotherhood organizations to front organizations, and organizations influenced by the Brotherhood.[26] During the same period, the German headquarters of the *Islamic Community Milli Görüş* (IGMG) also established a Europe-wide network of associations and mosques that is interwoven with the Muslim Brotherhood network. The IGMG, for example, has its own representative on the *European Fatwa Council*, and its youth organization IGMG *Gençlik* is a member of the Muslim Brotherhood's umbrella organization FEMYSO. This infrastructure proved to be decisive for the third phase of the Muslim Brotherhood's development: The establishment of Political Islam as a social force in Europe.

Third Phase: Social Recognition

After the first generation of Muslim Brothers had established its centers in Europe during the 1950s (first phase) and the second generation increasingly focused its political work on Europe in the 1980s through a widespread network (second phase), a third phase of the establishment of Political Islam in Europe was initiated after the turn of the millennium. This phase was triggered in the first decade of the 21st century by grave terrorist attacks (New York, Madrid, London) and the cartoon controversy.

September 11 marked a turning point for the establishment of Political Islam in Europe. Shocked by these grave events, the public was suddenly made aware of a phenomenon that had hitherto occupied only small circles of experts: the existence of a radical, fundamentalist current within Islam which would not stop at the gates of Western societies. This current pursues an Islamic-based counter-model to secularism, democracy, and pluralism. Within Islam, an extremist ideology had developed that, supported by its growing movement, wanted to carry into the world a culture war that could already be observed within the Islamic world during the past three decades.

The fact that some of the perpetrators of the attacks in New York, Madrid, and London had lived in Europe for several years, and three of the four London attackers had been born in the UK, was particularly shocking. This realization had two immediate consequences. First, Islamic studies, until then a niche university subject, received unexpected attention. Second, politicians and civil society organizations began to look for contacts and allies to identify extremist tendencies among rapidly growing Muslim communities and tried to develop de-radicalization strategies.

Since then, the process is often based on false premises. For example, a clear line has been drawn between violent Jihadists and non-violent groups because the phenomenon of Islamism is predominantly associated with violence and terrorism. But fundamentalist ideas of Islam also extend into the non-violent realm. Unlike the widely accepted assessment about the dangerous potential of right-wing extremist ideologies, in which cases both violent and non-violent currents receive equal attention, violent and non-violent "legalistic" Islamist tendencies are treated as two separate topics. Despite their anti-constitutional goals, this perception enabled actors of legalistic Political Islam to present themselves as representatives of the "Islam of the center". Considering that politicians and a shocked public were desperately searched for answers and solutions, Islamists had just to prove one thing: "not being Bin Laden."

Unlike right-wing or left-wing extremists, two factors helped them: A kind of migrant bonus and identity politics. Apart from a few converts, Muslims and their descendants either came as migrants or refugees to Europe. Some European societies carry with them a heavy historical burden of Fascism, National-Socialism, or Colonialism, which they try to confront critically. In their efforts not to be accused of racism, anti-democratic, and anti-pluralistic ideas, and even racist attitudes, among migrants are not recognized. To some extent, there exist double standards. Anti-democratic and anti-pluralistic attitudes among migrants and their descendants are not analyzed as critically as would be the case with other parts of society. Proponents of Political Islam succeed, through this double standard, in tapping into left-wing, alternative circles and the so-called post-Colonial discourse by exploiting the undifferentiated friend-foe thinking associated with it.

The situation is aggravated by a discourse on identity politics, supported primarily by parts of the left, which has increasingly pushed other political and social conflict lines into the background over the past decade. In this discourse, Muslims are viewed as an independent, special and, above all, homogeneous group and are locked into a kind of "identity corset" they are not to leave. Internal diversity disturbs this collectivist view of identity politics, which perceives Muslims only as victims of discrimination and exclusion. In the interplay of identitarian right-wing ideas on the one hand, and Islamist and left-wing identity politics on the other, "Muslim" became an inescapable identity marker.

While right-wing actors use this identitarian category to exclude Muslims, most actors from the left-wing define Muslims primarily as a group in need of protection from a racist society. Anti-democratic attitudes and problematic developments within Muslim communities and certain Muslim organizations thus become a crack in this projection of victimhood and are therefore readily ignored. In both cases, Muslims are culturalized, and being Muslim becomes an ethnic category. A more differentiating view would consider Muslims first and foremost as citizens and measure them by their concrete attitudes and actions.

The Polemic Battle Cry: Islamophobia

Such culturalist views on Muslims have ever brought forth an independent sub-category of racism.[27] "Islamophobia" was created in university discourse in the 1990s and has been able to increasingly penetrate social discourse since the beginning of the 2000s.[28] Unlike the term racism, however, the terms "Islamophobia" or "anti-Muslim racism" do not refer to the devaluation and discrimination of people based on their ethnic origin or other immutable characteristics. Instead, religious affiliation is defined as an innate and immutable characteristic, while any criticism of Islam, be it its particular currents or actors, is branded as racism and declared a phobia. The term "Islamophobia" does not differentiate between resentful agitation against people on the one hand, and criticism of religion inspired by enlightenment on the other hand. "Muslim-phobia" (*Muslimfeindschaft*) would be the right term to describe discrimination and hostility directed against Muslims, since it terminologically focuses specifically on the people concerned and not on their religion. Even a working group of the German Islam Conference proposed this term. Inherent in the term Islamophobia, on the other hand, is the confusion of criticism of Islam with the stigmatization and discrimination of believers. It functions as a polemical battle cry that tries to place any criticism of Islam, practices in conservative Muslim communities, or Islamic organizations under the suspicion of racism.

The European Islamophobia Report (EIR) shows clearly that this term is rather used as a tool to achieve hegemonic positions in political discourse than to contribute to academics. Published by "Islamophobia researcher" Farid Hafez together with Enes Bayrakli, in cooperation with SETA – a Turkish foundation close to Erdoğan – this annual publication strings together supposedly "Islamophobic" events, actions, and statements in a collection of country reports. In these reports, far-right activism and racist statements are lined up together with statements made by established journalists and academics criticizing Islam or Islamic organizations. Even criticism of the policies enacted by Turkish President Erdoğan and his supporters are deemed "Islamophobic" in these reports.[29] Erdoğan himself described the French parliament's decision to criminalize the denial of the Armenian genocide as "Islamophobic."[30]

Georges Bensoussan, a French historian and staff member of the Paris Shoah Memorial, was accused of "Islamophobia" for pointing out in his findings that Antisemitism among Muslims represents an emerging phenomenon in France. This kind of Antisemitism was concealed hitherto. All the 14 murders of French Jews in recent years have been committed by Muslims, according to him. Consequently, Bensoussan was sued by a Muslim association – the *Collectif contre l'islamophobie en France*. The court, however, acquitted him.[31]

The Hour of Political Islam

Activists of Turkish and Arab Islamist currents, as described above, were the first to organize on a larger scale in Europe because of their persecution in their countries of origin. This head start ensures their dominance in the major Islamic associations today. Their representatives sit at the table with policymakers, churches, and NGOs at the local, state, and EU levels. This success is also due to the start-up capital they brought with them to Europe: on the one hand, the well-organized structures in their countries of origin that had already existed for decades and, on the other, the financial support they received from Saudi Arabia, the Gulf states and, later, Turkey.

Finally, the rise of Political Islam, which has been observed in all majority-Islamic countries for about four decades, gave them an additional boost. Political Islam has become mainstream in most Islamic countries, perhaps with the exception of Turkey and Indonesia, which were dragged into this development with a time lag. The Syrian Islamic scholar Aziz Al-Azmeh has referred to this development as the "Islamization of Islam".[32]

When politicians, churches, and civil society organizations were looking for Muslim partners in the wake of the Islamist terrorist attacks and the rise of IS in Syria and Iraq, networks of Political Islam were ready and able to offer their associations and organizations as partners in the fight against extremism and terrorism at various levels. In the area of media relations, their level of organization also benefited them. They quickly realized that a kind of institutional laziness was prevalent within newsrooms; it was only a matter of addressing this through availability. Journalists writing about an Islamic or integration topic, especially in daily journalism, quickly need a quote, a statement from a Muslim. Organizations of Political Islam can serve this need of the media well through their structures. This continues to have the effect that people from Islamic organizations who usually come from the spectrum of Political Islam are overrepresented in almost all media. As a result, they shape the public image of Islam.

The Muslim Vote: Electoral Calculations

Also, the focus of political parties on the next election has favored the rise of actors from Political Islam. Apart from those on the right of the political spectrum, almost all political parties try to use Islamic organizations as door openers into Muslim communities to lure new votes with their help. The success of such attempts is not easy to assess, as several unknown factors exist. The Social Democratic Party Austria (SPÖ) nominated, for example, a member of the *Milli Görüş* movement, Resul Ekrem Gönültaş, for the 2013 parliamentary election. Gönültaş received over 12,000 preferential votes, a result that carries weight within the party. However, it is, on the one hand, impossible to determine how many of these 12,000 people would have voted for the SPÖ also without this candidate; on the other hand, it is impossible to determine whether people no longer vote for the SPÖ because of its uncritical attitude toward problematic Islamic organizations. Criticism of the SPÖ's cooperation with *Milli Görüş* and the far right *Grey Wolves* (Turkish Federation) has been voiced primarily in social networks, including by Muslims. Anyways, the goals of Political Islamic organizations such as *Milli Görüş* and a social democratic party could hardly be further apart.

In any case, the cooperation of political parties with Islamist organizations creates long-term costs for society. Evidently, Islamist organizations expect from parties favors in return for support in elections. With permits and state funding for educational institutions like kindergartens and schools, or the granting of facilities that benefit the long-term establishment of their organization, Islamist organizations try to pursue their own goals. Such political cooperation helps Islamists to achieve hegemony over the content and organizational form of Islam in their respective country.

The Underestimated Ideology

Organizations of Political Islam are currently firmly established in Europe. They are project partners of trade unions, churches, NGOs, and political decision-makers in a wide variety of areas. Their representatives are represented in Islam and integration conferences, and figure as part of interreligious dialogue forums and anti-racism initiatives. Members of Political Islamic organizations can be found in various political parties and NGOs. Even in prevention work against extremism and the deradicalization of Jihadists, individuals and organizations from the spectrum of Political Islamic are present.

Particularly in this field, the opinion sometimes prevails that moderate Islamism represents the best protection against violent Islamism. According to this view, religious extremists can best be deradicalized by non-violent adherents of Islamist ideas. The fact that such a thought is exclusively applied to Islamic extremism seems rather questionable. Nobody would think about using legalistic, right-wing organizations/parties such as the NPD, the Identitarian Movement, or the AfD for the purpose of deradicalizing violent neo-Nazis.

Most European Islamic associations and federations may condemn terror out of conviction, but they share one goal with the perpetrators of violence nonetheless: to prevent a critical public debate about Islam. Having it their way, Islam would be mentioned exclusively in a positive sense. That is why they attempt to censor plays, satire, exhibitions, and results of scientific research. Such attempts are not infrequently successful, in part because of a fear of being judged to be racist or "Islamophobic". The massive uproar among Muslims in Europe and worldwide due to the cartoons in Denmark and many subsequent threats and attacks on journalists, artists, and scientists had an intimidating effect.

The threatening fatwa issued by Iranian revolutionary leader Ayatollah Khomeini in 1989 against Salman Rushdie and the subsequent assassinations of publishers and translators of "The Satanic Verses" signified a green light for a global Islamist struggle against freedom of expression. The cartoon controversy of 2006 was another catalyst.[33] The latter provides a good illustration of the dynamic relationship between legalistic and violent Islamism.

In September 2005, the Danish newspaper *Jyllands Posten* printed twelve Muhammad cartoons. In response, several Danish Imams launched a campaign against the newspaper, which also involved embassies of several Islamic states. This campaign quickly went international. Thematically, the campaign referred first to the alleged aniconism in Islam that forbade the depiction of Muhammad; this is contradicted by Islamic art history, which features numerous depictions of Muhammad from all centuries;[34] this shows, however, that Islamists are increasingly succeeding in establishing their ideas of Islam as general rules. Seen in this light, the enforcement of a radical ban on images is part of the advance of Islamism. Museums of Islamic art in the Islamic world can no longer show parts of their art treasures if they contain representations of Muhammad. The argument that the cartoons ridiculed Muhammad and Islam and were "islamophobic" or even racist, weighed even more heavily in the Western cartoon controversy, however.

The cartoon controversy took a decisive turning point when the spiritus rector of the Muslim Brotherhood, the Qatar-based televangelist Yusuf al-Qaradawi, took the stage. In his popular weekly broadcast on Al-Jazeera, he called for a "Day of Rage" on the 3 February 2006. As a result, violent riots from Jakarta to Tripoli, in which the embassies of Denmark and other European countries were attacked, followed. About 150 people were killed. In the following years, the world experienced many more of these "Days of Rage".

The cartoon controversy showed that terror is used by representatives of Islamic organizations and associations as a not-too-hidden menace to lend weight to their demands. The Danish Imam Raed Hlayhel was involved in the campaign against the cartoonists; in an interview, he received broad attention due to an allusion he made to the murder of Theo van Gogh. This could be understood as a threat: "If you have seen what happened in Holland, and the cartoons are nonetheless printed, this is stupid."[35] In turn, then spokeswoman for the *Islamic Religious Community of Austria* (IGGÖ), Carla Amina Baghatjati, mentioned that the release of Geert Wilder's film "Fitna" could evoke "emotional reactions" among her coreligionists.[36] "Emotional reactions" was a euphemism, given the violent riots following the release of the film.

This massive use of violence fostered a discursive shift already apparent at the beginning of the cartoon controversy. The debate centered on the question of whether it was permissible to depict Muhammad despite Islamic bans on images. Hardly anyone asked the rather obvious question of why a religious ban should apply to people who do not adhere to this religion. As a result of this discursive shift, those who had drawn anger and hatred on themselves were blamed for escalations and violence: cartoonists, artists, filmmakers, and writers.

The printing of Muhammad cartoons and artworks within the Islamic tradition, such as ancient Persian or Ottoman illuminations, has since that moment repeatedly sparked protests from "moderate" or "legalistic" Islamists.[37] The reprint of the Danish cartoons triggered the first campaign against the satirical magazine *Charlie Hebdo*. The French Islamic umbrella organization *Conseil français du culte musulman* (CFCM) filed a lawsuit. In a trial that received much attention in France, the court ruled that the printing of the cartoons did not violate French law; but the campaign had brought *Charlie Hebdo* into the focus of fundamentalist circles.

After *Charlie Hebdo* announced in October 2011 that the upcoming issue would bear the title "Charia Hebdo" and that Prophet Muhammad would be its editor-in-chief, an arson attack on its offices was committed.[38] Finally, on 7 January 2015, there followed a devastating attack that claimed the lives of almost the entire editorial staff of the magazine. Two heavily armed Jihadists shot dead ten members of the editorial team and a policeman; at the same time, four more people died in a coordinated attack on a Jewish supermarket in Paris.

French teacher Samuel Paty's murder on 16 October 2020 once again illustrated the interplay between legalistic and Jihadist Islamists. During a lesson on the subject "the right to freedom of expression" Paty had discussed the Muhammad cartoons from *Charlie Hebdo* with his students. In response, the father of one of the students launched a smear campaign against the teacher on the Internet. In this, he was supported by Abdelhakim Sefrioui, a French Imam from Morocco with close ties to the Muslim Brotherhood.[39]

Like in the case of *Charlie Hebdo*, nonviolent Islamist actors had marked the target before violent Islamists took up arms. In other cases, the perpetrators were in direct contact with the Muslim Brotherhood. For example, one of the murderers of British soldier Lee Rigby, who was first hit by a car and then gruesomely killed with knives and a hatchet in London in 2013, had studied at the Welsh branch of the French Muslim Brotherhood university *Institut Européen des Sciences Humaines* (IESH) one year before the attack.[40]

In turn, the terrorist who killed five of his colleagues with a knife in October 2019 at the Paris police headquarters in which he worked, regularly attended a mosque whose main Imam belongs to a Muslim Brotherhood association, the *Conseil Théologique des Musulmans de France*.[41]

Jihadist violence is insidiously changing society. Numerous satirists, cabaret artists, and cartoonists admit to making jokes about everything except Islam. Hape Kerkeling and Harald Schmidt, for example, have frankly admitted that jokes about Islam are far too delicate for them; and Kaya Yanar remarked that he avoids jokes about Islam because he wants to live a little longer. Given the potential threat and past experiences, this fear is justified.[42] Many newspapers no longer dare to print cartoons referring to Islam, and teachers will probably be wary of discussing certain cartoons during class in the future. The latent and actual threat of Islamism creates the danger that pluralistic and democratic societies are increasingly undermined.

Conclusions

While the world remains gripped by Islamist terrorists who have ravaged Europe for 20 years and reached their temporary peak in the form of the IS, legalistic Islamists from Muslim Brotherhood circles and its partner organizations have set out to transform democratic societies from within. Their transnational organizations, such as the *Federation of Islamic Organizations* in Europe (FIOE) or the *Forum of European Muslim Youth and Student Organizations* (FEMYSO), are headquartered in Brussels and lobby at the EU level. Their national organizations, such as the *German Muslim Community* (DMG) or the *Islamic Community Milli Görüş* (IGMG), with their countless offshoots and sub-organizations, actively seek cooperation with politics and public administration, at the federal, state, and local levels, and benefit thereby from state and local funding.

The famous march through the institutions by legalistic Islamist forces has proven to be expedient, with terror playing into their hands. While the world was looking at Jihadism and terror, legalistic Islamists could count on ignorance and disinterest on the part of political decision-makers, the media, and the public; none of them seemed capable of meeting the new challenge of Islamic extremism, historically unknown in Europe, up to this point. Europe is still struggling with this challenge.

After two decades of Islamist terror in Europe, the focus should no longer be exclusively on Jihadism, but also on Political Islamic ideas that constitute an ideology not restricted to Jihadists. Political Islam should be taken as seriously as other totalitarian ideologies. Islamists of all shades share a dichotomous worldview that divides people hierarchically into believers and non-believers, Muslims and non-Muslims; they imagine an ideal Islamic world community, reject democracy based on constitutional rights, the separation of state and religion, and share a victim narrative that turns "non-believers" into aggressors and thus into enemies of Muslims. On this fundament, Jihadists can keep on building their propaganda in the future.[43]

Notes

1 Nina Scholz, Heiko Heinisch: Alles für Allah. Wie der politische Islam unsere Gesellschaft verändert, Vienna, 2019, p. 24 f, 69–73.

2 Antisemitism is a recurring theme in Islamist discourse, stretching from al-Banna to a strategy paper of the Muslim Brothers from 1981, and can be found in discourses of various actors of today's Political Islam.

3 Lorenzo Vidino: The Closed Circle. Joining and Leaving the Muslim Brotherhood in the West, New York, 2020, p. 41.

4 A copy of the document including an English translation can be found at: https://www.investigative-project.org/documents/misc/687.pdf [09.03.2022]. See further: Scholz, Heinisch: Allah, p. 44.

5 "2. Februar 1982: Das Massaker von Hama in Syrien, BPB, 01.02.2017: https://www.bpb.de/politik/hintergrund-aktuell/241689/massaker-von-hama [09.03.2022].

6 In this sense, Amar Lasfar, president of the umbrella organization of the French Muslim Brotherhood network, *Union des Organisations Islamiques de France* (renamed some years ago in Musulmans de France), in a speech: https://twitter.com/IslamismMap/status/1090581822872915969 [09.03.2022].

7 Hasan al-Banna: On Jihad: https://thequranblog.wordpress.com/2008/06/07/the-complete-works-of-imam-hasan-al-banna-10/ [09.03.2022].

8 cf. al-Banna: On Jihad. Sayyid Qutb: Zeichen auf dem Weg, Cologne, 2005, pp. 82, 95. Necmettin Erbakan speaks of Jihad as worship, in: Davam. Ne Yaptiysam Allah Rızası İçin Yaptım, Istanbul, 2017, p. 25.

9 "Rift Between Syrian National Coalition and Islamist Repel Deepens", AL-Monitor, 2013: https://www.al-monitor.com/originals/2013/09/isis-syria-rebels-fsa-azaz-aleppo.html [06.03.2022], Heiko Heinisch, Lorenzo Vidino: Organisationen des politischen Islam und ihr Einfluss in Europa und Österreich, Vienna, 2021, p. 32 f.

10 Vidino: Closed Circle, p. 79.

11 Attacked were offices of Charlie Hebdo in Paris, Copenhagen, Paris, Brussels, Nice, Berlin, Manchester, and Barcelona.

12 Stefan Meining: Eine Moschee in Deutschland. Nazis, Geheimdienste und der Aufstieg des politischen Islam im Westen, Munich, 2011, p. 159 f.

13 Meining: Moschee, p. 116 f.

14 Ian Johnson: Die Vierte Moschee. Nazis, CIA und der islamische Fundamentalismus, Stuttgart, 2011, p. 219 f.

15 cf. Meining: Moschee, p. 169.

16 Meining: Moschee, p. 120. cf. too: Lorenzo Vidino, Die Eroberung Europas durch die Muslimbruderschaft, MEW, 2015: https://www.meforum.org/758/die-eroberung-europas-durch-die-muslim [09.03.2022].

17 Stefan Luft: Die Anwerbung türkischer Arbeitnehmer und ihre Folgen, Bundeszentrale für politische Bildung 2014: https://www.bpb.de/internationales/europa/tuerkei/184981/gastarbeit [09.03.2022].

18 Ednan Aslan, Evrim Erşan Akkılıç, Jonas Kolb: Imame und Integration, Wiesbaden, 2015, p. 11.

19 Heiko Heinisch, Imet Mehmedi: Die Rolle der Moschee im Integrationsprozess, ÖIF Forschungsbericht, Vienna, 2017, p. 27

20 A particular norm system for Muslim minorities in non-Muslim countries.

21 Sarah Albrecht: Dār al-Islām Revisited Territoriality in Contemporary Islamic Legal Discourse on Muslims in the West, Leiden, 2018, p. 165 f.

22 Strategiepapier, a.a.O. cf. too: Elham Manea: Der alltägliche Islamismus. Terror beginnt, wo wir ihn zulassen, Munich, 2018, pp. 191–193. Scholz, Heinisch: Allah, pp. 43–46.

23 "Dschihad auf dem Bildungsweg", FAZ, 06.11.2020: https://www.faz.net/aktuell/feuilleton/debatten/islamisten-wollen-europa-ueber-die-bildung-erobern-17033192.html?premium [09.03.2022]. cf. The documentary made by: Saida Keller-Messahli: Welchen Islam wollen wir in Europa? Das Bildungsnetzwerk der Muslimbrüder, 2021: https://vimeo.com/401601506/634b8a9293 [09.03.2022]

24 Scholz, Heinisch: Allah, pp. 48–52.

25 Strategiepapier, a.a.O.

26 This differentiation of Muslim Brothers and their organizations and associations follows: Lorenzo Vidino: The Muslim Brotherhood in Austria, Washington/Vienna, 2017, pp. 8–10.

27 cf. for multiculturalism: Heiko Heinisch, Nina Scholz: Europa, Menschenrechte und Islam – ein Kulturkampf?, Vienna, 2012, pp. 29–45.

28 cf. for a deconstruction of the term: Heinisch, Scholz: Europa, pp. 17–27.

29 Enes Bayrakli, Farid Hafez (Hg.): European Islamophobia Report, 2016, pp. 22, 38.

30 "Erdoğan wirft Franzosen Völkermord in Algerien vor", Die Presse, 23.12.2011: https://www.diepresse.com/719251/erdogan-wirft-franzosen-voelkermord-in-algerien-vor [09.03.2022].

31 https://www.deutschlandfunk.de/antisemitismus-in-frankreich-du-bist-ein-dreckiger-jude-100.html.

32 Aziz al-Azmeh: Die Islamisierung des Islam. Imaginäre Welten einer politischen Theologie, Frankfurt, 1996.

33 A detailed description of the controversy can be found in: Heinisch, Scholz: Europa, pp. 99–116.

34 cf. for Islamic aniconism: Heinisch, Scholz: Europa, pp. 89–97.

35 http://jyllands-posten.dk/international/ECE3931400/Wie+der+Karikaturenstreit+sich+entwickelte/.

36 Kurier, 29. March 2008, p. 8.

37 cf. Nina Scholz, Heiko Heinisch: Charlie versus Mohammed. Plädoyer für die Meinungsfreiheit, Vienna, 2016, p. 23 f.

38 "French satirical paper Charlie Hebdo attacked in Paris", BBC, 02.11.2011: https://www.bbc.com/news/world-europe-15550350 [09.03.2022].

39 "Eine Hinrichtung mit Ansage", FAZ, 18.10.2020: https://www.faz.net/aktuell/politik/ausland/enthauptung-eines-lehrers-eine-hinrichtung-mit-ansage-17007774.html [09.03.2022].

40 "Welsh Muslim College that taught Lee Rigby's killer was under influence of radical preacher", Wales Online, 30.11.2014: https://www.walesonline.co.uk/news/wales-news/welsh-muslim-college-taught-rigbys-8197120 [09.03.2022].

41 "Der neue Dschihad und seine Mentoren", FAZ, 17.10.2019: https://www.faz.net/aktuell/feuilleton/debatten/islamistische-attentate-der-neue-dschihad-und-seine-mentoren-16436466.html. cf. too: "Le Conseil théologique musulman de France voit le jour", Le Point, 29.05.2015: https://www.lepoint.fr/societe/le-conseil-theologique-musulman-de-france-voit-le-jour-29-05-2015-1932201_23.php [09.03.2022].

42 Scholz, Heinisch: Charlie, pp. 37–39.

43 "Die unterschätzte islamistische Ideologie", Der Standard, 08.11.2020: https://www.derstandard.at/story/2000121508981/die-unterschaetzte-islamistische-ideologie [09.03.2022].

30

JIHADISM AND TRUE ISLAM

Discourses and Realities

Rüdiger Lohlker

"The battle for the soul of Islam" has been discussed in several recent publications.[1] For a better understanding, it may be necessary to analyze the other side of the battle line, the jihadi claims to be the only group who can understand Islam authentically.

We will focus on three case studies:

1 the discussion among jihadis about the strategy of jihadism, especially the establishment of a caliphate,
2 the internal debate of IS, and
3 the critique of the Taliban and Muslim Brotherhood as important politico-military actors of contemporary Islam.

Some data may illustrate the scope of the phenomenon discussed here.[2] Generally speaking, jihadi discourses against other Islamic worldviews are often framed as a critique of the "scholars of the rulers" (*'ulamā' al-salāṭīn*)[3] or "scholars of evil" (*'ulamā' al-sū'*),[4] tapping into a common discourse in the Arabic world of criticizing the ruling elites. Thus, jihadis declare non-jihadi Muslims as deviant, heretic (*murtadd*), and unbelieving. Not declaring a person who is an infidel as infidel amounts to being an infidel yourself, according to some jihadi authorities.[5]

The fundamental idea of jihadism is the need for a violent solution to all contemporary problems affecting the Muslim communities and the requirement of a fighting elite to implement this solution.

This elite will be the only group that will be saved at the end of the times. Thus, it is called 'the saved group' (*firqa najiyya*) or the 'victorious group' (*tā'ifa mansūra*). There is a long Islamic story about these ideas, but the crucial meaning is that there will be only *one* group that will be saved on the Day of Resurrection, and all jihadi groups claim to be this group. This is the fundamental dogma, a pressing apocalyptic need behind the infighting among jihadi groups. As Montgomery Watt aptly stated, "this is tantamount to saying that it is as a member of the Islamic community that a man achieves meaning or significance in his life or realizes genuine values."[6] Thus, protection of the community becomes necessary to ensure the salvation of the community of true Muslims. This can be done by a true jihadi – and nobody else, since there are no true Muslims outside the true jihadi community, the only one to be saved.

DOI: 10.4324/9781003326373-35

The Legitimacy of IS and Its Caliph

The "victorious group" is not the prerequisite for salvation *per se*, but it has to have a specific form: the caliphate. As al-Qaeda thinks of a long-term strategy to establish a caliphate sometime in the future after a long fight, and some jihadis may reflect upon the possibility that the Taliban and their leader may be the Sunni caliphate, the Islamic State decided to proclaim the caliphate as soon as possible.

The proclamation of the IS-caliphate in the summer of 2014 has been a crucial moment in the history of jihadism. There are several texts by supporters of the Islamic State saying that this caliphate meets all the requirements of the classical theory of the caliphate, especially the acceptance of being an enemy by the enemies of Islam.

Biographical accounts list the necessary requirements: the IS-caliph was a descendant from the tribe of Quraysh, an essential requirement for a caliph, being the author of scholarly works,[7] and leading a successful political and military fight for the supremacy of Islam. Establishing the caliphate is necessary and the proof of accomplishing this task is the fear instilled in the hearts of the enemies of Islam.[8] The successor of the first IS-caliph is also called a descendant of the Quraysh tribe, the tribe of the prophet.

As to other jihadi currents, the acceptance of the authority of the Taliban marks a completely different attitude. By calling the then-leader of the Taliban, Mullah Omar, the "commander of the faithful" (*amīr al-mu'minīn*) and clothing him in the supposed "mantle of the prophet" (*burda*), the Taliban claimed the leadership of the Islamic community that was accepted by al-Qaeda.[9] The plans for the proclamation of the caliphate by al-Qaeda itself were part of the hundred years perspective of the organization. The claim of the Taliban was criticized by IS (see below).

The proclamation of the IS-caliphate was also criticized by the Iraqi jihadi organization *Jaysh al-Mujāhidīn* which in 2014 published a book accusing IS among other things of declaring somebody as an unbeliever (*takfīr*) without justification, outright lying, and ignoring the binding Sharia rules for military jihad. The qualifications of the then IS-caliph are not accepted because he was not a *leader* of a jihadi group, just a rank and file member.

Prominent jihadi theoreticians like Abū Muhammad al-Maqdisī criticized IS for being extremist, straying from the right path, and not obeying more experienced leaders and scholars, such as those of al-Qaeda.[10]

The critique of IS after its split from al-Qaeda led to a debate about the strategy and tactics to be employed by jihadis on the ground, organizational rifts setting apart both organizations in Syria and beyond, and to ongoing propaganda warfare.

IS, for instance, published a series of short texts[11] titled "al-Qaeda in a few lines" (*al-Qā'ida fi l-sutūr*) with quotations from leading IS figures[12] saying that the "leadership of the al-Qaeda organization is straying away from the correct [theological] methodology (*minhāj*)," and that the leader of al-Qaeda Central, Ayman al-Zawāhirī is called the leader of the "Jews of Jihad."[13]

In a recent illustrated post (May 27, 2021) on the platform *Element*, we read: "How do we fight the evil (*tāghūt*)[14]? Al-Qaeda: 'We negotiate with them.' The [Islamic] State: 'Fight them and God will punish them by means of your hands and disgrace them, and he will grant you victory over them and heal the breasts of a believing people.'"[15]

Thus, the Islamic State implicitly tells the reader that al-Qaeda has the same intent as the Taliban (see below) to negotiate with the ultimate evil and enemy; the Islamic State as the antithesis is the true representative of Islam. In plain language, IS saying: We are representing Islam as it is represented in the Qur'an, al-Qaeda is betraying Islam to the enemy.

Consistently, an anti-al-Qaeda channel on *telegram* – now offline – run by a supporter of IS was called "the Jews of Jihad" (*yahūd al-jihād*). The IS-ecosystem, the online subculture of IS followers and supporters, is deeply rooted in the theology of IS and is structuring its worldviews and organizing its policies.

Dissidents opposing the new leadership of IS published on some media outlets formerly supporting IS a severe critique of the competence of this leadership to meet the requirements of their task.

To sum it up, we may analyze the debate on the caliphate among jihadis as the quest for legitimacy to be the supreme leader of the Islamic community, understood as the *fighting* community of *true* Islam.

Leaving aside the infighting inside the jihadi currents, e.g. the emerging new role of the Hay'at Tahrīr al-Shām (HTS) as a new actor fighting IS and opposing al-Qaeda, the logic of theological exclusivity leads to an ongoing fragmentation of the jihadi currents.

Taliban and Muslim Brotherhood

The recent policy of the Taliban[16] leadership and the treaty with the USA in 2020[17] have elicited reactions in the jihadi subcultures that range from praise to condemnation.

The Islamic State regards the Taliban as a movement that has left the fold of Islam and turned to a theologically flawed nationalist policy and is a collaborator of the Pakistani intelligence, thus part of the global evil.[18] It condemned the Taliban for allying with the "crusaders," i.e., the USA. Taking a purported alliance between the Taliban and the USA for granted, the new policy is understood to be aiming at the preparation for a fight against the Islamic State that may be joined by Shiites, apostates, and other unbelieving sects.

The agreement between the Taliban and the USA is portrayed in a different light by al-Qaeda. The organization has repeatedly – since 2014[19] – described the Taliban and the Islamic Emirate of Afghanistan as the future caliphate and the leader of the Taliban as the future caliph. Thus, the leader of al-Qaeda, Ayman al-Zawahiri, has pledged allegiance to all Taliban leaders since 2014, as he did to the former leader Mullah Omar. The alliance with the Taliban is essential for the jihadi project of al-Qaeda and its affiliates even in the Maghreb. Thus, the Taliban have to have the necessary Islamic credentials of being the seat of the future caliphate.

Although *Hay'at Tahrīr al-Shām* (HTS) rejected the idea of owing loyalty to the Taliban, the head of the Shari'a committee of HTS congratulated the Taliban for the start of the negotiations with the Afghan government. The statements of HTS made clear that the strategy of the Taliban is regarded as a successful model to be followed.

Senior scholars of the jihadi subcultures "have expressed both praise and concern for the Taliban's recent doings."[20]

This critique and support can be read as a claim of the jihadi subcultures to have the true Islamic position toward a leading power of unbelief at a global level. Thus, there is a competition among jihadis as to who can gain the pole position in the fight against the leading power of the West, perceived as the most imminent threat to Islam. The internal rift in jihadism noted for many years now[21] is mirrored toward the different positions.

Another critique is directed against the Muslim Brotherhood, illustrating the claim for absolute authority by some parts of the jihadi subcultures to be the most successful contemporary Islamic force. Thus, we read in a booklet published in 2017[22] that the Muslim Brotherhood has, since 1928, claimed to apply Islamic law (*sharī'a*) protecting the believer. They did not follow the right path, being called in this text "the community straying from the right path" (*jamā'a al-dalāl*), and were constantly lying and leading the people away from the true religion, especially, when they espoused a strategy of using elections as a tool to take power in Muslim countries. This amounts, from the point of view of IS, to pure unbelief (*kufr*). There are other booklets and statements, especially, by sources close to the Islamic state, severely criticizing the Muslim Brotherhood.

Since there is a whole set of theological arguments taken from a salafi (and not the ikhwani) context and used against the Muslim Brotherhood, it is erroneous to construct a basic agreement between both currents. These currents compete for Islamic legitimacy in a subset framed by the world of nation-states globalized, or better: glocalized. This competition depends on the regional and local conditions these currents are operating in.

One crucial aspect of jihadism is the claim that the organizations and subcultures represent the "fighting group"[23] of true Islam, led by the "fighting Imam" (*imām muqātil*)[24], that will become the "victorious group" or "saved sect" (*tā'ifa mansūra, firqa nājiyya*)[25] by virtue of fighting. IS, in particular, attacks other jihadi authors for being mere "armchair Jihadis."[26] Thus, the dissemination of material on technical and military matters[27] is an important element of jihadi communication.

A recent online publication[28] gives detailed information about how "to make detonator, timer and the explosives." This is contextualized as a competition with other violent actors like "the hypocrites of the Taliban" and the "divine aid from Allah in the form of a pandemic to weaken the Mushrik[29] Govts. of Al-Hind"[30]. Publishing these materials is a twofold part of the battle described in this text: 1) to claim to be a true fighting force not restricting itself to "cyberwar rooms" and 2) to discredit other fighting forces as non-Islamic, referring to the persons at the beginning of Islam who were inwardly concealing unbelief, outwardly posing as Muslim. They were said to have been trying to undermine the Islamic community.

These discussions may be regarded by some as mere religious window-dressing trying to conceal the 'real' interests of the actors. We demonstrated that these discourses are, indeed, a rational debate about the perspectives of contemporary violent and non-violent Islamic politics. Negotiating with the USA or not, fighting Shiites forces or cooperating, e. g., with Iran, attacking Saudi Arabia as part of the abode of unbelief and claiming that the true pilgrimage should not lead to Mecca, but to the front to fight the enemy of Islam, killing Sufis, etc, are to be understood as part of this ongoing battle for the soul of Islam.

The painstaking discussions about petty religious details are a way to organize the strategies, operational art, and tactics of jihadi warfare and activities according to their specific religious worldviews[31] and to be successful competitors in the global markets of violence. Ignoring the religious dimensions of jihadism means producing very limited research results.

The fundamental difference of the strategic approach of the Egyptian Muslim Brotherhood (and affiliate organizations) and that of the jihadi subcultures may be illustrated by an iconographic message issued in June 2021.[32] The message is in Arabic. On the right hand, the most important position in Arabic iconography, we read: "the peaceful way." Below we find a picture of the former Egyptian President Mohamed Morsi (d. 2019), affiliated with the Muslim Brotherhood, behind bars during his trial after he had been removed from office. On the left hand, we find the IS-Caliph Abu Bakr al-Baghdadi (d. 2019), and below we read: "the way of Jihad." The message is clear. IS has been successful by using violence and the Brotherhood has lost power after having turned to parliamentary elections. In the background there is the assumption that the true leader of Islam is the fighting group who will be saved on the day of resurrection and their leader; the Muslim groups following the parliamentary path are heretics and will lose power.

True IS Jihadism

The internal debates of IS are well known. The discussion from 2014 to 2017 focused, e. g., on the idea of excommunication of the excuser (*al-'udhr bi'l-jahl*) or the infinite regress of excommunication (*takfīr bi'l-tasalsul*), putting against one another two factions of IS authors/scholars.[33] These theological debates prove the importance of religious debates for the development of jihadi organizations. The doctrine of excommunication as espoused by IS a theological tool used inside subcultures like IS, leading to justifications of some extreme positions. Some statements even declared the IS-caliph Abu Bakr al-Baghdadi to be an unbeliever.

Other internal debates inside IS concern conduct, tactics, and strategy. In December 2015 some IS fighters in Yemen criticized the poor military performance of one commander. But IS central leadership declared this critique as unacceptable and classified this critique as a break of the pledge of allegiance to the IS-caliph of that time. This would amount to breaking away from IS – although the critics said they still have a pledge of allegiance to al-Baghdadi.[34]

Military Conflicts among Jihadis and Politico-Military Movements

Leaving the conflict arising from Hay'at Tahrīr al-Shām (HTS) in Syria and the conflict between the Taliban and the Islamic State's *wilāya* of Khorasan aside, West Africa is another important field of conflicts between jihadi organizations. In summer 2019 the tensions between IS-affiliated powers in the Sahel and al-Qaeda-affiliated became exacerbated, notwithstanding the local and regional influences. Between July 2019 and July 2020 there were 46 clashes between these powers.[35] According to the IS weekly *al-Nabā'*, these armed clashes continued.

Conclusion

Although seems to argue for the importance of the claim of transnational jihadism for supremacy in the field of violent and extremist Islam, there is a final argument to be discussed. Jihadism – understood as global, transnational Jihad – "is somewhat cosmopolitan and diverse but the limits and variation to this vary greatly depending on that union and the geographies under analysis."[36] For a comprehensive understanding of the conflicts in West Africa, Afghanistan, Southeast Asia, or Europe a globalized view is not adequate. A transcultural and transhistorical perspective has been criticized by Talal Asad, starting from the assumption of Louis Dumont that European medieval societies have witnessed changes in religion in the broadest sense[37]:

> According to this view, medieval religion, pervading or encompassing other categories, is nevertheless *analytically* identifiable. It is this fact that makes it possible that religion has the same essence today as it had in the Middle Ages, although its social extension and function were different in the two epochs. Yet the insistence that religion has an autonomous essence [...] invites us to define religion (like any essence) as a transhistorical and transcultural phenomenon. [...] Yet the separation of religion from power is a modern Western norm, the product of a unique post-Reformation history. The attempt to understand Muslim traditions by insisting that in them religion and politics (two essences modern society tries to keep conceptually and practically apart) are coupled must, in my view, lead to failure. At its most dubious, such attempts encourage us to take up an a priori position in which religious discourse in the political area is seen as a disguise for political power.[38]

All the categories we are discussing are affected by this "dubious" assumption that there is a transhistorical essence of religion. As there is no transhistorical or transcultural essence of this kind of religion in general, this holds true for jihadism. The premise to be accepted is "that exoticizing the jihad is a dangerous tendency and the default to globalize rather than localize our understanding of these conflicts, groups and individuals, undermines true analysis of the mixed local and global dynamics of jihad. Jihadism is not to be analyzed as a globalized phenomenon, its discourses and nothing else. The true analysis of the mixed local and global dynamics of jihad. This *glocalism* requires attention if we are to better understand the appeal of jihadism."[39] This is the way to pursue an evidence-based analysis of jihadism.

Hence, we will have to integrate evidence-based research of jihadism on a global level, including the Internet, with local developments, meaning a continuous feedback of global and local analysis to understand the realities framing the activities of jihadism.

On a conceptual level, we may understand the jihadi subcultures as a global phenomenon taking root in local environments and trying to stretch its rhizomatic web as far as possible.

Notes

1 Paradigmatically, a cartoon published on the platform *Hoop* in April 2021 shows a man in the garment of an Islamic scholar with a crosshairs symbol at his headgear and titles "*'ulamā'al-salātīn*" indicating the fate of these Islamic scholars.

2 A recent image published online on the platform *Element* called contemporary Islamic scholars from the Islamic world „the dogs of the dogs of the people doomed to hellfire", meaning the rulers of the Arabo-Islamic world supporting the USA.

3 Cf. Rüdiger Lohlker, „Die Gewalttheologie des IS: Gewalt, Kalifat und Tod", in Jan-Heiner Tück (ed.), *Sterben für Gott – Töten für Gott? Religion, Martyrium und Gewalt*, Freiburg i. Br.: Herder, 2015, pp. 70–89: 75–76.

4 William Montgomery Watt, *Islamic Political Thought*, Edinburgh: Edinburgh University Press, 1998: 90.

5 A questionable claim: a BA thesis, a MA thesis, a Ph.D. thesis, and another book on Quranic recitation not well known.

6 Lohlker Die Gewalttheologie, pp. 77–80 with references to jihadi sources.

7 There was an internal debate at jihadi online fora if the fall of the Taliban after 2001 is an indicator for the coming of the Last Days (cf. Rüdiger Lohlker, *Dschihadismus: Materialien*, Wien: Facultas/WUV, 2009, pp. 117–122).

8 Rüdiger Lohlker, *Theologie des Gewalt: Das Beispiel IS*, Wien: Facultas, 2016, pp. 141–142.

9 Published at the platform *telegram* in April 2019.

10 Both quotations are from texts by Abu Muhammad al-ʿAdnānī (killed 2016).

11 The name of a *telegram* group that is now offline.

12 In Jihadispeak *tāghūt* means everything evil: tyrants, non-Jihadi powers, devils, etc.

13 Translation: Seyyed Hossein Nasr (ed.), *The Study Quran: A New Translation and Commentary*, New York, NY: HarperCollins, 2015, p. 509.

14 For the Taliban and their worldview cf. Mona Kanwal Shaikh, *Guardians of God: Inside the Religious Mind of the Pakistani Taliban*, New Delhi: Oxford University Press, 2016.

15 Cole Bunzel, Jihadi Reactions to the U.S.-Taliban Deal and Afghan Peace Talks, in *Jihadica*, September 23, 2020 (http://www.jihadica.com/jihadi-reactions-to-the-u-s-taliban-deal-and-afghan-peace-talks/) (last retrieved May 30, 2021).

16 IS helped to create a local group fighting the Taliban called *wilāyat Khorasān*, the province of Khorasan, now split into three adding a *wilāyat Pakistan* and a *wilāyat Hind* (India); cf. Antonio Giustozzi, The Islamic State in Khorasan, London: Hurst, 2018.

17 There are statements in the same vein on the Internet fora even before 2014.

18 Bunzel, Jihadi Reactions.

19 Cf. Cole Bunzel, *Jihadism on its own Terms: Understanding a Movement*, Stanford, CA: Hoover Institution, 2017.

20 Muʿādh Ahmad (Kurkunt), *al-Tibyān fī kufr Jamāʿat al-Ikhwān*, Muʿassasat al-Wafāʾal-Iʿlāmiyya, 2017 (online publication); the text refers to a former article in the IS journal *Dabiq* but is rewritten for an Arabic language audience, demonstrating that the focus on English language publications of IS misleading since it fails to grasp the real discourses in IS subcultures.

21 One of the first Jihadi groups adopting this name was the Libyan Fighting Group (*al-jamāʿa al-libiyya al-muqātila*) established in the 1990s.

22 For the claim of the first IS-caliph al-Baghdadi (d. 2019) to be the fighting Imam cf. Rüdiger Lohlker, „Die Gewalttheologie des IS: Gewalt, Kalifat und Tod", in Jan-Heiner Tück (ed.), *Sterben für Gott – Töten für Gott?* Freiburg i. Br.: Herder, 2015, pp. 70–98: 78–79.

23 These terms have a hallowed history going back to early Islam. It is worth mentioning that there non-exclusive readings of these terms.

24 A case at hand may be the prominent author Abū Muhammad al-Maqdisī.

25 Rüdiger Lohlker: Jihadism Reconsidered: The Industrial Revolution of Terrorism, in Syed Munir Khasru (ed.), *The Digital Age, Cyber Space, and Social Media: The Challenges of Security & Radicalization*, Dhaka: IPAG, 2020, pp. 41–56 and Rüdiger Lohlker: Collective Organizers: Lone Wolves, Remote Control, and Virtual Leadership, in Rüdiger Lohlker (ed.), *World Wide Warriors*, Göttingen: Vienna University Press, 2019, pp. 9–41.

26 *The Making of a Bomb: Learn how to make Detonator, Timer and the Explosives. Preparation to Gazwa-e-Hind*, accessed May 31, 2021, on the platform *Element*. All the quotations are from this text.

27 A *munāfiq*, a hypocrite, is a person pretending to be a Muslim but not fulfilling the necessary prerequisites to be a *true* Muslim, i.e., for Jihadis, fighting the enemy (the Taliban are negotiating with the USA, criticized, esp. by IS). The term refers to the beginnings of Islam.

28 Al-Hind is the ancient Arabic name of South Asia now used for India. Since the publication is part of the communication of IS it may be regarded as a product of the *wilāyat al-hind* of IS.

29 For the analysis of worldviews and religious violence cf. Mona Kanwal Shaikh, „Worldview Analysis", in Mark Juergensmeyer/Manfred B. Steger/Saskia Sassen (eds.), *The Oxford Handbook of Global Studies*, Oxford: Oxford University Press, 2019, pp. 157–171.

30 The message was downloaded from the platform *Hoop* on June 6, 2021; evidently the message is a message punished some time ago since in older picture of the IS-caliph al-Baghdadi is shown who is thought to be in the position of the victorious leader.

31 Cf. Cole Bunzel, Caliphate in Disarray: Theological Turmoil in the Islamic State (posted October 3, 2017) (http://www.jihadica.com/caliphate-in-disarray/) (last retrieved June 6, 2021).

32 Cf. Aymenn Al-Tamimi, Dissent in the Islamic State: Abu al-Faruq al-Masri's 'Message on the Manhaj' (posted 31, 2016) (https://www.ctc.usma.edu/dissent-in-the-islamic-state-abu-al-faruq-,al-masris-message-on-the-manhaj%E2%80%A8/) (last retrieved June 6, 2021).

33 Héni Nasaibia/Caleb Weiss, „The End of the Sahelian Anomaly: How the Global Conflict between the Islamic State and al-Qa'ida Finally Came to West Africa", in *CTC Sentinel* 13vii (July 2020), pp. 1–14 from a global view not taking account of the local factors influencing these conflicts.

34 Tom Smith/Kirsten E. Schulze, „Introduction: Examining the Global Linkages of Asian and North American Jihadis, "in Tom Smith/Kirsten E. Schulze (eds.), *Exporting Global Jihad: Critical Perspectives from Asia and North America*, London: I. B. Tauris, 2020, pp. 1–14: 3.

35 Louis Dumont, Religion, Politics, and Society in the Individualistic Universe, in *Proceedings of the Royal Anthropological Institute of Great Britain and Ireland*, 1970, No. 1970 (1970), pp. 31–41: 32.

36 Talal Asad, *Genealogies of Religion: Discipline and Reasons of Power in Christianity and Islam*, Baltimore, MD: The Johns Hopkins University Press, 1993, pp. 28–29.

37 Smith/Schulze 2020, p. 3.

38 Paradigmatically, a cartoon published on the platform *Hoop* in April 2021 shows a man in the garment of an Islamic scholar with a crosshairs symbol at his headgear and titles „*ʿulamāʾal-salātīn*"indicating the fate of these Islamic scholars.

39 A recent image published online on the platform *Element* called contemporary Islamic scholars from the Islamic world „the dogs of the dogs of the people doomed to hellfire", meaning the rulers of the Arabo-Islamic world supporting the USA.

References

Muʾādh Ahmad (Kurkunt), al-Tibyān fī kufr Jamāʾat al-Ikhwān, Muʾassasat al-Wafāʾ al-Iʾlāmiyya, 2017 (online pubication).

Aymenn Al-Tamimi, Dissent in the Islamic State: Abu al-Faruq al-Masri's 'Message on the Manhaj' (posted 31, 2016) (https://www.ctc.usma.edu/dissent-in-the-islamic-state-abu-al-faruq-al-masris-message-on-the-manhaj%E2%80%A8/) (last retrieved June 6, 2021).

Talal Asad, *Genealogies of Religion: Discipline and Reasons of Power in Christianity and Islam*, Baltimore, MD: The Johns Hopkins University Press, 1993.

Cole Bunzel, Caliphate in Disarray: Theological Turmoil in the Islamic State (posted October 3, 2017) (http://www.jihadica.com/caliphate-in-disarray/) (last retrieved June 6, 2021).

Cole Bunzel, *Jihadism on its own Terms: Understanding a Movement*, Stanford, CA: Hoover Institution, 2017.

Cole Bunzel, Jihadi Reactions to the U.S.-Taliban Deal and Afghan Peace Talks, in *Jihadica*, September 23, 2020 (http://www.jihadica.com/jihadi-reactions-to-the-u-s-taliban-deal-and-afghan-peace-talks/) (last retrieved May 30, 2021)

James M. Dorsey, The Battle for the Soul of Islam (https://www.hudson.org/research/16463-the-battle-for-the-soul-of-islam) (last retrieved May 22, 2021).

Louis Dumont, Religion, Politics, and Society in the Individualistic Universe, in *Proceedings of the Royal Anthropological Institute of Great Britain and Ireland*, 1970, No. 1970 (1970), pp. 31–41.

Antonio Giustozzi, *The Islamic State in Khorasan*, London: Hurst, 2018.

Seyyed Hossein Nasr (ed.), *The Study Quran: A New Translation and Commentary*, New York, NY: Harper-Collins, 2015.

Rüdiger Lohlker, *Dschihadismus: Materialien*, Wien: Facultas/WUV, 2009.

Rüdiger Lohlker, "Die Gewalttheologie des IS: Gewalt, Kalifat und Tod", in Jan-Heiner Tück (ed.), *Sterben für Gott – Töten für Gott?* Freiburg i. Br.: Herder, 2015, pp.70–98.

Rüdiger Lohlker, *Theologie der Gewalt: Das Beispiel IS*, Wien: Facultas, 2016.

Rüdiger Lohlker, Collective Organizers: Lone Wolves, Remote Control, and Virtual Leadership, in Rüdiger Lohlker (ed.), *World Wide Warriors*, Göttingen: Vienna University Press, 2019, pp. 9–41.

Rüdiger Lohlker, Jihadism Reconsidered: The Industrial Revolution of Terrorism, in Syed Munir Khasru (ed.), *The Digital Age, Cyber Space, and Social Media: The Challenges of Security & Radicalization*, Dhaka: IPAG, 2020, pp. 41–56.

Héni Nasaibia/Caleb Weiss, „The End of the Sahelian Anomaly: How the Global Conflict between the Islamic State and al-Qa'ida Finally Came to West Africa", in CTC Sentinel 13vii (July 2020), pp. 1–14.

Mona Kanwal Shaikh, *Guardians of God: Inside the Religious Mind of the Pakistani Taliban*, New Delhi: Oxford University Press, 2016.

Mona Kanwal Shaikh, „Worldview Analysis", in Mark Juergensmeyer/Manfred B. Steger/Saskia Sassen (eds.), *The Oxford Handbook of Global Studies*, Oxford: Oxford University Press, 2019, pp. 157–171.

Tom Smith/Kirsten E. Schulze, „Introduction: Examining the Global Linkages of Asian and North American Jihadis", in Tom Smith/Kirsten E. Schulze (eds.), *Exporting Global Jihad: Critical Perspectives from Asia and North America*, London: I. B. Tauris, 2020, pp.1–14.

William Montgomery Watt, *Islamic Political Thought*, Edinburgh: Edinburgh University Press, 1998.

31

JIHADISM IN THE WEST

A Post-Caliphate Transitory Phase

Lorenzo Vidino

Jihadism has a four-decade long history in the West. Its initial, largely negligible presence dates back to the early 1980s, when scattered groups of jihad-enthusiasts throughout Western Europe and North America answered the call of Abdullah Azzam and traveled to Afghanistan to fight alongside various factions against the Soviet Union.

That first ripple was followed, in the 1990s, by the establishment of a larger jihadist presence in the West. Europe and, to a lesser degree, North America became the home of individual militants fleeing persecution in their home countries in the Middle East, and organizations such as the Egyptian Gamaa Islamiya and the Algerian Armed Islamic Group (GIA) created sophisticated logistical networks throughout Europe.[1] During this first phase of jihadism in Europe, most jihadist organizations showed no violent intent toward their new host countries, which they viewed only as temporary and extremely convenient bases of operations. Even though it was apparent from their propaganda that they strongly disapproved of Europe's foreign policies, secular societies, and perceived anti-Muslim biases, jihadists focused their violent activities on their countries of origin. Notable exceptions were the United States, which suffered a large attack in 1993 (against the World Trade Center), and France, which was the subject of a wave of attacks in the mid-1990s. This phase of Western jihadism was also characterized by the mobilization for Bosnia, which involved a much larger number of Western volunteers than the previous one for Afghanistan.

The 9/11 attacks– tellingly led by a small group of Middle Eastern-born militants who had been radicalized and recruited in Hamburg, a clear indication of the growing importance of the European jihadist scene – triggered important changes in Western jihadism. Firstly, it led authorities to devote substantial attention to a phenomenon they had largely ignored in previous years. At the same time, the number of Western residents captured by jihadist ideology, while still remaining, to be sure, statistically insignificant in relation to the overall Muslim population, grew significantly. Signifying an important demographic shift in European jihadism, many of these new adepts were European born, second generation immigrants or converts.

The 2000s decade was characterized by a fairly steady pace of jihadist mobilization. The 2003 invasion of Iraq triggered the departure of a relatively large contingent of European foreign fighters. And Europe suffered several terrorist attacks. Revealing the heterogeneous nature, also from an operational point of view, of Europe's jihadist scene, some of the attacks were sophisticated operations directly connected to al-Qaeda (chiefly, the March 2004 Madrid bombings and the

DOI: 10.4324/9781003326373-36

July 2005 London bombings), while others were perpetrated by individuals who embraced jihadist ideology but had no operational connections with any established group.

By the late 2000s and the early 2010s, the jihadist threat in the West seemed to have plateaued. Militant actors and networks were still very much present, conducting a broad range of activities, including terrorist attacks. But the intensity of the phenomenon seemed to have somewhat degraded compared to the early 2000s, and authorities had a much better grasp on the phenomenon. All this changed, though, by mid-2012 as the initially peaceful protests against the Syrian regime of Bashar al Assad quickly morphed into a civil war.[2] As jihadist militias began to play an increasingly central role in the Syrian conflict and broadcast their exploits and appeals to join them through a variety of online platforms, Western jihadist scenes mobilized. According to official estimates, some five thousand European and a few hundred American residents traveled to Syria, the vast majority of which joined the Islamic State and, to a lesser degree, Jabhat al Nusra.[3]

The other manifestation of the wave of jihadism that swept the West in conjunction with the developments that took place in Syria and Iraq (growth of several jihadist groups, influx of fighters, conquest of territory and declaration of the Caliphate by IS) was the surge in terrorist activities and attacks in the West. Tellingly, whereas in 2012 Europol counted 122 arrests for jihadist activities and zero attacks throughout Europe, in 2015 the number of arrests reached a whopping 687 with 150 people killed in 17 different attacks.[4] In total, Europe suffered 86 terrorist attacks of jihadist inspiration from the June 2014 declaration of the Caliphate until September 2020.[5] The United States suffered 21 attacks in the same time frame.[6] Attacks ranged widely in sophistication, most of them being fairly improvised and amateurish.

This phase of Western jihadism appears to be over. The downfall of the Caliphate and the substantial weakening of IS brought dramatic changes to jihadism worldwide and, of course, also in the West. Western jihadists no longer have a magnetic destination to which to travel as they did when IS controlled territory in Syria and Iraq – the number of Westerners who have traveled to "new" areas such as parts of Africa, Afghanistan or Southeast Asia is comparatively negligible. And even though 2020 registered more attacks (19), than 2018 (11) and 2019 (8), attacks on Western soil are quantitatively and qualitatively down compared to the middle of the previous decade, when the IS-related mobilization was at its peak.

If the IS/Caliphate-dominated phase is over, what is next for Western jihadism? What will the characteristics and trends of jihadism in Europe and North America be in the near future? Predictions on such a complex topic, which is dependent on the interaction of some potentially foreseeable and some objectively unforeseeable factors are extremely difficult to make.[7]

Yet, if the past yields any lesson, it is that the West is always home to pockets of sympathy for jihadist ideology. Those pockets vary in composition and size: while some are relatively large and tied to established recruitment pipelines, others are more spontaneous, constituted by isolated individuals and small groups of friends who radicalize independently. They are also geographically unevenly distributed, some countries and regions experiencing a much larger presence than others. And the jihadist groups operating outside of the West and those they support vary, from cluster to cluster and from time to time.

In substance, irrespective of these differences, it is fair to say that a jihadist scene is a permanent fixture in Europe and North America. But the size and direction of this diverse scene has always been determined largely by events taking place outside of the West. It has always been events such as the war in Afghanistan in the 1980s, the Bosnian war in the 1990s, 9/11 and the subsequent invasion of Afghanistan and Iraq, and finally, the surge of IS and its June 2014 declaration of a Caliphate that determined spikes in the numbers of jihadist sympathizers in the West, the activism of Western-based jihadist networks and their mobilization choices.

The vicissitudes of Western jihadism are therefore shaped by the interactions of two macro variables. The first is internal, and it is constituted by the characteristics of the Western jihadist scene, which is of course different from Western country to Western country. Various elements shape it, from the presence of radicalizing agents to the socio-economic marginalization of the local Muslim community, from the effectiveness of local counter-terrorism efforts to migration policies. The second element, which, as said, plays a major role in determining size and direction of the Western jihadist scene, is constituted by geopolitical events taking place outside of Europe. Based on this analysis, the rest of the article will survey the current status of both variables – arguably the best approach to assess the current state of Western jihadism and its potential progression in the near future.

The Global Scenario

What happened in Syria and Iraq in the middle years of the previous decade is, from a jihadist point of view, unprecedented and difficult to replicate. Various jihadist groups were fighting, at least at the onset of the conflict, a brutal enemy (the regime of Bashar al Assad) that was killing civilians and whose actions were easily frameable in a jihadist perspective as a sectarian conflict. They operated in a territory that is extremely iconic – the historical heart of the Arab world – and easily accessible from a logistical point of view. They could rely on the fact that large social media platforms like Facebook and Twitter had just gained widespread global reach and were still largely unprepared to patrol their space for extremist content. Moreover, the largest of the jihadist groups to operate in this favorable environment, IS, made the historical step of declaring a caliphate, an announcement that triggered a massive emotional response in Islamist circles.

In substance, what took place in Syria and Iraq between 2012 and, let's say, 2017, the year in which the fall of Mosul epitomizes IS' downfall, was a jihadist perfect storm. It is impossible to predict what geopolitical events might occur in the near future exactly like few would have been able, in 2010, to predict that just two years later Syria would have become a global jihadist hotbed. But, surveying the current geopolitical landscape, no dynamic seems to even closely mirror what took place in Syria and Iraq during the last decade.

Firstly, both IS and al-Qaeda, the two brand names of global jihadism, are severely weakened.[8] Both have suffered crippling blows to their leadership and neither appears to have the stature, manpower, territorial control, and ability to operate on a global scale, as they had done in their heydays (which, to be sure, occurred at different times). That is not to say that either group is vanquished or that they cannot regain some of their strength. But recently, the almost universal assessment is that both groups are at some of their lowest points in their history.

Both groups control a broad array of affiliates operating throughout the world. These affiliates have mixed fortunes. Interestingly, in various areas that have historically played a major role in global jihadism, such as Syria/Iraq and North Africa, they appear to be in relative disarray or, anyways, unable to pose a major challenge to local regimes and incapable of attracting large numbers of foreign fighters. Arguably, the epicenter of global jihadism has currently shifted to sub-Saharan Africa, with IS affiliates wreaking havoc in Nigeria and the Lake Chad Basin, the Democratic Republic of Congo and Mozambique. Similarly, al-Qaeda affiliate al Shabaab, despite various setbacks, remains an important force in Somalia. According to US military intelligence, it has the "capability to conduct high-profile attacks across the region, actively targets US and regional forces, and exploits Somalia's political turmoil and security gaps."[9]

These regional affiliates do receive the support of the mother groups and jihadist sympathizers throughout the world, including in the West. But it is difficult to think that any of them would have the ability to mobilize external supporters, particularly in the West, to the same degree that IS did almost a decade ago. Logistical difficulties in reaching those territories and a significantly less intense emotional appeal of their causes are important factors that make the jihads of Congo and Nigeria substantially less appealing to Western jihadists. In substance, there is no doubt that Western jihadists will express their sympathy for, let's say, Boko Haram or the Islamic State in Central Africa. Some individuals will also attempt to travel to those areas to join local jihadist groups. But it is unlikely that those groups will be able to mobilize, both in terms of foreign fighters fluxes and attacks, anything even remotely comparable to what IS did.

As a consequence, at this point the Western jihadist scene appears to be in a phase of strategic confusion. Actors and networks that support jihadist ideology are still very much present in all Western countries, but they have not mobilized with the same intensity as in the previous years. Travel for fighting purposes, also because of Covid-19 related restrictions, is not a feasible option. And while attacks in the West are still happening, albeit on a smaller scale and in lower numbers than in the recent past, there is nothing resembling the constant call for carrying out attacks coming from well-known and charismatic leaders that characterized the previous decade. In substance, as of today, there is no jihadist group or geopolitical event capable of catalyzing and directing the enthusiasm of Western jihadists to a degree even remotely comparable to a few years back.

Western Dynamics

The IS-triggered mobilization of the last decade was, by any parameter one would use to assess it, the largest to have ever occurred in the West. It was also extremely significant when compared to that of other regions. Tellingly, European Muslims are, after a population calculation, approximately 16 times overrepresented among the foreign fighters in Syria and Iraq compared to figures for Muslims traveling from other regions of the world.[10]

So, what were the features and triggers of the last wave of mobilization in the West that could help us better predict trends in the near future? During the last decade scholars and policymakers have been spending substantial energies in trying to understand what drives a statistically insignificant, yet still disturbing number of European Muslims to embrace jihadist ideology. While countless theories have been formulated, it is fair to say that most agree that radicalization is a highly complex and individualized process, often shaped by a poorly understood interaction of structural and personal factors.

In particular, there is a growing consensus that socio-economic factors, while unquestionably important elements should be taken into consideration, are often not the key drivers of radicalization. As Thomas Hegghammer puts it, while there is no doubt that most European jihadists are economic underperformers, the question is "to what extent there is a causal link" between their marginalization and their radicalization and, if such link exists, "what the precise mechanisms are and how economic deprivation interacts with other factors."[11] They do not explain, for example, why in each Western country there have been high concentrations of radicalized individuals in certain areas and not in others with similar, if not worse, socio-economic conditions.

Moreover, countries that have experienced some of the highest per capita numbers of foreign fighters are central and northern European countries (such as Sweden, Austria and Denmark) that tend to fare significantly better, using any of the indicators commonly used to assess integration and socio-economic performance (unemployment, access to education, etc.), at integration than southern European countries. Paradoxically though, Spain, Italy and the southern European countries have seen significantly lower levels of radicalization than their central and northern European countries.

An observation of recent mobilization dynamics has instead pointed to the importance of networks, radicalizing agents and personal connections. A 2008 analysis by the European Commission's Expert Group on Violent Radicalization perfectly expressed this view by arguing that radicalization takes place "at the intersection of an enabling environment and a personal trajectory."[12] If the "personal trajectory" refers to the psychological processes that shape the decisions of the radicalized individual, the "enabling environment" refers to the places, whether in the physical or virtual world, where individuals are first introduced to a radical ideology and where they can subsequently develop and nurture their devotion to it.

The process is extremely complex, and each trajectory is different. But evidence from the recent IS-related mobilization clearly shows that personal connections are crucially important. Examining the recent mobilization of foreign fighters in Germany, for example, Sean Reynolds and Mohammed Hafez have found "only modest support for the integration deficit hypothesis." "Instead," they argue, "the preponderance of evidence suggests that interpersonal ties largely drive the German foreign fighter phenomenon. Recruitment featured clustered mobilization and bloc recruitment within interconnected radical milieus, leading us to conclude that peer-to-peer networks are the most important mobilization factor for German foreign fighters."[13]

Similar dynamics were visible throughout Europe. In Belgium, the vast majority of foreign fighters who traveled to Syria were associated with Sharia4Belgium and two additional Salafist milieus, the so-called Resto Tawhid network of Belgian convert Jean-Louis Denis and the Zerkani network.[14] This dynamic also explains the uneven distribution on Belgian territory of the origin of Belgian foreign fighters, who hailed disproportionally from the areas in which said networks were most active.

A similar dynamic took place in neighboring Netherlands, where small, informal activist Salafist groups like Sharia4Holland, Straatdawah and Behind Bars became active in the early 2010s.[15] As the AIVD assesses years later, "the movement was led by jihadists, and it attracted supporters of the jihad. But there were no signs of any intention to commit acts of violence, and for a long time departures to join the struggle elsewhere were rare. Only with the emergence of Syria as a theatre of jihad did attention finally shift from dawah to actual participation in the holy war." Dutch security services conclude that "this is indicative of how blurred the line between radicalism and jihadism has become. These movements have created an environment in which people with similar ideas meet and develop radical ideas into jihadist ideologies."[16]

An analysis of the dynamics that led the southern French city of Toulouse to become one of the country's main jihadist hubs constitutes another example of this phenomenon.[17] Salafists and Muslim Brotherhood-linked networks began attracting a following in some of the city's more disadvantaged neighborhoods since the mid-1990s, largely taking over mosques controlled by the Tabligh and Muslim Brotherhood-linked networks. They attracted many local youths, in particular among individuals with a criminal background (the *salafo-délinquants*, as some in France refer to those who embrace Salafism but still engage in the criminal activities they had been carrying out before their conversion).

While many did not, several of the local youths who fell under the spell of Salafism eventually went on to engage in violence. One of the first ones was Mohamed Merah, who carried out a string of attacks in the Toulouse area in 2012 before dying in a shootout with French police. A wave of Toulousian foreign fighters then followed once the Syrian conflict exploded.

Basing their analysis on Toulouse and several other cases in the country, various French scholars have made the argument that urban environments in which Salafists are particularly active often become radicalization hubs. Bernard Rougier speaks of "écosystèmes islamistes" for small areas of European cities in which Salafist influences are pervasive.[18] The majority of people who live in these "Islamist ecosystems" will not engage in violence. But it is arguable that they constitute the ideal environments for jihadist messages, whether conveyed in person by recruiters or simply spread online.

And indeed, the internet is one of the defining elements that characterized the latest Western mobilization. One is hard-pressed to find a single case of a Western jihadist of the last decade who was not at least a consumer of online propaganda. And an ever-growing number of them are also, thanks to social media and increasing accessibility of relevant technological tools, also producers and disseminators of their own, independent jihadist propaganda. Supporter-generated content in various European languages, in fact, has come to compensate the decreased volume of IS official propaganda.[19]

For many Western jihadists online propaganda is a reinforcer; it complements the messages and inputs they receive from leaders and peers in their radicalized circles in the physical space. In these cases, online and offline radicalization complement one another, both contributing to the individual's further radicalization and, at times, commitment to mobilization. For others who might not have contacts in the physical space, online propaganda is their only lifeline to jihadism. The cases of people who radicalized without any connection in the physical space but solely through online consumption of propaganda and interactions with like-minded individuals have grown exponentially over the last few years. In substance, while many Western jihadists do radicalize "the old way" through personal interactions supplemented by online activities, a growing number of them do so exclusively online.

The Current Environment

The current Western jihadist environment is extremely heterogeneous. Radicalized individuals include men and women; recent arrivals to the West and third generation Western Muslims and converts; well-integrated and highly educated individuals and those at the margins of society; individuals who belong to structured networks with solid connections to IS, al-Qaeda or other groups operating outside of the West and, as the 2020 Europol report argues, "individuals or small groups [that] are observed to self-radicalize, principally on the internet, without being part of wider networks."[20] Moreover, there are substantial differences in all these aspects from Western country to country, and, not rarely, from region to region within the same country.

This immense diversity makes making predictions for the future a challenge. But a good starting point is constituted by observing that we are still living with a very direct legacy of the phase of Western jihadism that has just come to a close. While in itself over, the IS-related mobilization that characterized the previous decade still shapes the current state of jihadism and understanding how so is a key to predicting what might come. In substance, as Thomas Renard pointedly observed, the jihadist threat in Europe (but the same analysis applies to a large extent to the United States, Canada and Australia) currently has "two main dimensions: one linked to the caliphate's legacy; and the other stemming from fringe extremists.[21]

As for the former, there is little doubt that the West will have to deal with a very large number of consequences that stemmed from the IS-triggered mobilization of the previous decade. This phenomenon manifests itself, and will likely do so for several years to come, in various ways. There are, first of all, many individuals who have connections to IS and other groups, and there is evidence that they are still planning attacks, often coordinating their actions with their contacts outside of the West. That is the case, for example, of the groups of Tajik nationals arrested by German authorities in April 2020 who were accused of planning attacks against various US and NATO targets in the country.[22] The men were reportedly coordinating their actions with IS handlers in Syria and Iraq.

There are then individuals that, while not possessing any formal ties to IS or other groups, are fully radicalized and perceive themselves as part of these organizations' global membership. Many of them are so-called "frustrated travelers," isolated individuals or groups of like-minded individuals who attempted to travel to Syria (or, to a lesser degree, other locales where jihadist groups are active) but could not do so because authorities intercepted them or because favorable conditions to travel no longer existed. That is the case, among the many examples, of the perpetrator of the November 2, 2020 terror attack in Vienna, who had served a short prison term after having unsuccessfully attempted to travel to Syria.[23]

As the Vienna case shows, another legacy of the recent wave is the large number of individuals who are currently detained. Numbers vary from country to country, but throughout the West the surge of terrorism investigations and convictions of the last few years inevitably led to an increase in the number of terrorism-linked inmates. The phenomenon has two potentially problematic consequences. The first is constituted by these individuals' potential radicalizing impact on the larger prison population. The second relates to the fact that in most Western countries individuals connected to terrorism-related matters, unless there was direct involvement in an attack, generally receive fairly short sentences, often of a few years. This leads to the scenario in which, as we have started to see and in the coming years will see with even greater frequency, individuals convicted as part of the IS-related mobilization are being set free. There is of course the strong possibility that some of these individuals might not have de-radicalized and could re-engage in terrorist activities. The phenomenon is relevant also in the United States, where authorities could not always apply the historically extremely severe sentences applied to terrorists to individuals convicted for IS-related activities.[24]

Finally, the last legacy of the mobilization is the presence of returnees, individuals who traveled to Syria and Iraq, joined IS or other jihadist groups, and have either come back to Europe or North America or have been attempting to do so. Their statuses run the gamut: from those who have returned legally and suffered no consequences to those who are in jail and those who served time and are now free; from those who are still radicalized to those who have fully rejected their militancy. Moreover, a substantial number of Western jihadists are still detained by various entities in Syria and Iraq, and virtually all Western countries have debated what to do with them, with solutions ranging from proactive efforts to repatriate them to stripping them of their citizenship. Unquestionably, management of returnees and aspiring returnees will be a major issue Western countries will have to deal with over the next few years.

If all these elements are direct legacies of the previous wave, Western countries are starting to see the emergence of new radicalization trajectories. A growing number of individuals authorities have started to monitor or perpetrators of attacks in recent months have radicalized in recent years, after the fall of the Caliphate. They do embrace jihadist ideology with zeal, but given the partial leadership vacuum that currently characterizes global jihadism, they do not recognize themselves as members of any specific group. They are therefore an even more scattered and unpredictable threat, whose dangerousness is balanced in most cases by a high degree of operational amateurism.[25]

The different elements of the IS-related mobilization's legacy and the new radicalization trajectories often come together to form the West's complex current jihadist environment. As said, it is difficult to know how this scene will evolve in terms of size and direction. At the current moment, no geopolitical or local event has the characteristics to sway anything beyond a few marginal segments of the Western jihadist scene. But as proven by the previous mobilization during the Syrian conflict, a spark can take place in the most unforeseen of ways.

Parts of the Western general public have somewhat forgotten the threat it poses, or at least relegated it to a low priority. This has also been due to a strong resurgence, particularly in the United States and a few other countries, of right-wing extremism. But within law enforcement and intelligence agencies the widespread consensus is that we are simply going through a transitory phase of the now long history of Western jihadism, and one that can evolve in many directions.

Notes

1 Daniel Benjamin and Steven Simon, *The Age of Sacred Terror* (New York, NY: Random House, 2002); Lorenzo Vidino, *Al-Qaeda in Europe: The New Battleground for International Jihad* (Amherst, NY: Prometheus Books, 2006).

2 Charles Lister, *The Syrian Jihad: Al-Qaeda, the Islamic State and the Evolution of an Insurgency* (Oxford, Oxford University Press, 2015).

3 Data according to EU Counter-Terrorism Coordinator Gilles de Kerchove, in Raffaello Pantucci, "A View From the CT Foxhole: Gilles de Kerchove, European Union (EU) Counter-Terrorism Coordinator," *CTC Sentinel*, August 2020, Volume 13, Issue 8; for the United States, see Alexander Meleagrou-Hitchens, Seamus Hughes and Bennett Clifford, *The Travelers: American Jihadists in Syria and Iraq*, GWU Program on Extremism, February 2018.

4 Europol: *"TE-SAT 2012: EU Terrorism Situation and Trend Report"* (The Hague, Netherlands, 2012). Europol: *"TE-SAT 2016: EU Terrorism Situation and Trend Report."* (The Hague, Netherlands, 2016).

5 Database kept and regularly updated by the author and Francesco Marone. Numbers updated to November 2017 and methodology are available in Lorenzo Vidino, Francesco Marone and Eva Entenmann, *Fear Thy Neighbor: Radicalization and Jihadist Attacks in the West*, joint report by GWU's Program on Extremism, ISPI and ICCT The Hague, June 14, 2017. The number 86 is calculated as of May 2021.

6 Ibid.
7 The caveats listed by Thomas Hegghammer in a 2016 piece seeking to make predictions on the future of jihadis in Europe are [perfectly logical and applicable to this piece. See Thomas Hegghammer, "The Future of Jihadism in Europe: A Pessimistic View," *Perspectives on Terrorism*, Volume 10, Issue 6, 2016.
8 Statement by Scott Berrier, Lieutenant General, U.S. Army Director, Defense Intelligence Agency, before the US Senate Armed Forces Committee, April 2021.
9 Ibid.
10 Fernando Reinares, "Jihadist Mobilization, Undemocratic Salafism, and Terrorist Threat in the European Union." Georgetown Security Studies Review, 2017.
11 Thomas Hegghammer, *Revisiting the poverty-terrorism link in European jihadism*, lecture before the Society for Terrorism Research annual conference, Leiden, November 8, 2016.
12 *Radicalisation Processes Leading to Acts of Terrorism*, report prepared by the European Commission's Expert Group on Violent Radicalisation, May 15, 2008.
13 Reynolds, Sean C., and Mohammed M. Hafez, "Social Network Analysis of German Foreign Fighters in Syria and Iraq," *Terrorism and Political Violence 31 (4)*, pp. 1–26, 2017.
14 Van Ostaeyen, Pieter, "Belgian Radical Networks and the Road to the Brussels Attacks." *CTC Sentinel*, Volume 9, Issue 6, 2016, pp. 7–12.
15 *The Transformation of Jihadism in the Netherlands: Swarm Dynamics and New Strength*, AIVD, September 2014; Ineke Roex, "The rise of public dawa networks in the Netherlands: Behind Bars, Sharia4Holland, and Straatdawah," in Lorenzo Vidino, *Sharia4: Straddling political activism and jihad in the West*, al Mesbar Studies and Research Centre, Dubai, 2015.
16 *The Transformation of Jihad in the Netherlands: Swarm Dynamics and New Strength*, AIVD, 2014. Available at: https://english.aivd.nl/publications/publications/2014/10/01/the-transformation-of-jihadism-in-the-netherlands, p. 13.
17 Hugo Micheron, "Toulouse: la machine de prédication ou la fabrication sociale du jihadisme," in Bernard Rougier, *Les territoires conquis de l'islamisme* (PUF, 2020). pp. 225–251.
18 Bernard Rougier, *Les territoires conquis de l'islamisme* (PUF, 2020).
19 Europol TE-SAT, 2020, p. 33.
20 Ibid.

21 Thomas Renard, "The Caliphate's Legacy and Fringe Extremists," *ICCT*, January 18, 2021.
22 Nodirnek Soliev, "The April 2020 Islamic State Terror Plot Against U.S. and NATO Military Bases in Germany: The Tajik Connection," *CTC Sentinel*, Volume 14, Issue 1, January 2021.
23 https://www.bmi.gv.at/downloads/Endbericht.pdf
24 Lorenzo Vidino and Seamus Hughes, "America's Terrorism Problem Doesn't End with Prison—It Might Just Begin There," *Lawfare*, June 17, 2018.
25 Thomas Renard, "The Caliphate's Legacy and Fringe Extremists," *ICCT*, January 18, 2021.

32

BECOMING A JIHADIST

A Psychoanalytical Perspective

Jean-Luc Vannier

Perhaps we would say more correctly: the act happened through him[1]

(Theodor Reik, 1925)

In this chapter, we will try to recall the necessary consideration of the psychic and unconscious dimension of the jihadist terrorist and will study the resistance to take into account this specific approach. We will have a look at the difficulties French institutions have in correctly apprehending jihadism. Using several clinical examples, including those of our own cases, we will show how adolescents become the preferred target of jihadist recruiters mainly through the Internet. Finally, we will question the effective de-radicalization of detainees or persons on probation if the process remains at the surface and within behavioral psychology. The conclusion will open up further possible discussion on the need for recognition of the terrorist through video, the question of the meaning of mourning for the victims' relatives and that of the terrorist's criminal responsibility.

The kamikaze action has to do with psychiatry. Terrorism is a very complicated disease: among those we are looking for and tracking, some have religious motivations. But others have mostly psychiatric problems.

Loic Garnier

Some individuals, who may be sensitive and have psychological disorders at some point in their lives, are undoubtedly more susceptible to this kind of thesis and we would be irresponsible not to tackle this problem. Our idea is that we could have a better sharing of information with psychiatry.

Laurent Nunez

The first statement by Loic Garnier[2], head of the Anti-Terrorist Coordination Unit (Uclat) from 2009 to 2018, has received very little interest; probably even a strong resistance. Laurent Nunez[3], the French National Coordinator of Intelligence, is the author of the second declaration which followed, in April 2021, the Minister of the Interior's presentation of Bill No. 4104 to the Parliament, relating to the prevention of acts of terrorism and to intelligence.

DOI: 10.4324/9781003326373-37

Its article 6 wants "to extend the possibility of communication of information related to the admission of a person in psychiatric care, today limited to the only representative of the State in the department of the place of hospitalization, to the one in charge of the follow-up of this person, when they represent a further serious threat for the security and the public order because of their radicalization with terrorist characteristics. As a result, a loss of information for the administrative authority, departmental or national, in charge of monitoring the radicalization of the person concerned."[4]

It took five years for the French authorities to realize the need to include the psychic dimension to assess properly – not exclusively of course – jihadist terrorism.

The Psychic Dimension of Jihadist Terrorism

What matters as a psychoanalyst[5] are the joint articulations between psychic processes and individual pathways and how future terrorists find an unconscious means of shoring up and containing their impulsive chaos on the path of radicalization and in that of the accomplishment of the jihadist act.

Allow us to list all kinds of mechanisms between psychic processes and the progression toward jihadism:

- The weakening of the Ego as a result of a depreciation induced by the Ego Ideal with which the hero replaces the father, the first Ego Ideal,[6]
- The setting up of obsessive defensive mechanisms,
- The external search for a structured and salutary support,
- The resurgence of destructive drives.

According to the EU-Counter-Terrorism Coordinator Gilles de Kerchove,

"the perpetrators of the Brussels and Paris attacks, Salah Abdeslam or Abdelhamid Abaoud, were guys who spent time in bars, drank beer, smoked hashish. They did not know anything of religion. They were petty criminals. They were violent, had access to weapons and during their radicalization the excessive interpretation of radical Islam gave them a black-and-white justification to use violence."[7]

The candidate for jihad acts in such a manner because of his erratic psychic deconstruction that entirely escapes his control. Sporadic destruction is an essential condition for maintaining a psychological balance between feelings of well-being and contact with reality: "The criminal defends himself against a painful unconscious conflict by acting outside of this conflict, often by a heroic identification."[8] The jihadist offer allows the individual to find in radical Islam, including the extreme commitments leading to death, a means to weld the sexual drive of death defined as "the auto-aggressive or hetero-aggressive tendency that aims to destroy all life, disorganize everything together, either at the social level or at the level of the existence of the individual being."[9] From self-punishment, the subject moves on to self-destruction.

Many elements of such a radicalization – the sudden diehard devotion, the total destructiveness of the terrorist himself and that of his targets, the claim of paternity that provides necessary recognition in the aftermath – bring to light the archaic work of the drive. We have known for a long time "the pacifying function for the psychotic of a life regulated by severe constraints, such as those proposed by religious or military communities."[10]

To summarize this first part:

The future terrorist experiences more of a disintegration than a psychic conflict that would still serve him, even partially, as structure and support.

The absence of a solution to his psychic problems leads him to a kind of resolutory resignation which is not completely far from the register of submission, an enjoyment to be the object of the omnipotence of the other as a tutelary and charismatic figure on the model of the asymmetrical adult-child relation. This has to be put in connection with the fascinating attraction exerted on the human being by the submission[11]: "the states in which the subject falls are passive states... One does not reach it by making effort; on the contrary the essential is to abandon oneself in an almost passive way to the action of grace."[12]

The future terrorist connects to radicalism more by derivation, that is to say, rather by peripheral linking than by active research of adhesion.

The Resistance to Take into Account the Psychic Dimension and the Difficulties of the French Institutions in Properly Apprehending Jihadism

Let us recall a number of facts we learned over the course of investigations and press leaks. One of the Bataclan terrorists frequently used drugs while another was suffering from mental illness. In Valence, the judicial authority had difficulties in assessing the aggressor, who wanted to "knock over but not kill" the soldiers with his car. On the one hand, there were "questions about his mental health" and "inexplicable motivations." On the other hand, there were "images of jihadist propaganda but nothing about belonging to any network." As for the attack on the Goutte-d'Or district police station in Paris, the investigation mentioned the same aporia: "A fake explosive belt, the cries, the allegiance, these are signs that can be connected to a terrorist network, but at the same time they can be signs of mental imbalance." It appears that the terrorist from Nice 2016 worked as an escort, which confirms Freud's views of the psyche mixing desire and prohibition.[13]

The young German-Iranian fanatic, who committed the Munich bloodshed in July 2016, was suffering from psychiatric disorders. He was able, however, to prepare his murderous madness for an entire year. "A true preparation of the act does not prevent us from noting the binding nature of the drive coming from the unconscious."[14]

The Christmas market terrorist in Berlin in December 2016 escaped the attention of German counterintelligence because he was also a drug user and a dealer. The German authorities explained that, notwithstanding the fact that they had placed him under surveillance, his regular consumption of psychoactive substances appeared to be a factor capable of ruling him out as a potential terrorist: "the subject does not really premeditate his act but there is often an anxious forecast with struggle and doping."[15]

More recently in France, the investigation into the murder of the teacher Samuel Paty revealed that the murderer "was allegedly radicalized by playing *call of duty* online after being contacted by a recruiter...had the annoying habit of breaking windows...and his dream was to become a professional MMA fighter."[16] After his attack on the Basilica of Notre Dame in Nice in the same month, the Tunisian Brahim Aouissaoui invoked memory loss, which can be totally feigned or the result of a splitting of the Ego.[17] Concerning the assassination of a police officer,[18] the Prosecutor noted about the perpetrator, a Tunisian national, "a not very contestable radicalization...but the presence of certain personality disorders."

Distinguishing terrorist acts from mental imbalance is a denial of the fact that the "conflict lies at the heart of instinctual life."[19] We can easily perceive the resistance to comprehend the mysterious trajectory of the path to terrorism: an enigmatic genesis, almost indecipherable, and a culmination in the polar opposite, marked by a two-fold seal of reality and horror. This coexistence inside a sole human being of "both a fanaticism which verges on dementia and of a calculating sagacity which leaves nothing to chance"[20] highlights the difficulty to assess the psyche of jihadists and the illusory search for a "typical profile."

One of the most blatant examples of this resistance comes, surprisingly, from a terrorism specialist, Stefan Goertz[21], who writes that "Islamic terrorists do not suffer from pathological narcissism, paranoia, or authoritarian personality disorders, but are surprisingly normal in terms of mental health." He assessed further "that the mentally ill certainly cannot plan elaborate covert terrorist attacks."[22]

There is, on the contrary, a cold psychosis without decompensation or delusions. Even delirium is compatible with the exercise of the highest level of consciousness and "the most banal clinic allows us to observe that a delusional subject can exercise all kinds of professional activities"[23]. In any psychosis, even the deepest one, one can find the existence of two psychic attitudes: "one, which takes into account reality, the normal attitude, the other which under the influence of the drives, detaches the self from reality."[24] And one of the characteristics of this process is not to lead to the formation of a compromise between the two attitudes in presence – a detectable symptom – but "to maintain them simultaneously without establishing a dialectical relation between them."[25]

The psychic dimension includes sexuality. In a fascinating study, Peter Langman[26] provides a qualitative analysis of ten perpetrators of mass violence where he discusses the killers "in terms of body-related issues" and their acts as a way "to overcome their perceived inadequacy, framed as damaged masculinity."

Anxiety is irremediably linked to the emergence of sexual problems – infantile or pre-oedipian – repressed by the perpetrators;[27] an assertion still valid fifty years later.[28] It often happens that psychotic or schizophrenic patients have hallucinations or delusions characterized by sexuality[29].

This may be better understood by the following two examples. During a private exchange, a former German intelligence officer told me that after September 11, 2001, his superiors instructed him to follow the presumed Islamists, as he had previously been investigating revolutionary groups such as the RAF. He acknowledged, but only in the light of our discussions on the importance of the sexual factor, that each of the telephone conversations between jihadists or radicalized people brought up sexual problems that made the investigators smile but to which they did not give any kind of importance in the evaluation of the people tapped.

In the same vein, a study by psychoanalyst Ruth Stein mentions the following fact:

"One afternoon in Trafalgar Square, London, in November 2000, I heard a young British convert to Islam speak at a large demonstration of mujahideen. As I expected, the man's argument for converting to Islam and joining the mujahideen had to do with sexuality. He blasted the rottenness of Western society, which is 'poisoned by homosexuality, adultery, fornication, sexual licentiousness.' He shouted with rage and fear that sexual sin must end because it was destroying the world. The new light he saw, 'the Truth he had found in Islam', he said, helped him find a cure for the sexual diseases of British society. His discourse, centered on sexuality, was anti-sexual, anti-heterosexual, and patently anti-homosexual."[30]

By the way, some of the Bataclan terrorists wore genitalia protection guards.[31]

Teenagers Are the Preferred Target of Jihadist Recruiters

In a conference held in Nice a few months before the July 2016 massacre, a specialist from the General Directorate for Internal Security described the process of Islamist radicalization in three stages: seduction, deconstruction, reconstruction. Seduction is a key concept in psychoanalysis. The budding jihadist, especially if he is a teenager who is at this age often looking for new and glorious identifications, could be "seduced" by the recruiter. This seduction is marked by the asymmetry between the protagonists and recalls infancy. All this serves the aim of "stimulating identifications through guilt" and these identification processes are therefore even more funda- mental[32] as they are likely to "enhance criminal behaviour."[33]

Aimed towards the recruitment of young people, videos on the internet intelligently collate supposedly intangible, universal and even supernatural values in order to plunge the teenager into the infantile belief of his almighty power. These propaganda films include the required vis- ual effects: the projective identification with the hero obviously chosen for his friendly face, guilt based on the argument that others have given their lives for the jihadist cause, the exploitation of the feminine psychic side with the maternal softness of the afterlife's hazy limbo of paradise, the highlighting of the masculine and the virility galvanized by the song of war in the background music, and finally this glorious journey that awaits the martyr.

This manipulation by the jihadist recruiters also satisfies the three primary needs of adolescents:

- To distinguish oneself from adults,
- To win over the control of one's body, the physical pubertal reality being experienced as "alien,"
- To become one with the peer group by seeking new heroic identifications and group memberships.

The destructiveness of the teenager is an active attempt to restore a form of psychic homeosta- sis before collapsing, disappearing, and leaving this childhood behind; a Pomethean act of life.[34] Such acts are essential and match the triple quest of the teenager:

1. To free oneself from the felt psychic suffering by diverting this suffering toward self-inflicted physical pain,
2. To feel strong sensations and to feel alive, even at the risk of dying,
3. To signal oneself with insistence near adults in the secret expectation of being contained by them. Every delinquent act is a "signal that calls for a response from the environment."[35]

In our opinion, the act accomplished by the terrorist, jihadist or otherwise, focuses on a "need for punishment," a claim that something should happen for real: an act to allow the criminal to give substance to his unconscious feeling of guilt and to "escape his anxiety and unconscious fantasies."[36]

This notion of act remains nevertheless a major unthought in our culture[37]. The rational, meticulous, material preparation of the project would correspond to the "action." On the other hand, the act would correspond to the unconscious dimension of what is sought by the subject: the impulse stop. And this for at least two reasons: Firstly, a specific characteristic of the act lies in its potential capacity to introduce unpredictable adventure to any situation. Secondly, its po- tential power to transcend the subject beyond what his project consisted of. An increase in the "feeling of unconscious guilt can make a human become a criminal who finds the relief of being able to connect this feeling of unconscious guilt to something real and current."[38] Let us illustrate this feeling of guilt which "exists before the act and which is therefore not the consequence but the motive": During a session, a young Muslim said: "I would like to leave a historical trace in my family...I want them to remember me as someone who has always fought for success." Do we not detect the morbidity of a guilty subject, a melancholic indictment of self due to the debt vis-à-vis "a poor father born in the Moroccan Atlas" that would only be corrected by a great feat: social success…or death?

This feeling of guilt, basically an anxiety due to the aggression of our own impulses[39], can only be controlled with a system of symbolic representations: "expiation, reparation and forgiveness."[40] Two of our clinical cases will illustrate the encounter of the suffering adolescent with jihadist recruitment on the Internet.

The first case: The first one is a 14-year-old girl whose parents are both highly educated and even have some important academic responsibilities. In their first telephone contact with me, they were worried about an unusual speech held by their daughter about Islam, religion of peace and love.[41] This does not worry atheist and tolerant parents. More embarrassing for them is a tendency for the daughter to also avoid family gatherings, dinners and Sunday outings. The girl agrees to come to the session.

Her story is quite "simple": A first disappointed great love – to be interpreted as the first sexual experience – with humiliating consequences within her group of friends and the feeling of an immense psychic suffering. The young girl tries to overcome it by some scarifications whose physical pain failed to exceed the intensity of her moral pain. After having heard about the sites of jihadist recruitment, she tries to find them on the Web and, so she believes, to thwart her possible surveillance by the French services. An excitement – the forbidden combined with risk-taking – which finally allows her to forget the very painful experience of her love mourning.

These mechanisms of connection between her suffering and these prohibited investigations were the topic of her analysis. Then, abandoning these sites, she tried "an acting out" by applying for a job as an "au pair" in a far-away country in Central America. She is barely 15 years old, with a frail body and fragile appearance. Despite her unconscious morbidity, she cannot ignore that she could become a prey for predators on this distant horizon; It was a project on which I have, on a quite exceptional occasion of my intervention, put an absolute veto. Surprisingly, but not for the one who knows the faculties of displacement in the psyche, this young girl is today pursuing very brilliant studies of law and criminology.

The second case: It is after more than two years on the couch that this young woman of 19 years told of her voyage toward radical Islamism, since then abandoned.

Sexually touched at 7 years old, raped at 13, this young woman slowly became aware of a perverted and highly sexualized relationship with her father from her youngest age. A perverted relationship that triggered a precocious sexuality, a need to seduce, as she herself had been seduced. After many months, she recognized that her rape could have been avoided. Unfortunately, she had gotten an ambivalent reaction from her father following her rape: "There is no smoke without fire."

Some time later, she discovered a jihadist recruitment video on the Internet. She completely changed her clothes to cover her hair, adopted all the food practices and fundamentalist rituals of Islam, and refused to shake hands with boys/men. Her parents paid little attention to these changes during these two years, blaming them on teenage rebellion. She gradually gave up this radical form of Islam, finding the recommendations too "heavy" and "constraining" after all. Let us add that her entering into psychoanalysis coincided with a questioning of her concubinage for several years with a young Muslim whose verbal violence, just at the wrong time, replicated exactly the scenario of the perverse relationship that she had with her father.

In these two cases, one can see the anxiety as a form of desire of realization and compensatory satisfaction in the sense of a punishment. "Feeling guilty gives the right to punishment and therefore the right to the fear of punishment."[42]

On Effective De-Radicalization of Detainees or Persons on Probation

We have issued *ab initio* reservations on de-radicalization attempts, taken up in various places: They seem to fail if they do not go back to the deeper motives that led the person to be receptive, apparently in search of salvation, to the "jihadist reconstruction." Hence our doubts about attempts at "de-radicalization" based on a purely cognitive approach which strives to affect the conscious Ego of those concerned[43]. How can one explain then that the capacities of reason given to this Ego were unable to hinder pre-emptively the individual in his deadly approach? These attempts, based on deconstructing the religious language, consist of putting the radicalized in the presence of a Quran specialist who demonstrates to him that his interpretation is erroneous. A personal acquaintance who, out of social commitment, gives mathematics courses to inmates in a French prison as part of a rehabilitation program, explained to us that he had to ask for the exclusion of the radicalized inmates who followed his teachings, as they systematically contested the content of the course, claiming that it is not the "right book to read."

There is a reversal of values when we move from self-preservation to the sexual drive as "uilitarianism does not take the instinctual element of the delinquent into account"[44]. We will therefore endorse this conclusion of the English psychologist Christopher Dean, stating that "it can never be certain that attackers have been cured."[45]

Conclusion

We must question the meaning of the scoptophilic perspective when a jihadist takes selfies at his future crime scenes: Is it an issue of identity "containment"?[46] Is the recording of a video of allegiance evidence that the writing[47] now suffers from a deficit of reliability?

Attitudes after the attacks indicate the emergence of a mechanism of collective expiation to endorse a part of the other's crimes. One of our patients, Niçoise by birth, explained to us that "I could not accept what happened. For a week, it was as if these events had happened far away from me. I did not lose any of my relatives, nor any of my friends, but it sent me too violently back to my inner chaos." In the same perspective, we see the bereaved relatives of a victim awaiting a trial so that the murderer can reveal the motives of his act. But how could this criminal furnish them with a revelatory meaning of which he himself is ignorant?

If there were to be a cure, it should be, said Jacques Lacan, "only an integration by the subject of his true responsibility," even suggesting that it is sometimes "more human, with the punishment, to allow the subject himself to find this responsibility."[48]

Concluding, let us quote Hegel: "By considering that the sentence contains his right, we honor the criminal as a rational being…Punishment is the right of the criminal."[49]

Notes

1 Theodor Reik, « Geständniszwang und Strafbedürfnis", *Probleme der Psychoanalyse und der Kriminologie»* Suhrkamp Taschenbuch 167, Frankfurt am Main, 1974, S.126.

2 L'Obs. 6 January 2016, https://www.nouvelobs.com/societe/20160106.OBS2347/terrorisme-l-action-kamikaze-releve-de-la-psychiatrie.html.

3 Le Figaro, 26 April 2021, https://www.lefigaro.fr/flash-actu/antiterrorisme-nunez-prone-un-meilleur-partage-d-informations-avec-la-psychiatrie-20210426.

4 Projet de loi n° 4104 relatif à la prévention d'actes de terrorisme et au renseignement, Assemblée nationale, 28 April 2021, https://www.assemblee-nationale.fr/dyn/15/textes/l15b4104_projet-loi.

5 This text extends previous reflections: Jean-Luc Vannier, « Réflexions psychanalytiques sur le terrorisme djihadiste, de l'autopunition à l'autodestruction », *Radicalisation et Radicalité, Une Voie de la destructivité*, Psychiatrie Française, Vol. XXXXVIII, 2/17, pp. 91–110.

6 Sigmund Freud, « Psychologie des masses et analyse du moi », *Œuvres complètes, XVI, 1921–1923*, Presses Universitaires de France, 2003, p. 75.

7 Gilles de Kerkove, L'Orient Le Jour, 3 mars 2017, https://www.lorientlejour.com/article/1038398/-le-liban-travaille-avec-des-legislations-des-annees-60-du-siecle-dernier-.html.

8 Daniel Lagache, « Le psychologue et le criminel », *Œuvres II, 1947–1952*, Presses Universitaires de France, Coll. « Bibliothèque de psychanalyse », 1979, p. 188.

9 Jean Laplanche, *Le primat de l'autre en psychanalyse*, Champs Flammarion, 1997, p. 66.

10 Jean-Claude Maleval, *Logique du délire*, Presses Universitaires de Rennes, Coll. « Clinique Psychanalytique et Psychopathologique, Nouvelle édition revue et augmentée, 2011, p. 176.

11 « One gives oneself, so to speak, voluptuously in sacrifice » according to Sandor Ferenczi, « Réflexions sur le plaisir de la passivité », in *Réflexions sur le masochisme*, Petite Bibliothèque Payot, n° 871, 2012, p. 94.

12 Eugène-Bernard Leroy, *Nature des hallucinations*, Revue philosophique de la France et de l'étranger, tome LXIII, Paris, 1907, p. 609.

13 Sigmund Freud, Manuscrit K, *Lettres à Wilhelm Fliess, 1887–1904*, Presses Universitaires de France, 2007, pp. 210–211.

14 Claude Balier, *Psychanalyse des comportements sexuels violents*, Presses Universitaires de France, Coll. « Le fil rouge », 2008, p. 29.

15 Serge Lebovici, Pierre Mâle, Francis Pasche, *Psychanalyse et criminologie, Rapport Clinique*, Revue Française de Psychanalyse, Tome XV, n°1, janvier - mars 1951, p. 53.

16 About the psychic dimension of the MMA's: J.-L. Vannier, *Les Mixed Martial Arts sont-ils solubles dans la pulsion sexuelle de mort ?* Le Carnet Psy, 2014/3, n°79, pp. 30–38.

17 Sigmund Freud, « Le clivage du moi dans le processus de défense », *Œuvres complètes, XX, 1937–1939*, Presses Universitaires de France, 2014, p. 221.

18 April 2021 in Rambouillet.

19 Etienne de Greff, *Les instincts de défense et de sympathie*, Presses Universitaires de France, 1947, p. 9.

20 Philippe de Felice, *Foules en délire, Extases collectives, Essai sur quelques formes inférieures de la mystique*, Albin Michel, 1947, p. 358.

21 Jean-Luc Vannier, « A propos de *Islamistischer Terrorismus*, une lecture analytique », *Droit de l'enfant et psychiatrie*, Psychiatrie Française, Vol. L 4/19, Juillet 2020, pp. 94–99.

22 Stefan Goertz, *Islamistischer Terrorismus, Analyse – Definitionen – Taktik*, Kriminalistik, 2019, p. 35.

23 Jean-Claude Maleval, *Logique du délire, op. cit.*, p. 20, 21.

24 Sigmund Freud, « Abrégé de psychanalyse », *Œuvres complètes, XX, 1937–1939*, Presses Universitaires de France, 2014, p. 300.

25 Jean Laplanche et J.-B. Pontalis, *Vocabulaire de la psychanalyse*, Presses Universitaires de France, Coll. « Quadrige », 2014, p. 70.

26 Peter Langman, « Desperate identities: A bio-psycho-social analysis of perpetrators of mass violence », *Criminol Public Policy*, 19 (1); 1–24.

27 Angelo Hesnard and Rene Laforgue, *Les processus d'Autopunition en Psychologie des névroses et des Psychoses, en Psychologie criminelle et en Psychopathologie*, Rapport présenté à la Vème Réunion des Psychanalyses de langue française, Revue Française de Psychanalyse, t. IV, n°1, 1930–1931., p. 73.

28 Henri Grivois, *Urgence folie*, Synthélabo, Paris, 1993, p. 16.

29 Jean-Luc Vannier, « A propos du satanisme et de la sorcière », in *Malaise dans la culture libérale*, Le Coq Héron, 183/2005, Erès, p. 123.

30 Ruth Stein, *Le mal comme amour et libération: l'état d'esprit d'un terroriste religieux kamikaze*, Revue Française de Psychanalyse, 2002/3 Vol. 66, pp. 897–921, note p. 905.

31 According to an official of the Paris Fire Brigade.

32 Sigmund Freud, « Psychologie des masses et analyse du moi », *Œuvres complètes, XVI, 1921–1923*, Presses Universitaires de France, 2003, p. 45. The early Jacques Lacan considers it « as the most fundamental psychic phenomenon that psychoanalysis has discovered: identification, whose formative power is even proven by biology », Jacques Lacan et Michel Cenac, *Introduction théorique aux fonctions de la psychanalyse en criminologie*, Revue Française de Psychanalyse, 1951, *op. cit.*, p. 21.

33 Daniel Lagache, *Psychanalyse et criminologie*, Rapport clinique, Revue Française de Psychanalyse, tome XV, n°1, janvier-mars 1951, p. 111.

34 Philippe Jeammet, *Le temps, c'est la vie*, Filigrane, Vol. 22, n°2, automne 2013, p. 29.

35 D. W. Winnicott, *Conversations ordinaires*, Folio essais n°438, 2004, pp. 130–144. It would be of great interest to rediscover and re-study D.W. Winnicott's reflections on what he calls « antisocial », particularly with regard to the current phenomenon of gangs and their violence.
36 Gérard Mendel, *L'acte est une aventure, du sujet métaphysique au sujet de l'actepouvoir*, La Découverte, 1998, p. 397.
37 Metaphysics was built in the West on the intellectual devaluation of the act and a temptation to reduce the act to the corporeal.
38 Sigmund Freud, « Le moi et le ça », *Œuvres complètes, XVI, 1921–1923*, Presses Universitaires de France, 2003, p. 295.
39 « Every thought of crime is the crime itself » for the unconscious feeling of guilt. Jean Laplanche, *La révolution copernicienne inachevée*, Presses Universitaires de France, Coll. « Quadrige », 2008, p. 170.
40 Guy Rosolato, *Le sacrifice, Repères psychanalytiques*, Presses Universitaires de France, Coll. « Quadrige », 2002, p. 65.
41 The « weak signals » (note author).
42 René Laforgue, *De l'Angoisse à l'Orgasme*, Revue Française de Psychanalyse, 1930, Vol. 4, n° 2, p. 249.
43 It is useless to tell an anorexic that she is dangerously too thin when she is genuinely convinced that she is overweight: Jean-Luc Vannier, « Le pouce paternel, *Nahrungseinfuhr* d'une adolescente anorexique », *Autisme et psychoses infantiles*, Revue Psychiatrie Française, vol. XXXXV, 4/14, Septembre 2015, pp. 74–81.
44 Jean Laplanche, « Réparation et rétributions pénales », *La révolution copernicienne inachevée, 1967–1992*, Presses Universitaires de France, Coll. « Quadrige », 2008, p. 176.
45 Christopher Dean is the head of the Health Identity Intervention (HII), Interview with the BBC 2 January 2020, https://www.bbc.com/news/uk-50967100.
46 Serge Tisseron, *Psychanalyse de l'image*, Pluriel, 2010, pp. 255–258.
47 Jean-Luc Vannier, *Réflexions psychanalytiques sur quelques évolutions de la langue française*, Le Carnet Psy, 2020, https://www.carnetpsy.com/.
48 Jacques Lacan, *Introduction théorique aux fonctions de la psychanalyse en criminologie*, Revue Française de Psychanalyse, tome XV, n°1, janvier-mars 1951, p. 84.
49 G. W. F. Hegel, *Principes de la philosophie du droit*, Gallimard, 1940, pp. 97, 99, 100.

References

Claude Balier (2008), *Psychanalyse des comportements sexuels violents*, Presses Universitaires de France, Coll. « Le fil rouge ».
Philippe de Félice (1947), *Foules en délire, Extases Collectives*, Albin Michel.
Sandor Ferenczi (1930), « Réflexions sur le plaisir de la passivité », *Réflexions sur le Masochisme*, Petite Bibliothèque Payot.
Sigmund Freud (1896), *Lettres à Wilhelm Fliess, 1887–1904*, Presses Universitaires de France.
Sigmund Freud (1921), « Psychologie des masses et analyse du moi », *Œuvres complètes, XVI, 1921–1923*, Presses Universitaires de France.
Sigmund Freud (1923), « Le moi et le ça », *Œuvres complètes, XVI, 1921–1923*, Presses Universitaires de France.
Sigmund Freud (1938), « Le clivage du moi dans le processus de défense », *Œuvres complètes, XX, 1937–1939*, Presses Universitaires de France.
Sigmund Freud (1939), « Abrégé de psychanalyse », *Œuvres complètes, XX, 1937–1939*, Presses Universitaires de France.
Georg Wilhelm Friedrich Hegel (1821), *Principes de la philosophie du droit*, Gallimard.
Stefan Goertz (2019), *Islamistischer Terrorismus, Analyse – Definitionen – Taktik*, Kriminalistik.
Etienne de Greeff (1947), *Les instincts de défense et de sympathie*, Presses Universitaires de France.
Henri Grivois (1993), *Urgence folie*, Synthélabo, Paris.
Alain Hesnard; **René Laforgue** (1931), *Les Processus d'Autopunition en Psychologie des Névroses et des Psychoses, en Psychologie criminelle et en Pathologie générale*, Rapport présenté à la Vème Réunion des Psychanalystes de langue française, Revue Française de Psychanalyse, Tome IV, n°1.
Philippe Jeammet (2013), *Le temps, c'est la vie*, Filigrane, vol. 22, n°2.
Jacques Lacan (1951), Discussion des rapports théorique et clinique sur « Psychanalyse et criminologie », Revue Française de Psychanalyse, Tome XV, n°1.

Jacques Lacan; **Michel Cénac** (1951), *Introduction théorique aux fonctions de la psychanalyse en criminologie*, Revue Française de Psychanalyse, Tome XV, n°1.

René Laforgue (1930), *De l'Angoisse à l'Orgasme*, Revue Française de Psychanalyse, vol. 4, n° 2.

Daniel Lagache (1950), « Psychocriminogénèse », in « Le psychologue et le criminel », *Œuvres II, 1947–1952*, PUF, Coll. « Bibliothèque de psychanalyse », 1979.

Daniel Lagache (1951), *Psychanalyse et criminologie, Rapport clinique*, Revue Française de Psychanalyse, Tome XV, n°1.

Peter Langman (2019), « Desperate identities: A bio-psycho-social analysis of perpetrators of mass violence », *Criminol Public Policy 19 (1)*, 1–24.

Jean Laplanche (1977), « Les voies de la déshumanité », *La révolution copernicienne inachevée, 1967–1992*, Presses Universitaires de France, Coll. « Quadrige ».

Jean Laplanche (1982), « Réparation et rétributions pénales », *La révolution copernicienne inachevée, 1967–1992*, Presses Universitaires de France, Coll. « Quadrige ».

Jean Laplanche (1997), *Le primat de l'autre en psychanalyse*, Champs Flammarion.

Jean Laplanche; **Jean-Bertrand Pontalis** (1973), *The Language of Psychoanalysis*, W.W. Norton & Company, NY.

Serge Lebovici; **Pierre Mâle**; **Francis Pasche** (1951), *Psychanalyse et criminologie, rapport Clinique*, Revue Française de Psychanalyse, Tome XV, n°1.

Eugène-Bernard Leroy (1907), *Nature des hallucinations*, Revue philosophique de la France et de l'étranger, tome LXIII, Paris.

Jean-Claude Maleval (2011), *Logique du délire*, Presses Universitaires de Rennes, Coll. « Clinique Psychanalytique et Psychopathologie », Nouvelle édition revue et augmentée.

Gérard Mendel (1998), *L'acte est une aventure, du sujet métaphysique au sujet de l'actepouvoir*, La Découverte.

Guy Rosolato (1987), *Le sacrifice, Repères psychanalytiques*, Presses Universitaires de France, Coll. « Quadrige ».

Ruth Stein (2002), *Le mal comme amour et libération: l'état d'esprit d'un terroriste religieux kamikaze*, Revue Française de Psychanalyse, n°3, Vol. 66.

Serge Tisseron (1995), *Psychanalyse de l'image, Des premiers traits au virtuel*, Pluriel.

Jean-Luc Vannier (2005), « A propos du satanisme et de la sorcière », *Malaise dans la culture libérale*, Le Coq Héron, Erès, n°183.

Jean-Luc Vannier (2014), *Les Mixed Martial Arts sont-ils solubles dans la pulsion sexuelle de mort?* Le Carnet Psy, 2014/3, n°79.

Jean-Luc Vannier (2014), « Le pouce paternel, *Nahrungseinfuhr* d'une adolescente anorexique », *Autisme et Psychoses Infantiles*, Psychiatrie Française, Vol. XXXXV, 4/14.

Jean-Luc Vannier (2017), « Réflexions psychanalytiques sur le terrorisme djihadiste, de l'autopunition à l'autodestruction », in *Radicalisation et Radicalité, Une Voie de la destructivité*, Psychiatrie Française, Vol. XXXXVIII, n°2.

Jean-Luc Vannier (2019), « A propos de *Islamistischer Terrorismus*, une lecture analytique », *Droit de l'enfant et psychiatrie*, Psychiatrie Française, Vol. L, n° 4.

Jean-Luc Vannier (2020), *Réflexions Psychanalytiques sur quelques évolutions de la langue française*, Le Carnet Psy.

Donald Wood Winnicott (1967), *Conversations Ordinaires*, Folio Essais.

33

UNDERSTANDING THE MOTIVATIONS OF "LONE WOLF" TERRORISTS[*]

The "Bathtub" Model

Boaz Ganor

Introduction

Modern terrorism is a dynamic and evolving phenomenon that keeps morphing. Over the years, terrorists and terrorist organizations around the world have been using a wide range of attacks, sometimes mimicking successful attacks perpetrated by other terrorists in different arenas.

In general, terror attacks worldwide may be categorized as follows:

1   **Personal Initiative Attack** – attacks perpetrated by individual terrorists without operational connection to any terrorist organization ("Lone Wolf" attacks)
2   **Local Independent Networks** – attacks that involve a small number of terrorists, mostly family relatives or close friends who have been radicalized together and one day decided to conduct a terrorist attack. Here too, these terrorists lack an operational connection to a terrorist organization.
3   **Organized Attacks** – attacks perpetrated by a terrorist cell, which is a part of a terrorist organization. The cell members were recruited by the organization, trained by it, were sent by the organization to perpetrate the attack, received the required operational support, and perpetrated the attack on behalf of the organization.

Attacks within the first two categories may be inspired by a certain terrorist organization. The Lone Wolves and the Local Independent Networks may refer to themselves as IS, al-Qaeda or any other terrorist organization's activists even though they were never recruited, never trained by it or received operational support. The characteristics of the terrorists in each of the above groups differ from one another in their profile, background, modus operandi (at times) and their motives for the attack. Any of these different types of attacks may develop into a wave of attacks.

The ebb and flow of a terrorism wave may have multiple reasons and explanations, stemming, inter alia, from a change in the terrorists' set of beliefs, cost-benefit analysis of the perpetrators

---

[*] First published and adapted from Boaz, Ganor, Understanding the Motivations of "Lone Wolf" Terrorists: The "Bathtub" Model, *Perspectives on Terrorism* 15, no. 2 (April 2021): pp. 23–32.

DOI: 10.4324/9781003326373-38

or their dispatchers, from the level of their communities' social approval for their attacks, and the availability of operational means at their disposal.[1]

The "lone wolf" phenomenon is not new; throughout history, individual independent terrorists perpetrated attacks without any guidance, operational involvement, or organizational support of terrorist organizations.[2]

However, it would appear that the expanding use of the Internet has significantly contributed to the growth of this phenomenon.[3] The Internet has enabled terrorists around the world to be part of virtual communities of like-minded people, contributing to the radicalization of their members, educating one another on planning and executing attacks—all without ever physically meeting one another.[4] It has also enabled terrorist organizations to post and disseminate propaganda, and to offer instructions on how to produce weapons, ammunition, and explosives.[5] Members of such virtual communities and other potential "lone wolves" who are exposed to this material might be inspired to perpetrate terrorist attacks. The ability of the terrorist propagators (organizations and other entities) to directly communicate (locally and internationally) with radical youngsters all over the world enables them to further radicalize and also motivates these individuals to execute "lone wolf" attacks in different countries.[6]

Mark Sageman argues that the Internet has created a new generation of terrorists who carry out a "leaderless jihad."[7] However, it seems that the prevalence of recent years' "lone wolf" attacks stems, inter alia, from the objective difficulties faced by terrorist organizations in their attempt to execute "organized attacks" (i.e., attacks that are the culmination of initiative, preparation, and involvement of terrorist organizations). For example, ISIS's loss of territories in Syria and Iraq, al-Qaeda's weakness in various theaters around the world, and Hamas's operational limitations outside the Gaza Strip drove these organizations to call upon independent lone actors to perpetrate attacks inspired by, or even on behalf of, the above organizations. These organizations seek to create an atmosphere that supports "lone wolf" attacks via incitement and propaganda disseminated online, and enc-ge their supporters worldwide to attack locally.[8] Within this framework, Bruce Hoffman explains that "this new strategy of al-Qaeda is to empower and motivate individuals to commit acts of violence completely outside any terrorist chain of command."[9] Ramon Spaaij reinforces Hoffman's claim, noting that the number of attacks perpetrated by independent individuals inspired by radical Islam has been on the rise, inter alia due to the terrorist organizations' call to carry out such attacks.[10]

However, the "lone wolf" threat is not limited to global jihadi terrorism. Jeffrey Simon notes that "it would be wrong to assume that lone wolf terrorism is the exclusive domain of Islamic extremists."[11] As Daniel Byman argues, right-wing supremacists, anti-abortionists, and separatist movements have all used this strategy in various ways and with different levels of success.[12] Most notably, as Bakker and de Graaf suggest, there has been a growing fear of "lone wolf" attacks by right-wing extremists.[13] In a study conducted in 2011, Raffaello Pantucci examined Anders Behring Breivik's murder of 77 people in Oslo and Utoya (Norway) on 22 July 2011.

He argues that Breivik fits the "lone wolf" profile, while having connections to far-right communities around the world.[14] His findings on Breivik reveal the powerful role of the Internet in disseminating extremist ideologies that motivate like-minded individuals to perpetrate terrorist attacks.[15] In addition, a study conducted by Paul Gill and his colleagues on the use of the Internet by lone actors reveals that "extreme right-wing offenders" are "more likely than Jihadist-inspired offenders in the United Kingdom to learn and communicate online."[16] Similarly, Florian Hartleb argues that existing typologies of "lone wolf" terrorism should be reconsidered with greater attention given to the new phenomenon of "right-wing single actors."[17]

Terror attacks are the product of two main variables: (i) motivation to perpetrate an attack and (ii) the operational capability to execute it.[18] Foiling terrorism may therefore be the outcome of limiting the motivations that drive the attackers or, alternatively, curbing their capability to execute these attacks. Terrorism capabilities are usually assembled in a long process of preparations (e.g., procuring weapons, assembling explosive devices, and more) but these preparations have in many cases a clear "radar signature" available for intelligence detection.

Therefore, many intelligence agencies focus on locating and identifying the operational preparations for a terror attack, then attempting to foil it. This "signature" is absent in many "lone wolf" attacks which are often perpetrated with a cold weapon.[19] This kind of weapon can be found in every household (e.g., sharp objects, knives, screwdrivers, axes, vehicles). Therefore, the importance of understanding the motivation of the "lone wolves" is essential for the prevention of this type of attacks. However, the motivations of "lone wolves" are difficult to locate and to neutralize.

This chapter examines the motivations that drive lone wolves to perpetrate their attacks. This analysis is generic in nature and it addresses terrorists driven by radical Islamist motives (either global or local), as well as nationalist terrorists, or terrorists acting in the name of other extreme ideologies such as those found on the far right. The article proposes classifying the various motives at the core of these attacks into several categories as well as offering a model to analyze the cross influence of said categories on the decision to perpetrate a "lone wolf" attack. The generic model proposed in the article might serve therefore as a baseline for the formation of new counterterrorism and Counter–Violent Extremism (CVE) strategies in order to prevent or foil this kind of attack.

Defining the Phenomenon

Various scholars, such as Levitt, Byman, and Weimann, argue that the term "lone wolf" is a misnomer, as the *"wolf"* is not really *"lone."*[20] The attacker is influenced by, and operates within, a certain social atmosphere; he or she is in contact with others and shares his or her intentions with them; and s/he is even assisted by them.

The "lone wolves" might be inspired by a certain terrorist organization and see themselves as its operatives even if they were never recruited, nor received training, payments, or assistance from that organization.

Therefore, upon his or her arrest and interrogation, the "lone wolf" may claim that s/he was an activist of ISIS, al-Qaeda, or other organization s/he identifies with.[21] Moreover, after a "lone wolf" attack, some organizations might claim responsibility for the attack to boost their position and gain free "glory".

Brian M. Jenkins reviewed the 2004 FBI definition which states that a "lone wolf" is an individual who has no nexus to a foreign power or entity.[22] Jenkins argued that the term "lone wolf" does not accurately describe the phenomenon of terrorism, as the concept used to refer to a "hero operating outside the law, doing whatever is necessary to get the job done."[23] He therefore proposed to use the term "stray dog" instead of "lone wolf," noting that it better describes individuals involved in this type of terrorism.[24] According to Jenkins, "...the jihadists' behavior seems to more closely resemble that of stray dogs, who may be found alone or in packs, estranged from but dependent on society, streetwise but lacking social skills, barking defiantly, and potentially dangerous but at the same time, suspicious, fearful, skittish."[25]

Daveed Gartenstein-Ross and Nathaniel Barr criticized the quick and sometimes wrongful labeling of perpetrators as "lone wolves" in the aftermath of attacks. They suggested that only a small number of attackers designated as "lone wolf" truly meet that definition.[26] According to Gartenstein-Ross and Barr, "true" lone wolves are "individuals who strike without ever communicating with jihadist networks, either online or in person." On the other hand, Gabriel Weimann suggested that "'lone wolf' terrorists are not completely out of contact," as they communicate through the "Dark Web."[27] He argued that similar to "lone wolves" in the animal kingdom, individual terrorists also have their "virtual pack." Online platforms provide them with many opportunities, such as finding instructions on building homemade bombs or mapping potential targets.[28]

Daniel Byman added that the term "lone wolf" does not effectively describe the phenomenon, since most of the time one cannot ascertain how lonely and isolated from other terroristic elements the individual terrorist really was. He therefore suggested "lone-ish wolves," i.e., wolves that sometimes operate independently and sometimes within a very small "pack."[29] Clare Ellis and Raffaello Pantucci used the following definition of the term "lone-actor terrorist":

"The threat or use of violence by a single perpetrator (or small cell), not acting out of purely personal-material reasons, with the aim of influencing a wider audience, and who acts without any direct support in the planning, preparation and execution of the attack, and whose decision to act is not directed by any group or other individuals (although possibly inspired by others)."[30]

In a study conducted in 2020, Clemmow, Bouhana, and Gill concluded that such "cyclical" definitional debates are not necessarily productive, arguing that "lone-actor terrorists do not have to be defined wholly as lone or connected."[31]

In this article, the term "lone wolf" is used to define the phenomenon wherein an individual terrorist perpetrates an attack on his/her own or with the assistance or involvement of others (acquaintances, family) but without any operational connection to any specific terrorist organization.[32] In other words, even if the terrorist was in contact with others (online or in person) and was inspired by a specific terrorist organization, or even if s/he saw himself/herself as its operative, still, as long as no terrorist organization was involved in any of the stages of the attack perpetrated—the initiation, planning, preparation, or logistics of the attack—it will be considered under the suggested definition as a "lone wolf" attack.[33]

The proposed working definition points to the fact that the differential classification between this type of attack and many other attacks is the lack of operational involvement of a terrorist organization in any of the stages of the attack. In that, this definition does not contradict other definitions according to which many lone wolves interact with others, or even with terrorist organizations.

Since a terrorist organization is not involved in the preparatory stage of the attack, the "lone wolf" must independently procure all the required means and equipment to execute the attack. Therefore, the "lone wolf" mostly uses accessible and unsophisticated means and equipment. These include various cold weapons (such as knives, axes, or other sharp objects) for stabbing attacks; vehicles (such as passenger cars, trucks, or other heavy-duty vehicles) for car-ramming attacks; improvised explosives the attacker constructs on his/her own; or any other accessible firearms (such as purchased, stolen, or self-manufactured guns and rifles). In light of the above, attaining operational capability to execute the attack is usually a rather low hurdle to jump over and not an obstacle in the way of the attack.

The range of motivations affecting the decision of the "lone wolf" to perpetrate an attack is wide and varied. In his early typology of "lone wolf" terrorism, Raffaello Pantucci examined terrorists with religious (Islamist) motivations.[34] Other scholars such as Hamm and Spaaij included a wider range of political, religious, and ideological factors in their analysis.[35] In a study conducted in 2019, Jude McCulloch examined the "lone wolf" phenomenon through a gendered lens. Her research revealed that the criminal records and known biographies of numerous "lone wolf" terrorists include significant histories of violence against women.[36]

It is therefore hard to isolate a single motive of that entire spectrum as the one that drove the "lone wolf" to attack. In the case of organized attacks, the perpetrating organization usually announces the reasons for the attack, which are practically always associated with the organization's ideology. Even so, however, it is usually unclear what motivated the individuals who actually executed the attack to join the organization in the first place and then to carry out the particular attack in question.

The uncertainty about the motivation for the attack is much greater in the case of "lone wolf" assailants. In any case, a complete and valid assessment of the perpetrator's motives can only be obtained through a psychological and background investigation, preferably by direct interviews with him/her after arrest.[37]

In a research project conducted by Ariel Merari and Boaz Ganor, the motivations that drove Palestinian terrorists to perpetrate more than 550 "lone wolf" attacks in Israel between 2015–2017 were examined. It was found that the terrorists perpetrated the attacks as a result of widely varied motives, including: revenge for national, religious, or personal humiliation, desire to die or to get to paradise, national struggle, defense of the al Aqsa Mosque, to prove himself/herself, or to gain social esteem.[38] In light of these findings and the motivations'typologies offered by the above researchers, the "lone wolves'" motives may be classified into three groups: (i) ideological,[39] (ii) psychopathological,[40] and (iii) other personal circumstances.[41]

The "lone wolf's" decision to perpetrate an attack is therefore a unique personal combination of the above which may differ from one attacker to another. Each group of motivations may include several subgroups. For example, the ideological motives group may include, inter alia, devotion to radical ideologies such as nationalist-separatist, communist, anarchist, fascist, or other political motives.

The personal motivations group may include economic motives (such as poverty, low socio-economic status, and acute economic crises); inter-personal motives (such as crises in the "lone wolf's" relationship with his or her partner or another central figure in his/her life); and familial motives (including hardship within the family, problematic or complex relationship between family members or particular figures such as father, mother, older siblings, as well as the level of appreciation or disrespect the "lone wolf" gets from his or her family) or other personal motives (such as the desire for adventure, self image, or status improvement). The psychological motives group includes the terrorist's desire to commit suicide, which may be caused by mental instability, harsh experience, despair, or belief in an afterlife. As argued by Ramon Spaaij, lone wolves "tend to have a greater propensity to suffer mental health issues" in comparison to individuals who belong to a terrorist group.[42] Spaaij's findings on mental disorder seem to be in parallel with Emily Corner's and Paul Gill's research[43] on mental illness and lone-actor terrorism.[44]

Another psychological motive that the terrorist suffers from may be a psychological instability.[45] In addition, within the above variables, one should include the motives that stem from the terrorist's predisposition to the value of honor. These may include, among others, the terrorist's or his/her family's honor; women's or a specific female family member's honor; national, tribal or community honor; as well as the honor of the terrorist's religion or its religious symbols.

As depicted in Figure 33.1, the "lone wolf's" decision to attack is seldom driven by one sole motive; it is rather the outcome of an aggregate combination of ideological, personal, or psychological motives. Scholars have adopted different methods of classification and there are various ways to group each motive. For example, James Khalil argues that sociopsychological factors (such as the desire for adventure, a higher status, and vengeance) play a role in the individual's decision to perpetrate an attack.[46] The weight of each motive varies on the merits of every case and the personal circumstances of the terrorist, his/her mental structure, his/her exposure to incitement, and more.

In fact, one may visualize the "lone wolf's" decision-making process vis-a-vis the attack to a vessel (e.g., a bathtub) being filled up by various sources of water/faucets which are the

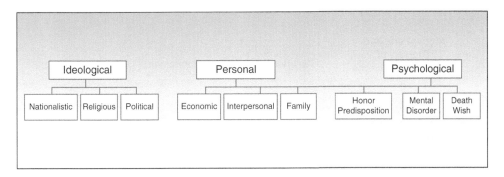

Figure 33.1 "The Bathtub" Model – Typology of "Lone Wolf" Motives.

Source: Author's Creation.

aforementioned various groups and subgroups of motivations (hereinafter: "The Bathtub Model").

Each of the various motives contributes its part to fill up the "motivation bath" at its own velocity and intensity. When the bathtub is full and cannot contain any more motivations, it overflows, and an attack occurs. This overflow reflects the maturation of the terrorist's decision to attack. Filling up the bathtub may be a slow process and the decision to attack may take many days; or, the bathtub may quickly be filled, in which case the decision to attack will be made within a very short time.

A decision to attack may be the outcome of one major motive (be it personal, psychological, or ideological) or a combination of motives. In the "Bathtub Model" this is akin to a situation where one faucet fills the tub while others are closed or just dripping. Thus, the different motives and their effects on the terrorist change from one person to another, but each contributes its relative portion to fill up the bathtub (i.e., arrive at a decision to attack).

The upper threshold of the "bathtub" is therefore the critical variable in the proposed model, as it determines that maximal level of the "lone wolf 's" ability to contain his/her motives, frustrations, emotions, and urges.

When this threshold is higher, the terrorist is able to contain more reasons and motives before s/he attacks. When the threshold is lower, the effect of the various "faucets"/motives carry more weight in the decision to attack and arriving at such a decision may be faster. Furthermore, the upper threshold therefore reflects the mental strength of the "lone wolf," his/her psychological stability, and ability to contain external influences and internal emotions.

It is important to note that the "Bathtub Threshold" (Figure 33.2) is not only unique to each person, but also dynamic and may change, depending on the circumstances, for the very same person, in accordance with his/her level of exposure to "concrete triggers" that might intensify his/her emotions and drive him/her to perpetrate the attack immediately or within a very short time. Those triggers include: (i) an exposure of the terrorist to an earlier attack perpetrated by another "lone wolf" and the desire to follow in that terrorist's footsteps and mimic him/her; (ii) an exposure to a traumatic event that generated extremely subjective feelings of anger, humiliation, and a desire for revenge. Such traumatic events may be the product of the personal circumstances or experiences of the attacker (such as a family or interpersonal crisis), or an incident which happened to another person that the attacker was exposed to through acquaintance with the individual, or through news or social media; (iii) an exposure to incitement messages from those calling for these types of attacks.

The trigger for action, whether a traumatic event or an exposure to certain information, can actually speed up the filling of the bathtub, release inhibitions, and overcome hesitations; and the

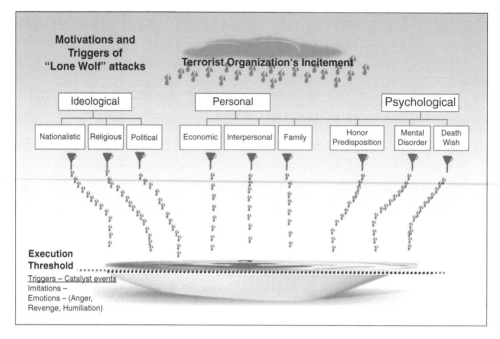

Figure 33.2 The "Bathtub Model" – "Lone Wolf" Attack Execution Threshold.

Source: Author's Creation.

extreme emotions that flood the terrorist's mind as a result of such release may instantly lower the Bathtub Threshold, creating an overflow, that is, a decision to attack sooner rather than later. In psychology, an "inhibition" is defined as the "conscious or unconscious constraint or curtailment of a process or behavior, especially of impulses or desires."[47]

In this study, the "lone wolf's" inhibitions are the product of his/her mental stability and his/her ability to contain crises, plus his/her value and belief system constraints, as well as his/her cost/benefit analysis. The basic premise in this context is that, apart from mentally ill people, the deliberate infliction of harm on others requires overcoming moral inhibitions stemming from the attacker's set of values and overcoming possible utilitarian considerations that may curb the desire to perpetrate an attack (such as the risk to the attacker himself/herself and the price s/he may pay if arrested after the attack).

The "lone wolf's" decision-making process to perpetrate an attack and the effect of the various triggers may therefore be presented in the following formula:

$$\mathbf{TA = (M + T) > I}$$

> **TA** (Terror Attack) = **Motivation** (Ideological + Personal + Psychological) + **Triggers** (Imitation + Trauma + Concrete Incitement, etc.) > **Inhibitions** (Psychological Stability + Value and Belief System + Cost/Benefit Analysis)

In other words, the "lone wolf's" decision to perpetrate the attack is the product of balancing the sum of the various motives (ideological, psychological, personal) and the sum of the various triggers s/he was exposed to (role model, traumatic event, incitement) against the terrorist's inhibitions (which are the product of his/her mental stability and his/her ability to contain crises, plus his/her value and belief system constraints as well as his/her cost/benefit analysis). When the sum of the triggers and motivations is greater than the inhibitions, then an attack will be perpetrated. If one can collect the relevant data, the above formula enables, prima facie, CT professionals to calculate the total motivations, triggers, and inhibitions that affect "lone wolves," prospectively or retrospectively (i.e., before or after the attack). It also enables the analyst to simultaneously examine the "lone wolf's" basic personality traits, the ideological set of beliefs, the societal effects that are at the core of his/her decision to attack, as well as to evaluate the role of triggers, personal events, and external circumstances that influenced the "lone wolf's" decision to attack. In that sense, the formula expresses the intensity of the drive to perpetrate the "lone wolf" attack.

The "Bathtub Model" also enables researchers to explore the central role that two other factors may have on the "lone wolf's" attack decision-making process: the terrorism incitement factor and government efforts and initiatives to prevent violent extremism.

It should be noted that terrorist organizations, Da'wa organizations, and radical lay leaders might have an important contribution to the "lone wolf's" decision to attack. Their incitement "fertilizes" over time the volatile atmosphere in the "lone wolves'" community and the explicit calls for attacks register in the "lone wolf's" mind, contributing to the filling of the "motivation bathtub." Incitement and propaganda have a direct influence on all of the ideological motivations, as well as on motivations based on honor, and also on some of the suicidal motivations (for example, there are cases in which attackers decided that they want to die in an attack in order to receive the heavenly rewards promised posthumously). As noted above, incitement might have a direct impact on the decision to attack, as it intensifies trigger events by praising prior attacks and attackers, or by deepening the attackers' sense of humiliation. Within this framework, the terrorist organizations may incite "lone wolves" to perpetrate attacks on certain dates (for example, during holidays or anniversaries of past terrorist attacks), under a certain modus operandi (including, for example, cold-weapon attacks, car-ramming attacks, shootings, and acts of railway sabotage), or against specific targets (such as "infidels," Western states, immigrant communities, or ethnic minorities).

On the other hand, one may infer from the "Bathtub Model" that a country dealing with terrorism and violent extremism has an ability to reduce the impact of some of the motivations of the "lone wolves" (these include, for example, ideological motivations, as well as motivations stemming from loss of honor and humiliation).

In that sense, every "bathtub" has a "drain." The "drain" is to a large extent controlled by the government. The government and security forces can open the drain and thus lower the level of "liquid" in the "motivation bathtub." The "drain" manifests the concrete actions taken by states as part of their Countering Violent Extremism (CVE) efforts and activities. It may include, among others, communication channels with leaders of the "lone wolves'" ideological, political, or ethnic communities; political reforms aimed at reducing tensions and appeasing these communities; as well as economic and educational reforms. All of these may be translated into an influence on the array of considerations of potential "lone wolves" and delay or even thwart their decision to attack.

Conclusions

In summation, understanding the characteristics, scope, and intensity of the "lone wolves'" motivations are essential for any attempt to prevent or thwart this kind of attack, even more than with other forms of attacks.

The proposed "Bathtub Model" enables one to map out the various motives, motivations, and triggers at the core of the attacks, and to identify the synergy between them.

The Bathtub Model is conceptual; however, it may carry many operational ramifications. As a theoretical model, it can serve as a basis for future research that will contribute to the understanding of the "lone wolves" terrorism phenomenon. Additional research may examine intersections between groups of motivations, such as: personal vs. ideological motives, honor, and humiliation vs. other groups of motivations. Interdisciplinary and multidisciplinary research that combine psychological, sociological, and political science approaches may use the model to examine a synergetic effect and influence that various types of motivations may have on "lone wolves'" decision to perpetrate attacks. The model may also assist with identifying potential triggers that may "lower bathtub walls" significantly and rapidly, (i.e., quick and dangerous reduction of the inhibitions that prevent potential "lone wolves" from perpetrating their attacks). However, this conceptual model may also have operative applications. The model may point out cross-linkages between different types of incitement and certain groups of motivations that generate "lone wolf" attacks and by doing so assist with counteracting and preventing such incitement. Furthermore, the model may point to an elevated likelihood for the occurrence of "lone wolf" attacks in certain time periods when there is an increase in incitement that may trigger an increase in the above motivations, or when statements made by political leaders are perceived by potential attackers as an affront to their culture, ideology, or religion. Another operational insight stemming from the proposed model is the need to put an effort into "lowering the water level in the tub," (i.e., enable potential lone wolves to contain harsh sentiments and motivations without acting on them), or alternatively find a way to neutralize some of these sentiments and motivations ("enlarging the drain of the bathtub"). These efforts to prevent the decision of the "lone wolf" to perpetrate an attack might be made via CVE activities within high-risk communities, via educational reforms, during counter-incitement campaigns, by means of social and economic reforms, combined with free psychological services and treatments offered to potential "lone wolves."

Acknowledgments

The author is thankful to the editors and anonymous reviewers, to Dr. Michael Barak, Lorena Atiyas-Lvovsky, Stevie Weinberg and Dafne Beri for their research and editing, and to Ofer Vilenko for his translation into English.

Notes

1 Alex P. Schmid, "Root Causes of Terrorism: Some Conceptual Notes, a Set of Indicators, and a Model", *Democracy and Security* 1, no. 2 (2005): pp. 127-136; 135.

2 Daniel L. Byman, "Can Lone Wolves Be Stopped?", (Brookings, March 15, 2017); URL: https://www.brookings.edu/blog/markaz/2017/03/15/can-lone-wolves-be-stopped/.

3 Gabriel Weimann, "Virtual Packs of Lone Wolves: How the Internet Made 'Lone Wolf' Terrorism a Misnomer". Wilson Center, February 28, 2014; URL: https://medium.com/its-a-medium-world/virtual-packs-of-lone-wolves-17b12f8c455a.

4 Tomaš Zeman, Jan Břeň, and Rudolf Urban, "Role of Internet in Lone Wolf Terrorism", *Journal of Security and Sustainability* 7, no. 2 (December 2017): pp. 185.192; 186.

5 Gabriel Weimann, "Lone Wolves in Cyberspace", *The Centre for the Study of Terrorism and Political Violence: Journal of Terrorism Research* 3, no. 2 (2012): pp. 75–90; URL: https://research-repository.st-andrews.ac.uk/bitstream/handle/10023/3981/405-950-1-PB.pdf?sequence=1&isAllowed=y.

6 Gabriel Weimann, "Chapter 3: Lone Wolves in Cyberspace"; in: *Terrorism in Cyberspace: The Next Generation* (NY: Woodrow Wilson Center Press, 2015).

7 Marc Sageman, *Leaderless Jihad: Terror Networks in the Twenty-First Century* (Philadelphia: University of Pennsylvania Press, 2008).

8 Miron Lakomy, "Recruitment and Incitement to Violence in the Islamic State's Online Propaganda: Comparative Analysis of Dabiq and Rumiyah", *Studies in Conflict & Terrorism*, February 2019; URL: https://doi.org/10.1080/1057610X.2019.1568008.

9 Bruce Hoffman, *Inside Terrorism* (New York, NY: Columbia University Press, 1999).

10 Mark S. Hamm and R. F. J. Spaaij, *The Age of Lone Wolf Terrorism* (New York, NY: Columbia University Press, 2017).

11 Jeffrey D. Simon, *Lone Wolf Terrorism: Understanding the Growing Threat* (Amherst, NY: Prometheus Books, 2016).

12 Daniel L. Byman, "Can Lone Wolves Be Stopped?", (Brookings, March 15, 2017); URL: https://www.brookings.edu/blog/markaz/2017/03/15/can-lone-wolves-be-stopped/.

13 Edwin Bakker and Beatrice de Graaf, "Preventing Lone Wolf Terrorism: Some CT Approaches Addressed", *Perspectives on Terrorism* 5, no. 6 (December 2011): pp. 43–50. See also Florian Hartleb, *Lone Wolves: The New Terrorism of Right-Wing Single Actors* (Cham: Springer, 2020).

14 See Raffaello Pantucci, "*A Typology of Lone Wolves: Preliminary Analysis of Lone Islamist Terrorists,*" The International Centre for the Study of Radicalisation and Political Violence (ICSR), March 2011, pp. 1–39; URL: https://icsr.info/wp-content/uploads/2011/04/1302002992ICSRPaper_ATypologyofLoneWolfes_Pantucci.pdf..

15 Raffaello Pantucci, *"What Have We Learned about Lone Wolves from Anders Behring Breivik?"*, *Perspectives on Terrorism*, 5, no. 5 (December 2011): pp. 27–42.

16 Paul Gill et al., "Terrorist Use of the Internet by the Numbers", *Criminology and Public Policy* 16, no. 1 (February 2017): pp. 99–117; URL: https://doi.org/10.1111/1745-9133.12249.

17 Florian Hartleb, *Lone Wolves: The New Terrorism of Right-Wing Single Actors* (Cham: Springer, 2020).

18 Boaz Ganor, *The Counter-Terrorism Puzzle: A Guide for Decision Makers* (New Brunswick, USA: Transaction Publishers, 2008), pp. 51–53.

19 Ariel Merari & Boaz Ganor (2020): *Interviews With, and Tests of, Palestinian Independent Assailants, Terrorism and Political Violence*, DOI: 10.1080/09546553.2020.1821668.

20 See Matthew Levitt, "The Lone-Wolf Terrorist is a Misnomer", mcall.com (The Morning Call, September 22, 2016); URL https://www.mcall.com/opinion/mc-new-york-bombing-terrorist-0923-20160922-story.html. See also: Gabriel Weimann, "Virtual Packs of Lone Wolves: How the internet made 'lone wolf 'terrorism a misnomer". Wilson Center, February 28, 2014; URL: https://medium.com/its-a-medium-world/virtual-packs-of-lone-wolves-17b12f8c455a. See as well: Daniel L. Byman, "Can Lone Wolves Be Stopped?", (Brookings, March 15, 2017), https://www.brookings.edu/blog/markaz/2017/03/15/can-lone-wolves-be-stopped/.

21 Bart Schuurman et al., "End of the Lone Wolf: The Typology That Should Not Have Been", *Studies in Conflict & Terrorism* 42, no. 8 (September 2018): pp. 771–778; URL: https://doi.org/10.1080/10576 10x.2017.1419554.

22 Brian Michael Jenkins, "Stray Dogs and Virtual Armies: Radicalization and Recruitment to Jihadist Terrorism in the United States Since 9/11". Santa Monica, CA: RAND Corporation, 2011,21. Accessed August 28, 2020; URL: http://www.jstor.org/stable/10.7249/op343rc.

23 Jenkins, B. M., Stray Dogs, op. cit., p. 21.

24 The term "stray dog" was coined by the Italian police in the 1970s and attributed in reference to the Red Brigades.

25 Jenkins, B. M., Stray Dogs, op. cit., p. 21.

26 Daveed Gartenstein-Ross and Nathaniel Barr, "The Myth of Lone-Wolf Terrorism: The Attacks in Europe and Digital Extremism", *Foreign Affairs*, July 26, 2016; URL: https://www.foreignaffairs.com/articles/western-europe/2016-07-26/myth-lone-wolf-terrorism.

27 Gabriel Weimann, "Virtual Packs of Lone Wolves: How the internet made 'lone wolf' terrorism a misnomer". Wilson Center, February 28, 2014; URL: https://medium.com/its-a-medium-world/virtual-packs-of-lone-wolves-17b12f8c455a.

28 Gabriel Weimann, "Chapter 3: Lone Wolves in Cyberspace", in *Terrorism in Cyberspace: The Next Generation* (NY: Woodrow Wilson Center Press, 2015).

29 Daniel L. Byman, "Can Lone Wolves Be Stopped?", (Brookings, March 15, 2017); URL:https://www.brookings.edu/blog/markaz/2017/03/15/can-lone-wolves-be-stopped/.

30 Clare Ellis et al., "Lone-Actor Terrorism: Final Report", *Royal United Services Institutes for Defence and Security Studies* (RUSI, 2016); URL:https://rusi.org/sites/default/files/201604_clat_final_report.pdf.

31 Caitlin Clemmow, Noemie Bouhana, and Paul Gill, "Analyzing Person-Exposure Patterns in Lone-Actor Terrorism: Implications for Threat Assessment and Intelligence Gathering", *Criminology & Public Policy* 19, no. 2 (2020): pp. 451–482; URL: https://doi.org/10.1111/1745-9133.12466.

32 Ariel Merari and Boaz Ganor, *Interviews With…*,op. cit., p. 2.

33 Ibid.

34 R. Pantucci, *A Typology of Lone Wolves*

35 Ramon Spaaij, *Understanding Lone Wolf Terrorism: Global Patterns, Motivations and Prevention*, vol. 3 (New York City, NY: Springer, 2012).

36 Jude McCulloch et al., "Lone Wolf Terrorism Through a Gendered Lens: Men Turning Violent or Violent Men Behaving Violently?", *Critical Criminology* 27 (July 2019): pp. 437–450; URL: https://doi.org/10.1007/s10612-019-09457-5.

37 See Merari and Ganor, *Interviews With, and Tests of, Palistinian Independent Assailants, op. cit.*

38 Idem., p. 9.

39 For a study on the ideological motives, see: Ramon Spaaij, *Understanding Lone Wolf Terrorism: Global Patterns.*

40 For a study on the role of psychopathology in terrorist behavior, see: Emily Corner, Noemie Bouhana, and Paul Gill, "The Multifinality of Vulnerability Indicators in Lone-Actor Terrorism", *Psychology, Crime & Law* 25, no. 2 (2019): pp. 111–132; URL: https://doi.org/10.1080/1068316x.2018.1503664.

41 For a study on personal (economic) circumstances, see: Peter J. Phillips and Gabriela Pohl, "Economic Profiling of the Lone Wolf Terrorist: Can Economics Provide Behavioral Investigative Advice?", *Journal of Applied Security Research* 7, no. 2 (March 2012): pp. 151–177; URL: https://doi.org/10.1080/19361610.2012.656250.

42 R. Spaaij, op. cit.

43 Emily Corner and Paul Gill, "A False Dichotomy? Mental Illness and Lone-Actor Terrorism". *Law and Human Behavior* 39, no. 1 (February 2015): pp. 23–34; URL: https://doi.org/10.1037/lhb0000102.

44 Daveed Gartenstein Ross, "What Does the Recent Spate of Lone Wolf Terrorist Attacks Mean?", *War on the Rocks* (Texas National Security Review, October 2014); URL: https://warontherocks.com/2014/10/what-does-the-recent-spate-of-lone-wolf-terrorist-attacks-mean/, accessed December 21, 2020.

45 For a study on psychology and lone wolf terrorism, see: Manon Prats, Sophie Raymond, and Ivan Gasman, "Religious Radicalization and Lone-Actor Terrorism: A Matter for Psychiatry?", *Journal of Forensic Sciences* 64, no. 4 (July 2019): pp. 1–6; URL: https://doi.org/10.1111/1556-4029.13992.

46 James Khalil, "Radical Beliefs and Violent Actions Are Not Synonymous: How to Place the Key Disjuncture Between Attitudes and Behaviors at the Heart of Our Research into Political Violence", *Studies in Conflict & Terrorism* 37, no. 2 (January 2014): pp. 198–211; URL: https://doi.org/10.1080/1057610X.2014.862902.

47 Encyclopaedia Britannica, accessed December 21, 2020; URL: https://www.britannica.com/science/inhibition-psychology.

34

EVOLVING PERSPECTIVES ON PSYCHOPATHOLOGY AND TERRORISM

Randy Borum

Psychology has always provided a popular lens for understanding terrorism and violent extremism. But sometimes it has been used like a blunt instrument. Early inquiry on the "psychology of terrorism" tended to focus on the clinical dimensions of the discipline. Psychology was not broadly applied as a science of human behavior, which would include both "normal" and "abnormal" psychological processes. From the late 1960s through the mid-1980s, when scholars started writing about (though not necessarily researching) the psychology of terrorism they often began with three (non-mutually exclusive) working assumptions/hypotheses:

- Terrorists engaged in terrorism because they were psychologically damaged and/or disordered
- Terrorists were often "psychopaths" who were pervasively antisocial and lacking in empathy and remorse
- Terrorists had a distinctive demographic and psychological profile that reliably distinguished them from non-terrorists

Generally speaking, those three assumptions were not borne out by any rigorous empirical investigation. The early studies tended to use broad, imprecise definitions of their concepts and often unsystematic measurements.

Psychological abnormality was invoked as a dichotomous construct, assuming that people either had a diagnosable psychological/psychiatric disorder underlying their behavior or they did not. The reality—as more recent research has clearly demonstrated—is that psychological problems can be much more nuanced; a range of psychological processes—not just diagnosable disorders—may be relevant; and that psychological factors can contribute much more to the study of terrorism than just hypotheses about psychopathology. But getting from there to here has been a rather slow, evolutionary process.

Early Studies of Psychological Disorders and Violent Extremism

Some of the earliest psychological musings about terrorist behavior were driven by psycho-analytic theory, arguing that terrorism was likely caused by early abuse and maltreatment, and

DOI: 10.4324/9781003326373-39

that terrorist motivations were largely unconscious and rooted in hostility toward their parents. The basic hypothesis was that terrorists behaved as they did because they were psychologically damaged in some way.

Ultimately, psychoanalytic speculation gave way to a more specific focus on psychopathology-mental illnesses and disorders. It is not difficult to see how behavior as extreme and infrequent as terrorism would elicit a presumption of abnormality to explain the question of "why". But as Corner and colleagues (Corner, Gill, & Mason, 2016; Gill & Corner, 2017) have pointed out, the assumed relationship was often based on a constrained notion of mental illness and a conflation of irrationality with mental disorder. This was particularly evident in discussions of suicide terrorism, where a terrorist's intention to kill or sacrifice himself was regarded as *prima facie* evidence of both irrationality and mental illness. Bouhana and Wikström (2010) note that "suicide terrorism is perceived as the greatest challenge to rational choice explanations, since no benefit could outweigh the ultimate cost of action (certain death)" (p. 41).

To investigate the link between mental disorders and violent extremism, researchers began to evaluate samples of incarcerated terrorists—mainly members of organized terrorist groups—or those referred for mental health evaluations using various assessment measures. Those studies, though lacking in precision and methodological rigor, generally found the prevalence of mental illness among samples of incarcerated terrorists to be generally comparable to rates in the general population (McCauley, 2002; Ruby, 2002; Sageman, 2004; Victoroff, 2005). When research failed to find what was expected, some scholars inferred that terrorists overall must be psychologically "normal" and that mental health problems were all but irrelevant to violent extremism. As a generalization, that may have been a leap too far.

Different measures of risk provide different kinds of information about the effects of risk factors and how they operate. It is easy but not uncommon to conflate those different perspectives. In epidemiology—the field of study concerned with the incidence and causes/determinants of diseases and health problems—at least three kinds of risk are frequently cited. The first is "absolute risk", which is simply the incidence or likelihood of an adverse outcome (such as terrorism) in a given population. The second is "relative risk", which comprises the ratio or risk difference in the incidence of an adverse outcome between those who carry or have been exposed to a risk factor and those who have not (a reference or comparison group). The third type is "attributable risk." Attributable risk, as the name suggests, measures the proportion of cases in which an adverse outcome is attributed specifically to the presence of a given risk factor. In other words, it represents the cases where the problematic outcome would not have occurred if the risk factor had not been present. These same perspectives from epidemiology can also be applied to understanding the incidence and determinants of other adverse behavioral outcomes, such as violence, or even violent extremism.

Corner, Gill, and Mason (2016) have argued that critiques of those early studies of mental disorders and terrorism (e.g., Borum, 2004, Horgan, 2005; Victoroff, 2005) were sometimes misinterpreted to suggest that the research evidence pointed to an absence of any relationship between mental health problems and terrorism. "In reality, what the reviews illustrated", Corner, Gill, and Mason (2016) have said, "was the lack of evidence to suggest that very specific forms of mental illness *caused* terrorism" (p. 560, emphasis in original). In essence, those early studies failed to provide evidence of attributable risk linking specific and narrowly defined mental disorders to specific and narrowly defined forms of terrorism (Corner & Gill, 2015). Of course the absence of evidence is not necessarily evidence of absence.

Second Generation Studies of Psychological Disorders and Violent Extremism

A second generation of studies emerged—many of which have appeared since 2010—exploring the prevalence of mental disorders among samples of violent extremists (Gill et al., 2021; Misiak et al., 2019; Trimbur et al., 2021). The study quality and the methodologies are somewhat improved, but remain inconsistent. Some of those more recent studies reported higher rates of mental health problems than the first generation inquiries, but the rates across those studies have varied significantly.

Prevalence estimates for psychopathology in any given sample or population vary due to differences in what is measured and how it is measured (the source of the evidence). Some studies have regarded psychopathology as being present only if there was a formal diagnosis. Others have used a broader definition of "mental health problems", which could include one or more "symptoms" or maladaptive behaviors, such as indications of suspiciousness or difficulties with anger management. If a given group of violent extremists is assessed for the presence of psychopathology, there will obviously be many more who have symptoms and problems than have formally diagnosable disorders. And if the examination only includes certain, specific disorders (as some of the early studies did) then prevalence estimates will be even lower. So, vastly different rates of psychopathology could be reported for the same group depending on the threshold and criteria the researchers choose to use.

Measuring Psychopathology in Group-Based Terrorists

To illustrate how estimated rates of psychopathology can vary according to the scope and method of measurement, consider again our notional group of violent extremists who are being assessed. The researchers may set a standard threshold or criteria to indicate psychopathology. The number and rate of reported problems, however, could vary depending on whether they were using structured clinical interviews, unstructured interviews, official records (e.g., mental health and/ or arrest records), collateral interviews, confirmatory sourcing (when two or more sources agree), or even—as a number of studies have done—using open source news reports. Using open source reporting can be especially tricky because the absence of symptoms is almost never reported; not all news reports systematically inquire about or look for evidence of mental health problems; and those that do typically have an idiosyncratic threshold for what kinds of behaviors they will report and what evidence they will regard as sufficiently reliable to warrant reporting.

Despite those ambiguities and limitations, studies have reported mental health problems or diagnosed mental disorders in about

- 8% of people arrested for a wide range of terrorist crimes in the United States (Hewitt, 2003)
- 12% of terrorist autobiographies (Corner & Gill, 2020)
- 4.5% of Jihadi terrorists in Europe (Bakker, 2006)
- 7.6% of U.S. extremists who had committed small-cell and group-motivated murders (Gruenewald, Chermak, & Freilich, 2013)
- 57% of extremists involved with white supremacist groups (Bubolz & Simi, 2019)
- 43.7% of individuals radicalized in the United States (cases in which mental illness status was known) (LaFree et al., 2018)
- 29% (for mood and anxiety disorders and mild intellectual disability) of 34 clients who were participating in a CVE program in Amsterdam, in the Netherlands. Also 35% had substance related disorders, 41% had personality disorders and 15% psychotic disorders) (Grimbergen & Fassaert, 2022).

The most comprehensive, systematic review of mental health problems and violent extremism at this point is a 2021 analysis by Gill and colleagues (2021). They examined 25 studies based on 28 samples and found prevalence to range between 0% and 57%. When they aggregated the studies with known sample sizes and used a more stringent criterion of a "confirmed diagnosis", the overall prevalence rate was between 14% and 17%, depending on the extent of available information.

For comparison, the point prevalence for <u>any</u> mental illness in 2020 among U.S. adults was 21%. The point prevalence for serious mental illness (those suffering serious functional impairment from their illness) was about 6% (Substance Abuse and Mental Health Services Administration, 2021). That rate is consistent with rates in at least half of 28 countries in a global WHO survey (Kessler et al., 2009).

These comparative rates, however, do not suggest that terrorists are more psychologically healthy than non-terrorists. To reiterate, prevalence rates will vary based on which diagnoses/disorders are included and how they are measured, but based on the available evidence, it does not appear that most samples of group-affiliated terrorists have substantially higher rates of serious mental illness than are found in the general population. But results from more recent studies do "largely dispel the myth there is no mental disorder present within terrorist samples" (Gill et al., 2021, p. 58).

Although there was little consistency among methodologies used in the second generation studies, those studies did begin to examine different types of mental disorders and different types of terrorism with a bit more granularity. Those shifts in focus changed the complexion of research evidence on the association between mental health problems and violent extremism.

Measuring Psychopathology in Lone Offender Terrorists

The type of terrorism appears to matter. As lone offender acts of terrorism became increasingly common (Richards et al., 2019) and case reports were highlighting the attacker's history of psychological problems, questions about the role of psychopathology in violent extremism re-emerged. Researchers systematically examined terrorism cases involving solo attackers. Those studies revealed a different trend than the early studies of terrorists who were primarily members of organized groups.

At least relative to other terrorists, psychological problems appear to be more common among lone/solo attackers. Typically, studies have found between one third and one half of lone offenders who engage in terrorism or mass targeted violence have mental health problems (Capellan & Anisin, 2018; COT, 2007; Fein & Vossekuil, 1999; Gill, Horgan, & Deckert, 2014; Gill et al., 2019; Gruenewald et al., 2013; Liem et al., 2018; Meloy et al., 2019; Trimbur et al., 2021; Zeman et al., 2018). The trend has been consistent in both solo attackers of public figures and solo attackers of other targets. With all of the caveats about limitations and differences among studies, here is a quick rundown:

- More than 60% of individuals known to have attacked, or approached to attack, a prominent public official or public figure in the United States had been evaluated or treated by a mental health professional and almost half (44%) had a history of serious depression or despair. A similar proportion (43%) was known to be delusional at the time of the principal attack/approach incident, and one in five had a history of auditory hallucinations (Fein & Vossekuil, 1999).
- Nearly half of those who attacked reigning monarchs or their families experienced delusions or hallucinations around the time of their attack (James et al., 2008).
- Nearly half of those who attacked elected politicians in Western Europe "were pursuing (to an irrational degree) an agenda of an idiosyncratic nature, usually but not always delusional in content" (James et al., 2007, p. 339).

- Nearly one third (31.9%) of the 119 lone actor terrorists in one larger-scale study had a history of mental health problems (Gill, Horgan, & Deckert, 2014).
- About half (49%) of attackers in U.S. cases involving firearm-related mass murders showed signs of "mental health issues" prior to their attack (Follman, Aronsen, & Pan, 2022). Among the 35 attackers who survived (and sampling of 20 that did not) the vast majority (87.5%) may have had "misdiagnosed and incorrectly treated or undiagnosed and untreated psychiatric illness" (Cerfolio et al., 2022).
- More than 40% of domestic (U.S.) extremist "loner" attackers had a known history of mental illness (Gruenwald et al., 2013).
- About 43% of mass shooters (both extremist and non-extremist) in one sample showed evidence of a "mental disturbance" (Capellan & Anisin, 2018).
- About 87.5% of 32 of mass shooters (killing three or more) in a U.S. sample who survived their attacks had been assessed to have a DSM-5 diagnosis—56% had been given a diagnosis of schizophrenia (Glick et al., 2021).
- Approximately one third (37%) of European lone actor terrorists (broadly defined) showed some indication of mental illness (Liem et al., 2018).
- About one third (32.7%) of lone actor terrorists in the United Kingdom had a known history of mental illness or personality disorder (Gill et al., 2019).
- About 43% of "lone wolf" attackers in an international sample had been diagnosed with some type of mental disorder before their attack and another 13% received a mental disorder diagnosis during their trials (Zeman et al., 2018).
- Nearly half (48%) of a small convenience sample of North American lone actor terrorists had a mental disorder (Meloy et al., 2019).
- About three quarters (75%) of persons listed in the European Terrorist Database who had been convicted of Jihadi terrorism between 2012 and 2021 and who had forensic mental health reports had some form of diagnosable psychopathology. Rates among youthful offenders (<21) were slightly higher than rates for adult offenders (73% vs. 81%) (Duits et al., 2022).

The pattern of findings above—consistent with other comparative analyses—has led some researchers to conclude "lone- and group-terrorists may appear to be two distinct groups of people in terms of their drivers and criminogenic needs" (Gill et al., 2021, p. 66). In any case, research on mental health problems among group-affiliated terrorists does not appear to be generally applicable to all terrorists, particularly to lone attackers.

Prevalence and Role of Psychopathology May Vary for Different Sub-Groups

Differences in causes, correlates, and risk factors may emerge for other subgroups as well, perhaps even subgroups of lone or solo offenders (Kenyon, Baker-Beall, & Binder, 2021; Zierhoffer, 2014). Researchers openly acknowledge the absence of any standard or consensus-based definition of terrorism generally or of a "lone offender" terrorist specifically (Borum, 2013; Borum, Fein, & Vossekuil, 2012; Kenyon, Baker-Beall, & Binder, 2021). Compounding this challenge is a shift in the boundaries of (a) what is publicly regarded as terrorism, or at least (b) who should be grouped together among lone/solo offenders.

Regarding the scope of who might be considered a terrorist, most formal definitions of terrorism include an essential provision that the act be committed to instill fear in a broader population in order to further a political, social, or religious cause (Schmid, 2023; Schmid & Jongman, 1988).

That has been a primary feature distinguishing terrorism from other forms of violence and murder. With many solo attacks, however, personal motives and grievances mix with ideological ones (Borum, Fein, & Vossekuil, 2012; Ellis et al., 2016; Gill et al., 2017). So, even where the attacker intended to cause fear, intimidation, and terror, the question of whether the act was committed primarily or solely "to further a political, social, or religious cause" or to influence the policy or conduct of a government is, at least, ambiguous.

Regarding the scope of who might be considered a "lone offender", assassins and public figure attackers, so-called "school shooters", ideologically driven mass shooters, non-ideologically driven mass shooters, and terrorist/extremist solo attackers have been lumped together or sometimes disaggregated and compared in various studies (Capellan, 2015). In an empirical comparison of assassins and school shooters, for example, McCauley and colleagues (McCauley, Moskalenko, & Van Son, 2013; McCauley & Moskalenko, 2014), found that actors in both groups engaged in significant pre-attack planning and that action was facilitated by means and opportunity. Those are operational factors and may certainly belie some operational similarities. They also reported, however, "four characteristics common for both school attackers and assassins: perceived grievance, depression, a personal crisis ('unfreezing'), and history of weapons use outside the military", and suggested that "these characteristics may be useful in distinguishing lone-wolves from group-based terrorists" (McCauley, Moskalenko, & Van Son, 2013, p. 4).

Even though these four characteristics may have been common to both groups (though they were measured differently in the two studies), the prevalence appeared to vary between them: "Perceived Grievance" was found in 81% of the school attackers, but in only 67% of the assassins; "Depression" was found in 78% of the school attackers, but in only 44% of the assassins; a personal crisis (unfreezing[1]) was found in 98% of the school attackers, and in "almost half" of the assassins. So, those factors may be useful for distinguishing lone from group-based terrorists, but the results do not necessarily imply that school attackers and assassins share common drivers and causes.

Type of Psychopathology May Affect Relevance

Not surprisingly, the type of disorder may also matter. Psychological disorders are quite diverse, ranging from impairments in intellectual and social development, mood, and thinking to problems with anxiety and reactions to trauma. That range of disorders is not evenly distributed in the general population or among violent extremists.

A few studies have sought to examine the prevalence of a wide range of specific psychological disorders among violent extremists and have reported those results, comparing different types of terrorists (e.g., group-affiliated, lone, mass-murderer) to one another and to the rates in the general population (Corner, Gill, & Mason, 2016; Corner et al., 2018; Duits, Alberda, & Kempes, 2022). Most disorders do not seem to be substantially more common among violent extremists. Although limited data are currently available, it is possible that Schizophrenia and Delusional Disorder may be exceptions. Those disorders were not reported to appear more prominently in earlier studies of group-affiliated terrorists, but, among lone attackers, mass shooters, and fixated individuals, higher rates have been reported. Depressive disorders have shown mixed findings (some higher and some lower than in the general population). The available evidence, however, does not seem to point to any "unique profile of psychopathology" (Misiak et al., 2019, p. 56).

Untangling effects of specific mental disorders, symptoms, or psychological problems can be incredibly complicated for several reasons: (a) many people who have one type of mental disorder also have more than one (co-morbidity); (b) underlying maladaptive personality traits (e.g., undue suspicion, anger, and hostility) can affect the types of symptoms that people with any given type of disorder may manifest; (c) many people with mental disorders also encounter more difficult life experiences (e.g., abuse), more stressful events (e.g., trauma), and more adverse social conditions (e.g., social isolation and alienation) than people without mental health problems; and (d) for some, being engaged with terrorism or violent extremism itself can precipitate or aggravate mental disorders.

Mental illnesses and psychological disorders do not provide a master explanation for terrorism, but they are also not irrelevant. For researchers, rather than asking whether terrorists are more likely than non-terrorists to have diagnosable mental disorders, it may be more useful to ask what roles psychological problems and factors may have for different forms of violent extremism, for different individuals, in different contexts. As Corner and Gill (2022) have insightfully noted, "We need more than an understanding of "presence", we need an understanding of 'relevance'" (p. 399).

For anti- and counter-terrorism professionals the key implication is that even in cases where mental disorders are present, ideologies and other motives may still be critical driving factors and the individual may be quite capable of organized thought and action (Atran, 2021). A person's ability to engage in goal-directed behavior and to act on his intentions (e.g., logical thinking, coherence and consistency of ideas, and self-regulation) are much more important than a diagnosis (Borum, 2013). More work remains to be done to better understand the role of psychopathology among lone attackers generally and among sub-groups of lone offenders specifically.

Psychopathy as an Explanation for Violent Extremism

Beyond exploring major mental illnesses in terrorist samples, some researchers and clinicians considered that such an extreme form of antisocial deviant behavior might arise from a syndrome of extreme antisocial personality traits. Psychopathy emerged as a likely candidate.

The psychological construct of psychopathy has a storied history and its definition has evolved over the years, but contemporary notions of psychopathy, which emerged from decades of research, center around two broad factors. The "Interpersonal/Affective" factor represents the psychopath's deficient emotional experiences (e.g., lack of guilt, empathy, and remorse) and interpersonal exploitativeness (e.g., callous, use of others, parasitic lifestyle). The "Lifestyle/Antisocial" factor represents a persistent pattern of antisocial (though not necessarily criminal) behavior and a highly impulsive lifestyle (Hare & Neumann, 2008).

Although psychopathy is discussed in the DSM-5 (the current American reference manual specifying criteria for psychiatric disorders), it is not an officially accepted clinical diagnosis, and it is generally not regarded as a mental illness, but more as a clinical syndrome (Jurjako, 2019). Associating psychopathy with violent extremism is not surprising since, as DeLisi (2019, p. i) noted, "For over two centuries, psychopathy has stood as perhaps the most formidable risk factor for antisocial behavior, crime, and violence."

Most published writing and analyses linking terrorism to psychopathy have been speculative and anecdotal. Some have scoped the psychopath moniker very broadly. Others have identified specific behavioral patterns commonly associated with psychopathy (e.g. antisocial behavior, lack of guilt and disregard for social norms) and inferred that they might be characteristic of terrorism (Martens, 2004). Pearce (1977), for example, in his early typology of hostage takers, suggested the "political terrorist" type "may be an aggressive psychopath, who has espoused some particular cause because extremist causes can provide an external focal point for all the things that have gone wrong in his life." The dynamic described here may be true for some terrorists, but there is no real empirical evidence linking it to psychopathy, specifically—at least as the concept of psychopathy is currently understood.

Corner et al. (2021) have conducted what is probably the most careful and comprehensive systematic review to date on the links between violent extremism and psychopathy-related constructs (and other personality factors). Among the hundreds of studies they reviewed, very few had any direct connection to psychopathy. The studies that do exist used online surveys with self-report measures of psychopathy among college student samples, and terrorism was not a specific focus.

In Jones (2013) study, psychopathy scores were significantly associated with narcissism, Machivellianism and social dominance orientation (believing some groups are better than others), but literally had a zero correlation with right-wing authoritarianism. In a study by Bélanger and colleagues (Bélanger et al., 2014) examining the "psychology of martyrdom", none of the facets of psychopathy had significant bivariate correlations with participants' willingness to self-sacrifice for "a cause that was very important to them" (p. 497).

A study of French female college students (Morgades-Bamba et al., 2018) found that callous/unemotional and remorseless traits had no direct effect on either radicalized cognitions (rated acceptability of various behaviors) or radicalized behaviors (self-report of how often in the past year they had engaged in those behaviors). An indirect/mediated relationship, however, was found when psychopathy interacted with dogmatism (cognitive rigidity). A further analysis of that sample found that the cluster of young women with the highest levels of sadistic, psychopathic, and Machiavellian traits, and moderate level of narcissistic traits had the highest levels of radicalized cognitions and radicalized behaviors (Chabrol et al., 2020). That finding is perhaps not surprising, but psychopathic traits were not separated out in this particular analysis, and prior analyses of the same sample found no direct relationship between psychopathic traits in isolation and radicalized cognitions or behaviors. Hare has concluded that "there is little credible research on how psychopathy—or other clinical constructs, disorders, or personality traits, for that matter—inform an understanding of terrorism" (Hare et al., 2022, p. 3).

Personality "Traits", Profiles, and Terrorism

Beyond the early theoretical, psychoanalytic focus on narcissism as a possible driver of terrorism (Crayton, 1983; Morf, 1970), researchers over the years have also considered that certain personality traits may help to explain terrorist behavior, and that perhaps a constellation of those traits might emerge comprising a unique terrorist profile.

The quest for a "terrorist personality" has a rather inauspicious history, but a couple of recent systematic reviews provide an exceptional view of the current state of science with regard to personality-related and psychological factors in violent extremism, while also highlighting some challenges in personality-related terminology. I would like to preface the summary of those reviews with two caveats:

- In the literature on terrorism and violent extremism, the terms "personality traits" and "psychological factors" are often used interchangeably. There is no precise, consensus-based definition for either or for marking a clear distinction between them. But conflating these terms or underlying concepts can cause confusion and inadvertently create the appearance of contradictory conclusions. The narrower definition of personality traits is what scholars in the field seem to have in mind when noting the absence of credible research linking personality traits with terrorism (Hare et al., 2022; Monahan, 2012). If "personality traits" are considered narrowly to represent the limited number of continuous (as opposed to dichotomous) "basic dimensions on which people differ" (Diener & Lucas, 2019, p. 279) in stable and consistent ways, and "psychological factors" are considered more broadly to represent other psychological features, characteristics, styles, and processes that affect thinking, emotion, and behavior, then it may be fair to say that, in general, the research evidence for personality traits is more limited, but the evidence for certain psychological factors is more promising.

- As Gill and Corner (2017) have pointed out in discussing research on the role of psychopathology in terrorism, it is possible to confuse claims and conclusions about the absence of good scientific evidence linking a phenomenon to terrorism and the presence of good scientific evidence for the absence of a link between the phenomenon and terrorism. We should be careful not to repeat that mistake in characterizing evidence for associations between personality traits or psychological factors and violent extremism.

With those caveats in mind, two rigorous, comprehensive research reviews provide an excellent "big picture" view of the current state of the scientific evidence on personality-related and psychological factors in violent extremism. One is a systematic review by Corner et al. (2021) examining the links between violent extremism and personality (as well as personality disorders, and psychopathy). The other is a systematic review and meta-analysis (combining results from multiple studies in a single analysis) by Wolfowicz and colleagues (Wolfowicz et al., 2021) examining individual-level risk and protective factors for cognitive and behavioral radicalization. Collectively, these analyses are instructive for understanding the current state of the research. Both studies also looked at a range of variables beyond the scope of what is addressed in this section, but we will summarize the results that are relevant to our themes.

Corner et al. (2021) reviewed 437 studies that had "an explicit goal of understanding the determinants of radicalisation or behaviour associated with a terrorist offence" (p. 382). The review included studies with both quantitative and qualitative measures. The research team pored through hundreds of studies examining a wide range of negative (maladaptive) and positive (common personality traits) personality characteristics. Study participants included adults and adolescents from around the world drawing from both extremist and non-extremist samples.

The authors encapsulated traits under the "negative" theme as features of the "Dark Tetrad" of psychopathy, narcissism, Machiavellianism, and sadism. The specific traits associated with each dimension were as follows:

- Psychopathy: sensation-seeking; low self-control; impulsivity; low empathy
- Narcissism: superiority; greed
- Machiavellianism: self-interest; weak morality; status seeking; moral neutralization; and inflexibility
- Sadism: moral disengagement; intolerance; and need for dominance

Of the four dimensions in this Tetrad, traits associated with psychopathy (sensation-seeking; low self-control; impulsivity; low empathy) carried the most robust empirical support with 14 studies, about 86% of which received the highest rating for methodological quality. The Tetrad's other three dimensions—narcissism (four studies), Machiavellianism (five studies), and sadism (four studies) collectively had 13 studies, distributed fairly evenly across the domains. Among the specific traits within the remaining domains, "superiority" (three studies) carried the most empirical support.

The authors encapsulated traits under the "positive" theme as features of the Five Factor Model of personality[2] (Openness, Conscientiousness, Extraversion, Agreeableness, and Neuroticism). The specific traits associated with each dimension were as follows:

- Openness: adventure-seeking; courage, passion; creativity
- Conscientiousness: fairness-seeking; goal commitment
- Extraversion: "No studies under review identified significant associations between traits associated with extraversion and radicalisation or terrorism" (Corner et al., 2021, p. 395).
- Agreeableness: altruism; bravery; belonging; selflessness
- Neuroticism: uncertainty; guilt; fear

Of the five factors in the model, traits associated with neuroticism carried the most robust empirical support with seven (7) studies, about one third of which received the highest rating for methodological quality. Within the Neuroticism dimension, the specific trait of uncertainty, with four studies, had the highest level of empirical support. For the Five Factor Model's other dimensions, no studies were found for extraversion, and the remaining three—openness (7 studies), conscientiousness (2 studies), and agreeableness (7 studies)—collectively have 16 studies across the domains. Among the specific traits in those other dimensions, most had only one or two studies each.

Overall, the Corner et al. (2021) systematic review found that the volume and quality of empirical research studies related to violent extremism were higher for psychological factors (e.g., sensation-seeking, low self-control) than for traditional personality traits (e.g., extraversion, conscientiousness, agreeableness).

Wolfowicz et al. (2021) conducted a meta-analysis of 127 studies (primarily cross-sectional), from 206 samples representing 20 OECD countries, producing 1302 effect sizes for more than 100 different individual-level factors. The review included only studies using quantitative measures and excluded qualitative studies. The authors selected studies

> whose outcome variable(s) were in line with at least one of three relevant outcomes derived from McCauley and Moskalenko's (2017) two pyramid model (TPM) of radicalization: (1) Radical attitudes: Justification/support for radical behaviors carried out in the name of a cause. (2) Radical intentions: Willingness/intentions towards engagement in radical behaviors in the name of a cause. (3) Radical behaviors: Actual involvement in violent radical behaviors in the name of a cause, including terrorism.
>
> *(p. 13)*

In this paper, we will only address findings for radical intentions and radical behaviors as the outcomes of interest. The authors reported the strength of the connection between each factor and radical intentions in tiers ranging from Very Small (weakest statistically significant relationship) to Small, to Moderate, to Large (strongest statistically significant relationship) (Wolfowicz et al., 2021).

Radical Intentions

For radical *intentions*, Very Small (but statistically significant) effects were found for the following personality-related and broader psychological risk factors[3]: Uncertainty; Neuroticism; Experiencing Discrimination; and Adjusted Personality Disorder[4]/Narcissism. Gender (Male) was also represented, though it is neither a personality trait nor a psychological/psychosocial factor. Age (negatively related)—though not a personality trait or a psychological/psychosocial factor—was also represented as a Protective Factor.

Small effects were found for the following risk factors: Quest for Significance; Extraversion; Individual Relative Deprivation; Religious Convert; Positive Affect; Harmonious Passion; Low Integration; Dark-triad personality traits Psychopathy, Narcissism, and Machiavellianism; Power Distance Orientation (PDO); In-group Connectedness; Personal Self-esteem; Anomie; In-group Identity; Realistic Threat; Perceived Injustice; and Symbolic Threat. Student and Gender (Male) were also represented, though neither is a personality trait or a psychological/psychosocial factor. In addition, Small effects were found for the following protective factors: Agreeableness; Conscientiousness; Openness; and Immigrant.

Moderate effects were found for the following risk factors: Past aAtivism; Collective Relative Deprivation; Moral Neutralizations; Perceived Discrimination; In--group Superiority; Anger; Commitment to a Cause; Activist Intentions; Negative Affect; and Radical Attitudes. Large effects were found for Obsessive Passion and Identity Fusion.

Radical Behaviors

For radical *behaviors*, Very Small (but statistically significant) effects were found for the following personality-related and broader psychological risk factors[5]: Bullying Victim; Welfare Recipient (not a personality trait or a psychological factor); Parental Abuse; and Parental Involvement. Age was negatively related as a Protective Factor, though not a personality trait or a psychological/psychosocial factor.

Small effects were found for the following risk factors: Low Integration; Experiencing Violence; Personal Injustice; Mental Health; Radical Family; Authoritarianism/Fundamentalism; Unemployment (not a personality trait or a psychological factor); Thrill-Seeking/Risk-Taking; Anger; and Low Self Control. Small effects were also found for the following protective factors (each is negatively related) as well: School Bonding; Law Legitimacy; and Law Abidance.

Moderate effects were found for the following risk factors: Deviant/Radical Peers; Radical Attitudes; Online Contact with Extremists; Past Military Service; Criminal History; Recent Job Loss; Gender (Male) was also represented, though it is neither a personality trait nor a psychological/psychosocial factor. A large effect was found for Previous Incarcerations.

Analyzing more than 100 potential risk and protective factors in samples from 20 different countries and with multiple ideologies is a massive undertaking. There were a few important differences found across different geographic regions and ideological groupings, however, overall, there was considerable consistency. The authors conclude that "[t]aken collectively, the results indicate that many risk factors may have universal relationships with radicalization outcomes in democratic countries and across ideologies, and be equally applicable across certain demographics (Wolfowicz et al., 2021, p. 71).

Both reviews highlight some interesting and potentially promising psychological factors for further investigation. Neither, however, points to a unique personality/psychological profile of the terrorist (see also Misiak et al., 2019). Corner et al. (2021) conclude that "the search for a single 'terrorist personality' was always overly ambitious, yet at the same time overly simplistic. It was doomed to failure from the start." (p. 298)

Summary and Conclusions

For more than 60 years, researchers have explored the psychological underpinnings of terrorist behavior at the individual level. Early efforts included some psychoanalytic speculation (often based on clinical or field experience), but there was also a working belief that perhaps terrorism—because it is such an extreme behavior—might best be understood as the product of a mental disorder or disease. The initial studies exploring rates of mental disorders among terrorist samples found rates comparable to the general population. But those efforts lacked scientific rigor and did not provide a credible scientific basis for any firm conclusions. Nevertheless, some inferred that mental health problems must be all but absent among terrorists and irrelevant to understanding violent extremism.

A second generation of studies using improved research methods also found that overall rates of most mental disorders were similar among samples of group-based terrorists and the general population, but a different pattern emerged for lone offenders, where mental health problems were regularly found in a third or more of the cases. If anyone was still clinging to the belief that mental disorders were not—or could not be—present in terrorist samples, a spate of studies provided research evidence to the contrary.

Another very early trend was speculation that the roots of violent extremism might be found in the construct of psychopathy. Although psychopathy is, without question, one of the most robust and consistent predictors and correlates of antisocial behavior generally, there has been very little empirical evidence suggesting that it is a major cause of terrorism. When mental disorders and clinical syndromes failed to offer a neatly packaged proposition for understanding the cause of terrorism, some researchers turned their attention to personality factors. The working hypothesis was that there must be a set of characteristics that could reliably distinguish terrorists from non-terrorists; perhaps those characteristics might even comprise a psychological profile of the violent extremist. But studies consistently failed to find a constellation of personality variables that characterized all terrorists or explained terrorist behavior. This is probably not, however, because there are no differences between terrorists and non-terrorists in their patterns of thought, emotion, and behavior, but because there are such vast differences among terrorists. Terrorism and terrorists are quite diverse (Alexander & Klein, 2005).

After decades of inquiry, it seems unlikely that a new understanding of terrorism and radicalization will be found in psychopathology or static, "trait-based" effects, but viewing terrorism as a complex and dynamic process seems much more promising (Emmelkamp, et al., 2020; Horgan, 2008; Vermeulen, et al., 2022). Ferguson and McAuley (2021) have observed that "research on how and why people become involved in violent extremism has moved away from answers based on psychopathology or personality profiles" (p. 6) to the roles of social and collective identity. Although it is clear that involvement in violent extremism is driven by multiple causes and that it is an outcome with multiple possible pathways, the concept of identities can provide an organizing framework for understanding how various vulnerabilities and propensities can affect individuals' pathways and decisions about engaging in violent extremism (Atran, 2021; Borum, 2014; Swann & Buhrmiester, 2015).

Notes

1 McCauley, Moskalenko, and Van Son (2013) define unfreezing as "a change in circumstances, especially a sudden change, that leaves an individual in some kind of personal crisis" and suggest that crisis creates "an opening in an individual's life that decreases the perceived cost of acting on a grievance and increases the value of acting to gain or regain status and respect" (McCauley, Moskalenko, & Van Son, 2013, p. 11).
2 The authors note that "[n]o studies under review specifically sought to examine the Five-Factor Model. However, 15 studies reviewed did identify significant variables that correspond to the personality traits within the five-factor model" (Corner et al., 2021, p. 395).

3 The authors note that, among the Protective Factors for Radical Intentions, "[t]he estimates for Education, Socioeconomic status (SES) and Outgroup friendships were not statistically significant" (Wolfowicz et al., 2021, p. 37). Among Risk Factors for Radical Intentions "[s]tatistically nonsignificant
   estimates were found for Unemployment, Social-Dominance Orientation (SDO), External political
   efficacy, and Perceived discrimination" (Wolfowicz et al., 2021, p. 37).
4 This variable is listed in the analysis as "Adjusted Personality Disorder (APD)" but the example description is "For example, DSM-IV personality disorders, Narcissistic Personality Inventory". Because
   (a) the term "Adjusted Personality Disorder" is uncommon; (b) the acronym "APD" is commonly used
   to refer to "Antisocial Personality Disorder", and (c) Antisocial Personality Disorder tends to be the
   more commonly studied Personality Disorder in research related to terrorism and violent extremism,
   the exact intended referent of "Adjusted Personality Disorder (APD)" is unclear.
5 The authors note that among the Protective Factors for Radical Behaviors, "[s]tatistically nonsignificant
   estimates were found for Marital status and Education" (Wolfowicz et al., 2021, p. 39). Among the Risk
   Factors for Radical Behaviors, "[s]tatistically nonsignificant estimates were found for Religious Up-
   bringing, Religious Convert, Immigrant Status, Relationship Problems, Anger, and Current Military
   Service" (Wolfowicz et al., 2021, p. 39).

References

Alexander, D., & Klein, S. (2005). The psychological aspects of terrorism: from denial to hyperbole. *Journal of the Royal Society of Medicine, 98*(12), 557–562. doi:10.1258/jrsm.98.12.557

Atran, S. (2021). Psychology of transnational terrorism and extreme political conflict. *Annual Review of Psychology, 72*, 471–501.

Bakker, E. (2006). *Jihadi terrorists in Europe: Their characteristics and the circumstances in which they joined the jihad: An exploratory study.* The Hague: Netherlands Institute of International Relations Clingendael.

Bélanger, J. J., Caouette, J., Sharvit, K., & Dugas, M. (2014). The psychology of martyrdom: Making the ultimate sacrifice in the name of a cause. *Journal of Personality and Social Psychology, 107*(3), 494–515.

Borum, R. (2004). *Psychology of terrorism.* Tampa, FL: University of South Florida.

Borum, R. (2013). Informing lone-offender investigations. *Criminology and Public Policy, 12*(1), 103–112.

Borum, R. (2014). Psychological vulnerabilities and propensities for involvement in violent extremism. *Behavioral Sciences & the Law, 32*(3), 286–305.

Borum, R., Fein, R., & Vossekuil, B. (2012). A dimensional approach to analyzing lone offender terrorism. *Aggression and Violent Behavior, 17*(5), 389–396.

Bouhana, N., & Wikström, P.-O. H. (2010). Theorizing terrorism: Terrorism as moral action. *Contemporary Readings in Law and Social Justice, 2*(2), 9–79.

Bubolz, B. F., & Simi, P. (2019). The problem of overgeneralization: The case of mental health problems and US violent white supremacists. *American Behavioral Scientist.* https://doi.org/10.1177/0002764219831746.

Capellan, J. A. (2015). Lone wolf terrorist or deranged shooter? A study of ideological active shooter events in the United States, 1970–2014. *Studies in Conflict & Terrorism, 38*(6), 395–413. https://doi.org/10.1080/1057610X.2015.1008341.

Capellan, J. A., & Anisin, A. (2018). A distinction without a difference? Examining the causal pathways behind ideologically motivated mass public shootings. *Homicide Studies, 22*(3), 235–255.

Cerfolio, N. E., Glick, I., Kamis, D., & Laurence, M. (2022). A retrospective observational study of psychosocial determinants and psychiatric diagnoses of mass shooters in the United States. *Psychodynamic Psychiatry, 50*(3), 1–16.

Chabrol, H., Bronchain, J., Morgades-Bamba, C. I., & Raynal, P. (2020). The dark tetrad and radicalization: Personality profiles in young women. *Behavioral Sciences of Terrorism and Political Aggression, 12*(2), 157–168. https://doi.org/10.1080/19434472.2019.1646301.

Corner, E., & Gill, P. (2015). A false dichotomy? Mental illness and lone-actor terrorism. *Law and Human Behavior, 39*(1), 23–34.

Corner, E., & Gill, P. (2020). Psychological distress, terrorist involvement and disengagement from terrorism: A sequence analysis approach. *Journal of Quantitative Criminology, 36*, 499–526.

Corner, E., & Gill, P. (2022). Psychopathy and terrorist involvement. In P. Marques, M. Paulino, & L. Alho (Eds.), *Psychopathy and criminal behavior* (pp. 389–402). Academic Press.

Corner, E., Gill, P., & Mason, O. (2016). Mental health disorders and the terrorist: A research note probing selection effects and disorder prevalence. *Studies in Conflict & Terrorism, 39*(6), 560–568.

Corner, E., Gill, P., Schouten, R., & Farnham, F. (2018). Mental disorders, personality traits, and grievance-fueled targeted violence: The evidence base and implications for research and practice. *Journal of Personality Assessment, 100*(5), 459–470.

Corner, E., Taylor, H., Van Der Vegt, I., Salman, N., Rottweiler, B., Hetzel, F., Clemmow, C., Schulten, N. & Gill, P. (2021). Reviewing the links between violent extremism and personality, personality disorders, and psychopathy. *The Journal of Forensic Psychiatry & Psychology, 32*(3), 378–407.

COT (ed.). (2007). Lone-Wolf Terrorism. Case study for Work Package 3. Citizens and governance in a knowledge-based society TTSRL. Retrieved May 2013 from www.transnationalterrorism.eu/tekst/publications/Lone-Wolf%20Terrorism.pdf.

Crayton, J. W. (1983). Terrorism and psychology of the self. In L. Z. Freedman, & Y. Alexander (Eds.), *Perspectives on terrorism* (pp. 33–41). Wilmington, Delaware: Scholarly Resources.

DeLisi, M. (Ed.). (2019). *Routledge international handbook of psychopathy and crime*. Routledge. https://doi.org/10.4324/9781315111476.

Diener, E. & Lucas, R. (2019). Personality traits. In L. Brewer (Ed.), *General psychology: Required reading*. Noba Textbook Series: Psychology.

Duits, N., Alberda, D. L., & Kempes, M. (2022). Psychopathology of young terrorist offenders, and the interaction with ideology and grievances. *Frontiers in Psychiatry, 239*, 1–14.

Ellis, C., Pantucci, R., de Roy van Zuijdewijn, J., Bakker, E., Smith, M., Gomis, B., & Palombi, S. (2016). Analysing the processes of lone-actor terrorism: Research findings. *Perspectives on Terrorism, 10*(2), 33–41.

Emmelkamp, J., Asscher, J. J., Wissink, I. B., & Stams, G. J. J. M. (2020). Risk factors for (violent) radicalization in juveniles: A multilevel meta-analysis. *Aggression and Violent Behavior, 55*, 101489. https://doi.org/10.1016/j.avb.2020.101489.

Fein, R. A., & Vossekuil, B. (1999). Assassination in the United States: an operational study of recent assassins, attackers, and near-lethal approaches. *Journal of Forensic Sciences, 44*(2), 321–333.

Ferguson, N., & McAuley, J. W. (2021). Dedicated to the Cause: Identity Development and Violent Extremism. *European Psychologist, 26*(1), 6–14.

Follman, M., Aronsen, G., & Pan, D. (2022). US mass shootings, 1982–2020: data from Mother Jones' investigation. Mother Jones. Available at: https://www.motherjones.com/politics/2012/12/mass-shootings-mother-jones-full-data/. Accessed May 20, 2022.

Gill, P., Clemmow, C., Hetzel, F., Rottweiler, B., Salman, N., Van Der Vegt, I., Marchment, Z., Schumann, S., Zolghadriha, S., Schulten, N., Taylor, H. & Corner, E. (2021). Systematic review of mental health problems and violent extremism. *The Journal of Forensic Psychiatry & Psychology, 32*(1), 51–78.

Gill, P., Corner, E., McKee, A., Hitchen, P., & Betley, P. (2019). What do closed source data tell us about lone actor terrorist behavior? A research note. *Terrorism and Political Violence*, 1–18. https://doi.org/10.1080/09546553.2019.1668781.

Gill, P., Horgan, J., & Deckert, P. (2014). Bombing alone: Tracing the motivations and antecedent behaviors of lone-actor terrorists. *Journal of Forensic Sciences, 59*(2), 425–435. https://doi.org/10.1111/1556-4029.12312.

Gill, P., & Corner, E. (2017). There and back again: The study of mental disorder and terrorist involvement. *American Psychologist, 72*(3), 231–241

Gill, P., Silver, J., Horgan, J., & Corner, E. (2017). Shooting alone: The pre-attack experiences and behaviors of US solo mass murderers. *Journal of Forensic Sciences, 62*(3), 710–714.

Glick, I. D., Cerfolio, N. E., Kamis, D., & Laurence, M. (2021). Domestic mass shooters: The association with unmedicated and untreated psychiatric illness. *Journal of Clinical Psychopharmacology, 41*(4), 366–369.

Grimbergen, C., & Fassaert, T. (2022). Occurrence of psychiatric disorders, self-sufficiency problems and adverse childhood experiences in a population suspected of violent extremism. *Frontiers in Psychiatry, 13*, 1–14.

Gruenewald, J., Chermak, S., & Freilich, J. D. (2013). Distinguishing "loner" attacks from other domestic extremist violence: A comparison of far-right homicide incident and offender characteristics. *Criminology & Public Policy, 12*(1), 65–91. https://doi.org/10 1111/1745-9133.12008.

Hare, R. D., León-Mayer, E., Salinas, J. R., Folino, J., & Neumann, C. S. (2022). Psychopathy and crimes against humanity: A conceptual and empirical examination of human rights violators. *Journal of Criminal Justice, 81*, 101901.

Hare, R. D., & Neumann, C. S. (2008). Psychopathy as a clinical and empirical construct. *Annual Review of Clinical Psychology, 4*, 217–246.

Hewitt, C. (2003). *Understanding terrorism in America*. New York, NY: Routledge.

Horgan, J. (2005). *The psychology of terrorism*. New York, NY: Routledge. https://doi.org/10.4324/9780203496961

James, D. V., Mullen, P. E., Meloy, J. R., Pathé, M. T., Farnham, F. R., Preston, L., & Darnley, B. (2007). The role of mental disorder in attacks on European politicians 1990–2004. *Acta Psychiatrica Scandinavica*, *116*(5), 334–344.

James, D. V., Mullen, P. E., Pathé, M. T., Meloy, J. R., Farnham, F. R., Preston, L., & Darnley, B. (2008). Attacks on the British royal family: The role of psychotic illness. *Journal of the American Academy of Psychiatry and the Law Online*, *36*(1), 59–67.

Jones, D. N. (2013). Psychopathy and Machiavellianism predict differences in racially motivated attitudes and their affiliations. *Journal of Applied Social Psychology*, *43*, E367–E378.

Jurjako, M. (2019). Is psychopathy a harmful dysfunction? *Biology & Philosophy*, *34*(1), 1–23.

Kenyon, J., Baker-Beall, C., & Binder, J. (2021). Lone-actor terrorism – A systematic literature review. *Studies in Conflict & Terrorism*, 1–24. https://www.tandfonline.com/doi/abs/10.1080/1057610X.2021.1892635

Kessler, R. C., Aguilar-Gaxiola, S., Alonso, J., Chatterji, S., Lee, S., Ormel, J., Ustün, T. B., & Wang, P. S. (2009). The global burden of mental disorders: An update from the WHO World Mental Health (WMH) surveys. *Epidemiologia e Psichiatria Sociale*, *18*(1), 23–33. https://doi.org/10.1017/s1121189x00001421.

LaFree, G., Jensen, M. A., James, P. A., & Safer-Lichtenstein, A. (2018). Correlates of violent political extremism in the United States. *Criminology*, *56*(2), 233–268.

Liem, M., van Buuren, J., de Roy van Zuijdewijn, J., Schönberger, H., & Bakker, E. (2018). European lone actor terrorists versus "common" homicide offenders: An empirical analysis. *Homicide Studies*, *22*(1), 45–69. https://doi.org/10.1177/1088767917736797.

Martens, W. H. (2004). The terrorist with antisocial personality disorder. *Journal of Forensic Psychology Practice*, *4*(1), 45–56.

McCauley, C. (2002). Psychological issues in understanding terrorism and the response to terrorism. In C. E. Stout (Ed.), *The psychology of terrorism: Theoretical understandings and perspectives*, Vol. 3, pp. 3–29).

McCauley, C., & Moskalenko, S. (2014). Toward a profile of lone wolf terrorists: What moves an individual from radical opinion to radical action. *Terrorism and Political Violence*, *26*(1), 69–85.

McCauley, C., Moskalenko, S., & Van Son, B. (2013). Characteristics of lone-wolf violent offenders: A comparison of assassins and school attackers. *Perspectives on Terrorism*, *7*(1), 4–24.

Meloy, J. R., Goodwill, A. M., Meloy, M. J., Amat, G., Martinez, M., & Morgan, M. (2019). Some TRAP-18 indicators discriminate between terrorist attackers and other subjects of national security concern. *Journal of Threat Assessment and Management*, *6*(2), 93–110. https://doi.org/10.1037/tam0000119

Misiak, B., Samochowiec, J., Bhui, K., Schouler-Ocak, M., Demunter, H., Kuey, L., Raballo, A., Gorwood, P., Frydecka, D., & Dom, G. (2019). A systematic review on the relationship between mental health, radicalization and mass violence. *European Psychiatry*, *56*(1), 51–59.

Monahan, J. (2012). The individual risk assessment of terrorism. *Psychology, Public Policy, and Law*, *18*, 167–205. https://doi.org/10.1037/a0025792.

Morf, G. (1970). *Terror in Quebec - case studies of the FLQ*. Toronto: Clark, Irwin.

Morgades-Bamba, C. I., Raynal, P., & Chabrol, H. (2018). Exploring the radicalization process in young women. *Terrorism and Political Violence*, *32*(7), 1–19. https://doi.org/10.1080/09546553.2018.1481051.

Pearce, K. (1977). Police negotiations: A new role for the community psychiatrist. *Canadian Psychiatric Association Journal*, *22*, 171–174.

Richards, L., Molinaro, P., Wyman, J., & Craun, S. (2019). *Lone offender: A study of lone offender terrorism in the United States (1972–2015)*. Quantico Virginia: National Center for the Analysis of Violent Crime, Federal Bureau of Investigation, Behavioral Analysis Unit.

Ruby, C. L. (2002), Are Terrorists Mentally Deranged?. Analyses of Social Issues and Public Policy, 2, 15–26.

Sageman, M. (2004). Understanding terror networks. Philadelphia: University of Pennsylvania Press.

Schmid, A. (March, 2023). *Defining Terrorism*. ICCT Report. International Centre for Counter-Terrorism. The Netherlands. Retrieved from: https://www.icct.nl/sites/default/files/2023-03/Schmidt%20-%20Defining%20Terrorism_1.pdf

Schmid, A. & Jongman, A. (1988). *Political Terrorism: A Research Guide to Concepts, Theories, Databases, and Literature*. New Brunswick, NJ: Transaction Books.

Substance Abuse and Mental Health Services Administration. (2021). Key substance use and mental health indicators in the United States: Results from the 2020 National Survey on Drug Use and Health (HHS Publication No. PEP21-07-01-003, NSDUH Series H-56). Rockville, MD: Center for Behavioral Health Statistics and Quality, Substance Abuse and Mental Health Services.

Swann Jr, W. B., & Buhrmester, M. D. (2015). Identity fusion. *Current Directions in Psychological Science*, *24*(1), 52–57. Administration. Retrieved from https://www.samhsa.gov/data/.

Trimbur, M., Amad, A., Horn, M., Thomas, P., & Fovet, T. (2021). Are radicalization and terrorism associated with psychiatric disorders? A systematic review. *Journal of psychiatric research*, *141*, 214–222.

Vermeulen, F., van Leyenhorst, M., Roex, I., Schulten, N., & Tuzani, N. (2022). Between psychopathology and ideology: Challenges and practices in interpreting young extremists experiencing mental illness in The Netherlands. *Frontiers in Psychiatry*, *12*, 2584.

Victoroff, J. (2005). The mind of a terrorist: A review and critique of psychological approaches. *Journal of Conflict Resolution*, *49*(1), 3–42. https://doi.org/10.1177/0022002704272040.

Wolfowicz, M., Litmanovitz, Y., Weisburd, D., & Hasisi B. (2021). Cognitive and behavioral radicalization: A systematic review of the putative risk and protective factors. *Campbell Systematic Reviews*, *17*, e1174. https://doi.org/10.1002/cl2.1174.

Zeman, T., Břeň, J., & Urban, R. (2018). Profile of a lone wolf terrorist: A crisis management perspective. *Journal of Security & Sustainability Issues*, *8*(1), 1. https://doi.org/10.9770/jssi.2018.8.1(1).

Zierhoffer, D. M. (2014). Threat assessment: Do lone terrorists differ from other lone offenders? *Journal of Strategic Security*, *7*(3), 48–62.

35

EUROPEAN APPROACHES TO RISK ASSESSMENT OF TERRORIST OFFENDERS

Andrew Silke

Background

Recent years have witnessed a number of high profile terrorist attacks carried out by perpetrators who had spent time in prison for previous terrorism-related offending. In London at the end of 2019 and beginning of 2020 there were two separate terrorist attacks carried out by former terrorist prisoners. In November 2019, Usman Khan attacked and killed two people and injured three others before being shot dead by police officers. Khan had spent eight years in prison after being convicted for planning terrorist attacks and had been released in December 2018. Just over two months later in February 2020, another released prisoner, Sudesh Amman injured two people in an attack in south London, before he too was shot dead by police officers who had him under close surveillance. Amman had been released from prison just ten days earlier. He had spent 20 months in prison after being convicted of possessing and disseminating documents useful to terrorists. In November 2020, Kujtim Fejzulai carried out a terrorist attack in Vienna, killing four people and injuring 23 more using firearms and a knife. He was shot dead by police responding to the attack. Fejzulai had been jailed in 2019 after a failed attempt to travel to join Islamic State in Syria. He spent 8 months in prison and carried out his attack eleven months after his release.

These, and other similar cases, starkly illustrate the potential dangers posed by released terrorist prisoners. Not surprisingly, when such attacks occur they fuel understandable debates and concern about risk assessment, de-radicalisation, re-integration and the impact of prison on terrorists. While the available evidence encouragingly suggests that re-offending rates for released terrorist prisoners overall are actually relatively low,[1] our understanding of the minority who do re-offend is poor. Current research does not provide much insight into the processes and risks around released prisoners who re-engage with terrorism, and in particular we lack information on what distinguishes offenders such as Khan, Amman and Fejzulai from the majority who do not re-engage.

These cases naturally draw particular attention to how risk assessment and risk management in relation to terrorist offenders in prison and probation contexts are carried out. Our understanding of the risk assessment of terrorists and extremists is overall still in its relative infancy, but there is no denying that we have witnessed enormous progress in the last 15 years. A 2019 review, for example, was able to identify 16 different potential risk assessment frameworks which had been developed for use with terrorist and violent extremist offenders.[2] Some of those frameworks

DOI: 10.4324/9781003326373-40

were designed for use with convicted offenders (both in custody and after release), whereas others were designed for use in a pre-offending space (e.g. with individuals who were considered potentially vulnerable to radicalisation).

The focus of this chapter is on frameworks which are used with convicted offenders in prison or probation settings. Overall progress in this area has been uneven and not all countries are as equally developed or sophisticated in their approach to risk assessment and management for these types of offenders. Such variation applies even in a European context, where, at least by wider international standards, prison and probation systems are comparatively well organised and resourced. Some European countries have invested resources in developing bespoke risk assessment frameworks for their terrorism and violent extremism-related offenders, while others have imported frameworks originally developed for use in other jurisdictions. The United Kingdom has arguably led the way in terms of bespoke development, though interestingly it's constituent nations have followed separate paths in responding to the problem. England and Wales, for example, developed the Extremism Risk Guidance 22+ (ERG) in 2011 which has become one of the most well-known and heavily researched risk assessment frameworks. Northern Ireland introduced a separate system, the Terrorism Risk Offender Dynamic Assessment (TRODA) in 2021, which has been designed to reflect some of the distinctive features and challenges faced in the Northern Irish context. In contrast, Scotland has used the Violent Extremist Risk Assessment protocol (VERA-2R), a risk assessment framework originally designed in Canada and first implemented in Australia, and which is now the system with the widest international use. A number of European countries, including Germany, Sweden, Austria, France, The Netherlands and Belgium have also used VERA-2R.[3] A major focus of this chapter will be to look at these three frameworks, particularly the two longer established ones about which there has been more attention and research.

It is very likely we will make even further progress on terrorist risk assessment over the next decade. The field has moved away from a position where such prisoners were very poorly understood in terms of risk assessment frameworks, and where the default position was to assume that such work was either almost impossible, or else that such prisoners would *always* be high risk. The legacy of both these misguided perspectives is still with us and there is no question that risk assessment of these types of prisoners faces unique and serious challenges. That said, sensible risk assessment is increasingly possible in these cases. The development of theoretically informed measures to do this certainly represents a significant step forward, as is the growing recognition and acceptance of the different issues which need to be considered for these prisoners.

Structured Professional Judgement and Terrorist Risk Assessment

Most of the terrorism-related risk assessment frameworks used with convicted offenders follow a structured professional judgement (SPJ) approach. This is certainly true of the three frameworks we will examine in more detail here: ERG, VERA-2R and TRODA. The SPJ approach to risk assessment was first introduced in 1993 when it was applied to violence risk assessment. It has since become one of the dominant models for risk assessment in a variety of contexts. A range of studies has found that risk assessments determined by SPJ approaches tend to outperform assessments using either actuarial approaches or unstructured clinical judgment frameworks.[4] While both of those alternative approaches continue to have advocates, SPJ is nonetheless now widely considered a "good practice" framework for assessing and managing risk.[5]

SPJ involves a combination of empirical knowledge and professional judgment.[6] The assessor identifies a risk level by considering a defined set of relevant risk factors using an evidence base and a pre-established rating system. SPJ protocols draw on diverse factors which are generally divided into a number of themes or domains. The factors are drawn from a systematic assessment of the relevant scientific knowledge base and from obtained empirical evidence.

One criticism which has been made of how terrorism risk frameworks have used the SPJ approach is that, as Logan and Lloyd have memorably phrased it, they have tended to adopt a "lite" version of SPJ rather than the "full-fat version." As assessed by Logan and Llyod, SPJ in the terrorism frameworks typically involves

the identification of risk (and protective, if applicable) factors in the individual case and then a summary risk rating of high, medium, or low risk – a judgement made on the evaluator's overall appraisal of risk based on the pattern of risk factors present in the case.[7]

It can miss out however on the scenario planning and formulation elements normally associated with a "full-fat" SPJ and which usually aims to achieve a comprehensive risk management.

Apart from this issue, it is worth noting that in general the main weaknesses of an SPJ approach are first, that in order to be carried out effectively the SPJ model assumes that the assessors have an appropriate level of knowledge and experience. SPJ approaches will not work well with inexperienced and/or insufficiently qualified assessors. Second, the SPJ approach also assumes that the risk factors being used are optimal.[8] This is a particular challenge in a context where a novel risk assessment framework is being developed for a new population and where the knowledge base may be uncertain or developing rapidly. Such a context certainly has applied in terms of the development of risk assessment frameworks for terrorist and violent extremist offenders since 2010. SPJ approaches are recognised as needing revision to reflect changes in the scientific evidence base. As a result, a reflective framework to allow for periodic assessment of changes in the knowledge base should be built into an SPJ framework. All three of the frameworks considered in this chapter have committed to reflective reviews in light of changes in the relevant scientific literature and we can expect that all will be periodically revised and updated as a result.

VERA-2R

The Violent Extremist Risk Assessment (VERA) framework is the oldest and geographically the most widely used risk assessment framework for terrorist and violent extremist offenders. Of the three frameworks considered here, VERA-2R is the only one which has been commercialised and is also the only one which has been translated into other languages beyond English. This has facilitated its adoption or use in a variety of countries, including Canada, Australia, Belgium and The Netherlands. The original iteration of VERA was first developed in 2009,[9] with a revised version appearing in 2010[10] and the latest iteration being published in 2018.[11] The original version of the framework used 25 factors, but the latest VERA-2R is built around assessing individuals on 45 factors which are organised into six domains. These domains are structured into:

Belief, attitudes and ideology
Social context and intention
History, action and capacity
Commitment and motivation
Protective and risk-mitigating indicators

The sixth domain is available for considering additional factors, including factors relating to criminal history, personal history and mental health disorder.

The factors used in VERA were selected primarily on the basis of a review of the relevant scientific literature in conjunction with expert review and consultation. This is similar to the approaches which broadly informed the development of the other frameworks, though ERG was also able to draw on insights from direct work with terrorist offenders. There is some overlap with many of the factors identified in the ERG,[12] though the VERA-2R factors notably also include 6 protective factors.

VERA-2R supplies an overall risk assessment score for the individual terrorist. The framework currently gives equal weighting to the different factors in arriving at this score though this approach may change at the some point in the future if follow-up data becomes available.

A small-scale study by Beardsley and Beech found that the VERA-2 factors appeared to be relevant and supported its use for risk assessment[13] but more robust evaluations are not available in the open literature. A study by Martine Herzog-Evans assessed that VERA-2 had intrinsic merit but overall concluded that the ERG would probably be a better fit for the French context.[14] A later study based on users' perceptions in a French context painted an often critical picture of VERA, with arguments that the framework was used to justify interpretations of radicalisation rather than potentially allowing for alternative explanations. The authors argued that VERA-2R was being used to give "scientific trappings to a labelling of dangerousness."[15] Some similar concerns were also raised by Australian users of VERA-2R, though there was also explicit recognition among that sample that, whatever the limitations, there was still a genuine need and role for tailored tools such as VERA-2R.[16] The effectiveness and suitability of VERA-2R has been source of debate in the Australian context where for example the Australian Parliamentary Joint Committee on intelligence and Security reported in 2021 that it:

> was not entirely convinced on the basis of the evidence provided to the inquiry that the VERA-2R tool is the most appropriate tool to determine the level of risk posed by a convicted terrorist offender. The Committee recommended … that an independent review of VERA-2R and alternatives be undertaken, with findings reported to the Parliament.[17]

A key factor in the doubt expressed around VERA-2R in this context was the lack of evidence available around the framework's validity, an issue to which we will return later in this chapter.

Extremism Risk Guidance (ERG 22+)

Prior to 2010, risk assessment in terrorism-related cases in England and Wales primarily relied on the Offender Assessment System (OASys).[18] OASys was developed in the 1990s and was intended to provide a "comprehensive assessment and planning instrument to give a systematic, reliable and evidence-based structure to the established sentence management process."[19] OASys provides an assessment of (1) an individual's risk of causing serious harm; and (2) an individual's risk of reconviction.

However, from the mid-2000s onwards, the National Offender Management Service (later renamed HM Prison and Probation Service (HMPPS)) increasingly recognised that a more tailored risk assessment framework was needed for terrorism-related offenders. The Extremism Risk Guidance 22+ (ERG 22+) was the result of that effort.[20] Developed by the Operational Intervention Services Group, the ERG was launched in 2011. The ERG currently assesses terrorism-related offenders on 22 factors which are believed to be related to extremist offending (the "+" in the title is a reflection that the model will consider other factors beyond the 22 if they are shown to be relevant to a particular case). These 22 factors are broken down into three domains: (1) engagement, (2) intent and (3) capability.[21]

The 22 specific factors are:

1 Need to redress injustice and express grievance
2 Need to defend against threat
3 Need for identity, meaning and belonging
4 Need for status
5 Need for excitement, comradeship or adventure
6 Need to dominate others
7 Susceptibility to indoctrination
8 Political/moral motivation
9 Opportunistic involvement
10 Transitional periods
11 Family and/or friends support extremist offending
12 Group influence and control
13 Presence of mental illness or personality disorder
14 Over-identification with an extremist group, cause or ideology
15 "Us and them" thinking
16 Dehumanisation of the enemy
17 Attitudes that justify offending
18 Harmful means to an end
19 Harmful end objectives
20 Individual knowledge, skills and competencies to commit extremist offences
21 Access to networks, funding and equipment to commit extremist offences
22 Criminal history

The specific ERG factors were selected on the basis of information from the then current "literature on risk assessment and terrorism, by casework with offenders convicted under terrorist legislation and by discussion with international peers."[22] Since the initial development of the ERG, further work has been undertaken to establish an evidence base around the framework. The original developers recognised that the ERG factors were essentially theoretical factors and that there was uncertainty regarding the strength of relationships with offending. As the developers highlighted at the time:

> The ERG factors are essentially working hypotheses to account for how an individual became engaged and to capture the features of their mind-set, their intentions and their capability for terrorism. None of these factors has a demonstrated link with future offending, so are as yet unproven. As such the ERG cannot predict risk with any certainty, but directs attention to aspects of the individual associated with their offending where intervention may be targeted or proportionate risk management approaches deployed.[23]

ERG 22+ does not provide a specific risk assessment score for an offender (in the same manner that a system such as OASys does) partly because the developers felt that the evidence base is weaker and the influence of the 22 factors on risk outcomes is not yet known. The 22 factors currently all carry a theoretical equal weighting at the start of an assessment (i.e. no factors are considered a priori as being more important than others). Once assessment begins, case formulation may result in particular factors being deemed especially relevant to the specific case in hand.

Much as VERA-2R has been the target of recent critical attention in Australia, the ERG has also been the focus of criticism. In particular, in the initial years following its implementation relatively little information was released regarding the ERG and this lack of information led to some accusations in the media that it was a secret and unscientific framework.[24] Such assessments were harsh but they did highlight that a lack of publically information around a new framework could be counterproductive. Thankfully, more recent years have seen a growing literature base regarding the ERG[25] and have also witnessed the emergence of research which is based on an analysis of ERG assessments.[26] Indeed, of all the risk assessment frameworks designed for use with convicted terrorist offenders, the ERG is now probably the framework with the most extensive and strongest published evidence base. There is still currently a lack of evidence around the predictive validity of the ERG, though it seems increasingly likely that the ERG will be the first framework to make such data available.

When used in the setting for which it was originally designed researchers have generally supported the use of the ERG. For example, Rita Augestad Knudsen recently concluded that the "actual use of the ERG in England and Wales' prisons has ... incorporated some relevant safeguards such as encouraging incorporation of context as well as vetting and training assessors, and it is promising that the tool is presently under review."[27] However, she criticised the manner in which the ERG factors had been co-opted in the design of the Vulnerability Assessment Framework (VAF), for example, which is used in the pre-offending space in England and Wales and which does not enjoy many of the safeguards associated with the ERG.

Terrorism Risk Offender Dynamic Assessment (TRODA)

A new risk assessment framework which was introduced in 2021 is the Terrorism Risk Offender Dynamic Assessment (TRODA). This was designed specifically for use in Northern Ireland and is focused on terrorism-related offenders within the Northern Irish prison and probation system. TRODA was designed to reflect the distinctive challenges and practical issues experienced in Northern Ireland with regard to these types of offenders, almost all of whom are connected to a range of paramilitary groups currently or formerly active in the region.

During the height of the Northern Ireland Troubles, it is estimated that somewhere between 20,000 and 32,000 men and women were incarcerated for terrorism-related offences between 1969–1998. From the 1970s onwards, terrorism related prisoners were concentrated primarily in Long Kesh (later called HMP The Maze). At its height, this prison held over 1000 prisoners and it remained the primary holding facility for such prisoners throughout the Troubles era.[28] (Bates-Gaston, 2003). Following the closure of HMP The Maze in 2000 as part of the Good Friday peace process, terrorism-related prisoners have since been mainly concentrated (but not exclusively so) at HMP Maghaberry, which is the prison designated within the Northern Ireland prison estate for high security inmates.

During the course of the Troubles, terrorism-related offenders developed a sophisticated doctrine to attempt to compromise the secure and safe operations of the prison estate. A range of issues emerged, including several escapes and attempted escapes, orchestrated mass riots, routine intimidation and harassment of staff (both in the prison and in the outside community), the murder of prison officers, the murders of other inmates, the deaths of ten prisoners on hunger strike, the smuggling in of firearms and explosives, etc. This was most clearly seen in the operation of HMP The Maze, but was also an issue at other locations where such prisoners were held (e.g. HMP Whitemoor and HMP Parkhurst in England).[29]

These prisoners and the groups they belonged to became very experienced in using interpersonal skills and other techniques to influence and manipulate staff.[30] In the post-Good Friday era, while terrorism-related prisoner numbers are greatly reduced, they have continued to use many of the same strategies and tactics within custody settings which were originally developed in the Troubles era. In this regard, such prisoners in Northern Ireland typically present a more challenging dynamic than that normally seen with regard to Islamist-inspired or far-right prisoners, who comprise the majority of terrorism-related prisoners in the rest of the United Kingdom prison estate, for example. The Northern Ireland prisoners are also distinctive because of the strong group dynamic which operates, including to the point where the prisoners have a command structure and follow orders from designated leaders. Added to this, there is still a significant degree of open support and tolerance for the prisoners within specific communities in Northern Ireland, which is in contrast to the experience of other types of terrorist offenders found in the rest of the United Kingdom.

TRODA was designed to reflect these distinctive characteristics of the Northern Ireland terrorism-related offender population and the challenges they posed. In common with the other major risk assessment frameworks discussed earlier, TRODA adopts a structured professional judgement (SPJ) for risk assessment. The TRODA framework provides 32 risk factors around which to build a structured risk assessment. These factors are organised into seven domains. The first six domains are concerned with "engagement" and are factors considered due to their potential role in increasing or sustaining engagement in terrorism related offending. The seventh domain is concerned with "disengagement" factors. These are factors with a potential role for increasing the likelihood of disengaging from terrorism related offending.

The first domain focuses on factors relating to psychology, identity & beliefs. The second domain focuses on intent and attitudes. The third domain covers social context factors relating to family and group association. The fourth section considers vulnerability factors linked to risk such as alcohol and drug abuse, mental health factors and social isolation. The fifth section looks at capacity and capability factors. The sixth section looks at factors concerned with staff & regime manipulation. The final section incorporates factors indicative of disengagement & desistence from terrorist related offending.

Issues for Consideration

Risk assessment of terrorists and extremists has experienced considerable progress in the past 15 years. The field has moved from a position where such prisoners were very poorly understood in terms of risk assessment frameworks, to one where there is greater understanding of the potential factors which play a role for these offenders compared to "ordinary" offenders. There is also clearer recognition that risk assessment of these types of prisoners faces unique and serious challenges. Added to this, the development of a range of theoretically informed measures to assist risk assessment, such as ERG 22+, VERA-2R and TRODA represent significant steps forward.

Nevertheless, very significant problems remain. There are substantial limitations in our knowledge and competence in working with such offenders. There are also serious gaps in the evidence base and it is likely to be some time before the current frameworks can be fully validated by solid research evidence. There are also particularly large gaps in risk assessment for certain types of terrorist prisoners and particular contexts. A great deal of recent effort has been focused on the needs and contexts of Islamist extremists and (to a lesser extent) far-right extremists, for example. In contrast, risk assessment for terrorism-related offenders of the type typical in Northern Ireland had been much more poorly explored before the development of TRODA. There was certainly a strong case for the development of a context specific framework. Northern

Ireland faces challenges in this area which are unique compared to the rest of the United Kingdom. As highlighted by Professor Jackie Bates-Gaston:

> There are capacity and cultural differences between the paramilitaries in Northern Ireland prisons and the Islamist Extremists in England and Wales. Both Loyalist and Republican prisoners have consistently refused to engage in work or any form of risk assessment, "rehabilitation or interventions." When released on Licence, they have successfully resisted supervision by the Probation Board or the Police Service Northern Ireland (CJINI response to NI Justice Committee, 2012) unlike in England and Wales where these prisoners are managed by the Multi Agency Public Protection Arrangements (MAPPA).[31]

Context *is* critical in considering risk assessment of terrorists and extremists. Many researchers, for example, have questioned the extent to which risk assessment frameworks developed in one context or region, or for one particular type of population, can be successfully applied to others.[32]

Certainly, not all terrorist and extremist offenders are the same. Terrorists are surprisingly heterogeneous and they defy simple categorization into one type or profile. This applies as much to entire terrorist movements as it does to individuals, and there is a potentially bewildering array of terrorist groups to deal with. Big categories such as Religious, Right wing, Anarchist and Nationalist/Separatist can be further split and divided into ultimately potentially hundreds of sub-categories. Naturally there is considerable variation between these different types of movements on important factors not least around the movement's structure, community support and membership, but also, crucially, around the level and nature of the violence the groups are prepared to encourage and engage in. As a result, each movement needs to be considered in its own political, social and aspirational context.

Similarly, just as there are differences between groups and ideologies, there are also significant differences between the individuals who belong to or are connected with these movements and causes. ERG22+, for example, was originally designed for use with individuals who had been convicted of terrorism-related offences and who were still in prison.[33] The factors, however, were then exported en masse to the Vulnerability Assessment Framework (VAF) which was used with individuals in community settings in a very different context and where the assessors do not have the same experience or qualifications as required for users of the ERG. This co-option of the ERG factors, for a population that it was not designed for, inevitably and understandably attracted considerable criticism.[34]

Gender Bias?

One concern with most of the risk assessment frameworks is that they were originally essentially designed primarily for use with male offenders. The literature they were derived from was focused mainly on male offenders, as was any case work (when that played a role in informing the development of the framework).[35] Further, initial testing around reliability issues also tended to be based on male cases.[36] As a result, the practical applicability of the frameworks for risk assessment with female subjects is unclear. Recently, there has been increasing recognition that most mainstream models of radicalisation are often very poor with regard to the experience of girls and women. Risk assessment frameworks which have been built on these models can potentially have significant blind spots when it comes to the experiences, pathways and trajectories of female terrorists. It is worth noting that recent years have seen the development of some new frameworks for understanding the decision-making, pathways and agency of women in terrorism, such as the "Gendered Radicalisation" model proposed by Pearson, Winterbotham & Brown (2021).[37] The Gendered Radicalisation model explores how gender operates as a variable within the radicalisation process to influence women and men's journeys to violent extremism and terrorism and it explicitly tries to examine how gender roles and relations shape terrorist activity. That type of perspective is largely absent from the domain and factor structures currently in use with the existing risk assessment models and this is certainly an area which needs attention.

Lack of Evidence around the Validity and Effectiveness of the Frameworks

A long running criticism of the different frameworks has been the lack of evidence around each framework's predictive validity and their overall effectiveness. In the early years of any new risk assessment framework – and particularly ones which are focused on what is a small offender population – a lack of validity data is not at all surprising and is to be expected. It takes time to build up relevant evidence.

Evidence is now emerging that the longer established risk assessment tools such as ERG and VERA-2R have demonstrated reliability. Inter-rater reliability between assessors, for example, looks good. What is currently relatively lacking, however, is evidence around validity. There is no evidence in the public domain around the predictive validity, for example, of any of the frameworks. Given that both VERA-2R and ERG have been in use for over a decade it is reasonable at this point to expect that more data should be available.

There are signs that such data is at least beginning to appear in the open literature in connection to the ERG. For example, in 2019, HMPPS published a study on the construct validity of the ERG. This was partly based on the analysis of 171 completed ERG assessments on offenders who had been convicted of Islamist extremism-related offences. The study found that the 22 risk factors used by ERG were generally consistent in their measurement of the overall risk. The review did flag that a case existed to change the current domain structure from three to five domains and made some other potential proposals for how the ERG might be revised.[38]

In contrast, there have been no similar or equivalent studies published in relation to VERA-2R. As a result, there is more uncertainty around how well the VERA-2R factors work in actual assessments and how much confidence can be placed in their validity.

A related concern for both tests is that no outcome data has been published yet. We do not know yet how good the frameworks are at identifying high risk offenders, for example, as measured by subsequent re-offending? Given the potential seriousness of re-offending of released terrorist prisoners this is clearly an important question but one on which almost no information is available.

Both ERG and VERA-2R have now been in use for over ten years and it is reasonable to now expect more data to be published. The ERG, for example, has been used on hundreds of offenders in England and Wales, significant numbers of whom have been released from prison and where data should be available with regard to subsequent re-offending. To date, information is only available in relation to a handful of cases such as in connection with the coroner inquests which followed Usman Khan's attack in 2019.[39]

Even less information and data are currently available in connection with VERA-2R. Indeed, it is unclear how many offenders have actually been assessed using the VERA-2R. Most of the countries which are reported as having used the VERA-2R have substantially smaller terrorist prisoner populations than England and Wales. Given that, it is possible that even though VERA-2R has been used in several countries, the total number of prisoners assessed using the framework may potentially be roughly equivalent to the ERG.

An additional problem facing evaluation of VERA-2R is that it is likely that there would be significant barriers in compiling assessments from across the different jurisdictions into one database. As a result, VERA-2R might struggle for some considerable time to be able to publish data equivalent to that which is now emerging in relation to the ERG. One consequence is that the evidence base with regard to validity and effectiveness will probably be much more clearly established for the ERG first.

Are Current Risk Assessment Factors Biased Towards Radicalisation?

A final potential concern to consider is whether the factors currently used in the risk assessment frameworks are top heavy with items connected to initial processes of radicalisation? John Horgan made the important point that it is useful to think about involvement in terrorism in terms of a life-cycle model composed of three stages (1) becoming involved in terrorism, (2) staying involved in terrorism, and, (3) leaving terrorism.[40] To this we can also add a fourth potential stage: (4) returning to terrorism.

All of the existing risk assessment frameworks have drawn on the research literature on radicalisation as part of the foundation for each framework. This literature, however, tends to be heavily focused on the first stage: *Becoming involved* in terrorism. In comparative terms, much less research energy has focused on the other stages. Leaving terrorism is a topic which has attracted growing interest and our understanding of disengagement and deradicalisation factors and processes is deepening.[41] However, staying involved and returning to terrorism have been relatively poorly studied and feature in only a very limited capacity in research to date. Yet, both of these elements theoretically look crucial to risk assessment in the context of prisoners and released offenders.

Conclusions

Risk assessment of terrorist prisoners is a work in progress. Though the picture is improving, it is still important to bear in mind the current limitations in our knowledge and competence in working with such offenders. There remain serious gaps in the evidence base and it is likely to be some time before the current risk assessment frameworks can be properly validated by solid research evidence. There are promising signs that such information is beginning to appear, particularly in relation to the ERG framework, but more is certainly needed.

In the long term, there is wide recognition that a great deal of further work is needed to identify the most reliable and valid factors on which to base risk assessment around terrorism-related offenders. It is unlikely there will be an endpoint to such labour. At one level, we can expect the scientific evidence base to keep evolving and this will impact on the risk assessment frameworks considered here – all of which are committed to a process of reflection and review based on changes in that evidence. Equally important, we can also expect to see significant changes in the nature of the terrorist threat itself – not least in terms of the motivations and the characteristics of the perpetrators. Context matters, and frameworks designed and tested on earlier generations of offenders should not be automatically expected to apply as well to future ones. Risk assessment in this field will be a dynamic process.

Nonetheless, it would be churlish not to end by noting that considerable progress has still been made in the past 15 years. Today, we are in a much better position to conduct risk assessments and formulate risk management in relation to terrorism-related offenders. One certainty is that this will remain a complex but vitally important issue as we go forward.

Notes

1 Silke, Andrew, and John Morrison. *Re-offending by released terrorist prisoners: Separating hype from reality.* International Centre for Counter-Terrorism, 2020.

2 Van der Heide, Liesbeth, Marieke van der Zwan, and Maarten van Leyenhorst. *The practitioner's guide to the galaxy: A comparison of risk assessment tools for violent extremism.* International Centre for Counter-Terrorism, 2019.

3 https://www.vera-2r.nl/international.

4 Lodewijks, Henny PB, Theo AH Doreleijers, Corine De Ruiter, and Randy Borum. "Predictive validity of the Structured Assessment of Violence Risk in Youth (SAVRY) during residential treatment." *International Journal of Law and Psychiatry* 31, no. 3 (2008): 263–271.

5 Pedersen, Liselotte, Kirsten Rasmussen, and Peter Elsass. "Risk assessment: The value of structured professional judgments." *International Journal of Forensic Mental Health* 9, no. 2 (2010): 74–81.

6 Hart, S. D., Douglas, K. S., & Guy, L. S. (2017). "The structured professional judgement approach to violence risk assessment: Origins, nature, and advances." In D. P. Boer, A. R. Beech, T. Ward, L. A. Craig, M. Rettenberger, L. E. Marshall, & W. L. Marshall (Eds.), *The Wiley handbook on the theories, assessment, and treatment of sexual offending* (pp. 643–666). Wiley Blackwell.

7 Logan, Caroline, and Monica Lloyd. "Violent extremism: A comparison of approaches to assessing and managing risk." *Legal and Criminological Psychology* 24, no. 1 (2019): 141–161.

8 Hart, Stephen D., Kevin S. Douglas, and Laura S. Guy. "The structured professional judgement approach to violence risk assessment: Origins, nature, and advances." *The Wiley handbook on the theories, assessment and treatment of sexual offending* 2 (2016): 643–666.

9 Pressman, D. Elaine. *Risk assessment decisions for violent political extremism.* (2009). Public Safety Canada, Government of Canada, Ottawa. Cat. No. PS3-1/2009-2-1E-PDF.

10 Pressman, D. Elaine, and John Flockton. "Violent extremist risk assessment: Issues and applications of the VERA-2 in a high-security correctional setting." In *Prisons, terrorism and extremism*, pp. 122–143. Routledge, 2014; Pressman, D. Elaine. "The complex dynamic causality of violent extremism: Applications of the VERA-2 risk assessment method to CVE initiatives." In *Disaster forensics*, pp. 249–269. Springer, Cham, 2016.

11 Pressman, Elaine, D. Duits, Thomas Rinne, and John Flockton. "VERA-2R a structured professional judgement approach." European Commission, 2018.

12 Höffler, Katrin, Miriam Meyer, and Veronika Möller. "Risk assessment—The key to more security? Factors, tools, and practices in dealing with extremist individuals." *European Journal on Criminal Policy and Research* 28 (2022): 1–27.

13 Beardsley, Nicola L., and Anthony R. Beech. "Applying the violent extremist risk assessment (VERA) to a sample of terrorist case studies." *Journal of Aggression, Conflict and Peace Research* 5, no. 1 (2013): 4–15

14 Herzog-Evans, Martine. "A comparison of two structured professional judgment tools for violent extremism and their relevance in the French context." *European Journal of Probation* 10, no. 1 (2018): 3–27.

15 Chantraine, Gilles, and David Scheer. "«Risques» et «radicalisation». Critiques savantes et professionnelles d'un outil d'évaluation criminologique." *Sociologies Pratiques* 1 (2020): 73–83.

16 Cherney, Adrian. "The release and community supervision of radicalised offenders: Issues and challenges that can influence reintegration." *Terrorism and Political Violence* 33, no. 1 (2021): 119–137.

17 https://www.aph.gov.au/Parliamentary_Business/Committees/Joint/Intelligence_and_Security/ReviewofAFPPowers/Report/section?id=committees%2Freportjnt%2F024517%2F73595.

18 HM Prison Service and The National Probation Service. *OASys guidance.* The Stationery Office, London, 2002. See also, Mehta, Anisha. "Fit for purpose: OASys assessments and parole decision s - A practitioner's view." *Probation Journal* 55, no. 2 (2008): 189–194.

19 HM Prison Service. *Offender assessment and sentence management – OASys.* (2003). https://www.justice.gov.uk/downloads/offenders/psipso/pso/PSO_2205_offender_assessment_and_sentence_management.doc.

20 Rehabilitation Services Group. *Extremism risk guidance 22+: Summary and overview.* National Offender Management Service, 2011.

21 Lloyd, Monica, and Christopher Dean. "The development of structured guidelines for assessing risk in extremist offenders." *Journal of Threat Assessment and Management* 2, no. 1 (2015): 40.

22 Interventions Services. *Extremism Risk Guidance (ERG) 22+: Structured Professional Guidelines for Assessing Risk of Extremist Offending*. HM Prison & Probation Service, 2019.

23 Rehabilitation Services Group. *Extremism risk guidance 22+: Summary and overview*. National Offender Management Service, 2011.

24 https://www.theguardian.com/uk-news/2016/sep/29/academics-criticise-prevent-anti-radicalisation-strategy-open-letter.

25 Powis, Beverly, Kiran Randhawa, and Darren Bishopp. "An examination of the structural properties of the Extremism Risk Guidelines (ERG22+): A structured formulation tool for extremist offenders." *Terrorism and Political Violence* 33, no. 6 (2021): 1141–1159.

26 Kenyon, Jonathan, Jens Binder, and Christopher Baker-Beall. "Understanding the role of the internet in the process of radicalisation: An analysis of convicted extremists in England and Wales." *Studies in Conflict & Terrorism* (2022): 1–25. https://www.tandfonline.com/action/showCitFormats?doi=10.1080%2F1057610X.2022.2065902&area=0000000000000001

27 Rita Augestad, Knudsen. Measuring radicalisation: Risk assessment conceptualisations and practice in England and Wales. *Behavioral Sciences of Terrorism and Political Aggression* 12, no. 1 (2020): 37–54.

28 Bates-Gaston, Jacqueline. "Terrorism and imprisonment in Northern Ireland: A psychological perspective." In Andrew Silke (Ed.), *Terrorists, Victims and Society: Psychological Perspectives on Terrorism and Its Consequences,*233–255, Wiley, 2003.

29 Bates-Gaston, Jacqueline. "Prisons and detention: Reflections on the Northern Ireland experience." In *Routledge handbook of terrorism and counterterrorism*, pp. 444–457. Routledge, 2018.

30 Silke, Andrew. *Prisons, terrorism and extremism*. Routledge, Oxford, 2014.

31 Bates-Gaston, Jacqueline. "Prisons and detention: Reflections on the Northern Ireland experience." In *Routledge handbook of terrorism and counterterrorism*, pp. 444–457. Routledge, 2018.

32 Herzog-Evans, Martine. "A comparison of two structured professional judgment tools for violent extremism and their relevance in the French context." *European Journal of Probation* 10, no. 1 (2018): 3–27.

33 Rehabilitation Services Group. *Extremism risk guidance 22+: Summary and overview*. National Offender Management Service, 2011.

34 Augestad Knudsen, Rita. "Measuring radicalisation: Risk assessment conceptualisations and practice in England and Wales." *Behavioral Sciences of Terrorism and Political Aggression* 12, no. 1 (2020): 37–54.

35 Lloyd Monica and Dean Christopher. The development of structured guidelines for assessing risk in extremist offenders. *Journal of Threat Assessment and Management* 2, no. 1 (2015): 40.

36 For example see Pressman, D. Elaine., and Flockton, John S. Violent extremist risk assessment: Issues and applications of the VERA 2 in a high-security correctional setting. In Andrew Silke (Ed.), *Prisons, terrorism and extremism: Critical issues in management, radicalisation and reform* (pp. 122–143). Routledge, Oxon, UK, 2014; and Powis, Beverly, Randhawa-Horne, Kiran and Bishopp, Darren (2019). The Structural Properties of the Extremism Risk Guidelines (ERG22+): A structured formulation tool for extremist offenders. London: Ministry of Justice.

37 Pearson, Elizabeth, Winterbotham, Emily, and Brown, Katherine E. *Countering violent extremism: Making gender matter*. Springer Nature, 2021.

38 Powis, Beverly, Randhawa-Horne, Kiran and Bishopp, Darren (2019). The Structural Properties of the Extremism Risk Guidelines (ERG22+): a structured formulation tool for extremist offenders. London: Ministry of Justice

39 https://fishmongershallinquests.independent.gov.uk/.

40 Horgan, John. *The psychology of terrorism*. Routledge, 2004.

41 For example Silke, Andrew, John Morrison, Heidi Maiberg, Chloe Slay, and Rebecca Stewart. "The Phoenix model of disengagement and deradicalisation from terrorism and violent extremism." *Monatsschrift für Kriminologie und Strafrechtsreform* 104, no. 3 (2021): 310–320.

36

A MODEL FOR COUNTERING VIOLENT EXTREMISM AND PROMOTING DISENGAGEMENT FROM TERRORISM

Joshua Sinai

The objective of governments' counterterrorism campaigns is to resolve and terminate terrorist insurgencies against them, whether domestically or overseas, by organized groups or lone actors. Generally, this is accomplished through two components. The first is the "hard component" of military, law enforcement, intelligence, and other related measures to defeat the insurgents on the ground and, increasingly, in cyberspace. The second consists of the "soft component" to employ appropriate narratives and related conflict resolution programs to counter the radicalization of susceptible individuals into the type of violent extremism that sustains terrorist groups and lone actors in order to promote their disengagement from terrorism into more constructive non-violent activities. To accomplish this "soft component" it is crucial to identify the appropriate measures that will prove effective in persuading such groups and lone actors, as well as their extremist sub-cultures in terms of activists and sympathizers, to adopt more peaceful means to express their grievances and objectives through constructive and peaceful means. In such a way, in best case scenarios, extremist terrorist groups and lone actors will be marginalized and will ultimately give up their violent activities, which will hopefully enable them to be eventually re-integrated into their societies as peaceful citizens.

Terrorist groups, lone actors, and their various types of adherents, operate in different types of political environments, ranging from authoritarian, failed states, to democratic systems, where the underlying conditions that give rise to terrorism differ, although they may cross over from one specific type of environment to another, for instance, in having a conflict in an authoritarian environment such as the Middle East influence adherents in a democratic country. As a result of such different political environments, with each requiring its own tailored governmental response measures, this approach focuses on countering violent extremism (CVE) in democratic societies, where constructive alternatives to engaging in violence are feasible, for example, through freedom of expression, political assembly, and voting in elections. In repressive authoritarian or failed states, however, the model presented in this article would need to be reconfigured to address the specific challenges presented by terrorist insurgencies that operate in such constrained political systems.

DOI: 10.4324/9781003326373-41

Countering Radicalization into Violent Extremism – The Pyramid of Radicalization Model

A government's campaign to counter violent extremist oppositionary movements in democratic societies involves persuading their susceptible individuals that more effective and useful non-violent alternatives to express themselves politically, religiously, or on other issues, are feasible. In this approach, a pyramid of radicalization model is employed to demonstrate the components and measures that are required for effective CVE.

Two components are required to be implemented in an integrated manner in an effective CVE campaign. The **first component** is to **identify the levels of the pyramid of radicalization** that need to be countered (see Figure 36.1). In this pyramid, the process of radicalization into violent extremism is comparable to ascending an increasingly narrow pyramid, where the majority **non-violent sympathizers** are located at its base and **violent extremists** (i.e., those who become terrorists) are at the smaller apex. Most individuals holding strong political beliefs, who can be characterized as sympathizers of extremist movements, are located at the **bottom of the pyramid**. They provide the pool for a minority of individuals who will ascend to become **activists** at the **middle of the pyramid**. The activists are non-violent extremists who are active on behalf of their extremist cause, for example, by participating in street demonstrations, handing out pamphlets, or managing extremist websites. In Islamist movements, such individuals would be active in extremist, yet largely non-violent organizations such as Hizb ut-Tahrir or the Muslim Brotherhood, both of which are outlawed in some countries. In far-right movements, they would be active in organizations such as the English Defence League (EDL). Within such extremist movements, a smaller minority might turn to terrorism, whether as members of terrorist groups such as the Islamic State (ISIS) or as lone wolf adherents of such groups. At **the apex** will be two types of violent extremists. The **first type** are those who support violent extremists in a direct way by providing them with financial or logistical support, weapons, and

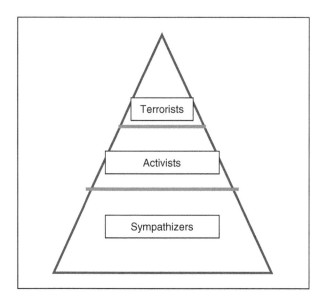

Figure 36.1 The Pyramid of Radicalization into Terrorism.
Source: Author's Creation.

other means of operational assistance. The **second type** are the violent extremists who engage in terrorist operations.

The **second component** involves **focusing a CVE campaign on** individuals who have become violent at **the apex of the pyramid**, but also those who become activists for their cause in **the middle of the pyramid** and who could potentially further ascend the radicalization pyramid into terrorism. The larger sub-culture of sympathizers at **the bottom of the pyramid** also needs to be focused on in a countering violent extremism campaign, because terrorists and activists depend on them for their support base.

An important point about countering violent extremism is that in a democratic and pluralistic society it is legitimate for sympathizers, at the bottom of the radicalization pyramid, to hold "radical" views as long as they are not expressed through violent means. Thus, expressing extremist ideas would not make one subject to arrest, but once an extremist sympathizer begins to explore the possibility of acquiring weapons and ammunition, then they would begin to cross the threshold into violence, making them liable for potential arrest. The objective in countering violent extremism campaigns, therefore, is to facilitate the disengagement of such extremist individuals from terrorist violence into peaceful activities, while recognizing that they might continue to harbor strong beliefs about their objectives that those holding moderate views may not necessarily agree with, but, most importantly, that they will remain non-violent in nature. When such possibilities for disengagement from terrorism exist, government and community programs need to find ways to rehabilitate and integrate such formerly extremist individuals into mainstream society, so that they can pursue their objectives within a competitive, pluralist, and democratic framework – while accepting the will of the majority for policies they may not necessarily agree with, but that can be contested through democratic means.

In countering extremism, it is crucial, therefore, to determine the degree of political, religious or other forms of extremism that is acceptable in a democratic society and the threshold where individuals and groups cross along the radicalization pyramid toward violent extremism, in order to identify the intervention points to mitigate any upward progression toward violent extremism and maximize the downward changes away from violence. As discussed earlier, countering violent extremism campaigns do not necessarily mean that extremist individuals will return to their pre-radicalized state. Rather, the goal of such programs is to facilitate the disengagement of extremist individuals from terrorist violence into peaceful activities.

Once the two components of the pyramid of radicalization are identified, seven measures are involved in effective CVE campaigns. These measures need to be addressed comprehensively and in an integrated manner, with different measures used to intervene throughout the base, middle and top levels of the radicalization pyramid.

First, the underlying conditions that give rise to radicalization into extremism need to be identified and addressed. The radicalization processes that may give rise to violent extremism do not emerge in a vacuum, but are the product of a confluence or coalescence of multiple inter-related drivers, whether in the societies where terrorist uprisings originate or in those of their targeted adversaries. The causes vary and change dynamically over time. In the case of the Islamic State, for example, a major driver is an ultra-puritanical interpretation of Islam that rejects tolerance and acceptance of other religions, including any secular beliefs and practices, with all of these declared enemies to be destroyed. Other drivers may include the alienation of such individuals from their societies, due to a variety of factors, including social and professional failures, with such ideologies promising to transform them into heroes for their cause. Thus, in the case of individuals who become violent jihadists, it is important to understand the effect of such genocidal ideologies in producing individuals who decide to implement them through violence.

Second, as with the underlying causal drivers, it is crucial to identify the ideological center of gravity within a radicalized social movement and its violently extremist offshoots (in the form of a terrorist group). Extremist political and religious ideologies mobilize individuals and groups to commit acts of terrorism and provide them with a guide for action to redress their grievances (whether these are justified or not).

A social movement's narrative constitutes an important ideological center of gravity. Such narratives generally consist of a perception that a movement's members have a great role to play in society, yet are marginalized by that society, that they are divinely ordained by a supreme being to impose their ideology and way of life on their society, that its adversary society and government are unjust and hypocritical, amongst other grievances.

Certain documents or tracts provide such extremist social movements with their ideological underpinning. For example, the 1980s Jewish Terrorist Underground and its Greater Land of Israel members were influenced by the ultra-nationalist and messianic writings of Rabbi Abraham Kook; William Luther Pierce's 1978 racist novel, *The Turner Diaries* inspires white supremacist groups; and Islamist extremists are influenced by Sayyid Qutb's Milestones, and other extremist publications.

Thus, an effective counter-narrative program needs to understand how to persuade extremists to turn away from such extremist ideological tracts toward more moderate and constructive ways of thinking about how to achieve objectives that fall within a society's legal boundaries.

Third, the radicalization process into extremism needs to be countered at a social movement's individual level at the earliest possible phase in the radicalization pyramid. For example, according to Arie Kruglanski, extremist ideologies appeal to individuals experiencing psychological uncertainty because such ideologies are "formulated in clear-cut, definitive terms" and provide "cognitive closure."[1] It is such extremist ideologies that provide the fertile ground for support of, and recruitment into, terrorist organizations.

Early intervention at the pyramid's three levels is more effective than having to react against an array of more mature extremist manifestations later on in the radicalization process.

It is here that governments and NGOs engaged in de-radicalization using violent extremism programs would focus on the question of "who is likely to become a non-violent or violent extremist." For example, once a group's narrative starts to resonate, for instance, in the case of jihadists with their adherents' belief that the opportunity has arrived to implement their quest for an Islamist Caliphate in a geographic location such as Syria, they will begin searching for groups that provide the comradeship, the sense of social belonging, status, excitement, and empowerment in achieving such objectives. These are the individuals in Western societies, for example, who travel to Syria to become foreign fighters on behalf of groups such as the Islamic State.

Fourth, the tipping points in radicalization from non-violent extremism into terrorism need to be identified and countered. In the case of the radicalization pyramid, these tipping points would take place when susceptible sympathizers become activists and then ascend to the pyramid's terrorism apex. While lots of individuals may share extremist beliefs at the bottom of the pyramid, few actually become violent extremists or operatives in a terrorist group. Thus, an effective de-radicalization strategy and campaign must focus on the tipping points from sympathizers to activists and then to becoming terrorists.

This is the part of the process of radicalization into terrorism, where formal groups, such as terrorist organizations, or informal extremist networks, such as "friends and family" (with many terrorists, especially in the West, operating with their family members or friends) begin to mobilize individuals to engage in violence to achieve their shared objectives. It is at such mobilization "tipping points" that de-radicalization measures need to be implemented at the earliest point of intervention.

In countering radicalization into violent extremism, it is crucial to identify. During the radicalization process, activities by such individuals and their associates that might leave detectable traces. Unlike operational terrorists, for whom avoiding detection is a high priority, facilitators of radicalization, such as extremist religious preachers, community leaders, and "friends and family," have to locate individuals within their communities who may be susceptible to becoming radicalized. Studying such recruiting processes, including how they are manifested on the Internet's social media sites, and recognizing their radicalizing techniques will result in a focused counter-extremism and de-radicalization intervention.

Fifth, individuals who have already become violent extremists at the apex of the pyramid (whether directly or through provision of various means of support) need to be de-radicalized in order to facilitate their disengagement from terrorism. Here, it may be easier to de-radicalize the pyramid's mid- and bottom-tier activists and sympathizers, because, unlike the apex's terrorists who are already set in their ways, those below them in the pyramid will likely be more susceptible to changing their minds about supporting those who promote terrorist warfare to achieve their objectives.

Since de-radicalizing an active, at large terrorist is a most difficult task, one locus for such de-radicalization efforts may lie in prisons, where many violent extremists, as well as criminals who might be susceptible to becoming terrorists, are incarcerated, giving authorities an opportunity to intervene. With prisons providing a large pool of potential terrorists, especially in Western Europe, this has become a major area for countering violent extremism programs in those countries.

In another area, even with violent extremists, some may become "worn out" by the difficult and grueling struggle of constantly remaining underground, or may not wish their families to suffer as a result of their terrorist activities, so an opportunity for de-radicalization intervention may be possible.

Sixth, it is crucial to use former and rehabilitated militants in a countering extremism campaign to serve as role models for the appeal and benefits of non-violence. Former extremists' extensive knowledge of an extremist ideology and how militant groups operate, particularly their problems, internal contradictions, and what often turn out to be false promises to their adherents, will have greater credibility than "establishment" types in attempting to persuade militants of the advantages of disengaging from violent extremism. It is also important to ensure that the former militants are fully rehabilitated, as there have been several cases of such "formers" later found to engage in illicit activities while claiming to have turned toward a new non-violent path.

Seventh, countering violent extremism campaigns need to be implemented on the "ground", where radicalizers and other agents of radicalization, such as "friends and family", operate as well as in cyberspace, where extremist websites and forums serve as radicalization influencers. It is here that effective counter-narratives that present a more constructive alternative future for extremists need to operate, either, if possible, on such extremist websites or in close proximity to them so that they will be viewed by extremists.

Metrics to Assess CVE Programmatic Effectiveness: Britain as a Case Study

Once governments' CVE campaign programs are implemented, to assess their impact, metrics of programmatic effectiveness need to be applied to historical and current cases of how governments conduct CVE campaigns to resolve the ideological components of the terrorist threats facing them.

In terms of metrics of effectiveness, although no such quantitative metrics have been developed in the CVE discipline to score levels of programmatic success, this model proposes a scale to score the success level of such programs in de-radicalizing and disengaging their targeted populations from terrorism. It is recognized that this scoring model is intended for illustrative purposes, as a way to spur further advances in consolidating it as a metric that can be used by other researchers in the field.

In this model, scoring the success of government CVE campaign programs in de-radicalizing and disengaging a targeted group from terrorism, whether as terrorists (group or lone actor), activists, or sympathizers, is proposed as: 90% to 100% (very high), 80% to 89% (high), 70% to 79% (moderate), 60% to 69% (low), and 50% to 59% (very low). A score of 0% to 49% would be considered as various degrees of "failure," since it would indicate that a terrorist insurgency, backed by a radical subculture, was likely to remain intact and protracted, whereas a baseline of 70% and higher would demonstrate the beginning of various levels of success.

It is important to note that a government's CVE campaign, by itself, is not sufficient to resolve a terrorist insurgency in a comprehensive manner. This is due to the fact that, as mentioned at the beginning of this article, an effective government counterterrorism campaign also requires certain "hard components," such as military, intelligence and law enforcement measures to ensure that an insurgency's physical manifestations are terminated as well.

In this chapter, the CVE campaign model's scoring system is applied to three prominent cases of past and current terrorist insurgencies. The first two cases are in the United Kingdom, with the PIRA insurgency resolved in the late 1990s and the current insurgency by the country's Islamists this is still ongoing. The conflict between Israel and its Palestinian terrorist adversaries is assessed in the third case. Note that these case studies are brief and written as preliminary illustrative cases, which require additional material to fully flesh them out.

Britain – PIRA

The British Government's counterterrorism campaign against the Provisional Irish Republican Army's (PIRA) insurgency, known as "the Troubles", lasted for about 30 years from the late 1960s to 1998. It was concluded when a peace agreement, known as the "Good Friday Agreement of 1998", was reached between the PIRA and the British Government, with the Irish Government also playing an important role in bringing the contending sides together. The United States Government also played an important mediator role to bring the two sides together. As an example of effective and quantifiable de-radicalization and disengagement from terrorism of terrorist combatants, activists, and their sympathizers, the 1998 Agreement resulted in the demobilization of the PIRA combat units, with their leadership, together with the leadership of Sinn Fein, their political front, integrated into the government of Northern Ireland as well as becoming elected representatives in the British Parliament. In accordance with this model's scoring system, the British-led counterterrorism campaign (and its CVE component) is given a score of "Very High" (90% - 100%), as its success has continued to last until the current period.

Britain and Islamist Extremists

While the British Government, together with the Republic of Ireland, successfully resolved the PIRA insurgency through an effective counterterrorism and CVE campaign, since around 2000, it has been challenged by a pervasive Islamist terrorist threat domestically, by groups and lone actors, with many of the Islamists having ties with their foreign terrorist groups. It was noted in a 2015 report, for example, that the British security services faced a domestic threat by 3,000 Islamist extremists.[2] With British Muslims estimated to number three million, and with an estimated ten percent (300,000) considered extremist [note that this is the author's guesstimate, since no publicly available estimates are available], it means that of the remaining

297,000 persons, with a further guesstimate proportion proposed by this author of terrorists to activists at 1:10, 30,000 could be considered as activists, and the remaining 267,000 considered as sympathizers. The British security services, as well as the government's CVE agencies, their investigators, analysts, and social workers, would therefore need to focus and prioritize their CVE resources on this overall radicalized subculture in British society, with the estimated 3,000 militants a top priority for monitoring and preemption. It would be valuable, therefore, to determine how many of the estimated 3,000 Islamist militants could be persuaded to de-radicalize and disengage from potential terrorism, how many of their "next-in-line" 30,000 activists could be influenced to cease supporting these militants, and how many of the remaining 267,000 sympathizers could be convinced to adopt a more moderate view of Islam and the benefits of non-violent political engagement.

Within this radicalized environment, the British Government introduced, in 2011, a Prevent program, which has been updated and revised several times since then. It is based on three strategies: "respond to the ideological challenge of terrorism and the threat we face from those who promote it; prevent people from being drawn into terrorism and ensure that they are given appropriate advice and support; and work with sectors and institutions where there are risks of radicalisation which we need to address."[3] Since implementing this counterterrorism/CVE strategy, the British Islamist militants have continued to mount terrorist attacks, although most were carried out by lone actors, with minimal linkages to organized terrorist groups. No statistics have been released by the British Government on the Prevent program's success in deradicalizing and disengaging the country's Islamist violent extremists, including the hundreds who are reportedly prison inmates for their terrorist crimes, so, for illustrative purposes, the program's effectiveness score is guessed at "Low" (60%–69%).

Israel – Israeli Arabs and Palestinians

The insurgency by Palestinian and Islamic State-related terrorists is a persistent challenge to the Israeli state. It is exacerbated by a type of insurgency by far-right-wing ultra-nationalist Jewish extremists, who are linked in some form to the Jewish settlers in the contested West Bank, which Israel has controlled since it was conquered in the June 1967 War. Some of the Jewish extremists are also active in the Israeli parliament, with members of the right-wing Jewish parties supporting (or, at least, tolerating) them to some degree. With successive Israeli governments since the breakthrough Oslo Accords of 1993–1995 between the Israeli Government and the Palestinian Authority unable or unwilling to resolve the Israeli-Palestinian conflict, no comprehensive CVE campaign has ever been implemented by an Israeli government. Making matters even worse, a significant portion of youth among Israel's Arab minority (estimated at around 20 percent of the total Israeli population) has become radicalized into Islamist activism, with no Israeli CVE campaign implemented to address their grievances and concerns. With no comprehensive Israeli CVE campaign established to address these two radicalized populations, the Israeli CVE programmatic effectiveness is scored as "Failure" (0%–49%).

Conclusion

In conclusion, in governments' countering violent extremism campaigns, even under the best of circumstances, one should not expect formerly violently extremist individuals to become completely de-radicalized. In such cases, the objective should be to facilitate their disengagement from terrorism into more peaceful and constructive activities, even as they might retain some element of extremism in their ideologies, since the sources of their grievances might still be unresolved. As long as political and military conflicts persist in areas under dispute, such as the Middle East, conflicts that produce a range of unresolved problems, perceptions of injustice, alienation, and anger, one cannot expect those who are sympathetic to their cause and grievance to suddenly give up such sentiments. Moreover, as terrorist groups such as the Islamic State continue to lose ground in Iraq and Syria, their areas of operations will likely shift to other regions, including intensifying their activities in the West. To counter the appeal of such terrorist groups, the goal of governments' counter- and de-radicalization programs in democratic societies should be to facilitate the disengagement of violent extremist individuals who believe that violence is the sole answer out of terrorism and into more constructive nonviolent paths where they can continue their oppositionary activism in a peaceful and legitimate way.

Notes

1 Arie Kruglianski, "Inside the Terrorist Mind," paper presented to the National Academy of Science annual meeting, Washington, DC, April 29, 2002.
2 http://www.express.co.uk/news/uk/606092/Islamist-Extremist-Islamic-State-ISIS-MI5-Britain-Andrew-Parker-Security-David-Cameron.
3 United Kingdom, Prevent Strategy, 2011, p. 14.

37

CRISIS AND CATASTROPHES, SECURITY AND RESILIENCE

On the Significance of Finding Definitions for Security Policy

Herfried Münkler

Introduction: Science and Politics

The definition of terms is one of the core tasks of science, especially for human sciences. Nevertheless, many non-scientists often regard this kind of work as a somewhat redundant engagement, an entertaining occupation with no political or social outcome. The general argument is that the current problem remains the same, regardless of its denomination and of any linguistic differentiations. But actually, problems and challenges alter depending on their terminological definitions and how these are made accessible for specific operative uses. In this regard, not only science works on understanding problems in its efforts to terminologically distinguish, differentiate and explore semantic areas and associative connections, but so does the language of administration where the meaning of generic and narrower terms becomes practically accessible to anyone involved in administrative processes. We are all connected in our daily use of terms, after all, and by using them we are able to create an "order of things" (M. Foucault) and bring structure to, our surroundings. The difference between everyday language and academic language is the traditional and literally naïve use of the first, whereas we consistently reflect on the direct and precise use of the terms in the second; thinking about whether the used words support the exact description of a fact and whether they enable and contribute to dealing with such facts. This means the scientific definition of terms is on a meta-level compared to the everyday language and to the use of terms in administration and politics. The definition of terms is therefore a reflection on the precision of their use, released from their operative use.

The abovementioned considerations are necessary also because terms like "security" or "insecurity" are so-called container terms where different things can be stored, which not only indicates various facts and circumstances but also requires forms of processing that vary from one another. Here a conflict between officialese and conceptualization in sciences can be observed, since the state and its administration use the term "security" differently than science does, free from any exigencies. Besides, this is also the case with terms such as "terror" and "terrorism". The immediate use of academic definition work consists in reviewing old and worn semantics of politics and administration, in yielding information on their enhancement and, in particular, in calling attention to the changes of facts below the terminological surface, which have most likely remained unnoticed due to holding on to trusted conceptions. The more established a certain

DOI: 10.4324/9781003326373-42

term is, the more insensitive the persons who work with them are toward changes. The following considerations can be understood in this sense.

Crises and Catastrophes

Crises and catastrophes are oftentimes mentioned in one breath. This can lead to the impression that both terms have the same meaning, separated only alliteratively by two different names. However, this is far from being the case. Even in the administrative state order, crisis prevention and civil protection are two separate areas, differentiated on the basis of their respective duration and the extent of damage. A catastrophe has the character of an event, irrespective of it being a natural calamity or a huge accident caused by human beings. The description "event" means that the occurrence is of limited duration – very often only a few minutes – whether it be an avalanche, a hurricane, an explosion, a major fire (which can of course last for several hours) or a multiple collision. Very often catastrophes cause deaths, whereas this is not necessarily the case with crises. The latter can indeed start with an event – such as the Great Depression in 1929 that began with the collapse of banks, or the global economic crisis in 2007 following the Lehman bankruptcy – but do not constitute events themselves but rather a long-lasting disturbance of the structural order. Unlike catastrophes, which usually occur over a short period of time (albeit their impact remains longer), crises last for a long time. This means that we can start with a damage survey and a cause analysis immediately after an event has ended. With crises, however, we never know when they are really over or if they will ever be, and if returning to the previous circumstances will even be possible. Very often this is not the case. Crises change structures and courses of action. Catastrophes on the other hand are eruptive breaks where the destructed situation can be restored or renewed after a certain period of time. They leave scars which remind us of their consequences, but they do not change the fundamental constellations – at least not in their short and sometimes repetitive occurrences, and as long as they do not become what we call a crisis, which almost always has disruptive consequences. Crises not only last longer but they also require a change from within the structure of societies, states, economic systems and so on until they can be ranked as hurdled. Catastrophes entail a cleanup after they have passed; crises require much effort to be able to overcome them. We can insure ourselves against catastrophes but not against crises.

This is how the order of terms has organized the structure of danger and risk until very recently. Thanks to this ordered use of terms, we have had a feeling of security. The terminological differentiation is a contribution in the quest of controlling the uncontrollable. The semantic separation between crises and catastrophe is (and has been) one of the most basic order of enlightened thinking in a world that no longer views every calamity and misery as judgment from above as a punishment for human misbehavior.[1] On the one hand, the definition and understanding of a "catastrophe" underwent a kind of risk assessment and actuarially was stripped of its threatening nature. On the other, crises became challenges for politics and society and required social change and adaptation, as well as new political instruments in order to be able to concentrate on crisis prevention. It was important not to confuse crises with catastrophes.

This order of terms – attendant on the "order of things", is rather morbid today: by way of example, we don't know whether we are currently faced with a climate catastrophe or a climate crisis, and the use of language is accordingly orderless. Also, scientific and technological development has enabled catastrophes that are uninsurable because their amount of loss clearly exceeds any possible benefit.[2] One example is the Fukushima nuclear disaster. In retrospect, the terminological differentiation between catastrophe and crisis had the function of narrowing down the contingency and to make the power of coincidence controllable.[3] This differentiation has therefore anticipated a socio-political behavior characterized by its knowing what is needed to be done. Today, this is not the case anymore, or at least it has become a lot more difficult to solidly differentiate between catastrophe and crisis. This complicacy is currently highlighted by the COVID-19 pandemic. Is the coronavirus a catastrophe or are we dealing with a crisis? In other words: Is the global spread of COVID-19 an event which lasts much longer than expected according to the conventional idea of catastrophes, but will in a more or less foreseeable future find an end, which will enable us to return to our previous ways of life and behaviors? Or is it a crisis which forces extensive changes in our economic system and our lifestyles upon us, including the reduction of global trade chains, the end of intercontinental tourism, less sociality and more domesticity?

The "catastrophe scenario" depends on the availability of a reliable vaccine and the rebuilding of immunity sufficient to contain the infection. The "crisis scenario" becomes reality when this immunity cannot be achieved, or other viruses soon cause a new pandemic. We are currently at a crossroads shaped by the fact that our trusted, terminological differentiations no longer work. This in turn implicates an odd uncertainty upsetting many people to a point where some believe they can resolve this uncertainty by simply denying the existence of the pandemic without further ado. This pandemic is turning into a crisis for all the assurances and securities that hold society together. This is becoming apparent with the rise of conspiracy theories connected with COVID-19, as they can be considered the strongest expression of a security crisis. Conspiracy theories have undoubtedly arisen oftentimes before, as they are a complementary companion of enlightenment. In their complementary appearance they superseded the biformity of God and Satan. As long as the order of terms organized the order of things, conspiracy theories only played a marginal role within politics and society. People wearing tin foil hats and watchers of jet trails in the sky generally provided general entertainment to others. The erosion of the semantic order, however, has now put them into the center of society and politics, giving them a stage to proclaim and promise to reestablish the order in our current situation of disorder. The trusted securities and assurances are slowly crumbling away, and orientation vanishes. One example of this is the joint demonstrations of right-wing radicals and people who actually consider themselves positioned on the political left wing against the measures of democratically elected and rule-of-law based governments to contain the pandemic.

Terrorist Attacks and Terrorism

A terrorist attack is an event which usually takes place within only a few seconds. It may cause great or little damage and lead to many or few victims – as an attack it remains an event. This is also true in the case of the attacks of 9/11 in the United States. However, individuals planning terrorist attacks actually want to overcome this kind of event character and permanently interfere with the mentality of a society and the politics of a country. This is their strategic motto, according to which they implement tactics and plan their attacks. Carrying out several attacks at the same time or their sequencing – the connecting of several events, resulting in the impression of those affected that the event is neither spatially nor temporally limited – serves this motto, for instance. Another tool for overcoming this character of event is the creation of images connected with the attack. Such images sink deep into the memory of people thanks to their enduring replication possibility, and therefore leap over the limitations of the terrorist event. On this level, the decisive conflict between terrorists and "counter-terrorists" takes place. As long as "counter-terrorists" are able to reduce terrorist attacks to occasional assaults – which do not reach a certain dimension of intensity – they interfere with the strategies of terrorists. Societies under attack are quite able to reduce the effects of attacks, or to limit the effects to the immediate event itself, as they are themselves inclined to grow indifferent to terrorist assaults which are aimed at the "collective mind" of a society, rather than its material infrastructure. This changes only when attacks are repetitive and begin to spread fear among people for days, or maybe even weeks or months, causing a society to drift into a state of emergency. In this case the hope of society returning to its normal state soon after the event has taken place fades, as does the expectation that everything will soon be as it was before. Just like nightmares are less impactful the next day, event-like terrorist attacks also fade away slowly. However, if their effects remain, the idea of changing fundamentally in order to leave behind all the fear caused by the attack hardens more and more, which means that society is in the depths of a severe crisis.

Several relevant studies have repeatedly shown that, strategically, terrorism does not aim at the physical consequences when committing attacks (such as blowing up a bridge, exploding vehicles or achieving the highest possible number of casualties), but at the psychological effects these assaults cause, either within certain groups or within the entire population. This fact significantly distinguishes terrorism from assassinations or guerilla wars – even though there are certain similarities between these phenomena, too. Assassinations can be a tactical means of terrorist strategy used within the framework of a revolutionary (or counter-revolutionary) project during the initial phase of a guerilla war, or at the beginning of a civil war. Terrorism became a main ingredient of political disputes around the end of the 19th century. As a strategy, terrorist acts belonged to the political left, and political disputes to the political right on the spectrum. Both sides considered terrorist acts a remedy for reaching the next level of escalation, be it the revolutionary small-scale war preparing for the military victory of the revolutionaries, or the civil war aimed at installing the "leading man" or an authoritarian order. As long as terrorism has followed these strategic aims, it is and always was an intermediate step within a larger project, with its options of planning attacks and the selection of targets being rather limited. There is every indication that right-wing terrorism has always had more options than left-wing terrorism. This could help to explain why state-led terrorism defense measures were a great deal more effective against the left than the right.

However, during the past two decades this dynamic has changed significantly. The more recent forms of terrorism are no longer a part of an overall strategy but have taken on a life of their own and are also aware of their aims and purposes.[4] This means that potential targets of terrorist attacks[5] have multiplied because it is no longer necessary to consider certain social or ethnic groups during the selection process. Because of this, police protection of prospective targets has become much more difficult to provide, since not only symbolic locations within a city, but also areas with many people gathering, or just individual people who have been selected as targets and who are present at a specific location by chance can be targets. Terrorists no longer attack certain groups (i.e. the social and political elite, civil servants or security personnel) in order to intimidate and to force a behavioral change upon them; rather, they want to create fear among whole societies. The forms of terrorism – which differentiated according to their diverse political goals – have become closer to each other and are today so alike as to be indistinguishable.

In conclusion, one can say that terrorism now aims at attacking the unstable collective mind of post-heroic societies[6] – which means that anything that is vulnerable becomes a target. Under these circumstances, security in an objective sense like the sense of security a society feels is more difficult to establish and to sustain than during the times when war threats or reciprocal nuclear hostage-takings in the East-West conflict were the main security policy-related challenges. Back then, the sense of security and threat that people felt developed depending on confrontation and relaxation. Today there is no longer a political barometer that compares with this dynamic. Attacks can happen at any time; the situation itself is rather vague, and therefore the terms used to describe this situation are accordingly undifferentiated.

Security and Resilience

"Resilience" as a term was initially used in the fields of psychology and engineering and has had a solid career during the past years. "Resilience" stands for the ability of individuals, systems and societies to deal with severe restrictions of areas of life or even their complete failure, and to survive unpredictable – unforeseen – restrictions of their capacities to act without a complete breakdown on all levels. The antonym of resilience is "vulnerability",[7] with regard to the vulnerability of individuals, systems and societies. This term must be differentiated from vulnerabilities that can be restricted and vulnerabilities that are impossible to restrict. The "costs" connected with the restriction of vulnerabilities play a decisive role, both regarding the immediate financial expenses as well as the restrictions of flexibility and spontaneous adaptability to changes, which is almost always connected with the creation of invulnerability. If this creation of invulnerability (in a twofold respect) becomes invaluable, a certain degree of vulnerability must be accepted. "Resilience "understood as resistance and persistence is a complementary element against the mere acceptance of vulnerability.

This clearly shows a fundamental paradigm change regarding security-related thinking: conventional central concepts such as "threat" or "determent" are increasingly taking a backseat and "vulnerability" and "resilience" the front one. Terrorists are difficult to scare off in fact, since they normally operate clandestinely and do not reclaim territories that could in turn become the targets of counterattacks. The Islamic State (IS) in Northern Iraq and parts of Syria has been an occasional, brief exception to this. By now this terrorist organization has returned to its model of a clandestine organization that operates from within the depths of social rooms. Adding cyber attacks on control systems and communication networks of whole societies to this, where the origin of the attack is usually hard to find and irrevocably verify, we can assume that aforementioned concepts of "threat" and "determent" are increasingly losing their significance today. It is generally known that hackers are mostly immune to threats of counterattacks, which means they pose a threat that cannot be nailed down and precisely defined, but remains an abstract danger. Therefore, it makes sense to position them rather on the side of society's own vulnerability than on the side of potential threats. The minute they are accounted for as vulnerabilities, however, an effective response or even a deterrent effect would be to cultivate resilience which accepts vulnerability by making it bearable. A threatened society reacts to an asymmetric challenge with an asymmetric response: if the former security promise has let society become particularly vulnerable, resilience acknowledges these vulnerabilities, tries to constrain them and reduce their significance in the process.

In this regard we can learn a lot from coping with COVID-19 and consider it a forerunner for future pandemics which are likely to occur more often in the future, especially also in view of the missing traditional war model which would serve as the intellectual framework for this challenge. One reliable indicator for this is the failed use of a war narrative to semantically frame this type of challenge produced by the pandemic and our reactions to it: the war semantics either disappeared again very rapidly or have led to catastrophic results in those cases where it remained, due to providing a wrong and definitely inept framework for the containment of the coronavirus pandemic.[8] These semantics included the identification of vulnerability and its containment if possible, as well as the building of resilience – be it as a long-term strategy by developing immunity or, in the short-term, by targeting the population's behavior in order to contain the spread of the virus and to build up resilience by creating a certain mentality among people which would support maintaining the economic and social lifestyle, even though no reliable medication for the treatment of the virus and no vaccines against COVID-19 had been available so far. Today, several arguments indicate that a society which develops the most reliable resilience against the pandemic will most likely perform best in handling the coronavirus. The ones likely to perform the worst in international comparison will probably be those still speaking of their victory over the virus and who orient their government actions along these semantics. This is most obvious when we look at the different reactions by governments toward the fast-spreading pandemic and conventionalize these ways of reaction into three different, ideal-typical models – in this text simply put as the Chinese, the American and the German models. With regard to the question of the significance of terms used for security policy-related strategies, the issue of specific development stages of countries which show why a certain type of government action has in particular, been formed, is not the focus of consideration. Instead, the models of action are to be examined together with their semantics and with the aim of determining how the order of terms is connected with the order of action.

The *Chinese Model* is mostly based on a paternalistic semantics, according to which the state and the political parties – and in particular Xi Jinping, the current and paramount leader of China and president of the PRC – are concerned with the security and the well-being of the Chinese population. In the case of fighting the coronavirus pandemic, both the political bodies and the Chinese state make use of scientific and academic expertise. The State and politics have both worked for a long time to make this expertise fundamentally available to them, and now they have it at their disposal. This fact accounts for the nature of China's academically founded political approach, where Marxism still plays an important role. The scientific nature must never be questioned or brought into discussion by civil society. For this reason, any expertise that is used by the government to base its actions upon is treated like a secret discipline, only available to the government. This is about the population's unconditional trust in the government which is only guaranteed if the expertise – upon which all actions are based – is considered unconditionally right and "true". The consequent government action derived from this order of knowledge is of course dependent on a number of material requirements, which are not naturally available: first, the unlimited competences of the government, which means that its measures are not questioned by independent courts or regional bodies equipped with certain authorities (as is the case in federal systems). Second, this includes considerable resources available to the government and put into use at will, such as the use of staff and goods in order to provide the population of a big city under quarantine with the essential goods, or the building of hospitals practically overnight. And finally, the government action highly depends on a population traditionally characterized by its high social discipline and used to following their government's instructions instead of claiming voluntaristic ideas of freedom. The Chinese people trust that their government is doing the right and necessary thing. Resilience in a more narrow sense is not necessary in this scenario because the entire order, including its semantics aims at coping with all challenges in an administrative way. The vulnerability of this type of government action consists in the population losing trust in their government, for instance if the expected or promised results never happen or massive doubts among the population arise (i.e. doubts as to whether the official COVID-19 figures actually reflect the reality of the situation).

The *American Model* is concentrated on the heroic attitude of the U.S. President and the environment close to him. For this reason, this model is based on the semantics of war, hostile attacks and brave resistance. The Western narrative where a single hero faces a superior number of enemies and eventually comes off victorious at the end of this fight is central. The semantics of the heroic American model includes the possibility of the leader not being guided by scientific or academic expertise, since this could perhaps reduce or question his heroism. For that reason alone, his public performance is characterized by putting the scientists providing him with expertise and consultations in their place, and even humiliating them. This does not necessarily mean that he never heeds their counsel in general; however, under all circumstances, he must avoid the impression that he is being directed by such experts, since this would contradict his heroic attitude. This heroic approach is in fact only an attitude for two reasons: first, because the presidential hero follows a script he must not deviate from, and second, because neither the necessary powers nor the resources for fighting the pandemic alone are available to him. As a result, several American state governors, as well as a number of courts, have seriously and repeatedly counteracted President Donald Trump's actions. From an operative perspective a grave weakness, the following is certainly the great advantage of this model, also with a view to its being imitable by third parties: the American model does not depend on material requirements but only requires one man as its leader who knows how to play his role in a convincing manner and follow the script of heroic resistance. We could almost bestow this model an award for the acting abilities of the politician selected for the leading role. Similar to the Chinese model, the American one does not generate social resilience, because the leader takes on everything necessary and becomes – following the Western narrative – the savior of a desponded and scared population. The vulnerability of this model lies in the danger of parts of the population losing trust in the narrative and its semantics, simply by the people watching its government's actions, comparing them with those of other governments and concluding that they have plainly been deceived. Academically speaking, this means that the semantics of war and battle are inadequate to meet the challenges of the pandemic and successfully restrain the spread of the coronavirus.

In contrast, the *German Model* completely abandons any claim to omniscience as well as any heroic attitude, and both approaches would be very difficult to combine with the style of rule of the former Chancellor of the Federal Republic of Germany, Angela Merkel. Without exception, all the measures taken to restrain the pandemic have been under the caveat of their reversibility, which in turn is oriented toward the advancement of science related to the virus as well as the level of infections. And, more importantly, all of this has not been happening covertly, but transparently and was communicated to the public. The government has drawn on scientific/academic expertise from different scientific disciplines ranging from virology to economics and from psychology to pedagogics, considers every counsel prospectively and according to their use or collateral damage, and then accordingly makes decisions that imply certain measures. In order to legitimize these measures, the government refers to scientific expertise, however, it does not follow it without limitations or conditions – therefore there can be no talk of a "rule of expertocracy". For a real expertocracy the government is actually lacking in both powers and resources. Any decision taken by the government can be reviewed by an independent court, and government actors might encounter resistance from within society, be it in the form of demonstrations to show resistance or diffuse forms of individual uncooperativeness. Therefore, it is at the core of all government actions to convince society of the adequacy of the measures taken and to create compliance with them. Both – acceptance of adequacy and social compliance – must be secured again and again through explanations and justifications, since only in this way can the people's trust in government measures be upheld. We can consider these efforts for social resilience and for flexible persistence, which become especially important as soon as it is recognized that the pandemic is no longer a temporary catastrophe, but rather a long-term crisis. This type of government action therefore counts on resilience, while acknowledging and repeatedly reassessing a vulnerability. However, this model also inherits its own vulnerability, consisting in the willingness of the majority of the population to listen to the government's explanations and to follow its advice. Followers of conspiracy theories direct their doings exactly against this and try to counteract both. At the end of the day, it is a battle of terms and their reasonableness, fought in an open arena.

The expectation of the observer of all three ideal types of government action in times of the coronavirus pandemic is the following: whoever handles the wrong terms will never be able to measure up to the challenges that approach him or her, because he does not understand them. Whoever bets on acting only will also fail. Only the fact that the acting model —which generally escapes any possibility of diligently dealing with terms – can easily be copied escapes this hope.

Notes

1 On this in detail Mathias Lindenau/Herfried Münkler, "Vom Orakel zur Risikoanalyse: Figurationen von Sicherheit und Risiko"; in: Lindenau/Meier Kressig (eds.), *Zwischen Sicherheitserwartung und Risiko-erfahrung*, Bielefeld 2012, pp. 21–74.

2 Cf. in Hempel/Bartels/Markwart (eds.), *Aufbruch ins Unversicherbare. Zum Katastrophendiskurs der Gegenwart*, Bielefeld 2013.

3 According to Becker/Scheller/Schneider (eds.), *Die Ungewissheit des Zukünftigen. Kontingenz in der Geschichte*, Frankfurt/New York 2016, and Böhme/Röcke/Stephan (eds.), *Contingentia. Transformationen des Zufalls*, Berlin/Boston 2016.

4 According to Clausewitz Vom Kriege (ed.), *Hahlweg*, Bonn 1980, p. 214ff., and The "goal" answers the question "what we want to achieve in the war" and the "purpose" answers the question "what we want to achieve with the war".

5 This concept of goal is not used in the Clausewitzian sense, but here "goal" stands for a specific group of people or a place.

6 On term and concept of the post-heroic society, see Münkler, *Kriegssplitter Die Evolution der Gewalt im 20. und 21. Jahrhundert*, Berlin 2016, pp. 169–187, On the change in terrorism, see Münkler, *Der Wandel des Krieges. Von der Symmetrie zur Asymmetrie*, Weilerswist 2006, pp. 211–247.

7 Dazu ausführlich Münkler/Wassermann, "Von strategischer Vulnerabilität zu strategischer Resilienz: Die Herausforderung zukünftiger Sicherheitsforschung und Sicherheitspolitik"; in: Gerhold/Schiller (eds.), *Perspektiven der Sicherheitsforschung*, Frankfurt am Main 2012, pp. 77–95.

8 In addidion Herfried und Marina Münkler, "Der Einbruch des Unvorhersehbaren und Wie Wir uns Zukünftig Darauf Vorbereiten Sollten"; in: Kortmann/Schulze (eds.), *Jenseits von Corona. Unsere Welt nach der Pandemie*, Bielefeld: transcript Verlag, 2020, pp. 101–108.

PART VI

COVID-19, Resilience and Terrorism

38

COVID-19 AND GLOBAL TERRORISM PANDEMICS

Boaz Ganor

INTRODUCTION

2020 will be written down in history as a turning point year. It is hard to predict where the global pivot will be, however, one thing is clear – what used to be will be no more. The health-care and economic challenges will change, tourism, work and daily routines will change, in-ternational, bilateral and multilateral relationships will change and similarly the security and counter-terrorism challenge will be shaped accordingly. The COVID-19 pandemic has been wielding great influence on the above, as well as many other global processes.

On the face of it many parallels may be drawn between these two pandemics, COVID-19 and global terrorism. In both cases these are lethal phenomena that endanger many people's lives, may cause significant bodily injury, negatively affect life routine and the collective, as well as personal, sense of safety. Yet, beyond the common aspects of the threat these two phenomena pose to the nations of the world, they both present a random challenge. No one on earth is immune to either terrorism or COVID-19. Both can strike anywhere at any time without an advance alert and hurt any person regardless of religion, creed, race or gender or location. An innocent civilian strolling in the mall or down a crowded street may be hurt by a random terror attack perpetrated in the area. Similarly, another person can contract the virus through an accidental chance exposure to a COVID-19 carrier. The random nature of both phenomena and the life threatening risks they pose to ordinary civilians evoke a great sense of fear and anxiety. By its nature, terrorism strives to terrorize various target audiences. This modus operandi intends to promote and achieve ideo-logical, political, social and other targets by spreading fear among the target community.[1] In the case of COVID-19, the fear and anxiety are the products of the scope of the risk coupled with the sense of insecurity and inability to defend oneself from this danger.

The fear factor that accompanies both pandemics is not just an outcome of their random na-ture but also a product of the media coverage of the damage they cause, especially the personal stories of the victims and their families. The latter, in and of themselves, intensify anxiety and create a sense that "by sheer chance, it wasn't me or someone close to me that was hurt. Next time I may not be so lucky."[2]

One of the prominent common denominators of both pandemics is their infectious quality. Both phenomena are contagious and spread rapidly and exponentially. If the COVID-19 virus

DOI: 10.4324/9781003326373-44

spreads through human contact and exposure to a sick person, the terrorism virus infects through the web and social media. The exposure of people to incitement and radicalization content via the web may cause a widespread infection of wide circles of people who may adopt radical points of view that encourage and lead to terror attacks.[3] In this sense a person may transfer incitement to terrorism messages, using his own laptop in one country and using websites, social media networks and other online platforms located in another country, and incite followers to perpetrate devastating attacks in their homelands around the globe. This phenomenon is especially evident in "lone wolf" attacks[4] that are in many cases inspiration for terror attacks – the perpetrator becomes a role model to others and inspires them to follow his lead. This kind of Propaganda of the Deed was typical for the activity of anarchists during the late 19th century and the beginning of the 20th century and is based on exponential infection.[5] And this leads to another common denominator – both phenomena are cross-border. Neither the COVID-19 virus, nor terrorist incitement, inspiration and activities, can be stopped by borders.

Considering the wider ramifications of the phenomena, one can observe many similarities here again: Both COVID-19 and terrorism cause severe economic harm. COVID-19 measures that require social distancing and quarantine have caused a significant decrease of the GDP of many countries as well as an unprecedent peak of unemployment rates.[6] Air traffic tourism and the leisure time industry were among the most severely affected. Similarly, following notorious terror atrocities such as 9/11 in the United States as well as other terrorism waves in different countries, these measures have caused severe damage to these and other industries and economies.[7] Moreover, both phenomena challenge and subvert the public's trust in its governments and decision-makers and destabilize law and order. This lack of trust may be manifested via harsh criticism of the way COVID-19 is being contended, the way these governments manage the crisis, as well as their decisions in response, especially in connection with social distancing and quarantine policies. Or, in the case of counter-terrorism, the public trust in their governments might be reduced when the public starts to question the government's determination or capability to protect them at all costs by taking all the necessary steps needed to prevent any terrorist's attacks.

One of the most difficult dilemmas regarding counter-terrorism is the "Democratic Dilemma," meaning the natural tension between the use of effective counter-terrorism measures and the need to preserve liberal-democratic values.[8] This tension intensifies in light of the fact that counter-terrorism measures are intended, at their core, to protect a basic human right – the right to live, hence these counter-terrorism measures are taken in order to save lives. However, employing some of the most effective counter-terrorism measures infringes to varying degrees on multiple other human and civil rights, such as freedom of speech, freedom of movement and assembly, the right to privacy and many others. This basic dilemma that marks the tension between the need to prevent the loss of lives and the infringement of democratic-liberal values is manifested in the way countries contend with COVID-19 as well. Is it the state's right, in the name of public health, to infringe on people's privacy by questioning patients about the way they live their lives and the people they meet with? Can it impose a widespread quarantine? Compel people to move wearing face masks? Isolate certain communities that have a high infection ratio or are considered high-risk groups (e.g. the elderly or certain ethnic minorities)? Can it prohibit demonstrations or group prayers? These questions become even more sensitive when the preventive measures include the deployment of technology such as advanced triangulation systems, applications that monitor the movements of cell phone owners, AI-based technologies and more. Such technologies serve as sources to locate sick people and to sever the infection chain (in the case of COVID-19) as soon as possible, or to locate the terrorists, their accomplices and supporters to prevent terror attacks.[9]

The Democratic Dilemma-challenges[10] in contending with terrorism or with COVID-19 require a regulatory regime that will govern the use of various measures, especially the use of advanced technology to prevent both phenomena. In both cases there is a paramount need to develop a system of checks and balances based on the separation of powers, which will include an effective monitoring system to verify that any branch of government exceeds its power. These essential checks and balances must be measured and sophisticated enough so as to leave enough room for an effective response for various enforcement agencies to be able to prevent either the spread of COVID-19 or a wave of terror attacks. The states must strike the required balance between the urgent need to effectively deal with the problem and their duty to examine, monitor and review these measures and prevent their abuse.

Moreover, effectively contending with both phenomena calls for tight cooperation, local as well as global. To effectively contend with COVID-19 requires ongoing cooperation among multiple government ministries (Finance, Health, HLS, Education and more), healthcare systems (Ministry of Health, hospitals, HMOs), private and public sector (importers and manufactures of healthcare equipment, technology and life sciences companies that develop vaccines and medicines), municipal and national governments, academia and government (consulting on healthcare, epidemiology, economy, crisis management and more), law enforcement agencies, and healthcare authorities (sharing of information and executing heightened enforcement) and many more. Similarly, to effectively contend with terrorism requires an inter-ministry, inter-agency and inter-sectorial cooperation.[11]

With both phenomena it is important to reach an understanding and collaboration between the government and decision-makers and the public at large and particular sectors of the public (high-risk communities) to achieve cooperation, compliance and assistance to the joint effort to thwart terrorism and the spread of the virus. However, due to the fact that both pandemics are infectious and cross-border in nature the need for cooperation is global on top of the local aspect. For example, if a certain country successfully manages to reduce the infection ratio within its territory and arrive at an effective control of the spread of the virus through enforcement of social distancing and quarantine, the moment it will open its borders to neighboring countries and resume marine and aerial international transportation, without cooperation with its neighbors and other countries on prevention regulation of the spread of the virus, the movement of people (tourists, businessmen, expats and relatives) will soon cause an increase of the infection ratio and worsen its position. The same is true with regards to terrorism. A country that takes effective counter-terrorism measures but leaves its borders open and has no close cooperation on counter-terrorism with its neighbors is risking terrorists infiltrating its territory and perpetrating attacks. This global regulatory cooperation has even greater importance whenever terrorists use online platforms in different countries and these countries do not work together to eradicate the phenomenon. An effective struggle against both phenomena requires therefore a cross-border, uniform use of counter-measures, mutual thresholds and common regulation, coordination and joint operations among the various enforcements agencies, as well as learning from the experience of other states.

That said, the learning process in and of itself is not enough. At the core of the effective struggle with both phenomena there is the fundamental stage of gathering intelligence, analyzing and processing it and arriving at actionable conclusions. The need for reliable and current intelligence when fighting terrorism is obvious.[12] Without intelligence one cannot thwart a specific attack cannot actively engage in an offensive or operative action against terror organizations, against their operatives and accomplices, or even establish effective policies and practices. Intelligence is also fundamental to an effective campaign against COVID-19. Policy makers and heads of the healthcare systems need to know as soon as possible who has been infected by the virus in order to cut any infection chain. They need to know how other healthcare systems in different countries operate and learn from their experience, and they need to learn about the developing dynamics of the pandemic's behavior and so on.

Moreover, with both phenomena it is important to enlist the public to fight the phenomenon and encourage them to comply with the health regulations and counter-terrorism agencies in various countries understood long ago the importance of recruiting the public for intelligence warnings and acted to heighten their awareness, inter alia through campaigns such as "If You See Something Say Something."[13] Similarly, various countries act to recruit the public to report an increase of COVID-19 symptoms through various means such as designated cellular apps to enable an early detection of infection clusters.

Based on the gathered intelligence one can compile the reference scenarios that will serve as the basis for the decision-makers' status review and assessment of possible ways to contend with the phenomenon. When dealing with terrorism, possible attack types and locations will be presented so that counter-terrorism agencies will know how to prepare for and deploy counter-measures to thwart them, whereas, when dealing with a healthcare crisis, possible scenarios are needed in order to identify and address the thresholds beyond which the healthcare system will collapse (e.g. number of patients, number of severely ill patients, number of ventilated patients). Based on the intelligence assessment and the reference scenarios, the required equipment to effectively battle the disease will be prepared and supplies procured, treatment protocols compiled, staff will be trained etc. The intelligence picture also forms a basis for setting the required regulatory regime – what laws and ordinances need to be enacted to define the authority of the various government agencies as well as the public's level of compulsory compliance.[14]

As mentioned above, enlisting the public to contend with the phenomenon is paramount; however, the way to recruit the public does not have to be via reinforcement and legal sanctions but rather through incorporation, persuasion, education and, above all, transparency. Only when the public will be convinced that the steps taken by the government are indeed needed to keep it healthy and save, it will comply. To achieve that, there is a need to develop an effective and professional interaction with the public; explaining the policy and the steps taken by the government is necessary. This interaction needs to gain the public's trust by disseminating current and reliable information coupled with clear and impartial instructions that do not favor or discriminate any sector of the public.

All of the above point to the fact that contending with COVID-19, as with terrorism, requires a professional, efficient and consistent decision-making process. The leaders must ensure the existence of a clear, hierarchal chain of command and a definite division of authority and responsibilities between all the relevant ministries and agencies, and, in synergetic fashion, refrain from unnecessary disputes, and avoid rivalries, politics and ego clashes (either personal or institutional).

In summation, the processes to contend with either COVID-19 or terrorism are very similar as both conform to the modus operandi required to contend with global crises and disasters (see diagram below). In the early stage (i.e. pre-crisis), one must gather as much intelligence as possible to understand the scope of the phenomenon, its nature, ramification, its vulnerabilities and more. On that basis one must strive to prevent the crisis from happening by increasing government agencies preparedness and readiness for either routine of emergency activities, increasing public resiliency and heightening public awareness to the possibility of such disaster happening. Should the preventive measures fail and the crisis (i.e. waves of pandemic or global terrorism) erupt the government should then switch gears and focus on the next stage – managing the crisis. The purpose of the latter is to minimize and mitigate the damage from the crisis, limit the number of casualties (dead, injured or sick) by delegating authority and dividing roles and

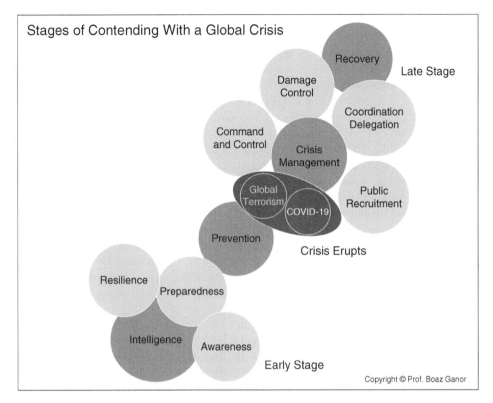

Figure 38.1   Stages of Contending with a Global Crisis.

Source: Author's Creation.

responsibilities among the various relevant emergency apparatuses, coordinating, controlling and commanding them, and enlisting the public to assist the above and comply with the regulations. Once the crisis has been contained then the last stage starts – recovery and resumption of pre-crisis normalcy. Here one must restore, as fast as possible, all the individual, community, municipality and national normal day-to-day activities (Figure 38.1).[15]

As explained above, both pandemics, COVID-19 and global terrorism, as well as the challenges that arise when fighting them, have multiple similarities. That said, it is important to acknowledge some fundamental differences between them. First, assuming the COVID-19 eruption was not manmade, both pandemics represent two different types of calamities – terrorism is a manmade calamity, executed by design in an attempt to achieve concrete ideological, political, social and other goals. COVID-19 is an unintended natural disaster.[16] The malice in terrorism is manifested, inter alia, in all the early stages of the attacks – initiation, planning and preparation, as well as in the attack itself. All of the above are meant to maximize the terror attack's impact in a way that will promote the aforementioned goals and interests of the perpetrators. That is not the case with COVID-19. Here, not only are there no plans or preparations to launch the pandemic, but it wasn't meant to promote anybody's interests. Moreover, unlike terror attacks, which are designed to target a special class of people, ethnic minority, ideological or political rivals, COVID-19 cannot be focused on any specific target population and avoid infecting other people at the same time. Therefore, it is very difficult to maliciously use the virus in the service of a state actor, terror organization or any other group for a pinpoint attack or a specific attack on an enemy or a specific rival.[17]

Another fundamental difference is associated with the way one combats each phenomenon. Whereas counter-terrorism effort is based on the "terrorism formula" whose variables are motivation and operational capability, i.e. a terror attack only happens when the perpetrator has both the motivation to execute the attack and the capability to carry it out, and an effective counter-terrorism effort requires either neutralizing the motivation (by CVE measures – Countering Violent Extremism[18]) or neutralizing the operational capabilities of the terrorists (CT), fighting the COVID-19 pandemic, the counter-measure efforts are totally focused on neutralizing the virus' ability to inflict massive harm.

Finally, it should be noted that like any other crisis, contending with either COVID-19 or terrorism entails many opportunities. For example, even though both phenomena have different life-threatening attributes, they both create an immediate and acute need to develop special modus operandi and technologies for handling them. The latter may even be one and the same, as we have seen with cell phone triangulation. Since need is the mother of all invention, one can hope that countering both phenomena will accelerate Research and Development (R&D) processes that not only assist the curbing and preventing of the phenomena in the future, but also may have other dual use advantages and provide a technological and conceptual springboard in many aspects of life.

Another opportunity involves the suffering caused to many innocent people around the world because of these phenomena. This global human suffering creates a sense of shared destiny, which may be directed (with the proper steering by the leadership in different countries) to mend fences, overcome differences and mute conflicts. This sense of shared destiny may even promote effective global cooperation that will help defeat terrorism and COVID-19. To effectively contend with terrorism one must form a global coalition to include all global relevant actors battling terrorism (decision-makers, governments, security and intelligence agencies, first responders, international organizations, civil organizations, academia and the public at large).[19] The same holds true when fighting COVID-19. Here too, we must form a global coalition and include all relevant actors to study and understand the disease better, identify the challenges it poses and develop effective ways and means to prevent and handle it, all the while learning from each others' experience, forming joint doctrines and global regulations for cross-border containment and the elimination of the virus. In fighting the new global phenomenon of the COVID-19 pandemic, we must learn the lessons of countering global terrorism and acknowledge that "it takes a network to defeat a network."[20]

Notes

1 Max, A. (2006). Why Terrorism Does Not Work. International Security, 31(2), 42–78. http://www.jstor.org/stable/4137516

2 Marin, I. (2009). The Role of the News Media in Connection with Global Terrorism. Geopolitics, History, and International Relations, 1(2), 159–163. https://www.jstor.org/stable/26804006

3 Gadarian, S. K. (2010). The Politics of Threat: How Terrorism News Shapes Foreign Policy Attitudes. The Journal of Politics, 72(2), 469–483. https://doi.org/10.1017/s0022381609990910

4 Ganor, B. (2021). Understanding the Motivations of "Lone Wolf" Terrorists: The "Bathtub" Model. Perspectives on Terrorism, 15(2), 23–32. https://www.jstor.org/stable/27007294

5 Colson, D. (2017). Propaganda and the Deed: Anarchism, Violence and the Representational Impulse. American Studies, 55/56, 163–186. http://www.jstor.org/stable/44982624

6 Kusumahadi, T. A., & Permana, F. C. (2021). Impact of COVID-19 on Global Stock Market Volatility. Journal of Economic Integration, 36(1), 20–45. https://www.jstor.org/stable/26985574

7 Chernick, H. (Ed.). (2005). Resilient City: The Economic Impact of 9/11. Russell Sage Foundation. http://www.jstor.org/stable/10.7758/9781610441216

8 Art, R. J., & Richardson, L. (Eds.). (2007). Democracy and Counterterrorism: Lessons from the Past. United States Institute of Peace.

9 National Academy Press. (2002). Making the Nation Safer: The Role of Science and Technology in Countering Terrorism.

10 Findley, M. G., & Young, J. K. (2011). Terrorism, Democracy, and Credible Commitments. International Studies Quarterly, 55(2), 357–378. http://www.jstor.org/stable/23019692

11 Romaniuk, P. (2010). Institutions as Swords and Shields: Multilateral Counter-Terrorism Since 9/11. Review of International Studies, 36(3), 591–613. http://www.jstor.org/stable/40783287

12 Schmid, A. P., Forest, J. J. F., & Lowe, T. (2021). Counter-Terrorism Studies: A Glimpse at the Current State of Research (2020/2021): Results from a Questionnaire Sent to Scholars and (Former) CT Practitioners. Perspectives on Terrorism, 15(4), 155–183. https://www.jstor.org/stable/27044241

13 Mueller, J., & Stewart, M. G. (2012). The Terrorism Delusion: America's Overwrought Response to September 11. International Security, 37(1), 81–110. http://www.jstor.org/stable/23280405

14 Aftergood, S. (2020, April 23). COVID-19 Highlights Need for Public Intelligence [web log]. Retrieved December 6, 2022, from https://fas.org/blogs/secrecy/2020/04/covid19-intelligence/.

15 William, C. N. (2007). Emergency Planning and Potential Liabilities for State and Local Governments. State & Local Government Review, 39(1), 44–56. http://www.jstor.org/stable/4355440

16 That of course discounts various theories blaming the Chinese government for the eruption of the pandemic, either negligently or by design.

17 The above statement obviously assumes that COVID-19 was not launched premeditatedly by the Chinese to inflict harm on the global economy and create opportunities for the Chinese market.

18 Feve, S., & Dews, D. (2019). ANALYZE. In National Strategies to Prevent and Counter Violent Extremism: An Independent Review (pp. 19–26). Global Center on Cooperative Security. http://www.jstor.org/stable/resrep20256.6

19 Romaniuk, P. (2010). Institutions as Swords and Shields: Multilateral counter-terrorism since 9/11. Review of International Studies, 36(3), 591–613. doi:10.1017/S0260210510000653.

20 Kleindorfer, P. R., Wind, Y., & Ganor, B. (2009). 26. In The Network Challenge: Strategy, Profit, and Risk in an Interlinked World (pp. 453–470). Essay, Wharton School Publ.

39

THE FALSE PROMISE OF SALAFI-JIHADISTS

Rhetoric and the Response to COVID-19

Seth G. Jones

As COVID-19 spread around the globe, the Islamic State, al-Qaeda, and other Salafi-jihadists attempted to take advantage of the crisis. They argued that the pandemic was a punishment against infidel regimes. As one al-Qaeda document summarized: "The truth remains, whether we like it or not, that this pandemic is a punishment of the Lord of the Worlds for the injustice and oppression committed against Muslims specifically and mankind generally by governments you elect."[1] Islamic State and al-Qaeda propaganda predicted that the pandemic would cripple Western economies, militaries, and societies, and it would allow them to revitalize attacks, recruitment, and fundraising across the globe.[2] In addition, some analysts agreed that COVID-19 might provide a boost to Salafi-jihadists.[3] As one article concluded, "COVID-19 will handicap domestic security efforts and international counter-ISIS cooperation, allowing the jihadists to better prepare spectacular terror attacks and escalate campaigns of insurgent warfare on battlefields worldwide."[4]

In light of these forecasts, this chapter asks two main questions. How did Salafi-jihadists attempt to take advantage of the COVID-19 crisis? How successful were they in achieving their objectives? To answer these questions, this chapter mostly relies on primary source documents—including statements—by Salafi-jihadists. It also examines quantitative data on al-Qaeda and Islamic State attacks to assess possible changes in the number and type of attacks.

This analysis has two primary findings. First, Salafi-jihadist groups and individuals hoped that COVID-19 would allow them to conduct several types of actions: increase terrorist attacks around the globe (including in the West), wage biological warfare, provide better governance than local regimes, recruit more supporters, and broadly weaken the West. Second, Salafi-jihadists generally *failed* to achieve most of their objectives—at least in the short-term. Their statements were largely rhetorical. These groups did not increase attacks (including in the West), they failed to outperform local regimes in responding to COVID-19, and their apocalyptic predictions about the collapse of the West did not materialize. Based on the unavailability of data in some areas—such as recruits—it is difficult to assess whether Salafi-jihadists were able to increase supporters. Still, al-Qaeda and the Islamic State did not appear to significantly benefit from COVID-19, despite their expectations and rhetoric.

The rest of this chapter is divided into three sections. The first provides an overview of the organizational structure of Salafi-jihadists. The second section outlines the major objectives of

DOI: 10.4324/9781003326373-45

Salafi-jihadist groups and individuals in response to COVID-19, from conducting attacks to recruiting new members. The third offers a brief conclusion and highlights the main challenges faced by Salafi-jihadists.

A Decentralized Landscape

The Salafi-jihadist global landscape is decentralized and can be divided into at least four categories: the Islamic State and affiliated provinces (or *wilayats*), al-Qaeda and affiliated groups, other Salafi-jihadist groups, and inspired individuals and networks. This diffuse structure ensured that there was a plethora of comments and predictions on COVID-19 by a diverse set of Salafi-jihadists across the globe.

First, the Islamic State's core remains in Iraq and Syria, though it lost virtually all the territory it once controlled in those countries. Led by Amir Muhammad Sa'id Abdal-Rahman al-Mawla, the Islamic State has approximately 10,000 fighters in Iraq and Syria and has utilized a desert, or *sahraa*, strategy to retake territory.[5] Its immediate objective is to restore the group's territorial control and administration, or *tamkin*, and conduct guerrilla attacks against Syrian and Iraqi government forces and their partners.[6] As one Islamic State document summarized, the organization is committed to "guerrilla warfare … against the disbelievers and apostates, preparing the way for lasting control of the land."[7] The Islamic State has increasingly delegated authority from its core in Iraq and Syria to remote provinces in such countries and regions as Afghanistan, the Philippines, Libya, Egypt, Yemen, Central Africa, and West Africa.[8]

Second, al-Qaeda's leadership structure remains primarily in Afghanistan and Pakistan, led by Ayman al-Zawahiri and Abdullah Ahmed Abdullah (also known as Abu Muhammad al-Masri).[9] Some other senior al-Qaeda figures, such as Saif al-Adel, are likely located in Iran.[10] Al-Qaeda core is largely in survival mode, and many of its leaders have been killed by U.S. and partner strikes. Yet al-Qaeda still retains affiliated groups across Africa, the Middle East, and Asia. Examples include al-Qaeda in the Arabian Peninsula (based in Yemen), Harakat al-Shabaab al-Mujahidin (based in Somalia), Jama'a Nusrat ul-Islam wa al-Muslimin (based in Mali and neighboring countries in the Sahel), al-Qaeda in the Islamic Maghreb (based in Algeria and neighboring countries), al-Qaeda in the Indian Subcontinent (based in Afghanistan and Pakistan), and Hurras al-Din (based in Syria). In addition, al-Qaeda retains close relations with other groups, such as Hay'at Tahrir al-Sham in Syria, which boasts an estimated 8,000 to 10,000 fighters.[11] Much like the Islamic State, al-Qaeda's affiliates operate largely autonomously from core leaders in their operations, tactics, recruitment, and fundraising.

Figure 39.1 provides an overview of Islamic State and al-Qaeda attacks between January and October 2020, based on data from the Armed Conflict Location and Event data Project (ACLED). It shows significant amounts of activity in countries like Somalia, Iraq, Syria, Nigeria, the Philippines, and Mali.

Third, there are a number of allied groups that have relationships with either al-Qaeda or the Islamic State. They have not become formal members and their leaders have not pledged *bay'at* (or loyalty) to either al-Qaeda or the Islamic State. The arrangement allows these groups to remain sovereign, but to work with the Islamic State or al-Qaeda when their interests converge. In addition, there are a substantial number of allied Salafi-jihadist groups across Africa (such as Ansar al-Sharia Derna and Ansar al-Sharia Benghzi), South Asia (such as Lashkar-e-Taiba and the East Turkestan Islamic Movement) and East Asia (such as Jemaah Islamiya).

Some groups do not have a Salafi-jihadist ideology but still cooperate with either the Islamic State or al-Qaeda. The Taliban's ideology, for example, is heavily influenced by the Hanafi

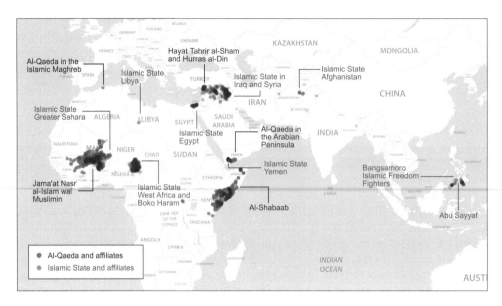

Figure 39.1 Al-Qaeda, Islamic State, and Affiliated Attacks, 2020.[12]

Source: Author's Creation. Based on the Armed Conflict Location and Event Data Project (ACLED), https://www.acleddata.com.

Deobandi religious tradition.[13] While the Taliban's ideology has been changing since the 1990s, Taliban leaders generally support the creation of a government that follows an extreme interpretation of sharia (Islamic law) and the establishment of an Islamic Emirate in Afghanistan.[14] Relations between the Taliban and al-Qaeda have persisted for nearly two and a half decades.[15] As a 2020 U.S. Department of Defense report noted, "Despite recent progress in the peace process, [al-Qaeda in the Indian Subcontinent] maintains close ties to the Taliban in Afghanistan, likely for protection and training."[16] Relations between al-Qaeda and Taliban-linked groups include long-standing personal connections, intermarriage, and a common history of struggle and jihad.[17]

Fourth, there are inspired individuals and networks that do not have direct contact with al-Qaeda or Islamic State members, but who are inspired by their ideology and incensed by the perceived oppression of Muslims in Iraq, Afghanistan, Syria, Palestinian territory, and other countries. They are frequently motivated by a hatred of the West and local regimes. Without direct support, many these individuals and networks are amateurs.[18]

Overall, the Salafi-jihadist movement has become increasingly diffuse. Relations between the Islamic State and al-Qaeda are competitive and sometimes violent, though they vary based on countries and specific localities. As the next section highlights, this decentralized landscape translated into a variety of projections from Salafi-jihadists across the globe about COVID-19.

Salafi-Jihadist Objectives

This section outlines the objectives of the Islamic State, al-Qaeda, and other Salafi-jihadists following the COVID-19 outbreak. Collectively, Salafi-jihadists focused on five main types of activities: increase terrorist attacks around the globe, conduct biological warfare, expand recruitment and other support, outperform local regimes, and weaken the West.

Increase the Number of Attacks

Salafi-jihadists boasted that they would use the outbreak of COVID-19 to ramp up terrorist attacks across the globe, including in the West after suffering setbacks. The Islamic State lost virtually all of the territory it once controlled in Iraq and Syria, and its leader, Abu Bakr al-Baghdadi, was killed by U.S. forces in October 2019. Al-Qaeda also experienced significant senior leadership losses and struggled to conduct or inspire major attacks in the West. In October 2020, Afghan special operations forces killed a senior al-Qaeda official, Hossam Abdul Al-Raouf (who used the nom de guerre Abu Muhsin al-Masri). In October 2020, U.S. special operations forces also killed several al-Qaeda operatives in Idlib Province of Syria, including Abu Mohammed al-Sudani.[19]

Because of these setbacks, Islamic State and al-Qaeda leaders hoped that an escalation in attacks could help revitalize their campaigns. In March 2020, for example, al-Qaeda's leadership announced that COVID-19 provided an unparalleled opportunity to conduct attacks overseas. "Now is the time to spread the correct Aqeedah [creed], call people to Jihad in the Way of Allah and revolt against oppression and oppressors," it noted.[20] Similarly, the Islamic State urged supporters across the globe to conduct attacks. In its publication *al-Naba*, the Islamic State noted that COVID-19 raised "the possibility of increasing the impact of attacks on people and property, and spreading chaos and confusion."[21] The article continued that these attacks could mirror previous ones in Paris, London, and Brussels. The group explained that it would be among the "worst nightmares of the Crusaders" if an attack occurred in the West, just as these countries faced bleak economies and overcrowded hospitals.[22] In Indonesia, Islamic State supporters called for attacks against "apostates in big cities" during the COVID-19 crisis while their enemies were distracted.[23] Islamic State supporters on Facebook encouraged supporters to attack and loot "kuffar" (disbelievers) in Indonesia during the pandemic.[24] In South Asia, a pro-Islamic State media outfit encouraged supporters in India to capitalize on their enemies' preoccupation with COVID-19 to conduct more attacks.[25] Islamic State supporters in the Philippines—including those that associated with the Bangsamoro Islamic Freedom Fighters—urged sympathizers to wage jihad to reopen mosques closed by COVID-19 restrictions.[26] Indeed, numerous Salafi-jihadists commented on digital platforms that they should conduct attacks against governments that closed mosques and implemented broader lockdown measures.[27] As Figure 39.2 highlights, however, the data show that both the Islamic State and al-Qaeda failed to increase the number of attacks in 2020, at least through September. There were virtually the same number of attacks across the globe in January 2020 (364 attacks) as there were in September 2020 (373 attacks). Indeed, the Islamic State and al-Qaeda attack tempo largely *flatlined* in 2020.

There were some exceptions. In May 2020, the Islamic State exploited gaps in Iraqi security forces caused by COVID-19 lockdowns to conduct attacks in Iraq.[29] But these numbers quickly dropped back down. There were also a handful of inspired attacks in Europe. On September 25, 2020, for example, a Salafi-jihadist conducted a knife attack at the former headquarters of the satirical magazine *Charlie Hebdo*. On October 16, Abdoullakh Anzorov beheaded a teacher in Paris after the victim showed controversial cartoons of the Prophet Muhammad to his students, and Brahim Aouissaoui killed three individuals in Nice nearly two weeks later.[30] On November 2, an Islamic State sympathizer killed four people in Vienna, Austria. In Germany, security agencies arrested a cell of suspected Islamic State members, who were Tajik nationals, for plotting attacks against U.S. forces in Germany.[31]

Yet the number of Salafi-jihadist attacks in Europe—and the West more broadly—did not significantly increase in 2020. In addition, COVID-19 had little or nothing to do with any of the

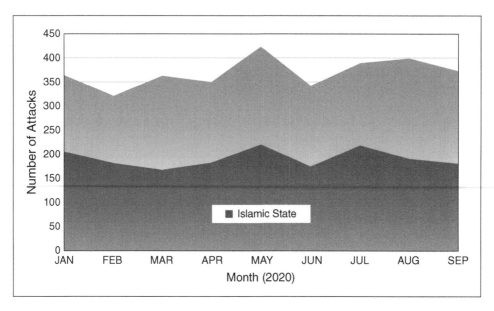

Figure 39.2 Number of Islamic State and Al-Qaeda Attack.[28]

Source: Author's Creation. Based on the Armed Conflict Location and Event Data Project (ACLED), https://www. acleddata.com.

attacks. In France, for instance, the terrorist attacks in September and October 2020 were tied to *Charlie Hebdo* and cartoons of the Prophet Muhammad, not COVID-19.

Conduct Biological Warfare

Salafi-jihadists also encouraged individuals to wage biological warfare against enemy governments. For example, an Islamic State online magazine encouraged sympathizers to weaponize COVID-19, noting that "every brother and sister, even children, can contribute to Allah's cause by becoming the carriers of this disease and striking the colonies of the disbelievers, wherever they find them." The article urged jihadist sympathizers to "strike the disbelievers with this disease which is a weapon." It also made a fallacious claim that "true" Muslims would not be infected since "no disease can harm even a hair of a believer who only lives to praise Allah and His benevolence."[32]

There has been a significant and justifiable concern that terrorists—including Salafi-jihadists—might conduct at an attack using biological, chemical, radiological, or even nuclear weapons.[33] Even a rudimentary or failed attack could incite substantial fear.[34] In addition, COVID-19 has showed that countries and their populations can be vulnerable to novel types of viruses and raised the prospect that a Salafi-jihadist or other terrorist group might use a pathogen or other biological agent to conduct an attack.[35] White supremacist and other violent far-right groups, for example, discussed the possibility of weaponizing COVID-19 and using biological agents to perpetrate attacks in light of COVID-19.[36]

With the possible exception of a Salafi-jihadist plot foiled by Tunisian security forces in April 2020 to use COVID-19 as a weapon, it does not appear that Salafi-jihadists systematically attempted to conduct deliberate biological attacks by spreading COVID-19.[37] There is also little evidence thus far that Salafi-jihadists attempted to jumpstart biological, chemical, radiological, or nuclear programs in response to COVID-19. As one United Nations counterterrorism report concluded, "While ISIL propaganda characterizes COVID-19 as a divine weapon, there have been no indications that ISIL is systematically attempted to weaponize the virus."[38] Instead, the Islamic State and al-Qaeda generally preferred to plan and inspire traditional attacks using explosives, firearms, knives, and vehicles—in part since these weapons and material were easier to acquire and use.[39]

Increase Recruitment and Supporters

Salafi-jihadists hoped to increase recruitment by taking advantage of COVID-19 quarantines, a rise in the number of individuals working and going to school from home, and a surge in online activity. Their goal was not just to radicalize Muslims, but to *convert* individuals to Islam. As one al-Qaeda document argued, "we would like to remind non-Muslims to utilize their time in quarantine for finding out more about Islam from authentic sources, reading, and reflecting on the merits that make Islam stand out from all other religions, isms and systems."[40] The rise in the number of individuals online—including young people—provided an opportunity for exposure to propaganda and extremist ideas. The Islamic State, al-Qaeda, and others had a potentially captive audience.[41] Consequently, the Islamic State utilized hashtags related to COVID-19 in an attempt to divert internet users to its propaganda.[42]

Some Salafi-jihadists tried to be creative, however disillusioned their attempts were. Their recruitment pitch was salvation from the pandemic. For example, a leader of a splinter group of the Bangsamoro Islamic Freedom Fighters urged individuals to join the group to save themselves from infection.[43] Yet there is little evidence that the Islamic State, al-Qaeda, or other Salafi-jihadists have increased recruitment because of—or even during—COVID-19.

Outperform Local Regimes

Some Salafi-jihadists argued that they were better prepared to respond to the COVID-19 crisis than local regimes. In areas where the local government's presence was limited, non-existent, or incompetent, Salafi-jihadists and other allied groups promised to provide more effective essential services and health care.[44]

One example was the Afghan Taliban. In response to COVID-19, the Taliban asserted that the government of Ashraf Ghani failed to curb the spread of the coronavirus and accused it of embezzling foreign assistance. Taliban leaders claimed they had helped safeguard Afghans from the virus and urged foreign health agencies and non-governmental organizations to provide assistance, promising that they would ensure the safety of all international aid workers.[45] In addition, the Taliban portrayed the COVID-19 pandemic as an "unprecedented opportunity" for wealthy Muslims to donate to the needy—especially during Ramadan. The group promoted the work of its Department for the Affairs of Needy, Orphans, and the Disabled.[46]

Yet there was little evidence that the Taliban or other groups were better able to provide services in response to COVID-19 than local regimes, though some countries used the COVID-19 outbreak to repress their populations.[47] Over the long term, these state actions could increase local grievances. After all, numerous countries in Africa, the Middle East, and Asia remain vulnerable to Salafi-jihadists and other insurgents because of local grievances and poor governance—though for reasons other than their response to COVID-19. Such countries as Iraq, Syria, Yemen, Afghanistan, Libya, Mali, Nigeria, and Somalia—which are all dealing with al-Qaeda or the

Islamic State—are at or near the bottom 10 percent of countries worldwide in terms of government effectiveness, according to the World Bank.[48] Based on such indicators, the conditions for terrorism and insurgency persist, regardless of COVID-19.

Weaken the West

Finally, Salafi-jihadists hoped that COVID-19 would fundamentally weaken Western countries. Al-Qaeda, the Islamic State, and other supporters offered apocalyptic predictions that COVID-19 would significantly undermine Western economic power, societal cohesion, and military might. These arguments generally fell into one of four categories.

First, some argued that COVID-19 would cause long-term economic damage and eventually trigger economic collapse. As one al-Qaeda assessment concluded, "With the emergence of COVID-19, the American economy has been struck by a powerful tsunami." It continued that "economies of major nations lie in ruin."[49] An article in the Islamic State publication *Al-Naba* argued that COVID-19 brought massive "misfortunes and calamities" to the United States.[50] More broadly, Salafi-jihadists hoped COVID-19 would trigger economic collapse in the West and countries across the Arab world.[51] "They are on the brink of a great economic disaster" pronounced one Islamic State article.[52] An Islamic State-aligned group made apocalyptic predictions about economic and societal breakdown around the globe: "In other parts of the world, where we find that the tyrannical ruling regimes are less stable and controlling, these regions will witness collapses and divisions at a faster pace, which will be associated with factors such as the Great Depression, public pressure, and poverty."[53]

Second, others argued that the pandemic would kill millions of civilians, more than any terrorist attack could ever kill. An Islamic State spokesperson argued that COVID-19 was divine punishment for Western "Crusaders," and he urged Allah to kill civilians and "empower the plague, the aches, and the sickness over the followers of Pharaoh, the tyrants from among Arabs and the foreigners, the enemies of Islam, because they did not leave a corruption that they did not use to fight the worshipers."[54] He equated Western countries with Pharaoh in the Biblical story of the ten disasters inflicted on Egypt, as Moses attempted to bring the children of Israel out of the country. In addition, al-Qaeda leader Ayman al-Zawahiri remarked that UK Prime Minister Boris Johnson "encouraged the spread of the pandemic so as to kill the largest possible number of non-productive sections of society."[55] It was, of course, a ludicrous assertion.

Third, some Salafi-jihadists argued that COVID-19 would exacerbate social, economic, and racial divisions in Western societies, including "worsening bloody racial politics."[56] As one article in *Al-Naba* claimed, the United States was headed toward a precipice because of COVID-19, and the existence of large-scale riots were signs of "feebleness" and "weakness."[57] In the summer of 2020, Salafi-jihadists attributed the demonstrations and riots in the United States following the death of George Floyd to punishment for corruption and unbelief. They made similar statements during protests in the fall of 2020.[58]

Fourth, Salafi-jihadists hoped that Western economic, health, and societal problems would cause their militaries to withdraw from Muslim lands.[59] As one group affiliated with al-Qaeda asked, "O French people … Would it not have been more judicious to announce the repatriation of the French military forces being in Sahel and Mali"?[60] Some Western states temporarily withdrew their military forces from Iraq as a protective measure in response to COVID-19.[61] As a U.S. State Department statement explained, "the unprecedented challenges posed by the COVID-19 pandemic to the Iraqi and Syrian people, and to our mission, led to temporary adjustments to protect the force during this period, in full coordination with the Iraqi authorities."[62]

The announcements corresponded with a decision by the UK, France, the United States, and several other countries to withdraw their forces from Iraq even before COVID-19.

Yet while Western countries certainly suffered economic, social, and other pressures from COVID-19—including spikes in infections and lockdowns—none were cataclysmic. In the United States, for example, gross domestic product (GDP) grew 7.4 percent in the third quarter of 2020, which was equivalent to 33.1 percent on an annualized basis.[63] In addition, the eurozone economy rose in the third quarter of 2020, with the combined GDP of the 19 eurozone members up 12.7 percent from the second quarter.[64]

Conclusion

COVID-19 has had a profound impact on international politics, killing millions of people, causing governments to establish quarantines and close their borders, and triggering an economic recession.[65] As Henry Kissinger remarked, "The coronavirus epidemic will forever alter the world order."[66] In examining the Islamic State and al-Qaeda responses to COVID-19, it should not be surprising that these entities resorted to apocalyptic predictions and outright fabrications. Their propaganda has always included significant disinformation, misinformation, and lies. Still, there were numerous analysts who believed that COVID-19 provided an opportunity for Salafi-jihadists to resurge and that it could undermine counterterrorism efforts. As one article summarized: "ISIS is likely to benefit in any case, as COVID-19 saps its enemies' strength."[67]

Despite these predictions, some Salafi-jihadists expressed veritable alarm about the pandemic and attempted to limit its spread. In Somalia, for example, al-Shabaab set up a "consultative forum" on jihad in East Africa and warned, "The Muslim society is hereby called upon to take caution against the infectious diseases that are now on the increase across the world, such as Coronavirus and HIV, whose spread is contributed to by the crusader forces who have invaded the country and the disbelieving countries that support them."[68] In Syria, the al-Qaeda-linked Hay'at Tahrir al-Sham and other groups expressed concern about individuals that tested positive for COVID-19 in Idlib and prayed for help. "Allah, Lord of Corona," one post read, "spare this liberated region from this epidemic, O Allah, heal our patients and protect our people."[69] Some al-Qaeda announcements urged supporters to ensure hygiene and cleanliness to prevent the spread of COVID-19, even as they characterized the pandemic as an act of God against the sins and corruption of infidel regimes.[70]

It is still too early to assess the long-term implications of COVID-19 on terrorism.

But Salafi-jihadists were unsuccessful in achieving most of their objectives—at least in the short term. They failed to increase the number of attacks (including in the West), failed to outperform local regimes in responding to COVID-19, and failed to weaken the West. In addition, COVID-19 created a host of problems for Salafi-jihadists.

First, government quarantines, social distancing requirements, and restrictions on freedom of movement within countries resulted in fewer possible transportation targets for attacks, such as trains, subways, and airports. Some of the most lethal Salafi-jihadist attacks have been transportation targets, such as those in Madrid in March 2004, London in July 2005, Mumbai in July 2006, Moscow in March 2010, and Brussels in March 2016. In addition, with sporting events, malls, restaurants, concerts, and outdoor events shut down, it was also difficult for terrorists to conduct attacks against large crowds. Examples included the Boston Marathon bombings in April 2013; Westgate Mall attack in Nairobi, Kenya in September 2013; coordinated attacks at restaurants, a football stadium, and other locations in Paris, France in November 2015; Bastille Day attack in Nice, France in July 2016; Christmas market attack in Berlin, Germany in December 2016; and Ariana Grande pop concert in Manchester, England in May 2017.

Second, there was a significant reduction in international travel as countries closed their borders. The decrease in foreign travel meant that there were fewer foreign tourist targets. In the past two decades, Salafi-jihadists have attacked numerous tourist destinations, such as Bali, Indonesia in October 2002 and October 2005; Sharm El Sheikh, Egypt in 2005; Dahab, Egypt in April 2006; Sousse, Tunisia in June 2015; and Barcelona, Spain in August 2017. The barriers to travel also impacted terrorist freedom of movement, including the travel of foreign fighters.[71]

Despite these challenges, however, there will likely be opportunities for Salafi-jihadists to conduct attacks and resurge in the future—regardless of COVID-19. Weak and ineffective governance, local grievances, and the withdrawal of Western counterterrorism forces will likely ensure that Salafi-jihadists remain a threat for the foreseeable future across Europe, Africa, the Middle East, and Asia. Following the September 11, 2001 terrorist attacks in the United States, the 9/11 predicted that the struggle against Salafi-jihadists would be "a generational challenge."[72] That reality has not changed.

Notes

1 Al-Qaeda, "The Way Forward: A Word of Advice on the Coronavirus Pandemic," As-Sahab Media Foundation, March 31, 2020, available at: https://ent.siteintelgroup.com/Jihadist-Threat-Statements/al-qaeda-central-advocates-islam-to-westerners-suffering-covid-19-pandemic-urges-muslims-embrace-religious-principles.html.

2 See, for example, "Coronavirus: Verily, It Is a Punishment Sent by Allah on Whom He Wished, and Allah Made It Mercy for the Believers," *The Voice of Hind*, No. 2, March 2020, p. 7, available at: https://ent.siteintelgroup.com/Jihadist-Threat-Chatter/2nd-issue-of-voice-of-hind-magazine-urges-indian-is-supporters-use-preoccupation-with-coronavirus-to-mount-attacks.html; "American Chaos After the Chinese Virus," *Al-Naba*, June 2020, available at: https://ent.siteintelgroup.com/Jihadist-Threat-Statements/is-regards-tinderbox-of-u-s-unrest-during-covid-19-pandemic-as-blessing-from-god-to-muslims.html.

3 See, for example, *Contending with ISIS in the Time of Coronavirus* (Brussels: International Crisis Group, March 31, 2020); Colin P. Clarke, "Remember Us? Islamic State Stays Active During Coronavirus," Foreign Policy Research Institute, May 8, 2020; European Union, *Terrorism Situation and Trend Report* (The Hague: European Union Agency for Law Enforcement Cooperation, 2020), p. 4; Gary Ackerman and Hayley Peterson, "Terrorism and COVID-19: Actual and Potential Impacts," *Perspective on Terrorism*, Vol. 14, No. 3, June 2020, pp. 59–73.

4 International Crisis Group: *Contending with ISIS in the Time of Coronavirus*, March 2020 p. 4., available at: https://www.crisisgroup.org/global/contending-isis-time-coronavirus.

5 On the Islamic State's desert strategy see Michael Knights, "The Islamic State Inside Iraq: Losing Power or Preserving Strength?" *CTC Sentinel*, Vol. 11, No. 11, December 2018, pp. 1–10; Hassan Hassan, "Insurgents Again: The Islamic State's Calculated Reversion to Attrition in the Syria-Iraq Border Region and Beyond," *CTC Sentinel*, Vol. 10, No. 11, December 2017, pp. 1–8. On the number of Islamic State fighters see United Nations Security Council, "Twenty-Sixth Report of the Analytical Support and Sanctions Monitoring Team Submitted Pursuant to Resolution 2368 (2017) Concerning ISIL (Da'esh), Al-Qaida and Associated Individuals and Entities," S/2020/717, July 23, 2020, p. 6.

6 Author interview with senior U.S. and Jordanian officials, Jordan, July 2019.

7 "The Temporary Fall of Cities as a Working Method for the Mujahideen," *Al-Naba*, April 2019. Aymenn Jawad Al-Tamimi translated Parts I, II, III, and IV into English at http://www.aymennjawad.org/2019/04/islamic-state-insurgent-tactics-translation. The quote is from Part I.

8 United Nations Security Council, "Twenty-Sixth Report of the Analytical Support and Sanctions Monitoring Team Submitted Pursuant to Resolution 2368 (2017) Concerning ISIL (Da'esh), Al-Qaida and Associated Individuals and Entities," S/2020/717, July 23, 2020, p. 6.

9 See, for example, Federal Bureau of Investigation, "Abdullah Ahmed Abdullah," accessed November 1, 2020.

10 See, for example, United Nations Security Council, "Twenty-Second Report of the Analytical Support and Sanctions Monitoring Team Submitted Pursuant to Resolution 2368 (2017) Concerning ISIL (Da'esh), Al-Qaida and Associated Individuals and Entities," S/2018/705, July 27, 2018, p. 8.

11 United Nations Security Council, "Twenty-Sixth Report of the Analytical Support and Sanctions Monitoring Team Submitted Pursuant to Resolution 2368 (2017) Concerning ISIL (Da'esh), Al-Qaida and Associated Individuals and Entities," S/2020/717, July 23, 2020, p. 7.

12 The data is based on the Armed Conflict Location and Event Data Project (ACLED), https://www.acleddata.com.

13 On the Taliban's religious and other views see Alex Strick van Linschoten and Felix Kuehn, eds., *The Taliban Reader: War, Islam and Politics* (New York, NY: Oxford University Press, 2018).

14 On the importance of an Islamic Emirate see, for example, "Weekly Comment," *Voice of Jihad*, September 19, 2020. "Afghan Taliban Alleges Islamic Governance is Desired by All Afghans, Not Just Itself," September 21, 2020, available at: https://ent.siteintelgroup.com/Jihadist-Threat-Statements/afghan-alleges-islamic-governance-is-desired-by-all-afghans-not-just-itself.html.

15 See such primary sources as "Letter to Mullah Muhammed 'Umar from Bin Laden," CTC Harmony Program, AFGP-2002-600321.

16 Department of Defense: *Enhancing Security and Stability in Afghanistan* (Washington, DC: U.S. Department of Defense, June 2020), p. 28. Available at: https://media.defense.gov/2020/Jul/01/2002348001/-1/-1/1/ENHANCING_SECURITY_AND_STABILITY_IN_AFGHANISTAN.PDF.

17 Antonio Giustozzi, *The Taliban at War: 2001–2018* (New York: Oxford University Press, 2019), pp. 81–83; "Eleventh Report of the Analytical Support and Sanctions Monitoring Team Submitted Pursuant to Resolution 2501 (2019) Concerning the Taliban and Other Associated Individuals and Entities Constituting a Threat to the Peace, Stability and Security of Afghanistan," United Nations Security Council, S/2020/415, May 27, 2020, p. 3.

18 Brian Michael Jenkins, *Stray Dogs and Virtual Armies: Radicalization and Recruitment to Jihadist Terrorism in the United States Since 9/11* (Santa Monica, CA: RAND, 2011).

19 Eric Schmitt, "Al Qaeda Suffers Losses to Leadership, Yet Remains Resilient," *New York Times*, October 28, 2020.

20 Al-Qaeda, "The Way Forward: A Word of Advice on the Coronavirus Pandemic," As-Sahab Media Foundation, March 31, 2020, available at: https://ent.siteintelgroup.com/Jihadist-Threat-Statements/al-qaeda-central-advocates-islam-to-westerners-suffering-covid-19-pandemic-urges-muslims-embrace-religous-principles.html.

21 "The Worst Nightmares of the Crusaders," *Al-Naba*, March 19, 2020, available at: https://ent.siteintelgroup.com/Jihadist-Threat-Statements/is-urges-jihadists-capitalize-on-paralysis-and-fear-amid-covid-19-pandemic-in-enemy-lands.html.

22 "The Worst Nightmares of the Crusaders," *Al-Naba*, March 19, 2020, available at: https://ent.siteintelgroup.com/Jihadist-Threat-Statements/is-urges-jihadists-capitalize-on-paralysis-and-fear-amid-covid-19-pandemic-in-enemy-lands.html.

23 "Indonesian IS Supporters Incite for Attacks During COVID-19 Crisis," March 30, 2020, available at: https://ent.siteintelgroup.com/Jihadist-Threat-Southeast-Asia/indonesian-is-supporters-incite-for-attacks-during-covid-19-crisis.html.

24 "Amid COVID-19 Pandemic, Indonesian IS Supporter Calls to Loot 'Kuffar' Goods," March 31, 2020, https://ent.siteintelgroup.com/Jihadist-Threat-Southeast-Asia/amid-covid-19-pandemic-indonesian-is-supporter-calls-to-loot-kuffar-goods.html.

25 "Coronavirus: Verily, It Is a Punishment Sent by Allah on Whom He Wished, and Allah Made It Mercy for the Believers," *The Voice of Hind*, No. 2, March 2020, p. 7, available at: https://ent.siteintelgroup.com/Jihadist-Threat-Statements/is-urges-jihadists-capitalize-on-paralysis-and-fear-amid-covid-19-pandemic-in-enemy-lands.html.

26 "Call for Violence to Reopen Philippine Mosques Closed by COVID-19 Restrictions," May 22, 2020, available at https://ent.siteintelgroup.com/Jihadist-Threat-Southeast-Asia/call-for-violence-to-reopen-philippine-mosques-closed-by-covid-19-restrictions.html; "BIFF Leader Calls for Violence and Followers to Attend Mosque Despite COVID-19," May 6, 2020, https://ent.siteintelgroup.com/Jihadist-Threat-Southeast-Asia/biff-leader-calls-for-violence-followers-to-attend-mosque-despite-covid-19.html.

27 See, for example, "Lockdown Terror," *The Voice of Hind* ("Lockdown Special"), June 2020, p. 9, available at: https://ent.siteintelgroup.com/documents/jihadist-threat/1255-site-lockdown-special/file.html. Also see SITE Intelligence Group, "Recent Global Jihad Updates on the COVID-19 Pandemic," May 6-12, 2020, available at: https://ent.siteintelgroup.com/Jihadist-News/recent-global-jihad-updates-on-the-covid-19-pandemic-may-6-12-2020.html

28 The data is based on the Armed Conflict Location and Event Data Project (ACLED), https://www.acleddata.com.

29 United Nations Security Council, "Twenty-Sixth Report of the Analytical Support and Sanctions Monitoring Team Submitted Pursuant to Resolution 2368 (2017) Concerning ISIL (Da'esh), Al-Qaida and Associated Individuals and Entities," S/2020/717, July 23, 2020, p. 6.

30 Nicolas Chapuis, "Après l'attentat de Nice, les zones d'ombre du parcours du suspect, arrivé récemment en Europe," *Le Monde*, October 30, 2020. Salafi-jihadists urged additional attacks. See, for example, "Defend Him by Cutting the Necks," Tarjuman Asawiriti, October 2020, available at: https://ent.siteintelgroup.com/Jihadist-Threat-Chatter/prominent-is-aligned-media-unit-urges-muslims-follow-example-of-french-teacher-beheading-in-avenging-prophet.html.

31 "Germany Arrests 5 Tajiks in Suspected ISIS Cell Planning Attacks on U.S. forces," *Associated France Presse*, April 15, 2020.

32 "Diseased World," *The Voice of Hind* ("Lockdown Special"), June 2020, p. 6, available at: https://ent.siteintelgroup.com/documents/jihadist-threat/1255-site-lockdown-special/file.html.

33 See, for example, Bruce Hoffman, *Inside Terrorism*, Third Edition (New York, NY: Columbia University Press, 2017), pp. 280–295.

34 See, for example, *Homeland Threat Assessment* (Washington, DC: U.S. Department of Homeland Security, October 2020), p. 17.

35 Council of Europe, "The Council of Europe Continues Working to Enhance Co-operation Against Terrorism, Including Bioterrorism," June 4, 2020.

36 "Neo-Nazi Channel Advocates Weaponization of COVID-19, Shares Instructions for Biological Weapon," July 14, 2020, available at: https://ent.siteintelgroup.com/Guide-Tracker/neo-nazi-channel-advocates-weaponization-of-covid-19-shares-instructions-for-biological-weapon.html; "Neo-Nazi User Promoted Using COVID-19 for Acts of Bioterrorism," April 3, 2020, available at: https://ent.siteintelgroup.com/Far-Right-/-Far-Left-Threat/neo-nazi-user-promoted-using-covid-19-for-acts-of-bioterrorism.html; "Minorities Targeted with Genetically Engineered Bioweapons," May 27, 2020, available at: https://ent.siteintelgroup.com/Bioterrorism-and-Public-Health/genetically-modified-biological-weapons-to-kill-minorities-explored.html; "Bubonic Plague Suggested to Kill Minorities, Spread Fear, Disrupt Economy," July 16, 2020, available at: https://ent.siteintelgroup.com/Bioterrorism-and-Public-Health/bubonic-plague-discussed-to-kill-minorities-spread-fear-disrupt-economy.html.

37 Ackerman and Peterson, "Terrorism and COVID-19," p. 65.

38 United Nations Security Council, "Twenty-Sixth Report of the Analytical Support and Sanctions Monitoring Team Submitted Pursuant to Resolution 2368 (2017) Concerning ISIL (Da'esh), Al-Qaida and Associated Individuals and Entities," S/2020/717, July 23, 2020, p. 22.

39 On the technical hurdles of CBRN for al-Qaeda and the Islamic State see Hoffman, *Inside Terrorism*, pp. 292–295.

40 Al-Qaeda, "The Way Forward: A Word of Advice on the Coronavirus Pandemic," As-Sahab Media Foundation, March 31, 2020, available at: https://ent.siteintelgroup.com/Jihadist-Threat-Statements/afghan-taliban-portrays-itself-as-better-able-to-manage-covid-19-pandemic-than-afghan-government.html.

41 United Nations, *The Impact of the COVID-19 Pandemic on Terrorism, Counter-terrorism and Countering Violent Extremism* (New York: United Nations Security Council, Counter-Terrorism Committee Executive Directorate, June 2020), p. 1.

42 Ackerman and Peterson, "Terrorism and COVID-19: Actual and Potential Impacts," p. 61.

43 "BIFF Faction Leader Calls for Recruitment Amid COVID-19 Pandemic," March 25, 2020, available at: https://ent.siteintelgroup.com/Jihadist-Threat-Statements/afghan-taliban-portrays-itself-as-better-able-to-manage-covid-19-pandemic-than-afghan-government.html.

44 United Nations, *The Impact of the COVID-19 Pandemic on Terrorism, Counter-Terrorism and Countering Violent Extremism* (New York, NY: United Nations Security Council, Counter-Terrorism Committee Executive Directorate, June 2020), p. 2.

45 Taliban, "The COVID-19 Pandemic and Our Shared Responsibilities," March 2020, available at: https://ent.siteintelgroup.com/Jihadist-Threat-Statements/afghan-taliban-portrays-itself-as-better-able-to-manage-covid-19-pandemic-than-afghan-government.html.

46 Taliban, "O My Servant! Spend (On Charity), I Shall Spend on You," May 2020, available at: https://ent.siteintelgroup.com/Jihadist-Threat-Statements/afghan-taliban-regards-covid-19-pandemic-during-ramadan-as-unprecedented-opportunity-for-charitable-giving.html.

47 Kars de Bruijne and Loic Bisson, "States, Not Jihadis, Exploiting Corona Crisis in West Africa," *Clingendael Spectator*, May 27, 2020.

48 World Bank Governance Indicators Data Set, 2020, available at: https://info.worldbank.org/governance/wgi/.

49 Al-Qaeda, "The Way Forward: A Word of Advice on the Coronavirus Pandemic," As-Sahab Media Foundation, March 31, 2020, available at: https://ent.siteintelgroup.com/Jihadist-Threat-Statements/is-says-covid-19-pandemic-debunks-myth-of-american-omniscience-and-power.html.

50 "Such As Have No Power Either for Benefit or for Harm to Themselves," *Al-Naba*, No. 227, March 2020, available at: https://ent.siteintelgroup.com/Jihadist-Threat-Statements/is-says-covid-19-pandemic-debunks-myth-of-american-omniscience-and-power.html.

51 "American Chaos After the Chinese Virus," *Al-Naba*, June 2020, available at: https://ent.siteintelgroup.com/Jihadist-Threat-Chatter/is-aligned-group-sees-economic-depression-regime-collapse-in-multiple-states-as-acts-of-god-worthy-of-praise.html.

52 "The Worst Nightmares of the Crusaders," *Al-Naba*, March 19, 2020, available at: https://ent.siteintelgroup.com/Jihadist-Threat-Chatter/is-aligned-group-sees-economic-depression-regime-collapse-in-multiple-states-as-acts-of-god-worthy-of-praise.html.

53 "And a Similar Fate Awaits the Disbelievers," Hadm al-Aswar Media Foundation, August 2020, available at: https://ent.siteintelgroup.com/Jihadist-Threat-Chatter/is-aligned-group-sees-economic-depression-regime-collapse-in-multiple-states-as-acts-of-god-worthy-of-praise.html.

54 Abu Hamza al-Qurashi, "And the Disbelievers Will Know Who Gets the Good End," Al-Furqan Foundation, May 2020, available at: https://ent.siteintelgroup.com/Jihadist-Threat-Statements/is-spokesman-echoes-jihadi-sentiment-of-covid-19-being-divine-punishment-vows-group-will-never-compromise-their-faith.html.

55 Ayman al-Zawahiri, "Together Towards Allah," As-Sahab Media Foundation, May 2020, available at: https://ent.siteintelgroup.com/Jihadist-Threat-Statements/aq-leader-zawahiri-critiques-value-neutral-irreligious-western-materialism-in-2nd-episode-of-anti-atheism-series.html.

56 Ayman al-Zawahiri, "Together Towards Allah," As-Sahab Media Foundation, May 2020, available at: https://ent.siteintelgroup.com/Jihadist-Threat-Statements/aq-leader-zawahiri-critiques-value-neutral-irreligous-western-materialism-in-2nd-episode-of-anti-atheism-series.html.

57 "American Chaos After the Chinese Virus," *Al-Naba*, June 2020, available at: https://ent.siteintelgroup.com/Jihadist-Threat-Chatter/2nd-issue-of-voice-of-hind-magazine-urges-indian-is-supporters-use-preoccupation-with-coronavirus-to-mount-attacks.html.

58 See, for example, "Jihadist Capitalizes on Racial Unrest in Philadelphia, U.S.," October 2020, available at: https://ent.siteintelgroup.com/Jihadist-Threat-Chatter/jihadist-capitalizes-on-racial-unrest-in-philadelphia-u-s.html.

59 "The Worst Nightmares of the Crusaders," *Al-Naba*, March 19, 2020, available at: https://ent.siteintelgroup.com/Jihadist-Threat-Statements/is-urges-jihadists-capitalize-on-paralysis-and-fear-amid-covid-19-pandemic-in-enemy-lands.html.

60 "Coronavirus and Takuba Cure," *Al-Kifah Media*, March 2020, available at: https://ent.siteintelgroup.com/Statements/pro-aq-french-unit-argues-france-should-focus-on-covid-19-expenditures-rather-than-military-abroad.html.

61 "U.S.-Led Coalition Pulls Trainers from Iraq Over Virus," *France 24*, March 19, 2020; "France to Withdraw All Troops from Iraq Due to Coronavirus Outbreak," *Reuters*, March 25, 2020.

62 Quoted in Bryant Harris, "Intel: Coronavirus Forces Partial U.S. Troop Drawdown in Iraq," *Al-Monitor*, March 23, 2020.

63 U.S. Department of Commerce, Bureau of Economic Analysis, "Gross Domestic Product, Third Quarter 2020," BEA 20–53, October 29, 2020.

64 Paul Hannon and Eric Sylvers, "Eurozone Economy Soars but France and Germany's Lockdowns Cast Covid-19 Shadow," *Wall Street Journal*, October 20, 2020. Available at: https://www.wsj.com/articles/eurozone-economy-soars-but-covid-19-resurgence-leaves-it-the-global-weak-spot-11604052146.

65 Hal Brands and Francis J. Gavin, eds., *COVID-19 and World Order: The Future of Conflict, Competition, and Cooperation* (Baltimore, MD: Johns Hopkins University Press, 2020).

66 Henry A, Kissinger, "The Coronavirus Pandemic Will Forever Alter the World Order," *Wall Street Journal*, April 3, 2020. Available at: https://www.wsj.com/articles/the-coronavirus-pandemic-will-forever-alter-the-world-order-11585953005.

67 *Contending with ISIS in the Time of Coronavirus* (Brussels: International Crisis Group, March 31, 2020), p. 5.

68 Shabaab al-Mujahideen Movement, "Communique from the Consultative Forum Regarding the Jihad in East Africa," 23 Rajab 1441 H [March 18, 2020], available at: https://ent.siteintelgroup.com/Statements/shabaab-convenes-consultative-forum-on-jihad-in-east-africa-civil-and-military-issues.html.

69 "First Recorded Case of COVID-19 Reported in Idlib, Syria," July 9, 2020, available at: https://ent.siteintelgroup.com/Jihadist-Threat-Chatter/first-case-of-covid-19-reported-in-idlib-syria.html.

70 Al-Qaeda, "The Way Forward: A Word of Advice on the Coronavirus Pandemic," As-Sahab Media Foundation, March 31, 2020, available at: https://ent.siteintelgroup.com/Jihadist-Threat-Statements/al-qaeda-central-advocates-islam-to-westerners-suffering-covid-19-pandemic-urges-muslims-embrace-religious-principles.html.

71 United Nations, *The Impact of the COVID-19 Pandemic on Terrorism, Counter-Terrorism and Countering Violent Extremism* (New York, NY: United Nations Security Council, Counter-Terrorism Committee Executive Directorate, June 2020), p. 2.

72 National Commission on Terrorist Attacks, *The 9/11 Commission Report: Final Report of the National Commission on Terrorist Attacks Upon the United States* (New York, NY: W.W. Norton, 2004), p. 361.

40

THE IMPACT OF THE COVID-19 PANDEMIC ON TERRORISM AND COUNTER-TERRORISM

Reassessing the Evidence

*Sam Mullins**

Following the first international reports of a novel coronavirus outbreak in China in January 2020, COVID-19 (as it was named on February 11th) has spread rapidly around the globe, bringing with it social, political and economic turmoil. Ever keen to exploit instability, violent extremists of all kinds rapidly seized upon the opportunity, putting their own spin on events in an attempt to promote their respective causes and regain some of the attention lost to the virus. Unfortunately, the international media has been all too willing to oblige, eagerly reporting on extremists' views of the pandemic and amplifying their messages far beyond their relatively small body of existing supporters.[1] At the same time, both successful and failed terrorist attacks alike have frequently been presented as evidence that terrorists are successfully exploiting the pandemic. In conjunction with this, the preponderance of expert commentary (to include both respected academics and seasoned practitioners), has tended to emphasize the potentially exacerbating effects that the pandemic may have on violent extremism and terrorism.[2] The picture that emerges is concerning, to say the least.

Yet, much of the discussion has been based on select, anecdotal evidence, logical inference and theoretical supposition, leaving many unanswered questions and a good deal of uncertainty. Although it is clear that violent extremists and terrorists have *tried* to exploit the pandemic, it is not readily apparent that they have been particularly successful. Similarly, there are often few details to substantiate that a given terrorist plot or attack actually involved deliberate exploitation of conditions arising from the pandemic, other than that the events in question took place since the outbreak began. Furthermore, relatively little attention has been paid to information or events that run contrary to the dominant, pessimistic narrative, or to the various challenges and difficulties that terrorists must contend with as a result of the spread of COVID-19.[3] It is therefore necessary to re-examine and re-evaluate the various assertions that have been made, with a view to offering a more balanced threat assessment. This is the goal of the present article. The paper proceeds with an examination of terrorist recruitment efforts during the pandemic,

---

* The views expressed in this article are those of the author alone and do not necessarily represent the official position of the Daniel K. Inouye Asia-Pacific Center for Security Studies, or the United States government.

DOI: 10.4324/9781003326373-46

followed by fundraising, health-related governance and conducting attacks. This is comple-
mented with an analysis of the impact on counter-terrorism (CT), followed by the summary
and conclusion.

Recruitment

As noted above, it did not take long for violent extremists and terrorists to seek to capitalize on
the pandemic for purposes of propaganda. Jihadist commentators have tended to emphasize that
COVID-19 is the work of God, seeing it as divine punishment, first of all for China's treatment
of Uighurs in Xinjiang; then, as the virus spread, for Iran's "blindness" and "insolence" as a Shia
theocracy; the United States' perceived oppression of Muslims worldwide; and eventually also
fellow Muslims for their ostensibly "sinful" behavior and laxity of faith.[4] ISIS adopted a predicta-
bly aggressive stance, declaring it an ideal time to conduct attacks, given the added burden placed
on security forces. By comparison, al-Qaeda took the opportunity to invite non-Muslims to
convert to Islam, but also continued to call for attacks against U.S. and Israeli targets worldwide.[5]

The other main set of actors to try to exploit the pandemic for extremist purposes have been
members of the far-right, most notably in the United States and Europe, who have promoted a
variety of competing conspiracy theories designed to undermine trust in government and engen-
der hatred and violence against ideological enemies. The Chinese, Jews, George Soros, Bill Gates
and the U.S. government have all been blamed for manufacturing and/or exploiting the virus
to advance their perceived agendas of domination and oppression, while homosexuals and immigrants have been respectively accused of inviting God's wrath and spreading the virus.[6] Right-
wing extremists were also especially quick to recognize that the virus itself might be weaponized
and began calling on supporters to deliberately infect their enemies even before the pandemic
was officially declared.[7] Meanwhile, left-wing extremists have called for social protests, rioting,
looting and violence against police.[8]

Besides simply seeking to maintain relevance in the midst of a global catastrophe that has all
but eclipsed them, there are at least three connected aims to all of this output: to galvanize existing supporters; to radicalize and recruit new ones; and to incite people to violence. The critical
question is, are they succeeding? Theoretically, conditions arising from the pandemic (the imposition of lockdowns, unemployment, economic hardship, loneliness, frustration and boredom)
could have potentially increased the vulnerability of large numbers of people to radicalization.
In the words of the UN, terrorists have been granted a "captive audience."[9] In support of this
theory, researchers have found that along with the proliferation of extremist groups on social media, the volume of related search-traffic and subscribers to these groups have also increased. In the
United States, there was a larger increase in searches for white supremacist material on Google in
states that had been under lockdown for a longer period of time.[10] Similarly, international traffic
to ISIS websites reportedly increased as lockdowns took effect globally.[11]

There are, however, limited inferences that we can draw from this. Though it might suggest
increased levels of interest in extremist propaganda during lockdowns, it does not constitute evidence of wide-spread radicalization, much less mobilization.[12] Of course, there are examples of
individuals who have become radicalized since the pandemic began. In one instance, a rail company employee named Eduardo Moreno deliberately crashed a train at the Port of Los Angeles
in an attempt to draw public attention to what he believed was a secret government conspiracy
surrounding COVID-19 and the *USNS Mercy* hospital ship, which was there to support the Los
Angeles coronavirus response.[13] In another case in the UK, a 14-year-old convert to Islam, accused of attempting to build an improvised explosive device (IED) in preparation for a jihadist

terrorist attack, was initially reported to have radicalized during the month of May when a national lockdown was in effect.[14]

Yet in cases such as these, it takes time before we have sufficient information to make an informed judgment. Although anti-government right-wing extremists have been pushing all manner of conspiracy theories, it is unclear how Moreno developed his own, apparently delusional, mindset and there has so far been no information to suggest that he was influenced by others. In the case of the 14-year-old British convert, it later transpired that he had been engaging with ISIS propaganda online since at least February, which was before the first lockdowns were introduced in the United Kingdom.[15] More importantly, he was eventually acquitted. In other cases (such as Timothy Wilson, who planned to blow up a hospital treating coronavirus patients in Missouri; or Aaron Swenson, who allegedly planned to livestream the murder of police officers in Texas), their descent into terrorism either began long before the pandemic, or else was driven by other events.[16]

Perhaps the clearest example of pandemic-inspired terrorism to date emerged in the United States in October, when 13 right-wing extremists were charged with plotting to kidnap the Governor of Michigan, Gretchen Whitmer, because they were angry at the "unconstitutional" lockdown measures she had enacted and wanted to start a civil war in order to overthrow the government. Yet again, there is information to suggest that the alleged conspirators had developed militant, anti-government beliefs and organizations before the pandemic began. The so-called Wolverine Watchmen, a "militia" to which at least seven of the men belonged, had been recruiting on Facebook since November 2019.[17] And it seems that as far back as May 2018 the apparent plot leader, Adam Fox, had railed against "corrupt self-serving politicians and lawmakers" on Twitter, warning them that "we will come for you and end your era of rule!!"[18] Thus, although the arrival of the pandemic seemingly helped spur the men to act, it was not the reason they had radicalized in the first place. Most of the alleged plotters have since been acquitted and, at the time of writing, only the two alleged ringleaders are facing a retrial.[19]

The bigger point here is that besides a relatively small number of individuals who radicalized and mobilized to terrorism as a more-or-less direct result of the current health crisis, it is not apparent that terrorist recruitment efforts have brought about a significant, quantitative increase in either radicalization or associated terrorist activity. Importantly, this gels with assessments made by the intelligence community. For example, in an assessment of the situation in the Philippines, the U.S. Defense Intelligence Agency (DIA) reported that there was insufficient information to tell whether ISIS East Asia (ISIS-EA) had significantly shifted its overall intensity of recruitment or attack, and that it "lacked information indicating whether [COVID-19 related terrorist propaganda in the Philippines] resulted in any increase in terrorist violence or recruitment."[20]

Looking at terrorist recruitment more broadly, a survey of 100 CT and security practitioners, mostly from the Indo-Pacific region (including the United States), found that 51% either disagreed or strongly disagreed that terrorists' pandemic-related propaganda had resulted in increased radicalization/recruitment, compared to 24% who agreed or strongly agreed.[21] A subsequent study conducted with a more diverse sample of 415 practitioners found almost identical results—50% disagreed or strongly disagreed with the above statement versus 24% who were of the opposite opinions.[22] Based on this, it appears that, although there have been some successes and the reality clearly varies according to location, on balance, terrorist recruitment efforts during the first two years of the pandemic have so far been largely unsuccessful.

Looking ahead, there is remaining concern about the long-term impact of the social and economic consequences of the pandemic, combined with deep-felt resentment of state-imposed restrictions.[23] Especially worrisome is the apparent, widespread growth in anti-government sentiment, exemplified by the *Querdenken* movement in Germany, which has been linked to various acts of political violence, including a plot to assassinate the premier of Saxony.[24] But whether the risk associated with these developments will outlast the pandemic, or if it has already peeked, remains to be seen.

Fundraising

Less has been written about terrorists' potential ability to exploit the pandemic in order to raise funds, though it remains a distinct possibility and at least one significant case has been uncovered so far. Commenting on this in April (just one month after the World Health Organization (WHO) declared a pandemic), the Institute for Policy Analysis of Conflict (IPAC) noted that Indonesian militants had long been operating charities that claim to provide "humanitarian assistance" and that the authorities should be on the look-out for fundraising efforts connected to the virus, including potentially bogus appeals for personal protective equipment (PPE) for health workers.[25] Of course, terrorists all over the world have raised money using fraudulent means for many years, including under the guise of charitable collections, and so this possibility is not unique to Indonesia.

Indeed, in August 2020, the U.S. Department of Justice announced that it had disrupted three different terrorist fundraising schemes, which had been soliciting donations in cryptocurrency on social media, seizing millions of dollars in the process.[26] One of these schemes was allegedly orchestrated by a Turkish-based ISIS facilitator named Murat Cakar, who operated a website (www.FaceMaskCenter.com), fraudulently claiming to provide "Surgical N95 respirators" and other PPE to protect against COVID-19.[27] Though claiming to have been in operation since 1996, FaceMaskCenter.com was established, using a Turkish IP address, on February 26th 2020. Cakar then used four different Facebook pages, which he had previously set up as early as 2014 (and ostensibly used to sell clothing) to advertise the new website.[28]

Despite claiming that its products were approved by the U.S. Federal Food and Drug Administration (FDA) and the National Institute for Occupations Safety and Health (NIOSH), in reality, the masks purportedly for sale were non-approved Turkish-made items. It remains unclear how many customers were duped by this scheme or how much money Cakar made, though it is noteworthy that a U.S.-based individual had contacted the site inquiring about PPE for hospitals, nursing homes and fire departments, thus illustrating its international reach as well as potentially deadly consequences.[29] Moreover, Cakar had been in contact with at least one U.S.-based ISIS sympathizer dating back to 2017: a 27-year-old Long Island woman named Zoobia Shahnaz, who knowingly sent approximately $100,000 to an alias of Cakar before being arrested, and in November 2018 pleading guilty to providing material support to ISIS.[30] The picture of Cakar that emerges is of a long-time, internationally connected and reasonably successful criminal/ISIS supporter who pounced on the opportunity to exploit the pandemic.

Although—to the author's knowledge—this is still the only public report of its kind to date, it would be naïve to think that other violent extremists and terrorists have not thought of this and at least attempted similar COVID-related schemes, even if most are likely to be on a smaller scale and less sophisticated. However, in the first survey of security practitioners mentioned above, nearly 70% of respondents were of the opinion that terrorists had *not* been able to raise more funds than usual because of the pandemic, with one person asserting that "Raising fund[s] [has] stopped due to the restriction[s] on movements."[31] Only 9% disagreed with this assessment. The second, larger survey also produced comparable results, with 59% of the opinion that fundraising had not increased versus just 12% who disagreed.[32]

These results suggest that successful exploitation of the pandemic by terrorists for financial gain has so far been the exception to the rule, or at the very least is yet to be effectively investigated. Besides the rather sophisticated example above, we have nothing in the way of hard evidence to demonstrate that this is happening on a widespread or large-scale basis. Furthermore, although we know that terrorists routinely employ all manner of extortion and illicit means to raise funds, much of this is predicated on a functioning economy and could well be disrupted in the wake of COVID-19, with serious implications for group finances, decision-making and organizational integrity.[33] Indeed, important fundraising activities—such as neo-Nazi music festivals—have had to be cancelled as a result of travel restrictions and lockdowns.[34] Thus, as much as the pandemic has presented potential fundraising opportunities for violent extremists and terrorists, it has also brought setbacks and challenges.

Health-Related Governance

A third way that terrorists are thought to have gained an advantage is in the area of health-related governance for groups that control territory. Specifically, by providing healthcare services and making an effort to control the spread of contagion, the pandemic is seen as an opportunity for terrorist and insurgent organizations to effectively win the "hearts and minds" of people under their control.[35] This is presumed to increase their perceived legitimacy in the eyes of the people and thus solidify, if not expand popular support.

Drawing on case studies of Hayat Tahrir al-Sham (HTS) in Syria and the Afghan Taliban, Marta Furlan argues that "rebel rulers are better positioned than governments to deal with emergencies [such as COVID-19] because they do not need to demonstrate governance capacity in *absolute* terms but rather governance capacity in *relative* terms vis-a-vis the government."[36] In the cases of HTS and the Taliban, they appear to have done just that. In contrast to the inept responses of the Syrian and Afghan governments at the time, the two militant organizations in question went to great lengths to show that they were proactively responding to the virus, conducting awareness campaigns and distributing PPE, while also establishing quarantine centers and enforcing checkpoints, lockdowns and other forms of control.[37]

On the face of it, such efforts are quite impressive, and it is possible they have had the desired effect. Nevertheless, caveats apply. Much of what we know about terrorist groups' responses to the pandemic comes in the form of carefully produced propaganda, which the groups have made themselves. According to the International Crisis Group (ICG), "the Taliban's public health scramble may be more window-dressing than substance."[38] This chimes with an assessment of terrorist responses to COVID-19 by Kabir Taneja and Rafaello Pantucci, who argue that the real worth of these activities lies more in their propaganda value than in altering reality on the ground.[39] These same authors point out that in the case of HTS, the group jeopardized its own ideological and internal cohesion by advising people to temporarily avoid going to mosque— effectively "choosing science over religious directives."[40] Others, including Hezbollah and Hamas have done the same.[41] In Syria, HTS' senior leader Abu Malik al-Tali briefly resigned in protest against this decision, while prominent jihadist ideologues such as Abu Muhammad al-Maqdisi have been outspoken in their criticism of orders to close mosques in response to the coronavirus.[42] What this shows is that, much like internationally recognized governments, jihadists governing during the pandemic are often faced with difficult decisions, whereby pragmatic measures to contain the spread of disease invoke significant negative reactions among some of their constituents.

In connection with this, we must be careful to distinguish between *outputs* and *outcomes*. Despite all the effort that HTS and others have made, it is not self-evident that these have been universally approved of by the populations in question, or that they have had an overall positive net effect. Even under democratically elected governments, a substantial proportion of the population has become frustrated and angry in reaction to shutdowns of business and other restrictions designed to protect them. There is no reason to believe that terrorists will be immune from the same, though such feelings are less likely to be publicly expressed for fear of reprisal. This brings us to yet another important point—the effect of any efforts made to contain the pandemic cannot be viewed in isolation from an insurgent organization's overall approach to governance. HTS, for instance, faced mass protests—which it harshly suppressed—for plans to open up a trade crossing with the Syrian regime in May.[43] According to one protestor who was interviewed, "the opening of the crossing showed HTS has little concern for the fate of the region's population."[44] In Lebanon, Hezbollah is faced with widespread resentment, despite mobilizing thousands of volunteers to assist with the pandemic.[45] Meanwhile, the Taliban are fiercely intolerant of any form of criticism or complaint and, before forcibly seizing power in August 2021, were responsible for more than 40% of civilian casualties in Afghanistan.[46] Millions now live on the brink of starvation under their draconian rule—facts that are likely to outweigh any sense of gratitude generated from the distribution of PPE during the pandemic. Many other militant groups are even less adept and even more reliant on fear as a means of coercing the people under their control. In Colombia, dissident members of the Revolutionary Armed Forces of Colombia (FARC) have taken an especially harsh approach, threatening people to maintain social distance and obey militant curfews on pain of death. As one human rights campaigner bluntly put it, "COVID is not killing us. Armed groups are killing us."[47]

All of this is not to say that terrorist and insurgent-administered health-related governance is entirely ineffective. However, we must be careful to conduct more comprehensive analyses that take into account the complexity of their respective operating environments. As with recruitment efforts (detailed above), numerous terrorist organizations have certainly tried to improve their image—not to mention their own operational security—by implementing pandemic-related controls. But the real impact is difficult to assess and it is equally true that the current crisis may expose their intrinsic limitations and inability to dispense effective governance.[48] Moreover, to the extent that the pandemic is a distraction and drain on resources for governments, the same is also clearly true for terrorists, in particular those involved in civil administration.

Conducting Attacks

A fourth area where terrorists potentially gained an advantage is in the planning and conducting of attacks. This line of reasoning stems, not only from the supposed increase in radicalization that some believe is taking place, but more directly from the contention that security forces are "distracted" by the coronavirus (or more specifically, that their manpower, resources and capabilities have been negatively impacted as a result of having to take on pandemic-related security duties, while also implementing force protection measures to prevent the spread of disease). The clear implication of this is that CT agencies will not be able to devote sufficient time and resources to effectively contain the terrorist threat, leaving gaps in security that terrorists will be able to exploit. Certainly, this is reflected in the thinking of right-wing violent extremists and jihadist terrorist organizations, as well as analytical assessments published by the likes of the highly esteemed Center for Strategic and International Studies (CSIS) and the ICG.[49]

The impact of the pandemic on CT will be examined below in greater detail. To begin with, it is important to question whether we have actually seen the implied increase in terrorist attacks, and if so, can it be clearly attributed to the effects of the pandemic? To be sure, there has been a significant number of relatively low-level acts of extremist-motivated violence and sabotage—for instance, attacks on Muslims, who are widely blamed for spreading the coronavirus in India, and the destruction of mobile phone towers, based on the mistaken belief that the virus is somehow spread by 5G technology in Europe.[50] However, it is something of a definitional stretch to regard these as acts of terrorism, which usually involve more serious levels of violence, deliberately calibrated to communicate with a mass audience, as well as more clearly articulated political/ ideological (as opposed to personally expressive or instrumental) goals.

Focusing on attacks by terrorist organizations, two commonly cited examples that have been depicted as proof that terrorists are exploiting COVID-related weaknesses in security, are Iraq and Sub-Saharan Africa. In the case of Iraq, there is some disagreement about the number of attacks that have occurred. Researchers Michael Knights and Alex Almeida reported that ISIS mounted at least 566 attacks in Iraq in the first three months of 2020, representing a staggering 94% increase from the previous year.[51] Yet according to Lt. Gen. Pat White, the American commander of the U.S.-led coalition to defeat ISIS, the number of attacks has been "very consistent" with 2019.[52] In addition, he noted that the attacks have become less sophisticated as the coalition has successfully degraded ISIS's capabilities.[53] Even if we accept that ISIS managed to step up its operations in Iraq in 2020, the group was reportedly already making a comeback by mid-2019, before the pandemic had begun.[54] In the view of Jason Blazakis, "it seems more likely that any ISIS resurgence [in Iraq] is tied to pre-existing counterterrorism strategies and decisions."[55] Significantly, Knights and Almeida appear to agree, concluding that "the endogenous factors that draw the most international attention—U.S-Iran tensions and COVID-19—are merely accelerants of an Islamic State recovery in Iraq that was already well underway in late 2019."[56]

A similar story can be seen in Sub-Saharan Africa. Though analysts have been quick to attribute attacks in the region to the onset of the pandemic, often no details are provided to clearly connect the two. For example, Emilia Columbo and Marielle Harris point to the massacre of 92 Chadian troops by Boko Haram at the end of March 2020 as evidence that terrorists in the region are "leveraging the Covid-19 crisis as an opportunity to intensify attacks."[57] However, at the time the attack occurred, just three coronavirus cases had been confirmed in Chad and the country had taken few steps to combat the virus, suggesting that whatever failures contributed to the attack in question, COVID-19 most likely had little to do with it.[58] Furthermore, any observed increases in terrorism in Sub-Saharan Africa must be seen within the context of a rise in attacks in the region dating back to 2004, which has dramatically surged, almost uninterrupted, since 2011.[59]

This speaks to a broader issue with much of the commentary on COVID-19 and terrorism: namely, the frequent neglect of existing trends, combined with a failure to distinguish between correlation and causation. Just because a given attack takes place within the context of the pandemic, does not necessarily mean it was enabled by COVID-related gaps in security. Melissa Pavlik of the Armed Conflict Location and Event Data Project (ACLED) makes a similar point in drawing attention to the fact that pre-pandemic trends, and not the coronavirus, are the most likely reasons for observed decreases in political violence in Syria and Afghanistan, and for increases in Libya and Yemen (though it has contributed to various forms of political violence elsewhere).[60]

Importantly, the first survey of security practitioners referred to above found that 78% of respondents (versus just 9%) either disagreed or strongly disagreed with the statement that "Because of the Coronavirus pandemic, terrorists in my country have been able to conduct more attacks than usual." Yet again, the results from the second survey were highly consistent at 68% versus 12%.[61] As noted by these practitioners, part of the reason why we have not seen an increase in terrorist attacks in most places is because terrorists must also contend with lockdowns and restrictions on movement, which make it harder for them to move around. Indeed, this is one of the reasons given by Lt. Gen. White for ISIS's relatively modest gains in Iraq.[62] This gels with the findings of the annual Global Terrorism Index, produced by the Institute for Economics and Peace, which found that "the evidence suggests that the pandemic has had very little impact on terrorism in 2020 and 2021."[63] Thus, whatever potential advantages terrorists may have gained as a result of the pandemic, it appears that in many cases, these have been offset by added security measures designed to halt the spread of disease.

The Impact on Counter-Terrorism

As already noted, it is generally believed that security services responsible for CT have been negatively impacted by the pandemic and that as a result, they have been rendered less effective.[64] There are indeed many examples of COVID-related impediments, largely relating to the redeployment of forces and/or implementation of force health protection measures, such as social distancing. For instance, in March 2020, the Philippines sent the 12th Marine Battalion, which had been preparing for CT duties in Sulu, to help support the pandemic response in Metro Manila instead.[65] Meanwhile, the anti-ISIS coalition multinational training mission, as well as operational support for Iraqi Security Forces (ISF) were temporarily suspended due to coronavirus concerns.[66] U.S. security cooperation activities were likewise put on hold in Africa and two multinational exercises scheduled to take place on the continent had to be canceled.[67] Another issue has been the impact on the intelligence community, whose members cannot work from home, given the need to be able to access classified documents and secure IT systems.[68] Finally, in the United Kingdom, the pandemic resulted in a significant drop in referrals to the national Prevent program, illustrating that efforts toward preventing and countering violent extremism (P/CVE) have also been affected.[69]

Yet as serious as these developments are, the reality is far from being a one-sided story. In the Philippines, security forces have maintained consistent pressure on terrorists operating in the country and, in July, President Duterte approved a new anti-terrorism law granting authorities expanded powers.[70] In Iraq, the ISF, assisted by coalition airpower and intelligence, surveillance and reconnaissance (ISR) capabilities, has likewise continued to engage in successful CT operations on a daily basis.[71] In Africa, Maj. Gen. Dagvin Anderson, Commander of U.S. Special Operations Command Africa (SOCAF), clarified that despite setbacks experienced at the outset of the pandemic, "[T]hroughout that entire period... U.S. Special Operations Forces stayed engaged and did not leave the continent. We did not walk away from our partners... We stayed engaged and continued to put pressure on these violent extremists."[72] Finally, members of the intelligence and P/CVE communities, though hobbled by the need to social distance, have nevertheless adapted, incorporating technological and organizational workarounds that enable them to keep working and, in some cases even "flourish."[73]

To draw once again on the survey data referred to several times above, the results confirm that although the pandemic has presented challenges, many of these appear to have been at least partially overcome. Thus, in the first survey, although 50% of respondents agreed or strongly agreed that CT has become more difficult during the pandemic (whether due to diversion of resources or having to implement social distancing), 33% were of the opposite opinion.[74] In the second, larger survey, the results were again almost identical, with 51% agreeing with this statement versus 34% who disagreed.[75] Most importantly, even those who agreed that CT had become more difficult explained that alternative working arrangements had been found, allowing them to continue functioning, as one person put it, "at full capacity in most aspects of our work."[76] It was furthermore pointed out that vastly reduced international travel and trade had effectively freed up some personnel to focus on other tasks, suggesting that CT resources may have even received a boost in some areas.[77] The bottom line is that despite the various difficulties, it is not readily apparent that CT has suffered sufficiently to grant terrorists a significant edge. To the contrary, the mostly limited increases in frequency of attacks (in particular, those which we can attribute to the pandemic), suggests that it has not.

Summary and Conclusion

This article set out to reevaluate the impact of the COVID-19 pandemic on terrorism and CT, taking into account information both for and against dominant narratives, which tend to emphasize the exacerbating effects of the virus on security. In each of the areas examined (recruitment, fundraising, health-related governance, conducting attacks, and the impact of the pandemic on CT), a somewhat similar story emerges. There is solid evidence to show that terrorists are attempting to exploit the ongoing crisis in order to advance their respective "campaign plans," while at the same time security services have been faced with additional challenges. But there is very limited information to demonstrate that terrorists are meeting their objectives, while at the same time, considerable evidence exists to suggest the contrary. Similarly, there is reason to believe that CT authorities have been able to adapt and continue functioning in an effective manner, in spite of the new and more challenging operating environment.

It is important to emphasize that this does not necessarily imply that the impact of the pandemic has been negligible overall. For example, in the case of Murat Cakar, FaceMaskCenter. com was seemingly able to raise large sums of money for ISIS. That alone is qualitatively significant. Likewise, although the added burden placed on security forces has not necessarily given terrorists the dramatic advantage that some fear, it is still a problem that should not be overlooked. It is also apparent that each particular context and terrorist organization is more or less unique. The impact of the pandemic on terrorism inside and outside of conflict zones, and in urban and rural areas, has not been the same, and of course it will also vary according to different groups and over time, for a multitude of reasons.[78] With these caveats in mind, it is important to note that it is not the aim of this article to provide firm conclusions on any of the issues discussed, but rather to promote a more balanced analytical approach to understanding the problem.

As things stand, it is still relatively early in the pandemic and we are generally lacking detailed and reliable information on key issues of concern. In time, COVID-induced stresses and related terrorist recruitment efforts may yet lead to a substantial increase in mobilization to terrorism; terrorists may become far more adept at generating funds based on lessons learned during the pandemic; HTS and others could potentially experience significant gains in public support, thanks in part to their handling of the coronavirus; and terrorist attacks might eventually increase as CT budgets are increasingly strained under the weight of economic recession. But for the time being, it has to be acknowledged that these have yet to pass and are far from inevitable outcomes.

Although there is a growing number of exceptions, public commentary on this issue has generally suffered from failing to give due consideration to conflicting information; ignoring existing, long-term trends and alternative, explanatory factors; conflating correlation with causation; relying too heavily on theoretically-driven inferences and making assumptions beyond the available data. By taking care to address these problems, analysts will produce far more nuanced and valuable insights that would improve our understanding of what is an incredibly complex set of interrelated and continually evolving problems. Indeed, this will be essential for enabling the successful adaptation of CT strategies in a post-pandemic world.

Notes

1 For example: James Gordon Meek, "Terrorist Groups Spin COVID-19 as God's 'smallest soldier' Attacking West" *ABC News*, April 1, 2020, https://abcnews.go.com/International/terrorist-groups-spin-covid-19-gods-smallest-soldier/story?id=69930563. Accessed April 1, 2020.

2 Paul Cruikshank and Don Rassler, (2020) "A View from the CT Foxhole: A Virtual Roundtable on COVID-19 and Counterterrorism with Audrey Kurth Cronin, Lieutenant General (Ret) Michael Nagata, Magnus Ranstorp, Ali Soufan, and Juan Zarate" *CTC Sentinel*, 13 (6), 1–15, https://ctc.usma.edu/june-2020/. Accessed June 29, 2020.

3 See, for example: Jessica Davis, "Terrorism During a Pandemic: Assessing the Threat and Balancing the Hype" *Just Security*, April 28, 2020, https://www.justsecurity.org/69895/terrorism-during-a-pandemic-assessing-the-threat-and-balancing-the-hype/. Accessed April 28, 2020; Sam Mullins, "Terrorism and COVID-19: Are We Over-Estimating the Threat?" *Small Wars Journal*, June 25, 2020, https://smallwarsjournal.com/jrnl/art/terrorism-and-covid-19-are-we-over-estimating-threat. Accessed June 25, 2020.

4 Nur Aziemah Azman, "'Divine Retribution': The Islamic State's COVID-19 Propaganda" *The Diplomat*, March 24, 2020, https://thediplomat.com/2020/03/divine-retribution-the-islamic-states-covid-19-propaganda/. Accessed March 24, 2020; Mina al-Lami, "Jihadists see COVID-19 as an Opportunity" *Global Network on Extremism and Technology*, June 1, 2020, https://gnet-research.org/2020/06/01/jihadists-see-covid-19-as-an-opportunity/. Accessed June 1, 2020; Steve Stalinsky, "What Jihadists Are Saying About the Coronavirus" *The Wall Street Journal*, April 6, 2020, https://www.wsj.com/articles/what-jihadists-are-saying-about-the-coronavirus-11586112043?mod=e2two. Accessed April 7, 2020.

5 Al-Lami, "Jihadists see COVID-19 as an Opportunity", op.cit.

6 "Coronavirus Crisis Elevates Antisemitic, Racist Tropes" *Anti-Defamation League*, March 17, 2020, https://www.adl.org/blog/coronavirus-crisis-elevates-antisemitic-racist-tropes?_ga=2.126157261.1542293471.1591735322-458039737.1591735322. Accessed March 20, 2020.

7 Ibid.

8 Simon Osborne, "Far Left Extremists Urge Riots, Looting and Violent Uprising Amid Coronavirus Chaos" *The Express*, March 19, 2020, https://www.express.co.uk/news/world/1257518/coronavirus-germany-far-left-extremists-riot-looting-violence. Accessed March 20, 2020; Jérémie Pham-Lê, Jean-Michel Décugis et Vincent Gautronneau, "Confinement : pourquoi le «jour d'après» inquiète les services de renseignement" *Le Parisien*, April 11, 2020, http://www.leparisien.fr/faits-divers/coronavirus-les-services-de-renseignements-craignent-l-embrasement-apres-le-confinement-11-04-2020-8298150.php. Accessed April 11, 2020.

9 "Twenty-sixth report of the Analytical Support and Sanctions Monitoring Team Submitted Pursuant to Resolution 2368 (2017) Concerning ISIL (Da'esh), Al-Qaida and Associated Individuals and Entities," *United Nations Security Council*, July 23, 2020, p. 6, https://undocs.org/S/2020/717. Accessed July 23, 2020.

10 "The Impact of Social Distancing on Engagement with Violent Extremist Content Online in the United States," *Moonshot CVE*, April 16, 2020, https://moonshotcve.com/social-distancing-white-supremacy/. Accessed April 16, 2020.

11 @MoustafaAyad (Moustafa Ayad), "1. Theories on likely upticks in online radicalization during #COVID19 lockdowns need evidence. To that end, I looked at traffic to #ISIS websites on the open web. Traffic began peaking in March as lockdowns took effect globally. One had 500,000+ visitors over 3 months. Thread." *Twitter*, June 16, 2020, https://twitter.com/MoustafaAyad/status/1272984693923708929. Accessed June 16, 2020.

12 Michael King and Sam Mullins, "COVID-19 and Terrorism in the West: Has Radicalization Really Gone Viral?" *Just Security*, March 4, 2021, https://www.justsecurity.org/75064/covid-19-and-terrorism-in-the-west-has-radicalization-really-gone-viral/. Accessed March 4, 2021.

13 Gino Spocchia, "Engineer Derails Train Near Navy Mercy Ship over Coronavirus Conspiracy Theory" *The Independent*, April 3, 2020, https://www.independent.co.uk/news/world/americas/coronavirus-navy-ship-conspiracy-theory-train-crash-usns-mercy-a9442586.html. Accessed September 9, 2020.

14 Andrew Gregory, "14-Year-Old Boy Accused of Making Bombs with Shrapnel for Islamist Terror Attack Appears in Court" *The Independent*, June 18, 2020, https://www.independent.co.uk/news/uk/crime/terror-attack-eastleigh-teenager-islamist-bomb-hampshire-old-bailey-latest-a9574226.html. Accessed September 9, 2020.

15 Lizzie Dearden, "Boy, 15, Cleared of Preparing for Isis-Inspired Terror Attack during Lockdown" *The Independent*, October 9, 2020, https://www.independent.co.uk/news/uk/crime/terror-plot-attack-uk-isis-teenage-boy-eastleigh-lockdown-not-guilty-b910016.html. Accessed December 17, 2020.

16 Emmanuel Felton, "A Self-Proclaimed "Boogaloo Boy" Was Arrested After Allegedly Livestreaming His Hunt To Kill A Police Officer" *Buzzfeed News*, April 22, 2020, https://www.buzzfeednews.com/article/emmanuelfelton/boogaloo-boy-arrested-texarkana-swenson. Accessed April 23, 2020; Steve Vockrodt, "FBI Records Detail Missouri man's Plot to Bomb Hospital" *The Kansas City Star*, April 16, 2020, https://www.securityinfowatch.com/healthcare/news/21134279/fbi-records-detail-missouri-mans-plot-to-bomb-hospital. Accessed April 18, 2020.

17 *State of Michigan v. William Null and Michael Null*, MI050015J, Affidavit, October 7, 2020, https://www.michigan.gov/documents/ag/Affidavit_michael_and_william_null_704638_7.pdf. Accessed October 9, 2020.

18 Adam Dean Fox (@adfox17) "Now is the time to end this monopoly against freedom! All you corrupt self serving politicians and lawmakers better be wary of the people you try so dearly to enslave! We are strong and you are weak! No more passive restraints, we will come for you and end your era of rule!!" May 29, 2018, 3.44am, Tweet, https://twitter.com/adfox17/status/1001459155121704960. Accessed October 10, 2020.

19 Tresa Baldas and Arpan Lobo, "2 Whitmer Kidnap Plot Suspects Found not Guilty; Mistrial Declared for other 2" *Detroit Free Press*, April 8 2022, https://www.freep.com/story/news/local/michigan/2022/04/08/jury-whitmer-kidnap-plot-jury-verdict/9510806002/. Accessed April 8, 2022.

20 *Operation Pacific Eagle-Philippines: Lead Inspector General Report to the United States Congress*, April 1, 2020–June 30, 2020 (United States Department of Defense, 2020), pp.8–10, https://media.defense.gov/2020/Aug/11/2002474708/-1/-1/1/LEAD%20INSPECTOR%20GENERAL%20FOR%20OPERATION%20PACIFIC%20EAGLE-PHILIPPINES%20APRIL%201,%202020%20-%20JUNE%2030,%202020.PDF. Accessed August 13, 2020.

21 Sam Mullins, "Assessing the Impact of the COVID-19 Pandemic on Terrorism and Counter-Terrorism: Practitioner Insights" *Security Nexus Perspectives*, August 7, 2020, https://apcss.org/wp-content/uploads/2020/08/N2515_Mullins-_Impact_Pandemic_Terrorism.pdf. Accessed August 7, 2020.

22 James K. Wither and Richard Mašek, "The COVID-19 Pandemic: Counterterrorism Practitioners' Assessments" *Small Wars Journal*, October 23, 2020, https://smallwarsjournal.com/jrnl/art/covid-19-pandemic-counterterrorism-practitioners-assessments. Accessed October 24, 2020.

23 "Denmark adds COVID-19 Extremism in Terror Assessment" *ABC News*, March 28, 2022, https://abcnews.go.com/Health/wireStory/denmark-adds-covid-19-extremism-terror-assessment-83736102. Accessed April 3, 2022; Mullins, "Assessing the Impact of the COVID-19 Pandemic on Terrorism and Counter-Terrorism, op.cit.

24 Daniel Heinke, (2022) "The Security Threat Posed by the Corona-Skeptic Querdenken Movement in Germany" *CTC Sentinel*, 15 (3), 18–24, https://ctc.westpoint.edu/the-security-threat-posed-by-the-corona-skeptic-querdenken-movement-in-germany/. Accessed April 3, 2022.

25 "IPAC Short Briefing No.1: COVID-19 AND ISIS IN INDONESIA" *Institute for Policy Analysis of Conflict*, April 2, 2020, http://file.understandingconflict.org/file/2020/04/Covid_ISIS.pdf.

26 "Global Disruption of Three Terror Finance Cyber-Enabled Campaigns" *U.S. Department of Justice*, August 13, 2020, https://www.justice.gov/opa/pr/global-disruption-three-terror-finance-cyber-enabled-campaigns. Accessed August 13, 2020.

27 *United States of America v. FaceMaskCenter.com and Four Facebook Pages*, Complaint, Case 1:20-cv-02142-RC, August 5, 2020, https://www.justice.gov/opa/press-release/file/1304296/download. Accessed August 13, 2020.

28 Ibid.

29 Ibid.

30 Ibid; *United States of America v. Zoobia Shahnaz, Indictment*, Case CR-17 0690, December 13, 2017, https://extremism.gwu.edu/sites/g/files/zaxdzs2191/f/Shahnaz%20Indictment.pdf, Accessed September 11, 2020.

31 Mullins, "Assessing the Impact of the COVID-19 Pandemic on Terrorism and Counter-Terrorism" op.cit.

32 Wither and Mašek, "The COVID-19 Pandemic: Counterterrorism Practitioners' Assessments" op.cit.

33 Christopher Hockey and Michael Jones, (2020) "The Limits of 'Shabaab-CARE': Militant Governance Amid COVID-19" *CTC Sentinel*, 13 (6), 33–39, https://www.ctc.usma.edu/the-limits-of-shabaab-care-militant-governance-amid-covid-19/. Accessed September 14, 2020.

34 Tim Hume, "It's Not All Bad: Coronavirus Shut Down Europe's Neo-Nazi Music Festival Scene" *Vice News*, May 7, 2020, https://www.vice.com/en_us/article/qj4dex/its-not-all-bad-coronavirus-shut-down-europes-neo-nazi-music-festival-scene. Accessed September 15, 2020.

35 Colin Clarke, "Yesterday's Terrorists Are Today's Public-Health Providers" *Foreign Policy*, April 8, 2020, https://foreignpolicy.com/2020/04/08/terrorists-nonstate-ungoverned-health-providers-coronavirus-pandemic/. Accessed April 8, 2020; Marta Furlan, (2020) "Rebel Governance at the Time of Covid-19: Emergencies as Opportunities for Rebel Rulers" *Studies in Conflict and Terrorism*, DOI:10.1080/1057610X.2020.1816681. Accessed September 13, 2020.

36 Furlan, (2020) "Rebel Governance at the Time of Covid-19" p. 2, op.cit.

37 Ibid.

38 Andrew Watkins, "COVID-19 in Afghanistan: Compounding Crises" International Crisis Group, May 6, 2020, https://www.crisisgroup.org/asia/south-asia/afghanistan/covid-19-afghanistan-compounding-crises. Accessed May 6, 2020.

39 Kabir Taneja and Rafaello Pantucci, "Beware of Terrorists Offering COVID19 Aid" *Observer Research Foundation*, April 17, 2020, https://www.orfonline.org/expert-speak/beware-of-terrorists-offering-covid19-aid-64731/. Accessed April 17, 2020.

40 Ibid.

41 Shaul Shay, "Jihad in the Shadow of the Coronavirus" *International Institute for Counter-Terrorism*, March 24, 2020, https://ict.org.il/jihad-in-the-shadow-of-the-coronavirus/.. Accessed September 15, 2020.

42 "Coronavirus and Sharia Law: Divide Over Closure of Mosques and ban of Friday Prayers in Idlib" *Enab Baladi*, April 16, 2020, https://english.enabbaladi.net/archives/2020/04/coronavirus-and-sharia-law-divide-over-closure-of-mosques-and-ban-of-friday-prayers-in-idlib/. Accessed September 14, 2020; Aymenn al-Tamimi, "Jihadist Perspectives on Coronavirus Pandemic: Primary Sources" *AymennJawad.org*, March 25, 2020, http://www.aymennjawad.org/2020/03/jihadist-perspectives-on-coronavirus-pandemic. Accessed March 25, 2020; Aaron Zelin, "The Jihadi-Backed Salvation Government and Covid-19 in Northwest Syria" *Italian Institute for International Political Studies*, March 15, 2020, https://www.ispionline.it/it/pubblicazione/jihadi-backed-salvation-government-and-covid-19-northwest-syria-26152. Accessed March 15, 2020.

43 "Syrians In Idlib Protest Opening Of Trade Link With Regime" *Barron's*, May 1, 2020, https://www.barrons.com/news/bank-stocks-negative-interest-rates-federal-reserve-coronavirus-loan-loss-reserves-51589404202. Accessed May 1, 2020.

44 Ibid.

45 Dave Gavlak, "Hezbollah Called to Reform Amid Protests, Political Pressure, Possible Sanctions" *Voice of America*, June 9, 2020, https://www.voanews.com/middle-east/hezbollah-called-reform-amid-protests-political-pressure-possible-sanctions. Accessed September 15, 2020.

46 Rahim Faiez, "UN says Afghan Civilian Casualties Down by 13% this Year" *ABC News*, July 27, 2020, https://abcnews.go.com/International/wireStory/afghan-civilian-casualties-13-year-72003990. Accessed September 14, 2020; *"You Have No Right to Complain": Education, Social Restrictions, and Justice in Taliban-Held Afghanistan*, (Human Rights Watch, 2020), https://www.hrw.org/sites/default/files/media_2020/06/afghanistan0620_web_0.pdf. Accessed September 14, 2020.

47 Emily Hart, "'Comply or die': Colombia's Guerrillas Impose their Own Covid-19 Lockdowns" *The Telegraph*, May 23, 2020, https://www.telegraph.co.uk/news/2020/05/23/comply-die-colombias-guerrillas-impose-covid-19-lockdowns/. Accessed May 23, 2020.

48 Hockey and Michael Jones, (2020) "The Limits of 'Shabaab-CARE'" op.cit.

49 Mina al-Lami, "Jihadists see COVID-19 as an Opportunity" *Global Network on Extremism and Technology*, June 1, 2020, https://gnet-research.org/2020/06/01/jihadists-see-covid-19-as-an-opportunity/. Accessed June 1, 2020; Emilia Columbo and Marielle Harris, "Extremist Groups Stepping up Operations during the Covid-19 Outbreak in Sub-Saharan Africa" *Center for Strategic and International Studies*, May 1, 2020, https://www.csis.org/analysis/extremist-groups-stepping-operations-during-covid-19-outbreak-sub-saharan-africa. Accessed May 1, 2020; "Contending with ISIS in the Time of Coronavirus" *International Crisis Group*, March 31, 2020, https://www.crisisgroup.org/global/contending-isis-time-coronavirus. Accessed March 31, 2020; "The Far-Right's Online Discourse on COVID-19 Pandemic" *SITE Intelligence Group*, March 2020.

50 Shweta Desai and Amarnath Amarasingam, "#Coronajihad: COVID-19, Misinformation, and Anti-Muslim Violence in India" *Strong Cities*, https://strongcitiesnetwork.org/resource/coronajihad-covid-19-misinformation-and-anti-muslim-violence-in-india/. Accessed May 27, 2020; "#5GCoronavirus:

How the Pandemic Gave Life to an Old Conspiracy Theory" *Moonshot CVE*, April 2020, https://moonshotcve.com/wp-content/uploads/2020/04/5GCoronavirus_Moonshot-Report.pdf. Accessed June 24, 2020.

51 Michael Knights and Alex Almeida, (2020) "Remaining and Expanding: The Recovery of Islamic State Operations in Iraq in 2019–2020" *CTC Sentinel*, 13 (5), 12–27, https://ctc.usma.edu/remaining-and-expanding-the-recovery-of-islamic-state-operations-in-iraq-in-2019-2020/. Accessed September 15, 2020.

52 Ryan Browne, "ISIS Seeks to Exploit Pandemic to Mount Resurgence in Iraq and Syria" *CNN*, May 8, 2020, https://www.cnn.com/2020/05/07/politics/isis-coronavirus-iraq-syria/index.html. Accessed September 15, 2020.

53 Ibid.

54 Knights and Almeida, (2020) "Remaining and Expanding" op.cit.

55 Jason Blazakis, "Is the Threat from ISIS Really more Significant because of COVID-19?" *The Hill*, May 13, 2020, https://thehill.com/opinion/national-security/497261-is-the-threat-from-isis-really-more-significant-because-of-covid-19. Accessed May 13, 2020.

56 Knights and Almeida, (2020) "Remaining and Expanding" op.cit.

57 Columbo and Harris, "Extremist Groups Stepping up Operations during the Covid-19 Outbreak in Sub-Saharan Africa", op.cit.

58 "COVID-19 Information" *U.S. Embassy in Chad*, March 25, 2020, https://td.usembassy.gov/covid-19-information-2/. Accessed September 15, 2020; "Management of the COVID-19 Crisis in Chad" *African Regional Organisation of the International Trade Union Confederation*, undated, https://www.ituc-africa.org/Management-of-the-COVID-19-Crisis-in-Chad.html. Accessed September 15, 2020.

59 The University of Maryland, (2020 *Global Terrorism Database*, Sub-Saharan Africa, https://www.start.umd.edu/gtd/search/Results.aspx?start_yearonly=2001&end_yearonly=2018&start_year=&start_month=&start_day=&end_year=&end_month=&end_day=&region=11&asmSelect0=&asmSelect1=&dtp2=all&success=yes&casualties_type=b&casualties_max=. Accessed September 15, 2020.

60 Melissa Pavlik, "A Great and Sudden Change: The Global Political Violence Landscape Before and After the COVID-19 Pandemic" *Armed Conflict Location and Event Data Project*, August 4, 2020, https://acleddata.com/2020/08/04/a-great-and-sudden-change-the-global-political-violence-landscape-before-and-after-the-covid-19-pandemic/. Accessed September 15, 2020.

61 Wither and Mašek, "The COVID-19 Pandemic: Counterterrorism Practitioners' Assessments" op.cit.

62 Shawn Snow, "ISIS Exploits COVID-19 with Little Success, U.S. Troop Deployments to Iraq on Track Despite Pandemic" *Military Times*, May 8, 2020, https://www.militarytimes.com/news/coronavirus/2020/05/08/isis-exploits-covid-19-with-little-success-us-troop-deployments-to-iraq-on-track-despite-pandemic/. Accessed September 15, 2020.

63 *Global Terrorism Index 2022:Measuring the Impact of Terrorism*, (Sydney: Institute for Economics and Peace, 2022), https://www.visionofhumanity.org/wp-content/uploads/2022/03/GTI-2022-web.pdf. Accessed April 3, 2022.

64 Daniel Byman and Andrew Amunson, "Counterterrorism in a Time of COVID" *Brookings*, August 20, 2020, https://www.brookings.edu/blog/order-from-chaos/2020/08/20/counterterrorism-in-a-time-of-covid/?preview_id=1015313. Accessed August 20, 2020.

65 Frances Mangosing, "Marines Diverted from War on Terror in Sulu to Fight COVID-19 in Luzon" *Inquirer.net*, March 25, 2020, https://newsinfo.inquirer.net/1248479/marines-diverted-from-war-on-terror-in-sulu-to-fight-covid-19-in-luzon. Accessed March 25, 2020.

66 *Operation Inherent Resolve: Lead Inspector General Report to the United States Congress: January 1, 2020–March 31, 2020* (United States Department of Defense, 2020), https://media.defense.gov/2020/May/13/2002298979/-1/-1/1/LIG_OIR_Q2_MAR2020_GOLD_508_0513.PDF. Accessed July 24, 2020.

67 *East Africa Counterterrorism Operation: North and West Africa Counterterrorism Operation: Lead Inspector General Report to the United States Congress: January 1, 2020–March 31, 2020*, (United States Department of Defense, 2020), https://media.defense.gov/2020/Jul/17/2002459044/-1/-1/1/LEAD%20IG%20EAST%20AFRICA%20AND%20NORTH%20AND%20WEST%20AFRICA%20COUNTER-TERRORISM%20OPERATIONS.PDF. Accessed July 24, 2020.

68 Warren Strobel and Dustin Volz, "Spies, Unable to Telework, Adapt Their Access to U.S. Secrets" *The Wall Street Journal*, April 6, 2020, https://www.wsj.com/articles/spies-unable-to-telework-adapt-their-access-to-u-s-secrets-11586177533. Accessed April 7, 2020.

69 "CTP Warn About Greater Risk of Radicalisation During Covid-19 Lockdown" *Counter Terrorism Policing*, April 22, 2020, https://www.counterterrorism.police.uk/ctp-look-to-bolster-prevent-referrals-during-lockdown/. Accessed September 15, 2020.

70 Andreo Calonzo, "Duterte Approves Anti-Terror Law Giving Authorities More Powers" *Bloomberg*, July 3, 2020, https://www.bloomberg.com/news/articles/2020-07-03/duterte-approves-anti-terror-law-giving-authorities-more-powers. Accessed September 15, 2020.

71 Chad Garland, "Coalition Strikes Pound ISIS Caves in Iraq" *Stars and Stripes*, May 1, 2020, https://www.stripes.com/coalition-strikes-pound-isis-caves-in-iraq-1.628042. Accessed May 1, 2020.

72 Africa Regional Media Hub, "Press Briefing on U.S. Efforts to Combat Terrorism in Africa with SOCAF Commander Maj. Gen. Anderson" *U.S. Department of State*, August 5, 2020, https://soundcloud.com/africa-regional-media-hub/press-briefing-on-us-efforts-to-combat-terrorism-in-africa-with-socaf-commander-maj-gen-anderson. Accessed August 5, 2020.

73 Sean Arbuthnot, "How COVID-19 Has Impacted Counter-Extremism Efforts" *Rantt Media*, July 24, 2020, https://rantt.com/how-covid-19-has-impacted-counter-extremism-efforts. Accessed July 25, 2020; Strobel and Volz, "Spies, Unable to Telework, Adapt Their Access to U.S. Secrets", op.cit.

74 Mullins, "Assessing the Impact of the COVID-19 Pandemic on Terrorism and Counter-Terrorism" op.cit.

75 Wither and Mašek, "The COVID-19 Pandemic: Counterterrorism Practitioners' Assessments" op.cit.

76 Ibid.

77 Ibid.

78 Mullins, "Assessing the Impact of the COVID-19 Pandemic on Terrorism and Counter-Terrorism" op.cit; "Twenty-sixth report of the Analytical Support and Sanctions Monitoring Team submitted pursuant to resolution 2368 (2017) concerning ISIL (Da'esh), Al-Qaida and associated individuals and entities" *United Nations Security Council*, July 23, 2020, https://undocs.org/S/2020/717. Accessed July 24, 2020.

41

A LEGACY OF DISORDER, DESPERATION, AND DEFIANCE

The Possible Effects of the Coronavirus Pandemic on the Future Course of Terrorism

Brian Michael Jenkins

What effect will the coronavirus pandemic have on the future course of terrorism? Will the pandemic presage new waves of bio-terrorist attacks? Will the massive death tolls caused by the pandemic inure the public to the comparatively minuscule violence of today's terrorism?

Do the death threats to health officials and political leaders in reaction to the control measures mandated to slow the spread of the virus foreshadow new terrorist campaigns?

Will the pandemic doom already fragile governments? Will it shatter the social order, plunging the world into violent anarchy? Or will it strengthen the hand of oppression?

For understandable reasons, the connection between the pandemic and political violence in an already turbulent world has become a subject of intense interest. The linkage has deep roots in faith and history. Pestilence, slaughter, famine, and death ride together in apocalyptic visions. Historically, war, disease, and famine often accompanied one another, causing widespread suffering and death. It is understandable that we should connect the pandemic and the particular mode of political violence that commands contemporary headlines and has contributed so much to recent alarms.

However, it may be difficult to discern direct cause and effect links between the pandemic and terrorism. The pandemic is a global event with broad economic, social, and political consequences. These will vary greatly from country to country. Some of the pandemic's effects may only become apparent years from now in as yet unpredictable ways. Although it is also a global phenomenon, terrorism is an artificially and narrowly defined mode of political expression and armed conflict. Its trajectory reflects political and technological developments. In many cases, terrorist tactics are part of a broader ideological struggle or political contest.

The pandemic theoretically may have some direct effects. For example, some terrorists are already speculating on how to weaponize the virus. The pandemic could encourage more extremists to think about biological weapons. They fill the Internet with their rants and scenarios. Some plots may emerge. It may be informative to also look at the pandemic's possible effects more broadly. How might the pandemic affect political stability? Will it create conditions that lead to political unrest? Could it increase international tensions?

Any inquiry will be necessarily speculative. As this is being written the pandemic is still underway, and in many parts of the world, it appears to be surging. It will not suddenly be over,

DOI: 10.4324/9781003326373-47

but will continue well into 2022 and is becoming endemic. And this pandemic differs from previous pandemics in history. Some similarities of behavior are observable over time, but much has changed since the Spanish Flu that afflicted the world in 1918 and 1919, and certainly since the great plague of the Middle Ages. Examining the effects of these earlier pandemics will offer clues, perhaps some hypotheses, but not provide a reliable template. And finally, the coronavirus pandemic is only one of many factors influencing the course of political events, and by extension, political violence.

The distinguished medieval historian, Samuel K. Cohn, Jr., warns us that "Pinning long-term effects on single events is hazardous in any case and more so with such factors as levels of violence, difficult to quantify or judge qualitatively over a landscape as vast as Western Europe." Nonetheless, the Black Death and its recurrences cannot be shown to have ushered in unequivocally a more "violent tenor of life" that supposedly ensued over the late 14th and 15th centuries. Instead, stability, not violence, followed in some places or with the growth of diplomacy and the balance of power between city-states in northern and central Italy during most of the fifteenth century.[1] His admonition carries even more weight as the effort here is to examine the consequences not just on one continent, but globally.

With these caveats in mind, the following chapter first looks at some of the already apparent direct effects of the pandemic on terrorist thinking. Then, looking at previous pandemics as a point of departure, the chapter will look at a range of possible effects, focusing on those that might contribute to or impact the nature of future political violence.

A Brief History of Modern Bio-Terrorism

The current pandemic does not offer terrorists or extremists new capabilities or point them to a path they hadn't already thought about before. The use of biological weapons in warfare has a long history. Actors outside of governments only on a few occasions have entered the realm of bio-terrorism, with little success.

In 1972, two college students in Chicago invented a terrorist group called R.I.S.E. and plotted to contaminate the city's water supply with *Salmonella typhi*, which causes typhoid fever. Their objective was to wipe out the human race "except for a select group of people [who would be inoculated in advance, and] who would live in harmony with nature."[2] The plot was interrupted by the FBI before any attempt was made.

In 1984, members of a religious cult in Oregon contaminated the salad bars of a town with *salmonellosis* in order to incapacitate people during a local election where they were trying to take control. More than 700 people were infected, but none died.

In 1990, the Aum Shinrikyo sect in Japan, which later carried out the nerve gas attack on Tokyo's subway system, attempted to disseminate *botulinum* toxin in the form of a mist sprayed from a moving vehicle at two U.S. military bases, Narita Airport, the Japanese Diet, and the Imperial Palace. The effort failed to produce any results.

The group carried out six more biological attacks in 1993. In June, Aum Shinrikyo operatives dispersed *botulinum* toxin in an attempt to infect guests at a royal wedding, again without results. The group then switched to *anthrax bacillus* for a second series of attacks in July. The first of these involved the dispersal of anthrax from a rooftop in Tokyo. The dispersal caused a foul odor but no documented cases of illness.[3] There were several more attempts to disperse anthrax in 1993.

For a final attempt in 1995, the group planned to disperse *botulinum* toxin from spray devices concealed inside briefcases, however, the individual in charge had second thoughts and replaced the toxic solution with water.[4]

These attempts were part of a broader effort to develop and use biological, chemical, and possibly even nuclear weapons. As in the 1972 Chicago case, the cult's leader had visions of provoking a nuclear war that would wipe out the world's population. Only he and selected followers would survive to create a new race that would then repopulate the planet.

The theme of chosen survivors who rebuild humanity in a post-apocalyptic world dates back to Noah's Ark in the Hebrew Bible and the Hindu Dharmasastra and recurs in contemporary science fiction and some terrorist plots involving weapons of mass destruction.

Al-Qaeda, who dedicated itself to the field of mass murder, also attempted to weaponize biological agents, including anthrax, *botulinum* toxin, and ricin, although there are also reports that it sought or acquired *Yersinia pestis* (plague), Ebola virus, and salmonella bacteria.[5] The effort failed, although there were a number of foiled terrorist plots and allegations of plots involving ricin in Europe, most recently in Germany in 2018. Al-Qaeda's leaders were not thinking about rebuilding humanity but felt entitled to kill millions of infidels in retaliation for their perceived aggression against Islam.

In 2001, a series of letters containing anthrax spores were mailed to news media outlets and Democratic senators, killing 5 people and infecting 17 others as well as contaminating facilities including a Senate office building. The attack, beginning a week after the 9/11 attacks, raised alarms that the United States now also faced terrorists armed with biological weapons and launched one of the FBI's largest investigations. A suspect was ultimately identified, but he killed himself before arrest.[6]

These plots materialized in the closed universes of cults and mental disorder—both the leader of the 1972 plot in Chicago and the suspected author of the 2001 anthrax letters had suffered mental problems. Apart from the very utilitarian aim of swinging a local election, their motives and ultimate objectives were unclear, grandiose, or bizarre. There is no proximity to or evidence of inspiration provided by previous pandemics.

Apart from the 2001 anthrax letters, most of the plots failed owing to the difficulty of weaponizing biological agents and the technical limitations of the perpetrators involved. Even groups with manifest intentions, significant funding, and access to scientists, like Aum Shinrikyo, were unable to successfully carry out a large-scale biological attack.

But technical limitations may not entirely explain the paucity of terrorist use of biological weapons. There also may be self-imposed constraints.

Jihadis may see the current pandemic as an ally, even though it has wreaked a toll on Muslim nations. The virus is an ally in that it has weakened or distracted security forces—jihadi attacks have intensified in a number of countries during the pandemic and jihadi-inspired terrorist attacks have occurred in Europe. But biological weapons, which kill the elderly, the infirm, and in some cases, young children, do not support the jihadis' image of themselves as warriors. Some terrorists may share the general revulsion that biological attacks provoke. Another factor is that contagious diseases spread quickly and are indiscriminate in who they kill. A group found responsible for a biological attack that spreads disease would quickly find itself reviled as an enemy of all humanity.

Notions of murdering millions appear to be more often associated with apocalyptic cults or religion-based and far right ideologies. Bio-terrorism scenarios in particular resonate with the genocidal fantasies of white supremacist and anti-Semitic extremists. A poster circulated on the Internet advised followers, "What to Do if You Get Corona 19: Visit your local mosque, visit your local synagogue, spend the day on public transport, spend time in your local diverse neighborhood." This is more an expression of attitude than a terrorist plot. However, there were several cases in the 1990s in which rightwing extremists in America were convicted of possessing plague, ricin or *botulinum* toxin. The intended targets were not always clear, but appear to have been government officials.[7]

Although most plots involving biological weapons were uncovered and the attacks that resulted from the plots missed by the authorities resulted in deaths or illness on only two occasions (the 1984 Oregon incident and the 2001 anthrax letters), the fact that the current pandemic may be inspiring thousands more people to even think about biological weapons is a not positive development. On the other hand, that the coronavirus pandemic may be prompting authorities to dust off forgotten plans for dealing with biological incidents is a good thing. Large-scale biological attacks remain difficult to pull off. Alarming hoaxes and low-level attacks are far more likely and, given the anxieties already caused by the pandemic, may cause greater alarm.

Rightwing extremists appear to be devoting more attention to conspiracy theories involving the origins and *purposes* of the pandemic. They see the coronavirus pandemic as a vast plot to impose government tyranny. Most of the online communications among rightwing extremists focus instead on the spread of the virus, including quarantines that are not only intended to frighten the public into accepting greater control, but are the forerunners of internment camps, where vast numbers of people who defy the government will be held. Efforts to trace contacts during the pandemic are a cover for the introduction of social surveillance technology. Vaccines will offer opportunities to insert tiny electronic devices that track people. This is the kind of paranoia that festers on the far right. The pandemic has given these conspiracy theories a much larger audience.

Resistance to public health measures to slow the spread of the virus—restrictions on assemblies, mandates to wear masks, temporary shutdowns, or new rules imposed on certain categories of business—has already led to denunciations of state tyranny, angry confrontations, and, more seriously, to death threats against public health officials and political leaders. A plot to kidnap and hold or kill the governor of the U.S. state of Michigan (connected with discussions to also kidnap the governor of the state of Virginia) indicates that extremists may be willing to initiate a violent campaign.

As contemporary terrorist enterprises have switched from traditional recruiting into small clandestine organizations, which required the careful vetting of volunteers to weed out infiltrators and unreliable operators, to "leaderless resistance" and remote recruiting by exhortation, many of today's terrorists are self-selecting and organizationally untethered. They may be inspired as much by visions of violence as by commitment to any specific ideology, which may act as a conveyor for their individual discontents. Many come with troubled personal histories of aggression, substance abuse, and mental problems. No bright shining line divides the political fanatics from the mentally disturbed.

The pandemic has increased their numbers. Deprived of their daily routines and personal relationships, many people are disoriented and disillusioned, creating a receptive audience for fringe ideas. These are the conditions that psychologists believe can accelerate radicalization. The end of the pandemic will not de-radicalize them. They add another layer of potential terrorist actors emerging from the pandemic.

The greater danger comes from state-backed projects. Conspiracy theories immediately linked the coronavirus to Chinese government laboratories. There is no concrete evidence supporting the theory, but the possibility exists that, under pressure of sanctions or during war, states or rogue elements within a state apparatus might consider a clandestine launching of a biological attack disguised as a natural outbreak.

The threat of a biological attack by a state is not new.[8] Both the United States and the United Kingdom considered this possibility during World War II and the Cold War, and prepared to respond in kind as a deterrent. The British program ended in the 1950s, the U.S. program in 1969. Iraq under Saddam Hussein began developing biological weapons in the early 1980s. Coalition forces sent to liberate Kuwait after its takeover by Saddam Hussein in 1990 were prepared for a biological attack, which never came. The full extent of Iraq's program became known after the First Gulf War and was considered to be largely dismantled by the late 1990s. However, allegations that Iraq was covertly continuing the effort were offered as one of the justifications for the U.S.-led invasion of Iraq in 2003. Post-invasion inspections showed that the biological weapons program had indeed been suspended.

The current pandemic theoretically could inspire some countries to consider the utility of biological warfare. If the coronavirus becomes endemic, it theoretically could also provide some cover for a covert operation. At the same time, however, the pandemic would also point to the risks that the virus might get out of control and harm the country that initiated the attack. In a post-pandemic environment, with hundreds of thousands already dead, the risks of retaliation would be extremely high, and affected nations might not wait for proof of culpability, but respond on suspicion. Here, the 2003 invasion of Iraq is instructive.

As this brief review shows, the coronavirus pandemic does not necessarily increase the likelihood of terrorists using biological weapons, although it may increase their appearance in hoaxes, extortionate threats, and possibly low-level incidents. Ascending to the greater danger posed by state-sponsored attacks, the calculations remain the same in a post-pandemic world. Biological weapons are not reliable. They are indiscriminate. Contagious diseases as opposed to toxins derived from plants or microorganisms are difficult to control. And they entail high risks of massive retaliation and regime change.

This brings us to a different formulation of the question: Will the pandemic affect the world in ways that make armed conflict and other forms of political violence, including terrorism, more likely? This is a broader inquiry. What do previous pandemics tell us?

The Coronavirus Compared to Previous Pandemics

It makes a difference whether a pandemic kills three percent or half of a population, and whether it subsides in a couple of years or becomes a recurring event over decades or centuries. The coronavirus pandemic thus far appears to be killing fewer people than the great pandemics of history. If this pattern continues its effects will come more from economic and social disruption than total deaths.

As of October 2020, the coronavirus has affected more than 40 million people worldwide, 1.2 million have died. Clearly, it is a major global event that has already had far-reaching consequences, especially its damage to the global economy. However, the pandemic's long-term effects on society may depend on whether it surges well beyond its current totals before vaccines contain its spread and numbers overwhelm medical capacity and the ability to administer treatment regimens that have already greatly reduced mortality. The COVID19 pandemic has a long way to go to match the death and devastation caused by some of history's worst pandemics.

The Plague of Justinian (541–542) eventually killed an estimated 30–50 million people, and even after it subsided in Byzantium, it continued to reappear in Europe, Africa, and Asia for several years, causing widespread devastation.

The Black Death (1347–1351) killed an estimated 200 million people—one-half of Europe's population at the time. The plague continued to reappear for several centuries in more localized outbreaks. The successive waves of the plague saw a change in popular attitudes. The first and worst outbreak provoked mass hysteria. People interpreted it as a sign of God's wrath from which there was no escape, medicine was useless. Chroniclers described events in apocalyptic terms, coloring their accounts of the plague's origins with venomous fumes, black smoke, thunder and lightning bolts. Processions of flagellants, whipping themselves with metal-tipped leather straps moved from city to city. Jews were blamed and persecuted.

Accounts of the successive waves of the plague discarded the supernatural and reflected growing confidence in preventive measures and cures. Although knowledge of how the plague spread was still primitive by today's standards, people were beginning to understand the consequences of overcrowded cities, unhygienic conditions, even epidemiology.

The so-called "Third Plague" (beginning in western China in 1855, spreading to Hong Kong in 1894, and emerging in India at the end of the 19th century) killed an estimated 12 million people, mainly in India.[9] It reached, but hardly affected Europe.

The Spanish Flu (1918–1919), the largest pandemic in modern times, killed an estimated 40–50 million people—between 2 and 3 percent of the world's population at that time.

The current death toll of the coronavirus pandemic compares with the Asian Flu (1957–1958), which killed an estimated 1.1 million, and the Hong Kong Flu (1968–1970), which killed a million people. However, the COVID19 pandemic is still in its first year. With daily death tolls averaging 5,000–6,000 worldwide, it could easily ascend above 2 million deaths. It could also presage an endemic problem with periodic recurrences. However, to match the proportion of the population killed by the 1918 Spanish Flu in today's world, the coronavirus would have to kill something on the order of 200 million people. That seems unlikely.

Smallpox, an endemic disease since ancient times, periodically exploded in large-scale outbreaks. Europeans brought it the Americas and Australia where it killed vast numbers of indigenous populations who had no natural immunity. Even in the 20th century, smallpox still killed between 300 and 500 million people worldwide before it was finally wiped out through vaccination.

Smallpox killed its victims quickly—about a third of those who were infected died within one or two weeks. In contrast, the HIV/AIDS virus took years to weaken its victims. Before effective treatments were developed, victims were doomed. Since 1981, AIDS has killed 39 million. Smaller-scale epidemics with fewer deaths also have caused local social and political upheavals.

Beyond pandemics, there are natural disasters—earthquakes, floods, volcanoes, typhoons— that in the worse cases may kill millions. And tens of millions have died in the 20th century's two world wars. What effects did they have?

These events may offer some clues about the kinds of social and political effects we might envision from the COVID19 pandemic. We group these into four broad categories: effects on society, economic effects, political repercussions, and psychological effects. Our focus in each category is on those aspects that relate to political violence.

Effects on Society

The immediate response to the threat of infectious disease is to seek safety. Some can do this by fleeing centers of danger, usually cities, to remote, unaffected areas. It is a solution available to today's mobile elite who can retreat to ranches in Wyoming or villas in the south of France, less so to those with regular jobs and families to take care of. A second course of action is to separate those not yet afflicted from contact with those who might carry the disease—quarantine and self-isolation. In the 14th century, walled cities closed their gates. The coronavirus pandemic has seen countries close their borders and restrict travel in other ways.

Outsiders become sources of suspicion. Nationalist tendencies intensify, encouraged by the tendency of politicians to deflect blame for their own helplessness or incompetence or further advance populist goals. Pandemics can be blamed on other countries or exploited to encourage nativism, xenophobia, hostility to minorities and immigrants.

Looking at wars between 1946 and 2004, researchers have found that "countries with high intensity of infectious disease stress, cultures are characterized by ethnocentric and xenophobic values," and that "countries characterized by high ethnocentrism and xenophobia experience greater intrastate armed conflict and civil war."[10] These findings would suggest that pandemics theoretically contribute to tendencies that correlate with internal armed conflict.

Public health authorities have sought to slow the spread of the coronavirus by encouraging people to self-isolate by working from home if possible. This works so long as there is a much larger support infrastructure of individuals who accept greater risks by going to work places and delivering essential goods to those isolating themselves. For some, this offers an opportunity to increase their income, but it essentially divides society, shifting risks to those lower on the economic scale.

Those lower on the economic scale, which in many cases, means ethnic minorities, are already at greater risk. They may live in more crowded conditions. In some countries, they may not have the same access to quality health care and as a consequence may already be unequally afflicted by pre-existing health conditions that make them especially vulnerable if they contract the virus. In the United States, minorities are disproportionately represented among the pandemic's victims.

With self-isolation comes hoarding, which is both prudent, but also encourages an every person for themselves attitude. We have seen numerous examples of bad behavior, altercations, and confrontations, but well below widespread looting, food riots or civil unrest.

In other words, the pandemic underscores and may accelerate the growth of economic inequality, which has already been cited as a concern. The pandemic may also sharpen the racial and ethnic inequality that is a persistent problem in a number of societies. At the same time, the pandemic rekindles old prejudices and promotes new ones. The pandemic in sum may produce a more divided society. Protests against racism and for economic justice have preceded, accompanied, and may be intensified by the pandemic.

The massive death tolls of Medieval pandemics cheapened life, which was already cheap. Some suggest that this led to increases in homicides, although other historians challenge this thesis.[11] Following the plague (another round of the Black Death), which struck Italy particularly hard in 1630, the erosion of social norms and hierarchy led to an outbreak of homicidal violence. Reportedly, the Spanish Flu prompted an increase in murder-suicides resulting from depression. "Newspapers on both sides of the Atlantic carried stories of men and women who attempted to slay their families."[12]

In Europe and the United States, crime, including violent crime, has declined overall around the world during the coronavirus pandemic,[13] but there has been an increase in shootings and killings in the United States, which historically has a comparatively high homicide rate.[14] The higher number of homicides may reflect the psychological problems caused by lockdowns and isolation. A more prosaic possibility is that spending more time in close quarters is promoting a higher volume of domestic violence, which is the explanation for most murders. It is, however, too early to see whether this is an anomaly or a trend.

Organized crime has always been quick to exploit scarcities and dislocations in the economy. Economic desperation may increase social tolerance of criminal activities. If the conclusion is that the pandemic has exposed the inherent unfairness of the political and economic systems, people will have less respect for the law.

Widespread unemployment may increase the number of recruits willing to join criminal enterprises. Loan sharking, counterfeit products, including hard-to-get medicines for treatment of the virus, thefts of vaccines and the distribution of counterfeit vaccines, as well as human trafficking are likely features of the pandemic and post-pandemic criminal landscape.

Cybercrime, which has been increasing over the years, is up.[15] How much of this is tied to the pandemic is uncertain. Cybercrime is opportunistic. Isolation has resulted in more people spending more time on the Internet and there have been reports of ransomware attacks on hospitals.

Economic Effects

The pandemic has had a disastrous impact on the global economy, causing widespread unemployment and suffering. The global cost associated with the economic impact could be $3.4 trillion a year. For the European Union, it may be about 5.6 percent in annual GDP, or approximately $983 billion. The United Kingdom has incurred a loss of about 4.3 percent of its annual GDP or an annual loss of about $145 billion at a time when the economic consequences of Brexit remain unclear. The United States has lost about 2.2 percent in annual GDP, or about $480 billion.[16] The global economic situation will continue to deteriorate.

It is not clear how quickly countries may recover, and some countries will recover quicker than others. Some assert that once the restrictions are lifted and an effective vaccine is widely administered, the economy and employment will recover quickly. But countries-especially developing economies-heavily dependent on exporting basic commodities or tourism may face far slower recoveries. Energy exporting countries have been bit hard. The increased hostility toward globalization, which existed before the pandemic, but has been intensified by the pandemic may further impede economic recovery.

The pandemic has pushed millions of people back below the poverty line. Past research has not been able to find direct causal effects between poverty and terrorism, one facet of political violence. Ted Robert Gurr, however, argued 50 years ago that poverty itself is not a root cause of political violence. His theory of relative deprivation instead argues that riots, rebellions, coups, or insurgencies are caused by the frustration that arises from the discrepancy between what people have and what they think they deserve.[17] In that case, being thrust back into poverty may be more frustrating than remaining poor. As in all hypotheses presented here, there are, of course other factors which influence behavior, including leadership, organization, the ability of the government to address grievances, and perceptions of government strength and probity.

The current pandemic has also put many governments in difficult economic straits as they have attempted to mitigate the economic effects of the pandemic and shutdowns on the population. Tax revenues have declined with the contraction in economic activity. Government deficits have grown. Great power competition, economic sanctions, and escalating tariff wars-trends that pre-date the current pandemic- complicate the situation. Distributing vaccines, improving public health, and subsidizing companies and industries at risk and the unemployed will take priority. Foreign assistance budgets will be especially vulnerable to cuts. Developing countries dependent on exports and foreign assistance will be hard hit.

The tendency of governments to follow their own interests in response to pandemics instead of pursuing a more globally coordinated approach could further impede economic recovery. Recent research by the RAND Corporation has found that "vaccine nationalism,"—a situation in which countries push to get first access to a supply of vaccines, potentially hoarding key components for vaccine production—could cost the global economy $1.2 trillion a year in GDP terms.[18] Underscoring the difficulty of a unified approach, even the European Union is having problems developing effective policies.

Uneven economic recovery and the re-impoverishment of some countries may accelerate migration of the desperate at a time when many economically advanced countries are determined to reduce their intake of migrants and refugees and take care of their own citizens.

Political Repercussions

The pandemic could provoke political instability in a variety of ways. Historical experience suggests that poorly-handled disasters erode faith in government leadership and institutions. In ancient China, calamities were seen as signs that the ruler had lost the mandate of heaven to rule and needed replacement. Rebels took up arms. Dynasties fell.

A devastating cyclone hit East Pakistan in 1970, killing a half million people. Angered by the government's failure to heed warnings and its bungled relief efforts, civil war broke out, leading to the permanent division of Pakistan into two countries—Pakistan and Bangladesh—a year later.

The 1972 earthquake in Nicaragua, which killed thousands, underscored the incompetence and corruption of the Somoza regime, which had ruled the country for decades. Outrage turned to armed opposition, contributing to a long civil war that ultimately brought down the government. The AIDS epidemic, which destroyed tourism in Haiti in the early 1980s, probably contributed to the fall of Jean-Claude Duvalier.[19]

The Black Death of the Middle Ages and subsequent outbreaks had different effects across Europe. In some cases, the Black Death was followed by social agitation, strikes, riots, even armed rebellions, but historians point out that these also featured in the years prior to the pandemic.

Some of the unrest, however, appears to be connected to the outbreaks. Disease significantly reduced the population. Smaller populations meant less economic production and fewer people to tax. Rulers tried to compensate for the loss of revenue by expanding the tax base and raising rates. Ordinary workers who, in a tight labor market, were earning more but who had previously been exempt from taxes were expected to pay their share. Poll taxes were imposed on everyone. Local lords increased their rents. These measures provoked popular resistance. The deaths of many of the rulers and government officials also contributed to instability.

Subduing the urban gangs that fought for various political factions and the brigands that roamed the countryside posed a major challenge to governments. Those who were able to successfully pacify the towns and the rural areas survived. Others were hounded out of office.

Many people opposed the restrictions on travel during the Black Death in the Middle Ages. Officials who enforced the measures were threatened. Another major plague pandemic that spread across Asia in the late 19th century heightened tensions between British rulers and Indian subjects who resisted the severe control measures imposed by the government. Local resistance ultimately led to the assassination of one of the senior British officials and his military aide.

The inability of governments to control pandemics or impose control measures on resistant populations creates a perception of weakness. Government authorities are not to be believed, are ineffectual, or worse, are evil and corrupt. Anecdotal accounts identify this as an issue in some of the past pandemics. It is clearly an issue in the current coronavirus pandemic.

Control measures intended to slow the spread of the current coronavirus pandemic have already resulted in death threats to public health officials and political leaders in the United States, and authorities recently uncovered a plot to kidnap the governor of Michigan and discussions to target the governor of Virginia. The very legitimacy of political authority has been challenged in a manner last seen in America in the 1960s.

Conspiracy theories that the pandemic is a political plot aimed at undermining the president, intern the government's opponents, or impose a tyranny by inserting microscopic electronic tracking chips in any vaccine, have flourished in the fevered political atmosphere in the United States, but also have appeared in Canada and elsewhere.

While epidemics may weaken armies enough to change the outcome of battles, we have few examples where pandemics so weakened affected countries that they invited foreign invasion.

439

One clear example would be the spread of smallpox brought by the Europeans to America the decimated native empires, making them easy prey for Spanish conquest.[20] Another possible (but partial) exception is the Manchurian plague that hit China in 1910 and 1911. Foreign powers already intent on carving China into zones of influence exploited the difficulties caused by the plague to advance their ambitions.[21]

Psychological Effects

Pandemics also inspire apocalyptic thinking, and may contribute to nihilism and reckless behavior. This could, in turn, foster an erosion of ethics and a decline in respect for the law. As Thucydides noted in his horrific account of the epidemic that killed up to a third of Athens' population in 431–430 BC and its immediate aftermath, the sudden wave of deaths left disorder in its wake. "Athens owed to the plague the beginnings of a state of unprecedented lawlessness. Seeing how quick and abrupt were the changes of fortune which came to the rich who suddenly died and to those who had previously been penniless but now inherited their wealth, people now began openly to venture on acts of self-indulgence...As for the gods, it seemed to be the same thing whether one worshipped them or not, when one saw the good and the bad dying indiscriminately. As for offenses against human law, no one expected to live long enough to be brought to trial and punished."[22] However, the psychological effects of past pandemics is an area where we have little empirical evidence, so any suggestions must remain in the realm of hypotheses.

In the current pandemic, more people are staying at home, spending more time in isolation, which psychologists believe can accelerate individual radicalization.[23] Deprived of their daily routines and personal relationships, people are disoriented and disillusioned, creating a receptive audience for fringe ideas. Although magical thinking is usually consigned to a pre-scientific age, it is noteworthy that conspiracy theories about the current pandemic have flourished.

One of the questions asked at the beginning of this chapter was whether the death tolls of the coronavirus pandemic would inure the public to the comparatively minuscule violence of today's terrorism. This requires a more detailed analysis.

As of November 2020, the coronavirus has killed approximately 1.2 million people worldwide, although this statistic may undercount the total volume of excess deaths resulting from the pandemic. The pandemic is ongoing, and, at the moment this is being written in the autumn of 2020, cases and deaths are surging. Some mathematical models indicate that by the spring of 2021, the coronavirus will have killed 2 million people worldwide. Thus far, in the United States, the pandemic has killed approximately 230,000 people. This is equivalent to the death toll of more than 76 attacks such as 9/11.

Immediately after 9/11, terrorism analysts and public health officials feared that terrorists would continue to escalate their violence, employing weapons of mass destruction, in particular, nuclear or biological agents to kill tens of thousands or hundreds of thousands of people. Smallpox was most frequently mentioned, but anthrax and plague were also included as Category A agents that theoretically could be used in a terrorist attack.[24]

Various scenarios were developed to examine the risks of various vaccination approaches in the United States. The most dangerous of the scenarios imagined a hostile government activating 40 sleeper agents who are given variola virus and equipped with nebulizers to disseminate it at the ten largest commercial airports across the country. Able to infect a hundred thousand persons, the estimated death toll was approximately 55,000 people.[25] The coronavirus probably will kill at least five to eight times that many in the United States,[26] although deaths from a terrorist attack have greater psychological impact.

As it turned out, the 2,977 lives lost on September 11, 2001 turned out to be a statistical outlier rather than an indicator of worse to come. Terrorist attacks continued after 9/11, but at pre-9/11 totals, with the worst cases involving around 200 fatalities. As pressure on al-Qaeda and its affiliates and spinoffs continued, there were fewer attacks of this scale outside of war zones (although this trend could easily reverse). But can terrorists hope to achieve the same psychological effect with attacks of this scale in a post-pandemic environment?

The terrorist stabbing attacks that occurred in France during the autumn of 2020—incidents involving four fatalities––and the November 3 shooting in Vienna––which left five dead–– suggest that the pandemic has not diminished the emotional impact of terrorist attacks with even a small number of fatalities. An event with a single fatality can still provoke alarm, anger, and have significant political effects. Where the attack takes place, the identity of the victim, the nature of the attack, and other factors outweigh the body count. The beheading of a French school teacher in October 2020 prompted a national response that will have far-reaching societal consequences.

The high anxiety already generated by the coronavirus also may make society emotionally even more vulnerable to low-level plots involving biological agents. The pandemic provides the amplifier.

Conclusions

From the Black Death of the 14th century to the 2020 coronavirus pandemic, we find that pandemics have been accompanied and followed by civil disobedience, social unrest, protests, riots, increases in violent crime, rebellions, and war. Governments often fell. Pandemics and wars revolve around each other like binary stars. It is tempting to look for and deceptively easy to see causality.

But caution is in order before we argue that the pandemics produced the turmoil. Armed rebellions, civil wars, and conflicts between nations are an almost constant feature of history. Global pandemics, with millions of deaths, occur more rarely, but local epidemics, some resulting in mass deaths, remain common. Theoretically, one could randomly scatter pandemics over the 700 years between the Black Death of the mid-14th century and the 1918 Spanish Flu and never be far from political unrest or armed conflict.

Effects of past plagues are complex, they may be immediate or become apparent years later. Some effects may appear to be direct consequences of the upheaval caused by the pandemic, others may appear over a longer term. They may be propelled by the pandemic or by its decline. Many other factors come into play. It is difficult to generalize.

Nevertheless, some issues seem to repeatedly emerge. One is popular resistance to the social controls and health requirements imposed by the authorities. Hoarding and battles over scarce resources is another recurring feature. Brief increases in violent crime seem to be common. More organized criminal activity may reflect economic dislocation or new opportunities. Pandemics may expose or reinforce existing problems—poor governance, societal divisions, prejudices, inequality, corruption. Existing social and political cleavages intensify. "Outsiders" are blamed and may become the targets of popular wrath, reflecting existing prejudices as well as the efforts of leadership to deflect blame. Displays of government incompetence, corruption, or simply indifference provoke outrage. Political violence in various forms may increase. Governments are brought down or fall. Political relationships realign.

But we cannot easily isolate the societal effects of pandemics from other factors that influence their course. Some of the recurring features mentioned above appear to be direct consequences of the pandemic. Other consequences appear to be one element of comorbidity involving the pre-existing social and political conditions of a society. A historical and cross-national analysis of pandemics and serious epidemics would produce endless variations.

What we can say is that pandemics, causing massive loss of lives and social and economic disruption, leave behind a legacy of disorder, desperation, and defiance. The pandemic and post-pandemic environment can lead to violence, a portion of which, in today's terminology, could be classified as terrorism.

Notes

1 Samuel K. Cohn, Jr., "The Black Death: End of a Paradigm," *The American Historical Review,* Volume 107, Number 3 (June 2002), pp. 703–738.
2 Michael Miner, "The terrorist mind—A look back at a 1972 plot to poison Chicago," *Chicago Reader,* September 25, 2012. https://chicagoreader.com/blogs/the-terrorist-mind-a-look-back-at-a-1972-plot-to-poison-chicago/; see also, W. Seth Carus, "R.I.S.E. (1972)," in Jonathan B. Tucker (ed.), *Toxic Terror: Assessing Terrorist Use of Chemical and Biological Weapons.* Cambridge, MA: MIT Press, 2000.
3 Hiroshi Takahashi, et.al., "Bacillus anthracis Bioterrorism Incident in Kameido, Tokyo, 1993," *Emerging Infectious Diseases,* Volume 10, Number 1 (January 2004). https://wwwnc.cdc.gov/eid/article/10/1/03-0238_article; see also, Kyle B. Olson, "Aum Shinrikyo: Once and Future Threat?," *Emerging Infectious Diseases,* Volume 5, Number 4 (August 1999). https://wwwnc.cdc.gov/eid/article/5/4/99-0409_article
4 Frerichs, et.al. op.cit.
5 Sammy Salama and Lydia Hansell, "Does Intent Equal Capability? Al-Qaeda and Weapons of Mass Destruction," *Nonproliferation Review,* Volume 12, Number 3 (November 2005). https://www.nonproliferation.org/wp-content/uploads/npr/123salama.pdf
6 Scott Decker, *Recounting the Anthrax Attacks: Terror, the Amerithrax Task Force, and the Evolution of Foensics in the FBI.* Louisville, CO: Roman and Littlefield Publishers, 2018.
7 Frerichs, et al. op.cit.
8 John Parachini, *Combating Terrorism: Assessing the Threat of Biological Terrorism.* Santa Monica, CA.: RAND Corporation, 2001. https://www.rand.org/pubs/testimonies/CT183.html
9 The numbers assigned to pandemics are confusing. There were successive waves of the Black Plague beginning with the first devastating outbreak in 1347–1351, a second in 1357–1358, a third in 1362, and a fourth in 1382, although there was also an outbreak in 1374. Further localized outbreaks of the pandemic continued into the 17th century. However, historians also describe the Bubonic plague that re-emerged in China in the mid-19th century and caused widespread death as the "Third Pandemic." This Third Pandemic also came in waves and continued until the middle of the 20th century.
10 Kenneth Letendre, Corey L. Fincher, and Randy Thornhill, "Does Infectious Disease Cause Globalization in the Frequency of Intrastate Armed Conflict and Civil War?" *Biological Reviews,* 2010, Volume 85, Number 3 (2010), pp. 669–683.
11 Norman F. Cantor, *In the Wake of the Plague: The Black Death and the World It Made.* New York: Simon & Schuster, 2001; Samuel K. Cohn, Jr. "The Black Death: End of a Paradigm," op.cit; David Herlihy, *The Black Death and the Transformation of the West.* Cambridge, MA: Harvard University Press, 1997 (The introduction by Samuel Cohn is especially useful.), and; John Kelly, *The Great Mortality: An Intimate History of the Black Death, the Most Devastating Plague of All Time.* New York: Harper Perennial, 2005. xenophobia
12 Catherine Arnold, *Pandemic 1918: Eyewitness Accounts from the Greatest Medical Holocaust in Modern History.* New York, NY: St. Martin's Griffin, 2018.
13 Ben Stickle and Marcus Felson, "Crime Rates in a Pandemic: The Largest Criminological Experiment in History," *American Journal of Criminal Justice*, Volume 45 (June 16, 2020). https://doi.org/10.1007/s12103-020-09546-0
14 Cheryl Corley, "Crime Has Declined Overall During The Pandemic, But Shootings And Killings Are Up," *NPR/KQED,* July 20, 2020. https://www.npr.org/2020/07/20/892418244/crime-has-declined-overall-during-the-pandemic-but-shootings-and-killings-areup#:~:text=Live%20Sessions,Crime%20Has%20Declined%20Overall%20During%20The%20Pandemic%2C%20But%20Shootings%20And,uptick%20in%20shootings%20and%20killings.

15 Europol, *Beyond the Pandemic—How COVID-19 Will Shape the Serious and Organized Crime Landscape in the EU.* April 30, 2020. https://www.europol.europa.eu/publications-documents/beyond-pandemic-how-covid-19-will-shape-serious-and-organised-crime-landscape-in-eu

16 Marco Hafner, et al. *COVID-19 and the Cost of Vaccine Nationalism.* Santa Monica, CA: The RAND Corporation, 2020. https://www.rand.org/pubs/research_reports/RRA769-1.html

17 Ted Robert Gurr, *Why Men Rebel.* Princeton, NJ: Princeton University Press, 1970; see also, Gurr, "Why Men Rebel Redux: How Valid are its Arguments 40 Years On?" *E-International Relations,* November 17, 2011. https://www.e-ir.info/2011/11/17/why-men-rebel-redux-how-valid-are-its-arguments-40-years-on/

18 Hafner, et.al. op.cit.

19 Richard J. Evans, "Epidemics and Revolutions: Cholera in Nineteenth Century Europe," *Past & Present.* August 1988. https://www.jstor.org/stable/650924

20 Richard Gunderman, "How smallpox devastated the Aztecs—and helped Spain conquer an American civilization," *PBS Newshour,* February 23, 2019. https://www.pbs.org/newshour/science/how-smallpox-devastated-the-aztecs-and-helped-spain-conquer-an-american-civilization-500-years-ago; Sarah Roller, "The Worst Epidemic in History? The Scourge of Smallpox in the Americas," *History HIT,* October 6, 2020. https://www.historyhit.com/europeans-smallpox-and-the-americas/

21 William C. Summers, *The Great Manchurian Plague of 1910–1911: The Geopolitics of an Epidemic Disease.* New Haven, CT: Yale University Press, 2012.

22 Thucydides, *The History of the Peloponnesian War,* Book II, Chapter 7; see also Gary Bass, "The Athenian Plague, A Cautionary Tale of Democracy's Fragility," *The New Yorker,* June 10, 2020. https://www.newyorker.com/culture/culture-desk/the-athenian-plague-a-cautionary-tale-of-democracys-fragility

23 Simona Trip, et al. "Psychological Mechanisms Involved in Radicalization and Extremism: A Rational Emotive Behavioral Conceptualization," *Frontiers in Psychology.* March 6, 2019. https://www.ncbi.nlm.nih.gov/pmc/articles/PMC6414414/

24 Anthony Fauci, *The Haskins Lectureship in Science Policy, November 15, 2002.* Santa Monica, CA: RAND Corporation. https://www.rand.org/pubs/papers/P8076.html

25 Samuel A. Bozette, et al., "A Model for a Smallpox-Vaccination Policy," *The New England Journal of Medicine,"* 348: 416–425 (January 30, 2003). https://www.nejm.org/doi/full/10.1056/NEJMsa025075

26 Institute for Health Metrics and Evaluation, *COVID-19 Projections (based on Current projection scenario by February 1, 2020.* Accessed on November 1, 2020. https://covid19.healthdata.org/global?view=total-deaths&tab=trend

42

HYBRID JIHAD

A Trend Scenario for Transnational Terrorism

Nicolas Stockhammer

Methodology and Scope

Derived from the functional methodological approach of the extended algorithm-processed trend and key factor analysis of transnational terrorism as continuously implemented on the virtual platform "Foresight Strategy Cockpit" (FSC), this research study seeks to examine what potential future outlook variants may evolve from each identified key factor and describes its likely manifestations, the degree of impact and the overall probability.

Therefore, resulting from a multi-faceted analytical process, current trends of (predominantly Islamist) terrorism that are expected to shape the phenomenon for the intermediate future, were identified. Consequently, the major influencing "key factors" were operationalized according to criteria like probability, impact and stability regarding appearance and dynamics. This had been elaborated on in the antecedent volume two of this edition.[1] In essence, these key factors reflect foresight-relevant drivers and developments that will very likely have a manifest impact over a period of approximately two to five years in the surrounding field ("*Umfeldanalyse*"). Such a 360-degree algorithm based strategic foresight research process ("connecting the dots") facilitated sketching possible scenario projections at an ambitious level of adaption and predictability. Methodologically, as nobody is able to generically predict the future of terrorism, scenario projections are experimental foresight determinations of possible developments for the years ahead and hence take into consideration sometimes pretty much deviant as well as very common, rather generic presumptions. These sometimes even extreme projections, substantiated by the key trends identified, are arranged in a matrix style format: on the horizontal x-axis, in most cases the degree of capability to influence, change or pertain etc. is classified, whereas on the vertical y-axis the intensity of intentionality to act or withstand etc. is measured. As there are four projections for each key factor, they are weighted against each other and categorized following the bipolar reference model as has been set out above. In this analysis, for the sake of reducing complexity and also in order to concentrate on the most relevant key factors, the seven most significant among them are operationalized in future projections (see Figure 42.1).

DOI: 10.4324/9781003326373-48

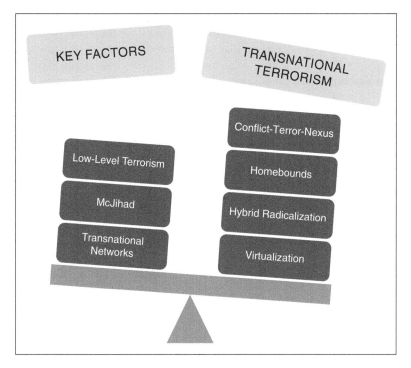

Figure 42.1 Key Factors Transnational Terrorism

Source: Author's Creation

Key Factor Analysis

Low–Level Terrorism

In Europe alone, some 90 Islamist attacks have been carried out or prevented by the security authorities since 2004.[2] As a result of the perpetrated Islamist attacks, there were more than 800 casualties and more than 3,800 have been injured, some of them seriously. In recent years, terrorist attacks in Europe were carried out by hit teams of Islamist terrorist organizations such as the Islamic State and al-Qaeda on the one hand, and by individual perpetrators on the other, with the latter being responsible for the majority of terrorist attacks in Europe. According to Petter Nesser, in fact most of the (West) European jihadist attacks since ISIS significantly lost territory and finally the military campaign in Syria and Iraq, "have been low-tech, conducted by single actors, using melee weapon or vehicles. We have not seen complex, mass casualty attacks, like those in Paris in November 2015, which involved a group of attackers, employing different weapons and tactics, such as suicide bombings and mass shootings".[3]

According to the terrorist logic of spreading fear and insecurity among the population through seemingly random violence, public transportation, transportation hubs, train stations, public squares and spaces are prototypical attack targets. Simultaneous and/or staggered explosions on trains or subways *per se* guarantee a high number of dead and injured as well as possible live coverage during rush hour. The sheer knowledge that any indiscriminate passenger may possibly become a victim of a terrorist attack in a public transport vehicle has a considerable psychological attrition-effect on the population. This effect is intended by the perpetrators and therefore part of the operational-tactical attack planning of Islamist terrorism.

Spontaneous low-level-attacks by radicalized (opportunistic) lone perpetrators have been the prevailing terrorist attack pattern in Europe since 2015. Low-level terrorism by individual perpetrators or micro-cells uses the simplest tactical principles and means of action, such as easily procured weapons or everyday objects – knives and cars – which could potentially also include drones in the near future.

An empirical analysis of the overall weapons used (or planned) in the Islamist attacks carried out or prevented by security authorities shows that both the hit teams of large jihadist organizations and jihadist individual perpetrators used explosives, firearms and vehicles as means of attack, although they were used more frequently by the hit teams. Jihadist lone attackers have also used vehicles and firearms for their attacks, but much more frequently cut and thrust weapons. Since 2017 no jihadist terrorist strike in Europe involved explosives.[4] Hence, knives and other stabbing and cutting weapons may well be described as the classic means of low-level terrorism at the moment.[5] It is remarkable that "every jihadi assault in Europe since 2017 has been carried out by a lone individual, suggesting that it has become very difficult plan group attacks".[6]

To sum it up, we are currently confronted with tactical approaches that go by the name of "opportunistic" or "occasional" terrorism. This category, which qualifies as "low-level" terrorism, actually comprises very different constellations, all of which merely have in common that the terrorist action (mostly a lone wolf variant) results from the combination of operational propaganda, which has been widely circulated by a jihadist organization such as ISIS, and a favorable environment. As a rule, there is no direct connection with ISIS, although in the majority of attacks since 2015, even in the category of "opportunistic bombers," there has been almost exclusive evidence of contact with a terrorist organization or even "remote control" by the same.[7]

Without doubt the low-level approach will continue to set the stage of Islamist terrorism for some time. Correspondingly as this manifests in a key factor, the outlook for the near future concerning this specific modus operandi category of Islamist attacks seems methodologically useful in order to determine its further relevance. As a matrix of examination, the degree of capability (*x-axis*) is contoured against the intentionality (*y-axis*). Following Boaz Ganor's (2015) counter-terrorism equation, according to which the formula "motivation times operational capability(s)" expresses the probability basis for the implementation of a terrorist attack, it can logically be assumed that if either of these factors is neutralized, i.e. if the operational (planning or logistical) capability is compromised, or if the intrinsic motivation decreases, it is almost certain that a terrorist attack will not (or no longer) occur.[8] Hence this categorization seems useful in order to determine the probability of occurrence and to evaluate the threat factor.

Regarding possible trend scenario projections for the development of low-level terrorism, four different alternative future projections, each with a different probability and impact have been identified with the help of an FSC research-based method (see Figure 42.2):

- **PROJECTION 1: HIGH–LOW (high ambition-low capabilities)**
- **PROJECTION 2: NON-STARTER (low ambition-low capabilities)**
- **PROJECTION 3: MUMBAI-SQUAD (high ambition-high capabilities)**
- **PROJECTION 4: BLACK MAMBA (low ambition-high capabilities)**

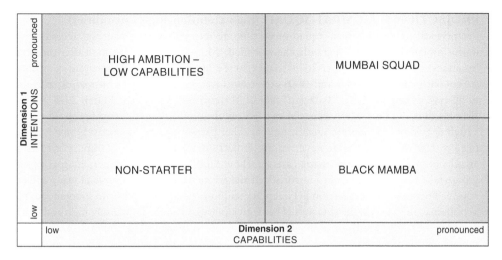

Figure 42.2 FSC – Projections for Key Factor "Low-Level Terrorism"

Source: Author's Creation

- **PROJECTION 1: HIGH – LOW (high ambition-low capabilities)**

  Prototypical for this projection is the discrepancy between the intrinsic motivation and tactical/logistical capabilities of the terrorist actors. In genealogical terms, this is usually a preliminary stage of a smaller-scale, improvised terrorist act to be launched following a progressive radicalization process. Symptomatic of this is the often desperate attempt to acquire logistical and tactical skills (this happens mainly in clandestine chat groups or on relevant extremist online forums) to execute an attack. As the desire to resort to violence is already pronounced, it is highly likely that the necessary capabilities will sooner or later follow. With increasing attempts to recruit potential attackers, plot attacks, identify possible targets and acquire weapons or skills, it becomes all the more presumable that due to the intensification of communication beforehand, counterterrorism ambitions will probably have a greater chance to succeed. However, given the small scale of the attacks at that specific level and its reduced complexity in preparation and planning, this may also turn out to be advantageous for the perpetrators. From the perspective of counterterrorism, time matters. It is, next to (intelligence) information, the crucial resource in that particular constellation. Such a high-low-projection may be considered as likely, but only transitional.

- **PROJECTION 2: NON-STARTER (low ambition- low capabilities)**

  Often observed as a reaction to disenchantment among war returnees (homebound jihadists), this projection corresponds with the disillusionment that political or ideological goals can hardly be achieved by a strategy of politically motivated violence. In line with this deeply rooted conviction that terrorism is no viable option, no corresponding logistical capabilities (such as armament) are sought by relevant actors in order to implement an attack scenario. It may also be the case that extremist attitudes still exist among radicals, but the strategy is regarded as false or ineffective. According to this disposition, subversion and propaganda promise more success.

  Nevertheless, theoretically the assumption exists that disillusioned former foreign fighters may reoffend and join extremist groups again, assist former comrades in arms or support ongoing attempts by other actors. The likelihood as well as the impact of this projection remain at a lower scale.

- **PROJECTION 3: MUMBAI-SQUAD (high ambition-high capabilities)**
  Prototypical for the Mumbai-Squad projection are terrorist attacks launched according to a multi-dimensional modus operandi, the so-called "Mumbai scheme", (named after the Mumbai attacks staged in November 2008[9] that became a blueprint[10] for simultaneous, coordinated strikes with automatic rifles and IEDs at various locations by different hit teams), as we had to observe during the Paris "Bataclan" plot of November 2015 and the March 2016 strikes in Brussels. But also lone-actor scenarios may follow this multi-faceted tactical proposition with a high degree of adaptability, suggesting that other parties may be supportively involved during any stage of execution. However, in this projection, the boundaries of improvised terrorist assaults to projected attack scenarios are somehow fluid. The individual perpetrators or small groups take concrete cues from a terrorist cell and create the basis for a simple plotting and execution. There is no contradiction between meticulously planned attacks and spontaneous plots as both may involve low-level tactics. The degree of motivation is immensely high and in itself a product of extreme radicalization. The Vienna terrorist attack of November 2, 2020 is symptomatic of this development – it should rather be categorized as improvised, but it corresponds with the characteristics of a "lone perpetrator plus"–scheme since it was possible to prove direct exchange with fellow Islamists concerning logistics, operative planning and immediate implementation before the act was finally committed. In addition, inspirational support from jihadist groups was also evident. However, a rather dilettante execution indicates the low-level character of the attack. Conclusively, the mix of articulated ambition and existing capabilities, which involve access to weapons is by far the most threatening scenario projection within the examined range. As recent attacks have demonstrated, the likeliness of such a culmination of motivation and the willingness to carry out a terrorist plot is clearly indicated, particularly if one takes into consideration the evidence generated in the aftermath of relevant attacks, where symptoms of this pathological constellation have become evident. Nevertheless, the strong counter-terrorism efforts in the West seem to render the operating environment of such squads tougher and the probability of this materializing quite low. But far from impossible.
- **PROJECTION 4: BLACK MAMBA (low ambition- high capabilities)**
  Like a Black Mamba, this group or lone perpetrator remains in a clandestine environment but already has acquired the necessary capabilities to implement an improvised terror scenario. Maybe there has been a former involvement in terrorism or a previous experience with politically motivated violence. Often this type of attacker has gone through paramilitary training or served in regular armed forces. Basically well aware of possible effects and opportunities, for many different reasons, they prefer to remain calm and inconspicuous. Perhaps the inner pressure and intrinsic motivation to make such a scenario effective is not yet developed enough, primarily due to external circumstances (e.g. the pandemic) or because of psychological problems or ideological concerns. This impacts the relatively low plausibility of the black mamba projection at the moment. Nevertheless, the threat posed by such a structure or lone actor should not be underestimated, as it doesn't take much of a trigger to set off violent action.

McJihad

What I initially termed as "*McJihad*" describes a very specific kind of franchise of terror that involves a lose network of lone wolves, bandwagoners and copy-cats, in most cases persons without a proven "track record" as jihadists.[11] As Marc Sageman rightly indicated, the protagonists of this terrorism facet are homegrown, self-trained, self-financed. He observes a global network of "homegrown wannabes", what he calls "*leaderless jihad*".[12] Obviously, this franchise phenomenon of homegrowns is closely related with prior criminal activity, commonly subsumed under the analytical concept model of "crime-terror-nexus"[13]. They are mostly low-level assaults that are staged by "gangster-jihadists", failed foreign terrorist fighters or would-be terrorists without prior affiliation or limited contact to a jihadist network, seeking to compensate their manifold shortcomings.[14] In the past, jihadist groups would have spurned petty criminals as recruits because their delinquent activity *in nuce* violates the tenets of Islam. But the success of law enforcement in cracking down on terrorist groups' traditional methods of recruitment has forced jihadists to look for alternative breeding grounds. Virtually anyone can step up at short notice and become part of this uncomplicated "join-in" venture, without lengthy acceptance procedures, any lead time or complex instructions. The basic jihadist pattern already exists, only the execution remains to be determined individually. Under that proposition, the perpetrator is fundamentally flexible in his tactics as well as completely detached from a command hierarchy, but somehow still connected and/or supported. At least the attackers are backed in the aftermath of the attack, where the terrorist organization suggests an allegiance or *ex-post*-dedication. Without doubt, this disposition benefits the essential element of surprise in terrorist attacks, which at the same time makes it extremely difficult to prevent or thwart them successfully. Such a loose franchise system has proven to be tremendously efficient. Terrorist action is handled under the primacy of spontaneity paired with unprecedented simplicity (low-level-attacks) in implementation and a minimum of communication beforehand. Anatomically, McJihad is fully connected with low-level terrorism, as its perpetrators take full advantage of unrelatedness and tactical independence.

Similarly, based on FSC methodology and systematic operationalization, four different possible trend scenario projections have been identified (see Figure 42.3):

- **PROJECTION 1: SEMIFLEX-TERROR (high ambition–low capabilities)**
- **PROJECTION 2: RIGID NETWORK (low ambition–low capabilities)**
- **PROJECTION 3: TROJAN HORSE (high ambition–high capabilities)**
- **PROJECTION 4: CLANDESTINE UNIT (low ambition–high capabilities)**

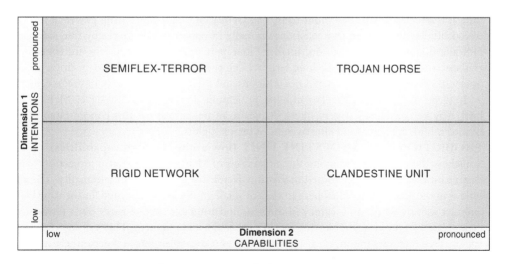

Figure 42.3 FSC – Projections for Key Factor "McJihad"

Source: Author's Creation

- **PROJECTION 1: SEMIFLEX-TERROR (high ambition–low capabilities)**
  Semiflex-Terror is characterized by the discrepancy between harboring great ambitions to commit an act of terrorism on the one hand and being limited in terms of capacity when it comes to executing it on the other. These limitations on the part of individual actors and loose terrorist cells affect both logistics and tactical implementation capabilities. According to this projection, the proponents of Islamist terrorism are confronted with massive counterterrorism campaigns and preventive measures. This notwithstanding, the level of radicalization is already advanced, and there is an unrelenting effort to compensate for the deficits in capabilities. In the most common cases, like-minded individuals and groups abroad are brought in with the provision of support or the promise of capabilities – either virtually, financially or in real terms – and also with a contribution of weapons or trained (battle-hardened) personnel. If they somehow succeed to acquire necessary logistic and tactical capabilities, then these groups or lone actors may manifest a serious terrorist threat. In such a constellation, the boundaries and transitions between the Semiflex and Trojan horse scenario projections are fluid, sometimes blurred.

- **PROJECTION 2: RIGID NETWORK (low ambition–low capabilities)**
  This projection is centered around conservative, organizationally inflexible and strongly hierarchically structured networks. In view of the government's increased efforts to defend itself against violent extremism, these networks lack the ambition to carry out a (planned) terrorist act, and even an opportunistic low-level attack seems unrealistic because it requires loose, i.e. flexible, structures. Due to the inherent tactical-operational rigidity of the groupings, their ability to carry out such attacks is also poorly developed. Particularly in view of the fact that the protection of the constitution and the intelligence services are heavily focused on preventing any activity by these old-fashioned organizations, it is highly unlikely that such terrorist actions will materialize. Conclusively, the impact of such structures remains modest.

- **PROJECTION 3: TROJAN HORSE (high ambition–high capabilities)**
  From the perspective of counterterrorism ambitions, this projection is the worst case scenario and at the same time the blueprint of the coming low-level-constellations in the field of Islamist violence against civilians. On the one hand, it is based on enormous intentionality and terrorist ambition; on the other hand, due to the volatile, almost fluid character of the loose organization, it is associated with enormous tactical flexibility and high penetrating power in the area of capabilities, which manifests itself operationally in opportunistic attacks by free riders and radicalized apologists. In addition, smaller "lone perpetrator plus" scenarios are covered by this spectrum, which will in the long term remain the preferred tactical variant in the modus operandi *"cheap and dirty"*, i.e. rapid fire weapons and explosives particularly in urban centers.

  In terms of probability the Trojan horse projection, a prototypical low-level-McJihad hybrid, may be considered as very likely. As it also relates to impact, this concentrated power results in both efficiency and effectiveness of terrorist plots.

- **PROJECTION 4: CLANDESTINE UNIT (low ambition–high capabilities)**
  Somehow the lurking tiger among the projections of McJihad, the scenario projection "clandestine unit" is substantially rooted in the time factor that determines intentionality. The ambitions of the jihadist individual perpetrators or small groups remain limited for the time being and in a waiting position in secrecy in order to find a suitable time to carry out a terrorist attack, in view of the close monitoring by CT authorities and instances. The waiting time is optimally used to ensure logistical capacities, as well as tactical planning and personnel capacities. The threat posed by this type of clandestine unit should not be underestimated. In the long term, this variant is highly explosive. Speaking of probability and impact, it may be justifiably assumed that this projection can be regarded as being both very likely and also immensely

effectual. Again, a dissolution of boundaries toward the Trojan horse is observable. The differentiating factor is time and the development that evolves from growing preparedness.

Transnational Networks

What does "transnational" in the context of (Islamist) terrorism mean? According to Martha Crenshaw, transnational terrorism "involves actions in which victims, perpetrators, and sites of violence represent different states and nationalities".[15] Furthermore, "transnational terrorist attacks may be initiated by local actors against foreign targets in the geographic conflict space, or by radicalized local residents or transnational networks against targets outside the combat zone".[16] With relation to terrorist networks, the term "transnational" reflects a network's ability to operationally transcend borders and bundle strengths to promote a common extremist purpose. Cross-border support can either target ideology, comprise logistical or tactical assistance, or any measure appropriate to substantiate the pursuit of common goals. In its current manifestations, cells rather than large networks determine the situation reports of intelligence services. They are distinctively referred to as a minor category (rather minor cells) in comparison with overarching terrorist groups. Case evidence[17] seems to support the thesis that in the jihadist segment predominantly small cells or lone actors plot or stage attacks in Europe.

In the recent case of the Viennese attack of November 2, 2020 such a supportive structure and further involvement of likeminded jihadis (obviously some kind of micro-network transcending the borders) in Switzerland and Germany may be assumed.[18] However this doesn't contradict the previously analyzed McJihad thesis, as there is rather strong evidence of a decoupled franchise with primarily ideological ties to the core organization of ISIS.

Again, four different possible trend scenario projections regarding the potential structure and development of transnational terrorist networks have been identified (see Figure 42.4):

- **PROJECTION 1: LOCAL CELLS (high international ambition–low capabilities)**
- **PROJECTION 2: LOCAL ISLANDS (low international ambition–low capabilities)**

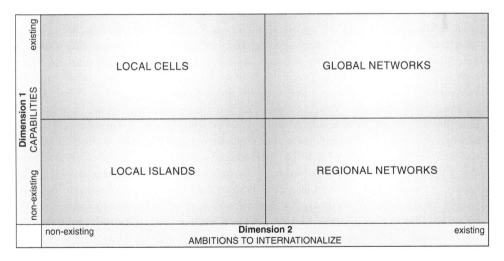

Figure 42.4   FSC– Projections for Key Factor "Transnational Networks"

Source: Author's Creation

- **PROJECTION 3: GLOBAL NETWORKS (high international ambition–high capabilities)**
- **PROJECTION 4: REGIONAL NETWORKS (low international ambition–high capabilities)**

- **PROJECTION 1: LOCAL CELLS (high international ambition–low capabilities)**
These (foremost small) structures are deliberately limited to the local level, although their capabilities would basically allow for transnationalization. Nevertheless, it cannot be assumed that they exist in isolation, and they are networked to varying degrees with other cells (especially in nearby countries) for the purpose of low-threshold cooperation or support. Often the local restriction is due to tactical considerations, for example, to avoid being targeted by foreign services. In addition, these clandestine groups tend to focus on realistic goals and quickly adapt their engagement to structural circumstances. It lies in their morphological and ideological nature that they may immediately turn outwards and expand their activities to the neighboring countries. So the probability to internationalize is high-particularly taking into consideration transnational virtual activity. In terms of impact, the cross-border-effectiveness of these structures highly depends on the degree of international involvement.

- **PROJECTION 2: LOCAL ISLANDS (low international ambition–low capabilities)**
In the foreground of this projection are the striking inability and also the constant lack of ambition that characterizes the structure. This may be due to insufficient resources but also to the absence of aspiration to build a sustainable transnational terrorist cell. Often it is the disillusionment of war returnees, the disappearance of the group (imprisonment, persecution by the security authorities, leaving the scene, drifting into other even more radical milieus, etc.), which in sum leads to the weakening, decimation and lack of perspective of such groups. To summarize, the potential is low, the likelihood that this entity emerges into an international stage is minimal and the impact it has is negligible.

- **PROJECTION 3: GLOBAL NETWORKS (high international ambition–high capabilities)**
Based on this projection, it can be assumed that there is a high degree of transnational networking – both virtually and in person. Such cells dispose of the necessary resources and capacities, and accordingly the intention to carry out a terrorist attack anywhere and at any given time is always virulent. Internationality and cooperative networking among likeminded extremist structures are seen as a manifest advantage and therefore instrumentalized. Such cells skillfully exploit the benefits of cross-border clandestinity and, like a snake wind their way through the security authorities' network. Even though the impact of global networks may be considerable, these structures seem likely to be less successful in the near future and therefore the probability of new global actors emerging will be low. Taking into consideration constant fragmentation and regionalization, the growing importance of the franchise imperative and the increasing organizational command principle of *"leaderless jihad"*, it is expected that globally active networks (currently, with some restrictions, al-Qaeda and ISIS) might sooner or later diminish or even disappear. Perhaps they may just exist further as ideological frameworks in the sense of global jihad, but not seek to project or transfer power.

- **PROJECTION 4: REGIONAL NETWORKS (low international ambition–high capabilities)**
In scenario projection four, low-level cross-border cooperation is cultivated. These regionally active networks pose a threat, especially with a view to the immediate future, and, whilst hoping to make up for deficits in motivational resources, these actors could extend

their scope occasionally. The degree of threat increases in direct proportion to the growing extremist ambitions and the resources available. Given this mechanism, CT institutions must pay particular attention to such groups. For the time being, this may become the model of choice in the sphere of jihadist network organization. The impact and vigor of regional networks and cells depends on local factors and specific objectives that refer to the individual scope. It is evident that Boko Haram has a very different ambition than al-Shabaab or the Taliban.

Conflict-Terror-Nexus

As elaborated in part one of this edition[19], a "direct connection between geopolitically relevant, regional conflicts (in particular in the Greater Middle East) and Islamist terrorism" can be presumed. As Thomas Hegghammer recently pointed out, "[…] the high number of armed conflicts in the Muslim world has fed grievances and offered operational space for jihadi groups to grow".[20] It is the exploitation of these grievances that instigates politically motivated extremist violence, at least concerning propaganda and motivation, a manifest nexus between regional conflicts in the Islamic world and international Salafi-jihadist terrorism exists and subversively sets the scene.[21] Jihadist perpetrators in Europe regularly take revenge for invasion or occupation or war in their home countries. Right in the aftermath of the US campaign in Iraq starting 2003, "the invasion and the occupation of Iraq has stirred a great deal of anger among jihadists in Europe".[22] Fragile statehood in the Greater Middle East as well as eroding societal cohesion in the region pave the way to extremist violence against the distant enemy. The main reason for this turning toward targets in the West is primarily rooted in the attention terrorist attacks attract there in comparison with constant violent eruptions in the region, that practically remain ignored or at least ineffective when it comes to triggering the desired change in policy making.

Foresight Strategy Cockpit analysis suggests four different scenario projections that are each weighted for the intentionality to carry out a terrorist attack as well as the degree of transnational networking (see Figure 42.5):

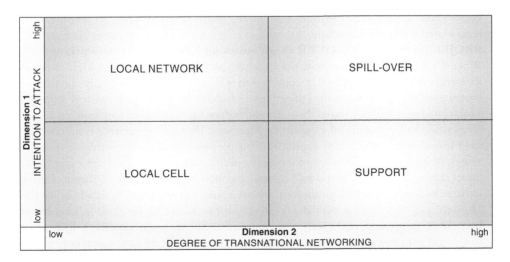

Figure 42.5   FSC– Projections for Key Factor "Conflict-Terror-Nexus"

Source: Author's Creation

- **PROJECTION 1: LOCAL NETWORK (high attack ambition–low networking)**
- **PROJECTION 2: LOCAL CELL (low attack ambition–low networking)**
- **PROJECTION 3: SPILL-OVER (high attack ambition–intense networking)**
- **PROJECTION 4: SUPPORT (low attack ambition– intense networking)**

- **PROJECTION 1: LOCAL NETWORK (high attack ambition–low networking)**
  The local network projection is based on the assumption that a (usually small) entity has a strong intention to resort to violent extremist action, but its desire to stage an attack is primarily rooted in a local or closer regional context and less connected with conflicts in the Muslim world. Accordingly, the immediate societal and political situation in the country where these extremists reside plays a major role in the sense of the genesis of the attack plot. Without direct intersection with foreign groups or ideological impact from abroad, local Islamist networks tend to favor the near enemy approach. The refusal to censor the Charlie Hebdo caricatures e.g. had a stronger impact on jihadist violence in France than any propaganda or ideological influence from outside the country. However, France is also regularly blamed for supporting apostate regimes and, particularly in Africa, France is seen as the spearhead against jihadist groups operating in the Sahel and Sahara, similarly "as is America in other regions of the world".[23] Therefore the terrorist backlash against the French is also related with this specific role, being seen as a colonialist and supporter of great power politics. Nevertheless, the proposition to stay local can turn out impactful and the probability to promote jihadist violence under that banner seems a pragmatic option.

- **PROJECTION 2: LOCAL CELL (low attack ambition–low networking)**
  Among the "Conflict-Terror-Nexus" trend scenario, the local cell projection is somehow a low-level constellation. In substance it centers on inability, powerlessness and non-existence of capability. Neither inspiration nor explicit tactical motivation, nor the aim of international networking exists. There is mostly no international infliction, contact or transnational inspiration, narrative or role-model approach. In terms of threat, a local cell of that kind is like a squib load, a systemic failure based on lacking capabilities and intentions. Referring to Boaz Ganor's counter-terrorism equation, as described above, this means that no imminent threat is associated with such a structure.

- **PROJECTION 3: SPILL-OVER (high attack ambition–intense networking)**
  When it comes to threat assessment, the spill-over projection symbolizes the high-alert mode. Essentially, this is what operative counter-terrorist ambitions are primarily focused on: a pronounced risk combined with a progressive capability to attack, international support and a substantial motivation. Usually these structures draw upon distinct inspiration, cross-border cooperation and transnational capabilities. Moreover, they seek inspiration from conflicts in the Muslim world, which they exploit in their propaganda, also with reference to terrorist action, where this revenge-narrative serves as a justification for indiscriminate violence. If the direct support of parties ("crusaders") in these conflicts is used as a pretext, then it is the narrative of non-involvement in connection with tolerance of cruelties committed against fellow Muslims, as it was the case with attacks in countries not directly involved in wars in Syria, Iraq and Afghanistan. Conclusively, this projection is highly toxic, very likely in manifestation and is expected to have a severe impact on political stability in the attacked countries. The Paris attacks of November 2015 can serve as a blueprint for this development. This case also shows how the involvement of returned foreign terrorist fighters may render a plot even more dangerous and efficient.

- **PROJECTION 4: SUPPORT (low attack ambition–intense networking)**
At a first glance it may seem paradoxical, but intense international affiliation and a constant recourse to victim-narratives related with conflicts in the Greater Middle East could also go hand in hand with reduced ambitions to attack in the West. There are several reasons for such a mindset: either the structure finds itself in the focus of CT activities, or is rebuilding its capacities, or is consolidating after prior exposition, or, in most cases is preparing for a strike. In usual terms, smaller cells are a very careful before they expose themselves as a jihadist entity.

   For them it takes a lot of preparation, resources and patience to plan and conduct an attack. Therefore, the motivation increases relatively to the capabilities and the reassurance of their ideological creed, nurtured by the victim-revenge-narrative. Any doubt or remorse must be discarded in the course of radicalization. Once this stage has been reached, the motivation to organize and carry out a terrorist attack increases dramatically. The affiliation with international fellow Islamists has a tremendous impact on that process. Simultaneously, the probability that such terrorist violence will emerge will then be about to increase exponentially. The impact of this is undeniable, even though it results from a second degree process that ultimately leads to terrorism.

Spillover of Homebounds

In the long term a manifest threat for European security also emanates from the increasing number of foreign terrorist fighters who have returned to their countries of origin from the war zones in Syria and Iraq or are returning home ("*homebound*"), some of whom could plan, orchestrate or carry out terrorist attacks using military means as they are equipped with combat know-how. As early as in 2016, James R. Clapper, then director of US-National Intelligence, warned in the aftermath of the Brussels attacks: "Foreign fighters who have trained in Iraq and in Syria might potentially leverage skills and experience to plan and execute attacks in the West. Involvement of returned foreign fighters in terrorist plotting increases the effectiveness and lethality of terrorist attacks."[24] Most of these fighters were born and raised in Europe and carried EU passports when they became radicalized and joined various extremist groups in the region. When they decided to return home, where they officially belong, this raised severe concerns in many European capitals, especially after terrorist attacks at Brussels and Istanbul airports and indiscriminate attacks on crowds in Paris, Berlin, London and many more, some of them involving returnees.[25] Jihadists trained in weapons, IEDs, and combat tactics can inflict significant damage, especially when operating in groups. Therefore, transnational spillover effects from ongoing violent theaters in Libya, Syria, Afghanistan and the like must be considered when developing counterterrorism strategies at home and abroad.[26]

   Reportedly, at least 15,000 people were able to flee the caliphate before it collapsed. Of that number, about 7,500 returned home, of whom only about half are detained or under active surveillance by local authorities; 5,000 others were deported by Turkey without notification to host states or the countries of which they are citizens; 2,500 more sought refuge in Sudan; and about 2,700 others infiltrated ISIS branches elsewhere.[27] The logistics of the returnees, who have combat experience and training and access to weapons or infrastructure and logistics, borrows from the principle of underground guerrilla warfare. The current terrorist trend is clearly moving in the direction of simple planning, rapid execution and appropriate armament of the attackers (rapid-fire rifles and explosive vests), since the logistical preparation hardly requires precise planning, nor greater resources. Nevertheless, we should not underrate the potential ability to stage projected attacks, including networks and cells that transcend the spectrum of limited low-level attacks involving homebound jihadists.

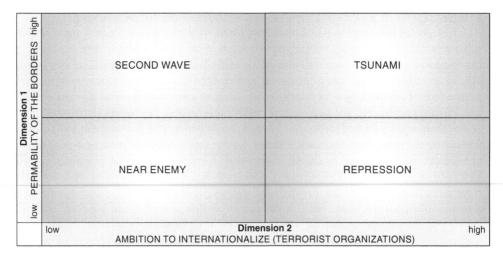

Figure 42.6 FSC– Projections for Key Factor "Spillover of Homebounds"
Source: Author's Creation

To further describe the potential development regarding the expected spillover of homebound foreign terrorist fighters (henceforth "FTFs") four different scenario projections have been laid out (see Figure 42.6):

- **PROJECTION 1: SECOND WAVE (high border permeability–low networking)**
- **PROJECTION 2: NEAR ENEMY (low border permeability–low networking)**
- **PROJECTION 3: TSUNAMI (high border permeability–intense networking)**
- **PROJECTION 4: REPRESSION (low border permeability–intense networking)**

- **PROJECTION 1: SECOND WAVE (high border permeability–low networking)**
  Based on the assumption that the Schengen borders will be as permeable as they had been before the pandemic, a further influx of foreign terrorist fighters that initially have been stuck in Turkey or elsewhere in the Greater Middle East or in the European periphery is to be expected.[28] As European intelligence services have their eyes on these homebound jihadists, they are rather defensive when it comes to transnational networking. Some of these former extremist peers (probably up to one third of them) may well be regarded as disillusioned or drifting. In a midterm perspective, the remaining two thirds may still be considered a major concern due to a spate of prison releases of fellow jihadists (some of them former comrades in Syria or Iraq) all over Europe, decreasing surveillance measures, as well as a potentially shifting focus (e.g. toward right wing extremists and conspiracy extremists) of security authorities. The probability of this projection is relatively high; even though the pandemic may still cause restrictions, at least locally the impact could be considerable.
- **PROJECTION 2: NEAR ENEMY (low border permeability–low networking)**
  As with other scenario projections previously elaborated with FSC methodology, "near enemy" describes a marginalized and low impact constellation. Characterized by an ongoing inability or discouragement to promote extremist action, homebound foreign terrorist fighters only play a subsidiary role in this projection. This can either be substantiated by a rigid border regime that prevents an influx of returning jihadist fighters or a minimal motivation to

include residing forces in terrorist plotting or violent action. Again, this projection is rooted in the belief that without intention and capabilities, no attack seems likely. The probability of this projection evolving into substantial action is very low.

- **PROJECTION 3: TSUNAMI (high border permeability-intense networking)**

  "Tsunami" epitomizes a gigantic wave of extremists that sweeps over to Europe. Behind the symbolism lies the assumption that due to permeable Schengen borders and intense networking within the local structures and abroad, a wave of returning FTFs may set the stage for terrorist attacks in European metropolises. They could be involved in operative planning, coordination and logistic support. Moreover, *homebounds* bring a sort of jihadist "street credibility" with them and are regarded as role models and combat heroes, no matter what their individual record may look like. This quality makes them a useful propaganda and recruitment tool that is skillfully used by terrorist organizations. Hypothesizing that these individuals may accept this active role and exploit their combat experience as well as their transnational networks, a substantial threat could emanate from these extremist ingredients. European security forces, however, closely monitor *homebounds*, a fact that contributes to a higher awareness concerning potential extremist activities that might evolve from them or their contact circles. As a whole, the tsunami projection reflects a high potential as well as a high probability and presumes a high degree of motivation, but also distinct awareness by security/counter-terrorist forces.

- **PROJECTION 4: REPRESSION (low border permeability-intense networking)**

  This projection relates to the assumption that due to the pandemic and stricter cross-border legislation, homebound FTFs are less likely to return to their country of origin. However, there is a firm intent among individuals of this category to contribute to transnational ambitions of likeminded groups in Europe, even if this is very likely administered from outside of Europe. Taking into consideration that such a repressive border management may be abandoned for the benefit of fiscal austerity or other strategic considerations, this could mean a substantial increase of risk, as these suspects may not be in the particular scope of European security bodies. Moreover, the purposeful transnational jihadist cooperation already implemented may subsequently turn out useful with regard to plotting and providing support in preparation of terrorist attacks. In terms of anticipation, preemption and prevention such a constellation is highly threatening, as action could evolve immediately following the return of some former foreign terrorist fighters that are armed with combat experience, skills in preparing terrorist attacks and supporting networks. And most significantly, they may bring a distinct extremist motivation to stage attacks with them. In a nutshell, this projection entails a mid-term high probability of threat as well as a large-scale extremist motivation.

Hybrid Radicalization

As elaborated in volume two of this edition[29], one of the recent major intellectual French discussions (Kepel vs. Roy) about radicalization centered on the question whether Salafi-jihadists radicalize within or toward Islamism. Based on the proposition of McJihad and the widespread system of affiliated franchise terrorist networks, there is substantial evidence that the latter variant (as advocated by Olivier Roy) will increasingly become the distinct pattern of radicalization for the near future. Phenomenologically this refers to a convergent (hybrid) process, where both traditional ideological approaches and postmodern (i.e. virtual) methods of exploitation are intentionally combined to facilitate the absorption of extremist convictions. The expected trajectory in this field suggests that there are (at least) four different potential future projections with different degrees of impact and probability(see Figure 42.7). The x-axis describes the degree of

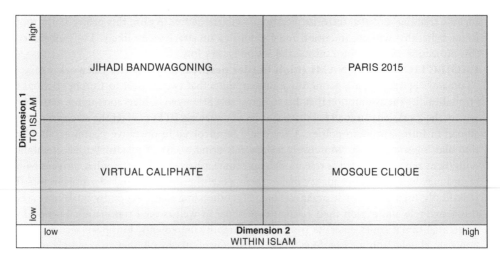

Figure 42.7 FSC– Projections for Key Factor "Hybrid radicalization"

Source: Author's Creation

radicalization toward (extremist) Islam, whereas the degree of radicalization within Islam toward Islamism is depicted on the y-axis.

- **PROJECTION 1: JIHADI BANDWAGONING (radicalization high to Islam-low within Islam)**
- **PROJECTION 2: VIRTUAL CALIPHATE (radicalization low to Islam-low within Islam)**
- **PROJECTION 3: PARIS 2015 (radicalization high to Islam-intense within Islam)**
- **PROJECTION 4: MOSQUE-CLIQUE (radicalization low to Islam-intense within Islam)**

- **PROJECTION 1: JIHADI BANDWAGONING (high to Islam-low within Islam)**
  Recent developments in the sphere of jihadist terrorism suggest an increasing decoupling of radicalization from extremist ideology as the single source of the multi-level process leading to terrorism. Accordingly, Salafi-jihadism may hence primarily be regarded as a justification for violence but not anymore as the sole substantial facilitating element. Conclusively, the end-means-relation between extremism and violence has gradually changed. So has radicalization. Extremist beliefs have for the highly technology-oriented 3G-jihadists (al-Suri)[30] become more a carrier for radicalization than its initial cause. Taking a closer look at the majority of European Islamist attacks since 2015, more and more so-called "gangster jihadists" (most of them being petty criminals) have been involved in these plots ("*crime-terror-nexus*")[31]. Extremist ideology has for them been more a justifiable aspiration than the catalyst or root cause. Not because of inherent extremist stances, but because of them being a useful purpose to distract from their perceived or real existence without perspective, adolescents felt pretty much attracted by Islamist propaganda. The majority of European jihadists resorted to violence because they were given a platform and they suddenly had something to identify with.[32] In essence, religion in its extremist reading was not the major driving force that made them commit atrocities, but rather the idea of exculpating themselves for their deeds as petty criminals and their wrong-headed quest for

significance. Salafi-jihadism is the ideology they chose and follow in a bandwagoning manner. Drawing on witness accounts and statistical evidence[33], the assumption suggests itself that the vast majority of these later perpetrators did not anymore have a substantial track record as fully fledged Islamists, nor did they have a deep-rooted religious sophistication before committing terrorist attacks, primarily in the name of ISIS. It was mostly remorse or a sense of revenge, rather than earthly motivations, that brought these young men to Salafi-jihadism and violence in the name of religiously motivated extremism. Their infliction with petty crime turned out to be a useful skill when it came to logistics and preparation. In sum, this projection seems to be the most likely variant for the next five years. Its impact on Islamist radicalization is considerable.

- **PROJECTION 2: VIRTUAL CALIPHATE (low to Islam–low within Islam)**
Taking into consideration the ongoing virtualization of extremism and its growing leverage on radicalization, this projection delineates a development that suggests a transfer of Islamist radicalization to a virtual sphere[34]. Jihad has gone online long ago, but its followers often prefer the aspect of propaganda of the deed and facticity over ideological (extremist) discussions. A "virtual caliphate" may be a designated goal of jihadists all over the world, but supporters are more likely to draw their inspiration from tangible examples of successful jihadist attacks than from abstract discussions about "true Islam". Their radicalization is a product of this fascination, but not that of ideological persuasion. It is directed toward an extremism of the deed and not so much toward an extremist ideology. Hence the question of whether there is an ideological predisposition within or whether the person radicalizes toward an extremist interpretation of Islam becomes secondary. However, the strong impact this projection has on individual radicalization should not be underestimated. Neither should the probability of this evolving.

- **PROJECTION 3: PARIS 2015 (high to Islam–intense within Islam)**
The Paris 2015 projection – named after the Parisian Bataclan attack of 13 November 2015 – is symptomatic for a two-folded radicalization, one from within and one from outside. The perpetrators of this terrorist scenario, most of them being petty criminals and outsiders, were radicalized within Islam toward Islamism but also from "nowhere" toward Islamism.

According to this constellation, supporters of jihad could draw their obsession for this kind of extremism either from their preexisting propensity or from an incitement that is directed from external catalysts. Or a combination of both. The double impact on radicalization is what makes this even more dangerous, as the strong claim for action is inherent. The probability of the Paris 2015 projection can be regarded as high.

- **PROJECTION 4: MOSQUE-CLIQUE (low to Islam–intense within Islam)**
Mosque-Clique describes the most common pattern of radicalization within Islam.[35] Mostly, this takes place in the supportive environment of radical mosques and follows traditional paths. That means that particularly young men, prone to extremist ideas, are exposed to Islamist ideology and people who reinforce, further stimulate and fuel these ideas. In such an environment, a Salafist reading of the Qur'an is exploited to radicalize, recruit and streamline young Muslims accordingly. This is exactly where the transition from the individual to the group takes place. Clark McCauley and Sophia Moskalenko point to the importance of (peer) groups in the radicalization process.[36] Radical imam preachers capitalize on the persuasibility of their followers and channel their radical views toward violent extremism. Quite obviously this is extended to the social environment of later perpetrators, where extremist narratives pave the way to terrorist violence. As security authorities all across Europe are aware of this dynamic, just as radical imams are aware of being observed, one may assume that the likelihood of this projection remains stable at a lower level. Concerning the immediate impact, the prediction suggests that it may be devastating in terms of its potential violent output.

Virtualization

The Internet (predominantly social media and encrypted messaging apps) plays a key role related to the entire value chain of terrorism: "An essential criterion along the terrorist 'value chain' and on all spectrums is the role of the Internet and the associated virtualization of terror – from the first contact with extremist propaganda, radicalization and recruitment through planning to logistical support including the exchange of experiences of how to effectively carry out a terrorist attack – almost everything takes place online.".[37] To illustrate that essential symbiosis, it should be added that "even afterwards the exploitative dissemination of the attack as ,propaganda of the deed' can be maintained on the net."[38] As Thomas Hegghammer, referring to the rise of ISIS and the recent Islamist terrorist wave in Europe from 2015–2017, rightly concluded: "Its (ISIS') propaganda spread so fast that state security services could not keep track of all its new sympathizers. This translated into one of the most serious waves terrorist violence in Europe's modern history. In three years, from 2015 to 2017 jihadis in Europe killed nearly 350 people, more than the number killed in jihadi attacks in the preceding 20 years [...]."[39] That was just an initial point in terms of the exploitation of virtualization, also regarding encryption: "Finally, the new online ecosystem offered rich opportunities for secret communication. Encrypted messaging apps proliferated, and jihadi communications spread over a wide range of platforms. It was a signals intelligence nightmare".[40] Going digital turned out to be a tactical advantage of jihadist entrepreneurs and radicals, as to some extent penetration and infiltration by security agencies requires hacking social media applications owned by giants like Facebook. Terrorists hence more and more take advantage of the vast opportunities that emerge from exploiting new cyber-related technologies and the anonymity of the Web, particularly the DarkNet.

Again, in the four projections referencing to this key trend, the ratio of virtual intentionality (y-axis) toward virtual capabilities of terrorist actors (x-axis) and their relative degree of specificity is the relevant value(see Figure 42.8).

- **PROJECTION 1: HI-LOW (intention high-low capability)**
- **PROJECTION 2: LOSERS OF PROGRESS (intention low-low capability)**

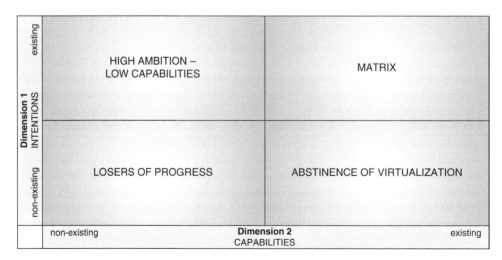

Figure 42.8 FSC – Projections for Key Factor "Virtualization"

Source: Author's Creation

- **PROJECTION 3: MATRIX (intention high–high capability)**
- **PROJECTION 4: ABSTINENCE OF VIRTUALIZATION (intention low-high capability)**

- **PROJECTION 1: HI-LOW (intention high-low capability)**

This projection resembles the *"want, but can't scenario"*. The pronounced discrepancy between intention and capabilities is symptomatic. Accordingly, extremists consider the opportunities of a progressive virtualization as a tactical advantage in the sense of multiplying options and diversifying methods. However, this is under the assumption that they do not yet have the technical skills to implement cyber operations and capitalize on them. Their reluctance to intensify efforts to gain significant capabilities is rooted in the awareness that any such attempt is closely monitored by security forces and intelligence bodies. It is quite easy to create social media channels to promote extremist propaganda and recruitment, but more complex to find stable and safe lines of internal communication. Establishing secure platforms for operative planning and logistic support is all the more difficult. Despite all that, it is very likely that organizations attempting to extend their virtual capabilities will somehow succeed. Success will always be evaluated in terms of quality and outreach. The impact of such a development toward exploitation of cyber-capabilities for extremist purposes is considerable and should definitely not be neglected.

- **PROJECTION 2: LOSERS OF PROGRESS (intention low-low capability)**

The "losers of progress" are neither capable nor willing to virtualize their extremist activities. According to this projection no attempts whatsoever are made to make use of the Internet in terms of promoting Islamist views or to further engage others. There are many different reasons for this retreat or concealment. Capabilities may be an issue, as tech-based circumventing abilities could be non-existing; with regards to ambition, several aspects (from personal drawbacks to organizational deficits) play a role. A major inhibiting factor may also be the constant fear of being revealed or the subject of intense investigation. Moreover, some disillusioned former FTFs may completely refrain from radical activities, both in real life as well as virtually.

As with similar projections related with other key factors, this one is a non-starter. The only threat risk emerging concerns a dramatic shift in intentionality or capabilities. However, such a projection is not very likely.

- **PROJECTION 3: MATRIX (intention high–high capability)**

The "Matrix" projection describes virtual high performance and the ability to conduct cyber-operations along the Jihadist "value-chain" ranging from providing platforms for propaganda to preparation of attacks. Capability and deep-rooted motivation go hand in hand as extremists take advantage of the manifold opportunities cyber-space offers them in any possible way regarding their activities. Anonymity and clandestinity are favoring organizations and lone actors that draw upon benefits from sub-conventional, asymmetric tactics and vice-versa. Based on the assumption that these jihadist proponents manage to escape or bypass the countering efforts of CT investigators, these extremists may create a virtual hub that allows them to adapt quickly and to use it as a weapon. In substance, the toxic combination of strong motivation and existing capabilities poses a constant threat to security. Unfortunately, the probability of the establishment of a "Matrix" is to be considered as relatively high.

- **PROJECTION 4: ABSTINENCE OF VIRTUALIZATION (intention low – high capability)**

Last but not least, the projection "abstinence of virtualization" suggests an (admittedly not very realistic) constellation, where Islamists dispose of cyber-capabilities, but do not have the ambition to materialize on them. This proposition is a rather hypothetic one, as extremists (almost) never seem to dismiss opportunities. Rather, they constantly work toward extending their outreach, capacities and capabilities. Essentially assuming that they have a weapon in their drawer without actually using it, does not have a logical substance. However, although the likelihood of this projection is very low, its evolving impact would be considerable based on the expectation that increasing the intentionality would mean a higher risk. This can be summarized in the risk potential formula: *motivation x capabilities=degree of risk*.

Trend Scenario "Hybrid Jihad"

The combination of the seven most likely projections for the next five years serves as the basis for the construction of a future trend scenario (named "Hybrid Jihad"), that depicts what has to be expected concerning jihadist violence in Europe in this period. Any kind of forecast analysis is predominantly based on assumptions of likelihood and sometimes also of impact. It goes without saying that external factors such as the development in the immediate security environment and conflicts involving Muslim countries are either a driving force or an inhibiting factor. Therefore, all of these considerations are to be regarded under a caveat. This also concerns the analytical method applied, as the projections are partly based on AI as well as human expertise and resemble more a keen forecast, than a fact-based status report. However, the underlying key factors claim to depict current developments and are substantiated in analytical observation.

Essentially, "Hybrid Jihad" is a system based on simplicity, practicability and both, effectiveness and efficiency. It is rooted in the assumption that jihadist terrorists seek tactical and operative success by reducing complexity. This can be achieved by anticipatively eliminating risk factors with reference to possible detection. Low-level attacks are easier to administrate as well as being more effective in terms of operative strategy. Even more, lose terrorist networks contribute to the amorphous principle of "leaderless jihad" (Marc Sageman). Current forms of radicalization add to this franchise and bandwagoning-dynamic. Islamist cross-border cooperation provides tactical flexibility, interoperability (e.g. Belgian attackers in France supported by locals) and supports clandestine preparations prior to projection of terrorist violence. Drawing on the idea of global jihad and referring to conflicts abroad strengthens ideological bonds within the peer group, particularly involving homebound FTFs. Last but not least, the transfer of communication, planning and plotting to the virtual (i.e. digital) sphere opens a wide range of possibilities along the entire value chain of jihadist violence. For the next two to five years this will constitute the most probable trend scenario.

1 *Low-Level-Terrorism ("Hi-Low")*
   With reference to the phenomenon of low-level-terrorism, the outlined *"Hi-Low"* projection, which stands for high ambition-low capabilities, will probably shape the threat scenario of smaller-scale terrorist violence mainly by jihadist lone-attackers in the near future. However, it has to be evaluated as a transitional projection. As the motivation is menacingly distinct and grievances may be further fueled by hybrid radicalization attempts, jihadists will continue to improve their capabilities. The projection clearly suggests a pattern of recurring single actor attacks following simple plots.

2 *McJihad ("Semiflex"/"Clandestine Unit")*
   Referring to the key factor McJihad, there is a broader range of possibilities that result from different factors: First, the regional aspect has to be considered. Counter-terrorism measures and ambitions may vary – especially in Europe. Also, the capabilities of unattached

jihadist networks depend on the people and structures, however lose, behind them. Second, McJihad is very much intertwined with other key factors. There is a manifest interdependence between McJihad and transnational networks, hybrid radicalization, homebound and virtualization, that makes at least two different projections seem possible: although there is a slight preference for the "*Semiflex-Terror*" projection, again reflecting high motivation, but low capabilities, also "*Clandestine Unit*", where it is basically the other way around, is within the range when it comes to plausibility. To some extent the worst-case projection "*Trojan Horse*" (high intentionality and high capabilities) is also thinkable. Gradually, the interplay with and the intensity of the other identified key factors influence the development within the scope of McJihad to a veritable degree. Therefore, this projection is unstable and relatively uncertain.

3   *Transnational Networks ("Regional Networks"/"Local Cells")*

With regards to Transnational Networks, a similar set of different probability options concerning the drafted projections applies. The most likely variant as of now is that of "*Regional Networks*" with a distinct level of motivation to internationalize, but limited capacities to engage properly. Even smaller network structures preferably recourse to trans-border cooperation and attempt to increase their operational influence, as e.g. the intense transnational activities (Germany, Switzerland, Balkans) prior to the Viennese attack of November 2020 suggest. This notwithstanding, it is conceivable, that "*Local Cells*" may also become the most likely projection for Europe in the medium run. This could be the case if regional ambitions of jihadist networks are limited by local CT initiatives and operations. Even though capabilities exist, they strategically refrain from staging projected attacks. Such a dynamic heavily depends on external factors such as counter measures by governments and regional conditions.

4   *Conflict-Terror-Nexus ("Local Network"/"Spillover")*

As it relates to the *Conflict-Terror-Nexus*, the intention to attack is contrasted with the degree of transnational networking. It can be seen as a contextual key factor that is clearly associated with that of transnational networks, as set out above. The main difference is the orientation of intentionality. If motivation is directed toward plotting and staging terrorist attacks and ideologically draws upon conflicts in the Muslim world, then it will be summarized under this proposition. When it comes to the projections, there is a strong tendency toward that of "*Local Network*". This concerns both the sphere of impact but also that of probability. Accordingly, the entity's desire to organize an attack is primarily rooted in a local context and less connected with conflicts abroad. A vast majority of jihadist attacks in the West have been rooted in the closer environment of the site. However, the jihadist narrative of revenge for conflicts involving the political sphere of Islam plays a rather subsidiary role. Against the backdrop of all this, the "*Spillover*" projection that significantly adds this dimension to the violent ambitions seems likely, provided that both propaganda activities and real capabilities go hand in hand.

5   *Homebounds ("Repression")*

The projection "*Repression*", basically substantiated in a low border permeability and simultaneous intense networking is for different reasons the most likely outlook variant among the key factor homebound jihadists. Both the rigid border regimes accompanying European Covid-19 policies as well as counterterrorism measures targeting the phenomenon of homebound foreign terrorist fighters, are a strong facilitator of repression. Any purposeful attempts of former FTFs to penetrate or infiltrate their citizenship country are suppressed by authorities. However, this may quickly change due to fiscal necessities or dynamics regarding the pandemic that render such a strict access-strategy obsolete. Also, a shift in attention, e.g., a stronger focus on right-wing-extremism, may contribute to a strengthening of jihadist ambitions to re- and allocate their former comrades and include them in strategic planning. To a certain degree, the projection "*Second Wave*" (high border permeability-low networking) is still among the possible, albeit of a limited probability given a potential loose border regime, since this mainly refers to the Schengen area and no substantial changes in terms of less strict border controls are to be expected there.

6 *Hybrid Radicalization ("Jihadi Bandwagoning")*

Taking into consideration the extremely fluid transitions between each projection emerging from the key factor "hybrid radicalization", here the decision to focus on one specific foresight option has been narrow. Without doubt the preference for "*Jihadi Bandwagoning*" (radicalization high to Islam-low within Islam) was not as analytically clear as those regarding the other key factors in this trend scenario. Yet the European dynamics of transnational terrorism in the past decade advocate a tendency toward this projection, particularly taking into consideration the key factor McJihad, as well as developments in the field of low-level terrorism. This is well intended. Lose franchise networks dynamics smoothly correspond with this form of radicalization and, reciprocally are directly connected with each other. Gangster jihadists are a result of this radicalization to Islamism as well as the system of McJihad is genetic for any form of jihadist violence involving this typology of entrepreneurs and perpetrators. Whereas homegrowns predominantly seem to follow the radicalization path of this category, homebounds are generically rather prone to radicalization within Islam- meaning the "classic" radicalization subsumed in the projections under "*Mosque-Clique*". Conversely, it is entirely possible that these two types, far from being exclusive, could merge and support radicalization patterns, including both methods and ways. As a worst case projection, that would encompass a convergent (thus hybrid) form of radicalization according to what has been called "*Paris 2015*" in this analysis. In a nutshell for the time being, however, the trend scenario sticks to the projection "*Jihadi Bandwagoning*", as currently the majority of extremist supporters may be classified according to this analytic pattern.

7 *Virtualization ("Matrix")*

Last but not least, given the fact that extremists all over the world take advantage of the pluriverse capabilities that virtualization, i.e. the exploitation of cyber-related technologies and services, offers, one may automatically assume the worst case. And even more so, tactical sophistication similarly, the desire and the ability to digitally operate along the value chain of extremist violence are permanently growing. We are already amidst the "*Matrix*", a virtual high performance projection that goes hand in hand with the ability to systematically conduct cyber-operations. Again, virtualization is the bond that keeps all the other key factors more or less together. Radicalization is driven by virtual activities, where it reaches a majority of potential followers. Social media and communication platforms offer a hub, where extremists communicate, recruit and disperse propaganda (including the concerted exploitation of conflicts in the Muslim world) - this refers to both homebounds and homegrowns. Any transnational activity involves a virtual communication or exchange. McJihad is the result of going virtual and spread by digital natives. Finally, the low-level terrorism is fueled by clandestine online sources, where instruction manuals and blueprints for attacks exist. The only inhibiting force could be that of security bodies improving their counter- and surveillance measures. Given these measures, that might be considered as the only restriction that could point toward the "*Hi-Low*"- projection. In essence, focusing on Europe, these jihadi-digital natives have managed to acquire substantial skills and are ready to use them in order to put jihadist violence into effect.

Conclusion

The future projections derived from the seven most prominent key factors of continuing FSC-analysis point toward different possible developments in each sphere (low-level-scenarios, McJihad, transnationalization, conflict-terror-nexus, homebounds, hybrid radicalization, virtualization). Being centered on the conjunction of intention and capabilities, each projection has been carefully weighted against these two variables (or others if they apply). Furthermore, the probability of each projection, as well as the potential impact have been evaluated. Without doubt, most of these key factors and respective scenarios are connected with each other. The nexus between jihadist transnational aspirations, the recourse on local conflicts in the Islamic world, the influx of homebound jihadists and new forms of Islamist radicalization cannot be separated from each other. On the contrary, they have to be all taken into account in a conclusive scheme that the author holistically describes as "hybrid jihad" in the sense of a trend scenario. This clearly indicates the interdependence and inevitability of certain developments centered on the seven key factors. However, it concedes and anticipates alternative foresight projections that culminate into one single horizon. Convergence is the driving force and the essential criterion that characterizes different aspects of transnational terrorism. Be it radicalization within Islam or toward Islamism, or the interplay between homebound and homegrown jihadists, the variation of terrorist combat tactics and *modi operandi* or the oscillation between real measures and virtual activities-pretty much any recent development of jihadist terrorism is centered on that convergent dynamic. We are facing an unprecedented structural phenomenological change that requires a tailored methodological approach in order to make sense of it. In essence, transnational terrorism has morphed into a multifaceted phenomenon with diverse options and different possible developments. Drawing upon the AI-based algorithms of FSC, any such analysis becomes more creative and substantial. Defining future projections is a highly innovative process, where analytical thinking is challenged by the necessity to literally think beyond the boundaries of the empirical safe ground. Some of the projections may, at a first glance seem rather unlikely or constructed. Without doubt, even though they are based upon expert assessments emerging from contributions in this edition and earlier volumes, some projections still bear the risk of uncertainty and unpredictability. Additionally, the selection of different development options or the consequential judgment could cause some dissent among scholars. Anyhow, within the framework of foresight analysis, it is the intellectual challenge to still think of constellations that at least superficially seem beyond imagination. Adhering to analytic commonplaces and walking along paths that have been hiked too many times before is no big deal. Perhaps this trend-scenario provides some thought-provoking impulse. Reflecting its work-in-progress-character, this will be further elaborated on and advanced in the following volume. In a next step, "Hybrid Jihad" is going to be examined in the context of the surrounding strategic field of transnational terrorism (e.g. conflicts in the euro-strategic environment), both regarding its manifestations and reciprocal influence. Consistently, the key trends defining the continuing development will be subject to a monitoring and reassessment process.

Notes

1 See Stockhammer, Nicolas (2023). *Key Trends in Transnational Terrorism. A Software-Based Key Factor Foresight Analysis*, in Part IV of this volume.
2 Goertz, Stefan (2017). *Der Neue Terrorismus. Neue Akteure, Strategien, Taktiken und Mittel.* Wiesbaden: Springer VS; Nesser, Petter (2018). *Islamist Terrorism in Europe.* Oxford: Oxford University Press; Nesser, Petter (2020). "*Introducing the Jihadi Plots in Europe Dataset (JPED).*" Draft Manuscript, cited by

Hegghammer, Thomas / Ketchley, Neil (2021). *Plots, Attacks, and the Measurement of Terrorism,* (Preprint), available at: https://osf.io/preprints/socarxiv/t72yj/ (accessed June 15, 2021).

3 See Nesser, Petter. *Foiled Versus Launched Terror Plots: Some Lessons Learned,* in Part IV of this volume.

4 See Hegghammer, Thomas (Sept/Oct 2021). *Resistance is futile. The war on terror supercharged state power,* in: Foreign Affairs, 100:5, p. 51.

5 Goertz, Stefan (2020). *Terrorismusabwehr. Zur Aktuellen Bedrohung Durch den Islamistischen Terrorismus in Deutschland und Europa.* Wiesbaden: Springer VS, p. 24.

6 Hegghammer (2021). p. 51.

7 https://www.welt.de/politik/deutschland/article158157889/Wie-der-IS-seine-Attentaeter-im-Westen-fernsteuert.html (accessed June 15, 2021).

8 Ganor, Boaz (2015). *Global Alert: The Rationality of Modern Islamist Terrorism and the Challenge to the Liberal Democratic World.* New York, NY: Columbia University Press, p. 94.

9 In 2008, on 26 November, 9 terrorists attacked the Taj Mahal Hotel, Oberoi Hotel and Nariman House, along with the main railway terminal, a Jewish cultural center, a café frequented by foreigners, a cinema house, and two hospitals in Mumbai killing almost 200 people; about 300 were seriously injured in these three places. It took three days for NSG commandos to overcome these terrorists. In the three days long fight, the commandos were able to kill 8 terrorists and captured one injured one.

10 Middle East- expert Bruce Riedel has published several articles or comments on that aspect: Riedel, Bruce (2009). *The Mumbai Massacre and its implications for America and South Asia,* in: Journal of International Affairs, FALL/WINTER 2009, 63:1, (Pakistan & Afghanistan: Domestic Pressures and Regional Threats), pp. 111–126; Riedel, Bruce (2008). *'A Nightmare We Cannot Afford in the 21st Century',* Der Spiegel, available at: https://www.spiegel.de/international/world/terror-expert-and-obama-advisor-bruce-riedel-a-nightmare-we-cannot-afford-in-the-21st-century-a-595148.html (accessed June 20, 2021); Riedel, Bruce (2015). *Modeled on Mumbai? Why the 2008 India Attack is the Best Way to Understand Paris,* Markaz Blog, Brookings Institution, available at: https://www.brookings.edu/blog/markaz/2015/11/14/modeled-on-mumbai-why-the-2008-india-attack-is-the-best-way-to-understand-paris/ (accessed June 20, 2021).

11 See Stockhammer, Nicolas (2023). *Introduction to Combined Expert Contributions: The Case of Hybrid Terrorism– Systemic Lessons from Recent European Plots,* in Part I of this volume.

12 Sageman, Marc (2008). *Leaderless Jihad: Terror Networks in the Twenty-First Century.* Philadelphia: University of Pennsylvania Press, preface VII.

13 Makarenko, Tamara / Mesquita, Michael (2014). *Categorising the crime–terror nexus in the European Union,* in: Global Crime, 15:3–4, pp. 259–274.

14 Llan, Jonathan / Sandberg, Sveinung (2019). *How 'gangsters' become jihadists: Bourdieu, criminology and the crime–terrorism nexus,* in: European Journal of Criminology, 16:3, pp. 278–294; BBC. *Brussels Attacks: Molenbeek's Gangster Jihadists,* available at: https://www.bbc.com/news/magazine-35890960 (accessed June 20, 2021).

15 Crenshaw, Martha (2020). "*Rethinking Transnational Terrorism: An Integrated Approach,*" Peaceworks (No. 158), United States Institute of Peace (February), p. 4., available at: https://www.usip.org/publications/2020/02/rethinking-transnational-terrorism-integrated-approach (accessed June 20, 2021).

16 Ibid p. 4.

17 For instance Vidino, Lorenzo / Marone, Francesco / Entenmann, Eva (2017). "*Fear Thy Neighbor: Radicalization and Jihadist Attacks in the West,*" Milan, Italy: Joint Program on Extremism, ICCT-The Hague, ISPI Report.

18 https://www.dw.com/en/vienna-terror-attack-police-search-suspects-homes-in-germany/a-58184610 (accessed July 14, 2021).

19 See Stockhammer, Nicolas (2023). *Key Trends in Transnational Terrorism. A Software-Based Key Factor Foresight Analysis,* in Part IV of this volume.

20 Hegghammer (2021). p. 52.

21 Nesser, Petter (2006). *Jihadism in Western Europe after the invasion of Iraq: Tracing motivational influences from the Iraq War on jihadist terrorism in Western Europe,* in: Studies in Conflict & Terrorism, 29:4, pp. 323–342.

22 ibid, p. 324.

23 Bindner, Laurence (2018). "*Jihadists' Grievance Narratives against France,*" ICCT Policy Brief February 2018, p. 5, available at: https://www.icct.nl/sites/default/files/import/publication/Bindner-Jihadists-Grievance-Narratives-Against-France-February2018.pdf (accessed July 14, 2021).

24 Clapper, James R. (Director of National Intelligence) (February 9, 2016)."*Statement for the Record: Worldwide Threat Assessment of the US Intelligence Community,*" Senate Armed Services Committee, pp. 4–5.

25 See Sadik, Giray (2023). *Terrorism and Hybrid Threats: Analyzing Common Characteristics and Constraints for Countermeasures*, in Part IV of this volume.

26 Peter Braun (2019). *"Fighting 'Men in Jeans' in the Grey Zone Between Peace and War,"* NDC Policy Brief No: 18, NATO Defense College.

27 See Hoffman, Bruce. *Jihadist Violence. New Terrorist Actors/Groups Emerging. Who Will be the Key Players in the Next Decade?* in Part I of this volume.

28 Dettmer, Jamie (2021). *"France, Britain Fearful of Resurgent Jihadist Threat After Lockdown,"* Voice of America News, available at: https://www.voanews.com/europe/france-britain-fearful-resurgent-jihadist-threat-after-lockdown (accessed July 14, 2021).

29 See Stockhammer, Nicolas (2023). *Key Trends in Transnational Terrorism. A Software-Based Key Factor Foresight Analysis*, in Part IV of this volume.

30 https://digital.freitag.de/2316/dritte-welle-des-dschihad (accessed September 20, 2021).

31 Makarenko, Tamara / Mesquita, Michael (2014). *Categorising the crime–terror nexus in the European Union*, in: Global Crime, 15:3–4, pp. 259–274; Ruggiero, Vincenzo (2019). *Hybrids: On the crime–terror nexus*, in: International Journal of Comparative and Applied Criminal Justice, 43:1, pp. 49–60.

32 Aslan, Ednan et al. (2017). *Islamistische Radikalisierung. Biografische Verläufe im Kontext der religiösen Sozialisation und des radikalen Milieus*, available at: https://iits.univie.ac.at/fileadmin/user_upload/p_iits/Pictures_colleagues/radikalisierung_2017_07_19_onlineversion_einzelseiten.pdf (accessed September 20, 2021).

33 D'Amato, Silvia (2019). *Islamization of criminal behaviour: The path to terrorism? Terrorist threat and crime in French counterterrorism policy-formulation*, in: European Journal of Criminology, 16:3, pp. 332–350; Ruggiero, Vincenzo (2019): *Hybrids: on the crime–terror nexus*, in: International Journal of Comparative and Applied Criminal Justice, 43:1, pp. 49–60.

34 See Stockhammer, Nicolas (2023). *Key Trends in Transnational Terrorism. A Software-Based Key Factor Foresight Analysis*, in Part IV of this volume.

35 Azzam, Maha (2007). *The radicalization of Muslim communities in Europe: Local and global dimensions,* in: Brown Journal of World Affairs, 13, p. 123.

36 McCauley, Clark / Moskalenko, Sophia (2008). *"Mechanisms of political radicalization: pathways toward terrorism,"* in: Terrorism and Political Violence, 20, pp. 418–428.

37 Neumann, Peter R / Stockhammer, Nicolas (2021). *Vorläufige Lektionen vom Terror in Wien,* EICTP Policy Brief 1/February 2021, available at: https://www.eictp.eu/wp-content/uploads/2021/01/FINAL_EICTP-Policy-Brief-Terror-and-lessons-learnt.pdf (accessed September 20, 2021).

38 See Stockhammer, Nicolas (2023). *Key Trends in Transnational Terrorism. A Software-Based Key Factor Foresight Analysis*, in Part IV of this volume.

39 Hegghammer (2021). p. 50

40 ibid, p. 50.

43

TERRORIST THREATS POST-COVID-19

Raffaelo Pantucci

It is too early at this stage to draw any definitive conclusions about the impact COVID will have upon terrorism, but some early sketches can be drawn of problems which appear to be exacerbated. The causal link to COVID is hard to prove. But there has been a noticeable shift in various terrorist ideologies in COVID's shadow, which merit a stock-take. The aim of this article is to dig into these shifts and try to offer some broad thoughts about the threat in terms of its longer-term trajectory..

What Have Terrorists Said about COVID-19?

As a starting point, it is useful to explore what terrorist groups have actually said and done about COVID. In the early days of the virus, groups were commenting on it in much the same way as everyone else was. In some cases, they drew the ideas into their larger conspiracies, seeking to explain it as part of a master plan to destroy the world and advance their ideology. Less apocalyptic responses focused instead on the practical things that groups could do to help populations fend off the virus. This form of social services was an attempt to win over hearts and minds to demonstrate how governments were failing. In many cases it built on a history of offering social services to their communities and merely served to further endear them. And yet others instead chose to make the strategically sensible point that the net result was likely to be less attention by security forces and distracted authorities, therefore offering a useful moment to strike or take territory.[1]

There was also considerable discussion around the idea of trying to weaponize the virus, though the evidence around this happening has been very thin. Extremist forums churned out propaganda about what could be done, but very few actually moved forward with their plans. One plan was dramatically uncovered in Tunisia, where a preacher was telling his followers to cough or sneeze on security forces in advance of an attack.[2] For the most part, security services have not reported much change in the threat picture as a result of COVID.[3] In the United States some people have been prosecuted under terrorism legislation for threatening to actively spread the virus, though it is not clear there was any political motive behind their act.[4]

Having said all of this, there has been a noticeable increase in the volume of noise around terrorist groups,[5] though it is not clear this has actually resulted in an increase in violence. While metrics are hard to get, using the data offered by the Armed Conflict Location & Event Data

DOI: 10.4324/9781003326373-49

Project (ACLED), it would appear that all of the conflict and political violence metrics that they follow are down year after year across the world, and in particular in regions where terrorist groups are dominant.[6] This is not an entirely surprising outcome. Given the general lockdowns and difficulties in traveling, it has become harder to practically mobilize in the same way as before. And while online activity has made the spread and virulence of extremist ideas and disinformation alongside it easier, it is not yet in a position to replace the physical act of violence.

But a lack of violence does not unfortunately necessarily equate to the absence of a problem. The underlying issues that can cause radicalization can take considerable time to turn into a visible terrorist threat. And the current immediate news environment can telescope our ability to properly assess the timeline required for problems to develop. As a result of the constant threats publicized by extremist groups ialongside the simultaneous constant reporting of threats globally, it can be harder to assess longer-term changes and patterns. The constant coverage gives an impression of an accelerating threat. This results in an expectation that threats materialize immediately, when in fact they can take time to mature.

This is not an entirely new phenomenon, nor is it one that is exclusive to the study of terrorism and political violence. In general, societal expectations around issues are wildly accelerated by a relentless news cycle that requires a constant digest of new information and news. The net result is a lack of patience in tracing consequences and the impact of specific actions. From an analytical perspective, it can make it more complicated to appropriately describe problems and threats, as the expectation is often that causal impact will be rapid and immediate. In fact, problems often take time to develop and ultimately articulate themselves in violence. The confusion that this reality creates is augmented in a static situation like that created by COVID-19, which has brought vast sections of human activity around the world to a standstill. Objectively, standing back, it is hard to assess that COVID-19 has materially changed for the better many situations that were affected by terrorism;, in fact, it can appear that the longer-term situation has likely been made worse.

A Current Stocktake

A complete overview of all terrorist threats globally for such a short paper would be by its nature incomplete and incorrect. Consequently, the author will focus on two dominant threat ideologies (violent Islamists and the extreme right wing) and provide a brief overview of their current status, with some broad analysis of how things are advancing in the shadow of COVID.

Within the violent Islamist cohort, al-Qaeda and ISIS affiliated organizations are the dominant representatives. And in both cases, an assessment with relation to the impact of COVID on them is fairly limited at this stage. Both groups continue to thrive in their different ways, though they appear to be facing issues related to their respective broader operating environments rather than anything linked specifically to COVID. Outside rhetoric, at this stage it is very difficult to find many studies that have conclusively pointed to any major change in behavior.[7]

For example, al-Qaeda recently marked the 19th anniversary of the September 11, 2001 attack. This was marked across al-Qaeda publications and media channels, though the outputs were for the most part repetitive of previous years and revealed little that was new. The key message from leader Ayman al Zawahiri was an attack on an Al Jazeera documentary made about the attack.[8] This reflects a broader stasis around the group, which, while not defunct, has largely faded from its high point of the past few decades. A useful overview of the organization by BBC Monitoring's Mina Al Lami showed how its affiliates in Mali and Somalia are its best beacons of success, while its other affiliates are under considerable pressure.[9]

Similarly, while ISIS continues to exist as a global organization, it is very different from the organization which dominated the airwaves during its peak years when controlling territory in Syria and Iraq. Its core entity in the Levant is a shrunken version of its former self, but it is gradually making gains on the ground, in Iraq in particular.[10] Its global network of affiliates remains loose, with different groups variously showing a greater or lesser degree of effectiveness and connection to the core. Some are reduced in effectiveness, while others appear ascendant.[11] As an overall organization, however, it appears to be in a stage of being an irritant in most of the environments in which it is present, rather than being the existential threat it was previously when controlling vast pieces of territory in the Levant.

This is certainly not to say that either organization is completely down. Key for the current paper, however, is the fact that neither group appears to have been impacted particularly by COVID. Rather, both persist on roughly the same trajectory that they did before the outbreak of the virus. The threat from them remains relatively constant, with some parts of the threat rising and others falling. The key point, however, is persistence, with security agencies still prioritising the threat from violent Islamist actors.[12]

More dynamic and impacted to a greater degree in some ways by the virus is the extreme right wing. A threat that was ascendant across Europe, North America and select parts of Asia, (Australia and New Zealand) before the outbreak of COVID-19, white supremacist terrorism was something that has been an escalating concern for some time. [13] However, in the shadow of the virus, the problem appears to have mushroomed in a number of different directions. Most prominently in the United States there has been a growth in prominence of a number of different groups, ideas and violence. Whilst their individual strains might be slightly different, there are key themes that appear to tie many of them together. From the anti-state Boogaloo Bois who are expecting an impending civil war, the now-prominent Proud Boys (a drinking club dedicated to fighting leftist protestors), to more classic far-right groups stoking race war or the constellation of new groups clustering around aspects of the far right like the Incel movement, QAnon conspiracy theorists or angry online communities gathering on sites like 8kun, 4chan or Gab, the world of the far right in the United States has achieved greater prominence recently.

Their presence has been exacerbated in recent times, though it is not clear whether this is related to the virus, or more simply American politics which have moved in a deeply divisive direction under President Trump. His active inflaming of racial tensions and anger toward left-wing protestors feeds the extreme right, groups of which he has actively promoted from his position as President of the United States of America. During the first Presidential debate, his comments about the Proud Boys group quite specifically brought prominence to them[14], while his earlier tweeting has brought international prominence to a far-right British group, Britain First.[15]

But he is not solely responsible for this rising right-wing. Under the auspices of COVID, some aspects of the acceleration of extreme right anger can be linked to the expansion of the state, something that has been happening in some parts of the country in response to COVID-19.[16] And there has been a growth in conspiracy theories linked to COVID-19 response – like fears around vaccines or the impact of 5G technology – which have often stoked some of the growing constellation of groups gathered on the extreme right.[17] This will be covered again later, but they are clearly playing into long-standing US narratives of an overbearing federal state which is seeking to disenfranchise groups, removing their guns, infringing on their liberties and generally becoming a menace to the free State as defined in the US constitution. Such Patriot or Sovereign Citizen groups have long been a feature of the American discourse, but recent political clashes, somewhat exacerbated by the further expansion of the state in response to COVID and polarized political narratives, have strengthened their hold amongst fringe communities.

In Europe, a more classic extreme right tends to dominate, with racist networks flourishing in the shadows of a growth of far-right political movements and a polarized debate around immigration. This phenomenon has been developing for some time, with Germany facing the National Socialist Underground (NSU) in the late 2000s, while angry protest groups like the United Kingdom's English Defence League (EDL) spawned imitators across Europe. Annual Europol reports point to a growing extreme right-wing threat in Europe, while individual security forces point to disrupted plots.[18] Renaud Camus' totemic text *The Great Replacement* has captured a particular mood across the continent[19], while mass violence associated with such ideas can be found earlier in Anders Behring Breivik's 2011 attack in Oslo and on Utoya Island.[20] Europe has also seem an emergence of conspiracy theorists, QAnon[21] and Incels,[22] and a growing rumbling of anti-government anger similar to that in the US.[23]

But similar to the narrative on the violent Islamist side, what has been happening on the extreme right is in many ways merely an extension of what was going on before. Extreme right-wing terrorism had been a growing phenomenon for the past few years and its fragmentation had started even before the outbreak of COVID-19 and the lockdowns that followed. For some countries, the return to dominance of the extreme right was a reflection of a balance of threat that existed pre-September 11, 2001.[24]

Future Threats

COVID has, however, changed how society is functioning and this will have some sort of effect on terrorist threats. In particular, the change to society that is going to be wrought in the longer time by the virus or existing issues whose impact was accelerated by the virus will have some effect on terrorist threats.

As stated at the outset, it is at this stage quite difficult to measure the exact causal effect, but some trends appear to be accelerated in the shadow of the virus, which points to how this moment might impact the longer-term threat picture. While life is returning to some semblance of normality, the constant fear of new waves of the virus and the consequent disruption to society that follows continues to hang over things. The economic damage done by the virus has still not been calculated and may be being artificially suppressed temporarily due to economic stimulus programs. But their impact will be felt in many different ways in terms of government budgets both at home and abroad. The abrupt shift online is likely to permanently change some industries and eliminate others. The effect on the workforces will be dramatic and abrupt, creating potentially large unemployed or underemployed communities.

The potential impact on political violence and terrorism is hard to gauge, but three areas stand out as potential spaces in which political violence may grow in the future, in part as a result of the impact of COVID-19 ravaging the planet. In many ways, these are also extensions of previous problems, but their acceleration against other trends impacted by COVID is potentially going to create greater problems than might otherwise have emerged.

A Web Spun by COVID

One of the biggest winners of COVID-19 is the Internet. With the advent of lockdowns and working from home, people found themselves increasingly spending time online. The impact of this on terrorism is complicated and goes in many different directions. In the first instance, there is the impact on online radicalization. Something that used to be seen as a peripheral aspect of the problem, with the majority of radicalization still requiring physical contact with other extremists, has, in the last few years, seen a growth in cases involving individuals who are choosing to move toward terrorist ideas and then into action solely on the basis of contacts or material they have found online.

In some cases, this is simply a shift online of what used to happen offline. The phenomenon of remote direction, as popularized by ISIS, is a shifting of the relationship between group and individual attackers online. Whereas previously, individuals would head to a training camp and then be directed to launch an attack back home, now the approach was to simply direct people from a distance to launch their attacks using the many encrypted applications that exist. Individuals like Junaid Hussain[25] or Rachid Kassim[26] became infamous for the networks of young westerners they directed from ISIS held territory to launch terrorist attacks.

But more recently this has developed differently, where people are now seemingly ready to launch attacks based on ideas, they have found online with little to no connection with the actual group itself. In some cases, the individuals are not even joining a group. In the case of something like Incel or QAnon, they are simply following an online phenomenon or chat group and stirring themselves onto violence. The connection between terrorist violence and organized networks and hierarchies is shifting. This has been described as "post-organizational" terrorist plotting, where groups, their links and structures are no longer as clear as they used to be.[27] While structured organizations still exist, the growth of ideologies online, which people can piece together themselves, connect with as imprecisely as they would like, and ultimately interpret in any way that they would like, has created a range of problems that lie beyond our current interpretations of political violence.

The expression of this can be found in how security services find themselves talking about threats. In the United Kingdom, there has been an increase in the number of individuals who are radicalising with an ideology, which appears to reflect a mix of contradictory issues and ideas that are being bracketed by the Home Office as being "mixed, unstable or unclear".[28] In the United States, terrorism is now handled by the Department for Homeland Security (DHS) alongside "Targeted Threats".[29] In Canada they talk of "ideologically motivated violent extremism".[30] The key point is that there is an increase of individuals who are acting out in a manner that is reminiscent of terrorism, and yet, when some investigation is done into their ideological motivation, it is unclear exactly what it is. It is even possible to question whether this should properly be called terrorism or whether it is in fact simply an expression of personal anger using the vernacular of terrorism to give it greater meaning.[31]

Whatever the case, this cohort of individuals is a growing phenomenon. There are a number of individuals who are becoming involved in terrorist activity who are suffering from mental health issues, others that are being identified as having autism spectrum disorders and a growing proportion of very young individuals being drawn into violent activity. Again, absolute numbers are hard to identify, but the number of studies looking into the question has grown, while security agencies have increasingly expressed concerns. And while none of these phenomena are new, there is some evidence that the cases are being exacerbated as a result of the lockdown because of COVID. In the United Kingdom, there is the case of the 14-year-old boy who reportedly became fascinated with ISIS videos while stuck at home in lockdown, and started to make bombs off models he found online (he was ultimately cleared by a court).[32] In Spain, a radical, who had been under observation by security services, was arrested after authorities started to grow concerned about the fact that he was radicalizsing further and moving toward action during lockdown.[33] Finally, there have been lower level cases, such as individuals who were going through periods of probation and suddenly found themselves underemployed and then turned back to online activity.

And this roster accounts only for those of violent Islamist inclination. There is a growing concern around these issues for other ideologies as well. Focusing on the United Kingdom, there has been the recent disturbing case of a deeply disturbed man arrested on charges relating to left-wing terrorist activity who committed suicide while incarcerated.[34] Online extreme right networks in Europe have been found to have been led by very young teenagers.[35] There have been Incels found in Europe making explosives, including very young teenagers who have been identified as suffering from autism spectrum disorders.[36] And then there is the confusing phenomena of very young individuals whose ideology appears to be a self-created mix of ideas drawing on a wide pool of extreme material they find online.

Such individuals who are self-assembling extremist ideas are often drawn toward conspiracy theories or dark holes on the Internet, where such ideas can lurk. And the strength and potency of such online conspiracies have only grown – enhanced by the uncertainty and instability that COVID and geopolitics have created. Conspiracy theories like fears of the dangers of 5G, and the threats from vaccines, and super-conspiracies like those underpinning QAnon about dark cabals of paedophiles ruling the world are all now circulating online amongst communities of people who are spending ever larger volumes of time online on social media. While work has gone into trying to change or break the algorithms, companies are still struggling to completely control them, and often these ideas grow in spaces beyond the big social media companies.

All of this is further exacerbated by active government disinformation campaigns that are working to stir up tensions online. In part this are directed against elections, but it is also simply a way of causing trouble. Sometimes it is not even clear the degree to which they are directed by states, rather than angry groups or bored children. But whatever the case, their impact is felt much more deeply, partly as a result of the general polarization that is taking place in politics, but also because of the fact that an ever increasing volume of people are spending time online.

The Left, Luddism and Environmentalism

Tracking all of this forwards, the time spent online is not only something which is transforming our methods of communication and absorption of information, but it is further likely to have longer-term repercussions on the shape of our economies and workforces. As lockdowns and restrictions continue, entire industries are suffering and are likely to close down. Physical retail, already in retreat thanks to the boom in online markets, is likely to take a further beating, while the food and beverage industry is going to continue to suffer for some time to come. The fundamental point is that a growing number of these services will shift online in some capacity, meaning that the physical jobs needed in shops or restaurants to serve people will not necessarily exist anymore. This will create a growing community of unemployed people, or people who end up under-employed or forced to take even more menial jobs. It is hard to gauge exactly what the volume of this shift will be, but it might start to inspire a backlash against the technology and firms that are abetting this shift.

Luddism, a concept first advanced in the 19th century by textile workers angry at the advance of modern technology that was rendering their jobs redundant, could make a comeback. This is not new. Theodore Kaczyinski, the infamous Unabomber, was an earlier Luddite whose anger at technology's dominance of society was something which led him to launch a one-man letter bombing campaign from 1978–1995 from a remote cabin in Montana.[37] His manifesto, "Industrial Society and Its Future" was published in September 1995 in the Washington Post and started with the premise that "the industrial revolution and its consequences have been a disaster for the human race."[38] He may have been twenty years early, but many of the issues he raises in his manifesto are relevant today. As we enter an ever more interconnected and online world, not only are we likely to see more people reacting negatively to it, but we will also see more people becoming disenfranchised as a result. Stories have already emerged about the horrors of working for some of the big online retail companies,[39] and these are likely to become more numerous in COVID's wake as we see them assume an even more dominant place within our society.

It is not only a modern form of Luddism that may emerge in reaction. Many of the ideas rejecting society or large industrial take over are reminiscent of ideas emanating from the left – where capitalism's imposing structures crush individuals in advance of profit. These fundamental ideas are often appropriated by groups on both sides. Consequently the massive expansion of some companies, of an Internet which is controlled by large firms and which is ultimately disempowering people and eliminating employment, has the potential to be attractive as an adversary to those on the far left as well. Anti-globalization groups that used to have prominence in the pre-September 11 world,[40] have in the past two decades been dominated by a terrorist narrative, which focuses on the threat from violent Islamist groups and latterly those on the extreme right-wing. The left has receded as a dominant threat, notwithstanding President Trump's declarations otherwise.[41] Yet, within the chaos wrought by COVID-19, it is possible to see a re-emergence of elements of a far-left threat, angry at the rampant far right and seeing inequality deepening.

Atop this, issues around environmentalism may have been pushed to one side due to COVID-19 concerns, but the problems remain. From a governmental perspective, there is still a need to resolve them, though the pace of change is one that is not happening fast enough for a number of activists. Whilst violence associated with the environmental movement is rare, the fall-out from COVID and the likely de-prioritization of environmental issues in favor of healthcare and repairing stricken economies, may stir more violence. An interesting phenomenon of the past few years has in fact been the mainstreaming of environmental anger into other ideologies. In some cases, like al Shabaab's banning of plastic bags, it appears banal and almost comical,[42] but in others, like the attackers in El Paso and Christchurch declaring they are eco-fascists,[43] it shows how environmental ideas can be absorbed into more mainstream violent ideologies in a way that enhances the narrative. This suggests, that for environmental issues to become a terrorist problem, they do not necessarily have to emerge solely from the environmental movement's mainstream or fringe. Played against the broader backdrop of instability and likely environmental degradation, which will continue in the post-COVID-19 world, it is possible such narratives will gain greater salience.

China

A final threat, which is likely to rise further, accelerated by COVID-19, is the growth of China as a target for violence and terrorism. Already a trend that was visible pre-COVID-19, it was something which was likely in part a product of China's rise to a preeminent place on the international stage, as well as a reaction to China's domestic and foreign policy. At home, the treatment of its Uighur minority has long spurred angry rhetoric against China, but it has generated surprisingly little terrorism. Domestic violence within China associated with Uighur extremism is often really expressions of anger at the state, with only some incidents justifiably considered terrorism.[44] China's heavy-handed crackdown has largely suppressed these instances of violence at home, but there have been a few abroad associated with Uighur networks.[45] More dominant has been the growing targeting of Chinese nationals and interests by groups elsewhere – more often than not local networks rather than international ones.

For example, in Pakistan, China has increasingly become the target of Baluchi and Sindhi separatists. While there is a consistent level of concern around violent Islamist groups within the country, they have for the most part not targeted the Chinese specifically.[46] When they have hit Chinese targets, it has tended to be incidental and as part of a larger assault against foreigners or the state. In contrast, Sindhi and Baluchi groups have specifically targeted Chinese institutions and repeatedly put out messaging saying that China was their target. Similarly, in Indonesia, there may be a long history of anti-Chinese sentiment, but recently there has been a growth in specific thinking about targeting Chinese nationals within the country by violent Islamist groups. In part, they consider this retribution for the treatment of Uighurs, but it also reflects an anger toward China as an invading colonial force.[47]

This particular anger is something that is only likely to grow going forwards. Beijing will find that, as China rises to become an ever more central pillar in international affairs, it will attract as many detractors as it will supporters. And some of these detractors will be infuriated enough by Chinese behavior to want to commit acts of violence against Chinese interests. This trend is likely to be accelerated by the COVID-19 moment the world is going through. Beijing's unapologetic response to its links to the origin of the virus, subsequent aggressive public relations diplomacy captured under the moniker "wolf warrior"[48] and a forceful posture on the world stage have done little to endear China to the international community.[49] All of this is likely to attract different levels of public anger, some of which is likely to articulate itself as terrorism.

In some parts of the world this has already taken something of an ugly twist with the growing targeting of East Asian nationals in racist attacks.[50] Taken alongside the growing levels of tension toward China, this is the sort of violence that has in other contexts ended up expressing itself through violence. China and ethnic East Asians are likely to increasingly find themselves potential targets of violence going forwards.

Conclusions

Much of this is of course speculative at this point. The world is still battling COVID with no clear timeline for when we will able to talk about being in a post-COVID world. And the longer the world suffers from COVID, the deeper the consequences touched upon in this paper are likely to be. The societal divisions, the economic damage, and the transformed economies and societies are all issues where impact is already visible, and this will only become more acute as more time passes. Society will change and this will have some sort of knock-on effect on the world of terrorism and political violence.

It will likely take some time, even years, before a clear causal link will be possible between the current events and the longer-term changes that might take place in terms of politically motivated violence and terrorism. Some of these effects might in fact be mere accelerations of what was already happening. This is something that is visible already in the growing prominence of the extreme right. Its rise was already visible pre-COVID, with the pattern tracing back years. But in the shadow of the disease and the societal, political and economic impact it has wrought, we are seeing its rise sped up and worsened. Of course this has to juxtaposed with the polarized political environment in Washington, DC, which has particularly amplified the noise around the far right, something that has also likely been made worse by COVID-19. The point being that separating out effects and causal links will be something that is going to be hard to measure and quantify.

One issue that is likely to change in the West in particular in the wake of COVID-19 is the role of the state in society. The massive bail-outs, new healthcare and security infrastructure that will be needed to ensure future pandemics are better managed, and the large public debt that will follow will require management. They will generate unhappiness in unexpected quarters, and in some cases, outright rejection. Given terrorism is at its root a form of anti-establishmentarianism, the massive growth of the state that is likely to result in a post-COVID world could be a key underlying issue to look at when trying to explore how terrorism might evolve in the future. This is already most prominently visible in the United States, where there is a long history of libertarian and anti-federal government activity, but it is possible that similar strains may start to emerge elsewhere. In some ways, the anti-Chinese anger that may become exacerbated is another expression of this, with China becoming such a dominant figure globally, that it is consequently attracting ire.

All of this needs to be kept in perspective of course. While COVID may have some effect on terrorism and political violence, its principal impact will most immediately and dramatically be felt in other aspects of human behavior. However, understanding how these ripples will echo in terrorism remains an important aspect to observe.

Notes

1 https://d2071andvip0wj.cloudfront.net/B004-covid-19-seven-trends.pdf
2 https://northafricapost.com/40082-terrorists-plotting-covid-19-contamination-attack-on-tunisian-security-forces-arrested.html
3 https://apcss.org/assessing-the-impact-of-the-covid-19-pandemic-on-terrorism-and-counter-terrorism-practitioner-insights/
4 https://abcnews.go.com/US/wireStory/us-charges-terror-crimes-threats-spread-virus-70052376
5 https://gnet-research.org/2020/04/27/comparing-jihadist-and-far-right-extremist-narratives-on-covid-19/
6 https://acleddata.com/#/dashboard
7 There has been considerable work, however, looking at the potential risks. For example, IPAC in Indonesia has written a number of useful papers looking at threats there: https://understandingconflict.org/en and the UN has summarized what has been happening in CT and CVE terms: https://www.un.org/securitycouncil/ctc/sites/www.un.org.securitycouncil.ctc/files/files/documents/2021/Jun/cted-paper-the-impact-of-the-covid-19-pandemic-on-counter-t_0.pdf, and finally, Abdul Basit has provided a useful summary of a number of trends across the terrorism space and the threat and opportunity it provides for terrorist organizations: https://www.tandfonline.com/doi/full/10.1080/18335330.2020.1828603
8 https://www.longwarjournal.org/archives/2020/09/zawahiri-asserts-al-qaedas-independence-in-new-message.php
9 https://www.bbc.com/news/world-54102404
10 https://www.crisisgroup.org/middle-east-north-africa/gulf-and-arabian-peninsula/iraq/when-measuring-isiss-resurgence-use-right-standard
11 ISIS Somalia has had a very bad year so far: https://public.tableau.com/profile/fddmaps#!/vizhome/SomaliaClaims/Dashboard1 while its affiliate group in Mozambique has been increasingly effective: http://www.open.ac.uk/technology/mozambique/sites/www.open.ac.uk.technology.mozambique/files/files/CEEI_Security_Brief_3.pdf
12 The US intelligence community is one prominent example: https://www.dni.gov/files/documents/Newsroom/Testimonies/20200917_HCHS_Miller_SFR_Final.pdf, though it is not clear that this applies internationally and domestically to the same degree. A recent DHS assessment pointed to an expanded White Supremacist Threat in particular at home: https://www.dhs.gov/sites/default/files/publications/2020_10_06_homeland-threat-assessment.pdf
13 Australia has recorded a particular rise: https://www.theguardian.com/australia-news/2020/sep/22/asio-reveals-up-to-40-of-its-counter-terrorism-cases-involve-far-right-violent-extremism as well as the United States: https://www.dhs.gov/sites/default/files/publications/2020_10_06_homeland-threat-assessment.pdf
14 https://edition.cnn.com/2020/09/30/politics/proud-boys-trump-debate-trnd/index.html
15 https://www.bbc.com/news/world-us-canada-42166663
16 The case of Eduardo Moreno is instructive in this regard: https://www.justice.gov/usao-cdca/pr/train-operator-port-los-angeles-charged-derailing-locomotive-near-us-navy-s-hospital
17 https://public-assets.graphika.com/reports/Graphika_Report_Covid19_Infodemic.pdf

18 file:///Users/raffaellopantucci/Downloads/european_union_terrorism_situation_and_trend_report_te-sat_2020_0.pdf

19 https://www.lemonde.fr/les-decodeurs/article/2019/03/15/la-theorie-du-grand-remplacement-de-l-ecrivain-renaud-camus-aux-attentats-en-nouvelle-zelande_5436843_4355770.html

20 https://www.bbc.com/news/world-europe-14259989

21 https://slate.com/technology/2020/09/qanon-europe-germany-lockdown-protests.html

22 https://www.telegraph.co.uk/men/the-filter/rise-women-haters-inside-dark-world-british-incels/

23 https://static1.squarespace.com/static/5a68981e914e6b64f13a443d/t/5be465b0cd8366d059af728a/1541694959474/SOURCE_D3.7_ASSR4.pdf

24 Australia is a case in point where far right violence was the dominant threat pre-9/11. Similarly, within Europe, while various separatist groups were the dominant terrorist threat, the far right was a problem that sometimes spilled into violence.

25 https://ctc.usma.edu/british-hacker-became-islamic-states-chief-terror-cybercoach-profile-junaid-hussain/

26 https://www.wsj.com/articles/how-islamic-state-weaponized-the-chat-app-to-direct-attacks-on-the-west-1476955802

27 https://www.orfonline.org/expert-speak/confronting-the-challenge-of-post-organisational-extremism/

28 https://assets.publishing.service.gov.uk/government/uploads/system/uploads/attachment_data/file/763254/individuals-referred-supported-prevent-programme-apr2017-mar2018-hosb3118.pdf

29 https://www.dhs.gov/tvtp

30 https://www.canada.ca/content/dam/csis-scrs/documents/publications/PubRep-2019-E.pdf

31 https://www.brookings.edu/blog/order-from-chaos/2020/09/22/who-is-a-terrorist-actually/; https://www.straitstimes.com/opinion/running-amok-in-an-age-of-meaningless-terror

32 https://www.bbc.com/news/uk-england-hampshire-54450013

33 https://www.catalannews.com/society-science/item/man-arrested-in-barcelona-for-allegedly-plotting-terrorist-attack

34 https://www.leeds-live.co.uk/news/leeds-news/dominic-noble-huddersfield-dies-prison-18812989

35 https://apnews.com/article/7067c03e1af0b157be7c15888cbe8c27

36 https://www.birminghammail.co.uk/news/uk-news/fantasist-obsessed-incels-jailed-over-17998017

37 https://www.fbi.gov/history/famous-cases/unabomber

38 https://www.washingtonpost.com/wp-srv/national/longterm/unabomber/manifesto.text.htm

39 https://www.theguardian.com/books/2018/mar/11/hired-six-months-undercover-in-low-wage-britain-zero-hours-review-james-bloodworth

40 https://www.theatlantic.com/business/archive/2014/01/the-dark-side-of-globalization-why-seattles-1999-protesters-were-right/282831/

41 https://www.ft.com/content/fdf5e423-4a4e-482c-8ca8-e0bf71fcfbcd, it is also worth noting that some left-wing terrorism still exists in parts of southern Europe – for example, Italy and Greece.

42 https://www.businessinsider.com/al-shabab-bans-plastic-bags-as-a-serious-threat-to-people-2018-7

43 https://www.gq.com/story/what-is-eco-fascism

44 https://raffaellopantucci.com/2014/07/24/chinas-domestic-insurgency/

45 https://www.rferl.org/a/kyrgyzstan-china-embassy-jailed/28583623.html and https://www.reuters.com/article/us-thailand-blast-idUSKBN13A0FR

46 https://www.scmp.com/news/china/diplomacy-defence/article/2160918/lesson-pakistan-suicide-attack-china-will-have-pay-high

47 https://www.scmp.com/week-asia/politics/article/3099151/indonesian-terrorists-planned-attack-shop-owners-areas-chinese

48 https://www.straitstimes.com/opinion/beware-the-spirit-of-the-wolf-warrior

49 https://www.pewresearch.org/global/2020/10/06/unfavorable-views-of-china-reach-historic-highs-in-many-countries/

50 https://www.bbc.com/news/world-us-canada-52714804

PART VII

Afghanistan, Al–Qaeda and Beyond

44

THE SECURITY SITUATION IN AFGHANISTAN AND ITS IMPLICATIONS FOR GLOBAL TERRORISM

Herfried Münkler

The great problem of coalition warfare has always been that the allies did not or could not sufficiently agree upon what goals and purposes they wanted to pursue in and with the war. In this context, purpose, according to Clausewitz' much-cited definition, answers the question of what is to be attained "with the war", while objectives provide information on what is to be attained "in the war". To develop an idea of the deployment of troops, resources and equipment required to enter the war and of how long it will take to achieve the objectives and enforce the purpose, it is necessary to find an approximately precise definition of the purposes and objectives of this war. Admittedly, the resistance to be expected from the other war party must also be taken into consideration in relation to the purposes and objectives pursued. This includes the fact that, in view of the assumed military deployment and the prospective duration of a war, the objectives and purposes will be modified, scaled back or expanded – during the preparation of a war or in the course of it. Accordingly, there is a dynamic interrelationship between the purposes and objectives on the one hand and the deployment of troops, resources and equipment – including its duration – considered necessary to fulfil these purposes and objectives on other hand.

Consequently, the fact that the size of the troops and the amount of resources and equipment deployed in Afghanistan kept changing and that the duration of the mission was extended time after time was by no means the main problem that caused the intervention to fail. The main problem was rather that these modifications took place without serious debate about the purposes and objectives pursued; instead, they were merely reactions to the changing situation in Afghanistan or due to the timeframes set by policy makers of intervention powers. This, in turn, had much to do with a disagreement between the intervention powers about the objectives and purposes of the war. Yet, a critical revision of these objectives and purposes during the mission would have inevitable called into question the entire mission because it would have been necessary to clarify retrospectively what should have been agreed upon at the beginning of the intervention – but was not agreed upon. This kind of debate should be avoided, and, for this very reason, they simply carried on as before. With the benefit of hindsight, it can be ascertained that right from the start many things went terribly wrong with the West's intervention in Afghanistan. The pictures of the disastrous withdrawal in the summer of 2021 have made this abundantly clear. If politicians subsequently claimed that the almost 20-year-long deployment of the armed

DOI: 10.4324/9781003326373-51

forces[1] had by no means been in vain, this must be examined in the light of the purposes pursued with the intervention and the objectives set for its course. In this context, it becomes clear that, from the very beginning, there was much uncertainty as to what purpose the West wanted to achieve in the Hindu Kush.

Three Possible Purposes: Dismantling of Al-Qaeda, Regime Change, Nation Building

When analyzing the statements of the years 2001 and 2002 made by the governments involved in the Afghanistan intervention, three purposes can be distinguished: Firstly, the sustained *dismantling of al-Qaeda's* bases and training camps, which was intended to prevent the repetition of terrorist attacks on Western countries, such as those on New York and Washington on September 11, 2001. For this purpose, the organization was to be destroyed, which had already claimed political responsibility for several attacks on U.S. facilities around the world and which had succeeded in the most spectacular operation with the attacks of September 11, 2001. Since the suicide bombers had died in these attacks, the U.S. administration's response was aimed at those politically responsible for them, namely those who, by their own admission, had given the order for the attacks: the al-Qaeda leadership staying in Afghanistan.[2]

When the U.S. government demanded that the ruling Taliban hand over the al-Qaeda leadership and immediately dismantle their bases, it kept the decision between *crime paradigm* and *war paradigm* open, i.e., it did not decide whether to treat the terrorist attacks as a criminal act or as a declaration of war. Whether this was merely a tactical move, while the leading key-figures of the Bush administration were already indulging in excessive war rhetoric – this question must remain unanswered. Only when the Afghan Taliban rejected U.S. demands or demanded proof of al-Qaeda's involvement in the attacks,[3] the United States committed to the war paradigm, combining the destruction of al-Qaeda's bases with the defeat of the Taliban regime, the terrorist organization's patron. In the early months of the war, military intervention consisted of a combination of arming Afghan warlords to fight the Taliban, heavy U.S. airstrikes on suspected al-Qaeda bases, and the use of U.S. Special Forces tasked with capturing or killing al-Qaeda leaders and locating hidden terrorist organization camps and marking them for airstrikes.

In this phase, the purpose of a permanent destruction of al-Qaeda was inevitably merged with the purpose of a regime change directed against the rule of the Taliban; however, it temporarily appeared as if both purposes could be pursued and achieved simultaneously. By the end of 2001/ beginning of 2002, this phase of the war was over: Taliban rule in Kabul and in large parts of the country had collapsed, al-Qaeda's bases and training camps had been destroyed, and yet the al-Qaeda leadership, namely Osama bin Laden and Ayman al-Zawahiri, had not been captured. Therefore, it was not possible to be sure whether the terrorist organization had actually been permanently dismantled.

In this situation, the decision should have had to be made as to whether the purpose of the war was to be limited to the destruction of al-Qaeda or whether ending Taliban rule in Afghanistan was included in the purposes of the war. Admittedly, if the former had been chosen, the overthrow of the Taliban regime might well have been regarded as an objective to be achieved to ensure the sustained dismantlement of al-Qaeda in Afghanistan. In this case, the end of the Taliban would have been a means to the end of the destruction of al-Qaeda. Furthermore, the intervention powers would have had to remain in the country for some time. Conversely, the decision to confine themselves to the military dismantlement of the al-Qaeda bases would have meant that the Western intervention coalition would have ended the fighting, withdrawn their troops and offered the allied warlords advice and support in consolidating their rule – and otherwise left the country to itself. Obviously, the termination of the intervention should have been accompanied by the threat that the invention powers would return and strike with all their might if al-Qaeda were once again able to use the Hindu Kush as a root cause for global terrorist attacks. In this case, the following would have been true: Whatever forces might prevail in Afghanistan – they would be accepted as long as they prevented al-Qaeda from rebuilding in the country. The political idea behind it was to turn the masters in the Hindu Kush into forced allies in the fight against al-Qaeda by making these alliance obligations a precondition for the continuation of their rule.

The intervention coalition did not opt for this solution because it was not sure whether al-Qaeda had actually been crushed or sustainably weakened, and because it wanted to prevent a repeat of what had happened in the late 1980s after the Soviets withdrew from Afghanistan, when the country sank in a mire of corruption and civil war. The civil war fought between the various warlords had finally ended with the Taliban taking power in Kabul. As a result, the purpose of the Western intervention shifted imperceptibly from the destruction of a terrorist organization to a permanent *regime change* in Afghanistan, and it soon seemed as if the fight against al-Qaeda had only provided an occasion to change the balance of political power and influence in the Hindu Kush. Thereby, genuine geopolitical aspects became more relevant, and the initial dominance of a military anti-terrorist operation receded into the background. This was reflected, among other things, in the fact that less and less distinction was made between the terrorist organization al-Qaeda and the Taliban: furthermore the Taliban took the place of al-Qaeda in the designation of the enemy against whom one was fighting. The attribution of the term terrorism was increasingly extended to the Taliban although their way of warfare was more akin to that of guerilla fighters.[4]

Regime change must be politically secured, and accordingly the main issue soon became how to generate the broadest possible support for the country's new government. Two aspects are relevant to the issues discussed in this article: On the one hand, the fact that the Afghanistan mission was a war in which one's own political will was to be enforced against an opposing will was forgotten for some time; as a result, the war paradigm was replaced by that of assistance in the installation of a functioning administration and material support for the reconstruction of the country. Accordingly, the question of enforcing one's own will was shaped by humanitarian semantics. The consequences of this form of self-suggestion were that people in the intervention states reacted with irritation when there was suddenly renewed and even to an increasingly extent talk of acts of war or attacks on Western troops in Afghanistan. On the other hand, the focus on the reconstruction of Afghanistan increased the vulnerability of the armed forces in the country insofar as they were no longer to a considerable extent in combat mode, but were carrying out support and aid measures in order to win the hearts and minds of the people in the country according to the much-quoted formula of British Field Marshal Templer. To put it more pointedly: The interveners became highly vulnerable and the hunters became driven. However, because the two competing purposes of the intervention were conflated, this change was for a long time not captured analytically; instead, there was only irritated talk of a general deterioration of the situation in Afghanistan.

Finally, the Afghanistan mission was further complicated by the fact that the purpose of *regime change*, i.e., the replacement of the government or, if necessary, the change of the political order, was supplemented by that of *nation building*, which was concerned with a fundamental reorganization of society, starting with the change of its economic foundations, such as a reduction in opium production, and followed by the transformation of the mentalities not only of the elites but also of the broad mass of the population. In fact, *regime change* and *nation building* cannot be precisely distinguished from each other. *Nation building* can be regarded as a necessary companion to *regime change*, just as *regime change* can be regarded as a precondition for *nation building*. In general, however, *nation building* involves a much greater investment of resources than *regime change*; furthermore, *nation building* involves a much longer duration of intervention. One can also say that *regime change* is a slimmed-down version of *nation-building*, or that *nation building* is something like the gold standard of *regime change*. The consequence of such formulas, however, is that the differences between the two approaches become blurred and, as a result, the difference in purpose is no longer adequately captured. In Afghanistan, this meant that the Europeans conceived of *regime change* more in sense of *nation building*, while the United States, when it spoke of *nation building*, did so primarily in sense of sustainable *regime change*.

The Doha Negotiations and the Restriction of Western Objections and Purposes

The negotiations held in Doha, Qatar, between the U.S. government and the Taliban (the European coalition partners, like the Afghan government, were not involved in the negotiations, but both were briefed – however completely and comprehensively – by the United States.) were officially about the modalities of the withdrawal of Western troops. It was not the "if" and "when" but only the "how" of the withdrawal that was negotiated in Doha. The U.S. government, as leader of the intervention coalition, had made this decision for its own forces, and there was no doubt that this would inevitably involve the withdrawal of the Europeans. The assumption was that the withdrawal would result in some form of power sharing between the existing government under President Ashraf Ghani and the Taliban – but the nature of the power sharing was to be negotiated between the two Afghan parties themselves; the United States did not want to influence this, and accordingly it was not an issue in Doha. The de facto result was a strong negotiating position for the Taliban, who only had to wait and give assurances that they would not disrupt the withdrawal of Western troops and would not attack their diminishing beachhead in Afghanistan and, most recently, Kabul. What they did afterwards was obviously of no concern to the United States.

Presumably, none of the U.S. negotiators expected the Afghan government and its security forces to collapse as quickly and completely as they actually did, but none of them could rule out a medium- or long-term takeover of power by the Taliban in view of the deteriorating military situation for the government forces. This was not without significance for the already publicly communicated purpose of the intervention that was coming to an end. In addition, this purpose is relevant for a further assessment of the intervention as "completely failed" or "partially successful". The rule of thumb was (and still is): the more the purposes are located in the area of *regime change* or even *nation building*, the more likely it is that the assessment amounts to a "complete failure"; the more one emphasizes the destruction of al-Qaeda as the actual purpose of the intervention, the more adequate it is to speak of a "partial success". Admittedly, the question rises why the intervention, if the later communicated purpose was indeed its initial purpose, was not terminated in 2002 or 2003. Was it possible that a war had been waged over a period of more than a decade and a half that was superfluous, i.e., pointless, in view of the purpose now being communicated?

The only possible answer in defense of the minimum-purpose solution is that the Taliban gave assurances in Doha that they would not allow al-Qaeda to take root again in Afghanistan, but that assurance could only be enforced in this way by the long presence of Western soldiers in the Hindu Kush. The second part of this hypothesis cannot be verified, and it remains to be seen whether the first part, the prevention of al-Qaeda's return to the Hindu Kush, might actually be true or merely be a political feint by the Taliban. The targeted killing of al-Qaeda leader Ayman al-Zawahri in July 2022 in Kabul not only revealed that Taliban never broke its ties with al-Qaeda. The U.S.-drone strike also demonstrated a slightly new counterterrorism approach by maintaining the fight against al-Qaeda, ISIS and associated forces from over the horizon as President Joe Biden outlined in October 2022 at the National Security Strategy. There are certainly indications that al-Qaeda's presence in Afghanistan will not be as strong as it was before 2001 – but due to Zawahiri´s franchising strategy al-Qaeda managed spread globally, but has certain drawbacks when it comes to mobilization – in Europe at least. In fact, today, there are more foreign terrorist groups than two decades ago – although it remains to be seen whether this is due to the Taliban's potential promises and its according compliance or whether this is the result of changes within Salafi-jihadism. There is some evidence in favor of the latter: While al-Qaeda was still the operationally predominant and the symbolically most influential force in Islamist terrorism before and, for some time, during the West's intervention in Afghanistan, this has no longer been the case for about a decade. Other groups, notably IS, have taken its place.[5]

Reasons for the Taliban's Abstinence from Global Terrorism

Accordingly, the question is whether the Taliban are only committed to preventing the return of al-Qaeda or whether they will fundamentally take actions against globally operating Islamist terrorist organizations. For the moment, there is much to suggest that they will take decisive actions against IS, which carried out several bombings in Kabul in the summer of 2021 and also 2022 to further exacerbate the chaotic situation that arose with the withdrawal of Western troops. As far as can be seen, the Taliban are largely in control of the situation in Afghanistan, and there is no reason to believe they would be willing to share power in the country with competing Islamist organizations or even with terrorist groups with a global reach.

In this development, it is of considerable importance how the relationship of the new masters of Afghanistan with the immediate neighboring states develops, especially with China and the Central Asian republics and Russia behind them, which could feel threatened by aggressive Islamism in the Hindu Kush. The relationship with China, with which Afghanistan only shares a comparatively short border, will probably be the litmus test for the Taliban regime's handling of jihadist groups on its territories. It concerns mainly the Uyghurs, a Turkic ethnic group with Muslim religious affiliation that has developed strong autonomy and independence aspirations in recent years, in Jinjiang Province, a province belonging to the People's Republic of China. As part of these efforts, there have been several bomb attacks and armed conflicts in Jinjiang. The Chinese government has reacted with a policy of brutal repression, cramming hundreds of thousands of Uyghurs into re-education camps and taking measures to reduce the Uyghur birth rate, which is significantly higher than that of the Han Chinese. For human rights organizations, Jinjiang Province is one of the most notorious areas of human rights violations in the world. The Chinese government justifies this policy with the danger of Islamist terrorism spreading to Jinjiang.

In view of the Chinese repression, support for Uighur resistance against Chinese repression by the Taliban or by jihadist groups operating from Afghanistan cannot be ruled out in principle. However, there are currently no indications of such a development. Rather, there seems to be an agreement between the Taliban and the Chinese leadership that the Taliban will not support the Uighurs and that China will accept the Taliban regime in Afghanistan and will not support any resistance to the Taliban. This can be described as a policy of non-interference in the "internal affairs" of the other, in line with previous international practice, a policy in which respect for human and civil rights in the other country plays no role.

An analogous, likewise informal, agreement by the Taliban can also be assumed with respect to the Central Asian republics of Turkmenistan, Uzbekistan, Kyrgyzstan and Tajikistan, as well as Russia, which stands in their background. The Central Asian republics mentioned above take a hard line against radical Islamism, and their prisons are overcrowded with people accused of sympathizing with or even supporting jihadist groups. Therefore, one might initially expect the Taliban to support various jihadist groups in the Central Asian republics on the basis of "ideological affinity", for example by providing explosives and weapons, as well as retreat and training camps. So far, however, nothing of the kind has become known. Apparently, the principle of mutual non-interference applies here as well. Compliance therewith is a prerequisite for the Taliban to consolidate their rule in Afghanistan and concentrate on the internal problems of the country, which has so far been largely sustained economically and financially by the West and international aid organizations. These problems are enormous, especially since the Taliban cannot count on the Islamic neighboring states of Iran and Pakistan[6] to take the place of the West as aid providers. They are all too busy with their own internal problems.

This, in turn, means that the Taliban regime, if it does not want to risk a catastrophic famine in Afghanistan, is highly dependent on the help of the United Nations and its subdivisions, international aid organizations as well as the West, and it will only receive this help as long as it does not serve as a base and retreat for international terrorist organizations. To put it bluntly, the Taliban regime's ability to survive depends on its compliance with the agreements reached in Doha. However, it is by no means dependent on the mere goodwill of the West because it can threaten that a flight movement will start from Afghanistan that would far exceed the capacity and willingness of Western countries to absorb it if medical aid and the most urgent food supplies are not delivered. Not the threat of terrorist attacks, but that of a mass exodus of its own population has become the Taliban's most important instrument in pursuing its interests and gaining acceptance for its rule. The irony is that it is only through twenty years of intervention in the Hindu Kush that the West has put itself in the position of having to take in large numbers of Afghan migrants and cannot, as it usually does, dismiss them as a problem of the Islamic world or at least of the immediate neighboring countries. Admittedly, this only works as long as Afghanistan plays no role in global terrorism.

If the political purpose of the Western intervention in Afghanistan was to create a constellation in which the country at the Hindu Kush no longer represents a place of retreat or a deployment area for global terrorism, this goal has been achieved, at least under the current constellation; admittedly, by completely different means and with substantially different means than those of a military intervention of long duration. Whether this result could have been achieved without military intervention, for instance, by trying to influence the political will of the Taliban regime, ruling Kabul in 2001, with diplomatic means and economic promises, remains to be seen. The transformation of a regime from a regional or global export of its ideas and ideologies to one that is focused on political construction and the implementation of its goals at home, the transformation of an extremely expansive network organization into a territorially fixed hierarchy is a difficult process in which the distribution of power at home and the political preferences associated with it are the decisive factors.

The domestication of the Cuban revolution at the beginning of the 1960s can be cited as a successful example of such a transformation. The Cuban revolutionaries had initially seen themselves as initiators of a political and social revolution in Central and South America and then gradually embraced the project of building a socialist society "in one country", namely Cuba, which allowed Cuba to fit into the international concept of peaceful coexistence of socialist and capitalist states. Cuba's great dependence on the Soviet Union played a role in this, as did the

United States' de facto renunciation of invasion and Fidel Castro's political separation from Che Guevara, who continued to adhere to the network model of revolution and failed in Bolivia. The caliphate state of the IS in northern Iraq and Syria took a completely different course since it was also possible to assume the territorial fixation of an organization that in principle sees itself as global. In principle, the West could have waited and observed whether a "Cuban development" would take place there as well, which means that the global aggressiveness of IS would have been increasingly absorbed by the challenges of building a territorial order. There were probably several reasons for not deciding to do so: the questioning of the political balance of power in the Middle East in general associated with the emergence of a new state, along with a disposability of all state borders drawn by Western powers after World War I, which would have thrown one of the world's most conflict-ridden regions into turmoil; in addition, the absence of a major an-nexing power that would have supported the construction of a caliphate state and provided some stabilization, as the Soviet Union did in the case of Cuba; and finally, the aggressively provocative appearance of IS itself and its ongoing involvement in terrorist attacks on a global scale, includ-ing the dissemination of execution videos. Accordingly, the West participated in crushing IS in the form of airstrikes and arming various militias to fight the battle on the ground, basically following the Afghan intervention model of fall 2001, but not in engaging in any longer-term transformation or reconstruction project. The price of this abstinence was that the Assad regime, allied with Russia, had carte blanche in reclaiming the Syrian territories previously held by IS and became the winner of the year-long civil war.

We will have to wait and see whether the West's plan for the Afghan Taliban (above all that of the United States, which played a leading role in Doha) will work out. The fact that the Tali-ban were not an Islamist network with a global sphere of action from the outset, but confined themselves to the Hindu Kush region, i.e., Afghanistan and the so-called Pakistani tribal areas, speaks in favor of this. They do not pursue a decidedly revolutionary project, but see themselves as preservers and defenders of a traditional way of life, which is why their armed struggle was directed primarily against the project of Western *nation building*, which, if it had been successful, would actually have amounted to a profound transformation of Afghan society – just like the modernization project pursued by the communist-declaring governments in Kabul during the 1970s and with the Soviet military intervention. Those who have suffered most from the Western withdrawal are the urban classes, and among them especially the women, who could be seen as the beneficiaries of this project and, to a considerable extent, have seen themselves as such. They will leave Afghanistan and seek refuge in the West or will have to bow to the expectations of the new masters, who are oriented toward a radically patriarchal way of life. They are not expected to put up any politically relevant or even armed resistance. The only potential for armed resist-ance will be in the countryside, away from the larger cities, if the economic situation continues to deteriorate. The economic situation, however, will depend not only on the resumption and continuation of aid deliveries, not least from the West, but also to a large extent on the sales opportunities for regional opium production and the global market for heroin. Changing this would have been one of the central goals of *nation building*.

Notes

1 Since this article only deals with the Western military intervention, the Soviet military intervention from 1979 to 1988 and the subsequent civil war in Afghanistan are not addressed, nor is the fact that lessons could have been learned from both missions in determining one's own objectives and purposes.

2 At the beginning of the terrorist attacks directed against the U.S., there was Usama bin Laden's "decla-ration of war" of 1996 which originated in Afghanistan.

3 The U.S. extradition request to the Taliban has been compared to Austria-Hungary's request to Serbia in June 1914 to extradite to Vienna the masterminds of the assassination of Archduke Franz Ferdinand in Sarajevo. Serbia did not comply with this request, which ultimately led to the First World War as a result of the alliance mechanisms. Here, too, it is disputed in the relevant literature whether the Habsburg Monarchy wanted the war against Serbia or whether the war could have been prevented if Belgrade had been more accommodating.

4 Accordingly, the lack of debate about the objections and purposes of the Afghanistan intervention is best exemplified by the colonization of strategic decisions by a semantics of political legitimacy. The term "terrorism" played a prominent role in the latter.

5 Whether the formation of IS is causally attributable to the wars of intervention in Afghanistan and especially in Iraq, as often claimed, or whether it rather grew out of the internal dynamics of jihadism cannot be discussed here. It is relevant for the assessment of military interventions as a whole but plays only a subordinate role for the assessment of the intervention in Afghanistan, where the IS plays only a supporting role – at least for the time being.

6 There are differences between Afghanistan and Pakistan because of the border between the two countries drawn by the British colonial rulers, which runs right through Pashtun territory. Pashtun nationalism has always called into the question this border. Its acceptance by the Taliban is a further test of their political will to stabilize.

45

AFGHANISTAN UNDER TALIBAN RULE

Consequences for Global Security and Terrorism Against the West

Seth G. Jones

In August 2021, the Taliban overthrew the Afghan government and proclaimed the "Islamic Emirate of Afghanistan," nearly two decades after they were toppled by the United States after the September 11, 2001 terrorist attacks in New York City and Washington, D.C. The West must now contend with a potentially serious resurgent terrorist threat emanating from Afghanistan. Both al-Qaeda and the Islamic State-Khorasan Province (ISIS-K) are active in Afghanistan and could pose a growing threat outside of the country.[1] As a 2022 United Nations Security Council report concluded, "terrorist groups enjoy greater freedom in Afghanistan than *at any time in recent history.*"[2]

The implications are significant. The narrative that the West—and especially the United States—was defeated by Islamic forces is being widely disseminated on extremist social media platforms. As-Sahab, al-Qaeda's core media organization, is urging Muslims to follow the Taliban's example and take up arms against the West.[3] For some countries, such as the U.S. and the United Kingdom, the threat is deeply concerning. For example, U.S. intelligence agencies assess that "both ISIS-K and al-Qaeda have the intent to conduct external operations."[4] The head of the United Kingdom's domestic intelligence agency, MI5, warned that Islamic extremists had been "hardened and emboldened" because of the Taliban victory, with some UK citizens traveling to Afghanistan to join terrorist groups.[5] For other countries, such as the Netherlands, the threat is worrying—though not imminent.[6]

As this chapter argues, the terrorist threat in Afghanistan is caused by two main factors. First, the Taliban government has close links with several terrorist groups, including al-Qaeda. These ties have allowed terrorist groups to rebuild and establish training camps in the country. Second, Afghanistan is a weak and failing state, which is a prerequisite for a terrorist sanctuary. The combination of a weak state and collapsing economy has at least two implications: terrorist groups have relative freedom to operate in the country, and there is a pool of potential recruits.

Despite the growing terrorist challenge, the United States and Europe have done far too little to deal with a threat that is likely to have grown. The rest of this chapter is divided into four sections. The first outlines the Taliban's ideology and objectives, including the challenge of Taliban governance. The second section discusses evolving terrorism concerns, particularly from al-Qaeda and ISIS-K. The third assesses policy options to counterterrorist groups in Afghanistan. And the fourth section provides policy recommendations.

DOI: 10.4324/9781003326373-52

The Taliban's Failing State

During the Taliban's last time in power from 1996 to 2001, Afghanistan was a failed state. The World Bank ranked Afghanistan at the bottom of its list of countries in the category of "government effectiveness" in 2000, with a score of 0 percent out of 100.[7] The collapse of governance provided an opportunity for terrorist groups, such as al-Qaeda, to establish roots. History is now in danger of repeating itself, with Afghanistan on the verge of an economic, humanitarian, and broader governance collapse.

The Taliban today is a different organization than it was during its last reign in Kabul, but its ideology remains deeply rooted in the Hanafi school of Islamic jurisprudence.[8] While the Taliban's ideology has been evolving since the movement's establishment in the 1990s, Taliban leaders today generally support the establishment of a government by Islamic law (sharia) and the creation of an extreme Islamic Emirate in Afghanistan.[9] The Taliban elevate the role of Islamic scholars (or ulema) that issue legal rulings (or fatwas) on all aspects of daily life. The ulema play a particularly important role in monitoring society's conformity with the prescriptions of Islam—at least the Taliban's version of Islam—and in conservatively interpreting religious doctrine.[10] The Taliban has also been described as a "nationalist" movement in the sense that its leaders advocate an Islamic Emirate in Afghanistan, rather than as part of a broader pan-Islamic caliphate.[11]

In addition, the Taliban's ideology includes an important component of Pashtunwali, an evolving system of customary law, culture, and conflict resolution followed by many ethnic Pashtun tribes in Afghanistan and Pakistan.[12] Pashtun tribal structure has undergone dramatic changes over the past several decades of war, and local versions of Pashtunwali (or nirkh) can differ significantly across areas.[13] Nevertheless, the Taliban has adopted some components of Pashtunwali. The Taliban strictly segregates the sexes, known as purdah, and an Afghan man's honor (or nang) is closely tied to how the women of his family are treated.[14] In addition, Taliban leaders generally disparage democracy as a corrupt invention of the West and dismiss as shams the elections held in Afghanistan after 2001.[15]

During the Taliban's time in power from the mid-1990s to 2001, the movement enforced a stringent interpretation of the Islamic dress code for men and women.[16] Men were forced to grow beards and avoid Western haircuts or dress. The Taliban closed cinemas and prohibited music.[17] The Taliban banned almost every conceivable kind of entertainment—such as television, videos, cards, kite-flying, and most sports—except a few such as public executions in Kabul's main soccer stadium. The Taliban also defaced and destroyed hundreds of cultural artifacts that it called polytheistic, including museums and private art collections.[18]

Over the past few years, the Taliban has moderated its views on some issues, such as the use of modern technology and digital platforms.[19] The Taliban Minister of Interior Affairs Sirajuddin Haqqani wrote that the Taliban would "build an Islamic system in which all Afghans have equal rights, where the rights of women that are granted by Islam—from the right to education to the right to work—are protected."[20] Since overthrowing the government of Ashraf Ghani in August 2021, however, the Taliban have prevented women from participating in the country's main political bodies, barred many women and girls from attending schools and working in most jobs, and prohibited women from traveling more than 45 miles from their house unless they have a male relative to accompany them.[21] In March 2022, the Taliban announced that girls' secondary schools were to remain indefinitely closed until the Taliban could implement policies that were compliant with the "principles of Islamic law and Afghan culture."[22] These steps were predictable. The Taliban has a well-documented record of repression, intolerance, and human rights abuses against women, foreigners, ethnic minorities, and journalists.[23] The Taliban's military victory also wiped out the country's short-lived experience in democracy, part of a larger global trend in which global freedom has now declined in 16 consecutive years.[24]

More concerning, however, is that Afghanistan under the Taliban is a failing state—a prerequisite for a terrorist sanctuary. The Taliban government has been unable to establish basic services, and the Afghan economy has shrunk by at least 40 percent since the United States and European withdrawal.[25] The poverty rate could skyrocket to 97 percent of the population and there are significant food security challenges.[26] Afghanistan jumped to the top of the International Rescue Committee's 2022 Emergency Watchlist as it nears collapse of virtually all basic services.[27] In addition, the Taliban does not control law and order outside of most cities. These conditions are likely to be suitable for terrorist groups to survive and flourish.

The Evolving Terrorism Problem

Since the departure of U.S. and European forces, the terrorist threat in Afghanistan has increased. According to U.S. intelligence estimates, the number of al-Qaeda operatives in Afghanistan has risen since the Taliban's overthrow of the regime.[28] In addition, the UK's domestic intelligence agency, MI5, assessed that the Taliban victory gave a "morale boost" to UK extremists and increased the likelihood of them "reconstituting themselves within Afghanistan and projecting the threat back at the West including the UK."[29] As one European assessment concluded, "the EU is concerned that Afghanistan could revert to being a safe haven for international terrorists who might target EU countries."[30] ISIS-K operatives have already been involved in plots in Europe, including the 2020 plot by four Tajik nationals in Germany to commit attacks against U.S. military forces and civilians in Germany. They had instructions to construct improvised explosive devices and had started procuring the necessary components.[31]

However, the threat to the West is not uniform. Some European countries have assessed that the short-term threat is limited. "The NCTV estimates that this could eventually become a risk but does not expect large numbers of Dutch people to travel there," concluded the Netherlands National Coordinator for Counterterrorism and Security. "Firstly, the Dutch jihadist movement is fragmented and lacks charismatic leaders, which means that it is probably unable to mobilise large numbers of sympathisers to join jihadist groups in Afghanistan at this time."[32] The rest of this section examines the threat posed by al-Qaeda, ISIS-K, and other terrorist groups in Afghanistan.

Al-Qaeda

The primary goal of al-Qaeda remains what is has always been: to establish a pan-Islamic caliphate and overthrow the corrupt "apostate" regimes across the Islamic world. Al-Qaeda today is comprised of disparate networks around the globe with uneven centralized control. Its main affiliates are located in the Middle East, including Hurras al-Din in Syria and al-Qaeda in the Arabian Peninsula in Yemen; Africa, including Jama'at Nasr al-Islam wal Muslimin in the Sahel and al-Shabaab in Somalia; and South Asia, including al-Qaeda's global leadership and local affiliate al-Qaeda in the Indian Subcontinent (AQIS).

In some countries, such as Yemen, al-Qaeda has been significantly weakened and appears to be on a declining trajectory in terms of popular support and capabilities. But Afghanistan is a central strategic node for al-Qaeda, where the group now has safe haven. Despite the death of Ayman al-Zawahiri in Kabul in August 2022 from a U.S. drone strike, several senior al-Qaeda leaders likely reside in Afghanistan, including Saif al-Adel and Amin Muhammad ul-Haq Saam

Khan. One of Usama bin Laden's surviving sons, Abdallah, visited Afghanistan in late 2021 to meet with Taliban leaders, according to a United Nations Security Council assessment.[33]

AQIS, al-Qaeda's local affiliate in Afghanistan, is led by Osama Mehmood and his deputy, Atif Yahya Ghouri, and aided by such senior leaders as Aziz Azam.[34] In early 2021, U.S. intelligence agencies estimated that al-Qaeda was the weakest it had been in years and included fewer than 200 members in Afghanistan.[35] Less than a year later, al-Qaeda's total numbers in Afghanistan—including core al-Qaeda and AQIS—likely doubled to roughly 500 fighters, with most of its members coming from Afghanistan, Bangladesh, India, Myanmar, and Pakistan.[36] AQIS is most active in such Afghan provinces as Ghazni, Helmand, Kandahar, Nimruz, Paktika, and Zabul.[37]

Afghanistan is different from any other country where al-Qaeda operates, since the group enjoys a sympathetic relationship with the Taliban regime. Al-Qaeda leaders have a particularly close historical relationship with some Taliban leaders—such as Sirajuddin Haqqani, the Taliban Minister of Interior Affairs and a U.S. designated terrorist.[38] Indeed, al-Qaeda leaders have pledged loyalty (or bayat) to every Taliban leader since the group's establishment, from Mullah Muhammad Omar to Mullah Akhtar Mansour and Mawlawi Haibatullah Akhunzada. In 2007, for example, Usama bin Laden remarked that the Taliban "are fighting America and its agents under the leadership of the Commander of the Believers, Mullah Omar, may Allah protect him."[39] Bin Laden likely pledged bayat, in part, to ensure that Afghans saw the insurgency as being led by Afghan mujahideen and not by foreign Arabs. Following Bin Laden's death in 2011, the Taliban praised him as a martyr that had fought "with great honesty and bravery, shoulder to shoulder with the Afghans."[40]

In August 2015, Ayman al-Zawahiri pledged bayat to newly-announced Taliban leader Mullah Akhtar Mohammad Mansour, who was eventually killed by a U.S. drone strike in Pakistan. "I, as the Emir of [al-Qaeda], present to you our pledge of allegiance, renewing the method of Sheikh Usama and his brothers the pure martyrs," al-Zawahiri said.[41] In June 2016, al-Zawahiri similarly pledged allegiance to Mansour's successor, Mawlawi Haibatullah Akhunzada, the current Taliban leader. "We pledge allegiance to you on jihad to liberate every inch of the lands of the Muslims that are invaded and stolen—from Kashgar to al-Andalus, from the Caucasus to Somalia and Central Africa, from Kashmir to Jerusalem, from the Philippines to Kabul, and from Bukhara to Samarkand," said al-Zawahiri[42].

With a safe haven in Afghanistan, al-Qaeda's threat to the West is likely to grow over time. Al-Qaeda operatives could conduct—or more likely *inspire*—attacks against U.S. and European interests overseas, such as embassies, bases, and other Western targets in South Asia, the Middle East, and Africa, as they did before 9/11. With a base in Afghanistan, al-Qaeda could also conduct or inspire attacks in Europe.

ISIS-K

The Islamic State's local affiliate, ISIS-K, also presents a threat. While ISIS-K is a sworn enemy of the Taliban and al-Qaeda, its goal is similar to that of al-Qaeda: to establish a pan-Islamic caliphate. ISIS-K was severely weakened through mid-2021 because of aggressive U.S. and Afghan counterterrorism operations, Taliban offensives, and internal divisions within ISIS-K. But the U.S. and European withdrawal has allowed the group to resurge. ISIS-K does not control significant territory, but its size has now doubled in less than a year, increasing from 2,000 to roughly 4,000 operatives following the release of several thousand prisoners from Bagram and Pul-e-Charkhi prison outside of Kabul.[43] Up to half of ISIS-K's operatives are foreign fighters.[44] The group received significant sums of money from ISIS core after the Taliban victory, in part to build an external attack capability.[45]

ISIS-K is led by Sanaullah Ghafari (also known as Shahab al-Muhajir), an Afghan national.[46] Other ISIS-K leaders include Sultan Aziz Azam, Maulawi Rajab Salahudin, and Aslam Farooqi. In addition, some former members of the Afghan military and Afghanistan's intelligence agency, the National Directorate for Security, joined ISIS-K since it is the most active opposition group to the Taliban in Afghanistan.[47]

ISIS-K has already demonstrated an ability to conduct high-profile and complex attacks in Afghanistan. Among the most notable was the August 27, 2021, attack at the Kabul airport that killed more than 180 people, including 13 U.S. service members. According to one estimate, ISIS-K carried out 76 attacks on Taliban forces between September 18 and November 30, 2021, a significant jump from 2020, when it conducted only 8 attacks during the entire year.[48] As one senior U.S. official noted in March 2022, "the Department of Defense assesses ISIS-K could establish an external attack capability against the United States and our allies in twelve to eighteen months, but possibly sooner if the group experiences unanticipated gains in Afghanistan."[49]

Other Terrorist Groups

In addition to al-Qaeda and ISIS-K, there are other regional and international terrorist groups operating in Afghanistan, such as the Tehreek-e-Taliban Pakistan, Eastern Turkistan Islamic Movement (ETIM), Islamic Jihad Group, Khatiba Imam al-Bukhari, and Islamic Movement of Uzbekistan. The ETIM, for example, has between 200 and 700 fighters and poses a particularly significant threat to China, against whom it is plotting terrorist attacks.[50] The Tehreek-e-Taliban Pakistan also retains a relatively large size, with between 3,000 and nearly 6,000 fighters.[51] Several groups, such as Jaish-e-Mohammed and Lashkar-e-Taiba, pose a significant threat to India and have conducted high-profile attacks in Mumbai, New Delhi, and other Indian cities.

More broadly, the Taliban's victory has inspired jihadists around the world. Groups in Africa, the Middle East, Asia, and other locations celebrated the Taliban's conquest of Kabul on chat rooms and other online platforms, pledging the revitalization of a global jihad. Al-Qaeda released a statement after the U.S. withdrawal congratulating the Taliban for its victory and calling it a "prelude" to other jihadist victories.[52]

Policy Options in Afghanistan

The main Western counterterrorism policy objective should be to prevent the reemergence of Afghanistan as a base for terrorist operations against the West and Western interests overseas. But the precipitous U.S. military withdrawal from Afghanistan—along with the rapid collapse of the Ghani government—created serious challenges to achieve this objective. The United States, for example, retained no military forces in Afghanistan and no military bases, such as Bagram or Kandahar Airfield, and it abandoned its local Afghan partners. Under these conditions, there are two main policy options to deal with the terrorism problem in Afghanistan.

The first is to develop a modus vivendi with the Taliban. This option might involve providing economic and humanitarian assistance—and potentially even intelligence—to the Taliban government in return for conducting an increasingly effective and sustained campaign against ISIS-K. When asked in 2021 whether the United States could work with the Taliban to combat ISIS-K, U.S. Chairman of the Joint Chiefs of Staff General Mark Milley responded that "it's possible."[53] A variant of this option might be for the United States and Europe to de facto leave counterterrorism operations to the Taliban—but provide little or no assistance.

However, there are at least two problems with this option. First, the Taliban has an active relationship with numerous terrorist groups in Afghanistan, including al-Qaeda. While the Taliban has conducted some operations against ISIS-K, Taliban leaders have shown little interest in countering a range of other terrorist groups. Consequently, this option fails to solve the broader terrorism problem—and may worsen it by aiding a government that supports terrorist groups. Second, the Taliban is unlikely to significantly weaken ISIS-K with or without Western help, since it lacks the capabilities and control of territory. The Taliban's Ministry of Interior Affairs and the General Directorate of Intelligence have attempted to better synchronize their efforts to combat ISIS-K's operations in urban areas, but ISIS-K has increased the number of attacks in Afghanistan.[54]

Doing nothing—and hoping that the Taliban becomes more effective—is also problematic for both of the reasons highlighted above. As the head of U.S. Central Command noted, "ISIS-K may gain strength and be emboldened to expand its operations and target neighboring countries" absent sustained pressure.[55]

A second policy option is to conduct a more effective over-the-horizon counterterrorism campaign. It would include monitoring terrorist groups using overhead assets and potentially periodically striking terrorist targets. But this option will be difficult to implement without local partners, intelligence assets, and bases. Between 2001 and 2021, successive U.S. and other Western administrations conducted aggressive counterterrorism operations in Afghanistan with the benefit of partner forces operating from bases across the country; a robust partner intelligence architecture, including human intelligence (HUMINT) and signals intelligence (SIGINT) collection capabilities; and close collaboration with Afghan military, intelligence, police, and militia partner forces.

Following the U.S. and European withdrawal, however, the West has none of these capabilities today. As its name implies, "over-the-horizon" involves the use of aerial platforms and satellites launched from afar to collect SIGINT and imagery intelligence (IMINT), as well as to conduct periodic strikes from fixed-wing aircraft and UAVs, such as the MQ-9A Reaper. The hope is that an over-the-horizon strategy does not require the deployment of any—or at least many—military forces, thus minimizing casualties, decreasing the financial costs of a large military deployment, and reducing political risks. U.S. National Security Advisor Jake Sullivan argued that the United States and other countries had developed a viable over-the-horizon strategy:

> We have to deal with the threat of terrorism in Yemen and Somalia and Syria. We have to deal with the threat of terrorism across the Islamic Maghreb.... And what we have shown is, in many of the countries I just mentioned, among others, we have been successful to date in suppressing the terrorist threat to the U.S. homeland in those countries without sustaining a permanent military presence or fighting in a war. And that is what we intend to do with respect to Afghanistan as well.[56]

Yet there are notable differences between most of these counterterrorist campaigns and Afghanistan today.

First, the United States and other European countries have no significant partner force on the ground in Afghanistan. In virtually every other counterterrorism campaign since 9/11, Western governments had a local partner. Various Western countries worked with the Iraqi government, including the Counter Terrorism Service, in Iraq; the Somali government, African Union Mission in Somalia (AMISOM) forces, and clan militias in Somalia; the Syrian Democratic Forces (SDF) in Syria; local security forces, such as the Libyan National Army (LNA), in Libya; the Malian government in Mali during Operation Barkhane; and militias aided by Saudi Arabia and the United Arab Emirates in Yemen. In Afghanistan today, however, the Taliban is not an ally, and anti-Taliban leaders and groups have fled the country, been killed by the Taliban, laid down their weapons, or even joined ISIS-K.

Second, the West has virtually no intelligence architecture in Afghanistan. U.S. and European intelligence organizations withdrew most of their intelligence collection capabilities. As the head of U.S. Central Command acknowledged in December 2021, "we're probably at 1 or 2 percent of the capabilities we once had to look into Afghanistan," making it "very hard" to understand what is happening in Afghanistan.[57]

Third, the United States and Europe have no bases in the region to fly aircraft for intelligence collection or strike missions. The United States withdrew from all bases in Afghanistan, such as Bagram Airfield and Kandahar International Airport, and do not have bases in Central Asia or South Asia. Instead, the United States has utilized locations such as Al Udeid Air Base in Qatar, which is approximately 2,500 miles from Kabul assuming Pakistan allows U.S. aircraft overflight rights. It takes an MQ-9A approximately 14 hours to fly round-trip, giving it limited time to loiter in Afghanistan before returning to Qatar.

The result is that the West is severely hamstrung in conducting counterterrorism operations in Afghanistan, with no partner forces, little intelligence, and no nearby bases. Under these conditions, the West will face significant difficulties in collecting intelligence about terrorist activities and orchestrating effective operations. The failed U.S. drone strike in Kabul against a supposed ISIS-K target on August 29, 2021, was a good example of the current counterterrorism challenges in Afghanistan. While President Biden and U.S. Chairman of the Joint Chiefs General Mark Milley initially lauded the attack as a textbook example of over-the-horizon capabilities, it was a failure.[58] The U.S. Department of Defense eventually acknowledged that the strike was a major mistake, which ultimately killed 10 Afghan civilians, including 7 children, rather than ISIS-K members.[59]

Over the Horizon

Without a more effective counterterrorism approach, Afghanistan has the potential to become an increasingly dangerous safe haven for al-Qaeda, ISIS-K, and other terrorist groups who can threaten the West. Any Western policy needs to include combating extremist social media activity. Social media remains the primary way for al-Qaeda and ISIS to radicalize individuals in the West, and the defeat of the United States and its European partners in Afghanistan has been a major recruitment boost online.[60] In addition, sanctions against al-Qaeda, ISIS-K, and other terrorists in Afghanistan—including new leaders—is important to undermine their ability to raise and move money. Customs, immigration, and intelligence-sharing steps are also important, including systematically checking biographic and biometric data of Afghans and others coming from Afghanistan and arriving at the U.S.'s and EU's external borders against all relevant databases (such as SIS, Eurodac Europol systems and databases, ECRIS-TCN, "No Fly" list, Selectee List, VIS, and Interpol databases).

However, the West may still face tough decisions about what to do against a growing terrorism problem in Afghanistan. The best option is to conduct a more effective over-the-horizon counterterrorism campaign, which could have three components.

First, the United States and European partners should work with locals inside and outside Afghanistan to rebuild the intelligence architecture in Afghanistan against terrorist groups. The U.S. military and CIA have a long history of working with local Afghan forces—including Uzbek, Tajik, Hazara, and some Pashtun militias—to collect intelligence.[61] Some of these U.S. activities were orchestrated as covert action programs under Title 50 of the U.S. Code, which allows the United States to conduct political, economic, and military activities abroad that are not acknowledged publicly.[62] During the 1990s, for example, the CIA provided covert funding and equipment to anti-Taliban groups, such as the Northern Alliance, to counter al-Qaeda.

The Biden administration's withdrawal of U.S. military forces does not preclude the United States from using CIA paramilitary units from the Special Activities Center or U.S. special operations forces operating under Title 50 authority to work with forces in Afghanistan and nearby countries. The main goal should *not* be to overthrow the Taliban regime, but rather to collect intelligence on terrorist groups and individuals operating in Afghanistan, such as al-Qaeda and ISIS-K. These partners—which might range from supporters of the National Resistance Front (NRF) to anti-Taliban Pashtun, Uzbek, Tajik, Hazara, and other networks—can provide valuable information on terrorist leaders, training camps, and other activities, which the West should supplement with intelligence collected from other sources. The United States and Europe can leverage such individuals as Ahmad Massoud, Amrullah Saleh, Bismullah Khan Mohammadi, Ali Nazary, and their networks. In addition, there is deep opposition to the Taliban among some Pashtun tribes and sub-tribes, such as Barakzais and Popalzais, that Western intelligence and military units could potentially leverage.

Intelligence from partners on the ground in Afghanistan is critical for "tipping and cueing," which refers to the process of monitoring an area or specific target of interest by a sensor. If there is evidence of terrorist activity, intelligence operatives can request "tipping" another complementary sensor platform—such as an MQ-9—to acquire "cueing" an imager over the same area. Effective HUMINT on the ground is critical for this process because it can provide more accurate information on the location and actions of a terrorist target. The tip-and-cue process allows countries to build an intelligence picture, which it then uses to conduct an action against a target, if feasible. Without partners on the ground in Afghanistan, however, U.S. intelligence is largely blind.

Second, the United States and Europe should negotiate basing access in the region, especially for intelligence, surveillance, and reconnaissance capabilities. The United States and Europe should jumpstart negotiations with countries in the region—such as Tajikistan, Uzbekistan, Kyrgyzstan, Pakistan, and possibly even India—to fly manned and unmanned aircraft to conduct intelligence, surveillance, and reconnaissance over Afghan territory. These discussions are ongoing and they will be difficult.[63] In addition, Russia and, to some extent China, have been cautious about allowing the U.S. and other countries to use bases in Central Asia.[64] The West's escalating tensions with Moscow over the war in Ukraine and broader geostrategic competition will make these negotiations difficult. But surveillance aircraft may be more politically palatable for some of these countries.

Third, the United States and Europe need to expand their over-the-horizon capabilities as part of Operation ENDURING SENTINEL. Given the mission requirements for Afghanistan, one of the best aircraft for the job is the unmanned MQ-9. The current U.S. MQ-9 inventory, however, is focused on the MQ-9A Reaper. But it takes a Reaper some 14 hours to fly round-trip from Al Udeid Air Base in Qatar to Afghanistan, giving it only 12–15 hours of operational coverage to collect intelligence and strike targets if necessary. The newest MQ-9 platform, the MQ-9B SkyGuardian, would be even better and allow the West to fly at least 15 additional hours over Afghanistan with a larger payload. Several countries, such as the United Kingdom and Australia, are buying the MQ-9B SkyGuardian. The West could complement its UAVs with manned aircraft—including F-15E strike fighters, F-16 fighter bombers, A-10 ground attack jets, and B-52 strategic bombers—to conduct strikes, if necessary. Some countries, such as the United States and United Kingdom, have indicated that could support strikes in Afghanistan if the Taliban failed to prevent the growth of international terrorist groups.[65]

A failure to significantly improve Western counterterrorism policies, capabilities, and posture will put the United States and Europe at growing risk of a terrorist attack. U.S. and other Western intelligence agencies now assess that al-Qaeda and ISIS-K may have external operations capabilities in 2022. This reality makes it important to move expeditiously and adopt a more effective counterterrorism campaign *before* the next attack.

Notes

1 Kenneth F. McKenzie, "Posture Statement," Hearing Before the Senate Armed Services Committee, March 15, 2022.

2 United Nations Security Council, "Fourteenth Report of the Secretary-General on the Threat Posed by ISIL (Da'esh) to International Peace and Security and the Range of United Nations Efforts in Support of Member States in Countering the Threat," S/2022/63, January 28, 2022.

3 Netherlands, *Terrorist Threat Assessment for the Netherlands* (Hague: National Coordinator for Counterterrorism and Security, Ministry of Justice and Security, October 2021).

4 "Hearing to Receive Testimony on Security in Afghanistan and in the Regions of South and Central Asia," U.S. Senate Committee on Armed Services, October 26, 2021.

5 The quote is from Dan Sabbagh, "MI5 Chief: Taliban Afghan Victory has Boosted Extremists," *Guardian*, September 10, 2021. Also see Rebecca Camber, "Afghanistan Is Becoming a Breeding Ground for Jihadis Again," *Daily Mail*, February 20, 2022.

6 Netherlands, *Terrorist Threat Assessment for the Netherlands* (Hague: National Coordinator for Counterterrorism and Security, Ministry of Justice and Security, October 2021).

7 World Bank Governance Indicators data set, available at http://info.worldbank.org/governance/wgi/, accessed April 4, 2022.

8 On the Taliban's religious and other views see the primary source Taliban documents in Alex Strick van Linschoten and Felix Kuehn, eds., *The Taliban Reader: War, Islam and Politics* (New York: Oxford University Press, 2018).

9 On the importance of an Islamic Emirate see, for example, "Weekly Comment," *Voice of Jihad*, September 19, 2020. Available at "Afghan Taliban Alleges Islamic Governance is Desired by All Afghans, Not Just Itself," SITE Intelligence Group, September 21, 2020.

10 Olivier Roy, *Islam and Resistance in Afghanistan*, Second Edition (New York: Cambridge University Press, 1990), p. 57; Gilles Kepel, *Jihad: The Trail of Political Islam* (Cambridge, MA: Harvard University Press, 2002), p. 58.

11 Anand Gopal and Alex Strick van Linschoten, *Ideology in the Afghan Taliban* (Kabul: Afghanistan Analysts Network, 2017).

12 On the Taliban and Pashtuns see, for example, Thomas Barfield, *Afghanistan: A Cultural and Political History* (Princeton, NJ: Princeton University Press, 2010), pp. 258–260; Anand Gopal and Alex Strick van Linschoten, *Ideology in the Afghan Taliban* (Kabul: Afghanistan Analysts Network, 2017). On historical overviews of the Pashtuns see Akbar S. Ahmed, *Millennium and Charisma Among Pathans: A Critical Essay in Social Anthropology* (New York: Routledge, 1976).

13 See, for example, Thomas Ruttig, *How Tribal Are the Taleban?* (Kabul: Afghanistan Analysts Network, 2010), p. 2.

14 Thomas H. Johnson, *Taliban Narratives: The Use and Power of Stories in the Afghanistan Conflict* (New York: Oxford University Press, 2017), pp. 27–30.

15 Jabir Numani, "Seven Threats to Jihad," *Al-Emera*, September 3, 2014, in Strick van Linschoten and Kuehn, *The Taliban Reader*, pp. 441–443; Osman, *A Negotiated End to the Afghan Conflict; Taking Stock of the Taliban's Perspectives on Peace*, p. 4.

16 Among the many primary source accounts of the Taliban in its early years is Abdul Salam Zaeef, *My Life with the Taliban* (London: Hurst, 2010).

17 Decree Announced by General Presidency of Amr Bil Maruf, Religious Police, Kabul, December 1996.

18 Ahmed Rashid, *Taliban: Militant Islam, Oil and Fundamentalism in Central Asia* (New Haven, Conn.: Yale University Press, 2000), pp. 68–76.

19 See the primary source interviews with the Taliban in Clarissa Ward, Najibullah Quraishi, and Salma Abdelaziz, "36 Hours with the Taliban," CNN, February 2019; *Taking Stock of the Taliban's Perspectives on Peace* (Brussels: International Crisis Group, August 11, 2020), p. 8.

20 Sirajuddin Haqqani, "What We, the Taliban, Want," *New York Times*, February 20, 2020.

21 Pamela Constable, "Taliban Cracks Down on More Rights While Demanding Western Aid," *Washington Post*, December 30, 2021.

22 Heather Barr, *Taliban Close Girls' Secondary Schools in Afghanistan, Again* (New York: Human Rights Watch, March 23, 2022).

23 See, for example, *"You Have No Right to Complain": Education, Social Restrictions, and Justice in Taliban-Held Afghanistan* (New York: Human Rights Watch, June 30, 2020).

24 Freedom House, *Freedom in the World 2022: The Global Expansion of Authoritarian Rule* (Washington: Freedom House, 2022).

25 Yaroslav Trofimov, "For a Taliban-Ruled Afghanistan, and the Rest of the World, a Crisis Looms," *Wall Street Journal*, December 13, 2021.

26 United Nations Development Programme, *Economic Instability and Uncertainty in Afghanistan after August 15: A Rapid Appraisal* (Kabul: UNDP Afghanistan, September 9, 2021); McKenzie, "Posture Statement."

27 International Rescue Committee, *2022 Emergency Watchlist* (New York: International Rescue Committee, December 15, 2021).

28 Robert Burns and Lolita C. Baldor, "U.S. Commander: Al-Qaida Numbers in Afghanistan Up 'Slightly,'" *Associated Press*, December 10, 2021.

29 Ken McCallum, head of MI5, gave an exclusive interview to the *Daily Mail*. See Rebecca Camber, "Afghanistan Is Becoming a Breeding Ground for Jihadis Again," *Daily Mail*, February 20, 2022.

30 European Parliament, *Security Situation in Afghanistan: Implications for Europe* (Brussels: European Parliament, 2021).

31 EUROPOL, *European Union Terrorist Situation and Trend Report 2021* (Luxembourg: European Union Agency for Law Enforcement Cooperation, 2021), p. 48.

32 Netherlands, *Terrorist Threat Assessment for the Netherlands* (Hague: National Coordinator for Counterterrorism and Security, Ministry of Justice and Security, October 2021), p. 21.

33 United Nations Security Council, "Twenty-Ninth Report of the Analytical Support and Sanctions Monitoring Team Submitted Pursuant to Resolution 2368 (2017) Concerning ISIL (Da'esh), Al-Qaida and Associated Individuals and Entities," S/2022/83, February 3, 2022.

34 See, for example, "ISIL/Da'esh and Al-Qaida: Two Groups and Two Individuals Added to the EU Sanctions List over Terrorism," European Council, Press Release, February 21, 2022; United Nations Security Council, "Twenty-Ninth Report of the Analytical Support and Sanctions Monitoring Team."

35 Scott Berrier, "Statement for the Record: Worldwide Threat Assessment," U.S. Senate Armed Services Committee, 2021.

36 Netherlands, *Terrorist Threat Assessment for the Netherlands* (Hague: National Coordinator for Counterterrorism and Security, Ministry of Justice and Security, October 2021), p. 21; United Nations Security Council, "Twenty-Ninth Report of the Analytical Support and Sanctions Monitoring Team."

37 United Nations Security Council, "Twenty-Ninth Report of the Analytical Support and Sanctions Monitoring Team."

38 Federal Bureau of Investigation, "Most Wanted: Sirajuddin Haqqani," Updated 2022.

39 Usama bin Laden, "Message to the Peoples of Europe," Released in November 2007.

40 "On the Martyrdom of the Great Martyr Sheikh Osama bin Laden," Al-Emera, May 6, 2011, in Strick van Linschoten and Kuehn, *The Taliban Reader*, pp. 365–366.

41 Ayman al-Zawahiri, "Zawahiri Pledges Allegiance to New Afghan Taliban Leader in Audio Speech," SITE Intelligence Group, August 13, 2015. Also see Olivier Roy and Tore Hamming, "Al-Zawahiri's Bay'a to Mullah Mansoor: A Bitter Pill But a Bountiful Harvest," *CTC Sentinel*, Vol. 9, No. 5, May 2016, pp. 16–20.

42 Ayman al-Zawahiri, "Al-Qaeda Leader Ayman al-Zawahiri Pledges to New Afghan Taliban Chief," Site Intelligence Group, June 11, 2016.

43 United Nations Security Council, "Twenty-Ninth Report of the Analytical Support and Sanctions Monitoring Team."

44 United Nations Security Council, "Fourteenth Report of the Secretary-General on the Threat Posed by ISIL (Da'esh) to International Peace and Security", 2022.

45 Office of the Director of National Intelligence, *Annual Threat Assessment of the U.S. Intelligence Community* (Washington, DC: Office of the Director of National Intelligence, February 2022); United Nations Security Council, "Fourteenth Report of the Secretary-General on the Threat Posed by ISIL (Da'esh) to International Peace and Security", 2022.

46 Antony J. Blinken, "Taking Action Against ISIS-K," U.S. Department of State, November 22, 2021.

47 Yaroslav Trofimov, "Left Behind After U.S. Withdrawal, Some Former Afghan Spies and Soldiers Turn to Islamic State," *Wall Street Journal*, October 31, 2021.

48 Tom Hussain, "ISIS-K Escalates Terror Attacks in Afghanistan and Pakistan in Show of Resistance Against Taliban," South China Morning Post, December 8, 2021.

49 McKenzie, "Posture Statement."

50 United Nations Security Council, "Twenty-Ninth Report of the Analytical Support and Sanctions Monitoring Team."

51 United Nations Security Council, "Twenty-Ninth Report of the Analytical Support and Sanctions Monitoring Team", 2022.

52 Jason Burke, "Al-Qaida: The Terror Group that Learned the Secret of Longevity," *Guardian*, September 9, 2021.

53 Quint Forgey, "Milley: 'It's Possible' U.S. Will Work with Taliban to Thwart ISIS-K," Politico, September 1, 2021.

54 McKenzie, "Posture Statement", 2022.

55 McKenzie, "Posture Statement", 2022.

56 Jake Sullivan, "Press Briefing," White House, August 17, 2021.

57 Robert Burns and Lolita C. Baldor, "U.S. Commander: Al-Qaida Numbers in Afghanistan Up 'Slightly,'" *Associated Press*, December 10, 2021.

58 Joseph Biden, "Remarks by President Biden on the End of the War in Afghanistan," White House, August 31, 2021; Helene Cooper and Eric Schmitt, "Pentagon Defends Deadly Drone Strike in Kabul," *New York Times*, September 17, 2021.

59 David Vergun, "Air Force Official Briefs Media on Deadly Drone Strike in Kabul," U.S. Department of Defense, November 3, 2021.

60 United Nations Security Council, "Twenty-Ninth Report of the Analytical Support and Sanctions Monitoring Team."

61 National Commission on Terrorist Attacks Upon the United States, *The 9/11 Commission Report* (New York: W.W. Norton, 2004).

62 50 U.S. Code § 3093, Presidential Approval and Reporting of Covert Actions.

63 Leo Shane III, "CENTCOM Needs More Resources to Counter Afghanistan Terror Threat: Nominee," *Defense News*, February 8, 2022.

64 McKenzie, "Posture Statement", 2022.

65 Dan Sabbagh, "MI5 Chief: Taliban Afghan Victory has Boosted Extremists," *Guardian*, September 10, 2021.

46

AFGHANISTAN AFTER THE WITHDRAWAL OF THE WEST

The Taliban, Al-Qaeda, and IS-K

Guido Steinberg and Aljoscha Albrecht

The withdrawal of all American and other coalition troops from Afghanistan in August 2021 allowed the Taliban to regain power is a major success for the global jihadist movement and is likely to boost its morale for years to come. After the defeat of the Soviet Union in 1989, it can credibly claim that its fighters have taken part in the ouster of the second superpower from Afghan soil. But although Usama bin Laden's al-Qaeda has been allied to the Taliban since 1996 and has operated together with the Afghan Islamists ever since, it remains far from certain that the jihadists will be able to benefit from its ally's success. The organization has long struggled to remain an international terrorist force to be reckoned with. It has failed to perpetrate any attacks of note in the West after 2005 and has mainly managed to remain relevant through its regional affiliates in more or less remote corners of Asia, Africa, and the Middle East. Between 2014 and 2017, Islamic State in Iraq and Syria (ISIS), from mid-2014 Islamic State (IS), has proved to be the much more powerful group, attracting fighters on a global scale, perpetrating attacks in many countries worldwide and establishing affiliate organizations all over the Muslim world, including IS Khorasan (IS-K), the local branch in Afghanistan. In spite of major setbacks since 2017, IS-K seems to be a more likely origin of major international attacks in the coming years than al-Qaeda, especially if it manages to form new alliances of Afghan, Pakistani and foreign jihadists on Afghan soil.

An Enduring Alliance: The Taliban and Al-Qaeda

The alliance between the Taliban and al-Qaeda has shaped the history of the jihadist movement since May 1996, when Bin Laden returned to Afghanistan from Sudan. Al-Qaeda quickly established its new headquarters in the country and started planning and organizing the 9/11 attacks in New York and Washington, D.C. After the American invasion and the defeat of the Taliban in late 2001, al-Qaeda withdrew to the Pakistani tribal areas, where it established a new headquarters in North Waziristan under the protection of the Haqqani organization, which by then operated as a part of the Afghan Taliban. Until 2012, the areas developed into the epicenter of international terrorism, with groups like al-Qaeda, the East Turkestan Islamic Movement (ETIM), the Islamic Jihad Union (IJU) and others taking part in the fight against the United States and its allies in Afghanistan, while others like the Pakistani Taliban (Tehrik-e Taliban Pakistan or TTP) and the Islamic Movement of Uzbekistan (IMU) focused on the fight against the Pakistani state.

DOI: 10.4324/9781003326373-53

Besides supporting the Taliban struggle in Afghanistan, al-Qaeda stuck to its strategy of attacks against the "far enemy", namely the United States and its European allies, in order to force them to withdraw from the Middle East. But Western counter-terrorism developed and grew more effective after 2001, so that the London bombings on 7 July 2005, which killed 52 people on a bus and in the subway in the British capital, were the last mass casualty al-Qaeda-attack in the Western world. In Europe, many plots were thwarted by the security authorities. Facing repeated setbacks, al-Qaeda made a major last-ditch effort to revive its activities in the West. In a string of events commonly labeled the "Europlot", al-Qaeda sent back to Europe several new recruits, who were supposed to carry out smaller attacks to demonstrate that al-Qaeda was still capable of fighting its enemies in the West. In the meantime, the organization hoped to gain some respite and manage to plan more strategic attacks against Western targets.[1]

The Düsseldorf cell led by the Moroccan Abdeladim El-Kebir was probably the most threatening part of the Europlot, but three of its four members were arrested in April 2011, so that the whole scheme collapsed. It might be interpreted as a sign of al-Qaeda's helplessness that the organization continued to propagate a strategy of "individual jihad" in a programmatic video in June 2011, shortly after Bin Laden was killed in Abbottabad on 2 May 2011. At that time, the idea of lone-actor-attacks had gained some support in jihadist circles, but all attempts remained a far cry from the mass casualty attacks al-Qaeda had perpetrated in its heyday from 1998 to 2001.[2] If the idea ever had any traction among jihadists worldwide, it was lost in the years between 2010 and 2012, when its major proponents were killed. Al-Qaeda did not only lose its founder-leader Usama bin Laden, but also many other senior commanders as a result of the relentless US drone war against its bases in Pakistan. In the following years, it became obvious that the organization had not been able to adequately replace seasoned leaders like Mustafa Abu l-Yazid (a.k.a. Sheik Said al-Masri, d. May 2010), Jamal al-Misrati (a.k.a. Atiyatallah al-Libi, d. August 2011), and Hasan Muhammad Qaid (a.k.a. Abu Yahia al-Libi, d. June 2012). Prominent leaders like Saif al-Adl and Abdallah Ahmad Abdallah (Abu Muhammad al-Masri, d. August 2020) were under house arrest or other forms of surveillance in Iran, while others (Abu al-Khair al-Masri, Khalid al-Aruri, and Sari Shihab) traveled to Syria to rebuild structures with the al-Nusra-Front (Jabhat al-Nusra) and later Hurras al-Din, where most of them were subsequently killed by American airstrikes. Perhaps even more importantly, the new but aging al-Qaeda leader Aiman al-Zawahiri (1951–2022) lacked the charisma of his predecessor and seems to have been isolated in some hideout in Pakistan and/or Afghanistan so that he gradually lost influence on the jihadist scene worldwide. This didn't change after the Taliban victory, when Zawahiri moved to Kabul and released new video messages, which refuted rumors of his demise. The al-Qaeda leader was subsequently killed in an American drone strike in the Afghan capital on 1 August 2022.

The fact that al-Qaeda has survived to this day, despite these serious difficulties, is arguably due to its penchant for alliance-building, most importantly with the Afghan Taliban and especially the Haqqani organization, with which the al-Qaeda leadership maintains close contact.[3] It was therefore hardly surprising that the group was quick to release a statement congratulating the Taliban on its power grab.[4] Although it was never stronger than a few hundred fighters, al-Qaeda played an outsize role in Afghanistan by supporting its allies with terrorist know-how, including the construction and use of improvised explosive devices (IEDs) and suicide attacks. Although the February 2020 agreement between the United States and the Taliban stipulated that the Taliban give up their support for al-Qaeda and other international terrorists, there is no evidence that the Taliban took any action whatsoever against the presence of the Arab organization and its affiliate, al-Qaeda in the Indian Subcontinent (AQIS), on Afghan soil. Quite in contrast, al-Qaeda structures seem to remain embedded in the Taliban and show a presence in several Afghan provinces.[5]

The long-standing alliance with the Taliban is also a potential source of weakness, though, because al-Qaeda depends on Taliban support for its very survival in the country and the Taliban's strategy remains unclear. As of yet (April 2022), there are no indications that the Taliban plan to give up their relationship with the Arab organization.

In spite of its apparent weakness, al-Qaeda remains a terrorist force to be reckoned with, especially if the Taliban decide – as seems to be the case – not to fulfil their commitments in the 2020 Doha agreement but instead honor their alliance with al-Qaeda. But more importantly, the US withdrawal severely limits the capabilities of an effective fight against jihadist activities in Afghanistan and Pakistan. US intelligence has lost its eyes and ears on the ground and the help of its local partners in the Afghan government. Furthermore, even if information continues to flow from Afghanistan, the US military and the CIA have not yet managed to gain access to bases close to the Afghan borders for drones and aircraft, making the aerial fight against the jihadists much more difficult than before. If al-Qaeda and its allied organizations manage to profit from the US withdrawal by attracting more personnel and finances, the threat from Afghanistan is likely to grow in the next months and years. While recent trends show that al-Qaeda has experienced serious difficulties in recruitment, especially among foreign fighters, it should be borne in mind that, unlike IS, al-Qaida has traditionally relied on attacks carried out by smaller numbers of highly trained assailants.

IS Khorasan against the Taliban

Al-Qaeda's difficulties have been partly caused by its own weaknesses, but these have been compounded by the emergence of IS as a powerful competitor. In 2014, the organization managed to conquer large parts of Iraq and Syria and could therefore plausibly claim to have implemented the model of an "Islamic state" that many jihadists worldwide had been waiting for. After IS's declaration of the caliphate in June 2014, thousands of young foreign fighters, among them many women, flocked to Syria to join the fledgling "state". Furthermore, IS was so rich and became so attractive to jihadists worldwide, that it managed to expand by establishing a network of affiliate organizations called "provinces" in many countries of the Islamic world starting in November 2014, among them IS Khorasan Province (Wilaya Khorasan or IS-K).

For the new organization, the Afghan theater was particularly challenging, because it had to hold its own against two far superior opponents. From the outset, IS Khorasan fought against the Taliban as it believes that there can be only one "Islamic state" and one legitimate caliph. Moreover, IS criticizes the Taliban for closely cooperating with the Pakistani military and frequently refers to the movement as an instrument of the Inter-Services Intelligence (ISI), Pakistan's military intelligence agency.[6] Moreover, it criticizes the cooperation between the Taliban and Iran's Islamic Revolutionary Guard Corps, whose joint efforts have expanded significantly since 2015 and have been directed, above all, against their common enemy, the United States.[7] Until August 2021, the presence of the US military in the Hindu Kush was another problem for IS, which, together with Afghan government troops, fought against the organization and repeatedly inflicted heavy losses on it.

Between 2014 and 2021, IS-K suffered high losses but always proved to be able to regenerate. One of the reasons seems to have been the varied social base of the organization in Afghanistan, which primarily consisted of Pakistanis, Afghans, and Central Asians (as opposed to al-Qaeda, which remains a strongly Arab organization). IS-K's leadership was dominated by Pakistani Pashtuns who had earlier belonged to TTP, an independent jihadist group dedicated to fighting the Pakistani state (unlike the Afghan Taliban movement, which is allied with Islamabad). Above all, it was the Pakistani Pashtuns from the tribal areas in Orakzai, Khyber, and Bajaur who professed allegiance to the new organization. The Afghan nationals who joined from 2014 onwards were largely former Afghan Taliban who had broken with their organization for ideological or personal reasons. Many were commanders who had remained marginal figures within the group because they were Salafists (which the Taliban are not) and criticized the Taliban movement for propagating non-religious tribal traditions, among other things. The third subgroup of IS Afghanistan is composed of Central Asian jihadists, mainly Uzbeks and Tajiks. Those who joined the organization in the early days were mainly fighters of IMU who, in the wake of a Pakistani Army offensive in 2014, had been forced to leave the sites in the Pakistani tribal areas to which they had retreated and flee to Afghanistan.[8]

Right from the start, IS-K's main opponent was the Taliban. While it was able to score major successes in the east of the country, taking over several districts in the southern part of Nangarhar Province, the Taliban launched their first large-scale offensive in fall 2015 and were able to drive IS out of many localities. From 2016 onwards, the US military stepped up its attacks, too. Again and again, the US government and its Afghan allies reported having carried out successful missions that left many IS militants dead. By the end of 2016, the group appeared to have been considerably weakened, – its numbers are reported to have shrunk from some 3,000 to 4,000 in 2015 to perhaps only 700 in late 2017 – but it proved able to offset heavy losses by enlisting new recruits. This became evident during the course of 2017, when it was once again able to expand its influence. Not even increased US air strikes and joint operations with allied Afghan security forces were able to prevent that from happening; on the contrary, IS-K continued its offensive.

Among its most remarkable achievements was IS-K's expansion from early 2017 onwards into the heavily Uzbek-populated provinces of Jawzjan, Sar-e Pol, and Faryab in the northwest of Afghanistan, where the group established a new base. At the same time, it stepped up its attacks in the urban centres of the country, targeting mainly the Shiite Hazara. A series of attacks in Kabul alone claimed the lives of hundreds of civilians. It was not until 2018 that IS began to suffer repeated defeats as it came under pressure from its opponents. In Jawzjan, the Taliban launched attacks that ended in July 2018 with the crushing of IS in the northwest of Afghanistan. A large-scale Taliban offensive against the IS strongholds in Nangarhar followed in mid-October 2018, although on this occasion the jihadists were able to defend themselves. In 2019, the number of defeats grew as both Taliban and Afghan government troops – the latter bolstered by US support – carried out attacks against IS in Nangarhar, inflicting heavy losses. In November 2019, the organization lost the last territories in the province to which it could retreat and the small number of fighters who had been able to escape from the clutches of the enemy fled farther north to Kunar. When, in March 2020, the Taliban announced that the last remaining safe havens in that province had been captured as well, IS Afghanistan appeared to have been defeated. However, repeated attacks in Kabul bore witness to the fact that the organization was still operating underground and thus continued to pose a danger for Afghanistan.

At the beginning of 2021, IS Afghanistan's numbers were back up to 1,000–2,200. During the course of 2021, it became increasingly clear that IS's options to act were growing as the pressure from the US troops eased. The number of its attacks grew slowly at first and then rapidly from August onwards. Especially headline-grabbing was the bombing of the airport in Kabul on 26 August 2021: amid all the turmoil shortly after the Taliban had captured the capital, a suicide bomber killed at least 183 people, including 13 US soldiers.[9] Meanwhile, it is estimated that some 2,000–3,000 IS inmates escaped in prison breakouts in 2021, which means the number of fighters may have increased significantly.[10] A UN report from early February 2022 suggests that the number could be approaching 4,000 once again, a figure last recorded in 2015.[11] In the following months, IS increased the frequency of its attacks in several parts of the country, often focusing on Shiite mosques. Places of worship were not only hit in Kabul but also in Kunduz and Kandahar, which suggests IS-K had expanded its area of operations. The attack in Kunduz on 8 October 2021, in which more than 50 people died, shows that IS also has a strong presence in this area close to the Uzbek and Tajik borders. And the attack on a Shiite mosque in the Taliban stronghold of Kandahar on 15 October, which left more than 60 people dead, illustrates that the organization is capable of operating in the Taliban heartland. In addition, there have been numerous attacks on Taliban "security forces" in Nangarhar Province and Kunar, where IS appeared to be gaining strength in the second half of 2021. Deborah Lyons, the UN Secretary-General's Special Representative for Afghanistan, warned in November 2021 that IS now had a presence in almost every Afghan province and had increased the number of its attacks from around 60 in 2020 to more than 330 in 2021.[12] For its part, IS has said it killed and wounded more than a dozen Taliban in Logar, Nangarhar and Kunar provinces in December 2021 and January 2022 alone.[13] On 4 March 2022, IS attacked a Shiite mosque in Pakistan, killing at least 62 people. [14] With this being one of the most devastating attacks the country has seen in several years, IS-K has shown that it is capable of carrying out large-scale attacks outside Afghanistan.

A Special Relationship: The Haqqani Organization and IS Khorasan

The withdrawal of US troops in August 2021 and the takeover of power by the Taliban changed the overall situation in Afghanistan and, along with it, the position of the jihadists in Afghanistan, especially IS. Things had already started to change by the time of the negotiations between the US administration under President Donald Trump and the Taliban, which began in Doha, Qatar, in 2018 and culminated in an agreement in February 2020. The document provided for a gradual reduction in US troops and a complete withdrawal from Afghanistan by 1 May 2021.[15] For the Taliban, it was a daring step to enter into negotiations with the infidel occupiers over a solution to the conflict. Some commanders and fighters criticized the pragmatism of the Taliban leadership, fueling hope within IS that more ideologically motivated individuals or even subgroups of the Taliban would defect and join the organization.[16] Although this danger does not seem to have materialized yet, the Taliban were clearly nervous about the rival organization. Around the same time as the Doha talks, the Taliban stepped up the military pressure on IS Khorasan, which led to the defeat of the latter in Nangarhar in November 2019 and in Kunar in March 2020. While the Taliban may have been aiming to crush the organization before its willingness to negotiate with the United States could be used by the enemy to enlist new recruits, IS was able to continue its activities underground, the defeats notwithstanding.

Since the Kabul airport bombing on 26 August 2021, the debate about potential defectors from the Taliban-al-Qaeda ecosystem to IS-K has focused on the Haqqani organization and the role it has played in the new fighting strength of IS in Afghanistan. Since its inception in the first half of the 1990s, the Taliban movement has never been monolithic and has comprised several sub-groups, of which the Haqqani organization is the most autonomous and powerful. It was founded by the Pashtun warlord Jalaluddin Haqqani (1939–2018), who fought against the Soviet occupation as early as the 1980s and thereafter served as the strongman in Pakistan's North Waziristan tribal area and Afghanistan's Paktia, Paktika, and Khost provinces, having reached an agreement with the Pakistani military, whose client the Haqqanis remain to this day. In 1996, Jalaluddin allied himself with the Taliban and subsequently provided sanctuary to Usama bin Laden and al-Qaeda – in fact, the organization's relations to the Haqqanis have always been stronger than to the rest of the Taliban movement. The alliance with the Arab jihadists held for the next two-and-a-half decades, during which their ideas spread among the Haqqanis. Jalaluddin handed over the leadership of the organization to his son Sirajuddin no later than 2012, by which time the Haqqanis (unlike the mainstream Taliban) were considered strictly jihadist. They were also regarded as particularly powerful – most major attacks in Kabul were attributed to them. During this period, Sirajuddin rose through the formal ranks of the Taliban; in 2015, he was appointed as one of two deputies of the Taliban leader Mullah Akhtar Mohammad Mansur (officially in office in 2015–2016) and then first deputy to the latter's successor, Haibatullah Akhundzada.[17]

From an early stage, there were commanders and fighters within the Haqqani organization who were well inclined toward IS. In November 2016, some 150 followers of Haqqani from Kabul are reported to have joined IS Afghanistan, and more defections followed later.[18] Moreover, there is information to suggest that the current IS Afghanistan leader, Shahab al-Muhajir, who was appointed to that post in June 2020, is a former mid-level-commander of the Haqqani organization.[19] These links to the Haqqanis may be one reason why IS has succeeded in carrying out so many attacks in the capital. Nevertheless, it can be assumed, based on IS activities in Kabul before August 2021, that there was some sort of cooperation with the Haqqani organization. Sirajuddin and his people controlled many access routes into the capital, where they were the strongest insurgent group until August 2021; this suggests that Sirajuddin and his troops harbor a certain ambivalence toward IS. In the new Taliban government formed in September 2021, Sirajuddin was appointed minister of the interior; thus, he is also responsible for Afghanistan's domestic security. Meanwhile, the devastating attack at Kabul airport in August 2021 highlighted just how dire the security situation was in the capital. If the Haqqani organization is not fully committed to fighting against IS, this would be an enormous advantage for the latter terrorist group.

The case of Sirajuddin Haqqani points to an even bigger problem: namely, the Taliban takeover of power could lead to a shakeup of the Islamist scene in the Hindu Kush. After decades of war and a long association with jihadist Arabs, Pakistanis and Central Asians, there is a strong jihadist current running through the Taliban – one that not only has a particularly large number of adherents in the Haqqani organization but is also influential in other Taliban units. After the takeover of power in Kabul, the jihadist goal is to expand the fight beyond Afghanistan to the neighboring states and the whole world. The number of Afghan, Pakistani and Central Asian fighters who feel committed to jihadism is probably in the low 10,000s.[20]

Thus, the Taliban face a dilemma. If they heed calls from abroad and promote a moderate policy at home, jihadist insurgents could turn their back on the movement and endanger the stability of the new regime. If, on the other hand, they pursue a more overtly ideological line, it will probably be impossible to attract aid from abroad, which is urgently needed because of the catastrophic economic and supply situation in Afghanistan. The strong position of the Haqqani organization in the new government can be seen as an indication that the Taliban want to accommodate jihadist forces. Moreover, there is no evidence that the Taliban are cutting ties with al-Qaeda, as provided for in the February 2020 agreement with the United States. Many initial measures suggest that the Taliban leadership is following an ambivalent course to generate support from abroad without losing the jihadists within its own ranks to IS. To a Western audience, it publicly promises moderation, while, in the country, repression of potential adversaries has been intensified. Reports about secret revenge killings, imprisonment and torture of former military and police personnel who have publicly been promised an amnesty by the Taliban are but one example of hardliners defining the actual policies of the Taliban government.[21] Increasingly repressive policies towards women are another.[22]

At the same time, the increasing activity of IS Afghanistan is a clear sign that the jihadists could become a growing threat for the Taliban, the neighboring states and worldwide. There are (as yet unconfirmed and probably exaggerated) reports that since August 2021, large numbers of foreign fighters from the Middle East, Central Asia, and Pakistan have gone to Afghanistan. If the country were indeed to become a magnet for jihadists from other regions, IS would likely be the more important final destination than al-Qaeda: the former's deeply ideological approach has led to tens of thousands of new recruits joining the organization since 2014, whereas the latter has had problems winning over young radicals. The extent to which IS can benefit from the influx of foreign jihadists depends heavily on just how strong the new Taliban state is and whether it will be in a position to contain IS militarily.

If IS continues to grow stronger, it is likely not only to remain a threat for Afghanistan but also to expand its activities to the immediate neighboring countries. Pakistan, Uzbekistan and Tajikistan are the main candidates, as the overwhelming number of IS fighters in Afghanistan come from these three states and IS maintains bases not far from the borders of those countries. Iran is another possible target of IS expansion. The country is particularly well suited for this purpose because the Taliban movement has so far maintained good relations with Tehran and because IS can distinguish itself from the Taliban by attacking Iranian targets. Moreover, it should be able to expect financial support for such a strategy from anti-Shiite donors in Pakistan and the Arab Gulf states.

The Threat to the West

The continuing strength of IS Khorasan also poses a threat to Western nations. As early as 2017–2018, there was growing evidence of European recruits heading to the Hindu Kush to join IS there – a number of French nationals were to be found during this period alongside IS militants in Jawzjan Province.[23] That Europe is another important target for IS terrorist activity was evident from the April 2017 attack in central Stockholm, which killed five people and injured many others. Sayvaly Shafiev (a.k.a (Abu) Muawiya), a Tajik leader of the Central Asians in IS Afghanistan had been in close contact with the attacker, Rakhmat Akilov, who is an ethnic Tajik (with Uzbek nationality).[24] In 2019, German law-enforcement officials revealed that, quite similarly, in 2018–2019, a Tajik IS cell in North Rhine-Westphalia had been communicating with a Central Asian IS cadre in Afghanistan named Umed Davlatov (a.k.a Shakhomat), who gave it religious-ideological lessons online. In January 2021, a member of the cell, the Tajik citizen Ravsan Bakaev, was convicted because he had taken part in forming an IS cell which planned to perpetrate attacks on behalf of the organization in Germany.[25]

In the planning of such attacks, IS Afghanistan is able to benefit from the fact that since 2015, its parent organization in Iraq and Syria has been developing an innovative approach to terrorist strikes directed from a distance. Between the perpetrator and the person planning the strike, there is only virtual contact, which is established and maintained via messaging services such as Telegram, in particular. The planner advises the prospective terrorist on religious-ideological issues as well as on the selection of a target and the means of carrying out the attack. In return, the attacker records a video before the act in which he states his commitment to what he is about to do and swears allegiance to the IS leader. He then sends this video to IS, which publishes it after the attack and claims responsibility for the deed.

For IS, terrorist attacks directed and led by the organization have the advantage of being more effective than conventional single-perpetrator attacks, which, though difficult to prevent, rarely claim many victims. At the same time, they have a distinct edge over large-scale, organized attacks, such as those in Paris in November 2015, because the logistical, personnel and financial costs are much lower and the terrorists do not have to cross national borders, which carries the risk of being discovered. Many IS attacks since 2016 have been directed from a distance, including the one in a Christmas Market in Berlin on 19 December 2016. Nevertheless, IS terrorist activity has slackened considerably since 2017, in part because of improved telecommunications surveillance by US security agencies, which have uncovered numerous plots in advance.

Another reason is likely to be the weakness of IS headquarters, which since 2016 has lost all the territory it held in the Middle East. The defeats have impaired the jihadists' ability to mobilize potential perpetrators of attacks – for example, key planners have been killed or captured. To successfully launch attacks from afar, IS needs a site to which its specialists can retreat and find new weak spots in telecommunications surveillance systems as well as build and maintain a network of international contacts. Perhaps equally important, the organization needs to demonstrate power and strength in a war zone following years of defeats so that it can attract new young recruits. Nowhere are the conditions better for doing so than in Afghanistan. If the strength of IS continues to grow in the Hindu Kush and the organization expands its armed struggle to the neighboring countries, it will likely soon pose a greater threat to Europe and the West once again.

Notes

1 This strategy was outlined in an internal al-Qaeda document loaded in a thumb drive that the Afghan-Austrian foreign fighter Maqsood Lodin – one of the fighters who was sent back from Pakistan – carried hidden in his body when he was arrested in Berlin on 16 May 2011. future_work.docx. n.p., n.d. [2009] (Document in the author's possession). Lodin carried related papers with him. On these and a strategic letter by Yunis al-Muritani, which was presented as evidence in the trial against the Düsseldorf cell in 2012 cp. Guido Steinberg, Gutachten zu den "Lodin-Papieren "von 2009 und dem Brief Yunis al-Muritanis an "Zamara'i" vom 28. März 2010 (Anlage 1 zum al-Qaida-Gutachten vom 10 August 2013) (Unpublished court testimony), Berlin, 14 August 2012, passim.
2 *La tukallaf illa nafsak* (Thou Art Only Held Responsible for Thyself), Part 1, Video (Al-Sahab Media, 3 June 2011).
3 United Nations Security Council (UNSC), Twenty-Sixth Report of the Analytical Support and Sanctions Monitoring Team Submitted Pursuant to Resolution 2368 (2017) Concerning ISIL (Da'esh), Al-Qaida and Associated Individuals and Entities (S/2020/717), 23 July 2020, p. 15, https://www.securitycouncilreport.org/atf/cf/%7B65BFCF9B-6D27-4E9C-8CD3-CF6E4FF96FF9%7D/s_2020_717.pdf.
4 United Nations Security Council (UNSC), Twenty-Ninth Report of the Analytical Support and Sanctions Monitoring Team Submitted Pursuant to Resolution 2368 (2017) Concerning ISIL (Da'esh), Al-Qaida and Associated Individuals and Entities (S/2022/83), 3 February 2022, p. 15, https://documents-ddsny.un.org/doc/UNDOC/GEN/N21/416/14/PDF/N2141614.pdf?OpenElement.
5 Asfandyar Mir, "Twenty Years After 9/11: The Terror Threat from Afghanistan Post the Taliban Takeover", *CTC Sentinel*, September 2021, Volume 14, Issue 7, pp. 19–43, https://www.ctc.usma.edu/twenty-years-after-9-11-the-terror-threat-from-afghanistan-post-the-taliban-takeover/.
6 Zahid Hussain, "Daesh in Afghanistan", Between War & Peace – The Afghanistan Essays, Jinnah Institute, Islamabad, 15 January 2018, https://jinnah-institute.org/publication/the-afghanistan-essays-daesh-in-afghanistan/.
7 Ali Fathollah-Nejad and Hamidreza Azizi, "Iran and the Taliban after the US fiasco in Afghanistan", *Middle East Institute*, 22 September 2021, https://www.mei.edu/publications/iran-and-taliban-after-us-fiasco-afghanistan.
8 On the three subgroups in detail cp. Giustozzi, *The Islamic State in Khorasan*, p. 132.
9 Helene Cooper, Eric Schmitt, and Thomas Gibbons-Neff, "As U.S. Troops Searched Afghans, a Bomber in the Crowd Moved in", *New York Times*, 27 August 2021 (updated 1 September 2021), https://www.nytimes.com/2021/08/27/us/politics/marines-kabul-airport-attack.html.
10 Amira Jadoon, Abdul Sayed, and Andrew Mines, "The Islamic State Threat in Taliban Afghanistan: Tracing the Resurgence of Islamic State Khorasan", *CTC Sentinel*, January 2022, Volume 15, Issue 1, pp. 33–35 (p. 37), https://ctc.usma.edu/wp-content/uploads/2022/01/CTC-SENTINEL-012022.pdf.

11 United Nations Security Council (UNSC), Twenty-Ninth Report of the Analytical Support and Sanctions Monitoring Team Submitted Pursuant to Resolution 2368 (2017) Concerning ISIL (Da'esh), Al-Qaida and Associated Individuals and Entities (S/2022/83), 3 February 2022, p. 16, https://documents-ddsny.un.org/doc/UNDOC/GEN/N21/416/14/PDF/N2141614.pdf?OpenElement.

12 Jonathan Landay, "U.N. Envoy Says Islamic State Now Appears Present in All Afghan Provinces", *Reuters*, 17 November 2021, https://www.reuters.com/world/asia-pacific/un-envoy-says-islamic-state-now-appears-present-all-afghan-provinces-2021-11-17/?utm_source=iterable&utm_medium=email&utm_campaign=3226629_.

13 Asena Karacalti and Katerina Bozhinova, "Regional Overview: South Asia and Afghanistan 11 December 2021–7 January 2022", *ACLED*, 13 January 2022, https://acleddata.com/2022/01/13/regional-overview-south-asia-and-afghanistan-11-december-2021-7-january-2022/.

14 Ismail Khan and Salman Masood, "ISIS Claims Bombing of Pakistani Mosque, Killing Dozens", *New York Times*, 4 March 2022, https://www.nytimes.com/2022/03/04/world/middleeast/pakistan-peshawar-mosque-explosion.html.

15 Joint Declaration between the Islamic Republic of Afghanistan and the United States of America for Bringing Peace to Afghanistan, February 2020, p. 3, https://www.state.gov/wp-content/uploads/2020/02/02.29.20-US-Afghanistan-Joint-Declaration.pdf.

16 United Nations Security Council (UNSC), Twenty-Sixth Report of the Analytical Support and Sanctions Monitoring Team Submitted Pursuant to Resolution 2368 (2017) Concerning ISIL (Da'esh), Al-Qaida and Associated Individuals and Entities (S/2020/717), 23 July 2020, p. 6, https://www.securitycouncilreport.org/atf/cf/%7B65BFCF9B-6D27-4E9C-8CD3-CF6E4FF96FF9%7D/s_2020_717.pdf.

17 For a short overview of the Haqqani organization cp. Jeff M. Smith, "The Haqqani Network: The New Kingmakers in Kabul", *War on the Rocks*, 12 November 2021, https://warontherocks.com/2021/11/the-haqqani-network-afghanistans-new-power-players/. For a deeper historical analysis cp. Vahid Brown and Don Rassler, *Fountainhead of Jihad. The Haqqani Nexus, 1973–2012*, London: Hurst 2013, passim.

18 Giustozzi, 2022, *The Islamic State in Khorasan*, p. 109.

19 United Nations Security Council (UNSC), Twelfth Report of the Analytical Support and Sanctions Monitoring Team Submitted Pursuant to Resolution 2557 (2020) Concerning the Taliban and other Associated Individuals and Entities Constituting a Threat to the Peace Stability and Security of Afghanistan (S/2021/486), 1 June 2021, pp. 3–4, 16–17, https://www.ecoi.net/en/file/local/2053487/S_2021_486_E.pdf.

20 Author's Interview with Military Intelligence Official, Berlin, December 2021.

21 Barbara Marcolini, Sanjar Sohail and Alexander Stockton, "The Taliban Promised Them Amnesty. Then They Were Executed", *New York Times*, 12 April 2022, https://www.nytimes.com/interactive/2022/04/12/opinion/taliban-afghanistan-revenge.html?searchResultPosition=7.

22 Safiullah Padshah and Christina Goldbaum, "Taliban Renege on Promise to Open Afghan Girls' Schools", *New York Times*, 23 March 2022, https://www.nytimes.com/2022/03/23/world/asia/afghanistan-girls-schools-taliban.html?searchResultPosition=2.

23 Cp. e.g. "French, Uzbek Daesh Militants Killed in Jawzjan Air Operation", *Tolo News*, 2 January 2018, https://tolonews.com/afghanistan/french-uzbek-daesh-militants-killed-jawzjan-air-operation.

24 Police Interrogation of Rakhmat Akilov (in German translation), Stockholm, 19 May 2017, pp. 18–19. On Shafiev, see UNSC, Twenty-Fourth Report of the Analytical Support and Sanctions Monitoring Team Submitted Pursuant to Resolution 2368 (2017) Concerning ISIL (Da'esh), Al-Qaida and Associated Individuals and Entities (S/2019/570), 15 July 2019, p. 15, https://documents-dd-ny.un.org/doc/UNDOC/GEN/N19/199/15/PDF/N1919915.pdf?OpenElement; Giustozzi, *The Islamic State in Khorasan*, pp. 197–198.

25 Oberlandesgericht Düsseldorf, Urteil gegen Ravsan Bakaev, Düsseldorf, 26 January 2021, passim. The other members of the Tadjik IS cell were convicted to prison terms between four and nine and a half years in May 2022, but the verdict remained subject to revision at the time of writing this article.

47

GLOBAL JIHAD

Al-Qaeda and the Islamic State's Struggle for Power and Global Dominance

Katherine Zimmerman

Al-Qaeda and the Islamic State remain locked in a struggle to transform the Muslim world according to their own vision and in a competition with each other, vying to lead the global jihad. They have sought, as part of the Salafi-jihadi movement, to replace the so-called apostate regimes of Muslim-majority countries and spread their fundamentalist interpretation of Islam. They have also sought to weaken the United States, Europe, Russia, and others who have combated them or supported Muslim regimes. Yet while al-Qaeda and the Islamic State share a vision for the Muslim world, they also contest the other's claim to be the vanguard of the Salafi-jihadi movement. They thus compete to lead the movement and at times have come into direct conflict. Neither has lost yet, and despite their competition, the global Salafi-jihadi movement continues to strengthen.

The modern Salafi-jihadi movement is, in short, the ideological current that cohered during the jihad against the Soviets in Afghanistan. Its core principle holds that violent jihad is an individual obligation (*fard 'ayn*) for Muslims to defend and restore Islam, with the objective of building an Islamic society under the restored caliphate. Its adherents also believe that they must purify Islam's practice of innovations (*bid'a*) to return it to the Islam the Prophet Muhammad and his followers (the *salaf*) observed. The Afghan jihad served as a melting pot for leaders and scholars engaging on the question of jihad. They forged the core Salafi-jihadi doctrine with which all of today's Salafi-jihadi groups engage. The premature death of Abdallah Azzam, the "father of jihad," in 1989 and Osama bin Laden's dominating presence at the center of the emergent movement eclipsed an ongoing discourse within the movement over theological particulars that continues today.

Winning or Losing? The Salafi-Jihadi Movement's Struggle

The global Salafi-jihadi movement has engaged in a decades-long effort to transform the Muslim world by co-opting and leading local revolutions against so-called apostate regimes and attacking the West and others to weaken their influence in Muslim lands. A recent tapering off of the jihadi terror threat in the United States and Europe has fostered a false sense of accomplishment in the West. Certainly, two decades of investment in a worldwide counterterrorism apparatus to disrupt transnational terror plots has paid off—the ability for al-Qaeda and the Islamic State to carry out another major terror attack has been greatly diminished. Al-Qaeda and the Islamic State are currently losing on the terrorism front. Yet their expansion within the Muslim world, a strategic

DOI: 10.4324/9781003326373-54

aim that they had sought to advance through terrorism, shows long-term strengthening even though the vast majority of Muslims continue to reject Salafi-jihadism. Today, the Salafi-jihadi movement stretches across more territory with more fighters who have more expertise than ever before, and it can point to the Taliban's return in Afghanistan as proof of success.

The global COVID-19 pandemic helped Salafi-jihadi groups in active conflict zones. It has had little impact on Salafi-jihadi operations, which have continued apace, whereas states diverted scarce resources from counterterrorism operations—including security forces—to respond to the pandemic and pandemic restrictions, affecting the Western counterterrorism response. Broadly, Salafi-jihadi groups took the new pandemic challenge in their stride and adjusted their narratives accordingly, blaming the West and nonbelievers for the virus, which they described as punishment for the injustices committed against Muslims.[1] Al-Shabaab, al-Qaeda's Somalia-based affiliate that administers territory, established a committee to monitor the virus, and in 2021 it warned followers against the vaccine and advised taking medications prescribed in the Qur'an instead.[2] The pandemic and state responses to it exacerbated many of the conditions that Salafi-jihadi groups have exploited to gain influence in communities, including anti-government grievances, competition for scarce resources, and intergroup tensions.[3] The general retraction of Western foreign assistance programs and force deployments created additional opportunities for Salafi-jihadi groups to become stronger. Salafi-jihadi groups thus gained influence in the gaps that local governments and Western states left behind.

The Salafi-jihadi movement has expanded into new areas—particularly in Africa—taking advantage of conditions ripe for its success. These conditions include the presence of anti-government grievances, active or potential intercommunal conflict, and weak or exploitative security forces. The Islamic State spread into a local insurgency in Cabo Delgado, Mozambique, in 2020, dramatically changing the nature of the fight.[4] A multinational military intervention to support Mozambican forces has yet to quell the insurgency, and neighboring countries remain concerned about the possibility that the Islamic State will spread into their territories.[5] The Islamic State also insinuated itself into the Allied Democratic Forces' insurgency in the Democratic Republic of the Congo and was behind a renewed terrorism threat in Uganda.[6] In West Africa, the Islamic State has surged and reorganized in Nigeria and the Lake Chad Basin after killing Boko Haram's leader in clashes, though its branch's growth in the Sahel stagnated after that branch's leader died in August 2021.[7] Al-Qaeda's West African affiliate and associated groups have strengthened across the Sahel and are pushing into Benin, Côte d'Ivoire, Ghana, Senegal, and Togo.[8]

Salafi-jihadi groups have also shifted increasingly toward focusing efforts on providing local governance where they have consolidated power. Al-Shabaab has strengthened as counterterrorism pressure has eased and has even begun reissuing calls to followers to emigrate (make *hijra*) to live under its rule in Somalia.[9] As the dust settles in the aftermath of the US withdrawal from Afghanistan, the Taliban will probably issue a similar call as Salafi-jihadi groups rebound. Regardless, the Taliban's takeover of the country is a major victory for the Salafi-jihadi movement, which sees the return of the Islamic Emirate to power as a step forward in the global fight.[10] Hayat Tahrir al-Sham, based in Idlib, Syria, is transforming its image from a gun-bearing group to a governing one as it consolidates its hold, and it almost certainly looks to the Taliban as a source of emulation.[11] Salafi-jihadi groups measure their success by the number of people under their influence. By this measure, they are succeeding.

The Salafi-jihadi movement's successes have not been easily won, however. They have come at a noteworthy cost to the leaders of the various organizations, who find themselves hunted globally by the United States and its counterterrorism partners. Such sustained counterterrorism pressure has disconnected remaining leaders from their followers and hindered regrowth. For example, the late Islamic State leader, Abu Ibrahim al-Qurayshi,[12] kept a low profile during his two years at the helm of the organization, never once revealing himself to or communicating directly with his followers. And yet, Qurayshi met the same fate as his predecessor, Abu Bakr al-Baghdadi—death by suicide vest during a US counterterrorism raid in February 2022.[13] Time has proven al-Qaeda's and the Islamic State's resilience to a decapitation strategy, and the threat of death has not deterred current or future terrorist leaders. Yet the timing of Qurayshi's death may prove a more serious setback for the Islamic State after Iraqi security forces captured the most senior deputy leader, Sami Jasim Mohammad al-Jaburi, in November 2021.[14] The removal of key Islamic State figures from the battlefield, including over summer 2022, and the likelihood that Jaburi provided additional intelligence on the organization's operations may slow the Islamic State's ability to regroup after its collapse.

Al-Qaeda's leadership has similarly suffered under counterterrorism pressure. It has lost a number of senior leaders, especially the leaders of its affiliates in Yemen, North Africa, and the Indian subcontinent, over the past few years.[15] The ongoing targeting of al-Qaeda's leaders globally has further eliminated key individuals from the ranks, including those operating in Syria.[16] When a US airstrike killed a high-ranking official within al-Qaeda in the Arabian Peninsula's media wing, its channels fell silent and then displayed noticeable quality differences when they came back.[17] Few of al-Qaeda's top regional leaders have contact with the rank-and-file members for fear of being targeted—al-Shabaab's leader has not been seen in public for five years. The effect of leadership deaths on al-Qaeda and harm to the network even pushed al-Qaeda's main media arm to emphasize operational security in a March 2022 video.[18]

The most significant blow to al-Qaeda has been the August 2022 death of Osama bin Laden's successor, Ayman al-Zawahiri. Already, Zawahiri and his deputies' inability to communicate directly with followers and respond in a timely fashion to major events probably hindered al-Qaeda's ability to attract new followers and mobilize supporters. Zawahiri retreated from public view for lengthy periods, which generated speculation about his ability to lead the organization, his actual influence over the decentralized al-Qaeda network, and, even premature rumors of his death in fall 2020.[19] A flurry of videos featuring Zawahiri released after the Taliban regained control of Afghanistan reinforced criticism of him as a detached leader because he did not touch on current events.[20] Only in spring 2022 did Zawahiri respond directly to developments, citing an event in India that went viral in February 2022.[21] Yet his reappearance on the global stage was to be short-lived, ending with his death in August 2022. As of November 2022, however, al-Qaeda has yet to name its next leader, leading to predictions of al-Qaeda's end. Some prominent ideologues have even called for its dissolution,[22] though the transnational network will probably persist through the regional affiliates for some time—formal or not.

Significant counterterrorism pressure has weakened parts of the Salafi-jihadi movement, especially in East Asia, Iraq and parts of Syria, and Yemen. Counterterrorism operations in Indonesia and the Philippines have seemingly dismantled the Islamic State's network and disrupted recent plots.[23] Similarly, Emirati and US counterterrorism operations have degraded al-Qaeda in Yemen considerably since its peak strength in 2015 and prevented the Islamic State from ever gaining more than a token foothold in the country.[24] Al-Qaeda's Yemen-based affiliate still pursues transnational attack capabilities, however.[25] Counterterrorism operations have reduced the Islamic State in Iraq and Syria to a fraction of its former strength. Yet it retains numerous supporters in internally displaced persons camps and detention facilities in northeast Syria—those who had once lived in its physical "caliphate"—and has recently sought to reconstitute its forces.[26] Such counterterrorism gains against Salafi-jihadi groups have been reversed in the past when attention and resources shift elsewhere or conditions deteriorate. The challenge the

Salafi-jihadi movement poses is that once it surfaces, its networks have proven extremely difficult to eradicate, requiring constant counterterrorism pressure to keep them from regenerating.

Losses in places like Iraq, Syria, and Yemen have also taken a toll on the global Salafi-jihadi movement. The elimination of the Islamic State's so-called caliphate in Iraq and Syria stanched the global surge of Salafi-jihadi-inspired terrorism. Difficulty in running recruiting networks and organizing attacks certainly plays a role. Yet the influence of Salafi-jihadi groups on would-be recruits in the West seems to be declining, even as these groups have steadily consolidated their influence in places in Africa, northwestern Syria, and Afghanistan. Two key indicators of this influence, foreign-fighter travel and inspired-or directed-terror attacks in the West, are trending downward. None of the active theaters for jihad are drawing foreign fighters in any numbers. Salafi-jihadi terror plots are also well below their peak, which was in 2016.[27] Western intelligence services' capability to identify would-be recruits and prevent their travel or participation in terror attacks is one reason for such a decline. Europe's crackdown following the Islamic State's terror wave landed many Salafi-jihadis in prison, taking the immediate threat off the streets. The COVID-19 pandemic might have also artificially deflated the numbers by making it much more difficult to travel and to recruit new members, fundraise, and plot attacks because of various restrictions put in place. It is quite possible that these two indicators could resurge rapidly as pandemic restrictions ease, including the activation of preplanned attacks formed during the lockdown.[28]

Al-Qaeda or the Islamic State? Claiming the Vanguard

The Salafi-jihadi movement has never been monolith, but it was not until June 2014 that al-Qaeda's position as the vanguard force was challenged directly. The Islamic State declared the reestablishment of the caliphate and announced its leader, Abu Bakr al-Baghdadi, as both caliph and *emir al-mumineen* (commander of the faithful).[29] It also announced that any Muslim who refused to swear allegiance to the caliph was an apostate, the punishment for which is death. Al-Qaeda leaders contested the validity of the declaration, which they argued had been made without proper consultation and before the correct conditions were in place.[30] Yet the Islamic State's message had resonated with those Salafi-jihadis who held even more fundamentalist beliefs than al-Qaeda but who had previously been held in check. The Islamic State's sudden eruption on the global stage revealed a deep schism in Salafi-jihadism that persists to this day. Al-Qaeda and the Islamic State remain locked in battle for primacy in the global jihad over key ideological differences, and while al-Qaeda seems to be persevering, the Islamic State has not given up the fight.

Al-Qaeda's leadership knew the founder of what would eventually become the Islamic State, Abu Mus'ab al-Zarqawi, disagreed with al-Qaeda's methodology (*minhaj*) and strategic approach and sought to persuade him otherwise by supporting and engaging with him in debate. Saif al-Adel, al-Qaeda's military commander, convinced Bin Laden to provide Zarqawi—a former petty criminal—with seed money to establish a training camp in Herat in western Afghanistan, in 1999, and set about trying to overcome known differences between Zarqawi and al-Qaeda's creed (*'aqida*) and practice.[31] Bin Laden and Zarqawi met in 2000, when Bin Laden sought—and failed—to receive a *bay'a* pledge from Zarqawi.[32] Necessity pushed Bin Laden and Zarqawi together, however, after the Taliban regime fell in Afghanistan. Zarqawi had fled to Iraq, where he established new training camps. His group rose to prominence rapidly in 2003, but he needed the funding and jihadi legitimacy that Bin Laden could confer.[33] Bin Laden needed a win for al-Qaeda, and so despite the pair's ongoing disagreements, he accepted Zarqawi's allegiance in 2004. Zarqawi pressed on with his own strategic vision for the jihad in Iraq. Al-Qaeda's frustrated leadership sought to rein him in, unsuccessfully, through a series of written private admonishments and reprimands from its hideouts. It was not until after Bin Laden's death, when both al-Qaeda and the Islamic State were thriving, that the issue came to a head, as al-Qaeda sought to impose its method again on the Islamic State.[34]

The very public split between al-Qaeda and the Islamic State that began in April 2013 and continues through today removed any pretense of unity within the Salafi-jihadi movement and created a rift essentially between those who cleaved toward al-Qaeda's interpretation and those who cleaved toward the Islamic State's. The two groups did not dispute basic Salafi-jihadi tenets but rather disagreed on issues related to *takfir*—the act of declaring other Muslims to be infidels—and requirements for establishing a state under *shari'a* that had real-world implications for their respective strategic approaches. The Islamic State holds that it is the *only* faction on the correct path and rejects any form of compromise with those who do not accept its ways immediately, who it says can be killed. It thus believes that it must build Islamic states under its fundamentalist interpretation of *shari'a* as the group expands its control. Al-Qaeda, meanwhile, takes a more gradualist approach, transforming societies according to its image over time and focusing on unity (*tawhid*) among Muslims over factionalism and the eventual formation of a state when factions are strong enough to defend it against Western attacks. Al-Qaeda thus emphasizes proselytizing (*da'wa*) over pressure, building relationships and broad alliances over coercion, and fighting the far enemy (the United States and the West) over near enemies (local regimes). Both the Islamic State and al-Qaeda readily denounce each other: the Islamic State for being too puritanical, for being today's *kharijites*,[35] and al- Qaeda for being too populist, for allowing so-called deviant factions to hold power.

The Islamic State became the new force for global jihad by 2015–2016, but it lost its edge as it lost its physical caliphate in the years that followed. It delivered for Salafi-jihadis what al-Qaeda could not, and then would not: a government under *shari'a* and then a physical caliphate. Al-Qaeda's previous forays into running emirates had been ill-fated, including the recent attempts in southern Yemen and northern Mali, which both collapsed rapidly under counterterrorism pressure. Such failures fed al-Qaeda's reticence to govern openly, and fear of becoming isolated from the local population due to resistance to al-Qaeda's interpretation of *shari'a* or its inability to fill all the roles of the state compounded this reluctance. In direct contrast, the Islamic State brazenly raised its flag over territory it administered in Iraq, Syria, and later, Libya, and it issued a clarion call for Muslims to rise up in its name. An unprecedented number answered, flooding into Iraq and Syria. The Islamic State's global network expanded as new groups and smaller al-Qaeda splinter groups publicly declared their allegiance to the new caliph. Al-Qaeda had faded from the headlines, but its affiliates continued to strengthen during this time.[36] Counterterrorism operations focused on the Islamic State rolled back its gains and weakened the global network, shifting the balance toward al-Qaeda again.

Al-Qaeda and the Islamic State groups have battled each other in their struggle. In Syria, fighting broke out between Jabhat al-Nusra and the Islamic State in late 2013 and lasted into fall 2014.[37] The contentious relationship between the Islamic State and Jabhat al-Nusra, which it had helped found, became heated as Jabhat al-Nusra factions in Syria, especially those comprised of foreign fighters, defected to the Islamic State and mediation attempts failed.[38] Jabhat al-Nusra ultimately lost the ground fight in eastern Syria, but its successor—Hayat Tahrir al-Sham—outlasted the Islamic State and governs in northwestern Syria.[39] In Yemen, the Islamic State never gained more than a token foothold, held in check at first by its foreignness in the country and US counterterrorism operations. It later essentially picked a fight with al-Qaeda, sparking a multiyear back-and-forth between the two groups that has weakened the jihad in Yemen.[40] In the

Sahel, the Islamic State had splintered from al-Qaeda's Jama'at Nusrat al-Islam wa al-Muslimeen (JNIM) in 2015 and loosely cooperated with JNIM until spring 2020, when the two began competing directly for influence over key terrain and access to resources.[41] The intra-jihadi conflict is ongoing in the region, though the local Islamic State branch has suffered operational setbacks due to counterterrorism operations that killed senior leaders.[42]

Today, the primary battlefield between al-Qaeda and the Islamic State is Afghanistan. Al-Qaeda recognizes the Taliban's leader as commander of the faithful (*emir al-mumineen*), and al-Qaeda's members have celebrated the Taliban's takeover as a victory for Islam and proof that al-Qaeda's "path of jihad" ultimately led to success. The Taliban's relationship with al-Qaeda, complicated by the terms negotiated with the US, still favors al-Qaeda's strengthening, as the public reemergence of Bin Laden's security chief Amin al-Haq in Nangarhar province in late August 2020 shows.[43] Meanwhile, the Islamic State perceives the Taliban's newfound position as one gained through compromise with (American) infidels—and the Taliban administration no more Islamic than the Afghan government.[44] The Islamic State has thus remained "relentlessly committed" to targeting the Taliban, and thereby weakening al-Qaeda, in Afghanistan.[45] Disenchanted Taliban members have been drawn to the more radical Islamic State, as have some former Afghan security force members, who see the Islamic State as the strongest force opposing the Taliban.[46] The Islamic State's attacks in Afghanistan can serve to spoil the Taliban's victory and diminish its value for al-Qaeda.

Looking Ahead: Jihad after Afghanistan

The Taliban's return to power in Afghanistan marks the start of a new chapter for the global Salafi-jihadi movement that will further refine the contours of the external struggle to change the Muslim world while also affecting the internal dynamics. First, the Taliban's takeover, besides fueling conflict between the Taliban and the Islamic State, reopens the question of whether al-Qaeda or the Islamic State promotes an effective strategy to achieve their aims. Second, the opening of Afghanistan to jihad no doubt favors al-Qaeda while also reigniting the global movement, though the focus may remain on local jihad. Finally, the US decision to adopt an "over-the-horizon" counterterrorism posture while realigning resources inevitably changes the nature of the global effort to counter al-Qaeda and the Islamic State, and the Salafi-jihadi movement's prioritization of the "near" over the "far" war.

The Taliban's triumph in Afghanistan and al-Qaeda's quiet successes worldwide show that al-Qaeda's approach, embodied in the Taliban's struggle, delivered an Islamic government over the long term. The fact that the West has decided not to intervene against the Taliban further underscores the value of a long-term strategy that bleeds the enemy of resources and wears down the enemy's resolve to fight. The Islamic State's dazzling feats after it declared its so-called caliphate in June 2014, seizing control of large swathes of Iraq and Syria, attracted thousands of followers, as nothing breeds success like success. Yet al-Qaeda's warnings that the Islamic State's caliphate would collapse rang true as losses compounded entering 2019. Al-Qaeda and the Islamic State each claim to follow the true path of jihad, which ultimately leads to victory for Islam in the restoration of the global caliphate. The differences between their creed (*'aqida*) and methodology (*minhaj*) have informed distinct strategies. The Islamic State has not yet been able demonstrate a full recovery from its losses, whereas al-Qaeda can point to the Afghanistan victory as proof of its strategy's effectiveness.

Al-Qaeda's global position strengthened after the Taliban's rise to power in Afghanistan, raising al-Qaeda's profile again in the Salafi-jihadi movement. The return of the Taliban's Islamic

Emirate of Afghanistan accomplishes one of al-Qaeda's main aims, which is the establishment of *shari'a*-based governance in the Muslim world. The Taliban's deal also creates a precedent that other groups, especially Somalia's al-Shabaab, could follow and risks al-Qaeda achieving this aim elsewhere. Essentially, the Taliban has charted a course for local jihad to deliver the success transnational terror attacks never did. In Afghanistan, al-Qaeda has already expanded—it was present in at least 15 provinces by June 2021 with up to 500 members[47] and was running new training camps by June 2022.[48] Zawahiri's death may give al-Qaeda's senior leaders pause about their security in Afghanistan, but they will guide the next phase of its jihad globally under the new conditions. Finally, even without a call for *hijra*, Afghanistan will become a destination for Salafi-jihadis as Syria and Iraq once were.[49]

The ongoing easing of counterterrorism pressure on Salafi-jihadi groups operating in local contexts will create more space for them to strengthen. The overall emphasis in the Salafi-jihadi movement on local dynamics has made it more difficult for Western states to justify ongoing counterterrorism operations abroad without a clear terrorism threat at home, prompting the rightsizing of counterterrorism resources and creating more space for Salafi-jihadi groups to expand. Waning enthusiasm for the African Union peacekeeping mission in Somalia and al-Shabaab's enduring threat may make a negotiated Taliban-like settlement more appealing, even after US forces reentered to support Somali counterterrorism operations.[50] In Afghanistan, the over-the-horizon strike that killed Zawahiri in downtown Kabul, Afghanistan, showed America's counterterrorism reach, but its ability to respond to emergent threats dropped significantly after the August 2021 withdrawal, even as formerly imprisoned fighters rejoining the ranks along with new recruits have reinvigorated groups.[51] And now in the Sahel, the French have announced their withdrawal from Mali after a nine-year campaign against jihadists, prompting similar announcements from European and other African countries contributing to counterterrorism and peacekeeping missions in Mali.[52] Mali instead has turned to Russia to help with counterterrorism, but the military demands of the war in Ukraine are now affecting Wagner group operations in the country, creating friction between the partners and opportunities again for Sahelian Salafi-jihadi groups to expand. The global Salafi-jihadi movement will benefit from these local developments.

The competition between al-Qaeda and the Islamic State to lead the Salafi-jihadi movement perseveres, and the two groups are unlikely to resolve their differences.[53] Al-Qaeda has begun to reemerge as leading the global jihad in the aftermath of Afghanistan, but the Islamic State remains in position to claim this back. It has not stopped its attacks on al-Qaeda's positions— both rhetorically and physically—nor has it shied from headline-grabbing terror attacks against civilians, unlike al-Qaeda.[54] Today, the Islamic State is strongest where al-Qaeda had weak or nonexistent ties, and its growth has fundamentally occurred where al-Qaeda is absent. The result is the Salafi-jihadi movement's expansion and progress in its broader struggle, even as al-Qaeda and the Islamic State compete to determine the future of the fight.

Notes

1 BBC Monitoring, "Al-Qaeda Invites 'Western Nations' to Islam Amid Covid-19," April 1, 2020; and BBC Monitoring, "New IS Leadership Message Says Covid-19 is God's Punishment on West," May 28, 2020.

2 Thomas Joscelyn, "Shabaab Recommends Black Seed and Honey to Combat Coronavirus," Long War Journal, April 1, 2021, https://www.longwarjournal.org/archives/2021/04/shabaab-recommends-black-seed-and-honey-to-combat-coronavirus.php; and BBC Monitoring, "Covid-19 Society: Somalia's al-Shabab Forms Coronavirus Monitoring Committee," May 13, 2020.

3 Mercy Corps, A Clash of Contagion: The Impact of COVID-19 on Conflict in Afghanistan, Colombia, and Nigeria, June 2021, https://www.mercycorps.org/sites/default/files/2021-06/Clash-of-Contagions-Full-Report-June-2021.pdf.

4 Jessica Trisko Darden and Emily Estelle, "Confronting Islamist Insurgencies in Africa: The Case of the Islamic State in Mozambique," *Orbis* 65, no. 3, Summer 2021, https://doi.org/10.1016/j.orbis.2021.06.007; and Emily Estelle, "The Islamic State Resurges in Mozambique," Foreign Policy, June 16, 2021, https://foreignpolicy.com/2021/06/16/mozambique-islamic-state-terrorism-france-total/.

5 Vicky Start, "South Africa Sending Fresh Troops to Mozambique to Fight Islamist Insurgents," Voice of America, February 22, 2022, https://www.voanews.com/a/south-africa-sending-fresh-troops-to-mozambique-to-fight-islamist-insurgents-/6454195.html; and UN Security Council, "Twenty-Ninth Report of the Analytical Support and Sanctions Monitoring Team Submitted Pursuant to Resolution 2368 (7017) Concerning ISIL (Da'esh), Al-Qaida and Associated Individuals and Entities," February 3, 2022, 7, https://www.undocs.org/S/2022/83.

6 Liam Karr, "Africa File: Islamic State Bombings in Uganda Challenge East Africa Counterterrorism Response," Critical Threats Project at the American Enterprise Institute, December 13, 2021, https://www.criticalthreats.org/briefs/africa-file/africa-file-islamic-state-bombings-in-uganda-challenge-east-africa-counterterrorism-response; and UN Security Council, "Twenty-Ninth Report of the Analytical Support and Sanctions Monitoring Team," 6–7.

7 UN Security Council, "Twenty-Ninth Report of the Analytical Support and Sanctions Monitoring Team," 9–10.

8 Michael M. Phillips, "Militants Are Edging South Toward West Africa's Most Stable and Prosperous States," *Wall Street Journal*, March 2, 2022, https://www.wsj.com/articles/sahel-based-militants-edging-south-toward-west-africas-most-stable-and-prosperous-states-11646221800; and Rahma Bayrakdar, "Al Qaeda's Growing Threat to Senegal," Critical Threats Project at the American Enterprise Institute, February 18, 2021, https://www.criticalthreats.org/analysis/al-qaedas-growing-threat-to-senegal.

9 For example, Al-Kataib Foundation for Media Productions, "An Inspire the Believers #15," January 18, 2022, https://jihadology.net/2022/01/19/new-video-message-from-%e1%b8%a5arakat-al-shabab-al-mujahidin-and-incite-the-believers-15/.

10 Katherine Zimmerman, "Afghanistan Is Set to Become a Sanctuary for Extremists," The Hill, September 2, 2021, https://thehill.com/opinion/national-security/570416-afghanistan-is-set-to-become-a-sanctuary-for-extremists.

11 Nagwan Soliman, "The New Jihadists and the Taliban Model," Carnegie Endowment for International Peace, December 20, 2021, https://carnegieendowment.org/sada/86049.

12 The UN Monitoring Team established his name as Amir Mohammad Said Abdul Rahman al-Salbi. He had previously been known under the name of al-Mawla, a nickname. UN Security Council, "Twenty-Ninth Report of the Analytical Support and Sanctions Monitoring Team," 5.

13 Eric Schmitt and Ben Hubbard, "Raid Targeting ISIS Leader Came After Months of Planning," February 4, 2022, https://www.nytimes.com/2022/02/03/us/politics/isis-leader-killed-syria.html.

14 UN Security Council, "Twenty-Ninth Report of the Analytical Support and Sanctions Monitoring Team," 5.

15 Tore Refslund Hamming, "Al-Qaeda After Ayman al-Zawahiri," Lawfare Blog, April 11, 2021, https://www.lawfareblog.com/al-qaeda-after-ayman-al-zawahiri.

16 Aaron Y. Zelin, "Jihadis 2021: ISIS & al Qaeda," The Islamists, March 17, 2021, https://www.wilsoncenter.org/article/jihadis-2021-isis-al-qaeda; US Central Command, "U.S. Strike in the Vicinity of Suluk, Syria, October 22, 2021," press release, October 22, 2021, https://www.centcom.mil/MEDIA/STATEMENTS/Statements-View/Article/2820408/us-strike-in-the-vicinity-of-suluk-syria-oct-22-2021/; and Jeff Seldin, "US Strike Targets al-Qaida in Syria," Voice of America, September 20, 2021, https://www.voanews.com/a/us-strike-targets-al-qaida-in-syria-/6236468.html.

17 Elisabeth Kendall, "Twenty Years After 9/11: The Jihadi Threat in the Arabian Peninsula," CTC Sentinel 14, no. 7, September 2021, 68, https://ctc.usma.edu/wp-content/uploads/2021/09/CTC-SENTINEL-072021.pdf.

18 Al-Sahab Media Foundation, "'Stop Them; Indeed, They Are to Be Questioned: Security and Awareness with Responsibility," March 1, 2022, https://jihadology.net/2022/03/01/new-video-message-from-al-qaidah-and-stop-them-indeed-they-are-to-be-questioned-security-and-awareness-with-responsibility/.

19 Bruce Riedel, "Where in the World Is al-Qaida's Leader?" Brookings Institution, August 10, 2015, https://www.brookings.edu/blog/markaz/2015/08/10/where-in-the-world-is-al-qaidas-leader/; Charles Lister, "How al-Qa`ida Lost Control of Its Syrian Affiliate: The Inside Story," CTC Sentinel 11, no. 2, February 2018, 2, https://ctc.usma.edu/wp-content/uploads/2018/02/CTC-Sentinel_Vol11Iss2-2.pdf; and Hassan I. Hassan (@hxhassan), "#exclusive #breaking Ayman Zawahiri, al-Qaeda leader & Osama bin Laden successor, died a month ago of natural causes in his domicile. The news is making the rounds in close circles. - I realize the issue wt such claims but corroborated it wt sources close to AQ (Hurras al-Din)," Twitter, November 13, 2020, 1:02 p.m., https://twitter.com/hxhassan/status/1327310792383983616.

20 Zawahiri's statements through early 2022 only provided proof of life as recent as early 2021, sufficient to dispel the rumor of his death but not the image of him as an incapable leader. UN Security Council, "Twenty-Ninth Report of the Analytical Support and Sanctions Monitoring Team," 5.

21 Ayman al-Zawahiri, "The Noble Woman of India," Al-Sahab Media Foundation, April 5, 2022.

22 For in-depth analysis, see Cole Bunzel, "'Dissolve Al-Qaida': The Advice of Abu Mariya al-Qahtani," Jihadica, August 24, 2022.

23 UN Security Council, "Twenty-Ninth Report of the Analytical Support and Sanctions Monitoring Team," 17.

24 Elisabeth Kendall, "Where is AQAP Now?" Sana'a Center for Strategic Studies, October 21, 2021, https://sanaacenter.org/publications/analysis/15357; and Katherine Zimmerman, "Taking the Lead Back in Yemen," statement before the House Committee on Foreign Affairs Subcommittee on Middle East, North Africa, and International Terrorism, March 6, 2019, https://www.aei.org/research-products/testimony/testimony-taking-the-lead-back-in-yemen/.

25 UN Security Council, "Twenty-Ninth Report of the Analytical Support and Sanctions Monitoring Team," 13.

26 UN Security Council, "Twenty-Ninth Report of the Analytical Support and Sanctions Monitoring Team," 6; and Jane Arraf and Ben Hubbard, "As Islamic State Resurges, U.S. Is Drawn Back into the Fray," New York Times, January 25, 2022, https://www.nytimes.com/2022/01/25/world/middleeast/isis-syria.html.

27 Jytte Klausen, "Why Jihadist Attacks Have Declined in Europe," Foreign Affairs, December 19, 2018, https://www.foreignaffairs.com/articles/europe/2018-12-19/why-jihadist-attacks-have-declined-europe.

28 UN Security Council, "Twenty-Ninth Report of the Analytical Support and Sanctions Monitoring Team," 5.

29 Al-Qaeda recognizes the leader of the Taliban as *emir al-mumineen*.

30 Katherine Zimmerman, "Competing Jihad: The Islamic State and al Qaeda," Critical Threats Project at the American Enterprise Institute, September 1, 2014, https://www.criticalthreats.org/analysis/competing-jihad-the-islamic-state-and-al-qaeda.

31 Vahid Brown, "A Profile of Saif al-Adel," Combating Terrorism Center at West Point, January 1, 2008, 4, https://ctc.usma.edu/a-profile-of-saif-al-adel/.

32 Loretta Napoleoni, "Profile of a Killer," Foreign Policy, October 20, 2009, https://foreignpolicy.com/2009/10/20/profile-of-a-killer/.

33 Napoleoni, "Profile of a Killer."

34 The Islamic State's spokesman in 2014 addressed this issue directly. Abu Mohammed al-Adnani, "Apologies, Amir of al-Qaidah," al-Furqan Media, May 11, 2014, https://jihadology.net/2014/05/11/al-furqan-media-presents-a-new-audio-message-from-the-islamic-state-of-iraq-and-al-shams-shaykh-abu-mu%e1%b8%a5ammad-al-adnani-al-shami-sorry-amir-of-al-qaidah/.

35 The term "*Kharijite*" refers to a historical group that held such extremist positions that they rejected Ali as caliph because he submitted the decision of whether he should rule to human arbitration, holding that such judgment belongs to Allah alone. They separated from other Muslims and are widely perceived to have been heretics.

36 Katherine Zimmerman, "Al Qaeda's Strengthening in the Shadows," statement before the House Homeland Security Committee Subcommittee on Counterterrorism and Intelligence, July 13, 2017, https://docs.house.gov/meetings/HM/HM05/20170713/106235/HHRG-115-HM05-Wstate-ZimmermanK-20170713.pdf.

37 Tore Hamming, "The Failure of Jihadi Conflict Resolution," War on the Rocks, February 15, 2021, https://warontherocks.com/2021/02/the-failure-of-jihadi-conflict-resolution/.

38 Aaron Y. Zelin, "The War Between ISIS and al-Qaeda for Supremacy of the Global Jihadist Movement," Washington Institute, June 26, 2014, https://www.washingtoninstitute.org/policy-analysis/

war-between-isis-and-al-qaeda-supremacy-global-jihadist-movement; and Hamming, "The Failure of Jihadi Conflict Resolution."

39 Soliman, "The New Jihadists and the Taliban Model."

40 Kendall, "Twenty Years After 9/11: The Jihadi Threat in the Arabian Peninsula," 65.

41 Katherine Zimmerman, "Salafi-Jihadi Ecosystem in the Sahel," American Enterprise Institute, April 22, 2020, https://www.aei.org/research-products/report/salafi-jihadi-ecosystem-in-the-sahel/; Heni Nsaibia and Caleb Weiss, "The End of the Sahelian Anomaly: How the Global Conflict Between the Islamic State and al-Qa'ida Finally Came to West Africa," CTC Sentinel 13, no. 7, July 2020, https://ctc.usma.edu/the-end-of-the-sahelian-anomaly-how-the-global-conflict-between-the-islamic-state-and-al-qaida-finally-came-to-west-africa/; and Lina Raafat, "The Schism of Jihadism in the Sahel: How Al-Qaeda and the Islamic State Are Battling for Legitimacy in the Sahelian Context," Middle East Institute, October 13, 2021, https://www.mei.edu/publications/schism-jihadism-sahel-how-al-qaeda-and-islamic-state-are-battling-legitimacy-sahelian.

42 A March 2022 Islamic State infographic highlighted that it had killed 36 al-Qaeda militants in the preceding four months, e.g. Laith Alkhouri (@MENAanalyst), "#ISIS claims that over the past 4 months it has killed and wounded 204 people in the Sahel region (Mali, Burkina Faso, Niger) including 36 alleged Al-Qaeda militants - mostly in Mali - as both groups compete for dominance of the jihadi landscape in the region," Twitter, March 4, 2022, 11:56 a.m., https://twitter.com/MENAanalyst/status/1499790961685184513; and UN Security Council, "Twenty-Ninth Report of the Analytical Support and Sanctions Monitoring Team," 10.

43 Bill Roggio, "Osama bin Laden's Security Chief Triumphantly Returns to Hometown in Afghanistan," Long War Journal, August 30, 2021, https://www.longwarjournal.org/archives/2021/08/osama-bin-ladens-security-chief-triumphantly-returns-to-hometown-in-afghanistan.php.

44 For more, see Cole Bunzel, "Al Qaeda versus ISIS: The Jihadi Power Struggle in the Taliban's Afghanistan," Foreign Affairs, September 14, 2021, https://www.foreignaffairs.com/articles/afghanistan/2021-09-14/al-qaeda-versus-isis.

45 Amira Jadoon, Abdul Sayed, and Andrew Mines, "The Islamic State Threat in Taliban Afghanistan: Tracing the Resurgence of Islamic State Khorasan," CTC Sentinel 15, no. 1, January 2022, 41, https://ctc.usma.edu/the-islamic-state-threat-in-taliban-afghanistan-tracing-the-resurgence-of-islamic-state-khorasan/.

46 Yaroslav Trofimov, "Left Behind After U.S. Withdrawal, Some Former Afghan Spies and Soldiers Turn to the Islamic State," Wall Street Journal, October 31, 2021, https://www.wsj.com/articles/left-behind-after-u-s-withdrawal-some-former-afghan-spies-and-soldiers-turn-to-islamic-state-11635691605; and Peter Mills, "Afghanistan Warning Update: IS-KP in Afghanistan Is Expanding Faster than Anticipated," Institute for the Study of War, October 27, 2021, http://www.iswresearch.org/2021/10/afghanistan-warning-update-is-kp-in.html.

47 Asfandyar Mir, "Twenty Years After 9/11: The Terror Threat from Afghanistan Post the Taliban Takeover," CTC Sentinel 14, no. 7, September 2021, 33, https://ctc.usma.edu/twenty-years-after-9-11-the-terror-threat-from-afghanistan-post-the-taliban-takeover/.

48 Gordon Lubold, "U.S. Courts Central Asian Nations to Combat Potential Terrorism from Afghanistan," Wall Street Journal, June 23, 2022, https://www.wsj.com/articles/u-s-courts-central-asian-nations-to-combat-potential-terrorism-from-afghanistan-11655976600.

49 Rita Katz, "The Taliban's Victory Is al Qaeda's Victory," Foreign Policy, September 13, 2021, https://foreignpolicy.com/2021/09/13/taliban-victory-afghanistan-al-qaeda-victory-911/.

50 The Somali forces countering al-Shabaab found themselves outgunned after US forces withdrew from the country in January 2021. US President Joe Biden approved the redeployment of US forces to Somalia in May 2022. Charlie Savage and Eric Schmitt, "Biden Approves Plan to Redeploy Several Hundred Ground Forces into Somalia," New York Times, May 16, 2022, https://www.nytimes.com/2022/05/16/us/politics/biden-military-somalia.html; and John Vandiver, "US Withdrawal in Somalia Has Strengthened Hand of al-Shabab Terrorists, Top Officials Say," Stars and Stripes, February 17, 2022, https://www.stripes.com/theaters/africa/2022-02-17/somalia-al-qaida-africa-united-states-5056544.html.

51 Robert Burns and Lolita Baldor, "US Commander: Al-Qaida Numbers in Afghanistan Up 'Slightly,'" Associated Press, December 9, 2021, https://news.yahoo.com/us-commander-al-qaida-numbers-015036806.html.

52 Norimitsu Onishi, Ruth Maclean and Aurelien Breeden, "France Announces Troop Withdrawal from Mali After 9-Year Campaign," New York Times, February 17, 2022, https://www.nytimes.

com/2022/02/17/world/africa/mali-france-withdrawal.html; and Reuters, "Ivory Coast to Withdraw from Mali Peacekeeping Force -Letter," November 15, 2022, https://www.reuters.com/world/africa/ivory-coast-withdraw-un-peacekeeping-mission-mali-letter-2022-11-15/.

53 Saif al-Adel is a likely candidate to succeed Ayman al-Zawahiri. It is possible that Adel's more hardline views persist and that his personal rejection of justifications for compromise could align al-Qaeda and the Islamic State more closely.

54 The Islamic State claimed a recent attack on a Shi'a Mosque in Peshawar, Pakistan, that killed over 60 people and injured nearly 200 more, for example. Sophia Saifi and Saleem Mehsud, "ISIS Claims Responsibility for Blast Killing Dozens at Shia Mosque in Pakistan's Peshawar," CNN, March 5, 2022, https://www.cnn.com/2022/03/04/asia/pakistan-peshawar-blast-intl/index.html.

48

AL-QAEDA—20 YEARS
AFTER 9/11

Bruce Hoffman

Al-Qaeda won. With the Taliban's re-conquest of Afghanistan and the United States' ignomini-
ous withdrawal from that country, al-Qaeda triumphed over America and its allies in this final
spasm of the war on terror that commenced twenty years ago with the attacks on September 11,
2001. Al-Qaeda outlasted the U.S. commitment to build a free and democratic Afghanistan. And
in concert with its Taliban brothers-in-arms overcame both the United States and the International Security Assistance Force (ISAF)—the multinational military mission in Afghanistan that
had already begun to wind down in 2010 and formally ended in 2014 when active U.S. combat
operations in the country also ceased.[1]

The Taliban's victory delivered everything that al-Qaeda sought in supporting its longtime
ally. The Taliban was restored to power and its extreme interpretation of Islamist Shari'a law was
reimposed over Afghanistan. Al-Qaeda's safe haven in the country was thus both resurrected and
ensured—at least for the immediate future. Apart from the Taliban's vague assurances to restrain
al-Qaeda from using Afghanistan as a base to stage September 11th-like international attacks, al-
Qaeda has no limits nor constraints on its existence and operations in that country.[2] Regardless,
the Taliban's assurances on this issue will likely prove as meaningless as they were in the years
prior to 2001.[3]

The Taliban has already violated nearly every pledge it made during the negotiations with
the United States in Doha. And, it has installed in its most critical ministries terrorist luminaries
whose close ties to al-Qaeda and other regional terrorist movements effectively vitiate its undertakings to abjure from supporting international terrorist activities.[4] These senior Taliban officials
include the interior minister, Sirajuddin Haqqani, who now occupied the most important government post overseeing Afghanistan's police, borders, and attendant security apparata. Haqqani,
the leader of the eponymous network that has been designated a foreign terrorist organization
by the U.S. Department of State since 2012,[5] has been sanctioned by both the United Nations
and the United States as a designated terrorist. The State Department for years has offered a
$10 million reward to anyone who provides information facilitating Haqqani's apprehension.
Sirajuddin Haqqani's uncle, Khalil al-Rahman Haqqani, is the Taliban's minister of refugees. He
has been similarly sanctioned by the U.N. and United States and the State Department has long
offered a $5 million reward for his capture. Both Abdul Haq Wasiq, the director of intelligence,
and Khairullah Khairkhwa, the minister of information and culture, are also sanctioned by the

DOI: 10.4324/9781003326373-55

UN and spent years imprisoned at the U.S. prison facility for enemy combatants at Guantanamo before their release in 2014 as part of the deal that freed U.S. Army deserter Sergeant Bowe Berg- dahl from captivity.[6] The UN Security Council reports that Wasiq was responsible for overseeing foreign fighters under al-Qaeda's aegis and their training camps in Afghanistan.[7] Khairkhwa has similarly longstanding ties with al-Qaeda, including with its deceased founder and one-time emir, Usama bin Laden.[8] The U.N. cites another Haqqani, Yahya, as having been the network's key point of contact for liaison with al-Qaeda since 2009.[9]

The continued strength of these historically close bonds between al-Qaeda and the Taliban were underscored at a meeting that reportedly took place in the Sarwan Qal'ah District of Hel- mand Province in the spring of 2019. According to the United Nations, a delegation of senior Taliban leaders met with Hamza Usama Muhammad bin Laden, the late al-Qaeda leader's son and heir apparent "to reassure him personally that the Islamic Emirate would not break its histor- ical ties with Al-Qaeda for any price."[10] And, in May 2019, Ayman al-Zawahiri, al-Qaeda's then leader and emir, released a video containing a eulogy for the Haqqani Network's paterfamilias, Jalaluddin, thus further underscoring the close bonds between al-Qaeda and the Taliban.[11] As a 2021 UN assessment noted of the depth and strength of al-Qaeda-Taliban relations,

> The senior leadership of Al-Qaida remains present in Afghanistan, as well as hundreds of armed operatives, Al-Qaida in the Indian Subcontinent, and groups of foreign terrorist fighters aligned with the Taliban… Relations between the Taliban, especially the Haqqani Network, and Al-Qaida remain close, based on friendship, a history of shared struggle, ideological sympathy and intermarriage. The Taliban regularly consulted with Al-Qaida during negotiations with the United States and offered guarantees that it would honour their historical ties. Al-Qaida has reacted positively to the agreement, with statements from its acolytes celebrating it as a victory for the Taliban's cause and thus for global militancy. The challenge will be to secure the counter-terrorism gains to which the Taliban have committed, which will require them to suppress any international threat emanating from Al-Qaida in Afghanistan.[12]

The warmth of Taliban-al-Qaeda relations should come as no surprise given the force multi- plying role the latter played in the former's 2021 victory. Key al-Qaeda Central Asian franchises like the Islamic Jihad Union, Eastern Turkistan Islamic Movement, Jammat Ansarullah, and the Khatiba Imam al-Bukhari provided critical support to the Taliban throughout the offensive that reconquered Afghanistan. Members of these groups were rewarded by the Taliban with impor- tant administrative duties along Afghanistan's northern border and in provinces elsewhere in the country.[13] Through one of the al-Qaeda movement's newer franchises, AQIS (al-Qaeda in the Indian Subcontinent), al-Qaeda loyalists are reportedly comfortably ensconced in at least eight Afghan provinces, including Helmand, Kandahar, Nimruz, Zabul, Ghazni, Nangahar, Kunar, and Nuristan provinces.[14]

Al-Qaeda is therefore arguably better positioned today than at any time since before Septem- ber 11th to carry on the war that Bin Laden declared against the United States in 1996, 1998, and 2001. The problem, however, is that the United States, against all evidence, has repeatedly—and precipitously—declared victory over al-Qaeda in the war on terror. Every American president since 2003 has done so. Speaking at the U.S. Military Academy's commencement that June, President Trump took credit for "ending the era of endless wars."[15] During the 2020 presidential campaign perhaps the only thing that both candidates agreed on was ending that war. Joe Biden was clear on this point in his rumination on U.S. foreign policy, titled "Why America Must Lead

Again," that appeared in *Foreign Affairs* in March 2020, right after he clinched the Democratic Party's nomination. "It is past time to end the forever wars, which have cost the United States untold blood and treasure," Biden wrote. "As I have long argued, we should bring the vast majority of our troops home from the wars in Afghanistan and the Middle East ..."[16] And, once in office, President Biden made good on that pledge. "Bin Laden is dead, and al-Qaeda is degraded in Iraq—in Afghanistan," he stated in April 2021. "And it's time to end the forever war."[17]

It's not difficult to understand the reasoning behind this argument. In addition to the killings of Bin Laden in 2011 and other senior al-Qaeda leaders both before and after, during the final two years of the Trump administration an astonishing array of top al-Qaeda commanders were eliminated either in U.S. air strikes, on the ground assassinations, or by indigenous security forces allied with and supported by the United States In 2019 alone, they included

- Hamza bin Laden, as previously mentioned, who was killed in what President Trump described as a U.S. "counterterrorism operation in the Afghanistan/Pakistan region" at least two months before;[18]
- Qassim al-Rimi, the emir of Al-Qaeda in the Arabian Peninsula (AQAP) and another reputed heir apparent to al-Zawahiri, who perished in a U.S. air strike that took place in Yemen;[19] and,
- Murad al-Shayeb, a senior al-Qaeda commander serving in al-Qaeda's Uqba bin Nafi Battalion (KUBN) closely linked with al-Qaeda in the Islamic Maghreb (AQIM, who was killed by Tunisian troops near the border with Algeria.[20]

And, in 2020, four more senior al-Qaeda leaders or commanders were eliminated, including:

- Abdelmalek Droukdal, AQIM's emir, who was killed in a gun battle in Mali near the Algerian border by French special forces operatives. The U.S. Africa Command reportedly provided intelligence and additional support to the French units operating in this lawless corner of the Sahel;[21]
- Khaled Al-Aruri, the leader of al-Qaeda's Syrian franchise, Tanzim Hurras al-Din, who was killed in a U.S. missile strike;[22]
- Abu Mushin al-Masri, the deputy commander of AQIS, who perished in combat with Afghan special operations units;[23] and,
- Abdullah Ahmed Abdullah (aka Abu Muhammad al-Masri), reputedly al-Zawahiri's deputy and indicated by the U.S. for his role in the 1998 East Africa suicide bombings, who was killed in Teheran, Iran in what was reported to be a joint U.S.-Israeli clandestine operation.[24]

The most consequential targeted assassination arguably was the U.S. drone strike in July 2022 that killed al-Zawahiri.[25] Although at the time of writing his successor is still unknown, as the past twenty years have repeatedly demonstrated, al-Qaeda has a deeper bench than has often been assumed both in terms of its leadership cadre and its ability to attract new fighters into its ranks. Al-Qaeda's succession planning is necessitated by the continued attrition of senior leaders and commanders as new loyalists are consistently elevated to succeed their deceased predecessors.

Today the al-Qaeda universe comprises approximately 20,000 fighters. In Syria, a hardcore of some 1,000–3,000 hardcore combatants remain in the movement's principal catspaw in that country, Hurras al-Din, along with between 1,000 and 3,000 ETIM foreign fighters. Longstanding Arabian Peninsula franchise AQAP retains perhaps as many as 3,000 men-at-arms while al-Shabaab in Somalia has between 7,000–12,000 fighters. AQIM can boast of at least a few hundred operatives and there were at least 200–400 al-Qaeda personnel in Afghanistan. Although the number of al-Qaeda assets in West Africa and the Sahel is not known, the most recent UN threat assessment nonetheless noted that its affiliates in both places "appear to have made decisive progress by exploiting local grievances, overwhelming stretched security forces and navigating complex interrelationships between armed groups."[26]

Irrespective of the numbers, the Salafi-Jihadi ideology underpinning al-Qaeda clearly continues to resonate and spread. Today, for instance, there are four times as many Salafi-Jihadi groups designated as Foreign Terrorist Organizations by the U.S. State Department as there were on September 10, 2001.[27] The same upward trajectory has been tracked by independent think-tanks such as the London-based Tony Blair Institute for Global Change and the Center for Strategic and International Studies in Washington, D.C.[28]

Both al-Qaeda and the Taliban thus share the same worldview. It is based on the call to arms in defense of Muslim lands that the Palestinian scholar and cleric Abdullah Azzam first issued four decades ago. As Azzam argued, members of the umma, the Sunni Muslim community, have an obligation to rally to the defense of their fellow Muslims—wherever and whenever they are threatened. Azzam termed this collective obligation *fard kifayah* and declared that it was incumbent upon Muslims to come to the aid of imperiled fellow Muslims. His message was pivotal in galvanizing the mujahideen—"holy warriors"—that included the foreign fighters from throughout the world who came to Afghanistan in the 1980s and fought against the Soviet Union's occupation of that country.[29].

Azzam's view still strongly resonates among al-Qaeda, its franchise, and its Taliban allies. The United States and the West are seen as waging a predatory, aggressive war against Islam. According to this collective mindset, the Muslim world is enmeshed in an existential conflict against both the Western democratic liberal states as well as the Western-backed local regimes that resist the imposition of the Salafi-Jihadi interpretation of Shari'a. In this unavoidable clash of civilizations, jihad is the only defense against Islam's perfidious enemies.[30] That al-Qaeda and its allies and others now see the United States in decline and retreat as a superpower will likely infuse new momentum into their struggles.[31] The "war against the US will be continuing on all other fronts unless they are expelled from the rest of the Islamic world," two senior al-Qaeda operatives insisted in an interview with the U.S.-based cable news network CNN, months before the Taliban returned to power in Afghanistan. "Thanks to Afghans for the protection of comrades-in-arms, many such jihadi fronts have been successfully operating in different parts of the Islamic world for a long time," one of them enthused.[32]

The big question of course is if and when al-Qaeda will re-commence its long dormant campaign of international terrorism. There are some nascent signals that this plotting has already resumed. In 2020, for instance, U.S. air strikes killed two senior al-Qaeda commanders. Both Abu Yahya al-Uzbeki and Safina al-Tunisi were believed to have been charged with re-building al-Qaeda's external operations capacity in order to project terrorism beyond the Levant.[33] In this respect, the tragic shooting at the Naval Air Station Pensacola in Florida just before Christmas 2019 was a timely reminder that al-Qaeda remains intent on striking targets in the West—and specifically in the United States That attack involved a sleeper agent, a Saudi Air Force pilot trainee affiliated with AQAP, who killed three U.S. Navy sailors and wounded eight others. It was the first lethal terrorist attack in the United States orchestrated by a foreign terrorist organization since September 11, 2001.[34]

More evidence of al-Qaeda's intentions to revive its external operations surfaced in July 2021 when Indian police disrupted a plot by al-Qaeda's Kashmir franchise, Ansar Ghazwat ul-Hind, to carry out simultaneous suicide attacks in Lucknow, India and other densely-populated cities. The series of planned attacks was meant to coincide with that country's independence day celebrations.[35] For the time being at least, al-Qaeda's focus appears to be on destabilizing South Asia through the fomenting of new crises along the lines of the 2008 Mumbai attacks perpetrated by Pakistan's Lashkar-e-Toiba, a longtime al-Qaeda ally. Al-Qaeda thus seems devoted to strengthening its presence across the Indian subcontinent—in Pakistan, India, Bangladesh, Myanmar, and the Maldives. One potentially significant indicator of an impending recommencement of international terrorist attacks would possibly entail the movement of al-Qaeda commanders from Syria back to Afghanistan.

Meanwhile, al-Qaeda and its loyalists appear to be laying the foundations for a new campaign of international terrorism focusing again on commercial aviation. Their hope is that some new, dramatic, and spectacular strike will catapult the movement back into the limelight and recreate the global insecurity and fear and anxiety that existed in the time following the September 11, 2001 attacks. Al-Qaeda's obsession with crashing the world's economy by disrupting air travel accounts for its long-held fixation with this particular target set. Al-Qaeda's catspaw in its bid to resume targeting commercial aircraft is curiously its least technologically sophisticated franchise, al-Shabaab. Al-Qaeda's unlikely reliance on this group may also explain why each of three serious aviation-related plots linked to al-Shabaab all failed. The first occurred on February 2, 2016 when a bomb concealed in a laptop computer exploded aboard a Daallo Airlines flight en route from Mogadishu, Somalia to Djibouti. The flight had been delayed, so the device detonated before the aircraft could reach cruising altitude——thus averting a disaster. The pilot was thus able to safely return the aircraft to Aden Adde International Airport. The only fatality was the alleged bomber.[36] The second involved the 2019 arrest of an al-Shabaab operative in the Philippines. This person was taking the same kind of flying instruction that the four al-Qaeda hijacker-pilots had undergone before the September 11, 2001 attacks. The would-be pilot had also conducted research both on aviation security generally and on America's tallest buildings as part of a plan whose genesis dated back to at least 2016.[37] The third plot was uncovered in 2020 when yet another al-Shabaab terrorist found and arrested in an undisclosed African country while also taking flying lessons.[38]

Clearly, despite either wishful thinking or deliberately ignoring the facts, neither al-Qaeda nor its affiliates have given up their global terrorist ambitions, including resurrecting their ability to attack in both the West and the United States Emboldened by the American withdrawal from Afghanistan, al-Qaeda likely sees new opportunities for growth and expansion. As the former acting director of the Central Intelligence Agency, Michael Morell, warned in an interview shortly after the United States departed from Afghanistan, "The reconstruction of al-Qaeda's homeland attack capability will happen quickly, in less than a year, if the U.S. does not collect the intelligence and take the military action to prevent it."[39]

Notes

1 See "ISAF's mission in Afghanistan (2001–2014), *North Atlantic Treaty Organization*, 19 August 2021 at: https://www.nato.int/cps/en/natolive/topics_69366.htm.

2 "Twenty-ninth report of the Analytical Support and Sanctions Monitoring Team submitted pursuant to resolution 2368 (2017) concerning ISIL (Da'esh), Al-Qaida and associated individuals and entities," United Nations Security Council, 3 February 2022, pp. 5–6.

3 See Kate Bateman, Asfandyar Mir, Ambassador Richard Olson, and Andrew Watkins, "Taliban Seek Recognition, But Offer Few Concessions to International Concerns," USIP, 28 September 2021 at: https://www.usip.org/publications/2021/09/taliban-seek-recognition-offer-few-concessions-international-concerns; Kamran Bokhari, "Taliban Unlikely to Abide by a Deal with the United States," Newlines Institute For Strategy And Policy, 21 August 2019 at: https://newlinesinstitute.org/afghanistan/taliban-unlikely-to-abide-by-a-deal-with-the-united-states/; Center for Preventive Action and Contingency

Planning for Future Crises, "What to Know About the Afghan Peace Negotiations," cfr.org, 11 September 2020 at: https://www.cfr.org/article/what-know-about-afghan-peace-negotiations; Driss El-Bay, "Afghanistan: The Pledge Binding Al-Qaeda to the Taliban," BBC News, 7 September 2021 at: https://www.bbc.com/news/world-asia-58473574; and, Barbara Elias, "The Taliban Won't Compromise al Qaeda. Here's Why," ForeignPolicy.com, 21 September 2021 at: https://foreignpolicy.com/2021/09/21/taliban-al-qaeda-afghanistan-ties-terrorism/.

4   "Twenty-Ninth Report of the Analytical Support and Sanctions Monitoring Team," p. 6.

5   Bureau of Counterterrorism, "Foreign Terrorist Organizations," U.S. Department of State (no date), at: https://www.state.gov/foreign-terrorist-organizations/.

6   Mujib Mashal, "Once Jailed in Guantanamo, 5 Taliban Now Face U.S. at Peace Talks," New York Times, 26 March 2019 at: https://www.nytimes.com/2019/03/26/world/asia/taliban-guantanamo-afghanistan-peace-talks.html.

7   "Abdul-Haq Wassiq," United Nations Security Council at: https://www.un.org/securitycouncil/sanctions/1988/materials/summaries/individual/abdul-haq-wassiq. See also, Toby Harnden, "The Taliban Are Telling Us They Haven't Changed at All," New York Times, 10 September 2021 at: https://www.nytimes.com/2021/09/10/opinion/taliban-new-government.html.

8   "Khairullah Khairkhwa," Counter Extremism Project (no date) at: https://www.counterextremism.com/extremists/khairullah-khairkhwa.

9   "Eleventh Report of the Analytical Support and Sanctions Monitoring Team Submitted Pursuant to Resolution 2501 (2019) Concerning the Taliban and Other Associated Individuals and Entities Constituting a Threat to the Peace, Stability and Security of Afghanistan," United Nations Security Council, 30 April 2020, 12 at: https://www.securitycouncilreport.org/atf/cf/%7B65BFCF9B-6D27-4E9C-8CD3-CF6E4FF96FF9%7D/s_2020_415_e.pdf.

10 "Eleventh Report of the Analytical Support and Sanctions Monitoring Team Submitted Pursuant to Resolution 2501 (2019) Concerning the Taliban and Other Associated Individuals and Entities Constituting a Threat to the Peace, Stability and Security of Afghanistan," United Nations Security Council, 30 April 2020, p. 12.

11 Ibid.

12 Ibid., p. 3

13 See Mumin Ahmadi, Mullorajab Yusufi, and Nigorai Fazliddin, "Exclusive: Taliban Puts Tajik Militants Partially in Charge Of Afghanistan's Northern Border," Radio Free Europe/Radio Liberty, 27 July 2021 at: https://www.rferl.org/a/taliban-tajik-militants-border/31380071.html; Center for Preventive Action, "Countering a Resurgent Terrorist Threat in Afghanistan," cfr.org, 14 April 2022 at: https://www.cfr.org/report/countering-resurgent-terrorist-threat-afghanistan; Tanya Mehra and Matthew Wentworth, "The Rise of the Taliban in Afghanistan: Regional Responses and Security Threats," International Centre for Counter-Terrorism, 27 August 2021 at: https://www.icct.nl/publication/rise-taliban-afghanistan-regional-responses-and-security-threats; Farangis Najibullah and Mumim Ahmadi, "Taliban Said To Have Rearmed Tajik Militants And Moved Uyghur Fighters From Chinese Border," Radio Free Europe/Radio Liberty, 4 October 2021 at: https://gandhara.rferl.org/a/taliban-tajik-china-uyghur/31492147.html; and, "Khatiba Imam al-Bukhari," United Nations Security Council (no date) at: https://www.un.org/securitycouncil/sanctions/1267/aq_sanctions_list/summaries/entity/khatiba-imam-al-bukhari-%28kib%29

14 Various discussions with U.S. government analysts, January through April 2022.

15 Quoted in Steve Holland, "Trump to West Point grads: 'We are ending the era of endless wars'," Reuters, 13 June 2020 at: https://www.reuters.com/article/us-usa-trump-wars/trump-to-west-point-grads-we-are-ending-the-era-of-endless-wars-idUSKBN23K0PR

16 "Joseph R. Biden, Jr., "Why America Must Lead Again," Foreign Affairs, March/April 2020 at: https://www.foreignaffairs.com/articles/united-states/2020-01-23/why-america-must-lead-again

17 White House, "Remarks by President Biden on the Way Forward in Afghanistan," Speeches and Remarks, 14 April 2021 at: https://www.whitehouse.gov/briefing-room/speeches-remarks/2021/04/14/remarks-by-president-biden-on-the-way-forward-in-afghanistan/

18 "Statement from the President," The White House, 14 September 2019; "Remarks by President Trump in Press Conference," 25 February 2020 at: https://trumpwhitehouse.archives.gov/briefings-statements/remarks-president-trump-press-conference-4/; and, Alex Horton, "Osama bin Laden's son, once the probable heir to al-Qaeda's leadership, killed in U.S. operation, Trump confirms,"

14 September 2019 at: https://www.washingtonpost.com/national-security/2019/09/14/hamza-bin-laden-once-possible-heir-al-qaeda-was-killed-us-operation-trump-says/.

19 "Statement from the President," The White House, 6 February 2020 at: https://trumpwhitehouse.archives.gov/briefings-statements/statement-from-the-president-13/; and, Phil Helsel, "White House Says US Killed Qassim Al-Rimi, Leader of Al-Qaeda in Yemen," NBC News, 6 February 2020 at: https://www.cnbc.com/2020/02/07/white-house-says-us-killed-qassim-al-rimi-leader-of-al-qaeda-in-yemen.html.

20 "French Forces Killed Al-Qaeda's North Africa Chief in Mali, defence Minister Says," France24, 6 May 2020 at: https://www.france24.com/en/20200605-french-forces-kill-al-qaeda-s-north-africa-chief-in-mali-ministry-says; Caleb Weiss, "Al-Qaeda leader reported killed in Tunisia," Threat Matrix: A Blog of FDD's Long War Journal, 20 October 2019 at: https://www.longwarjournal.org/archives/2019/10/al-qaeda-leader-reported-killed-in-tunisia.php. See also, Aaron Y. Zellin, Andrew Lebovich, and Daveed Gartenstein-Ross, "Al-Qa'ida in the Islamic Maghreb's Tunisia Strategy," CTC Sentinel, vol. 6, issue 7, July 2013, at: https://www.ctc.usma.edu/al-qaida-in-the-islamic-maghrebs-tunisia-strategy/.

21 Benjamin Roger and Farid Alilat, "How AQIM leader Abdelmalek Droukdel was killed in Mali, The Africa Report, 8 June 2020 at: https://www.theafricareport.com/29482/how-aqim-leader-abdelmalek-droukdel-was-killed-in-mali/.

22 Eric Schmitt, "U.S. Used Missile With Long Blades to Kill Qaeda Leader in Syria," New York Times, 24 June 2020 at: https://www.nytimes.com/2020/06/24/world/middleeast/syria-qaeda-r9x-hellfire-missile.html.

23 "Senior al-Qaeda leader Abu Muhsin al-Masri killed in Afghanistan," Al Jazeera, 25 October 2020 at: https://www.aljazeera.com/news/2020/10/25/senior-al-qaeda-leader-abu-muhsin-al-masri-killed-in-afghanistan.

24 Adam Goldman, Eric Schmitt, Farnaz Fassihi and Ronen Bergman, "Al-Qaeda's No. 2, Accused in U.S. Embassy Attacks, Was Killed in Iran," New York Times, 13 November 2020 at: https://www.nytimes.com/2020/11/13/world/middleeast/al-masri-abdullah-qaeda-dead.html. See also, "Most Wanted Terrorists," Federal Bureau of Investigation (no date), at: abdullah-ahmed-abdullah.pdf

25 Bruce Hoffman, "What Zawahiri's Killing Means for al-Qaeda," Council on Foreign Relations, 2 August 2023 at: https://www.cfr.org/in-brief/what-zawahiris-killing-means-al-qaeda

26 "Twenty-Ninth Report of the Analytical Support and Sanctions Monitoring Team," pp. 8–13.

27 "Foreign Terrorist Organizations," Bureau of Counterterrorism, U.S. Department of State (as of 22 April 2022), at: https://www.state.gov/foreign-terrorist-organizations/.

28 See Tony Blair Institute for Global Change, Violent Islamist Extremism: A Global Problem, 13 September 2018, pp. 9 & 13–14 at: https://institute.global/insight/co-existence/violent-islamist-extremism-global-problem.; and, Seth G. Jones, et al., The Evolution of the Salafi-Jihadist Threat: Current and Future Challenges from the Islamic State, Al-Qaeda, and Other Groups (Washington, DC: CSIS Transnational Threats Project, November 2018). p. iv at: https://www.csis.org/analysis/evolution-salafi-jihadist-threat.

29 Among Azzam's seminal books on this specific issue are: In Defence of Muslim Lands: The First Obligation after Faith (London: Maktabah Publications, 2002); Join the Caravan (London: Maktabah Publications, 2001); and, The Lofty Mountain (London: Maktabah Publications, no date).

30 Eleventh Report of the Analytical Support and Sanctions Monitoring Team," p. 12.

31 See, for example, the observations of Hassan Nasrallah, the Secretary-General of Hezbollah a Shi'a terrorist organization in Aaron Boxerman and AFP, "Hezbollah chief: Israel should learn from Afghanistan that US is unreliable," Times of Israel, 18 August 2021 at: https://www.timesofisrael.com/hezbollah-head-israel-should-learn-from-afghanistan-that-us-is-unreliable/.

32 Quoted in Nic Robertson and Saleem Mehsud, "Al Qaeda promises 'war on all fronts' against America as Biden pulls out of Afghanistan," CNN World, 30 April 2021 at: https://www.cnn.com/2021/04/30/asia/al-qaeda-afghanistan-biden-intl-cmd/index.html.

33 Dave Makichuk, "Deadly 'flying Ginsu' weapon used again in Syria," Asia Times, 18 August 2020 at: https://asiatimes.com/tag/idlib-province/; Aymenn Jawad Al-Tamimi, "The Tunisian Jihadists Assassinated by the Americans in Idlib," Aymenn Jawad Al-Tamimi's Blog, 16 September 2020 at: https://aymennjawad.org/2020/09/the-tunisian-jihadists-assassinated-by.

34 Eric Tucker, "FBI: Shooter at Pensacola Navy base coordinated with Al-Qaida," Military Times, 18 May 2020. For more on the attack, see Colin Clarke, "The Pensacola Terrorist Attack: The Enduring

Influence of al-Qaʿida and its Affiliates," *CTC Sentinel*, vol. 13, issue 3, March 2020 at: https://ctc.usma.edu/pensacola-terrorist-attack-enduring-influence-al-qaida-affiliates/.

35 See India TV News Desk, "Big I-Day Terror Plot Foiled: Al-Qaeda Terrorists were Planning to Use 'Human Bombs' in Lucknow, other Cities," India TV News, 11 July 2021 at: https://www.indiatvnews.com/news/india/al-qaeda-terrorists-arrested-lucknow-plan-uttar-pradesh-crowded-markets-target-bomb-explosions-pakistan-handler-718468; and, "3 more arrested in U.P. claiming they had links with Al-Qaeda," The Hindu, 16 July 2021 at: https://www.thehindu.com/news/national/other-states/3-more-terrorists-arrested-in-up/article35332916.ece.

36 Greg Botelho and Robyn Kriel, "Blast Blows Hole in Commercial Plane over Somalia; one Falls and Dies," CNN.com, 3 February 2016 at: https://www.cnn.com/2016/02/02/africa/somalia-airplane-explosion/index.html; and, "Daallo Airlines blast: Somalia sentences two to life in prison," BBC News, 30 May 2016 at: https://www.bbc.com/news/world-africa-36411555.

37 Jonathan Dienst and Tom Winter, "Man with ties to terror group indicted in alleged plot to stage 9/11-style attack," NBC News, 16 December 2020, and Benjamin Weiser, "Kenyan Planned 9/11-Style Attack After Training as Pilot, U.S. Says," New York Times, 16 December 2020.

38 Eric Schmitt and Abdi Latif Dahir, "Al Qaeda Branch in Somalia Threatens Americans in East Africa—and Even the U.S.," New York Times, 21 March 2020 at: https://www.nytimes.com/2020/03/21/world/africa/al-qaeda-somalia-shabab.html.

39 Quoted in Paul Cruickshank, Don Rassler, and Kristina Hummel, "Twenty Years After 9/111: Reflection from Michael Morell, Former Acting Director of the CIA," *CTC Sentinel*, vol. 14, issue 7, September 2021 at: https://ctc.usma.edu/twenty-years-after-9-11-reflections-from-michael-morell-former-acting-director-of-the-cia/.

49

THE TALIBAN-AL-QAEDA NEXUS

Brothers in Arms

Ali Fisher and Nico Prucha

"God has promised us victory. Bush promised us defeat.
We shall see, which promise is most sincere."

Mullah Muhammad Omar[1]

From the perspective of al-Qaeda (AQ), Afghanistan is a success story – and continues to be one, with the Taliban taking over the country in August 2021. AQ and the Taliban have a deep relationship that intensified over the Taliban's refusal to hand over Usama bin Laden to the United States after the 11 September 2001 terrorist attacks. AQ referred to Taliban leader Mullah Muhammad Omar as "the leader of the faithful" (amir al-mu'minin), a title traditionally reserved for the highest-ranking Islamic leader. Usama bin Laden in his speeches referred to Mullah Muhammad Omar as amir al-mu'minin,[2] just as AQ of 2022 continues to refer to Omar's current successor Hibatullah Akhundzada as such.[3] AQ is a supporter of the Taliban's Islamic Emirate and fought common enemies in Afghanistan when the United States invaded to oust the Taliban as a consequence of 9/11 and their refusal to extradite Usama bin Laden.[4] Both groups, AQ as well as the Taliban, became outspoken and prolific producers of content that is disseminated online as much as offline – allowing an insight into their ideological proximity to one another despite being of different backgrounds. AQ emerged out of a setting dominantly influenced by Wahhabi-Hanbali, while the Taliban are Deobandi of the Hanafi legal school.[5] However, over the course of time since the Taliban emerged in 1994 and declared the Islamic Emirate in 1996, with Mullah Muhammad Omar "wrapped in the Cloak of the Prophet Mohammed," assuming "the right to lead not just all Afghans, but all Muslims,"[6] the Taliban and AQ switched from building an Islamic state to a two-decade long insurgency – thriving on a shared meaning of theology as their motivation, as both groups express frequently in their writings. The Taliban are focused on developing their Islamic state – the Islamic Emirate of Afghanistan – within the borders of modern-day Afghanistan, while AQ follows it's agenda of global jihad. For both groups the shared meaning of theology is the unifying factor. For the Taliban, the reach is local, which AQ underpinned in February 2022, hoping the Islamic Emirate can help in "defending the Islamic land of Afghanistan and to build a strong military force, a presence which would be felt in the region in the future."[7]

DOI: 10.4324/9781003326373-56

AQ as well as the Taliban are prolific producers of often highly professionally made content. This content is often in the same online space, especially since the terrorist attacks of 11 September 2001 that triggered the invasion of Afghanistan led by the United States and the subsequent insurgency against the West and their allies in Afghanistan, that would last nearly 20 years. AQ and Taliban materials have often appeared within the same online forums in the 2000s where users could easily find and download the newest releases of both groups. With AQ in the 2000s frequently releasing new videos of the media institute as-Sahab, Afghanistan was featured in the continuing jihad against American and NATO forces as well as the Western backed Afghan government.[8]

Videos by the Taliban appeared increasingly within the online flora and fauna of AQ,[9] with selected videos featuring Arabic subtitles or voice-over narration[10] to further outline the shared effort of fighting for a common cause against a common enemy inside Afghanistan. While the Taliban remain very active and present on Twitter, not facing account suspensions such as AQ, the current shared space for Taliban and AQ is on Telegram and WhatsApp.[11] On Telegram, Taliban groups exist, with some of these having over 10,000 members alongside AQ groups that are often connected via the shared content. The monthly magazine of the Taliban, al-Somood, is published in Arabic and was made available within the AQ-dominated online forums of the 2000s and today on Telegram, Twitter and elsewhere. Al-Somood, "a monthly Islamic magazine by the central media of the Islamic Emirate of Afghanistan" has been published monthly for 17 years and has been made available on Twitter and classical websites[12] as of 2022. The Arabic main account of the Taliban (@alemara_ar) on Twitter has over 172,000 followers and the Twitter handle of the Taliban's Arabic monthly magazine has 6,800 followers.

For AQ, the Taliban are brothers, as they, as rulers of Afghanistan – past and present – "implement the Islamic shari'a," Islamic law.[13] The common objective is to support and enable a state – or body of governance – based on shari'a law, for which the Taliban stand for, despite being opposed by other factions in Afghanistan. "The cause of fighting alongside the Taliban is to support this newborn Islamic state, for the first time allowing such a state for Sunni Muslims after a very long time. This state is the fruit of the jihad by the Afghan people for over twenty years to this day."[14] AQ and its branches worldwide clearly state that "the organization [AQ] is connected to the Islamic Emirate of the Taliban, who, despite being exposed to American violence, have implemented shari'a and have not conceded any principles of religion."[15] The theology of the "principles of religion" (usul al-din) is the fundamental basis on which AQ and the Taliban act on core theological issues of what an Islamic state is about. A core tenet is the "oneness of God" (tawhid). Tawhid stands in contrast to shirk - the practice of idolatry that violates tawhid. For jihadis, the distinction of as being the most pious servants of God runs along the line of clearly defining shirk and who is a mushrik (someone practicing idolatry) and thus a legitimate target. Following this understanding, the Taliban in March 2001 ordered the Buddhi statues of Bamiyan to be demolished: "Based on the verdict of the clergymen and the decision of the Supreme Court of the Islamic Emirate (Taliban), all the statues around Afghanistan must be destroyed. All the statues in the country should be destroyed because these statues have been used as idols and deities by non-believers before. They are respected now and may be turned into idols in future too. Only Allah, the Almighty, deserves to be worshipped, not anyone or anything else."[16]

AQ circles approved the destruction of the Buddha statues of Bamiyan by the Taliban in 2001, praising amir al-mu'minin Mullah Muhammad Omar as he "challenged the entire world by destroying the statues (Bamiyan Buddhas), acting upon the shari'a of [prophet] Muhammad, which was sent for this purpose,"[17] comparing Mullah Muhammad Omar to the line of the historical successors of prophet Muhammad. Omar ibn al-Khattab: "The 'Umar of this time is in Afghanistan, enforcing humiliation and subjugation upon the disbelievers (kuffar) in his land!"[18]

The Supreme Court of the Islamic Emirate in 2001 was led by Chief Justice Abd al-Hakim al-Haqqani, a specialist in Islamic jurisprudence and fluent in Arabic. The victory by the Taliban in August of 2021 also marked the return to power of Abd al-Hakim al-Haqqani, who has been reinstated as Chief of Justice of the Supreme Court in Kabul and is the current Minister of Justice. In June 2022 he published a new book in Arabic to underpin his scholarly status by addressing sources (in Arabic) of the Qur'an and Sunna, "The Islamic Emirate and its System."[19] In his book he reaffirms many core theological components as the integral element for the Islamic Emirate. The foreword is penned by the current leader of the Taliban, Hibatullah Akhundzada, who clarifies that "Islam is a wholesome all comprising system for the servant of God for all aspects of human life, leading to absolute fulfillment in this world (dunya) and the afterlife (al-akhira), rightly guiding to the creed (aqida) and worship, to noble morals and sovereignty, calling for social solidarity and sincerity in one's behavior."[20] Akhundzada praises al-Haqqani as "a professor of the ulama, an epochal scientist of Islamic traditions of religious jurisprudence, a Mujahid on the path of God."[21]

Afghanistan as a Launching Pad for the University of Global Jihad and Local Statehood

The invasion of Afghanistan, a Sunni-Muslim majority country, by the Soviet Union in 1979 was a major shock. The fear was voiced by some that Afghanistan would be the next Islamic country where Muslims are forced to turn away from their religion, as some conservative and extremist circles attested to the status of Palestine.[22] The trauma of the loss of Palestine and the declaration of the state of Israel, referred to in Arab circles as the *nakba* (catastrophe), must never be repeated. This trauma coincides with the motivation of being a vanguard to protect other Islamic territories and is evident in the motivation of foreign fighters joining the jihad in the 1980s against the Red Army in Afghanistan and was later voiced in regards of other conflicts such as Bosnia, where the fear of losing Islamic territory is is tied into the threat of "de-Islamization" of this very ground.[23] The Soviet invasion of Afghanistan was framed as an attack by "an atheist state that has come with destruction,"[24] in the words of foreign fighters that wanted to preserve Afghanistan as a Muslim society – and ideally construct an Islamic state.[25] The Soviet Union invaded Afghanistan on 24 December 1979 to install a Moscow-friendly regime headed by Babrak Karmal.[26] Kamal failed to gather popular support from the Afghan people – and his government in Kabul was facing a spreading rebellion and insurgencies in the tribal as well as urban space. The destruction brought by Soviet forces and their local allied Afghan forces intensified the nation-wide resistance against both the occupation forces as well as the Afghan regime headed by Babrak Karmal. The increasing insurgency was dominantly Islamic in orientation[27] and, from around the world, young Muslims started coming to Afghanistan to support the Muslim population of Afghanistan against the non-Muslim occupiers. Afghanis who took up arms against the Soviet occupiers as well as the regime of Karmal often referred to themselves as Mujahideen, organized in parties,[28] fighting on the path of God.[29] With Arab Muslims arriving in Afghanistan, there arose a new faction that would transform into al-Qaeda in the years to come. Of the many factions in Afghanistan, the Maktab al-Khidmat, or Services Bureau, was established to recruit Arab Muslims into an organized force – and to keep them away from the chaos of the many Afghan resistance groups. The Services Bureau was headed by Abdallah Azzam, a scholar of Islamic jurisprudence who became the spiritual leader of modern jihad.[30] Abdallah Anas, a companion of Azzam, describes the situation: "We set up the Services Bureau together with a group of the brothers, while you had been gone. Among them was Usama bin Laden.

We founded the Services Bureau to organize the participation in the Afghan jihad for Arabs. We do not want them to stay in various Afghan guesthouses. We want to offer independent locations that can be used by them without excluding anyone of them."[31]

Azzam's service had the intention to transform the Arab recruits into a fighting unit, organizing military training in camps and offering religious studies as well as providing spiritual guidance, establishing the modus operandi of jihadi groups for generations to come by combining military training, outlined as a religious obligation and duty, with jihad as the ultimate service for God, with religious education. This led to a religious education sector within the ongoing war in Afghanistan. Part of this educational sector of the Services Bureau was dominated by the launch in December 1984, of the first edition of the Arabic language bi-monthly magazine "al-Jihad," just three months after the Services Bureau itself had been set up.[32]

This sparked the articulation – and global dissemination in print – of the core jihadi theology, ignited by Abdallah Azzam in his many articles, books and the worldwide rollout of al-Jihad magazine. As early as July 1991, the use of Macintosh computers to advance the media work had been recommended.[33] The plea to establish an independent "Islamic media" to educate Muslims worldwide, free of any religious misguidance or disinformation, set the foundations for what would become the very basis of online jihadi activists and media departments in the decades to come.[34] This "open global university of jihad," as Reuven Paz referenced it in 2004,[35] served as the basis to project influence on theological grounds, with the ambition to initiate new members into the jihadi mindset. In 2003 Ahmad al-Wathiq bi-l llah, deputy director of the Global Islamic Media Front (GIMF), presented AQ as an "organization, state, and university."[36] In an AQ forum, the Mohajroon Forum, where Taliban content was also part of the matters discussed,[37] the "university of al-Qaeda" was outlined: "Do you remember how the beginning of al-Qaeda was, in the Mujahid land of Afghanistan? It began at the Services Bureau, and the house of the ansar (the supporters), and the al-Faruq training camp.[38] (…) Some brothers asked us why do we not label it "the sciences of terrorism" instead of "sciences of jihad"? And our answer was today whosoever wages jihad in the path of God and challenges America and Zionism and other enemies of God – in the eyes of the hypocrites and the enemies of Islam, this person is a "terrorist." This is the political jargon for jihad.[39]

Military handbooks and training materials, known as the "encyclopedia of jihad,"[40] that appeared in this context would in the 2000s inspire AQ on the Arab Peninsula, in Saudi Arabia, to establish an electronic magazine dedicated to military tactics and handiwork.[41] The famed "encyclopedia of jihad" itself resurfaced in mid-2002 within AQ and Taliban networks online,[42] digitalized and professionally made as a PDF instead of a copy of a paper version. It was re-released as "The Islamic Emirate Afghanistan – Services Bureau – Military Leadership," conveying the legacy of the Services Bureau. Eight parts of the encyclopedia had been re-published, detailing various rifle types, the fabrication and handling of explosives and general military-tactical procedures. Each of these documents has an introduction outlining the theological necessity to follow the divine command to "prepare for jihad" and to follow the advice of the lessons learned by "the Arab mujahidin during the days of their jihad against the Soviets in Afghanistan. The mujahidin documented their special experience and expertise in the long-lasting battle fields of jihad in this encyclopedia."[43]

Each volume begins with a verse of the Qur'an, Sura al-Anfal, verse 60: "Prepare against them whatever forces you [believers] can muster, including warhorses,[44] to frighten off [these] enemies of God and of you, and warn others unknown to you but known to God. Whatever you give in God's cause will be repaid to you in full, and you will not be wronged."[45] Ribat, a reference to the warhorses, the ribat al-khayl, has two main aspects in contemporary jihadi literature. First, the complete 60th verse of the Qur'an is often stated in introductions to various theological and military handbooks or videos.[46] This verse in particular is used as "proof" to dedicate oneself to fighting the enemies of God. The introduction of the encyclopedia of jihad continues: "everyone today knows that the Islamic world is occupied from East to West, from North to South. The armies of the disbelievers and of atheism do as they please with Muslims (…). Anyone asking how can we step towards establishing the obligation of jihad while we are in this weak and dire position finds the answer in the speech of God: obey God and His Messenger, and do not quarrel with one another, or you may lose heart and your spirit may desert you. Be steadfast: God is with the steadfast."[47] And God says: "Prepare against them whatever forces you [believers] can muster."[48]

The Taliban emerged from Kandahar in 1994 and had taken took over most of Afghanistan, including Kabul, by 1996. The Islamic Emirate of Afghanistan was declared on 27 September of that year and, shortly after the AQ attacks of 11 September 2001 on New York and Washington, the Taliban had been forced from power and into a full-blown insurgency when the United States with the United Kingdom invaded Afghanistan on 7 October 2001.[49] According to Yusuf al-Uyairi, a key theologian and leader of al-Qaeda on the Arab Peninsula in the early 2000s,[50] the chaos and quarrels among various warlords and former allies in Afghanistan "led to the birth of the Taliban."[51] The deteriorating conditions among in Afghanistan forged the foundation of the Taliban in Kandahar, under the lead of Mullah Omar. According to Ahmed Rashid, the basic tenets of the foundation of the Taliban had been to

> restore peace, disarm the population, enforce Shari'a law and defend the integrity and Islamic character of Afghanistan. As most of them were part-time or full-time students at madrassas, the name they chose for themselves was natural. A talib is an Islamic student, one who seeks knowledge, compared to the mullah, who is one who gives knowledge. By choosing such a name the Taliban (plural of Talib) distanced themselves from the party politics of the Mujaheddin and signalled that they were a movement for cleansing society rather than a party trying to grab power. All those who gathered around Omar were the children of the jihad but deeply disillusioned with the factionalism and criminal activities of the once idealised Mujaheddin leadership. They saw themselves as the cleansers and purifiers of a guerrilla war gone astray, a social system gone wrong and an Islamic way of life that had been compromised by corruption and excess. Many of them had been born in Pakistani refugee camps, educated in Pakistani madrassas and had learnt their fighting skills from Mujaheddin parties based in Pakistan. As such, the younger Taliban barely knew their own country or history, but from their madrassas they learnt about the ideal Islamic society created by the Prophet Mohammed 1,400 years ago, and this is what they wanted to emulate.[52]

Yusuf al-Uyairi's account is similar, adding that, by 1995 the "Taliban movement emerged in Kandahar and the global media started reporting the news of a new force, that had spread in one year across five or six Afghan provinces (wilaya) in the Southwest of Afghanistan, having taken control and chased away armed militants. [The Taliban] began to implement the authority of shari'a law and persecuted thieves."[53] Al-Uyairi is described by Roel Meijer as a prolific writer who "managed to publish hundreds of pages on topics ranging from open letters (…) to several political analyses of the American presence in the Middle East, the jihad in Chechnya, the Abu Sayyaf group in Philippines, and the Taliban in Afghanistan," noting al-Uyairi "comes across a well-informed, clear-headed, and down to earth analyst."[54] In al-Uyairi's writing on the Taliban, he emphasizes two elements that are of great importance: First, the Taliban emerged as a force to bring order and an end to random kidnappings and rape among other crimes in Afghanistan, and second, the Taliban are students of shari'a science and hence united in their view of what type of system can bring order to the chaos.[55] He claims that several

women of the family of Mullah Muhammad Omar had been kidnapped. He led several students of shari'a science in Kandahar backed by Islamic scholars who issued legal decrees allowing to fight the offenders in the absence of the Rabbani[56]-appointed governor of Kandahar doing anything; Mullah Muhammad Omar and eleven of his men went to the village of Singesar, killing several of the robbers and taking ten prisoners. Two bodies of the missing women were found with them, and they confessed to killing them. Therefore, Mullah Muhammad Omar and his men implemented the physical punishment (hadd punishment) upon them, killing everyone who was involved in the crime. Their weapons had been taken as loot (ghanima) and they started to cleanse out the remaining robbers and thieves.[57]

Upon returning to Kandahar, Mullah Muhammad Omar demanded that the governor resigns and to gives up the means needed to successfully fight against the freely roaming criminals – leading, according to al-Uyairi, to the development of the Emirate and "declaring the implementation of shari'a law in Kandahar, forcing the thieves to flee and providing security to the people who returned to their normal daily affairs of life."[58] The core demands by Mullah Muhammad Omar had been shari'a law as the norm to which all warlords must comply and to expulsion of all communists from their ranks. "On 26 September 1996, the Taliban attacked Kabul and took it at night in a quick sweep due to the disunity of the remaining warlords, forcing them to flee to the North."[59]

In Their Words: Selected AQ Reactions Worldwide to the Victory of the Taliban

AQ groups responded to the victory of the Taliban after the fall of Kabul in August 2021. Every statement was released in Arabic and within the shared space online, ranging from Telegram to Element.[60] The statements re-affirm the validity of the Taliban and praise the victory as proof of jihad being the only possible solution to what is referred to as an ongoing "war against Islam."

Al-Thabat Newsletter

AQ praised the victory of the Taliban in their electronic newsletter "Thabat" after the fall of Kabul. The newsletter, which is a document of several pages featuring news from places around the world where AQ is fighting, such as Somalia, Syria, or the Sahel, was launched on 20 August 2021. On the cover, a picture of former US-president George W. Bush is framed in English and Arabic in big white and red letters with "After 20 Years of War... America has been Defeated."[61] The headline of the main story "The Islamic Emirate rules all of Afghanistan" is visually enhanced with a screengrab of an al-Jazeera news reporting showing the Taliban leadership inside the presidential palace in Kabul on the day of the taking-over of Kabul.[62] "After 20 years of jihad against more than 40 Crusader states, the Mujahidin of the Islamic Emirate had been able to enter the Afghan capital of Kabul and territorially control all of Afghanistan. The Mujahidin hosted a news conference from inside the presidential palace in Kabul and started the news conference by reading from the Sura al-Fath."[63] Sura al-Fath states a treaty given to prophet Muhammad by God securing peace with the opposing Meccan ruling tribe of the Quraysh. The sura is significant as it reassures the believers that their self-restraint and obedience to the prophet were inspired by God. The Sura affirms "those who pledge loyalty to you [the Prophet] are actually pledging loyalty to God Himself,"[64] while condemning the hypocrites (munafiqin) of Medina and the idolators of Mecca. The AQ newsletter emphasizes what Taliban media have emphasized time and again[65]: "Islamic shari'a will rule Afghanistan as re-affirmed by the Islamic Emirate. This will be the ruling system in Afghanistan, not a western democracy."[66] How the Islamic Emirate envisions this Islamic State was further detailed in a book published in Arabic by current Taliban Minister of Justice and Chief Justice of the Supreme Court Abd al-Hakim al-Haqqani.

Global Islamic Media Front

GIMF is a decades old electronic AQ media outlet that publishes mostly documents and statements in Arabic but also other languages.[67] GIMF is used to release "statements by the general leadership" (bayan min al-qiyyadat al-'ama) of AQ. Current Taliban leader Hibatullah Akhundzada, who inherited the function of "leader of the faithful" from Mullah Muhammad Umar, is praised as a steadfast believer in consequently fighting against the Americans and NATO. "What began twenty years ago, with US aircraft viciously bombing the country and forcing the Islamic Emirate (Taliban) to withdraw to the mountains, ended with the Islamic Emirate triumphantly returning to Kabul, and the Americans and its Afghan stooges hastily running away and taking flight."[68] Afghanistan is highlighted, again and again, as the most important Islamic territory, where "the path of jihad and martyrdom" has ended in the military victory for the "third time." With the defeat of the Soviet occupation that lasted from 1979–1989 by the Mujahidin factions and the take-over of Kabul by the Taliban in 1996, this defeat of Western-led forces in August 2021 is marked as the third victory. Citing Mullah Muhammad Umar, "God promised us victory, Bush promised us defeat; we shall see, which promise is most sincere." Following a classical jihadi rhetoric, the GIMF statement addresses "our Muslim umma," claiming that to "unite, arm and fight on the path of God to defend the umma's religion, sanctities,[69] land and possessions" is the only way forward – with the victory in Afghanistan overcoming "well-equipped and numerically superior enemies." The dominant Arabic writings and books by AQ are filled with references to the Qur'an and Sunna, whereas AQ considers itself as being guided by the "book of God" (kitab allah, the Qur'an) and the method of prophethood (documented in the Sunna[70]).[71] No enemy ever has been able to overcome a true community of believers "guided by their Prophet Muhammad – peace and blessings upon him[72] – and his noble companions in their jihad against the kuffar[73] and the hypocrites,[74] fighting to rule by the shari'a of Islam on earth. [As God says:] "God has made a promise to those among you who believe and do good deeds: He will make them successors to the land, as He did those who became before them; He will establish the religion He has chosen for them; He will grant them security to replace their fear. "They will worship Me and not join[75] anything with Me." Those who are defiant[76] after that will be the rebels."[77,78] For AQ the victory of the Taliban and the return of the Islamic Emirate to the urban space mean a liberation of Afghanistan from anti-Islamic forces and a chance to serve, again, as a beacon for Muslims worldwide. "With the help of God this historic victory will open the way for Muslim masses to achieve liberation from the despotic rule of tyrants who have been imposed by the West on the Islamic world. God willing, the victory of the Muslim umma in Afghanistan shall prove to be a prelude to the liberation of Palestine from the Zionist occupation. America and NATO's Afghan debacle marks the beginning of the end of the dark era of Western hegemony and military occupation of Islamic lands."[77] The statement concludes by marking the importance of having won militarily to "establish God's law in Afghanistan and protect the interests of Islam and Muslims." Jihad is the means to victory, "just as Afghanistan was liberated from American occupiers and their allies, oh God, may you rid Palestine from the Zionists, the Islamic

Maghreb from French and allied occupation, Syria, Somalia, Yemen, Kashmir and all Islamic lands from their enemies."[78]

Al-Qaeda on the Arab Peninsula, Yemen

Just as the AQ central leadership, al-Qaeda on the Arab Peninsula (AQAP) refers to the leader of the Taliban as amir al-mu'mineen (the leader of the faithful). AQAP congratulates "the leader of the faithful and his brothers of the Islamic Emirate as well as all Mujahideen worldwide" for pre-vailing in their fight against the Americans.[79] "After two decades of jihad and resistance[80] against the Western Crusader forces, the Americans and local enemies" and after "the defeat of the Soviet Union about 30 years ago," AQAP announces this as the beginning "to rid all Muslim lands of the tyrants." AQAP calls the victory in Afghanistan with the Taliban occupying the Afghan cities and Kabul within days a "victory and empowerment for us, as it shows that jihad and combat is the path of shari'a and of Sunni tradition, the real way to recuperate our rights and drive tyrants as well as occupiers out and to make the word of God the highest."[81] AQAP states, based on scripture and religious texts, which are the "basis of proof of the jihadis' actions, the Taliban have proven God's commands in their fight to re-implement divine law." The religious texts refer to "several verses of the Qur'an and hadith[82] and are proof" that is hence often cited in jihadi publications to legitimize actions and explain their doings. Jihadis are tuned to leading the fight until either judgment day or the establishment of an Islamic State. "We ask God that he may stand with our brothers the Taliban to rule by the divine law and to establish the creed of loyalty and dissociation"[83] and emphasize the importance of the principle of "commanding what is right and forbidding what is wrong."

AQ Reactions in the Sahel and North Africa

On 23 August, 2021, Jabhat Nusra al-Islam wa-l Muslimin (JNIM) and AQ in the Islamic Maghrib (AQIM) issued a joint statement congratulating the Taliban. JNIM is mostly active in the Sahel and is notorious for attacking international as well as local forces in Mali and maintains a functioning media outlet called "al-Zallaqa." AQIM mostly operates in Algeria and North Africa and has been maintaining its media outlet "al-Andalus" since the mid-2000s. The joint state-ment of al-Zallaqa and al-Andalus opens with the citation of the Qur'an 33:25: "God sent back the disbelievers along with their rage – they gained no benefit."[84] After enduring "two decades of brutal occupation and blatant transgression against religion, sanctities ('ird) and land, and after two decades of jihad, of combat and sacrifice, the Afghan Muslim people are victorious against the international coalition of disbelief led by the Americans and the British."[85]

From resisting the English and the Russians and now the Americans, the joint statement issues praise to deceased Taliban leader Mullah Omar, who is referred to as the leader of the faithful, citing his famous statement "we have promised Bush defeat, god has promised us victory, we shall see which of the two promises is more sincere."[86] Having defeated the world's most power-ful army, jihad is pitched as a reality based on the divine commandment that enables the true believers to overcome all odds and implement sharia law as the basis for a Afghan-Islamic society.

Kurdistan

The AQ-affiliated Brigade of Kurdistan in Iraq and Iran, praises the Taliban for "reaping the fruits of victory after 20 years of combat and resistance against the invading Crusaders."[87] Prais-ing the path of jihad set by prominent leaders and theologians, the Brigade praises Abdallah

Azzam, Mullah Omar, Usama bin Laden and Attiyatullah al-Libi, who set the Islamic umma worldwide on the path of righteousness to restore Islamic dignity and might, while emphasizing that "more than a hundred Kurds are fighting against the Crusaders in Afghanistan as well."

AQ on the Indian Subcontinent

In the past years, AQ has established a persistent presence in India. On 19 August, an Arabic statement was issued congratulating the Taliban, referring to them "as having renewed their seat of governance in Kabul, bringing peace and joy to the heart of every Muslim worldwide."[88] Praising the "leader of the faithful who also is a scholar of hadith and Qur'anic studies Hibatullah and his second in command, Mullah Abd al-Ghani Baradar" and expressing special cheers to the leader of the Haqqani network, Siraj al-Din Haqqani.

The victory in Afghanistan is "a special message to the Islamic umma," and a special message "to every Muslim as the victory of the Islamic Emirate demonstrates the only path to drive out and defend the Islamic community against unjust aggressors is to apply jihad and to head out and join the fight."

AQ Central

On 31 August 2021, as-Sahab, the main media outlet of AQ Central, released a written statement. The statement opens with a citation from the Qur'an and frames the Taliban as those, who are acting upon God's command of "enforced obligatory prayers, the giving of alms (zakat), and are those who are commandeering good and forbidding what is wrong."[89] The last part is a direct reference to the principle of "commanding what is right and forbidding what is wrong." In this claim, the group seeks to draw on the authority of Qur'an 3:104: "Be a community that calls for what is good, urges what is right, and forbids what is wrong. Those who do this are the successful ones."[90]

The victory in Afghanistan, in the words of AQ, in the name "of the Islamic community, is a historic victory."

AQ Central praises the endurance of resistance against non-Muslim aggressors, referencing a statement made by Prophet Muhammad, that believers engage with their "bodies, their wealth, their blood, their worldly belongings," continuing to engage in wars against the disbelievers, "generation after generation." Knowing "no surrender," Afghanistan is a vital battlefield for true believers, being tested "on the path of jihad and martyrdom," making the Afghan Islamic community the best one of the global Islamic community. This is the global appeal for groups such as AQ operating in cahoots with local jihadi forces such as the Taliban: Liberating Islamic territory in a jihadi mindset to govern accordingly by Islamic law, while AQ is in charge of global affairs with the ambition to enable Muslims in other parts of the world (for example Somalia with al-Shabab) to liberate territory with the primary objective of jihad to implement divine law as the common rule. Hence, as the other AQ outlets, AQ Central refers to the leader of the Taliban as "the leader of the faithful" and as such as the 'supreme commander' of all Muslims worldwide, with AQ in charge of roles under the Taliban leadership. Deceased Taliban leader Mullah Omar is praised and his statement about Bush is framed by AQ as the legacy: "God has granted the Mujahidin victory."

As jihadis have proven in Afghanistan, AQ Central emphasizes continuing jihad with the objective of implementing divine – sharia – law as the only possibility for Muslim people worldwide in order to free themselves from repression and tyranny. AQ underlines its mission to free Muslims, especially in Palestine, stating that, after defeating America and NATO in Afghanistan, everything is possible, "having ended the era of American and European arrogance." The end of this era, according to AQ Central, will end the occupation of Muslims lands.

This notion was re-affirmed and emphasized in the lengthy praise of the Taliban in the AQ magazine, One Umma.[91]

AQ Electronic Magazine "One Umma"

The 6th edition of the magazine "One Umma" was published in February 2022. The cover depicts a photoshop-enhanced portrait photo of Mullah Muhammad Omar in the prime of his life with the sun rising over a mountain in the background. His infamous statement "God has promised us victory. Bush promised us defeat. We shall see…" appears besides him, with "which promise is most sincere!" written in big Arabic letters. Below that is stated: "amir al-mu'minin al-imam Muhammad Omar Mujahid, may God have received him." The editorial of the magazine is dedicated to the Taliban victory, showing the leadership at the presidential palace, an image taken from al-Jazeera that was used before by the Thabat newsletter. The first part of Sura 48, al-Fath, that the Taliban recited at the presidential desk, is the title of the editorial: "Truly We have opened a path to clear triumph."[92] The editorial[93] opens with the citation of Qur'an 65, starting with the last sentence of the second part: "God will find a way out for those, who are mindful of Him, and will provide for them from an unexpected source; God will be enough for those who put their trust in Him. God achieves His purpose; God has set a due measure for everything."[94]

Addressing the Taliban leadership as well as the Islamic umma, the lengthy editorial praises victory as "having driven out all occupying Crusader soldiers from Afghanistan and fully cleaning the Muslim Afghan soil from the Crusader filth."[95] Congratulating Hibatullah Akhundzada and emphasizing his status as a scholar of Qur'anic exegesis (tafsir) and of hadith studies,[96] "we had never had any doubt that the sacred jihad of our sacred umma will conclude in victory. This is the divine promise, with its fulfillment only being a question of time."[97] This defeat "is a lesson for the international forces of evil they shall never forget and not repeat with the people of Islam, God willing. The gist of the lesson that the Islamic Emirate's experience has to offer is that core of jihad as well as the principles of belief (iman) are firmly established and deeply rooted and can be seen in the confrontation against the Crusader coalition."[98]

The editorial addressed several key themes as outlined below:

Governance and Islamic Statehood

"May God help the leadership of the Islamic Emirate establish the system of shari'a, govern by Gods book (Qur'an) and the teachings of the Messenger (Sunna), and give the Afghan nation the rights due to them. May God guide the Islamic Emirate to deal with the entire Afghan nation with mercy and kindness, establish justice within Afghan society and ensure that the masses are guaranteed an honorable and decent life under the shade of the shari'a."[99]

"On this historic occasion, we would like to honor the memory of all those who lit the flame of freedom, led the way with their tremendous sacrifices and helped the umma attain this stunning victory. We would like to express our deep love and utmost respect for all those who offered sustained support and help to the honorable Afghan nation and the Islamic Emirate in their noble Jihad."[100]

"Thousands of God-fearing, pious and noble people worked in obscurity for years, took great risks, and offered extraordinary sacrifices for the realization of this remarkable feat. And it is in great part due to their unflinching support that stood the test of time that the mujahidin were able to prevail over the forces of disbelief."[101]

"We have a humble piece of advice to offer to the honorable imams of the Jihad in the Islamic Emirate of Afghanistan. God has entrusted you with power and authority. Above all, He has honored you with the heritage of prophethood. So may God see in you a befitting example of humility and mercy towards His servants. May God help you establish the shari'a and govern the affairs of the people in line with shari'a-based policies. We have no doubt that you are worthy and truly capable of shouldering this grave responsibility. Repose your trust in God, seek guidance from the collective wisdom of the great Imams of the recognized schools of Islamic law-especially in the field of shari'a politics-so that an Islamic political system is established in accordance with the prevailing school of Islamic law in Afghanistan."[102]

Foreign Fighters

"We have not forgotten and shall never forget the caravans of faith, of hijra and jihad that heeded to the call of God and His messenger to support their brothers in Afghanistan, to aid them in religion and creed (aqida). Arriving from different corners of the world, they offered their souls and wealth for this cause, in the hope to attain what God has in store as reward on the Day of Judgment. The entire land of Afghanistan bears witness to their martyrdom operations and their faith-inspired sacrifices. Thousands of graves across Afghanistan are a witness to the fact that the Muslim youth did not betray the cause of this sacred Jiihad. The pure blood that was shed on Afghan soil is a testimony to the profitable trade they engaged in with their Lord. We pray to God to accept their sacrifices, reward them for their Jiihad on the day that they meet Him and recompense them with His paradise in the Hereafter."[103]

Da'wa – Religious Educational Sector and Missionary Operations

"The efforts of the scholars and students of Islamic sciences equally deserve recognition in this respect. Sincere God-fearing scholars, callers to God, writers, and learned people all played a critical role in rallying support for this noble cause. To them we say: May God support you just as you supported your brothers in faith. May God bless your hands that held the weapon in the battlefield and the pen in the field of media and da'wa.

Your articles, statements, religious decrees (fatawa) – from the very beginning of the invasion to the day that the Afghan soil was cleansed of the Crusaders – played a valuable role in helping the umma reach this stage. Your efforts are a witness to your commitment and sincerity and to the fact that throughout these years there was no dearth of support and encouragement from you for the mujahidin. We value your efforts and hold you in great esteem. And even if we were to differ in our opinions at times, you are one of us and we are one of you; in fact, we are for you. So have faith in our unbound love for you; a love that springs from the common bond of faith. May God grant you success. May God protect you and guide you every step of the way. May we all rejoice together on coming victories in other parts of the Islamic world."[104]

Recommendations to the Islamic Emirate of Afghanistan

"In this respect, we would strongly encourage those who have been burdened with the responsibility of administering the affairs of Muslims in the beloved land of Afghanistan to:

1 Build a strong, Islamic, Jihad-oriented army for the Islamic Emirate; a versatile and dynamic military force that excels in all fields and whose rank and file are strong in their faith and

commitment to the Islamic cause. One of the blessings of God is that He has blessed the army of the Islamic Emirate with abundant supplies of weapons and an arsenal left behind by the Western Crusader forces. This arsenal should undoubtedly help in defending the Islamic land of Afghanistan and building a strong military force, the presence of which, God-Willing, would be felt in the region in the future.

2 Build a modern, dynamic educational system that is capable of producing efficient specialized cadres from all segments of the Afghan society in diverse fields, including Islamic sciences, medicine, and engineering.

3 Build a resilient self-sustaining economic system based on Islamic principles; a system that is usury-free, fights all forms of interest-based exploitative transactions and invests the resources and mineral wealth of Afghanistan in line with Islamic economic principles. It is through the wise exploitation of Afghanistan's resources that the Islamic Emirate should be able to provide the people with their economic rights and revive the duty of Zakat (giving alms)."[105]

Warning against Democracy

"We would like to use this opportunity to offer a short piece of advice to our brothers who, even after seeing the living miracle that Afghanistan and the Islamic Emirate represent, still believe in democracy as the appropriate method of empowering Islam. You have never achieved anything by pinning your hopes on democracy and neither will you achieve anything meaningful in the future by sticking to the same futile course. The one and only successful way to empower Islam is by the bullet, not the ballet. It is only through fulfilling the duty of Jihad in the Way of God – a Jihad that is strictly in accordance with the teachings and laws of the shari'a – that establishing an Islamic government is practically possible."[106]

Global Jihad Continues to Counter Western Hegemony

"After the return of the beloved land of Afghanistan to the merciful shade of Islam, we would like to reassure the Islamic umma that even though attacks directed at the bastion of Zionism – America – have for now ceased on the soil of Afghanistan, this blessed Jihad against the Empire of Evil will continue from other parts of the world.

God has promised us his favors and bounty, and we shall continue to persevere in our efforts on the battlefields in different parts of the Islamic world, specifically lands that are under attack from the Crusader enemy. With our trust firmly reposed in God, our quest for justice shall continue. We will continue to hunt down America and its allies until they desist from interference in the affairs of the Islamic World and end their oppression of Muslims across the globe. Our decades-old program of weakening Western Crusader hegemony over the Islamic World and breaking the enemy's will to fight until all Islamic lands are liberated – just as Kabul was liberated – shall continue unabated. Our priorities in this regard remain unchanged: the purification of the Holy Land of Palestine from Zionist filth, the liberation of all Muslim prisoners-from Guantanamo to those languishing behind bars in the authoritarian systems imposed by the West across the Muslim World-and pushing America back behind the seas and oceans until it learns to mind its own business and stops meddling in the affairs of the Muslim World. The Afghan experience should suffice as a lesson for the West that the Muslim World has zero-tolerance for all types of interference and that the West would be far better off if it puts its own house in order and maintains a hands-off policy vis-à-vis the Islamic World.

Lastly, we promise our Islamic umma that it will see the same lessons learned in Afghanistan being applied in all the theatres of Jihad had across Muslim lands: a sincere commitment to Jihad, strict adherence to the principles of the shari'a, and a preference for granting general clemency and showing mercy to people after attaining power, for we consider ourselves students of the school of the imam, the Mujahid, the leader of the faithful, Mullah Muhammad Umar, may God, the Lord of the Worlds, have received him."[107]

Conclusion

The Taliban and al-Qaeda have had an intertwined and intimate relationship. The Taliban refused to extradite Usama bin Laden, claiming to not do so "without evidence" of the AQ attacks on 11 September 2001.[108] The Taliban instead endured a hard removal from power and over 20 years of occupation. AQ and the Taliban have shared the online space where both released their videos from the Afghan battlefields fighting a common enemy. The content of the videos revealed a growing approximation of their theology, their understanding of jihad, and the enemies they are fighting inside Afghanistan for the Taliban and on a global scale, including neighboring Pakistan in the case of AQ in the 2000s. When the Taliban recaptured Kabul and re-established the rule of the Islamic Emirate of Afghanistan inside the urban space, having fought a resistance from the rural countryside for nearly two decades, AQ was elaborate and outspoken in outlining what the victory of the Taliban means. AQ groups worldwide responded to the victory and the lengthy editorial in AQ's electronic magazine "One Umma" gave a deeper insight. In parallel, the book published by the Taliban's acting Minister of Justice and Chief Justice of the Supreme Court, Abd al-Hakim al-Haqqani, provides a clear structured understanding of the Taliban's vision of statehood, showing theological overlap with AQ writings of the past decades. AQ chief Ayman al-Zawahiri was killed in an American drone strike in Kabul, almost a year after the withdrawal of American and NATO forces,[109] with analysts responding in clearly naming the Taliban as being "a protecting power for AQ."[110] The Taliban during the first Islamic Emirate of Afghanistan had established the Ministry of "Commanding what is right and forbidding what is wrong," which can be loosely translated as the "virtue" ministry. In 2021, this ministry was reinstated,[111] making it clear, as in the book on Islamic governance by al-Haqqani, what is allowed and what will be persecuted within the tight framework of shari'a law and what types of physical punishment are set for what types of offenses. Yusuf al-Uyairi, the AQ theologian and leader of AQ on the Arab Peninsula until his death in 2003, in his analysis of the Taliban, republished interviews with the Taliban leadership, including their selected statements and religious decrees, citing an interview with the first Minister of the "Commanding what is right and forbidding what is wrong" Ministry: "The Taliban movement will not forget the role of our brothers, the Arab Mujahidin." He continues: "we as Afghans have a natural love for Arabs, for our Prophet – peace and blessings upon him – was an Arab. His native tongue was Arabic. The Qur'an was revealed in Arabic. Because of their endeavors [of early Muslims under the leadership of prophet Muhammad], this great religion came to us when Islam spread from Mecca and Medina. We do not forget that the language of the people of paradise is Arabic. This is why I have great passion for the brothers, the Arab mujahidin who spread among the people what they see of us in terms of applying shari'a law. This land is their land, this state is their state. We ask God that he may receive those who engage in hijra and jihad."[112]

Notes

1 Taliban statement fatahat Afghanistan wa-intisar al-Islam, 16 August 2021, citing Mullah Muhammad Omar 2001. The statement with a picture of Mullah Muhammad Omar was featured on the electronic AQ magazine "one umma" to celebrate the Taliban victory in Afghanistan. Umma Wahida (2022), sixth edition, February.

2 For example: Osama bin Laden (2006), Ritha al-shaykh Abu Mus'ab al-Zarqawi.

3 Akhundzada is portrayed as a "scholar of Qur'an exegesis and hadith scholar" according to AQ magazine One Ummah, number 6, February 2022.

4 Taliban are back – what next for Afghanistan? https://www.bbc.com/news/world-asia-49192495?piano-modal (accessed 11 June 2022).

5 Yusuf al-Uyairi (2001), Al-Mizan l-haraka Taliban, electronic version in authors possession, provides an AQ angle on the Taliban as a Deobandi group with the allegation only some are Salafis while others are not, pp. 5–7. What matters is what overlaps in terms of a) the theological format into b) practical means such as establishing an Islamic state governed by Shari'a law, with hudud punishments part thereof or the question of allowing graves (some Taliban follow that) and the matters of destroying symbols and sites of idolatry.

6 Ahmed Rashid (2008), Taliban – The Power of Militant Islam in Afghanistan and Beyond (London, New York: I.B. Tauris), electronic book version.

7 Umma Wahida (2022), AQ magazine, sixth edition, February.

8 For example, Improvised Explosive Ordnance attack on a German Armored Car in the province of Kunduz (2009), as-Sahab Media, or (in Urdu) Kharat kay rabi (2014), featuring the daily lives of the Mujahidin in the Afghan frontlines, including religious sermons and study courses led by 'frontline preachers'.

9 For example, the video Afghan Victors (2013), Released by "the Cultural Commission of the Islamic Emirate through al-Imara Studio", made available in the AQ vb/bulletin forum Ansar al-Mujahidin, a forum that is defunct as of writing.

10 For example: The Caravan of Heroes series (2013), Made available in Arabic and English or the video series "True Men" (2020), available in Pashto, Farsi, Arabic and English via Manba' al-Jihad media, part of the Cultural Commission of the Islamic Emirate.

11 Ali Fisher, Nico Prucha (2022), The Salafi-Jihadi Online Ecosystem in 2022 – Swarmcast 2.0, European Institute for Counter Terrorism and Prevention, July 2022, https://eictp.eu/en/the-salafi-jihadi-online-ecosystem-2022-swarmcast-2-0/ (accessed 1 August 2022).

12 The archive of all editions: https://alsomood.af/?page_id=16785
Twitter: https://twitter.com/sumoodmag (both accessed 27 June 2022).

13 Omar Abd al-Hakim (Abu Mus'ab al-Suri) (1998), Afghanistan wa-Taliban wa-ma'rakat al-Islam al-yawm, part 1, (Markaz al-Ghuraba' li-l dirasat al-Islamiyya), p. 3.

14 Ibid.

15 Tanzim qa'idat al-jihad fi jazirat al-arab (2021), al-Malahem Media.

16 Agent France Presse Kabul, March 2001, via https://buddhism-guide.com/buddha-statues-of-bamiyan/ (accessed 10 June 2022).

17 Hamud ibn Uqla al-Shu'aybi, Sulayman ibn Nasir al-Ulwan, Ali ibn Khudhayr al-Khudayr (2002), Letter to Mullah Muhammad Umar from the scholars (English translation), at-Tibyan Publications, pp. 7–8.
Hamud ibn Uqla al-Shu'aybi, a Saudi scholar who died there in prison in 2002 was important for AQ theologians and the first generation of al-Qa'ida on the Arab Peninsula, operating in Saudi Arabia. Nico Prucha (2010), Die Stimme des Dschihad – al-Qa'ida erstes Online-Magazin (Hamburg: Verlag Dr. Kovac), pp. 78–91.

18 Ibid. The "Letter to Mullah Muhammad Umar" was also featured in a lengthy publication with the title "The Martyrs of Afghanistan" that gained popularity within the AQ online worlds in 2003, with the war in Afghanistan having started after the 9/11 attacks.

19 Abd al-Hakim al-Haqqani (2022), Al-Imarat al-Islamiyya wa-nizamha (Maktabat Dar al-Ulum al-Shar'iya), with a foreword by amir al-mu'minin, al-shaykh Hibatullah Akhundzada.

20 Ibid., pp. 5–6.

21 Ibid., p. 6.

22 The implications and consequences in the collective perception of loosing an integral part of identity with the occupation of Palestine by non-Muslim actors for the dynamic of global jihad is analyzed in: Hazim al- Amin (2011), al-Salafi al-yatim – al-wajha al-filastini li-"jihad al-alimi" wa-"l qa'ida" (Beirut, London: Dar al-Saqi).

23 Nico Prucha (2013), Arab Foreign Fighters in Bosnia – The Roads to Europe, in: Gunther Hauser, Franz Kernic, Sven Gareis: "The European Union - a Global Actor?" (Opladen, Berlin, Toronto: Budrich Publishers), pp. 334–350.

24 Al-Jihad Magazine (December 1985, number 14), p. 46.

25 Zaynab al-Ghazali, "Afghanistan is the dream for the future and the beacon of life – the path to the Islamic Caliphate from Afghanistan", al-Jihad Magazine (December 1985, number 14), pp. 38–40.

26 Ahmed Rashid (2008), Taliban – The Power of Militant Islam in Afghanistan and Beyond (London, New York: I.B. Tauris), electronic book version.

27 Afghanistan is described as a traditional conservative Islamic society by Hafiz Allah Haqqani. The author lists "ten most important parties that committed to jihad against the Soviet forces", including the Jama'at al-Islamiyya headed by Ahmad Shah Mas'ud (established 1973) also lists al-Jabhat al-Qawmiyya, the only Shia-led party (headed by Sayyid Ahmad Jilani). Hafiz Allah Haqqani (1997), Taliban Afghanistan min Hulm Mullah ila Imarat al-Mu'mineen, (Islamabad: Institute of Policy Studies), pp. 42–56.

28 This support was not necessarily to engage in combat or violence.

29 See for example the magazine "al-Mujahid", January 1980, part of the resistance lead by Ahmad Shah Mas'ud, who would be known as the leader of the "Northern Alliance" in the late 1990s in opposition to the Taleban.

30 Thomas Hegghammer (2020), The Caravan Abdallah Azzam and the Rise of Global Jihad (Cambridge: Cambridge University Press), pp. 77–87.

31 'Abdallah Anas (2002), Waladat al-Afghan al-'Arab Sira 'Abdallah Anas bayna Mas'ud wa-'Abdallah 'Azzam, (Beirut, London: Dar al-Saqi), p. 34.

32 Thomas Hegghammer (2020), The Caravan Abdallah Azzam and the Rise of Global Jihad (Cambridge: Cambridge University Press), p. xi.

33 The magazine had a P.O. box address in Peshawar and maintained a network of P.O. boxes for subscribers from New York City to London, to Yemen, Saudi Arabia, Bahrain, Jordan, UAE, Sudan, Oman, Qatar. Al-Jihad Magazine (1991), i'lan ham, al-Jihad Magazine no. 80, July/August 1991.

34 Nur al-Din (1985), Mafhum al-sadq fi l-ilam al-Islami, al-Jihad Magazine no. 12, pp. 26–31.

35 Reuven Paz (2004), Who Wants to Email Al-Qaeda, PRISM Series of Global Jihad, No.2/2, July 2004.

36 Ali Fisher (2018), Netwar in Cyberia: Decoding the Media Mujahidin, USC Center on Public Diplomacy (Los Angeles: Figueroa Press), p. 44. Ali Fisher cites Reuven Paz (2007), Reading Their Lips: The Credibility of Jihadi Web Sites as 'Soft Power' in the War of the Minds, PRISM and GLORIA Center, vol. 5, no. 5.

37 As was common for the forums of that era, the Taliban had their designated section divided into "al-Imara:::Taliban" where the latest news, statements and memoranda had been made available in Arabic and other languages.

38 The camp is detailed in: The 9/11 Commission Report, National Commission on Terrorist Attacks Upon the United States, by the US-government, https://911commission.gov/report/ (accessed 2 August 2022).

39 Saqr Quraysh (2006), The University of al-Qa'ida for the sciences of jihad – Now Accepting Applications, shabakat al-Muhajirun. An archived thread of the posting is in the authors archives.

40 'Abdallah Anas (2002), Waladat al-Afghan al-Arab Sira 'Abdallah Anas bayna Mas'ud wa-'Abdallah 'Azzam (Beirut, London: Dar al-Saqi), pp. 33–36.

41 The magazine was named Mu'askar al-Battar and focused on attacks within urban settings.

42 In the early 2000s AQ and Taliban utilized online forums where both AQ media globally as well as Taliban statements and videos had been released frequently. As these forums had been dominantly for Arabic users, the Taliban released Arabic translations there while maintaining their own websites in multiple languages (i.e. Farsi, Arabic, Pashto and partially in English). Twitter is an important hub which the Taliban use extensively and without facing account suspensions or bans. See for example the Islamic Emirate Twitter account, https://twitter.com/TalibanUpdates (accessed 29 June 2022).

43 Mawsu'at al-Jihad (Encyclopedia of Jihad), pp. 3–4.

44 *Ribat al-khayl*

45 Qur'an 8:60. Translation by: M.A.S. Abdel Haleem (2010), The Qur'an (Oxford: Oxford University Press), p. 185.

46 Nico Prucha (2009), Jihadists'use of Quran's *ribat* concept, *Jane's* Islamic Affairs Analyst, (August).

47 Qur'an 8:46, Translation by: M.A.S. Abdel Haleem (2010), The Qur'an (Oxford: Oxford University Press), p. 184.

48 Mawsu'at al-Jihad (Encyclopedia of Jihad), p. 3.

49 A timeline of events: https://edition.cnn.com/2013/10/28/world/operation-enduring-freedom-fast-facts/index.html (accessed 25 June 2022).

50 Nico Prucha (2010), Die Stimme des Dschihad – al-Qa'ida erstes Online-Magazin (Hamburg: Verlag Dr. Kovac), pp. 14–17; 36–40.

51 Yusuf al-Uyairi (2001), Al-Mizan l-haraka Taliban, electronic version in authors possession, p. 28.

52 Ahmed Rashid (2008), Taliban – The Power of Militant Islam in Afghanistan and Beyond (London, New York: I.B. Tauris), electronic book version.

53 Yusuf al-Uyairi (2001), Al-Mizan l-haraka Taliban, electronic version in authors possession, p. 29.

54 Roel Meijer (2006), Re-Reading al-Qaeda, Writings of Yusuf al-Ayiri, ISIM Review 18 (Autumn), https://scholarlypublications.universiteitleiden.nl/handle/1887/17089 (accessed 12 June 2022).

55 Yusuf al-Uyairi (2001), Al-Mizan l-haraka Taliban, electronic version in authors possession, pp. 31–37.

56 Burhanuddin Rabbani who was allied with Ahmad Shah Mas'ud and held Kabul until the Taliban pushed them out, according to al-Uyairi (2001).

57 Yusuf al-Uyairi (2001), Al-Mizan l-haraka Taliban, electronic version in authors possession, p. 31.

58 Ibid.

59 Ibid. p. 31. The Northern Alliance was later established under the leadership by Ahmad Shah Mas'ud who would be assassinated by AQ operatives two days before the 11 September 2001 attacks.

60 Built on Matrix, "An open network for secure, decentralized communication", Element | Secure collaboration and messaging (accessed 24 July 2022).

61 Sahifa Thabat, number 30, 20 August 2021. The newsletter features "the most prominent news of the mujahideen in every Islamic country" and solely features AQ and Taliban operations.

62 The image was used in AQ's "one umma" magazine as well. For the Al-Jazeera exclusive story – and image: Hamza Mohamed, Ramy Allahoum (2021), Taliban enters Afghan presidential palace after Ghani flees, Al-Jazeera, 15 August 2021, https://www.aljazeera.com/news/2021/8/15/taliban-continues-advances-captures-key-city-of-jalalabad (accessed 22 June 2022).

63 Sahifa Thabat, number 30, 20 August 2021, p. 2.
The event was covered by Aljazeera, https://www.youtube.com/watch?v=5FDFLPOXrEM, 15 August 2021 (accessed 15 August, 2021).

64 Qur'an 24:55. Translation by: M.A.S. Abdel Haleem (2010), The Qur'an (Oxford: Oxford University Press), pp. 512–513.

65 For example Mullah Baradar at the Moscow conference to broker a peace deal between the Taliban and the Afghan government on March 18, 2021 made clear in the opening of his speech that jihad will continue to implement shari'a law and that only a nationwide Islamic form of governance can ensure a lasting ceasefire. Al Somood (2021), Monthly Magazine by the Taliban in Arabic, March 2021, pp. 2–4.

66 Sahifa Thabat, number 30, 20 August 2021, p. 2.

67 Guido Steinberg: "Jihadismus und Internet: Eine deutsche Perspektive", Stiftung Wissenschaft und Politik, October 31, 2012, https://www.swp-berlin.org/en/publication/jihadismus-und-internet (accessed 17 June 2022).

68 Global Islamic Media Front (2021), Bayan tahani'a wa-mubaraka bi-munasibat al-fath fi Afghanistan, 25 August, 2021, authors copy.

69 The Arabic 'ird is used in to relate sanctities such as religious sites no non-Muslim should be allowed to and the status of Muslim women. Jihadis position themselves as being the sole defenders for religion and for theologically determined status of the true Muslima who, by her behavior and dress code, is to be shielded and protected from non-male family members. Jihadis for decades have been outspoken on how occupying or non-Muslim forces have trampled on Muslimas and why it is the duty of any able bodied man to respond and join the call.

70 The Sunna documents the deeds and saying of Prophet Muhammad and his companions (sahaba).

71 Rüdiger Lohlker (2019), Al-Nabi al-dawlawi? On the Role of the Prophet in IS and other jihadi Subcultures, in: Rüdiger Lohlker and Tamara Abu-Hamdeh (eds.), Jihadism Revisited Rethinking a Well-Known Phenomenon (Berlin: Logos Verlag).

72 In traditional religious circles peace and blessings upon him is added when mentioning Prophet Muhammad.

73 Disbelieving non-Muslims.

74 In Arabic: munafiqin. Both terms, kuffar and munafiqin are derived of Qur'and Sunna to communicate to the target audience that contemporary jihadis are fighting against internal (munafiqin) as well as external enemies. Kuffar is used to refer to local non-Muslim enemies and likewise for soldiers of NATO countries in Afghanistan or US Forces in Iraq as well as for non-Muslim civilians worldwide.

75 In Arabic: la yushrikuna bi-ya: in the jihadi mindset this is reference to the sacrosanct importance to worship God and only God while actively combatting any form of 'polytheism'. Hence, when the Taliban destroyed the Buddha statues of Bamiyan, the justification was based on the understanding of annihilating any form of shirk (which can loosely be translated as polytheism).

76 In Arabic: wa-man kafara ba'd: in jihadi reading, "those who remain disbelievers nonetheless" and as such must be confronted violently.

77 Ibid.

78 Ibid.

79 Al-Malahem (2021), Tahani'a wa-mubaraka bi-l fath wa-l tamkin fi Afghanistan, 18 August 2021.

80 In Arabic: sumud – the name of the monthly Arabic language magazine by the Taliban.

81 A popular slogan that appeared in the 1980s in the magazine al-Jihad and gained prominence in the late 2000s with the emergence of AQ in Iraq lead by Abu Mus'ab al-Zarqawi.

82 Documented sayings and deeds by prophet Muhammad.

83 Al-wala' wa-l bara', which is used to differentiate between true believers who are loyal to God and everyone else. In jihadis understanding, any Muslim who serves for a government that is deemed as unislamic is disloyal to God and thus a legitimate target.

84 Translation by: M.A.S. Abdel Haleem (2010), The Qur'an (Oxford: Oxford University Press), p. 422. Haleem notes that this refers historically "to the sandstorm that caused the disbelievers to go back without success." In Jihadi videos, sandstorms are sometimes shown as a reference thereto, in an attempt to further their image of being the only true believers and active servants for God and thus being backed by divine force.

85 Al-Zallaqa and Al-Andalus (2021), Bayan tahani'a wa-mubarakam, 23 August 2021.

86 Ibid.

87 Bayan tahani'a li-imara Afghanistan al-Islamiyya, 20 August 2021.

88 Bayan tahani'a bi-munasiba fath wa-nasr al-imara al-islamiyya fi ard Afghanistan, 19 August 2021.

89 Ibid.

90 Embedded in this citation of the Qur'an is the deeper meaning of *applied theology* – referenced in the Qur'an in Arabic as *ya'murun bi-l-ma'ruf wa-yanhun bi-l-munkir.*

91 Umma Wahida (2022), sixth edition, February.

92 Qur'an 48: 1. Translation by: M.A.S. Abdel Haleem (2010), The Qur'an (Oxford: Oxford University Press), p. 512.

93 Umma Wahida (2022), sixth edition, February, p. 4.

94 Qur'an 65: 2–3. Translation by: M.A.S. Abdel Haleem (2010), The Qur'an (Oxford: Oxford University Press), p. 559.

95 Umma Wahida (2022), sixth edition, February, p. 5.

96 Umma Wahida (2022), sixth edition, February, p. 6.

97 Ibid.

98 Ibid.

99 A slogan often used by Islamist and jihadi groups.

100 Umma Wahida (2022), sixth edition, February, p. 6.

101 Umma Wahida (2022), sixth edition, February, p. 7.

102 Umma Wahida (2022), sixth edition, February, pp. 8–9.

103 Umma Wahida (2022), sixth edition, February, p. 7.

104 Umma Wahida (2022), sixth edition, February, p. 8.

105 Umma Wahida (2022), sixth edition, February, pp. 9–10.

106 Umma Wahida (2022), sixth edition, February, p. 9.

107 Umma Wahida (2022), sixth edition, February, p. 11.

108 Taliban Won't Turn Over Bin Laden - CBS News, 11 September 2001 (accessed 26 June 2022).

109 https://www.bbc.co.uk/news/world-asia-62387167, 2 August 2022 (accessed 9 August 2022).

110 Guido Steinberg in an interview with WELT, 2 August 2022, https://www.youtube.com/watch?v=FNfWfsPYImY (accessed 3 August 2022).

111 https://nypost.com/2021/09/13/taliban-brings-back-virtue-ministry-stoning-and-amputations-for-major-sins/, 13 September 2021 (accessed 4 August 2022).
See also: https://www.washingtonpost.com/world/2021/09/08/afghan-vice-virtue-ministry/, 8 September 2021 (accessed 4 August 2022).

112 Yusuf al-Uyairi (2001), Al-Mizan l-haraka Taliban, electronic version in authors possession, p. 97.

INDEX